73-38293

D1265634

USEFUL REFERENCE SERIES NO. 97

Index to Women

of the World

from Ancient to Modern Times:

Biographies and Portraits

By

NORMA OLIN IRELAND

Author of Index to Scientists; Index to Full Length
Plays (1944-1964); The Picture File; etc.

F. W. FAXON COMPANY, INC.
WESTWOOD, MASSACHUSETTS
1970

International Standard Book Number 0-87305-097-5

Library of Congress Card Number 75-120841

PRINTED IN THE UNITED STATES OF AMERICA

A THREEFOLD DEDICATION

to

(1) My husband, Dave Ireland, who has always encouraged me in my work and who has given unstintedly of his time and effort — to help me accomplish my goals. He has driven many miles to libraries, carried unlimited boxes of books, checked and re-checked my manuscript, and helped to make the final completion of this work possible.

(2) My mother, sisters and grandmothers, all of whom combined professions with homemaking and motherhood, with successful accomplishment. And to my father and grandfathers who also appreciated the contributions of womanhood outside of the home, and provided the education to make it possible.

(3) The PIONEER WOMEN of the world, especially of American history, including some of my antecedents included in this book: Hannah Chapin Sheldon, Frances Dighton Williams, Margaret Hicks, "Widow" Walker and the Pilgrim *Mothers* (Chilton, Rogers). To all of these who "blazed the trail" that we, today, might lead better lives. And lastly to my many friends, those "working girls and wives" who have been MODERN PIONEERS in their various professions and occupations.

TABLE OF CONTENTS

FOREWORD

This work was compiled because we felt that a comprehensive index to women, their biographies and chief contributions, was long overdue. It is, also, a companion to our *Index to Scientists,* and, similar to that volume, it includes personalities of the world from ancient to modern times. Altho we have tried not to emphasize any group, perhaps we have been partial to "pioneers," both in history and occupation, who have made possible our progress of today. We believe that such a work is timely, considering the current stress on equality of "race, creed and color," but certainly equality on the basis of "sex and age" is also necessary! We still have far to go, even in the United States, when women astronauts are not accepted, and a female jockey has to fight to ride a horse in a race! Perhaps our "Introduction" may open some eyes as to the accomplishments of women, and our references to biographies reveal some leaders whom history has recorded but later history books have ignored.

We have analyzed 945 collective biographies including a few magazine multiple volumes. Approximately 13,000 women are included. Not only general compilations have been indexed, but also collections in special fields. In general, we have indexed mostly "circulating books," published in the United States and Great Britain, with some exceptions. Some small volumes have been included such as books for younger readers, to make the book useful to small libraries and schools. Most encyclopedias, biographical dictionaries and reference books have been omitted as well as large compilations (such as the wonderful Kunitz series of authors) because of lack of space. We have endeavored to include the latest editions of most volumes, but in some cases inclusion has necessarily been limited to representative books in the series if all are not available.

We have included a few magazine series of special value, not otherwise completely indexed in other sources: *Current Biography,* 1940–1968, *New Yorker's* Profiles," 1925–1968, *Time's* "Cover stories," 1924–1968 and *Bulletin of Bibliography's* special features on librarians and authors, v. 8-24. Compilation of the index ended in 1968 except for a few recent books. We have, in no way, however, tried to duplicate the complete coverage of the excellent *Biography Index,* but have tried to include additional older books not indexed in this work.

All periods of history have been covered, from Biblical times, as we felt that inclusion of Bible women, saints, etc. would increase the book's usefulness.

Omission of names has one main reason: not included in the 945 books we indexed. We have not tried to make it a modern "Who's Who" because there are many reference books available for this purpose, altho we have tried to cover today's great women, as far as possible. Altho we had hoped to make an occupational supplement, lack of space has prevented. Instead, we have made a percentage summary of general and special fields, based on the type of books indexed. It must be remembered that "General" includes all fields, as they are compilations of famous women of all kinds. Here is a breakdown, therefore, based on the 945 volumes we indexed, showing subjects covered:

General	33.2 percent
History and Pioneers	20.0
Literature	13.4
Science	6.8
Religion	5.9
Theater	5.9
Music	5.0
Special classes	3.3
(some duplication under other subjects, e.g. Negro musicians under Music)	
Art	2.1
Social work and Reform	1.9
Dance	1.5
Education	.5
Athletics	.5

It is interesting to compare these percentages with the occupational group tables in *Who's Who in America*, 1901–1902, 1926–1927 and 1948–1949, as given in Larson's summary.[1] Altho his summary is for both *men and women* and has a limited coverage, he rates their inclusion as follows: authors and artists head all lists; actors, musicians, social reformers, scientists, educators and journalists were in the top twelve of all years.

Users of our book will also be interested to know the percentage of books indexed, according to date of publication. At first, we planned to include only books published in the last twenty years, but we soon discovered that some of the most useful books, especially in the category of history, were written earlier. Biographical subjects are never outdated and we considered the fact that if libraries keep these older books on their shelves, then they must be currently useful. We have tried to emphasize later publications, of course, and indexed current books up to the time the manuscript went to press. Our percentages are as follows:

---

[1] Larson, Cedric A. *Who.* Sixty years of eminence. The story of Who's Who in America N.Y., McDowell, Obolensky, 1958. 389p

1960–1968 books	23.1 per cent
1950's	26.6
1940's	17.3
1930's	12.3
1900's, 1910's, 1920's	17.2
Previous to 1900, "n.d."	3.5

We have tried to use our best judgment in indexing each book, especially when material was uneven and scattered throughout the book. We have evaluated biographical material on the basis of its importance and length, in each particular book. We examined a great many books we did not include because (1) material was insufficient, (2) only one woman included, (3) not suitable for indexing. Perhaps we have missed some good volumes and some important women, but one cannot achieve absolute completeness. Indexing of individual volumes was usually complete but selective when insufficient material was given for some individuals. Inclusive paging is given, except in the case of periodicals. Paging of portraits is not given in this book, to save space, since inclusive paging usually includes the portrait.

ARRANGEMENT AND HEADINGS

Arrangement of names is alphabetical by letter, as is usually found in biographical dictionaries. Dates of life, nationality and occupations are given for each woman, followed by symbols for analyzed references. We have used the easy-to-remember abbreviated key-word system rather than letter combinations. We have checked many biographical dictionaries and other reference books to determine exact dates of lives, but in some cases there is variance by authorities and in many cases, fragmentary dates. We have included some either/or dates, as books differ, but this is no reflection on the personalities, altho we do offer apologies for some of our sex who conceal birthdates. We have given dates of marriage, graduation, or time "flourished" if exact birthdate is not found; "n.d." usually means current dates, altho birthdate unknown. "Flourished" is not entirely inclusive, but probably most active years, as judged by biographies found. Christian names are given, rather than husbands' names, except in some instances when former is not known. We hope we have not inadvertently included any males, by error, but if so, they are in good company! We have included many cross-references, when women are well-known under both names.

We have tried for consistency in occupational headings, insofar as possible, as well as for exactness. We have not broken down titles, in all classes, however, because of overlapping. For instance, too many actresses are known in motion picture, stage and television work, so just the word *actress* is used. We have not indicated races or special classes, because inclusion in this volume is based on accomplishment alone. We have, however, indexed every possible worthwhile book in every sort of special class or grouping, including the handicapped.

ACKNOWLEDGMENTS

We wish to thank the librarians of the many libraries we consulted, as follows: Altadena, Chula Vista, Glendale, Los Angeles, Pasadena and San Diego libraries. We are especially grateful for the interlibrary loan service given by the Altadena Public Library including service from California State Library and many other libraries in California. We especially thank the Chula Vista Library, including Mrs. Ruth Jamison and Mrs. Blume Levine, who made all resources available to us at the beginning of this work, when we lived in San Diego county.

We appreciate the kindness of the editors of various publications and organizations who sent us lists and other helpful aids: Miss Anne Sutherland, formerly editor of *Bulletin of Bibliography;* Marian Powers of *Time* magazine; Fred Keefe of *The New Yorker* and Leta Bradley of The United Christian Missionary Society. We also thank Mrs. Doris Shirar and Mrs. Lilian DeLey of Altadena, and Mrs. Winifred Irving of Sierra Madre for their help in extra typing, checking and transportation.

CONCLUSION

To conclude, we urge you to judge the women who are included in this work for their conductions to history rather than as current "celebrities." But only time can prove their worth, as is so well expressed in the little verse by Elizabeth Barrett Browning:

> ... *"Measure not the work*
> *Until the day's out and the labour done;*
> *Then bring your gauges. If the day's work is scant*
> *Why call it scant; affect no compromise;*
> *And, in that we have nobly striven at least,*
> *Deal with us nobly, women though we be,*
> *And honour us with truth if not with praise."*

— NORMA OLIN IRELAND
1024 Alpine Villa Drive
Altadena, California, 91001

INTRODUCTION

I. WOMEN AS PIONEERS

This volume is fundamentally an index to women pioneers: pioneers in all ages and in all fields. We have included notable women of yesterday and today, women who have influenced history, religion, the arts, literature, science and invention. Unfortunately we have had to include the bad along with the good, but it is a well-known fact that many king's mistresses influenced the course of history and we cannot deny that certain "wild" characters played a part in the history of our own West.

We use the term "pioneer" in two ways: (1) in a general sense, as first or early workers in all fields of knowledge, (2) as early settlers of America. Altho we have made no attempt to duplicate today's "Who's Who's," we have tried to cover the centuries of world history, and especially the decades of American history. For instance, we have endeavored to show that the famous actresses of the eighteenth and nineteenth centuries should be remembered, not because they were superior (according to modern standards), but because they laid the groundwork for the American theatre of today. Likewise, we have included many Revolutionary and Civil War nurses who were well-known only in their time, but who were pioneers in nursing as it is known today.

IN EARLY AMERICA

Specifically, we have sought to list famous women pioneers in America, forgotten in most biographical dictionaries, but without whom there would be no America today. First of all, we have the Pilgrims, those wives and mothers who braved the ultimate in hardships in order to help in the founding of this country. "Fifteen of the twenty-nine women who sailed from England and Holland," states Marble,[1] "were buried on Plymouth hillside during the winter and spring . . . nearly twice as many men as women died during those fateful months of 1621. Can we 'imagine' the courage required by the few women who remained after the devastation, as the wolves were heard howling in the night, the food supplies were fast disappearing, and the houses of shelter were delayed in completion by 'frost and much foul weather,' and by the very few men in physical condition to rive timber or to thatch roofs?"

"Mrs. Ernestine Potowski Rose was one of the first to point with pride to the Pilgrim Mothers as opposed to the Pilgrim Fathers," says Lillian O'Connor.[2] "This she did at the First National Convention for Women's Rights

[1] Marble, Annie Russell. *The Women who came in the Mayflower.* Pilgrim, 1920. p12-13
[2] O'Connor, Lillian. *Pioneer women orators.* Columbia University Press, 1954. p75

in 1850. 'Who has ever heard of the Pilgrim Mothers?' she asked. 'Did they not endure all — as the Pilgrim Fathers did?' "

WOMEN OF THE WEST

The sturdy Colonial pioneers came next, then the Westward Movement brought the pioneers of the West who had to be just as hardy, sometimes even more so. William Hard is quoted by Inez Irwin,[3] as follows: "The Colonial gentleman had to have his soap kettles and candlemoulds and looms and smokehouses and salting tubs and spinning wheels operated by somebody if he was going to get his food and other necessities cheap. The pioneer woman must work at a pace which seems fabulous nowadays, and she must breed."

"For the most part the early West — by which is meant West Virginia, Kentucky and Tennessee, was settled from the frontiers of Virginia and the Carolinas, and by people of the so-called Scotch-Irish race," Bruce[4] tells us. us. "The women of this stock were a strong-limbed, clear-eyed folk. Their predominant trait was a stubborn, unflinching courageousness manifest alike in times of great crises, and in the ordinary vicissitudes of life. When Mrs. Joseph Davis of Virginia, to give an illustration, broke her arm at the crossing of the Cumberland River, but continued on the road to Kentucky, riding her horse and carrying her baby as though no injury had befallen her, she but typified the innate pluck and determination common to the women who settled the West. There were no weaklings among them — weaklings would never have crossed the well-nigh trackless mountains, to say nothing of withstanding the ordeals of the wilderness existence.

"They were, too, wonderfully self-reliant women, and women in whom the spirit of initiative was strongly developed, as we already know from our study of the border women of the 'forgotten half-century.' Many were instrumental in inducing their husbands and sons to seek new homes in the West."

Women of the far West had an even greater part to play in the conquest of the wilderness and the making of our country. Unfortunately their heroism has been little stressed in history books. "The crossing was hazardous," so states Hargreaves.[5] "Two thousand miles in a summer with an ox team hitched to a springless wagon! This was the prospect ahead of a wife whose husband decided to 'go west' in the 1840's. . . . The suffering of the crossing has been recounted over and over. The work of building homes in a wild new country where the family must depend almost entirely upon its own resources for the first hard years was bravely undergone. The women's side of the great colonizing movement has never been greatly stressed, but in reality, at least an equal share of the subduing of the wilderness fell upon their capable

[3] Irwin, Inez Haynes. *Angels and Amazons.* Doubleday, Doran, 1933. p.13

[4] Bruce, H. Addington. *Woman in the making of America.* New rev. ed. Little, Brown, 1928. p151-152

[5] Hargreaves, Shelba *in* Binheim, Max, ed. *Women of the West.* Publishers' Press, 1928. p153-154

shoulders. The law and order from which civilization springs on a frontier came with the silent, unassuming women with babies in their arms and little children clinging to their skirts.

"Government must be firmly established if women and children were to live in safety. Schools and churches must be maintained. The mental and moral welfare of the settlement must be attended to for the sake of children. Women insisted on this. Women have been the civilizing influence."

The pioneer woman had to be versatile, and there was no job that she didn't do. Fowler[6] puts it this way: "Sometimes a hunter and trapper and again a mariner; now we see her performing the rugged work of a farm, and again a fighter, stoutly defending her home."

STATUES IN HONOR OF . . .

We are compiling a list of statues and other monuments in honor of women, and shall be glad if our readers would send postcards of such statues in their area. There have been a few statues, in some of the states, to commemorate the pioneer woman, but very few. One in the Middlewest is the pioneer mother statue in Penn Valley Park, Kansas City, Missouri, inscribed with the "Whither thou goest" theme. There is a chain of twelve monuments across the country honoring pioneer mothers and one of these is "The Madonna of the Trail" in Upland, California erected to honor the "Pioneer Mothers of the Covered Wagon Days."

Irene Welch Grissom is quoted in the book by Binheim[7] as follows: "Many statues have been erected to commemorate the pioneer men, who conquered the wilderness by the help of their women. But as yet no heroic figure, carved in stone, honors the West as it gives homage to the memory of the pioneer woman."

One monument in the West, however, is an exception to the rule. "Utah's Seagull Monument," says Mrs. Amy Brown Lyman, also in Binheim's Book,[8] "was erected to the memory of the gulls, which in early days saved the first crops from destruction by omniverous western crickets. It portrays in a group of pioneer figures at its base, the pioneer women. This woman, the inspiration of the group in which she is placed, stands erect beside the man, who, with drooping head and relaxed muscles, is plainly disheartened. The children are listless and weary; but the woman, with head up and muscles tense, is plainly dominated by mother-love and by the basic instincts of life and race preservation. She alone shows indominable courage and determination. This woman is typical of the Western pioneer women, who arm in arm with the men, helped to blaze the trails across the great American Desert and to found an empire in the West."

[6] Fowler, William F. *Woman on the American frontier.* Scranton, 1877. p67
[7] Binheim, *op. cit.* p114
[8] *Ibid.,* p167

We especially like the poem by Elizabeth Yarborough, in Tooni Gordi's book,[9] which so well expresses the pioneer American women's sacrifices and endurance:

AMERICAN WOMEN

"With only night for succor,
With only wind for cloak,
They walked beside their husbands
Until the long day broke.
They walked with tender slippers
Upon the blackened earth,
They sat down on the hillsides
To give their children birth.
They saw the weevil eating
Into the heart of wheat.
They saw the cyclone coming,
Terrible and fleet.
They heard in dead of winter
The wild wolves at the door;
Their homes were built of matchsticks,
The dark earth was their floor.
They felt the wind come flying
With keen and ragged teeth.
They stood beside the dying
And heard the last short breath.
They saw the hills and valleys,
They saw the rivers flow,
As if they were a legend
That happened long ago.
They felt the redskins' arrows,
They plucked them from their bones,
They buried children tomahawked
Upon their own hearthstones.
They saw their sons go walking
In their proud husbands' way,
They saw their daughters following,
They had no words to say.
These women were America,
They buried their own dead,
And sat beside them singing
With proud, uplifted head."

[9] Gordi, Tooni. *Contemporary women poets.* H. Harrison, 1936. p260

II. WOMEN IN HISTORY

Historians have long neglected women, and it is high time some revision is made in this regard. Mrs. John King Van Rensselaer, as quoted by Green,[1] expressed it this way: "History is generally written by man, who dwell on politics, wars, and the exploits of their sex. Household affairs, woman's influence, social customs and manners, are seldom chronicled and are only to be discovered underlying what are deemed the important events of life, more by inference than from anything that is actually written about them."

Although, according to one definition by Webster, history is "the branch of knowledge that records and explains past events," yet it is both men and women themselves who really make history. L. M. McCraith has this to say on the subject:[2] "History is the study of great principles, rather than of great men and women, but it is the study of great men and women which gives history its interest. Personalities have even been inextricably connected with great ideas, and principles, and upon personalities have turned the great events of the world."

WOMEN IN HISTORY BOOKS

"Admittedly all normal girls and boys are hero worshippers and are molded by their ideals," states Jane McCallum.[3] "Historians place before them the heroic part that has been played by our forefathers in the 'history of a people whose beginning was a great adventure and whose life has been a great toil.' They record man's part in the discovery and colonization of our continent, in the religious controversies of New England, in the fights for freedom of speech and conscience, for education, for temperance, and for the ballot; and they go into lengthy detail in recording the military achievements of these men. I would not blot out one word that has been written in praise of the men who helped make our nation, but why only a half-told tale — a play presented as it were, with only half of the actors on the stage? What were the women doing throughout these toilsome, adventurous years? 'Strong minds, great hearts, true faith, and willing hands' they must have had, or they could not have borne and reared the sons upon whose lives historians love so long to dwell. In 1831 de Tocqueville, in writing of his visit to this country said, 'If I were asked to what the singular prosperity and growing strength of the American people ought mainly to be attributed, I should reply — to the superiority of their women'."

Mary Beard[4] also has had much to say on the lack of material about women in history books: "An examination of the standard history textbooks in use in our schools raises the pertinent question whether women have ever made a contribution to American national progress that is worthy of record.

---

1 Green, Harry Clinton. *Pioneer mothers of America*, v. 1. Putnam, 1912. p153
2 McGrath, L. M. *The Romance of Irish heroines*. Longmans, Green, 1913. p.ix
3 McCallum, Jane Y. *Woman pioneers*. Johnson, 1929. p5
4 Beard, Mary. *Women as force in history*. Macmillan, 1946. p58

If the silence of the historians is taken to mean anything it would appear that one-half of our population have been negligible factors in our country's history. Ancient histories, however, surprisingly often gave women the credit they deserved! Certainly the original sources," continues Beard,[5] "which scholars use for the study of men in long and universal history, often mention and even recount stories or give elaborate data of many kinds about women. For example, Heroditus, whom historians of the modern age have called 'the father of history' deliberately included women in his history. Tacitus, the Roman, also observed and commented on the women of his time. Indeed ancient writers in various societies often thought it necessary to consider women and among their works are to be found statements respecting women's force of character, learning, physical energy, military and political power, and creative intelligence — statements made by the contemporaries of such women."

Turning back the pages of history to ancient times, we, of course, find women of the Bible of great influence on history. We find other women, long before Christ, who are described by Charles S. Muir[6] as makers of history including Tomyris, queen of Scythia in the 6th century B.C. who conquered Cyrus the Great, conqueror of the world at that time: "It is almost inconceivable that a woman could train an army and out-general one of the world's most celebrated military leaders. But the 'female of the species' is indeed a force to be reckoned with in the world — sometimes she conquers with an indomitable, fighting spirit and again she is most docile and overcome by love, which is the greatest force in the world."

ASPASIA

Aspasia of Miletus, 5th century B.C., was another woman important in ancient history. "She was most brilliant and a very eloquent speaker," continues Muir. "Her home became the rendezvous of all the distinguished people in Athens. Her influence, both social and political, was widespread. The greatest philosophers and statesmen sought her advice and considered her their trusted confidante. Even Socrates, the wisest of men, would often visit her in order to drink in some of her learning . . . Socrates would return again and again to the feet of Aspasia, that fountain of wisdom, and there he would have his philosophy refreshed and rejuvenated. But Socrates was not the only one that sat at Aspasia's feet and imbibed her wisdom, for she had all Athens at her feet. No one in that city wielded a greater influence than she did. The people regarded her as a sort of oracle. Even in important disputed matters she was called upon to render decisions and her decisions were considered as final, as though rendered in a court of justice. She could discuss the fine arts with a brilliance that could not be equalled, and for this reason her companionship was sought on all occasions. Some historians state that Aspasia

---

[5] *Ibid.*, p273
[6] Muir, Charles S. *Women, the makers of history.* Vantage, 1956. p35-37

was so influential that wars were brought about at her instigation. Due to her urging, the Samian and Peloponnesian conflicts are said to have been started."

H. J. Mozans goes even further in *his* praise of Aspasia:[7] "In many respects she was the most remarkable woman Greece ever produced. Of rare talent and culture, of extraordinary tact and finesse, of a fascinating personality combined with the grace and sensibility of her sex, together with a masculine power of intellect, this gracious Ionian stands with Sappho on the pinnacle of Hellenic culture, each in her own field the highest feminine representative of an aesthetic race. . . . Her house became the resort of all the great men of Athens. Socrates was often there. Phidias and Anaxagoras were intimate acquaintances, and probably Sophocles and Euripides were in constant attendance. Indeed, never had any woman such a salon in the whole history of man. The greatest sculptor that ever lived, the grandest man of all antiquity, philosophers and poets, sculptors and painters, statesmen and historians, met each other and discussed congenial subjects in her rooms. And probably hence has arisen the tradition that she was the teacher of Socrates in philosophy and politics and Pericles in rhetoric. Her influence was such as to stimulate men to their best, and they attributed to her all that was best in themselves . . .

"She is said to have written some of the best speeches of Pericles — among them his noted funeral oration over those who died in battle before the walls of Potidaea. As to Socrates, he himself explicitly refers to her, in the 'Memorabilia,' as his teacher. She is a notable character in the Socratic dialogues and appears several times in those of Aeschines, while there is every reason to believe that she strongly influenced the views of Plato, as expressed by him in the *Republic* respecting the equality of woman with man. She was continually consulted regarding affairs of state, and her influence in social and political matters was profound and far-reaching. This is evidenced by the abuse heaped upon her by the comic dramatists of the time. . . . But, however great her influence, we are warranted in asserting that it was never exercised in an illegitimate manner. She was ever, as history informs us, the good, the wise, the learned, the eloquent Aspasia. It was her goodness, her wisdom, her rare and *varied* accomplishments, her clear insight and noble purposes that gave her the wonderful power she possessed and which enabled her, probably more than any one person, to make the age of Pericles not only the most brilliant age of Greek history, but also the most brilliant age of all time."

OTHER WOMEN OF ANTIQUITY

Anna de Koven[8] also tells us of the influence of other women of antiquity; "Like distant peaks raising their heads among the enveloping clouds of history and legend, the women of antiquity exemplify 'the power, the martyrdom, the vengeance and the unshakeable will' of women . . ." She tells of Semiramis

---

[7] Mozans, H. J. *Woman in science.* Appleton, 1913. p12-14
[8] Koven, Anna de. *Women in cycles of culture.* Putnam, 1941. p1-2

of Babylonia as the first example of the governing power of the woman back of the king, controlling his policies, herself the ruler of Assyria and Babylonia. Then, of Theodora, wife of Justinian[9] "She too exemplified the power, the passion, and the vengeance of woman when raised to the throne. She possessed the eminent qualities of a ruler, masculine firmness and a calm courage under no matter what difficulties. When a riot threatened the palace and the emperor wished to fly, her reply was one of the noblest ever pronounced by a sovereign: 'When nothing remains but safety in flight, I say I will not fly. Those who have worn the Crown should never survive its Cross. Never shall I see the day that I shall no longer be called empress. Caesar, it is well! The vessels are ready, the sea is open, but as for me, I remain. I love that old maxim that the purple is a splendid shroud." So Theodora saved the empire; and while Justinian was occupied with the religious dissention of his capitol, she conducted the wars and the diplomacy of the empire, appointed and degraded the heads of the church, and even contradicted the orders of the emperor. She had a clear view of the necessities of government, and her political sagacity was worthy of any emperor."

The story of Cleopatra is well known. Muir[10] describes how this woman's beauty, charm and influence changed the course of history: "The glamorous personality of Cleopatra involved not only her extraordinary beauty but also forcefulness of character had made her crave power and glory. Vested in philosophy, she was a gifted musician as well. She changed history, for the Battle of Actium which she caused Antony to lose decided the mastery of the world."

In the first century we find Boadicea. Muir continues:[11] "At the foot of Westminster Bridge, in London, and facing both Houses of Parliament, there is a beautiful piece of sculpture depicting a woman, Boadicea, standing in her war chariot drawn by two magnificent horses. The English do well to remember this courageous queen for she challenged the whole Roman Empire because of its dastardly crimes . . . Boadicea is said to have commanded an immense army — some authorities giving the number as 150,000, others claiming 250,000."

In 270 A.D. we find Zenobia, Queen of Palmyra, as outstanding. Again Muir:[12] "She was a woman of great courage, high spirits and strikingly beautiful; with purity of morals in private life, she combined prudence, justice and liberality in her administration. Her literary acquirements were considerable; she spoke Latin and Greek as well as the Oriental languages with fluency."

WOMEN OF ANCIENT ROME

Ancient Rome had many women of unusual intellect who were noteworthy as makers of Roman history. Among others, these included Cornelia,

[9] *Ibid.*, p13
[10] Muir, *op. cit.*, p48
[11] *Ibid.*, p53-54
[12] *Ibid.*, p55

wife of Pompey the Great; Aurelia, mother of Julius Caesar; Livia, wife of Augustus and mother of Tiberius; Laelia, mother-in-law of Cicero; Agrippina, wife of Germanicus. "Woman had her part in the making, as well as the unmaking of Rome," states Joseph McCabe.[13] "In the earlier days, when her work was confined within the walls of the home, no consul ever guided the momentous fortune of Rome, no soldier ever bore its eagles to the bounds of the world, but some woman had taught his lips to frame the syllables of his national creed." Of the Roman empress Julia Domna, he says: "We know that at Rome she rebuilt the temple of Vesta, and the numerous provincial inscriptions suggest a much wider interest. Under her lead the women of Rome were encouraged to look beyond their homes. Sabina had erected or dedicated, a meeting hall for women in the Forum of Trojan, but it has fallen into decay. Julie restored this early 'Women's Club,' and no doubt introduced into it her enthusiasm for letters and philosophy which she still had. Her 'circle,' as Philostratus calls it, probably included the historian Dio, who was still at Rome and the poet Appian, who had some years before described her as 'the great Domna.' Philostratus himself, a Greek writer and rhetorician, one of the most learned men of the time, was closely associated with her. It was at her request that he wrote his famous 'Life of Apollonius of Tyrana.' In his 'lives of the Sophists' (Philiscus) he speaks of her as 'Julia the Philosopher,' and in one of his letters he refers with high appreciation to her learning."

Muir[14] refers to Roman women thusly: "In the 5th Century, B.C., two women, Veturia and Volumnia, mother and wife of Coriolanus, saved the city of Rome from destruction. Plutarch writes: "But the joy and transport of the whole city of Rome was chiefly remarkable in the honors and marks of affection paid to the women, as well as by the Senate as the people in general. And the Senate passed a decree that whatsoever they would ask in the way of favor or honor should be allowed and done for them." Subsequently the Romans erected a beautiful temple to show their gratitude to these two women for saving their city."

"Among the pioneers of the intellectual movement in Rome," states Mozans,[15] "and one of the most beautiful types of the learned women of her time, was the celebrated daughter of the elder Scipio Africanus — Cornelia, mother of the Gracchi. She is famous on account of her devotion to her two sons, Tiberius and Caius. She was their teacher; and it was her educated and refined mind that, more than anything else, contributed to the formation of those splendid characters for which they were so highly esteemed by their countrymen . . ." Then there was Livia.[16] "So great was her influence and so persistent was her activity in government affairs, that it is sometimes asserted that she was the prime mover of most of the public acts of both these rulers.

[13] McCabe, Joseph. *Empresses of Rome.* Holt, 1911. p2
[14] Muir, *op. cit.*, p39
[15] Mozans, *op. cit.*, p21-22
[16] *Ibid.*, p24-25

Then there was the gracious, the virtuous, the self-sacrificing Octavia, sister of the Emperor Augustus, who was so successful in composing grave differences between her brother and her husband, and who so exerted her influence of peace during the troublous times in which she lived that she lives in history as a peacemaker" . . . and "energetic and heroic Agrippina, the wife of Germanicus. In many respects she was the most commanding personality of her age, and exhibited in an eminent degree those stirling qualities which we are wont to associate with the strong, dignified, courageous women of ancient Rome . . ." "She was," as Tacitus informs us, "a greater power in the army than legates and commanders, and she, a woman, had quelled a mutiny which the emperor's authority could not check."

Balsdon tells us of the depicting of famous women of Rome:[17] "The women who are known to us from literature, in the main from the historians and the poets, were those who belonged to, or who interested, the upper class of society in the city of Rome itself. But the artist and the stone-cutter between them have left a different record, and a record which covers a far wider social range. All over Italy and in much of Europe, even in America today the museums are full of their portrait busts. And, for the women of the Caesars, there are coins — coins which, by convention, dispensed in portraiture with the flattering of idealism which was expected of a sculptor. Women were depicted on the wall paintings of since-resurrected houses and villas at Pompeii and elsewhere."

WOMEN IN FRANCE

The influence of certain women on the destinies of their countries is most enlightening. Among such women was Blanche of Castile, queen of France and wife of Louis VIII. According to Muir,[18] she "was an exceptionally talented woman and displayed remarkable executive ability. She personally looked after all the government departments, including the army. With an iron hand she succeeded in quelling numerous revolts that threatened the country. When she surrendered her regency the country was flourishing. . . . No man could have ruled with more ability. Her strength of character made a great impression on France. She was considered one of the most illustrious characters of her time."

We all know the story of Joan of Arc who led France to victory, and we shall not repeat it here. Another woman, born in 1754, was also influential in France's history: Madame Roland. "She swayed the deliberations of statesmen and shook the very throne of France," says Muir.[19] She was a leader of the Girondists. "Her husband, Jean Marie, was also one of the leaders of the Girondists; however, when the mob became rampant he was overcome by despair and fled from the city, leaving his courageous wife to face the menacing populace. She did not know what fear was." Later, when they

[17] Balsdon, John. *Roman women, their history and habits.* Day, 1963. p16
[18] Muir, *op. cit.*, p78
[19] *Ibid.*, p120-212

tried to compel her to disclose the hiding place of her husband, she refused. She is the author of the famous quotation:[20] "O Liberty! How many crimes are committed in thy name!" Madame Roland's husband did not long survive her, for when he heard of his wife's death he took his own life."

Julie Recamier defied Napoleon; Madame Theresa Tallien delivered France from the Reign of Terror. Eleanor, divorced wife of Louis VII of France and wife of Henry II, is said to have "had more influence on the course of history than any other great lady of her time,"[21] according to Stenton. Women controlled France for a long period. Muir expresses it well:[22] "According to the laws of France, a woman cannot rule that country . . . but how the weaker sex must have smiled inwardly when it was aware of how it did rule that country for many years in the manner just described." Eighteenth century France was especially known for its influential women. "As it was," says Kavanagh,[23] "their part was still great and striking. They gave more grace to wit, more daring to philosophy, more generosity to political contests, and more heroism to defeat and death. For those who know how to look beyond the mere surface of history, the action of women in France during the 18th century will not soon be forgotten. She appears in that age — the most remarkable since that of the Reformation — connected with every important question. We behold her giving a stronger impulse to literature and thought; and, like man, earnestly seeking, through all the mists and errors of human knowledge, to solve the great social and political problems which still agitate us in our day: the legacy of the past to the future."

During the reign of the later Valois, women also played an important part, according to Imbert de Saint-Amand:[24] "At no epoch in French history have women played a greater part than under the reigns of the later Valois. Their influence pervades politics, letters, and the arts. They direct public affairs, make and break treaties, share in every intrigue, hazard, and danger of the civil wars. The sovereigns are ruled by women: Francis I, by the Duchess of Étampes, Henry II by Diana of Poitiers, Francis II by Mary Stuart, Charles IX by Catherine de Medici. Mingling in all the pleasures of the court, passionately fond of hunting, riding like intrepid amazons, assisting at tourneys and even duels, chiefly as the occasion of them, plunging headlong into the most audacious enterprises, the women throughout the dramatic and picturesque period, lead a brilliant unquiet life, full of passions, adventures, and perils."

For almost a hundred years France was really ruled by the kings' mistresses, including Madame de Pompadour, Madame de Maintenon and Mistress DuBarry.

[20] *Ibid.*, p122

[21] Stenton, Doris May. *The English woman in history.* Macmillan, 1957. p37

[22] Muir, *op. cit.*, p125

[23] Kavanagh, Julia. *Women in France during the 18th century.* Putnam, 1893, v. 2. p259

[24] Saint-Amand, Imbert de. *Women of the Valois court.* Scribner, 1895. p123

MORE GREAT QUEENS AND ADVISORS

There are many great queens whose reigns have been outstanding for good works and great accomplishment. Martia, queen of the Britons, was one of these. "She was the widow of Gutiline, King of the Britons," says Muir,[25] "and was surnamed Proba, or the Just. She was left protectress of the realm during the minority of her son. Perceiving much in the conduct of subjects which needed reformation, she devised sundry wholesome laws, which the Britons after her death named Martian statutes. Alfred caused these laws to be restored in the realm. These Martian laws embraced trial by jury and the just descent of property. It is no wonder Alfred the Great saw how fair and impartial these laws were, and even though they were devised by a woman, he used them as a basis for the just laws he is always given so much credit for. Edward the Confessor said: 'There is every reason to suppose that the common law of England, attributed to Alfred the Great, was by him derived from the laws first established by a British queen, Martia.'"

"One of the most brilliant reigns in English history was that of the Queen Anne . . ." says Muir.[26] "It was through her efforts that the union between England and Scotland was effected." The reign of Elizabeth I is well-known for its glory, and Muir describes her reign:[27] "For 45 years she wielded the sceptre, and during that time England grew and flourished like a bay tree, and its prestige rose mightily. While Elizabeth held the helm, the ship of state was guided through many tempestuous seas and brought at last to a haven of greatness the nation had never known before."

William Pitt is known for his greatness, but how many know the power back of his accomplishment? Muir[28] tells us that William Pitt "was the most dominant figure in the English politics that had arisen in many generations, yet back of that power were the hands and mind of a remarkable woman. This woman advised Pitt on all state matters and she was his trusted confidante; he allowed her full scope in the exercise of his imperious will. During Pitt's incumbency in office it was actually a woman that guided England!" This woman was Lady Hester Stanhope, who later ruled over wild Arab tribes on Mt. Lebanon in Palestine.

Of Austria's famous queen, Maria Theresa, Muir says:[29] "She was one of the great queens of history. Elizabeth is probably the most famous, Victoria, the most beloved, Catherine of Russia, the most brilliant, but for courage, intellect and sincerity, none surpassed the great Maria Theresa of Austria; while as a wife and mother her record is scarcely approached by any queen. . . . the only woman ruler of the Hapsburg dynasty, but she accomplished more than any of the others, for she prevented the disintegration

[25] Muir, *op. cit.*, p69-70
[26] *Ibid.*, p111
[27] *Ibid.*, p95
[28] *Ibid.*, p139-140
[29] *Ibid.*, p133-134

of the empire . . . It is noteworthy that it was a woman who raised Austria to one of the greatest powers of the civilized world. Without a doubt she wrote the most brilliant chapter in the history of that nation. Her antagonist, Frederick II, said of her: 'She prepared in the secrecy of the cabinet thought-projects, which she afterwards carried into execution. She introduced an order of accounting into her finances unknown to her ancestors. To introduce better discipline into her army she formed camps and personally visited them that she might animate her troops. The army required such a degree of perfection as it had never attained under any of her predecessors, and a woman thus accomplished designs worthy of a great man.' "

Russia has had two remarkable queens, Catherine I and Catherine II, both of whom raised that country to new heights. About Catherine II, the Great, Muir tells us:[30] "She soon won their admiration by the vigor and brilliance of her administration, and by the way she built up the military and political strength of her country. Under her, Russia was established as the leading power in the Near East and in the Crimea."

---

[30] *Ibid.*, p130

III. WOMEN AS PATRIOTS AND MILITARY LEADERS

Since ancient times women have taken part in wars. They have never shirked from actual participation in war when necessary, and they have been heroines. They have planned, executed and taken part in many battles, unbelievable though this may be. Joan of Arc and Molly Pitcher are probably the only ones stressed in history books. Mary Beard[1] tells us of ". . . efforts on the part of many women in ancient times to use war as an instrument of policy in defending themselves and their realms against the overweening military power of imperial Rome. But if Cleopatra is to be singled out, so also must be Zenobia, Queen of Palmyra on the border of the Arabian desert. Zenobia admired Cleopatra but Zenobia operated more directly in actual military exploits, and was more spectacular in her flaming determination to extend her dominions. . . . She was however not an arm-chair strategist, for she donned military attire, joined her troops, and 'shared their toils on horseback and on foot. Besieged in Palmyra and refusing to make a compromise peace, Zenobia fell into Roman hands."

"Nor were all women passive observers," continues Beard,[2] "and silent victims of the numerous wars waged under the sanction of religion in far-off times and places. The love of power and strife that motivated Zenobia likewise characterized women of Arabia in the Islamic age. With a fury that may be fairly described as tigerish, women waged holy wars for and against the faith proclaimed by Mohammed. While the Prophet was still alive, one of his fiercest foes was a woman of a great clan called Hind, Hind-al-Hunud, 'the Hind of Hinds' . . . Imperial power[3] required the backing of physical force and actual or potential warfare. Among the women who did not shrink from war when their power was at stake was Julia Maesa, aunt of Caracella. . . . Julia Maesa knew how to procure her army and how to hold the soldiers together and make them fight successfully if attacked by the troops of Macrinus. When her men seemed to be wavering in their allegiance to her, Maesa inflamed their loyalty by ordering one of her daughters, Seemis, to hold aloft in their presence her little lad, Varius Avitus . . . At a crucial point in this course, Julia Maesa and her daughters left their chariots and lashed their troops into a hotter tempo, if only by their tongues and frantically waving arms. At the end the day was won for Julia Maesa. . . ."

Balsdon tells us of certain formidable women of Britain[4] who, when they opposed a Roman landing in Anglesey in A.D. 60, "brandished torches and looked like Furies, clad in black, their hair in disorder, or the chaste women of Germany, such women as Caracella's captives who, asked if they preferred death or slavery, replied 'Death,' and when they were sold into slavery, cheated their purchasers by killing themselves and their children too."

[1] Beard, Mary. *Women as force in history.* Macmillan, 1946. p284
[2] *Ibid.,* p283
[3] *Ibid.,* p297
[4] Balsdon, John. *Roman women, their history and habits.* Day, 1963. p18

OTHER FEMALE PATRIOTS

There have been female patriots in every country and age. Minna Schmidt[5] tells us of many. First there was Lascarina Bouboulina, Greek patriot and famous sea heroine who "took over command of fleet, blockaded the seacoast, pursued the Turkish ships, defended the women with sword in hand." Then we have Susanna Lorantffy, Hungarian:[6] "She established boarding-schools, founded scholarships and endowment funds and invited outstanding scientists from other countries as professors . . ." She endowed colleges, established printing presses, "backed" several authors. "Aside from being very kind and generous she was also very devout and did a great deal for better morals. She often assembled her scientists and arranged discussions about religious matters. During the warfare of 1644-45 she was the organizer of the army. She supervised the military operations, she took care of the defense of fortresses, of the care of prisoners."

Ranee of Jhansi (Lakshmi Bai) was an Indian patriot.[7] ". . . Lakshmi Bai became one of the leaders of this Battle of Independence of India against the British, and dressed herself as a man and marched at the head of a highly disciplined army. It was stated by the British general who fought against the army of Lakshmi Bai that never in his life had he seen a greater hero than the general of this army. He did not know it was a woman who was the leader of the opponent. Lakshmi Bai was killed in battle."

Kenau Hasselaer was a Dutch patriot of the Spanish War in 1568. Schmidt tells of her exploits:[8] "The burghers of the town, among them women and children, fought shoulder to shoulder beside those of the garrison. . . . Foremost among these women was Kenau Hasselaer, sprung from a patrician family of Haarlem. History records how she and her sister, Amaron, resisted the assailants with harness on and sword in hand, how they fought in the ramparts and even outside in the thick of the fight, firing the men by their example . . ."

Emilja Plater was a Polish patriot. Schmidt continues:[9] ". . . War was declared with Russia. On hearing the news, Emilja, then 25 years old, rode furiously to the little town of Dusiaty where, by her fiery speeches, the men of the locality were carried away on a wave of patriotism. Here she organized her first detachment; that under her brilliant leadership that was an inspiration not only to them, but to all the others fighting for the freedom of their country, won a series of battles with the Russian regulars, who outnumbered them greatly. She was always at the head of her troops, leading them in the thick of battle." She received commissions as Lieutenant, Captain and Colonel.

[5] Schmidt, Minna. *400 outstanding women of the world.* The author, 1933. p218
[6] *Ibid.*, p228
[7] *Ibid.*, p237
[8] *Ibid.*, p296-297
[9] *Ibid.*, p325

WOMEN OF SCOTLAND

The women of Scotland are notorious for their courage and patriotism. An example is the Marchioness of Hamilton. Anderson describes one of her exploits:[10] "When her son James, marquis, afterward Duke of Hamilton, who sided with Charles I, against the covenanters, conducted an English fleet to the Forth, in 1639, to overawe them, she appeared on horseback, with two pistols by her side, at the head of a troop of horses, among the intrepid thousands who lined the shores of Leith on that occasion, to resist the landing; and, drawing one of her pistols from her saddle-bow, declared she would be the first to shoot him should he presume to land and attack the troops of the covenant. It is said that she even loaded her pistols with balls of gold; but this rests on doubtful authority. It is certain, however, that when the marquis cast anchor in the Forth, near Leith, loitering for the king, whose army was marching into Scotland to his assistance, she paid him a visit on board his vessel. The particulars of this interview have not been recorded; but the people anticipated from it the most favorable results. 'The son of such a mother,' they said 'will do us no harm.' Nor did they suffer any harm. The spirited conduct and intercession of his mother, it is supposed, was one cause which prevented the marquis's debarkation of his troops."

In Harry Graham's *A Group of Scottish Women*,[11] we hear more of Scottish feminine courage. "Women were often to be seen upon the battlefields of those days. King Edward I of England used, it is said, to summon the ladies, as well as the earls and barons of his kingdoms to attend him in war. . . . Even as late as the middle of the 18th century, we find an example of a woman taking a personal part in actual warfare. The Duke of Perth would never have espoused Prince Charles's cause so warmly but for his mother, the duchess, who proclaimed the Chevalier from the battlements of Castle Drummond and recruited a regiment in his behalf. She herself accompanied the Scottish army to England, and at Carlisle, when the expected reinforcements failed to put in an appearance, threatened to lead the troops in person against the enemy. . . .

"Since that day more than one Scotswoman has turned amateur recruiting sergeant. The regiment of Gordon Highlanders was raised by a woman, Jane, Duchess of Gordon. Another Duchess, Elizabeth, Duchess-Countess of Sutherland, when a girl of 12 years, raised a Sutherland regiment, at the time of the American Declaration of Independence, declaring that she was only sorry she could not herself command it.

"This brave child subsequently reviewed her troops, one thousand strong, from the windows of her aunt's house in Edinburgh, and later, in 1793, when she had reached womanhood, exerted herself to raise another corps of "Fencibles" which was eventually embodied in the famous "93rd" Regiment. In our time the successful enlistment of a body of Scottish Horse, which did

10 Anderson, James. *The Ladies of the covenant.* Armstrong, 1880. p35
11 Graham, Harry. *A Group of Scottish women.* Duffield, 1908. p26-28

splendid work in South Africa during the war, was largely due to the exertions and influence of a woman."

But the most memorable siege in Scottish history is said to be that of Black Agnes, 1338, who defended the Castle of Dunbar for five months. "Whenever the fight was the hottest," relates Muir,[12] "Black Agnes could be seen encouraging the men and keeping them at their stations. She repulsed every attack and ignominiously defeated the noted Earl of Salisbury, who was chagrined to find all of his plans checkmated by a woman."

COURAGE IN WARTIME

The story of the "Dames of Weinsberg" is another account of women's courage in wartime, and of the sacrifice women have always made for their men. The Emperor Conrad III was at war with Welf, Duke of Bavaria, and the latter was compelled to surrender. Conrad decided to destroy the town of Weinsberg. Muir describes what followed:[13] "But the women of the town implored him to be merciful, and as a result he finally consented to allow the women their freedom and the privilege of taking with them whatever valuables each one could carry on her back. Imagine the surprise of everybody when, instead of seeing the women emerge with packs of silverware, jewelry, trinkets, and clothing, each woman came out with a man on her back. These brave women considered their husbands, brothers and sweethearts to be their most valuable possessions. The Emperor was much affected by this most extraordinary performance by these loyal women, and the tears came to his eyes as he hastened to assure them that he would keep his word. . . . After this he offered very favorable peace terms to the Guelphs for the settlement of the war and gave credit to these remarkable women for their part in bringing it about."

Agustina Saragoza was the Spanish heroine in the siege of Saragossa by the French in 1808. "The fighting was fiercest around the gate Portillo;" Schmidt relates,[14] "when Agustina arrived with food, not one man was alive. The guns were deserted but some distance away stood a group of men who still remained on duty. Agustina picked up a match from the hand of a dead gunner and fired off a 620 pounder and vowed she would not leave that gun until the end of the siege. Her splendid courage and brilliant example inspired the hesitant group and they rushed to her side to renew the battle. The many attacks against the gate Portillo were always repulsed, but with terrific slaughter on both sides. Agustina remained at her post though the siege lasted 50 days."

The tale of Wanda, queen of Poland during the time of the invasion by German tribes, is another story of great courage:[15] ". . . at the head of her

---

[12] Muir, *op. cit.*, p79
[13] *Ibid.*, p76-77
[14] Schmidt, *op. cit.*, p355
[15] *Ibid.*, p315

army, she repulsed the enemy in several battles. . . . She summoned the council and leaders of the army, and declared her intention of giving her life for the sake of the people. In spite of their entreaties, she threw herself from the battlements of the Castle of Kraków into the river below, the Wisla, and sacrificed herself for the good of her nation. Wanda shall live forever in the memories of her people not only as a queen and a successful leader in battle, but as a true woman, to whom no sacrifice is too great. And through the entire history of Poland, for more than a thousand years, the heroic deeds of Polish women have become immortal."

Doris Stenton tells us of Britain's patriots.[16] "It is clear that women could ride as well as men, plan campaigns, and direct the defenses of a castle. In 1075 Emma, wife of the rebel Earl of Norfolk, was left in her husband's castle of Norwich while he escaped oversea. She held the castle until she was given a safe-conduct to leave the country. Twenty years later the wife of the rebel Earl of Northumbria only surrendered Bamburgh Castle to William II because he threatened to blind her husband, whom he captured. Nichola de la Haia, the wife of Gerard de Camville, Sheriff of Lincoln, had brought to her husband the hereditary office of constable of Lincoln Castle. With him she was besieged in Lincoln in 1191, and twenty-five years later, as a widow, she herself held the castle against the king's rebels."

"Charlotte Stanley," Lady Stenton continues,[17] "proved herself a competent commander in war by her successful defense of Lathom House in 1644 against a Parliamentarian army."

Margaret of Anjou, British queen who championed the cause of her husband, Henry VI of England, in the War of Roses, was another English patriot. "Margaret would never accept defeat," says Muir,[18] "but fought battle after battle in an effort to maintain her husband's rights and to preserve the throne for her son. She was the very heart and soul of the struggle and was always an inspiration to her troops. Due to her valiant efforts the Lancasterians were enabled to continue their fighting for many years."

France has had many heroines, including the great Joan of Arc. Julia Kavanagh[19] tells of a few of them: "Madame de Beauglie, attired like an amazon, a carbine in her hand commanded 30 cavaliers, equipped and salaried at her expense, on the coast of La Vendee. The young and handsome Madame de Fief, distinguished herself in the army of Charrettel who, without joining the great body of insurgents, kept up a brisk and separate warfare on the sea-shore. Of the peasant women who thus took up arms, only one survived the civil war: her real name was Joanne Bordereau; she was generally called L'Angevin, from the province of Anjou, whence she came."

---

[16] Stenton, op. cit., p37
[17] Ibid., p152
[18] Muir, op. cit., p85
[19] Kavanagh, Julia. Women in France during the 18th century. Putnam, 1893, v. 2. p198

AMERICAN WOMEN IN WARS: THE REVOLUTION

American women have always adapted themselves to conditions of war-time and met all emergencies that have arisen. They have aided men in every way humanly possible, and in the early wars of the nation they some-times played an active part in America's defense. The story of Molly Pitcher is perhaps the best known and we shall briefly tell it, according to Muir:[20] "Her husband was gunner in the Revolution. When he fell she took up his gun. She did it with such skill and accuracy that General Greene permitted her to continue her efficient firing. Her efforts contributed greatly toward the winning of the battle, and saved the cannon from capture by the British." General Washington gave her a lieutenant's commission and placed her name on the Roll of Honor.

Our favorite story of the Revolution is little-known, but thrilling, and should be in every history book. William F. Fowler relates it in his book:[21] "The winter at Valley Forge was the darkest season in the Revolutionary struggle. The American army were sheltered by miserable huts, through which the rain and sleet found their way upon the wretched cots where the patriots slept. By day the half-famished soldiers in tattered regimentals wandered through the camp, and the snow showed the bloody tracks of their shoeless feet. Mutinous mutterings disturbed the sleep of Washington, and one dark, cold day, the soldiers at dusk were on the point of open revolt. Nature could endure no more, and not from want of patriotism, but from want of food and clothes, the patriotic cause seemed likely to fail. Pinched with cold and wasted with hunger, the soldiers pined beside their dying camp-fires. Sud-denly a shout was heard from the sentinels who paced the outer lines, and at the same time a cavalcade came slowly through the snow up the valley. Ten women in carts, each cart drawn by ten pairs of oxen, and bearing tons of meal and other supplies, passed through the lines amid cheers that rent the air. Those devoted women had preserved the army, and Independence from that day was assured."

Another memorable incident of the Revolution shows the patriotic daring of women. Retold from Butler's *History of Groton,* Elizabeth Ellet gives us the story in her book:[22] "The patriotism of the women in these times 'which tried men's souls,' must not be passed over in silence. After the departure of Colonel Prescott's regiment of 'minutemen,' Mrs. David Wright of Pepperell, Mrs. Job Shattuck of Groton, and the neighboring women, collected at what is now called Jewett's Bridge, over the Nashua, between Pepperell and Groton, clothed in their absent husbands' apparel, and armed with muskets, pitchforks, and such other weapons as they could find; and having elected Mrs. Wright their commander, resolutely determined that no foe to freedom, foreign or

---

[20] Muir, *op. cit.,* p145
[21] Fowler, William F. *Women on the American frontier.* Scranton, 1877. p136-137
[22] Ellet, Elizabeth R. *The Women of the American Revolution.* George W. Jacobs & Co., 1900, v. 2. p295

domestic, should pass that bridge. For rumors were rife, that the regulars were approaching, and frightful stories of slaughter flew rapidly from place to place, and from house to house.

"Soon there appeared one on horseback, supposedly to be treasonably engaged in conveying intelligence to the enemy. By the implicit command of Sergeant Wright, he is immediately arrested, unhorsed, searched, and the treasonable correspondence found concealed in his boots. He was detained prisoner, and sent to Oliver Prescott, Esquire, of Groton, and his despatches were sent to the Committee of Safety. . . . The officer thus taken prisoner being a politic gentleman, and probably experienced in the tactics of gallantry, endeavored, when thus arrested and disarmed, to win his way by kissing his fair captors. But they were proof against his arts as well as his arms."

And so, we have given you a few examples of courage and patriotism, but there are many, many more obscure stories not found in the usual history books. For instance, there is the story of Tymicha, the Greek philosopher, who bit off her tongue rather than reveal the secrets of her tormenting tyrant; Lacna, an Athenian, did likewise. And in the modern age, what story can match the courage of Mrs. Isidor Straus, who turned back from a lifeboat of the sinking *Titanic* and rejoined her husband, to die, saying "We have been together many years; where you go I will go."

IV. WOMEN IN RELIGION

From ancient to modern times, women have had an active part in religion, both as foundresses and active participants. Edith Deen gives her opinion on their lack of recognition in church literature:[1] "Because I often had to search so far and so hard to run down a paragraph of information, I realized all the more than the contribution of women to the life and witness of the Church has never received just treatment in the hands of church historians. The reason may well be that while men discussed and disputed, the women continued quietly to witness and instruct their children in the faith.

"I also began to realize," continued Miss Deen, "as I worked with women of many kinds of faith and work — Catholics and Protestants, mystics and missionaries, writers and mothers — that lead to God but all have the same goal. I saw too that these women were real apostles, for there is no apostleship without the acceptance of suffering, isolation, misunderstanding and solitariness. Christ moves and oftentimes amid such conditions. I saw too that it is individuals sometimes little sung in history, working through God-given spiritual power, who supremely guide civilization."

Charles Muir tells of the influence of two women in the Christian and Mohammedan religions:[2] "The Virgin Mary has been idolized by the people, and down through the ages musicians, architects, poets and artists have vied with one another in celebrating her praise and according her the greatest honor. . . . Mary was and will ever be the one type of perfect motherhood. She was the greatest, noblest, sweetest of women. Her prediction '. . . from henceforth all generations shall call me blessed,' has been fulfilled, for untold millions in every land the world over have honoured and even worshipped her." In connection with the Mohammedan religion, he says:[3] ". . . the chances are that there would be no Mohammedan religion today if Mohammed had not married Khadija, a wealthy widow. When Mohammed propounded his new doctrine it was not well received, and when he announced that he was the prophet sent from God, the people were disgusted with him. However, he finally made one convert, and she was his devoted and faithful wife. Khadija dearly loved her husband, and when everyone else was ridiculing him, she boldly stated that she believed in him and his new religion. She was the first to acknowledge her faith in Mohammedanism, and to prove her loyalty she turned over her entire wealth to him to use in the propagation of his new doctrine."

WOMEN WITH CHRIST

Other writers turn to the crucifixion and the courageous part women played in Christ's ordeal. Michael Faulhaber in his book states:[4] "But without

---

[1] Deen, Edith. *Great women of the Christian faith.* Harper, 1959. pXIII, XIX, Preface
[2] Muir, Charles. *Women, the makers of history.* Vantage, 1956. p49, 53
[3] *Ibid.,* p68
[4] Faulhaber, Michael Cardinal. *The Women of the Bible.* Newman Press, 1955. p184-185, 187-188

any exaggeration we may well assert that the women stood the test of the hour of the Passion better than the men and gave brave witness to their knowledge of the Cross-bearer. He has given us no words spoken by the women; it was their deeds which bore witness to the Crucified. In that tremendous hour of the world's history, therefore, there stood more women than men at His side, at the side of the Lamb of the Sacrifice. On this account the group around the Crucifixion has remained a memorial of honour to the world of women . . ."

"Along with them, however, he was accompanied by another group of women, and their tears wore a courageous confession of faith in the Cross-bearer, and open defense of his innocence, an open protest against the judicial murder of the God-Man who had healed their sick and blessed their children. . . . Veronica, a lady of rank, without troubling about the mockery of the crowd in front of her villa, offered our Saviour her own veil to wipe the blood and sweat from His Face, and our Saviour with a look of thanks gave her back the veil with His portrait painted in His Blood upon it.

"Thus were the very first Easter tidings given to women, and women were chosen to carry to the apostles the joyful messages with the Easter greeting from Him who had arisen. . . . Those who had been loyal to him till his death, should be the first to sing the Allelulia for his Life. One of the truest of the true from Good Friday 'til Easter Day was Mary of Magdelan. . . . And behold — really, Magdalen was permitted to be the first to see and worship Him arisen."

Muir[5] mentions another: "At the time of Christ's trial, when all others had forsaken Him, it was one lonely woman that had a good word to say for Him and tried to save Him from death." This was Procula, wife of Pontius Pilate. . . . "And then at the cross . . . the three Marys stood by Him to the last."

About another little-known woman of the Bible, an interesting fact is given by Eveleen Harrison:[6] ". . . Anna — called the mother of the Temple. Our interest in her story is focused on the supreme historical fact that she is recorded as the first woman publicly to recognize and acknowledge Jesus Christ as the Messiah, the Anointed One of God."

CHRISTIANS CHANGE HISTORY

Other Christian converts who changed the course of history included another Anna, wife of Vladimir, who turned Russia to Christianity. According to Muir,[7] "Vladimir was likened to Solomon. Not only was he wise but history informs us he had many wives, in addition to 800 concubines. Even though he was interested in the welfare of the people, he was profligate and his licentiousness knew no bounds. But a remarkable and unbelievable change

[5] Muir, *op. cit.*, p225
[6] Harrison, Eveleen. *Little known women of the Bible.* Round Table Press, 1936. p102
[7] Muir, *op. cit.*, p72

came over the King due to the influence of one woman." He married Anna, sister of Constantine IX, who married him provided he become a Christian. "Seldom has a ruler been more loved, and since his death in 1015 he has been venerated as a saint and declared to be equal to an apostle. Such was his record. Back of it all was Anna, his Christian wife, with whom he lived happily for 23 years, and to whom should be given the honor of bringing about this good."

Another early woman whose religious influence was great was Theodora, the "Senatrix," not to be confused with the Theodora who was born 508 A.D. "This Theodora," says Muir,[8] "was not a ruler, but her influence was so great in the 10th century, that popes were seated in the papal chair or deposed at her bidding. Never before or since has a woman gained such ascendancy over papal affairs."

To a woman, also, must be given the credit of turning France from Paganism: Clotilda. "To her," continues Muir,[9] "belongs the honor of making France a Christian nation. The Frankish king had married Clotilda, the daughter of the Burgundian King. She was a Christian, and for 3 years after her marriage had made every effort to have her pagan husband turn to her religion without success. Finally, in 496, when engaged in a great battle at Tolbiac, and being hard-pressed, as a last resort he invoked the aid of Clotilda's God and promished to become a Christian if the Lord would give him his victory." He won, and the religious history of France was changed.

Hilda, Abbess of Whitby, was an Englishwoman of religion who wielded great influence and at least one ancient historian gave her credit. She was "the foundress and ruler of a large double monastery at Whitby," says Lady Stenton.[10] "Few English women have ever exercised a more far-reaching influence on the world they knew. Her reputation brought her visitors from far and wide for advice and help. But it is the educational work carried out under her direction which sets her apart from other women of her rank and calling. In an age when the spread of Christianity in England was hindered by the fewness of priests, many of Hilda's monks were brought to a degree of learning adequate to the priesthood. Bede, the greatest of Anglo-Saxon historians, states that he had known 5 bishops each of whom had been educated at Whitby in her time. No record of her personality has survived, but it is at least clear that she was sensible and sympathetic when Caedmon, a cowherd on her estate, suddenly found himself capable of composing sacred verse. It was with her encouragement that he became the first religious poet in the English language."

"It is not generally known," states Muir,[11] "but it is true nevertheless, that England was Christianized through the influence of one woman." That

[8] Muir, *op. cit.*, p65-66
[9] Muir, *op. cit.*, p62
[10] Stenton, Doris Mary. *The English woman in history.* Macmillan, 1957. p13
[11] Muir, *op. cit.*, p7

woman was Queen Bertha, a Christian princess, who married King Ethelbert in 560 A.D.

Mozans describes the religious contributions of two other great women:[12] "Special mention should be made of Paula and her daughter Eustochium; for it is probable that, had it not been for their influence on Jerome, and their active cooperation in his great life work, we should not have the Latin version of the Scriptures that is today known as the Vulgate. . . . They aided him not only by their sympathy and by purchasing for him, often at a great price, the manuscripts he needed for his colossal undertaking, but also assisted him by their thorough knowledge of Latin, Greek and Hebrew in translating the Sacred books from the original Hebrew into Latin. So great was Jerome's confidence in their scholarship and so high was his appreciation of their ability and judgment that he did not hesitate to submit his translations to them for their criticism and approval. . . . And they did read and compare and criticize. And more than this, they frequently suggested modifications and corrections, which the great man accepted with touching humility and incorporated in a revised copy."

Anna De Koven tells us that the[13] "Bringer of Christianity to the first kingdom of France, Clothilde, may well be included among the women who have wrought revolution in the history of mankind."

SAINTS OF GREAT INFLUENCE

We find many saints of great influence in the history of religion. St. Hildegarde was one of these. H. J. Mozans[14] tells us that she "was for a third of a century the abbess of the convent of St. Rupert at Ningen. So great was her reputation for sanctity and for the extent and variety of her attainments that she was called "the marvel of Germany." She is without doubt one of the most beautiful and imposing as well as one of the greatest figures of the Middle Ages — great beside such contemporaries as Abelard, Martin of Tours and Bernard of Clairvaux. People from all parts of the Christian world sought her counsel; and her convent at Bingen became a Mecca for all classes and women. But nothing shows better the immense influence which she wielded than her letters of which hundreds have been preserved. Among her correspondents were people of the humble walks of life as well as the highest representatives of Church and State. There were simple monks and noble abbots, dukes, kings and queens; archbishops and cardinals and no fewer than four Popes. . . . It is safe to say that no woman during the Middle Ages exercised a wider or more beneficent influence than did this humble Benedictine abbess of Bingen on the Rhine and had unsought so large a number of distinguished correspondents. And, if we accept the criterion that influence is measured by the number and nature of one's relations, it would be

[12] Mozans, H. J., pseud. *Woman in science.* Appleton, 1913. p46-47
[13] Koven, Anna De. *Women in cycles of culture.* Putnam, 1941. p10
[14] Stenton, Doris May . *The English woman in history.* Macmillan, 1957. p13

difficult to find in any age relations that were more select or more cosmopolitan. But her astonishing collection of letters is the slightest product of her intellectual activity. She is without doubt the most voluminous woman writer of the Middle Ages. Her works on theology, Scripture and science make no less than six or eight huge octavo volumes . . ."

Another saint of unusual influence was Catherine of Siena. Deen describes her:[15] "No woman in history understood church matters better than the fourteenth-century saint, Catherine of Siena, who was born at a time of nearly unequalled church corruption. No woman was more uncompromising or more relentless in carrying out what she felt was the will of God. She influenced kings and queens and popes alike, and her last six years were a long martyrdom of service to the Church. Her prayers, miracles, healings, writings, and her life — all place her among the great women saints of history. No Christian woman has surpassed Catherine of Siena in sacrifice and devotion. No one has borne more flaming witness to the Unseen, to its inexhaustible fountains of Love. No one has fought against vice, disease and death with greater courage. No woman has attacked church corruption with such vigor. Catherine of Siena's life reveals an extraordinary blend of mystical faith and practical Christian service."

In Italy lived the great Saint Clara. "She was," says Mozans,[16] "as is well known, the ardent cooperator of St. Francis of Assisi in his great work of social and religious reform which has contributed so much toward the welfare of humanity. But it is not generally known what an important part she had in this great undertaking, and how she sustained the Poverello during long hours of trial and hardship. . . . She defended Francis not only against others but also against himself. In those hours of dark discouragement which so often and so profoundly disturb the noblest souls and sterilize the grandest efforts ,she was beside him to show the way. . . ."

NEW DENOMINATIONS

The work and influence of women in the formation of new denominations is great. "Jane Corneigle Campbell (1763-1835), wife of Thomas Campbell and mother of Alexander Campbell, founders of the Christian Church (Disciples of Christ), imparted to her husband and son the bold independence of her French Huguenot ancestry" states Deen.[17] "From the time of their marriage in 1787 she was an inspiration to her husband Thomas. . . . To her son, whose practical leadership and zeal as a reformer helped to develop the Christian churches (Disciples of Christ), the first major Protestant movement nurtured in America, she gave respect for individual rights, love for liberty and dauntless courage." Her son wrote of her: 'She made a nearer approximation beau ideal of a truly Christian mother than any one of her sex with whom I have had the pleasure of forming a special acquaintance . . . Mother Campbell,

---

[15] Deen, *op. cit.*, p50, 60
[16] Mozans, *op. cit.*, p358
[17] Deen, *op. cit.*, p375, 378

in sympathy with the afflicted, the poor, the orphan, and the friendless, was, in my area of observation, rarely equaled, and seldom, if ever, surpassed.' Her son also added that 'Woman, next to God, makes the living world of humanity. She makes man what he is in the world, and very frequently makes him what he shall hereafter be in the world to come.' Such a woman was Jane Corneigle Campbell."

"How much the Kingdom of God has owed to godly women!" states Principal D. W. Lambert.[18] "We think of Monica, the saintly mother of Augustine, of Susanna Wesley, whose wise counsel and training meant so much to the founder of Methodism, and of Catherine Booth, without whose practical sagacity and faith the Salvation Army would never have come into being. To these names must be added Margaret Fell, who has rightly been described as "The Mother of Quakerism!" '

Antoinette Brown Blackwell was another religious pioneer, the first woman in all the Christian world to become a regular clergyman.

Mabel Peyton and Lucia Kinley[19] describe Susanna Wesley: "Mrs. Wesley had read much, and thus both logic and metaphysics had formed part of her studies . . . she gave spiritual wealth to her well-beloved family. There is no doubt that it was her careful early training of them which developed their sterling characters."

In regard to the founding of American Methodism, Inez Irwin states:[20] "Some historians call Barbara Heck of New York the real founder of Methodism in the United States. At least, she inspired her kinsman, Robert Strawbridge, to begin preaching the Wesleyan doctrine and to organize in 1766 our first Methodist Episcopal Church. Very likely, having as yet no governing body of male theologians to prevent, she herself preached."

Last but not least is the great founder of Christian Science, Mary Baker Eddy. Deen[21] quotes Norman Vincent Peale in a recent thought-provoking statement: "Years ago, all sorts of smart people laughed unroariously at the statement of Mary Baker Eddy that matter did not exist, that it was an error of mortal mind. But only a few yesterdays ago, man split the atom and discovered, indeed, that there is no such thing as matter: that energy is all. Whether or not we agree with Mrs. Eddy's theology, we cannot deny that somehow, if only by accident or coincidence, she anticipated the most important scientic discovery of our age."

We conclude our summary of women's place in religion by quoting two lines from Proverbs:[22]

> "Give her the fruit of her hand
> And let her works praise her in the gates."

[18] Lambert, Principal D. W. *The Quiet in the land.* Epworth Press, 1956. p21

[19] Peyton, Mabel Bartlee and Lucia Kinley. *Mothers, makers of men.* Dodge, 1927. p86, 88

[20] Irwin, Inez Haynes. *Angels and Amazons.* Doubleday, Doran, 1933. p56

[21] Deen, *op. cit.*, p219

[22] *Bible*, Proverbs, Chap. 31, line 31

V. WOMEN IN THE FINE ARTS

In the fine arts, women have made outstanding contributions, not only as participants, but also as influential wives and mothers of great artists and musicians. In the earlier days, women were sometimes prohibited from participation, and, in many cases not recognized if they did achieve greatness. Several of our most important male artists and musicians published works of women, especially relatives, under their own names.

Arthur Elson[1] gives a good history of such discrimination, dating from ancient times. In ancient Egypt, for instance, he says . . . "women were not allowed to play the flute, but could indulge in the tabor and other instruments." "The early Christian church, too,"[2] he continues, "afforded no encouragement for women to exert their musical abilities. When the earliest meetings occurred in catacombs, the female members of the congregation took their part in singing the hymns, but, when organized choirs were formed, they were allowed no place. The singing-schools founded in Rome by the Popes Sylvester I and Hilary, at the end of the fourth century, were devoted solely to the training of male voices . . . the custom of permitting women to join with men in the singing was abolished by the Synod of Antioch in the year 379."

FAMOUS ARTISTS AND PATRONS

"Isabelle D'Este . . . was acclaimed by her contemporaries as 'the first lady of the world' according to H. J. Mozans.[3] "She has been described as one who secured everything to which she took a fancy. She had but to hear of the discovery of a beautiful antique, a rare work in bronze or a marble uncovered by the spade of the excavator, when she forthwith made an effort to procure it for her priceless collection. She aimed at supremacy in everything artistic and intellectual, and would be content with nothing short of perfection . . ."

Clara Waters, who writes of women in the fine arts[4] tells us: "Laya, who lived about a century before the Christian era, is important. She is honored as the original painter of miniatures, and her works are greatly esteemed."

Waters continues, telling of the varied practices in different countries[5] . . . "the advantages of the American Art Academy in Rome are not open to women. The fact that for centuries women have been members and professors in the Academy of St. Luke . . . the narrowness of the American Academy in the Eternal City is especially pronounced. One can but approve the encouragement afforded women artists in France, by the generosity with which their excellence is recognized. To be an officer in the French Academy is an

---

[1] Elson, Arthur and Everett E. Truelt. *Woman's work in music.* New rev. ed. Page, 1931. p18
[2] *Ibid.,* p36-37
[3] Mozans, H. J. *Woman in science.* Appleton, 1913. p310-311
[4] Waters, Clara. *Women in the fine arts.* Houghton Mifflin, 1904. p.xii
[5] *Ibid.,* p2

honor surpassed in France by the Legion of Honor only. Within a twelve month 275 women have been distinguished, 28 of them being painters and designers."

An example of a talented French artist was Mrs. Felicité Chastanier Thurwanger who achieved greatness in spite of early discouragement. Waters writes:[6] "Mme. Thurwanger was the pupil of Delaroux during five years. The master unconsciously did his pupil an injury by saying to her father: 'That daughter of yours is wonderfully gifted, and if she were a man I would make a great artist of her.' Hearing this, the young artist burst into tears and her whole career was clouded by the thought that her sex prevented her being a really great artist, and induced in her an abnormal modesty. This remarkable artist . . . when 84 years old, sent to the exhibition at Nice — which is, in a sense, a branch of the Paris salon — three portraits which she had just finished. They were hung in the place of honor and unanimously voted to belong to the first class."

Many famous artists credit their mother with the influence and encouragement which made them great. Benjamin West is one of these. "It was the encouragement he got from his mother that stimulated Benjamin's interest in painting . . ." states Archer Wallace,[7] "it was his mother, who, more than any other person, influenced Benjamin and encouraged him in every way. . . . Her name was Sarah Pearson West."

Peyton and Kinley quote John Ruskin as saying about his mother's influence:[8] "I am sure that being forced to make all I could out of very little things, and to remain long contented with them, not only in great part formed the power of close analysis in my mind, and the habit of steady contemplation, but rendered the power of greater art over me, when I first saw it, as intense as that of magic, so that it appeared to me like a vision out of another world . . . She taught him the lesson of hard work, developed in him intellectual sincerity and love of justice. His life work consisted chiefly in the appreciation of beauty and its interpretation for those less richly endowed."

"Recent investigations," says Waters,[9] "make it probable that certain pictures which have for generations been attributed to Frans Hals were the work of Judith Leyster."

We shall make no attempt to list the great women artists, as the large number listed in this book speak for themselves, including Rosa Bonheur and countless others.

"UNSUNG" MUSICIANS

Fanny Mendelssohn, sister of Felix Mendelssohn, was a wonderful musician. Elson and Truelt tell us:[10] "Like her brother, she was a composer of

[6] *Ibid.*, p336

[7] Wallace, Archer. *Mothers of famous men.* Smith, 1931. p37-38

[8] Peyton, Mabel Bartlett and Lucia Kinley. *Mothers, makers of men.* Dodge, 1927. p91-92, 96

[9] Waters, *op. cit.*, p382

[10] Elson, *op. cit.*, p127

note. At first, however, he objected to her publishing her works, on account of her sex, and half a dozen of her songs without words were brought out among his own[11] . . . it is only in the last few decades that woman's inalienable right to compose has been established. The trials of Carlotta Ferrari in getting her first opera performed are an example in point. The opposition of Mendelssohn to the publication of even a few minor works is another instance of the attitude formerly taken by even the greatest composers. The life of Chaminade affords still another case of this opposition. When Rubinstein heard a few of her early compositions, upon which he was asked to pass an opinion, he could not gainsay their excellence, but insisted on adding that he thought women ought not to compose. . . . The cases of Clara Schumann, Alice Mary Smith (Mrs. Meadows-White) and Ingeborg von Bronsart afford ample proof, to say nothing of our own Mrs. Beach."

History is full of examples of mothers and wives of famous men who have aided them in their own field and given up their own ambitions. Elson[12] gives the stories of some of them, including Bach's second wife, Anna Magdalena Wulken who was a fine musician and a Cöthen court singer for twenty-one years. "She was a good musician and did much to enliven the domestic circle by her beautiful soprano voice. Not content in merely taking part in her husband's work, she learned from him to play the clavier and read figured bass, and rendered him invaluable aid by copying music for him. Soon after her marriage, Bach and his wife started a manuscript book, entitled 'Clavier Büchlein von Anna Magdalena Bach, Anno 1720.' "

Carl Maria Von Weber married the excellent singer Caroline Brandt. "At first," Elson continues,[13] "she was not willing to sacrifice her career, but did — when he obtained a life position as conductor in Dresden. The newly wedded pair made a triumphant concert tour, and settled down to a life of domestic felicity in Dresden. It can hardly be said that Weber lived happily ever afterward, for he found many troubles in connection with his new post. But his married life was such a constant joy to him that he felt always inspired with fresh energy to overcome all difficulties. It was during his married career that he won those immense popular successes . . .

"Ludwig Spohr was another composer who possessed a musical wife. He came of a musical family, his father being a flutist, while his mother played the piano and sang . . . he met Dorette Scheidler, the famous harpist, whom he afterward married. Her influence is seen in his later compositions for he wrote for her a number of sonatas for harp and violin, as well as a good many harp solos. The musical pair went on many tours, always sharing the honours of the performances."

Another musical wife of a famous composer was Wilhelmina (or Minna)

---

[11] *Ibid.*, p234
[12] *Ibid.*, p69
[13] *Ibid.*, p79-81

Planer, first wife of Cosima Wagner. "Their natures," says Elson,[14] "were different in many respects. While he displayed many of the vagaries of genius, she was patient and practical, and, if not wholly understanding the highest side of his nature, she gave up her own career to help him through his days of poverty and struggle." But unfortunately, the marriage ended in divorce.

"Of composers gifted with musical wives," continues Elson,[15] "the most prominent is Richard Strauss . . . at her best when singing her husband's songs."

But one of the happiest of marriages between musicians was probably that of Robert Schumann and Clara Wieck, the latter who was recognized as a musician before her husband but who devoted her life to furthering his recognition as well. "They lived for each other, and for their children," states Elson.[16] "He molded his compositons on lines to suit her artistic nature, and she threw herself ardently into the task of giving these works to the world. Her days were spent in winning fame for him, or in shielding his sensitive and irritable nature from too rude contact with the world. Through Schumann's genius, that of his wife was influenced, and Clara Schumann became far greater than Clara Wieck had ever been. She became a true priestess of art. She did not rest until she gave the world a clear understanding of the depth of thought in his great works. She made her fame serve his, and considered the recognition of his qualities her own reward. Yet it still happened at times that this recognition came slowly, and in Vienna, as late as 1846, he was spoken of merely as the husband of Clara Wieck, and after the court concert given by her, someone turned to him with the question: "Are you musical, too?"

Sybil Sanderson, the operatic singer,[17] "inspired Jules Massenet to produce many of his best works, notably the opera "Esclurmonde," which was written with her in view as performer."

In answer to the criticism that there has been no first rank female composer, Elson had this to say:[18] ". . . in explanation of this is the fact that women have not been generally at work in this field until the last century, while men have had considerably more time."

"These are but a few of the more important instances[19] in musical history, which go to show that woman's influence is responsible for many works in connection with which her name does not appear at first glance. The actual woman composers, however, form a long and honorable list, and are by no means confined to the present period of female emancipation."

[14] *Ibid.*, p86
[15] *Ibid.*, p88
[16] *Ibid.*, p105-106
[17] *Ibid.*, p130
[18] *Ibid.*, p272
[19] *Ibid.*, p130

GREAT ACTRESSES; MISCELLANEOUS

In the acting profession, it is obvious that some of the greatest have been women, such as Sarah Bernhardt, Helena Modjeska, Sarah Kemble Siddon, Helen Hayes. It is also interesting to note that the ancestral tables of many families in America show famous actors and actresses in the family, including Booth, Southern, Boucicault, Hackett, Drew, Barrymore, Wallack, Davenport, Holland and Power. Is it not ridiculous that man, born of woman, should be the reason for greatness in this or any other profession, rather than the factor of heredity? Montrose Moses has this to say:[20] "A record of the famous actor-families in America necessarily includes a survey of the stage in America during practically one hundred years. . . . A student perhaps will take these data and scientifically exemplify, according to Galton, the principles upon which the doctrine of hereditary genius is founded."

In the dance, the names of great feminine artists are perhaps even better known than those of the male, including such names as Pavlova, Isadora Duncan and many ballerinas of today.

Women sculptors should not be forgotten: names such as Vinnie Ream Hoxie, for instance, who modeled the statue of Lincoln in the Capitol Rotunda, as well as the statue of Admiral Farragut. Then there were Harriet Goodhue Hosmer, Mary Frances Thornycroft, Marie Tussaud, Malvina Hoffman, and many others.

It is interesting that the most beautiful building in the world, "the one faultless edifice that has ever been reared," says Charles Muir,[21] "was the result of one woman's noble life." That was the exquisite Taj Mahal, inspired by Mumtz Mahal. How could there be a more appropriate memorial to woman, in art?

[20] Moses, Montrose, F. *Famous actor-families in America.* Crowell, 1906. p12-13
[21] Muir, Charles S. *Women, the makers of history.* Vantage, 1956. p107

VI. WOMEN IN LITERATURE

It may come as a surprise, as it did to us, to learn that the world's first novel, *The Tale of the Genji,* a product of eleventh century Japan, was authored by a woman — Lady Murasaki!

Although the place of women in literature is well recognized today, it wasn't true, at least in English-speaking countries, a few centuries ago. A few women chose to use male pseudonyms to assure the recognition which they could not receive otherwise.

RECOGNITION OF WOMEN WRITERS

B. G. MacCarthy expresses this opinion:[1] ". . . but there was another consideration, which, from the beginning of women's literary adventuring had loomed large, and greatly affected their work and their status. This was the condemnatory attitude of the reading public towards women writers. Masculine condemnation of women's quill-driving was "compounded of many simples" but chiefly of a double fear: fear that women's new occupation might change their attitude towards domestic and social duties, and fear that women's achievements might eclipse those of men. For countless ages women have been given the sort of education which fitted them to become wives and mothers in this world, and saints either here or hereafter. These activities were conducive towards man's happiness, and were no encroachment on the territory he was accustomed to consider as peculiarly his own. But if women were to realize themselves in some separate way, if they, like men, should have an intellectual life, which, of necessity, must be led alone and which, as man knew, was richly self-rewarding, might not women become intolerable from the man's point of view? That is to say, not merely preoccupied with other than domestic details, but no longer looking up to man as the arbiter of her fate."

Agnes Rogers gives her viewpoint:[2] "I don't think you can measure their various accomplishments by the same yardstick. However, when one comes upon a field where the performance of women may be justly compared with that of man, it is interesting to see the results. By "justly" I mean that no artificial or extraneous conditions enter the picture. This is particularly true in the field of writing. Granted that some women formerly thought it advisable to use a masculine nom de plume for purposes of modesty or whatever, there is no real discrimination in training, wages, or working conditions in the writing of books. It may be significant that the best-selling books in the United States between 1852 and 1861 were equally divided between the sexes, twelve authors were women, twelve were men. (The titles included *Uncle Tom's Cabin, Walden, John Halifax, Gentleman,* and *East Lynne.*)"

[1] MacCarthy, G. B. *Women writers, their contribution to the English novel, 1621-1744.* Cork University Press, 1944. p19
[2] Rogers, Agnes. *Women are here to stay.* Harper, 1949. p39

The greatest Englishwoman living in the 18th century was Hannah More. Muir[3] quotes John Lord's opinon of her: " 'No one woman in England or the United States ever occupied such an exalted position or exercised such a broad and deep influence on the public mind in the combined character of woman of society, author and philanthropist. Her labors have become historical. She was the representative of the greatest movement of modern times — that which aims to develop the mind and soul of women and give to her the dignity of which she has been robbed by paganism and narrow-minded men.' She was idolized by the people of Great Britain and was famous in the United States also. Her theory was, 'God made man and woman in one flesh and we should not point out any fundamental inferiority or superiority between them.' She was a poetess, writer on moral and religious subjects, lively conversationalist. She taught in a girls' school and started many schools for poor children . . . had so well used the talents that had been entrusted in her."

THE GREATEST POET

Sappho, born 600 B.C., has been called by Swinburne "the greatest poet that ever lived." "This strangely gifted woman," states Muir,[4] "after a lapse of twenty-five centuries, is still said to be the one poet in all the world whose every line has the seal of absolute perfection." Her *Song of Songs* is in the Bible.

"So great was her renown," says Mozans,[5] "among the ancients that she was called 'the Poetess,' as Homer was called 'the Poet.' Solon, on hearing one of her songs sung at a banquet, begged the singer to teach it to him at once that he might learn it and die. Aristotle did not hesitate to endorse a judgment that ranked her with Homer and Archilochus, while Plato, in his Phaedras, exalts her still higher by proclaiming her 'the tenth muse.' Horace and Ovid and Catullus strove to reproduce her passionate strains and rhythmic beauty; but their efforts were little better than paraphrase and feeble imitation. Her features were stamped on coins, 'though she was but a woman,' and, after her death, altars were raised and temples erected in honor of this 'flower of the Graces' . . ."

INFLUENCE ON MALE AUTHORS

Once again is seen the influence and help of women in the lives of successful men. One of these is the aunt of Ralph Waldo Emerson. "Her influence upon the boy's plastic mind," says R. F. Dibble,[6] "can never be accurately known; it is possible, and even probable, that without it he might, like his forefathers, have been just another Reverend Emerson. All his life, she constantly scourged and prodded him to essay higher things. 'Scorn trifles, lift your aims; do what you are afraid to do.' "

[3] Muir, Charles. *Women, the makers of history.* Vantage, 1956. p135-136
[4] *Ibid.,* p31
[5] Mozans, H. J. *Woman in science.* Appleton, 1913. p5-6
[6] Dibble, R. F. *Life of Aunt Mary Emerson* in Balch, Marston, ed. *Modern short biographies.* Harcourt, Brace and Co., 1945. p239

Margaret Isabella Stevenson is credited with the success of Robert Louis Stevenson, according to Peyton and Kinley.[7] "It was, however, to his clever and cultured mother who formed his taste. Perhaps he is indebted to her for his story-telling instinct, for she possessed to the end of her days the art of fascinating her listeners with a simple tale. No wonder the child grew up to be a master of romance, for all the early influences surrounding him fostered this tendency. His mother used to read to him constantly until he learned to read for himself. He was not strong enough to be sent to school until he was nine, and even then his attendance was irregular."

"It is, of course, a matter of literary history,"[8] says Cornelia Otis Skinner, "that the grande homme Léontine de Caillavet discovered, adopted and cultivated . . . Anatole France . . . His success, his fame, was the chief goal of her life . . . took Anatole France firmly in her steady hand and educated him from the ground up. She was responsible for the success of all but three or four of his many books and it was through her efforts that he was eventually admitted to the Academy. She turned herself into a secretary extraordinary for him, editing everything he wrote, gathering endless research material for him, translating useful articles from foreign publications, for she was an accomplished linguist. She took notes during his conversations, and filed them for future use. She brought him new ideas, new facets of erudition, new plots for his novels, new topics for his essays. She worked along with him, and literally so, her writing desk next to his, writing his prefaces for him, sometimes entire chapters of his novels. She herself was a fine author, and could imitate his style. It is not unlikely that France occasionally imitated hers, for he would unconsciously borrow her turn of phrases, accept her ideas, work with them, put them down on paper and eventually believe them to be his own.

"France was well aware of her invaluable assistance and duly grateful. His dedication to *Crainquebille* reads: 'To Mme. de Caillavet, his book which I should not have written without her help, for, without her help, I should not write books.'"

"Anatole France and his Egeria (Mme. de Caillavet) traveled much through Europe.[9] Madame, an avid and scholarly sightseer, would visit every museum, every cathedral, every palace and chateau. In her zeal for expanding her already wide knowledge of art and history, she'd do masses of research — the local libraries, ferreting out new facets of information, any and everything that might prove useful for her great man. The fruitful result of their stay in Florence was France's most popularly successful novel, *The Red Lily*."

THE PRESENT

Margaret Lawrence expresses the present outlook, altho her book was

[7] Peyton, Mabel Bartlett and Lucia Kinley. *Mothers, makers of men.* Dodge, 1927. p105

[8] Skinner, Cornelia Otis. *Elegant wits and horizontals.* Houghton, 1962. p159-160

[9] *Ibid.*, p165-166

written a few decades ago:[10] "After women have put down all the pent-up sorrows of womanhood in a world made for men by men; and after they have satisfied themselves that they can hold whatever they want to get in that world, we shall be racially much further on, no matter what conclusions we may draw, tentatively, or finally, about women and their work.

"For the present we are in the middle of a period of commercial feminism which would have astonished Plato, who in the memory of the race was the first man to take up the cause of women to mind. And what it would do to John Stuart Mill, who in the nineteenth century championed women, is an idea for idle cogitation."

[10] Lawrence, Margaret. *The school of femininity.* Stokes, 1936. p11

VII. WOMEN IN SCIENCE AND INVENTION

"There is no place on earth or in Heaven,
There is no task to mankind given,
There is no joy, there is no woe,
There is no death, there is no birth,
Without a woman in it." . . .
— MINNA MOSCHEROSCH SCHMIDT [1]

And thus we find women prominent in all phases of science and invention since very early times. "Women, as a rule, love science for its own sake," says H. J. Mozans,[2] "and, unlike the specialists in question, they are, in its pursuit, rarely actuated by any selfish or mercenary interests, or by the hope of financial reward. Precise and never-ending observations with the microscope and spectroscope, which at best give them but a superficial knowledge of certain details of science, while it leaves them in ignorance of the greater part of it, do not appeal to them. They prefer general ideas to particular facts, and love to roam over the whole realm of science rather than confine themselves to one of its isolated corners."

VERSATILITY IN SCIENCE; THE ANCIENTS

Women seem to have the capacity for versatility in science which is an unusual trait in this field. A few scientists who worked in more than one field include Emile du Châtelet (astronomy, mathematics, physics), Celia Grille Borromeo (mathematics, languages); Hypatia of Alexandria (mathematics, philosophy, physics, invention), and Saint Hildegard (religion, astronomy, physics).

There are some great names in the ancient world of science, and among them is Hypatia, who lived in the 4th century B.C. Mozans states:[3] ". . . it is certain that she commanded the admiration and respect of all for her great learning, and that she bore the mantle of science and philosophy with so great modesty and self-confidence that she won all hearts. A letter addressed to 'The Muse,' or to 'The Philosopher' was sure to be delivered to her at once. In addition to her works on astronomy and mathematics, Hypatia is credited with several inventions of importance, some of which are in daily use. Among these are an apparatus for determining the specific gravity of liquids — what we should now call an aerometer. Besides these apparatus, she was likewise the inventor of an astrolabe and a planisphere."

"The father of Hypatia," Charles Muir tell us,[4] "Theon, was an astronomer, mathematician and noted teacher of philosophy in Alexandria, Egypt.

---

[1] Schmidt, Minna Moscherosch. *400 outstanding women of the world.* The Author, 1933. p542
[2] Mozans, H. J. *Women in science.* Appleton, 1913. p409
[3] *Ibid.,* p138, 140
[4] Muir, Charles. *Women, the makers of history.* Vantage, 1956. p58

Hypatia became so proficient in philosophy and mathematics that she was able to take her father's place as a teacher of these subjects. A Neoplatonist in her philosophy, and the head of that school, she gave lectures to learned men from all over the East who came to hear her. Hypatia lived a spotless life in a corrupt age. Her constant aim was to inspire others with the love of truth. The people of Alexandria respected and loved her for her learning and the beauty of her character. Even the judges of her courts considered her so wise that they consulted her and sought her advice on the cases submitted to them for adjudication."

"In science," Mozans continues,[5] "Hypatia was among the women of antiquity what Sappho was in poetry and what Aspasis was in philosophy and eloquence — the chiefest glory of her sex. In profundity of knowledge and variety of attainments, she had few peers among her contemporaries, and she is entitled to a conspicuous place among such luminaries of science as Ptolemy, Euclid, Apollonius, Diophantus and Hipparchus."

Two of the great "Seven Wonders of the World" were built by women! Semiramis, in the 9th century B.C., is credited with building the "Hanging Gardens," one of the seven wonders of the world. Another of the great wonders of the world, the Great Mausoleum at Halicarnassus, was built by Artemisia, queen of Caria, in memory of her husband, Mausolus.

"Artemisia was a very learned woman," states Muir.[6] "She had the reputation of being a noted botanist, a medical researcher, and the discoverer and namer of several herbs." (She is not to be confused with the other Artemisa, however, queen of Halicarnassus and Cos.) ". . . the genial author of the Decameron gives special praise to one Arete of Cyrene," Mozans tells us,[7] "for the breadth and variety of her attainments. She was the daughter of Aristippus, the founder of the Cyrenaic school of philosophy, and is represented as being a veritable prodigy of learning. For among her many claims to distinction she is said to have publicly taught natural and moral philosophy in the schools and academies for thirty-five years, to have written forty books, and to have counted among her pupils one hundred and ten philosophers. She was so highly esteemed by her countrymen that they inscribed on her tomb an epitaph which declared that she was the splendor of Greece and possesses the beauty of Helen, the virtue of Thirma, the pen of Aristippus, the soul of Socrates, and the tongue of Homer."

EXPLORERS IN GEOGRAPHY, AVIATION

Inez Irwin[8] tells us of The Society of Women Geographers which lists women discoverers and travellers . . . "Delia Akeley and her long, loving careful study of Africa, Annie S. Peck, most intrepid of women mountain climbers, Harriet Chalmers Adams, Mary Hastings Bradley, Gertrude Emer-

---

[5] Mozans, op. cit., p141
[6] Muir, op. cit., p40
[7] Mozans, op. cit., p197-198
[8] Irwin, Inez. Angels and Amazons. Doubleday, Doran, 1933. p438

son, Marguerite Harrison, Ellen La Motte, Jean Kenyon Mackenzie, Margaret Mead, Muna Lee, Blair Niles, Grace Thompson Seton, Gertrude Selby, Caroline Singer. And for an individual feat, let me cite just one — the exquisite achievement of Amelia Earhart . . . a supreme proof of women's equality in nerve, or verve, mechanical skill and courage."

We should like to add the name of Anne Lindbergh, whom we admire most of all women of today, not only because of her great accomplishment in aeronautics, but also because of her versatility and beauty of soul as expressed in her writing.

It is also interesting to note many other records and "firsts" in the field of aviation, in which women were among the pioneers. Yet women have had to fight harder for equality and recognition in this field of science, perhaps, than in any other. They have been denied the privilege of being full astronauts today in the United States, altho eminently qualified except for superficial requirements. But in Antarctic sea study, we were pleased to learn that two women scientists were allowed to join the recent bacteria-hunting expedition sponsored by the National Science Foundation. In oceanography, also, opportunities are opening for women, and there are some well-known marine biologists and oceanographers making places for themselves in this new frontier.

OTHER SCIENTISTS, ASSISTANTS

Jane Loudon, Englishwoman, was the wife of John Claudius Loudon, famous horticulturist, and did much to aid his work because he only had one arm. "Jane married John Claudius Loudon," according to Buckner Hollingsworth,[9] "just in time to help him with his 4th major work, 'The Architecture of cottage, farm and villa architecture." As soon as she married him Jane became his amanuensis. In place of a honeymoon she took his dictation which she transcribed into the manuscript of the bulky encyclopedia which ran when published to 1,150 pages of fine print. Jane was to recount later how for months they sat up all night, night after night, working and drinking strong coffee to keep themselves awake. It would have been a vigorous beginning for any marriage."

Many other scientific women, including American pioneers, achieved their goals under the most difficult of situations. We especially like the story of Mary Richardson Walker, pioneer and missionary of early Oregon, who was interested in botany and taxidermy, as told by Nancy Wilson Ross[10] "Here was a woman of the liveliest intelligence; a human creature so interested in the world around her that she could not find time enough in a sixteen-hour working day to satisfy her curiosity about rocks, birds, flowers, trees, animals, vegetables, minerals, fish, Indians, human beings, God, the Bible, her children. There were not many minds comparable to her own in a pioneer society — or, for that matter, in any society." . . . In later years her mind failed. Why?

[9] Hollingsworth, Buckner. Her garden was her delight. Macmillan, 1962. p.87
[10] Ross, Nancy Wilson. Westward the women. Knopf, 1944. p75-76

Perhaps because . . . "Her appetite for knowledge and for the tools of knowledge — books, scientific instruments, exchange of thought — was forever unappeased. . . . Mary gave her mind, to the great experiment that made it possible for white woman by the thousands to follow after them, daring the solitude and deprivations of pioneer life."

INVENTORS

It is amazing when you read of the various types of inventions patented by women, and *not* just simple devices for use in the home, but many of them complicated scientific inventions. Mozans expresses it thus:[11] "What particularly arrests one's attention in reading the Patent Office reports is not only the very wide range of the devices which they embrace . . . The following story well-illustrates the prevailing ignorance regarding the part women have taken in the invention of certain articles that are so common that most people think they were never patented. "I was out driving once with an old farmer in Vermont," writes Mrs. Ada C. Bowles, "and he told me 'You women may talk about your rights, but why don't you invent something!' I answered 'Your horse's feed bag and the shade over his head were both invented by women.' The old fellow was so taken aback that he was barely able to gasp, 'Do tell'." (In today's transportation, I wonder how many people know that the white line on roads was first suggested by a woman?)

"The government report of the early year of 1888 credited women with over one thousand patents. How many more are there where men took advantage of the women who did not know the ropes, or had no cash to pay the preliminaries to take out a patent?

"The first woman to receive a patent in the U.S. was Mary Kies. It was issued May 5, 1809 for a process of straw-weaving with silk or thread . . . But by far the most remarkable of woman's inventions during the period (1841-1851) was a submarine telescope and lamp, for which a patent was awarded in 1845 to Sarah Mather."

The assistance of women to male inventors is a subject within itself. Among such instances is the little-known story of the woman who helped Eli Whitney with his invention of the cotton gin: Catherine Greene, widow of General Greene. Mary Ormsbee Whitton[12] tells us: "Thither in 1792 came by chance a young graduate of Yale, who had supposed himself engaged as a tutor by some neighboring family. The Yankee youth found the position filled, and himself stranded, practically penniless. Learning of his plight, the widow of Mulberry Grove invited him to stay at her home until another position could be obtained. The young tutor was Eli Whitney.

"Planters in the region were then discussing the possibilities of mechanical aid in ginning short-fibred cotton. The stranded tutor, who had been a

11 Mozans, *op. cit.*, P344-347, 540
12 Whitton, Mary Ormsbee. *These were the women, U.S.A.*, 1776-1860. Hastings House, 1954. p48

mechanic before entering Yale, agreed to make a try, fitting up a workshop in the basement of Kitty Greene's house. Tradition shows her standing beside him with a brush, cleaning the metal prongs of Whitney's first model, an action that suggested a mechanical improvement to the young inventor, a second cylinder to prevent the massing of material."

From a list of prominent women inventors we have picked the following at random, from among the older inventions made by women: pneumatic tire, heating and ventilating apparatus for buildings, railroad cars, air-cooling fans, digging machine, snow plow, snow shovel and scraper, stage scenery, paving blocks (several), fire escapes.

WOMEN IN MEDICINE

Women have perhaps overcome more odds in medicine than in any other field of science, and it is a well-known fact that such women were once stoned as witches. Isabella Taves[13] quotes Dr. Connie Guion in this regard: 'Today, much of the old prejudice against women's holding important medical positions is gone. The men in hospitals have had to admit that women make excellent doctors, and executives. It remains now, only for women to break down a few outmoded customs that have obstructed their progress in medicine.' Taves continues: "Dr. Guion feels that women, when they become doctors, have a personal obligation to their sex. A bad woman doctor can work irreparable damage to the future of women in medicine, for if she is not satisfactory, she is not just a bad doctor, but 'a bad woman doctor.' She feels that in her own case, and in the situation of hundreds of other women who are practicing physicians, that her sex makes no difference."

"Madame Marie Bovin," says Mozans,[14] "possessing extraordinary insight as an investigator and marvelous sagacity as a diagnostician . . . achieved the distinction of being the first really great woman doctor of modern times."

Esther Pohl Lovejoy writes:[15] "One of the least publicized women in American history, Ann Preston, was born of Quaker parents at the family homestead in Westgrove, Pennsylvania. Her schooling was limited, but her natural gifts transcended education. A keen observer, with a touch of genius, she had learned a lot about life from experience and was not impressed by academic arguments regarding woman's sphere. . . . Armed with a pen, she defended the college and the cause of women in medicine, especially against the active opposition of the Philadelphia Co. Medical Society. . . . This influence was carried beyond Philadelphia — to New York, Boston, Edinburgh, and other centers where women were struggling for a place in medicine . . ."

We are familiar with the names of the early pioneers in medicine, including Emily Blackwell and others, but we must not forget the modern pioneers in the related fields of specialization. Nurses should also be noted, and we

---

[13] Tavens, Isabella. *Successful women.* Dutton, 1943. p237-238
[14] Mozans, *op. cit.,* p. 294
[15] Lovejoy, Esther Pohl. *Women doctors of the world.* Macmillan, 1957. p31, 35

like the tribute paid to Mary Adelaide Nutting, nurse, educator and author, according to Meta Pennock:[16] "When Professor Phelps presented Miss Nutting to the president of Yale University in 1922, on the occasion of her receiving the honorary degree of Master of Arts, he named her 'one of the most useful women in the world.' His estimate stands today." Florence Nightingale and others pioneered the course; Mary Adelaide Nutting and others "carried on."

AMONG THE GREATEST . . .

We shall not repeat the well-known story of Marie Curie, physical chemist, who was awarded the Nobel prize for chemistry for work on radium and its compounds, nor is it necessary to relate the work of Maria Mitchell, astronomer, who discovered a comet and several nebulae. But it is interesting to note that the U.S. Coast Survey employed her to do their mathematical calculations. She was an educator, novelist and poet as well! At least these two have been honored on stamps, altho they are not given separate mention in all biographical dictionaries.

Only twenty American women have been personally honored by U.S. postage stamps, and nearly all of these stamps were issued after women were given the right to vote! Approximately 200 women have been honored, altogether, on the world's stamps; a *tiny* percentage of all the great women since the beginning of time!

[16] Pennock, Meta. *Makers of nursing history* . . . Lakeside, 1949. p39

VIII. SUMMARY: THE FUTURE

"Equality of women" is a subject which has been discussed since Biblical times, but the resolution of the problem seems closer today than it has ever been before. With Congressional resolutions, various women's groups and other means, women are fighting for the rights which they have long deserved.

IN ANCIENT TIMES

We find the earliest legal example in the Bible. According to Schmidt,[1] "The case of Zelophehad was the oldest decided case that is still cited as an authority: — the daughters of Zelophehad were in a predicament. Why, because they were daughters, should they be *deprived* of their father's property. He had no sons. They brot a suit in court — one of the earliest reported law suits, more than 3000 years ago. They received the judgment — and the fundamental policy of the state was altered — and now women could be numbered!"

According to Evaleen Harrison,[2] Deborah was . . . "the only woman in the history of the Hebrews raised to political power by consent of the people, and, centuries before the days of woman's rights, elected as judge over the nation . . ."

In ancient Rome, we read of the problem in Balsdon's book:[3] "Once women had achieved this equality in marriage, it was ridiculous that they should not acquire such independence as men possessed in the administration of their own property. . . . Certain changes in the law were made, it is true, in women's interest. The restrictions imposed by the Lex Voconia on a woman's inheriting property, for instance, were abolished after the time of Augustus, and the humanistic spirit of the lawyers of the Empire was shown in their administration of the law as it stood . . ."

Women were long interested in the legal profession. Balsdon continues:[4] "And it is evident that, from the late Republic onwards a number of women in Rome were very well educated indeed. The distinguished orator of Q. Hortensius, who died in 50 B.C. had a daughter who was probably the wife of Q. Servilius Caepio, who adopted M. Brutus. Despite the fact that women could not plead at the bar at Rome, she interested herself in her father's profession to such a degree that a critical moment in Roman history she pleaded, and with success. This was in 42 B.C., when Antony's wife Fulvia refused to champion the cause of the wives of the proscribed on whom the triumvirs had imposed a crippling burden of taxation. Hortensia argued their case in a memorable speech which posterity preserved and read — because it was a good speech, and not because it was made by a woman."

"By the law of 'Couverte de Baron' of 1419," states Leonard, Drinker, and

[1] Schmidt, Minna. *400 outstanding women of the world.* The Author, 1933. p33-35
[2] Harrison, Evaleen. *Little known women of the Bible.* Round Table Press, 1936. p38
[3] Balsdon, John. *Roman women, their history and habits.* Day, 1963. p28
[4] *Ibid.*, p56

Holden,[5] "English women had the right to carry on productive enterprises, as 'Feme Sole.' This right was evident in all the English colonies. The women from Holland had long had similar rights, German and French women had comparable opportunities; so women are found in occupational life in all of the colonies."

"The first time we read of the right of citizenship bestowed upon a woman," says Schmidt,[6] "is when Henry VIII of England divorced his first wife Catherine of Aragon; he signed an allowance and a Letters Patent of English Citizenship."

WOMEN'S SUFFRAGE

We shall not go into the Women's Suffrage Movement, which was successfully culminated in the Nineteenth Amendment to the Constitution. But we should always acknowledge the contributions of those leaders who dedicated their lives to making life easier for the women who were to follow them. Although these women were called "feminists," often they were criticized because some of them seemed to drop their femininity when they had to fight for their rights. Isabella Taves gives her viewpoint:[7] "It is hard to believe, in these days of lady vice-presidents, and female tycoons, that women doctors were once stoned as witches; that women's parts in the theatre were played by simpering young boys; that women writers, if they had any kind of a strong message, preferred to write under masculine pen-names. . . . It seems incredible that, even as recently as a generation ago, women went into business with chips on their shoulders, and that, to get ahead, they became such violent feminists that they, temporarily at least, lost much of their charm. That isn't true today. I think that if I were to list one quality which all truly successful women now have in common, it would be their femininity. They haven't attempted to step over the mangled bodies of men to climb into drivers' seats. They don't in any way want to supplant men in business. On the contrary, they have succeeded largely because they have brought womanly quickness, sensitivity and understanding to jobs where it was needed."

SUMMARY

Over the centuries we have seen the evolution of the so-called "weaker sex," until now their power can no longer be denied. "We have seen," says Muir,[8] "how such women as Semiramis, Tomyris, Boadicea and Joan of Arc became famous military leaders, and how they out-generaled and defeated the greatest men strategists of their times; we have seen how Queen Elizabeth, Catherine the Great, Victoria and Tseu-Hi took their places as rulers over vast kingdoms; we have seen how Aspasia, Cleopatra, Anna, Clotilda, Catherine

---

[5] Leonard, Eugene Andruss, Sophie Hutchinson Drinker and Miriam Young Holden. *The American woman in colonial and Revolutionary Times, 1565-1800.* University of Pennsylvania Press, 1962. p36
[6] Schmidt, *op. cit.,* p537
[7] Taves, Isabella. *Successful women.* Dutton, 1943. p11
[8] Muir, Charles. *Women, makers of history.* Vantage, 1956. p228

de Medici, Madame Maintenon, Hester Stanhope and Theodora exercised such power that political leaders were compelled to do their bidding; in science such women as Madame Curie and Lisa Meitner have brought about the most wonderful achievements; in human betterment no one has equalled the work of Florence Nightingale or Elizabeth Fry; nor can any courage be likened to that of Grace Darling; and Sappho stands supreme among the poets; in fact, in whatever field of endeavor they have chosen to enter, women have risen to the greatest heights and have not only matched but have surpassed their male competitors, in many cases putting them to shame. As men have made practically all the wars and are seemingly unable to effect a lasting peace, would it not be a good idea to let the women try their hand at it? They are more pacific in their nature. . . . It is not preposterous to think of such a thing, for history records that it has actually happened. It was in 1529 that two women negotiated the Peace of Cambrai, and the peace has been referred to as the 'ladies' peace.'"

WOMEN TODAY, AND IN THE FUTURE

We have seen many "firsts" in the achievement of women during the first few years. We have seen the first woman to head a member concern of th New York Stock Exchange, although no woman has yet achieved trading privileges. We have seen women rise to the prime ministership, the first being in Ceylon. We have seen the first woman try for the U. S. vice-presidency. We have seen women take part in oceanography and other new fields. We have only skimmed the surface, and some fields such as athletics have seen women reach many top records.

There are several modern feminist organizations today which are trying to break down the traditional barriers of equality. One group, of long standing, is called "Woman for President," and its members expect to see a woman president at some not-so-distant date. They will start with the vice-presidency. Another organization is NOW which stands for the National Organization for Women. This and other women's groups relate that one-third of American workers are women who hold a disproportionate number of menial, low-salaried jobs. Women are paid from 50 to 60% of what men are paid, in the *same* occupations. In professions it is the same: for instance, women chemists with Ph.D.'s earn less than male chemists who have only bachelor degrees. In 1966 the full-time working woman earned a median salary of $3973, as compared to $6848 for a man. Women are too often told that they must choose between motherhood and a career; how many men are asked to choose between fatherhood and a career?

Recently Bob Wilson of San Diego, California, introduced a resolution in Congress (H.J. Res. 512, March 3, 1969) that would amend the Constitution to guarantee equal rights for women: "Equality of rights under the law shall not be denied or abridged by the United States or any state on account of sex . . ." To date, no action has been scheduled by the House and

Senate Judiciary Committees, who have jurisdiction over the matter, but it is getting good support in Congress. Senators Louise Gore, John Tower and Eugene McCarthy are among its supporters. A poll shows 68 senators and 220 House members are in favor of the Amendment. If it passes Congress, it will have to be ratified by three-quarters of the state legislatures.

Grant Overton[9] quotes Zona Gale in her definition of feminine success. "Success for a woman means a harmonious adjustment to life." But as long as man's quest for a harmonious adjustment is not interrupted by having babies, woman's handicap is only too apparent."

One of our favorite quotes concerning the woman's cause is from Mozan's book,[10] and perhaps it summarizes everything in a few lines: "The romantic idea of treating woman as a clinging vine, and thus eliminating half the energies of humanity, is rapidly disappearing and giving place to the idea that the strong are for the strong — the intellectually strong; that the evolution of the race will be complete only when men and women shall be associated in perfect unity of purpose, and shall, in fullest sympathy, collaborate for the attainment of the highest and the best. . . . Then will men and women for the first time fully supplement each other in their aspirations and endeavors and realize somewhat of that oneness of heart and mind . . . The woman's cause is man's; they rise or sink together, dwarfed or godlike, bond or free."

Our final tribute to women is the poem "Heritage" by Lytton Cox, as quoted in McCallum's work:[11]

HERITAGE

"A highway runs beside my door —
Just a broad, straight road and nothing more —
Except when the westering sun droops low
Till the dust in the air takes a golden glow
Like a veil or a web, and within its sheen
The present fades as the past is seen.

Then like a dream down the broad highway
Pass women of old and of yesterday:
Spartan mother, a jeweled queen,
Peasant martyr and Magdalene;
Fair young faces marked by years,
Sad eyes faded and dimmed from tears;
Brave, strong shoulders unbent by loss,
Old backs bowed from a long-borne cross,
Rank on rank, a mighty throng.

[9] Overton, Grant. *The Women who make our novels*. New and rev. ed. Dodd, Mead, 1928. p158

[10] Mozans, *op. cit.*, p416

[11] McCallum, Jane Y. *Women pioneers*. Johnson, 1929. p3

They march to the beat of an unheard song;
Mothers of men they have toiled and wept
That a dream might live and a flame be kept.

Then from afar, like the whir of wings,
A voice in majestic paen sings:
"These are they who have journeyed through;
They have kept the faith, they have builded true,
And the way will never be quite so long
Because they have wrought so fair and strong."

The vision fades . . . and the road once more
Is only a road by my open door.
Through a mist of tears I lift mine eyes
To the first faint star in the twilight skies,
And breathe my prayer on the evening breeze:
"Thank God for my heritage from these!" "

INDEX TO ABBREVIATIONS, ETC.

* Especially suitable for younger readers.

M
m.	— married
Madag.	— Madagascarian
Mesop.	— Mesopotamian
Mex.	— Mexican
Mon.	— Monacan
Monte.	— Montenegrian
Moroc.	— Moroccan
Morav.	— Moravian

N
N.	— North
N. Afric.	— North African
n.d.	— no date
Nether.	— Netherlander
New Z.	— New Zealander
Newfound.	— Newfoundlander
Nor.	— Norwegian

O

P
p.	— page
pa.	— paper
Pak.	— Pakestanian
Palest.	— Palestinian
Palm.	— Palmyrian
Pan.	— Panamanian
Pers.	— Persian
Peru.	— Peruvian
Phil.	— Philippino
Pol.	— Polish
Pomer.	— Pomeranian
por.	— portrait
Port.	— Portuguese
pseud.	— pseudonym
Puert.Ric.	— Puerto Rican

Q

R
Rev.	— Revolutionary
Rom.	— Roman
Rum.	— Rumanian
Russ.	— Russian

S
S.	— South
S. Afr.	— South African
Salv.	— Salvadorian
Sardin.	— Sardinian
Scan.	— Scandinavian
Scot.	— Scottish
Serb.	— Serbian
Siam.	— Siamese
Sic.	— Sicilian
Siles.	— Silesian
Slov.	— Slovenian
Sp.	— Spanish
supp.	— supplement
Swed.	— Swedish

T
Tas.	— Tasmanian
Thail.	— Thailandian
Transyl.	— Transylvanian
Trin.	— Trinidadian
Turk.	— Turkish
TV	— Television

U
U.N.	— United Nations
unp.	— unpaged
Urug.	— Urugayian

V
Venez.	— Venezuelan
Virgin Isl.	— Virgin Islander

W
W.	— West
W. Ind.	— West Indian

X

Y
Yugoslav.	— Yugoslavian

Z

LIST OF COLLECTIONS

ANALYZED IN THIS WORK

AND

KEY TO SYMBOLS USED

ABBOT—NOTABLE
Abbot, Willis J. Notable women in history. Winston, 1913. 448p

ABRAMOWITZ—GREAT
Abramowitz, Isidore, ed. The great prisoners. Dutton, 1946. 879p

ADAMS—GREAT
Adams, Russell L. Great Negroes, past and present. Afro-American, 1963. 182p

*ADAMS—HEROINES
Adams, Elmer C. and Warren Dunham Foster. Heroines of modern progress. Macmillan, 1926. 324p

*ADAMS—SKY
Adams, Jean and Margaret Kimball. Heroines of the sky. Doubleday, Doran, 1942. 295p

ADDAMS—EXCELLENT
Addams, Jane. The excellent becomes the permanent. Macmillan, 1932. 162p

ADELMAN—FAMOUS
Adelman, Joseph. Famous women. Lonow, 1926. 328p

AIKMAN—CALAMITY
Aikman, Duncan. Calamity Jane and the lady wildcats. Holt, 1927. 347p

ALLEN—ADVENT
Allen, Devere, ed. Adventurous Americans. Farrar & Rinehart, 1932. 346p

AMERICA'S 12
America's twelve great women leaders during the past hundred years. Associated Authors Service, 1933. 35p

AMES—THESE
Ames, Noel, comp. These wonderful people. Peoples Book Club, 1947. 495p

AMORY—PROPER
Amory, Cleveland. Proper Bostonians. Dutton, 1947. 381p

ANDERSON—LADIES
Anderson, James. The Ladies of the Covenant. Armstrong, 1880. 494p

ANDREWS—WOMEN
Andrews, Mathew Page, comp. The women of the South in wartimes. Norman, Remington, 1920. 466p

ANTHOLOGIA—POETS
Anthologia Graeca. The poets of the Greek anthology. George Routledge & Sons, Ltd., n.d. 259p

ARMITAGE—CENT.
Armitage, Angus. A century of astronomy. Sampson Low, 1950. 256p

ARMOUR—IT
Armour, Richard Willard. It all started with Eve. McGraw-Hill, 1956. 137p

ARSENIUS—DICT.
Dictionary of biographies over personalities, depicted on the world's postage stamps. Oloffson Bros., 1937. 207p. pa.

ASCAP
The Amer. Soc. of Composers and the ASCAP biographical dictionary of composers, authors, and publishers. 2nd ed. Crowell, 1952. 636p

ASQUITH—MYSELF
Asquith. Countess of Oxford, and ed. Myself when young. Frederick Muller, Ltd., 1938. 422p

ATKINSON—DANCERS
Atkinson, Margaret F. and May Hillman. Dancers of the ballet, Knopf, 1955. 174p

AUBREY—BRIEF
Aubrey, John. Aubrey's brief lives, ed. . . . by Oliver Lawson Dick. Univ. of Mich., 1957. 341p

lxi

AUCHINCLOSS—PION.
Auchincloss, Louis. Pioneers and care-takers. A study of 9 Amer. women novelists. Univ. of Minn., c. 1961, 1965. 202p

AYSCOUGH—CHINESE
Ayscough, Florence. Chinese women yesterday and today. Houghton Mifflin, 1937. 324p

BACON—PURITAN
Bacon, Martha Sherman. Puritan prom-enade. Houghton Mifflin, 1964. 160p

BAKELESS—IN
Bakeless, Katherine Little. In the big time. Lippincott, 1935. 208p

BALCH—MODERN
Balch, Marston, ed. Modern short biog-raphies and auto-biographies. Har-court, Brace, 1945. 589p

BALD—WOMEN
Bald, Marjory Amelia. Women writers of the 19th cent. Russell, 1963. 288p

BALSDON—ROMAN
Balsdon, John Percy Vyvian Dacre. Roman women: their history and habits. 1st Amer. ed. Day, 1963. 351p

BARKER—SAINTS
Barker, William P. Saints in aprons and overalls. Fleming H. Revell, 1959. 128p

BARNETT—WRITING
Barnett, Lincoln. Writing on life. Wm. Sloane Associates, 1951. 383p

BARTLETT—MOTHERS
Bartlett, Mabel and Sophia Baker. Moth-ers—makers of men. 2d. rev. ed. Exposition Press, c1927, 1952. 100p

BARTLETT—THEY
Bartlett, Robert M. They dared to live. Association Press, 1948. 135p

BARTON—CELEB.
Barton, George. Celebrated spies and famous mysteries of the Great War. Page, 1919. 345p

BARTON—WOMEN
Barton, William Eleaser. The women Lincoln loved. Bobbs-Merrill, 1927. 377p

BEARD—AMER.
Beard, Mary A., ed. America through women's eyes. Macmillan, 1933. 558p

BEARD—WOMAN
Beard, Mary A. Woman as force in history. Macmillan, 1946. 369p

BEATON—PERSONA
Beaton, Cecil and Kenneth Tynan. Per-sona Grata. Putnam, 1954. 99p

BEAUMONT—COMPLETE
Beaumont, Cyril W. Complete book of ballets. Garden City Pub., Inc., 1949. 900p

BECKWITH—CONTEMP.
Beckwith, John A. & Geoffrey Coope. Contemporary American biography. Harper, 1941. 347p

*BEEBE—SAINTS
Beebe, Catherine. Saints for boys and girls. The Bruce Pub. Co., 1959. 147p

BELL—STORM.
Bell, E. Moberly. Storming the citadel. The rise of the woman doctor. Con-stable & Co., Ltd., 1953. 200p

BELL—WOMEN
Bell, Margaret. Women of the wilder-ness. Dutton, 1938. 384p

*BENET—AMER. POETS
Benet, Laura. Famous American poets. Dodd, Mead, 1950. 183p

*BENET—FAMOUS POETS
Benet, Laura. Famous poets for young people. Dodd, Mead, 1964. 160p

*BENET—HUMORISTS
Benet, Laura. Famous American humor-ists. Dodd, Mead & Co., 1959. 190p

BENJAMIN, LEWIS. *See* MELVILLE, LEWIS

BENNETT—AMER.
Bennett, Helen Christine. Amer. women in civic work. Dodd, Mead, 1915. 277p

BENNETT—SIX
Bennett, H. S. Six medieval men and women. Cambridge Univ. Press, 1955. 177p

BENSON—QUEEN
Benson, Edward Frederic. Queen Vic-toria's daughter. D. Appleton-Century, 1938. 315p

BENSON—WOMEN
Benson, Mary Sumner. Women in eighteenth-century America. Col-umbia Univ. Press, 1935. 343p

BEST—REBEL
Best, Mary A. Rebel saints. Harcourt, Brace, 1925. 333p

BINHEIM—WOMEN
Binheim, Max, ed. Women of the West. Publishers' Press, 1928. 223p

BLACK—NOTABLE
Black, Helen C. Notable women authors of the day. Maclaren, 1906. 342p

BLANCH—WILDER
Blanch, Lesly. The wilder shores of love. Simon & Schuster, 1954. 332p

BLEACKLEY—LADIES
Bleackley, Horace. Ladies frail and fair. Dodd, Mead, 1926. 328p

BLEI—FASC.
Blei, Franz. Fascinating women, sacred and profane. Simon & Schuster, 1928. 225p

BLUM—GREAT
Blum, Daniel. Great stars of the American stage. Greenberg, 1952. 152p

BLUM—TELEVISION
Blum, Daniel. Pictorial history of television. Chilton Co., Book division, Pub., 1959. 288p

BLUNT—GREAT
Blunt, Hugh Francis. Great wives and mothers. Devin-Adair, 1917. 424p

BOCCACCIO—CONC.
Boccaccio, Giovanni. Concerning famous women. Tr. by Guido A. Guarino. Rutgers Univ. Press, 1963. 257p

BODEEN—LADIES
Bodeen, Dewitt. Ladies of the footlights. The Pasadena Playhouse Assoc., 1937. 133p

BOLITHO—BIOG.
Bolitho, Hector. A biographer's notebook. Macmillan, 1950. 213p

BOLITHO—TWELVE
Bolitho, Wm. Twelve against the gods. The Press of The Readers Club, c1929, 1941. 356p

*BOLTON—AUTHORS
Bolton, Sarah K. Famous American authors. Rev. by Wm. A. Fahey. Crowell, 1954. 248p

*BOLTON—FAMOUS LEADERS
Bolton, Sarah K. Famous leaders among women. Crowell, 1895. 356p

*BOLTON—LIVES
Bolton, Sarah K. Lives of girls who became famous. Crowell, 1949. 343p

BONTE—AMER.
Bonte, George Willard. America marches past. D. Appleton-Century, 1936. 196p

*BORER—WOMEN
Borer, Mary Cathcart. Women who made history. Frederick Warne, 1963. 192p

BOTTRALL—PERS.
Bottrall, Margaret. Personal records. A gallery of self-portraits. Day, 1962. 234p

BOWIE—WOMEN
Bowie, Walter Russell. Women of light. Harper & Row, 1963. 205p

*BOYD—RULERS
Boyd, Mildred. Rulers in petticoats. Criterion Books, 1966. 224p

*BOYNICK—PIONEERS
Boynick, David King. Pioneers in petticoats. Crowell, 1959. 244p

BOYNTON—SOME
Boynton, Percy Holmes. Some contemporary Americans, Univ. of Chicago, 1924. 289p

BRADFORD—DAU.
Bradford, Gamaliel. Daughters of Eve. Boston, c1928, 1930. 304p

BRADFORD—PORTRAITS
Bradford, Gamaliel. Portraits of American women. Houghton Mifflin, 1919. 276p

BRADFORD—WIVES
Bradford, Gamaliel, Jr. Wives. Harper, 1925. 298p

BRADFORD—WOMEN
Bradford, Gamaliel. Portraits of women. Houghton Mifflin, 1916. 202p

BREIT—WRITER
Breit, Harvey. Writer observed. World Pub., 1956. 286p

BRENNER—POETS
Brenner, Rica. Poets of our time. Harcourt, Brace, 1941. 411p

*BRENNER—TEN
Brenner, Rica. Ten modern poets. Harcourt, Brace, 1930. 278p

*BRIDGES—HEROES
Bridges, Thomas C. & H. H. Tiltman.
Heroes of modern adventure. Lit-
tle, Brown, c1927, 1937. 277p

BRIGHAM—JOURNALS
071 . Brigham, Clarence S. Journals & jour-
B856J   neyman. Univ. of Pa., 1950. 114p

BRITTAIN—WOMEN
Brittain, Vera Mary. The women at
Oxford, a fragment of history. Mac-
millan, c1960. 272p

BROCKETT—WOMAN'S
Brockett, L. P. and Mrs. Mary C.
Vaughan. Woman's work in the
LAC   Civil War: A record of heroism,
14251   patriotism and patience. Zeigler,
McCurdy, 1867. 799p

BROOKS—MASTERS
Brook, Donald. Masters of the key-
board. Rockliff, 1946. 183p

BROOK—SINGERS
Brook, Donald. Singers of today. 2d.
ed. rev. Rockliff, 1958. 200p

BROOKS—COLONIAL
Brooks, Geraldine. Dames and daughters of colonial days. Crowell, 1900.
284p

BROOKS—THREE
Brooks, Gladys Rice (Billings). Three
wise virgins. Dutton, 1957. 244p

BROOKS—YOUNG
Brooks, Geraldine. Dames and daughters of the young republic. Crowell,
1901. 287p

BROWN—DARK
Brown, Ivor. Dark ladies. Collins, 1957.
319p

BROWN—GENTLE
Brown, Dee. The gentle tamers: women
of the old wild west. Putnam, 1958.
317p

BROWN—HOME.
Brown, Hallie Q. Homespun heroines
and other women of distinction.
Aldine, 1926. 248p

BROWN—UPSTAGE
Brown, John Mason. Upstage. Norton,
1930. 276p

BRUCE—WOMAN
Bruce, H. Addington. Woman in the
making of America. New and rev.
ed. Little, Brown, 1928. 347p

BRUERE—LAUGH.
Bruère, Mrs. Martha. Laughing their
way; women's humor in America.
Macmillan, 1934. 295p

BRUNDIDGE—TWINKLE
Brundidge, Harry T. Twinkle, twinkle,
movie star. Dutton, 1930. 284p

BRYANT—AMER.
Bryant, Lorinda Munson. American pictures and their painters. Lane,
1921. 307p

BUCHANAN—WOMEN
Buchanan, Isabella Reid. Women of the
Bible. Colwell, 1924. 112p

*BUCKMASTER—WOMEN
Buckmaster, Henrietta. Women who
920.073 shaped history. Collier Bks., 1966.
B926W   152p

BUL. OF BIBL.
P   Bulletin of Bibliography. Faxon Co., v.8
to 27.

BURGE—ENCY.
Burge, C. G. Encyclopaedia of aviation.
Putnam, n.d. 642p

BURNETT—AMER.
Burnett, Will & Charles E. Slatkin.
American authors today. Ginn,
1947. 560p

BURNETT—FIVE
301.41 Burnett, Constance Buel. Five for free-
B965f   dom. Abelard, 1953. 317p
1968
BURNETT—THIS
Burnett, Whit. This is my best. Dial,
1942. 1180p

BURT—PHILA.
Burt, Struthers. Philadelphia, holy experiment. Doubleday, Doran, 1945.
396p

BURTON—LOVELIEST
Burton, Doris. The loveliest flower.
Academy Guild, 1959. 186p

BURTON—NOTABLE
Burton, Margaret E. Notable women of
modern China. Revell, 1912. 271p

BURTON—VALIANT
Burton, Doris. Valiant achievements.
Great Christians of our day. Henry
Regnery, 1956. 184p

CAFFIN—VAUD.
Caffin, Caroline. Vaudeville. Pictures
by Marius de Zayas. Mitchell Ken-
nerley, 1914. 231p

CAHN—LAUGH.
Cahn, William. The laugh makers. Putnam's Sons, 1957. 192p

CAJORI—HIST.
Cajori, Florian. A history of mathematics. Macmillan, 1929. 516p

CALDER—SCIENCE
Calder, Ritchie. Science in our lives. Mich. State College, 1954. 186p

CANNING—100
Canning, John, ed. 100 great modern lives. Hawthorn Books, 1965. 640p

CANTOR—AS
Cantor, Eddie. As I remember them. Duell, Sloan & Pearce, 1963. 144p

CAREY—TWELVE
Carey, Rosa Nouchette. Twelve notable good women of the XIXth century. Dutton, 1902. 380p

*CARMER—CAVAL
Carmer, Carl Lamson. Cavalcade of America: the deeds and achievements of the men who made our country great. Brown, 1956. 382p

*CARMER—YOUNG
Carmer, Carl Lamson. A cavalcade of young Americans. Lothrop, Lee & Shepard, 1958. 256p

CARNEGIE—BIOG.
Carnegie, Dale. . . . Biographical roundup. Greenberg, 1945. 233p

CARNEGIE—FIVE
Carnegie, Dale. . . . Five minute biographies. Permabooks, 1949. 187p, pa.

CARNEGIE—LITTLE
Carnegie, Dale. Little known facts about well known people. The World's Work, Ltd., c1947, 1949. 208p

CASTIGLIONI—HIST.
Castiglioni, Arturo. A history of medicine. 2nd ed. rev. & enl. Knopf, 1947. 1192p

*CATHER—GIRLHOOD
Cather, Katherine Dunlap. Girlhood stories of famous women. Century, 1924. 336p

*CATHER—YOUNGER
Cather, Katherine Dunlap. Younger days of famous writers. Century, 1925. 325p

CAVANAH—WE
Cavanah, Frances, ed. We came to America. Macrae Smith, 1954. 307p

CHAMBERS—DICT.
Chambers's dictionary of scientists, by A. V. Howard. Dutton, 1958. 499p

*CHANDLER—FAMOUS
Chandler, Anna Curtis. Famous mothers and their children. Stokes, 1938. 329p

*CHANDLER—MEDICINE
Chandler, Caroline. Famous men of medicine. Dodd, 1950. 140p

CHAPPELL—FEM.
Chappell, Clovis G. Feminine faces. Abington-Cokesbury, 1942. 219p

*CHERRY—PORTRAITS
Cherry, Gwendolyn, Ruby Thomas and Pauline Willis. Portraits in color. Pageant, 1962. 224p

CHURCH—BRITISH
Church, Richard. British authors. Longmans, Green, 1948. 145p

CLARK—CHIANGS
Clark, Elmer T. The Chiangs of China. Abington-Cokesbury, 1943. 123p

CLARK—GREAT
Clark, Barrett H. Great short biographies of the world. McBride, 1929. 1407p

CLARK—INNOCENCE
Clark, Emily. Innocent abroad. Knopf, 1931. 270p

CLARKE—SIX
Clarke, Mary. Six great dancers. Hamilton, 1957. 190p

CLUB—PRINTING
Club of Printing Women of New York. Antique, modern and swash. The Club, c.1955. 60p

*CLYMER—MODERN
Clymer, Eleanor. Modern American career women. Dodd, Mead, 1959. 178p

COAD—AMER.
Coad, Oral Sumner. American stage. (Pageant of America, vol. 14) Yale University, 1929. 362p

COCROFT—GREAT
Cocraft, Thoda. Great names and how they are made. Dartnell, 1941. 270p

CODE—GREAT
Code, Joseph B. Great American foundresses. Macmillan, 1929. 512p

*COFFMAN—AUTHORS
Coffman, Ramon Peyton and Nathan G. Goodman. Famous authors for boys and girls. Barnes, 1943. 167p

*COFFMAN—KINGS
Coffman, Ramon. Famous kings and queens for young people. Barnes, 1947. 128p

COLE—WOMEN
Cole, Margaret. Women of today. Thomas Nelson & Sons, Ltd., 1938. 311p

COLLINS—BIOG.
Collins, Joseph. The doctor looks at biography. Doran, 1925. 344p

COLLINS—GREAT
Collins, Charles W. Great love stories of the theatre. Duffield, 1911. 327p

COLLINS—LITERATURE
Collins, Joseph. The doctor looks at literature. Doran, 1923. 317p

*COMMAGER—CRUS.
Commager, Henry Steele. Crusaders for freedom. Doubleday, 1962. 240p

CONCANNON—DAU.
Concannon, Mrs. Thomas. Daughters of Banba. M. H. Gill & Son, Ltd., 1922. 275p

COOK—OUR
Cook, Howard Willard. Our poets of today. 3d rev. ed., Moffat, Yard, 1923. 421p

COOK, ROYAL E. *See* THORNTON, COOK E.

COOLIDGE—SIX
Coolidge, Julian L. Six female mathematicians. Reprint from Scripta Mathematics, V. 17, #1-2. Mr.-Je. 1951. p20-31. pa.

COOPER—AUTHORS
Cooper, Anice Page. Authors and others. Doubleday, 1927. 190p

*COOPER—TWENTY
Cooper, Alice Cecilia & Chas. A. Palmer. Twenty modern Americans. Harcourt, Brace, & World, Inc., 1942. 404p

COPE—SIX
Cope, Zachary. Six disciples of Florence Nightingale. Pitman Medical Pub. Co., Ltd., 1961. 76p

CORKRAN—ROMANCE
Corkran, Alice. The romance of women's influence. New ed. Blackie & Son, Ltd., n.d. 377p

CORYN—ENCHANT.
Coryn, Marjorie. Enchanters of men. The Naldrett Press, 1954. 224p

*COURNOS—BRITISH
Cournos, John and Sybil Norton. Famous British novelists. Dodd, Mead, 1952. 130p

COURNOS—FAMOUS
Cournos, John and Sybil Norton. Famous modern American novelists. Dodd, Mead, 1958. 181p

COURTNEY—ADVEN.
Courtney, Janet Elizabeth H. The adventurous thirties. Oxford Univ., 1933. 279p

CR '59
Celebrity Register. (International celebrity register.) Celebrity Register Ltd., U.S. ed., 1959. 864p

CR '63
Celebrity register. (formerly International celebrity register.) Harper & Row, 1963. 677p

CRAWFORD—LITTLE
Crawford, Marian. The little princesses. Harcourt, Brace, 1950. 314p

CROWLE—ENTER
Crowle, Eileen Georgina Beatrice. Enter the ballerina, by Pigeon Crowle (pseud.). Pitman, 1955. 178p

CULVER—WOMEN
Culver, Elsie Thomas. Women in the world of religion. Doubleday, 1967. 340p

CUNEY-HARE—NEGRO
Cuney-Hare, Maud. Negro musicians and their music. Associated Publishers, Inc., 1936. 439p

CUPPY—DECLINE
Cuppy, Wm. Jacob. Decline and fall of practically everybody. Holt, 1950. 230p

CUR. BIOG.
Current Biography. Wilson, 1940-1968.

*DODGE—STORY
Dodge, Bertha (Sanford). Story of nursing. Little, 1954. 243p

DOLAN—GOODNOW'S
Dolan, Josephine A. Goodnow's history of nursing. 11th ed. W. B. Saunders Co. 1963. 360p

*DOLIN—WORLD
Dolin, Arnold. World-famous great American heroines. Hart, 1960. 191p. pa.

DONALDSON—RADIO
Donaldson, Charles E. Popular radio stars. Wash. Service Bureau, 1942. 30p. pa.

DONOVAN—WOMEN
Donovan, Frank. Women in their lives; the distaff side of the Founding Fathers. Dodd, 1966. 339p

DORLAND—SUM
Dorland, Wm. A. Newman. The sum of feminine achievement. Stratford, 1917. 237p

DOUGLAS—REMEMBER
Douglas, Emily Taft. Remember the ladies. Putnam, 1966. 254p

DOWNES—OLIN
Downes, Olin. Olin Downes on music. Schuster, 1957. 473p

DREER—AMER.
Dreer, Herman. American literature by Negro authors. Macmillan, 1950. 334p

DREWRY—POST
Drewry, John E. Post biographies of famous journalists. Univ. of Ga. (Random House), c1928, 1942. 518p

DRINKER—MUSIC
Drinker, Sophie. Music and women. Coward-McCann, 1948. 323p

DRURY—FIRST
Drury, Clifford M. First white woman over the Rockies. Arthur H. Clark Co., 1963, 3 vol. v. 1-280p—1963. v. 2-382p—1963. v. 3-321p—1966

DuCANN—LOVES
DuCann, Chas. Garfield Lott. Loves of George Bernard Shaw. Funk, 1963. 300p

DUNAWAY—TREAS.
Dunaway, Philip and Mel Evans. A treasury of the world's great diaries. Doubleday, 1957. 586p

DUNAWAY—TURN.
Dunaway, Philip and George de Kay. Turning point. Random House, 1958. 432p

DWIGGINS—THEY
Dwiggins, Don. They flew the Bendix race. Lippincott, 1965. 198p

EARHART—FUN
Earhart, Amelia. Fun of it; random records of my own flying and of women in aviation. Harcourt, 1932. 218p

EARLE—COLON.
Earle, Alice Morse. Colonial dames and good wives. Frederick Ungar, 1962. 315p

EATON—ACTOR'S
Eaton, Walter Prichard. The actor's heritage. Atlantic Mo., 1924. 294p

*EBY—MARKED
Eby, Lois Christine. Marked for adventure. Chilton, 1960. 122p

EDMAN—THEY
Edman, Victor Raymond. They found the secret . . . Zondervan, 1960. 159p

EHRLICH—CELEB.
Ehrlich, A. pseud. (Payne, A.) Celebrated violinists, past and present. 3rd ed. Scribners, 1913. 287p

EICHBERG—RADIO
Eichberg, Robert. Radio stars of today. Page, 1937. 218p

ELGIN—NUN
Elgin, Kathleen. Nun. A gallery of sisters. Random House, 1964. 141p

ELIOT—HEIRESSES
Eliot, Elizabeth. Heiresses and coronets, the story of lovely ladies and noble men. McDowell, Obolensky, 1959. 282p

ELLET—PIONEER
Ellet, Mrs. Elizabeth Fries (Lummis). The pioneer women of the West. Porter & Coates, 1852. 434p

ELLET—WOMEN (1)
Ellet, Elizabeth F. The women of the American Revolution. Vol. 1. Geo. W. Jacobs, 1900. 396p

ELLET—WOMEN (2)
Ellet, Elizabeth F. The women of the American Revolution. Vol. II. Geo. W. Jacobs, 1900 359p

ELSON—WOMAN'S
Elson, Arthur and Everett E. Truelt.
Woman's work in music. New rev.
ed. Page, 1931. 301p

°ELSON—SIDE (1)
Elson, Henry William. Side lights on
American history. Vol. 1. Macmil-
lan, 1929. 349p

EMBREE—13
Embree, Edwin R. 13 against the odds.
Viking, 1944. 261p

ENCY. BRIT.—AMER.
The Encyclopoedia Britannica. Collec-
tion of contemporary American
painting. Written and edited by
Grace Papano. Ency. Britannica,
Inc., 1946. 126p

ENGLEBERT—LIVES
Englebert, Omer. The lives of the Saints.
Tr. by Christopher and Anne Fre-
mantle. David McKay, c. 1951,
1960. 532p

EPSTEIN—PEOPLE
Epstein, Beryl (Williams). People are
our business. Lippincott, 1947. 180p

EPSTEIN—YOUNG
Epstein, Beryl (Williams). Young faces
in fashion. Lippincott, 1956. 176p

ERSKINE—OUT
Erskine, Helen Worden. Out of this
world. Putnam, 1953. 300p

EUSTACE—INFINITY
Eustace, Cecil John. An infinity of ques-
tions. Dennis Dobson Ltd., 1946.
170p

EUSTIS—PLAYERS
Eustis, Morton. Players at work. Theatre Arts, Inc., 1937. 127p

EWART—WORLD'S
Ewart, Andrew. The world's wicked-
est women. Taplinger, 1964. 288p

EWEN—AMERICAN
Ewen, David. American composers today. Wilson, 1949. 265p

EWEN—ENCY.
Ewen, David. Encyclopedia of the opera.
Wyn, 1955. 594p

EWEN—LIVING
Ewen, David, comp. and ed. Living
musicians. Wilson, 1940. 390p

EWEN—MEN
Ewen, David. Men and women who
make music. Merlin, c. 1939, 1949.
233p

EWEN—POPULAR
Ewen, David. Popular American composers from revolutionary times to
the present. Wilson, 1962. 217p

FABRICANT—WHY
Fabricant, Noah D. Why we became
doctors. Greene & Stratton, 1954.
182p

FAIRFAX—LADIES
Fairfax, Beatrice (Marie Manning).
Ladies now and then. Dutton, 1944.
254p

FARBER—NOBEL
Farber, Edward. Nobel prize winners
in chemistry, 1901-1950. rev. ed.
Abelard-Schuman, 1963. 341p

°FARJEON—KINGS
Farjeon, Eleanor and Herbert. Kings
and queens. Lippincott, 1932. 87p

°FARMER—BOOK
Farmer, Lydia. A book of famous queens.
Rev. by Willard Heaps. Crowell,
1964. 264p

FARMER—WHAT
Farmer, Lydia Hoyt, ed. What America
owes to women. Moulton, 1893.
505p

FARRAR—LITERARY
Farrar, John, ed. The literary spotlight. Doran, 1924. 356p

FAULHABER—WOMEN
Faulhaber, Michael Cardinal. The
women of the Bible. Newman,
1955. 248p

FELLOWES—HEROES
Fellowes-Gordon, Ian. Heroes of the
twentieth century. Hawthorne
Books, 1966. 288p

FELSTEAD—STARS
Felstead, S. Theodore. Stars who made
our halls. T. Werner Laurie, 1946.
187p

FERRERO—WOMEN
Ferrero, Gugliemo. The women of the
Caesars. Century, 1912. 337p

°FERRIS—FIVE
Ferris, Helen J. comp. Five girls who
dared. Macmillan, 1931. 270p

*FERRIS—GIRLS
Ferris, Helen J. and Virginia Moore.
Girls who did. Dutton, 1927. 308p

FERRIS—GREAT (1)
Ferris, G. T. Great singers, from Faustina Bordoni to Henrietta Sontag.
Vol. 1. rev. ed. Appleton, 1907.
220p

*FERRIS—WHEN
Ferris, Helen J., ed. When I was a girl.
Macmillan, 1930. 301p

FESTING—ON
Festing, Gabrielle. On the distaff side;
portraits of four great ladies. Pott,
1903. 281p

FIFTY—FAMOUS
Fifty famous women; their virtues and
failings, and the lessons of their
lives. Ward & Lock, n.d. 312p

FINDLAY—SPINDLE
Findlay, Jessie P. The spindle-side of
Scottish song. Dutton, 1902. 200p

FISHER—AMER.
Fisher, Dorothy Canfield. American portraits. Holt, 1946. 317p

FISHER—BALL
Fisher, Hugh. Ballerinas of Sadler's
Wells. Macmillan, 1954. 32p

FITZGIBBON—MY
Fitzgibbon, Robert and Ernest V. Heyn,
ed. My most inspiring moment.
(From a series in Family Weekly
Magazine.) Doubleday, 1965. 270p

FITZHUGH—CONCISE
Fitzhugh, Harriet Lloyd and Percy K.
Fitzhugh. Concise biographical dictionary. Grosset & Dunlap, 1935.
777p

*FLEISCHMAN—CAREERS
Fleischman, Doris E. (Bernays, Doris
Elsa Fleischman.) Careers for
women. Garden City, 1928. 514p

*FLEMING—DOCTORS
Fleming, Alice. Doctors in petticoats.
Lippincott, 1964. 159p

FLEMING—GREAT
Fleming, Alice. Great women teachers.
Lippincott, 1965. 157p

*FOLEY—FAMOUS
Foley, Rae. Famous American spies.
Dodd, Mead, 1962. 158p

*FORSEE—AMER.
Forsee, Aylesa. American women who
scored firsts. Macrae Smith, 1960.
251p

FORSEE—MY
Forsee, Aylesa. My love and I together.
Macrae Smith, 1961. 208p

*FORSEE—WOMEN
Forsee, Aylesa. Women who reached
for tomorrow. Macrae Smith, 1960.
203p

FORTUNE—100
Fortune, Editors of. 100 stories of business success . . . Bantam Books,
1957. 162p. pa.

FOSTER—RELIGION
Foster, Warren Dunham. Heroines of
modern religion. Sturgis & Walton,
1913. 275p

*FOWLER—GREAT
Fowler, Mary Jane. Great Americans.
Fideler, 1966. 128p

FOWLER—WOMAN
Fowler, Wm. F. Woman on the American frontier. Scranton, 1877. 527p

FRANK—TIME
Frank, Waldo ("Search Light"). Time
exposures. Boni & Liveright, 1967.
188p

*FRASER—HEROES
Fraser, Chelsea. Heroes of the air.
Crowell, 1939. 846p

FREDERICK—TEN
Frederick, Pauline. Ten first ladies of
the world. Meredith, 1967. 174p

*FREEDMAN—TEEN.
Freedman, Russell. Teenagers who made
history. Holiday House, 1961. 272p

FUNKE—ACTORS
Funke, Lewis and John E. Booth. Actors
talk about acting. Random House,
1961. 469p

FURNISS—SOME
Furniss, Harry. Some Victorian women;
good, bad, and indifferent. Dodd,
Mead, 1923. 226p

GADE—UNDER
Gade, John A. Under the golden lilies.
Brill, 1955. 287p

GALLICO—GOLDEN
Gallico, Paul. The golden apple. Doubleday, 1965. 315p

*GALLOWAY—ROADS
Galloway, Louise. Roads to greatness. Crowell-Collier, 1962. 374p

GAMMOND—DICT.
Gammond, Peter and Peter Clayton. Dictionary of popular music. Philosophical Library, 1961. 274p

GARDINER—POR.
Gardiner, Alfred G. Portraits and portents. Harper, 1926. 306p

GARRATY—UNFOR.
Garraty, John Arthur. The unforgettable Americans. Chanel, 1960. 338p

GELATT—MUSIC
Gelatt, Ronald. Music makers. Knopf, 1953. 286p

*GELFAND—THEY
Gelfand, Ravina and Letha Patterson. They wouldn't quit. Lerner, 1962. 56p

*GELMAN—YOUNG
Gelman, Steve. Young Olympic champions. Norton, 1964. 191p

GERLINGER—MIS.
Gerlinger, Irene Hazard. Mistresses of the White House. French, c. 1948, 1950. 123p

*GERSH—WOMEN
Gersh, Harry. Women who made America great. Lippincott, c1962. 224p

GILDER—ENTER
Gilder, Rosamond. Enter the actress, the first women in the theatre. Houghton Mifflin, 1931. 313 p

GOFF—WOMEN
Goff, Alice C. Women can be engineers. The Author, 1946. 277p

GOLDING—GREAT
Golding, Claud. Great names in history 356 B.C.-1910 A.D. Lippincott, n.d. 300p

GOLDSMITH—SEVEN
Goldsmith, Margaret. Seven women against the world. Methuen, 1935. 236p

GOODSELL—PIONEERS
Goodsell, Willystine, ed. Pioneers of women's education in the United States. McGraw-Hill, 1931. 311p

GOSS—MODERN
Goss, Madeleine. Modern music-makers. Dutton, 1952. 499p

GOULD—MODERN
Gould, Jean. Modern Amer. playwrights. Dodd, Mead, 1966. 302p

GOULDER, GRACE. See IZANT, GRACE GOULDER

GRAEF—MYSTICS
Graef, Hilda C. Mystics of our times. Hanover House, 1962. 240p

GRAHAM—GROUP
Graham, Harry. A group of Scottish women. Duffield, 1908. 343p

GREBANIER, FRANCES. See WINWAR, FRANCES, pseud.

*GREEN—AUTHORS
Green, Roger Lancelyn. Authors and places—a literary pilgrimage. Putnam, 1963. 191p

GREEN—PIONEER (1) (2) (3)
Green, Henry Clinton and Mary Wolcott Green. The pioneer mothers of America. 3 vol. Putnam, 1912. 485p

GUEDALLA—BONNET
Guedalla, Philip. Bonnet and shawl; an album. Putnam, 1928. 204p

GUERBER—EMPRESSES
Guerber, H. A. Empresses of France. Dodd, Mead, 1901. 416p

*HAGEDORN—BOOK
Hagedorn, Hermann. The book of courage. Winston, 1942. 427p

HAGGARD—REMARK.
Haggard, Andrew C. P. Remarkable women of France (from 1431 to 1749). Paul, 1914.

HAHN—LOVE
Hahn, Emily. Love conquers nothing. Doubleday, 1952. 315p

HALL—MOTHS
Hall, Geoffrey F. Moths round the flame. Holt, 1936. 364p

HAMMERTON
Hammerton, Sir J. A. Concise universal biography. Amalgamated Press Ltd., n.d. 1452p

HAMPTON—OUR
Hampton, William Judson. Our presidents and their mothers. Cornhill, 1922. 255p

HANAFORD—DAU.
Hanaford, Phebe A. Daughters of America; or, Women of the century. True, n.d. 750p

HARGRAVE—SOME
Hargrave, Mary. Some German women and their salons. Brentano's, n.d. 290p

HARKINS—FAMOUS
Harkins, Edward Francis. Famous authors (women). Page, c1901, 1906. 343p

HARKINS—LITTLE
Harkins, Edward Francis and C. H. L. Johnston. Little pilgrimages among the women who have written famous books. Page, 1902. 343p

HARKNESS—HEROINES
Harkness, David James. Heroines of the Blue and Gray. Univ. of Tenn. Newsletter, Vol. 34, No. 4, Aug., 1960. 14p

HARRISON—LITTLE
Harrison, Eveleen. Little known women of the Bible. Round Table Press, 1936. 135p

HASKELL—BALLET
Haskell, Arnold L. Ballet decade. Macmillan, 1951. 224p

°HASKELL—SAINTS
Haskell, Arnold L. Saints alive. Roy, 1953. 148p

HASKELL—VIGNET.
Haskell, Arnold L. Ballet vignettes. Allyn, 1948. 80p

HASTED—UNSUCCESS.
Hasted, Jane-Eliza. Unsuccessful ladies . . . An intimate account of the aunts (official and unofficial) of the late Queen Victoria. Hale Ltd., 1950.

HASTINGS—GREATER
Hastings, James, ed. The greater men and women of the Bible. Clark, c1914, 1940. 520p

°HAYWARD—BOOK
Hayward, Arthur L. A book of kings and queens. Roy, n.d. 228p

HAZELTINE—WE
Hazeltine, Alice Isabel. We grew up in America. Abingdon, 1954. 240p

HEAPS—FIVE
Heaps, Isabel Warrington. Five Marys. Abingdon-Cokesbury, 1942. 101p

°HEATH—AUTHORS
Heath, Monroe. Great American authors at a glance. (Great American Series, Vol. III). Pacific Coast, 1966. 34p. pa.

HEATH—WOMAN
Heath, Sophie Mary and Stella Wolfe Murray. Woman and flying. Long, 1929. 223p

°HEATH—WOMEN (4)
Heath, Monroe. Great American women. Great Americans at a glance. Vol. IV. Pacific Coast, 1957. 32p. pa.

°HEIDERSTADT—INDIAN
Heiderstadt, Dorothy. Indian friends and foes. McKay, 1958. 130p

HEINMULLER—MAN'S
Heinmuller, John. Man's fight to fly. Funk & Wagnalls, 1944. 366p

HELLER—STUDIES
Heller, Otto. Studies in modern German literature. Ginn, 1905. 301p

.HELLMAN—MRS.
Hellman, Geoffrey. Mrs. De Peyster's parties. Macmillan, 1963. 421p

HENDERSON—CONTEMP.
Henderson, Archibald. Contemporary immortals. Appleton, 1930. 209p

HERMAN—HOW
Herman, Hal, comp. and ed. How I broke into the movies. The Author, 1930. 127p

HEROLD—LOVE
Herold, J. Christopher. Love in five temperaments. Atheneum, 1961. 337p

HETHERINGTON—42
Hetherington, John. Forty-two faces. Cheshire, 1962. 250p

HINCKLEY—LADIES
Hinckley, Laura L. Ladies of literature. Hastings House, 1946. 374p

HIPSHER—AMER.
Hipsher, Edward Ellsworth. American opera and its composers. Presser, 1927. 408p

HOEHLING—WOMEN
Hoehling, A. A. Women who spied. Dodd, Mead, 1967. 204p

HOLBROOK—DREAMERS.
Holbrook, Stewart Hall. Dreamers of the American dream. Doubleday, 1957. 369p

HOLBROOK—LITTLE
Holbrook, Stewart Hall. Little Annie Oakley and other rugged people. Macmillan, 1948. 238p

HOLLINGSWORTH—HER
Hollingsworth, Buckner. Her garden was her delight. Macmillan, 1962. 166p

HOLMES—SEVEN
Holmes, Winifred. Seven adventurous women. Bell, 1953. 206p

°HOLMES—SHE
Holmes, Winifred. She was queen of Egypt. Bell, 1959. 175p

HOLROYD—FIFTY
Holroyd, George H. Fifty famous lives. Collins, n.d. 255p

HORAN—DESPERATE
Horan, James David. Desperate women. Putnam, 1952. 336p

°HOROWITZ—TREAS.
Horowitz, Caroline and Tom Leonard (pseud.), (Strong, Joanne, pseud.). A treasury of the world's great heroines, by Joanna Strong (pseud.) and Tom B. Leonard (pseud.). Hart, c1951. 190p

HORTON—WOMEN
Horton, Robt. F. Women of the Old Testament. Whittaker, 1897. 291p

HOWARD, A. V. See CHAMBERS—DICT.

HOWARD—OUR
Howard, John Tasker. Our American music. Crowell, 1946. 841p

HOWE—GALAXY
Howe, Bea. A galaxy of governesses. Verschoyle, 1954. 206p

HOWE—MEMORIES
Howe, M. A. DeWolfe. Memories of a hostess; a chronicle of eminent friendships . . . Atlantic Mo., 1922. 312p

HOYLE—TAR
Hoyle, Bernadette. Tar heel writers I knew. Blair, 1956. 215p

HUBBARD—LITTLE
Hubbard, Elbert. Little journeys to the homes of famous people. Putnam, c1897, 1922. 429p

HUFF—FAMOUS (2nd)
Huff, Warren and Edna Lenore Webb Huff. Famous Americans. Second series. Webb, 1941. 641p

HUGHES—FAMOUS
Hughes, Elinor. Famous stars of filmdom. (Women.) Page, 1931. 341p

°HUGHES—FIRST
Hughes, Langston. The first book of Negroes. Watts, 1952. 69p

HUGHES—MOTHERS
Hughes, Elmer R. Famous mothers from the Bible and history. Exposition, 1963. 156p

HUGHES—MUSIC
Hughes, Langston. Famous Negro music makers. Dodd, Mead, 1955. 179p

°HUGHES—NEGROES
Hughes, Langston. Famous Amer. negroes. Dodd, Mead, 1954. 147p

HUME—GREAT
Hume, Ruth Fox. Great women of medicine. Random House, 1964. 268p

°HUMPHREY—ELIZABETHS
Humphrey, Grace. The story of the Elizabeths. Penn., 1924. 206p

°HUMPHREY—JANES
Humphrey, Grace. The story of the Janes. Penn, 1928. 232p

°HUMPHREY—MARYS
Humphrey, Grace. The story of the Marys. Penn, 1923. 203p

°HUMPHREY—WOMEN
Humphrey, Grace. Women in American history. Bobbs-Merrill, 1919. 222p

HUMY, FERNAND E. D'. See D'HUMY, FERNAND E.

HUROK—IMPRES.
Hurok, S. . . . with Ruth Goode. Impresario. Random House, 1946. 291p

HUSSLEIN—HEROINES
Husslein, Joseph Casper. Heroines of Christ. Bruce, 1939. 186p

HYDE—MODERN
Hyde, Marietta A., comp. and ed. Modern biography. Harcourt, 1926. 345p

ICR. See CR

IMBERT—VALOIS
Imbert de Saint-Amand. Women of the Valois court. Tr. by Elizabeth Gilbert Martin. Scribner, 1895. 356p

INNIS—CLEAR
Innis, Mary Quayle. The Clear spirit: twenty Canadian women and their times. Univ. of Toronto, 1966. 301p

INTERNATIONAL CELEBRITY REGISTER. See CELEBRITY REGISTER

IREMONGER—AND
Iremonger, Lucille. And his charming lady. Secker and Warburg, 1961. 239p

IRWIN—ANGELS
Irwin, Inez Haynes. Angels and amazons. Doubleday, Doran, 1933. 531p

IZANT—OHIO
Izant, Grace Goulder. Ohio scenes and citizens. World, 1964. 253p

IZARD—HEROINES
Izard, Forrest. Heroines of the modern stage. Sturgis & Walton, 1915. 390p

JACKMAN—AMER.
Jackman, Rilla Evelyn. American arts. Rand McNally, 1928. 561p

*JACOBS—FAMOUS
Jacobs, Helen Hull. Famous American women athletes. Dodd, Mead, c1964. 121p

JANIS—THEY
Janis, Sidney. They taught themselves. Dial, 1942. 236p

JAZZ—PANORAMA
Jazz Review. Jazz panorama . . . Edited by Martin T. Williams. Crowell-Collier, c1958, 1962. 318p

JENKINS—HEROINES
Jenkins, John S. Heroines of history. Miller, 1889. 520p

JENKINS—SIX
Jenkins, Elizabeth. Six criminal women. Duell, 1949. 224p

JENKINS—TEN
Jenkins, Elizabeth. Ten fascinating women. Odhams, 1955. 208p

JENSEN—REVOLT
Jensen, Oliver. The revolt of American women. Harcourt, Brace, 1952. 224p

JENSEN—WHITE
Jensen, Amy LaFollette. White House and its 33 families. McGraw, 1962. 278p

JESSUP—FAITH
Jessup, Josephine Lurie. The faith of our feminists. Smith, 1950. 128p

JOHNSON—LUNATIC
Johnson, Gerald White. The lunatic fringe. Lippincott, 1957. 248p

*JOHNSON—SOME
Johnson, Dorothy M. Some went West. Dodd, 1965. 180p

JOHNSON—SOME CONTEMP.
Johnson, Reginald Brimley. Some contemporary novelists (women). Parsons, 1920. 220p

JOHNSON—WOMEN
Johnson, Reginald Brimley. The women novelists. Scribner, 1919. 299p

JONES—HEROINES
Jones, Katherine M. Heroines of Dixie. Bobbs-Merrill, 1955. 430p

*JONES—MODERN
Jones, George J. and Emily F. Sherman. Modern world setting for Amer. history. Heath. 1925. 295p

JONES—QUAKERS
Jones, Rufus M. The Quakers in the American colonies. Russell & Russell, 1962. 603p

*KAHN—TOPS
Kahn, Steve. Tops in pops. McFadden, 1961. 136p. pa.

KANE—SPIES
Kane, Harnett Thomas. Spies for the Blue and Gray. Hanover House, 1954. 311p

KARSH—FACES
Karsh, Yousuf. Faces of destiny. Ziff-Davis, 1946. 159p

KAVANAGH—WOMEN (1) (2)
Kavanagh, Julia. Women in France during the 18th century. Putnam, 1893. v. 1-232p. v. 2-250p

KELEN—MIST.
Kelen, Betty. The mistresses. Random House, 1966. 341p

KELLY—REPORTERS
Kelly, Frank K. Reporters around the world. Little, Brown, 1957. 242p

KEMBLE—IDOLS
Kemble, James. Idols and invalids. Doubleday, Doran, 1936. 328p

KENWORTHY—12
> Kenworthy, Leonard S. Twelve citizens of the world. Doubleday, c1944, 1953. 286p

*920
K38t*

KEYES—LIVES
> Keyes, Rowena K. Lives of today and yesterday. Appleton. 1931. 297p

KEYES—THREE
> Keyes, Frances Parkinson. Three ways of love. Hawthorn Books, 1963. 299p

*KIRKLAND—ACHIEVED
> Kirkland, Winifred M. and Frances Kirkland. Girls who achieved. Smith, 1931. 132p

*KIRKLAND—ARTISTS
> Kirkland, Winifred M. and Frances Kirkland. Girls who became artists. Harper, 1934. 115p

*KIRKLAND—GOOD
> Kirkland, Winifred M. and Frances Kirkland. Girls who made good. Smith, 1930. 120p

*KIRKLAND—WRITERS
> Kirkland, Winifred M. and Frances Kirkland. Girls who became writers. Harper, 1933. 121p

KITTLER—PROFILES
> Kittler, Glenn D. Profiles in faith. Coward-McCann, 1962. 318p

KLEIN—GREAT
> Klein, Herman. Great women singers of my time. Dutton, 1931. 244p

*KNAPP—NEW
> Knapp, Sally. New wings for women. Crowell, 1946. 179p

*KNAPP—WOMEN
> Knapp, Sally. Women doctors today. Crowell, 1947. 184p

*KOBBÉ—HOMES
> Kobbé, Gustav. Famous actresses and their homes. Little, Brown, 1905. 243p

*KOMROFF—TRUE
> Komroff, Manuel. True adventures of spies. Little, Brown, 1954. 220p

KOVEN—WOMEN
> Koven, Anna De. Women in cycles of culture. Putnam, 1941. 333p

LADER—BOLD
> Lader, Lawrence. The bold Brahmins; New England's war against slavery; 1831-1863. Dutton, 1961. 318p

LADIES'—AMER. 12
> Ladies' Home Journal, and The Christian Science Monitor. America's twelve great women leaders during the past hundred years as chosen by the women of America. Associated Authors Service, 1933. 55p

LAHEE—FAMOUS
> Lahee, Henry Charles. Famous singers of today and yesterday. Page, 1898. 337p

LAHEE—GRAND
> Lahee, Henry Charles. The grand opera singers of today. Page, 1912. 543p

LAMBERT—QUIET
> Lambert, Principal D. W. The quiet in the land. Epworth, 1956. 101p

*LAMM—BIOG.
> Lamm, Lucian. Biographical sketches in American history. College Entrance, 1931. 168p

LAMPARSKI—WHAT.
> Lamparski, Richard. Whatever became of . . . ? Crown, 1967. 208p

*920.073
238W*

LAMSON—FEW
> Lamson, Peggy. Few are chosen. American women in political life today. Houghton Mifflin, 1968, 240p

*301.4129
L242F*

*LARSEN—SCRAP.
> Larsen, Egon, (Egon Lehrburger). Inventor's scrapbook. Drummond, 1947. 216p

*LAUWICK—HEROINES
> Lauwick, Hervé. Heroines of the sky. Translated by James Cleugh. Muller, 1960. 221p.

LAW—CIVILIZ.
> Law, Frederick Houk. Civilization builders. Appleton-Century, 1939. 356p

LAWRENCE—SCHOOL
> Lawrence, Margaret. The school of femininity. Stokes, 1936. 382p

*823.09
L4225
1966*

LEARY—GOLDEN
> Leary, Francis. The golden longing. Scribner, 1959. 358p

LEE—WIVES
> Lee, Elizabeth. Wives of the prime ministers, 1844-1906. Dutton, n.d. 252p

LEETCH—REVEILLE
> Leetch, Margaret. Reveille in Washington, 1860-1865. Harper, 1941. 483p

LEONARD—AMER.
Leonard, Eugene Andruss, Sophie Hutchinson Drinker and Miriam Young Holden. The American woman in colonial and Revolutionary times, 1565-1800, Univ. of Penn., 1962. 169p

LeROY—MUSIC
LeRoy, George. Music hall stars of the nineties. British Technical and General Press, 1952. 70p

*LEVINGER—GREAT
Levinger, Elma Ehrlich. Great Jewish women. Behrman, 1949. 159p

LEWIS—PORTRAITS
Lewis, Ethel Clark. Portraits of Bible women. Vantage, 1956. 252p

LIFTON—WOMAN
Lifton, Robert Joy. The woman in America. Houghton Mifflin, 1965. 293p

301.412
L723w

LIPMAN—PRIMITIVE
Lipman, Jean and Alice Winchester. Primitive painters in America, 1750-1950. Dodd, Mead, 1950. 182p

759.13
L764p

LLEWELLYN—CHINA'S
Llewellyn, Bernard. China's courts and concubines. Allen and Unwin, 1956. 214p

LOFTS—WOMEN
Lofts, Norah. Women in the old testament. Macmillan, 1949. 178p

220.9
L821w

LOGAN—LADIES
Logan, Logna B. Ladies of the White House. Vantage, 1962. 194p

LOGAN—PART
Logan, Mary Simmerson. The part taken by women in American history. Perry-Nalle, 1912. 927p

LOGGINS—HEAR
Loggins, Vernon. I hear America. Literature in the United States since 1900. Crowell, 1937. 378p

*LOGIE—CAREERS
Logie, Iona. Careers in the making. Harper, 1935. 381p

*LOGIE—CAREERS (2nd)
Logie, Iona. Careers in the making. 2nd series. Harper, 1942. 243p

LONGWELL—AMER.
Longwell, Marjorie R. America and women. Dorrance, 1962. 205p

LORD—GREAT
Lord, F. Townley. Great women of the Bible. Harper, n.d. 207p

LOTZ—JEWS
Lotz, Philip Henry. Distinguished American Jews. (Creative Personalities, Vol. VI.) Association Press, 1945. 107p

920.073
L885d
1970

LOTZ—UNUSED
Lotz, Philip Henry, ed. Unused alibis. Association Press, 1951. 120p

LOTZ—WOMEN
Lotz, Philip Henry. Women leaders. (Creative Personalities, Vol. II.) Association Press, 1946. 149p

LOVE—FAMOUS
Love, Cornelia Spencer. Famous women of yesterday and today. Rev. ed. Univ. of North Carolina, 1936. 52p

LOVEJOY—WOMEN
Lovejoy, Esther Pohl. Women doctors of the world. Macmillan, 1957. 413p

610.69
L897w

LOVEJOY—WOMEN PHYS.
Lovejoy, Esther Pohl. Women physicians and surgeons. Livingston, n.d. 246p

LOWNSBERY—SAINTS
Lownsbery, Eloise. Saints and rebels. Longmans, Green, 1937. 356p

McCABE—EMPR.
McCabe, Joseph. The empresses of Rome. Holt, 1911. 357p

920
M123e

*McCALLUM—WOMEN
McCallum, Jane Y. Women pioneers. Johnson, 1929. 251p

*MacCARTHY—LATER
MacCarthy, Bridget. The later women novelists. 1744-1818. Cork Univ., 1947. 296p

MacCARTHY—WOMEN
MacCarthy, Bridget. Women writers. Cork Univ., 1944. 288p

MACARTNEY—GREAT
Macartney, Clarence Edward. Great women of the Bible. Abingdon-Cokesbury, 1942. 207p

McCLINTOCK—NOBEL
McClintock, Marshall. The Nobel prize treasury. Doubleday, 1948. 612p

°McCONNELL—FAMOUS
McConnell, Jane (Tompkins). Famous ballet dancers. Crowell, 1955. 176p

°McCONNELL—OUR
McConnell, Jane (Tompkins) and Burt Morton McConnell. Our first ladies; from Martha Washington to Jacqueline Lee Bouvier Kennedy. Crowell, 1961. 358p

McCOY—PORTRAITS
McCoy, Guy, comp. and ed. Portraits of the world's best women musicians. Presser, 1946. 251p

McCRAITH—ROMANCE
McCraith, L. M. The romance of Irish heroines. Longmans, Green, 1913. 174p

°McKOWN—HEROIC
McKown, Robin. Heroic nurses. Putnam, 1966. 320p

MacNALTY—PRINCES
MacNalty, Sir Arthur Salusbury. The princes in the tower. Johnson, 1955. 212p

✓ MACQUEEN-POPE—LADIES
Macqueen-Pope, Walter James. Ladies first; the story of woman's conquest of the British stage. Allen, 1952. 384p

192.0942
M174 ℓ

✓McSPADDEN—SCULPTORS
McSpadden, Joseph Walker. Famous sculptors of America. Dodd, Mead, 1927. 377p

730.922
M176f
1968

°MacVEAGH—CHAMPLIN
MacVeagh, Lincoln, ed. The new Champlin cyclopedia for young folks. Holt, 1924. 630p

MADISON—CRITICS
Madison, Charles A. Critics and crusaders. Holt, 1947. 534p

MAHONY—ILLUS.
Mahony, Bertha E., Louise Payson Latimer and Beulah Folmsbee. Illustrators of children's books, 1744-1945. Horn, c1947, 1961. 527p

MAITLAND—KNIGHTS
Maitland, Lester J. Knights of the air. Doubleday, Doran, 1929. 338p

✓ MANTLE—AMER.
Mantle, Robt. Burns. Amer. playwrights of today. Dodd, Mead, 1929. 324p

927. q
M319a

MANTLE—CONTEMP.
Mantle, Burns. Contemporary American playwrights. Dodd, Mead, 1938. 357p

MARBLE—WOMEN
Marble, Annie Russell. The women who came in the Mayflower. Pilgrim, 1920. 110p

MARBLE—WOMEN, BIBLE
Marble, Annie Russell. Women of the Bible. Century, 1923. 315p

✓MARCUS—MEMOIRS (1) (2)
Marcus, Jacob Rader. Memoirs of American Jews, 1775-1865, v. 1, 2. Jewish Pub. Soc. of Amer., 1955. vl-375p v2-387p.

LAC
23868-
69

MARINACCI—LEAD.
Marinacci, Barbara. Leading ladies; a gallery of famous actresses. Dodd, 1961. 206p

MARKS—GLAMOUR
Marks, Edward B. They all had glamour. Messner, 1944. 448p

✓MARSHALL—AMER.
Marshall, John David. An American library history reader. Shoe String, 1961. 464p

027.073
M369a

MARTIN—PETE
Martin, Thornton (Pete). Pete Martin calls on . . . Simon & Schuster, 1962. 510p

MARTINDALE—SOME
Martindale, Hilda. Some Victorian portraits. Allen & Unwin, 1948. 106p

MASSINGHAM—GREAT
Massingham, H. J. The great Victorians. London, 1932. 507p

✓ °MATTHEWS—DAUNT.
Matthews, Winifred. Dauntless women. Friendship, 1947. 170p

266.023
M429d
1970

MATZ—OPERA
Matz, Mary Jane. Opera stars in the sun. Farrar, Straus & Cudahy, 1955. 349p

MAURICE—MAKERS
Maurice, Arthur B. Makers of modern American fiction. The Mentor. Dept. of Literature, Vol. 7, #13. (Serial No. 185.) 12p (Plus #1-6)

°MAY—WOMEN
May, Charles Paul. Women in aeronautics. Nelson, 1962 260p

*MAYNARD—AMER.
Maynard, Olga. Amer. modern dancers. Little, Brown, 1965. 218p

MAYNARD—GREAT
Maynard, Theodore. Great Catholics in American history. Hanover House, 1957. 261p

MAYNARD—SAINTS
Maynard, Theodore. Saints for our times. Appleton - Century - Crofts, 1952. 296p

MAYNE—ENCHANT.
Mayne, Ethel Colburn. Enchanters of men. Putnam, 1925. 358p

MEAD—250
Mead, Frank S. 250 Bible biographies. Harper, 1934. 250p

MEAD—MEDICAL
Mead, Kate Campbell Hurd. Medical women of America. Froben, 1933. 95p

MEANS—WOMAN
Means, Marianne. The woman in the White House: the lives and times of twelve notable first ladies. Random House, 1963. 299p. pa.

MEARS—THEY
Mears, Louise Wilhelmina. They come and go. Christopher, 1955. 122p

MEINE—GREAT
Meine, Franklin and Harris Gaylord Warren, ed. Great leaders of the world. University of Knowledge, 1940. 383p

MELIKOV—IMMORT.
Melikov, Gregor. The immortals of America in the Hall of Fame. The Author, 1942. 224p

MELVILLE—MAIDS
Melville, Lewis (Lewis Saul Benjamin). Maids of honour. Doran, 1917. 314p

MELVILLE—MORE
Melville, Lewis (Lewis Saul Benjamin). More stage favourites of the eighteenth century. Hutchinson, 1929. 286p

MELVILLE—REGENCY
Melville, Lewis (Lewis Saul Benjamin). Regency ladies. Doran, 1926. 300p

MELVILLE—STAGE
Melville, Lewis (Lewis Saul Benjamin). Stage favourites of the 18th century. Doubleday, Doran, 1929. 13-288p

MELVILLE—WINDSOR
Melville, Lewis (Lewis Saul Benjamin). The Windsor beauties. Houghton, 1928. 285p

MERSAND—AMER.
Mersand, Joseph. The American drama since 1930. Modern Chapbooks, 1951. 188p

*MEYER—CHAMPIONS
Meyer, Edith Patterson. Champions of peace. Little, Brown, 1959. 216p

*MEYERS—CHAMP.
Meyers, Barlow. Champions all the way. Whitman, 1960. 210p

MICHIGAN—BIOG.
Michigan State Library. Biographical sketches of American artists. Mich. State Lib., 1924. 370p

MILLER—HANDI.
Miller, Basil. Ten handicapped people who became famous. Zondervan, 1951. 73p

MILLER—TEN
Miller, Basil. Ten girls who became famous. Zondervan, 1956. 72p

*MILLER—WEST.
Miller, Helen Markley. Westering women. Doubleday, 1961. 240p

*MILLETT—AMER.
Millett, Fred B. Contemporary American authors. Harcourt, Brace, 1940. 716p

MILLETT—BRIT.
Millett, Fred B. Contemporary British literature. 3rd rev. & enl. Harcourt, Brace, 1939. 555p

MINNIGERODE—SOME
Minnigerode, Meade. Some American ladies. Putnam, 1926. 287p

MIZWA—GREAT
Mizwa, Stephen P., ed. Great men and women of Poland. Macmillan, 1942. 397p.

*MODEROW—PEOPLE
Moderow, Gertrude. People to remember. Scott, Foresman, 1960. 296p

*MONTGOMERY—STORY
Montgomery, Elizabeth Rider. The story behind great medical discoveries. McBride, 1945. 247p

MOORE—DISTING.
Moore, Virginia. Distinguished women writers. Dutton, 1934. 253p

*MOORE—MODERN
Moore, John Travers and Rosemarian V. Staudacher. Modern crusaders. Farrar, Straus & Cudahy, 1957. 190p

*MOORE—WHEN
Moore, Rebecca Deming. When they were girls. Owen, 1923, 1937. 192p

MOORE—WOMEN
Moore, Frank. Women of the war. Scranton, 1867. 596p

MORELLO—HALL
Morello, Theodore. The Hall of Fame for great Americans at New York University. N.Y. Univ., 1962. 192p. pa.

MORGAN—WRITERS
Morgan, H. Wayne. Writers in transition: seven Americans. Hill & Wang, 1963. 170p

MORRIS—400
Morris, Richard, ed. Four hundred notable Americans. Harper & Row, c1953, 1965. 279p. pa.

MORTON—WOMEN
Morton, Henry. Women of the Bible. Dodd, Mead, 1954. 204p

MOSES—FAMOUS
Moses, Montrose F. Famous actor-families in America. Crowell, 1906. 341p

MOTT—GALLERY
Mott, Frank Luther. A gallery of Americans. A Mentor book. New Amer. Library, 1951. 224p. pa.

MOZANS—WOMAN
Mozans, H. J. (John Zahm). Woman in science. Appleton, 1913. 452p

*MUIR—FAMOUS
Muir, Jane. Famous dancers. Dodd, 1956. 159p

MUIR—WOMEN
Muir, Chas. Stothard. Women, the makers of history. Vantage, 1956. 234p

*MUIR—WRITERS
Muir, Jane. Famous modern Amer. women writers. Dodd, 1959. 171p

MURROW—THIS (1)
Murrow, Edward R. This I believe. (1st series.) Simon & Schuster, 1952. 200p. pa.

MURROW—THIS (2)
Murrow, Edward R. This I believe. (2d series.) Simon & Schuster, 1954. 231p

*NATHAN—WOMEN
Nathan, Dorothy. Women of courage. Random House, 1964. 188p

NATIONAL—CONTEMP.
National Sculpture Society, N.Y. Contemporary American sculpture. The Society, 1929. 352p

NELSON—BIBLE
Nelson, Hazel McCurdy. Bible women come alive. Abington, 1952. 144p

NEWQUIST—SHOW.
Newquist, Ray. Showcase. Morrow, 1966. 412p

NEW YORK
New Yorker. Profiles from the New Yorker. Knopf, 1938. 400p

N.Y. MUSEUM—NEW
New York, Museum of Modern Art. The new decade. Edited by Andrew Carnduff Ritchie. The Museum, 1955. 111p

NEW YORKER
New Yorker. "Profiles" 1925-1968

*NIDA—PILOTS
Nida, Wm. L. and Stella H. Nida. Pilots and pathfinders. Macmillan, 1928. 411p

NIGG—GREAT
Nigg, Walter. Great saints. Translated by Wm. Stirling. Regnery, 1948. 286p

*NISENSON—MINUTE
Nisenson, Samuel and Wm. A. DeWitt. Illustrated minute biographies. Grosset & Dunlap, 1949. 160p

*NISENSON—MORE MINUTE
Nisenson, Samuel and Alfred Parker. More minute biographies. Grosset & Dunlap, 1933. 160p

NOBEL—MAN
Nobel Foundation, ed. Nobel, the man and his prizes. Univ. of Oklahoma, 1950. 620p

*NOLEN—SPIES
Nolen, Barbara, ed. Spies, spies, spies. Watts, 1965. 250p

O'BRIEN—50
O'Brien, Edward J., ed. 50 Best American short stories. Literary Guild, 1939. 868p

O'BRIEN—ROAD
O'Brien, John Anthony. Road to Damascus. Doubleday, c1949, 1950. 248p

OCKENGA—WOMEN
Ockenga, Harold John. Women who made Bible history. Zonderman, 1962. 239p

°O'CLERY—QUEENS
O'Clery, Helen. Queens, queens, queens. Watts, 1965. 195p

O'CONNELL—OTHER
O'Connell, Charles. The other side of the record. Knopf, 1947. 332p

O'CONNOR—PIONEER
O'Connor, Lillian. Pioneer women orators. Columbia Univ., 1954. 264p

O'HIGGINS—AMER.
O'Higgins, Harvey J. and Edward H. Reede. The American mind in action. Harper, 1924. 336p

OLIPHANT—WOMEN
Oliphant, Mrs., and others. Women novelists of Queen Victoria's reign. Hurst & Blackett, 1897. 311p

100 GREAT
One hundred great lives. Edited by John Allen. Greystone, 1945. 790p

ORCUTT—CELEB.
Orcutt, William Dana. Celebrities off parade. Willett, Clark, 1935. 287p

ORMSBEE—BACK.
Ormsbee, Helen. Backstage with actors. Crowell, 1938. 343p

ORR—FAMOUS
Orr, Lyndon. Famous lovers of history. Harper, c1909, 1912. 368p

ORR—FAMOUS AFFIN.
Orr, Lyndon. Famous affinities of history. (4 vols. in 1.) Harper, 1912. 186p

OSBORN—FRAGMENTS
Osborn, Herbert. Fragments of entomological history. The Author, Columbus, 1937. 394p

OVERTON—AUTHORS
Overton, Grant. Authors of the day. Doran, 1924. 390p

OVERTON—WOMEN
Overton, Grant. The women who make our novels. New and rev. ed. Dodd, Mead, 1928. 352p

OVINGTON—POR.
Ovington, Mary White. Portraits in color. Viking, 1927. 241p

PADOVER—CONFESS
Padover, Saul K., ed. Confessions and self-portraits. Day, 1957. 362p

PAPASHVILY—ALL
Papashvily, Helen (Waite). All the happy endings . . . Harper, 1956. 231p

PARKHILL—WILDEST
Parkhill, Forbes. The wildest of the West. Holt, 1951. 310p

PARKINSON—LAW
Parkinson, C. Northcote. A law unto themselves. Houghton Mifflin, 1966. 232p

°PARKMAN—HEROINES
Parkman, Mary R. Heroines of service. Century, 1917. 322p

PARSHALLE—KASH.
Parshalle, Eve. The Kashmir bridge—women. Oxford, 1965. 231p

PARTON—DAU.
Parton, James. Daughters of genius. Hubbard, 1885. 563p

PARTON—NOTED
Parton, James. Noted women of Europe and America. Bay State, 1884. 646p

PATRICK—PROFILES
Patrick, Sam and George Getze. Profiles in science. Times-Mirror Syndicate, 1962. 59p

PATTEE—FEM.
Pattee, Fred Lewis. The feminine fifties. D. Appleton-Century, 1940. 339p

PAXTON—WOMEN
Paxton, Annabel. Women in Congress. Dietz Press, 1945. 131p

PEARSON—MARRY.
Pearson, Hesketh. The marrying Americans. McCann, 1961. 313p

PEARSON—PILGRIM
Pearson, Hesketh. The Pilgrim daughters. Heinemann, 1961. 343p

PEATTIE—JOURNEY
Peattie, Donald Culross. Journey into America. Houghton Mifflin, 1943. 276p

PECKHAM—CAPT.
Peckham, Howard H. Captured by Indians. Rutgers Univ., 1954. 238p

*PECKHAM—WOMEN
Peckham, Betty. Women in aviation. Nelson, 1945. 31p

PELTZ—SPOT.
Peltz, Mary Ellis. Spotlight on the stars. Metropolitan Opera Guild, 1943. 114p

PENNOCK—MAKERS
Pennock, Meta Rutter. Makers of nursing history. . . . Lakeside, 1940. 142p

PETERSON—GREAT
Peterson, Houston. Great teachers, portrayed by those who studied under them. Rutgers Univ., 1946. 351p

PEYRE—FRENCH
Peyre, Henri. French novelists of today. Oxford, 1967. 484p

PEYTON—MOTHERS
Peyton, Mabel Bartlett and Lucia Kinley. Mothers, makers of men. Dodge, 1927. 144p

PHELPS—MEN '58 (1)
Phelps, Robert H., ed. Men in the news — 1958. Lippincott, 1959. 269p

PHELPS—MEN '59 (2)
Phelps, Robert H., ed. Men in the news: 2. Lippincott, 1960. 320p

PHILA.—WOMEN
Philadelphia Women's Stamp Club. Women on stamps. Feb., 1953. unp. pa.

PHILLIPS—33
Phillips, Emma M. 33 women of the restoration. Herald House, 1960. 197p

PLANCK—WOMEN
Planck, Charles E. Women with wings. Harper, 1942. 33p

PLEASANTS—GREAT
Pleasants, Henry. Great singers; from the dawn of opera to our own time. Simon & Schuster, 1966. 382p

*PLUMB—LIVES
Plumb, Beatrice. Lives that inspire. Denison, 1962. 219p

POMEROY—LITTLE
Pomeroy, Sarah Gertrude. Little-known sisters of well-known men. Estes, 1912. 304p

POOL—FAMOUS
Pool, John P. Famous women of India. Gupta, 1954. 150p

POOLE—ASTRONAUTS
Poole, Lynn and Gray. Scientists who work with astronauts. Dodd, Mead, 1964. 172p

*POOLE—OUTDOORS
Poole, Lynn and Gray. Scientists who work outdoors. Dodd, 1963. 178p

POPULAR RECORD
Popular record directory, by Lyle Kenyon Engel. Fawcett, 1958. 144p

*POWER—MORE
Power, Rhoda and Eileen Power. More boys and girls of history. Cambridge, 1928. 273p

PRINDIVILLE—FIRST
Prindiville, Kathleen. First ladies. Macmillan, c1932, 1962. 309p

*PRINGLE—WHEN
Pringle, Patrick. When they were girls. Roy. n.d. 208p

PROCHNOW—GREAT
Prochnow, Herbert V. Great stories from great lives. 4th ed. Harper, 1944. 404p

PROGRESS—SCIENCE
The progress of science. A review of 1941. Grolier Society, 1942. 404p

PROUT—PETTICOAT
Prout, Denton, pseud. and Fred Feely. Petticoat parade. Rigby, 1965. 252p

RABLING—UNDER
Rabling Harold and Patrick Hamilton. Under the Southern Cross. St. Martin's 1962. 114p

RAVENEL—WOMEN
Ravenel Florence Leftwich. Women and the French tradition. Macmillan 1918. 234p

READER'S—GREAT
Reader's Digest. Great lives, great deeds. Reader's Digest Assoc. 1964. 576p

REAVEY—NEW
Reavey, George, ed. and tr. New Russian poets, 1953-1966. October House, 1966. 292p

*REED—FOLLOW
Reed, Dena. Follow your star. Teen Age Books, c1948, 1957. 153p

REIS—COMPOSERS
Reis, Claire R. Composers in America. Rev. & enl. Macmillan, 1947. 399p

RIBALOW—AUTO.
Ribalow, Harold U. Autobiographies of American Jews. Jewish Pub. Soc. of Amer., 1965. 496p

*RICHARDSON—GREAT
Richardson, Ben. Great American negroes. Rev. by Wm. A. Fahey. Crowell, c1945, 1956. 339p

*RICHMOND—IMMIG.
Richmond, Jack. Immigrants all—Americans all. Comet, 1955. 141p

*RIEDMAN—MEN
Riedman, Sarah R. Men and women behind the atom. Abelard-Schuman, 1958. 228p

*RIEDMAN—PORTRAITS
Riedman, Sarah R. and Elton T. Gustafson. Portraits of Nobel laureates in medicine and physiology. Abelard-Schuman, 1963. 343p

RIEGEL—AMER.
Riegel, Robert E. American feminists. Univ. of Kansas, 1963. 223p

RIVKIN—HELLO
Rivkin, Allen and Laura Kerr. . . . Hello, Hollywood! Doubleday, 1962. 571p

ROBINSON—HIST.
Robinson, Wilhelmina S. Historical Negro biographies. Publishers, 1967. 291p

ROBINSON—100
Robinson, Donald. The 100 most important people in the world today. (A Cardinal ed.) Pocket Books, 1952. 427p. pa.

RODERICK—20
Roderick, Colin A., de. 20 Australian novelists. Angus & Robertson, 1947. 323p

ROGERS—GALLANT
Rogers, Cameron. Gallant ladies. Harcourt, Brace, 1928. 363p

ROGERS—WOMEN
Rogers, Agnes. Women are here to stay. Harper, 1949. 220p

*ROLLINS—FAMOUS
Rollins, Charlemae. Famous American negro poets. Dodd, Mead, 1965. 96p

*ROLLINS—ENTER.
Rollins, Charlemae. Famous Negro entertainers of stage, screen, and TV. Dodd, Mead, 1967. 122p

ROOSEVELT—LADIES
Roosevelt, Eleanor and Lorena A. Hickok. Ladies of courage. Putnam, 1954. 312p

ROOT—CHAPTER
Root, Mary Philotheta. Chapter sketches. Connecticut. Daughters of the American Revolution. Judd, 1901. 531p

ROSEN—FOUR
Rosen, George and Beate Caspari-Rosen. 400 years of a doctor's life. Schuman, 1947. 429p

ROSENBAUM—MODERN
Rosenbaum, Sidonia Carmen. Modern women poets of Spanish America. Hispanic Institute, 1945. 273p

ROSENTHAL—SOPRANOS
Rosenthal, Harold. Sopranos of today. Calder, 1956. 103p

ROSS—CHARMERS
Ross, Ishbel. Charmers and cranks. Harper & Row, 1965. 306p

*ROSS—HEROINES
Ross, Nancy Wilson. Heroines of the early West. Random House, c1944, 1960. 182p

*ROSS—KNOW
Ross, George E. Know your presidents and their wives. McNally, 1960. 72p

ROSS—LADIES
Ross, Ishbel. Ladies of the press. Harper, 1936. 622p

ROSS—PLAYER
Ross, Lillian and Helen Ross. The player, a profile of an art. Simon & Schuster, 1962. 459p

ROSS—WESTWARD
Ross, Nancy Wilson. Westward the women. Knopf, 1944. 199p

ROURKE—ROOTS
Rourke, Constance. The roots of American culture. Harcourt, Brace, 1942. 305p

RUSSELL—GLIT.
Russell, Phillips. The glittering century.
Scribner, 1936. 326p

RYDER—ARTISTS
Ryder, John. Artists of a certain line.
The Bodley Head, 1960. 125p

SACKVILLE-WEST—EAGLE
Sackville-West, Victoria. The eagle and
the dove. Doubleday, Doran, 1944.
175p

SALE—OLD
Sale, Edith Tunis. Old time belles and
cavaliers. Lippincott, 1912. 286p

SALESKI—JEWISH
Saleski, Gdal. Famous musicians of Jewish origin. Bloch, 1949. 716p

SALESKI—WANDER.
Saleski, Gdal. Famous musicians of a
wandering race. Bloch, 1927. 463p

SANDERS—CANADIAN
Sanders, Byrne Hope. Canadian portraits
. . . famous women. Clarke, Irwin,
1958. 145p

SANDERS—INTIMATE
Sanders, Margaret. Intimate letters of
England's queens. Museum Press,
1957. 234p

SARGENT—PIONEERS
Sargent, Shirley. Pioneer in petticoats;
Yosemite's early women, 1856-1900.
Trans-Anglo Books, 1966. 80p

SATURDAY REV.
The *Saturday Review Gallery* . . . Selec-
ted from the complete files by Jerome Beatty, Jr. and the Editors of
Saturday Review. Simon & Schuster, 1959. 481p

*SCHERMAN—AMER.
Scherman, David Edward. America; the
land and its writers. Dodd, Mead,
1952, 1956. 80p

SCHERMAN—LITERARY
Scherman, David E. Literary America.
Dodd, Mead, 1952. 176p

SCHICKEL—STARS
Schickel, Richard. The stars. Dial, 1962.
287p

SCHMIDT—400
Schmidt, Minna Moscherosch. 400 out-
standing women of the world. The
Authors, 1933. 583p

SCHNITTKIND, HENRY. *See* THOMAS
SCHONBERG—GREAT
Schonberg, Harold C. The great pian-
ists. Simon & Schuster, 1963. 448p

SEITZ—UNCOMMON
Seitz, Don Carlos. Uncommon Americans; pencil portraits of men and
women who have broken the rules.
Bobbs-Merrill, 1925. 328p

SERVIEZ—ROMAN (1) (2)
Serviez, Jacques Boergas de. The Roman empresses. Dingwall-Rock,
1925. 2 vol.

SETTEL—RADIO
Settel, Irving. A pictorial history of
radio. Citadel, 1960. 176p

*SEVENTEEN—IN
Seventeen. In my opinion. The Seventeen book of very important per-
sons. Macmillan, 1966. 211p

SEWELL—BRIEF
Sewell, W. Stuart. Brief biographies of
famous men and women. Permabooks, 1949. 244p. pa.

SHAPIRO—CONTEMP.
Shapiro, Charles, ed. Contemporary
British novelists. University Press,
1965. 164p

SHAPIRO—JAZZ
Shapiro, Nat and Nat. Hentoff, eds. Jazz
makers. Rinehart, 1957. 368p

SHARKEY—POP.
Sharkey, Don and Sister Loretta Clare.
Popular patron saints. Bruce, 1959.
233p

SHAW—STORY
Shaw, Anna Howard. The story of a
pioneer. With the collaboration of
Elizabeth Jordan. Harper, 1915.
338p

SHERMAN—WORLD'S
Sherman, Robert. World's great love
letters. World Pub., 1943. 242p

*SHIPPEN—BRIDLE
Shippen, Katherine Binney. A bridle
for Pegasus. Viking, 1951. 192p

*SHIPPEN—DESIGN
Shippen, Katherine Binney. Bright design. Viking, 1949. 207p

*SICKELS—CALICO
Sickels, Eleanor. In calico and crino-
line; true stories of American wom-
en, 1608-1865. Viking, 1935. 270p

SICKELS—TWELVE
Sickels, Eleanor. Twelve daughters of democracy. Viking, 1941. 256p

SILVER—PROFILES
Silver, Lily Joy. Profiles in success. Fountainhead, 1965.

SIMKINS—WOMEN
Simkins, Francis Butler and James Welch Patton. The women of the confederacy. Garrett & Massie, 1936. 306p

SIMONHOFF—JEW.
Simonhoff, Harry. Jewish notables in America 1776-1865. Greenberg, 1956. 402p

SIMONHOFF—SAGA
Simonhoff, Harry. Saga of American Jewry, 1865-1914. Arco, 1959.

SINGER—3000
Singer, Kurt, ed. 3000 yrs. of espionage. Prentice-Hall, 1948. 384p

SINGER—WORLD (II)
Singer, Kurt. Spies and traitors of World War II. Prentice-Hall, 1945. 295p

SINGER—WORLD'S
Singer, Kurt. The world's 30 greatest women spies. Funk, 1951. 321p

SITWELL—WOMEN
Sitwell, Edith. English women. Hastings House, 1932. 48p

16 AMER.
16 American health heroes. (Vol. XXV. of the Health Bulletin for teachers). Metrop. Life Ins., n.d. 75p. pa.

SKINNER—ELEGANT
Skinner, Cornelia Otis. Elegant wits and grand horizontals. Houghton, 1962. 262p

SMITH—HIST. (I)
Smith, David Eugene. History of mathematics. Vol. 1. Ginn, 1958. 596p

SMITH—ORIGINALS
Smith, Warren Hunting. Originals abroad. Yale Univ., 1952. 205p

SMITH—ROMANCES
Smith, Bessie White. The romances of the presidents. Lothrop, Lee & Shepard, 1932. 400p

SMITH—TORCH
Smith, Henry Monmouth. Torchbearers of chemistry. Academic, 1949. 270p

SMITH—WHITE
Smith, Marie and Louise Durbin. White House brides. Acropolis Books, 1966. 208p

SMITH—WOMEN'S
Smith, Lewis, ed. Women's poetry today . . . with biographical notes and comment by Alice Carey Weitz. Sully, 1929. 237p

SNOW—WOMEN
Snow, Edward R. Women of the sea. Dodd, Mead, 1962. 272p

SNYDER—TREAS.
Snyder, Louis L., ed. A treasury of intimate biographies. Greenberg, 1951. 384p

SOPER—THESE
Soper, David Wesley. These found a way. Westminster, 1951. 175p

SORLEY—KING'S
Sorley, Janetta C. King's daughters. Cambridge Univ., 1937. 287p

SPENCER—WORKERS
Spencer, John. Workers for humanity. Harrap, 1962. 106p

SPRUILL—WOMEN'S
Spruill, Julia Cherry. Women's life and work in the Southern colonies. Univ. of N. Carolina, 1938. 426p

SPURGEON—SERMONS
Spurgeon, Charles Haddon. Sermons on women of the Old Testament. Zondervan, 1960. 256p

STAMBLER—ENCY.
Stambler, Irwin. Encyclopedia of popular music. St. Martin's, 1965. 359p

STEBBINS—LONDON
Stebbins, Lucy Poate. London ladies. Columbia Univ., 1952. 208p

STEBBINS—VICTORIAN
Stebbins, Lucy Poate. Victorian album. Columbia Univ., 1946. 226p

*STEEDMAN—WHEN
Steedman, Amy. When they were children. Stokes, 1914. 387p

STENTON—ENGLISH
Stenton, Doris Mary (Parsons), Lady. The English women in history. Macmillan, 1957. 363p

STERN—AND
Stern, Gladys Bronwyn. And did he stop and speak to you? Regnery, 1958. 202p

STERN—WE
  Stern, Madeleine B. We the women:
  Career firsts of 19th cent. America.
  Schulte, 1963. 403p

STERN—WOMEN
  Stern, Elizabeth Gertrude (Levin). The
  women in Gandhi's life, by Eleanor
  Morton, pseud. Dodd, Mead, 1953.
  304p

*STEVENS—HUMAN.
  Stevens, William Oliver. Famous hu-
  manitarians. Dodd, Mead, 1953.
  131p

*STEVENS—WOMEN
  Stevens, William Oliver. Famous women
  of America. Dodd, 1950. 174p

STEVENSON—NOBEL
  Stevenson, Lloyd G. Nobel prize winners in medicine and physiology,
  1901-1965. Abelard-Schumann,
  1967. 464p

STEWART—45
  Stewart, Virginia. 45 contemporary Mex-
  ican artists. Stanford Univ., 1951.
  167p

STEWART—MAKERS
  Stewart, Kenneth and John Tebbel.
  Makers of modern journalism. Pren-
  tice-Hall, 1952. 514p

STILES—POSTAL
  Stiles, Kent B. Postal saints and sinners.
  Theo. Gaus' Sons, 1964. 295p

STIRLING—ODD
  Stirling, A. M. W. (Anna Maria Diane
  Wilhelmenia). Odd lives. Macmil-
  lan, 1959. 168p

*STODDARD—TOP.
  Stoddard, Anne. Topflight. Junior Lit.
  Guild & Nelson, 1946. 224p

*STONE—HEROES
  Stone, David. Heroes and heroines.
  Watts, 1961. 51p

STONE—WE
  Stone, Irving, ed., with Richard Ken-
  nedy. We speak for ourselves.
  Doubleday, 1950. 462p

STRANG—ACTRESSES
  Strang, Lewis C. Famous actresses of
  the day in America. Page, 1899.
  360p

STRANG—PRIMA
  Strang, Lewis C. Prima donnas and sou-
  brettes of light opera and musical
  comedy in America. Page, 1900.
  270p

*STRONG—HEROES
  Strong, Joy. Heroes and heroines of
  many lands. Hart, 1965. 191p

*STRONG—OF
  Strong, Joy. Of courage and valor. Hart,
  1955. 318p

STUART—IMMORT.
  Stuart, Ray. Immortals of the screen.
  Sherbourne, 1965. 224p

STUMP—CHAMP.
  Stump, Al J. Champions against odds.
  Smith, 1952. 255p

STURGES—CELEB.
  Sturges, Dwight C. Celebrities off parade. Willett, Clark, 1935. 287p

*SWEETSER—FAMOUS
  Sweetser, Kate Dickinson. Famous girls
  of the White House. Crowell, 1930.
  299p

SWINSON—DANCERS
  Swinson, Cyril, ed. Dancers and critics.
  Adam and Charles Black, 1950. 80p

SWINSON—GREAT
  Swinson, Cyril. Great ballerinas of today. Black, 1960. 32p

TAFT—WOMEN, MENTOR (172) #1-6
  Taft, Lorado. Women sculptors of Amer-
  ica. Mentor Assoc., 1919. 12p. Also
  Mentor (separates) #1-6

TALLENTYRE—WOMEN
  Tallentyre, S. G. The women of the
  salons. Putnam, 1926. 235p

TALMEY—DOUG
  Talmey, Allene. Doug and Mary and
  others. Macy-Masius, 1927. 181p

TANNER—HERE
  Tanner, Louise. Here today . . . Crowell, 1959. 311p

*TAPPAN—HEROES
  Tappan, Eva M. Heroes of progress.
  Houghton Mifflin, 1928. 273p

TAVES—SUCCESS.
  Taves, Isabella. Successful women. Dutton, 1943. 319p

TEBBEL—INHER.
  Tebbel, John. The inheritors. Putnam,
  1962. 310p

TERHUNE—SUPER.
  Terhune, Albert Payson. Superwomen.
  Fiction Lib., 1916. 271p

*TERKEL—GIANTS
Terkel, Studs (Louis). Giants of jazz. Crowell, 1957. 215p

*TERRY—STAR
Terry, Walter. Star performances; the story of the world's great ballerinas. Doubleday, 1954. 224p

THEY—WENT
They Went to Africa. Biographies of missionaries . . . The United Christian Missionary Society, 1952. 147p

THOMAS—CANAD.
Thomas, Clara. Canadian novelists. 1920-1945. Longmans, Green, 1946. 129p

THOMAS—CRUSADERS
Thomas, Dana. Crusaders for God. Wyn, 1952. 340p

THOMAS—50
Thomas, Henry and Dana Lee Thomas. 50 great Americans. Doubleday, 1958. 468p

THOMAS—LIVING WOMEN
Thomas, Henry and Dana Lee Thomas. Living biographies of famous women. Blue Ribbon Books, c1942, 1959. 313p

THOMAS—MODERN
Thomas, Henry and Dana Lee Thomas. 50 great modern lives. Hanover House, 1956. 502p

THOMAS—RULERS
Thomas, Henry and Dana Lee Thomas. Living biographies of famous rulers. Garden City Pub., 1940. 310p

THOMAS—VITAL
Thomas, Lowell Jackson. Vital sparks; 101 outstanding lives. Doubleday, 1959. 480p

THOMSON—QUEENS
Thomson, Katherine Byerley. (Grace and Philip Wharton, pseuds.) The queens of society. Harper, 1861. 488p

THORNTON-COOK—ROYAL
Thornton-Cook, E. Royal Marys. Dutton, 1930. 247p

THORP—FEMALE
Thorp, Margaret Farrand. Female persuasion. Yale Univ., 1949. 253p

TIME
Time Magazine. 1924-1968 (cover stories).

TOWLE—VIGIL.
Towle, Virginia Rowe. Vigilante woman. Barnes, 1966. 182p

TREASE—SEVEN
Trease, Geoffrey. The seven queens of England. Vanguard, 1953. 254p

*TREASE—SEVEN STAGES
Trease, Geoffrey. Seven stages. Vanguard, 1964. 194p

TROWBRIDGE—SEVEN
Trowbridge, W. R. H. Seven splendid sinners. Unwin, c1908, 1924. 320p

TRUETT—FIRST
Truett, Randle Bond. The first ladies in fashion. Hastings House, 1954. 80p

TUCKERMAN—BOOK
Tuckerman, Henry T. Book of the artists. Carr, 1967. (Reprint ed. of 1867 pub.) 639p

TURNER—SAM
Turner, Martha Anne. Sam Houston and his twelve women. . . . Pemberton, 1966. 96p

TV GUIDE—ROUNDUP
TV Guide-Roundup. By the Editors of TV Guide. Popular Library, c1960, 1961. 207p

TV—PERSON. (1)
TV personalities. Vol. 1. TV Personalities, 1954. 158p. pa.

TV—PERSON. (2)
TV Personalities. Vol. 2. TV Personalities, 1956. 158p. pa.

TV—PERSON. (3)
TV Personalities. Vol. 3. TV Personalities, 1957. 158p. pa.

*ULRICH—FAMOUS
Ulrich, Homer. Famous women singers. Dodd, Mead, 1953. 127p

*UNSTEAD—PEOPLE
Unstead, Robt. John. People in history. Macmillan, 1957. 512p

UNTERMEYER—LIVES
Untermeyer, Louis. Lives of the poets. Simon & Schuster, 1959. 758p

UNTERMEYER—MAKERS
Untermeyer, Louis. Makers of the modern world. Simon & Schuster, 1955. 809p

*UNTERMEYER—PATHS
Untermeyer, Louis. The paths of glory. Delacorte, 1966. 251p

U.S.—BIOG., SOVIET
U.S. Joint Publications Research Service. Biographical sketches of Soviet scientific personalities. Distrib. by Office of Tech. Services, U.S. Dept. of Commerce, 1960. 387p

U.S.—WOMEN—(65th-79th). *See* PAXTON—WOMEN

U.S.—WOMEN—(87th)
U.S. Women's Bureau. Women of the 87th Congress, 1961. 45p. pa.

U.S.—WOMEN (88th)
U.S. Women's Bureau, Women of the 88th Congress, 1963. 29p. pa.

*VANCE—HEAR
Vance, Marguerite. Hear the distant applause! Dutton, 1963. 154p

*VANCE—LAMP
Vance, Marguerite. Lamp lighters; women in the Hall of Fame. Dutton, 1960. 254p

VAN DER VELDE—SHE
Van der Velde, Frances. She shall be called woman. Grand Rapids International, 1957. 258p

VAN DOREN—AMER.
Van Doren, Carl. Contemporary American novelists, 1900-1920. Macmillan, 1923. 176p

VAN GELDER—WRITERS
Van Gelder, Robert. Writers and writing. Scribner, 1946. 381p

WAGENKNECHT—MOVIES
Wagenknecht, Edward. The movies in the age of innocence. Univ. of Oklahoma, 1962. 280p

WAGENKNECHT—SEVEN
Wagenbnecht, Edward. Seven daughters of the theater; Jenny Lind, Sarah Bernhardt, Ellen Terry, Julia Marlowe, Isadora Duncan, Mary Garden, Marilyn Monroe. Univ. of Okla., 1964. 234p

WAGENKNECHT—WHEN
Wagenknecht, Edward. When I was a child. Dutton, 1946. 477p

WAGNALLS—OPERA
Wagnalls, Mabel. Opera and its stars. Funk & Wagnalls, 1924. 410p

*WAGNER—FAMOUS
Wagner, Frederick and Barbara Brady. Famous Amer. actors and actresses. Dodd, 1961. 159p

WAGNER—PRIMA
Wagner, Alan. Prima donnas and other wild beasts. Argonaut Books, 1961. 250p

WALLACE—FABULOUS
Wallace, Irving. The fabulous originals. Knopf, 1955. 317p

WALLACE—MOTHERS
Wallace, Archer. Mothers of famous men. Smith, 1931. 105p

WALLACE—SQUARE
Wallace, Irving. The square pegs. Knopf, 1957. 315p (& xiii plus index)

WARFEL—AMER.
Warfel, Harry R. American novelists of today. Amer. Book, 1951. 478p

WATERS—WOMEN
Waters, Clara Erskine Clement. Women in the fine arts, from the seventh century B.C. to the 20th century A.D. Houghton Mifflin, 1904. 395p

WATSON—40
Watson, Ernest. Forty illustrators and how they work. Watson-Guptill, 1946. 318p

WATSON—SOME
Watson, Paul Barron. Some women of France. Coward-McCann, 1936. 269p

WEBB—FAMOUS
Webb, Mary Griffin and Edna Lenore Webb. Famous living Americans. Webb, 1914. 594p

WEEKS—DISCOVERY
Weeks, Mary Elvira. Discovery of the elements. (6th ed.) Journal of Chem. Education, 1956. 910p

WEIGALL—PERSON.
Weigall, Arthur. Personalities of antiquity. Garden City, 1928. 235p

WEINER—PARVENU
Weiner, Margery. The Parvenu princesses, Elisa, Pauline and Caroline Bonaparte. Murray, 1964. 274p

WELCH—SIX
Welch, Alice Kemp. Of six medieval women. Macmillan, 1913, 1963. 188p

WELLINGTON—WOMEN
Wellington, Amy. Women have told. Little, Brown, 1930. 204p

WESTCOTT—CALEN.
Wescott, Glenway. A calendar of saints for unbelievers. Harper, 1933. 215p

WHITING—WHALING
Whiting, Emma Mayhew and Henry Beetle Hough. Whaling wives. Houghton, Mifflin, 1953. 293p

WHITTON—FIRST
Whitton, Mary Ormsbee. First first ladies. Hastings House, 1948. 341p

WHITTON—THESE
Whitton, Mary Ormsbee. These were the women, U.S.A. 1776-1860. Hastings House, 1954. 288p

WILLIAMS, BERYL. See EPSTEIN, BERYL (WILLIAMS)

WILLIAMS—GREAT
Williams, Henry Smith. Great astronomers. Simon & Schuster, 1930. 618p

WILLAMS—OUR
Williams, Blanche Colton. Our short story writers. Moffat, Yard, 1920. 357p

WILSON—ALL
Wilson, John Harold. All the King's ladies. Univ. of Chicago, 1958. 206p

WILSON—NBC
Wilson, Earl. The NBC book of stars. Pocket Books, 1957. 185p

*WINDHAM—SIXTY
Windham, Joan. Sixty saints for girls. Sheed & Ward, 1962. 376p

WINN—QUEEN'S
Winn, Godfrey. The Queen's countrywomen. Hutchinson, 1956. 280p

WINWAR—POOR
Winwar, Frances. Poor splendid wings. Little, Brown, 1933. 413p

*WITHAM—PAN.
Witham, W. Tasker. Panorama of American literature. Daye, 1947. 389p

WOMEN—ACHIEVE.
Women of achievement. House of Field, 1940. 213p

WOOD—CARLYLE. See TV PERSONALITIES

WOODWARD—BOLD
Woodward, Helen Beal. The bold women. Farrar, Straus & Young, 1953. 373p

WOODWARD—WAY
Woodward, W. E. The way our people lived. Dutton, 1944. 402p

WOODY—HIST. (1)
Woody, Thomas. A history of women's education in the United States. v. 1. The Science Press, 1929. 608p

*WORCESTER—MAKERS
Worcester, Donald E. Makers of Latin America. Dutton, 1966. 222p

WRIGHT—FORGOT.
Wright, Richardson. Forgotten ladies. Lippincott, 1928. 307p

*WRIGHT—GREAT
Wright, Helen and Samuel Rapport. Great adventures in nursing. Harper, 1960. 288p

WRITERS—PARIS
Writers at work. The Paris Review interviews. Viking, 1963. 368p

WYNDHAM—CHORUS
Wyndham, Horace. Chorus to coronet. British Technical and General Press, 1951. 184p

YARMOLINSKY—TREAS.
Yarmolinsky, Avrahm, ed. Treas. of Russian verse. Macmillan, 1949. 314p

YEAR—PIC.
Year, Editors of. A pictorial history of science. Year, n.d., 257p

*YOST—FAMOUS
Yost, Edna. Famous Amer. pioneering women. Dodd, Mead, 1961. 158p

*YOST—NURSING
Yost, Edna. American women of nursing. Lippincott, 1947. 197p

*YOST—WOMEN MOD.
Yost, Edna. Women of modern science. Dodd, Mead, 1959. 176p

*YOST—WOMEN SCI.
Yost, Edna. American women of science. Lippincott, 1943. 232p

YOUNG—WOMEN
Young, Agatha. The women and the crisis. McDowell, Obolensky, 1959. 389p

ZAHM, JOHN. See MOZANS, H. I. pseud.

ZIEROLD—CHILD
Zierold, Norman J. The child stars. Coward-McCann, 1965. 250p

ZOLOTOW—NEVER
Zolotow, Maurice. Never whistle in a dressing room. Dutton, 1944. 319p

* For younger readers.

INDEX TO WOMEN

A

Aahhotep I (c. 1580 B.C.)
Egypt. queen
Hammerton pl

Aahmes-Nefertari (c. 1600 B.C.)
Egypt. queen
Hammerton pl,por.

Aalberg, Ida Emelia (1857-1915)
Fin. actress
Stiles—Postal pl

Aarestrup, Marie Helene (b. 1829)
Norw. painter
Waters—Women pl

Abarca, Marie De (d. 1656)
Sp. painter
Schmidt—400 p535,por.

Abbatt, Agnes Dean (1847-1917)
Amer. painter
Waters—Women pl

Abbema, Louise (1858-1927)
Fr. painter
Waters—Women pl-2

Abbot, Sarah (fl. 1820's-1830's)
Amer. educator
Woody—Hist. I p356-357,por.

Abbott, Abigail. See Ellsworth, Abigail Wolcott

Abbott, Berenice (1898-   )
Amer. photographer
Cur. Biog. '42 p1-3por.
Women—Achieve. p148,por.

Abbott, Cynthia (1908-   )
Eng. illustrator
Ryder—Artists p43

Abbott, Edith (1876-1957)
Amer. social worker, educator
Cur. Biog. '41,p3-4por.
Cur. Biog. '57p1

Abbott, Eleanor Hallowell (b. 1872)
Amer. novelist
Maurice—Makers p11,por.
Overton—Women pl
Wagenknecht—When p166-179

Abbott, Emma (1849/50-1891)
Amer. singer
Adelman—Famous p227
Dorland—Sum p18,162-163
Ewen—Ency. p3
Lahee—Famous p195-198
Logan—Part p768
McCoy—Portraits pl,por.
Schmidt—400 p16-17

Abbott, Grace (1878-1939)
Amer. social worker, govt. official
Allen—Advent. p333-346,por.
Hammerton p4
Huff—Famous (2nd) p33-40,por.
*Logie—Careers p226-235
Rogers—Women p71,por.

Abbott, Helen Probst (fl. 1930's)
Amer. feminist, humanitarian
Women—Achieve. p151,por.

Abbott, Jane Ludlow Drake (1881-   )
Amer. novelist
Warfel—Amer. p3,por.

Abbott, Maude E. (1869-1940)
Can. physician
Castiglioni—Hist. p835,992,1115,1127
Innis—Clear p142-157,por.
Lovejoy—Women p114-116,por.
Mead—Medical p59

Abel, Hazel Hempel (c1888-1966)
Amer. senator, educator, civic leader
Parshalle—Kash. p100-104,por.

Abell, Mrs. Edwin F. (fl. 1900's)
Amer. religious worker
Logan—Part p616

Abelson, Josephine May (fl. 1930's)
Amer. dental surgeon
Women—Achieve. p159,por.

Aberconway, Lady Laura Pochn (d. 1933)
Scot. feminist
Hammerton p7,por.

Aberdeen and Temair, Ishbel Maria Marjoribanks, Godron, Marchioness of (1857-1939)
Brit. feminist, political hostess
Furniss—Some p196-197,por.
Hammerton p9,por.

Abi (Biblical)
daughter of Zechariah
Deen—All p245

1

Abiah (Biblical)
    wife of Hezron
    Deen—All p245

Abigail (1) (Biblical)
    wife of Nabal, David
    Buchanan—Women p53-55
    Culver—Women p32
    Deen—All p101-106
    Hammerton p10
    Horton—Women p175-187
    Lewis—Portraits p48-50
    Macartney—Great p105-120
    *MacVeagh—Champlin p3
    Marble—Women p64-68
    Mead—250 p86
    Morton—Women p119-126
    Ockenga—Women p101-109

Abigail (2) (Biblical)
    sister of David
    Deen—All p245-246

Abihail (1) (Biblical)
    wife of Abishur
    Deen—All p246

Abihail (2) (Biblical)
    daughter of Eliah
    Deen—All p246

Abimelech's mother (Biblical)
    Deen—All p340

Abington, Frances (Fanny) Barton (1737-1815)
    Eng. actress
    Dorland—Sum p22,70,165
    Hammerton, p10,por.
    MacQueen—Pope p267-272,por.
    Melville—More p13-70,por.

Abishag (Biblical)
    Deen—All p246-247
    Hammerton p10
    Lewis—Portraits p54-55

Abital (Biblical)
    Deen—All p247

Aborn, Lora (n.d.)
    Amer. composer
    McCoy—Portraits pl,por.

Abott, Bessie (1878-1919)
    Amer. singer
    Lahee—Grand p54-57,por.

Abouchdid, Edna (fl. 1930's)
    Lebanese physician
    Lovejoy—Women p216

Abrams, Norma (fl. 1920's)
    Amer. journalist
    Ross—Ladies p296-298

Abrescia, Donna (fl. 1960's)
    Amer. parachutist
    *May—Women p59

Abreu de Estévez, Marta (1845-1909)
    Cub. philanthropist, patriot,
      humanitarian
    Phila.—Women, unp.
    Stiles—Postal p2

Acarie, Madame Barbe (1566-1618)
    Fr. Christian
    Deen—Great p348-349

Acca Laurentia (c. 634 B.C.)
    Rom. nurse, beauty
    Balsdon—Roman p22

Accoramboni, Vittoria (c. 1557-1585)
    It. beauty
    Hammerton p13

Ace, Jane Sherwood (1905-   )
    Amer. radio actress
    Cur. Biog. '48 p6-8,por.
    Eichberg—Radio p22-24,por.

Acerrona (fl. 15-50 A.D.)
    Rom. matron
    Balsdon—Roman p110-111

Achelis, Elisabeth (n.d.)
    Amer. organization official, calendar
      reformer
    Cur. Biog. '54 p5-7,por.
    New Yorker, Dec.30,1939,p.21-25,por.
      (Profiles)

Acheson, Sarah C. (b. 1844)
    Amer. social reformer
    Logan—Part p384

Achille-Fould, Mlle. Georges (b. 1865)
    Fr. painter
    Waters—Women p2-4

Achilles, Edith Mulhall (fl. 1930's)
    Amer. educator
    Women—Achieve. p193

Achsah (Biblical)
    Buchanan—Women p32
    Deen—All p247
    Hammerton p14
    Lewis—Portraits p104-106
    Mead—250 p54

Achurch, Janet (1864-1916)
    Eng. actress
    Hammerton, p14,por.

Ackermann, Louise Victorine Choquet (1813-1890)
    Fr. poet
    Dorland—Sum p24,179

Ackland, Harriet, Lady Christina Henrietta
    Caroline (1750-1815)
        Eng. heroine
    Ellet—Women (1) p171-179,por.
    *MacVeagh—Champlin, p4

Acklen, Adelicia (fl. 19th cent.),
        Amer. social leader
    Logan—Part p260

Ackley, Edith Flack (fl. 1930's)
        Amer. marionette expert
    Women—Achieve. p119,por.

Ackté-Jalander, Aino (1876-1944)
        Fin. singer
    Ewen—Ency. p5
    Hammerton p14
    Lahee—Grand p25-26
    McCoy—Portraits pl.por.
    Wagner—Prima p237

Acland, Harriet.
    See Ackland, Harriet, Lady Christina
        Henrietta Caroline

Acosts, Aïda de (fl. 1900's)
        Cub. aviatrix
    *May—Women p40
    Planck—Women p6-8,10-14

Acosta, Mercedes de (n.d.),
        Amer. author
    Cook—Our p270-273

Acosta-Sison, Honoria (fl. 1900's)
        Phil. physician
    Lovejoy—Women p242-245,por.

Acquillon, Duchess of (1604-1675)
        Fr. philanthropist
    Blunt—Great p173-174

Acte, Claudia (fl. 50-60 A.D.)
        Rom. friend of Nero
    Balsdon—Roman p108,124-125,128

Acton, Eliza (1799-1859)
        Eng. author
    Adelman—Famous p136

Adah (1) (Biblical)
        wife of Lamech
    Deen—All p248
    Mead—250 p6

Adah (2) (Biblical)
        wife of Esau
    Deen—All p248-249

Adair, Bethenia Angelina Owens (1840-
        1926)
        Amer. physician
    *Johnson—Some p85-99,por.
    Lovejoy—Women p107
    Ross—Westward p155-171

Adair, Ellen (fl. 19th cent.)
        Amer. belle
    Logan—Part p261

Adair, Janice, pseud. (Beatrice Duffy) (n.d.)
        Eng. actress
    Hammerton p16,por.

Adair, Mildred (d. 1943)
        Amer. composer
    McCoy—Portraits pl,por.

Adam, Jean (1710-1765)
        Scot. poet
    Hammerton p16

Adam, Juliette Lamber (1836-1936)
        Fr. author
    Adelman—Famous p275
    Dorland—Sum p107,115
    Hammerton p16,por.
    Watson—Some p217-269,por.

Adam, Madame Nanny (fl. 1900's)
        Fr. painter
    Waters—Women p4-5

Adamowska, Antoinette
    See Szumowska, Antoinette

Adams, Abby (fl. 1910's)
        Amer. organization official
    Logan—Part p354-355

Adams, Abigail (Mrs. William Stephens
        Smith) (b. 1765)
        Amer. belle
    Sale—Old p169-185,por.

Adams, Abigail Smith (1744-1818)
        Amer. first lady
    Adelman—Famous p86-87
    Amory—Proper, pl45,152-156
    Bartlett—Mothers p15-21
    Beard—Amer. p59-72
    Benson—Women p147, 171, 219, 246-
        247, 250, 255-256
    Bradford—Portraits pl-31,por.
    Brooks—Colonial, p169-214
    *Chandler—Famous p79-98
    DAR Mag. '55:389,portrayal,390
    *Daugherty—Ten p17-31,por.
    Donovan—Women p16-17,152-204,por.
    Douglas—Remember p7,49-52,por.
    Ellet—Women (2) p31-37,por.
    Farmer—What p65-71,107
    Gerlinger—Mis. p8-10,por.
    Green—Pioneer (2) p19-20
        (3) p32-59,149-150,por.
    Hampton—Our p42-51
    Hanaford—Dau. p46,72-75,215
    Jensen—White p10-11,por.
    Leonard—Amer. p111
    Logan—Ladies p15-21
    Logan—Part p214-217

(Continued)

Adams, Abigail Smith—*Continued*

  *McConnell—Our p17-32,por.
  Means—Woman p29-51,por.,cover
  Minnigerode—Some p47-88,por.
  Mott—Gallery p183-187
  Peyton—Mothers p7-17
  Prindiville—First p14-26
  *Ross—Know p7,por.
  Schmidt—400 p6-7 (por.7)
  Smith—Romances p29-37,por.
  Truett—First p10,por.
  Wallace—Mothers p42-47
  Whitton—First p20-38,por.
  Whitton—These p9-10

Adams, Agnes Jones (1858-1923)
  Amer. club leader
  Brown—Home. p200-204

Adams, Anne (fl. 1770's)
  Amer. Rev. war patriot
  Green—Pioneer (3) p467,por.

Adams, Annette Abbott (1877-1956)
  Amer. judge
  Rogers—Women p113,por.

Adams, Bertha Leith Grundy (d. 1912)
  Eng. author
  Black—Notable p286-298,por.

Adams, Carrie B. (1859-1940)
  Amer. composer, organist, educator
  McCoy—Portraits, 1,por.

Adams, Clara (fl. 1920's,1930's)
  Amer. aviatrix
  Planck—Women p77-79,por.
  Women—Achiev. p160,por.

Adams, Diana (1926-   )
  Amer. ballet dancer
  Atkinson—Dancers p3-6,por.
  Cur. Biog. '54 p7-9,por.
  Haskell—Vignet. p65
  *Terry—Star p193

Adams, Edith (Edie) (1927-   )
  Amer. actress
  Cr '59 p3-4,por.
  Cr '63 p3,por.
  Cur. Biog. '54 p9-10,por.
  TV—Person (3) p38-40,por.

Adams, Elizabeth Checkley (d. 1757)
  Amer. patriot
  Green—Pioneer (3) p59-62

Adams, Elizabeth Kemper (1872-1948)
  Amer. educator, editor
  Beard—Woman p22-24

Adams, Elizabeth Wells (d. c1808)
  Amer. patriot
  Green—Pioneer (3) p62-80

Adams, Eva Bertrand (1908-   )
  Amer. govt. official, lawyer
  CR '63 p3,por.
  Cur. Biog. '62 p1-3,por.

Adams, Evangeline Smith (c1872-1932)
  Amer. astrologist
  New Yorker Oct. 27, 1928, p29-32

Adams, Hannah (1755-1831)
  Amer. historian, essayist
  Beard—Amer. p174-181
  Benson—Women p171
  Dexter—Career p91-92
  Dorland—Sum p29,175
  Douglas—Remember p48
  Hammerton p19
  Hanaford—Dau. p215-216
  Irwin—Angels p21-22
  Leonard—Amer. p106-107,111
  Logan—Part p793-794
  Whitton—These p54 57

Adams, Harriet C (fl. 1916)
  Amer. explorer, lecturer
  Adelman—Famous p308

Adams, Helen Balfour (1848-1950)
  Amer. Civil war humanitarian
  Brockett—Woman's p636-639

Adams, Jane Kelley (b. 1852)
  Amer. educator
  Logan—Part p724

Adams, Juliette Aurelia Graves (b. 1858)
  Amer. composer, pianist, teacher,
    author, lecturer
  Howard—Our p583

Adams, Leónie Fuller (1899-   )
  Amer. poet
  *Millett—Amer. p212-213

Adams, Louisa Catherine Johnson (1775-1852)
  Amer. first lady
  Amory—Proper p157
  Farmer—What p78-80
  Gerlinger—Mis. p21-23,por.
  Green—Pioneer (3) p493-498,por.
  Hanaford—Dau. p78-80
  Jensen—White p42,44-45,por.
  Logan—Ladies p35-40
  Logan—Part p229-234
  *McConnell—Our p71-82,por.
  Minnigerode—Some p133-181,por.
  Prindiville—First p54-65
  *Ross—Know p15,por.
  Smith—Romances p83-91,por.
  Truett—First p20-21,por.
  Whitton—First p91-115,por.

Adams, Martha (fl. 1860's)
  Amer. Civil war nurse
  Brockett—Woman's p789

Adams, Maude (1872-1953)
  Amer. actress
  Adelman—Famous, p314
  Blum—Great p7,por.
  Coad—Amer. p283,por.
  Dorland—Sum p169
  Hammerton p20
  Izard—Heroines p324-346,por.
  *Kobbé—Homes p1-42,por.
  Logan—Part p772-773
  *MacVeagh—Champlin p6
  Ormsbee—Back p202-207,por.
  Strang—Actresses p11-26,por.
  *Vance—Hear p131-154,por.
  *Wagner—Famous p89,por.

Adams, Mildred (fl. 1930's)
  Amer. journalist
  Ross—Ladies p163-164

Adams, Sarah Fowler (1805-1848)
  Eng. poet, hymn writer
  Adelman—Famous p135
  Deen—Great p308
  Dorland—Sum p27,72,185
  Hammerton p20

Adams, Susanna Boylston (fl. 1700's)
  mother of John Adams
  Donovan—Women p11-17
  Hampton—Our p15-24

Adams, Suzanne (1872-1953)
  Amer. opera singer
  Ewen—Ency. p6
  McCoy—Portraits pl,por.

Adamson, Joy (n.d.), Kenyan author
  Fitzgibbon—My p255-261

Addams, Dawn (1930-   )
  Eng. actress
  C.B. '59 p5,por.

Addams, Jane (1860-1935)
  Amer .social worker, humanitarian
  *Adams—Heroines p280-307,por.
  Adelman—Famous p293-294,por.
  Allen—Advent. p141-153,por.
  America's 12 p9-11,por.
  Ames—These p279-297
  Bartlett—They p31-34
  Bennett—Amer. p69-90,por.
  *Bolton—Lives p1-14,por.
  Bonte—Amer. p155,por.
  Bowie—Women p90-111
  Bruce—Woman p337,por.
  *Carmer—Caval. p314-316,por.
  *Commager—Crus. p101-108
  *Cooper—Twenty p349-364,por.
  *Curtin—Gallery pl,por.
  Dolan—Goodnow's p263
  *Dolin—World p154-161,por.
  Dorland—Sum p120,128
  Douglas—Remember p188-199,205-210,
    por.

*Ferris—When p164-222,por.
*Fowler—Great p76-80,por.
  Hammerton p21,por.
*Heath—Woman p22,por.
  Henderson—Contemp. p119-133,por.
*Humphrey—Janes p103-125
  Irwin—Angels p227,415-417
  Jensen—Revolt p82,212,por.
*Kirkland—Good p55-62
  Ladies'—Amer. 12 p9-11,por.
*Lamm—Biog. p103
  Lifton—Woman p247-266
  Logan—Part p596-597
  Lotz—Women p1-10
  Love—Famous p9
  MacVeagh—Champlin p6
  Mears—They p31-33
  Meine—Great p17-20,por.
*Meyer—Champions p102-114,por.
*Moore—When p15-21
  Morris—400 p21
  Mott—Gallery p200-205
  Murrow—This (2) p213-215
*Nathan—Women p40-73
*Nida—Pilots p371-375
  Nobel—Man p547-550
*Parkman—Heroines p297-322,por.
  Phila.—Women unp.,por.
  Rogers—Women p69,por.
  Schmidt—400 p542,por.
*Stevens—Human p108-110,por.
*Stevens—Women p167-170,por.
  Stiles—Postal p3
  Stone—We p443-448
  Thomas—50 p330-338
  Thomas—Living Women p261-273,por.
    por.
  Wagenknecht—When p136-148
  Webb—Famous p20-33,por.

Addington, Sarah (1891-1940)
  Amer. author
  Cur. Biog. '40 p4
  Women—Achieve. p180,por.

Addison, Adele (n.d.)
  Amer. singer
  *Cherry—Portraits p199

Additon, Henrietta Silvis (1887-   )
  Amer. social worker, educator
  Cur. Biog. '40 p5-6
  Women—Achieve. p81,por.

Adela (d. 735)
  Nether. saint, grandmother of St.
    Gregory of Utrecht
  Deen—Great p327-328

Adela of Blois (c1062-1137)
  Fr. Christian
  Deen—Great p327-328

Adelaide (931-999)
  It. queen
  Hammerton p23

Adelaide, La Petite (fl. 1910's)
Fr. ballet dancer, actress
Caffin—Vaud. p104,por.

Adelaide, Madame (1732-1800)
Fr., aunt of Louis XVI
Haggard—Remark. p332-334

Adelaide, Saint (931-999)
Burgundian queen
Adelaman—Famous p31
Blunt—Great p86-87
Englebert—Lives p476-477
Sharkey—Pop. p59-62

Adelaide of Saxe Meiningen (1792-1849)
Eng. queen
Hammerton p23,por.
Hasted—Unsuccess. p112-136,por.
Sanders—Intimate p194-201,por.

Adelaide of Susa (1091-1150)
It. rel. leader
Schmidt—400 p246-247,por.

Adelsparre, Sophie Albertine (1808-1862)
Swed. painter
Waters—Women p5

Adkins, Bertha Sheppard (1906-   )
Amer. govt. official, politician
Cur. Biog. '53 p1-2,por.
Phelps—Men '58(1) p16
Roosevelt—Ladies p31-37

Adkison, Harriet Brown (fl. 1900's)
Amer. W. pioneer
*Miller—West p224-240

Adler, Polly (1900-1962)
Pol.-Amer. hostess
CR '59 p7,por.

Adoree, Renee (d. 1933)
Fr. actress
Brundidge—Twinkle p129-135,por.
Herman—How p121,por.
Stuart—Immort. p18-19,por.

Adrienne (fl. 1940's)
Ger.-Amer. spy
Singer—World's p292-303

Adsit, Nancy H. (b. 1825)
Amer. lecturer, insurance agent
Logan—Part p784

Ady, Cecilia Mary (d. 1958)
Eng. historian
Brittain—Women p113-114,162-164,
166,245

Aebutia (fl. 196 B.C.)
Rom. matron
Balsdon—Roman p38-39

Aelfgifu of Northampton.
See Northampton, Aelfgifu of

Aelfled. See Elfled

Aelia Flaccilla. See Flaccilla, Aelia

Aelia Pulcheria Augustus. See Pulcheria

Aemilia, Tertia (fl. 210 B.C.)
Rom., mother of Cornelia
Balsdon—Roman p47,187,215

Aesha (fl. 1650's)
E. Ind., dau. of Sultan Sujah
Pool—Famous p113-120

Aethelburg (fl. 680's-700's)
Eng. queen
Stenton—English p2

Aethelfleda. See Elfled

Aethelthryth (fl. 672)
Eng., wife of Ecgfrith
Stenton—English p10

Afra, Saint (d. 304)
Ger. saint
Wescott—Calen. p117-118

Agar (Biblical)
Deen—All p249

Agassiz, Elizabeth Cabot (1822-1907)
Amer. teacher, sci. writer
Adelman—Famous p236-237
Hanaford—Dau. p289
Irwin—Angels p125-126

Agatha, Saint (d. 251/253)
Sic. Christian martyr
Englebert—Lives p51
Hammerton p29
Phila.—Women unp.,por.
Sharkey—Pop. p35
Stiles—Postal p229
Wescott—Calen. p20
*Windham—Sixty p44-48

Ageloff, Sylvia (fl. 1930')s
Russ. spy
Singer—World's p307-312

Aglaonice (Ancient)
Gr. astronomer
Mozans—Woman p167

"Agnes" (fl. 1820's)
Amer. Civil war diarist
Jones—Heroines p201-203,316-317

Agnes, Saint (291-304)
Sic. Christian martyr
*Beebe—Saints p16-22

(Continued)

Agnes, Saint—*Continued*

Culver—Women p76
Englebert—Lives p28
Hammerton p30,por.
Husslein—Heroines p1-16
Keyes—Three p19-37,por.
Sharkey—Pop. p35
Wescott—Calen. p11-12
*Windham—Sixty p85-91

Agnes of Assisi (d. 1253)
It. saint
Englebert—Lives p436-437

Agnes of Bohemia, Blessed (d. 1280/1282)
Bohem. queen-saint
Blunt—Great p80-81
Englebert—Lives p91

Agnes of Dunbar (Black Agnes) (1312/13-1369)
Scot. heroine
Graham—Group p31-37
Muir—Women p78-79

Agnes of France.
See **Ann**, consort of Alexius II

Agnes of Meran (d. 1201)
Fr. queen
Hammerton p30

Agnes of Monte Pulciano (d. 1317)
It. saint, abbess
Wescott—Calen. p56

Agnes of Poitiers (d. before 589)
Fr. saint
Englebert—Lives p187

Agnes, Maria Gaetana (1718-1799)
It. mathematician, linguist, philosopher, inventor
Cajori—Hist. p250
Coolidge—Six p21-23
Dorland—Sum p20,76,132,141
Elson's—Woman's p123-124
Hammerton p30
Mozans—Woman p143-151
Smith—Hist. I p519,por.

Agostina (Agustina, Augustina) the maid of Saragossa (1788-1857)
Sp. heroine
Adelman—Famous p96
*Deakin—True p316-328
Dorland—Sum p96

Agoult, Marie Catherine Sophie de Flavigny, Comtesse d' (Daniel Stern, pseud.) (1805-1876)
Fr. historian, feminist
Dorland—Sum p40,175
Hammerton p30
Watson—Some p181-216

Agreda, Maria de (Maria Fernandez Coronel) (1602-1664)
Sp. nun, essayist, abbess
Dorland—Sum p131,172
Hammerton p30

Agrelo, Isabel Calvimontes de (1790-1855)
Argent. patriot
Schmidt—400 p32,por.

Agrippina I, the Elder (c. 13 B.C.-33 A.D.)
Rom. empress, wife of Germanicus
Balsdon—Rom p17,60,63,75,80,88,95-96,116,por.
Boccaccio—Conc. p200-201
Hammerton p31,por.
McCabe—Empr. p33,37,41-42,46,por.
MacVeagh—Champlin p9
Mozans—Woman p24-25,28

Agrippina II, the Younger (c15-59 A.D.)
Rom. empress, mother of Nero, wife of Claudius
Abbott—Notable p15-19
Balsdon—Roman p17-18,63,107-114,116-129,273,277
Beard—Woman p295-297
Boccaccio—Conc. p205-208
Ewart—World's p48-60
Ferrero—Women p134-211,276-337,por.
Hammerton p31
McCabe—Emer. p54,65,67,79-104,por.
MacVeagh—Champlin p9
Muir—Women p100-101
Serviez—Roman (1) p177-225

Agrippina Vipsania (fl. c. 11/12 B.C.)
Rom., wife of Tiberius
Balsdon—Rome p71-72,74,80

Aguilar, Grace (1816-1847)
Eng. novelist
Dorland—Sum p23,73,195
Hammerton p32,por.
*Levinger—Great p121-125

Agujari, Lucrezia (1743-1783)
It. singer
Hammerton p32,por.

Agustina. See **Agostina**

Ahern, Mary Elieen (c. 1865-1938)
Amer. librarian, editor, teacher
Bul. of Bibl. May-August 1925,p125,por.
Logan—Part p875
Marshall—Amer. p448

Ahinoam (1) (Biblical)
wife of Saul
Buchanan—Women p50
Deen—All p249-250
Lewis—Portraits p120

Ahinoam (2) (Biblical)
wife of David
Deen—All p250

Ahlai (Biblical)
Deen—All p250

Ahlers, Anny (1906-1933)
Ger. actress
Hammerton p33,por.

Ahlgren, Mildred Carlson (1902-   )
Amer. organization official
Cur. Biog. '52 p7-9,por.

Ahok, Mrs. (fl. 1890's, 1900's)
Chin. Christian worker
Burton—Notable p73-111,por.

Aholibah (Biblical)
Deen—All p251

Aholibamah (Biblical)
Deen—Ali p251-252

Ahrens, Ellen Wetherald (b. 1859)
Amer. painter
Michigan—Biog. p22
Waters—Women p5-6

Aiguillon, Marie Madeleine de Wignerod
du Pont de Courlay, Duchess d'
(1604-1675)
Fr. philanthropist
Hammerton p35

Aiken, Lizzie (fl. 1860's),
Civil war nurse
Moore—Women p478-484

Aikenhead, Sister Mary (1787-1858)
Irish nun, nurse, foundress, phi-
lanthropist
Dolan—Goodnow's p205
Hammerton p35
Stiles—Postal p4

Aikens, Amanda L. (1833-1892)
Amer. philanthropist, editor
Logan—Part p528-529

Aikin, Anna Letitia.
See Barbauld, Anna L(a)etitia

Aikin, Lucy (1781-1864)
Eng. historical writer
Adelman—Famous p110
Hammerton p35

Ailesbury, Dorothy Julia.
See Tester, Dorothy Julia

Airy, Anna (b. 1882)
Brit. painter
Hammerton p36

Aisha, Lalla (1930-   )
Moroc. princess
Time, Nov.11,1957,p32,por.,cover

Aissé, Mademoiselle (c1694-1733)
Circassian, Fr. letter-writer, beauty
Haggard—Remark. p120-214
Hammerton p37
Herold—Love p63-115,por.
Kavanagh—Woman (1), p76-85

Aitken, Jane (fl. 1800')s
Amer. printer
Club—Printing p19
Dexter—Career p106-107
Hanaford—Dau. p709

Akeley, Delia Denning (fl. 1920's)
Amer. explorer
Rogers—Women p141,por.

Akeley, Mary L. Jobe (1886-   )
Amer. educator, botanist, explorer,
author
Women—Achieve. p48,por.

Akers, Susan Grey (1889-   )
Amer. librarian, author, educator
Bul. of Bibl. Sept.-Dec.1958,p145-146,
por.

Akhmatoua, Anna, pseud.
See Gorenko, Anna Andreyevna

Akins, Zoe (1886-1958)
Amer. poet, playwright
Adelman—Famous p323
Mantle—Amer. p123-125
Mantle—Contemp. p27-32
*Millett—Amer. p216-217

Akmadulina (1937-   )
Russ. poet
Reavey—New p129

Alacoque, Marguerite Marie (1647-1690)
Fr. saint, nun, foundress
Hammerton p38
Husslein—Heroines p110-117
Stiles—Postal p4

Alband, Marie Louise (b. 1852)
Amer. singer
Logan—Part p616-617

Albanese, Licia (1913-   )
It.-Amer. singer
CR '59 p10,por.
CR '63 p6,por.
Cur. Biog. '46 p6-9,por.
Ewen—Ency. p12
Matz—Opera p3-8,por.
Peltz—Spot, p13,por.

Albanesi, Madame M. Henderson (fl. 1900's)
Brit. novelist
Hammerton p40,por.

Alden, Cynthia Westover (b. 1858)
Amer. linguist, inventor, humanitarian
Logan—Part p846

Alden, Esther (b. c. 1847)
Amer. Civil war diarist
Jones—Heroines p237-239

Alden, Isabella MacDonald ("Pansy," pseud.)
(1841-1930)
Amer. author
Logan—Part p846-847
Papashvily—All p186-197

Alden, Priscilla Mullins (m. 1621)
Amer. Pilgrim
Bell—Women p20-21,46-47,212-213,
220,301-307,por.
Green—Pioneer (1) p113-133
Logan—Part p33
Marble—Women p71-80
Schmidt—400 p2,por.
*Unstead—People p290-302,349

Alden, Sarah. See Standish, Sarah Alden

Alder, Emily (fl. 1860's)
Amer. Civil war nurse
Logan—Part p374

Alderson, Nannie Tiffany (1860-1946)
Amer. W. pioneer
*Johnson—Some p137-150,por.

Aldington, Hilda Doolittle.
See Doolittle, Hilda

Aldrich, Annie Reeve (1866-1892)
Amer. poet, novelist
Dorland—Sum p180

Aldrich, Bess Streeter (1881-1954)
Amer. author
Mears—They p90-93
Warfel—Amer. p6-7,por.

Aldrich, Clara. See Thomas, Clara Chaplin

Aldrich, Flora L. (b. 1859)
Amer. physician
Logan—Part p743

Aldrich, Madame Mariska (b. 1881)
Amer. singer
Lahee—Grand p213-215

Aldrich, Mildred (d. 1928)
Amer. journalist
Ross—Ladies p484-485

Aldridge, Amanda Ira ("Montague Ring")
(b. 1866)
Eng. composer, pianist, teacher
Cuney-Hare—Negro p314-318

Aldridge, Luranah Ira (b. 1860)
Eng. singer
Cuney-Hare—Negro p315,por.

Al-Durr, Shadjar (fl. 1250-1257)
Egypt. queen
Schmidt—400 p116-117,por.

Aleksyeevna, Sophia (1657-1704)
Russ. tszarevna, regent
Dorland—Sum p22

Alencon, Emilienne (fl. 19th cent.)
Fr. courtesan
Skinner—Elegant p221,227-229,231

Alexander, Annie.
See Hector, Annie Alexander

Alexander, Madame Beatrice (1895-   )
Amer. doll manufacturer
Cur. Biog. '57 p13-15,por.
Women—Achieve, p168,por.

Alexander, Catherine (Lady Kitty Duer) (m.
1779)
Amer. beauty
Green—Pioneer (2) p154-156, 158,por.
Sale—Old p152-157,por.

Alexander, Francesca (1837-1917)
It. artist
Waters—Women p6-7

Alexander, Grace (b. 1848)
Amer. soc. reformer
Logan—Part p589

Alexander, Janet (d. 1845)
Amer. midwife
Dexter—Career p35-36

Alexander, Jemima.
See Sharpe, Jemima Alexander

Alexander, Mary (Polly) Spratt Provoost
(1694-1760)
Amer. bus. woman, social leader
Dexter—Colonial p105-106,184
Green—Pioneer (1), p193-196
Leonard—Amer. p111

Alexander, Ruth (n.d.)
Amer. economist, lecturer
Cur. Biog. '43 p6-8,por.

Alexander, Sadie (1923-
Amer. lawyer
*Cherry—Portraits p158-159

Alexander, Sarah Livingston, Lady Stirling.
See Jay, Sarah Van Brugh Livingston

Alexandra (1844-1925)
Eng. queen
Adelman—Famous p274
Arsenius—Dict. p11,por.
Hammerton p56-57,por.
Stiles—Postal p7

Alexandra (1921-   )
Yugoslav. queen
CR '59 p13,por.

Alexandra, Elizabeth Olga Christabel
(1936-   )
Eng. princess
CR '59 p12-13,por.

Alexandra Feodorovna (1872-1918)
Russ. empress
Arsenius—Dict. p11,por.
Hammerton p57,por.

Alexandrine (1879-1952)
Dan. queen
Phila.—Women, unp.,por.
Stiles—Postal p7

Alexandrine of Taxis (1589-1666)
Belg. countess
Stiles—Postal p7

Alfonso, Arthémise.
See Goertz, Arthémise

Alford, Joanna (fl. 1785)
Amer. philanthropist
Hanaford—Dau. p647

Alger, Ellice Murdock (1870-1945)
Amer. ophthalmologist
Cur. Biog. '45 p3

Algeranova, Claudie (1924-   )
Eng. dancer
Davidson—Ballet p3-4

Ali, Safieh (fl. 1920's)
Turk. physician
Lovejoy—Women p213

Alice (fl. 999 A.D.)
Fr. saint
*Windham—Sixty p241-247

Alice ("Fatima") (1843-1878)
Eng. princess, grand duchess of
Hesse
Benson—Queen see index,por.
Carey—Twelve p295-330,por.

Alice, (Alix) Marie Anne Antonia Charlotte
Gabrielle (1929-   )
Luxem. princess
Arsenius—Dict. p13,por.
Stiles—Postal p8

Alice of Althone (b. 1883)
Eng. princess
Phila.—Women, unp.,por.
Stiles—Postal p8

Aliger, Margarita I. (fl. 1930's)
Russ. poet
Yarmolinsky—Treas. p283

Alippi-Fabretti, Quirina (b. 1849)
It. painter
Waters—Women p7

Alison, Isabel of Perth (d. 1681)
Scot. heroine
Anderson—Ladies p272-288

Alix. See Alice

Allan, Elizabeth (1910-   )
Eng. actress
Hammerton p61,por.

Allan, Maud (b. 1879)
Eng. dancer
Hammerton p61,por

Allan—Despréaux, Louise (1810-1856)
Fr. actress
Hammerton p61

Allee, Marjorie Hill (1890-1945)
Amer. author
Cur. Biog. '45 p2

Alleine, Theodosia (fl.1662)
Eng. author
Stenton—English p195-196

Allen, Adrienne (1907-   )
Eng. actress
Hammerton p62,por.

Allen, Ann (fl. 1824)
Amer. W. pioneer
Ellet—Pioneer p382

Allen, Barbara Jo (n.d.)
Amer. radio actress
Eichberg—Radio p112

Allen, Betsy. See Cavanna, Betty

Allen, Eliza. See Houston, Eliza Allen

Allen, Elizabeth (b. 1716)
Amer. patriot, W. pioneer
Ellet—Pioneer p382-385
Green—Pioneer (3) p512,515-516

Allen, Elizabeth Chase (1832-1911)
Amer. poet
Hanaford—Dau. p253-254

Allen, Florence Ellinwood (1884-1966)
 Amer. judge
 Cur. Biog. '41, p17-19,por.
 Cur. Biog. '63, p6-8,por.6
 Cur. Biog. '66 p462
 °Forsee—Amer. p92-106
 Irwin—Angels p300-301
 °Kirkland—Good p94-110
 Murrow—This (2) p2-3
 Parshalle—Kash. p152-156,por.
 Roosevelt—Ladies p195-198
 Schmidt—400 p542,por.

Allen, Frances Buchanan (m. 1784)
 Amer., wife of Ethan Allen
 Ellet—Women (2) p237-244
 Green—Pioneer (2) p162-164

Allen, Gracie (1905-1964)
 Amer. radio, TV actress
 Blum—Television p91,por.
 Cahn—Laugh p9,146,por.
 CR '59 p14,por.
 CR '63 p10,por.
 Cur. Biog. '40 p12-13
 Cur. Biog. '51 p75-77,por.
 Cur. Biog. '64 p3
 Eichberg—Radio p56-58,por.
 Settel—Radio p90-91,por.
 Stuart—Immort. p26-27,por.
 TV—Person (1) p14-15,por.

Allen, Helen. See Howe, Helen

Allen, Jayne. See Meadows, Jayne

Allen, Judith (fl. 1930's)
 Amer. actress
 Women—Achieve, p108,por.

Allen, Louise (fl. 1920's)
 Amer. sculptor
 National—Contemp. p13

Allen, Margaret Newton (1994/95-)
 Amer. sculptor
 National—Contemp. p10

Allen, Maria (fl. 1770's)
 Amer. Rev. war heroine
 °Carmer—Young p62-67

Allen, Marion (1862-1941)
 Amer. artist
 Cur. Biog. '42 p14-15

Allen, Martha Frances (1906-)
 Amer. organization official
 Cur. Biog. '59 p8-9,por.

Allen, Mary Brownson (b. c. 1733)
 Amer., Mrs. Ethan Allen
 Green—Pioneer (2) p159-164

Allen, Mary Gray (d. 1928)
 Eng. philanthropist
 Brittain—Women p141,173-174,259

Allen, Naomi (fl. 1950's)
 Brit. aviatrix, glider pilot
 °May—Women p222

Allen, Phebe (fl. 1860's)
 Amer. Civil war nurse, teacher
 Brockett—Woman's p502

Allen, Priscilla. See Smith, Priscilla Allen

Allen, Samantha. See Holley, Marietta

Allen, Sara (1764-1849)
 Amer. relig. worker
 Brown—Home. p11-12,por.

Allen, Viola (1869-1948)
 Amer. actress
 Blum—Great p19,por.
 Coad—Amer. p281,por.
 Hammerton p63
 °Kobbé—Homes p178-180,por.
 Strang—Actresses p134-146,por.

Allen, Vivian Beaumont (d. 1962)
 Amer. philanthropist
 Phelps—Men '58 (1) p21

Allerton, Fear Brewster (d. 1634)
 Amer. Pilgrim
 Bell—Women p114-115
 Green—Pioneer (1) p140

Allerton, Mary Norris (fl. 17th cent.)
 Amer. Pilgrim
 Bell—Women p17-18,24-25
 Green—Pioneer (1) (p151
 Hanaford—Dau. p34
 Logan—Part p32
 Marble—Women p56-57

Allerton, Remember (c. 1614-1652/56)
 Amer. Pilgrim
 Logan—Part p32

Allgood, Sara (1883-1950)
 Irish actress
 Hammerton p65,por.

Alliluyeva, Svetlana Stalina (1926-)
 Russ. author, daughter of Joseph
  Stalin
 Cur. Biog. '68 p18-20,por.

Allingham, Helen Paterson (b. 1848)
 Eng. artist
 Furniss—Some p79-82
 Waters—Women p7-9

Allis, Marguerite (c. 1887-1958)
 Amer. novelist
 Warfel—Amer. p9-10,por.

Allison, Emma (fl. 1880's)
 Amer. inventor
 Hanaford—Dau. p646

Allison, Frances (Fran) (n.d.)
Amer. TV actress
Blum—Television p185,por.
TV Person (1) p108-109,por.

Allitsen, Frances (Mary Frances Bumpus)
(1849-1912)
Eng. singer, composer
Elson—Woman's p148-149
McCoy—Portraits p2,por.

Allston, Margaret.
See Bergengren, Anna Farquhar

Allyson, June (1923-   )
Amer. actress
CR '59 p15-16,por.
CR '63 p11,por.
Cur. Biog. '52 p13-15,por.
Schickel—Stars p222-223,por.

Alma-Tadema, Lady Laura Therese (fl.
1870-1900)
Eng. artist
Furniss—Some p82-83,por.
Waters—Women p9-10

Almeida, Brites de (d.c. 1386)
Port. heroine, patriot
Arsenius—Dict. p13,por.
Phila.—Women unp,por.
Stiles—Postal p9

"A.L.O.E." See Tucker, Charlotte Maria

Alonso, Alicia (1921-   )
Cub. ballet dancer
Atkinson—Dancers p7-11,por.
CR '59 p16,por.
Cur. Biog. '55 p15-17,por.
Davidson—Ballet p4-6
*Eby—Marked p50-56
Haskell—Vignet. p.64
Swinson—Great p6,por.
*Terry—Star p177-185,por.

Aloysia, Sister (fl. 1840's)
Amer. W. pioneer, nun
Ross—Heroines p126-155
Ross—Westward p77-92

Alphand, Nicole (Bunau-Varilla) (n.d.)
Fr. hostess
Time Nov. 22, 1963, p21-25,por.,(Cover)

Alphonsa, Mother Mary.
See Lathrop, Rose Hawthorne

Alsen, Elsea (1892-   )
Pol. singer
Ewen—Living 13-14,por.

Alston, Margaret, pseud.
See Bergengren, Anna Farquhar

Alston, Theodosia. See Burr, Theodosia

Al-Taymuriyya, Ayesha (1840-1902)
Egypt. author, feminist
Schmidt—400 p119,por.

Alten, Bella (fl. 1900's-1910's)
Ger. singer
Lahee—Grand p277-278,por.

Alter, Belle Thompson (fl. 1860's)
Amer. Civil war nurse
Logan—Part p364

Alter, Martha (1904-   )
Amer. composer, teacher, pianist
Howard—Our p535
Reis—Composers p3-4

Altissimi, pseud. See Joris, Agnese

Altman, Thelma (fl. 1940's)
Amer. singer
Peltz—Spot. p106,por.

Alumbaugh, Goldie P (fl. 1920's-1950's)
Amer. missionary
They—Went p56-57

Alvarez, Marguerite d'.
See D'Alvarez, Marguerite

Amadeus, Mother. See Dunne, Sarah Theresa

Amalasuntha (Amalasventha) (c. 498-c. 535)
Russ. (Ostrogorth) queen
Hammerton p73,por.

Amalie, Marie Friederika Amalie (1818-
1875)
Gr. queen
Stiles—Postal p10

Amara, Lucine (1927-   )
Armen.-Amer. singer
Matz—Opera p91-95,por.
Wagner—Prima p237

Amaya, Carmen (fl. 1940's)
Sp. gypsy dancer
Stiles—Postal p10

A. M. B., Miss (fl. 1860's)
Amer. Civil war diarist
Jones—Heroines p78-79

Ambrose, Alice (fl. 1660's)
Amer. colonial religious worker
Jones—Quakers p103-105,130,276

Ambrosius, Johanna (fl. 19th cent.)
Ger. poet
Heller—Studies p293

"Amelia." See Welby, Amelia Ball Coppuck

Amelia (fl. 7th cent.)
Belg. saint
Blunt—Great p149-150

Amelia Sophia Eleanora (1710-1786)
Eng. princess
Festing—On p181-281

Amélie (1865-1951)
Port. queen consort
Hammerton p75,por.

Amen, Marion Cleveland (fl. 1930's)
Amer. bus. executive
Women—Achieve. p171,por.

Amenardes (718-655 B.C.)
Egypt. princess
Schmidt—400 p124-125,por.

American, Sadie (b. 1862)
Amer. lecturer, club leader
Logan—Part p642-646

Ames, Elinor (fl. 1930's)
Amer. lecturer, teacher, editor
Women—Achieve. p127,por.

Ames, Fannie B. (b. 1840)
Amer. industrial reformer
Logan—Part p589

Ames, Louise Bates (c. 1906-   )
Amer. psychologist
Cur. Biog. '56 p299-300,por.

Ames, Mary Clemmer (1839-1884)
Amer. author
Adelman—Famous p201
Dorland—Sum p39,117
Hanaford—Dau. p688

Ames, Minerva Ross (m. 1875)
Amer. club leader
Logan—Part p469-470

Ames, Nabby Lee (b. 1771)
Amer. pioneer
Green—Pioneer (3) p520-521

Ames, Sarah Fisher (1817-1901)
Amer. sculptor
Hanaford—Dau. p320

Amherst, Alicia-Margaret, Baroness Rockley.
See Rockley, Alicia-Margaret, Amherst

Amsden, Elizabeth (gr. 1892)
Amer. singer
Lahee—Grand p390-391,413,por.

Amsterdam, Birdie (1902-   )
Amer. justice
Cur. Biog. '40 p16-17,por.

Anacaona (fl. 1562)
Dom. R. Indian queen
Stiles—Postal p11

Anah (Biblical)
Deen—All p252

Anastasia, Grand duchess (1901-   )
Russ.-Amer. hostess
CR '59 p19-20,por.

Anastasia (1), Saint (d. c. 303/304)
Rom. martyr, philanthropist
Blunt—Great p23
Culver—Women p76

Anastasia (2) (d. 68)
Rom. saint
Westcott—Calen. p54

Anastasia (3) the Patrician, Saint (d. 567)
Gr. lady-in-waiting
Englebert—Lives p97

Ancher, Anna Kristine (1859-   )
Ger. artist
Waters—Women p16-17

Anders, Merry (1934-   )
Amer. actress
TV—Person (2) p13-14,por.

Andersen, Ane Marie (1767-1833)
Dan., mother of Hans Christian Andersen
*Chandler—Famous p143-168

Andersen, Stell (1897-   )
Amer. pianist
Ewen—Living p19,por.
McCoy—Portraits p3,por.

Anderson, Dame Adelaide Mary (1863/64-
1936)
Austral. feminist, social reformer
Martindale—Some p46-51

Anderson, Audentia Smith (b. 1872)
Amer. relig. writer, Mormon pioneer, genealogist
Phillips—33 p132-138

Anderson, Barbara Tunnell (1894-   )
Amer. author
Warfel—Amer. p11-12,por.

Anderson, Caroline Virginia (b. 1848)
Amer. physician
Robinson—Hist. p45-46

Anderson, Constance Myers (1898-   )
Amer. organization official
Cur. Biog. '48 p14-16,por.

Anderson, Eleanor Copenhaver (fl. 1930's)
Amer. YWCA secretary
Women—Achieve. p184,por.

Anderson, Elizabeth Garrett (1836-1917)
Eng. pioneer physician
Adelman—Famous p220
Bell—Storm p46-61,84-87,126-139,por.
Chambers—Dict. col.15
Cole—Women p131-159,por.
Dorland—Sum p145-148
Hammerton p82,por.
Hume—Great p84-123,por.
Lovejoy—Women p132-143,158-161,
por.

Anderson, Erica Kellner Collier (1914-   )
Aust.-Amer. photographer
Cur. Biog. '57 p15-17,por.

Anderson, (Helen) Eugenie Moore A. (1909-)
Amer. ambassador
Cur. Biog. '50 p4-6,por.
*Heath—Woman p32
Jensen—Revolt p206-207,por.
Lamson—Few p165-194,por.
Roosevelt—Ladies p213-216

Anderson, Gertrude E. Fisher (1894-   )
Amer. bus. executive
Robinson—Hist. p156-157

Anderson, Dame Judith (1898-   )
Austral. actress
Blum—Great p98,por.
CR '59 p20,por.
CR '63 p14,por.
Cur. Biog. '41 p24-24,por.
Cur. Biog. '61 p9-11,por.
Time Dec.21,1942,p45,por.(Cover)

Anderson, Katherine Watson (fl. 1930's)
Amer. journalist
Ross—Ladies p473-474

Anderson, Lucy Philpot (1790-1878)
Eng. pianist
Adelman—Famous p142-143

Anderson, Marian (1902/1908-   )
Amer. singer
Adams—Great p154,por
Ames—These p213-226
Bakeless—In p91-109,por.
*Bolton—Lives p29-41,por.
*Cherry—Portraits p64-71,por.
CR '59 p21,por.
CR '63 p15,por.
Cuney-Hare—Negro p356-357,por.
Cur. Biog. '40 p17-19,por.
Cur. Biog. '50 p8-10,por.
Downes—Olin p432-434
Embree—13 p139-152,por.
Ewen—Ency. p19
Ewen—Living p19-21,por.
Ewen—Men p80-89
Fisher—Amer. p315-318,por.
*Forsee—Amer. p9-35
*Hughes—First p45,por.
Hughes—Music p125-131,por.
*Hughes—Negroes p131-135,por.

Hurok—Impres. p237-261,por.
*Logie—Careers (2nd) p160-166
McCoy—Portraits p3,por.
Matz—Opera p53-55,por.
Parshalle—Kash. p173-180,por.
Phelps—Men 58 (1) p24-25
Pleasants—Great p337-339,por.
*Reed—Follow p75-83,por.
*Richardson—Great p15-23,por.
Robinson—Hist. p157-158,por.
*Rollins—Enter. p25-31,por.
*Stoddard—Top p146-160
Thomas—Modern p479-488
Time Dec.30,1946,p59,por.
*Ulrich—Famous p97-100,por.

Anderson, Mary (1872-1964)
Amer. govt. official
Cur. Biog. '40 p19-20,por.
Cur. Biog. '64 p3

Anderson, Mary Antoinette (Mary de Navarro)
(1859-1940)
Eng.-Amer. actress
Adelman—Famous p293
Bodeen—Ladies p111-115
Coda—Amer. p267,por.
Cur. Biog. '40 p612
Farmer—What p414
Furniss—Some p62-63,por.
Hammerton p83,por.
Izard—Heroines p230-264,por.
*Kirkland—Achieved p115-116
Logan—Part p781-782
*Vance—Heart p44-67,por.

Anderson, Mary Reid Macarthur (1880-1921)
Scot. soc. worker, labor organizer
Cole—Women p89-129,por.
Hammerton—935

Anderson, Michael (n.d.)
Amer. hostess
Time July 2,1965,p38,por. (Cover)

Anderson, Mrs. (fl. 1800's)
Amer. W. pioneer
Ellet—Pioneer p373
Logan—Part p95

Anderton, Margaret (n.d.)
Eng. pianist, teacher, lecturer
McCoy—Portraits p3,por.

André, Valérie Edmée (c. 1925-   )
Fr. aviatrix, surgeon, pioneer heli-
copter pilot
Lovejoy—Women p372-374,por.
*May—Women p204-205,por.

Andreas-Salomé, Lou (1861-1937)
Russ.-Ger. philosopher, biographer,
psychoanalyst
Heller—Studies p283

Andreé, Elfrida (1844-1929)
　　Swed. organist, composer
　　Elson—Woman's p220

Andreini, Isabella (1562-1604)
　　It. actress
　　Gilder—Enter p67-81,por.
　　MacQueen—Pope p24

Andress, Mary Vail (1877-1964)
　　Amer. banker
　　Parshalle—Kash. p133-134
　　Women—Achieve. p193

Andrews, Eliza Frances (fl. 1860's)
　　Amer. Civil war diarist
　　Jones—Heroines p405-409,por.
　　Simkins—Women p65-66,190,249-250,
　　　255

Andrews, Emma (fl. 1860's)
　　Amer. Civil war worker
　　Brockett—Woman's p83-84

Andrews, Jane (1833-1887)
　　Amer. story-writer
　　Dorland—Sum p46-189

Andrews, Judith Walker (b. 1826)
　　Amer. philanthropist
　　Logan—Part p529

Andrews, Julie (1935-　　)
　　Eng. actress, singer
　　CR '59 p23,por.
　　CR '63 p16,por.
　　Cur. Biog. '56 p16-18,por.
　　Newquist—Show. p31-43,por.
　　Stambler—Ency. p6-7,por.
　　Time Dec.23,1866 p53-57,por. (Cover)
　　TV—Person (3) p68-69,por.

Andrews, La Verne (1916-1967)
　　Amer. singer
　　CR '59 p24,por.
　　CR '63 p16-17,por.
　　Donaldson—Radio p5
　　Popular Record p9,por.
　　Stambler—Ency. p7-8

Andrews, Mary Garard (b. 1852)
　　Amer. clergyman
　　Logan—Part p736

Andrews, Mary Raymond Shipman (d. 1936)
　　Amer. novelist
　　Maurice—Makers p8

Andrews, Maxine (1918-　　)
　　Amer. singer
　　CR '59 p24,por.
　　CR '63 p16-17,por.
　　Donaldson—Radio p5
　　Popular Record, p9,por.
　　Stambler—Ency. p7-8

Andrews, Patti (1921-　　)
　　Amer. singer
　　CR '59 p24,por.
　　CR '63 p16-17,por.
　　Donaldson—Radio p5
　　Popular Record p9,por.
　　Stambler—Ency. p7-8

Angel, Heather (1909-　　)
　　Eng. actress
　　Hammerton p88,por.

Angela Merici (c1474-1540)
　　It. saint
　　Englebert—Lives p209
　　Phila.—Women, unp.,por.
　　Sharkey—Pop. p131-135
　　Stiles—Postal p230
　　°Windham—Sixty p345-350

Angela of Foligno (1250-1309)
　　It. saint
　　Culver—Women p103
　　Englebert—Lives p6
　　Wescott—Calen. p2

Angelau, Grace (fl. 1930's)
　　Amer. singer
　　Women—Achieve. p94,por.

Angeles, Victoria de Los (1924-　　)
　　Sp. singer
　　Brook—Singer p16-20
　　CR '59 p24,por.
　　Cur. Biog. '55 p18-20,por.
　　Davidson—Treas. p23-27,por.
　　Ewen—Ency. p108-109
　　Matz—Opera p110-114,por.
　　Rosenthal—Sopranos p9-10,por.

Angeli, Pier (1933-　　)
　　Sardin.-Amer. actress
　　CR '59 p24-25,por.

Angelique, Mere.
　　See Arnauld (Jacqueline) Angelique

Angelus, Muriel (1909-　　)
　　Eng. actress
　　Hammerton p90,por.

Anglin, Margaret Mary (1876-1958)
　　Can.-Amer. actress
　　Adelman—Famous p317
　　Blum—Great p21,por.
　　Coad—Amer. p301,por.
　　Cocroft—Great p13-16,55-80,por.
　　Hammerton p91,por.
　　Izard—Heroines p353-356
　　°Kobbé—Homes p181,por.
　　Logan—Part p779
　　Strang—Actresses p270-272

Anguisciola, Lucia (d. 1565)
　　It. painter
　　Waters—Women p10

Anne of Beaujeu (c. 1462-1522)
Fr., dau. of Lewis XI
Koven—Women p87-89

Anne of Bohemia (1366-1394)
Eng. queen
Culver—Women p117-119
Hammerton p93-94

Anne of Brittany (1476/77-1514)
Fr. queen
Hammerton p94,por.

Anne of Cleves (1515/17-1557)
Eng. queen
Hammerton p94,por.
Sanders—Intimate p22-26,por.

Anne of Denmark (1574-1619)
Eng. queen
Hammerton p94,por.
Sanders—Intimate p87-93,por.

Anne of Savoy (1320-c. 1353)
Byzant. empress
Diehl—Byzant. p287-308

Anne Neville (1456-1485)
Eng. queen
Hammerton p94
Leary—Golden p243-244,289-292

Annesley, Lady Constance Mary.
See O'Neil, Constance Mary, Lady Annesley

Annesley, Susanna.
See Wesley, Susanna Annesley

Annette (Funicello) (1942-   )
Amer. singer, actress, dancer
Stambler—Ency. p9

Annia Faustina. See Faustina, Annia Galeria

Annia Lucilla (m. 164)
Rom. empress
Balsdon—Roman p142-147,148,155
McCabe—Empr. p175,179,183-184,por.
Serviez—Roman (2) p72-90

Anning, Mary (1799-1847)
Eng. collector
Hammerton p95

Ansell, Mary.
See Cannan, Mary Ansell Barrie

Anselma, Madame.
See Gessler de Lacroix, Alejandrena

Anspach, Elizabeth Berkeley, Margravine
of (1750-1828)
Eng. playwright
Hammerton p97,por.97
Melville—Regency p186-207,por.

Anstruther, Joyce. See Struther, Jan, pseud.

Anthony, C. L., pseud. (   )
Eng. playwright
Hammerton p98,por.

Anthony, Katharine Susan (1877-1965)
Amer. author
Women—Achieve. p84

Anthony, Sarah Porter Williams (fl. 1830's)
Amer. bus. woman
Dexter—Career p216-218

Anthony, Susan Brownell (1820-1906)
Amer. social reformer, humanitarian, feminist
Abbot—Notable p268-273,por.
Adelman—Famous p170-171
America's 12, p12-15,por.
Beard—Amer. p226-229
*Bolton—Lives p43-59,por.
*Boynick—Pioneers p27-58
Bruce—Women p227-228,233,304,por.
Burnett—Five p177-256
*Carmer—Caval. p157-160,por.
*Commager—Crus. p158-160,168-170
Culver—Women p179-180
*Curtin—Gallery p2,por.
*Daugherty—Ten p108-122,por.
Dexter—Career p6-7
*Dolin—World p111-119,por.
Dorland—Sum p26,81,127,135-136
Douglas—Remember, p156-158,160-162
165-166,por.
Green—Pioneer (3) p92
Hanaford—Dau. p366,370,690
*Heath—Woman (4) p13,por.
Holbrook—Dreamers p85-86,193-202,
205,208,210-215,218
*Horowitz—Treas. p76-81
Irwin—Angels see index
Jensen—Revolt p49-53,55-56,por.
Ladies'—Amer. 12 p12-15,por.
*Lamm—Biog. p99-100
Logan—Part p570-573
Longwell—Amer. p91-120
*McCallum—Women p171-198
*MacVeagh—Champlin p29-30
Mears—They p75-76
*Moore—When p30-36
Morello—Hall p63,por.
Morris—400 p23-24
Muir—Women p177-180
*Nathan—Women p3-39
O'Connor—Pioneer p35,46,79-81,83,
156,166-167,183
Phila.-Women unp.,por.
Riegel—Amer. p65-81,90-91,149-150
Rogers—Women p36,por.
Roosevelt—Ladies p2,4,6-9,291
*Ross—Heroines p168-169
Schmidt—400 p11-12,por.
Seitz—Uncommon p147-155,por.
Sewell—Brief p183-184

(Continued)

Anthony, Susan—*Continued*

    Shaw—Story p189-237,por.
    *Stevens—Women p95-96,por.
    Stiles—Postal p13
    *Strong—Of p210-215
    Thomas—50 p194-202
    Thomas—Living Women p163-175,por.
    Untermeyer—Makers p60-65
    *Vance—Lamps p155-196,por.
    Whitton—These p146-147

Anthusa (c. 347-c. 407)
    Syrian Christian, mother of John
    Chrysostom
    Deen—Great p26-28

Antigna, Marie-Benezit Hélène (fl. 1861-
    1880)
    Fr. artist
    Waters—Women p17-18

Antin, Mary (1881-1949)
    Russ.-Amer. author
    Ames—These p129-133
    Cavanah—We p228-234
    *Parkman—Heroines p185-208,por.
    Ribalow—Auto. p51-71
    Stone—We p166-171

Antoine, Josephine (1908-   )
    Amer. singer
    Cur. Biog. '44 p13-15,por.
    Ewen—Living p22,por.
    McCoy—Portraits p4,por.
    Peltz—Spot. p15,por.
    Women—Achieve. p140,por.

Antoinette, Marie. See **Marie Antoinette**

Antonia, Claudia (d. 66 A.D.)
    Rom., dau. of Claudius
    Balsdon—Roman p43-44,107,122-123,
    127-128

Antonia (Gainaci), Blessed (1407-1507)
    It. saint
    Englebert—Lives p407

Antonia Caenis. See **Caenis, Antonia**

Antonia Major (fl. 1st cent., A.D.)
    Rom. dau. of Mark Antony
    Balsdon—Roman p70-71,74
    Boccaccio—Conc. p198-199
    Ferrero—Women p96-99

Antonia Minor (36 B.C.-37 A.D.)
    Rom. mother of Nero
    Balsdon—Roman p70-71,74,79-80,95-96

Antonia O.S.D. Fischer, Mother (b. 1849)
    Ger.-Amer. mother
    Logan—Part p619-620

Anyte of Tegea (fl. c. 300 B.C.)
    Gr. poet
    Anthologia—Poets p85-93

Apfelbeck, Marie Louise Bailey (b. 1876)
    Amer. artist
    Logan—Part p764-765

Apolionia, Saint (d. 249)
    Alex. saint
    Englebert—Lives p57

Apphia (Biblical)
    Deen—All p252

Appia, Madame Thérèse (fl. 1900's)
    Fr. painter
    Waters—Women p18

Applegarth, Margaret Tyson (b. 1886)
    Amer. playwright, editor, children's
    author
    Women—Achieve. p151,por.

Appleton, Adeline Carola (b. 1886)
    Amer. composer, teacher
    Hipsher—Amer. p62-63

Appleton, Anna E. (b. 1825)
    Amer. poet, translator
    Hanaford—Dau. p243-268

Appleton, Mattie H. (fl. 1870's)
    Amer. librarian
    Hanaford—Dau. p719

Appolonia, Jagiello (b. 1825)
    Lith. heroine
    Schmidt—400 p284-285,por.

Aqua, Eva Dell' (fl. 1930's)
    It. composer
    Elson—Woman's p212

Aquila (fl. 51 A.D.) (Biblical)
    Culver—Women p57-59

Aquinas, Sister.
    See Thomas Aquinas, Sister (Agnes
    O'Neill)

Aquino, Iva Ikuko Toguri d' (Tokyo Rose)
    (b. 1916-   )
    Japan. spy
    Singer—World's p216-221

Aquitaine, Eleanor d' (1122-1204)
    Fr., mother of Richard the Lion
    Hearted
    *Cather—Girlhood p79-99
    Schmidt—400 p171-172,por.

Aragona, Tullia. See **D'Aragona, Tullia**

Aranyi, Yelly d' (1895-   )
    Hung. violinist
    Ewen—Living p22-23,por.
    Hammerton p105,por.
    McCoy—Portraits p31,por.

Arblay, Madame d'. See Burney, Fanny

Arc, Joan of. See Joan of Arc

Arcane, Mrs. J. B. (fl. 1840's)
    Amer. pioneer
    Whitton—These p240-241

Archer, Alma (fl. 1930's)
    Amer. fashion expert, editor, author
    Women—Achieve. p58,por.

Archibald, Anne (fl. 1930's)
    Amer. bus. executive
    Planck—Women p217-218

Archibald, Edith Jessie (b. 1854)
    Can. novelist
    Thomas—Canad. p.3-4

Arden, Elizabeth (Florence Nightingale Graham) (1884-1966)
    Can. cosmetician, bus. executive
    CR '59 p27-28,por.
    CR '63 p18-19,por.
    Cur Biog. '57 p19-21,por.
    Cur. Biog. '66 p462
    New York. p329-341
    New Yorker, April 6,1935 p24-30 (Profiles)
    Rogers—Women p198-199,por.
    Time May 6,1946 p57,por.(Cover)

Arden, Eve (1912-   )
    Amer. radio, TV actress
    Blum—Television p96,por.
    CR '59 p28,por.
    CR '63 p19,por.
    Cur. Biog. '53 p31-33,por.
    TV—Person. (2), p124-125,por.

Arden, Joan, pseud.
    See Jourdaine, Clare Melicent

Arden, Toni (n.d.)
    Amer. singer
    Popular Record p12,por.

Arenal de Garcia Carrasco, Dona Concepcion (1820-1893)
    Sp. feminist, humanitarian, novelist
    Arsenius—Dict. p17,por.
    Phila.—Women, unp.,por.
    Stiles—Postal p15

Arencibia, Marta Abreu y (1845-1919)
    Cub. patriot
    Schmidt—400 p84-85,por.

Arendt, Hannah (1906-   )
    Ger. author, educator
    Cur. Biog. '59 p14-16,por.

Arete of Cyrene (fl. 370's-340's B.C.)
    Gr. physicist, philosopher
    Beard—Woman p318
    Mozans—Woman p197-199

Argentinita (Encaracion Lopez) (1905-1945)
    Sp. dancer
    Cur. Biog. '42 p28-31,por.
    Cur. Biog. '45 p10
    Hammerton p110,por.
    Hurok—Impres. p280-284,por.

Arguello, Concha Maria de Concepcion (1791-1857)
    Sp.-Amer. nun, pioneer
    DAR Mag. July 1921 p392,portrayal
    °Sickels—Calico p141-155
    Whitton—These p258-259

Argyll, Jane Warbuton (fl. 1710)
    Eng., maid of Queen Anne
    Stenton—English p252

Argyll, Louise Caroline, Duchess of.
    See Louise Caroline Alberta, Duchess of Argyll

Argyll, Pearl (1910-c. 1948)
    Eng. dancer
    Fisher—Ball. p10,por.
    Hammerton p110
    Haskell—Vignet. p22,por.

Ariki, Makea Takau. See Makea, Takau Ariki

Arkin, Frances S. (fl. 1930's)
    Amer. psychiatrist
    Women—Achieve. p128,por.

Arlen, Jeanne Burns (1917-   )
    Amer. composer, author
    ASCAP p13

Arletty (Leonie Bathiat) (1898-   )
    Fr. actress
    CR 59 p29,por.

Arman de Caillavet, Léontine Charlotte Lippman (1844-1910)
    Fr. salonist, author, editor
    Skinner—Elegant p17,153-168

Armani, Vincenza (fl. 1560's)
    It. actress
    Gilder—Enter p58-59

Armer, Laura Adams (1874-1963)
    Amer. author, illustrator
    Mahony—Illus. p268
    °Millett—Amer. p225-226

Armfield, Anne Constance.
    See Smedley, Constance

Armond, Isabel d' (fl. 1910)
  Amer. actress
  Caffin—Vaud. p212-213,por.

Armor, Eleanor.
  See Smith, Eleanor Armor

Armor, Mary Harris (fl. 1890's-1910's)
  Amer. social reformer
  Logan—Part p668-669

Arms, Julia (fl. 1900's)
  Amer. social reformer
  Logan—Part p670

Armstrong, Carman Neal.
  See Barnes, Carman Neal

Armstrong, Charlotte (1905-   )
  Amer. author, playwright
  Cur. Biog. '46 p16-17,por.

Armstrong, Helen Billington.
  See Billington, Helen

Armstrong, Margaret Neilson (1867-1944)
  Amer. author, illustrator
  Cur. Biog. '44 p18

Armstrong, Ruth (fl. 1900's)
  Amer. social reformer
  Logan—Part p670

Armstrong, Sarah B. (gr. 1880)
  Amer. physician, teacher
  Logan—Part p743

Arnaud, Yvonne (1892-1958)
  Fr. actress
  Hammerton p119,por.

Arnauld (Jacqueline) Angelique (1591-1661)
  Fr. abbess
  Adelman—Famous p68
  Hammerton p119,por.

Arne, Sigrid (n.d.)
  Amer. journalist
  Cur. Biog. '45 p15-16,por.

Arne, Susanna. See Cibber, Susanna Maria

Arnett, Hannah White (1733-1824)
  Amer. Rev. war patriot
  Green—Pioneer (3) p348-349

Arnim, Countess of.
  See Russell, Elizabeth Mary Annette
  Beauchamp

Arnold, Alma Cusian (b. 1871)
  Ger.-Amer. chiropractor
  Women—Achieve. p90,por.

Arnold, Annie R. Merrylees (fl. 1900's-1930's)
  Scot. painter
  Waters—Women p19-20

Arnold, Birch, pseud.
  See Bartlett, Alice Elinor

Arnold, Margaret (1912-   )
  Amer. club leader
  Parshalle—Kash. p229-231,por.

Arnold, Margaret Shippen (1760-1804)
  Amer. Rev. patriot, wife of Bene-
    dict Arnold
  Bradford—Wives p53-88,por.
  Donovan—Women p265-266
  Ellet—Women (2) p245-253
  Logan—Part p186-188
  Parton—Dau. p194-210
  Parton—Noted p194-210
  Sale—Old p158-168,por.
  Whitton—These p18-19,28-29

Arnold, Mary (fl. 1930's)
  Amer. social worker
  Women—Achieve. p113,por.

Arnold, Mary Ellen (fl. 1860's)
  Amer. Civil war diarist
  Jones—Heroines p351-352

Arnold, Mary Penrose (m. 1820)
  Eng., wife of Thomas Arnold
  Guedalla—Bonnet p69-95,por.

Arnold, Pauline (fl. 1910's-1930's)
  Amer. market research worker
  Women—Achieve. p111 (por.)

Arnold, Polly (1906-   )
  Eng. composer, author
  ASCAP p14-15

Arnold, Sarah Louise (1859-   )
  Amer. educator
  Logan—Part p721

Arnoldson, Sigrid (1860-1943)
  Swed. singer
  Lahee—Famous p252-253

Arnoul, Françoise (1932-   )
  Alger.-Fr. actress
  CR '59 p32,por.

Arnould (Madeline) Sophie (1744-1902/03)
  Fr. singer
  Dorland—Sum p29,70,167
  Ewen—Ency. p25
  Ferris—Great p55-85
  Hammerton p123,por.
  Lahee—Famous p20-22,23
  Mayne—Enchant. p109-122,por.
  Schmidt—400 p179,por.
  Wagner—Prima p238

Arnould-Plessy, Jeanne Sylvania (1819-1897)
  Fr. actress
  Dorland—Sum p19,68
  Hammerton p123

Arnow, Harriette Louise Simpson
(1908-   )
Amer. author
Cur. Biog. '54 p35-36,por.
Warfel—Amer. p14-15,por.

Aronson, Naoum (c. 1782-1943)
Russ. sculptor
Cur. Biog. '43 p14

Arral, Blanche (fl. 1910's)
Belg. singer
Lahee—Grand p307-309

Arria, the elder (d. A.D. 42)
Rom. heroine
Adelman—Famous p26
Balsdon—Roman p58
Hammerton p124

Arria, the younger (m. 56 A.D.)
Rom. matron
Balsdon—Roman p58

Arron, Cecilia Francisca Josefa de.
See Caballaro, Fernan Böhl von Faber,
pseud.

Arsinöe (fl. c. 200-300 B.C.)
Egypt. princess, mother of Ptolemy I
Hammerton p124

Artemisia (1) (5th cent., B.C.)
Halicaenassus & Cos queen
Muir—Women p40-41

Artemisia (2) (d.c. 350 B.C.)
Caria botanist, builder queen
Boccaccio—Conc. p123-127
Hammerton p125
MacVeagh—Champlin p38
Muir—Women p40

Arthur, Ellen Lewis Heendon (1837-1880)
Amer. first lady
Hanaford—Dau. p107-109
Logan—Ladies p118-120
*McConnell—Our p213-219
Prindiville—First p175-178
*Ross—Know p45,por.
Smith—Romances p286-290

Arthur, Jean (1908-   )
Amer. actress
CR '59 p33-34,por.
Cur. Biog. p17-18,por.

Arthur, Julia (Ida Lewis) (b. 1869)
Can. actress
Strang—Actresses p161-173,por.

Arthur, Melvina Stone (fl. 1800's)
Amer., mother of Chester A. Arthur
Hampton—Our p164-169

Arthur, Mrs. William (fl. 1820's)
Amer. frontier reformer
Aikman—Calamity p313-316

Artigas de Ferreira, Rosalie (1809-1891)
Urug. patriot, philanthropist
Schmidt—400 p412-413,por.

Artner, Marie Therese ("Theone," pseud.)
(1772-1829)
Hung. poet, playwright
Schmidt—400 p226,por.

Artois, Countess of.
See Mahaut, Countess of Artois and of
Burgundy

Artôt, Marguerite Josephine Désirée (1835-
1907)
Fr. singer
Ewen—Enc. p27
Lahee—Famous p113-114

Arundale, Sybil (b. 1897)
Eng. actress
Hammerton p127,por.

Arundel, Isabella, Countess of (d. 1282)
Eng. countess
Stenton—English p54-55

Arusmont, Frances Wright D'.
See Wright, Frances (Fanny) D'Arusmont

Arvède, Barine, pseud. (Mme. Charles Vin-
cens) (1840-1908)
Fr. author, critic
Ravenel—Women p39-63

Arvey, Verna (1910-   )
Amer. pianist, musical writer
ASCAP p15

Arville, Camille d' (Neeltye Dykstra) (b.
1863-   )
Dutch-Amer. singer, actress
Strang—Prima p208-221,por.

Aecue, Anne. See Askew, Anne

Asenath (Biblical)
Buchanan—Women p23-24
Culver—Women p21
Deen—All p253
Hammerton p129
Lewis—Portraits p58

Ashbridge, Elizabeth (fl. 18th cent.)
Brit. teacher, clergyman
Benson—Women p266

Ashburton, Harriet Montagu Baring
Baroness (1805-1857)
Eng. salonist
Courtney—Advent. p262-274,por.

Ashcroft, Dame Peggy (1907-   )
        Eng. actress
    Beaton—Peesona p11-13,por.
    Cur. Biog. '63 p10-13,por.
    Hammerton p130,por.

Ashford, Emma Louise (1850-1930)
        Amer. composer, teacher
    Adelman—Famous p283
    McCoy—Portraits p4,por.

Ashley, Grace (fl. 1930's)
        Amer. fashion designer
    Women—Achieve. p63,por.

Ashley, Grace Bosley (b. 1874)
        Amer. politician, club leader
    Women—Achieve. p63,por.

Ashley, Katherine (d. 1565)
        Eng. governess
    Howe—Galaxy p25-33,por.

Ashley, Minnie. See **Chanler, Beatrice Ashley**

Ashley, Lady Sylvia (1904-   )
        Eng. social leader
    CR '59 p34-35,por.

Ashmun, Margaret Eliza (d. 1940)
        Amer. author
    Cur. Biog. '40 p28,por.
    Women—Achieve. p193

Ashton, Elizabeth (fl. c. 1700)
        Eng. author
    Stenton—English p139

Ashton, Winifred. See **Dane, Clemence**

Ashur-Sharrat (c. 650 B.C.)
        Assyr. queen
    Schmidt—400 p125-126,por.

Ashwell, Len, Lady Simson (n.d.)
        Br. actress
    Hammerton p131-132,por.

Ashworth, Mrs. (fl. 1860's-1870's)
        Eng., mother of John Ashworth
    Wallace—Mothers p101-105

Askew, Alice J. de C. (d. 1917)
        Brit. novelist
    Hammerton p132

Askew (or Ascue, Ayscough), **Anne** (1521-
        1546)
        Eng. Protestant martyr
    Deen—Great p346-348
    Dorland—Sum p25,132
    Fifty—Famous p93-99
    Hammerton p132
    Stenton—English p125

Askew, Sarah B. (1863-1942)
        Amer. pioneer librarian
    Marshall—Amer. p448-449

Askwith, Margaret Long (fl. 1930's)
        Amer. teacher, bus. woman
    Women—Achieve. p135,por.

Aspasia (1) (470-410 B.C.)
        Gr. scholar, wife of Pericles
    Abbott—Notable p20-24,por.
    Adelman—Famous p21-23
    Hammerton p132,por.
    Lovejoy—Women p3
    °MacVeagh—Champlin p40
    Mozans—Woman p12-14
    Muir—Women p36-37
    Schmidt—400 p214,por.
    Weigall—Person. p135-143

Aspasia (2) (c. 400 B.C.)
        Pers. queen
    Hammerton p132-133

Asquith, Margot.
    See **Oxford and Asquith, Margot Ten-
        nant,** Countess of

Assche, Amélie van (b. 1804)
        Belg. painter
    Waters—Women p20

Assche, Isabel Catherine van (b. 1794)
        Belg. painter
    Waters—Women p20-21

Astaire, Adele (1899-   )
        Amer. dancer
    Barnett—Writing p32-38
    CR '63 p23-24,por.
    Hammerton p134,por.
    Lamparski—What, p74-75,por.
    Wyndham—Chorus p123-124

Astell, Mary (1666/68-1731)
        Eng. pioneer educator, polemical
            writer
    Benson—Women p28-33,39-40
    °Borer—Women p17-20
    Stenton—Englishp214,219-225,227-238,
        242,259,261

Aston, Mary A. (fl. 1860's)
        Amer. Civil war nurse
    Logan—Part p363

Astor, Alice. See **Bouverie, Alice Astor**

Astor, Caroline Webster Schermerhorn (c.
        1821-1908)
        Amer. social leader
    Eliot—Heiresses p48-60,por.
    Tebbel—Inher. p59-63

Astor, Eleanor Elise Robson.
    See **Belmont, Eleanor Elise Robson**

Astor, Mary (1906-   )
    Amer. actress
    CR '59 p37,por.
    CR '63 p25,por.
    Cur. Biog. '61 p16-18,por.
    Hammerton p135

Astor, Mary Dahlgren Paul (m. 1878)
    Amer. social leader
    Tebbel—Inher. p59-63

Astor, Lady Nancy Witcher Langhorne
        (1879-1964)
    Anglo-Amer. politician
    Adelman—Famous p319
    CR '59 p37,por.
    CR '63 p24-25,por.
    Cur. Biog. '40 p29-31,por.
    Cur. Biog. '64 p15
    Gardiner—Por. p188-195, por.
    Hammerton p135,por.
    Iremonger—And p192-210,por.
    *Kirkland—Good p63-68
    Pearson—Marry p246-263,por.
    Pearson—Pilgrim p258-274
    Tebbel—Inher. p65

Astrid (1932-   )
    Nor. princess
    CR '59 p37-38,por.

Astrid, Sofia Lovisa Thyra (1905-1935)
    Belg. queen
    Phila.—Women, unp., por.
    Stiles—Postal p17

Atarah (Biblical)
    Deen—All p253

Athaliah (Biblical)
    Jerusalem queen
    Boccaccio—Conc. p109-113
    Buchanan—Women p62-63
    Deen—All p140-142
    Hammerton p135
    Lewis—Portraits p127-130
    Marble—Women, Bible p201-205
    Mead—250 p127
    Muir—Women p99

Athanasia (d.860)
    Gr. saint
    Englebert—Lives p312

Athanasia. See also Anastasia

Athanasiu, Jean (1885-1938)
    Rum. singer
    Stiles—Postal p18

Athenais-Eudocia. See Eudocia

Atherton, Eva Havens (fl. 1920's-1950's)
    Amer. missionary
    They—Went p61-62

Atherton, Gertrude Franklin Horn (1857-
        1948)
    Amer. novelist
    Adelman—Famous p288
    Bindheim—Women p19,por.
    Cur. Biog. '40 p31-33,por.
    Cur. Biog. '48 p28
    Hammerton p136,por.
    Harkins—Famous p205-221,por.
    Harkins—Little p205-221,por.
    Logan—Part p805
    Love—Famous p37
    Maurice—Makers #4,por.
    Millett—Amer. p226-229
    Overton—Women p2-7
    Stone—We p77-83

Athes-Perrelet, Louise (fl. 1880's-1900's)
    Swiss painter, sculptor
    Waters—Women p21

Athol, Katherine Marjory, Duchess of (1874-
        1960)
    Eng. philanthropist
    Hammerton p137,por.

Athy, Margaret (c. 1506)
    Irish church-builder
    Concannon—Dau. p88

Atkins, Mary (1817-1882)
    Amer. educator
    Whitton—These p254-258

Atkinson, Dorothy (1892-   )
    Amer. W. pioneer
    Sargent—Pioneers p54,por.

Atkinson, Eleanor Stackhouse (1863-1942)
    Amer. author
    Cur. Biog. '43 p16

Atkinson, Nellie (1865-   )
    Amer. W. pioneer
    Sargent—Pioneers p53-54,56,58

Atkinson, Oriana Torrey (1894-   )
    Amer. author
    Cur. Biog. '53 p34-35,por.

Atossa (fl. 16th cent.)
    Pers. queen
    *MacVeagh—Champlin p41

Atwood, Donna (1962-   )
    Amer. ice skater
    Cur. Biog. '54 p47-48,por.

Atwood, Elizabeth Gordon (1882-   )
    Amer. educator
    Women—Achieve. p181,por.

Aubernon, Euphrasia Héloise Lydie (1825-
        1899)
    Fr. salonist
    Skinner—Elegant p146-151,153-156

Aubigné, Françoise de.
　See Maintenon, Françoise D'Aubigné,
　　Marquise de

Aubigny, Louise, Duchess of.
　See Kéroualle, Louise Renée de,
　　Duchess of Portsmouth and Aubigny

Aubin, Penelope (fl. 1720's)
　Eng. author
　MacCarthy—Women p253-254

Auchincloss, Janet Lee Bouvier (c. 1908-　)
　Amer., mother of Jacqueline
　　Kennedy
　CR '63 p26,por.

Aud, Queen (fl. 874-900)
　Arsenius—Dict. p20,por.
　Ice. queen
　Phila.—Women unp,por.
　Stiles—Postal p18

Audougard, Olympe (1830-1890)
　Fr. author, feminist
　Dorland—Sum p28

Audoux, Marguerite (b. 1880)
　Fr. novelist
　Hammerton p140

Audrey, Saint. See Ethel(d)reda (Audrey)

Audry, Colette (fl. 1940's-1950's)
　Fr. novelist
　Peyre—French p286

Auger, Ginette. See Genevieve

Augusta (n.d.), Saint
　Wescott—Calen. p44

Augusta, Duchess of Cambridge (1797-1889)
　Eng. hostess
　Hasted—Unsuccess. p222-252,por.

Augusta Marie Luise Katharina (1811-1890)
　Ger. empress
　Hammerton p141
　Schmidt—400 p200-201,por.

Augusta of Saxe-Coburg-Gartha,
　(1719-1772)
　Eng. princess, consort of
　　Frederick, Prince of Wales
　Melville—Maids p267-283,por.
　Trowbridge—Seven p151,por.

Augusta Victoria (1858-1921)
　Ger. empress
　Arsenius—Dict. p20
　Hammerton p141
　Schmidt—400 p204-205,por.

Auguste, Phillipe (1164-1225)
　Fr. nurse, nun
　Schmidt—400 p390,por.

Augustina. See Agustina

Augustine, Mother O.C.D. (fl. 1893)
　Amer. foundress
　Logan—Part p617

Augustine, Delmira (1880/87-1914)
　Urug. poet
　Rosenbaum—Modern p57-167

Aulaire, Ingri d'Mortenson (1904-　)
　Nor. author, illustrator
　Cur. Biog. '40 p34-36,por.
　Mahony—Illus. p297

Aulnoy, Marie Catherine Jumelle de Berne-
　　ville, Countess D' (c. 1650-1705)
　Fr. author
　Dorland—Sum p37,105
　Hammerton p144,por.
　*MacVeagh—Champlin p44

Ault, Marie (b. 1870)
　Eng. actress
　Hammerton p144-145

Aumale, Hawisa (m. 1180)
　Eng. countess
　Stenton—English p35-36,54,56

Aumale and Devon, Isabella de Forz (d.
　　1293)
　Eng. countess
　Stenton—English p54-55

Aurela (d. 54 B.C.)
　Rom., mother of Julius Caesar
　Balsdon—Roman p46-47,244-245

Auriol, Jacqueline Douet (1917-　)
　Fr. aviatrix
　CR '59 p40,por.
　Cur. Biog. '53 p35-37,por.
　*Lauwick—Heroines, p202-216,por.
　May—Women p174-177,por.

Aus der Ohe, Adele.
　See Ohe, Adele Aus der

Aussem, Cecilie (1910-　)
　Ger. lawn tennis player
　Hammerton p146

Austen, Alice (1866-1952)
　Amer. photographer
　Jensen—Revolt p15-26,por.

Austen, Jane (1775-1817)
　Eng. novelist
　Abbott—Notable p367-371
　Adelman—Famous p101-102

(Continued)

Austen, Jane—*Continued*

Bald—Women p1-27
*Borer—Women p54-72,por.
Bradford—Women p45-66,por.
*Cournos—British p17-25,por.
Dorland—Sum p33,75
Hammerton p146-147,por.
Hinckley—Ladies p59-118
Hubbard—Little p323-354,por.
*Humphrey—Janes p63-81
Johnson—Women p66-104
Lawrence—School p32-59,por.
MacCarthy—Later p235-281
MacCarthy—Women p41-43
*MacVeagh—Champlin p44
Maurice—Makers p12
Moore—Disting. p97-107
Schmidt—400 p146-147,por.

Austen, Winifred (fl. 1900's)
Eng. painter
Waters—Women p21-22

Austin, Ann (d. 1665)
Amer. colonial missionary
Dexter—Colonial p146
Jones—Quakers p4,26-29
Leonard—Amer. p111

Austin, Jane Goodwin (1831-1894)
Amer. novelist
Dorland—Sum p30
Farmer—What p36,201,por.

Austin, Kay (fl. 1930's)
Amer. journalist
Women—Achieve. p179,por.

Austin, Margretta Stroup (1907-   )
Amer. govt. official
Cur. Biog. '54 p49-51,por.

Austin, Mary Hunter (1868-1934)
Amer. novelist
Adelman—Famous p309
Farrar—Literary p165-174,308-309
Hammerton p147,por.
Logan p789
Maurice—Makers p10,por.
*Millett—Amer. p229-231
Overton—Women p8-22
Smith—Women's p1
Van Doren p140-143
Wagenkncht—When p385-399

Austin, Sarah (1793-1867)
Eng. author, translator
Dorland—Sum p25

Austral, Florence Wilson (1894-   )
Austral. singer
Davidson—Treas. p30-32
Ewen—Ency. p27-28
Ewen—Living p23-24,por.
Hammerton p147,por.
McCoy—Portraits p5,por.

Auten, Mary (1898-   )
Amer. entomologist
Osborn—Fragments p246,por.

Autriche, Anne D' (1601-1666)
Fr. sister, wife, mother, daughter of
kings
Schmidt—400 p175,por.

Auzon, Pauline (1775-1835)
Fr. painter
Waters—Women p22

Ava, Frau (fl. 12th cent.)
Aust. poet, nun
Schmidt—400 p41,por.

Avary, Myrta Lockett (fl. 1910's)
Amer. sociologist, editor, politician,
author
Logan—Part p831-832,854-855

Avedon, Doe (n.d.)
Amer. actress
TV—Person ( ) p69-70,por.

Avellaneda, Carmen Nobrega de (1837-1899)
Argent. patriot
Schmidt—400 p35,por.

Avellaneda y Arteaga, Gertrudis Gomez
(c. 1814-1873)
Cub. author, poet
Arsenius—Dict. p21,por.
Hammerton p148
Phila.—Women unp.,por.
Schmidt—400 p83-84,por.
Stiles—Postal p19

Avery, Deborah.
See **Putnam, Deborah Lothrop**

Avery, Nina Horton (c. 1840-1930)
Amer. club leader
Farmer—What p50,por.

Avery, Phyllis (1924-   )
Amer. actress
TV—Person (1) p64-65,por.

Avery, Rachel Foster (b. 1858)
Amer. feminist
Logan—Part p586-587

Avery, Rosa Miller (b. 1830)
Amer. social reformer
Logan—Part p589

Avice (fl. 1155)
Eng., daughter of Randulf the Sher-
iff
Stenton—English p32-33

Axelson, Mary MacDougal (fl. 1930's)
Amer. playwright
Mantle—Contemp. p199

Axley, Martha Frances (fl. 1930's)
Amer. artist
Women—Achieve. p112,por.

Axman, Gladys (fl. 1930's)
Amer. singer
Women—Achieve. p136,por.

Axtell, Lady Rebecca (fl. 1700's)
Amer. Colonial planter
Spruill—Women's p305-306

Ayers, Lucy C. (b. 1865)
Amer. nurse
Pennock—Makers p125,por.

Ayesha (or Ayeshah) (611-677/78)
Arab., wife of Mahomet
Hammerton p150

Aylett, Mary Macon (m. 1776)
Amer. pioneer
Green—Pioneer (3) p238

Aylward, Gladys (c. 1903-   )
Eng. missionary, heroine
*Deakin—True p152-172

Aylward, Ida (fl. 1930's)
Amer. author, painter
Women—Achieve. p154,por.

Ayres, Agnes (1898-1940)
Amer. actress
Cur. Biog. '41,p33

Ayres, Ruby Mildred (1883-1955)
Eng. novelist
Hammerton p151

Ayrton, Hertha Marks (1854-1923)
Eng. physicist
Chambers—Dict. col.28
Hammerton p151
Law—Civil. p240-241
Mozans—Woman p212-230

Ayrton, Matilda Chaplin (1846-1883)
Brit. pioneer physician
Chambers—Dict. col.27

Ayscough, Anne. See Ascue, Anne

Azubah (1) (Biblical)
1st wife of Caleb
Deen—All p253

Azubah (2) (Biblical)
dau. of Shilhi
Deen—All p254

Azuma, Tokuho (c. 1910-   )
Japan. dancer
CR '59 p43,por.
Cur. Biog. '54 p51-53

B

Baara (Biblical)
Deen—All p254

Babcock, Clara Maria (fl. 1880's)
Amer. clergyman
Hanaford—Dau. p490

Babcock, Harriet Sprague (d. 1952)
Amer. psychologist
Women—Achieve. p77,por.

Babcock, Lucille (fl. 1930's)
Amer. advertising executive, fashion expert, editor
Women—Achieve. p122,por.

Babiano y Mendez Nuñez Carmen (fl. 1870's-1880's)
Santiagon painter
Waters—Women p22

Babson, Naomi Lane (1895-   )
Amer. author
Cur. Biog. '53 p29-31,por.
Warfel—Amer. p17

Babushka. See Breshkovsky, Catherine

Bacall, Lauren (1924-   )
Amer. actress
CR '59 p43,por.
CR '63 p28,por.
Time July 29,1966,p50-54,por.(Cover)

Bacciochi, Marie Anne.
See Bonaparte, Marie Anne (later Elisa)

Bach, Anna Magdalena Wulken (1700-1760)
Ger. singer, wife of Johan Sebastien Bach
Elson—Woman's p69-70

Bach, Florence Julia (b. 1887)
Amer. artist
Ency. Brit.—Amer. p2,por.

Bach, Maria Barbara (d. 1720)
Ger., 1st wife of Johan Sebastien Bach
Elson—Women's p68-69

Bachauer, Gina (1913-   )
Gr. pianist
Cur. Biog. '54 p53-55,por.
Schonberg—Great p424

Bache, Sarah (d. 1798)
Amer. Rev. war heroine
Ellet—Women (I) p379-396,por.

Bache, Sarah Franklin (1744-1808)
Amer. philanthropist, dau. of Benjamin Franklin

(Continued)

Bache, Sarah Franklin—*Continued*

Adelman—Famous p87
Green—Pioneer (2) p14
Green—Pioneer (3) p179-192,279-280,
    por.
Hanaford—Dau. p54,141
Leonard—Amer. p112
Logan—Part p150-152,202

Bachrach, Elise Wald (1899-1940)
    Amer. artist
    Cur. Biog. '40 p39

Backer-Grondahl, Agatha (1847-1907)
    Nor. pianist
    Schonberg—Great p336-337

Backster, Margery (fl. 1428)
    Eng. accused heretic
    Culver—Women p113

Bacon, Albion Fellows (1865-1933)
    Amer. social reformer
    Adelman—Famous p302
    Bennett—Amer. p115-137,por.

Bacon, Anne Cooke (c1528-1610)
    Eng. travel writer
    Stenton—English p131-132,136

Bacon, Delia (1811-1859)
    Amer. author, Shakespearean critic
    Bacon—Puritan p95-118,por.
    Izant—Ohio p171-182
    Wallace—Square p168-222,por.
    Woodward—Bold p116-148

Bacon, Gertrude (1874-1949)
    Eng. aero, pioneer
    Hammerton p157-158,por.
 *May—Women p21-29,41-43,61-62,210
    por.

Bacon, Josephine Dodge Daskam (1876-
    1961)
    Amer. humor writer, Girl Scout ex-
        ecutive
    Bruère—Laugh p149,278
    Maurice—Makers p11,por.
    Women—Achieve. p189,por.

Bacon, Katherine (1896-   )
    Eng. pianist
    Ewen—Living p25,por.

Bacon, Peggy (1895-   )
    Amer. artist, author
    Cur. Biog. '40 p39-40,por.
    Mahoney—Illus. p271-272
    Women—Achieve. p170,por.

Bacon, Virginia (n.d.)
    Amer. society leader
    CR '63 p29,por.

Baddeley, Angela (1904-   )
    Eng. actress
    Hammerton p159,por.

Baddeley, Hermione (1906-   )
    Eng. actress
    Hammerton p159-160,por.

Baddeley, Sophia Snow (1745-1786)
    Eng. actress, singer
    Hammerton p100,por.

Baden-Powell, Olive St. Clair, Lady (1889-)
    Eng. Girl Scout executive
    Cur. Biog. '46 p19-21,por.

Bader, Golda Maude E. (fl. 1930's)
    Amer. lecturer
    Women—Achieve p104,por.

Badger, Mrs. (fl. 1859)
    Amer. artist, author
    Hanaford—Dau. p295

Baer, Leone Cass (fl. 1930's)
    Amer. journalist, reviewer, critic
    Ross—Ladies p409

Baez, Joan (1941-   )
    Amer. singer
    CR '63 p29-30,por.
    Cur. Biog. '63 p13-15,por.
    Time Nov.23,1962 p.54,por.(Cover)

Baggallay, Olive (fl. 1930's)
    Eng. nurse
    Dolan—Goodnow's

Bagley, Sarah G. (fl. 1836-1846)
    Amer. pioneer telegrapher and re-
        former
    Stern—We p79-94

Bagnold, Enid Algerine (1889-   )
    Eng. author
    CR '59 p45,por.
    Cur. Biog. '64 p17-19,por.

Bai, Mira (fl. 16th cent.)
    Ind. poet, song writer
    Schmidt—400 p235-236

Bailey, Abigail.
    See **Morgan, Abigail (Abbie) Bailey**

Bailey, Ann ("Mad Ann") (c. 1742-1825)
    Amer. patriot, heroine, scout and
        Ind. fighter)
    Dexter—Career p185-187
    Ellet—Pioneer p245-253
 *Dolin—World p22-29
    Green—Pioneer (2) p383-390,451
    Logan—Part p64-67
 *Stevens—Women p9-12

Bailey, Anna Warner ("Mother Bailey")
(1758-1850/51)
Amer. Rev. war patriot
Ellet—Women (2) p291-295
Fowler—Woman p131-132
Green—Pioneer (3) p349-354,357-358,
por.
Hanaford—Dau. p50-51
Logan—Part p174-175
Root—Chapter p353-364

Bailey, Carolyn Sherwin (1875-   )
Amer. author
Cur. Biog. '48 p31-32,por.

Bailey, Consuelo Northrop (1899-   )
Amer. govt. official
Cur. Biog. '54 p57-59,por.
Parshalle—Kash. p205-206,por.

Bailey, Edna Watson (fl. 1930's)
Amer. teacher
*Ferris—Girls p133-149

Bailey, Florence Augusta Merriam (1863-
1948)
Amer. ornithologist
Hammerton p163
Logan—Part p842

Bailey, Florence E. (fl. 1930's)
Amer. advertising executive, jewel-
ry designer
Women—Achieve. p178,por.

Bailey, Hannah J. (b. 1839)
Amer. philanthropist, social reformer
Logan—Part p529

Bailey, Jean Iris Murdock (gr. 1942)
Eng. author, tutor
Brittain—Women p247

Bailey, Lydia R. (d. 1869)
Amer. printer
Dexter—Career p107

Bailey, Margaret L. (b. 1812)
Amer. poet, journalist
Hanaford—Dau. p265,702

Bailey, Mary Westenra, Lady (1890-1960)
Brit. aviatrix
Burge—Ency. p625
Hammerton p163,por.
*Heath—Woman p203-217,por.
*May—Women p101-102

Bailey, Pearl (1918-   )
Amer. singer
*Cherry—Portraits p105-108
CR '59 p45,por.
CR '63 p30,por.
Cur. Biog. '55 p34-36,por.
New Yorker Dec. 1,1952 p89,por. (Pro-
files)
Popular Record p19,por.

Bailey, Temple (d. 1953)
Amer. novelist
Overton—Women p23-24

Baillie, Grizel, Lady (1665-1746)
Scot. poet
Graham—Group p90-112,por.
Hammerton p163-164,por.

Baillie, Isobel (1895-   )
Scot. singer
Brook—Singers p27-32,por.

Baillie, Joanna (1762-1851)
Scot. playwright, poet
Dorland—Sum p35,72,82,180
Findlay—Spindle p153-182
Hammerton p164,por.
Stenton—English p324,326-327

Baillie-Saunders, Margaret Elsie Crowther
(1873-1949)
Eng. novelist
Hammerton p164

Bailly, Elizabeth Donovan (fl. 1930's)
Amer. social welfare worker
Women—Achieve. p193

Baily, Caroline A. B. (fl. 1900's)
Amer. artist
Waters—Women p22

Bainbridge, Katherine (1924-   )
Eng.-Amer. poet, song-writer
ASCAP p18-19

Bainter, Fay (1891/92-1968)
Amer. actress
Blum—Great p91,por.

Baird, Cora Eisenberg (1912-1967)
Amer. puppeteer
CR '63 p30-31,por.
Cur. Biog. '54 p59-61,por.
Cur. Biog. '68 p451
TV—Person (1) p37-38,por.

Baird, Dorothea (1873-1933)
Eng. actress
Hammerton p166,por.

Baird, Irene (fl. 1919)
Eng.-Can. author, club leader
Thomas—Canad. p5-6

Baissac, Lise de (fl. 1940's)
Eng. spy
Hoehling—Women p139-141

Baker, Alexina Fisher (fl. 1850's)
Amer. actress
Coad—Amer. p181

Baker, Ann (n.d.)
Amer. actress
TV—Person p25,por.

Baker, Anna H. (fl. 1860's)
Amer. Civil war nurse
Logan—Part p369

Baker, Belle (1898-1957)
Amer. singer, actress
Settel—Radio p98,por.

Baker, Bessie (fl. 1920's-1930's)
Amer. nurse
Pennock—Makers p95,por.

Baker, Bonnie (1918-   )
Amer. singer
Donaldson—Radio p6

Baker, Carroll (1931-   )
Amer. dancer, actress
CR '59 p45-46,por.
CR '63 p31,por.

Baker, Delphine P. (b. 1828)
Amer. Civil war humanitarian
Brockett—Woman's p754-759

Baker, Dorothy Dodds (1907-1968)
Amer. author
Cur. Biog. '43 p16-18,por.
Cur. Biog. '68 p451
Warfel—Amer. p17-18,por.

Baker, Mrs. E. H. (fl. 1860's)
Amer. Civil war spy, Pinkerton
detective
Kane—Spies p71-74

Baker, Eliza. See Paine, Harriet Eliza

Baker, Elizabeth Bradford Faulkner (1885-)
Amer. educator, economist
Women—Achieve. p83,por.

Baker, Elizabeth Gowdy (1860-1927)
Amer. painter
Michigan—Biog. p28-29
Waters—Women p22-23

Baker, Ellen Kendall (d. 1913)
Amer. painter
Michigan—Biog. p29

Baker, Etta Iva Anthony (fl. 1930's)
Amer. author
Women—Achiev. p103,por.

Baker, Frances (fl. 1670's)
Eng. actress
Wilson—All p110

Baker, Grace Green (fl. 1930's)
Amer. club leader
Women—Achieve. p193

Baker, Harriette Newell Woods
Amer. author
Dorland—Sum p33,78,188

Baker, Josephine (1906/07-   )
Amer. dancer, singer
*Cherry—Portraits p109-111
CR '59 p46,por.
CR '63 p31,por.
Cuney-Hare—Negro p136,164
Cur. Biog. '64 p19-22,por.
Robinson—Hist. p159,por.
Rollins—Enter p39-43,por.

Baker, Katherine (fl. 1670's)
Eng. actress
Wilson—All p110

Baker, Lavern (c. 1922-   )
Amer. singer
Popular Record p20,por.

Baker, Lelia Barber (fl. 1930's-1950's)
Amer. missionary
They—Went p99-100

Baker, Louise Maxwell (1909-   )
Amer. author
Cur. Biog. '54 p61-62,por.
*Eby—Marked p100-101
Lotz—Unused p5-20
Warfel—Amer. p18,por.

Baker, Martha Susan (1871-1911)
Amer. painter
Michigan—Biog. p29

Baker, Mary (1897-   )
Eng. author, illustrator
Mahony—Illus. p272

Baker, Nina Brown (1888-1957)
Amer. author
Cur. Biog. '47 p31-32,por.
Cur. Biog. '57 p35

Baker, Rhoda (fl. 18th cent.)
Amer. colonial leather-worker
Earle—Colonial p235-239

Baker, Lady Samuel (fl. 1830's-1870's)
Eng. explorer, wife of Sir Samuel
Baker
Mozans—Woman p374

Baker, Sara Josephine (1873-1945)
Amer. pediatrician, public health
worker
Cur. Biog. '45 p30
Dolan—Goodnow's p292
Fabricant—Why p129-131
*Fleischman—Careers p78
Irwin—Angels p291-292
Lovejoy—Women p70,380
Rosen—Four p127-130,226-231,289-291
16 Amer. p65-68

Bakhuyzen, Juffrouw Gerardina Jacoba van
de Sande (1826-1895)
Nether. painter
Waters—Women p23-25

Bakhtadze, Kseniya Yermolayevna (1899-)
Russ. geneticist, plant selectionist,
academician
U.S.—Biog., Soviet p58

Bakwin, Ruth Morris (fl. 1930's)
Amer. pediatrician
Women—Achieve. p116,por.

Balbilla, Julia (fl. 100's A.D.)
Rom. poet
Balsdon—Roman p140

Balbina (fl. 2d cent.)
Rom., dau. of Quirinus, saint
Wescott—Calen. p46

Balch, Emily Greene (1867-1961)
Amer. economist, sociologist
Cur. Biog. '47 p32-34,por.
Cur. Biog. '61 p20
Irwin—Angels p187,310
Nobel—Man p549-550,566,569

Baldridge, Alice Boarman (fl. 1930's)
Amer. lawyer
Women—Achieve. p149,por.

Baldridge, Elizabeth Lee (fl. 1860's)
Amer. Civil war nurse
Logan—Part p364

Baldridge, "Tish" (1926-)
Amer. social secretary
CR. '63 p32,por.

Baldwin, Alice (fl. 1770's)
Amer. Rev. author
Beard—Amer. p83-86

Baldwin, Anne. See Chase, Anne Baldwin

Baldwin, Edith Ella (fl. 1890's-1900's)
Amer. painter
Waters—Women p25

Baldwin, Eunice Jennison (fl. 1760's-1770's)
Amer. patriot
Green—Pioneer (3) p486-489

Baldwin, Faith (1893-)
Amer. author
CR '59 p47,por.
CR '63 p32,por.
Overton—Women p25-26
Van Gelder—Writers p311-314
Warfel—Amer. p18-21,por.

Baldwin, Maria Louise (1856-1922)
Amer. teacher
Brown—Home p182-193,por.

Baldwin, Mary Briscoe (1811-1877)
Amer. missionary
Logan—Part p514-515

Baldwin, Milicent.
See Camp, Milicent Baldwin Porter

Baldwin, Tillie (c. 1888-1958)
Amer. W. pioneer, cowgirl
Brown—Gentle p188-189,por.

Baldwin, Verona (fl. 1883-1887)
Amer. W. pioneer
Parkhill—Wildest p50-54

Balestier, Caroline.
See Kipling, Caroline Starr Balestier

Balfour, Betty (1903-)
Eng. actress
Hammerton p174

Balfour, Frances Campbell, Lady (1858-
1931)
Scot. feminist
Hammerton p174,por.

Balfour, Margaret Ida (d. 1945)
Eng. physician
Lovejoy—Women p254-255

Balfour, Margaret Isabella (fl. 1800's)
Scot., mother of Robert Louis
Stevenson
Bartlett—Mothers p80-85

Balin, Ina (1937-)
Amer. actress
CR '63 p33,por.

Balkis. See Sheba, Queen of

Ball, Caroline Peddle (b. 1869)
Amer. sculptor
Waters—Women p25

Ball, Erna D. (fl. 1930's)
Ger.-Amer. neurologist
Women—Achieve. p146,por.

Ball, Frances (fl. 1857)
Amer. pioneer
Green—Pioneer (1) p483

Ball, Isabel Worrell (b. 1855)
Amer. journalist
Ross—Ladies p331-332

Ball, (Widow) Johnson (Mrs. Joseph) (fl.
1700's)
Amer., mother of Mary Ball
Washington
Green—Pioneer (1) p456-457

Ball, Lucille (1911-)
Amer. actress, comedienne, TV per-
sonality
Blum—Television p80,por.
CR '59 p48,por.

(Continued)

Ball, Lucille—*Continued*

CR '63 p33-34,por.
Cur. Biog. '52 p34-37,por.
Time May 26,1952 p62,por.
TV—Person (1) p62-63,por.

Ball, Mary. See Washington, Mary Ball

Ball, Ruth Norton (fl. 1920's)
Amer. sculptor
National—Contemp. p20

Ballard, Emily (fl. 1830's)
Amer. sea heroine
Snow—Women p86-101

Ballard, Kay (n.d.)
Amer. singer
CR '63 p34,por.
TV—Person (2) p88-89,por.

Ballard, Mary (fl. 1755)
Amer. colonial hotel hostess
Dexter—Colonial p12-13

Ballaseyus, Virginia (1893-   )
Amer. composer, author
ASCAP p20

Balle, Maria (d.c. 1940)
Ger. printer, type designer
Club—Printing p17

Ballinger, Violet Margaret L. Hodgson (gr. 1917)
Brit. politician
Brittain—Women p144-251

Ballou, Addie L. (fl. 1860's)
Amer. Civil war nurse, author, artist, lawyer
Logan—Part p362

Ballou, Eliza (fl. 1800's)
Amer., mother of James Garfield
Bartlett—Mothers p86-90

Ballou, Ella Maria (b. 1852)
Amer. court reporter
Logan—Part p899

Balsan, Consuelo Vanderbilt (1877-   )
Amer. philanthropist, hostess
CR '59 p48-49,por.
CR '63 p34,por.
Eliot—Heiresses p177-178,188-194
Pearson—Pilgrim p85-95,por.
Tebbel—Inher. p117,123-125

Baltimore, Annie E. (1836-1922)
Amer. musician
Brown—Home p127

Bampton, Rose Elizabeth (1909-   )
Amer. singer
CR '59 p49,por.
Cur. Biog. '40 p44-46,por.
Ewen—Ency. p32
Ewen—Living p29-30,por.
McCoy—Portraits p6,por.
Peltz—Spot p19,por.
Women—Achieve. p61,por.

Bampton, Ruth (1902-   )
Amer. composer, choral director
McCoy—Portraits p6,por.

Bancroft, Anne (1931-   )
It.-Amer. singer, actress
CR '59 p49,por.
CR '63 p34-35,por.
Cur. Biog. '60 p13-15,por.
Funke—Actors p437-469,por.,end-paper
Time Dec.21,1959 p46,por.(Cover)

Bancroft, Hester (1889-   )
Amer. sculptor
National—Contemp. p22

Bancroft, Jane M. (fl. 1880's)
Amer. club leader
Irwin—Angels p223,225-226

Bancroft, Marie Effie Wilton, Lady (1839-1921)
Eng. actress
Hammerton p180,por.
MacQueen—Pope p345-350,por.

Bandaranaike, Sirimavo (1916-   )
Ceylon prime minister
Cur. Biog. '61 p23-25,por.

Banfield, Mary (fl. 1850's)
Amer. pioneer
Whitton—These p250-254,256

Bang, Maia (1877-1940)
Nor. violinist, teacher, author
McCoy—Portraits p7,por.

Bang, Nina Henriette Wendeline (1866-1928)
Dan. politician
Hammerton p181

Banister, Zilpah P. Grant.
See Grant, Zilpah P.

Bankes, Mary Hawtrey, Lady (d. 1661)
Eng. heroine
Hammerton p182

Bankhead, Tallulah Brockman (1902/03-1968)
Amer. actress
Blum—Great p119,por.
CR '59 p49-50,por.

(Continued)

Bankhead, Tallulah—*Continued*

    CR '63 p35,por.
    Cur. Biog. '41 p36-39,por.
    Cur. Biog. '53 p42-44,por.
    Hammerton p182,por.
    Time Nov.22,1948, por.,cover
    Women—Achieve. p71,por.

Banks, Elizabeth L. (1870-1938)
    Amer. author, journalist
    Hammerton p182
    Ross—Ladies p17-18

Banks, Isabella Varley (1821-1897)
    Eng. poet, novelist
    Dorland—Sum p47,197
    Hammerton p182

Banks, Margaret (fl. 1910's)
    Amer. singer
    Lahee—Grand p368

Banks, Nancy Huston (b. 1850)
    Amer. novelist
    Maurice—Makers p10

Banks, Sarah A. Gertrude (fl. 1870's)
    Amer. physician
    Mead—Medical p48-49

Banky, Vilma (fl. 1920's-1930's)
    Hung.-Amer. actress
    Schickel—Stars p74,76-77,por.

Bannerman, Helen (d. 1946)
    Scot. illustrator, author
    Mahony—Illus. p272,274

Bannerman, Margaret (b. 1896)
    Brit. actress
    Hammerton p183,por.

Banning, Margaret Culkin (1891-   )
    Amer. novelist
    CR '63 p35,por.
    Cur. Biog. '40 p47-48,por.
    Overton—Women p27-30
    Warfel—Amer. p21-22,por.

Bannister, Constance (1919-   )
    Amer. photographer
    Cur. Biog. '55 p36-37,por.

Bannon, Laura (d. 1963)
    Amer. illustrator, author
    Mahony—Illus. p274

Banti, Brigitta Giorgi (1756-1806)
    It. singer
    Pleasants—Great p106-108,por.

Bañuelos, Antonia (fl. 1870's-1880's)
    Sp. painter
    Waters—Women p25

Baptista Varani (1458-1527)
    It. abbess, saint
    Englebert—Lives p210

Bara, Theda (1890-1955)
    Amer. actress
    Rogers—Women p103,por.
    Schickel—Stars p31,por.
    Stuart—Immort. p36-37,por.
    Wagenknecht—Movies p179-181

Baraloo, Lemma (fl. 1870's)
    Amer. lawyer
    Irwin—Angels p173

Baranamtarra (c2500 B.C.)
    Mesop. philanthropist, wife of
      priest-king
    Schmidt—400 p121,por.

Barbara, Duchess of Cleveland (1640-1709)
    Eng., friend of Charles Stuart
    Abbot—Notable p217-221,por.

Barbara (fl. 3d cent.)
    Nicomedian saint
    *Beebe—Saints p23-26
    Englebert—Lives p461-462
    Hammerton p184,por.
    Muir—Women p54-55
    Sharkey—Pop. p35
    Stiles—Postal p230
    Wescott—Calend. p191-192
    *Windham—Sixty p70-76

Barbauld, Anna Letitia (Laetitia)
    Eng. author, educator
    Adelman—Famous p99-100
    Dorland—Sum p35,111,180
    Hammerton p184
    MacVeagh—Champlin p51
    Stenton—English p299,317,327

Barber, Ann (fl. 1800's)
    Amer. publisher
    Dexter—Career p109

Barber, Edith Michael (1892-1963)
    Amer. home economist, author
    Taves—Success p275-292,por.
    Women—Achieve. p131,por.

Barber, Elsie Marion Oakes (1914-   )
    Amer. author
    Warfel—Amer. p22,por.

Barber, Jerusha (1789-1860)
    Amer. religious worker
    Blunt—Great p294-319

Barber, Mary Isabel (c. 1887-1963)
    Amer. dietician
    Cur. Biog. '41 p39-40,por.
    Cur. Biog. '63 p17

Barber, Mrs. Thomas W. (fl. 1850's)
Amer. pioneer
Fowler—Woman p247-260

Barbieri, Fedora (1919/20-   )
It. singer
CR '59 p51,por.
Cur. Biog. '57 p35-37,por.
Ewen—Ency. p35

Barbour, Ella (fl. 1940's)
Amer. home economist, restaurant
owner
Taves—Success. p299-320,por.

Barbour, Florence Newell (1866-1946)
Amer. pianist, composer
McCoy—Portraits p7,por.

Barbour, Joyce (1901-   )
Eng. actress
Hammerton p185

Barbour, Peggy Lee. See Lee, Peggy

Barclay, Florence Louisa Charlesworth
(1862-1921)
Brit. novelist
Hammerton p186

Bard, Mary Ten Eyck (1904-   )
Amer. author
Cur. Biog. '56 p29-30,por.

Bardot, Brigitte (1934-   )
Fr. actress
CR '59 p51-52,por.
Cur. Biog. '60 p17-19,por.
Wagenknecht—Movies p241-243

Barger, Myrtle King (fl. 1910's-1930's)
Amer. missionary
They—Went p48-50

Bariatinski, Lydia Yavorska, Princess (1874-
1921)
Russ. actress
Hammerton p187,por.

Bari-Dussot, Comtesse ("Mlle. Petite")
(fl. 1914-1918)
Fr. philanthropist, nurse
Dorland—Sum p126

Barine, Arvède. See Arvède Barine

Barkalow, Helena (d. 1870)
Amer. lawyer
Hanaford—Dau. p667

Barker, Ama (fl. 1922)
Amer. journalist
Ross—Ladies p291-292

Barker, Carol (1938-   )
Eng. illustrator
Ryder—Artists p47

Barker, E. Florence (d. 1897)
Amer. officer, Women's Relief Corps
Logan—Part p347

Barker, E. Frye (fl. 1910's-1930's)
Amer. advertising writer, dramatic
critic
Women—Achieve. p151,por.

Barker, Eliza Harris Lawton (fl. 1870's)
Amer. club leader
Logan—Part p409

Barker, Ellen Blackmar (Ellen Blackmar
Maxwell, pseud.) (fl. 1880's)
Amer. author
Logan—Part p853

Barker, Helen Huntington.
See Granville-Barker, Helen Gates

Barker, Jane (fl. 1715)
Eng. novelist
MacCarthy—Women p251-252

Barker, Sarah (fl. 1800's)
Amer. pioneer steamboat passenger
*Carmer—Young p99-105

Barker, Mrs. Stephen (fl. 1860's)
Amer. Civil war humanitarian,
nurse
Brockett—Woman's p200-211
Dannett—Noble p375-376
Logan—Part p311
Moore—Women p245-253

Barker, Tommie Dora (1888-   )
Amer. librarian, author, educator
Bul. of Bibl. Sept.-Dec.1940, p41-42,por.

Barker, Widow (fl. 1830's)
Amer. actress, friend of Sam Hou-
ston
Turner—Sam p54-56

Barlow, Arabella Griffith (fl. 1860's)
Amer. Civil war nurse
Brockett—Woman's p225-233
Logan—Part p311
Young—Women p276-278,327

Barlow, Rebecca Sanford (fl. 1770's)
Amer. Rev. war patriot
Ellet—Women (2) p297-301
Logan—Part p173-174

Barnard, Anne, Lady (1750-1825)
Scot. poet
Dorland—Sum p26,181
Graham—Group p257-278,por.
Hammerton p189

Barnard, Anne Hawkins (fl. 1930's)
Amer. club leader
Women—Achieve. p193

Barnard, Charlotte Allington ("Claribel")
       (1830-1869)
       Eng. ballad writer
       Dorland—Sum p51,181-182
       Howard—Our p646

Barnard, Elinor M. (c. 1872-1942)
       Amer. artist
       Cur. Biog. '42 p55

Barnard, Hannah (fl. 1798)
       Amer. clergyman
       Dexter—Career p57

Barnard, Kate (b. 1885)
       Amer. philanthropist, social
          reformer
       Adelman—Famous p322
       Bennett—Amer. p91-113,por.

Barnard, Margaret Witter (fl. 1930's)
       Amer. physician
       Women—Achieve. p150,por.

Barnard, Sophye (fl. 1910's)
       Amer. actress
       Caffin-Vaud. p80-81,por.

Barnard, Tissayac (b. 1878)
       Amer. pioneer, mountain climber
       Sargent—Pioneers p48,por.

Barnato, Diana (fl. 1944)
       Amer. aviatrix
       *May—Women p144

Barnell, Jane ("Lady Olga"), (b. 1871)
       Amer. circus personality
       New Yorker Aug.3,1940 p20

Barnes, Carman Neal (1912-   )
       Amer. novelist
       Warfel—Amer. p22-23
       Women—Achieve. p86,por.

Barnes, Florence Lowe ("Pancho") (1909-)
       Amer. aviatrix, resort owner
       Dwiggins—They p50,80,113,133-134,
          149
       Earhart—Fun p150

Barnes, Frances Julia (fl. 1890's)
       Amer. social reformer
       Farmer—What p354,por.
       Logan—Part p670-671

Barnes, Gertrude (fl. 1910's)
       Amer. actress
       Caffin—Vaud. p74-75,por.

Barnes, Hattie Delaro (fl. 1880's-1910's)
       Amer. singer, actress
       Marks—Glamour p277

Barnes, Jane (fl. 1810's)
       Amer. W. pioneer
       Brown—Gentle p13-14,75-80

Barnes, Mrs. John (b. 1816)
       Amer. actress
       Coad-Amer. p73,por.

Barnes, Margaret Ayer (b. 1886)
       Amer. author
       Lawrence—School p222-226
       Mantle—Contemp. p266-267
       *Millett—Amer. p234-235

Barnes, Margaret Campbell (1891-   )
       Amer. author
       Cur. Biog. '54 p45-46,por.

Barnett, Alice (b. 1888)
       Amer. composer, song writer
       ASCAP p23
       Howard—Our p563

Barnett, Clara Kathleen (Clara Doria, pseud.)
       (fl. 1850's-1920's)
       Eng.-Amer. singer, composer
       Elson—Woman's p203

Barnett, Claribel Ruth (1872-1951)
       Amer. librarian
       Bul. of Bibl. May-Aug. '44 p73-74,por.

Barnett, Henrietta (fl. 1950's)
       Eng. WRAF air commandant
       *May—Women p189

Barnett, Ida B. Wells (1862-1931)
       Amer. Civil Rights worker
       Robinson—Hist. p48,por.

Barnett, Mary. See Jack, Mary Barnett

Barney, Maginel Wright (c. 1887-   )
       Amer. illustrator
       Mahony—Illus. p274

Barney, Susan Hammond (fl. 1850's)
       Amer. social reformer
       Logan—Part p669-670

Barnhart, Nancy (1889-   )
       Amer. illustrator
       Mahony—Illus. p274

Barnum, Charlotte P. Acer (b. 1865)
       Amer. club leader
       Logan—Part p409-410

Barnum, Lucy Wolcott (1762-1799)
       Amer. patriot
       Green—Pioneer (3) p524-525

Baroni-Cavalcabo, Julie von (fl. 19th cent.)
       Pol. pianist, composer
       Elson—Woman's p228-229

Baronova, Irina (1919-   )
       Russ. ballet dancer
       Davidson—Ballet p22-25

(Continued)

Baronova, Irina—*Continued*

Hammerton p193
Haskel—Vignet. p34-35,por.
*Terry—Star p133-137,por.

Barr, Amelia Edith Huddleston (1831-1919)
Amer. novelist
Adelman—Famous p255-256
Hammerton p193,por.
Harkins—Famous p125-139,por.
Harkins—Little p125-139,por.
Logan—Part p803-804

Barrantes Manuel de Aragon, Maria del
Carmen (fl. 1810's)
Sp. painter
Waters—Women p25-26

Barratt, Louise Bascom (fl. 1930's)
Amer. editor, author
Women—Achieve. p93,por.

Barrault, Madeleine Renaud.
See **Renaud, Madeleine**

Barrett, Ann Henry (m. 1825)
Amer. actress
Coad—Amer. p80

Barrett, Janie Porter (b. 1865)
Amer. educator
Daniel—Women p53-78,por.
Ovington—Por. p181-193
Sickels—Twelve p190-208,254-255

Barrett, Kate Waller (1859-1929)
Amer. philanthropist, social worker,
lecturer
Logan—Part p532

Barrett, Meliscent (Milly) (fl. 1770's)
Amer. Rev. heroine
Green—Pioneer (2) p288-290

Barrie, Margaret Ogilvy (d. 1895)
Scot., mother of Sir James Barrie
*Chandler—Famous p269-285
Corkran—Romance p20-21
Hammerton p195,por.
Wallace—Mothers p88-94

Barrie, Mary. See **Cannan, Mary Ansell Barrie**

Barrie, Wendy (1913-   )
Amer. actress
CR '59 p53,por.

Barrientos, Maria (1884-1946)
Sp. singer
Ewen—Ency. p35-36

Barrington, Emily Dunning (1876-1961)
Amer. surgeon, gynecologist
Cur. Biog. '40 p56,por.

Cur. Biog. '61 p31
Fabricant—Why p101-103
Fleming—Doctors p39-54
Women—Achieve. p85,por.

Barrington, E. See **Beck, Lily Adams**

Barrington, Emilie Isabel (1842-1933)
Eng. author
Hammerton p196,por.

Barrios, Marie Jeanne (fl. 1920's)
Amer. air hostess
*May—Women p233

Barron, Marjorie Wilson (m. 1952)
Amer. missionary
They—Went p142

Barrow, Frances Elizabeth ("Aunt Fanny")
(1822-1894)
Amer. author
Dorland—Sum p40,189

Barrows, Ellen B. (fl. 1860's)
Amer. Civil war patriot
Brockett—Woman's p737

Barrows, Isabel C. (1845-1913)
Amer. pioneer stenographic reporter
Stern—We p178-204,por.

Barrows, Katherine Isabel (1845-1913)
Amer. editor, penologist
Adelman—Famous p246

Barry, Ann Street (1734-1801)
Eng. actress
Dorland—Sum p15-167

Barry, Elizabeth (c1658-1713)
Eng. actress
Collins—Great p55-81
Dorland—Sum p31
Eaton—Actor's p189-190,por.
Hammerton p197,por.
MacQueen—Pope p92-101
Ormsbee—Back p61-62
Wilson—All p110-117

Barry, James (or Miranda) (1795-1865)
Scot. physician
Lovejoy—Women p275-282,por.

Barry, Joan (1901-   )
Eng. actress
Hammerton p197

Barry, Katie (fl. 1910's)
Eng. actress
Caffin—Vaud. p167

Barry, Susan E. Hill (fl. 1860's)
Amer. Civil war nurse
Logan—Part p374

Barrymore, Diana (1921-   )
Amer. actress
CR '59 p54,por.

Barrymore, Elaine Barrie (fl. 1930's-1940's)
wife of John Barrymore
Lamparski—What. p48-49,por.

Barrymore, Ethel (1879-1959)
Amer. actress
Adelman—Famous p318-319
Blum—Great p56,por.
Caffin—Vaud. p122,por.
Coad—Amer. p300,por.
Cur. Biog. '41 p45-46,por.
Cur. Biog. '59 p25
*Ferris—Girls p49-59
Hammerton p198,por.
Izard—Heroines p350-353
*Kobbé—Homes p43-65,por.
Logan—Part p773-774
*MacVeagh—Champlin p54
Marinacci—Lead. p215-240,por.
Marks—Glamour p277
Moses—Famous p191-194,por.
Rogers—Women p44,por.
Stuart—Immort. p45-47,por.
Time Nov.10,1924, p15,por,cover
*Wagner—Famous p63-73,por.

Barrymore, Georgiana Drew (1856-1893)
Amer. actress
Coad—Amer. p249,por.
Moses—Famous p187,por.

Barstow, Norah. See Lee, Norah

Barstow, Vera (1893-   )
Amer. violinist
McCoy—Portraits p7,por.

Bartelme, Mary Margaret (fl. 1866-1954)
Amer. judge
Schmidt—400 p544,por.

Bartet, Jeanne Julia Regnault (1854-1941)
Fr. actress
Hammerton p198

Bartholomew, Ann S. Mounsey (1811-1891)
Eng. organist, pianist
McCoy—Portraits p8,por.

Bartholomew, Elizabeth (1749-1833)
Amer. pioneer
Logan—Part p54-55

Bartlett, Alice Elinor (Birch Arnold, pseud.)
(1848-1920)
Amer. journalist, poet
Logan—Part p844

Bartlett, Dorothy D. (fl. 1920's)
Amer. journalist
Ross—Ladies p515-517

Bartlett, Ella Elizabeth (fl. 1870's)
Amer. clergyman
Hanaford—Dau. p451

Bartlett, Ethel (1901-   )
Eng. pianist
Ewen—Living p37-38,por.

Bartlett, Floy Little (m. 1908)
Amer. composer
Elson—Woman's p262

Bartlett, Hanna Gray (d. 1807)
Amer. pioneer
Green—Pioneer (3) p206-207

Bartlett, Jennie E. (fl. 1880's)
Amer. artist
Hanaford—Dau. p306

Bartlett, Madeleine A. (fl. 1920's)
Amer. sculptor
National—Contemp. p22

Bartlett, Mary (d. 1789)
Amer. patriot
Green—Pioneer (3) p10-14

Bartley, Nalbro (b. 1888)
Amer. novelist
Overton—Women p41

Bartok, Eva (1929-   )
Hung. actress
CR '59 p54,por.

Barton, Betsey (1918-1962)
Amer. author
CR '59 p54,por.
*Eby—Marked p95,105
Lotz—Unused p13-20

Barton, Clara Harlowe (1821-1912)
Amer. nurse
Abbott—Notable p924-928
*Adams—Heroines p147-177,por.
Adelman—Famous p197-198
America's 12 p16-18,por.
Arsenius—Dict. p24,por.
Beard—Amer. p212-226
*Bolton—Lives p61-78,por.
Bonte—Amer. p163,por.
Brockett—Woman's p111-132,por.
Bruce—Woman p208-209,213
*Carmer—Caval. p311-313,por.
*Curtin—Gallery p5,por.
D'Humy—Women p227-277
*Dodge—Story p59-74
Dolan—Goodnow's p234,245,por.
*Dolin—World, p126-131,por.
Dorland—Sum p20,74,82-83,125
Douglas—Remember p139-141,147
Ency. Brit.—Amer. p3,por.
*Fowler—Great p70-75,por.
*Hagedorn—Book p199-212

(Continued)

Barton, Clara Harlowe—*Continued*

Hammerton p201
Hanaford—Dau. p184,203-204
*Heath—Women (4) p15,por.
*Horowitz—Treas. p66-70
*Humphrey—Women p189-206
Irwin—Angels p106,148-150
Jensen—Revolt p43,por.
Ladies'—Amer. 12 p16-18,por.
*Lamm—Biog. p102-103
Leetch—Reveille p61,218,325,431
Logan—Part p316-325
*McCallum—Women p127-138
*McKown—Heroic p101-120,por.
*MacVeagh—Champlin p55
*Moore—When p37-44
Morris—400, p30-31
Muir—Women p172-173
*Nida—Pilots p320-326
*Nisenson—Minute p20,por.
*Nisenson—More Minute p18,por.
*Parkman—Heroines p61-85,por.
Pennock—Makers p21,por.
Phila.—Women unp,por.
Popular Record p22,por.
Prochnow—Great p178-185
Schmidt—400 p396-397,por.
Sewell—Brief p144-145
*Stevens—Human. p77-79,por.
*Stevens—Women p75-80,por.
Stiles—Postal p24
*Strong—Of p192-196
*Tappan—Heroes p140-146
Young—Women (see index), por.

Barton, Elizabeth (The "Holy Maid of
    Kent") (c. 1506-1534)
    Eng. visionary
Fifty Famous p204-206
Hammerton p201

Barton, Frances.
    See Abington, Frances (Fanny) Barton

Barton, Kate (fl. 1870's)
    Amer. inventor
Hanaford—Dau. p652

Bary, Gertrude (fl. 1930's)
    Ger.-Amer. pianist
Women—Achieve. p177,por.

Barzillai's daughter (Biblical)
Deen—All p314

Bascom, Florence (fl. 1880's)
    Amer. geologist
Adelman—Famous p304

Bascom, Ruth Henshaw (c. 1772-1841)
    Amer. artist
Lipman—Primitive p31-38,por.
Whitton—These p192,205

Baseden, Yvonne (c. 1922-   )
    Eng. spy
Hoehling—Women p138-139

Bashemath (Biblical)
Deen—All p255

Bashkirtsev (Bashkirtseff) Marie (1860-1884)
    Russ. painter, diarist
Adelman—Famous p225-226
Dunaway—Treas. p16-20
Hammerton p202,por.
Moore—Disting. p11-28
Schmidt—400 p350,por.
Waters—Women p26-33

Basilissa (d. 68)
    Rom. saint
Wescott—Calen. p54

Basmath (Biblical)
Deen—All p255

Bass, Mary (fl. 1770's)
    Amer. colonial midwife
Dexter—Colonial p67-68

Bassani, Signora (fl. 19th cent.)
    It. inventor, lacemaker
Mozans—Woman p337

Bassett, Elizabeth.
    See Harrison, Elizabeth Bassett

Bassett, Karolyn Wells (1892-1931)
    Amer. composer, pianist
ASCP p26

Bassett, Sara Ware (1872-   )
    Amer. author
Cur. Biog. '56 p33-34,por.
Warfel—Amer. p25-26,por.

Bassi, Laura Maria Catarina (1711-1778)
    It. physicist, philosopher, scholar
Mozans—Woman p78-79,202-210

Bastié, Maryse (1898-1952)
    Fr. aviatrix
*Lauwick—Heroines p104-121,por.
*May—Women p127-128,por.
Stiles—Postal p25

Batchelder, (Mary) Evelyn.
    See Longman, (Mary) Evelyn Beatrice

Batcheller, Mrs. Tryophosa Bates (b. 1878)
    Amer. club leader, singer
Jensen—Revolt p91,por.

Batchelor, Emma (fl. 20th cent.)
    Amer. recluse
Erskine—Out p255-266

Batchelor, Rosa (fl. 20th cent.)
    Amer. recluse
Erskine—Out p255-266

Batchelor, Rosanna (d. 1942)
Amer. recluse
Erskine—Out p255-266

Bateman, Georgia (fl. 1920's-1950's)
Amer. missionary
They—Went p83-84

Bateman, Isabel Mary (1855-1934)
Eng. actress
Hammerton p1446

Bateman, Kate Josephine (1842/43-1917)
Amer. actress
Adelman—Famous p252-253
Coad—Amer. p226,por.
Hammerton p205

Bateman, Martha (fl. 1919-1950's)
Amer. missionary
They—Went p55-56

Bates, Blanche (1873-1941)
Amer. actress, singer
Blum—Great p34,por.
Coad—Amer. p306,por.
Cur. Biog. '42 p57
Marks—Glamour p279
Strang—Actress p243-247,por.

Bates, Charlotte Fiske (Mme. Rogé, pseud.)
(1838-1916)
Amer. poet
Logan—Part p844

Bates, Mrs. D. B. (n.d.)
Amer. W. pioneer
Brown—Gentle p86-87,115

Bates, Daisy Hunt O'Dwyer (1861-1951)
Brit., ethnologist
Holmes—Seven p155-176

Bates, Daisy Lee Gatson (1919/22-   )
Amer. Civil Rights worker
Cherry—Portraits p180-187,por.
Robinson—Hist. p162-163,por.

Bates, Katharine Lee (1859-1929)
Amer. poet, educator
Cook—Our p143-145
Smith—Women's p4

Bates, Lila Curtis (fl. 1930's)
Amer. pianist, teacher, poet
Women—Achieve. p143,por.

Bates, Mary E. (1863-1954)
Amer. surgeon
Lovejoy—Women p93

Bates, Mary E. (d. 1956)
Amer. librarian, editor
Bul. of Bibl. Jan.-Apr.1945 p121-122,
por.

Bates, Sylvia Chatfield (n.d.)
Amer. author
Warfel—Amer. p27,por.

Bateson, Margaret. See Mead, Margaret

Bateson, Mary (1865-1906)
Eng. historian
Hammerton p205

Bathemath (Biblical)
Deen—All p254-255

Bathiat, Leonie. See Arletty

Bathilda (Bathilde) (d. c. 678)
Fr. queen-saint
Blunt—Great p82-84
Deen—Great p323-324
Dolan—Goodnow's p91
Englebert—Lives p41

Bathory, Elizabeth (d. 1614)
Hung. princess, criminal
Hammerton p205
Muir—Women p97-98

Bathsheba (1040-1015 B.C.)
Israeli queen, mother of Solomon,
wife of King David
Adelman—Famous p18
Buchanan—Women p55-57
Culver—Women p32-33
Deen—All p112-117
Hammerton p205
Hughes—Mothers p115-127
Lewis—Portraits p50-54,121-122
Lofts—Women p111-121
MacVeagh—Champlin p56
Marble—Women p68-70
Mead—250 p97
Ockenga—Women p111-123
Schmidt—400 p267,por.

Batson, Flora. See Bergen, Flora Batson

Battelle, Phyllis (n. d.)
Amer. journalist
CR '63 p40,por.

Batten, Jean (1910-   )
New Z. aviatrix
*Fraser—Heroes p771-775
Hammerton p1446
Lauwick—Heroines p111-112,186-201,
por.
*May—Women p117-123-124

Battia, Villana (fl. 14th cent.)
It. saint
Wescott—Calen. p30

Battistella, Sophia L. C. (fl. 1930's)
Pol.-Amer. lawyer
Women—Achieve. p96,por.

Battle, Laura Elizabeth Lee (b. 1855)
Amer. religious worker
Logan—Part p617

Bauck, Jeanne Maria Charlotte (b. 1840)
Swed. painter
Waters—Women p33-34

Bauer, Florence Ann Marvyne (n.d.)
Amer. author
Warfel—Amer. p27-28,por.

Bauer, Karoline Philippine A. (1807-1878)
Ger. actress
Hammerton p207

Bauer, Marion Eugenie (1887-1955)
Amer. composer, editor, critic
Ewen—American p20-22,por.
Goss—Modern p129-140,por.
Howard—Our P435-436
McCoy—Portraits p8,por.
Reis—Composers p19-20
Saleski—Jewish p7-8,por.
Women—Achieve. p68,por.

Baum, Mrs. A. (d. 1910)
Ger.-Amer. Civil war patriot
Logan—Part p491

Baum, Vicki (1888-1960)
Aust.-Amer. novelist
CR '59 p57,por.
Hammerton p207,por.
Warfel p28-29,por.

Baumann, Anny (fl. 1930's)
Ger.-Amer. physician
Women—Achieve. p193

Baumer, Marie (1906-   )
Amer. author
Cur. Biog. '58 p34-35,por.

Baumgartner, Leona (1902-   )
Amer. physician, govt. official
Cur. Biog. '50 p22-24,por.
*Fleming—Doctors p130-143
Lovejoy—Women p381-382,por.
Women—Achieve. p130,por.

Baupré, Mlle. (fl. 1600's)
Fr. actress
Gilder—Enter p94-96

Baur, Bertha (d. 1940)
Amer. music educator
Cur. Biog. '40 p63
McCoy—Portraits p8,por.

Baur, Clara (d. 1912)
Ger. music educator
McCoy—Portraits p8,por.

Bausher, Mildred. See Jordan, Mildred

Bauviere, Isabeau de (fl. 1368-1400's)
Fr. queen
Koven—Women p180-184
Watson—Some p23-43

Baxter, Alice (fl. 1900's)
Amer. club leader
Logan—Part p501-502

Baxter, Anne (1923-   )
Amer. actress
CR '59 p57,por.
CR '63 p40-41,por.

Baxter, Annie White (m. 1888)
Amer. politician, clerk of court
Logan—Part p898-899

Baxter, Lucy E. Barnes (1835/37-1902)
Eng. art writer
Dorland—Sum p28,174

Baxter, Margaret Charlton (1636-1681)
Eng., wife of Richard Baxter
Balch—Modern p322-327

Baxter, Martha Wheeler (b. 1869)
Amer. sculptor, painter
Michigan—Biog. p36

Baxter, Susan Phinney (fl. 1820's)
Amer. tailor
Dexter—Career p217-218

Bay, Josephine Holt Perfect (1900-   )
Amer. financier, philanthropist
CR '59 p58,por.
Cur. Biog. '57 p41-43,por.

Bayes, Nora (1880-1928)
Amer. actress
Blum—Great p41,por.
Caffin—Vaud. p27-29,por.

Baylis, Lilian Mary (1874-1937)
Eng. composer, philanthropist,
theatre manager, heroine
De Morny—Best p156-162
*Horowitz-Treas. p179-181

Bayliss, Lillian (b. 1875)
Amer. painter
Michigan—Biog. p36

Bayliss, Marguerite Farleigh (1895-   )
Amer. author, scientist
Warfel—Amer. p29-31,por.

Bayly, Ada Ellen (Edna Lyall, pseud.)
Eng. novelist, feminist, politician
Black—Notable p133-144,por.
Dorland—Sum p36
Hammerton p932

Bayley, Gertrude Arthur (fl. 1860's)
   Amer. W. pioneer, mountain
     climber
Sargent—Pioneer p48

Bayne, Nannette Gude (fl. 1930's)
   Amer. linguist, social leader
Women—Achieve p47,por.

Bazan, Emilia Pardo.
   See Pardo Bazan, Emilia

Bazanova, Naylya Urazoulovna (1911-   )
   Russ. physiologist, academician
U.S.—Biog. Soviet p46-47

Bazelli, Madame. See Tetrazzini, Luisa

Beach, Amy Marcy Cheney (1867-1944)
   Amer. composer, pianist
Adelman—Famous p307-308
ASCAP p28
Cur. Biog. '45 p39-40
Dorland—Sum p161
Elson—Woman's p195-201,237,242-243,
   por.
Howard—Our p319-323,por.
McCoy—Portraits p9,por.
*Moore—When p45-51
Reis—Composers p21

Beach, Cora M. (b. 1878)
   Amer. author
Bindheim—Women p213,por.

Beaconsfield, Mary Anne Evans Disraeli,
   Viscountess (1792-1872)
   Eng., wife of Benjamin Disraeli
Cockran—Romance p93-96,por.
Hammerton p211,por.

Beale, Betty (c. 1912-   )
   Amer. journalist
CR '63 p41-42,por.

Beale, Dorothea (1831-1906)
   Eng. educator
Adelman—Famous p236
Brittain—Women (see index), por.
Hammerton p212,por.

Beale, Mary (1632-1697)
   Eng. painter
Waters—Women p34-35

Beales, Hannah (fl. 1760's)
   Amer. colonial bus. woman
Dexter—Colonial p54

Beales, Iris (n.d.)
   Amer. pioneer airline traffic man-
     ager
*Peckham—Women p95

Beam, Lura (1887-   )
   Amer. educator, author
Women—Achieve. p77,por.

Bean, Theodora (d. 1926)
   Amer. journalist
Ross—Ladies p257-259

Beard, Mary (1876-1946)
   Amer. Red Cross nurse
Dolan—Goodnow's p317,por.
Pennock—Makers p66,por.

Beard, Mary Ritter (1876-1958)
   Amer. author, historian
Cur. Biog. '41 p51-54,por.
Cur. Biog. '59 p32

Beard, Miriam (fl. 1920's)
   Amer. humor writer, feminist
Bruère—Laugh p60-61

Bearden, Bessye J. (c. 1891-1943)
   Amer. club leader
Cur. Biog. '43 p33

Beaton, Isabella (1870-   )
   Amer. pianist, composer
McCoy—Portraits p9,por.

Beaton, Maude Hill (fl. 1940's)
   Can. author
Thomas—Canad. p9

Beatrice (A.D. 303)
   Gr. saint
*Windham—Sixty p77-85

Beatrice Kristina (1909-   )
   Sp. princess
Arsenius—Dict. p25,por.
Phila.-Women unp.,por.
Stiles—Postal p26

Beatrice Marie Victoria Feodora (1857-1944)
   Eng. princess
Benson—Queen (see index)
Cur. Biog. '44 p37
Hammerton p213,por.

Beatrice Portinari (1266-1290)
   It., friend of Dante
Adelman—Famous p39-40
Corkran—Romance p349-360
Davenport—Great p107-113
*MacVeagh—Chaplin p57-58,por.

Beatrix (1938-   )
   Nether. princess
Phelps—Men (2) '59 p25-26
Stiles—Postal p26

Beatrix da Silva (1424-1490)
   Sp. saint
Englebert—Lives p315

Beatrix D'Este (d. 1262/70)
   Eng. foundress, nun, saint
Englebert—Lives p28
Wescott—Calen. p67-68

Beattie, Jessie Louise (1896-   )
    Can. author
    Thomas—Canad. p9-10

Beatty, Bessie (1886-1947)
    Amer. radio commentator, journalist, author
    Cur. Biog. '44 p37-40,por.
    Cur. Biog. '47 p39
    Ross—Ladies p580-583
    *Stoddard—Top p200-211
    Women—Achieve, p120,por.

Beauchamp, Frances E. (fl. 1880's)
    Amer. social reformer, lecturer
    Logan—Part p662-663

Beauchamp, Sarah. See Churchill, Sarah

Beauchateau, Mlle. (fl 1600's)
    Fr. actress
    Gilder—Enter p95

Beaufort, Jane (c. 1396-1445)
    Eng. hostess
    *Humphrey—Janes p149-168

**Beaufort, Margaret, Countess of Richmond
    and Derby** (1441/43-1509)
    Hammerton p215,1146,por.
    Schmidt—400 p131-132,por.
    Sorley—King's p171-242
    Stenton—English p57,122

Beauglie, Madame de (fl. 18th cent.)
    Fr. soldier
    Kavanagh—Woman (2) p198

Beauharnais, Hortense Eugenie de (1783-1837)
    Nether. queen
    *MacVeagh—Champlin p59

Beauharnais, Josephine de.
    See Josephine de Beauharnais

Beauharnais, Marie Anne Francoise Mouchard, Countess de (1738-1813)
    Fr.salonist,poet
    Kavanagh—Woman (2) p23-24

Beauharnais, Stephanie de (b. 1789)
    Fr. duchess of Baden, Ger.
    Phila.—Women, unp,por.

Beaumesnil, Henriette Adelaide Villard (1748-1803)
    Fr. singer, composer
    Elson—Woman's p187

Beaupré, Enid (fl. 1930's)
    Welsh-Amer. advertising executive
    Women—Achieve. p179

Beaury-Saurel, Amélie, Madame (fl. 1880's-1900's)
    Fr. artist
    Waters—Women p35

Beausoleil, Martine, Baroness De (1602-1640)
    Fr. mineralogist
    Mozans—Woman p238-240

Beauvoir, Simone de (1908-   )
    Fr. author
    CR '59 p59,por.
    Peyre—French p275-307,450

Beaux, Cecilia (1863-1942)
    Amer. painter
    Adelman—Famous p299
    Bryant—Amer. p203-206
    Cur. Biog. '42 p62
    Hammerton p217
    Jackman—Amer. p225-228
    *Kirkland—Artists p58-68
    Logan—Part p750
    Love—Famous p31
    *MacVeagh—Champlin p59
    Michigan—Biog. p37-39
    *Moore—When p52-57
    Waters—Women p35-38

Becher, Eliza O'Neill, Lady
    See O'Neill, Eliza, Lady Blecher

Beck, Anne Landsbury (n.d.)
    Amer. music educator
    McCoy—Portraits p9,por.

Beck, Béatrix (1914-   )
    Fr. novelist
    Peyre—French p401,450

Beck, Carol H. (1859-1908)
    Amer. painter
    Waters—Women p38-39

Beck, Lily Adams (E. Barrington, Louis Moresby, pseuds.) (d. 1931)
    Eng. novelist
    Overton—Women p31-40
    Thomas—Canad. p10-11

Beck, Mildred Buchwalder (1914-   )
    Amer. assoc. director
    Cur. Biog. '50 p32-33

Beck, Mrs. (fl. 1860's)
    Amer. Civil war patriot
    Brockett—Woman's p157,159,485,713

Becker, Angela (n.d.)
    Amer. pianist, composer, music
    teacher, organist
    McCoy—Portraits p9,por.

Becker, Grace (fl. 1940's)
    Amer. violoncellist
    McCoy—Portraits p9,por.

Becker, Helen. See Tamiris, Helen

Becker, Lucy Greenbaum.
    See Freeman, Lucy Greenbaum

Becker, May Lamberton (1873-1958)
        Amer. author, critic, editor, journal-
            ist
    Cur. Biog. '41 p55-56,por.
    Cur. Biog. '58 p36
    *Ferris—Girls p181-196

Beckford, Lydia C. (1703-1804)
        Amer. nurse
    Dexter—Career p33-34

Beckham, Mrs. (fl. 1770's)
        Amer. Rev. war heroine
    Ellet—Women (1) p335-337

Beckington, Alice (b. 1868)
        Amer. painter
    Michigan—Biog. p39

Beckley, Zoë (fl. 1910's)
        Amer. journalist
    Ross—Ladies p97-105,por.,back cover

Bedell, Grace (fl. 1860's)
        Amer., friend of Lincoln
    *Carmer—Young p202-209

Bedell, Leila Gertrude (fl. 1860's)
        Amer. physician
    Lovejoy—Women p94

Bedells, Phyllis (1893-   )
        Eng. dancer
    Hammerton p220,por.

Bedford, Anne, Duchess of (1402-1430)
        Fr., daughter of John the Fearless
    Leary—Golden p13

Bedford, Duchess of (fl. 1920's)
        Eng. aviatrix
    *May—Women p102,por.

Bee, Molly (n.d.)
        Amer. TV singer
    TV—Person (3) p50-51,por.

Beebe, Carolyn Harding (d. 1951)
        Amer. pianist, Society foundress
    Women—Achieve. p59,por.

Beebe, Mrs. William. See Niles, Blair Rice

Beeby, Nell V. (1896-1957)
        Amer. nurse, editor
    Dolan—Goodnow's p303-304,por.

Beech, Olive Ann Mellor (1903-   )
        Amer. aviation executive, industri-
            alist
    Cur. Biog. '56 p41-43,por.

*May—Women p182-183,por.
    Parshalle—Kash. p53-54,por.
*Peckham—Women p58-59,por.

Beecher, Catherine Esther (1800-1878)
        Amer. educator, author, social
            reformer
    Adelman—Famous p129-130
    Bacon—Puritan p73-93,por.
    Brown—Gentle p226-227,285
    Dexter—Career p23-25
    Dorland—Sum p43-44,77,111-112
    Douglas—Remember p89-90
    Goodsell—Pioneers p113-226,por.
    Hanaford—Dau. p524
    Irwin—Angels p29,32-35
    Jensen—Revolt p44-45,por.
    Logan—Part p725
    Thorp—Female p11-55
    Whitton—These p108-111,123
    Woody—Hist (1) p319-328,354-355,
        375-378,por.

Beecher, Harriet.
    See Stowe, Harriet Elizabeth Beecher

Beecher, Mrs. Henry Ward (fl. 1800's)
        Amer., wife of Henry Ward Beecher
    Farmer—What p123-124,182-184,por.

Beecher, Isabella.
    See Hooker, Isabella Beecher

Beecher, Roxanna Foote (d.c. 1816)
        Amer., mother of Henry Ward
            Beecher, Harriet Beecher Stowe
    Davis—Mothers p13-24

Beechman, Marie A. (fl. 1930's)
        Amer. railroad worker
    Women—Achieve. p181,por.

Beek, Alice D. Engley (b. 1876-   )
        Amer. painter, author, lecturer
    Bindheim—Women p189,por.

Beekman, Cornelia (c. 1752-1847)
        Amer. social leader
    Ellet—Women (2) p221-236
    Green—Pioneer (2) p279-288,por.
    Hanaford—Dau. p142-143
    Logan—Part p190-194

Beernaerts, Euphrosine (fl. 1870's)
        Aust. painter
    Waters—Women p39

Beers, Ethel Lynn Eliot (1827-1879)
        Amer. poet, lyricist
    Dorland—Sum p35,181

Beeton, Isabella Mary Mayson (1836-1865)
        Eng. author
    *Borer—Women p113-132,por.

Began, Luise Parmentier (m. 1877)
Aust. painter
Waters—Women p39-40

Begga (or **Begha**) (fl. 7th cent.)
Belg., abbess, foundress, saint
Englebert—Lives p413
Phila.—Women unp,por.
Schmidt—400 p55,por.
Stiles—Postal p230

Begtrup, Bodil Andreasen (1903-   )
Dan. feminist, U.N. delegate
Cur. Biog. '46 p31-32,por.

Behn, Aphra (Afra or Aphara) (1640-1689)
Eng. novelist, pioneer playwright
Gilder—Enter p173-201,por.
Hammerton p225,por.
MacCarthy—Women p25-27,148-188,
274-278
MacQueen—Pope p136-142,por.
Stenton—English p200-202,214,232,297
Untermeyer—Lives p216-217

Behrend, Jeanne (1911-   )
Amer. pianist, composer
Ewen—Living p44,por.
McCoy—Portraits p9,por.
Reis—Composers p25-26

Behrman, Beatrice.
See Alexander, Madame Beatrice

Beilby, Elizabeth (fl. 1870's-1880's)
Eng. physician
Bell—Storm p115-116,125

Beinhorn, Elly (fl. 1930's)
Ger. aviatrix
*May—Women p105,por.

Béjart, Armande Grésinde Claire Elizabeth
(1642-1700)
Fr. actress, wife of Molière
Gilder—Enter p100-131,por.

Béjart, Madeleine (1618-1672)
Fr. actress
Gilder—Enter p100-131

Bekker, Elizabeth (Betje) (1738-1804)
Nether. author
Dorland—Sum p54,198
Schmidt—400 p301,por.

Belais, Diana (fl. 1900's)
Amer. social reformer, sociologist
Logan—Part p594

Belcher, Hilda (1881-1963)
Amer. painter
Michigan—Biog. p41

Belcher, Marjorie Celeste.
See Champion, Marge Celeste

Belden, Ruth. See Wyllys, Ruth Belden

Bel Geddes, Barbara.
See Geddes, Barbara Bel

Belgiojoso, Cristina (1808-1871)
It. princess, patriot
Hammerton p226

Belinda (A.D. 698)
Belg. saint
*Windham—Sixty p193-197

Bell, Ann (fl. 1930's)
Amer. author, beauty
Women—Achieve. p177,por.

Bell, Dame Florence Evelyn Eleanore (1851-
1930)
Brit. author
Hammerton p227

Bell, Gertrude Margaret Lowthian (1868-
1926)
Eng. traveler, archaeologist, govt.
official, author, scholar, naturalist
Brittain—Women p73,76-77,248
Hammerton p227-228
Keyes—Lives p132-144
*Kirkland—Good p19-24
Sitwell—Women p45-46

Bell, Helen Olcott Choate (1830-1918)
Amer., dau. of Rufus Choate
Amory—Proper p126-129

Bell, Lilian (Mrs. Arthur Hoyt Bogue)
(1867-1929)
Amer. author
Harkins—Famous p239-254
Harkins—Little p239-254,por.
Logan—Part p806

Bell, Mabel Gardner (Mrs. Alexander Gra-
ham Bell) (m. 1877)
Amer. aviation patron
Planck—Women p41-42

Bell, Margaret Elizabeth (1898-   )
Amer. author
Cur. Biog. '52 p43-44,por.

Bell, Marilyn (1937-   )
Can. swimmer
Cur. Biog. '56 p47-49,por.

Bell, Mary E. (fl. 1860's)
Amer. Civil war nurse
Logan—Part p364

Bell, Ruth Moench (fl. 1920's)
Amer. teacher
Bindheim—Women p172,por.

Bell, Vanessa (1879-1961)
Eng. painter
Hammerton p229

Bellamy, George Anne (c. 1731-1788)
Eng. actress
Bottrall—Pers. p137-138,216
Hammerton p229
MacQueen—Pope p203-213,por.
Melville—Stage 241-279,por.

Bellamy, Madge (fl. 1920's)
Amer. actress
Herman—How p127,por.

Belle, Mlle. Andrée (fl. 1900's)
Fr. painter
Waters—Women p40-41

Belle, Barbara (1922-   )
Amer. composer, author
ASCAP p29

La Belle Cordière.
See Labé, Louise Charlin Perrin

Bellenden, Mary (d. 1736)
Eng. maid of honor
Melville—Maids p199-205

Beller, Mary Linn (n.d.)
Amer. actress
TV—Person (1) p105-106,por.

Belleville-Oury, Anne Caroline de (1808-
1880)
Ger. pianist
Schonberg—Great p105

Bellido, Maria Parado de Andrea (d. 1882)
Peru. patriot
Arsenius—Dict. p26
Phila.—Women unp,por.
Stiles—Patriot p27

Bellincioni, Gemma (1864-1950)
It. singer
Ewen—Ency. p41

Belloc, Bessie Rayner Parkes (fl. 1850's)
Eng. feminist
Bell—Storm. p15-17

Belloc, Marie Adelaide (Mrs. Belloc Lown-
des, pseud.) (b. 1868)
Eng. novelist
Hammerton p926

Bellwood, Bessie (Elizabeth Mahoney) (b.
1860)
Eng. singer
Felstead—Stars p68-69,por.
Leroy—Music p41-42,por.

Belmont, Alva E. Smith (d. 1933)
Amer. philanthropist, feminist,
politician
Adelman—Famous p284-285
Irwin—Anels p358,421

Belmont, Caroline Slidell (fl. 1850's-1860's)
Amer. daughter of Commodore
Perry
Tebbel—Inher. p149

Belmont, Eleanor Elise Robson (b. 1879)
Eng.-Amer. actress, author,
philanthropist, nurse
CR '59 p65,por.
Cur. Biog. '44 p40-43
Logan—Part p779-780
Pennock—Makers p51,por.

Belmont, Jessie Robbins Sloane (d. 1935)
Amer. hostess
Tebbel—Inher. p150-151,por.

Belmore, Alice (c. 1870-1943)
Eng. actress
Cur. Biog. '43 p36
Marks—Glamour p279

Belocca, Anna de (1854-   )
Russ. singer
Lahee—Famous p308-309

Beloff, Leah Norah (gr. 1940)
Eng. journalist
Brittain—Women p187,254

Bel-Shalti-Narrar (c. 540 B.C.)
Babyl. priestess
Schmidt—400 p127,por.

Belshazzar's mother (Biblical)
Deen—All p345-346

Beltrain, Manuel (fl. 1700's)
Colom. patriot
Schmidt—400 p77-78

Bemis, Lalu Nathoy ("China Polly") (1852-
1933)
Chin.-Amer. W. pioneer
Horan—Desperate p310-314,por.
*Miller—West p120-128

Benato-Beltrami, Elizabeth (fl. 1850's)
It. painter
Waters—Women p41

Benbridge, Letitia Sage (1770-1787)
Amer. painter
Leonard—Amer. p112

Benchley, Belle Jennings (1882-   )
Amer. zoo director
Cur. Biog. '40 p68-70,por.

Bender, Lauretta (1897-   )
Amer. physician, psychiatrist
*Knapp—Women p79-93,por.

Benedict, Hannah.
See Carter, Hannah Benedict

Benedict, Ruth (1887-1948)
　　Amer. anthropologist, educator,
　　author
　Cur. Biog. '41 p65-66,por.
　Cur. Biog. '48 p44
　Progress—Science p66-67,por.
　Women—Achieve. p144,por.

Benesh, Joan Dorothy (1920-   )
　　Eng. choreographer
　Cur. Biog. '57 p48-50,por.

Benet, Adelaide George (b. 1848)
　　Amer. botanist
　Logan—Part p879

Benét, Laura (n.d.)
　　Amer. poet
　Cook—Our p310

Benét, Rosemary Carr (1898-1962)
　　Amer. poet
　*Benét—Famous Poets p129-134,por.

Benger, Elizabeth Ogilvy (1778-1827)
　　Eng. historical writer
　Dorland—Sum p46,176

Bengless, Catherine H. Griffith (fl. 1860's)
　　Amer. Civil war nurse
　Logan—Part p374

Benham, Ida Whipple (b. 1849)
　　Amer. social reformer
　Logan—Part p598

Benham, Mrs. (fl. 1940's)
　　Amer. patriot
　Fowler—Woman p263-270

Benitez, Maria Bibiana (b. 1783)
　　Puert. Ric. playwright
　Schmidt—400 p332-333,por.

Benito y Tejada, Benita (fl. 1870's-1880's)
　　Sp. artist
　Waters—Women p41

Benizelos, Philothéy ("Kera" or "Kalogréza),
　　(fl. 1650's)
　　Gr. foundress, nun
　Schmidt—400 p216-217,por.

Benjamin, Louise Paine (fl. 1930's)
　　Amer. editor
　Women—Achieve. p177,por.

Benjamin, Mary A. (n.d.)
　　Amer. autograph dealer
　New Yorker Dec.5,1959 p57,por.
　　(Profiles)

Benjamin, Peggy Haskell (fl. 1930's)
　　Amer. naturalist
　Women—Scientist p193

Benjamin, Sarah Matthews (c. 1744-1861)
　　Amer. Rev. war patriot, nurse
　Green—Pioneer (3) p458

Bennett, Alice (b. 1851)
　　Amer. physician
　Hanaford—Dau. p575
　Irwin—Angels p140-141
　Logan—Part p743-744
　Mead—Medical p53

Bennett, Constance (1905/06-1965)
　　Amer. actress
　CR '59 p66,por.
　CR '63 p46-47,por.
　Hammerton p233,por.
　Hughes—Famous p3-24,por.
　Stuart—Immort. p224,por.

Bennett, Dorothy (1906-   )
　　Amer. playwright
　Mantle—Contemp. p304

Bennett, Dorothy Graham (1893-1959)
　　Amer. author
　Warfel—Amer. p181-182,por.
　Women—Achieve. p164,por.

Bennett, Eve (fl. 1930's)
　　Amer. fashion designer, editor
　Women—Achieve. p193

Bennett, Helen Christine (b. 1881)
　　Amer. author
　Women—Achieve. p79,por.

Bennett, Joan (1910-   )
　　Amer. actress
　CR '59 p67,por.
　CR '63 p47,por.

Bennett, Laura (fl. 1870's-1890's)
　　Amer. actress
　Marks—Glamour p279

Bennington, Long Lincs Christina of (d. c.
　　1283)
　　Eng. agriculturist
　Stenton—English p86-87,91

Bennis, Virginia (fl. 1940's)
　　Amer. glider pilot
　*May—Women p218-219

Benson, Clover (fl. 1930's)
　　Amer. advertising display designer
　Women—Achieve. p193

Benson, Marguerite (fl. 1930's)
　　Amer. social hygiene worker
　Women—Achieve. p96,por.

Benson, Sally (Sara) Smith (1900-   )
　　Amer. author
　Cur. Biog. '41 p69-70,por.
　O'Brien—50 p865
　Van Gelder—Writers p181-184

Benson, Stella (1892-1933)
Eng. author
Collins—Literature p181-186,por.
Hammerton p235,por.
*Johnson—Some Contemp. p161-174
Millett—Brit. p137-138

Bent, Ann (1768-1857)
Amer. merchant
Dexter—Career p38,141,156-158

Bentley, Elizabeth T. (gr. 1930)
former Russ. spy
Singer—World's p90-100,por.

Bentley, Inez A. (fl. 1940's)
Amer. physician
Lovejoy—Women Phys. p54

Bentley, Irene (1870-1940)
Amer. singer, actress
Cur. Biog. '40 p73

Bentley, Phyllis Eleanor (1894-   )
Eng. novelist
Lawrence—School p231-233
Millett—Brit. p138-139

Benton, Helen (fl. 1940's)
Russ. spy
Singer—World's p242-250

Benton, Louisa Dow (b. 1831)
Amer. lecturer
Logan—Part p788

Benton, Mrs. (fl. 1860's)
Amer. missionary, lecturer
Hanaford—Dau. p343-344

Bentron, Thérèse. See Blanc, Marie Thérèse

Benvenuta Bojani (fl. 13th cent.)
It. saint
Wescott—Calen. p169

Benzell, Mimi (n.d.)
Amer. singer
CR '59 p69,por.
CR '63 p49,por.

Bera, Frances (fl. 1950's)
Amer. aviatrix
*May—Women p188

Beranger, Clara (d. 1956)
Amer. screen writer
Women—Achieve. p153,por.

Berckman, Evelyn (1900-   )
Amer. composer
Howard—Our p535
Reis—Composers p28

Berengaria (d.c.1230)
Eng. queen
Hammerton p237
*MacVeagh—Champlin p65

Berenice (Julia Berenice) (28-after 75 A.D.)
Chalcis queen
Balsdon—Roman p132-133
*MacVeagh—Champlin p65

Berenice (fl. 67-81)
Cappadocian queen
Boccaccio—Conc.p158-159

Berg, Gertrude (1899-1966)
Amer. actress, author, playwright,
producer
Blum—Television p84,por.
Cahn—Laugh p174,por.
CR '59 p70,por.
CR '63 p49, por.
Cur. Biog. '41 p71-72
Cur. Biog. '60 p26-28,por.
Cur. Biog. '66 p462
Settel—Radio p66,por.
TV—Person (2) p122-123,por.
Women—Achieve. p63,por.

Berg, Patricia Jane (1918-   )
Amer. golfer
CR '59 p70,por.
CR '63 p49,por.
Cur. Biog. '40 p75-77,por.

Berganza, Teresa (1933/36-   )
Sp. singer
Pleasants—Great p351-352

Bergen, Flora Batson (1870-1906)
Amer. singer
Cuney-Hare—Negro p219-220,por.

Bergen, Polly (1930-   )
Amer. singer, actress
CR '59 p70-71,por.
CR '63 p50,por.
Cur. Biog. '58 p38-39,por.
TV—Person (2) p48-49,por.

Bergen, Sarah Rapelje.
See Bogaert, Sarah Rapelje Bergen

Bergengren, Anna Farquhar (Margaret Alston, pseud.) (b. 1865)
Amer. author, singer, journalist
Harkins—Famous p267-281,por.
Harkins—Little p267-281,por.
Logan—Part p806-807

Berger, Erna (1900-   )
Ger. singer
Ewen—Ency. p44

Berger, Hulda E. (fl. 1930's)
Amer. dentist
Women—Achieve. p117,por.

Bergman, Ingrid (1917-)
Swed. actress
Barnett—Writing p218-242
CR '59 p71-72,por.
CR '63 p50,por.
Cur. Biog. '40 p77-78,por.
Cur. Biog. '65 p34-37,por.
Ross—Player p38-42,por.
Schickel—Stars p229-230,por.
Time Aug.2,1943 p55,por.(Cover)
Time Jan.8,1945 p39,por.(Cover)
TV Guide—Roundup p32-35

Bergner, Elisabeth (1898/1900-)
Aust. actress
Hammerton p238,por.
Lamparski—What p54-55,por.

Beriosova, Svetlana (1932-)
Lith. ballet dancer
Crowle—Enter p151-172,por.
Cur. Biog. '60 p30-32,por.
Davidson—Ballet p25-27,por.
Fisher—Ball. p30,32,por.

Berkeley, Sister Xavier (1861-1944)
Eng. missionary
Burton—Valiant p1-19

Berlin, Ellin Mackay (1904-)
Amer. author
Cur. Biog. '44 p43-44,por.
Warfel—Amer. p36,por.

Berliner, Constance Hope (fl. 1930's)
Amer. bus. executive
Women—Achieve. p186,por.

Berlioz, Harriet Constance.
See Smithson, Harriet Constance

Bernadette of Lourdes (1844-1879)
Fr. saint
Deen—Great p404-406
Englebert—Lives p147-148
*Haskell—Saints p29-57,por.
Husslein—Heroines p61-82
Sharkey—Pop. p198-204
Stiles—Postal p231
*Windham—Sixty p362-371

Bernard, Madame Marie (fl. 1930's)
Amer. fashion designer
Women—Achieve. p164,por.

Bernard-Beere, Fanny Mary (1856-1915)
Eng. actress
Hammerton p240

Bernardino, Minerva (1907-)
Dom. R. minister to U.N.
Cur. Biog. '50 p41-43,por.

Bernardone, Sister Pica (fl. 12th, 13th cent.)
It., mother of St. Francis of Assisi
*Chandler—Famous p1-20

Bernardy, Amy Allemand (b. 1880)
It.-Amer. soc. reformer
Logan—Part p855

Bernauer, Agnes (d. 1435)
Ger. heroine
Hammerton p240

Berners, Dame Juliana (b. c. 1388)
Eng. pioneer author, prioress
Culver—Women p111-112
Hammerton p241

Bernhardt, Rachel (b. 1821)
Fr. actress
Muir—Women p167-168

Bernhardt, Sarah (1844-1923)
Fr. actress
Abbot—Notable p352-356
Adelman—Famous p268-269,por.
Blum—Great p3,por.
Bodeen—Ladies p71-82,por.
Bradford—Dau. p241-282,por.
Brown—Gentle p184-185
Caffin—Vaud. p25,por.
Coad—Amer. p296,por.
De Morny—Best p137-144,por.
Dorland—Sum p70,168-169
Felstead—Stars p114,por.
Fitzhugh—Concise p53-55
Hammerton p241-242,por.
Izard—Heroines p3-51,por.
Love—Famous p35-36
*MacVergh—Champlin p68
Marinacci—Lead. p125-152,por.
Meine—Great p45-48,por.
Phila.—Women, unp,por.
*Pringle—When p165-176
Schmidt—400 p187-188,por.
Sherman—World's p234-235
Skinner—Elegant p118-142,por.
Stiles—Postal p29
Thomas—Living Women p211-225,por.
Wagenknecht—Seven p53-88,por.
Waters—Women p41-43

Bernheim, Alice Rheinstein (fl. 1930's)
Amer. surgeon
Women—Achieve. p186,por.

Bernice (Biblical)
Deen—All p233-238
Lewis—Portraits p142-143
Marble—Women Bible p101-103

Bernice. See also Berenice

Bernie, Rose L. (fl. 1930's)
Amer. realtor, health expert
Women—Achieve. p125,por.

Bernstein, Aline Frankau (1881-1955)
Amer. author, scenic designer
Warfel—Amer. p36,por.

Bernstein, Elsa. See Rosmer, Ernst

Bernstein, Theresa (n.d.)
Amer. artist
Bryant—Amer. p278-279

Berri (or Berry), Marie Louise Elisabeth
d'Orleans (1695-1719)
Fr., granddaughter of Madame
D'Orleans
Kavanagh—Woman (1) p32-35

Berridge, Rachel, Countess of Clonwell (m.
1901)
Eng. actress
Wyndham—Chorus p112,por.

Berry, Agnes (1764-1852)
Eng., friend of Horace Walpole
Melville—Regency p92-108

Berry, Duchess of.
See Marie-Caroline Ferdinande Louise,
Duchess de Berry

Berry, Martha McChesney (1866-1942)
Amer. educator, foundress
Bartlett—They p7-10
Cur. Biog. '40 p80-81,por.
Cur. Biog. '42 p79
*Fleming—Great p115-130
*Forsee—Women p178-202
Huff—Famous (2nd) p41-52,por.
*Kirkland—Achieved p1-8
Logan—Part p539
Love—Famous p42
Mears—They p51-53

Berry, Martia L. Davis (b. 1844)
Amer. feminist, missionary, club
leader
Logan—Part p509

Berry, Mary (1763-1852)
Eng. author
Melville—Regency p92-108
Stenton—English p221,324-326,330

Berry, Mrs. Sidney (fl. 1770's)
Amer. Rev. war patriot
Bruce—Woman p87-88

Berteaux, Hélène Herbert (1825-1909)
Fr. sculptor
Adelman—Famous p218

Bertha (1) (d. 612)
Eng. Christian queen
Culver—Women p79
Deen—Great p322-323
Hammerton p244
Muir—Women p67-68

Bertha (2) (d.c. 725)
Fr. saint
Blunt—Great p151-152
Englebert—Lives p257-258

Bertha (2) (d. end of 6th cent.)
Fr. saint
Englebert—Lives p170

Berthod, Madeleine (n.d.)
Swiss skier
Stiles—Postal p30

Bertille (d.c. 705-713)
Fr. saint
Englebert—Lives p420

Bertin, Célia (1921-   )
Fr. novelist
Peyre—French p402-403

Bertin, Louise Angelique (1805-1877)
Fr. poet, composer
Adelman—Famous p143
Dorland—Sum p54,77,160,180
Elson—Woman's p182-183

Bertola, Mariana (fl. 1920's)
Amer. physician, educator, child
welfare worker
Bindheim—Women p24,por.

Beruria (fl. 1210's-1280's)
Ger., wife of Rabbi Meir
*Levinger—Great p97-100

Berwin, Bernice (fl. 1930's)
Amer. actress
Eichberg—Radio p109

Berzelius, Betty Poppius, Baroness (1811-
1884)
Swed., wife of Jon Jacob Berzelius
Weeks—Discovery p315,707,por.

Besant, Annie Wood (1847-1933)
Eng. theosophist and Ind. pol.
leader
Adelman—Famous p279-280
Cole—Women p191-232,por.
De Morny—Best p130-136
Du Cann—Loves p97-117,por.
Hammerton p245,por.
Stern—Women p33-39,por.
Stiles—Postal p30

Beskow, Elsa Maartman (b. 1874)
Swed. illustrator, author
Mahony—Illus. p278

Best, Allena Champlin (Anne M. Erick-
Berry, pseud.) (1892-   )
Amer. illustrator, author
Mahony—Illus. p278

Best, Edna (1900-   )
Eng. actress
CR '59 p76,por.
Cur. Biog. '54 p80-82,por.
Hammerton p246,por.

Best, Molly (fl. 1920's)
  Amer. humorist, journalist, author
  Bruère—Laugh p234

Beston, Elizabeth. See Coatsworth, Elizabeth

Betancourt, Ana (fl. 1850's)
  Cub. feminist, patriot
  Schmidt—400 p86,por.

Betham-Edwards, Matilda Barbara (1836/
    38-1919)
  Eng. author
  Black—Notable p120-132,por.
  Hammerton p246,por.

Bethel, Woman of (Biblical)
  Nelson—Bible p58-60

Bethlen, Katherine (1700-1759)
  Hung. scientific writer
  Schmidt—400 p224,por.

Bethlenfalve, Elsa von, Baroness Gutman (b.
    1875)
  Liech. princess
  Arsenius—Dict. p61,por.
  Phila.—Women unp.,por.

Bethsabee (Biblical)
  Faulhaber—Women p146-149

Bethune, Louise (b. 1856)
  Amer. pioneer architect
  Logan—Part p787-788
  Stern—We p61-67,por.
  Waters—Women p43

Bethune, Mary McLeod (1875-1955)
  Amer. educator, govt. employee
  Adams—Great p96,por.
  Bowie—Women p118-127
  *Cherry—Portraits p18-20
  Cur. Biog. '42 p79-81,por.
  Cur. Biog. '55 p46
  Daniel—Women p79-106,por.
  Embree—13 p9-24,por.
  Fleming—Great p71-85
  *Galloway—Roads p72-93,por.
  *Gersh—Women p32-48
  *Hughes—First p64,por.
  *Nathan—Women p74-116
  *Richardson—Great p178,por
  Robinson—Hist. p163,por.

Betkyn, the maidservant (d. 1563)
  Eng., Christian martyr
  Culver—Women p120-122

Betterton, Mary Saunderson (c. 1637-
    1710/12)
  Eng. actress
  Gilder—Enter p144-172
  MacQueen—Pope p44-50,96-97
  Marinacci—Lead. p1-22
  Ormsbee—Back p59-60,66,258
  Wilson—All p117-120

Bettignies, Louise Marie Jeanne Henriette de
    (1880-1918/19)
  Fr. spy
  Hoehling—Women p45-74,por.
  *Komroff—True p128-152
  Singer—3000 p245-270

"Bettina," pseud.
  See Russell, Elizabeth Mary Annette
  Beauchamp, Countess von Arnim

Bettis, Valerie Elizabeth (1919-   )
  Amer. ballet dancer
  CR '59 p76,por.
  CR '63 p54,por.
  Cur. Biog. '53 p65-67,por.

Betts, Helen M. (b. 1846)
  Amer. physician
  Hanaford—Dau p572-573

Betz, Pauline (1919-   )
  Amer. tennis player
  Time Sept.2,1946 p7,por. (Cover)

Bevan, Jennie. See Lee, Jennie

Bevans, Gladys Huntington (fl. 1930's)
  Amer. journalist, editor
  Women—Achieve. p178,por.

Beveridge, Kühue (m. 1899)
  Amer. sculptor
  Waters—Women p43-44

Bevier, Isabel (1860-1942)
  Amer. home economist, educator,
    lecturer, author
  Cur. Biog '42 p81

Bevier, Mrs. J. (fl. 1770's)
  Amer. Rev. patriot
  Ellet—Women (2) p205-207

Bevins, Mrs. Okey (d. 1942)
  Amer glider pilot
  *May—Women p216

Bialk, Elisa (1912-   )
  Amer. author
  Cur. Biog. '54 p82-83,por.

Bianco, Pamela 1906-   )
  Eng. illustrator
  Kirkland—Artists p13-22
  Mahony—Illus. p278

Bibiana (or Vivian) (d. 363)
  Rom. saint
  Englebert—Lives p459

Bickerdyke, Mary Ann ("Mother") (1817-
    1901)
  Amer. Civil war nurse
  Brockett—Woman's p172-186,por.

(Continued)

Bickerdyke, Mary Ann—*Continued*

    Bruce—Woman p206-208,por.
    Dannett—Noble p231-232,317,388,390,
      393,por.
    *Dodge—Story p75-81
    Dolan—Goodnow's p234-235
    Dorland—Sum p126
    Douglas—Remember p146-147
    Darkness—Heroines p13
    Logan—Part p326-329
    *McKown—Heroic p77-100,por.
    Moore—Women p465-471,por.
    Schmidt—400 p540
    *Sickels—Calico p235-270
    *Wright—Great p208-237
    Young—Women p367,por.

Bicking, Ada Elizabeth (d. 1953)
    Amer. music educator
    McCoy—Portraits p11,por.

Bicknell, Anna (fl. 1852)
    Eng. governess
    Howe—Galaxy p151-152

Bicknell, Mrs. (fl. 18th cent.)
    Eng. actress, comedienne
    MacQueen—Pope p162

Bickum, Dorothy (fl. 1930's)
    Amer. saleswoman
    Women—Achieve. p35,por.

Biddle, Mary Duke (1887-1960)
    Amer. humanitarian, philanthropist
    Women—Achieve. p27,por.

Biddle, Rebecca (fl. 1770's)
    Amer. Rev. war patriot
    Ellet—Women (2) p271-274

Biddulph, Jessie Catherine Vokes (1851-
    1884)
    Eng.Amer. actress, singer
    Coad—Amer. p245,por.

Bidlack, Mrs. Gore (fl. 1770's)
    Amer. Rev. war patriot
    Ellet—Women (2) p198-199

Bieloverskaia, Maria (fl. 1910's)
    Russ. soldier, heroine
    Dorland—Sum p99

Biffin, Sarah (1784-1850)
    Eng. handicapped painter
    Hammerton p249
    Waters—Women p44-45

Bigelow, Mrs. R. M. (fl. 1860's)
    Amer. Civil war humanitarian
    Brockett—Woman's p738-740

Bihet, Mlle. (fl. 1950's)
    Belg. nurse
    Dolan—Goodnow's p301,por.

Bijna (or Byns), Anna (c. 1494-1575)
    Flem. poet
    Hammerton p250

Bilbro (Anne), Mathilde (fl. 1910's-1950's)
    Amer. composer, music teacher,
      author
    Howard—Our p582
    McCoy—Portraits p11,por.

Bilders, Marie van Bosse (1837-1900)
    Nether. painter
    Waters—Women p45, 373-375

Bildersee, Adele (fl. 1930's)
    Amer. educator
    Women—Achieve. p112,por.

Bilhah (Biblical)
    Deen—All p255-256

Bilinska, Anna (1858-1893)
    Pol. painter
    Waters—Women p45

Billiart, Julie, Blessed (1751-1816)
    Fr. nun
    Elgin—Nun p72-75,por.
    Englebert—Lives p138
    Sharkey—Pop. p179-183

Billing, Rose M. (d. 1865)
    Amer. Civil war nurse
    Brockett—Woman's p460,738-739,742

Billington, Elizabeth Weichsel (1768-1818)
    Eng. singer.
    Dorland—Sum p36,68,162
    Ferris—Great (1) p86,por.
    Hammerton p251,por.
    Lahee—Famous p29-33
    Pleasants—Great p108-111,por.
    Wagner—Prima p107-108,238

Billington, Helen (fl. 1600's)
    Amer. pilgrim
    Bell—Women p20
    Green—Pioneer (1) p142-145
    Logan—Part p34-35
    Marble—Women p69-71

Bellini, Maria Nicolasa (1839-1903)
    Dom. R. educator
    Schmidt—400 p103-104,por.

Billwiller, Henrietta. See Hudson, Henrietta

Bilton, Belle, Countess of Clancarty (c. 1868-
    1906)
    Eng. actress, singer
    Wyndham—Chorus p93-94,100,por.

Binder, Pearl (1904-   )
    Eng. illustrator
    Mahony—Illus. p279

Binger, Delphine (fl. 1930's)
    Amer. bus. executive
    Women—Achieve. p136,por.

Bingham, Ann Willing (d. 1801)
    Amer. hostess, social leader
    Burt—Phila. p231,257-258,301
    Hanaford—Dau. p140
    Sale—Old p169-177,por.

Bingham, Jemima (m. 1769)
    Amer. missionary
    Logan—Part p510-511

Bingham, Millicent Todd (1880-1968)
    Amer. geographer, conservationist,
        author, editor
    Cur. Biog. '61 p55-57,por.

Bingham, Mrs. William (fl. 1790's)
    Amer. social leader
    Douglas—Remember p46

Binner, Madame (fl. 1930's)
    Aust.-Amer. bus. executive
    Women—Achieve. p62,por.

Biondi, Nicola (b. 1866)
    It. painter
    Waters—Women p45

Birch, Carroll (1896-   )
    Amer. physician
    Lovejoy—Women p227,por.

Birchard, Dora E. (n.d.)
    Amer. nurse
    *Wright—Great p43-45

Birch-Pfeiffer, Charlotte Karoline (1793/
        1800-1868)
    Ger. actress, playwright
    Dorland—Sum p31,166
    Heller—Studies p250-251

Bird, Clementine (d. 1775)
    Amer. printer
    Hanaford—Dau. p710

Bird, Isabella Lucy.
    See Bishop, Isabella Lucy Bird

Bird, Rachel. See Wilson, Rachel

Biresak, Thusnelda (n.d.)
    Amer. organist, pianist
    McCoy—Portraits p12,por.

Birgitta. See Bridget.

Birkhead, May (fl. 1927's-1930's)
    Amer. journalist
    Ross—Ladies p449-450

Biro, Sari (fl. 1940's)
    Hung. pianist
    McCoy—Portraits p12,por.

Birute (fl. 1300's)
    Lith. duchess
    Arsenious—Dict. p28

Bischoff, Ilse Marthe (1903-   )
    Amer. illustrator
    Mahony—Illus. p279

Bischoff, Marie. See Brandt, Marianne

Biscott, Jeanne (1601-1664)
    Fr. nurse
    Dolan—Goodnow's p150-151,por.

Bishop, Ann Rivière (1810-1884)
    Eng. singer
    Marks—Glamour p112-118,por.

Bishop, Emily Montague Mulkin (b. 1858)
    Amer. teacher, lecturer
    Logan—Part p785

Bishop, Harriet E. (1817-1883)
    Amer. pioneer teacher
    Whitton—These p210-211

Bishop, Hazel (1906-   )
    Amer. industrial chemist,
        manufacturer
    Cur. Biog. '57 p56-58,por.

Bishop, Isabella Lucy Bird (1831/32-1904)
    Eng. traveller, lecturer, travel writer
    Adelman—Famous p213
    Dorland—Sum p29,78,113
    Hammerton p255,por.
    *Johnson—Some p100-115

Bishop, Mary Axtell (b. 1859)
    Amer. religious worker, author
    Logan—Part p832

Bisland, Elizabeth.
    See Wetmore, Elizabeth Bisland

Bismarck, Johanna von (1824-1894)
    Ger., wife of Bismarck
    Schmidt—400 p203,por.

Bissell, Abigail. See Williams, Abigail

Bissell, Lucy J. (fl. 1860's)
    Amer. Civil war nurse
    Brockett—Woman's p788-789

Bissell, Sabra Trumbull (1742-1768)
    Amer. patriot
    Green—Pioneer (3) p508-509
    Root—Chapter p321-323

Bithiah (Biblical)
    Deen—All p256

Bixby, Allene K. (d. 1947)
    Amer. organist, composer and music
        teacher
    McCoy—Portraits p12,por.

Bixby, Diana (fl. 1940's)
    Amer. aviatrix
  *May—Women p184

Black, Jane. See Thomas, Jane

Black, Jean Ferguson (1900-   )
    Amer. playwright
  Mantle—Contemp. p304

Black, Jennie Prince (1868-1945)
    Amer. composer
  ASCAP p40

Black, Ruby Aurora (1896-1957)
    Amer. journalist, author
  Ross—Ladies p347-349

Black, Winifred (d. 1936)
    Amer. journalist
  Kelly—Reporters p113-136
  Ross—Ladies p60-67,por.,cover

Blackburn, Helen (1842-1903)
    Irish feminist
  Hammerton p257-258

Blackburn, Katherine (fl. 1900's)
    Amer. missionary
  They—Went p28

Blackburn, Victoria Grace (Fan-Fan, pseud.)
    (d. 1928)
    Can. journalist
  Thomas—Canad. p13-14

Blackmar, Miss (fl. 1860's)
    Amer. Civil war nurse
  Brockett—Woman's p429-430

Blackwell, Alice Stone (1857-1950)
    Amer. feminist, author, social
      reformer
  Adelman—Famous p287
  Bruce—Woman p225
  Irwin—Angels p46,259-261
  Logan—Part p672

Blackwell, Antoinette Brown (1825-1921)
    Amer. pioneer clergyman, teacher
  Adelman—Famous p262-263
  *Boynick—Pioneers p90-120
  *Commager—Crus. p166
  Culver—Women p172-174
  Deen—Great p394-396
  Douglas—Remember p96, 99-100
  Hanaford—Dau. p247,288,363,442-445
  Irwin—Angels p58-59,91,299
  Logan—Part p737
  O'Connor—Pioneer p73,206
  Riegel—Amer. p116-119

Blackwell, Betsy Talbot (n.d.)
    Amer. editor
  CR '63 p59,por.
  Cur. Biog. '54 p89-91,por.
  Women—Achieve. p137,por.

Blackwell, Elizabeth (1821-1910)
    Eng.-Amer. pioneer physician
  Adelman—Famous p219-220
  Bell—Storm. p26-45,92-93,por.
  *Bolton—Lives p81-91,por.
  *Buckmaster—Women p71-98,por.
  *Carmer—Caval. p204-206,por.
  Castiglioni—Hist. p917
  *Chandler—Medicine p53-57,por.
  *Commagar—Crus. p165-168
  Culver—Women p181
  *Curtin—Gallery p7,por.
  Dannett—Noble p54-57,59
  Dexter—Career p40-41
  Dolan—Goodnow's p221
  *Dolin—World p120-125,por.
  Dorland—Sum p47,80,109,128-129,147
  Douglas—Remember p96-99,141
  Fabricant—Why p63-65
  Farmer—What p383-385
  *Gersh—Women p164-184,por.
  Hammerton p258
  Hanaford—Dau. p552-555
  *Heath—Women (4) p14,por.
  *Horowitz—Treas. p43-47
  Hume—Great p1-47,por
  Irwin—Angels p46-50,150-151
  Jensen—Revolt p110,por.
  Logan—Part p742-743
  Lovejoy—Women p41-70,130-134,por.
  Mead—Medical p21-24,por.
  Mozans—Woman p300-304
  Patrick—Profiles p9
  *Pringle—When p132-147
  Rosen—Four p87-89,182-185,336-337
  16 Amer. p17-20
  *Strong—Of p150-154
  *Yost—Famous p89-97,por.
  Young—Women p20,72-76,367-368

Blackwell, Emily (1826-1910)
    Eng.-Amer. pioneer physician
  Bell—Storm. p41-42
  Castiglioni—Hist. p917
  Douglas—Remember p98-99
  Hanaford—Dau. p554
  Hume—Great p36-37,132,197-200
  Irwin—Angels p46-49
  Lovejoy—Women p41-50,70-72,por.
  Mead—Medical p24-25,por.

Blackwell, Lucy Stone. See Stone, Lucy

Blagg, Henrietta Maria (m. 1675)
    Eng. maid of honor
  Melville—Windsor p133-134

Blagge, Margaret.
  See Godolphin, Margaret Blagge

Blaha, Louise (1850-1926)
    Hung. actress
  Schmidt—400 p231-232,por.

Blahetka, Marie Leopoldine (1811-1887)
    Aust. pianist
  Elson—Woman's p160-161

Blaine, Harriet Stanwood Blaine (1828-1903   )
Amer., wife of James G. Blaine
Bradford—Wives p235-270

Blaine, Vivian (1924-   )
Amer. actress
CR '59 p82,por.
CR '63 p59,por.
TV—Person. (20) p36-37,por.

Blair, Janet (1921-   )
Amer .actress
CR '59 p82,por.
CR '63 p60,por.
TV—Person. (1) p28-29

Blaisdell, Elinore (n.d.)
Amer. illustrator
Mahony—Illus. p279

Blaisdell, Mary Frances (b. 1874)
Amer. author
Logan—Part p843

Blake, Amanda (n.d.)
Amer. actress
CR '63 p60-61,por.
TV—Person. (2) p113-114,por.

Blake, Doris (n.d.)
Can.-Amer. journalist
Cur. Biog. '41 p85-87,por.
Jensen—Revolt p196-197,por.
Ross—Ladies p428-430
Women—Achieve. p100,por.

Blake, Dorothy Gaynor (fl. 1940's)
Amer. composer, music educator
McCoy—Portraits p12,por.

Blake, Florence G. (1907-   )
Amer. nurse, educator
*Yost—Nursing p119-134

Blake, Katherine Devereux (1857-1950)
Amer. eductaor
Women—Achieve. p180,por.

Blake, Lillie Devereaux (1835-1913)
Amer. feminist, social reformer
Adelman—Famous p205
Hanaford—Dau. p377
Logan—Part p578-579
Riegel—Amer. p194-195

Blake, Louisa Aldrich (fl. 1890's)
Eng. physician
Bell—Storm. p130,168-169,176

Blake, Sophia Jex (1840-1912)
Eng. physician
Mead—Medical p35-37

Blakely, Gwendolyn. See Brooks, Gwendolyn

Blakeslee, Myra Allen (c. 1888-1953)
Amer. advertising executive, social welfare leader
Women—Achieve. p167,por.

Blakeway, Sarah (fl. 1741)
Amer. colonial planter, bus. woman
Spruill—Women's p307

Blalock, Mrs. L. M. (fl. 1860's)
Amer. Civil war soldier
Simkins—Women p80

Blalock, Ruby Wooten (1905-   )
Amer. organization official
Cur. Biog. '50 p56-57,por.

Blamire, Susanna (1747-1794)
Scot. poet, song-writer
Dorland—Sum p29,180-181
Findlay—Spindle p56-58

Blanc, Marie Thérèse (Thérèse Bentron) (1840-1907)
Fr. journalist, novelist, translator
Dorland—Sum p30,116,177

Blanch, Doris. See Lee, Doris Emrick

Blanchard, Hazel Ann (1920-   )
Amer. educator, organization official
Cur. Biog. '63 p36-38,por.

Blanchard, Helen Augusta (fl. 1870's)
Amer. inventor
Logan—Part p889

Blanchard, Madame Sophie (d. 1819)
Fr. pioneer aeronaut, balloonist
Earhart—Fun p195-197
*Lauwick—Heroines p20-24,por.
*May—Women p13-14
Planck—Women p1-5

Blanchard, Theresa Weld. See Weld, Theresa

Blanche of Castile (c. 1187-1252)
Fr. queen
Adelman—Famous p35-36
Beard—Woman p214-218
Blunt—Great p156
Hammerton p261,por.
Muir—Women p77-78

Blanchfield, Florence A. (1884-   )
Amer. army nurse
Cur. Biog. '43 p53-55,por.

Bland, Frances.
See Tucker, Frances Bland Randolph

Bland, Joyce (1906-   )
Eng. actress
Hammerton p261

Blandina (fl. 177 A.D.)
Fr. Christian martyr
Culver—Women p75

Blanding, Sarah Gibson (1898-   )
Amer. educator
CR '63 p61,por.
Cur. Biog. '46 p55-57,por.
Rogers—Women p112,por.

Blaney, Norah (1896-   )
Eng. actress
Hammerton p262

Blankenburg, Lucretia M. Longshore (1845-
1937)
Amer. club leader
Bennett—Amer. p207-227,por.

Blankers-Koen, Fanny (1918-   )
Nether. athlete (track)
Stiles—Postal p32

Blanshard, Julia (d. 1934)
Amer. journalist
Ross—Ladies p435-436

Blatch, Harriet Stanton (1856-1940)
Amer. feminist, lecturer
Adelman—Famous p286
Cur. Biog. '41 p87
Logan—Part p587

Blau, Tina (1845/47-1916)
Aust. painter
Schmidt—400 p51-52,por.
Waters—Women p45-46

Blavatsky, Elena (Helena) Hahn Petrovna
(1831-1891)
Russ. traveler, theosophist, editor
Adelman—Famous p223
Dorland—Sum p25,118,134
Hammerton p262,por.
Padover—Confess. p326-329

Bledsoe, Katherine Montgomery (fl. 1800's)
Amer. pioneer
Green—Pioneer (3) p460,463

Bledsoe, Mary (d. 1808)
Amer. W. pioneer
Ellet—Pioneer p13-28
Logan—Part p69-72

Bleecker, Ann Eliza (1752-1783)
Amer. colonial poet
Ellet—Women (2) p281-284,por.
Leonard—Amer. p112

Bleicher, Blanche O. (fl. 1930's)
Amer. bus.woman
Women—Achieve.p112,por.

Blennerhassett, Margaret Agnew (c. 1788-
1892)
Irish-Amer.pioneer
Whitton—These p96

Blessington, Marguerite Power, Countess of
(1789-1849)
Irish author, salonist
Abbot—Notable p212-216
Courtney—Adven. p248-262
Dorland—Sum p44,107
Hammerton p262,por.
Jenkins—Ten p151-178,por.
Orr—Famous p337-353
Orr—Famous Affin. III p61-82
Terhune—Super. p204-229

Blind, Mathilde (1841-1896)
Eng.-Ger. poet
Adelman—Famous p202-203
Dorland—Sum p22,172
Hammerton p263,por.

Blinova, Yekaterina Nikitichna (1906-   )
Russ. meteorologist
U.S.—Biog., Soviet p75-76

Bliss, Eleanor Albert (1899-   )
Amer. bacteriologist, physician
*Montgomery—Story p128-130

Bliss, Elizabeth Taylor.
See Dandridge, Elizabeth (Betty) Taylor Bliss

Bliss, Ethel House (c. 1880-1946)
Amer. educator
Women—Achieve. p127,por.

Bliss, Mrs. George (fl. 1890's)
Amer. philanthropist
Logan—Part p533

Blitch, Iris Faircloth (1912-   )
Amer. congresswoman
Cur. Biog. '56 p57-58,por.
U.S.—Women (87th) p9,por.

Blixen, Karen, Baroness.
See Dinesen, Isak

Bloch, Blanche (fl. 1920's-1930's)
Amer. pianist, conductor
Women—Achieve. p194

Bloch, Madame Elisa (b. 1848)
Siles. painter
Water—Women p46-47

Bloch, Lucienne (1909-   )
Swiss illustrator
Mahony—Illus. p279

Bloch, Suzanne (1907-   )
Swiss musician
Ewen—Living p49-50,por.

Block, Anna Scott (fl. 1900's)
  Amer. club leader
  Logan—Part p458-459

Blodgett, Katharine Burr (1898-   )
  Amer. research physicist, chemist
  Cur. Biog. '40 p90-91,por.
  Cur. Biog. '52 p55-57,por.
  Goff—Women p177-182
  °Yost—Women Sci. p196-213

Blondell, Joan (1909-   )
  Amer. actress
  CR. '59 p83,por.
  CR '63 p62,por.

Blondin, Catharine F. (fl. 1930's)
  Amer. designer, bus. executive
  Women—Achieve. p59,por.

Blood, Mrs. K. E. (fl. 1910's-1930's)
  New Z. philanthropist
  Women—Achieve. p194

Bloodworth, Bess (fl. 1930's)
  Amer. bus. executive, personnel and
    production expert
  Women—Achieve. p55,por.

Bloom, Claire (1931-   )
  Eng. actress
  Beaton—Persona p19-20,por.
  CR '59 p84,por.
  CR '63 p62,por.
  Cur. Biog. '56 p59-60,por.
  Ross—Player p282-289,por.
  Time Nov.17,1952 p80,por.(cover)

Bloom, Vera (c. 1898-1959)
  Amer. author, lyricist
  ASCAP p44

Bloomer, Amelia Jenks (1818-1894)
  Amer. feminist, social reformer
  Dorland—Sum p24,130
  Douglas—Remember p158-159
  Furniss—Some p183
  Hammerton p264,por.
  Hanaford—Dau. p703
  Holbrook—Dreamers p181-184
  Jensen—Revolt p45,por.
  Logan—Part p576-578
  O'Connor—Pioneer p76-79,127,162,168
  Riegel—Amer. p51-53,por.
  Thorp—Female p107-142,por.
  Whitton—These p141-143,213-214

Bloomfield, Georgiana, Lady (1822-1905)
  Eng. author, maid of honor
  Parton—Dau. p219-224
  Parton—Noted p219-224

Bloomfield-Zeisler, Fannie (1863-1927)
  Aust.-Siles. pianist
  McCoy—Portraits p236,por.

Saleski—Jewish p448-449
  Saleski—Wander. p294-295,por.
  Schonberg—Great p334-335,por.

Blount, Martha (1690-1762)
  Eng., friend of Alexander Pope
  Hammerton p264

Blow, Mary Elizabeth Thomas (b. 1863)
  Amer. religious worker
  Logan—Part p617

Blower, Elizabeth (b. 1763)
  Eng. novelist
  Hammerton p264

Blum, Florence A. (c. 1872-1959)
  Amer. club leader
  Women—Achieve. p131,por.

Blumenschein, Mary Shepard Greene
    (b. 1869)
  Amer. painter, illustrator, sculptor
  Michigan—Biog. p51

Blunt, Katharine (1876-1954)
  Amer. chemist, educator
  Cur. Biog. '46 p57-59,por.
  Cur. Biog. '54 p99

Bly, Nellie, pseud. (Elizabeth Cochrane Sea-
    man) (1867-1922)
  Amer. journalist
  Beckwith—Contemp. p134-147
  Kelly—Reporters p71-84
  Rogers—Women p56,por.
  Ross—Charmers p196-216,292-293,por.
  Ross—Ladies p48-49,por.

Blyth, Anne (1928-   )
  Amer. actress, singer
  CR '59 p85,por.

Boadicea (Boudicca) (d. 62 A.D.)
  Brit. queen of Iceni, heroine
  Beard—Women p281
  °Boyd—Rulers p41-47
  °Deakin—True p21-31
  Hammerton p266
  °Hayward—Book p19-30
  °MacVeagh—Champlin p76
  Muir—Women p53-54
  °Nisenson—More Minute p22,por.
  Schmidt—400 p129-130,por.
  °Unstead—People p19-24
  Weigall—Person. p45-52

Boardman, Eliza Henderson.
  See **Otis, Eliza Henderson**

Boardman, Frances (fl. 1930's)
  Amer. journalist
  Ross—Ladies p556-557

Boardman, Mabel Thorp (c. 1861-1946)
 Amer. Red Cross executive, nurse
 Cur. Biog. '44 p49-51,por.
 Cur. Biog. '46 p59
 Pennock—Makers p46,por.

Bock, Vera (fl. 1930's-1940's)
 Russ. illustrator
 Mahony—Illus. p281

Bodanya, Natalie (fl. 1930's-1940's)
 Amer. singer
 Ewing—Living p50,por.
 Wagner—Prima p238

Bodichon, Barbara Leigh-Smith (1827-1891)
 Eng. feminist, educator, editor
 Bell—Storm. p15-17
 Brittain—Women p27,31,67
 Dorland—Sum p37,109,138
 Hammerton p267
 Stenton—English p336,346-347

Bodine, Helen K. (fl. 1910's-1930's)
 Amer. fashion editor
 Women—Achieve. p135,por.

Boehm, Mildred Witt (fl. 1930's)
 Amer. bus. woman
 Women—Achieve. p156,por.

Boehringer, Cora Louise (fl. 1920's)
 Amer. educator, journalist
 Bindheim—Women p5-6,por.

Boemm, Ritta (fl. 1890's-1900's)
 Hung. painter
 Waters—Women p47

Bogaert, Sarah Rapelje Bergen (1625-1685/
 1700)
 Amer. pioneer
 Green—Pioneer (1) p198

Bogan, Louise (1897-   )
 Amer. poet
 CR '59 p85,por.
 CR '63 p64,por.
 Millett—Amer. p253-254
 Smith—Women's p6

Bogardus, Annetje Jane (d.c. 1663)
 Amer. pioneer
 Green—Pioneer (1) p155-171,173-175

Bogert, L. Jean (fl. 1930's)
 Amer. physiological chemist
 Women—Achieve. p126,por.

Bogle, Sarah C. N. (d. 1932)
 Amer. pioneer librarian
 Marshall—Amer. p449

Bogue, Lilian. See Bell, Lilian

Böhlau, Hélène (1859-1940)
 Ger. novelist
 Hammerton p269
 Heller—Studies p273-279

Boice, Margaret McIntosh (n.d.)
 Amer. social reformer
 Parshalle—Kash. p223-226

Boileau, Ethel, Lady (c. 1882-1942)
 Eng. novelist
 Cur. Biog. '42 p93

Bois-Berenger, Madame de (fl. 18th cent.)
 Fr. nurse
 Kavanagh—Women (2) p232-233

Boissevain, Edna.
 See Millay, Edna St. Vincent

Boissevain, Inez Milholland (1886-1916)
 Amer. feminist, lawyer
 Adelman—Famous p251-252

Boissonnas, Madame Caroline Sordet
 (1890's-1900's)
 Swiss painter
 Waters—Women p47

Boivin, (Marie) Anne (1773-1841)
 Fr. midwife
 Adelman—Famous p123
 Dorland—Sum p17,147
 Lovejoy—Women p159

Bokor, Margit Wahl (1909-1949)
 Hung. singer
 McCoy—Portraits p14,por.

Boland, Adrienne (fl. 1910-1920's)
 Fr. pioneer aviatrix
 Heinmuller—Man's p310,por.
 *Lauwick—Heroines p30-44,por.

Boland, Mary (1886-1965)
 Amer. actress
 Blum—Great p76,por.
 Stuart—Immort. p54-55,por.

Boley, Jean (1914-   )
 Amer. novelist
 Warfel—Amer. p40,por.

Boleyn, Anne (1507-1536)
 Eng. queen
 Abbot—Notable p59-64,por.
 Adelman—Famous p49-50
 Coryn—Enchant. p9-70
 Dorland—Sum p24
 Fifty—Famous p293-296
 Hahn—Love p65-70
 Hammerton p271-272,por.
 *MacVeagh—Champlin p29
 *Nisenson—More Minute p23,por.
 Sanders—Intimate p13-19,por.

Bolin, Jane Matilda (1908-   )
  Amer. judge
  Robinson—Hist. p164,por.

Bollmann, Mary O'R. (fl. 1930's)
  Amer. bus. executive, broker
  Women—Achieve. p176,por

Bolton, Anne Vaughan, Duchess of (fl. 18th cent.)
  Eng., daughter of Earl of Carbery
  MacQueen—Pope p169-170,por.

Bolton, Frances Payne Bingham (1885/86-)
  Amer. Congresswoman, nurse
  CR '59 p88,por.
  CR '63 p65,por.
  Cur. Biog. '40 p96-97,por.
  Cur. Biog. '54 p105-107,por.
  Dolan—Goodnow's p325-326,por.
  Lamson—Few p33-57,por.
  Paxton—Women p63-73,128,por.
  Pennock—Makers p55-56,por.
  Roosevelt—Ladies p168-177
  U.S.—Women (87th),p11,por.
  U.S.—Women (88th),p5,por.

Bolton, Isabel, pseud.
  See Miller, Mary Britton

Bolton, Lavinia, Duchess of.
  See Fenton, Lavinia, Duchess of Bolton

Bolton, Mary Katherine, Lady Thurlow (c. 1790-1830)
  Eng. actress
  MacQueen—Pope p262-263
  Wyndham—Chorus p41-43,por.

Bolton, Sarah (1815-1893)
  Amer. poet, essayist, social reformer
  Dorland—Sum p49,77,174,181
  Hanaford—Dau. p423,por.

Bompas, Charlotte Selina Cox (1830-1917)
  Eng. missionary
  Thomas—Crusaders p3-21

Bompiani-Battaglia, Clelia (b. 1847)
  It. painter
  Waters—Women p47-48

Bonaparte, Caroline. See Caroline Bonaparte

Bonaparte, Hortense Eugene (1783-1837)
  Nether. queen
  Hammerton p273

Bonaparte, Mrs. Jerome Napoleon (fl. 1930's)
  Amer. social leader, dog fancier
  Women—Achieve. p137,por.

Bonaparte, Maria Annunciata (later Carolina) (1782-1839)
  Fr. archaeologist
  Mozans—Woman p311-312

Bonaparte, Maria Letizia Ramolino (1750-1836)
  Fr. salonist, mother of Napoleon
  *Chandler—Famous p99-116
  Dark—More p199-217
  Dorland—Sum p20
  *MacVeagh—Champlin p78,por.
  Tallentyre—Women p170-203,por.
  Weiner—Parvenu (see index), por.

Bonaparte, Maria Paulina Borghese (originally Carolina) (1780-1825)
  Fr., sister of Napoleon
  Hammerton p274,por.
  Mayne—Enchant. p179-197,por.
  Orr—Famous p251-263
  Orr—Famous Affin. II p135-151
  Stiles—Postal p35
  Weiner—Parvenu p124-125,por.

Bonaparte, Marie Anne (later Elisa) (Elisa Bacciochi) (1777-1820)
  Fr. grand-duchess, sister of Napoleon
  Hammerton p154
  Weiner—Parevnu (see index), por.

Bond, Alice Dixon (n.d.)
  Amer. book reviewer, lecturer
  CR '63 p65-66,por.

Bond, Carrie Jacobs (1862-1946)
  Amer. composer, author, publisher
  ASCAP p45
  Bindheim—Women p25,por.
  Bonte—Amer. p119,por.
  Carnegie—Little p103-106,por.
  Elson—Woman's p265-266,por.
  Ewen—Popular p33-34,por.
  Howard—Our p574-575
  McCoy—Portraits p14,por.
  *Stevens—Women p143-147,por.

Bond, Elizabeth Powell (b. 1841)
  Amer. educator
  Logan—Part p727-728

Bond, Helen Judy (1892-   )
  Amer. home economist
  Women—Achieve. p153,por.

Bond, Jessie (1853-1942)
  Eng. pianist
  Cur. Biog. '42 p95
  Marks—Glamour p282

Bond, Rosalie B. De Solms (b. 1843)
  Amer. religious worker
  Logan—Part p617

Bond, Wilhelmina.
  See Cadwalader, Wilhelmina Bond

Bondfield, Margaret Grace (1873-1953)
  Eng. politician, labor leader
  Hammerton p274,por.

Bonehill, Bessie (fl. 1800's)
  Eng. dancer, actress
  Felstead—Stars p69,por.

Bonelli, Mona Modini (1903-   )
  Amer. author, song-writer
  ASCAP p46

Bonetti, Mary (1902-   )
  Amer. singer
  Women—Achieve. p194

Bonfanti, Marie (1851-1921)
  It. ballet dancer
  *Terry—Star p95-99,por.

Bonfield, Lida (fl. 1930's)
  Amer. bus. executive
  Women—Achiev. p185,por.

Bonfils, Winifred. See Black, Winifred

Bonham, Mildred A.(b. 1840)
  Amer. social reformer
  Logan—Part p537-538

Bonheur, Juliette, Madame Peyrol
  (c. 1830-1891)
  Fr. painter
  Waters—Women p48

Bonheur, Rosa (Marie Rosalie) (1822-1899)
  Fr. painter
  Abbot—Notable p372-376
  Adelman—Famous p192-194,por.
  *Bolton—Lives p93-104,por.
  Dorland—Sum p26,74,78,154
  Fitzhugh—Concise p61-63
  Furniss—Some p77-78
  Hammerton p275,por.
  Hubbard—Little p173-212,por.
  *Kirkland—Good p109
  *MacVeagh—Champlin p80
  Muir—Women p202-203
  Schmidt—400 p186-187,por.
  *Steedman—When p315-334
  Waters—Women p48-54,por.

Bonhomme, Yolande (fl. 1541-1556)
  Fr. pioneer printer
  Club—Printing p10-11

Bonhote, Elizabeth (1744-1818)
  Eng. author
  MacCarthy—Later p63-64

Bonita (fl. 10th cent.)
  Fr. saint
  *Windham—Sixty p248-253

Bonna (d. 1207)
  It. saint
  Englebert—Lives p207

Bonne D'Armagnac, Blessed (1439-1462)
  Fr. princess, saint
  Englebert—Lives p406

Bonner, Hypatia Bradlaugh (b. 1858)
  Eng. author
  Hammerton p275

Bonner, Mary Graham (1895-   )
  Amer. author
  Cur. Biog. '50 p59-60,por.
  Thomas—Canad. p14

Bonner, Sherwood, pseud.
  See MacDowell, Katherine Sherwood
    Bonner

Bonney (Bonny), Anne (1700-1720)
  Eng. pirate
  Rogers—Gallant p53-84

Bonney, Sarah E. (fl. 1880's)
  Amer. ornithologist
  Hanaford—Dau. p282-283

Bonney, (Mabel) Thérèse (n.d.)
  Amer. photographer, journalist
  Cur. Biog. '44 p51-54,por.
  Women—Achieve. p194

"Bonny Kate." See Sevier, Catherine Sherrill

Bonomi, Maria (Anna Olga Luiza)
  (1935-   )
  Brazil. artist
  Cur. Biog. '60 p46-48, por.

Bonsall, Elizabeth Fearne (b. 1861)
  Amer. painter
  Waters—Women p54

Bonsall, Mary M. (fl. 1900's)
  Amer. painter
  Waters—Women p54

Bonte, Paula (b. 1840)
  Ger. painter
  Waters—Women p54-55

Bonum, Elizabeth Johnson (fl. 1700's)
  Amer. pioneer
  Green—Pioneer (1) p457,464

Bonynge, Virginia, Lady Deerhurst (m. 1894)
  Amer. heiress
  Eliot—Heiresses p199-202

Bonzel, Mother Mary Theresia (1830-1905)
  Ger. foundress, nurse, nun
  Pennock—Makers p22

Booker, Edna Lee (n.d.)
  Amer. journalist, author
  Cur. Biog. '40 p97-99,por.

Boole, Ella Alexander (1858-1952)
  Amer. social reformer
  Logan—Part p667
  Women—Achieve. p169,por.

Boone, Jemima (b.c. 1762)
 Amer. pioneer, daughter of Daniel
 Boone
 Bruce—Woman p124-125
 Carmer—Young p48-54
 Peattie—Journey p116-123

Boone, Rebecca B. (c. 1775-1813)
 Amer. pioneer, wife of Daniel Boone
 Bruce—Woman p119,122-123,126,152-
 153
 DAR Mag. 55:392-393,July 1921,
 portrayal
 Ellet—Pioneer p42-61
 Ellet—Women (2) p303-304
 Green—Pioneer (2) p440-444
 Logan—Part p67

Boote, Rose, Marchioness of **Headfort,**
 (1878-1958)
 Irish actress
 Wyndham—Chorus p110-112,por.

Booth, Agnes (Marian Agnes Land Rookes)
 (1846-1910)
 Austral.-Amer. actress
 Farmer—What p415
 Logan—Part p793

Booth, Alice (fl. 1930's)
 Amer. author
 Women—Achieve. p142,por.

Booth, Almida (fl. 1880's)
 Amer. educator
 Hanaford—Dau. p534-535

Booth, Catherine Mumford (1829-1890)
 Eng. clergyman, "mother" of Salva-
 tion Army
 Adelman—Famous p195-196
 °Bolton—Famous Leaders p159-211,por.
 Corkran—Romance p103-113,por.
 Culver—Women p191
 Dark—More p261-285
 Deen—Great p237-245

Booth, Evangeline Cory (1865-1950)
 Eng.-Amer. Salvation Army execu-
 tive, orator, musician, poet
 Carnegie—Five p87-91
 Cur. Biog. '41 p90-91,por.
 Cur. Biog. '50 p60
 Hammerton p1446
 °Horowitz—Treas. p171-178
 °Kirkland—Achieved p45-51
 Lotz—Women p11-21
 °Moore—When p58-65
 Muir—Women p191-193
 New Yorker June 21,1930 p22-25
 °Stevens—Human p87-90,por.
 °Strong—Heroes p148-156
 °Strong—Of p255-262
 Thomas—Living Women p277-286,por.

Booth, Mary Devlin (1840-1863)
 Amer. actress
 Moses—Famous p42-43

Booth, Mary F. McVicker (1849-1881)
 Amer. actress
 Moses—Famous p49-52,por.

Booth, Mary Louise (1831-1889)
 Amer. journalist, translator, histor-
 ian, editor, author
 Adelman—Famous p200-201
 Dorland—Sum p18,115,134,176
 Hanaford—Dau. p686-687

Booth, Maude Ballington (1865-1948)
 Eng.-Amer. evangelist, social re-
 former
 Adelman—Famous p303-304
 Foster—Religion p222-257,por.
 Webb—Famous p49-57,por.

Booth, Mrs. (fl. 1860's)
 Amer. Civil war patriot
 Brockett—Woman's p769

Booth, Shirley (1907/09-   )
 Amer. actress
 Beaton—Persona p19,por.
 Blum—Great p125,por.
 CR '59 p89,por.
 CR '63 p66,por.
 Cur. Biog. '42 p96-97,por.
 Cur. Biog. '53 p81-84,por.
 Time Aug. 10,1953,p58,por.,cover

Boothe, Clare. See Luce, Clare Booth

Boott, Elizabeth (fl. 1870's-1900's)
 Amer. painter
 Waters—Women p55-56

Boozer, Mary (fl. 1860's)
 Amer. Civil war patriot
 Simkins—Women p63-64

Bora, Katherina Von (1499-1552)
 Ger. Christian, wife of Martin Luther
 Deen—Great p90-98

Borden, Ann
 See Hopkinson, Ann Borden McKean

Borden, Helen, Sister (fl. 1870's)
 Amer. nurse
 Irwin—Angels p157-158

Borden, Lucille Papin (b. 1873)
 Amer. novelist
 Women—Achieve. p41,por.

Borden, Mary (1) (b. 1886)
 Eng.-Amer. author
 Cooper—Authors p145-159,por.
 Hammerton p277
 Lawrence—School p265-268
 Overton—Women p42-48

Borden, Mary (2).
 See McKean, Mary (Maria) Borden

Borden, Mrs. (fl. 1770's)
 Amer. Rev. war patriot
 Ellet—Women (2) p352-253

Borden, Olive (c. 1907-1947)
 Amer. actress
 Herman—How p113,por.

Borden, Sylvia (1899-   )
 Amer. parachutist
 *May—Women p52,54

Bordereau, Jeanne ("L'Angevin"), (fl. 18th
   cent.)
 Fr. soldier
 Kavanagh—Women (2) p198

Bordoni, Faustina (Faustina Hasse) (1700-
   1793)
 It. singer
 Ferris—Great p7-32
 McCoy—Portraits p75,por.
 Wagner—Prima p71-74,238

Bordoni, Irene (c. 1893-1953)
 Fr.-Amer. actress
 Blum—Great p97,por.
 Settel—Radio p75,por.

Borg, Madeleine Beer (1878-1956)
 Amer. social worker humanitarian
 Women—Achieve. p194

Borghese, Pauline
 See Bonaparte, Maria Paulina Borghese

Borgia, Lucrezia, Duchess of Ferrara (1480-
   1519)
 It. politician
 Armour—It p60-68
 Cuppy—Decline p96-105
 Dorland—Sum p29
 Ewart—World's p103-110
 Hammerton p278,por.
 Kemble—Idols p79-90
 MacVeagh—Champlin p82

Borgia, Mary Borgia, Sister (fl. 1930's)
 Eng. nun
 Elgin—Nun p112-113,por.

Bori, Lucrezia (b. 1888)
 Sp. singer
 Even—Ency. p56-57
 Ewen—Living p53-55,por.
 McCoy—Portraits, p14,por.
 Time June 30, 1930 p34,por.,cover
 Women—Achieve. p51,por.

Boris, Ruthanna (1918-   )
 Amer. ballet dancer
 Atkinson—Dancers p16-18,por.

Bork, Florence L. Holmes (b. 1869)
 Amer. author
 Logan—Part p832

Borkh, Inge (1921/24-   )
 Ger. singer
 CR '59 p90,por.
 Rosenthal—Sopranos p11-12,por.

Borluut, Isabella (d. 1443)
 Belg. philanthropist
 Schmidt—400 p55-56

Borrero, Juana (1878-   )
 Cub. poet
 Rosenbaum—Modern p46-49

Borromeo, Clelia Grillo (fl. 17th-18th cent.)
 It. mathematician, linguist
 Mogans—Woman p77,142

Bortolan, Rosa (fl. 1840's)
 It. painter
 Waters—Women p56-57

Borzino, Leopoldina (fl. 1880's)
 It. painter
 Waters—Women p57

Bosboom-Toussaint, Anna Louise Geertruida
   (1812-1886)
 Nether. novelist
 Dorland—Sum p44,198

Boscawen, Frances (b. 1719)
 Eng. bluestocking
 Stenton—English p270-271

Boselli, Elizabeth (fl. 1950's-1960's)
 Fr. pioneer aviatrix
 *Lauwick—Heroines p29
 *May—Women p174

Bosio, Anigiolana (1830-1859)
 It. singer
 Lahee—Famous p88-89

Bosmans, Henriette (1895-1952)
 Nether. pianist, composer
 McCoy—Portraits p14,por.

Bosomworth, Mary Musgrove (1700-1760)
 Amer. colonial land negotiator
 Leonard—Amer. p112
 Spruill—Women's p242-243

Bosone, Reva Beck (n.d.)
 Amer. congresswoman, lawyer
 Cur. Biog. '49 p62-63,por.
 Roosevelt—Ladies p93-101

Bossidy, Mary (fl. 1930's)
 Amer. advertising executive
 Women—Achieve. p122,por.

Bostelmann, Else W. von Roeder (c. 1882-
1961)
Ger.-Amer. illustrator
Mahoney—Illus. p281

Boswell, Connee (fl. 1930's)
Amer. singer, actress
Donaldson—Radio p7-8
Lamparski—What. p186-187,por.

Boswell, Florence (fl. 1940's)
Amer. aviatrix
°May—Women p135-136

Boswell, Hazel (b. 1882)
Can. illustrator
Mahony—Illus. p281-282

Boswell, Martha (c. 1909-1958)
Amer. singer, actress
Lamparski—What. p186-187

Boswell, Vet (fl. 1930's)
Amer. singer, actress
Lamparski—What. p186-187,por.

Boteler, Helen (fl. 1860's)
Amer. Civil war musician
Andrews—Women p197-199

Bothwell, Jean (n.d.)
Amer. author
Cur. Biog. '46 p65-66,por.

Botssi, Despo (fl. 18th-19th cent.)
Gr. heroine
Schmidt—400 p219-220

Botta, Anne Charlotte Lynch (1820-1891)
Amer. author, foundress
Adelman—Famous p178
Dorland—Sum p39-40,77,109,172
Hanaford—Dau. p265-266

Bottome, Phyllis (1884-1963)
Eng. author
Lawrence—School p233-236

Bottomshaw, Mrs. (fl. 1746)
Amer. inventor
Club—Printing p16

Botume, Elizabeth Hyde (fl. 1860's)
Amer. Civil war patriot, teacher
Young—Women p304-305,368

Bouboulina, Laskarina (Lascarina) (1783-
1825)
Gr. patriot, sea heroine
Arsenius—Dict. p32, por.
Phila.—Women unp,por.
Schmidt—400 p218-219,por.
Stiles—Postal p36

Boucher, Hélène (d. 1934)
Fr. aviatrix
Lauwick—Heroines p13,160-179
°May—Women p125-127,por.

Boucherett, Jessie (fl. 1850's)
Eng. feminist
Bell—Storm p18-19

Bouchier, Dorothy (1910-   )
Eng. actress
Hammerton p283

Boucicault, Agnes Robertson (1832-1916)
Scot.-Amer. singer, actress
Coad—Amer. p202,por.
Moses—Famous p122-128,por.

Boudevska-Gantcheva, Adriana (b. 1878)
Bulg. actress
Stiles—Postal p37

Boudicca. See Boadicea, Queen

Boudinot, Annis.
See Stockton, Annis Boudinot

Bouguereau, Elizabeth Jane (1851-1922)
Amer. painter
Michigan—Biog. p54-55
Waters—Women p138

Bouillon, Duchesse of (fl. 1740's)
Fr., mistress of Maurice de Saxe
Haggard—Remark. p307-310

Boulanger, Lili (1893-1918)
Fr. composer
Elson—Woman's p249

Boulanger, Marie Elizabeth (b. 1810)
Fr. painter
Waters—Women p57

Boulanger, Nadia (b. 1887)
Fr. conductor, pianist, music teacher,
composer
CR '59 p91,por.
Cur. Biog. '62 p47-49,por.
Elson—Woman's p248-249
Ewen—Living p55-56,por.
McCoy—Portraits p15,por.

Bouquey, Madame (fl. 18th cent.)
Fr. religious leader
Kavanagh—Women (2) p193-194

Bourgeois, Florence (1904-   )
Amer. illustrator
Mahony—Illus. p282

Bourgeoys, Marguerite (1620-1700)
Can. Christian
Deen—Great p360

Bourgogne, Duchesse de (fl. 17th cent.)
Fr., sister-in-law of Philip V of
Spain
Haggard—Remark. p187-188,192-193

Bourignon, Antoinette (1616-1680)
Flem. visionary
Dorland—Sum p55,76,132

Bourke-White, Margaret (1906-   )
Amer. photographer
CR '59 p91-92
CR '63 p68,por.
Cur. Biog. '40 p862-863,por.
*Gersh—Women p185-204,por.
*Kirkland—Artists p34-35
Parshalle—Kash. p123-126,por.
*Stoddard—Top. p163-178
Taves—Success. p32-49,por.
Women—Achieve. p42-por.

Bourniquel, Camille (1918-   )
Fr. novelist
Peyre—French p406

Bourrillon-Tournay, Jeanne (1867-1932)
Fr. painter
Waters—Women p57-58

Boursetts, Madeline (fl. 1541-1556)
Fr. painter
Club—Printing p11

Boutell, Elizabeth (fl. 1663-1696)
Eng. actress
Wilson—All p120-122

Boutet, Anna Françoise.
See "Mars, Mlle," Ann Françoise
Hippolyte Boutet

Bouverie, Alice Astor.
See Obolensky, Alice Astor

Boves, Josefina (n.d.)
Amer. lawyer, politician
*Cherry—Portraits p166-168

Bovey, Catharine (1669-1726)
Eng. philanthropist
Stenton—English p236-237

Bovin, Madame Marie (fl. 18th cent.)
Fr. physician
Mozans—Woman p293-295

Bovy, Vina (1900-   )
Belg. pianist, singer
Ewen—Living p57-58,por.
McCoy—Portraits p15,por.

Bow, Clara (1905-1965)
Amer. actress
Brundidge—Twinkle p1-22,por.
CR '59 p92,por.

Hammerton p286,por.
Herman—How p9,por.
Wagenknecht—Movies p238-241,por.

Bowen, Ariel Serena Hedges (1849-1904)
Amer. musician, teacher
Schmidt—400 p28-29,por.

Bowen, Catherine Shober Drinker (1897-   )
Amer. author, lecturer
CR. 59 p92,por.
CR '63 p68,por.
Cur. Biog. '44 p61-63,por.

Bowen, Elizabeth Dorothea (1899-   )
Irish author
Breit—Writer p107-109
CR '59 p92-93,por.
Millett—Brit. p149-150

Bowen, Lota (fl. 1890's-1900's)
Eng. painter
Waters—Women p58-59

Bowen, Louise Hadduck deKoven (1859-1953)
Amer. philanthropist, social welfare
leader
*Ferris—Five p41-86,por.

Bowen, Marjorie.
See Long, Gabrielle Margaret Vere
Campbell

Bowen, Mary (fl. 1770's)
Amer. Rev. war patriot
Ellet—Women (2) p338

Bower, Bertha Muzzy, pseud. (1871-1940)
Amer. author
Cur. Biog. '40 p102-103,por.

Bowers, Eilley Orrum (1826-1903)
Amer. W. pioneer
*Miller—West p102-118

Bowers, Elizabeth (1830-1895)
Amer. actress
Logan—Part p778-779
Lotz—Unused p29-34

Bowers, Mrs. Faubion.
See Rama Rau, Santha

Bowers, Gladys Irene (m. 1944)
Amer. missionary
They—Went p138-139

Bowers, Sarah Sedgwick (fl. 1850's)
Amer. singer
Cuney-Hare—Negro p199

Bowie, Edith Hawks (fl. 1920's)
Amer., wife of Frank Hawks
Planck—Women p45

Bowles, Mrs. A. Lincoln (Nancy Hanks)
(fl. 1900's)
Amer. journalist
Ross—Ladies p482-483

Bowles, Ada C. (b. 1836)
Amer. clergyman, lecturer
Hanaford—Dau. p342,451

Bowman, J. Beatrice (gr. 1922)
Amer. Navy nurse
Pennock—Makers p61,por.

Bowne, Eliza Southgate (d. 1809)
Amer. diarist
Benson—Women p178,184-186

Bowron, Elizabeth Moore (fl. 1890's)
Amer. organization official
Logan—Part p466

Boyce, Westray Battle (1901-   )
Amer., Director of Women's Army
Corps
Cur. Biog. '45 p68-69,por.

Boyd, Anna Tomlinson (b. 1879)
Amer. pianist, music teacher
McCoy—Portraits p15,por.

Boyd, Christian, Lady **Hamilton** (d. 1646)
Scot. covenanter
Anderson—Ladies p36-49

Boyd, Elizabeth A. (n.d.)
Amer. accountant
MacCarthy—Women p36,255

Boyd, Belle (1844-1900)
Amer. spy, Civil war heroine
*Deakin—True p232-247
*Foley—Famous p106-121
Harkness—Heroines p3-4
Hoehling—Women p19-21,por.
Horan—Desperate p56-98,por.
Jones—Heroines p172-175,254-258,por.
Kane—Spies p129-155
Leetch—Reveille p156-158,274-275
432-433
*Sickels—Calico p209-253
Simkins—Women p79-80,273
Wright—Forgot p256-286,por.

Boyd, Louise Arner (b. 1887)
Amer. sci. explorer, geographer
Cur. Biog. '60 p48-49,por.

Boyd, Marion (fl. 1930's)
Amer. personnel director
Women—Achieve. p172,por.

Boy-Ed, Ida (1852-1928)
Ger. novelist
Hammerton p287

Boyer, Beatrice Alexander (m. 1919)
Amer. missionary
They—Went p62-63

Boyer, Lucienne (fl. 1930's)
Fr. singer
Hurok—Impres. p177-179

Boyer, Margaret (fl. 1860's)
Amer. Civil war patriot
Brockett—Woman's p736

Boyer, Sophie Ames (fl. 1930's)
Amer. club leader
Women—Achieve. p169,por.

Boyington, Mary K. (fl. 1860's)
Amer. Civil war nurse
Logan—Part p364

Boyle, Kay (1903-   )
Amer. author
Burnett—This p1125
CR '59 p94-95,por.
CR '63 p70,por.
Cur. Biog. '42 p101-104,por.
Lawrence—School p278,280
*Millett—Amer. p67-68,256-257
O'Brien—50 p860
Van Gelder—Writers p193-196
Warfel—Amer. p44-46

Boyle, Lady.
See **Henrietta, Countess of Rochester**

Boylston, Helen Dore (1895-   )
Amer. author
Cur. Biog. '42 p104-105,por.

Boylston, Sarah (fl. 1760's)
Amer. colonial businesswoman
Dexter—Colonial p109-110

Boynton, Helen Mason (m. 1871)
Amer. organization official
Logan—Part p460

Bozarth, Mrs. (fl. c. 1779)
Amer. pioneer, heroine
Fowler—Woman p97

Boznanska, Hélène Olga (b. 1865)
Pol. painter
Waters—Women p375

Bozzino, Candida Luigia (b. 1853)
It. painter
Waters—Women p59

Bracegirdle, Anne (c. 1663-1748)
Eng. actress
Collins—Great p85-107,por.
Dorland—Sum p167
Eaton—Actor's p192—195,por.
Izard—Heroines p373,375
MacQueen—Pope p101-108,por.
Wilson—All p122-127

Braceti, Mariana (fl. 1868)
    Puert. Ric. patriot
    Schmidt—400 p333-334,por.

Bracken, Clio Hinton Huneker (1870-1925)
    Amer. sculptor
    Taft—Women, Mentor #6

Bracken, Julia M.
    See Wendt, Julia M. Bracken

Brackenridge, M. Eleanor (fl. 1890's)
    Amer. feminist, humanitarian
    Logan—Part p420

Brackenridge, Marian (1903-   )
    Amer. sculptor
    National—Contemp. p32

Bracquemond, Marie (fl. 1870's)
    Fr. ceramic artist
    Waters—Women p60

Braddock, Amelia (fl. 1930's)
    Eng.-Amer. singer, teacher
    Women—Achieve. p144,por.

Braddock, Elizabeth (Bessie) Margaret
        Bamber (1899-   )
    Brit. politician
    Cur. Biog. '57 p66-68,por.

Braddon, Mary Elizabeth (1837-1915)
    Eng. novelist
    Adelman—Famous p214-215
    Dorland—Sum p37
    Hammerton p289,por.

Bradford, Alice (c. 1590-1670)
    Amer. Pilgrim
    Bell—Women p121-123,125,300-301
    Green—Pioneer (1) p113-142
    Marble—Women p101-105

Bradford, Charlotte (fl. 1860's)
    Amer., Civil war humanitarian
    Brockett—Women's p316, 731-732

Bradford, Cornelia (d. 1772)
    Amer. colonial publisher
    Brigham—Journals p75-76
    Dexter—Colonial p169
    Earle—Colonial p67-68
    Hanaford—Dau. p709
    Leonard—Amer. p112

Bradford, Dorothy (c. 1597-1620)
    Amer. Pilgrim
    Bell—Women p25-26
    Green—Pioneer (1) p141-142
    Logan—Part p32
    Marble—Women p54-55

Bradford, Mary (fl. 1860's)
    Amer., Civil war heroine
    Simkins—Women p71-72

Bradford, Susan (b. c. 1846)
    Amer., Civil war heroine
    Jones—Heroines p4-11,258-269,276-
        277,por.

Bradlee, Sarah. See Fulton, Sarah Bradlee

Bradley, Amy M. (fl. 1860's)
    Amer., Civil war nurse, teacher
    Brockett—Woman's p212-224
    Logan—Part p311
    Moore—Women p415-452

Bradley, Lillian Trimble (b. 1875)
    Amer. playwright
    Mantle—Amer. p274-275

Bradley, Lucretia (fl. 1850's)
    Amer. balloonist
    *May—Women p16-19,por.

Bradley, Mary Hastings (fl. 1940's)
    Amer. explorer
    Rogers—Women p141,por.

Bradley, Ora Lewis (fl. 1930's)
    Amer. teacher, artist, author
    Women—Achieve. p106,por.

Bradnox, Mary (fl. 1648)
    Amer. colonial physician
    Spruill—Women's p267-268

Bradstreet, Anne (1612-1672)
    Amer. colonial, pioneer poet
    Bell—Women p177-192,361-366
    Dexter—Colonial p126-130
    Dorland—Sum p47,181
    Douglas—Remember p34-36
    Hammerton p290
    Leonard—Amer. p103,112
    *McCallum, Women p33-40
    Witham—Pan. p19-20

Bradstreet, Martha (m. 1799)
    Amer. pioneer landholder
    Dexter—Career p195-196

Bradwell, Myra R. (1831-1896)
    Amer. pioneer lawyer
    Douglas—Remember p101
    Farmer—What p394-395,405
    Hanaford—Dau. p663,665,670
    Irwin—Angels p172-173
    Logan—Part p745-746
    Schmidt—400 p14-15,por.

Brady, Alice (1892-1939)
    Amer. actress
    Blum—Great p96,por.
    Marks—Glamour p282

Brady, Mary A. (1821-1864)
    Irish-Amer. philanthropist, Civil
        war humanitarian
    Brockett—Woman's p647-649
    Moore—Women p36-53

Brae, June (1918-   )
    Eng. ballet dancer
    Davidson—Ballet p28-29
    Haskell—Vignet. p49-50

Braeme (Brame), Charlotte Monica.
    See Clay, Bertha M.

Braeunlich, Sophia (b. 1860)
    Amer. govt. employee, secretary
    Logan—Part p863-864

Bragdon, Helen Dalton (1895-   )
    Amer. educator, organization official
    Cur. Biog. '51 p57-59,por.

Bragg, Mabel Caroline (1870-1945)
    Amer. health pioneer
    16 Amer. p69-72

Braham, Frances.
    See Waldegrave, Frances Elizabeth
    Anne Braham, Countess

Brahdy, Mina S. See Rees, Mina S.

Brainard, Bertha (fl. 1920's)
    Amer. radio personality
    Settel—Radio p47-48,por.

Braithwaite, Dame Lilian (1873-1948)
    Eng. actress
    Hammerton, p292,por.

Braman, Ella Frances (b. 1850)
    Amer. lawyer
    Logan—Part p746

Brambilla, Marietta Cassano D'Adda (1807-1875)
    It. singer, composer, music
        teacher
    Pleasants—Great p215,por.

Brame, Charlotte Monica.
    See Clay, Bertha M.

Branch, Anna Hempstead (c. 1875-1937)
    Amer. poet
    Cook—Our p154-155

Branch, Hazel E. (fl. 1918-1926)
    Amer. entomologist, teacher
    Osborn—Fragments p251,por.

Brandeis, Antoinetta (b. 1849)
    Bohem. painter
    Waters—Women p60-61

Brandram, Rosina (1846-1907)
    Eng. actress
    Hammerton p293

Brandström, Elsa (1888-1948)
    Swed. army nurse, humanitarian
    Phila.—Women, unp.,por.
    Stiles—Postal p38

Brandt, Caroline.
    See Weber, Caroline Brandt von

Brandt, Hilda. See X, Hilda

Brandt, Isabella (1591-1626)
    Belg., wife of Peter Paul Rubens
    Phila.—Women, unp,por.
    Stiles—Postal p38

Brandt, Marianne (Marie Bischof) (1842-c. 1921)
    Aust. singer
    Klein—Great p194-198
    Lahee—Famous p302-304
    Wagner—Prima p181,239

Brandt, Mary Elizabeth (fl. 1930's)
    Amer. author
    Women—Achieve. p194

Brandt, Molly (fl. 1760's)
    Amer. pioneer
    Logan—Part p49-50

Brandwein, Gertrude (fl. 1930's)
    Amer. insurance executive
    Women—Achieve. p181,por.

Brannan, Sophie Marston (fl. 1930's)
    Amer. artist
    Women—Achieve. p194

Branscombe, Gena (b. 1881)
    Can.-Amer. composer, author,
        conductor
    ASCAP p50-51
    Elson—Woman's p249-251
    Ewen—American p39-41,por.
    Goss—Modern p82-90,por.
    Howard—Our p565
    McCoy—Portraits p15,por.
    Reis—Composers p47-48

Brants, Mrs. Gerard Carl (fl. 1940's)
    Aust., wife of physician
    Phila.—Women, unp.,por.

Branzell, Karin Maria (1891-   )
    Swed. singer
    Cur. Biog. '46 p70-73,por.
    Ewen—Living p59-60,por.
    McCoy—Portraits p16,por.
    Peltz—Spot. p21,por.

Brash, Marion (n.c.)
    Amer. actress
    TV—Person. (3) p44,por.

Brasher, Judith (fl. 1737)
    Amer. colonial bus. woman
    Dexter—Colonial p44

Blaslau, Sophie (1892-1935)
    Amer. singer

    (Continued)

Braslau, Sophie—*Continued*

Ewen—Ency. p61
McCoy—Portraits p16,por.
Saleski—Jewish p582-583,por.
Saleski—Wander. p395-397,por.

Brastow, Virginia (c. 1872-1952)
Amer. journalist, editor
Ross—Ladies p583-584

Bratton, Martha (d. 1816)
Amer. Rev. war heroine
Ellet—Women (1) p271-284
Green—Pioneer (2) p390-395
Hanaford—Dau. p61
Logan—Part p183-185

Brault, Kay. See Boyle, Kay

Braun, Annette Frances (b. 1884)
Amer. entomologist
Osborn—Fragments p251,por.

Braunwald, Nina Starr (1928-   )
Amer. surgeon
Silver—Profiles p47-53,por.

Bravo, Florence (Florence Campbell Ricardo)
(m. 1875)
Eng. criminal
Jenkins—Six p177-224

Braxton, Elizabeth Corbin (fl. 1770's)
Amer. pioneer, patriot
Green—Pioneer (3) p257-258

Braxton, Judith Robinson (d. 1757)
Amer. pioneer, patriot
Green—Pioneer (3) p256-257

Braxton, Mary Carter (fl. 1770's)
Amer. pioneer, patriot
Green—Pioneer (3) p258

Braxton, Mrs. (fl. 1840's)
Amer. pioneer
Fowler—Woman p263-274

Bray, Anna Eliza Kempe (1790-1883)
Eng. novelist
Dorland—Sum p37,83

Brayton, Lily (1876-1953)
Eng. actress
Hammerton p294,por.

Brayton, Mary Clark (fl. 1860's-1880's)
Amer. social reformer, Civil war
humanitarian
Brockett—Woman's p545-552
Hanaford—Dau. p418

Breck, Carrie Ellis (1855-1934)
Amer. author, song-writer
ASCAP p51-52

Breckinridge, Aida de Acosta (1884-1962)
Amer. organization official
Cur. Biog. '54 p114-116,por.
Cur. Biog. '62 p52
Women—Achieve. p62,por.

Breckinridge, Margaret Elizabeth (fl.
1860's)
Amer. Civil war nurse
Brockett—Woman's p187-199,por.
Jones—Heroines p312-313,por.
Logan—Part p311
Moore—Women p75-90

Breckinridge, Mary (c. 1877-1965)
Amer. nurse
Dolan—Goodnow's p319-320,por.
*McKown—Heroic p169-188
*Wright—Great p118-132

Breckinridge, Mary Hopkins Cabell
(fl. c. 1768)
Amer. pioneer
Logan—Part p68-69

Breckinridge, Mary Marvin (fl. 1930's)
Amer. photographer, politician
Women—Achieve. p125,por.

Breen, May Singhi (1949-   )
(Malia Rosa)
Amer. composer, author
ASCAP p52

Breen, Mrs. Patrick (fl. 1840's)
Amer. pioneer
Whitton—These p234,236-237

Breintnall, Hannah (fl. 1750's)
Amer. colonial merchant
Dexter—Colonial p28-29

Brema, Marie (Minny Fehrmann) (1856-
1825)
Eng. singer
Davidson—Treas. p34-36
Lahee—Famous p310-311

Bremer, Frederika (1801-1865)
Swed. novelist
Adelman—Famous p144-145
Dorland—Sum p31
Fifty—Famous p285-288
Hammerton p295,por.
Schmidt—400 p368-370,por.
Whitton—These (see index)

Bremer, Hester (b. 1887)
Fr. sculptor
National—Contemp. p32

Brennan, Ella (1925-   )
Amer. restaurant manager
CR '63 p73,por.

Brenner, Dora (fl. 1930's)
    Amer. club leader
    Women—Achieve. p65,por.

Brennig, Marie Coudert (fl. 1930's)
    Amer. wedding consultant
    Women—Achieve. p152,por.

Brent, Margaret (1600/03-1661/70)
    Amer. feminist
    Beard—Amer. p21-22
    Brooks—Colonial p59-73
    Bruce—Woman p26-28
    Dexter—Colonial p98-100
    Douglas—Remember p36-37
    Earle—Colon. p45-49
    Green—Pioneer (1) p283,299-311
    Irwin—Angels p5-6,173
    Leonard—Amer. p26,112-113
    Logan—Part p43-49
    Longwell—Amer. p1-30
    McCallum—Women p43-46,por.
    Spruill—Women p236-241

Brent, Mary (fl. 1638-1650's)
    Amer. colonial landed proprietor,
        colonizer
    Dexter—Colonial p98-99

Breshkovsky, Catherine ("Babushka")
    Russ. patriot
    Adelman p276-277
    *Hagedorn—Book p317-331
    Hammerton p295
    Lownsbery—Saints p46-79,por,cover
    Thomas—Living women p195-207,por.

Breslau, (Marie) Louisa Catherine (1856-
        1927)
    Swiss painter
    Waters—Women p61-63

Breslin, Patricia (n.d.)
    Amer. actress
    TV—Person (2) p42-43,por.

Bressler-Gianoli, Madame (1875-1912)
    Swiss singer
    Lahee—Grand p127,144-146

Breton, Ruth (n.d.)
    Amer. violinist
    McCoy—Portraits p16,por.

Brett, Catheryna (fl. 1700's-1720's)
    Amer. pioneer
    Green—Pioneer (1) p410-425

Brett, Margaret (fl. 1730's)
    Amer. pioneer
    Green—Pioneer (1) p418

Breval, Lucienne (1869-1935)
    Ger.-Swiss singer
    Ewen—Ency. p61-62
    McCoy—Portraits p16,por.

Brevard, Mrs. (fl. 1770's)
    Amer. Rev. war heroine
    Ellet—Women (1) p343-344

Brewer, Mrs. Griffith (fl. 1900's)
    Eng. pioneer balloon passenger
    *May—Women p30

Brewer, Theresa (1931-   )
    Amer. singer
    CR '59 p99-199,por.
    CR '63 p74,por.
    Popular Record p29,por.
    Stambler—Ency. p32-33
    TV—Person (1) p9-10,por.

Brewster, Cora Belle (b. 1859)
    Amer. surgeon, editor, author
    Logan—Part p739

Brewster, Fear.
    See Allerton, Fear Brewster

Brewster, Margaret fl. 1670's)
    Amer. colonial religious worker
    Jones—Quakers p109-110

Brewster, Mary (c. 1569-1627)
    Amer. Pilgrim
    Bell—Women p15-16
    Green—Pioneer (1) p139-140
    Logan—Part p32
    Marble—Women p11,60-61

Brewster, Patience (d. 1634)
    Amer. pioneer
    Green—Pioneer (1) p140

Brewton, Rebecca.
    See Motte, Rebecca Brewton

Brewton, Mrs. Robert (fl. 1770's)
    Amer. Rev. war patriot
    Ellet—Women (2) p89-92

Brett, Zena. See Dare, Zena

Brian, Mary (fl. 1920's)
    Amer. actress
    Brundidge—Twinkle p101-109,por.

Briant, Nila Mack (fl. 1930's)
    Amer. radio director
    Women—Achieve. p195

Bricci (or Brizio), Plautilla (fl. 17th cent.)
    Rom. painter, architect
    Waters—Women p63-64

Brice, Fanny Borach (1891-1951)
    Amer. actress, singer
    Blumce—Great p99,por.
    Cahn—Laugh p66-67,82,por.
    Cantor—As p33-36,por.
    Cur. Biog. '46 p73-75,por.

(Continued)

Brice, Fanny—*Continued*

    Cur. Biog. '51 p59
    Donaldson—Radio p8
    New Yorker Apr.29,1929 p25-27
    Settel—Radio p84-85,148,por.

Brick, Katherine (fl. 1950's)
    Amer. aviatrix
    *May—Women p195

Brickdale, Eleanor Fortescue.
    See Fortescue-Brickdale, Eleanor

"Bricktop" (Ada Smith) (1895-   )
    Amer. singer, dancer, cabaret owner
    CR '59 p100,por.
    CR '63 p74,por.

Brico, Antonia (1902-   )
    Amer. conductor, pianist
    Cur. Biog. '48 p61-63,por.
    Ewen—Living p60-61,por.
    McCoy—Portraits p16,por.
    Women—Achieve. p71,por.

Bridekirk, Lady (fl. 16th cent.)
    Scot. soldier
    Graham—Group p23

Bridewell, Carrie (c. 1879-1955)
    Amer. singer, actress
    Lahee—Grand p10-11

Bridge, Edith McKenney (fl. 1930's)
    Amer. club leader
    Women—Achieve. p55,por.

Bridge, Elizabeth Stirling.
    See Stirling, Elizabeth

Bridges, Ethel (1897-   )
    Amer. composer
    ASCAP p53

Bridges, Fidelia (1834-1923)
    Amer. painter
    Hanaford—Dau. p299
    Michigan—Biog. p57
    Waters—Women p64

Bridget (or Birgitta) (1302/03-1373)
    Swed. saint
    Blunt—Great p159-161
    Deen—Great p331-333
    Englebert—Lives p382-383
    Hammerton p297.por.
    Muir—Women p59-60
    Phila.—Women, unp.,por.
    Schmidt—400 p363-364,por.
    Sharkey—Pop. p105-110
    Stiles—Postal p231

Bridgman, Laura Dewey (1829-1889)
    Amer. blind, deaf-mute
    Dorland—Sum p24

    Holbrook—Dreamers p264,271-273
    Logan—Part p698
    Parton—Dau. p243-255,por.
    Parton—Noted p243-255,por

Briga (fl. 490's-520's)
    Irish, mother of St. Comghall
    Concannon—Dau. p48-50

Briggs, Berta N. (fl. 1930's)
    Amer. artist
    Women—Achieve. p120,por.

Briggs, Cora S. (n.d.)
    Amer. composer, organist, music
      teacher
    McCoy—Portraits p16,por.

Briggs, Dorothy Bell (n.d.)
    Amer. composer
    McCoy—Portraits p16,por.

Briggs, Mrs. M. M. (fl. 1860's)
    Amer. Civil war nurse
    Logan—Part p365

Briggs, Margaret Perkins (fl. 1900's-1920's)
    Amer. poet
    Smith—Women's p21

Briggs, Mary Blatchley (b. 1846)
    Amer. journalist, poet
    Logan—Part p861

Brigham, Susan S. (b. 1811)
    Amer. patriot
    Logan—Part p437

Bright, Dora Estella (b. 1863)
    Eng. pianist, composer, music
      teacher
    Elson—Woman's p138-139

Brigid (fl. 15th cent.)
    Irish saint
    Concannon—Dau. p32-38

Brigid of Kildare (c. 453-523)
    Irish saint
    Culver—Women p78-79
    Deen—Great p320-321
    Dolan—Goodnow's p88,por.
    Hammerton p299
    McCraith—Romance p18-25
    Schmidt—400 p241,por.
    *Windham—60 p156-158

Brill, Jeannette Goodman (c. 1888-1964)
    Amer. judge
    Women—Achiev. p75,por.

Brillon, Madame (fl. 1700's)
    Amer., friend of Benjamin Franklin
    Donovan—Women p85-89,91-93

Briney, Nancy Wells (1911-   )
    Amer. publisher, editor
    Cur. Biog. '54 p116-118,por.

Brink, Carol Ryrie (1895-   )
    Amer. author
    Cur. Biog. '46 p75-76,por.

Brinkley, Nell (c. 1888-1944)
    Amer. artist, journalist
    Cur. Biog. '44 p66
    Ross—Ladies p416-420

Brinton, Mary Williams (fl. 1940's-1950's)
    Amer. missionary, nurse
    *Dodge—Story p176-177,216-217,219-
    221

Brinvilliers, Marie Madeleine D'Aubray,
        Marquise de (c. 1630-1676)
    Fr. pioneer
    Haggard—Remark p148-152, 154-157
    Hammerton p300

Bristol, Margaret (n.d.)
    Amer. composer, singer, conductor,
        author, music teacher
    ASCAP p53-54

Bristow, Gwen (1903-   )
    Amer. author
    Cur. Biog. '40 p108-110,por.
    Warfel—Amer. p52,por.

Britain, Radie (1903/04-   )
    Amer. composer
    ASCAP p54
    Goss—Modern p347-359,por.
    Howard—Our p535
    McCoy—Portraits p17,por.
    Reis—Composers p51-53

Britt, May (n.d.)
    Swed. actress
    CR '63 p75, por.

Brittain, Vera (c. 1893-   )
    Eng. author
    Hammerton p300-301,por.

Brittano, Susannah (d. 1764)
    Amer. colonial teacher,
        philanthropist
    Dexter—Colonial p82

Brittany, Duchess of.
    See d'Ambrose, Frances, Duchess of
        Brittany

Britton, Barbara (1925-   )
    Amer. actress
    TV—Person (1) p105,por.

Britton, Pamela (n.d.)
    Amer. actress
    TV—Person (3) p28,por.

Brizio, Plautilla. See Bricci, Plautilla

Bro, Marguerite Harmon (1894-   )
    Amer. author
    Cur. Biog. '52 p70-71,por.

Broadbent, Bessie May (1895-   )
    Amer. entomologist
    Osborn—Fragments p252

Broadfoot, Eleanor.
    See Cisneros, Eleanora de

Broadhurst, Jean (1873-1954)
    Amer. author, bacteriologist,
        teacher
    Women—Achieve. p176,por.

"Broadway Rose" (fl. 1940's)
    Amer. professional beggar
    Zolotow—Never p13-28

Broadwick, Tiny (fl. 1910's)
    Amer. parachutist
    *May—Women p52

Brochester, Ruth (fl. 1930's)
    Amer. lawyer
    Women—Achieve. p170,por.

Brock, Blanche Kerr (b. 1888)
    Amer. composer, hymn writer
    ASCAP p54-55

Brock, Emma Lillian (b. 1886)
    Amer. author, illustrator
    Mahony—Illus. p285

Brockman, Zoe Kincaid (1893-   )
    Amer. poet, journalist, poet
    Hoyle—Tar p11-13,por.

Brockway, Marion T. (fl. 1900's)
    Amer. nurse
    Pennock—Makers p88,por.

Brod, Ruth. See Hagy, Ruth Geri

Brode, Mildred Hooker (1900-   )
    Amer. librarian, organization
        official
    Cur. Biog. '63, p45-47,por.

Brody, Catherine (fl. 1930's)
    Amer. journalist
    Ross—Ladies p116-117

Broglie, Albertine Ida Gustavine de Staël,
        Duchesse de (1797-1838)
    Fr. author
    Ravenal—Women p189-196,por.

Brohan, Augustine Susanne (1807-1887)
    Fr. actress
    Hammerton p302,por.

Broido, Mademoiselle (gr. 1903)
    Fr.-Russ. pioneer ship physician
    Lovejoy—Women p256

Brokaw, Katherine F. (fl. 1920's-1930's)
    Amer. pediatrician
    Women—Achieve. p97,por.

Bromall, Anna E. (fl. 1880's)
    Amer. physician
    Hanaford—Dau. p557

Bromhall, Winifred (fl. 1920's-1940's)
    Eng.-Amer. illustrator
    Mahony—Illus. p285

Bromley, Dorothy Dunbar (1896-   )
    Amer. editor, author, journalist
    Cur. Biog. '46 p76-78,por.
    Women—Achieve. p44,por.

Bronsart, Ingeborg von (1840-1913)
    Russ. composer, pianist
    Elson—Woman's p220-225,238,por.
    McCoy—Portraits p17,por.

Bronson, Betty (fl. 1920's)
    Amer. actress
    Wagenknecht—Movies p229,por.

Brontë, Anne (1820-1849)
    Eng. novelist
    Adelman—Famous p138
    Bald—Women p35-37
    *Cournos—British p53-59,por.
    *Green—Authors p82-84
    Hammerton p303,por.
    Howe—Galaxy p105-111
    Johnson—Women p184-186
    Oliphant—Women p1-59
    *Pringle—When p86-102,por.
    Wellington—Women p37-42,por.

Brontë, Charlotte (1816-1855)
    Eng. novelist
    Abbott—Notable p392-396
    Adelman—Famous p139-140
    Bald—Women p28-34,38-76
    *Cournos—British p53-59
    Dorland—Sum p47,195
    Fifty—Famous p249-256,por.
    Fitzhugh—Concise p69-70
    *Green—Authors p81-85,por.
    Hammerton p303,por.
    Hinckley—Ladies p121-172
    Howe—Galaxy p93-99
    Hubbard—Little p115-144,por.
    Johnson—Women p164-178
    Lawrence—School p60-88,por.
    Love—Famous p15
    *MacVeagh—Champlin p88-89
    Massingham—Great p47-58
    Maurice—Makers p12
    Moore—Disting. p123-132

Oliphant—Women p1-59
Parton—Dau. p28-48
Parton—Noted p624-646,por.
*Pringle—When p86-102,por.
Schmidt—400 p150-151,por.
Stebbins—Victorian p49-91,210-213
*Steedman—When p279-288
Thomas—Living Women p97-110,por.
Wellington—Women p42-48,por.

Brontë, Emily Jane (1818-1848)
    Eng. novelist
    Adelman—Famous p138
    Bald—Women p28-34,77-99
    *Cournos—British p53-59
    Fitzhugh—Concise p69-70
    Hammerton p303,por.
    Hinckley—Ladies p175-211
    Howe—Galaxy p99-105
    Johnson—Women p179-184
    Lawrence—School p60-88,por.
    MacCarthy—Women p14
    Massingham—Great p59-74
    Moore—Disting. p109-121
    Oliphant—Women p1-59
    Parton—Dau. p28
    Parton—Noted p624-646
    *Pringle—When p86-102
    Sitwell—Women p35-36,por.
    Untermeyer—Lives p515-518
    Wellington—Women p49-57,por.

Brooke, Frances Moore (1724-1789)
    Eng. author
    Hammerton p304
    MacCarthy—Later p70-73

Brooks, Erica May (fl. 1920's-1930's)
    Eng.-Amer. athlete, lecturer
    Women—Achieve. p92,por.

Brooks, G. Anne (fl. 1930s)
    Amer. playwright, play producer
    Women—Achieve. p148,por.

Brooks, Geraldine (1925-   )
    Amer. actress
    TV—Person. (1) p30-31,por.

Brooks, Gwendolyn (1917-   )
    Amer. poet
    Adams—Great p128,por.
    *Cherry—Portraits p153-155
    CR '63 p76,por.
    Cur. Biog. '50 p72-74,por.
    Dreer—Amer. p89
    Robinson—Hist. p167,por.
    *Rollins—Famous p14, 87-91,por.

Brooks, Harriet (1876-1933)
    Can. chemist
    Weeks—Discovery p815,por.

Brooks, Maria Gowan (Maria del Occidente, pseud) (c. 1794-1845)
Amer. poet
Dexter—Career p95

Brooks, Marie Sears (d. 1893)
Amer. poet
Logan—Part p856

Brooks, Mary Frances (fl. 1860's)
Amer. Civil war diarist
Jones—Heroines p171-172

Brooks, Matilda Moldenhauser (n.d.)
Amer. physiologist, biologist
Cur. Biog. '41 p108-109,por.

Brooks, Nona L. (fl. 1930's)
Amer. clergyman
Bindheim—Women p108,por.

Brooks, Rosa Paul (n.d.)
Amer. librettist
Dreer—Amer. p90

Broomall, Anna E. (1847-1931)
Amer. physician
Mead—Medical p29-31,por.

Broomhall, Mrs. Addison F. (fl. 1900's)
Amer. club leader
Logan—Part p402-403

Brophy, Sallie (c. 1930-   )
Amer. actress
TV—Person (1) p35,por.

Brosnan, Mary (fl. 1930's)
Amer. business executive, window
display designer
Women—Achieve. p157,por.

Broster, Dorothy Kathleen (1877-1950)
Eng. author
Brittain—Women p105,156,249

Brothers, Joyce (1928-   )
Amer. psychologist
CR '59 p104,por.
CR '63 p77,por.

Brotherton, Alice Williams (d. 1930)
Amer. author, lecturer
Logan—Part p811

Brough, Elizabeth. See **Dare, Helen,** pseud.

Brough, Louise Althea (1923-   )
Amer. tennis player
CR '59 p104,por.
Cur. Biog. '48 p69-72,por.

Brough, Mary (1863-c. 1934)
Eng. actress
Hammerton p305,por.

Broughton, Elizabeth (fl. 17th cent.)
Eng. courtesan
Aubrey—Brief p40-41

Broughton, Julia (n.d.)
Amer. organist, music teacher
McCoy—Portraits, p17,por.

Broughton, Phyllis (c. 1862-1926)
Eng. actress, dancer
Wyndham—Chorus p164-165,por.

Broughton, Rhoda (1840-1920)
Eng. novelist
Black—Notable p37-44,por.
Hammerton p306

Brouwenstijn, Gré (1915-   )
Nether. singer
Davidson—Treas. p36-37,por.
Rosenthal—Sopranos p13-14,por.

Brower, Harriette (1869-1928)
Amer. pianist, music teacher, author
McCoy—Portraits p17,por.

Brown, Agnes (fl. 1920's)
Amer. painter
Waters—Women p66

Brown, Alberta Louise (1894-   )
Amer. librarian
Cur. Biog. '58 p63-65,por.

Brown, Alice (1857-1948)
Amer. author
Adelman—Famous p288
Cook—Our p152-154
Maurice—Makers p3
Overton—Women p49-54
Williams—Our p1-21

Brown, Annie Florence (fl. 1920's)
Amer. club leader
Binheim—Women p28,por.

Brown, Annie Williams (fl. 1940's)
Amer. singer
Cuney-Hare—Negro p385-386,por.

Brown, Antoinette.
See **Blackwell, Antoinette Brown**

Brown, Barnetta (1859-1938)
Amer. author, music-writer
ASCAP p57

Brown, Mrs. Charles S. (fl. 1890's)
Amer. golfer
Rogers—Women p60

Brown, Charlotte Blake (gr. 1874)
Amer. physician
Lovejoy—Women p58,103-106,129,por.

Brown, Charlotte Goudrey (n.d.)
Amer. gardener
*Ferris—Girls p119-130

Brown, Charlotte Harding.
See Harding, Charlotte

Brown, Charlotte Hawkins (1883-1961)
Amer. educator
*Cherry—Portraits p30-34
Daniel—Women p133-163,por.
*Hughes—First p45,por.
Robinson—Hist. p167-168,por.

Brown, Corinne Stubbs (b. 1849)
Amer. sociologist, teacher
Logan—Part p593

Brown, Demetra Vaka. See Vaka, Demetra

Brown, Dianthe (d. c. 1832)
Amer., wife of John Brown
Izant—Ohio p183-225

Brown, Dame Edith Mary (1864-1956)
Eng. physician
Lovejoy—Women p226

Brown, Eleanor Stockstrom (fl. 1930's)
Amer. interior decorator, business
executive
Women—Achieve. p186,por.

Brown, Elizabeth Carolyn Seymour
(fl. 1890's-1900's)
Amer. club leader
Logan—Part p473

Brown, Emma Crane (fl. 1930's)
Amer. club leader
Women—Achieve. p195

Brown, Esther Lucile (fl. 1940's)
Amer. nurse, educator
Dolan—Goodnow's p331-334,por.

Brown, Frances Fowke (m. 1710)
Amer. pioneer
Green—Pioneer (3) p221-223

Brown, Frances Jane (1819-1914)
Amer. social reformer
Brown—Home. p71-80,por.

Brown, Hallie Quinn (1849-1949)
Amer. teacher
Robinson—Hist. p168-169,por.

Brown, Hannah (fl. 1770's)
Amer. innkeeper
Dexter—Career p116-117

Brown, Helen Dawes (1857-1941)
Amer. author
Cur. Biog. '41 p113-114

Brown, Helen Gurley (1922-   )
CR "63 p78,por.

Brown, Ida Prescott Bigelow Eldredge
(c. 1864-1950)
Amer. social welfare leader
Lotz—Unused p35-42

Brown, Ina Corinne (fl. 1950's)
Amer. educator, anthropologist
Murrow—This (1) p17-18

Brown, Jane Gillespie (b. 1740)
Amer. W. pioneer
Ellet—Pioneer p79-106
Logan—Part p76-82

Brown, Justine (fl. 1930's-1940's)
Amer. mariner
Snow—Women p235-239

Brown, Kate Louise (1857-1921)
Amer. author, composer
Logan—Part p859

Brown, Katharine (fl. 1930's)
Amer. motion picture executive,
editor
Women—Achieve. p125,por.

Brown, Katharine Holland (fl. 1900's-1910's)
Amer. novelist
Maurice—Makers p11,por.

Brown, Laura A. (1874-1924)
Amer. politician, club leader
Brown—Home p237-239,por.

Brown, Lilian Mabel Alice Roussel, Lady
Richmond (c. 1883-1946)
Eng. explorer
*Bridges—Heroes p19-31,por.

Brown, Maria Foster (fl. 1800's)
Amer. W. pioneer
Beard—Amer. p91-102

Brown, Marion (1908-   )
Amer. author
Hoyle—Tar p15-19,por.

Brown, Martha McClellan (1838-1916)
Amer. social reformer
Logan—Part p672

Brown, Mary. See Crowell, Mary

Brown, Mary Anne Day (1816-1884)
Amer. pioneer, wife of John Brown
Izant—Ohio p183-225
Whitton—These p154

Brown, Mary Buckman (1740-1824)
Amer. Rev. war heroine
Logan—Part p120

Brown, Mary Helen (d. 1937)
Amer. composer
McCoy—Portraits p17,por.

Brown, Mary Somerville (gr. 1925)
Eng. controller, BBC
Brittain—Women p177,252

Brown, Nancy (c. 1870-1948)
Amer. journalist
°Plumb—Lives p173-194
Ross—Ladies p84, 532-534

Brown, Nancy M. Nelson (fl. 1860's)
Amer. Civil war nurse
Logan—Part p364

Brown, Olympia (1835-1926)
Amer. clergyman, feminist
Douglas—Remember p99-100
Hanaford—Dau. p349,367-368,445-446
Riegel p119-120,189

Brown, Pamela (1917-)
Eng. actress
CR '59 p106,por.
Time Nov. 20, 1950 p28,por.,cover

Brown, Rachel Fuller (1898-)
Amer. biochemist
°Yost—Women Mod. p64-79,por.

Brown, Sarah (fl. 1750's)
Amer. colonial business woman
Dexter—Colonial p44-45

Brown, Sarah J. (fl. 1930's)
Amer. sales manager
Women—Achieve. p170,por.

Brown, Sonia Gordon (1890-)
Russ. sculptor
National—Contemp. p35

Brown, Susan L. McLaughlin (fl. 1860's)
Amer. Civil war nurse
Logan—Part p364-365

Brown, Tabitha Moffat (b. 1780)
Amer. W. pioneer
°Miller—West. p32-44

Brown, Vanessa (1928-)
Amer. actress
TV—Person (2) p76-77,por.

Brown, Willa B. (fl. 1930's-1940's)
Amer. aviatrix
°May—Women p170
°Peckham—Women p35-36,por.

Brown, Winifred (1900-)
Eng. pioneer aviatrix
Hammerton p308,por.
°May—Women p103-104

Brown, Winnifred (fl. 1930's)
Amer. educator
Women—Achieve. p76,por.

Brown, Zaidee Mabel (1875-1950)
Amer. librarian, editor, lecturer
Bul. of Bibl. Sept.-Dec. '45 p169-170,por.

Brown-Potter, Cora Urquhart (b. 1859)
Amer. actress
Hammerton p311
Pearson—Marry. p168

Browne, Charlotte (fl. c. 1750's)
Amer. colonial nurse
Leonard—Amer. p113

Browne, Coral Edith (1913-)
Austral. actress
Cur. Biog. '59 p49-51,por.

Browne, Henrietta Bouteiller (1829-1901)
Fr. painter
Waters—Women p66-67

Browne, Irene (1896-1965)
Eng. actress
Hammerton p308

Browne, Mary Mumpere Shaver.
See Shaver, Mary Mumpere

Browne, Matilda (b. 1869)
Amer. sculptor, painter
National—Contemp. p34
Waters—Women p65-66

Browne, Nina Eliza (b. 1860)
Amer. librarian, editor
Logan—Part p719

Browne, Dame Sidney Jane (1850-1941)
Brit. nurse
Cur. Biog. '41 p114

Brownell, Gertrude Hall (b. 1863)
Amer. novelist
Smith—Women's p100

Brownell, Kady (b. 1842)
Amer. Civil war soldier, heroine
Brockett—Woman's p773-774
Hanaford—Dau. p196-197
Harkness—Heroines p11
Leetch—Reveille p69,106
Moore—Women p54-64,por.
Young—Women (see index), por.247

Brownfield, Abigail. See Phillips, Abigail

Browning, Elizabeth Barrett(1806/09-
1861)
Eng. poet
Abbot—Notable p377-381
Adelman—Famous p141-142,por.

(Continued)

Browning, Elizabeth Barrett—*Continued*

Bald—Women p209-232
*Bolton—Lives p107-119,por.
Bottrall—Pers. p109-111,217
Cockran—Romance p370-377
Davenport—Great p147-154
Dorland—Sum p28,178
Fitzhugh—Concise p73-75
*Galloway—Roads p298-313,por.
Hammerton p309,por.
Hinckley—Ladies p215-276
Hubbard—Little p5-39,por.
*Humphrey—Elizabeths p108-130
*MacVeagh—Champlin p90-91,por.
Moore—Disting. p175-187
Muir—Women p176-177
Parton—Dau. p61-70
Schmidt—400 p149-150,por.
Sewell—Brief p153-154
Sherman—World's p192-200
Thomas—Living Women p129-143,por.
Untermeyer—Lives p478-493
Untermeyer—Path p162-170,por.
Wellington—Women p21-33

Browning, Lady.
See Du Maurier, Daphne, Lady Browning

Browning, Lucielle (1913-   )
Amer. singer
McCoy—Portraits p18,por.
Peltz—Spot. p101

Browning, Marge (fl. 1930's)
Amer. milliner
Women—Achieve. p170,por.

Browning, Sarah Anna Wiedemann (d. 1849)
Eng., mother of Robert Browning
Peyton—Mothers p60-68

Browning, Sarianna (d. 1903)
Eng., sister of Robert Browning
Pomeroy—Little p143-179

Brownlow, Kate (fl. 1745)
Irish-Amer. colonial teacher
Dexter—Colonial p82-83

Brownscombe, Jennie (b. 1850)
Amer. artist
Waters—Women p64-65

Brownson, Josephine Van Dyke (1880-1942)
Amer. educator, cathechist
Burton—Valiant p93-111
Cur. Biog. '40 p113-114,por.

Brozia, Zina (fl. 1910's)
Fr. singer
Lahee—Grand p387-388,413-414

Bruce, Alice Moore (d. 1951)
Eng. educator
Brittain—Women p62,90-91,180,210

Bruce, Azealia (fl. 1880's)
Amer. W. pioneer
Sargent—Pioneers p62,por.

Bruce, Elizabeth M. (fl. 1880's)
Amer. clergyman, author, editor
Hanaford—Dau. p451

Bruce, Mrs. Victor (m. 1926)
Brit. sportswoman
Hammerton p312

Bruch, Hilde (fl. 1930's)
Amer. physician
Women—Achieve. p182,por.

Bruenn, Anna Rosa (fl. 1930's)
Amer. dentist
Women—Achieve. p188,por.

Bruff, Nancy (n.d.)
Amer. author
Warfel—Amer. p56,por.

Brunauer, Esther Caukin (1901-1959)
Amer. govt. official, U.N. official
Cur. Biog. '47 p71-72,por.
Cur. Biog. '59 p53

Brune, Aimée Pagès (1803-1866)
Fr. painter
Waters—Women p68

Brunhilde (Brunehaut, Brunhild) (d. 613)
Austrasian queen
Arsenius—Dict. p35,por.
Hammerton p313
Muir—Women p101-104

Brunton, Laura May (fl. 1930's)
Amer. aviatrix, glider pilot
Planck—Women p276-279,por.

Brunton, Louisa, Countess of Craven
(c. 1785-1860)
Eng. actress
MacQueen—Pope p261-262,por.
Wyndham—Chorus p41

Brupbacher, Alice (fl. 1930's)
Swiss-Amer. bus. executive
Women—Achieve. p181,por.

Brush, Katherine Ingham (1902-1952)
Amer. author
Dodd—Celeb. p378-382
Lawrence—School p176-179
Van Gelder—Writers p296-298
Warfel—Amer. p56-57,por.

Bruson, Mary Blackmar (fl. 1860's)
Amer. physician
Dannett—Noble p343-345

Bruttia Crispina (fl. 180 A.D.)
  Rom., wife of Commodus
  Balsdon—Roman p147-148

Brux, Lady (fl. 16th cent.)
  Scot. soldier, patriot
  Graham—Group p23-24

Bryan, Mary Edwards (b. 1844)
  Amer. editor, club leader
  Logan—Part p874-875

Bryan, Sarah. See Chinn, Sarah Bryan

Bryant, Alys McKey (fl. 1910's)
  Can. aviatrix
  °May—Women p100
  Planck—Women p35-37,por.

Bryant, Anita (n.d.)
  Amer. singer
  °Kahn—Tops p36-43,por.

Bryant, Felice (1925-   )
  Amer. song-writer
  Stambler—Ency. p35

Bryant, Lane. See Malsin, Lane Bryant

Bryant, Louise (m. 1923)
  Amer. journalist
  Ross—Ladies p111,377-378

Bryant, Mary Broad (fl. 1790's)
  Brit. sea heroine
  Prout—Petticoat p53-56

Bryant, Rebecca.
  See Boone, Rebecca B.

Bryant, Sarah Snell (fl. 1780's-1790's)
  Amer., mother of William Cullen
  Bryant
  Peyton—Mothers p69-74

Bryant, Sophie (1850-1922)
  Brit. educator
  Hammerton p314,por.

Bryce, Elizabeth Marion, Viscountess
  (1853-1939)
  Eng. humanitarian
  Cur. Biog. '40 p115

Bryner, Edna (fl. 1930's)
  Amer. author
  Women—Achieve p133,por.

Buccleuch and Monmouth, Anne, Duchess of
  (1651-1732)
  Scot. literary patron
  Graham—Group p113-127,por.

Bucge (fl. 730's)
  Eng. abbess
  Stenton—English p16-18

Buchan, Elspeth Simpson (1738-1791)
  Scot foundress, religious leader
  Graham—Group p199-225
  Hammerton p315

Buchanan, Anna Elizabeth (b. 1836)
  Amer. editor
  Logan—Part p832

Buchanan, Annabel Morris (b. 1888)
  Amer. composer, editor, author,
  lecturer
  ASCAP p62-63

Buchanan, Annie R. (fl. 1930's)
  Amer. patriot, club leader
  Women—Achieve. p171,por.

Buchanan, Elizabeth Speer (fl. 1700's)
  Amer., mother of James
  Buchanan
  Hampton—Our p114-120

Buchanan, Ella (d. 1951)
  Amer. sculptor
  National—Contemp. p36

Buchanan, Frances.
  See Allen, Frances Buchanan

Buchanan, Mary Elizabeth (fl. 1930's)
  Amer. editor
  Women—Achieve. p82,por.

Buchanan, Mrs. Robert (fl. 1890's)
  Amer. club leader, organization
  official
  Logan—Part p475-476

Buchwalter, Mrs. Edward L. (fl. 1890's)
  Amer. club leader
  Logan—Part p402

Buck, Dorothea Dutcher (1887-   )
  Amer. organization official
  Cur. Biog. '47 p72-74,por.

Buck, Pearl Sydenstricker (1892-   )
  Amer. author
  Ames—These p157-163
  Beard—Woman p30-31,33-36
  Burnett—Amer. p546,por.
  Burnett—This p1126
  °Cooper—Twenty p291-307,por.
  °Cournos—Famous p85,por.
  CR '59 p110-111,por.
  CR '63 p82-83,por.
  Cur. Biog. '56 p82-84,por.
  Dodd—Celeb. p342-346
  Fitzgibbon—My p7-14
  °Heath—Women (4) p30,por.
  °Kirkland—Writers p39-52
  Lawrence—School p318-323
  McClintock—Nobel p602
  °Millett—Amer. p266-268

(Continued)

Buck, Pearl Sydenstricker—*Continued*

  *Muir—Writers p103-115,por.
  Murrow—This (1) p21-22
  Nobel—Man p127
  Parshalle—Kash. p219-221,por.
  Rogers—Women p108,por.
  *Seventeen—In p137-140,por.
  Van Gelder—Writers p26-28
  Warfel—Amer. p58-60,por.
  Witham—Pan. p306-308,por.

Buckland, Mrs. Frank (fl. 19th cent.)
    Eng., wife of naturalist
  Mozans—Woman p374-375

Buckley, Lettie E. Covell (fl. 1860's)
    Amer. Civil war nurse
  Logan—Part p363

Bucklin, Sophronia (fl. 1860's)
    Amer. Civil war humanitarian,
      teacher, nurse
  Brockett—Woman's p791
  Dannett—Noble (see index)

Buckmaster, Henrietta (1909-   )
    Amer. author, journalist
  Cur. Biog. '46 p79-80,por.
  Warfel—Amer. p60-61,por.
  Women—Achieve. p178,por.

Buckrose, J. E. (d. 1931)
    Eng. author
  Hammerton p317

Budevska, Adriana (fl. 1940's)
    Bulg. actress
  Phila.—Women, unp.,por.

Budny, Lorraine Girouard (n.d.)
    Amer. costume designer
  Epstein—Young p155-176

Budzinski—Tylicka, Justine (gr. c. 1900)
    Pol. physician
  Lovejoy—Women p173

Buechmann, Helene (b. 1849)
    Ger. painter
  Waters—Women p68

Buell, Sarah (fl. 1820's)
    Amer. author, editor
  Logan—Part p797

Bueno, Maria Ester Audion (c. 1940-   )
    Brazil. tennis player
  Cur. Biog. '65 p59-62,por.

Buff, Charlotte (1753-1828)
    Ger., friend of Goethe
  Hammerton p317

Bugbee, Emma (fl. 1910's-1920's)
    Amer. journalist
  Ross—Ladies p122-126,315-317,por.

Bugbee, L. A. (d. 1917)
    Amer. composer, music teacher
  McCoy—Portraits p18,por.

Bugg, Catharine Smiley.
  See Cheatham, Kitty

Buie, Mary Ann (fl. 1860's)
    Amer. Civil war patriot
  Simkins—Women p21

Bulette, Julia (1832-1867)
    Amer. W. pioneer
  Brown—Gentle p13,80-85,por.

Bull, Eliza (fl. 1840's)
    Amer. W. pioneer
  Ellet—Pioneer p374
  Logan—Part p95

Bull, Joyce (fl. 1950's)
    Russ. aviatrix
  *May—Women p237-238

Bull, Sarah Wells (fl. 1630's)
    Amer. pioneer landowner
  Green—Pioneer (1) p398-410

Bullard, Jennie Matthewson (fl. 1860's)
    Amer. Civil war nurse
  Logan—Part p365

Bullinger, Anna (c. 1504-1564)
    Swiss Christian
  Deen—Great p342-344

Bulloch, Martha Bulloch.
  See Roosevelt, Martha Bulloch

Bulloch, Mary Deveaux (m.c. 1760)
    Amer. Rev. war patriot
  Green—Pioneer (3) p320-322

Bumbry, Grace (1937-   )
    Amer. singer
  Cur. Biog. '64 p60-62,por.

Bumpus, Mary Frances.
  See Allitsen, Frances

Bumpus, Mercy Lavinia See Warren, Lavinia

Bunche, Olive Agnes Johnson (1885-1917)
    Amer., mother of Ralph Bunche
  Davis—Mothers p131-141

Bunker, Rachel (d. 1796)
    Amer. midwife
  Dexter—Career p36-37

Bunker, Zaddie (b. 1887)
    Amer. aviatrix
  *May—Women p199

Bunnell, Mrs. Henrietta S. T. (fl. 1860's)
    Amer. Civil war nurse
  Logan—Part p369

Bunting, Mary Ingraham (1910-   )
  Amer. microbiologist, educator
  CR '63 p84-85,por.
  Cur. Biog. '67 p46-48,por.
  Time Nov.3,1961 p68,por.(cover)

Bunyan, Elizabeth (d. 1691/92)
  Eng. Christian, wife of John Bunyan
  Deen—Great p367-369

Bunzel, Ruth (fl. 1930's)
  Amer. anthropologist
  Women—Achieve. p118,por.

Buonsigniori, Madonna Giovanna (fl. 1350's)
  It. philosopher, linguist
  Farmer—What p392

Burchenal, Elizabeth (gr. 1902)
  Amer. folklorist
  Women—Achievement p135,por.

Burdett, Clara Bradley (m. 1878)
  Amer. club leader
  Logan—Part p725

Burdett-Coutts, Angela Georgina (1814-
      1906)
  Eng. philanthropist
  Adelman—Famous p203
  Carey—Twelve p157-168,por.
  Courtney—Advent. p207-232,por.
  Dorland—Sum p49,83,130-131,133-134
  Furniss—Some p144-145
  Hammerton p321
  Parton—Dau. p151-158
  Parton—Noted p151-158,por.

Burdick, Nellie Follis (fl. 1920's-1930's)
  Amer. actress, feminist,
      philanthropist
  Women—Achieve p67,por

Burford, Beatrice (fl. 1930's)
  Amer. harpist
  Women—Achieve. p57

Burge, Dolly Sumner Lunt (b. 1817)
  Amer. Civil war essayist
  Dunaway—Treas. p283-284

Burgess, Abbie (b. 1839)
  Amer. lighthouse keeper
  Snow—Women p162-166

Burgess, Elizabeth Chamberlain (1877-1949)
  Amer. nurse, educator
  Pennock—Makers p94-95,por.
  Women—Achieve. p122,por.

Burgess, Hannah Rebecca Crowell
      (b. c. 1835)
  Amer. sea navigator
  Snow—Women p137-161

Burgh, Elizabeth de (d. 1360)
  Eng., The Lady of Clare,
      granddaughter of Edward I
  Sorley—King's p29-64

Burgh (or Burgo), Honora de (fl. 1680's-
      1700's)
  Irish heroine
  McCraith—Romance p154-172
  Concannon—Dau. p211-217

Burgundofara of Fara (d. 667)
  Fr. saint
  Englebert—Lives p131

Burgundy, Countess of.
  See Mahaut, Countess of Artois and
      of Burgundy

Burgwyn, Mebane Holoman (1914-   )
  Amer. author
  Hoyle—Tar p21,por.

Burke, B. Ellen (b. 1850)
  Amer. teacher, lecturer, editor,
      publisher
  Logan—Part p862

Burke, Billie (1885-   )
  Amer. actress
  Blum—Great p66,por.
  CR '59 p113,por.
  CR '63 p86,por.

Burke, Fielding, pseud.
  See Dargan, Olive Tilford

Burke, Hilda (fl. 1920's-1930's)
  Amer. singer
  Ewen—Living p66,por.
  McCoy—Portraits p19,por.

Burke, Marie (1894-   )
  Eng. actress
  Hammerton p325,por.

Burke, Marion E. (fl. 1950's)
  Amer. aviatrix, flying-school owner
  *May—Women p195-196,por.

Burke, Martha Jane Canary.
  See "Calamity Jane"

Burke, Maud Alice.
  See Cunard, Maud Alice Burke, Lady

Burke, Mildred (fl. 1930's)
  Amer. journalist, librarian
  Ross—Ladies p474-476

Burkhard, Julia L. (n.d.)
  Amer. music educator
  McCoy—Portraits p19,por.

Burks, Amanda (fl. 1860's)
  Amer. W. pioneer
  *Miller—West p194-203

Burks, Frances (fl. 1930's)
Amer. author
Women—Achieve. p195

Burleigh, Celia (fl. 1880's)
Amer. clergyman
Hanaford—Dau. p490-492

Burleigh, Mildred Cooke Cecil, Lady
(d. 1589)
Eng., dau. of Sir Anthony Cooke
Stenton—English p131-134

Burleson, Evelyn (fl. 1930's)
Amer. aviatrix
Planck—Women p174-175

Burlingame, Edith (fl. 1900's)
Amer. feminist
Woodward—Way p374-375,386,389-390

Burlingame, Lettie L. (gr. 1886)
Amer. lawyer
Irwin—Angels p177

Burnell, Helen M. (fl. 1860's)
Amer. Civil war nurse
Logan—Part p364

Burnet, Elizabeth (1661-1708/09)
Eng. religious author
Fifty—Famous p210-216

Burnett, Carol (1934-)
Amer. singer, actress
CR '63 p86,por.
Cur. Biog. '62 p64-66,por.

Burnett, Cynthia S. (fl. 1870's-1880's)
Amer. social reformer
Logan—Part p672-673

Burnett, Frances Eliza Hodgson (1849-1924)
Amer. author
Adelman—Famous p270-271
Hammerton p326
Harkins—Famous p27-42,por.
Harkins—Little p27-42,por.
Johnson—Women p7-34
Logan—Part p792,800-801
Maurice—Makers #1,por.
*Moore—When p66-73
Overton—Women p55-57

Burnett, Hallie Southgate (1908-)
Amer. author, editor
Cur. Biog. '54 p136-137,por.

Burney, Fanny (Frances Burney d'Arblay)
(1752-1840)
Eng. novelist
Adelman—Famous p114-115
Benson—Women p77-78
Bottrall—Pers. p138-139,217

Bradford—Women p67-87,por.
Dorland—Sum p39,74,82,174
Dunaway—Treas. p374-383
Fifty—Famous p134-145,por.
Hammerton p326-327,478,por.
Hinckley—Ladies p3-56
Keyes—Lives p203-218
*Kirkland—Writers p1-12
MacCarthy—Later p87-128
MacCarthy—Women p37-39,41
*MacVeagh—Champlin p33
Maurice—Makers p12
Melville—Regency p31-50
*Pringle—When p32-54,por.
Stenton—English p250-251,271-272,296

Burnham, Clara Louise (d. 1927)
Amer. novelist
Overton—Women p58-60

Burnham, Mary (b. 1881)
Amer. editor, librarian
Women—Achieve. p103,por.

Burns, Ann (fl. 1950's-1960's)
Brit. aviatrix, aeronautical engineer,
glider pilot
*May—Women p222-223,por.

Burns, Annelu (1889-1942)
Amer. violinist, music teacher,
music author
ASCAP p67

Burns, Eveline Mabel (1900-)
Eng. economist, educator
Cur. Biog. '60 p64-66,por.
Women—Achieve. p118,por.

Burns, Jean (1767-1834)
Scot., wife of Robert Burns
Hammerton p328,por.

Burns, Lucy (fl. 1910's)
Amer. feminist
Irwin—Angels p354-355,385-387

Burns, Marcia.
See Van Ness, Barcia Burns

Burr, Abigail. See Hall, Abigail Burr

Burr, Amelia Josephine (b. 1878)
Amer. poet
Cook—Our p195-196
Smith—Women's p8

Burr, Elizabeth.
See Jumel, Elizabeth Bowen

Burr, Eunice Dennie (1729-1805)
Amer. patriot
Green—Pioneer (3) p503-507,por.
Root—Chapter p65-78,por.

Burr, Frances (fl. 1930's)
    Amer. artist, mountaineer
    Women—Achieve. p108,por.

Burr, Kate (fl. 1930's)
    Amer. journalist
    Ross—Ladies p524

Burr, Theodosia Alston (1783-1813)
    Amer., daughter of Aaron Burr
    Abbot—Notable p263-267
    Bradford—Wives p89-124,por.
    Brooks—Young p84-129
    *Elson—Side (1) p146-148
    Logan—Part p251-253
    Orr—Famous Affin. II p56-59
    Sale—Old p247-258,por.

Burr, Theodosia Prevost (d. 1794)
    Amer., wife of Aaron Burr
    Orr—Famous p187,188
    Orr—Famous Affin. II p55-56

Burra (or Burroughs), Ann (fl. 1600's)
    Amer. pioneer
    Green—Pioneer (1) p97-100

Burroughs, Edith Woodman (1871-1916)
    Amer. sculptor
    Michigan—Biog. p61
    Taft—Women, Mentor (172) p10-11;
        #4,6

Burroughs, Marie (fl. 1890's)
    Amer. actress
    Strang—Actresses p291-298,por.

Burroughs, Nannie Helen (b. 1883)
    Amer. educator, bookkeeper, club
        leader
    Daniel—Women p107-132,por.

Burrows, Christine Mary Elizabeth (1872-
        1959)
    Eng. educator
    Brittain—Women p104,127,161,179

Burrows, Frances L. Peck (fl. 1880's)
    Amer. club leader
    Logan—Part p294

Burstein-Arber, Rebecca (fl. 1920's)
    Russ.-Israeli pianist
    Saleski—Jewish p705

Burt, Alene (fl. 1930's)
    Amer. business executive
    Women—Achieve. p178,por.

Burt, Katharine Newlin (b. 1882)
    Amer. author
    Warfel—Amer. p65-66,por.

Burt, Mary T. (fl. 1870's-1880's)
    Amer. social reformer, publisher
    Hanaford—Dau. p427,por.

Burton, Emma (1844-1927)
    Amer. missionary, author
    Phillips—33 p65-69

Burton, Isabel Arundel, Lady (1831-1896)
    Eng. traveller, author
    Blanch—Wilder p1-132,por.
    Bottrall—Pers. p113-116,217-218

Burton, Jean (n.d.)
    Can.-Amer. author
    Cur. Biog. '48 p81-82,por.

Burton, Virginia Lee (1909-1968)
    Amer. author, illustrator
    Cur. Biog. '43 p89-90,por.
    Mahony—Illus. p287

Burwell, Rebecca (fl. 1800's)
    Amer., friend of Thomas Jefferson
    Donovan—Women p206-209

Busa, (Paulina) of Canusium
        (fl. 220's B.C.)
    Apulian patriot
    Boccaccio—Conc. p150-151

Busbey, Katharine Graves (1872-1959)
    Amer. author, social reformer
    Logan—Part p856-857

Busch, Mae (c. 1902-1946)
    Austral. actress
    Brundidge—Twinkle p213-220,por.

Bush, Grace (n.d.)
    Amer. composer, poet, pianist,
        lecturer
    McCoy—Portraits p19,por.

Bush, Katharine Jeanette (b. 1855)
    Amer. zoologist
    Adelman—Famous p285
    Logan—Part p880

Bush, Sally (fl. 1800's)
    Amer., stepmother of Abraham
        Lincoln
    Parton—Dau. p19-27,por.

Bushnell, Adelyn (1894-   )
    Amer. actress, author
    Warfel—Amer. p68-70,por.

Bushnell, Sophie Walker Hyndshaw
        (m. 1878)
    Amer. organization official
    Logan—Part p456-457

Buss, Frances Mary (1827-1894)
    Eng. educator
    Hammerton p330

Bussenius, Luellen T. (fl. 1930's)
    Amer. author
    Women—Achieve. p67,por.

Bussiere, Tadema Whaley (1898-   )
Amer. playwright
Mantle—Amer. p277

Bustabo, Guila (1919-   )
Amer. violinist
Ewen—Living p69,por.
McCoy—Portraits p19,por.

Butcher, Fanny (b. 1888)
Amer. poet, journalist
CR '63 p89,por.
Ross—Ladies p407-408

Bute, Mary Wortley Montagu, Lady
(fl. 1700's)
Eng. hostess
Stenton—English p263-266

Butler, Lady Arthur (fl. 1890's)
Amer.-Anglo. beauty
Furniss—Some p159-160

Butler, Behethland (b. 1764)
Amer. Rev .war patriot
Ellet—Women (2) p111-123

Butler, Mrs. Benjamin (d. 1877)
Amer. actress, social leader
Logan—Part p286-287

Butler, Charlotte (fl. 1680's-1690's)
Eng. actress
Wilson—All p127-129

Butler, Clarissa (fl. 1880's)
Amer. educator, historian
Hanaford—Dau. p539,733

Butler, Eleanor, Lady (c. 1745-1829)
Irish recluse
Hammerton p330-331

Butler, Elizabeth Southerden Thompson
(1850-1933)
Eng. painter
Furniss—Some p92-93,por.
Hammerton p331
Waters—Women p68-70

Butler, Fanny.
See Kemble, Frances Anne ("Fanny")

Butler, Ida Fatio (1868-1949)
Amer. Red Cross nurse
Pennock—Maker p67,por.

Butler, Josephine Elizabeth (1828-1906)
Eng. social reformer
Hammerton p331
Schmidt—400 p157-159,por.

Butler, Lorine Letcher (fl. 1930's)
Amer. nature writer
Women—Achieve. p123,por.

Butler, Mary Newport (fl. 1830's)
Amer. physician
Dexter—Career p39-40

Butler, Mildred Anne (b. 1858)
Irish painter
Waters—Women p68

Butler, Rehethland Foote (b. 1764)
Amer. Rev. war patriot
Logan—Part p142-143

Butler, Sally (1891-   )
Amer. lawyer, organization official
Cur. Biog. '46 p86-88,por.

Butler, Sarah Hildreth (1816-1870)
Amer., wife of Benjamin Butler
Bradford—Wives p199-234,por.

Butler, Sydney Elizabeth Courtauld (d. 1954)
Eng., wife of Richard Austen Butler
Winn—Queen's p236-244,por.

Butler, Mrs. William (fl. 1850's)
Amer. missionary
Logan—Part p522

Butt, Dame Clara (1873-1936)
Eng. singer
Hammerton p332,por.
McCoy—Portraits p19,por.

Butterfield, Frances W. (fl. 1930's)
Amer. teacher
Women—Achieve. p174,por.

Butts, Mrs. (fl. 1880's)
Amer. journalist
Hanaford—Dau. p688

Buxton, Eugenia (fl. 1930's)
Amer. pianist
Ewen—Living p70,por.
McCoy—Portraits p19,por.

Byard, Dorothy Randolph (fl. 1930's)
Amer. artist, poet
Women—Achieve. p114,por.

Byerlee, Victoria Ann (fl. 1920's-1950's)
Amer. missionary
They—Went p59-61

Byers, Margaretta (1901-   )
Amer. fashion designer, author
Cur. Biog. '41 p124-125,por.

Byers, Ruth (fl. 1910's)
Amer. journalist
Ross—Ladies p180-182

Byington, Spring (1893-   )
Amer. actress
Blum—Television p109,por.

(Continued)

Byington, Spring—*Continued*

CR '59 p118,por.
CR '63 p90,por.
Cur. Biog. '56 p94-95,por.
TV—Person. (1) p148-149

Byns, Anna. See Bijns, Anna

Byrd, Evelyn (b. 1709)
Amer. colonial belle
Green—Pioneer (2) p35-36,80,por.
Sale—Old p56-63,por.

Byrd, Lucy Parke (c. 1704)
Amer. pioneer
Green—Pioneer (2) p80

Byrd, Mary Willing (fl. 18th cent.)
Amer. colonial bus. executive,
plantation manager
Spruill—Women's p307-308

Byrne, Catherine (c. 1897-)
Irish politician
Phelps—Men (2) '59 p42-43

Byrne, Doris I. (fl. 1940's-1950's)
Amer. politician
Roosevelt—Ladies p74-75

Byrne, Mabel (n.d.)
Amer. politician
Roosevelt—Ladies p69-75

Byron, Brook (n.d.)
Amer. actress
TV—Person. (1) p44-45,por.

Byron, Katharine Edgar (fl. 1940's)
Amer. Congresswoman
Paxton—Women p128

Byson, Mary (fl. 1860's)
Amer. Civil war diarist
Jones—Heroines p72-74,275-276

C

Caballaro, Fernan Bohl von Faber, pseud.
(1796-1877)
Sp. author
Schmidt—400 p356-357,por.

Caballé, Montserrat (1933-)
Sp. singer
Cur. Biog. '67 p50-53,por.
Pleasants—Great p351-352,por.

Cabot, Elizabeth Higginson (d. 1791)
Amer., wife of ship-owner
Dexter—Career p194-195

Cabot, Ella Lyman (gr. 1904)
Amer. teacher, author
Logan—Part p719

Cabot, Lydia Dodge (fl. 1790's)
Amer. landowner
Dexter—Career p195

Cabrini, Frances Xavier (1850-1917)
It.-Amer. saint
°Beebe—Saints p54-63
Burton—Loveliest p132-150
Deen—Great p406-407
Maynard—Great p211-222
Pennock—Makers p23
Thomas—Modern p274-282

Caccia (b. 1759)
Rom. composer
Dorland—Sum p159

Caccini, Francesca (la Cecchina) (b. 1581)
It. singer, composer, poet
Elson—Woman's p64-65

Caceres de Arismendi, Luisa (1800-1866)
Venez. patriot
Schmidt—400 p417,por.

Cadell, Jean (b. 1884)
Scot. actress
Hammerton p335-336

Cadell, (Violet) Elizabeth (1903-)
Brit. author
Cur. Biog. '51 p84-85,por.

Cadillac, Marie Therese Guyon (m. 1687)
Amer. Rev. war patriot
Green—Pioneer (3) p458-459

Cadwalader, Elizabeth Lloyd (fl. 1770's)
Amer. pioneer
Green—Pioneer (2) p198-199

Cadwalader, Wilhelmina Bond (m. 1779)
Amer. pioneer
Green—Pioneer (2) p199

Cadwalader-Guild, Emma Marie (b. 1843)
Amer. painter, sculptor
Michigan—Biog. p61-62

Cadwise, Mrs. David (fl. 19th cent.)
Amer. humanitarian, philanthropist
Farmer—What p362-363

Cady, Hannah McIntosh (1809-1911)
Amer. patriot
Green—Pioneer (3) p523-524

Caecilia Metella, "the bad" (fl. 45 B.C.)
Rom., daughter-in-law of
P. Lentulus Spinther
Balsdon—Roman p55,264

Caecilia, Metella, "the good" (fl. 90 B.C.)
Rom. prophetess
Balsdon—Roman p249

Caenis, Antonia (fl. 50 A.D.)
Rom., concubine of Vespacian
Balsdon—Roman p131,232

Caesonia, Milonia (fl. c. 30-40 A.D.)
Rom. empress
McCabe—Empr. p55-56,59
Serviez-Roman (1) p138-145

Caetani-Bovatelli, Donna Ersilia (fl. 1870's)
It. archaeologist
Mozans—Woman p324-327

Cafritz, Gwen Detre de Surnay (1912-   )
Hung.-Amer. hostess
CR '59 p120-121,por.
CR '63 p93,por.

Cahal, Mary (fl. 1860's)
Amer. Civil war diarist
Jones—Heroines p191-193

Cahill, Mary (fl. 1740's)
Amer. colonial dressmaker
Dexter—Colonial p41-42

Cahier, Sarah Jane Layton-Walker (1875-
1951)
Amer. singer
Lahee—Grand p328-329,351,por.
McCoy—Portraits—p20,por.

Cahill, Marie (1874-1933)
Amer. actress
Blum—Great p43,por.

Cahill, Mary F. (fl. 1930's)
Amer. teacher
Women—Achieve. p145,por.

Caillavet, Leontine.
See Arman de Caillavet, Leontine
Charlotte Lippman

Cain's wife (Biblical)
Lewis—Portraits p33

Caird, Alice Mona(d. 1932)
Brit. author
Hammerton p338-339

Cairns, May Emily Finney, Countess of
(m. 1884)
Eng. actress
Wyndham—Chorus p160-164

Calahan, Mary A. (fl. 1860's)
Amer. educator
Logan—Part p304

"Calamity Jane" (Martha Jane Canary;
Mary Jane Burke) (1850/52-
1903)
Amer. W. pioneer

Aikman—Calamity p3-127
Deakin—True p173-189
Brown—Gentle p256-257,por.
Holbrook—Little p31-38
Horan—Desperate p171-200,por.
Rogers—Gallant p345-363
Rogers—Women p55,por.

Calandrini, Madame (fl. 18th cent.)
Fr., friend of Mlle. Aisse
Kavanagh—Woman (1) p80-82

Calderone, Mary Steichen (1904-   )
Amer. physician
Cur. Biog. '67 p53-56,por.

Caldwell, Anne (1876-1936)
Amer. song-writer
Logan—Part p789

Caldwell, Mrs. Erskine.
See Bourke-White, Margaret

Caldwell, Hannah (d. 1780)
Amer. Rev. war patriot
Ellet—Women (2) p125-133
Green—Pioneer (2) p364-371
Green—Pioneer (3) p309
Logan—Part p172-173

Caldwell, Mary Gwendolin, Marquise of
Montriers-Merinville (m. 1896)
Amer. heiress
Eliot—Heiresses p157-163

Caldwell, Mary Letitia (fl. 1930's)
Amer. chemist
Women—Achieve. p180,por.

Caldwell, Mira (fl. 1870's-1880's)
Amer. editor
Hanaford—Dau. p618

Caldwell, Rachel (c. 1739-1825)
Amer. Rev. war patriot
Ellet—Women (2) p177-186

Caldwell, Sarah Campbell (1904-   )
Amer. organization official,
educator
Cur. Biog. '53 p104-105,por.

Caldwell, Taylor (1900-   )
Eng.-Amer. author
CR '59 p122,por.
CR '63 p95,por.
Cur. Biog. '40 p137-138,por.
Fitzgibbon—My p1-6
Warfel—Amer. p78-79,por.

Calegari, Cornelia (b. 1644)
It. singer, organist
Elson—Woman's p65-66

Calhoun, Eleanor, Princess Lazarovich-
    Hrebelianovich (c. 1864-1957)
    Amer.-Serb. author
    Hammerton p340
    Women—Achiev. p102,por.

Calhoun, Floride Calhoun (1792-1866)
    Amer. hostess
    Whitton—These p173-176

Calhoun, Rebecca. See Pickens, Rebecca

Calkins, Mary Whiton (1863-1930)
    Amer. philosopher, psychologist,
        author
    Logan—Part p793

Call, Annie Payson (b. 1853)
    Amer. author
    Logan—Part p859

Call, Emma Louise (fl. 1880's)
    Amer. physician
    Mead—Medical p48

Callaghan, Domini (1923-   )
    Brit. ballet dancer
    Davidson—Ballet p29-31

Callanan, Mrs. (fl. 1870's-1880's)
    Amer. lecturer, feminist
    Hanaford—Dau. p342

Callas, Maria Meneghini (1923-   )
    Gr. singer
    Brook—Singers p43-47
    CR '59 p123,por.
    CR '63 p96,por.
    Cur. Biog. '56 p98-100,por.
    Davidson—Treas. p38-39
    Ewen—Ency. p68-69
    Pleasants—Great p141-142,350-352,
        por.
    Rosenthal—Sopranos p15-16,25,por.
    Time Oct.29,1956 p60,por.,cover
    Wagner—Prima p5-6,239

Callaway, Inez. See Robb, Inez Callaway

Callcott, Maria, Lady (Maria Graham; Maria
        Dundas)
    Eng. governess, author
    Howe—Galaxy p136-151,por.

Callery, Mary (1903-   )
    Amer. sculptor
    Cur. Biog. '55 p97-98,por.

Callirhöe. See Kora

Calloway, Blanche (1902-   )
    Amer. orchestra leader
    *Cherry—Portraits p128-131,por.

Calloway-Byron, Mayme (fl. 1917)
    Amer. singer
    Cuney-Hare—Negro p234

Callowhill, Hannah.
    See Penn, Hannah Callowhill

Calpurnia (1) (from 59 B.C.)
    Rom. empress, wife of Julius Caesar
    Hammerton p341
    Serviez-Roman (1) p3-27

Calpurnia (2) (fl. 1st cent.)
    Rom., wife of younger Pliny
    Balsdon—Roman p195,206

Calvé, Emma 1858-1942)
    Fr. singer
    Adelman—Famous p300-301
    Cur. Biog. '42 p130
    Davidson—Treas. p40-42
    Downes—Olin p31-32
    Ewen—Ency. p69
    Ewen—Living p71,por.
    Hammerton p342
    Klein—Great p149-155,por.
    Lahee—Famous p236-243,por.
    McCoy—Portraits p20,por.
    Pleasants—Great p303-308,por.
    *Ulrich—Famous p35-41,por.
    Wagnalls—Opera p291-296,por.
    Wagner—Prima p80,104-105,239

Calvert, Adelaide (1836-1921)
    Eng. actress
    Hammerton p342

Calvet, Corinne (1925-   )
    Fr.-Amer. actress
    CR '59 p123-124,por.

Cam, Helen Maud 1885-1968)
    Eng. educator, historian
    Cur. Biog. '48 p88-89,por.
    Cur. Biog. '68 p453

Cama, Madame Bhikaiji (1861-1936)
    Ind. revolutionary
    Stiles—Postal p44

Camacho, Maria de Luz (n.d.)
    Mex. Christian heroine
    Husslein—Heroines p17-26

Camargo, Marie Anna de Cuspide (1710-
        1770)
    Belg.-Fr. ballet dancer
    Dorland—Sum p27,166
    Hammerton p343,por.
    *Terry—Star p26-36,por.

Cambridge, Augusta.
    See Augusta, duchess of Cambridge

Cameron, Anne (n.d.)
    Amer. author
    Bruère—Laugh. p177

Cameron, Kate (fl. 1930's)
    Amer. journalist
    Ross—Ladies p413-414

Cameron, Katharine (fl. 1940's)
Scot. illustrator
Mahony—Illus. p289

Cameron, Mrs. Lovett (fl. 1890's)
Brit. author.
Black—Notable p96-106

Cameron, Violet (1870's-1880's)
Eng. actress
Furniss—Some p55,por.

Cammaerts, Émile (1878-1953)
Belg. poet, patriot
Hammerton p344

Camp, Milicent Baldwin Porter (1750-1824)
Amer. patriot
Green—Pioneer (3) p500
Root—Chapter p291-297

Campan, Jeanne Louise Henriette Genet
(1752-1822)
Fr. educator
Dorland—Sum p17,110

Campbell, Ada. See Irwin, May

Campbell, Amelia M. (fl. 1930's)
Amer. business woman
Women—Achieve. p162,por.

Campbell, Grace MacLennan Grant (1895-1963)
Can. novelist
Cur. Biog. '48 p89-90,por.
Cur. Biog. '63 p56
Thomas—Canad. p18-20

Campbell, Helena E. Ogden (fl. 1930's)
Amer. painter
Women—Achieve. p152,por.

Campbell, Jane, Lady Kenmure (c. 1594)
Scot. covenanter
Anderson—Ladies p62-86

Campbell, Jane Cannon (1743-1836)
Amer. Rev. war patriot
Ellet—Women (2) p209-220

Campbell, Janet Montgomery (fl. 15th cent.)
Scot. religious reformer
Culver—Women p122-123

Campbell, Charlotte, Lady (1775-1861)
Eng. lady-in-waiting
Melville—Regency p109,por.

Campbell, Jane Corneigle (1763-1835)
Fr.-Scot. Christian leader
Deen—Great p375-378

Campbell, Jeanne Sanford (n.d.)
Amer. fashion designer
Epstein—Young p27-45

Campbell, Margaret (Margaret Bowen)
(fl. 1930's)
Eng. author
Asquith—Myself p41-64,por.

Campbell, Patricia Platt (1901-   )
Amer. author
Cur. Biog. '57 p95-96,por.

Campbell, Mrs. Patrick (Beatrice Stella
Tanner) (1865/67-1940)
Eng. actress
Blum—Great p32,por.
Coad—Amer. p295,por.
Cur. Biog. '40 p140,por.
Dodd—Celeb. p106-110
DuCann—Loves p260-274,por.
Eaton—Actor's p190-191
Hammerton p345,1447,por.
Marks—Glamour p283-284

Campbell, Ruth Elizabeth (fl. 1930's)
Amer. editor
Women—Achieve. p147,por.

Campbell, Toni (1944-   )
Amer. actress
TV—Person (3) p12-13,por.

Campbell, Valeria (fl. 1860's)
Amer. Civil war humanitarian,
author
Brockett—Woman's p594-595

Campbell-Bannerman, Sarah Charlotte Bruce,
Lady (m. 1860)
Eng., wife of Sir Henry Campbell-Bannerman
Iremonger—And p227-229,por.
Lee—Wives p233-248,por.

Canary (Canarry), Martha Jane.
See "Calamity Jane"

Candace (Biblical)
Deen—All p257

Canfield, Dorothy.
See Fisher, Dorothy Canfield

Canfield, Martha (fl. 1860's)
Amer. Civil war nurse
Brockett—Woman's p495

Caniglia, Maria (1906-   )
It. singer
Davidson—Treas. p43-44

Cannan, Mary (fl. 1763)
Amer. colonial business woman
Dextrer—Colonial p45

Cannan, Mary Ansell Barrie (d. 1950)
Eng. actress
Hammerton p195

Canaanite woman.
See Syro-Phoenician woman

Canning, Elizabeth (1734-1773)
Eng. perjurer
Hammerton p348

Cannon, Annie Jump (1863-1941)
Amer. astronomer
Adelman—Famous 299
Cur. Biog. '41 p132
Dorland—Sum p142
Hammerton p349
Progress—Science p86-87
*Yost—Women Sci. p27-43

Cannon, Ida Maud (1877-1960)
Amer. nurse, social worker, author
Dolan—Goodnow's p320-321,por.
Pennock—Makers p98-99,por.

Cannon, Josephine.
See Johnson, Josephine Winslow

Cannon, Mary H. (m. 1871)
Amer. whaling voyager
Whiting—Whaling p215,285

Cannon, Poppy (n.d.)
S. Afr.-Amer. food columnist
CR '63 p98,por.

Canova, Judy (1916-   )
Amer. singer
CR '59 p126,por.
Lamparski—What. p130-131,por.

Canth, "Minna" Ulrika Wilhelmina Johan-
sson (1844/48-1897)
Fin. author, feminist
Phila.—Women unp,por.
Schmidt—400 p166,por.
Stiles—Postal p45

Canziani, Estella L. M. (b. 1887)
Eng. illustrator
Mahony—Illus. p289

Cape, Judith (fl. 1940's)
Can. novelist
Thomas—Canad. p20

Capello (or Capello) Bianca (1542/48-1587)
It. courtesan
Mayne—Enchant. p18-36,por.

Cappe, Catharine Harrison (1744-1821)
Eng. hostess
Stenton—English p113-114,230,302-306

Cappello, Biana. See Capello, Bianca

"Captain Molly" (fl. 1770's)
Amer. Rev. heroine
Bruce—Woman p90-91

Cara (fl. 400's, A.D.)
Irish, mother of Brendan the
Voyager
Concannon—Dau. p52-53

Caraway, Glenrose Bell (fl. 1930's)
Amer. club leader
Women—Achieve. p105,por.

Caraway, Hattie Wyatt (1878-1950)
Amer. Senator
Cur. Biog. '45 p89-92,por.
Cur. Biog. '51 p93
*Heath—Woman p32
Paxton—Women p15-28,128

Carden, Mae (fl. 1930's)
Amer. educator
Women—Achieve. p160,por.

Cardwell, Sue Webb (fl. 1940's-1950's)
Amer. missionary
They—Went p113-115

Carelli, Emma (1877-1928)
It. singer
Wagner—Prima p239

Carere, Christine (1931-   )
Fr. actress
CR '59 p128-129

Carey, Annie Louise (b. 1942)
Amer. singer
Logan—Part p768

Carey, Emma Forbes (b. 1833)
Amer. humanitarian, author
Logan—Part p833

Carey, Ernestine Moller Gilbreth (1908-   )
Amer. author, retail executive
Cur. Biog. '49 p224-226,por.

Carey, Helen A. (fl. 1930's)
Amer. teacher, author
Women—Achieve. p160,por.

Carey, Ocean Daily (fl. 1930's)
Amer. educator
Women—Achieve. p132,por.

Carey, Rosa Nouchette (1840-1909)
Eng. author
Black—Notable p145,por.
Dorland—Sum p18,197
Hammerton p352,por.

Carl, Ann Baumgartner (fl. 1940's)
Amer. aviatrix
*May—Women p171

Carl, Katharine Augusta (f. 1890's-1900's)
Amer. artist
Logan—Part p758
Waters—Women p71-72

Carlén, Emilie Smite (1807-1892)
    Swed. novelist, feminist
    Adelman—Famous p156

Carlin, Dorothy A. (fl. 1930's)
    Amer. civil engineer
    Women—Achieve. p74,por.

Carlin, Mary (m. 1851)
    Amer. whaling voyager
    Whiting—Whaling p21-24,61-63,64-69

Carlingford, Frances.
    See Waldegrave, Frances Elizabeth
    Anne Braham, Countess

Carlisle, Alexandra (b. 1886)
    Eng. actress
    Hammerton p353

Carlisle, Anne (d. 1680)
    Eng. painter
    Waters—Women p72-73

Carlisle, Helen Grace (1898-   )
    Amer. author
    Lawrence—School p259-264
    *Millett—Amer. p289

Carlisle, Kitty (1914-   )
    Amer. actress, singer
    CR '59 p129,por.
    CR '63 p101,por.

Carlisle, Rosalind Frances Stanley Howard,
    Countess of (1845-1921)
    Eng. feminist
    Hammerton p353,por.

Carlon, Fran (n.d.)
    Amer. actress
    TV—Person. (1) p155-156,por.

Carlotta, Marie Charlotte Amelie (1840-
    1927)
    Mex. empress
    Hammerton p388
    MacVeagh—Champlin p115
    *O'Cleary—Queens p140-155

Carlyle, Jane Baillie Welsh (1801-1866)
    Eng. author, wife of Thomas Carlyle
    Adelman—Famous p151-152
    Bottrall—Pers. p170-172,218
    Guedalla—Bonnet p11-37,por.
    Hammerton p354-355,por.
    *Humphrey—James p169-189
    Orr—Famous Affin. IV p43-69
    Parton—Noted p172-193
    Ravenel—Women p50-52
    Sitwell—Women p30-32,por.
    Stebbins—London p159-189
    Steedman—When p103-109
    Winwar—Poor p200-203,291-292

Carman, Dorothy Walworth (1900-   )
    Amer. novelist
    Overton—Women p75

Carmichael, Amy (fl. 1900's)
    Irish poet
    Edman—They p37-43

Carmichael, Anne (d. 1840)
    Amer. belle
    Sale—Old p273-280,por.

Carnarvon, Countess of. See Losch, Tilly

Carnegie, Dorothy Reeder Price (1912-   )
    Amer. educator, author
    Cur. Biog. '55 p102-103,por.

Carnegie, Hattie (1889-1956)
    Aust.-Amer. fashion designer
    Cur. Biog. '42 p136-138,por.
    Cur. Biog. '56 p102
    Jensen—Revolt p98,102,por.
    New Yorker Mar.31,1934 p23-37,por.
    Profiles
    Women—Achieve. p58

Carnegie, Margaret Morrison (1810-1886)
    Scot., mother of Andrew Carnegie
    *Chandler—Famous p249-268
    Peyton—Mothers p136-144

Carney, Kate (1869-1950)
    Eng. actress, singer
    Leroy—Music p25-26

Carol, Martine (1924-   )
    Fr. actress
    CR '59 p131,por.

Caroline Bonaparte (Caroline Murat)
    (1783-1838)
    Fr., consort of Joachim Murat,
    King of Naples
    Weiner—Parvenu (see index), por.

Caroline Louise Marguerite (1957-   )
    Mon. princess
    Stiles—Postal p47

Caroline Matilda (1751-1775)
    Dan.-Nor. queen
    MacNalty—Princes p128-161

Caroline of Anspach (Wilhelmina Carolina)
    (1683-1737)
    Eng. queen
    Hammerton p357,por.
    Melville—Maids p11-60,por.
    Melville—Regency p74-91,121-147,256-
    276,por.
    Sanders—Intimate p161-170,por.
    Stenton—English p241-253-256

Caroline of Brunswick (Amelia Elizabeth
Caroline) (1768-1821)
Eng. queen
Dark—Royal p317-339,por.
*MacVeagh—Champlin p117
Sanders—Intimate p181-193,por.

Caron, Leslie (1933-   )
Fr. ballet dancer
Atkinson—Dancers p19-22,por.
CR '59 p131-132,por.
Cur. Biog. '54 p157-158,por.
*McConnell—Famous p95-106,por.

Carosio, Marghuerita (fl. 1920's-1950's)
It. singer
Davidson—Treas. p45-47

Carothers, Mina Hall (fl. 1930's)
Amer. advertising executive
*Ferris—Girls p93-104

Carpara, Clara H (fl. 1930's)
Amer. music teacher
Women—Achieve. p195

Carpenter, Caroline A. (fl. 1870's-1880's)
Amer. educator
Hanaford—Dau. p530-533

Carpenter, Mrs. Leslie (1920-   )
Amer. govt. employee, speech-writer
CR '63 p103,por.

Carpenter, Margaret Sarah (1793-1872)
Eng. painter
Dorland—Sum p45,155
Waters—Women p73-74

Carpenter, Mary (fl. 1600's)
Amer. pioneer
Bell—Women p122

Carpenter, Mary (1807-1877)
Eng. philanthropist, editor
Adelman—Famous p183-184
Dorland—Sum p37,120
Hammerton p357-358

Carpenter, Mildred Carver (fl. 1930's)
Amer. researcher, genealogist
Women—Achieve. p65,por.

Carpenter, Mrs. Philip (fl. 1900's)
Amer. club leader, lawyer
Logan—Part p403

Carpentier, Madeleine (b. 1865)
Fr. painter
Waters—Women p74

Carr, Alice G. (fl. 1930's)
Amer. nurse
Pennock—Makers p128,por.

Carr, Charlotte E. (1890-1957)
Amer. personnel manager, social
worker
Women—Achieve. p125,por.

Carr, Deborah Edith Wallbridge (b. 1854)
Amer. librarian, statistician
Bul. of Bibl. May-Aug.1924,p65-66,por.

Carr, Emily (1871-1945)
Can. painter
Innis—Clear p221-241,por.
Sanders—Canadian p3-43,por.

Carr, Emma Perry (1880-   )
Amer. chemist
Cur. Biog. '59 p55-57,por.

Carraway, Gertrude Sprague (1896-   )
Amer. organization official, editor,
author
Cur. Biog. '54 p159-160,por.

Carré, Micheline (fl. 1930's-1940's)
Fr. spy
Singer—World's p162-177,por.

Carreau, Margaret (1899-   )
Amer. composer
ASCAP p77

Carreño, Teresa (1853-1917)
Venez. pianist, composer, singer
Adelman—Famous p253
Elson—Woman's p231-233,por.
Hammerton p358
McCoy—Portraits p21,por.
Phila.—Women unp.,por.
Schonberg—Great p328-332,por.
Stiles—Postal p47

Carreras, Maria Avani (b. 1872)
It. pianist
Ewen—Living p72,por.

Carrick, Jean Warren (fl. 1940's)
Amer. pianist, teacher, author
McCoy—Portraits p21,por.

Carriera, Rosalba (1675-1757)
It. painter
Adelman—Famous p253
Dorland—Sum p31,80,156
Hammerton p358,por.
Schmidt—400 p252-253,por.
Waters—Women p74-76

Carrington, Elaine Sterne (1892-1958)
Amer. author
Cur. Biog. '44 p85-87,por.
Cur. Biog. '58 p74

Carrington, Eva, Lady de Clifford (m. 1906)
Eng. actress, singer
Wyndham—Chorus p113,por.

Carrington, Margaret Irwin (d. 1867)
Amer. W. pioneer
Brown—Gentle p12-13,52-53,56-58

Carroll, Anna Ella (1815-1893)
Amer. Civil war heroine, military
genius
Harkness—Heroines p11
Young—Women p143-147,369,por.
Logan—Part p875-876

Carroll, Christina (fl. 1940's)
Rum.-Amer .singer
Peltz—Spot. p106,por.

Carroll, Consolata, pseud (Sister Mary Con-
solata (1892-   )
Amer. author, educator
Warfel—Amer. p82-83,por.

Carroll, Diahann (1935-   )
Amer. singer, actress
CR '63 p103,por.
Cur. Biog. '62 p74-76,por.

Carroll, Gladys Hasty (1904-   )
Amer. novelist
Warfel—Amer. p83-84,por.

Carroll, Harriet Chew (fl. 1790's)
Amer. pioneer
Green—Pioneer (3) p228,232

Carroll, Madeleine (1906-   )
Eng. actress
CR '59 p133,por.
CR '63 p104,por.
Cur. Biog. '49 p94-97,por.
Hammerton p359

Carroll, Mary Darnell (c. 1747-1782)
Amer. patriot
Green—Pioneer (3) p225-233

Carroll, Nancy (1906-1965)
Amer. actress
Hammerton p359
Herman—How p41,por.

Carroll, Ruth (fl. 1930's-1950's)
Amer. author
Hoyle—Tar p33-37,por.

Carroll, Ruth Robinson (1899-   )
Amer. illustrator, author
Women—Achieve. p149,por.

Carse, Matilda B. (fl. 1850's-1870's)
Amer. philanthropist, social
reformer, financier
Farmer—What p352-354,426-430

Carson, Ann Baker (fl. 1800's)
Amer. beauty
Burt—Phila. p308-309,318-319

Carson, Jeannie (n.d.)
Amer. actress
TV—Person (3) p136-138,por.

Carson, Luella Clay (b. 1856)
Amer. educator
Logan—Part p717-718

Carson, Mindy (1927-   )
Amer. singer, actress
CR '59 p133-134,por.
CR '63 p104,por.
Popular Record p34,por.

Carson, Nellie (fl. 1930's)
Can. aviatrix
*May—Women p100-101

Carson, Rachel Louise (1907-1964)
Amer. biologist, author
CR '59 p134,por.
CR '63 p104-105,por.
Cur Biog. '51 p100-102,por.
Cur. Biog. '64 p71

Carstairs, Janet Mure (b. 1625)
Scot. covenanter
Anderson—Ladies p124

Carswell, Catherine MacFarlane (1879-
1946)
Eng. author
Hammerton p359

Carter, Amy (n.d.)
Amer. aircraft factory instructor
Peckham—Women p58

Carter, Ann Shaw (fl. 1940's)
Amer. aviatrix, pioneer helicopter
pilot
*May—Women p203,205,por.

Carter, Artie Mason (n.d.)
Amer. musician, foundress, music
patron
Parshalle—Kash. p81-84,por.

Carter, Cora C. C. (fl. 1930's)
Amer. club leader
Women—Achieve. p195

Carter, Elizabeth (1717-1806)
Eng. poet, translator
Adelman—Famous p84
*Borer—Women p31-32
Dorland—Sum p18,76,176-177
Fifty—Famous p305-309
Hammerton p359
Stenton—English p267,270,286-295,
307,309,318

Carter, Frances Ann Tasker (1737-1797)
Amer. agriculturist
Leonard—Amer. p113
Spruill—Women's (see index)

Carter, Hannah Benedict (1733-1780)
Amer. Rev. war patriot
Green—Pioneer (3) p483-484
Root—Chapter p315-320

Carter, Helene (1887-1961)
Can.-Amer. illustrator
Mahony—Illus. p290

Carter, Leslie Dudley (1862-1937)
Amer. actress
Blum—Great p11,por.
Coad—Amer. p291-292,por.
Kobbé—Homes p185,226-228,por.
Marks—Glamour p284-285
Rogers—Women p44,por.
Strang—Actresses p193-205,por.

Carter, Mabel Ogilvie (fl. 1930's)
Amer. cosmetic executive
Women—Achieve. p31,33,por.

Carter, Mary Gilmore (b. 1867)
Amer. author
Logan—Part p833

Carter, Mrs. (fl. 1800's)
Amer. W. pioneer
Ellet—Pioneer p272-273

Carter sisters (fl. 1800's)
Amer. pioneers
Fowler—Woman p316-322

Cartwright, Ellen M. (1815-1873)
Amer. singer
Hanaford—Dau. p596-597

Cartwright, Emily J. Avery (fl. 1860's)
Amer. Civil war nurse
Logan—Part p368

Cartwright, Julia (d. 1924)
Eng. author
Hammerton p360

Carus, Emma (1879-1927)
Ger.-Amer. actress
Caffin—Vaud. p85

Carvajal, Luisa de (1568-1614)
Sp. missionary
Hammerton p360-361

Carvalho, Domitilia de (fl. 1950's)
Port. physician, poet
Lovejoy—Women p206

Carvalho, Marie Caroline Félix Miolan
(1827-1895)
Fr. singer
Lahee—Famous p106-107

Carver, Katherine (fl. 1600's)
Amer. Pilgrim
Bell—Women p14-15,54
Green—Pioneer (1) p147-148,151
Logan—Part p31
Marble—Women p57-58

Cary, Alice (1820-1871)
Amer. poet
Adelman—Famous p176-177
Dorland—Sum p16,178,185
Hanaford—Dau. p234,por.
Irwin—Angels p216-218
Logan—Part p810
Pattee—Fem. p58-66,por.
Whitton—These p68-69

Cary, Anna (Annie) Louise (1842-1921)
Amer. singer
Adelman—Famous p263
Lahee—Famous p304-308
McCoy—Portraits p22,por.
Whitton—These p197,200-201

Cary, Constance (fl. 1860's)
Amer. Civil war diarist
Jones—Heroines p79-81,145-149

Cary, Mary Ann Shadd (1823-1893)
Amer.-Can. pioneer
Brown—Home p92-96,por.

Cary, Mary Rande (fl. 1650's)
Eng. author
Stenton—English p171-175

Cary, Phoebe (1824-1871)
Amer. poet
Adelman—Famous p177
Bruère—Laugh. p106
Dorland—Sum p16,178,185
Hanaford—Dau. 234-235,por.
Irwin—Angels p216-217
Logan—Part p810
Pattee—Fem. p58-66,por.
Whitton—These p68-69

Casa, Lisa Della. See Della Casa, Lisa

Casalis, Jeanne de (1897-   )
Brit. actress
Hammerton p361,por.

Case, Alice Montague (b. 1870)
Amer. missionary, pioneer
Phillips—33 p114-120

Case, Anna (b. 1889)
Amer. singer
Lahee—Grand p309-310
McCoy—Portraits p22,por.

Casey, Margaret Elizabeth (b. 1874)
Amer. religious worker
Logan—Part p619

Cash, Azubah Bearse Handy (b. 1820)
　　Amer. whaling wife
　　Snow—Women p71-84,por.

Cashin, Bonnie (1915-　　)
　　Amer. fashion designer
　　CR '63 p107,por.
　　Epstein—Young p129-154

Casilda (d.c. 1007)
　　Sp. saint
　　Englebert—Lives p139
　　Stiles—Postal p231

Casilda (d. 458)
　　Christian saint
　　Wescott—Calen. p51

Caspary, Vera (1903/04-　　)
　　Amer. author, playwright
　　Cur. Biog. p100-101,por.
　　Mantle—Contemp. p307

Cass, Erna W. (fl. 1930's)
　　Amer. journalist
　　Women—Achieve. p189,por.

Cass, Peggy (1925-　　)
　　Amer. TV performer
　　CR '63 p107,por.

Cassatt, Mary (1845-1926)
　　Amer. painter
　　Adelman—Famous p278-279
　　Bryant—Amer. p209-212
　*Curtin—Gallery p14,por.
　　Douglas—Remember p181-184,por.
　　Hammerton p362
　*Heath—Woman p20,por.
　　Jackman—Amer. p167-169
　*MacVeagh—Champlin p120
　　Michigan—Biog. p65-66
　　Schmidt—400 p17-18,por.
　*Stevens—Women p137-140,por.
　　Waters—Women p76-78

Cassidy, Claudia (c. 1905-　　)
　　Amer. music, ballet and drama
　　　　critic
　　CR '59 p136,por.
　　CR '63 p107,por.
　　Cur. Biog. '55 p107-108,por.

Cassidy, Mary Q. (fl. 1930's)
　　Amer. educator
　　Women—Achieve. p195

Castagna, Bruna (1908-　　)
　　It. singer
　　Ewen—Ency. p78-79
　　Ewen—Living p76-77,por.
　　McCoy—Portraits p22,por.
　　Peltz—Spot. p98,por.

Castagnetta, Grace (1912-　　)
　　Amer. pianist, composer
　　Cur. Biog. '54 p160-162,por.
　　McCoy—Portraits p22,por.

Castellane, Anna Gould, Marquise de
　　　　(b.c. 1876)
　　Amer., daughter of Sam Gould
　　Pearson—Marry p128-143,por.

Castiglione, Countess (1835-1899)
　　It.-Fr. beauty, friend of Napoleon
　　Kelen—Mist. p106-118,330-331,por.

Castile, Blanche De (1188-1252)
　　Fr. queen
　　Schmidt—400 p172-173,por.

Castille, Johanna (b. 1479)
　　Sp. queen (Castile)
　　Phila.—Women unp.,por.

Castle, Barbara Anne Betts (1911-　　)
　　Brit. politician
　　Cur. Biog. '67 p58-60,por.

Castle, Irene Foote (1893/98-1969)
　　Amer. dancer
　　Caffin—Vaud. p103
　　CR '59 p137,por.
　　CR '63 p108,por.
　　Lamparski—What. p128-129,por.

Castle, Marian Johnston (1898-　　)
　　Amer. author
　　Warfel—Amer. p85,por.

Castlemaine, Countess of.
　　See Villiers, Barbara, Countess of
　　　　Castlemaine

Castro, Ines (Inez, Agnes) de (d. 1355)
　　Sp., wife of Dom Pedro
　*MacVeagh—Champlin p121-122

Castro, Rosalia De (1837-1885)
　　Sp. poet
　　Schmidt—400 p357-358

Castro-Carro sisters (fl. 1950's)
　　Puert. Ric. physicians
　　Lovejoy—Women p276,por.

Caswell, Mary McIlweane (m. 1750)
　　Amer. Rev. war patriot
　　Green—Pioneer (3) p318-319

Catalani, Angelica (1780-1849)
　　It. singer
　　Adelman—Famous p123
　　Ewen—Ency. p79
　　Ferris—Great (1) p132-170,por.
　　Hammerton p365
　　Lahee—Famous p37-40
　　Pleasants—Great p119-121,por.
　　Wagner—Prima p119-121,239

Catchpole, Margaret (1873-1941)
Eng. adventuress
Hammerton p365

Cather, Willa Sibert (1873-1947)
Amer. novelist
Auchincloss—Pion. p92-122
*Bolton—Authors p175-190
Boynton—Some p162-177
Burnett—This p1129
*Cournos—Famous p11-18,por.
*Curtin—Gallery p15,por.
Hammerton p365,por.
Heath—Authors p30,por.
*Heath—Women (4) p25,por.
Huff—Famous (2nd) p121-132,por.
Jensen—Revolt p101,por.
Jessup—Faith p54-75,126-128
*Kirkland—Writers p103-112
Lawrence—School p355-364
Loggins—Hear p207-216
Mears—They p87-89
*Millett—Amer. p25-27,280-292
Morgan—Writers p60-81
Morris—400 p53
*Muir—Writers p41-51,por.
New Yorker Aug.8,1931 p19-22,por.
(Profiles)
O'Brien—50 p859
Overton—Women p76-97
Rogers—Women p109,por.
Saturday Rev. p351-352
*Scherman—Amer. p68-70
Scherman—Literary p120-122
Time Aug.3,1931 p47,por.(cover)
Van Doren—Amer. p113-122
*Witham—Pan. p236-239,por.

Catherine I (1684/85-1727)
Russ. empress
Adelman—Famous p72-73
Hammerton p365
*MacVeagh—Champlin p122
Muir—Women p128

Catherine II (Catherine the Great) (1729-1796)
Russ. empress
Abbott—Notable p108-117
Adelman—Famous p80-81,por.
Armour—It p97-106
Arsenius—Dict. p104,por.
*Bolton—Famous Leaders p55-91,por.
*Boyd—Rulers p163-173,por.
Bradford—Dau. p155-197,por.
Carnegie—Little p33-35,por.
Cuppy—Decline p141-148
Dark—Royal p253-272,por.
Dorland—Sum p42
Ewart—World's p192-204
*Farmer—Book p113-126
Fitzhugh—Concise p105-106
Hammerton p306,por.
Jenkins—Heroines p393-444,por.

Kemble—Idols p221-243
*MacVeagh—Champlin p122,por.
Muir—Women p129-131
*Nisenson—Minute p31,por.
*O'Clery—Queens p123-139
100 Great p175-181
Orr—Famous p145-160
Orr—Famous Affin. II p3-22
Phila.—Women, unp.,por.
Russell—Glit. p168-177,por.
Schmidt—400 p343-344,por.
Sewell—Brief p79-80
Stiles—Postal p49
Thomas—Rulers p167-184
Trowbridge—Seven p96-147,por.

Catherine, Sister (fl. 1840's)
Amer. W. pioneer
*Ross—Heroines p128,149-150,153,155

Catherine de Medicis (1519-1589)
Fr. queen
Abbott—Notable p180-188
*Boyd—Rulers p91-100,por.
Dark—Royal p11-53,por.
Dorland—Sum p26
Ewart—World's p156-174
*Farmer—Book p57-68
Haggard—Remark, p16-19
Hammerton p980-981,por.
Imbert—Valois p123-348,por.
Koven—Women p175-180,193-211,231-235,241,por.
Love—Famous p24
*MacVeagh—Champlin p122-123
Muir—Women p93-94
*Terry—Star p12-16
Thomas—Vital p258-261

Catherine dei Ricci (1519-1589)
It. saint
Wescott—Calen. p18

Catherine Labouré (1806-1875)
Fr. saint
Englebert—Lives p496-497
Sharkey—Pop. p184-190

Catherine of Alexandria (d.c. 307)
Egypt. saint
*Beebe—Saint p29-35
Englebert—Lives p448-449
Hammerton p365
Husslein—Heroines p142-150
Stiles—Postal p231
Wescott—Calen. p184-185

Catherine of Aragon (Katheryn Howard)
(1485-1536)
Eng. queen
Abbot—Notable p50-58
Adelman—Famous p48-49
Dorland—Sum p53
Fifty—Famous p303-304

(Continued)

Catherine of Aragon—*Continued*

Hahn—Love p62-65,71-72
Hammerton p366-367,por.
*O'Clery—Queens p60-65
Sanders—Intimate p1-12,por.

Catherine of Bologne (1413-1463)
It. saint
Englebert—Lives p95

Catherine of Braganza (1638-1705)
Eng. queen
Hammerton p367,por.
Sanders—Intimate p110-112,por.

Catherine of Genoa (1447-1510)
It. saint
Beard—Woman p266
Blunt—Great p165
Deen—Great p336-338
Englebert—Lives p353
Wescott—Calen. p139-140

Catherine of Siena (1347-1380)
It. saint
Adelman—Famous p40-41
Beard—Woman p263-266
Blunt—Great p161-162
Culver—Women p111-112
Deen—Great p50-60
Dolan—Goodnow's p110-111
Englebert—Lives p167
Hammerton p365
Husslein—Heroines p83-104
Keyes—Three p127-265,por.
Maynard—Saints p60-78
Phila.-Women—unp.,por.
Schmidt—400 p247-248,por.
Stedman—When p19-26
Stiles—Postal p231-232
Wescott—Calen. p61-62
*Windham—Sixty p304-309

Catherine of Sweden (c. 1331-1380)
Swed. saint
Englebert—Lives p116
Wescott—Calen. p43

Catherine of Valois (1401-1437)
Eng. queen
Hammerton p367

Catherine of Würtemberg (1788-1819)
Ger. queen
Schmidt—400 p199-200,por.

Catherine. See also **Katherine**

Catherwood, Mary Hartwell (1847-1902)
Amer. novelist
Dorland—Sum p47

Catley, Anne (1745-1789)
Eng. singer, actress
MacQueen—Pope p214-222,por.

Catlin, Ida (fl. 1930's)
Austral. real estate broker,
advertising executive
Women—Achieve. p102,por.

Cato, Nancy (1917-   )
Austral. author
Hetherington—42 p177-182,por.

Catt, Carrie Chapman Lane (1859-1947)
Amer. feminist, lecturer
Adelman—Famous p307
Allen—Advent. p165-178,por.
America's 12 p19-21,por.
Beard—Amer. p376-384
Bonte—Amer. p155,por.
Burnett—Five p257-315
*Commager—Crus. p168-170
Cur. Biog. '40 p150-152,por.
Cur. Biog. '47 p101
Douglas—Remember p168-171
Hammerton p368
*Heath—Women p21,por.
Holbrook—Dreamers p217-219,221-223
Huff—Famous (2nd) p133-144,por.
Irwin—Angels (see index)
Ladies'—Amer. 12 p19-21,por.
Logan—Part p585-586
*MacVeagh—Champlin p124
Phila.—Women, unp.,por.
Riegel—Amer. p178,182,200,por.
Rogers—Women p62,por.
Roosevelt—Ladies p9-10
Schmidt—400 p544,por.
Shaw—Story p284-288
Stiles—Postal p49
*Stoddard—Top p181-197
Time June 14,1926 p8(cover)
Women—Achieve. p195

Cattaneo, Maria (fl. 1870's)
It. artist
Waters—Women p78

Cattell, Hettie (fl. 1930's)
Amer. journalist
Ross—Ladies p301-302

"Cattle Kate." See **Watson, Ella**

Caudill, Rebecca (1899-   )
Amer. author
Cur. Biog. '50 p86-87,por.

Cauer, Minna (1841-1922)
Ger. editor, feminist
Dorland—Sum, p134-135
Schmidt—400 p207-209,por.

Caulfield, (Beatrice) Joan (1922-   )
Amer. actress
Cur. Biog. '54 p164-166,por.
TV—Person (1) p52-53,por.

Caux, Mimi (1823-1906)
Hung. singer, actress
Schmidt—400 p226,por.

Cavalieri, Lina (1874-1944)
It. singer
Ewen—Ency. p80
Lahee—Grand p73-74,84-89
McCoy—Portraits p22,por.

Cavanah, Frances Elizabeth (1899-   )
Amer. author
Cur. Biog. '54 p166-167,por.

Cavanna, Betty (Betsy Allen) (1909-   )
Amer. author
Cur. Biog. '50 p87-88,por.

Cavell, Edith Louisa (1865-1915)
Eng. nurse
Adelman—Famous p249
Barton—Celeb. p21-43,por.
Bowie—Women p128-139
Canning—100 p285-291
Cole—Women p65-87,por.
*Deakin—True p190-202
Fellowes—Heroes p24-37,por.
*Hagedorn—Book p332-342
Hammerton p369,por.
Lotz—Women p22-29
*McKown—Heroic p145-167,por.
*MacVeagh—Champlin p124
Muir—Women p151-152
Phila.—Women, unp.,por.
*Reader's—Great p292-297
Stiles—Postal p50
*Wright—Great p238-261

Cavendish, Ada (1839-1895)
Eng. actress
Furniss—Some p49-52,por.

Cavendish, Margaret, Duchess of Newcastle
(c. 1624-1674)
Eng. author
Adelman—Famous p65
Bottrall—Pers. p126-128,218-219

Cavis, Helen (fl. 1930's)
Amer. aviatrix, aviation instructor
Planck—Women p163-164,por.

Caylus, Marie Marguerite Le Valois de Vil-
lete de Murcay, Comtesse de
(1674-1729)
Fr. social leader
Adelman—Famous p70

Cayvan, Georgia (1858-1906
Amer. actress
Coad—Amer. p274,por.

Cebotari, Maria (1910-1949)
Rum. singer
Ewen—Ency. p81-82

Cecil, Mary (1885-1940)
Amer. actress
Cur. Biog. '41 p143

Cecilia (d.c. 230)
Rom. saint
Deen—Great p313-314
Drinker—Music p263-282
Elson—Woman's p11-12
Englebert—Lives p444-445
Hammerton p371
Husslein—Heroines p27-43
McCoy—Portraits p22,por.
*MacVeagh—Champlin p124-125
Sharkey—Pop. p34-35
Stiles—Postal p232
Wescott—Calen. p182-183
*Windham—Sixty p48-57

Cederström, Baroness. See Patti, Adelina

Ceionia Fabia (fl. 135-136 A.D.)
Rom. matron
Balsdon—Roman p141,148

Celeste (Celeste-Elliot), Celine (1815/18-
1882)
Fr. dancer, actress
Coad—Amer. p98,por.

Celeste, Maria, Sister (d. 1642)
It. nun, dau. of Galileo
Mozans—Woman p363-369

Celeste, Marie (fl. 1890's)
Amer. singer, actress
Strang—Prima p156-171,por.

Cenci, Beatrice (1577-1599)
Rom., dau. of Francisco Cenci
*MacVeagh—Champlin p125

Center, Stella Stewart (b. 1878)
Amer. educator, lecturer
Women—Achieve. p107,por.

Centlivre, Susannah (c. 1667-1723)
Amer. playwright, actress
Hammerston p372
MacQueen—Pope p132-136,por.

Cerito, Fanny (1821-c. 1899)
It. ballet dancer
Beaumont—Complete p374-382,por.
*Terry—Star p81-83,por.

Césniece-Freudenfelde, Zelma (1892-1929)
Lat. physician
Schmidt—400 p276-277,por.

Chacón, Rosario Orrego de (1834-1879)
Chile. novelist
Schmidt—400 p422,por.

Chadwick, Florence (1918/19-   )
Amer. swimmer
CR '59 p139,por.
Cur. Biog. '50 p88-89,por.
Davis—100 p15,por.

Chadwick, Helene (1897-1940)
   Amer. actress
   Cur. Biog. '40 p153,por.

Chaffee, Allen (fl. 1900's-1930's)
   Amer. author
   Women—Achieve. p195

Chalmers, Audrey (1893/99-1957)
      Can.-Amer. illustrator, author
   Mahoney—Illus. p290

Chamberlain, Jeannie (b. 1865)
   Amer. heiress
   Eliot—Heiresses p202-209

Chamberlain, Mary Endicott (b.c. 1864)
      Amer., wife of Joseph Chamberlain
   Pearson—Marry p153-165,por.
   Pearson—Pilgrim p151-169

Chamberlin, Georgia Louise (c. 1862-1943)
      Amer. educator, author
   Cur. Biog. '43 p117

Chambers, Mrs. Lambert (fl. 1900's-1910's)
      Eng. lawn-tennis player
   Hammerton p376,por.

Chaminade, Cecile Louise Stéphanie (1861-
      1944)
      Fr. composer, pianist
   Adelman—Famous p296
   Cur. Biog. '44 p89
   Dorland—Sum p160
   Elson—Woman's p174-177,234,236,
      238,273,por.
   Gammond—Dict. p43
   Hammerton p377
   McCoy—Portraits p23,por.
   Schonberg—Great p337

Champion, Deborah (b. 1753)
      Amer. pioneer, heroine
   Beard—Amer. p72-75
   Green—Pioneer (2) p406-414

Champion, Marge Celeste (Marjorie Celeste
      Belcher) (1925-   )
      Amer. dancer
   CR '59 p141,por.
   Cur. Biog. '53 p110-112,por.
   TV—Person (3) p148-149,por.

Champion de Crespigny, Rose (m. 1878)
      Eng. author
   Hammerton p377

Champmeslé, Marie DesMares (1642-1698)
      Fr. actress
   Collins—Great p29-51
   Hammerton p377-378
   Stiles—Postal p51

Chanaanite woman (Biblical)
   Faulhaber—Women p165-169

Chandler, Anna Curtis (fl. 1910's-1930's)
      Amer. educator
   Women—Achieve. p145,por.

Chandler, Dorothy Buffum (1901-   )
      Amer. journalist
   CR '63 p112,por.
   Cur. Biog. '57 p101-102,por.
   Time Dec.18,1964 p46,56-58,por.
      (cover)

Chandler, Elizabeth Margaret (1807-1834)
      Amer. poet, author
   Hanaford—Dau. p263

Chandor, Valentine (fl. 1920's-1930's)
      Amer. educator
   Time Oct. 8, 1934 p59,por.(cover)

Chandy, Anna (1905-   )
      Ind. judge
   Cur. Biog. '60 p86-88,por.

Chanel, Gabrielle Bonheur ("Coco")
      Fr. fashion designer
   Asquith—Myself p65-73,por.
   CR '59 p142,por.
   Cur. Biog. '54 p169-171,por.
   New Yorker Mar.14,1931 p25-28
      (Profiles)

Chang, Widow (d. 1931)
      Chin. warrior
   Ayscough—Chinese p226

Chanler, Beatrice Ashley (Minnie Ashley)
      (1875-1946)
      Amer. actress,, sculptor, author,
      singer
   Logan—Part p759
   Strang—Prima p134-146

Chanler, Margaret (fl. 1910's)
      Amer. philanthropist
   Logan—Part p540

Channing, Carol (1921-   )
      Amer. actress
   Blum—Great p145,por.
   CR '59 p142-143,por.
   CR '63 p112,por.
   Cur. Biog. '64 p76-78,por.
   Time Jan.9,1950 p50,por.(cover)

Channing, Mrs. (fl. 1770's)
      Amer. Rev. war heroine
   Fowler—Woman p126

Chantal, Jeanne François Fremiot, Baronne
      de (1572-1641)
      Fr. saint
   Blunt—Great p169-173
   Deen—Great p352-354
   Dolan—Goodnow's p143

Chantrey, Mrs. (d.c. 1826)
    Eng., mother of Sir Francis Chantrey
    Wallace—Mothers p82-87

Chao Yun (fl. 1080's-1090's)
    Chin. concubine
    Llewellyn—China's p142

Chapelle.
    See La Chapelle, Marie Louise Dugès

Chapellin, Emilia, Mother (1858-1890)
    Amer. foundress, nun
    Schmidt—400 p418-419,por.

Chapin, Alice Delafield (fl. 1930's)
    Amer. educator
    Women—Achieve. p195

Chapin, Anne Morrison (d. 1967)
    Amer. playwright
    Mantle—Contemp. p307

Chapin, Augusta J. (fl. 1870's)
    Amer. clergyman
    Hanaford—Dau. p446-447

Chapin, Cornelia Van A. (fl. 1930's)
    Amer. sculptor
    Women—Achieve. p122,por.

Chapin, Hannah (Mrs. Hannah Sheldon)
    (fl. 1700's)
    Amer. pioneer, heroine
    Green—Pioneer (1) p250,255-256,275,
    278

Chapin, Mrs. Hermon (fl. 1860's)
    Amer. Civil war patriot
    Young—Women p300-301

Chapin, Katharine Garrison (1890-   )
    Amer. poet
    Cur. Biog. '43 p121-123,por.

Chapin, Lauren (1945-   )
    Amer. actress
    TV—Person (1) p44,por.

Chapin, Lucy (fl. 1800's)
    Amer. W. pioneer
    Ellet—Pioneer p370-371

Chapin, Mary E. (fl. 1870's-1880's)
    Amer. educator
    Hanaford—Dau. p549-550

Chapin, Sylvia (fl. 1800's)
    Amer. W. pioneer
    Ellet—Pioneer p367-368
    Logan—Part p95

Chapman, Blanche (c. 1850-1941)
    Amer. actress
    Cur. Biog. '41 p147
    Marks—Glamour p285

Chapman, Caroline (fl. 1830's-1850's)
    Amer. actress, W. pioneer
    Coad—Amer. p152,187

Chapman, Ceil (1912-   )
    Amer. fashion designer
    CR '59 p144,por.
    CR '63 p113,por.

Chapman, Elizabeth (fl. 1860's)
    Amer. Civil war nurse
    Logan—Part p361-362

Chapman, Ethel (fl. 1920's-1940's)
    Can. editor, novelist
    Thomas—Canad. p21-22

Chapman, G. D. (fl. 1860's)
    Amer. Civil war patriot
    Brockett—Woman's p714

Chapman, Helen Louise Busch (1904-   )
    Amer. organization official
    Cur. Biog. '55 p112-114,por.

Chapman, Maria Weston (1806-1885)
    Amer. feminist, philanthropist
    Hanaford—Dau. p175
    Irwin—Angels p76-77

Chapman, Maristan.
    See Chapman, Mary Hamilton Ilsley

Chapman, Mary Hamilton Ilsley (1895-   )
    Amer. novelist
    Warfel—Amer. p86-87,por.

Chapman, Mrs. Wood-Allen (gr. 1895)
    Amer. social reformer
    Logan—Part p661

Chapone, Hester Mulso (1727-1801)
    Eng. essayist, feminist
    Benson—Women p59-61,67,72-75
    Stenton—English p295-296

Chapone, Sally Kirkham (Sappho) (fl. 1770's)
    Eng. hostess
    Stenton—English p241-244,295

Chappel, Mrs. (fl. 1760's-1780's)
    Amer. W. pioneer
    Ellet—Pioneer p387

Chappelle, Mrs. B. F. (1897-   )
    Amer. psychologist
    Bindheim—Women p139,por.

Chard, Marie L. (1868-1938)
    Amer. physician
    Lovejoy—Women Phys. p53,por.

Charisse, Cyd (1923-   )
    Amer. dancer
    CR '59 p144,por.
    CR '63 p114,por.
    Cur. Biog. '54 p171-172,por.

Charke, Charlotte Cibber (c. 1710-1760)
    Eng. actress, playwright
    Bottrall—Pers. p57-60,219
    MacQueen—Pope p241-250
    Melville—Stage p123-150,por.

Charles, Elizabeth Rundle (1828-1896)
    Eng. author
    Dorland—Sum p25,196
    Hammerton p388

Charles, Joan, pseud.
    See Underwood, Charlotte

Charlesworth, Maria Louisa (1819-1880)
    Eng. author
    Hammerton p388

Charlesworth, Violet (fl. 1910's)
    Amer. actress
    Felstead—Stars p54

Charlick, Edith (fl. 1920's-1930's)
    Amer. nurse, bus. executive
    Women—Achieve. p149,por.

Charlotte (1898-   )
    Mon. princess
    Phila.—Women, unp.,por.
    Stiles—Postal p53

Charlotte.
    See also Carlotta Marie Charlotte Amelie

Charlotte Aldegonde Elise Marie Wilhelmine
        (1919-1964)
    Luxem. grand duchess
    Arsenius—Dict. p45,por.
    Cur. Biog. '49 p105-107,por.
    Hammerton p388
    Phila.—Women, unp.,por.
    Stiles—Postal p53

Charlotte Augusta (1796-1817)
    Brit. princess
    Hammerton p388
    Melville—Regency p155-175

Charlotte de Grammont.
    See Grammont (or Gramont) Charlotte
    de

Charlotte Sophia (1744-1818)
    Eng. queen
    Hammerton p388,por.
    Melville—Regency p13-21
    Sanders—Intimate p171-180,por.

Charmon ("The perfect woman") (p. 1910's)
    Amer. actress, acrobat
    Caffin—Vaud. p181,por.

Charnaux, Madeleine (d. 1939)
    Fr. sculptor, aviatrix
    °Lauwick—Heroines p122-146,por.

Charpentier, Constance Marie (1767-1849)
    Fr. sculptor
    Waters—Women p78

Charques, Dorothy Taylor (1899-   )
    Eng. author
    Cur. Biog. '58 p87-88,por.

Charrat, Janine (1924-   )
    Fr. ballet dancer, choreographer
    Haskell—Ballet p86-87
    Haskell—Vignet. p78

Charretie, Anna Maria (1819-1875)
    Eng. painter
    Waters—Women p79

Chartres, Mademoiselle de ("Mother
        Bathilda") (fl. 18th cent.)
    Fr., granddaughter of Madame
        D'Orleans
    Kavanagh—Woman (1) p36

Chase, Adelaide Cole (b. 1868)
    Amer. painter
    Waters—Women p79

Chase, Ann (1809-1874)
    Amer. patriot
    Hanaford—Dau. p57

Chase, Anne Baldwin (m. 1762)
    Amer. pioneer, patriot
    Green—Pioneer (3) p217-219

Chase, Anya. See Seton, Anya

Chase, Barrie (1934-   )
    Amer. dancer
    CR '63 p114,por.

Chase, Deborah (b. 1760)
    Amer. Rev. war patriot
    Snow—Women p107-111

Chase, Edna Woolman (1877-1957)
    Amer. editor
    Cur. Biog. '40 p160-161,por.
    Cur. Biog. '57 p108

Chase, Elizabeth B. (fl. 1870's-1880's)
    Amer. philanthropist
    Hanaford—Dau. p181

Chase, Hannah Kilty (m. 1783)
    Amer. pioneer
    Green—Pioneer (3) p218

Chase, Helen Frances (fl. 1930's)
    Amer. musician, music teacher
    Women—Achieve. p119,por.

Chase, Ilka (c. 1905-   )
    Amer. actress, author
    CR '59 p145,por.
    CR '63 p114,por.
    Cur. Biog. '42 p143-146,por.
    TV—Person. (1) p142,por.

Chase, Kate (Kate Chase Sprague) (1840-1899)
Amer. hostess, belle
Leetch—Reveille p52,204,453,454

Chase, Kate Fowler (1871-1951)
Amer. teacher, lecturer, club leader
Women—Achieve. p121,por.

Chase, Lucetta (fl. 1930's)
Amer. club leader
Women—Achieve. p135,por.

Chase, Lucia (1907-   )
Amer. ballet dancer, director
CR '59 p145,por.
CR '64 p114-115,por.
Cur. Biog. '47 p103-104,por.
Haskell—Vignet. p66

Chase, Mary (fl. 1840's)
Amer. pioneer
Fowler—Woman p224-235

Chase, Mary Coyle (1907-   )
Amer. author, playwright
CR '59 p145-146,por.
Cur. Biog. '45 p98-100,por.

Chase, Mary Ellen (1887-   )
Amer. author, educator
Burnett—This p1128-1130
°Cournos—Famous p59-65,por.
Cur. Biog. '40 p161-162,por.
°Logie—Careers (2nd) p3-11
Love—Famous p40-41
°Millett—Amer. p292-294
Stone—We p280-287
Taves—Success. p92-95
Wagenknecht—When p306-316
Warfel—Amer. p88,por.

Chase, Mary Maria (1822-1852)
Amer. poet, botanist
Hanaford—Dau. p261-262

Chase, Mary Wood (b. 1868)
Amer. pianist, educator, author
McCoy—Portraits p23,por.

Chase, Nelly M. (fl. 1860's)
Amer. Civil war soldier
Moore—Women p536-540

Chastain, Madye Lee (1908-   )
Amer. author, illustrator
Cur. Biog. '58 p88-89,por.

Chateauroux, Marie Anne De Mailly-Nesle,
Duchesse de (1717-1744)
Fr., friend of Louis XV
Haggard—Remark. p284-286,289-300
Hammerton p390
Kavanagh—Woman (1) p109-115

Chatelet, Emilie, Marquise du (Gabrielle
Emilie Le Tonnelier de Breteuil)
(1706-1749)
Fr., mathematician, astronomer,
physicist
°Coolidge—Six p23-25
Hammerton p390
Kavanagh—Woman (1) p119,122-140,
por.
Mozans—Woman p151-153,175-177,
201-202
Smith—Hist. (1) p477-478,por.

Chatfield, Ena Lyle Brown (m. 1932)
Amer. missionary
They—Went p140-141

Chatterton, Ruth (1893/1900-1961)
Amer. actress
Blum—Great p84,por.
CR '59 p146,por.
Hammerton p391
Hughes—Famous p25-46,por.
°May—Women p136
Stuart—Immort. p62-63,por.

Chauchet, Charlotte (1878-   )
Fr. painter
Waters—Women p79-81

Chausseraie, Mademoiselle de la (fl. 18th
cent.)
Fr., friend of Louis XIV
Kavanagh—Woman (1) p12-13

Chauvin, Mademoiselle (fl. 1880's)
Fr. lawyer
Adelman—Famous p308

Chauvire, Yvette (1917-   )
Fr. ballet dancer
Atkinson—Dancers p23-27,por.
Davidson—Ballet p37-40,por.
Haskell—Ballet p20-21,por.
Haskell—Vignet. p75-77,por.
Swinson—Dancers p54-56,por.
Swinson—Great p8,por.

Chazel, Mrs. (fl. 18th cent.)
Eng. orchestral conductor
Elson—Woman's p133

Cheatham, Adelicia Hayes (fl. 1870's-1880's)
Amer. social leader
Hanaford—Dau. p148-149

Cheatham, Kitty (Catharine Smiley Bugg)
(c. 1864-1946)
Amer. singer, composer, author,
lecturer
Cur. Biog. '46 p113
McCoy—Portraits p23,por.
Women—Achieve. p161,por.

Cheer, Margaret (m. 1768)
Amer. colonial actress
Dexter—Colonial p160-161,211-212

Chellier-Fumat, Mrs. (fl. 1890's-1900's)
Fr. physician
Lovejoy—Women p256

Chemet, Réné (b. 1888)
Fr. violinist
Ewen—Living p81-82,por.
McCoy—Portraits p23,por.

Cheney, Ednah Dow (1824-1904)
Amer. lecturer, author
Dorland—Sum p34,127,137-138
Hanaford—Dau. p247,340-341,489

Cheney, Frances Neel (1906-   )
Amer. librarian, author
Bul. of Bibl. May-Aug. 1963 p1-3,por.

Cheney, Harriet V. (fl. 1870's-1880's)
Amer. author
Hanaford—Dau. p233-239

Chen Fei, Pearl (fl. 1880's)
Chin. concubine
Llewellyn—China's p194,196,198-199

Chenoweth, Caroline Van Dusen (1846-   )
Amer. author
Logan—Part p843-844

Chérot, Elizabeth Sophie (1648-c. 1711)
Fr. painter
Waters—Women p81-83

Cherrill, Virginia (m. 1937)
Amer. actress
Wyndham—Chorus p141

Cherry, Addie Rose Alma (c. 1859-1942)
Amer. actress
Cur. Biog. '42 p149

Cherry, Emma Robinson (b. 1859)
Amer. painter
Waters—Women p83

Chesbro, Frances M. (b. 1824)
Amer. poet
Hanaford—Dau. p258-259

Chesnut, Mary Boykin (1823-1886)
Amer. Civil war diarist
Dunaway—Treas. p239-257
Jones—Heroines p55-61
Simkins—Women (see index)

Chesser, Elizabeth Sloan (1878-1940)
Eng. physician, lecturer
Asquith—Myself p75-96,por.
Cur. Biog. '40 p166

Chester, Eliza, pseud.
See Paine, Harriet Eliza

Chetwynd, Mrs. Henry (m. 1858)
Brit. author
Black—Notable p247-259,por.

Chevalier, Elizabeth Pickett (1896-   )
Amer. author
Cur. Biog. '43 p125-126,por.
Warfel—Amer. p88-89,por.

Chevers, Sarah (fl. 1650's)
Eng. missionary
Best—Rebel p117-135
Culver—Women p149

Chevigne, Laure de Sade, Comtesse de
(d. 1936)
Fr. hostess, friend of Proust
Skinner—Elegant p50-52

Chevreuse, Marie de Rohan-Montbazon
(1600-1679)
Fr., enemy of Cardinal Richelieu
Haggard—Remark. p31-33,35
*MacVeagh—Champlin p136

Chew, Harriet. See Carroll, Harriet Chew

Chew, Peggy (b. 1759)
Amer. belle
Sale—Old p139-144,por.

Cheylesmore, Leonora Parke, Lady
(m. 1916)
Tas. actress
Wyndham—Chorus p171-172

Chiang Kai-Shek, Madame Mayling Soong
(1898-   )
Chin. political leader
Carnegie—Biog. p133-138
Clark—Chiangs p40-52,72-120,por.
CR '59 p148-149,por.
Cur. Biog. '40 p168-170,por.
Karsh—Faces p38,por.
Miller—Ten p43-48
Phelps—Men '58 (1) p57-58
Stiles—Postal p55
Thomas—Living Women p301-313,por.
Time, Oct.26,1931 p21; Jan.3,1938 p12;
Mar. 1, 1943 p23,por.(covers)

Chidester, Ann (1919-   )
Amer. author
Warfel—Amer. p89,por.

Chiesa, Vivian Della (fl. 1930's)
Amer. singer
McCoy—Portraits p24,por.

Chiesman, Lydia (fl. 1670's)
Amer. politician
Spruill—Women's p234

Child, Julia McWilliams (1912-   )
Amer. home economist,
TV personality
Cur. Biog. '67 p66-68,por.
Time Nov.25,1966 p74-87,por.(cover)

Child, Lydia Maria Francis (1802-1880)
    Amer. social reformer, author, editor
Adelman—Famous p176
Bruce—Woman p174-178
Dexter—Career p101-102
Dorland—Sum p21,74,79,116,127
Douglas—Remember p58-61
Farmer—What 196,205-206
Hanaford—Dau. p168-170,184,263,352-354,696
Irwin—Angels p7,22,77
Logan—Part p794-796
Parton—Noted p26-43,por.
Riegel—Amer. p98-100
Thorp—Female p215-253,por.
Whitton—These p112-114,123

Chiles, Marietta (fl. 1800's)
    Amer. teacher
Brown—Home. p247

Chilia, Elvira Rey (fl. 1940's)
    Cub. physician
Lovejoy—Women p273

Chilton, Mary.
See Winslow, Mary Chilton

Chilton, Susanna (1634-c. 1676)
    Amer. Pilgrim
Green—Pioneer (1) p147
Logan—Part p34

Chimay, Jeanne Marie Ionace Thérèse de Cabarrus, Princess of (Madame Tallien) (1773-1835)
    Fr. patriot
Muir—Women p123-124

"China Polly."
See Bemis, Lalu Nathey ("China Polly")

Chinn, Sarah Bryan (m.c. 1784)
    Amer. W. pioneer, patriot
Ellet—Pioneer p361-367
Green—Pioneer (3) p502-503
Logan—Part p95

"Chipeta" (c. 1842-1924)
    Amer. Ind. heroine
Binheim—West p102-103

Chipp, Beatrice A. See Hicks, Beatrice A.

Chisholm, Caroline Jones (1810-1877)
    Austral. philanthropist, social reformer, author
Adelman—Famous p150
Fifty—Famous p152-157,por.
Prout—Petticoat p75-93,por.
Rabling—Under p37,por.
Schmidt—400 p37,por.

Chittenden, Elizabeth Meigs (m. 1750)
    Amer. Rev. war patriot
Green—Pioneer (3) p322

Ch'iu Chin (fl. 20th cent.)
    Chin. warrior
Ayscough—Chinese p223

Chizick, Sarah (fl. 1940's)
    Russ.-Israeli religious worker
*Levinger—Great p156-159

Chloe (Biblical)
Deen—All p257
Mead—250 p246

Choate, Anne Hyde (fl. 1920's-1930's)
    Amer. Girl Scout executive
Women—Achieve. p195

Choiseul, Madame de (1734-1801)
    Fr. social leader
Bradford—Women p155-176,por.

Cholmondeley, Mary (Pax, pseud.)
    (d.) 1925
    Eng. novelist
Hammerton p397

Chouteau, Yvonne (1929-   )
    Amer. ballet dancer
Atkinson—Dancers p28-30,por.

Christian, Linda (1923-   )
    Mex.-Amer. actress
CR '59 p150,por.
CR '63 p117,por.

Christiana. See Nina (saint)

Christians, Mady (1900-1951)
    Aust. actress
Cur. Biog. '45 p102-105,por.
Cur. Biog. '51 p107

Christie, Agatha Mary Clarissa Miller (c. 1891-   )
    Eng.-Amer. author
CR '59 p150,por.
Cur. Biog. '40 p172-173,por.
Cur. Biog. '64 p78-80,por.
Hammerton p399

Christie, Julie (1941-   )
    Brit. actress
Cur. Biog. '66 p47-49,por.

Christie, Winifred (n.d.)
    Scot. pianist
McCoy—Portraits p24,por.

Christina (1626-1689)
    Swed. queen
Abbott—Notable p118-126
Adelman—Famous p65-67
Blei—Fasc. p105-129,por.
*Boyd—Rulers p141-153,por.
Dark—Royal p155-171,por.
Dorland—Sum p37

(Continued)

Christina—*Continued*

   Fifty—Famous p108-111,por.
   Hammerton p399-400,por.
   MacNalty—Princes p79-91
   Orr—Famous p73-88
   Orr—Famous Affin. I p97-118
   Phila.—Women unp.,por.
   Ravenal—Women p43-44,por.
   Schmidt—400 p364-366
   Stiles—Postal p56
   Thomas—Living Women p67-68,por.

Christina, Maria (1858-1929)
   Sp. queen
   Hammerton p400

Christina, Mary (1806-1878)
   Sp. queen
   Hammerton p400

Christina of Stommeln (1242-1313)
   Ger. saint
   Englebert—Lives p423

Christina the Astonishing (1150-1224)
   Belg. saint
   Englebert—Lives p284
   Wescott—Calen. p108-109
   *Windham—Sixty p263-268

Christine (d. c. 1716)
   Ger.-Russ. princess, or imposter
   Earle—Colon. p160-165

Christine of Pisan (c. 1363-1431)
   Fr. poet, feminist, scholar
   Beard—Woman p258-259
   Lownsbery—Saints p294-316
   Welch—Six p116-146,por.

Christman, Elisabeth (n.d.)
   Amer. labor leader
   Cur. Biog. '47 p104-106,por.

Chubbuck, Emily.
   See Judson, Emily Chubbuck

Chudleigh, Elizabeth, Countess of Bristol,
      Duchess of Kingston (1720-1788)
   Eng. poet
   Rogers—Gallant p145
   Trowbridge—Seven p148-195,por.

Chudleigh, Mary, Lady (1656-1701)
   Eng. poet
   Stenton—English p206-208,215

Church, Angelica Schuyler (1877-1954)
   Amer. artist, sculptor
   Donovan—Women p278-280

Church, Ellen (fl. 1920's-1940's)
   Amer. airline hostess, "flying" nurse
   Knapp—New p73-78,por.

*May—Women p158-159,230,por.
*Peckham—Women p20-21
Planck—Women p190

Church, Marguerite Stitt (1892-   )
   Amer. Congresswoman, politician
   Cur. Biog. '51 p107-108,por.
   U.S.—Women (87th) p13,por.

Church, Sandra (1943-   )
   CR '63 p118,por.
   Amer. actress

Churchill, Bonnie (1937-   )
   Amer. journalist
   CR '63 p118,por.

Churchill, Clementine Ogilvy Hozier Spen-
      cer, Lady (1885-   )
   Eng., wife of Winston Churchill
   Cur. Biog. '53 p114-116,por.
   Forsee—My p172-208

Churchill, Elizabeth K. (fl. 1870's-1880's)
   Amer. lecturer
   Hanaford—Dau. p340

Churchill, Jeanette (Jennie) Jerome, Lady
      Randolph (1850-1921
   Amer. heiress, mother of Winston
      Churchill
   Eliot—Heiresses p61-77,por.
   Pearson—Marry. p52-85,por.
   Pearson—Pilgrim p44-79,por.

Churchill, Odette Mary Celine Brailly San-
      som (Odette Marie Sansom;
      "Lise") (c. 1912-   )
   Brit. spy.
   Hoehling—Women p133-136
   Singer—World's p228

Churchill, Reba (1934-   )
   Amer. journalist
   CR '63 p118,por.

Churchill, Sarah (1914-   )
   Eng. actress, dau. of Winston
      Churchill
   CR '59 p151,por.
   Cur. Biog. '55 p120-122,por.
   Jenkins—Ten p64-83,por.
   *Unstead—People p329-338,350

Chu Shu-Chên (fl. 1126-1200)
   Chin. poet
   Ayscough—Chinese p195-198

Chute, Beatrice Joy (1913-   )
   Amer. author
   Cur. Biog. '50 p91-92,por.

Chute, Marchette Gaylord (1909-   )
  Amer author
  CR '63 p119,por.
  Cur. Biog. '50 p92-93,por.
  °Muir—Writers p141-148

Cianchettini, Veronica Elizabeth Dussek
  (1779-1833)
  Bohem. composer, teacher
  Elson—Woman's p226

Ciano, Edda (b.c. 1911)
  It., dau. of Mussolini
  Time July 24,1939 p19,por.(cover)

Cibber, Susannah Maria (1714-1766)
  Eng. actress
  Dorland—Sum p25,164
  MacQueen—Pope p180-181,193-194
  Melville—Stage p193-239,por.

Cigna, Gina (1904-   )
  Fr. singer
  Ewen—Living p82-83,por.
  McCoy—Portraits, p24,por.

Cisneros, Eleanora de (Eleanor Broadfoot)
  (1878-1934)
  Fr. singer
  Lahee—Grand p127,146-147,por.
  McCoy—Portraits p24,por.

Claessens, Maria (b. 1881)
  Belg. singer
  Lahee—Grand p370,384

Claflin, Roxie (fl. 1850's-1860's)
  Amer. feminist, religious worker,
    mother of Tennessee and
    Victoria Claflin
  Davenport—Ladies p109-111-112,114,
    116,121

Claflin, Tennessee (1846-1923)
  Amer. feminist, broker, editor,
    journalist
  Davenport—Ladies p110-114,116,121,
    123-124
  Eliot—Heiresses p148-150,por.
  Riegel—Amer. p145-150
  Ross—Charmers p110-136,289-290,por.
  Ross—Ladies p27,31-35

Claflin,Victoria.
  See **Woodhull, Victoria Claflin**

Claghorn, Ethelinda (Ethelinda Lewis)
  (m. 1858)
  Amer. whaling voyager
  Whiting—Whaling p134-142,146-147

Claghorn, Lydia. See West, Lydia

Clair, Joan (fl. 1930's)
  Amer. cosmetic business executive
  Women—Achieve. p97,por.

Claire, Ina Fagan (1892-95-   )
  Amer. actress
  Blum—Great p92,por.
  Caffin—Vaud. p78
  Coad—Amer. p329,por.
  CR '59 p153,por.
  CR '63 p119,por.
  Cur. Biog. '54 p178-180,por.
  Eustis—Players p74-88,por.
  Hammerton p404
  Time Sept.30,1929 p20,por.(cover)

Clairmont, Claire (c. 1797-1879)
  Eng. governess, friend of Shelly and
    Lord Byron
  Howe—Galaxy p126-136
  Wallace—Fabulous p46-90

Clairon, Mademoiselle (Claire Josephe Léris)
  (1723-1803)
  Fr. actress
  Adelman—Famous p83
  Hammerton p404,900
  Herold—Love p261-327,por.

Clancy, Mary Baptist, Mother (fl. 1810's)
  Irish author
  Concannon—Dau. p153-156

Clap, Mary. See Wooster, Mary Clap

Clapp, Anna L. (fl. 1860's)
  Amer. Civil war humanitarian,
    teacher
  Brockett—Woman's p634-636

Clapp, Margaret Antoinette (1910-   )
  Amer. educator, author
  Cur. Biog. '48 p105-107,por.
  Time Oct.10,1949,por. (cover)

Clappe, Louise Amelia Knapp Smith ("Dame
    Shirley," pseud.) (1819-1906)
  Amer. author, pioneer
  Whitton—These p246-250
  Brown—Gentle p13,138,141,150,158,
    291
  °Miller—West p84-99

Clapper, Olive Ewing (1896-1968)
  Amer. author, lecturer
  Cur. Biog. '46 p115-117,por.

Clarahan, Virg Binns (fl. 1930's)
  Amer. public relations worker
  Women—Achieve. p188,por.

Clara Isabella Fornari, Blessed (1697-1744)
  Rom. nun
  Englebert—Lives p468

Clare (or Clara) (1194-1253)
  It. saint
  Blunt—Great p155-156
  Corkran—Romance p247-253

(Continued)

Clare—*Continued*

Culver—Women p93-95
Deen—Great p38-40
Dolan—Goodnow's p108,por.
Elgin—Nun p26-27,por.
Englebert—Lives p309-310
Mozans—Woman p358-359
Sharkey—Pop. p83-87
Stiles—Postal p232
Wescott—Calen. p120-121
°Windham—Sixty p281-289

Clare, Mary (1894-   )
Eng. actress
Hammerton p405

"Claribel." See Barnard, Charlotte Allington

Clark, Alicia Purdom (193?-   )
Pol. millionairess
CR '63 p119-120,por.

Clark, Amy Ashmore (1924-   )
Can. composer, author
ASCAP p85

Clark, Anne. See Hooper, Anne Clark

Clark, Bell Vorse (fl. 1860's)
Amer. Civil war nurse
Logan—Part p365

Clark, Charlotte A. (fl. 1800's)
Amer. W. pioneer
Ellet—Pioneer p350-357
Logan—Part p94-95

Clark, Deener (n.d.)
Amer. TV personality
CR '63 p120,por.

Clark, Dorothy Park ("Clark McMeekin,"
pseud.) (1899-   )
Amer. author
Cur. Biog. '57 p347-349,por.
Warfel—Amer. p295,por.

Clark, Elizabeth
See Zane, Elizabeth ("Betty")

Clark, Eugenie (1922-   )
Amer. ichthyologist
Cur. Biog. '53 p120-122,por.

Clark, Frances Eliot (1860-1958)
Amer. music educator
McCoy—Portraits p25,por.

Clark, Frances Hurd (fl. 1930's)
Amer. metallurgist
Women—Achieve. p131,por.

Clark, Genevieve Bennett (m. 1881)
Amer. patriot
Logan—Part p289-290

Clark, Georgia Neese (1900-   )
Amer. govt. official, U.S. treasurer
Cur. Biog. '49 p114-116,por.
Jensen—Revolt p103,por.
Roosevelt—Ladies p216-220

Clark, Helen (m. 1862)
Amer. whaling voyager
Whiting—Whaling p115-133,277

Clark, Helen Mary (n.d.)
Amer. aviatrix
°May—Women p   ,por.

Clark, Hilda (fl. 1890's)
Amer. singer, actress
Strang—Prima p253-259

Clark, Isabella P. (fl. 1870's)
Amer. pioneer
Sargent—Pioneers p56,por.

Clark, Julia (d. 1912)
Amer. pioneer aviatrix
Planck—Women p18

Clark, Katherine (fl. 1640's)
Amer. colonial business woman
Dexter—Colonial p3

Clark, Lois Pinney (fl. 1930's)
Amer. club leader
Women—Achieve. p132,por.

Clark, Lotti. See Moon, Lottie

Clark, Marguerite (1887-1940)
Amer. actress
Cur. Biog. '40 p179,por.
Wagenknecht—Movies p226-229,por.

Clark, Martha. See Wolcott, Martha Pitkin

Clark, Martha Hull (fl. 1790's)
Amer. landholder, mother of James
Freeman Clark
Dexter—Career p194

Clark, Mary (fl. 1650's)
Eng.-Amer. colonial religious worker
Jones—Quakers p48,57

Clark, Mary Augusta (fl. 1930's)
Amer. public health worker
Women—Achieve. p133,por.

Clark, Mary Chase (fl. 1920's-1930's)
Amer. lawyer
Women—Achieve. p103,por.

Clark, Mary Gail (1914-   )
Amer. composer, music teacher
McCoy—Portraits p25,por.

Clark, Mary S. (fl. 1870's-1880's)
Amer. lecturer
Hanaford—Dau. p344

Clark, Nancy Talbot (1825-1901)
    Amer. pioneer physician
    Lovejoy—Women p82-84
    Mead—Medical p45-46

Clark, Sarah Hatfield (b. 1728)
    Amer. patriot
    Green—Pioneer (3) p147-149

Clark, Susan Carrington (1831-1895)
    Amer. philanthropist
    Root—Chapter p412-416,por.

Clark, Verne (fl. 1930's)
    Amer. cosmetic bus. executive
    Women—Achieve. p99,por.

Clarke, Alva J. (fl. 1930's)
    Amer. employment agency manager
    Women—Achieve. p183,por.

Clarke, Amy (fl. 1860's)
    Amer. soldier
    Simkins—Women p80

Clarke, Edith (n.d.)
    Amer. electrical engineer
    Goff-Women p50-65

Clarke, Hannah (c. 1737-1827)
    Amer. Rev. war patriot
    Green—Pioneer (3) p474

Clarke, Helen Archibald (n.d.)
    Amer. author, editor
    Logan—Part p830-831

Clarke, Marian Williams (1880-1953)
    Amer. Congresswoman
    Paxton—Women p128

Clarke, Mary Anne Thompson (c. 1776-1852)
    Eng., mistress of Frederick, Duke
        of York
    Hammerton p407
    Hasted—Unsuccess p54-79,por.
    Melville—Regency p236-244,por.

Clarke, Mary Cowden.
    See Cowden-Clarke, Mary Victoria

Clarke, Mary Francis, Mother (d. 1887)
    Irish foundress
    Code—Great p254-291

Clarke, Maude Violet (1892-1935)
    Eng. historian
    Brittain—Women p143,191,206,246

Clarke, Nancy See Bruff, Nancy

Clarke, Rebecca (1886-   )
    Amer. composer
    ASCAP p87

Clarke, Rebecca Sophia ("Sophie May,"
        pseud.) (1833-1906)
    Amer. author
    Dorland—Sum p37,189

Clarke, Sarah (1808-1896)
    Amer. painter
    Hanaford—Dau. p302

Clarke, Sara Jane.
    See Greenwood, Grace, pseud.

Clarke, Virginia (fl. 1920's-1950's)
    Amer. missionary
    They—Went p85-86

Claudia (1) (Biblical)
    Deen—All p257-258
    Wescott—Calen. p118

Claudia (2) (fl. c. 143 B.C.)
    Rom., daughter of Claudius Pulcher
    Boccaccio—Conc. p135-136

Claudia (3) (fl. 1st cent.)
    Rom., wife of Statius
    Balsdon—Roman p207

Claudia Acte. See Acte Claudia

Claudia Marcella. See Marcella Claudia

Claudia Procula (Biblical)
    wife of Pontius Pilate
    Harrison—Little p112-123
    Marble—Women p98-99
    Mead—250 p223

Claudia, Quinta (fl. 204 B.C.)
    Rom., probably sister of Appius
        Claudius Pulcher
    Balsdon—Roman p32
    Boccaccio—Con. p168-169

Claussen, Julia (1879-1941)
    Swed. singer
    Cur. Biog. '41 p155
    Ewen—Ency. p89
    McCoy—Portraits p25,por.
    *Richmond—Immig. p17-18

Clauss-Szarvady, Wilhelmine (1834-1907)
    Czech. pianist
    Schonberg—Great p239

Clavering, Mary.
    See Cowper, Mary Clavering

Claxton, Kate (1849-1924)
    Amer. actress
    Coad—Amer. p254,por.

Clay, Bertha M., pseud. (Charlotte M.
        Braeme, or Brame) (1836-1884)
    Eng. novelist
    Dorland—Sum p39

(Continued)

Cleopatra—*Continued*

> Brown—Dark p160-252
> Carnegie—Little p13-17,por.
> °Coffman—Kings p25-32,por.
> Coryn—Enchant. p9-38
> Cuppy—Decline p55-60
> Dark—More p13-35
> Davenport—Great p66-74
> Ewart—World's p61-75
> °Farmer—Book p13-30
> Fitzhugh—Concise p130-131
> Hahn—Love p37-57
> Hammerton p410-411,por.
> °Hayward—Book p1-18
> °Holmes—She
> Jenkins—Heroines p11-49,por.
> Kemble—Idols p93-104
> Koven—Women p3-4
> °MacVeagh—Champlin p144-145,por.
> Muir—Women p42-49
> °Nisenson—Minute p40,por.
> °O'Clery—Queens p25-49
> 100 Great p149-156,por.
> Orr—Famous p3-16
> Orr—Famous Affin. I p3-21
> Phila.—Women unp.,por.
> Reader's—Great p163-168,por.
> Schmidt—400 p114-115,por.
> Sewell—Brief p13-14
> Stiles—Postal p58
> Terhune—Super. p135-155
> Thomas—Living Women p3-15,por.
> Thomas—Vital p61-66
> Weigall—Person. p96-103

Cleopatra Selene (b. 40 B.C.)
> Egypt., dau. of Cleopatra and
> Antony
> Balsdon—Roman p69,71,74-75

Clere, Elizabeth (fl.c. 1450's)
> Eng., wife of Robert Clare
> Stenton—English p98

Clerke, Agnes Mary (1842-1907)
> Irish astronomer
> Adelman—Famous p237
> Dorland—Sum p34,76,142
> Hammerton p411

Cleveland, Anne Neal (fl. 1800's)
> Amer., mother of Grover Cleveland
> Hampton—Our p170-182

Cleveland, Barbara Villiers.
> See **Villiers, Barbara,** Countess of
> Castlemaine

Cleveland, Clarissa.
> See **Dexter, Clarissa L.**

Cleveland, Duchess of
> See **Villiers, Barbara,** Countess of
> Castlemaine, Duchess of
> Cleveland

Cleveland, Emeline Horton (1829-1878)
> Amer. physician, surgeon, lecturer
> Hanaford—Dau. p571-572
> Lovejoy—Women p38-39
> Mead—Medical p63

Cleveland, Frances Folsom (1864-1947)
> Amer. wife of Grover Cleveland
> Farmer—What p100-101,145,por.
> Gerlinger—Mis. p70-72,por.
> Hanaford—Dau. p109-118,por.
> Jensen—White p134-137,por.
> Logan—Ladies p127-133
> Logan—Part p277-279
> °McConnell—Our p221-227,por.
> Prindiville—First p179-184
> °Ross—Know p47,por.
> Smith—Romances p298-304,por.
> Smith—White p105-117,por.
> °Sweetser—Famous p229-237,por.
> Truett—First p54,por.

Cleveland, Harriet (m. 1841)
> Amer. whaling voyager
> Whiting—Whaling p38-42

Cleveland, Rose Elizabeth (1846-1918)
> Amer., sister of Grover Cleveland
> Hanaford—Dau. p109-110
> Logan—Ladies p126
> Logan—Part p275-276

Clews, Mrs. James Blanchard (fl. 1910)
> Amer. religious worker
> Logan—Part p619

Clifford, Anne, Lady, Countess of Dorset
> (1590-1676)
> Eng. author, philanthropist
> Stenton—English (see index)

Clifford, Camille (m. 1906)
> Scan. dancer
> Wyndham—Chorus p113-116

Clifford, Elizabeth, Lady.
> See **De La Pasture, Elizabeth Lydia
> Rosabelle Bonham**

Clifford, Lucy Lane (d. 1929)
> Brit. novelist
> Hammerton p412,por.

Clifford, Mrs. (fl. 1870's)
> Amer. traveler
> Hanaford—Dau p737

Clifford, Rosamond ("Fair Rosamund"),
> (d. 1777)
> Eng., mistress of Henry II
> Jenkins—Ten p84-100
> MacVeagh—Champlin p219

Clifton, Fanny. See **Stirling, Mary Anne**

Clifton, Josephine (1813-1847)
    Amer. actress
    Coad—Amer. p99,por.

Cline, Genevieve Rose (b. 1879)
    Amer. judge
    Women—Achieve. p91,por.

Cline, Maggie (fl. 1910's)
    Irish actress
    Caffin—Vaud. p62-66,por.

Clinton, Catharine.
    See **Van Cortlandt, Joanna Livingston**

Clinton, Cornelia. See **Genet, Cornelia**

Clinton, Cornelia Tappen (m. 1770)
    Amer. Rev. war patriot
    Green—Pioneer (3) p300-302

Clinton, Doris (n.d.)
    Amer. mechanical, aeronautical
      engineer
    *Peckham—Women p129

Clithorow, Margaret Middleton (1556-1586)
    Eng. martyr
    Blunt—Great p224-249
    Hammerton p413

Clive, Caroline Meyse-Wigley (1801-1875)
    Eng. novelist
    Oliphant—Women p161-175
    Stebbins—Victorian p12-15,205

Clive, Catherine ("Kitty") R. (1711-1785)
    Irish actress, singer
    Dorland—Sum p20,69,164
    Hammerton p413
    MacQueen—Pope p289-290,por.
    Melville—Stage p51-107,por.

Clodia ("Lesbia") (b.c. 94 B.C.)
    Rom. beauty
    Balsdon—Roman p54-55,214,226,295

Cloke, Elizabeth Cook (Coke).
    See **Cook, Elizabeth**

Clooney, Betty (n.d.)
    Amer. singer
    TV—Person (1) p145,por.

Clooney, Rosemary (1928-   )
    Amer. singer
    CR '59 p157,por.
    CR '63 p123-124,por.
    Cur. Biog. '57 p113-115,por.
    Popular Record p36,por.
    Stambler—Ency. p50
    Time Feb.23,1953 p54,por.(cover)

Close, Elizabeth Stuart (fl. 1930's)
    Amer. fashion designer
    Women—Achieve. p187,por.

Clotilda (Clotilde) (c. 475-c. 545)
    Fr. saint
    Blunt—Great p75-78
    Cather—Girlhood p3-23
    Culver—Women p81-82
    Deen—Great p318-320
    Dolan—Goodnow p90
    Englebert—Lives p215
    Fifty—Famous p287-288
    Hammerton p414
    Koven—Women p10-11
    Muir—Women p62-63
    Wescott—Calen. p81

Cloud, Mrs. Roe (fl. 1950's)
    Amer. Ind. missionary
    Davis—Mothers p179

Clough, Anne Jemima (1820-1892)
    Eng. educator
    Brittain—Famous p35,59
    Dorland—Sum p46,77,109

Clowes, Evelyn May.
    See **Mordaunt, Elinor**

Clyde, Mrs. (fl. 1770's)
    Amer. pioneer
    Green—Pioneer (3) p149

Clymer, Elizabeth Meredith (m. 1765)
    Amer. Rev. war patriot
    Green—Pioneer (3) p195-197

Coale, Virginia (fl. 1930's)
    Amer. retail executive
    Women—Achieve. p93,por.

Coate, Mary (gr. 1915)
    Eng. tutor
    Brittain—Women p188,206,246

Coates, Edith (1908-   )
    Eng. singer
    Brook—Singers p48-54,por.
    Davidson—Treas. p67-71,por.

Coates, Florence Earle (1850-1927)
    Amer. poet
    Cook—Our p193-195

Coates, Ruth Keezel (fl. 1940's-1950's)
    Amer. missionary, nurse
    They—Went p142

Coats, Alice M. (1905-   )
    Eng. illustrator
    Mahony—Illus. p292

Coatsworth, Elizabeth (1893-   )
    Amer. poet, novelist
    Warfel—Amer. p93,por.

Cobb, Buff (1927-   )
    Amer. actress
    TV—Person (1) p145-146,por.

Cobb, Jerrie (Geraldine M.) (1931-)
    Amer. aviatrix
    CR '63 p124,por.
    Cur. Biog. '61 p106-107,por.
    *May—Women p44-55,247,250
    Silver—Profiles p63-72,por.

Cobb, Lydia (Lydia Leonard) (fl. 1770's)
    Amer. Rev. war patriot
    Green—Pioneer (3) p469

Cobb, Zoe Desloge (b. 1850)
    Amer. religious worker
    Logan—Part p619

Cobbe, Frances Power (1822-1904)
    Irish author, philanthropist
    Adelman—Famous p234

Cobble, Alice Dunning (fl. 1930's-1950's)
    Amer. missionary
    They—Went p97-98

Cobbs, Susan Parker (fl. 1950's)
    Amer. educator
    Murrow—This (1) p31-32

Coburn, Eleanor Habawell Abbot (b. 1872)
    Amer. author
    Logan—Part p851

Coca, Imogene (1908-)
    Amer. actress
    Blum—Television p21,25,por.
    CR '59 p158-159,por.
    CR '63 p124-125,por.
    Cur. Biog. '51 p115-117,por.
    TV—Person p83-84,por.

Cochran, Dewees (1902-)
    Amer. artist, doll maker
    Women—Achieve. p89,por.

Cochran, Jacqueline (1906/10-)
    Amer. aviatrix, business executive
    *Adams—Sky p239-253,por.
    Clymer—Modern p160-168,por.
    CR '59 p159,por.
    CR '63 p125,por.
    Cur. Biog. '40 p181-183,por.
    Cur. Biog. '63 p77-80,por.
    Dwiggins—They (see index),por.
    Heinmuller—Mans p352,por.
    *Lauwick—Heroines p45-54,por.
    *May—Women p152-155,163,171-174,
      176-177,198,por.
    *Peckham—Women p6,10
    Planck—Women p97-102,113,258-260,
      por.
    Women—Achieve. p74,por.

Cochran, Margaret.
    See Corbin, Margaret Cochran

Cochran, Nannie M. (fl. 1860's)
    Amer. Civil war nurse
    Logan—Part p365

Cochrane, Grizel (fl. 17th cent.)
    Scot. heroine
    Muir—Women p79-80

Coci, Claire (fl. 1930's-1940's)
    Amer. organist
    McCoy—Portraits p26,por.

Cockburn, Alicia (Alison Rutherford)
    (1713-1794)
    Scot. song-writer, poet
    Dorland—Sum p30-80-81,107
    Findlay—Spindle p26-45,por.
    Graham—Group p178-198,por.
    Hammerton p417

Cockburn, Catharine Trotter (1679-1749)
    Eng. playwright, poet, philosopher
    Stenton—English p231-234

Cockerton, Ina (1891-1952)
    Amer. nurse
    Phillips—33 p186-190

Cockrell, Marian (1909-)
    Amer. novelist
    Warfel—Amer. p94-95,por.

Cody, Mrs. S. F. (fl. 1900's)
    Amer. pioneer air passenger
    *May—Women p60

Coe, Emma Robinson (fl. 1850's-1860's)
    Amer. lawyer, feminist, lecturer
    O'Connor—Pioneer p90-91,183-184,
      301-303

Coe, Ethel Louise (n.d.)
    Amer. painter
    Michigan—Biog. p73-74

Coffey, Phyllis C. (fl. 1930's)
    Amer. teacher, humanitarian
    Women—Achieve. p148

Coffin, Dionis Stevens (fl. 1640's-1660's)
    Amer. colonial business woman
    Dexter—Colonial p50,208-209

Coffin, Keziah Folger (m. 1740)
    Amer. Rev. war merchant
    Dexter—Career p160
    Snow—Women p104-105

Coffin, Mrs. C. F. (fl. 1870's)
    Amer. philanthropist
    Hanaford—Dau. p182

Coffin, Lucretia. See Mott, Lucretia Coffin

Coffin, Mary Starbuck (fl. 1870's-1880's)
    Amer. poet
    Hanaford—Dau. p262

Coffin, Mrs. Peter (fl. 1770's)
    Amer. Rev. war patriot
    Bruce—Woman p102-104

Coggins, Caroline (fl. 1930's)
Amer. journalist, editor
Women—Achieve. p172,por.

Coghill, Mrs. Henry (fl. 19th cent.)
Eng. author
Furniss—Some p36-37

Coghlan, Rose (1853-1932)
Eng.-Amer. actress
Coad—Amer. p258,por.
Marks—Glamour p285-286
Strang—Actresses p258-269

Cogswell, Alice (fl. 18th-19th cent.)
Amer., deaf-mute, dau. of
Dr. Mason F. Cogswell
Holbrook—Dreamers p262-263

Cohen, Barbara (1901-   )
Amer. recording co. executive
Cur. Biog. '57 p115-117,por.

Cohen, Harriet (1901-   )
Eng. pianist
Brook—Masters p151-152,por.
Ewen—Living p86-87,por.
McCoy—Portraits p26,por.
Saleski—Jewish p463-464

Cohen, Katherine M. (1859-1914)
Amer. sculptor, painter
Taft—Women, Mentor #2
Waters—Women p84

Cohen, Octavia (b.c. 1718)
Amer. Civil war patriot
Logan—Part p496-497

Coillard, Christina (1829-1891)
Scot. pioneer missionary
*Matthews—Daunt. p73-101

Coit, Dorothy (1889-   )
Amer. dramatic coach, director and
teacher
Women—Achieve. p186,por.

Coit, Elizabeth (fl. 1930's)
Amer. architectural executive
Women—Achieve. p153,por.

Coit, Lottie Ellsworth (fl. 1940's)
Amer. music educator, violinist
McCoy—Portraits p26,por.

Coit, Margaret Louise (1919-   )
Amer. author, journalist
CR '63 p126,por.
Cur. Biog. '51 p124-126,por.

Coke, Mary Campbell, Lady (b. 1726)
Eng. hostess, dau. of Duke of Argyle
Stenton—English p266-268
Stirling—Odd p99-115

Coker, Elizabeth Boatwright (1909-   )
Amer. author
Cur. Biog. '59 p77-78,por.

Colbert, Claudette (1907-   )
Fr.-Amer. actress
CR '59 p160,por.
CR '63 p126,por.
Cur. Biog. '45 p115-116,por.
Cur. Biog. '64 p83-86,por.
Hammerton p419
Hughes—Famous p47-67,por.
Schickel—Stars p158,por.

Colbran, Isabella (1785-1845)
Sp. singer
Derwent—Rossini p124-126,170-171,
274-279,por.
Ewen—Ency. p90
Lahee—Famous p44-45

Colburn, Joan (fl. 1930's)
Amer. fashion commentator, radio
broadcasting executive
Women—Achieve. p130,por.

Colby, Anita (1914-   )
Amer. actress, model, technical
adviser, journalist, editor
CR '59 p160-161,por.
CR '63 p127,por.
Time Jan.8,1945 p39,por(cover)

Colby, Marie F. (fl. 1930's)
Amer. humanitarian
Women—Achieve. p196

Colby, Mary Colgate (d. 1938)
Amer. recluse
Erskine—Out p91-99

Colby, Nathalie Sedgwick (1875-1942)
Amer. essayist, poet, novelist
Cur. Biog. '42 p159
Overton—Women p98-102

Colby, Sarah A. (b. 1824)
Amer. physician
Hanaford—Dau. p561-563

Colcord, Joanna Carver (1882-1960)
Amer. social worker
Snow—Women p196-211,por.

Colcord, Mabel (b. 1872)
Amer. librarian, bibliographer,
entomologist
Bul. of Bibl. May-Aug.1949 p225,por.

Colden, Jane (1724-1766)
Amer. colonial botanist
Beard—Amer. p33
Dexter—Colonial p118-119
Earle—Colon. p86-87
Hollingsworth—Her p23-34
Leonard—Amer. p115

Cole, Celia Caroline (fl. 1930's)
Amer. beauty editor
Women—Achieve. p110,por.

Cole, Helen Brainard (fl. 1860's)
Amer. Civil war nurse
Logan—Part p371

Cole, Helen D. (fl. 1930's)
Amer. fashion designer
Women—Achieve. p196

Cole, Jessie Duncan Savage (1858-1940)
Amer. painter
Cur. Biog. '40 p183

Cole, Katherine.
See **Gaylord, Katherine Cole**

Cole, Miriam M. (fl. 1870's-1880's)
Amer. lecturer, feminist, author,
journalist
Hanaford—Dau. p345,703

Cole, Rebecca (gr. 1867)
Amer. physician
Lovejoy—Women p63,121

Cole, Ruth. See **Hart, Ruth Cole**

Cole, Ulric (1905-   )
Amer. composer
Ewen—American p64-65,por.

Coleman, Alice Blanchard (b. 1858)
Amer. missionary
Logan—Part p517-519

Coleman, Ann (fl. 1660's)
Amer. colonial religious worker
Jones—Quakers p103-105

Coleman, Georgia (1912-1940)
Amer. diver
Cur. Biog. '40 p183

Coleman, Louise Macpherson (fl. 1890's-
1900's)
Can.-Amer. nurse
Pennock—Makers p132,por.

Coleman, Mrs. (fl. 1650's)
Eng. pioneer actress
MacQueen—Pope p26-27
Stenton—English p202

Coleman, Satis Narrona (b. 1878)
Amer. music author
Women—Achieve. p112,por.

Coleridge, Sara Henry (1802-1852)
Eng. translator, poet
Adelman—Famous p137
Dorland—Sum p27,178,189
Hammerton p421,por.
°MacVeagh—Champlin p147

Coles, Izabel M. (fl. 1920's-1930's)
Amer. jewelry designer
Women—Achieve. p118,por.

Colet, Louise Révoil (1810-1876)
Fr. author, salonist
Dorland—Sum p46,106-107

Colette (1381-1447)
Fr. saint
Englebert—Lives p90-91
Wescott—Calen. p34

Colette, Sidonie Gabrielle Claudine
(1873-1954)
Fr. author
Beaton—Persona p29-30,por.
Hammerton p421
Peyre—French p276-278,452

Colfax, Harriet R. (fl. 1860's)
Amer. Civil war nurse
Brockett—Woman's p395-399

Colgan, Eleanor (fl. 1900's)
Amer. educator
Logan—Part p721

Collart (Collaert), Marie (b. 1842)
Belg. painter
Waters—Women p84-85

Collett (Collette), Camilla Wergeland
(1813-1895)
Nor. novelist, feminist
Schmidt—400 p308-309,por.
Stiles—Postal p59

Collett, Glenna (1903-   )
Amer. golf player
Jensen—Revolt p132,por.
New Yorker Sept. 17,1927 p26-28,
(Profiles)
Rogers—Women p131,por.

Collier, Constance Hardie (1878/1880-1955)
Eng. actress
Blum—Great p47,por.
Cur. Biog. '54 p193-196,por.
Cur. Biog. '55 p132
Hammerton p422

Collier, Lucille Ann. See **Miller, Ann**

Collin, Mademoiselle (fl. 1920's)
Fr. war nurse, parachutist
°May—Women p55

Collinge, Patricia (1894-   )
Irish actress
Blum—Great p115,por.

Collins, Dorothy (1926-   )
Can. singer
CR '59 p162,por.
TV—Person (2) p112,por.

Collins, Ellen (fl. 1860's)
    Amer. Civil war patriot
    Brockett—Woman's p79,533-534,536

Collins, Jennie C. (fl. 1870's-1880's)
    Amer. philanthropist
    Hanaford—Dau. p179

Collins, Joan (1933-   )
    Eng.-Amer. actress
    CR '59 p162,por.
    CR '63 p128,por.

Collins, José (1887-1958)
    Eng. actress, singer
    Caffin—Vaud. p79
    Hammerton p423,por.

Collins, Libby Smith (1844-1921)
    Amer. W. pioneer, cattle queen,
        vigilante
    Rogers—Women p55,por.
    Sickels—Twelve p112-129,253-254
    Towle—Vigil. p46-72,por.

Collitz, Klara Hechtenberg (d. 1944)
    Ger.-Amer. philologist
    Dorland—Sum p144

Collver, Nathalia S. (fl. 1930's)
    Amer. educator
    Women—Achieve. p176,por.

Colman, Benita Hume (n.d.)
    Eng.-Amer. actress
    TV—Person (1) p48,por.

Colman, Jane (fl. 1770's)
    Amer. author
    Benson—Women p110-111,113-114,
        116-118,123

Colman, Julia (fl. 1910's)
    Amer. social reformer
    Logan—Part p672

Colonna, Vittoria (1490/92-1547)
    It. poet
    Adelman—Famous p45-46
    Blunt—Great p398-404
    *Cather—Girlhood p187-211
    Corkran—Romance p259-293
    Deen—Great p75-81
    Dorland—Sum p17,179
    Koven—Women p113-121
    *MacVeagh—Champlin p149
    Schmidt—400 p250-251,por.

Colt, Henrietta L. Peckham (b. 1812)
    Amer. Civil war humanitarian
    Brockett—Woman's p609-613,por.

Colt, Miriam Davis (fl. 1850's)
    Amer. author, club leader
    Holbrook—Dreamers p50-51

Colt, Mrs. (fl. 1870's-1880's)
    Amer. philanthropist
    Hanaford—Dau. p183

Colt, Susan (d. 1863)
    Amer. whaling voyager
    Whiting—Whaling p81-93,por.

Coltman, Constance M. (gr. 1911)
    Amer. clergyman
    Brittain—Women p250

Colton, Elizabeth Sweetzer (fl. 1910's-1930's)
    Amer. Orientalist, linguist
    Dorland—Sum p144

Columba of Sens (d.c. 374)
    Sp. saint
    Englebert—Lives p496

Colver, Alice Mary Ross (1892-   )
    Amer. author
    Warfel—Amer. p97,por.

Colvill, Margaret Wemyss, Lady
        (fl. 1660's-1680's)
    Scot. covenanter
    Anderson—Ladies p241-252

Colvin, Mamie White (1883-1955)
    Amer. organization official
    Cur. Biog. '44 p104-106,por.
    Cur. Biog. '56 p124
    Women—Achieve. p186,por.

Colwell, Eileen Hilda (1904-   )
    Eng. librarian
    Cur. Biog. '63 p84-86,por.

Colwell, Elizabeth (fl. 1910's)
    Amer. printer, type designer
    Club—Printing p18

Colwell, Ethel (n.d.)
    Can. aviatrix
    *Knapp—New p117-128,por.
    *Peckham—Women p73-74

Coman, Charlotte Buell (1833-1924)
    Amer. painter
    Logan—Part p755
    Michigan—Biog. p74-75
    Waters—Women p85

Coman, Katherine (1857-1915)
    Amer. educator, economist,
        historian, social reformer
    Dorland—Sum p41,121,175
    Logan—Part p720

Coman, Martha (d. 1959)
    Amer. journalist
    Ross—Ladies p126-129

Comb, Helen (fl. 1870's)
    Amer. lawyer
    Hanaford—Dau. p668

Comber, Elizabeth Chow. See Han Suyin

Combs, Sarah Richardson (fl. 1800's)
    Amer. W. pioneer
    Ellet—Pioneer p62

Comden, Betty (1915/19-   )
    Amer. author, musician, actress
    ASCAP p92-93
    CR '59 p163,por.
    CR '63 p129,por.
    Cur. Biog. '45 p117-119,por.
    Stambler—Ency. p53

Comerre-Paton, Jacqueline (b. 1859)
    Fr. painter
    Waters—Women p85

Comfort, Annabel (fl. 1940's)
    Amer. composer, writer
    McCoy—Portraits p26,por.

Coming, Affra Harleston (d. 1699)
    Amer. colonial agronomist
    Leonard—Amer. p113

Commena, Anna (1083-1148)
    Gr., historian, Byzantine princess
    Culver—Women p92
    Dorland—Sum p174
    Koven—Women p14-16
    Schmidt—400 p215-216,por.

Compson, Betty (fl. 1920's)
    Amer. actress
    Brundidge—Twinkle p61-70,por.

Compton, Fay (1894-   )
    Eng. actress
    Hammerton p427,por.

Compton, Otelia Catherine Augspurger
        (d. 1944)
    Amer., mother of Compton brothers
    Davis—Mothers p74-78

Compton-Burnett, Ivy (1892-   )
    Eng. author
    Beaton—Persona p33,por.
    CR '59 p164-165,por.

Comstock, Anna Botsford (1854-1930)
    Amer. naturalist, wood-engraver,
        educator
    Osborn—Fragments p178,por.
    °Yost—Famous p121-129,por.

Comstock, Elizabeth L. (1815-1891)
    Eng.-Amer. social reformer
    Hanaford—Dau. p433,441,por.

Comstock, Harriet (b. 1860)
    Amer. novelist
    Overton—Women p103-104

Comstock, Mrs. (fl. 1800's)
    Amer. W. pioneer
    Ellet—Pioneer p401

Comstock, Nanette (fl. 1880's-1890's)
    Amer. actress
    Marks—Glamour p288

Comstock, Sarah Davis (fl. 1830's)
    Amer. missionary
    Hanaford—Dau. p510

Conan, Laure (1845-1924)
    Can. author
    Innis—Clear p91-102 (in French), por.

Conant, Helen C. (fl. 1870's-1880's)
    Amer. author
    Hanaford—Dau. p247

Conant, Helen S. (1839-1899)
    Amer. entomologist, author
    Hanaford—Dau. p288

Conant, Isabel La Howe Fiske (b. 1874)
    Amer. poet
    Smith—Women's p27

Conath, Estelline (fl. 1500's)
    It. pioneer printer
    Club—Printing p10

Concepcion, Arenal (1820-1893)
    Sp. publicist, social worker,
        humanitarian
    Schmidt—400 p358-360,por.

Conde, Bertha (n.d.)
    Amer. author
    Women—Achieve. p156,por.

Condorcet, Sophie de Grouchy de (1765-
        1822)
    Fr., wife of Marquis de Condorcet
    Kavanagh—Woman (2) p73-74,91-92

Cone, Helen Gray (1859-1934)
    Amer. educator, poet
    Cook—Our p220-221

Cone, Mary (fl. 1870's)
    Amer. author
    Sargent—Pioneers p20,30

Conger, Mrs. Al. (fl. 1900's)
    Amer. humanitarian, club leader
    Logan—Part p481

Conise, Annette (fl. 1870's)
    Amer. notary public
    Hanaford—Dau. p669

Conkey, Elizabeth A. Loughran (c. 1883-
        1963)
    Amer. politician
    Roosevelt—Ladies p102-110

Conklin, Jennie M. Drinkwater (1841-1900)
Amer. author, philanthropist, club
leader
Dorland—Sum p48,73-74,125,189

Conkling, Grace Walcott Hazard (1878-
1958)
Amer. poet
Cook—Our p319-321
Smith—Women's p30

Conkling, Hilda (1910-   )
Amer. poet
Cook—Our p330-334

Conkling, Julia Catherine (1827-1893)
Amer. organization official
Logan—Part p472

Conkling, Mabel (b. 1871)
Amer. sculptor
National—Contemp. p56
Taft—Women, Mentor #6

Connelly, Cornelia Auguste Peacock, Mother
(1809-1879)
Amer. foundress
Code—Great p406-436,por.

Conner, Nadine (1913-   )
Amer. singer
Cur. Biog. '55 p134-136,por.
Matz—Opera p107-109,por.
Peltz—Spot. p104

Conneray (Connarray), Martha.
See "Calamity Jane"

Conners, Grace (1900-   )
Amer. philanthropist
Time May 25,1931 p31,por.(cover)

Connolly, Maureen Catherine (1934-1969)
Amer. tennis player
CR '59 p166,por.
Cur. Biog. '51 p132-134,por.
Davis—100 p21,por.

Connolly, Sybil (1921-   )
Welsh-Irish fashion designer
CR '59 p167,por.

Connor, Emily E. (fl. 1930's)
Amer. printer, typographer
Club—Printing p24-25,por.

Connor, Marcia (fl. 1930's)
Amer. journalist, advertising
specialist
Women—Achieve. p134,por.

Conquest, Ida (1882-1937)
Amer. actress
Strang—Actresses p69-71

Cons, Emma (1838-1912)
Eng. philanthropist
Hammerton p432,por.

Consolata, Mary, Sister.
See Carroll, Consolata, pseud.

Constance (fl. 4th cent.)
Rom. saint
*Windham—Sixty p123-130

Constance of Hohenstaufen (d. 1313)
Byzant. empress
Diehl—Byzant. p259-275

Constance of Sicily (1152-1198)
Sic. queen, Rom. empress
Boccaccio—Conc. p239-241

Constantia (d.c. 330)
Rom. empress, wife of Licinius
McCabe—Empr. p288-293
Serviez—Roman (2) p406-426

Constantia, Augusta (d.c. 354)
Rom. saint, niece of Emperor
Constantine
Englebert—Lives p68

"Constantia." See Murray, Judith Sargent

Contat, Louise Françoise (1760-1813)
Fr. actress
Dorland—Sum p43,69,167

Conti, Italia (c. 1873-1946)
Eng. actress, dramatic teacher
Hammerton p436

Convers, Dorothea (b. 1873)
Irish author
Hammerton p437

Converse, Thelma, Lady Furness (fl. 1930's-
1940's)
Amer. social leader, business woman
Pearson—Pilgrim p231-240,por.

Conway, Anne Finch (fl. 1670's)
Eng. viscountess
Stenton—English p194-195

Conway, Shirl (1916-   )
Amer. actress
CR '63 p134,por.

Conyngham, Anne (fl. 1770's)
Amer. Rev. war patriot
Ellet—Women (2) p356-359

Conyngham, Lady (d. 1861)
Eng., friend of George IV
Melville—Regency p277-284

Coogan, Harriet Gardiner Lynch (1861-
1947)
Amer. recluse
Erskine—Out p223-235

Coogan, Jessie (fl. 1930's)
Amer. recluse
Erskine—Out p226-227,229-230,232-
235

Cook, Barbara (1927-   )
Amer. actress
CR '63 p135,por.
Cur. Biog. '63 p86-88,por.

Cook, Eliza (1818-1889)
Eng. poet, editor, publisher
Dorland—Sum p119
Hammerton p437

Cook, Elizabeth (fl. 1740's-1770's)
Amer. Rev. war patriot
Blei—Fasc. p181-184
Green—Pioneers (3) p516-517

Cook, Fannie Bruce (1893-1949)
Amer. author
Cur. Biog. '46 p129-130,por.
Cur. Biog. '49 p123
Sargent—Pioneers p32
Warfel—Amer. p98-99,por.

Cook, Mrs. Hosea (fl. c. 1790's)
Amer. pioneer, heroine
Bruce—Woman p135
Fowler—Woman p95-96

Cook, Jessie (fl. 1790's)
Amer. pioneer, heroine
Bruce—Woman p135-136
Fowler—Woman p95-96

Cook, Maria (fl. 1820's)
Amer. clergyman
Dexter—Career p62-63

Cook, Mary Elizabeth (b. 1881)
Amer. sculptor
National—Contemp. p52

Cook, Miss (fl. 1700's)
Amer. pioneer, heroine, Indian
captive
Fowler—Woman p86-87

Cook, Nancy (fl. 1930's)
Amer. designer, politician
Women—Achieve. p137,por.

Cook, Sarah (fl. 1670's)
Eng. actress
MacQueen—Pope p121-122

Cook, Susan. See Glaspell, Susan

Cooke, Demaris Hopkins (m. 1647, d. before
1669)
Amer. Pilgrim
Green—Pioneer (1) p140-141
Logan—Part p33-34

Cooke, Grace McGowan (b. 1863)
Amer. author
Logan—Part p847

Cooke, Hannah Sabin (b. 1722)
Amer. Rev. war patriot
Green—Pioneer (3) p300

Cooke, Hope.
See Hope Namgyal, Maharani of Sikkim

Cooke, Kate Walsh (d. 1903)
Amer. dancer, friend of John Henry
Cooke
Wyndham—Chorus p73-77-79

Cooke, Marjorie Benton (1876-1920)
Amer. monologist
Maurice—Makers p7,por.

Cooke, Rose Terry (1827-1892)
Amer. author
Bruère—Laugh. p9
Dorland—Sum p54,182

Cooke, Sarah (d. 1688)
Eng. actress
Wilson—All p130-131

Cookesley, Margaret Murray (fl. 1890's)
Eng. painter
Waters—Women p85-86

Cookman, Helen Cramp (fl. 1930's)
Amer. fashion designer, bus.
executive
Women—Achieve p138,por.

Cooley, Anna Maria (1874-1955)
Amer. home economist, author
Women—Achieve. p115,por.

Cooley, Winnifred Harper (fl. 1930's)
Amer. author, lecturer, radio
personality
Women—Achieve. p78,por.

Coolidge, Elizabeth Sprague (1864-1953)
Amer. pianist, music patron,
philanthropist
Cur. Biog. '41 p169-170,por.
Cur. Biog. '54 p204
McCoy—Portraits p27,por.

Coolidge, Emelyn Lincoln (1873-1949)
Amer. pediatrician, editor
Women—Achieve. p110,por.

Coolidge, Grace Anna Goodhue (1879-
1957)
Amer., wife of Calvin Coolidge
Fairfax—Ladies p202-203
Fowler—Woman p408-415
Gerlinger—Mis. p95-96,por.
Jensen—White. p224-228,por.
Logan—Ladies p174-182
*McConnell—Our p285-294,por.
New Yorker May 15,1926,p17-18,por.
(Profile)
Prindiville—First p229-235
*Ross—Know p61,por.
Smith—Romances p381-387,por.
Time Sept.17,1928,p7,por.

Coolidge, Mary Elizabeth Burroughs Rob-
erts Smith (b. 1860)
Amer. sociologist
Logan—Part p847

Coombs, Mrs. Fairfax. See Caldwell, Taylor

Coombs, Lucinda (gr. 1873)
Amer. physician, missionary
Lovejoy—Women p230-231

Coon, Harriet. See Cleveland, Harriet

Cooney, Barbara (1917-   )
Amer. illustrator
Mahoney—Illus. p293

Cooper, Alice (fl. 1920's)
Amer. sculptor
Taft—Women, Mentor #2

Cooper, Ann. See Whitehall, Ann Cooper

Cooper, Diana, Lady (Diana Mathers, pseud.)
(1893-   )
Eng. actress, beauty
CR '59 p169-170,por.

Cooper, Edna May (fl. 1920's)
Amer. aviatrix
*May—Women p254

Cooper, Elizabeth (b. 1877)
Amer. author
Dorland—Sum p174

Cooper, Emma Lampert (d. 1920)
Amer. painter
Jackman—Amer. p286
Michigan—Biog. p76
Waters—Women p86-87

Cooper, Gladys (b. 1888)
Eng. actress
CR '59 p170-171,por.
Cur. Biog. '56 p125-126,por.
Hammerton p440,por.
Wyndham—Chorus p154-155

Cooper, Humility (fl. 1600's)
Amer. Pilgrim
Logan—Part p34
Marble—Women p59-60

Cooper, Lenna Frances (fl. 1930's)
Amer. dietician
Women—Achieve. p127,por.

Cooper, Louise Field (1905-   )
Amer. author
Cur. Biog. '50 p99-100,por.
Warfel—Amer. p99,por.

Cooper, Susan Fenimore (1815-1894)
Amer. author
Hanaford—Dau. p239

Copeland, Bernice Rose (fl. 1940's)
Amer. composer, music teacher
McCoy—Portraits p27,por.

Copeland, Jo (1903-   )
Amer. fashion designer
CR '59 p171-172,por.
CR '63 p136,por.

Copeland, Katherine (n.d.)
Amer. actress
TV—Person. (2) p68-69,por.

Copley, Heather (1918-   )
Eng. illustrator
Ryder—Artists p55

Copley, Mary Singleton (d. 1789)
Irish-Amer. colonial merchant
Dexter—Colonial p20,206-207

Coplon, Judith (fl. 1920's-1940's)
Russ. spy
Singer—World's p113-127,por.

Copp, Evelyn Fletcher (d. 1945)
Amer. music educator
McCoy—Portraits p27,por.

Copp, Laura Remick (d. 1934)
Amer. pianist, music teacher
McCoy—Portraits p27,por.

Coppage, Grace (fl. 1930's)
Amer. cosmetician
Women—Achieve. p124,por.

Coppedge, Ione (fl. 1930's)
Amer. aviatrix
*May—Women p136

Coppin, Fanny M. Jackson (1835-1912)
Amer. educator
Brown—Home. p119-126,por.
Robinson—Hist. p67,por.

Corazzi, Giulitta (b. 1866)
It. painter
Waters—Women p87-88

Corbeaux, Fanny (1812-1883)
Eng. artist
Adelman—Famous p184

Corbett, Elizabeth Francis (b. 1887)
Warfel—Amer. p99-101,por.

Corbett, Gail Sherman (m. 1905)
Amer. sculptor
Jackman—Amer. p409-410
National—Contemp. p61

Corbett, Leonora (1908-   )
Eng. actress
Hammerton p442

Corbin, Caroline Elizabeth (b. 1835)
Amer. author
Logan—Part p833

Corbin, Edythe Patten (fl. 1900's)
Amer. social leader, linguist
Logan—Part p619
National—Contemp. p619

Corbin, Elizabeth.
See Braxton, Elizabeth Corbin

Corbin, Elizabeth T. (fl. 1750's)
Amer. pioneer
Green—Pioneer (3) p255,257

Corbin, Hazel (fl. 1920's)
Can.-Amer. nurse
Pennock—Makers p92,por.

Corbin, Margaret Cochran (1751-1800)
Amer. Rev. war heroine, patriot
Fowler—Woman p125-126
Green—Pioneer (2) p223-227
Hanaford—Dau. p63-64
Leonard—Amer. p113

Cochran, Katherine.
See Herne, Katherine Corcoran

Corday, Charlotte (Marie Anne Charlotte
Corday D'Armont) (1769-1793)
Fr. patriot
Abbot—Notable p156-159,por.
Adelman—Famous p93-94,por.
Clark—Great p1000-1013
Dobson—Four p1-27
Dorland—Sum p22
Fifty—Famous p83-92,por.
Goldsmith—Seven p1-30
Hammerton p442,por.
Kavanagh—Woman (2) p141-156,por.
Love—Famous p11-12
*MacVeagh—Champlin, p158,por.
Muir—Women p122-123
*Nisenson—More Minute p42,por.
Orr—Famous p217-227
Orr—Famous Affin. II p95-108

Corelli, Marie, pseud. (Mary Mackay)
(1855/64-1924)
Eng. author
Adelman—Famous p272
Black—Notable p329-335
Furniss—Some p40-41
Hammerton p443,por.

Corey, Catherine (fl. 17th cent.)
Eng. actress
MacQueen—Pope p62-64
Wilson—All p132-134

Corey, Dorothy Dudley (n.d.)
Amer. marketing, advertising
executive
Parshalle—Kash. p87-91,por.

Corey, Jill (1935-   )
Amer. actress, por.
TV—Person. (2) p90-91,por.

Corey, Martha (fl. 1690's)
Amer. accused witch
Green—Pioneer (1) p227

Cori, Gerty Theresa Radnitz (1896-1957)
Czech. biochemist, educator
Cur. Biog. '37 p135-137,por.
Cur. Biog. '58 p101
Lovejoy—Women p197-198,por.
Nobel—Man p226,271-272
*Riedman—Portraits p194-198
Stevenson—Nobel p255,por.
Year—Pic. p221,por.
*Yost—Women Mod. p1-16,por.

Corinna of Tanagro (fl. B.C. c. 490)
Gr. poet
Anthologia—Poets p84
Drinker—Music p103
Elson—Woman's p28

Corio, Ann (n.d.)
Amer. dancer, actress
CR '63 p137,por.
Newquist—Show. p45-56,por.

Cork, Mary, Countess of.
See Monckton, Mary

Cormier, Lucia (b. 1912)
Amer. politician
Time Sept.5,1960 p13,por.(cover)

Cornaro-Lusignano, Caterina (1454-1510)
It. (Cyprus) queen
Hammerton p443,por.
Schmidt—400 p248-249,por.

Cornelia (1) (fl. 169 B.C.-2nd cent., B.C.)
Rom. matron, mother of the Gracchi
Abbot—Notable p25-29,por.
Adelman—Famous p23-24
Balsdon—Roman p43-47,174,193,196

(Continued)

Cornelia—*Continued*

    Beard—Women p289-290
    Hammerton p444
    *MacVeagh—Champlin p158-159,por.
    Mozans—Woman p22,25-26
    Muir—Woman p41-42
    Schmidt—400 p245,por.

Cornelia (2) (d.c. 67 B.C.)
    Rom. matron, wife of Pompey
    Balsdon—Roman p47,56,209
    Hanaford—Dau. p25

Cornelia (3) (fl. 83 A.D.)
    Rom. vestal virgin
    Balsdon—Roman p241-242

Cornelia, Sister (fl. 1840's)
    Amer. W. pioneer
    *Ross—Heroines p126-155

Cornell, Katherine (1898-   )
    Amer. actress
    Ames—These p441-455
    Bakeless—In p3-22,por.
    Blum—Great p109,por.
    *Bolton—Lives p121-138,por.
    Brown—Upstage p124-128
    Coad—Amer. p328,por.
    CR '59 p172-173,por.
    CR '63 p137-138,por.
    Cur. Biog. '41 p171-174,por.
    Cur. Biog. '52 p125-127,por.
    Dodd—Celeb. p60-65
    Eustis—Players p59-73,por.
    Fisher—Amer. p291-293,por.
    *Forsee—Amer. p107-135
    Frank—Time p167-173,por.
    Funke—Actors p197-233,por.
    Hammerton p444
    Hazelton—We p74-82
    New Yorker Feb.14,1931,p23-25,por.
    (Profiles)
    Ormsbee—Back. p234-238
    Rogers—Women p175,por.
    Ross—Player p193-197,por.
    *Stoddard—Top p13-26
    Taves—Success. p59-68,por.
    Time Dec.21,1942 p45,por.(cover);
    Dec. 26,1932 p15,por.(cover)
    *Wagner—Famous p123-130,por.
    Women—Achieve. p68,por.

Cornell, Sophia S. (b. 1875)
    Amer. educator, author
    Hanaford—Dau. p539-540

Cornett, Alice (1911-   )
    Amer. composer
    ASCAP p98

Cornificia (fl. 40's-50's B.C.)
    poet
    Boccaccio—Conc. p188

Cornish, Nellie C. (fl. 1910's-1930's)
    Amer. music educator
    McCoy—Portraits p28,por.
    Women—Achieve. p196

Cornwall, Edith. See Parsons, Mary L.

Cornwallis, Caroline Frances (1786-1858)
    Eng. author
    Adelman—Famous p109-110
    Hammerton p444-445

Corona, Leonora (fl. 1920's)
    Amer. singer
    McCoy—Portraits p28,por.

Coronel de Agreda, Maria, Sister.
    See Agreda, Maria de, Sister

Corr, Mary Bernardine (b. 1858)
    Amer. author, teacher
    Logan—Part p721

Correia, Elisa (gr. 1889)
    Port. pioneer physician
    Lovejoy—Women p205

Correlli, Clementina (b. 1840)
    It. painter, sculptor
    Waters—Women p88

Corson, Juliet (1842-1897)
    Amer. educator, author, cookery
    reformer
    Dorland—Sum p25,151

Cort, Catherine. See Whitcomb, Catharine

Cort, Mabel Gibson (fl. 1915)
    Amer. missionary
    Culver—Women p156-158

Cortez, Leonora (fl. 1940's)
    Amer. pianist
    McCoy—Portraits p28,por.

Cory, Fanny Young (fl. 1870's)
    Amer. illustrator, cartoonist
    Michigan—Biog. p77

Cosgrave, Jessica Garretson Finch (d. 1949)
    Amer. foundress, educator
    New Yorker Apr.13,1946 p35-40,por.
    (Profiles)
    Women—Achieve. p150,por.

Cost, March (n.d.)
    Eng. novelist
    Cur. Biog. '58 p103-104,por.

Costa, Olga (1913-   )
    Stewart—45 p125-128,por.

Coste, Marie Ravenel de la (fl. 1860's)
Amer. Civil war poet
Jones—Heroines p247-249

Costello, Dolores (1906-   )
Amer. actress
Herman—How p53,por.
Hughes—Famous p68-88,por.
Schickel—Stars p60-61,65,por.

Cosway, Maria Cecelia Louise Hadfield
(1759-1838)
Irish-It. painter, musician
Donovan—Women p230-241,334,por.
Waters—Women p88-91

Cotes, Sarah Jeanette (b. 1862)
Can. journalist, author, traveller
Schmidtt—400 p76,por.

Cottel, Adelaide. See Mayhew, Adelaide

Cottin, Marie Sophie Risteau (1770-1807)
Fr. novelist
Dorland—Sum p50,193

Cottlow, Augusta (1878-1954)
Amer. pianist
McCoy—Portraits p28,por.

Cotton-Marshall, Grace (fl. 1940's)
Amer. composer
McCoy—Portraits p28,por.

Cottrell, Ida Dorothy Wilkinson (1902-
1957)
Austral. author
Cur. Biog. '55 p140-141,por.
Cur. Biog. '57 p117
Roderick—20 p71-80

Couch, Hilda Juanita (fl. 1930's)
Amer. journalist, editor
Women—Achieve. p157,por.

Coudert, Amalia Küssner (1876-1932)
Amer. painter
Logan—Part p752-753
Michigan—Biog. p72
Waters—Women p91

Coudreau, Octavie (fl. 1890's)
Fr. sci. explorer
Mozans—Woman p258-264

Countryman, Gratia Alta (1866-1953)
Amer. librarian
Bul. of Bibl. May-Aug.1922 p137,por.

Counts, Belle (fl. 1860's)
Amer. Civil war nurse
Logan—Part p368

Courcy, Florence de (fl. 1910's)
Amer. opera singer
Lahee—Grand p293-294,414

Courland, Dorothea of (fl. 1780's-1790's)
Fr., friend of Talleyrand
Blei—Fasc. p168-172,por.

Courtneidge, Cicely (1893-   )
Eng. actress
Hammerton p449-450,por.

Courtney, Janet Hogarth (fl. 1880's-1900's)
Eng. author, indexer
Brittain—Women p43,72,74-77,102-248

Courtney, Kate (m. 1862)
Amer. whaling voyager
Whiting—Whaling p142-146,208-213

Courtney, Kathleen, Dame (gr. 1900)
Eng., United Nations official
Brittain—Women p98,249

Cousin, Germaine (d. 1601)
Fr. saint
Englebert—Lives p230-231

Cousins, (Sue) Margaret (1905-   )
Amer. editor, author
Cur. Biog. '54 p209-211,por.

Coutan-Montorgueil, Laure Martin (fl. 1890's
1900's)
Fr. sculptor
Waters—Women p91-92

Coutts, Harriot. See Mellon, Harriot

Couvent, Madame Bernard (d. 1936)
Amer. philanthropist
Robinson—Hist. p68

Couzzins, Adaline (fl. 1860's)
Amer. humanitarian, lecturer
Hanaford—Dau. p659-661

Couzzins, Phebe W. (fl. 1860's)
Amer. lawyer
Hanaford—Dau. p658-659

Coveney, Harriet (fl. 19th cent.)
Eng. actress
Furniss—Some p53-54,por.

Cover, Juel Reed (n.d.)
Amer. journalist
*Plumb—Lives p39-48

Cowan, Minna Galbraith (n.d.)
Scot. organization official, social
worker
Cur. Biog. '48 p116-118,por.

Cowan, Ruth Baldwin (n.d.)
Amer. journalist
Ross—Ladies p549-551

Cowden-Clarke, Victoria (1809-1898)
    Eng. scholar, essayist
    Adelman—Famous p178-179
    Dorland—Sum p40,172

Cowell, Hannah (d. 1713)
    Amer. colonial nurse
    Dexter—Colonial p65

Cowell, S. Emma (fl. 1870's-1880's)
    Amer. dramatic reader
    Hanaford—Dau. p593

Cowham, Hilda. See Lander, Hilda Cowham

Cowham, Mrs. Neil. See Provines, June

Cowie, Laura (1892-   )
    Brit. actress
    Hammerton p451

Cowl, Jane Cowles (c. 1884-1950)
    Amer. actress
    Blum—Great p74,por.
    Coad—Amer. p327,por.
    Dodd—Celeb. p201-205
    Hammerton p451
    Mantle—Contemp. p293-294

Cowles, Cecil (1901-   )
    Amer. composer
    Howard—Our p580-581

Cowles, Fleur Fenton (1910-   )
    Amer. painter, editor, author, busi-
        ness woman
    CR '59 p176-177,por.
    CR '63 p141,por.
    Cur. Biog. '52 p129-131,por.
    Jensen—Revolt p99,por.

Cowles, Genevieve Almeda (b. 1871)
    Amer. painter, stained glass
        decorator
    Michigan—Biog. p79
    Waters—Women p92-93

Cowles, Maud Alice (1871-1905)
    Amer. painter, stained glass
        decorator
    Michigan—Biog. p79
    Waters—Women p93

Cowles, Virginia Spencer (n.d.)
    Amer. journalist, author
    Cur. Biog. '42 p160-162,por.

Cowley, Hannah Parkhouse (1743-1809)
    Eng. playwright
    Adelman—Famous p99
    Hammerton p452

Cowley, Mary (fl. 1741)
    Amer. colonial business woman
    Dexter—Colonial p54

Cowper, Emily.
    See Palmerston, Emily Mary Lamb, Lady

Cowper, Mary Claverling, Lady (1685-
        1723/24)
    Eng. maid of honor
    Melville—Maids p142-156,por.
    Stenton—English p253-256

Cox, Dinah (1804-1909)
    Amer. racial leader
    Brown—Home. p30-31,por.

Cox, Elizabeth (fl. 1670's-1680's)
    Eng. actress
    Wilson—All p134-135

Cox, Hannah (1796-1876)
    Amer. social reformer
    Hanaford—Dau. p375-376

Cox, Jane Cannon (fl. 1870's)
    Eng. criminal
    Jenkins—Six p188-224

Cox, Louise Howland King (1865-1945)
    Amer. painter, sculptor
    Adelman—Famous p301
    Michigan—Biog. p80
    Waters—Women p93-94,375

Cox, Lucy Ann (fl. 1860's)
    Amer. Civil war heroine
    Logan—Part p492

Cox, Margaret (fl. 1800's)
    Eng., mother of John Ruskin
    Bartlett—Mothers p70-74

Cox-McCormack, Nancy (b. 1885)
    Amer. sculptor
    National—Contemp. p62

Coxe, Margaret (fl. 1870's-1880's)
    Amer. author, botanist, educator
    Hanaford—Dau. p239,287

Coyle, Kathleen (1886-1952)
    Irish novelist
    Wagenknecht—When p261-272

Cozbi (Biblical)
    Deen—All p258-259
    Lewis—Portraits p168

Crabb, Mary (fl. 1730's)
    Amer. colonial needleworker, busi-
        ness woman
    Dexter—Colonial p43

Crabtree, (Charlotte) Lotta (1847-1924)
    Amer. actress
    Adelman—Famous p270
    Bodeen—Ladies p19-25,por.
    Brown—Gentle p14,175-178,por.
    Cahn—Laugh. p42,por.
    Coad—Amer. p183,por.
    Whitton—These p201-203

Craddock, Charles Egbert, pseud.
See Murfree, Mary Noailles

Craft, Ellen (fl. 1860's)
Amer. slave
Robinson—Hist. p69,por.

Craft, Mabel (fl. 1890's-1900's)
Amer. journalist
Ross—Ladies p6-7,65,577-579

Craig, Edith (1869-1947)
Eng. actress
MacQueen—Pope p367

Craig, Mary Marsden Young (fl. 1930's)
Amer. actress, playwright, director
Women—Achieve. p196

Craig, Elizabeth May (n.d.)
Amer. journalist
CR '59 p179,por.
CR '63 p143,por.
Cur. Biog. '49 p127-128,por.
Ross—Ladies p335-336

Craighill, Margaret D. (1898-   )
Amer. physician, army medical officer
Lovejoy—Women p366

Craighton, Elizabeth (fl. 1720's)
Amer. printer
Club—Printing p14-15

Craigie, Pearl Mary Teresa (John Oliver
        Hobbes, pseud.) (1867-1906)
Amer. novelist, essayist
Blunt—Great p424
Dorland—Sum p25,172
Furniss—Some p24-25,por.
Hammerton p454
Harkins—Famous p223-238
Harkins—Little p223-238,por.
Logan—Part p805-806

Craigin, Mary (fl. 1840's)
Amer. cult leader
Holbrook—Dreamers p5-6

Craik, Dinah Maria Mulock (1826-1887)
Eng. novelist
Adelman—Famous p194
Dorland—Sum p54,195
*Green—Authors p59-60
Hammerton p454
Johnson—Women p186-188
Oliphant—Women p217-248
Stebbins—Victorian p29-32,197,207-208

Crain, Jeanne (1925-   )
Amer. actress
Cur. Biog. '51 p142-145,por.

Cram, Nancy Gore (fl. 1810's)
Amer. clergyman
Dexter—Career p58-59

Cramer, Harriet Laura Barker (1848-1922)
Amer. journalist, philanthropist,
editor
Logan—Part p533

Cramm, Helen L. (d. 1939)
Amer. composer, music teacher
McCoy—Portraits p29,por.

Cramsie, Mary Isabel (b. 1844)
Amer. club leader
Logan—Part p722

Cranch, Mary (d. 1811)
Amer. pioneer
Ellet—Women (2) p39-40

Cranch, Mrs. Richard (fl. 1770's)
Amer. Rev. war patriot
Logan—Part p131

Crandall, Almira (fl. 1830's)
Amer. educator
Douglas—Remember p106,108-109,112

Crandall, Ella Phillips (d. 1938)
Amer. public health nurse
Pennock—Makers p54-55,por.

Crandall, Prudence (1803-1889/90)
Amer. educator, social reformer,
philanthropist
Bruce—Woman p181-184
*Buckmaster—Women p23-44,por.
Douglas—Remember p105-114,por.
Hanaford—Dau. p175
Parton—Noted p44-70

Crandall, Mrs. L. R. G. ("Margery")
(fl. 1920's)
Amer. spiritualist medium
Rogers—Women p117,por.

Crane, Caroline Bartlett (b. 1858)
Amer. clergyman, editor, teacher
Bennett—Amer. p1-45,por.
Irwin—Angels p167-169
Logan—Part p738

Crane, Jocelyn (1909-   )
Amer. zoologist
*Yost—Women Mod. p108-123,por.

Crane, Julia E. (1855-1923)
Amer. music educator
McCoy—Portraits p29,por.

Crane, Nathalia Clara Ruth (1913-   )
Amer. poet
Bruère—Laugh. p100
Women—Achieve. p133,por.

Crapsey, Adelaide (1878-1914)
Amer. poet
Cook—Our p312-314

Crathorne, Mary (fl. 1760's)
    Amer. colonial manufacturer
    Dexter—Colonial p47-48

Craven, Elizabeth.
    See Anspach, Elizabeth Berkeley,
        Margravine of

Craven, Florence Lees (fl. 1870's-1890's)
    Ger. nurse
    Schmidt—400 p400-401,por.

Craven, Louisa Brunton, Countess of.
    See Brunton, Louisa, Countess of Craven

Craven, Pauline (1808-1891)
    Fr. novelist
    Blunt—Great p380-395
    Dorland—Sum p35

Cravens, Kathryn (fl. 1930's)
    Amer. radio commentator
    Women—Achieve. p147,por.

Crawford, Carole Joan (1944-   )
    Jam. beauty
    Stiles—Postal p63

Crawford, Cheryl (1902-   )
    Amer. theatrical producer
    CR '59 p179,por.
    CR '63 p143-144,por.
    Cur. Biog. '45 p120-122,por.
    New Yorker May 8,1948,p34-38,por.
        (Profiles)

Crawford, Connie (fl. 1930's)
    Amer. aviation radio operator
    Planck—Women p227

Crawford, Gretchen C. (fl. 1930's)
    Amer. educator
    Women—Achieve. p116,por.

Crawford, Joan (1908-   )
    Amer. actress
    Brundidge—Twinkle p79-90,por.
    CR '59 p180,por.
    CR '63 p144,por.
    Cur. Biog. '46 p132-134,por.
    Cur. Biog. '66 p59-61,por.
    Hammerton p457
    Herman—How p25,por.
    Hughes—Famous p89-111,por.
    Mott—Gallery p210-216
    Ross—Player p66-72,por.
    Schickel—Stars p66-69,por.
    *Seventeen—In p51,por.
    TV—Person. (2) p53-54,por.
    Women—Achieve. p71,por.

Crawford, Mimi (m. 1934)
    Eng. actress
    Wyndham—Chorus p140,por.

Crawford, Miss (fl. 1880's-1900's)
    Eng. governess
    Howe—Galaxy p154

Crawford, Phyllis (1899-   )
    Amer. author, librarian, editor
    Cur. Biog. '40 p203-204,por.
    Women—Achieve. p166,por.

Crawford, Ruth (1901-   )
    Amer. composer, pianist, music
        teacher
    Howard—Our p532-533
    Reis—Composers p84-85

Credle, Ellis (1902-   )
    Amer. illustrator
    Mahony—Illus. p295

Creelman, Lyle (fl. 1940's-1950's)
    Can. nurse
    Dolan—Goodnow's p338,por.

Creemer, Lucy M. (fl. 1870-1880's)
    Amer. poet, religious worker
    Hanaford—Dau. p619-620

Créquy, Renée Caroline, Marquise de (1714-
        1803)
    Fr. author
    Hammerton p458

Crescentia, Sister (fl. 1960's)
    Brit. nun, nurse
    Elgin—Nun p76-77,por.

Crespo de Reignon, Asuncion (fl. 1840's-
        1860's)
    Sp. painter
    Waters—Women p94-95

Cresson, Margaret (1889-   )
    Amer. sculptor
    Jackman—Amer. p449-450
    National—Contemp. p64

Crews, Julia Lesser (n.d.)
    Amer. politician
    Roosevelt—Ladies p59-68

Crews, Laura Hope (1880-1942)
    Amer. actress
    Cur. Biog. '43 p154
    Izard—Heroines p359-361
    Marks—Glamour p290

Crippen, Abbie (b. 1860)
    Amer. W. pioneer
    Sargent—Pioneers p46,51,por.

Crippen, Effie Maude (b. 1868)
    Amer. W. pioneer
    Sargent—Pioneers p46-48,por.

Crippen, Fannie (b. 1806)
    Amer. W. pioneer
    Sargent—Pioneers p46-48,por.

Crippen, Kate (b. 1864)
Amer. W. pioneer
Sargent—Pioneers p46-47,por.

Crispilla, Quintia (fl. c. 200 A.D.)
Rom. empress, wife of Pupienus
Serviez—Roman (2) p290

Crispina (1) (fl. c. 180-190 A.D.)
Rom. empress, wife of Commodus
Serviez—Roman (2) p93-97
McCabe—Empr. p183-184,por.

Crispina (2) (fl. 4th cent.)
Afr. saint
Blunt—Great p22

Cristina, Beatrice. See Beatrice Kristina

Christina, Maria. See Maria Kristina

Crittenden, Elizabeth Moss (m. 1853)
Amer. social leader
Hanaford—Dau. p146
Logan—Part p256-257

Crittenden, Lucy (fl. 1910's)
Amer. social leader
Logan—Part p258

Crocker, Hannah Mather (1765-1847)
Amer. author, pioneer, feminist
Riegel—Amer. p7-8

Crocker, Lucretia (fl. 1870's-1880's)
Amer. educator
Hanaford—Dau. p540,543

Crockett, Elizabeth (d. 1860)
Amer. pioneer
Whitton—These p222-223

Crockett, Lucy Herndon (1914-   )
Amer. author
Cur. Biog. '53 p129-130,por.
Mahoney—Illus. p295

Croly, Jane Cunningham (Jennie June,
pseud.) (1829/31-1901)
Amer. author, journalist, editor
Adelman—Famous p204
Bruce—Woman p243-245
Dorland—Sum p38-39,111,115,137
Farmer—What p206,305,307,por.
Hanaford—Dau. p687
Irwin—Angels p213,215-219,227,233
Logan—Part p401
Ross—Ladies p16,39,43-46,por.

Cromartie, Anne, Countess of (1829-1888)
Scot. heiress, also Duchess of
Sutherland
Hammerton p460-461

Cromenburch, Anna von (fl. 16th cent.)
Neth. painter
Waters—Women p95

Crommelin, May (fl. 1890's)
Eng. author
Black—Notable p210-222

Cropper, Anna McLane (b. 1859)
Amer. club leader
Logan—Part p619

Crosby, Frances (Fanny) Jane (1820-1915)
Amer. blind hymn-writer
Adelman—Famous p215-216
Bonte—Amer. p119,por.
Deen—Great p306-307
Dorland—Sum p20,72,84,184-185
Foster—Pilgrim p115-133,por.
Hammerton p464
Miller—Ten p61-66
Muir—Women p195-196

Crosby, Katherine Van Rensellaer (1897-   )
Amer. sculptor
National—Contemp. p64

Crosby, Marie (fl. 1940's)
Amer. composer, music teacher
McCoy—Portraits p29,por.

Crosman, Henrietta (1861-1944)
Amer. actress
Blum—Great p15,por.

Crosman, Mrs. J. Heron (fl. 1900's)
Amer. organization official
Logan—Part p457-458

Cross, Joan (1900-   )
Eng. singer
Brook—Singers p55-60,por.
Davidson—Treas. p73-77,por.
Rosenthal—Sopranos p28-30,por

Cross, Mary Evans. See Eliot, George

Cross, Sarah B. (fl. 1860's)
Eng.-Amer. Civil war nurse
Logan—Part p368

Crossan, Clarissa Watters (fl. 1860's)
Amer. Civil war nurse
Logan—Part p368

Crosse, Mary Fisher Bayley (1624-1690)
Amer. colonial missionary
Leonard—Amer. p113
Spruill—Women's p249-250

Crossland, Mary (fl. 1870's)
Amer. nurse
Dolan—Goodnow's p229

Crossley, Ada (1874-1929)
Austral. singer
Hammerton p464,por.

Crossley, Winnie (fl. 1940's)
Eng. aviatrix, circus performer
*May—Women p142

Crothers, Rachel (1878-1958)
  Amer. playwright
  Coad—Amer. p335,por.
  Dodd—Celeb. p167-171
  Hammerton p464
  Logan—Part p792
  Mantle—Amer. p119-121
  Mantle—Contemp. p103-108
  Mersand—Amer. p158-159
  Millett—Amer. p110-111,307-308

Crouch, Mary (fl. 1780's)
  Amer. colonial printer
  Club—Printing p12
  Dexter—Career p102-103,108,109
  Dexter—Colonial p174
  Earle—Colon. p64
  Hanaford—Dau. p710-711

Crowe, Bonita (fl. 1940's)
  Amer. composer, organist, pianist
  McCoy—Portraits p29,por.

Crowe, Catherine Stevens (c. 1800-1876)
  Eng. novelist
  Dorland—Sum p41,194
  Hammerton p464
  Oliphant—Women p149-160
  Stebbins—Victorian p20-22,206

Crowe, Jocelyn (1906-   )
  Eng. illustrator
  Mahony—Illus, p295

Crowell, Annie L. (fl. 1930's)
  Amer. pianist, music teacher
  Women—Achieve. p196

Crowell, Dorothy. See Walworth, Dorothy

Crowell, Gertrude (fl. 1890's)
  Amer., child of whaling voyager
  Whiting—Whaling p268-269

Crowell, Grace Noll (b. 1877)
  Amer. poet
  Davis—Mothers p179
  *Plumb—Lives p119-144
  Smith—Women's p36

Crowell, Mary (m. 1886)
  Amer. whaling voyager
  Whiting—Whaling p268-269

Crowfoot, Dorothy Mary (gr. 1932)
  Eng. tutor, fellow
  Brittain—Women p247

Crowley, Mary Catherine (fl 1900's)
  Amer. editor, historian
  Logan—Part p833

Crowley, Mary M. (fl. 1930's)
  Amer. bus executive
  Women—Achieve. p173,por.

Crowley, Teresa M. (fl. 1930's)
  Amer. teacher
  Women—Achieve. p163,por.

Crowne, Dorothy (fl. 1930's)
  Amer. public relations expert
  Women—Achieve. p181,por.

Crownfield, Gertrude (1877-1945)
  Amer. author
  Cur. Biog. '45 p124

Crowninshield, Mary Bradford (d. 1913)
  Amer. author
  Logan—Part p858

Crusinberry, Jane (fl. 1940's)
  Amer. script writer
  Taves—Success. p106-114,por.

Cruz, Manuelita de la (d. 1955)
  Colom. nurse
  Stiles—Postal p64

Culbert-Browne, Grace (fl. 1940's-1950's)
  Austral. physician
  Lovejoy—Women p251-252

Culbertson, Belle Caldwell (b. 1857)
  Amer. missionary
  Logan—Part p520

Cull, Betty (n.d.)
  Amer. army aerial observer, bomb
    tester
  *Peckham—Women p41

Cullis, Winifred Clara (1875-1956)
  Eng. physiologist, educator, feminist
  Cur. Biog. '43 p158-159,por.
  Cur. Biog. '57 p123

Cullman, Marguerite (m. 1935)
  Amer. theatrical producer
  CR '63 p149,por.

Culp, Julia (b. 1881)
  Nether. singer
  Ewen—Living p94,por.
  McCoy—Portraits p30,por.

Culver, Essae Martha (n.d.)
  Amer. librarian, organization official
  Cur. Biog. '40 p213-214,por.

Culver, Helen (b. 1832)
  Amer. philanthropist, teacher
  Logan—Part p532

Cumberland, Duchess of
  See Frederica of Meckenburg-Strelitz

Cumings, Prudence.
  See Wright, Prudence Cumings

(Continued)

Curie, Marja—*Continued*

°MacVeagh—Champlin p166,por.
Meine—Great p126-130,por.
Mizwa—Great p333-343,por.
°Moderow—People p191-215,por.
°Montgomery—Story p121-126
Mozans—Woman p221-232
Muir—Women p196-200
Murrow—This (2) p216-217
°Nisenson—Minute p47,por.
°Nisenson—More Minute p43,por.
Nobel—Man p343-344,408-411
°Parkman—Heroines p267-293,por.
Patrick—Profiles p11
Phila.—Women, unp.,por.
°Pringle—When p177-192,por.
Reader's—Great p69-80,por.
°Riedman—Men p17-45,por.
Sewell—Brief p218-219
°Shippen—Design p185-191
Smith—Torch. p.55,por.
Stiles—Postal p64
°Strong—Of p269-275
Thomas—Modern p329-340
Time Feb.12,1940 p24,por.(cover)
Untermeyer—Makers p368-378
Weeks—Discovery p560,802-811,813,
  829-830,por.
Year—Pic p208,por.

Curran, Pearl Gildersleeve (1875/76-
    1941)
  Amer. composer, song-writer
  Cur. Biog. '41 p192
  Howard—Our p566-567
  McCoy—Portraits p30,por.

Curran, Sarah (1783-1806)
  Irish heroine, dau. of Richard
    Curran
  Schmidt—400 p243-244,por.

Curre, Sanja (c. 1920-1943)
  Alb. patriot
  Stiles—Postal p65

Currer, Elizabeth (fl. 1670's-1680's)
  Eng. actress
  MacQueen—Pope p120-121
  Wilson—All p135-136

Curry, Anne Ogilvie (fl. 1930's)
  Amer. cosmetic executive
  Women—Achieve. p31,33,por.

Curry, Jennie Foster (d. 1948)
  Amer. W. pioneer
  Sargent—Pioneers p73-76,por.

Curry, Peggy Simson (1912-   )
  Scot.-Amer. author
  Cur. Biog. '58 p106-107,por.

Curry, Sadie (fl. 1860's)
  Amer. Civil war nurse
  Logan—Part p498-499

Curtin, Phyllis (c. 1922-   )
  Amer. singer
  Cur. Biog. '64 p97-100,por.

Curtis, Ann (1926-   )
  Amer. swimmer
  Cur. Biog. '45 p128-129,por.

Curtis, Georgina Pell (1859-1922)
  Amer. author, social worker,
    educator
  Logan—Part p616,852

Curtis, Harriet F. (fl. 1840's)
  Amer. editor
  Hanaford—Dau. p226

Curtis, Jessie (fl. 1870's-1880's)
  Amer. illustrator
  Hanaford—Dau. p299

Curtis, Maynie Rose (fl. 1930's)
  Amer. research physiologist
  Women—Achieve. p162,por.

Curtis, Natalie (1875-1921)
  Amer. composer, pianist, lecturer
  Howard—Our p617
  McCoy—Portraits p30,por.

Curzon, Grace Elvina Trillia Hinds (1879-
    1958), Marchioness
  Eng. social leader
  Pearson—Marry p118-126

Curzon of Kedleston, Mary Victoria Leiter
    Curzon, Baroness (1868-1906)
  Amer. heiress
  Eliot—Heiresses p118-147,por.
  Pearson—Marry p104-116,por.
  Schmidt—400 p162-163,por.

Cusack, Mary Frances (Nun of Kenmare)
    (1820-1899)
  Irish author
  Adelman—Famous p180

Cushier, Elizabeth (1837-1932)
  Amer. physician
  Meda—Medical p85-95

Cushing, Catherine Chisholm (d. 1952)
  Amer. playwright
  Mantle—Amer. p280
  Mantle—Contemp. p308

Cushman, Beulah (fl. 1950's)
  Amer. physician, educator
  Lovejoy—Women p384,por

Cushman, Charlotte Saunders (1816-1876)
  Amer. actress
  Abbott—Notable p323-327,por.
  Adelman—Famous p158-159,por.
  Coad—Amer. p107-108,por.

(Continued)

Cushman, Charlotte Saunders—*Continued*

Dorland—Sum p26,69,165
Eaton—Actor's p105-107
Hammerton p469
Hanaford—Dau. p576-585
Howe—Memoires p219-222,por.
Logan—Part p770-772
Marinacci—Lead. p79-96,por.
Melikov—Immort. p91-171,por.
Morello—Hall p140,por.
Morris—400 p66-67
Parton—Dau. p311-321,por.
Parton—Noted p603-613,por.
*Stevens—Women p121-125,por.
Vance—Hear p17-43,por.
*Vance—Lamp p92-127
Whitton—These p184,186-189

Cushman, Emma (b. 1862)
Amer. nurse, humanitarian
*Kirkland—Achieved p59-65

Cushman, Mary. See **Allerton, Mary Norris**

Cushman, Pauline (1833/35-1895)
Amer. actress, Civil war spy
Bodeen—Ladies p26-30
Harkness—Heroines p10
Hoehling—Women p25-26
Horan—Desperate p99-123,por.
Kane—Spies p177-191
Moore—Women p170-175
Young—Women p235-244,369-370,por.

Cushman, Susan (fl. 1830's-1840's)
Amer. actress
Hanaford—Dau. p578-582

Custer, Elizabeth Bacon (1842-1933)
Amer. W. pioneer
Brown—Gentle p14,19,36,46-48,67-73,
117,123,144,por.
*Johnson—Some p115-128,por.
*Miller—West p130-147

Custin, Mildred (1906-   )
Amer. bus. executive
Cur. Biog. '67 p87-89

Custine, Madame de (fl. 18th cent.)
Fr. patriot
Kavanagh—Women (2) p218-219

Custis, Eleanor Parke.
See **Lewis, Eleanore Parke Custis**

Custis, Eliza Parke (c. 1794)
Amer. belle
Sale—Old p224-233,por.

Custis, Martha.
See **Washington, Martha Dandridge
Custis**

Cutbert, Susan Stockton (fl. 1770's)
Amer. patriot, pioneer
Green—Pioneer (3) p136

Cuthbert, Margaret Ross (1890-1968)
Can.Amer. radio executive
Cur. Biog. '47 p145-147,por.
Cur. Biog. '68 p453

Cuthburge (fl. 800's)
Eng. queen, saint, wife of Alfred
of Northumbria
Blunt—Great p81

Cuthrell, Mrs. Hugh. See **Baldwin, Faith**

Cutler, Bessie Ingersoll (fl. 1910's-1920's)
Amer. nurse, author
Pennock—Makers p127,por.

Cutler, H. M. Tracy (fl. 1870's-1880's)
Amer. lecturer
Hanaford—Dau. p345

Cutler, Kate (1870-1955)
Eng. actress
Hammerton p469

Cutler, Mary M. (fl. 1890's)
Amer. physician
Lovejoy—Women p239

Cutting, Mary Stewart (1851-1924)
Amer. author
Maurice—Makers p8,por.

Cuzzoni, Francesca (c. 1700-1770)
It. singer
Ferris—Great (1) p20-21
Pleasants—Great p97-100,por.
Wagner—Prima p71-74,240

Cynethryth (757-796)
Eng., wife of Offa, king of the
Mercians
Stenton—English p2-3

Cynthia of Propertius (Hostia)
(fl. c28 B.C.)
Rom. courtesan
Balsdon—Roman p192,260,262

Cyrus, Diana (fl. 1940's-1950's)
Amer. aviatrix
Dwiggins—They p125,127-129

Czartoryska, Isabela Fleming (1746-1835)
Pol. princess
Schmidt—400 p319,por.

D

Daché, Lilly (1904-   )
Fr.-Amer. milliner, fashion designer
Cavanah—We p81-92
CR '59 p188-189,por.
CR '63, 152,por.
Cur. Biog. '41 p198-199,por.
New Yorker Apr.4,1942,p20-24,por.
(Profiles)
Women—Achieve. p55,por.

Dacier, Anne Lebre (1654-1720)
Fr. classical scholar, translator
Adelman—Famous p68-69
Dorland—Sum p25-176
Mozans—Woman p82-83

Dada, Hatte A. (fl. 1860's)
Amer. Civil war nurse
Brockett—Woman's p431-439,por.

Dade, Barbara Bates (m. 1941)
Amer. missionary
They—Went p135-137

Dagget, Mrs. (fl. 1780's)
Amer. pioneer
Fowler—Woman p327-336

Daggett, Helen M. (fl. 1930's)
Amer. interior decorator, editor
Women—Achieve. p163,por.

Daggett, Maud (b. 1883)
Amer. sculptor
National—Contemp. p70

Daggett, Polly (fl. 1770's)
Amer. Rev. war heroine
*Carmer—Young p62-67

Dagmar (Virginia Ruth Egnor) (c. 1920-)
Amer. actress
CR '59 p189,por.
CR '63 p153,por.

D'Agoult, Marie.
See Agoult, Marie Catherine Sophie de
Flavigny, Comtesse d'

Dagover, Lil (1894-   )
Nether. actress
Hammerton p471

Dahl, Arlene (1927-   )
Amer. actress
CR '59 p189,por.
CR '63 p153,por.
TV—Person (2) p109,por.

Dahlgren, Madeleine Vinton (b. 1835)
Amer. author, scholar, translator,
social leader
Logan—Part p814

Dahn-Fries, Sophie (1835-1898)
Ger. painter
Waters—Women p95

Dakin, Florence (fl. 1900's-1930's)
Amer. nurse
Pennock—Makers p130,por.

Dalassena, Anna (d.c. 1105)
Byzant. statesman, mother of
Emperor Alexis
Diehl—Portraits p300-325

d'Albret, Jeanne. See Albret, Jeanne d'

d'Albrizzi, Contessa.
See Albrizzi, Isabella Teotochi,
Contessa d'

Dale, Margaret (1922-   )
Brit. ballet dancer
Haskell—Vignet. p55

Dale, Maureen (fl. 1960's)
Eng. airline hostess
*May—Women p239

D'Alencon, Emilienne.
See Alencon, Emilienne D'

Dalgliesh, Alice (1893-   )
Amer. editor, author
Women—Achieve. p157,por.

Dall, Caroline Wells Healy (1822-1912)
Amer. feminist, social reformer
Hanaford—Dau. p355-368
Riegel—Amer. p156-163
O'Connor—Pioneer p85,147,170

Dallam, Helen (fl. 1940's-1950's)
Amer. composer, author
ASCAP p106
Howard—Our p581
McCoy—Portraits p30,por.

Dalmas, Priscilla (fl. 1930's)
Amer. architect
Women—Achieve. p196

Dalossy, Ellen (fl. 1920's)
Czech. singer
Saleski—Wander. p401,por.

Dalrymple, Jean (1910-   )
Amer. theatrical publicist, producer,
director
CR '59 p190-191,por.
CR '63 p154,por.
Cur. Biog. '53 p140-142,por.
*Seventeen—In p93-97

Dalrymple, Martha (fl. 1920's)
Amer. journalist
Ross—Ladies p373-375

Dalton, Mrs. (fl. 1860's)
Amer. pioneer
Fowler—Woman p288-304

D'Alvarez, Marguerite (1896-1953)
Eng. singer
Ewen—Ency. p100

Daly, Maureen Patricia (1921-   )
Irish-Amer. author, editor
Cur. Biog. '46 p137-138,por.
Warfel—Amer. p109,por.

Damala, Rosine Bernard.
    See Bernhardt, Sarah

Damari, Shoshana (1922-   )
    Israeli singer, actress
    Saleski—Jewish p705-706,por.

Damaris (Biblical)
    Deen—All p259-260

Damayanti, Princess (   )
    E. Ind., dau. of King Bhima,
      wife of Nala
    Polo—Famous p34-35

d'Amboise, Frances, Duchess of Brittany
    (1447-1485)
    Fr. saint
    Blunt—Great p165-166

Dame Shirley, pseud.
    See Clappe, Louise Amelia Knapp Smith

Dame Trot. See Trotula of Salerno

Damer, Anne Seymour Conway (1749-1828)
    Eng. sculptor, actress, social leader
    Stenton—English p324
    Thomson—Queens p383-401,por.
    Waters—Women p96-100

Damerel, Donna (1912-1941)
    Amer. actress
    Cur. Biog. '41 p200

Damita, Lily (1906-   )
    Fr. actress
    Brundidge—Twinkle p249-255,por.
    Hammerton p474
    New Yorker Oct.26,1929 p30-33,por.
    (Profiles)

Damon, Ruth Augusta (fl. 1860-1870's)
    Amer. clergyman
    Hanaford—Dau. p449-450

Damrosch, Gretchen Finletter (1901-   )
    Amer. playwright
    Mantle—Contemp. p308

Dana, Elizabeth (b. 1751)
    Amer. pioneer
    Green—Pioneer (3) p90

Dana, Emily W. (fl. 1860's)
    Amer. Civil war nurse
    Moore—Women p373-381

Dana, Mrs. (fl. 1770's)
    Amer. Rev. war patriot
    Ellet—Women (2) p199-200

Dana, Mrs. William Starr (1862-1952)
    Amer. author, gardener
    Hollingsworth—Her p155-158

Danby, Frank, pseud. (Julia Frankau)
    (1863-1916)
    Brit. novelist
    Hammerton p475

Dancer, Alice (1854-1944)
    Amer. religious worker
    Phillips—33 p85-88

Dancer, Ann. See Barry, Ann Stranger

d'Andrea, Novella (fl. 14th cent.)
    It. scholar, beauty
    Cockran—Romance p122-123

Dandridge, Dorothea.
    See Henry, Dorothea Dandridge

Dandridge, Dorothy (1924-   )
    Amer. actress, singer
    CR '59 p192,por.
    CR '63 p155,por.

Dandridge, Elizabeth (Betty) **Taylor Bliss**
    (1824/26-1909)
    Amer., dau. of Zachary Taylor
    Gerlinger—Mis. p42-43
    Logan—Part p244-266
    Truett—First p34-35,por.

Dandridge, Martha.
    See Washington, Martha Dandridge

Dane, Clemence, pseud. (Winifred Ashton)
    (1861-1965)
    Eng. novelist
    Hammerton p475, por.
    Johnson—Some Contemp. p185-195
    Lawrence—School p364-373
    Millett—Brit. p190-191

Danforth, Abbie Ellsworth (b. 1836)
    Amer. clergyman
    Hanaford—Dau. p451

Danforth, Clarissa H. (m. 1822)
    Amer. clergyman
    Dexter—Career p60-61

Danforth, Ruth (fl. 1860's)
    Amer. Civil war nurse
    Logan—Part p369

Daniell, Tania. See Long, Tania

Daniels, Angela B. (fl. 1930's)
    Amer. production manager, bus.
      executive
    Women—Achieve. p173,por.

Daniels, Bebe (1901-   )
    Amer. actress
    CR '59 p192,por.
    Hammerton p476
    Herman—How p93,por.

(Continued)

Daniels, Bebe—*Continued*

Hughes—Famous p112-133,por.
Lamparski—What p192-193,por.
Wagenknecht—Movies p208-209,
213-214

Daniels, Frances D. (fl. 1860's)
Amer. Civil war nurse
Logan—Part p368

Daniels, Grace Baird (fl. 1950's)
Amer. organization official
Cur. Biog. '59 p85-86,por.

Daniels, Mabel Wheeler (b. 1879)
Amer. composer
ASCAP p108
Elson—Woman's p246-248
Ewen—American p77-78
Goss—Modern p61-69,por.
Howard—Our p394-395
McCoy—Portraits p31,por.
Reis—Composers p92

Danielson, Mrs. Jacques. See Hurst, Fannie

Danielson, Sarah Williams (b. 1737)
Amer. Rev. war patriot
Root—Chapter p303-304

Danilova, Alexandra Alicia (1907-   )
Russ. ballet dancer
Atkinson—Dancers p35-41,por.
CR '59 p193,por.
CR '63 p156,por.
Crowle—Enter p43-64,por.
Davidson—Ballet p42-48
Hammerton p476
Haskell—Vignet. p36,por.
Swinson—Dancers p49-53,por.
*Terry—Star p143-153,por.

d'Anjou, Marguerite.
See Anjou, Marguerite d'

Danner, Louise Rutledge (c. 1863-1943)
Amer. welfare worker, YWCA
official
Cur. Biog. '43 p159

Danser, Fanny Root (fl. 1930's)
Amer. club leader, missionary,
social reformer
Women—Achieve. p152,por.

Danvin, Catherine.
See Radziwill, Catherine, Princess

d'Aquino, Iva.
See Aquino, Iva Ikuko Toguri d'

d'Aquitaine, Eleanor.
See Aquitaine, Eleanor d'

D'Aragona, Tullia (1505-1556)
It. courtesan, poet
Mayne—Enchant. p81-94

d'Aranyi, Yelly. See Aranyi, Yelly d'

Darbishire, Helen (gr. 1903)
Eng. educator
Brittain—Women (see index)

d'Arblay, Madame. See Burney, Fanny

Darby, Abiah Maude Sinclair (fl. 1740's-
1760's)
Eng. author
Bolitho—Biog. p148-153

Darby, Deborah (fl. 1790's)
Eng. author
Bolitho—Biog. p153-157

Darby, J. N., pseud.
See Govan, Christine Noble

Darby, Joan (fl. 18th cent.)
Eng., wife of John Darby
Davenport—Great p127-128

Darby, Mary Sargent (fl. 1700's)
Eng. religious worker
Bolitho—Biog. p143-144

d'Arc, Jeanne. See Joan of Arc

Darcel, Denise (1925-   )
Fr.-Amer. singer, actress
CR '63 p156,por.

Dare, Helen (fl. 1920's)
Amer. journalist
Ross—Ladies p576-577

Dare, Phyllis (1890-   )
Eng. actress
Hammerton p478

Dare, Violet (fl. 1910's)
actress
Caffin—Vaud. p139

Dare, Virginia (Eleanor White) (b. 1587)
Amer., first Eng. child b. in
America
Green—Pioneer (1) p8-9,97
Leonard—Amer. p113
*MacVeagh—Champlin p173
Stiles—Postal p66

Dare, Zena (b. 1887)
Eng. actress
Hammerton p478,por.
Wyndham—Chorus p153-154

Darerca (fl. 490's-520's)
Irish, mother of Saint Ciaran
Concannon—Dau. p55-57

Dargan, Olive Tilford (fl. 1900's-1930's)
      Amer. poet, novelist
   Cook—Our p156-157
   Smith—Women's p38
   Warfel—Amer. p61-62,por.

Daringer, Helen Fern (1892-   )
      Amer. author
   Cur. Biog. '51 p152-153,por.

Darley, Ellen Westray (1779-1848)
      Amer. actress
   Coad—Amer. p64,por.

Darling, Flora Adams (1840-1910)
      Amer. organization official,
         foundress
   Dorland—Sum p23

Darling, Grace Horsley (1815-1842)
      Eng. heroine
   Carey—Twelve p279-292,por.
   Dorland—Sum p20,129
   Fifty—Famous p126-133,por.
   Hammerton p479
   *Horowitz—Treas. p139-141
   Muir—Women p157-159
   Parton—Noted p576-582,por.
   Sitwell—Women p33-34,por.
   *Strong—Heroes p113-115
   Strong—Of p155-157

Darlington, Hannah (fl. 1870's-1880's)
      Amer. social reformer
   Hanaford—Dau. p376-377

d'Armont, Marie Anne Charlotte Corday.
   See Corday, Charlotte

Darnell, Linda (1923-1965)
      Amer. actress
   CR '59 p193,por.
   CR '63 p157,por.
   Stuart—Immort. p72-73,por.

Darnell, Mary. See Carroll, Mary Darnell

Darrach, Mrs. Marshall (fl. 1900's)
      Amer. journalist
   Ross—Ladies p455-456

Darrah (Darragh), Lydia (1728-1789)
      Amer. Rev. war heroine
   Bruce—Woman p109-112
   DAR Mag.July 1921 p384-385
      (portrayal)
   Dexter—Colonial p73-77
   Ellet—Women (1) p199-206
   Fowler—Woman p139-141
   Green—Pioneer (2) p237-247,342-343,
      por.
   Hanaford—Dau. p55-56
   Hoehling—Women p3-17
   Komroff—True p25-41
   Leonard—Amer. p114

   Logan—Part p154-156
   Muir—Women p148-150
   Nida—Pilots p203-204
   *Sickels—Calico p73-95
   Singer—3000 p47-56

Darré, Jeanne-Marie (1905-   )
      Fr. pianist
   Schonberg—Great p423

Darrell, Maisie (1901-   )
      Eng. actress
   Hammerton p480

Darrieux, Danielle (1917-   )
      Fr. actress
   CR '59 p193,por.

D'Arusmont, Frances
   See Wright, Frances (Fanny)
   D'Arusmont

Darwell, Jane (c. 1880-1967)
      Amer. actress
   Cur. Biog. '41 p203-205,por.
   Cur. Biog. '67 p474

Darwin, Elinor M. (d. 1954)
      Irish illustrator
   Mahony—Illus. p296

Dashwood, Edmée Elizabeth Monica de la
      Pasture.
   See Delafield, Elizabeth Hanenkamp

Da Silva, Viera.
   See Vierira da Silva, Maria Helena

Daskkova (Dashkoff), Ekaterina Romanova,
         Princess (1743/44-1810)
      Russ. author
   Adelman—Famous p81-82
   Hammerton p481-482
   Trowbridge p119-124,por.

Dassel, Herminie (d. 1857)
      Ger.-Amer. painter
   Hanaford—Dau. p296
   Waters—Women p100-101

Daston, Sarah (b.c. 1613)
      Amer., accused witch
   Green—Pioneer (1) p234

d'Aulaire, Ingri.
   See Aulaire, Ingri d'Mortenson

Dauser, Sue Sophia (1888-   )
      Amer. nurse
   Cur. Biog. '44 p141-142,por.
   Pennock—Makers p61,por.

d'Autriche, Anne. See Autriche, Anne d'

Dauvray, Helen (fl. 1880's)
Amer. actress, theatrical manager
Coad—Amer. p272

Davenant, Mrs. John (fl. 16th cent.)
Eng., possible "Dark Lady" of
Shakespeare
Brown—Dark p282-285,287,289-293

Davene, Mrs. William (fl. 1800's)
Amer. circus acrobat
Marks—Glamour p292

Davenport, Elizabeth Wooley (fl. 1650's)
Amer. colonial property manager,
bus. woman
Dexter—Colonial p111-112
Earle—Colon. p52-55
Leonard—Amer. p114

Davenport, Esther (fl. 1890's-1930's)
Amer. journalist
Ross—Ladies p521-522

Davenport, Fanny (Frances) (1850-1898)
Amer. actress
Adelman—Famous p228
Bodeen—Ladies p83-86
Coad—Amer. p239,por.
Dorland—Sum p27,69-70,167
Moses—Famous p242-249-254,por.
Wilson—All p137

Davenport, Frances Gardiner (b. 1870)
Amer. historian, teacher
Logan—Part p865

Davenport, Hester (c. 1641-1717)
Eng. actress
Wilson—All p137-139

Davenport, Jane (1897-   )
Amer. sculptor
National—Contemp. p73

Davenport, Jean.
See Lander, Jean Margaret Davenport

Davenport, Louise M. (fl. 1930's)
Amer. club leader
Women—Achieve. p179,por.

Davenport, Marcia (1903-   )
Amer. author, music critic
CR '59 p194-195,por.
CR '63 p158,por.
Cur. Biog. '44 p142-144,por.
Van Gelder—Writers p343-348
Warfel—Amer. p109-110,por.

Davenport, Mrs. (b. 1642)
Eng. actress
MacQueen, Pope p37-39,por.

Davenport, Viola (fl. 1900's)
Amer. singer
Lahee—Grand p372

David, mother of (Biblical)
Nelson—Bible p41-42

Davidson, Hannah Amelia (b. 1852)
Amer. teacher, author, lecturer,
publisher
Logan—Part p849-850

Davidson, Lucretia Maria (1808-1838)
Amer. poet
Hanaford—Dau. p263-264
Logan—Part p797-798

Davidson, Margaret Miller (1823-1838)
Amer. poet
Hanaford—Dau. p263-264

Davie, Eugenie M. L. (fl. 1930's)
Amer. politician
Women—Achieve. p87,por.

Davie, May Preston (m. 1930)
Amer. politician
Phelps—Men '58 (1) p68-69

Davies, Blodwen (1897-   )
Can. author
Thomas—Canad. p30-31

Davies, Cecilia (1740-1836)
Eng. singer
Pleasants—Great p110

Davies, Christian (1667-1739)
Irish soldier
Hammerton p484-485

Davies, Clara Novello Davies (1861-1943)
Welsh choral director
McCoy—Portraits p31,por.

Davies, Eleanor Audley, Dame (1603-1652)
Eng. author, imposter
Fifty—Famous p206-209

Davies, Eleanor Trehawke (fl. 1910's)
Eng. pioneer aviation passenger
*May—Women p66-67

Davies, Emily (1830-1921)
Eng. social reformer, foundress
Brittain p32-36,67
Stenton—English p346-347

Davies, Fanny (1861-1934)
Eng. pianist
Hammerton p485,por.
Schonberg—Great p336

Davies, Florence (fl. 1930's)
Amer. journalist
Ross—Ladies p235,535

Davies, Llewela (fl. 1890's-1930's)
Welsh composer
Elson—Woman's p153

Davies, Marion (1900-1961)
Amer. actress
CR '59 p195,por.
Hammerton p485
Herman—How p33,por.
Stuart—Immort. p80-81,por.
Tebbel—Inher. p182-185

Davies, Marjorie Post Close Hutton
(fl. 1930's)
Amer. social leader
New Yorker Feb.4,1939 p23,28,por.,
Feb. 11,1939 p23-27, Feb.18,1939
p24-27(Profiles)

Davies, Mary ("Moll") (d. 1687)
Eng. actress
MacQueen—Pope p50-56
Wilson—All p139-141

Davies, Mary Carolyn (fl. 1920's)
Amer. poet, song-writer
ASCAP p110-111
*Benet—Amer. poets p177-180
Cook—Our p217-219
Smith—Women's p45

Davies, Sarah Emily (1830-1921)
Brit. educator, feminist
Hammerton p485
Lovejoy—Women p136-137,140

Daviess, Maria Thompson (1872-1924)
Amer. novelist
Maurice—Makers p10-11

Daviess, Mrs. (fl. 1770's)
Amer. Rev. war heroine
Ellet—Women (2) p310-311

Daviess, Mrs. Samuel (fl. 1780's)
Amer. pioneer
Fowler—Woman p199-203

Davis, Agnes (fl. 1920's-1940's)
Amer. singer
Ewen—Living p96-97,por.
McCoy—Portraits p32,por.

Davis, Ann Scott (1805-1891)
Irish-Can. Amer. pioneer, heroine
Phillips—33 p28-32

Davis, Anne B. (1926-   )
Amer. actress
TV—Person (2) p144-145,por.

Davis, Arlene Palsgraff (d. 1964)
Amer. aviatrix, business executive
*May—Women p163-186,por.

Davis, Bette (1908-   )
Amer. actress
CR '59 p196-196
CR '63 p158,por.
Cur. Biog. '41 p206-208,por.
Cur. Biog. '53 p144-146,por.

New Yorker Feb.20,1943 p19-24,por.
(Profiles)
Schickel—Stars p147-149,por.
Time Mar.28,1938 p44,por.(cover)

Davis, "Bun" (fl. 1930's)
Amer. airline hostess
Planck—Women p192

Davis, Caroline Dawson (n.d.)
Amer. labor leader
Jensen—Revolt p99,por.

Davis, Catharine. See Whitcomb, Catherine

Davis, Clara (fl. 1860's)
Amer. Civil war nurse
Brockett—Woman's p400-403

Davis, Dorothy (1922-   )
Amer. politician
Roosevelt—Ladies p84-85,88-93

Davis, Edith Smith (m. 1884)
Amer. social reformer
Logan—Part p669

Davis, Fay (1872-1945)
Amer. actress
Hammerton p485,por.
Strang—Actresses p273-284

Davis, Fay Simmons (d. 1942)
Amer. pianist, composer, music
teacher
McCoy—Portraits p32,por.

Davis, Frances (fl. 1910's-1920's)
Ross—Ladies p570-571

Davis, Frances (2). See Alda, Frances

Davis, Mrs. G. T. M. (fl. 1860's)
Amer. Civil war nurse,
humanitarian
Brockett—Woman's p352-356

Davis, Gail (n.d.)
Amer. actress
TV—Person. (1) p31-32,por.

Davis, Genevieve (1889-1950)
Amer. composer
ASCAP p111

Davis, Gladys Rockmore (1901-   )
Amer. artist
Cur. Biog. '53 p146-148,por.
Cur. Biog. '67 p474
Ency. Brit.-Amer. p32,por.

Davis, Hannah (fl. 1830's)
Amer. bus. woman, manufacturer
Hanaford—Dau. p613
Whitton—These p192-193

Davis, Jane (fl. 1940's-1950's)
    Amer. missionary
    They—Went p143

Davis, Janette (n.d.)
    Amer. singer
    TV—Person (1) p118,por.

Davis, Jessie Bartlett (b. 1860)
    Amer. singer
    Strang—Prima p88-103,por.

Davis, Joan (1912-1961)
    Amer. actress, comedienne
    Blum—Television p103,por.
    Cur. Biog. '45 p138-139,por.
    Cur. Biog. '61 p120
    Stuart—Immort. p89-91,por.
    TV—Person (1) p150-151,por.

Davis, Julia Margaret Hubman (m. 1948)
    Amer. missionary
    They—Went p139-140

Davis (or Davies), Katherine (fl. 1680's-
        1690's)
    Eng. actress
    Wilson—All p139

Davis, Katherine Bement (1860-1935)
    Amer. sociologist, penologist,
        philanthropist
    Dorland—Sum p122
    Logan—Part p538
    *Moore—When p74-81

Davis, Katherine K. (1892-   )
    Amer. composer, author
    ASCAP p112

Davis, Katherine McGrath (fl. 1950's)
    Amer. politician
    Jensen—Revolt p64,por.

Davis, Louise Taylor (fl. 1930's-1940's)
    Amer. advertising executive
    Taves—Success. p188-201,por.
    Women—Achieve, p165,por.

Davis, Mrs. M. E. (fl. 1890's)
    Amer. club leader
    Logan—Part p469

Davis, Marguerite (b. 1889)
    Amer. illustrator
    Mahony—Illus. p297-298

Davis, Maxine (1) (fl. 1920's)
    Amer. aviatrix
    *May—Women p81

Davis, Maxine (2) (fl. 1930's)
    Amer. journalist
    Ross—Ladies p354-356

Davis, Minerva M. (fl. 1930's)
    Amer. lawyer
    Women—Achieve. p98,por.

Davis, Minnie S. (fl. 1880's)
    Amer. author
    Hanaford—Dau. p239-240

Davis, Nelle (fl. 1930's)
    Eng.-Amer. pharmacist
    Women—Achieve. p189,por.

Davis, Nevada Victoria (fl. 1910's)
    Amer. journalist
    Ross—Ladies p425-426

Davis, Newell Trimble (fl. 1920's-1950's)
    Amer. missionary
    They—Went p70-72

Davis, Paulina Wright (1813-1876)
    Amer. feminist, social reformer,
        journalist, lecturer
    Hanaford—Dau. p697-702
    O'Connor—Pioneer p85-86,200
    Riegel—Amer. p128-130

Davis, Rebecca Harding (1831-1910)
    Amer. author
    Adelman—Famous p202

Davis, Tobé Collier (c. 1893-   )
    Amer. fashion designer, bus.
        executive
    Cur. Biog. '59 p88-90
    Women—Achieve. p64,por.

Davis, Varina Howell (1826-1906)
    Amer. Civil war diarist, wife of
        Jefferson Davis
    Bradford—Wives p161-198,por.
    Harkness—Heroines p1-2
    Jones—Heroines p14-15,27-29,67-79,
        285-286,389-392,por.
    Logan—Part p488-490
    Simkins—Women p178-180,184-186

Davison, Edith (fl. 1900's)
    Eng. governess
    Howe—Galaxy p188-192

Davison, Eloise (fl. 1930's-1940's)
    Amer. home economist
    *Logie—Careers (2nd) p145-151
    Women—Achieve. p82,por.

Davys, Mary (fl. 1750's)
    Eng. novelist
    MacCarthy—Women p35-36

Daw Thein Tin (Madame U. Thant)
        (m. 1934)
    Burmese, wife of U. Thant
    Frederick—Ten p138-156,por.

Dawes, Helen B. Palmer (m. 1890's)
    Amer. teacher, club leader
    Schmidt—400 p544-546,por.

Dawes, Mrs. James H. (fl. 1840's)
    Amer. seafarer
    Snow—Women p124-128

Dawes, Kathleen, Duchess of Manchester
    (m. 1931)
    Eng. actress
    Wyndham—Chorus p146

Dawes, Sophia, Baronne de Feuchères
    (1790-1840)
    Eng., mistress of Duke of Bourbon
    Coryn—Enchant. p177-202
    Hammerton p487,588-589

Dawn, Hazel (1891/94-   )
    Amer. actress, singer
    Blum—Great p102,por.

Dawson, Sarah Morgan (b.c. 1841)
    Amer. Civil war diarist
    Dunaway—Treas. p264-267

Dawson-Scott, Catharine Amy.
    See Scott, Catherine Amy Dawson

Day, Doris (1924-   )
    Amer. actress, singer
    CR '59 p196-197,por.
    CR '63 p161,por.
    Cur. Biog. '54 p225-227,por.
    Popular Record p43,por.
    Rivkin—Hello p250-253
    Stambler—Ency. p66-67,por.

Day, Dorothy (1897-   )
    Amer. journalist, social worker
    Cur. Biog. '62 p94-96,por.
    New Yorker Oct. 4,1952 p37(por);
    Oct.11,1952 p37 (Profiles)

Day, Edith (1896-   )
    Amer. actress
    Hammerton p487

Day, Emma V. (1853-1894)
    Amer. missionary
    Logan—Part p515-516

Day, Enid (n.d.)
    Amer. nursing asst.
    *Wright—Great p9-42

Day, Juliana (fl. 1960's)
    Amer. Civil war nurse
    Brockett—Woman's p789-790

Day, Laraine (1920/29-   )
    Amer. actress
    CR '59 p197,por.
    CR '63 p161-162,por.
    Cur. Biog. '53 p150-153,por.

Day, Martha (1813-1833)
    Amer. author
    Bacon—Puritan p133-135

Day, Olivia (d. 1853)
    Amer. editor
    Bacon—Puritan p135,151-153

Dayton, Dorothy (fl. 1920's)
    Amer. journalist
    Ross—Ladies p225-228

Dayton, Katharine (1890-1945)
    Amer. journalist, playwright
    Mantle—Contemp. p9,178-180

Dazie, Mademoiselle (fl. 1910's)
    Fr. dancer
    Caffin—Vaud. p104

De Abarca. See Abarca, Marie De

De Acosta See Acosta

Dealy, Jane Mary.
    See Lewis, Jane Mary Dealy, Lady

Dean, Julia (1830-1868)
    Amer. actress
    Blum—Great p60,por.
    Bodeen—Ladies p62-66
    Coad—Amer. p173,por.

Dean, Rebecca Pennell (1821-1890)
    Amer. pioneer educator
    Stern—We p147-177

Dean, Vera Micheles (1903-   )
    Russ.-Amer. author, lecturer
    Cur. Biog. '43 p160-162,por.

Deane, Margaret (b. 1831)
    Amer. teacher
    Logan—Part p834

Deane, Martha (1).
    See McBride, Mary Margaret

Deane, Martha (2). See Young, Marian

De Angeli, Marguerite (b. 1889)
    Amer. illustrator, author
    Cur. Biog. '37 p151-152,por.
    Mahony—Illus. p298

De Angelis, Clotilde (f. 1870's)
    It. painter
    Waters—Women p102

de Arrom, Cecelia Francesca Josefa.
    See Caballaro, Fernan Böhl von Faber

Deasy, Mary Margaret (1914-   )
    Amer. author
    Cur. Biog. '58 p114-115,por.

De Barker, Lorraine (fl. 1930's)
    Amer. cosmetician, bus. woman
    Woman—Achieve. p70,por.

De Beauharnais. See Beauharnais

Debay, Caroline Louise Emma (1809-1832)
    Fr. artist
    Dorland—Sum p21,154-155

Deberdt, Esther. See Reed, Esther Deberdt

Debillemont-Chardon, Gabrielle (b. 1865)
    Fr. artist
    Waters—Women p102

Deborah (Biblical)
    judge, prophetess
    Buchanan—Women p39-41
    Chappell—Fem. p63-75
    Culver—Women p25-26
    Deen—All p69-74
    Faulhaber—Women p74-93
    Hammerton p488
    Harrison—Little p38-52
    Hastings—Greater p441-457
    Horton—Women p119-133
    *Levinger—Great p35-37
    Lofts—Women p66-76
    Lord—Great p47-58
    *MacVeagh—Champlin p177
    Marble—Women, Bible p170-178
    Mead—250
    Morton—Women p85-91
    Schmidt—400 p266-267,por.
    Van der Velde—She p93-99

Deborah (2) (Biblical)
    Rebekah's nurse
    Deen—All p260
    Hammerton p488
    Lewis—Portraits p167-168,174-176

De Bourk, Mademoiselle (b.c. 1710)
    Amer. seafarer
    Snow—Women p19-28

De Camp, Rosemary (b. 1889)
    Amer. actress
    TV—Person (2) p145-146,por.

De Carlo, Yvonne (1922-   )
    Can.-Amer. actress
    CR '59 p198-199,por.
    CR '63 p163,por.

De Carvajal, Luisa. See Carvajal, Luisa de

De Casa Yrujo, Sarah McKean, Marchioness
        (b. 1777)
    Amer. pioneer
    Green—Pioneer (3) p281
    Sale—Old p219-223,por.

De Castro, Ines. See Castro, Ines de

De Cevee, Alice (1904-   )
    Amer. composer, pianist
    ASCAP p113

Decker, Sarah Platt (d. 1912)
    Amer. educator, organization
        official
    Logan—Part p420,718

Declan, Mother (n.d.)
    Afr. missionary, nun
    Moore—Modern p157-166

Dee, Ruth (n.d.)
    Amer. actress
    CR '63 p164,por.

Dee, Sandra (1942-   )
    Amer. actress
    CR '63 p164,por.

Dee, Sylvia (1914-1967)
    Amer. author, song-writer
    ASCAP p114
    Warfel—Amer. p115,por.

Deere, Mary Little Dickinson (m. 1862)
    Amer. club leader
    Logan—Part p481

Deffand, Marie de Vichy-Chamrond,
        Marquise Du (1697-1780)
    Fr. salonist
    Adelman—Famous p75-76
    Blei—Fasc. p149-153,por.
    Bradford—Women p133-154,por.
    Dorland—Sum p106
    Gade—Under p130-153,por.
    Hammerton p490
    Kavanagh—Woman (1) p164-182
    Tallentyre—Women p1-21,por.
    Thomson—Queens p403-432,por.
    Watson—Some p45-95,por.

De Forest, Jane O. (fl. 1880's)
    Amer. lecturer
    Hanaford—Dau. p341

De Frece, Matilda Alice, Lady.
    See Tilley, Vesta

De Galard-Terraube, Geneviève.
    See Galard Terraube, Geneviève de

De Gaulle, Yvonne Vendroux (1900-   )
    Fr., wife of Charles De Gaulle
    Frederick—Ten p54-77,por.

Degnan, Bridget Dixon (d. 1940)
    Irish-Amer. W. pioneer
    Sargent—Pioneers p70-73,por.

Degnan, Mary Ellen (b.c. 1887)
    Amer. W. pioneer
    Sargent—Pioneers p73

De Haas, Alice Preble Tucker (fl. 1900's)
 Amer. painter
 Waters—Women p103-104

Dehan, Richard, pseud.
 See Graves, Clotilde Inez

Deharme, Lise (1902-   )
 Fr. novelist
 Peyre—French p410

Dehaviland, Olivia (1916-   )
 Amer. actress
 CR '59 p200,por.
 CR '63 p164,por.
 Cur. Biog. '44 p211-215,por.
 Cur. Biog. '66 p74-76,por.
 Time Dec.20,1948 p44,por.

de Horvath, Cecile (fl. 1940's)
 Amer. pianist
 McCoy—Portraits p33,por.

Deianira. See De Janira

Deimer, Catherine (d. 1761/62)
 Amer. colonial bus. woman
 Dexter—Colonial p69

Déjazet, Pauline Virginia (1797/98-1875)
 Fr. actress
 Dorland—Sum p41,69,79,164
 Hammerton p492

De Jong, Dola (1911-   )
 Nether. author
 Cur. Biog. '47 p154-155,por.

De Kay, Helena (f. 1870's)
 Amer. painter
 Waters—Women p105

Deken, Aagji (1741-1804)
 Nether. poet, novelist
 Phila.—Women unp.,por.
 Schmidt—400 p302-303,por.
 Stiles—Postal p69

De Kroyft, (Susan) Helen Aldrich
  (1818-1915)
 Amer. blind author, lecturer
 Hanaford—Dau. p347-349

Delacroix, Caroline, Baroness de Vaughan
  (n.d.)
 Belg., mistress of Leopold II,
  King of Belgium
 Kelen—Mist. p172-189,332-333

Delacroix-Garnier, Madame P. (fl. 1890's-
  1900's)
 Fr. painter
 Waters—Women p105

De La Cruz, Sor Juana Ines (1651-1695)
 Mex. poet, linguist
 Schmidt—400 p288-289,por.

Delafield, Ann (fl. 1930's)
 Amer. cosmetician, dietician,
  teacher
 Women—Achieve. p34,por.

Delafield, Edmée Monica, pseud. (Mrs.
  de la Pasture; Dashwood),
  (1890-1943)
 Brit. novelist, playwright
 Cur. Biog. '44 p149
 Hammerton p492,por.
 Johnson—Some Contemp. p175-184
 Lawrence—School p301-303
 Millett—Brit. p195-197

Delafield, Elizabeth Hanenkamp (fl. 1800's)
 Amer. club leader
 Logan—Part p461

Delamare, Delphine Conturier (d. 1848)
 Flaubert's "Madame Bovary"
 Wallace—Fabulous p259-267

DeLancey, Alice (m. 1767)
 Amer. belle
 Sale—Old p109-116,por.

Deland, Margaret Wade (1857-1945)
 Amer. novelist
 Adelman—Famous p288-289
 Cur. Biog. '45 p145
 Dodd—Celeb. p151-156
 Logan—Part p859
 Maurice—Makers #3,por.
 Overton—Women p105-107
 Rogers—Women p39,por.
 Williams—Our p129-145

Delaney, Adelaide Margaret (b. 1875)
 Amer. lecturer, editor, author
 Logan—Part p834

Delaney, Catherine A. (1822-1894)
 Amer. racial leader
 Brown—Home. p90-91,por.

Delaney, Shelagh (1939-   )
 Brit. playwright
 Cur. Biog. '62,p99-101,por.

De Lange, Cornelia Catharina (b. 1871)
 Nether. physician
 Lovejoy—Women p185

Delano, Jane Arminda (1862-1919)
 Amer. nurse, Red Cross official
 DAR Mag. Nov. 1921,p649
 Dolan—Goodnow's p305
 Hammerton p493
 Pennock—Makers p47-48,por.
 Schmidt—400 p405-406,por.

Delany, Mary Granville (1700-1788)
 Eng. author
 Stenton—English p241-244,253,258,
  262,272,283,295.

De La Pasture, Edmée Elizabeth Monica.
   See Delafield, Edmée Monica, pseud.

De La Pasture, Elizabeth Lydia Rosabelle
      Bonham (b. 1866)
      Brit. author
   Hammerton p493,por.

De la Ramée, Marie Louise. See Ouida

De La Roche, Baroness (fl. 1910's)
      Fr. aviatrix
   *May—Women p62

De La Roche, Mazo (1879/85-1961)
      Can. novelist
   Burnett—Amer. p547,por.
   Innis—Clear p242-259,por.
   Lawrence—School p293-296
   Millett—Brit. p200-201
   Overton—Women p108-112
   Thomas—Canad. p31-33

De Larrocha, Alicia.
   See Larrocha, Alicia de

Delasalle, Angèle (b. 1867)
      Fr. painter
   Waters—Women p105-107

De la Torre(-Bueno), Lillian (1902-   )
      Amer. author
   Cur. Biog. '49 p141-142,por.

De Lavallade, Carmen (1931-   )
      Amer. dancer
   Cur. Biog. '67 p92-95,por.
   *Maynard—Amer. p205,por.

De La Vallière, Duchess.
   See La Vallière, Louise Baume Le
      Blanc de

Delbo, Helvig (d. 1944)
      Nor. spy, mistress of Pelving
   Singer—World (II) p168-173

De Leath, Vaughn (1896-1943)
      Amer. singer, song-writer
   Settel—Radio p58,por.

Deledda, Grazia (1875-1936)
      It. novelist, gardener
   Hammerton p494,por.
   McClintock—Nobel p602
   Nobel—Man p121
   Phila.—Women, unp,por.
   Stiles—Postal p69

Delilah (Biblical)
   Armour—It p13-24
   Buchanan—Women p42-43
   Chappell—Fem. p76-88
   Culver—Women p27
   Davenport—Great p57-59

   Deen—All p78-81
   Ewart—World's p21-24
   Faulhaber—Women p102-119
   Hammerton p494
   Hastings—Greater p514-517
   Lewis—Portraits p144-147
   Lofts—Women p77-86
   Macartney—Great p86-104
   *MacVeagh—Champlin p179
   Mead—250 p72
   Morton—Women p93-99
   Ockenga—Women p63-74
   Spurgeon—Sermons p81-93

De Lima, Sigrid (1921-   )
      Amer. author
   Cur. Biog. '58 p115-117,por.

Dell, Ethel M. (f. 1939)
      Brit. novelist
   Hammerton p494

Della Casa, Lisa (1921-   )
      Swiss-Amer. singer
   Cur. Biog. '56 p146-147,por.
   Matz—Opera p68-70,por.
   Rosenthal—Sopranos p26-27,por.

Della Chiesa, Vivian (c. 1915-   )
      Amer. singer
   Cur. Biog. '43 p164-165,por.

Delleglace, Mademoiselle (fl. 18th cent.)
      Fr. patriot
   Kavanagh—Woman (20) p189

Delmar, Irene (1903-   )
      Amer. journalist, editor
   Women—Achieve. p172,por.

Del Mondo, Fé (fl. 1950's)
      Phil. physician
   Lovejoy—Women p244-254,375,por.

Delna, Marie Ledan (1875-1932)
      Fr. singer
   Lahee—Grand p314-317

Del Occidente, Maria.
   See Brooks, Maria Gowan

De Long, Emma J. Wotton (1851-1940)
      Amer. author, editor
   Cur. Biog. '41 p218

De Long, Sally (n.d.)
      Amer. pioneer airline draftsman
   *Peckham—Women p95

Delorme, Bertha (fl. 1900's)
      Fr. painter
   Waters—Women p107-108

Delorme (or De Lorme) Marion
        (1611/13-c. 1650)
    Fr. courtesan
    Hammerton p495

De los Angeles, Victoria.
    See Angeles, Victoria de los

Delphina (1283-1360)
    It. saint
    Blunt—Great p150
    Englebert—Lives p450

Delpine, Margarita (fl. 17th-18th cent.)
    Eng. singer
    MacQueen—Pope p123

del Riego, Teresa (fl. 1940's)
    Eng. composer
    McCoy—Portraits p33,por.

Del Rio, Dolores (1905-   )
    Mex. actress
    CR '59 p202-203,por.
    CR '63 p166,por.
    Herman—How p65,por.
    Schickel—Stars p58,60,por.

Delysia, Alice (b. 1889)
    Anglo-Fr. actress
    Hammerton p495

De Mar, Paul, pseud. See Foley, Pearl

De Marco, Renee (fl. 1940's)
    Amer. dancer
    New Yorker Jan.6,1940 p22-27,por.
        (Profiles)

De Marco sisters (fl. 1930's-1950's)
    Amer. singers
    Reed—Follow p123-129

De Medicis, Catherine.
    See Catherine de Medicis

Demeur, Anne Arsène Charton (1842-1892)
    Fr. singer
    Ewen—Ency. p109-110

De Mille, Agnes George (c. 1905-   )
    Amer. dancer, choreographer
    °Clymer—Modern p150-159,por.
    CR '59 p203,por.
    CR '63 p166,por.
    Cur. Biog. '43 p165-167,por.
    °Forsee—Amer. p65-91
    Hazeltine—We p215-224
    °McConnell—Famous p117-132,por.
    °Muir—Famous p115-124,por.
    Newquist—Show. p91-104,por.
    New Yorker Sept.14,1946 p32-36,
        por. (Profiles)

Deming, Dorothy (1893-   )
    Amer. nurse, author
    Cur. Biog. '43 p167-168,por.

De Miramion, Madame (1629-1694)
    Fr. humanitarian, beauty, heiress
    Parton—Dau. p417-422

Demjanovich, Miriam Teresa (1901-1927)
    Amer. religious worker
    Maynard—Great p235-242

Demont-Breton, Virginie Elodie (b. 1859)
    Fr. painter
    Waters—Women p108-109

De Morgan, Emily Pickering (fl. 1870's)
    Eng. painter
    Waters—Women pj376-377

De Mott, Marjorie Mahon (fl. 1930's)
    Amer. bus. woman
    Women—Achieve. p188,por.

Deneke, Helena Clara (fl. 1910's)
    Eng. tutor
    Brittain—Women p125,142,146,150

Deneke, Margaret (fl. 1930's)
    Eng. choirmaster
    Brittain—Women p184,186,260

Denham, Elizabeth Brooke, Lady (c. 1647-
        1667)
    Eng. beauty
    Melville—Windsor p154-165,por.

Denis, Louise Mignot (c. 1710-1790)
    Fr., niece, companion of Voltaire
    Kavanagh—Woman (1) p152

Denis, Mrs. (fl. 1760's)
    Amer. W. pioneer
    Ellet—Pioneer p110-111

Denise (234-250)
    Gr. saint
    Englebert—Lives p189

Denison, Elsa (b. 1889)
    Amer. social reformer
    Logan—Part p604

Denne, Elizabeth (fl. 1700's)
    Amer. pioneer
    Green—Pioneer (1) p399-400,402-403

Denni, Gwynne (1882-1949)
    Amer. author, actress, musician,
        song-writer
    ASCAP p117

Dennie, Eunice. See Burr, Eunice Dennie

Dennis, Hannah (fl. 1700's)
    Amer. pioneer, Indian captive
    Bruce—Woman p74-79

Dennis, Olive Wetzel (1885-1957)
    Amer. engineer, inventor, r.r.
        executive
    Cur. Biog. '41 p220-221,por.
    Goff—Women p3-18

Dennis, Sandy (1937-   )
    Amer. actress
    Time Sept.1,1967 p54-57,por. (Cover)

Denny, Edith Litchfield (fl. 1920's-1930's)
    Amer. airship pilot
    *May—Women p43-44

Denny, Mary Frances (b. 1797)
    Amer. actress
    COAD—Amer. p128,por.

Densford, Katharine Jane (1890-   )
    Amer. nurse, educator
    Cur. Biog. '47 p166-168,por.

Densmore, Frances (1867-1957)
    Amer. ethnologist, musician
    Howard—Our p617-619,621

Denton, Anne (fl. 1650's)
    Eng. hostess
    Stenton—English p168

Denvir, Joan (1925-   )
    Brit. illustrator
    Ryder—Artists p57

De Onis, Harriet.
    See Onis, Harriet Vivian Wishnieff De

De Palencia, Isabel.
    See Palencia, Isabel de

De Peyster, Cornelia Lubbetse (d. 1725)
    Amer. colonial property manager
    Beard—Amer. p24-25
    Dexter—Colonial p103-105
    Green—Pioneer (1) p187-188,196

De Peyster, Maria.
    See Provost, Maria de Peyster Schrick
        Spratt

De Pina, May Frances (fl. 1930's)
    Venez.-Amer. model school director
    Women—Achieve. p148,por.

D'Épinay, Louise.
    See Épinay, Louise Florence
        Petronille de la Live d'

De Ponce de León, Dona Inés (c. 1475-
        c. 1515)
    Puert. Ric. humanitarian
    Schmidt—400 p331-332,por.

Deppen, Jessie L. (b. 1881)
    Amer. pianist
    ASCAP p118

Derby, Charlotte Stanley, Countess of
        (fl. 1640's)
    Eng. hostess
    Stenton—English p152

Derby, Elizabeth, Countess of.
    See Farren, Elizabeth

Derby, Mary (fl. 1810's)
    Amer. pioneer artist
    Whitton—These p193

De Reimer, Emily True (fl. 1900's)
    Amer. organization official
    Logan—Part p476

De Reszke, Josephine (1855-1891)
    Pol. singer
    Ewen—Ency. p112

Dereyne, Fay (fl. 1900's)
    Fr. singer
    Lahee—Grand p365-366,por.

Dermot, Jessie. See Elliott, Maxine

De Roquer, Emma. See Calvé, Emma

Derscheid, Marie (gr. 1893)
    Belg. physician
    Lovejoy—Women p187

Dervorgilla (d. 1193)
    Irish heroine
    McCraith—Romance p51-60

Dervorguilla (1213-1290)
    Scot. philanthropist
    Graham—Group p1-20,por.

De St. Julien, Elizabeth.
    See Moultrie, Elizabeth St. Julien

Desbordes-Valmore, Marceline (1786-1859)
    Fr. poet
    Stiles—Postal p70

Deschly, Irene (fl. 1900's)
    Rum. painter
    Waters—Women p377-378

de Sélincourt, Anne.
    See Sedgwick, Anne Douglas

Desgranges, Gisette.
    See Ennery, Madame d'

De Sevigné, Marie de.
    See Sevigné, Marie de Rabutin-Chantal,
        Marquise de

Desgarcins, Magdaleine (1769-1797)
    Fr. actress
    Dorland—Sum p50,168

Desgranges, Gisette.
    See Ennery, Madame d'

Desha, Mary (d. 1910)
Amer. foundress, teacher
Green—Pioneer (3) p405,463
Logan—Part p453-454

De Sherbinin, Betty (1917-   )
Can. author
Cur. Biog., '48 p140-141por.

Deshoulières, Antoinette du Ligier
(1638-1694)
Fr. poet
Dorland—Sum p57,105,178

Desislava (fl. 11th cent.)
Belg. Tsarina
Phila.—Women unp.,por.
Stiles—Postal p70

Desmond, Astra (fl. 1940's)
Eng. singer
Brooks—Singer p64-69,por.

Desmond, Florence (1907-   )
Eng. actress
Hammerton p501,por.

Desmoulins, Lucile (fl. 18th cent.)
Fr. Rev. war martyr
Kavanagh—Woman (2) p220-222,238

Desnoyer, Madame (fl. 1760's)
West Ind. seafarer
Snow—Women p128-136

Despard, Charlotte (b. 1844)
Brit. social reformer
Hammerton p501

Desroys, Alexis François (fl. 19th cent.)
Fr., mother of Lamartine
Bartlett—Mothers p43-45

De Staël, Madame.
See Staël, Anne Louise Germaine
Necker, Baronne de

D'este, Isabelle. See Este, Isabella d'

Destinn, Emily Kitti (1878-1930)
Bohem. singer
Davidson—Treas. p82-84
Ewen—Ency. p113
Hammerton p501
Lahee—Grand p266-272,por.
McCoy—Portraits p34,por.
Stiles—Postal p70

D'Estrées, Gabrielle.
See Estrées, Gabrielle D'

Detourbey, Jeanne.
See Loynes, Detourbey, Comtesse de

D'Etreillis, Baroness (fl. 1930's)
Fr. fashion designer
Women—Achieve. p196

Dethridge, Luvena Wallace (fl. 1930's)
Amer. singer
Cuney-Hare—Negro p379-380

De Treville, Yvonne. See Treville, Yvonne de

de Tuscan, Bela (fl. 1930's)
Amer. aviatrix, gyro-cycle pilot,
fencer
*May—Women p210

Detzliffin, Anna Sophia (1738-1776
Ger. soldier
Schmidt—400 p192-193,por.

Deutsche, Babette (1895-   )
Amer. poet
Cook—Our p221-223
Smith—Women's p49

Deutsche, Elizabeth (1937-   )
Aust.-Amer. student
Murrow—This (2) p52-53

Deutsche, Naomi (1890-   )
Aust.-Amer. nurse
Pennock—Makers p63

De Valois, Ninette (1898-   )
Irish ballet dancer, choreographer,
foundress
CR '59 p206,por.
Cur. Biog. '49 p146-148,por.
New Yorker Sept.16,1950 p32,por.
(Profiles)

Deveau, Mrs. Harvey J. ("Tugboat Mary")
(fl. 1950's)
Amer. seafarer
Snow—Women p234-235

Deveaux, Mary.
See Bulloch, Mary Deveaux

Devereux, Margaret Green (fl. 1920's-
1930's)
Amer. interior decorator, editor
Women—Achieve. p87,por.

Devi, Dewal (fl. 1290's)
E. Ind. princess of Guzerat
Pool—Famous p135-142

Devi, Gayatri. See Jaipur, Maharani of

Devilliers, Mademoiselle.
See La Villiers, Mademoiselle.

Devonshire, Georgiana Cavendish, Duchess
of (1757-1806)
Eng. social leader, beauty
Furniss—Some p156-159
Hammerton p503
Thomson—Queens p125-143,por.

Devore, Ella (1849-1920)
Amer. missionary
Phillips—33 p74-78

Devote (286-303/304)
Mon. saint
Stiles—Postal p232

Devotion, Martha.
See Huntington, Martha Devotion

De Vries, Margaret.
See Philipse, Margaret Hardenbroeck
De Vries

Dewey, James.
See McNeilly, Mildred Masterson

Dewey, Mary Elizabeth (b. 1821)
Amer. author
Hanaford—Dau. p217
Logan—Part p859

Dewhirst, Susan Lucretia (b. 1876)
Amer. missionary
Logan—Part p664-665

Dewing, Elizabeth R.
See Kaup, Elizabeth Bartol Dewing

Dewing, Maria Richards (1845-1927)
Amer. painter
Michigan—Biog. p96

De Wolf sisters (fl. 1910's)
Amer. singers
Cuney-Hare—Negro p214-215

De Wolfe, Elsie (1865-1950)
Amer. actress
Adelman—Famous p303
Strang—Actresses p248-257,por.

Dewson, Mary Williams (1874-1962)
Amer. govt. official, politician,
economist
Roosevelt—Ladies p11-21
Women—Achieve. p81,por.

Dexter, Almira E.
See Luce, Almira E.

Dexter, Clarissa L. (d. 1856)
Amer. whaling voyager
Whiting—Whaling p57-64

d'Hardelot, Guy. See Rhodes, Mrs.

Dharmapala, Anarharika (b. 1864)
Ceylon patriot
Stiles—Postal p71

Dhible, Madame (fl. 1780's)
Fr., pioneer air passenger
*Lauwick—Heroines p19-20

Diamant, Gertrude (1901-   )
Amer. author
Cur. Biog. '42 p200-201,por.

Diana (Biblical)
Mead—250 p240

Diana of Andolo (d. 1236)
It. saint
Englebert—Lives p224

Diane of Poitiers, Duchess of Valentinois
Fr., mistress of Henry II
Hammerton p504
Imbert—Valois p167-170,175-182,190,
339,por.

Diblan, Makbule (fl. 1940's)
Turk. physician, politician
Lovejoy—Women p214-215,por.

Dibrell, Ella Dancy (fl. 1900's)
Amer. club leader
Logan—Part p502-506

Di Cajanello, Duchess.
See Edgren-Leffler, Anne Charlotte

Dick, Dorothy (1900-   )
Amer. author, song-writer
ASCAP p121

Dick, Gladys R. H. (b. 1881)
Amer. physician
Castiglioni—Hist. p974,1019,1127

Dick, Jane (fl. 1790's)
Amer. W. pioneer
Ellet—Pioneer p193

Dickens, Mary (fl. 1890's-1900's)
Eng. author
Hammerton p506

Dickenson, Jean (1914-   )
Can.-Amer. singer
Donaldson—Radio p11
Women—Achieve. p109,por.

Dickerman, Julia Elida (b. 1859)
Amer. teacher, organist
Logan—Part p765

Dickerman, Marion (fl. 1930's)
Amer. educator
Women—Achieve. p174,por.

Dickerson, Nancy Hanschman.
See Hanschman, Nancy Conners

Dickerson, Susanna (fl. 1830's)
Anglo-Amer. pioneer, heroine
*Sickels—Calico p157-172

Dickey, Annamary (fl. 1930's-1940's)
Amer. singer
Peltz—Spot. p100,por.

Dickey, Jane K. (fl. 1930's)
Amer. organization official
Women—Achieve. p188,por.

Dickens, Marguerite (fl. 1870's-1880's)
Amer. organization official
Logan—Part p473-474

Dickinson, Anna Elizabeth (1842-1932)
Amer. social reformer, lecturer,
author, actress
Beard—Amer. p197-203
Dorland—Sum p168
Douglas—Remember p126-127
Hanaford—Dau. p337-340,591
Logan—Part p831
Riegel—Amer. p151-153
Roosevelt—Ladies p6-7
Woodward—Bold p231-232
Young—Women p310,370

Dickinson, Clare Joseph (1755-1830)
Eng. foundress
Code—Great p36-69

Dickinson, Emily Elizabeth (1830-1886)
Amer. poet
Adelman—Famous p200
*Benet—Amer. Poets p75-80,por.
Bonte—Amer. p177,por.
Bradford—Portraits p227-257,por.
Bruère—Laugh p97-98
Douglas—Remember p172-180,por.
Hammerton p506
*Heath—Authors p19,por.
Heath—Woman (4) p17,por.
Hyde—Modern p89-102
Loggins—Hear p14-22
Love—Famous p28
*MacVeagh—Champlin p186
Moore—Disting. p145-160
Morris—400 p72
*Muir—Writers p17-26,por.
*Scherman—Amer. p52-53
Scherman—Literary p68-69
Untermeyer—Lives p579-590
Untermeyer—Makers p132-138
Untermeyer—Paths p205-212
*Witham—Pan. p145-150,por.

Dickinson, Lavinia (fl. 1840's-1860's)
Amer. sister of Emily Dickinson
Douglas—Remember p179-180

Dickinson, Lucy Jennings Dickinson (1882-)
Amer. club leader
Cur. Biog. '45 p149-151,por.

Dickinson, Mary
See Mattoon, Mary Dickinson

Dickinson, Mary Lowe (1839-1914)
Amer. author, educator
Logan—Part p713-715

Dickinson, Sarah (fl. 1770's)
Amer. patriot
Green—Pioneer (3) p517-518

Dickinson, Susan E. (fl. 1870's-1890's)
Amer. journalist
Farmer—What p205,por.

Dickinson, Velvalee (c. 1893-   )
Amer., Japan. spy
Hoehling—Women p111-114
*Komroff—True p152-170
*Nolen—Spies p157-168
Singer—World II p173-185
Singer—World's p184-197,por.

Dickson, Dorothy (1896-   )
Amer. actress
Hammerton p507

Dickson, Marguerite Stockman (1873-1953)
Amer. author
Cur. Biog. '52 p147-148,por.
Cur. Biog. '54 p233

Dickson, Mary (fl. 1820's)
Amer. printer, publisher, bookseller
Dexter—Career p104-105,144-145

Dido (or Elissa) (9th cent., B.C.)
Carthag. queen, foundress
Adelman—Famous p18-19
Boccaccio—Conc. p86-92
Davenport—Great p44-48
Muir—Women p29-31
Schmidt—400 p123,por.

Didrikson, Mildred Babe.
See Zaharias, Mildred (Babe) Didrikson

Didziulis, Liudvika (1856-1925)
Lith. author
Schmidt—400 p280-281,por.

Dieffenbacker, Frances A. (fl. 1860's)
Amer. Civil war nurse
Logan—Part p368

Diehl, Anna Randall (fl. 1880's)
Amer. author, editor
Hanaford—Dau. p593

Diehl, Dena Shelby (fl. 1940's)
Amer. mother of year
Davis—Mothers p178

Diehl, Edith (1876-1953)
Amer. bookbinder
Women—Achieve. p196

Diehl, Frances White (1888-   )
Amer. organization official
Cur. Biog. '47 p169-171,por.

Diehl, Mary (fl. 1930's)
Amer. teacher, bus. executive,
personnel director
Women—Achieve. p141,por.

Dietrich, Adelheid (b. 1827)
Ger. painter
Waters—Women p109-110

Dietrich, Amalie (1821-1891)
Ger.-Austral. botanist
Mozans—Woman p243-244

Dietrich, Jan (fl. 1960's)
Amer. space woman
*May—Women p247

Dietrich, Marion (fl. 1960's)
Amer. space woman
*May—Women p247

Dietrich, Marlene (1904-   )
Ger.-Amer. actress
Beaton—Persona p37-38
CR '59 p209,por.
CR '63 p170,por.
Cur. Biog. '53 p158-161,por.
Cur. Biog. '68 p112-115,por.
Hammerton p508,por.
Huhes—Famous p134-158,por.
Jensen—Revolt p172,por.
Schickel—Stars p129-131,por.
Time Nov.30,1936 p39,por.(cover)

Dietrichsen, Mathilde Bonneire (b. 1847)
Nor. painter
Waters—Women p110

Dieulafoy, Jeanne Paule Henriette Rachel
Magre (1851-1916)
Fr. archaeologist
Mozans—Woman p318-321

Di Gallotti, Stephanie, Baroness (b. 1840)
Amer., W. pioneer, Queen Victoria's
cousin
Parkhill—Wildest p142-150

Digby, Jane Elizabeth ("Iantha," or
"Ianthe") (1807-1881)
Eng. social leader
Blanch—Wilder p133-203,por.
De Morny—Best p230-244

Digby, Venetia (1600-1633)
Eng. notorious woman
Aubrey—Brief p100-101

Digges, Elizabeth (d. 1699)
Amer. colonial planter, plantation
owner and manager
Beard—Amer. p27-28
Leonard—Amer. p114
Spruill—Women's p305

Dighton, Frances.
See Williams, Frances Dighton

Dike, Victoria (fl. 1930's)
Amer. musical, art director
Women—Achieve. p127,por.

Dilke, Emilia Frances Strong, Lady (1840-
1904)
Eng. art critic, journalist
Dorland—Sum p46,117-118

Dill, Marie (fl. 1930's)
Amer. fashion expert
Women—Achieve. p85,por.

Dillard, Mrs. (fl. 1770's)
Amer. Rev. war heroine
Ellet—Women (1) p331-334

Dillaye, Blanche (d. 1931)
Amer. painter, etcher, sculptor
Michigan—Biog. p98
Waters—Women p110-111

Diller, Angela (b. 1877)
Amer. music teacher, author
McCoy—Portraits p35,por.

Diller, Phyllis (1917-   )
Amer. entertainer
CR '63 p171,por.
Cur. Biog. '67 p98-100,por.

Dilling, Mildred (fl. 1920's-1930's)
Amer. harpist
Ewen—Living p99-100,por.
McCoy—Portraits p35,por.
New Yorker Feb.3,1940 p25-29,por.
(Profiles)
Women—Achieve. p69,por.

Dillon, Fannie Charles (1881-1947)
Amer. composer, pianist
ASCAP p122-123
Howard—Our p578
McCoy—Portraits p35,por.

Dillon, Hester A. (b. 1845)
Amer. patriot
Logan—Part p377

Dillon, Mary Elizabeth (b. 1885)
Amer. bus. executive
Women—Achieve. p82,por.

Dimitrova, Anastasie (1856-1894)
Bulg. heroine
Phila.—Women unp.,por.
Schmidt—400 p67-68,por.

Dimitrova, Liliana (fl. 1940's)
Bulg. heroine
Stiles—Postal p72

Dimock, Susan (1847-1875)
Amer. physician, surgeon
Dolan—Goodnow's p248,por.
Hanaford—Dau. p555-556
Lovejoy—Women p86-87

Di Murska, Ilma (1836-1889)
Hung. singer
Pleasants—Great p207-208,por.
Wagner—Prima p170-171,241

Dina, Elisa (fl. 1880's)
It. painter
Waters—Women p111

Dina Abdul Hamid (1928-   )
Jord. princess, m. King Hussein
Stiles—Postal p72

Dinah (Biblical)
Culver—Women p20
Deen—All p37-40
Lewis—Portraits p100-102
Van Der Velde—She p64-69

Dinesen, Isak, pseud. (Baroness Karen
Blixen) (1885-1962)
Dan. author
CR '59 p211,por.

Dingman, Margaret Christian (fl. 1930's)
Can.-Amer. retail buyer
Women—Achieve. p132,por.

Dinnies, Anna Peyre (fl. 1840's)
Amer. poet
Hanaford—Dau. p264

Dinsdale, Mary (1920-   )
Eng. illustrator
Ryder—Artists p59

Dionne sisters (1934-   ; Emilie d. 1954)
Can. quintuplets
Time May 31,1937 p54,por. (Cover)

Dircken, Lysbert (fl. 1840's-1850's)
Amer. colonial midwife
Dexter—Career p49

Dirks, Lysken (m. 1549)
Belg. religious reformer
Culver—Women p122-123

Di Savoia, Maria Adelaide (1822-1855)
It. (Sardinian) queen
Schmidt—400 p259-260,por.

Disney, Doris Miles (1907-   )
Amer. author
Cur. Biog. '54 p234-235,por.

Dissoway, Mrs. (fl. 1770's)
Amer. Rev. war patriot
Ellet—Women (2) p334-335

d'Istria, Dora, pseud. (Elena Ghika)
(1829-1888)
Rum. author
Adelman—Famous p182
Schmidt—400 p339-340,por.

Dithridge, Rachel L. (fl. 1930's)
Amer. poet, teacher
Women—Achieve. p196-197

Diver, Katherine Maud (m. 1896)
Eng. author
Hammerton p510

Divers, Bridget (fl. 1860's)
Irish-Amer. Civil war nurse
Brockett—Woman's p771-773
Hanaford—Dau. p194-196
Moore—Women p109-112
Young—Women p94-95,327-328

Divine, Grace (fl. 1920's)
Amer. singer
McCoy—Portraits p35,por.

Dix, Beulah, Marie.
See Flebbe, Beulah Marie Dix

Dix, Dorothea Lynde (1802-1887)
Amer. philanthropist, social
reformer, Civil war nurse
Adelman—Famous p150-151
Brockett—Woman's p97-108
Brooks—Three p3-80
Bruce—Woman p203-205
*Buckmaster—Women p1-21,por.
Castiglioni—Hist. p1085
Culver—Women p181
Dannett—Noble (see index)
*Daugherty—Ten p80-94
Deen—Great p385-388
*Dodge—Story p49-58
Dolan—Goodnow's p211-212,235-236,
por.
*Dolin—World p74-83,por.
Dorland—Sum p52,74-75,81,129
Douglas—Remember p130-139,142-
144,por.
Farmer—What p367-369
Hammerton p510
Hanaford—Dau. p176-179
*Heath—Woman (4) p7,por.
Holbrook—Dreamers p186,227-235
*Horowitz—Treas. p29-36
Irwin—Angels p148
*Lamm—Biog. p100-101
Leetch—Reveille p209-211
Logan—Part p523-525
*McCallum—Women p93-108
Morris—400 p73-74
Pennock—Makers p17-18,por.
*Stevens—Human. p33-40,por.
*Stone—Heroes p27-29
*Strong—Of p158-166
Whitton—These p111-112,161
*Yost—Famous p59-67,por.
Young—Women (see index)

Dix, Dorothy, pseud. (Elizabeth Meriwether
Gilmer (1870-1951)
Amer. journalist

(Continued)

Dix, Dorothy — *Continued.*

    Carnegie—Biog. p181-186
    Cur. Biog. '40 p249-251,por.
    Cur. Biog. '52 p151
    Drewry—Post p29-47
    Jensen—Revolt p196-197,por.
    Ross—Ladies p74-79,por.

Dix, Eulabee (1878-1961)
    Amer. artist
    Women—Achieve. p115,por.

Dixie, Florence Caroline Douglas, Lady
    (1857-1905)
    Eng. explorer, traveler, feminist
      author
    Adelman—Famous p235
    Dorland—Sum p52,113
    Hammerton p510

Dixon, Adèle 1908-   )
    Eng. actress
    Hammerton p510

Dixon, Jane (c. 1882-1960)
    Amer. journalist
    Ross—Ladies p191-194,por.

Djanel, Lily (1909-   )
    Belg. singer
    McCoy—Portraits p35,por.
    Peltz—Spot. p31,por.

Djanira (1914-   )
    Brazil. painter
    Cur. Biog. '61 p132-134,por.

Dmitrova, Anastasie.
    See Dimitrova, Anastasie

Doane, Peagie (1906-   )
    Amer. illustrator
    Mahony—Illus. p301

Dobbs, Mattiwilda (1925-   )
    Amer. singer
    Cherry—Portraits p92-96,por.
    CR '59 p213,por.
    CR '63 p174,por.
    Cur. Biog. '55 p172-173,por.

Doble, Frances (1902-   )
    Can. actress
    Hammerton p511

Dock, Lavinia Lloyd (1858-1956)
    Amer. nurse, author, feminist
    Dolan—Goodnow's p254,262,316-317
    Pennock—Makers p108-109,por.

Dodd, Carolyn G. (fl. 1930's)
    Amer. interior decorator,
      employment agency executive
    Women—Achieve. p168,por.

Dodd, Martha Eccles (1908-   )
    Amer. author
    Cur. Biog. '46 p148-149,por.

Dodd, Mary Ann Hammer (b. 1813)
    Amer. poet
    Hanaford—Dau. p239

Doamna, Maria (fl. 1300's)
    Rum. patriot
    Phila.—Women unp.,por.

Dodge, Cynthia Dodge (fl. 1940's)
    Amer. composer
    Elson—Woman's p260
    McCoy—Portraits p36,por.

Dodge, Delphine (fl. 1930's-1940's)
    Amer. heiress
    Tebbel—Inher. p82-84,por.

Dodge, Grace Hoadley (1857-1914)
    Amer. social reformer, philanthropist
    Adelman—Famous p248
    Culver—Women p193
    *Kirkland—Achieved p93-106
    *Moore—When p82-89

Dodge, Gregg Sherwood (1923-   )
    Amer. beauty, wife of
      Horace Dodge
    CR '63 p175,por.
    Tebbel—Inher. p85-87,por.

Dodge, Mabel. See Luhan, Mabel Dodge

Dodge, Mary Abigail (1833-1896)
    Amer. author, humorist
    Bruère—Laugh p23-24
    Dorland—Sum p30,189
    Hanaford—Dau. p245

Dodge, Mary Elizabeth Mapes (Gail
    Hamilton) (1831/38-1905)
    Amer. author, editor
    Adelman—Famous p217
    Bruère—Laugh p21-22
    *Cather—Younger p171-182
    *Coffman—Authors p85-89,por.
    Dorland—Sum p52,116,188
    Farmer—What p190,200,por.
    Furniss—Some p37-39,por.
    Hanaford—Dau. p689
    Logan—Part p851
    Ross—Ladies p327,329-331
    *Stevens—Women p159-163,por.
    Woody—Hist. (1) p356
    *Yost—Famous p99-107,por.

Dodge, Mary Hewes (fl. 1940's)
    Amer. violinist, pianist, music
      teacher, composer
    McCoy—Portraits p36,por.

Dodge, Nancy. See Linn, Nancy Hunter

Dodson, Sarah Paxton Ball (1847-1906)
Amer. painter
Michigan—Biog. p99-100

Dodson, Wilma Joy Livingston (m. 1950)
Amer. missionary
They—Went p144

Doe, Doris (fl. 1930's)
Amer. singer
Ewen—Living p100-101,por.
McCoy—Portraits p36,por.
Peltz—Spot. p103

Doggett, Kate Newell (1827-1884)
Amer. teacher, social leader,
translator, art critic
Farmer—What p370-372
Hanaford—Dau. p306
Irwin—Angels p212,214

Dolgoruky, Katherine (1846-1922)
Russ., wife of Alexander II
Kelen—Mist. p121-156,331-332

D'Olisva, Mademoiselle.
See La Motte, Jeanne de Saint-Rémy
de Valois

Dollar, Lynn (n.d.)
Amer. TV performer
TV—Person (3) p46-47,por.

Dolley, Sarah R. Adamson (1829-1909)
Amer. physician
Hanford—Dau. p567
Mead—Medical p42-43

Dolly, Jenny (1892-1941)
Amer. dancer
Cur. Biog. '41 p228

Dolly, Roszcika (fl. 1910's)
actress
Caffin—Vaud. p106,por.

Dolores, Donna (fl. 1500's)
Sp.-Amer., friend of Ponce de Leon
DAR Mag July 1921 p391-392
(Portrayal)

Dolson, Hildegarde (fl. 1930's)
Amer. fashion designer
Women—Achieve. p173,por.

Dolz, Luisa Maria (b. 1854)
Cub. educator, feminist
Stiles—Postal p74

Dombrovskaya, Yuliya Fominichna (1891-)
Russ. pediatrician
U.S.—Biog., Soviet p194

Dombrowski zu Papros und Krusvic, Käthe
Schönberger von (K.O.S., pseud.)
Aust. artist, author
Cooper—Authors p185-190
Mahony—Illus. p301

Domitia (fl. 40's A.D.)
Rom., sister of Domitia Lepida,
wife of Passienus Crispus
Balsdon—Roman p117,120-121

Domitia Lepida (d. 53 A.D.)
Rom. empress, wife of Galba
Balsdon—Roman p102,118-120
Serviez—Roman (1) p299-306

Domitia Longina (fl. 70's (A.D.)
Rom. empress, wife of Domitian
Balsdon—Roman p131-132
McCabe—Emp. p130-135,por.
Serviez—Roman (1) p343-354

Domitia Paulina (fl. 100's A.D.)
Rom., wife of L. Julius Servianus
Balsdon—Roman p139

Domitilla (d. end of 1st cent.)
Rom. saint, mother of Domitian and
Titus
Englebert—Lives p184-185
Serviez—Roman (1) p324-335

Dommet, Mrs. John (fl. c. 1730)
Amer. colonial teacher
Dexter—Colonial p89

Domna, Julia. See Julia Domna
McCabe—Empr. p194-209,por.

Domnina (fl. 3rd cent.)
Rom. saint
Blunt—Great p21

Donahue, Elinor (1937-   )
Amer. actress
TV—Person (1) p147-148

Donald, Mary Jane (fl. 1900's)
Amer. geologist
Dorland—Sum p150

Donalda, Pauline Mischa Léon (b. 1884)
Can. singer
Hammerton p514
Lahee—Grand p127,143-144
McCoy—Portraits p36,por.

Donaldson, Alice Willits (c. 1885-1961)
Amer. artist
Women—Achieve. p172,por.

Donaldson, Elizabeth W. (fl. 1930's)
Amer. traveler, author, sports-
woman
Women—Achieve. p49,por.

Donelson, Emily Jackson (fl. 19th cent.)
Amer. social leader, President
Jackson's niece, hostess
Hanaford—Dau. p133-134
Jensen—White p51-55,por.

(Continued)

Donelson, Emily Jackson—*Continued.*

*Sweetser—Famous p100-115
Truett—First p22,por.

Donelson, Rachel.
See Jackson, Rachel Donelson Robards

Doner, Mary Frances (1893-   )
Amer. author
Warfel—Amer. p121-122,por.

Donez, Ian (1891-   )
Amer. composer, author
ASCAP p125

Donlevy, Alice Heighes (1846-1929)
Eng.-Amer. artist
Hanaford—Dau. p319

Donlon, Mary Honor (fl. 1930's-1940's)
Amer. judge, govt. official
*Clymer—Modern p99-108
Cur. Biog. '49 p162-164,por.
Women—Achieve. p183,por.

Donne, Maria Dalle (fl. 1800's)
It. physician, surgeon
Mozans—Woman p299-300

Donnelley, Frances (m. 1906)
Eng. singer
Wyndham—Chorus p116-117

Donnelly, Antoinette.
See Blake, Doris, pseud.

Donnelly, Dorothy (1880-1928)
Amer. author, librettist, actress
ASCAP p125-126
*Kobbé—Homes p237-243,por.

Donnelly, Norah (fl. 1890's-1900's)
Amer. journalist
Ross—Ladies p19-20

Donner, Eliza (fl. 1840's)
Amer. pioneer
Whitten—These p237-238

Donner, Mrs. Jacob (fl. 1846)
Amer. pioneer
Fowler—Woman p466-468

Donner, Vyvyan (fl. 1930's)
Amer. journalist, artist, fashion
designer
Women—Achieve. p105,por.

Donniges, Hélène Von (fl. 19th cent.)
Ger., friend of Ferdinand Lassale
Orr—Famous III p147-167

Doolittle, Hilda ("H.D.", pseud.) (1886-
1961)
Amer. poet
Burnett—This p1139-1140
Cook—Our p255-258
*Millett—Amer. p328-329
Smith—Women's p51

Dooly, Ismay (d. 1921)
Amer. journalist, humanitarian
Ross—Ladies p594-595

Dopp, Katherine Elizabeth (b. 1863)
Amer. educator
Logan—Part p718

Dora, Sister (Dorothy Wyndlow Pattison)
(1832-1878)
Eng. nurse, philanthropist
Adelman—Famous p185
Carey—Twelve p215,por.
Dorland—Sum p21,131
Foster—Religion p134-159,por.

Doran, Mildred (fl. 1920's)
Amer. aviatrix
Planck—Women p69

Dorcas (or Tabitha) (Biblical)
Buchanan—Women p98-99
Deen—All p218-221
Faulhaber—Women p191-194
Lewis—Portraits p172
Marble—Women, Bible p 286-288
Nelson—Bible p106-107
Ockenga—Women p221-229
Schmidt—400 p268-269,por.
Van Der Velde—She p227-233

Doree, Doris (n.d.)
Amer. singer
Peltz—Spot. p104,por.
Saleski—Jewish p585,por.

D'Orémieulx, Mrs. T. (fl. 1860's)
Amer. Civil war patriot
Brockett—Woman's p531

Doremus, Mrs. R. Ogden (fl. 1880's-1890's)
Amer. club leader
Logan—Part p464-465

Doremus, Sarah Platt Haines (1802-1877)
Amer. philanthropist, missionary,
humanitarian
Adelman—Famous p166
Deen—Great p388-390
Farmer—What p335-339,362
Irwin—Angels p55
Logan—Part p512-513

Doren, Electra Collins (1861-1927)
Amer. librarian
Marshall—Amer. p270-278

Dorfmann, Ania (1905-   )
    Russ. pianist
    Ewen—Living p102-103,por.
    Saleski—Jewish p464,por.

Doria, Augusta, pseud. (fl. 1900's-1910's)
    Amer. singer
    Lahee—Grand p215-217

Doria, Clara, pseud.
    See Barnett, Clara Kathleen

Dorion, Marie (1786/1791-c. 1850)
    Amer. pioneer, heroine
    Defenbach—Red p145-223,por.

D'Orleans, Henriette.
    See Orleans, Henrietta Anne, Duchess d'

d'Orleans, Isabel Braganza (1846-1921)
    Brazil. princess
    Phila.—Women unp.,por.

Doro, Marie (1882-1956)
    Amer. actress
    Blum—Great p48,por.

Dorothea (Dorothy of Montaw) (1347-1394)
    Ger. saint
    Englebert—Lives p411

Dorothy (d.c. 311)
    Turk. saint
    Sharkey—Pop. p36
    Wescott—Calen. p21
    *Windham—Sixty p62-70

Dorr, Julia Caroline Ripley (1825-1913)
    Amer. poet
    Dorland—Sum p53,82,181

Dorr, Rheta Childe (c. 1866-1948)
    Amer. feminist, journalist
    Collins—Biog. p326-327
    Riegel—Amer. p173-177
    Ross—Ladies p109-116,por.

Dors, Diana (c. 1928-   )
    Eng. actress
    CR '59 p215-216

Dorset, Countess of.
    See Elizabeth Bagot, Countess of
    Falmouth

Dorsey, Anna Hanson McKenney (1815-
    1896)
    Amer. novelist
    Blunt—Great p423

Dorsey, Ella Loraine (b. 1853)
    Amer. author
    Logan—Part p853-854

Dorsey, Sarah Ann (1829-1879)
    Amer. author, Civil war patriot
    Logan—Part p491

Dorsey, Susan M. (1845-1919)
    Amer. educator
    Mears—They p79-80

Dorval, Marie (c. 1798-1849)
    Fr. actress
    Collins—Great p293,por.

D'Ossoli, Margaret Fuller.
    See Fuller (Sarah) Margaret
    Marchioness Ossoli

Doty, Katharine S. (fl. 1930's)
    Amer. personnel worker
    Women—Achieve. p185,por.

Dougherty, Dora Jean (1921-   )
    Amer. aviatrix, psychologist,
      helicopter pilot
    Cur. Biog. '63 p111-112,por.
    *May—Women p208

Dougherty, Mary (fl. 1910's-1920's)
    Amer. journalist
    Ross—Ladies p432-433

Dougherty, Patricia (fl. 1920's)
    Amer. journalist
    Ross—Ladies p548-549

Doughty, Ann Graves Cotton Eaton
    (fl. c. 1625)
    Amer. historian
    Leonard—Amer. p114

Douglas, Alice May (b. 1865)
    Amer. missionary, author
    Logan—Part p857

Douglas, Amanda Minnie (1831-1916)
    Amer. author
    Papashvily—All p183-186

Douglas, Donna (n.d.)
    Amer. actress
    CR '63 p177-178,por.

Douglas, Edna Mae (n.d.)
    Amer. civic leader
    *Cherry—Portraits p57-62,por.

Douglas, Emily Taft (1899-   )
    Amer. congresswoman, politician,
      Red Cross worker
    Cur. Biog. '45 p158-160,por.
    Paxton—Woman p107-110,128

Douglas, Helen Mary Gahagan (1900-
    Amer. actress, congresswoman,
      politician
    CR '59 p216-217,por.
    Cur. Biog. '44 p169-172,por.
    Dodd—Celeb. p101-105
    Lamparski—What. p34-35,por.
    Paxton—Women p111-116,128,por.
    Rogers—Women p65,por.
    Roosevelt—Ladies p47-57,58-59

Douglas, Jane. See Downs, Jane Douglas

Douglas, Laura Virginia O'Hanlon (b. 1889)
"Virginia" Santa Claus letter-writer
Phelps—Men (2) '59 p72-73

Douglas, Loretta Mooney, Lady (m. 1895)
Eng. actress
Wyndham—Chorus p105-106

Douglas, Margaret, Lady, Marchioness of
Argyll (c. 1610-1677)
Scot. covenanter
Anderson—Ladies p86-110

Douglas, Marjory Stoneman (1890-   )
Amer. author
Cur. Biog. '53 p162-164,por.

Douglas, Mary Stoneman (1890-   )
Amer. poet
Smith—Women's p54

Douglass, Anna Murray (m. 1840/41)
Amer., wife of Frederick Douglass
Adams—Great p29,por.

Douglass, Sarah Hallam (d. 1773)
Amer. colonial actress
Coad—Amer. p18-19,por.
Dexter—Colonial p158-163,212,por.
Leonard—Amer. p114
Spruill—Women's p260-261

Dove, Billie (fl. 1920's)
Amer. actress
Herman—How p13,por.

Dovima (1927-   )
Amer. fashion model
CR '59 p219

Dow, Betsy (fl. 1830's)
Amer. religious teacher
Culver—Women p215-216

Dowd, Alice Casey (c. 1889-1964)
Amer. fashion consultant, publicist
Women—Achieve. p146,por.

Dowd, Mary Hickey (b. 1866)
Amer. teacher, lecturer
Logan—Part p722

Downes, Anne Miller (d. 1964)
Amer. author
Warfel—Amer. p127-128,por.

Downey, Mary E. (fl. 1940's)
Amer. organist, composer
McCoy—Portraits p37,por.

Downing, Eleanor (fl. 1930's)
Amer. author, educator
Women—Achieve. p158,por.

Downs, Mrs. George Sheldon (b. 1843)
Amer. author
Logan—Part p860

Downs, Jane Douglas (fl. 1770's)
Amer. pioneer
Green—Pioneer (3) p512

Downs, Sallie Ward Lawrence Hunt
Armstrong. See Ward, Sallie

Downsbrough, Margaret (fl. 1950's)
Amer. glider pilot
*May—Women p220,por.

Doyle, Agnes Catherine (fl. 1900's)
Amer. librarian, author
Logan—Part p834

Doyle, Mrs. John H. (b. 1851)
Amer. club leader
Logan—Part p480

Doyle, Martha Claire MacGowan (b. 1869)
Amer. author
Logan—Part p834

Doyle, Peggy (fl. 1910's)
Amer. journalist
Ross—Ladies p489-491

Draga Maschin (1867-1914)
Serb. queen
Ewart—World's p228-242
Kelen—Mist. p225-267,333-334,por.

Dragomir (fl. 1200's)
Dan. queen
*Cather—Girlhood p55-75

Dragonette, Jessica (fl. 1920's-1930's)
Brit.-Amer. radio singer
Donaldson—Radio p11
Eichberg—Radio p72-73,por.
Ewen—Living p103-104,por.
Lamparski—What p66-67,por.
McCoy—Portraits, p37,por.
Settel—Radio p63,por.

Drake, Debra Bella (Debbie) (1932-   )
Amer. phys. education teacher,
author
CR '63 p181,por.

Drake, Lucy R. (fl. 1870's)
Amer. religious worker
Hanaford—Dau. p621-622

Drake, Sarah. See Wolcott, Sarah Drake

Drake-Brockman, Henrietta (1901-   )
Austral. author
Hetherington—42 p60-65,por.

Drane, Augusta Theodosia (1823-1894)
Eng. historian, poet, religious
worker
Dorland—Sum p30,133

Draper, Mrs. Amos G. (gr. 1877)
Amer. club leader
Logan—Part p470

Draper, Anna Palmer (fl. 1880's)
Amer. astronomer, philanthropist
Farmer—What p273-275,279

Draper, Betty (fl. 1750's)
Amer. pioneer, Indian captive
Green—Pioneer (1) p426-427,429,485

Draper, Dorothy Catherine (fl. 1840's)
Amer. pioneer photography-subject
Bonte—Amer. p104

Draper, Dorothy Tuckerman (1889-1969)
Amer. interior decorator
CR '63 p181,por.
Cur. Biog. '41 p237-238,por.

Draper, Helen F. (fl. 1900's)
Amer. Red Cross nurse
Pennock—Makers p135,por.

Draper, Margaret (d.c. 1800)
Amer. colonial printer, publisher
Club—Printing p11-12
Dexter—Colonial p177
Earle—Colon. p67
Hanaford—Dau. p647

Draper, Mary Aldis (c. 1718-1810)
Amer. Rev. war patriot, heroine
Bruce—Women p86,104-105
Ellet—Women (1) p135-140
Green—Pioneer (3) p378-383
Logan—Part p128-130
Wright—Forgot. p93-94

Draper, Muriel Gurdon Sanders (1886-1952)
Amer. feminist, humanitarian
Women—Achieve. p171,por.

Draper, Ruth (1884-1956)
Amer. monologist
Dodd—Celeb. p290-294
Hammerton p521

Dransfield, Hedwig (1871-1925)
Ger. editor, author
Schmidt—400 p205-206

Draves, Vicki Manalo (1924-   )
Amer.-Phil. diver
Stump—Champ. p33-43

"Dreamer." See Lowell, Amy

Dreier, Ethel E. (fl. 1920's-1930's)
Amer. humanitarian, club leader
Women—Achieve. p77,por.

Dresser, Louise (1882-1965)
Amer. actress
Stuart—Immort. p100-101,por.

Dresser, Marcia (fl. 1910's)
Amer. singer
Lahee—Grand p26

Dressler, Marie (1869/1873-1934)
Can.-Amer. actress
Blum—Great p37,por.
Cahn—Laugh. p119,121-122,por.
Dorland—Sum p169
Hammerton p522
Hughes—Famous p159-179,por.
Schickel—Stars p134,por.
Strang—Prima p181-191,por.
Stuart—Immort. p110-112,por.
Time Aug.7,1933 p23,por.

Drever, Miss (fl. 1900's)
Eng. pioneer balloonist
*Lauwick—Heroines p25

Drew, Doris (n.d.)
Amer. singer
TV—Person. (2) p103

Drew, Louisa Lane (1820-1897)
Eng.-Amer. actress
Adelman—Famous p207
Burt—Phila. p190-191
Coad—Amer. p198,220,por.
Dorland—Sum p39,79,166
*Wagner—Famous p57-61

Drexel, Katharine, Mother (1858-1955)
Amer. foundress, educator,
humanitarian
Burton—Loveliest p151-168
Kittler—Profiles p280-305
Logan—Part p722

Dreydel, Anne (fl. 1940's)
Eng. tutor
Brittain—Women p222-223

Dreyfus, Berta E. (fl. 1920's)
Amer. nurse
Pennock—Makers p80,por.

Dringlinger, Sophie Friedericke (1736-1791)
Ger. painter
Waters—Women p111

Drinker, Elizabeth Sandwith (1743-1807)
Amer. colonial diarist
Burt—Phila. p45,281,294
Leonard—Amer. p114

Dripetrua (fl. 130's-90's B.C.)
Laodicean queen
Boccaccio—Conc. p165

Driscoll, Louise (b. 1875)
Amer. poet
Smith—Women's p56

Driscoll, Marjorie (fl. 1910's)
Amer. journalist
Ross—Ladies p589-590

Drogheda, Kathleen, Countess of (fl. 1910's)
Eng. pioneer aviatrix, sportswoman
*May—Women p64
Planck—Women p15-16

Drogheda, Olive Mary Meatyard Moore,
Countess of (d. 1947)
Eng. dancer
Wyndham—Chorus p135-136,por.

Droste-Hülshoff, Annette Elisabeth Frelin
von (1797-1848)
Ger. poet
Adelman—Famous p131
Dorland—Sum p55,180
Heller—Studies p246-248
Stiles—Postal p76

Droucher, Sandra (fl. 1920's)
Aust. pianist
Saleski—Wander. p305,por.

Drouet, Bessie Clarke (1879-1940)
Amer. author, painter, sculptor
Cur. Biog. '40 p259

Dru, Joanne (1923-   )
Amer. TV performer
CR '63 p182,por.

Drummond, Sarah Prescott (fl. c. 1670's)
Amer. colonial politician, lecturer
Leonard—Amer. p114

Drusilla (d. A.D. 38) (Biblical)
Rom., dau. of Herod
Balsdon—Roman p96,117,250-251
Deen—All p233-238
Lewis—Portraits p142-143
McCabe—Empr. p51
Marble—Women, Bible p99-101

Druzbacka, Elzbieta (1695-1765)
Pol. poet
Schmidt—400 p317,por.

Duarte, Rosa (1828-1888)
Dom. R. patriot
Schmidt—400 p102-103,por.

DuBarry, Marie Jeanne Bécu, Comtesse
(1743/46-1793)
Fr. courtesan
Abbot—Notable p207-211,por.
Adelman—Famous p91
Blei—Fasc. p136-143,por
Cuppy—Decline p122-131
Dorland—Sum p57
Hammerton p524,por.
Kavanagh—Woman (1) p225-230,por.
Kavanagh—Woman (2) p101-102

Love—Famous p13
Mayne—Enchant. p123-136,por.
*Nisenson—More Minute p50,por.
Padover—Confess. p128-135
Sherman—World's p79-82
Terhune—Super. p175-203

Dublin, Mary (fl. 1930's)
Amer. economist, humanitarian
Woman—Achieve. p178,por.

Dubois, Alice.
See Bettignies, Louise Marie Jeanne
Henriette de

Dubois, Consuelo (fl. c. 1810's)
Fr. seafarer
Snow—Women p48-57

Dubois, Mary Constance (1879-1959)
Amer. author
Women—Achieve. p90,por.

Dubois, Yvonne Pene (fl. 1930's)
Amer. sculptor
Hanaford—Dau. p293-294

Dubourg, Victoria.
See Fantin-Latour, Victoria Dubourg

Dubray, Charlotte Gabrielle (fl. 1870's)
Fr. sculptor
Waters—Women p112

Dubre (Dubrey, Duberry), Hannah
(fl. 1750's)
Amer. colonial agriculturist
Dexter—Colonial p114

Dubrow, Angelica (Helen Holborn)
(fl. 1930's)
Ger. spy
Singer—World's p273-282

Dubucq de Rivery, Aimée (1763-1817)
Fr. sultana, adventurer
Blanch—Wilder p205-282,por.

Ducas, Dorothy (1905-   )
Amer. journalist
Ross—Ladies p210-213,por.

Ducas, Irene (m. 1077)
Byzant. empress
Diehl—Byzant. p198-225

Duchesne, Janet (1930-   )
Eng. illustrator
Ryder—Artists p63

Duchesne, Rose Philippine (1769-1852)
Fr. foundress
Code—Great p206-229,por.

Duckett, Elizabeth Waring (fl. 1860's)
    Amer., author, Civil war spy
    Andrews—Women p31-65
    Kane—Spies p163-165
    Simkins—Women p52-53

Duckwitz, Dorothy Miller (fl. 1920's)
    Amer. pianist
    McCoy—Portraits p38,por.

Duclaux, Madame.
    See Robinson, Agnes Mary

Ducoudray, Madame (fl. 18th cent.)
    Amer. inventor
    Hanaford—Dau. p647

Ducoudray, Mademoiselle M. (fl. 1890's-
        1900's)
    Fr. sculptor
    Waters—Women p112

Ducray, Anne (fl. 1760's)
    Amer. colonial business woman,
        needlewoman
    Dexter—Colonial p42-43

Du Deffant (or Deffand), **Madame**
        (1697-1780)
    Fr. blind salonist
    Abbot—Notable p222-226

Dudevant, Armandine Lucile Aurore Dupin.
    See Sand, George

Dudevant, Solange (b. 1828)
    Fr., daughter of George Sand
    Ravenel—Women p197-205

Dudley, Ann (1898-   )
    Amer. pioneer
    Green—Pioneer (1) p296-297

Dudley, Gertrude. See Millar, Gertie

Dudley, Helena Stuart (1898-   )
    Amer. social reformer
    Logan—Part p593-594

Dudley, Jane, Lady.
    See Grey, Jane, Lady

Dudley, Lady (fl. 1870's)
    Eng. belle
    Furniss—Some p153-154,por.

Dudley, Mary (fl. 1630's-1650's)
    Amer. pioneer
    Green—Pioneer (1) p295-296

Dudley, Mrs. Simon.
    See Bradstreet, Anne

Duer, Catharine, Lady.
    See Alexander, Catharine

Dufau, Clementine Helene (b. 1879)
    Fr. painter
    Waters—Women p112-113

Dufau, Jennie (d. 1924)
    Fr.-Amer. singer
    Lahee—Grand p434

Duff, Mary Ann Dyke (1794/95-1857)
    Eng. actress
    Coad—Amer. p84,por.
    Dexter—Career p85
    Dorland—Sum p21,166

Duff-Gordon, Lucie, Lady (1821-1869)
    Eng. author, translator
    Dorland—Sum p18
    Hammerton p527

Duggan, Grace Hinds (m. 1902)
    Lady Curzon
    Amer.-Eng. hostess
    Pearson—Pilgrim p114-115,por.

Duhem, Marie (fl. 1890's-1900's)
    Fr. painter
    Waters—Women p113-114

Du Jardin, Rosamond Neal (1902-   )
    Amer. author
    Cur. Biog. '53 p164-165,por.

Duke, Doris (1912-   )
    Amer. heiress, journalist, fashion
        editor
    CR '59 p223-224,por.
    CR '63 p184,por.
    Tebbel—Inher. p92-98,por.

Duke, Nanaline Holt Inman (m. 1907)
    Amer., mother of Doris Duke
    Tebbel—Inher. p92,por.
    Time Apr.27,1931 p25,por.(cover)

Duke, Patty (1946-   )
    Amer. actress
    CR '63 p184-185,por.
    Cur. Biog. '63 p117-119
    Ross—Player p150-155
    Time Dec.21,1959 p46

Duke, Winifred (fl. 1920's-1930's)
    Eng. author
    Hammerton p527

Dulaney, Evalina (fl. 1860's)
    Amer. Civil war patriot
    Andrews—Women p105-111

Dulany, Ida (fl. 1860's)
    Amer. plantation manager,
        Civil war patriot
    Simkins—Women p112,114,174

Dulce, Sister (Maria Rita Lopes Pontes)
　　　　(c. 1913-　　)
　　　Brazil. social worker
　　Elgin—Nun p120-121,por.
　°McKown—Heroic p291-309,por.

Dulles, Eleanor Lansing (1895-　　)
　　　Amer. govt. worker, economist
　　Cur. Biog. '62 p115-117,por.

Dumas, Sarah J. Steady (fl. 1860's)
　　　Amer. Civil war nurse
　　Logan—Part p364

Du Maurier, Daphne, Lady Browning
　　　　(1907-　　)
　　　Eng. author
　　Church—British p139-141,por.
　　CR '59 p224-225,por.
　　Cur. Biog. '40 p262-264,por.
　　Lawrence—School p179-182

Dumbrille, Dorothy (1898-　　)
　　　Can. author
　　Thomas—Canad. p37

Dumée, Jeanne (fl. 1680-1685)
　　　Fr. astronomer
　　Mozans—Woman p171

Dumesnil, Marie Françoise (Marie
　　　　Françoise Marchand) (1711/13-
　　　　1803)
　　　Fr. actress
　　Adelman—Famous p82-83

Dumont, Eleanore ("Madame Moustache")
　　　　(d. 1879)
　　　Amer., W. pioneer
　　Aikman—Calamity p280-307
　　Brown—Gentle p89-90
　　Towle—Vigil. p88-103

Dunaeva, Maria Biconish "McMillin"
　　　　(fl. 1940's)
　　　Russ. spy.
　　Singer—World's p305-306,por.

Dunaway, Faye (b. 1941)
　　　Amer. actress
　　Time Dec.8,1967 p66-76,por.(Cover)

Dunbar, "Black Agnes" of.
　　See Agnes of Dunbar

Dunbar, Lilias (b.c. 1657)
　　　Scot. covenanter
　　Anderson—Ladies p313-339

Dunbar, Matilda J. (1848-1934)
　　　Amer., mother of Paul Lawrence
　　　　Dunbar
　　Brown—Home. p156-159,por.

Duncan, Eleanor Folliott (fl. 1930's)
　　　Amer. editor
　　Women—Achieve. p197

Duncan, Irma (1897-　　)
　　　Amer. dancer
　　Women—Achieve. p82,por.

Duncan, Isadora (1878-1927)
　　　Amer. dancer
　　Adelman—Famous p321
　　Bolitho—Twelve p309-331,por.
　　Caffin—Vaud. p98
　　Davison—Ballet p63-68
　　Douglas—Remember p184-187
　　Hammerton p530-531,por.
　　Hurok—Impres. p89-127,por.
　　Jensen—Revolt p88,por.
　°Maynard—Amer. p30-69,por.
　　Morris—400 p80
　°Muir—Famous p57-70,por.
　　New Yorker Jan.1,1927 p17-18,por.
　　　(Profiles)
　　Ross—Charmers p217-251,293-294,por.
　　Stone—We p130-135
　　Thomas—Living Women p229-241,por.
　　Untermeyer—Makers p522-532
　　Wagenknecht—Seven p139-158,por..

Duncan, Margaret (fl. 18th cent.)
　　　Amer. colonial merchant, church
　　　　builder
　　Earle—Colon. p75

Duncan, Rena Buchanan Shore (fl. 1930's)
　　　Amer. club leader, author
　　Women—Achieve. p104,por.

Duncan, Vivian (1902-　　)
　　　Amer. composer, author, publisher
　　ASCAP p133

Dundas, Maria. See Callcott, Maria, Lady

Dungan, Olive (1903-　　)
　　　Amer. composer, pianist
　　ASCAP p133

Dunham, Charlotte Corday (b.c. 1829)
　　　Amer. whaling voyager
　　Whiting—Whaling p69-75,por.

Dunham, Katherine (1910-　　)
　　　Amer. dancer, choreographer,
　　　　anthropologist
　　Adams—Great p137,por.
　　CR '59 p225,por.
　　CR '63 p185-186,por.
　　Cur. Biog. '41 p245-246,por.
　　Haskell—Ballet p37-38
　　Hurok—Impres. p284-287,por.
　°McConnell—Famous p133-142,por.
　°Richardson—Great p69-78,por.
　　Robinson—Hist. p188,por.

Dunham, (Bertha) Mabel (b. 1881-　　)
　　　Can. author, librarian
　　Thomas—Canad. p37-39

Dunham, Mrs. (fl. 1790's)
Amer. W. pioneer
Ellet—Pioneer p76-77

Dunham, Stelle Secrest (fl. 1930's)
Amer. club leader
Women—Achieve. p197

Duniway, Abigail Jane Scott (1834-1915)
Amer. pioneer, feminist, journalist,
editor
DAR Mag. July 1921 p394 (portrayal)
*Gersh—Women p75-96,por.
Hanaford—Dau. p704-711
Holbrook—Dreamers p206-210
Ross—Heroines p156-178
Ross—Westward p137-154

Dunlap, Anne (m. 1919)
Amer. journalist
Ross—Ladies p183-186

Dunlap, Hope (b. 1880)
Amer. illustrator
Mahony—Illus. p302-303

Dunlap, Mary Stewart (n.d.)
Amer. painter
Michigan—Biog. p102-103

Dunlevy, Mary Craig (b. 1765)
Amer. W. pioneer
Ellet—Pioneer p226-239
Logan—Part p55-59

Dunlop, Florence S. (d. 1963)
Can. pioneer educator
Fleming—Great p131-143

Dunn, Fannie Wyche (1879-1946)
Amer. editor
Women—Achieve. p169,por.

Dunn, Hilda S. (fl. 1930's)
Amer. humanitarian
Women—Achieve. p171,por.

Dunn, Loula Friend (n.d.)
Amer. social worker
Cur. Biog. '51 p175-176,por.

Dunn, Rose (Rose of the Cimarron) (b.c.
1878)
Amer. W. pioneer, outlaw
Horan—Desperate p242-266

Dunne, Irene (1904-   )
Amer. actress
CR '59 p225-226,por.
CR '63 p186,por.
Cur. Biog. '45 p160-163,por.
Hammerton p532
Lamparski—What. p170-171,por.

Dunne, Sarah Theresa (Amadeus, Mother
Mary of the Heart of Jesus)
(1846-1917)
Amer. foundress
Code—Great p437-471,por.

Dunnigan, Alice Allison (1906-   )
Amer. journalist, educator,
economist
*Cherry—Portraits p200-201

Dunning, Carre Louise (1860-1929)
Amer. music teacher
McCoy—Portraits p38,por.

Dunning, Wilhelmina Frances (fl. 1930's)
Amer. physician
Women—Achieve. p197

Dunnock, Mildred (1906-   )
Amer. actress
CR '59 p226,por.
CR '63 p186,por.
Cur. Biog. '55 p175-177,por.

Dupee, Mary A. (fl. 1860's)
Amer. Civil war nurse
Brockett—Woman's p464-465
Moore—Women p485-490

Duperrault, Terry Jo (c. 1950-   )
Amer. sea heroine
Snow—Women p251-259,por.

Dupeyron, Madame (fl. 1910's)
Fr. pioneer aviatrix
*Lauwick—Heroines p28

Dupin, Amandine Aurore Lucie.
See Sand, George

Du Plessis, Marie (Rose Alphonsine Plessis)
(1824-1847)
Fr., friend of Alexander Dumas
Davenport—Great p155-158
Wallace—Fabulous p267-276

Du Pont, Alicia Bradford (d. 1920)
Amer. hostess
Tebbel—Inher. p202-203,205-206

Du Pont, Allaire (fl. 1930's)
Amer. glider pilot
*May—Women p216-217

Du Pont, Ethel (Mrs. Roosevelt, Mrs. Warren)
(c. 1916-1965)
Amer. social leader
Smith—White p169-172
Time June 28,1937 p24, por.(Cover)

Du Pont, Margaret Osborne (1918-   )
Amer. tennis player
Parshalle—Kash. p35-37,por.

Dupré, Amalia (1845-1928)
    It. sculptor
    Waters—Women p114

Duprez, May Moore (fl. 1900's)
    Eng. singer
    Felstead—Stars p43

Durack, Mary (1913-   )
    Austral. author
    Hetherington—42 p146-152,por.

Durand, Alice Celeste Fleury (Henry
        Greville, pseud.) (1841/42-1902)
    Fr.-Russ. novelist
    Dorland—Sum p32,199

Durant, Susan D. (d. 1873)
    Eng. sculptor
    Waters—Women p114-115

Duras, Marguerite (1914-   )
    Fr. novelist
    Peyre—French p412-413,453

Durbin, Deanna (1922-   )
    Can. singer, actress
    CR '59 p228,por.
    Cur. Biog. '41 p246-248
    Zierold—Child p190-205,por.

Durell, Marion (gr. 1908)
    Amer. nurse
    *Ferris—Girls p21-32

Durham, Margaret Mure (1618-1692/93)
    Scot. covenanter
    Anderson—Ladies p118-123

Durkin, Mrs. Douglas. See Ostenso, Martha

Durlach, Theresa Mayer (fl. 1930's)
    Amer. feminist, politician
    Women—Achieve, p144,por.

Durocher, Marie Josefina (1809-1895)
    Fr.-Brazil. obstetrician
    Lovejoy—Women p261-262

Durocher, Mary Rose, Mother (1811-1868)
    Can. foundress
    Code—Great p379-405

Durof, Madame (fl. 1870's)
    Fr. pioneer balloonist
    *Lauwick—Heroines p24-25

Duse, Eleanora (1859-1924)
    It. actress
    Adelman—Famous p271-272,por.
    Bodeen—Ladies p87-95,por.
    Coad—Amer. p296,por.
    Cocroft—Great p102-119,por.
    Collins—Biog. p225-231,por.
    Dorland—Sum p169

Fitzhugh—Concise p183-184
Hammerton p535-536,por.
Izard—Heroines p171-202,por.
*MacVeagh—Champlin p196-197
Marinacci—Lead. p153-183,por.
Schmidt—400 p257-258,por.
Snyder—Treas. p319-324
Stiles—Postal p77
Time July 30,1934,p15,por.(Cover)

Dussek (or Dusek), Josepha Hambacher
    (b. 1756)
    Czech. singer
    Stiles—Postal p78

Dustin, Hannah (b. 1657/60)
    Amer. pioneer, heroine
    Bruce—Woman p13-16,por.
    Green—Pioneer (1) p375-387,por.
    Hanaford—Dau. p37-38
    Schmidt—400 p2-3,por.

Dutcher, Sally L. (fl. 1870's)
    Amer. W. pioneer
    Sargent—Pioneers p45

Dutrieu, Hélène (c. 1896-1961)
    Fr. pioneer aviatrix
    *Lauwick—Heroines p28
    *May—Women p62-63,78,80
    Planck—Women p15-17

Dutt, Toru (1856-1877)
    Ind. poet, musician, essayist, scholar
    Hammerton p536
    Parton—Dau. p530-545,por.
    Parton—Noted p530-545,por.
    Schmidt—400 p238-239,por.

Dutton, Theodora (fl. 1940's)
    Amer. pianist, composer
    McCoy—Portraits p39,por.

Duvall, Betty (fl. 1860's)
    Amer. Civil war spy
    Kane—Spies p32-33

Duvall, Evelyn Ruth Millis (1906-   )
    Amer. social counselor
    Cur. Biog. '47 p184-186,por.

Duvall, Mrs. (fl. 1860's)
    Amer. social leader
    Logan—Part p258

Duveyrier, Anne Honoré Joseph (Mélesville,
        pseud) (1787-1865)
    Fr. playwright, librettist
    Ewen—Ency. p312

Dux, Claire (fl. 1910's-1920's)
    Pol. singer
    McCoy—Portraits p39,por.

D'Uzès, Madame La Duchesse (b. 1847)
Fr. sculptor
Waters—Women p115

Dwight, Elizabeth Baker (b. 1808)
Amer. missionary
Hanaford—Dau. p507-508

Dwight, Ellen (m. 1852)
Amer. social leader
Pearson—Pilgrim p18-43

Dwight, Mary Elizabeth (fl. 1930's)
Amer. artist, club leader
Women—Achieve. p49,por.

Dwyer, Florence P. (1902-   )
Amer. congresswoman, politician
U.S.—Women (87th) p15,por.
U.S.—Women (88th) p7,por.

Dyar, Mary. See Dyer, Mary

Dyas, Ada (1843-1908)
Eng. actress
Coad—Amer. p247,por.

Dye, Clarissa F. (fl. 1860's)
Amer. Civil war nurse
Logan—Part p362-363

Dye, Eva Emery (b. 1855)
Amer. author
Binheim—Women p159,por.

Dye, Marie (1891-   )
Amer. educator, nutrition research
worker, organization official
Cur. Biog. '48 p169-170,por.

Dye, Mrs. Royal J. (d. 1951)
Amer. missionary
They—Went p17-19

Dyer, Mary (d. 1660)
Amer. religious martyr
Bell—Women p260-264,379-384
Best—Rebel p215-257
Bruce—Woman p35-42
DAR Mag. July 1921 p370(portrayal)
Deen—Great p362-364
Douglas—Remember p25-26,38-39
Earle—Colon. p119-120
Green—Pioneer (1) p216,237
Jones—Quakers (see index)
Leonard—Amer. p114-115
°McCallum—Women p25-30
Muir—Women p109-110

Dyhrenfurth, Hettie (fl. 1930's)
Amer. teacher, author
Women—Achieve. p90,por.

Dykeman, Wilma (fl. 1950's)
Amer. author
Hoyle—Tar p57-59,por.
Parshalle—Kash. p145-146,por.

Dympna (Dymphna) (fl. 9th cent.)
Irish saint, princess
Dolan—Goodnow's p91,por.

D'Youville, Mother (1701-1771)
Can. foundress
Code—Great p1-35
Elgin—Nun p68-71,por.
Pennock—Makers p24-25

Dysart, Lady.
See Lauderdale, Elizabeth, Murray
Maitland, Duchess of

E

Eadburga (fl. 800's)
Eng., wife of Beorhtric, King of
Wessex
Stenton—English p3

Eadgyth. See Edith

Eadie, Noël (1901-1950)
Scot. singer
McCoy—Portraits p39,por.

Eads, Laura Krieger (fl. 1920's-1930's)
Amer. teacher, psychologist
Women—Achieve. p197

Eagar, Miss (fl. 1890's)
Eng. governess
Howe—Galaxy p178-183

Eagels, Jeanne (1890/94-1929)
Amer. actress
Blum—Great p80,por.
Coad—Amer. p329,por.

Eager, Gertrude (m. 1893)
Amer. whaling voyager
Whiting—Whaling p263,266-267,por.

Eakin, Vera O. (1900-   )
Amer. composer, pianist, organist
ASCAP p136

Eames, Elizabeth Jessup (m. 1837)
Amer. poet
Hanaford—Dau. p266

Eames, Emma Hayden (1865/67-1952)
Amer. singer
Adelman—Famous p308-309
Ewen—Ency. p130
Ewen—Living p105-106,por.
Lahee—Famous p254-258,por.
McCoy—Portraits p39,por.
Pleasants—Great p278-279
Wagnalls—Opera p259-265,por.
Wagner—Prima p79-80,187-191,241

Eames, Jane (1816-1894)
Amer. traveler, author
Hanaford—Dau. p736-737

Eangyth (fl. 720's)
Eng. abbess
Stenton—English p16-17

Earhart, Amelia (1898-1937)
Amer. pioneer aviatrix
*Adams—Sky p157-176,por.
America's 12 p37-40,por.
*Bolton—Lives p161-177,por.
*Boynick—Pioneers p178-208
*Cooper—Twenty p65-82,por.
*Dolin—World p173-180,por.
Dwiggins—They (see index),por.
Earhart—Fun p3-139,por.
*Ferris—Five p3-40,por.
*Forsee—Amer. p136-158
*Fraser—Heroes p545-547,629-637,701-
711,por.
Hammerton p537,por.
Heath—Women (4) p31,por.
Heinmuller—Man's p115-125,330,por.
*Horowitz—Treas. p109-114
Jensen—Revolt p89,por.
Ladies'—Amer. p37-40,por.
Lauwick—Heroines p75-96,por.
*Logie—Careers (2nd) p23-31
Lotz—Women p40-47
Maitland—Knights p314-315
*May—Women (see index),por.
Muir—Women p203-204
*Nathan—Women p117-146
Planck—Women p108,119-138,por.
Rogers—Women p138-139,por.
Schmidt—400 p546,por.
*Shippen—Bridle p140-146
Stiles—Postal p78
*Strong—Of p300-305
*Yost—Famous p143-153,por.

Earl, Maud (fl. 1880's-1900's)
Eng. painter
Waters—Women p115-116

Earle, Alice Morse (1853-1911)
Amer. author
Adelman—Famous p245

Earle, Genevieve Beavers (1883-1956)
Amer. city official, politician
Women—Achieve. p52,por.

Earle, Honor. See Matthews, Honor

Earle, Katherine (Kitty) (fl. 1800's)
Amer. hostess
Woodward—Way p167,170-192

Earle, Mary Orr (b. 1858)
Amer. club leader
Logan—Part p472

Earle, Virginia (b. 1873)
Amer. singer
Strang—Prima p21-29,por.

East, Henrietta Maria (fl. 1760's)
Amer. colonial business woman,
needlewoman
Dexter—Colonial p42

Eastin, Mary (d. 1847)
Amer., wife of Lucius Polk
Smith—White p45-48,por.

Eastman, Abigail (fl. 1760's-1780's)
Amer., mother of Daniel Webster
Bartlett—Mothers p22-25

Eastman, Elaine Goodale (1863-1953)
Amer. author, editor, humorist
Logan—Part p858

Eastman, Elizabeth (1905-   )
Amer. novelist
Warfel—Amer. p131,por.

Eastman, Julia Arabella (1837-1911)
Amer. novelist
Logan—Part p843

Eastman, Linda A. (1867-1963)
Amer. librarian
Bul. of Bibl. Sept.-Dec.1926 p1-2,por.

Eastman, Mary F. (fl. 1880's)
Amer. lecturer
Hanaford—Dau. p342

Eastman, Mary Huse (1879-1963)
Amer. librarian, author
Bul. of Bibl. Sept.-Dec.1953, p25-26,por.

Easton, Florence Gertrude (1884-1955)
Eng. singer
Ewen—Ency. p130-131
Ewen—Living p106-107,por.
McCoy—Portraits p40,por.

Eastwood, Alice (1859-1953)
Amer. botanist, author, adventurer
Hollingsworth—Her p126-138

Easty, Mary (d. 1692)
Amer., accused witch
Leonard—Amer. p115

Eaton, Evelyn Sybil Mary (1902-   )
Can. novelist
Thomas—Canad. p40-42
Warfel—Amer. p131-132,por.

Eaton, Genevieve (d. 1942)
Amer. aviatrix, glider pilot
*May—Women p216

Eaton, Mrs. J. S. (fl. 1860's)
Amer. Civil war worker
Brockett—Woman's p463,507-508

Eaton, Margaret (Peggy) O'Neale
(or O'Neill) (1796-1879)
Amer., wife of Secy. Eaton)
Jensen—White p51-54,por.
Minnigerode—Some p241-287,por.
Whitton—These p176-177,183

Eaton, Sarah (fl. 1610's-1620's)
Amer. Pilgrim
Green—Pioneer (1) p151
Logan—Part p34

Eaves, Elsie (1898-   )
Amer. civil engineer
*Fleischmann—Careers p150
Goff—Women p77-81
Women—Achieve. p150,por.

Ebel, Isabel Caroline (1908-   )
Amer. aeronautical engineer
Knapp—New p169-179,por.
*May—Women p168

Eberhardt, Isabelle (1877-1904)
Fr. adventurer
Blanch—Wilder p283-325,por.

Eberhart, Nelle Richmond (1871-1944)
Amer. composer, music writer
ASCAP p137

Eberle, Abastenia St. Leger (1878-1942)
Amer. sculptor
Jackman—Amer. p442-443
Michigan—Biog. p105-106
National—Contemp. p84
Taft—Women, Mentor #5 (172),p9

Eberle, Irmengarde (1898-   )
Amer. author
Cur. Biog. '46 p170-171,por.

Eberly, Angelina (d. 1860)
Amer., friend of Sam Houston
Turner—Sam p58-61

Ebner-Eschenbach, Marie von, Baroness
(1830-1916)
Aust. author
Adelman—Famous p212-213
Hammerton p538
Heller—Studies p259-261
Schmidt—400 p48-49,por.

Eccles, Mrs. George E. (fl. 1920's)
Amer. missionary
They—Went p64-65

Eccleston, Sarah Chamberlain (fl. 1860's)
Amer. Civil war nurse
Logan—Part p374

Eckles, Ann (fl. 1950's)
Amer. space scientist
*May—Women p243

Eckley, Sarah. See Coxe, Sarah Eckley

Ed, Ida. See Boy-Ed, Ida

Eddy, Eliza Jackson (d.c. 1882)
Amer. philanthropist
Holbrook—Dreamers p210-211

Eddy, Lillian E. (c. 1902-1966)
New Z.-Amer. industrial designer
Women—Achieve. p134,por.

Eddy, Mary Baker (1821-1910)
Amer. religious leader, foundress
Abbot—Notable p313-317
Adelman—Famous p242-243,por.
America's 12 p22-27,por.
Bonte—Amer. p155,por.
*Buckmaster—Women p123-152
Canning—100 p106-112
Culver—Women p187-188
Deen—Great p218-229
De Morny—Best p123-130
D'Humy—Women p279-338
Dorland—Sum p20,133
Douglas—Remember p100
Fitzhugh—Concise p184-186
Hammerton p539,por.
*Heath—Women (4) p16,por.
Irwin—Angels p169-170
Kittler—Profiles p90-110
Ladies'—Amer. 12 p22-27,por.
Logan—Part p701-705
Longwell—Amer. p121-149
Lovejoy—Women p216
*MacVeagh—Champlin p200
Morris—400 p82-83
Muir—Women p189-191
Orcutt—Celeb. p53-60,por.
Seitz—Uncommon p276-290,por.
Sewell—Brief p187
Stewart—Makers 363-365
Sturges—Celeb. p53-60,por.
Untermeyer—Makers p73-81
Whitton—These p181

Eddy, Olive Tyndale (fl. 1930's)
Amer. humanitarian
Women—Achieve. p197

Eddy, Sarah Hershey (m. 1879)
Amer. singer
Logan—Part p769

Eddy, Sarah James (b. 1851)
Amer. sculptor
National—Contemp. p87

Ede, Janina (1937-   )
Eng. illustrator
Ryder—Artists p65

Eden, Emily (1797-1869)
Eng. novelist, traveler
Courtney—Adven. p113-136
Stebbins—Victorian p43-44,210

Eden, Irene (fl. 1940's)
Ger. singer
McCoy—Portraits p40,por.

Ederle, Gertrude Caroline 1900/08-   )
Amer. swimmer
CR '59 p231-232,por.
Davis—100 p36
Gallico—Golden p47-65,por.
Hammerton p539
Jensen—Revolt p89
Lamparski—What. p72-73,por.
New Yorker Aug.28,1926,p15-16,por.
(Profiles)
Rogers—Women p131,por.

Edey, Birdsall Otis (1852-1940)
Amer. organization official, feminist
Cur. Biog. '40 p269,por.

Edgar, Rachel (fl. 1770's)
Amer. Rev. war heroine
DAR Mag. July 1921, p373(portrayal)

Edge, Rosalie Barrow (1877-1962)
Amer. conservationist
New Yorker April 17, 1958 p31-36,por.
(Profiles)

Edgerly, Anne R. (fl. 1930's)
Amer. business executive
Women—Achieve. p107,por.

Edgerly, Mira (Countess Korzybska)
(b. 1879)
Amer. painter
Michigan—Biog. p106

Edgeworth, Maria (1767-1849)
Irish novelist
Adelman—Famous p122-123
Dorland—Sum p32,197
Hammerton p539-540,por.
Johnson—Women p60-63
MacCarthy—Later p216-229
Maurice—Makers p12
Schmidt—400 p143-145,por.
Stenton—English p317,324,327

Edginton, May (n.d.)
Brit. author
Hammerton p540

Edgren, Anne Charlotte Leffler, Duchess di
Cajanello (1849-1892)
Swed. novelist, playwright
Adelman—Famous p224
Dorland—Sum p54,198

Edison, Nancy Elliott (1810-1871)
Amer., mother of Thomas Edison
Bartlett—Mothers p91-94
Chandler—Famous p231-248
Peyton—Mothers p130-135
Schmidt—400 p21-22,por.

Edith (Eadgyth) (c962-984)
Eng. saint
Englebert—Lives p354
Wescott—Calen. p140
*Windham—Sixty p227-233

Edmonds, (Sarah) Emma (Franklin
Thompson, pseud.) (1841-1898)
Can.-Amer. nurse, spy
Dannett—Nobel (see index), por.
*Foley—Famous p122-133
Harkness—Heroines p11-12
Singer—3000 p122-133

Edmondson, Belle (fl. 1860's)
Amer. Civil war diarist
Jones—Heroines p270-275

Edmonston, Catherine Ann (fl. 1860's)
Amer. Civil war letter writer
Simkins—Women p20,120,223,225

Edson, Sarah P. (fl. 160's)
Amer. Civil war nurse, author
Brockett—Woman's p440-447

Edvina, Marie Louise Lucienne Martin
(1885-1948)
Can. singer
Davidson—Treas. p88-89

Edwardes, Paula (fl. 1890's)
Amer. actress
Strang—Prima p113-119,por.

Edwards, Amelia Ann Blanford (1831-1892)
Eng. author, Egyptologist
Adelman—Famous p196
Dorland—Sum p50,73
Hammerton p546
Oliphant—Women p249-274
Stebbins—Victorian p35-39,208

Edwards, Clara (1925-   )
Amer. composer, pianist, singer,
author
ASCAP p138-139
Howard—Our p567
McCoy—Portraits p40,por.

Edwards, Edna Eck (fl. 1900's-1950's)
Amer. missionary
They—Went p38-40

Edwards, Henrietta (1849-1933)
Can. politician, feminist
Innis—Clear p172-173

Edwards, India (1895/98-   )
Amer. journalist, politician
CR '59 p232,por.
Cur. Biog. '49 p186-187,por.
Jensen—Revolt p60-61,por.
Roosevelt—Ladies p25-31

Edwards, Joan (1920-   )
Amer. composer, author, singer,
song-writer
ASCAP p139-140
Cur. Biog. '53 p173-174,por.

Edwards, June (fl. 1960's)
Amer. aviatrix, helicopter pilot
°May—Women p207

Edwards, Lena Frances (1900-   )
Amer. obstetrician
°Knapp—Women p47-61,por.

Edwards, Lottie (fl. 1930's)
Can. personnel director, dancer
Women—Achieve. p145,por.

Edwards, Matilda Betham.
See Betham-Edwards, Matilda Barbara

Edwards, Mrs. (fl. 1780's-1790's)
Amer. W. pioneer
Ellet—Pioneer p304

Edwards, Mrs. Ninian (fl. 1850's-1860's)
Amer. social leader
Logan—Part p285-286

Edwards, Ruth Hamilton (fl. 1940's-1950's)
Amer. missionary
They—Went p109-111

Eells, Myra Fairbanks (1805-1878)
Amer. pioneer
Drury—First p47-121,por.

Eggerth, Martha (c. 1916)
Hung. singer, actress
Cur. Biog. '43 p194-196,por.

Eggleston, Marjorie E. (fl. 1930's)
Amer. security saleswoman
Women—Achieve. p179,por.

Eggleston, Sarah Dabney (b.c. 1838)
Amer. World War I patriot
Andrews—Women p321,por.
Simkins—Women p222

Eglah (Biblical)
Deen—All p261

Eglinton, Susannah Kennedy, Countess of
(d. 1780)
Scot. art, literature patron
Graham—Group p165-177,por.

Egloffstein, Julia, Countess (1786-1868)
Ger. painter
Waters—Women p116

Egner, Marie (fl. 1890's)
Aust. painter
Waters—Women p116

Egnor, Virginia Ruth. See **Dagmar**

Ehlers, Alice (1890-   )
Aust. harpsichordist
Ewen—Living p109

Eibenschütz, Ilona (b. 1872)
Hung. pianist
Schonberg—Great p336

Eide, Kaja Hansen. See Noréna, Eidé

Eilers, Sally (1908-   )
Amer. actress
Hammerton p548

Einselen, Anne. See **Paterson, Anne,** pseud.

Einstein, Elsa Einstein (d. 1936)
Amer., wife of Dr. Albert Einstein
Time Dec.22,1930 p18,por.(cover)

Einzig, Susan (1922-   )
Eng. illustrator
Ryder—Artists p67

Eis, Alice (fl. 1910's)
Amer. actress
Caffin—Vaud. p101

Eisenhower, Barbara Jean (1926-   )
Amer. civic worker, wife of
John Eisenhower
Phelps—Men (2) '59 p78-79

Eisenhower, Ida Elizabeth Stover (1862-
1946)
Amer., mother of Dwight
Eisenhower
Davis—Mothers p166-174

Eisenhower, Mamie Geneva Doud (1896-   )
Amer., wife of Dwight Eisenhower
CR '59 p234-235,por.
CR '63 p191,por.
Cur. Biog. '53 p181-183,por.
Jensen—White p265-268,por.
Logan—Ladies p194
°McConnell—Our p325-334,por.
Means—Woman p242-263,por.
Prindiville—First p279-294
°Ross—Know p69,por.
Time Jan.19,1953 p17,por.
Truett—First p80,por.

Eisenschneider, Elvira (1924-1944)
Ger. patriot
Stiles—Postal p80

Eisenstein, Rosa von (b. 1844)
Aust. painter
Waters—Women p116-117

Eisgruber, Elsa (fl. 1920's-1940's)
Ger. illustrator
Mahony—Illus. p305

Eithne, Princess (fl. 840's-890's)
Irish wife of King Cormac
Concannon—Dau. p50-52,109-111

Ekberg, Anita (1931-   )
    Swed. actress
    CR '59 p235,por.
    CR '63 p192,por.

Elder, Ruth (1904-   )
    Amer. pioneer aviatrix
    Heinmuller—Man's p326,por.
    Maitland—Knights p314
    *May—Women p91-92
    Planck—Women p69,83-84

Elderkin, Anne Wood (1722-1804)
    Amer. patriot
    Green—Pioneer (3) p516
    Root—Chapter p55-64

Eldred, Edith Lillia Byers (d. 1912)
    Amer. missionary
    They—Went p22-23

Eldred, Maria Olmstead (fl. 1860's)
    Amer. Civil war nurse
    Logan—Part p368

Eldridge, Florence (1901-   )
    Amer. actress
    CR '59 p235-236,por.
    CR '63 p192,por.
    Cur. Biog. '43 p493-496,por.

Eleanor of Aquitaine (or of Guienne)
    (c. 1122-1204)
    Fr., queen of Henry II of England
    Beard—Women p214-218
    *Boyd—Rulers p57-58,por.
    Culver—Women p91
    Elson—Woman's p50-55,por.
    Hammerton p551
    Koven—Women p45-62,por.
    *MacVeagh—Champlin p204-205
    O'Clery—Queens p50-59
    Stenton—English p37-38

Eleanor of Castile (d. 1290)
    Eng. queen of Edward I
    Hammerton p551
    *MacVeagh—Champlin p205
    Schmidt—400 p130,por.
    Sorley—King's p1-28

Eleanor of Provence (d. 1291)
    Eng. queen of Henry III
    Hammerton p551

Elena. See Helen, Rum. queen

Elène, Madame (fl. 1930's)
    Aust. cosmetologist
    Women—Achieve. p175,por.

Elfled (Ethelfleda, Aethelflaed, or Aelfled)
    Eng. princess, dau. of Alfred the
    Great
    Hammerton p569
    Stenton—English p4,147,199

Elias, Leona Baumgartner.
    See Baumgartner, Leona

Elias, Rosalind (1931-   )
    Amer. singer
    CR '63 p192,por.
    Cur. Biog. '67 p105-107,por.
    Matz—Opera p250-252

Eliasoph, Paula (fl. 1930's)
    Amer. artist
    Women—Achieve. p133,por.

Eliot, Ann (fl. 1600's)
    Amer. missionary
    Logan—Part p510

Eliot, Anne Mumford (fl. 1630's-1640's)
    Amer. pioneer
    Bell—Women p240-243

Eliot, Frances (1901-   )
    Amer. illustrator
    Mahony—Illus. p305

Eliot, George, pseud. (Mary Ann, or Marian
    Evans) (1819-1880)
    Eng. novelist
    Abbott—Notable p382-386,por.
    Adelman—Famous p191-192
    Bald—Women p162-208
    *Cournos—British p63-71,por.
    De Morny—Best p181-189
    Dorland—Sum p15,194
    Fitzhugh—Concise p150-152
    Hammerton p552-553,por.
    Hinckley—Ladies p279-361
    *Humphrey—Marys p146-157
    Johnson—Women p204-225
    Lawrence—School p89-125,por.
    Love—Famous p17
    MacCarthy—Women p17,40
    *MacVeagh—Champlin p205-206,por.
    Massingham—Great p167-175
    Moore—Disting. p203-218
    Muir—Women p175-176
    Oliphant—Women p61-115
    Parton—Dau. p91-112
    Parton—Noted p91-112
    Ravenel—Women p53-55
    Schmidt—400 p153-154,por.
    Sitwell—Women p37-38,por.
    Stebbins—Victorian p131-152,214
    *Steedman—When p303-308
    Thomas—Living Women p113-125,por.
    Wellington—Women p59-76

Eliot, Grace Dalrymple (c. 1754-1823)
    Eng., daughter of Hugh Dalrymple
    Bleakley—Ladies p189-244,305-307,por.

Eliot, Martha May (1891-   )
    Amer. physician, govt. official,
      public health worker
    Cur. Biog. '48 p184-186,por.

Eliot, Max. See Ellis, Anna M. B.

Eliott, Susannah Smith (fl. 1700's)
Amer. pioneer
Green—Pioneer (2) p300-301

Elisha's mother (Biblical)
Deen—All p343

Elisheba (Biblical)
Deen—All p261-262
Lewis—Portraits p59-60

Elissa. See Dido

Elizabeth (1) (Biblical)
mother of John the Baptist
Buchanan—Women p77-79
Deen—All p168-172
Englebert—Lives p421
Hammerton p553
Harrison—Little p79-793
Hughes—Mothers p143-156
Lewis—Portraits p92-95
MacVeagh—Champlin p206
Marble—Women p153-155
Mead—250 p187
Ockenga—Women p156-169
Van Der Velde—She p149-156

Elizabeth (2) (1635-1650)
Eng. princess
Hammerton p556

Elizabeth (3) (1890-1945)
Fr. heroine, Mother Superior
Stiles—Postal p81

Elizabeth (4) (1922-   )
Luxem. princess
Arsenius—Dict. p58,por.
Stiles—Postal p80

Elizabeth." (5)
See Russell, Elizabeth Mary Annette
Beauchamp, Countess Von Arnim

Elizabeth (6) (1876-1965)
Belg. queen
Arsenius—Dict. p57,por.
Hammerton p554,por.
Phila.—Women, unp.,por.
Stiles—Postal p81

Elizabeth (7) (1900-   )
Eng., queen of George VI
Arsenius—Dict. p58,por.
CR '59 p237-238,por.
Phila.—Women unp.,por.
Stiles—Postal p81
Time Jan.12,1925 p8,por.;Aug.11,1930
p24,por. Oct.9,1939 p20,por.(Cover)

Elizabeth (8) (1602-1644)
Sp. queen
Adelman—Famous p62-63

Elizabeth I (1533-1603)
Eng. queen
Abbot—Notable p98-107,por.
Adelman—Famous p52-53,por.
Armour—It p69-78
Arcesenius—Dict. p58,por.
*Boyd—Rulers p115-126,por.
*Cather—Girlhood p215-240
*Coffman—Kings p83-89,por.
Cuppy—Decline p172-179
Dark—More p107-129
D'Humy—Women p137-177
Dorland—Sum p47
*Farjeon—Kings p52,por.
*Farmer—Book p69-88
Fifty—Famous p289-292
Fitzhugh—Concise p193-195
Golding—Great p79-83,por.
*Hagedorn—Book p101-110
Hammerton p554-556,por.
*Humphrey—Elizabeths p11-38
Jenkins—Heroines p269-322,por.
Jenkins—Ten p36-63,por.
Koven—Women p175,192,231-245,por.
Love—Famous p26
*MacVeagh—Champlin p206-207,por.
Meine—Great p150-154,por.
Muir—Women p95-97
Murrow—This (2) p180-181
*Nisenson—Minute p58.por.
*O'Clery—Queens p66-85
100 Great p163-168
Orr—Famous p39-52
Orr—Famous Affin. I p51-70
Parton—Dau. p161-171,por.
Parton—Noted p483-493,por.
Phila.—Women, unp.,por.
Sanders—Intimate p59-86,por.
Schmidt—400 p134-135,por.
Sewell—Brief p51-52
Sitwell—Women p9-10,por.
*Steedman—When p43-51
Stenton—English p57-60,123,126-131,
134,203,251
Stiles—Postal p81
Thomas—Rulers p117-134,por.
Thomas—Vital p266-270,por.
Trease—Seven p76-114
Unstead—People p244-254,348

Elizabeth II (1926-   )
Eng. queen
Arsenius—Dict. p58
*Boyd—Rulers p207-216,por.
CR '59 p237,por.
Crawford—Little p1-314,por.
Cur. Biog. '44 p187-190,por.
Cur. Biog. '55 p178-180,por.
*Farmer—Book p219-238
Karsh—Faces p64,por.
*O'Clery—Queens p185-195
Phila.—Women, unp.,por.
Stiles—Postal p81
Time April 29,1929 p27,por.; Mr.31,
1947 p29,por.; Feb.18,1952 p28,por.;

(Continued)

Ellenborough, Jane Elizabeth Digby,
Countess (1807-1881)
Eng. eccentric
Stirling—Odd p116-122
Wallace—Fabulous p81-125

Ellenrieder, Anna Marie (1791-1863)
Ger. painter
Waters—Women p117

Ellerman, Amy (c. 1888-1960)
Amer. singer
McCoy—Portraits p41,por.

Ellery, Abigail Carey (d. 1793)
Amer. patriot, pioneer
Green—Pioneer (3) p91-92

Ellery, Ann Remington (m. 1750)
Amer. patriot, pioneer
Green—Pioneer (3) p89-91

Ellery, Elizabeth. See Dana, Elizabeth

Ellery, Mary Goddard (fl. 1800's)
Amer. pioneer
Green—Pioneer (3) p92

Ellet, Elizabeth Fries Lummus (1818-1877)
Amer. author
Beard—Amer. p77-84
Hanaford—Dau. p224-225,264
Whitton—These p27-28

Ellet, Mary (1779-   )
Amer., war heroine
Hanaford—Dau. p191-192

Ellicott, Rosalind Frances (1857-1924)
Eng. composer
Elson—Woman's p140

Elliot, Jean (1727-1805)
Scot. poet, song-writer
Findlay—Spindle p46-55,por.
Hammerton p557

Elliot, Kathleen Morrow (1897-1940)
Amer. author
Cur. Biog. '40 p275-276,por.

Elliot, Nancy.
See Edison, Nancy Elliot

Elliot, Rebekah Ward (fl. 1930's)
Amer. hotel executive
Women—Achieve. p144,por.

Elliott, Ann (c. 1762-1848)
Amer. Rev. war heroine, patriot
Ellet—Women (2) p104-108
Fowler—Woman p137-138
Logan—Part p142

Elliott, Charlotte (1789-1871)
Eng. poet, hymn-writer
Deen—Great p304
Dorland—Sum p53,80,185-186
Hammerton p557

Elliott, Elizabeth Shippen Green.
See Green, Elizabeth Shippen

Elliott, Gertrude.
See Forbes-Robertson, Gertrude Elliott,
Lady

Elliott, Grace Loucks (fl. 1930's)
Amer. editor, author
Women—Achieve. p123,por.

Elliott, Harriet Wiseman (1884-1947)
Amer. educator, govt. official
Cur. Biog. '40 p276-277,por.
Cur. Biog. '47,p194

Elliott, Mabel E. (fl. 1920's)
Amer. physician
Lovejoy—Women p325-332
Lovejoy—Women Phys. p97-108,por.

Elliott, Maxine (Jessie Dermot) (1871-1940)
Amer. actress
Blum—Great p17,por.
Cur. Biog. '40 p277-279,por.
Kobbé—Homes p182-183,211-215
por.
Logan—Part p776-777
Strang—Actresses p104-112,por.

Elliott, Melcenia (fl. 1860's)
Amer. Civil war nurse
Brockett—Woman's p380-384

Eliott, Sabrina (fl. 1770's)
Amer. Rev. war patriot
Ellet—Women (2) p97-100
Logan—Part p131

Elliott, Susannah Smith (fl. c. 1750)
Amer. Rev. war patriot
Ellet—Women (2) p93-97
Logan—Part p140-141

Elliott, Victoria (1922-   )
Eng. singer
Davidson—Treas. p89-92

Ellis, Anna M. B. (Max Eliot) (1860-1911)
Amer. author, journalist
Dorland—Sum p31,118-119

Ellis, Cecil Osik (b. 1884)
Amer. composer
McCoy—Portraits p42,por.

Ellis, Edith (1876-1960)
Amer. playwright
Logan—Part p791-792
Mantle—Amer. p282-283
Mantle—Contemp. p309

Ellis, Margaret Dye (fl. 1870's)
　　Amer. social reformer
　　Logan—Part p667

Ellis, Mehetable (fl. 1760's)
　　Amer. colonial teacher
　　Dexter—Colonial p82

Ellis, Mina A. (fl. 1900's)
　　Can. explorer, author
　　Adelman—Famous p318

Ellis, Vivian (1904-　　)
　　Eng. composer
　　Hammerton p557

Ellis-Leebold, Nancy Lorna (fl. 1950's)
　　Austral. aviatrix
　　*May—Women p198

Elliston, George (Miss) (fl. 1920's)
　　Amer. poet
　　Smith—Women's p61

Ellsworth, Abigail Wolcott (1756-1818)
　　Amer. Rev. war patriot
　　Green—Pioneer (3) p459-460,por.
　　Root—Chapter p79-90,por.

Elmendorf, Mary J. (fl. 1920's)
　　Amer. poet
　　Binheim—Women p192,por.

Elmendorf, Theresa Hubbell West (1855-
　　1932)
　　Amer. librarian, editor
　　Bul. of Bibl. May-Aug. '31 p93-94,por.
　　Marshall—Amer. p300,451

Elmer, Emily Rowell (fl. 1860's)
　　Amer. Civil war nurse
　　Logan—Part p368

Elmore sisters (Ellen, Grace) (fl. 1860's)
　　Amer. plantation managers
　　Simkins—Women p113-114,165

Elsa de Guttman von Eros (1875-1947)
　　Liech. princess, wife of Francis I
　　Stiles—Postal p81

Elsie, Lily (1886-1962)
　　Eng. actress
　　Hammerton p558

Elsie-Jean.
　　See Stern, Elizabeth Gertrude Levin

Elsom, Katharine O'Shea (1903-　　)
　　Amer. physician, nutritionist
　　*Knapp—Women p109-122,por.

Elssler, Fanny (1810-1884)
　　Aust. dancer
　　Adelman—Famous p144
　　Coad—Amer. p111,por.
　　Hammerton p558
　　Schmidt—400 p47-48,por.
　　*Terry—Star p66-73,por.

Elssler, Therese (1808-1878)
　　Aust. dancer
　　Adelman—Famous p144

Elstob, Elizabeth (1683-1756)
　　Eng. governess, author
　　Howe—Galaxy p39-51,por.
　　Stenton—English p238-245

Elsworth, Annie (fl. 1840's)
　　Amer. secretary, pioneer telegraph
　　　　message writer
　　Muir—Women p161-162

Elvin, Violetta (1925-　　)
　　Russ. dancer
　　Crowle—Enter p114-136,por.
　　Davidson—Ballet p76-78
　　Fisher—Ball p22,por.

Ely, Helena Rutherfurd (1858-1920)
　　Amer. author, landscape-gardener
　　Hollingsworth—Her p139-142

Elzy, Ruby (c. 1910-1943)
　　Amer. singer
　　Cur. Biog. '43 p198

Embury, Emma Catherine (1806-1863)
　　Amer. author
　　Hanaford—Dau. p225

Emerson, Anita Loos. See Loos, Anita

Emerson, Faye (1917-　　)
　　Amer. actress
　　Blum—Television p163,por.
　　CR '59 p239,por.
　　CR '63 p194-195,por.
　　Cur. Biog. '51 p184-186,por.
　　Smith—White p165,por.
　　TV—Person. (3) p75,por.

Emerson, Gladys (1903-　　)
　　Amer. biochemist
　　*Yost—Women Mod. p140-155

Emerson, Mary (fl. 1760s')
　　Amer. colonial merchant, joiner
　　Dexter—Colonial p51

Emerson, Mary Moody (1774-1863)
　　Amer., aunt of Ralph Waldo
　　　　Emerson
　　Balch—Modern p237-246
　　Garraty—Unfor. p121-126

Emerson, Sybil (1895-　　)
　　Amer. illustrator, painter, teacher
　　Mahony—Illus. p306

Emery, Anne Eleanor McGuigan (1907-　　)
　　Amer. author
　　Cur. Biog. '52 p172-173,por.

Emery, Isabel Winifred Maud (1862-1924)
　　Eng. actress
　　Hammerton p559

Emig, Lelia Dromgold (fl. 1890's-1900's)
Amer. social reformer, philanthropist
Logan—Part p663-664

Emily Bicchiere (1238-1314)
It. saint
Englebert—Lives p173
Wescott—Calen. p122

Emma (1) (1836-1885)
Haw. Isl. queen, consort of
Kamehameha IV
Arsenius—Dict. p59,por.
Phila.—Women unp.,por.

Emma (2) (d.c. 1050)
Ger. saint
Englebert—Lives p151-152

Emma Adelheid Wilhelmine Therese (1858-
1934)
Nether. queen
Arsenius—Dict.p59,por.
Hammerton p559-560
Phila.—Women unp.,por.
Stiles—Postal p82

Emmerich, Anna Katharina (1774-1824)
Ger. visionary
Hammerton p560

Emmet, Evelyn Violet Elizabeth (n.d.)
Brit. U.N. Delegate
Cur. Biog. '53 p184-186,por.

Emmet, Lydia Field (1866-1952)
Amer. artist
Jackman—Amer. p230-231
Michigan—Biog. p108-109
Waters—Women p117-118

Emmet, Rosina.
See Sherwood, Rosina Emmet

Emmet, Mrs. Thomas Addis (fl. 1800's)
Amer. social leader
Logan—Part p259

Emrick, Jeanette Wallace (b. 1878)
Amer. author, lecturer, humanitarian
Women—Achieve. p181,por.

Enaneul (fl. c. 2100 B.C.)
Babyl. priestess
Schmidt—400 p121-122,por.

Enclos, Ninon de L'.
See L'enclos, Ninon de

Endicott, Annie T. (fl. 1870's-1880's)
Amer. philanthropist
Hanaford—Dau. p179-180

Endicott, Mary.
See Chamberlain, Mary Endicott

Endor, Witch of (Biblical)
Buchanan—Women p51
Deen—All p106-109
Horton—Women p134-147
Lofts—Women p122-128
°MacVeagh—Champlin p209
Marble—Women, Bible p232-235
Mead—250 p81
Morton—Women p101-108
Nelson—Bible p43-45

Engberg, Mary Davenport (b. 1880)
Amer. violinist, composer,
conductor
Binheim—Women p192,por.
McCoy—Portraits p42,por.

Engdahl, Olga Pauline Pearson (1896-   )
Amer. mother of the year
Parshalle—Kashe. p107-111,por.

Engel, Birgit (fl. 1920's)
Ger. singer
McCoy—Portraits p43,por.

Engelhard, Georgia (fl. 1940's)
Amer. mountaineer
Rogers—Women p135,por.

Engle, Flora Pearson.
See Pearson, Flora Engle

Engle, Marie (b.c. 1860)
Amer. singer
Lahee—Famous p251-252

Engle, Mary (fl. 1810's-1820's)
Amer. inn-keeper
Dexter—Career p116,120

Englefield, Cicely (1893-   )
Eng. illustrator
Mahony—Illus. p306

English, Mrs. William D. See Kelly, Judith

Ennery, Madame d' (Gisette Desgranges)
(m. 1882)
Fr. hostess
Skinner—Elegant p205-207

Enright, Elizabeth (1909/10-   )
Amer. illustrator, author
Cur. Biog. '47 p196-197,por.
Mahony—Illus. p306

Enriqueta, Maria (b. 1875)
Mex. poet
Rosenbaum—Modern p42-46

Enters, Angna (1907-   )
Amer. dancer, painter, author
CR '63 p195-196,por.
Cur. Biog. '40 p279-281,por.
Cur. Biog. '52 p173-176,por.
Hammerton p561

Enthoven, Gabrielle Romaine (1868-1950)
Eng. theater historian
Hammerton p561

Entragues. (Catherine) Henriette de
Balzac d' (1579-1633)
Fr., mistress of Henry IV
Haggard—Remark. p22-25

Entwistle, Sarah (m. 1781)
Irish actress
MacQueen-Pope p307-311

Eodias (Biblical)
Deen—All p262-263

Ephah (Biblical)
Deen—All p262

Ephrath (Ephratah) (Biblical)
Deen—All p262

Epinay, Louise Florence Pétronille de la
Live d' (1726-1783)
Fr. author, salonist
Adelman—Famous p84-85
Dorland—Sum p15,105
Hammerton p562,por.
Kavanagh—Woman (1) p152-159
Russell—Glit. p161-164
Tallentyre—Women p62-87,por.

Eppes, Maria Jefferson (1778-1804)
Amer. first lady
Prindiville—First p27-35

Eranso, Catolina (fl. 15th cent.)
Sp. spy
Muir—Women p150

Erb, Letitia H. (1895-   )
Amer. Chamber of Commerce
executive
Binheim—Women p121,por.

Erb, Mae-Aileen Gerhart (fl. 1940's)
Amer. composer, music teacher
McCoy—Portraits p43,por.

Ercole, Velia (fl. 1930's)
Austral. author
Roderick—20 p110-125

Erdman, Loula Grace (n.d.)
Amer. author, educator
Warfel—Amer. p136,por.

Erickson, Barbara Jane (fl. 1930's)
Amer. aviatrix, flying instructor
Planck—Women p246-247

Erinna (4th or 6th cent., B.C.)
Greek poet
Anthologia—Poets p84-85

Eriphila. See Erythrae

Eristoff-Kasak, Marie, Princess (d. 1934)
Russ. artist
Waters—Women p378

Ermesinde (or Ermensinde), Countess of
(fl. 1196-1247)
Luxem. philanthropist
Arsenius—Dict. p60,por.
Phila.—Women, unp.,por.
Stiles—Postal p83

Ermolova.
See Yermolova, Mariya Nikolayevna

Ernst, Jessie (1893-   )
Amer. playwright
Mantle—Contemp. p310

Erskine, Dorothy (1906-   )
Amer. novelist
Warfel—Amer. p136-137,por.

Erskine, Mrs. Steuart (fl. 1920's)
Brit. traveller, author
Hammerton p565

Ertmann, Dorothea von (1781-1849)
Ger. pianist
Schonberg—Great p86-87

Ertz, Susan (c. 1894-   )
Amer. novelist
Hammerton p565
Overton—Women p113-119

Erving, Anne Princess (fl. 1860's)
Amer. Civil war nurse
Logan—Part p365

Erwin, June Collyer (n.d.)
Amer. actress
TV—Person. (2) p62,por.

Erxleben, Dorothea Christin.
See Leporin-Erxleben, Dorothea Christin

Escallier, Eléonore (fl. 1850's-1880's)
Fr. painter
Waters—Women p118

Esch, Mathilde (b. 1820)
Bohem. artist
Waters—Women p118-119

Esfandiari, Soraya. See Soraya Esfandiari

Esinger, Adèle (b. 1846)
Aust. painter
Waters—Women p119

Eskelin, Karolina (gr. 1896)
Fin. physician, surgeon
Lovejoy—Women p175

Eskey, Elizabeth (fl. 1930's)
Amer. journalist
Ross—Ladies p97,174

Eslick, Willa B. (fl. 1930's)
    Amer. Congresswoman
    Paxton—Women p128

Espy, Jean (d. 1781)
    Amer. Rev. war patriot
    Green—Pioneer (3) p467-468

Essex, Countess of.
    See Stephens, Catherine, Countess of
    Essex

Essipov (or Essipoff), Annette (1851-1914)
    Russ. pianist
    McCoy—Portraits p44,por.
    Schonberg—Great p332-334,por.

Estaugh, Elizabeth Haddon (1680/82-1762)
    Amer. colonial foundress, pioneer
    Beard—Amer. p22-23
    Best—Rebel p296-312
    Burt—Phila. p96-97
    Dexter—Colonial p100-101
    Earle—Colon. p49-50
    Fowler—Woman p203-217
    Jones—Quakers p388-389
    Leonard—Amer. p115

Este, Isabella d', Marchioness of Mantua
    (1474-1539)
    It. archaeologist, beauty, diplomat,
    literary patron
    Koven—Women p99-112,por.
    Mozans—Woman p310-311
    Schmidt—400 p249-250,por.

Estelle, Helen G. H. (fl. 1930's)
    Amer. teacher, social reformer
    Women—Achieve. p166,por.

Esterhazy, Caroline, Countess (fl. 19th cent.)
    Ger., friend of Franz Schubert
    Elson—Woman's p124-125

Estes, Eleanor Ruth Rosenfeld (1906-   )
    Amer. librarian, author
    Cur. Biog. '46 p185-186,por.
    Warfel—Amer. p138,por.

Estes, Huldah (d. 1875)
    Amer. social reformer
    Hanaford—Dau. p423-424,427

Estévez, Marta Abreu.
    See Abreu de Estévez, Marta

Esther (Biblical)
    Adelman—Famous p21
    Buchanan—Women p67-69
    Chappell—Fem. p128-140
    Culver—Women p43-45
    Deen—All p146-152
    Faulhaber—Women p98-101
    Hammerton p568
    *Horowitz—Treas. p115-121

Horton—Women p276-291
*Levinger—Great p67-74
Lewis—Portraits p131-137
Lofts—Women p163-178
Lord—Great p83-93
MacArtney—Great p24-42
*MacVeagh—Champlin p213-214
Marble—Women, Bible p209-213
Mead—250 p263
Morton—Women p143-149
Muir—Women p27-29
Nelson—Bible p74-80
Ockenga—Women p147-155
*O'Clery—Queens p19-24
Schmidt—400 p268,por.
Spurgeon—Sermons p196-212
*Strong—Heroes p33-40
*Strong—Of p22-28
Van Der Velde—She p123-132

Estrées, Gabrielle d' (1573-1599)
    Eng., mistress of Henry IV
    Hammerton p568-569
    Mayne—Enchant. p37-51,por.

Estrela, Marie Augusta Generoso (gr. 1881)
    Brazil. physician
    Lovejoy—Women p67,262-263

Ethel, Agnes (1852-1903)
    Amer. actress
    Coad—Amer. p238,por.

Ethel(d)reda (Audrey) (c. 630-679)
    Eng. saint
    Blunt—Great p78-80
    Englebert—Lives p241
    Hammerton p569
    Wescott—Calen. p91
    *Windham—Sixty p170-177

Ethelfleda. See Elfled

Etheridge, Annie (fl. 1860's)
    Amer. Civil war heroine, nurse,
    humanitarian
    Brockett—Woman's p747-753,por.
    Hanaford—Dau. p192
    Harkness—Heroines p13-14
    Moore—Women p513-518
    Young—Women p113,125,200-201,322,
    371-372

Etheridge, May (m. 1913)
    Eng. dancer
    Wyndham—Chorus p146

Etruscilla, Herennia (fl. 190's-250's A.D.)
    Rom. empress
    Serviez—Roman (2) p312

Ets, Marie Hall (1895-   )
    Amer. illustrator, author
    Mahony—Illus. p306-307

Etting, Ruth (1907-   )
    Amer. singer
    Settel—Radio p88,por.

Etzenhouser, Ida Pearson (1872-1936)
    Eng.-Amer. religious worker
    Phillips—33 p126-131

Eudocia (Athenais) (c. 401-c. 460)
    Byzant. empress, mystic,
        philanthropist
    Blunt—Great p40-41
    Diehl—Byzant. p22-43
    Diehl—Portraits p24-48
    Hammerton p570
    McCabe—Empr. p334-338
    Schmidt—400 p213-214,por.

Eudoxia (d. 404)
    Rom. empress
    Hammerton p570
    McCabe—Empr. p325-332,por.

Eudoxia Lopukhina (c. 1669-1731)
    Russ. czarina
    Hammerton p570

Eugenia (1) (d.c. 258)
    Rom. saint
    Englebert—Lives p488

Eugenia (2) (fl. 1699)
    Eng. author
    Stenton—English p205-207,210,215

Eugénie Marie de Montijo de Guzman
    (1826-1920)
    Fr. empress
    Adelman—Famous p220-222
    Guerber—Empresses p250-416,por.
    Hammerton p570-571,por.
    Kelen—Mist. p91-119
    Love—Famous p14
    *MacVeagh—Champlin p215-216
    *Nisenson—More Minute p56,por.
    Parton—Dau. p288-303
    Parton—Noted p288-301
    Schmidt—400 p185,por.

Eulalia dei Catalini (fl. 4th cent.)
    Sp. saint
    Husslein—Heroines p105-109
    Wescott—Calen. p128

Eulalia of Media (d. 303/04)
    Sp. saint
    Englebert—Lives p61,469

Eunice (Biblical)
    Barker—Saints p81-90
    Buchanan—Women p107-110
    Deen—All p238-241
    Hughes—Mothers p192-130
    Lewis—Portraits p96-97
    Nelson—Bible p126-130
    Van Der Velde p251-257

Euphemia (fl. 1226-1257)
    Eng. abbess, hospital designer
    Dolan—Goodnow's p116

Euphemia (Flavia Aelia Marcia) (fl. 518)
    Rom. empress
    McCabe—Empr. p348,por.

Euphrasia (d.c. 412)
    It. saint
    Englebert—Lives p100-101

Euphrasia Mary (1796-1868)
    Fr. saint, foundress
    Burton—Loveliest p58-76

Europe, Mary L. (fl. 1900's)
    Amer. pianist
    Cuney-Hare—Negro p246-247

Eusebia, Aurelia (c. 330-c. 360)
    Rom. empress
    McCabe—Empr. p294-301,303

Eustis, Dorothy Harrison (fl. 1930's)
    Amer. humanitarian, foundress
    Women—Achieve. p87,por.

Eustis, Helen White (1916-   )
    Amer. author
    Cur. Biog. '55 p187-188,por.

Eustis, Jane (fl. 1755-1759)
    Amer. colonial merchant
    Dexter—Colonial p35

Eustochium of Padua, Blessed (1444-1469)
    Rom. translator, scholar, mystic
    Mozans—Woman p31-34

Euston, Kate Walsh.
    See Smith, Kate Walsh Fitzroy, Countess
    Euston

Eutropia Galeria Valeria (fl. 300's A.D.)
    Rom. empress
    Serviez—Roman (2) p371-375,403

Eutropia McMahon, Mother (fl. 1900's)
    Amer. nun
    Logan—Part p621

Eva (fl. 1939-1940's)
    Russ. spy
    Singer—World's p209-215

Evans, Alice Catherine (b. 1881)
    Amer. bacteriologist
    Castiglioni—Hist. p1127
    Cur. Biog. '43 p198-200,por.

Evans, Anne (1869-1941)
    Amer. civic leader, art patron
    Cur. Biog. '41 p264

Evans, Augusta Jane (1835-1909)
    Amer. novelist
    Dorland—Sum p21,195
    Jones—Heroines p211-214
    Logan—Part p839-850
    Papashvily—All p154-168,180-183
    Pattee—Fem. p120-122,125
    Whitton—These p223

Evans, Dale. See Rogers, Dale Evans

Evans (Dame) Edith (1888-   )
    Eng. actress
    Beaton—Persona p40-41,por.
    CR '59 p241-242,por.
    Cur. Biog. '56 p166-168,por.
    Hammerton p573,por.
    Murrow—This (1) p49-50
    Newquist—Show p107-120,por.

Evans, Joan (gr. 1916)
    Eng. antiquarian
    Brittain—Women p79,114-115,145,190,
    222,250

Evans, Katherine (fl. 1650's)
    Eng. missionary
    Best—Rebel p117-135
    Culver—Women p149

Evans, Lillian. See Evanti, Lillian

Evans, Margaret B. (fl. 1940's-1950's)
    Amer. printer
    Club—Printing p27-28

Evans, Mary Ann or Marian).
    See Eliot, George

Evans, May Garrettson (fl. 1880's)
    Amer. journalist
    Ross—Ladies p493-496

Evans, Orrena Louise (fl. 1910's)
    Amer. editor, librarian
    Marshall—Amer. p99-101

Evanti, Lillian (Lillian Evans)
    Amer. singer
    Cuney-Hare—Negro p357-358,por.

Evatt, Harriet Torrey (1895-   )
    Amer. author, illustrator
    Cur. Biog. '59 p111-112,por.

Eve (Biblical)
    Armour—It p1-12
    Boccaccio—Conc. p1-3
    Davenport—Great p1-9
    Deen—All p3-7
    Hammerton p573
    Horton—Women p1-15
    Hughes—Mothers p29-34
    Lewis—Portraits p11-15
    Lord—Great p11-22

*MacVeagh—Champlin p216
    Mead—250 p2
    Morton—Women p1-15
    Ockenga—Women p9-18
    Schmidt—400 p269-270,por.
    Van De Velde—She p13-21

Eve, Fanny Jean Turing, Lady (d. 1934)
    Eng. politician
    Hammerton p573

Eve, Sarah (fl. 1770's)
    Amer. colonial author
    Dexter—Colonial p139

Eveleigh, Mary.
    See Rutledge, Mary Shubrick Eveleigh

Evelyn, Judith (1913-1967)
    Amer. actress
    Blum—Great p135,por.
    CR '59, p242,por.

Everett-Green, Evelyn (1856-1932)
    Eng. author
    Hammerton p574

Everson, Mary Dahl (b. 1855)
    Nor.-Amer. W. pioneer
    Sickels—Twelve p132-147,254

Ewing, Elizabeth Wendell (fl. 1860's)
    Amer. Civil war nurse
    Logan—Part p369

Ewing, Ella Campbell (fl. 1900's)
    Amer. missionary
    They—Went p27-28

Ewing, Juliana Horatio Gatty (1841-1885)
    Eng. author
    Dorland—Sum p23,188
    Green—Authors p77-79
    Hammerton p574
    *MacVeagh—Champlin
    Oliphant—Women p291-312

Ewing, Lucia Chase (fl. 1930's)
    Amer. ballet dancer
    Women—Achieve. p107,por.

Ewing, Mary Emilie (b. 1872)
    Amer. author
    Logan—Part p834

Eyck, Margaretha von (d. 1430)
    Flem. painter
    Waters—Women p xvi,119-120

Eyre, Elizabeth (fl. 1920's)
    Amer. painter
    Bryant—Amer. p285-286

Eyre, Katherine Wigmore (1901-   )
Amer. author
Cur. Biog. '47 p192-193,por.
Cur. Biog. '57 p175-176,por.

Eyre, Louisa (1872-1953)
Amer. sculptor
National—Contemp. p94

Eytinge, Rose (1835-1911)
Amer. actress
Coad—Amer. p225,227,por.

Ezekiel's wife (Biblical)
Deen—All p335
Horton—Women p269-275
Lewis—Portraits p170

F

Fabian, Alberta. See Simonetta

Fabiola (d.c. 399/400)
Rom. saint, philanthropist,
foundress, nurse
Blunt—Great p34-35
Deen—Great p315-316
Dolan—Goodnow's p73,por.
Englebert—Lives p491
*McKown—Heroic p14-15
Mozans—Woman p272-274
Schmidt—400 p387,por.

Fabray, Nanette (1922-   )
Amer. actress
CR '59 p243,por.
CR '63 p199,por.
Cur. Biog. '56 p168-170,por.
TV—Person. (2) p114-115,por.

Fachira, Adila d'Arányi (b. 1888/89)
Hung. violinist
Hammerton p576

Facius, Angelika (1806-1887)
Ger. engraver
Waters—Women p120

Fages (Dona) Eulelia de Callis y
(fl. c. 1780's)
Amer. colonial pioneer·
Leonard—Amer. p115

Faget, Maxine A. (n.d.)
Amer. engineer
Poole—Astronauts p8,91-101

Fagniani, Maria ("Mie-Mie") (1711-1856)
Eng., wife of Lord Yarmouth
Melville—Regency p176-185

Fair, Ethel Marion (b. 1884)
Amer. librarian, editor, author,
lecturer
Bul. of Bibl. Jan.-Apr.'51 p81-82

Fair, Laura D. (fl. 1850's-1870's)
Amer. W. pioneer
Brown—Gentle p260-262,por.

Fair maid of Kent. See Joan, Eng. princess

Fairbank, Janet Ayer (1878-1951)
Amer. author, feminist
Overton—Women p120-122

Fairbanks, Cornelia Cole (d. 1913)
Amer. club leader
Logan—Part p454-455

Fairbrother, Louisa (c. 1816-1890)
Eng. actress
Wyndham—Chorus p60-66,por.

Fairbrother, Sydney (b. 1872)
Eng. actress
Hammerton p597,por.

Fairchild, Salome C. (1855-1921)
Amer. pioneer librarian
Marshall—Amer. p452

Fairclough, Ellen (1905-   )
Can. govt. official, accountant
Cur. Biog. '57 p177-178

Fairet, Marie (f. 1540's)
Fr. actress
Gilder—Enter p86-89

Fairfax, Beatrice (c. 1878-1945)
Amer. journalist, author
Cur. Biog. '44 p193-196,por.
Cur. Biog. '46 p188
Fairfax—Ladies p9-250
Ross—Ladies p80-83

Fairfax, Lady (fl. 17th cent.)
Eng. hostess
Stenton—English p169-170

Fairfax, Mary. See Somerville, Mary Fairfax

Fairfax, Sally Cary (fl. 1770's)
Amer., friend of George Washington
Donovan—Women p94,100-103,111-
115,125

Fairfield, Cicily Isabel.
See West, Rebecca, pseud.

Fairley, Grace M. (fl. 1900's)
Scot. nurse
Pennock—Makers p134,por.

Fairman, Agnes Rowe (fl. 1930's)
Amer. interior decorator
Women—Achieve. p129,por.

Fairweather, Margie (fl. 1940's)
Amer. aviatrix, navigator
*May—Women p142

Faithfull, Emily (1835-1895)
    Eng. philanthropist, foundress,
        businesswoman, lecturer, editor
    Adelman—Famous p198-199
    Dorland—Sum p47,117,120-121
    Hammerton p578,por.

Faithfull, Lilian Mary (gr. 1887)
    Eng. educator
    Brittain—Women p64,73,83-84,150,
        211,248

Falcon, Marie Cornélie (1812-1897)
    Fr. singer
    Ewen—Ency. p143

Falconer, Pearl (n.d.)
    Scot. administrator
    Ryder—Artists p69

Fales, Almirah L. (d. 1868)
    Amer. Civil war philanthropist
    Brockett—Woman's p279-283
    Young—Women p37,201-202

Falkenburg, Jinx (1919-   )
    Amer. actress
    CR '59 p245,por.
    CR '63 p201,por.
    Cur. Biog. '53 p392-395,por.

Falkland, Elizabeth Tanfield, Viscountess
        (1585-1639)
    Eng. hostess
    Stenton—English p137

Falkland, Lettice Morrison (d. 1647)
    Eng. hostess
    Stenton—English p140,187

Falmouth, Countess of.
    See Elizabeth Bagot, Countess of
    Falmouth

Fan-Fan, pseud.
    See Blackburn, Victoria Grace

Fanning, Anne Brewster (1753-1813)
    Amer. Rev. war patriot
    Root—Chapter p324,por.
    Elgin—Nun p48-51,por.

Fanny Allen, Sister (fl. 1700's)
    Amer. nun

Fanshawe, Anne Harrison, Lady (1625-1680)
    Eng. author
    Botrall—Pers. p124-126,221
    McCarthy—Women p107-121
    Stenton—English p68,153-155

Fantin-Latour, Victoria DuBourg (1840-
        1926)
    Fr. painter
    Waters—Women p111-112

Faralla, Dana (1909-   )
    Amer. novelist
    Warfel—Amer. p140,por.

Farell, Marita (fl. 1930's-1940's)
    Eng. singer
    Peltz—Spot. p98

Farida (1921-   )
    Egypt., queen of King Farouk
    Phila.—Women, unp.,por.
    Stiles—Postal p87

Faris, Bessie Homan (m. 1901)
    Amer. missionary
    They—Went p13-16

Farjeon, Eleanor (1881-1965)
    Eng. author
    *Benet—Famous Poets p113-118,por.

Farley, Elizabeth (fl. 1660's)
    Eng. actress
    Wilson—All p142-144

Farmer, Fannie Merritt (1857-1915)
    Amer. home economist, author
    Logan—Part p860
    Rogers—Women p39,por.

Farmer, Hannah (fl. 1870's-1880's)
    Amer. religious worker, poet
    Hanaford—Dau. p619

Farmer, Lydia Hoyt (1842-1903)
    Amer. author
    Farmer—What p19,204,por.

Farncomb, Caroline (fl. 1900's)
    Can. artist
    Waters—Women p120-121

Farnell, Vera (gr. 1914)
    Eng. librarian, educator
    Brittain—Women (see index)

Farnham, Amanda C. (fl. 1860's)
    Amer. Civil war patriot
    Young—Women p186,213

Farnham, Eliza Woodson Burnhans (1815-
        1864)
    Amer. author, philanthropist
    Adelman—Famous p166
    Riegel—Amer. p137-140
    Woodward—Bold p337-356

Farnham, Elizabeth (fl. 1840's)
    Amer., W. pioneer
    Brown—Gentle p13,228-229

Farnham, Mary Frances (fl. 1880's-1890's)
    Amer. educator
    Logan—Part p733-735

Farnham, Mateel Howe (m. 1910)
    Amer. novelist
    Overton—Women p123-125

Farnham, Sally James (1876-1943)
  Amer. sculptor
  Jackman—Amer. p443-444
  Logan—Part p760
  Michigan—Biog. p112-113
  Taft—Women Mentor #2,#3,172,por.

Farnsworth, Eunice.
  See Moor, Eunice Farnsworth

Farnsworth, Helen.
  See Sawyer, Helen Alton

Farquhar, Anna.
  See Bergengren, Anna Farquhar

Farquhar, Jane. See Colden, Jane

Farquharson, Martha, pseud.
  See Finley, Martha Farquharson

Farr, Florence (d. 1917)
  Eng. actress
  Du Cann—Loves p73-96,por.

Farr, Virginia (fl. 1930's)
  Amer. aviation instructor
  Planck—Women p161-162

Farr, Wanda Kirkbride (1895-   )
  Amer. biochemist
  *Yost—Women Sci. p139-157

Farrand, Rhoda Smith (fl. 1770's)
  Amer. Rev. war patriot
  Green—Pioneer (3) p457

Farrar, Eliza Ware (1791-1870)
  Amer. author
  Hanaford—Dau. p239

Farrar, Geraldine (1882-   )
  Amer. singer
  Adelman—Famous p321
  ASCAP p149
  CR '59 p246-247,por.
  Davidson—Treas. p96-98,por.
  Ewen—Ency. p146
  Ewen—Living p115-116,por.
  Lahee—Grand p73-84,por.
  Logan—Part p766
  McCoy—Portraits p46,por.
  Pleasants—Great p313-318,por.
  Time Dec.5,1927 p36,por.(Cover)
  *Ulrich—Famous p69-75,por.
  Wagenknecht—Movies p170-172,por.
  Wagenknecht—When p149-157
  Wagnalls—Opera p206-210,por.
  Wagner—Prima p51,101-102,241

Farrar, Margaret Petherbridge (1897-1967)
  Amer. puzzle editor
  Cur. Biog. '55 p193-195,por.

Farrell, Eileen (1920-   )
  Amer. singer
  CR '59 p246-247
  CR '63 p201-202,por.
  Cur. Biog. '61 p152-154,por.
  New Yorker May 23,1959 p47,por
    (Profiles)
  *Seventeen—In p207-211,por.
  Wagner—Prima p241

Farrell, Suzanne (1945-   )
  Amer. ballet dancer
  Cur. Biog. '67 p112-115,por.

Farren, Elizabeth, Countess Derby (c. 1759-
    1829)
  Eng. actress
  Hammerton p582,por.
  MacQueen—Pope p254-260,por.
  Melville—More p184-185,208
  Wyndham—Chorus p37-40,por.

Farren, Ellen ("Nellie") (1848-1904)
  Eng. actress
  Furniss—Some p55-58
  Hammerton p582,por.

Farren, Maria Ann Russell (fl. 1830's)
  Amer. actress
  Coad—Amer. p170,por.

Farrenc, Jeanne Louise (1804-1875)
  Fr. composer
  Elson—Woman's p181-182

Farrington, (Mary) Elizabeth Pruett (1898-)
  Amer. Congresswoman
  Cur. Biog. '55 p195-197,por.

Farrington, Mary (fl. 1730's-1740's)
  Eng. maid of honor
  Melville—Maids p205-206

Farron, Julia (1922-   )
  Eng. ballet dancer
  Haskell—Vignet. p53-54,por.

Fassett, Cornelia Adèle Strong (1831-1898)
  Amer. painter
  Waters—Women p121-123

Fatima (c. 606-632)
  Arab., dau. of Mohammed
  Hammerton p582
  *MacVeagh—Champlin p221

Fatima, Umm Zaynab (d.c. 1314)
  Egypt. foundress
  Schmidt—400 p118,por.

Faucit, Helen(a) Saville (1817/20-1898)
  Eng. actress
  Adelman—Famous p186
  Dorland—Sum p37,165
  Hammerton p582
  MacQueen—Pope p331-336,por.
  Wyndham—Chorus p16-17

Faugeres, Margaretta (fl. 1790's)
    Amer. poet
    Ellet—Women (2) p284

Faulds, Mrs. David (m. 1885)
    Amer. businesswoman
    Farmer—What p423-425

Faulkner, Nancy (1906-   )
    Amer. author
    Cur. Biog. '56 p176-177,por.

Faulkner, Virginia L. (fl. 1930's)
    Amer. journalist, editor, author
    Women—Achieve. p118,por.

Fauset, Jessie Redmon (1884-1961)
    Amer. author, educator, editor
    Cherry—Portraits p142-144
    Dreer—Amer. p255,por.

Fausta, Flavia Maxiamiana Fausta (289-326
        A.D.)
    Rom. empress
    Balsdon—Roman p167,169-170
    McCabe—Empr. p271,278-282

Faustina, Annia Galeria (1) (The Elder)
        (c. 104-141 A.D.)
    Rom. empress, wife of Antoninus
        Pius
    Hammerton p583,por.
    McCabe—Empr. p163-168,por.
    *MacVeagh—Champlin p221
    Serviez—Roman (2) p18-37

Faustina, Annia Galeria (2) (The Younger)
        (125-175 A.D.)
    Rom. empress, wife of Marcus
        Aurelius
    Balsdon—Roman p142-147,por.
    Hammerton p583
    McCabe—Empr. p169-178,por.
    *MacVeagh—Champlin p221
    Serviez—Roman (2) p38-71

Faustina, Annia Galeria (3d) (fl. 200's-220's)
    Rom. empress, wife of Heliogabalus
    Serviez—Roman (2) p233-237

Faustina Augusta, The Elder (d.c. 140/141
        A.D.)
    Rom. empress
    Balsdon—Roman p142,144-145,257
    Boccaccio—Conc. p221-222

Faustina (Bordoni) (1693-1783)
    It. singer
    Pleasants—Great p97-100,por.

Faustina, Maxima (m. 360)
    Rom. empress, wife of Constantius
    McCabe—Empr. p304-305,308-309

Fauveau, Féliciede (1799-1886)
    Fr.-It. sculptor
    Waters—Women p123

Faux-Froidure, Eugénie Juliette (fl. 1890's-
        1900's)
    Fr. painter
    Waters—Women p124-215

Favart, Justine (d. 1772)
    Fr. actress
    Collins—Great p161-186

Fawcett, Millicent Garrett (1833-1884)
    Eng. feminist, politician
    Furniss—Some p115-117,por.
    Iremonger—And p172-191,por.
    Lovejoy—Women p132,137
    Schmidt—400 p160-161,por.

Fawziya (Fawzia) (1921-   )
    Iran empress, Egypt. princess
    Phila.—Women, unp.,por.
    Stiles—Postal p87

Fay, Amy (1844-1928)
    Amer. pianist
    McCoy—Portraits p46,por.

Fay, Delia A. B. (fl. 1860's)
    Amer. Civil war nurse
    Logan—Part p369

Fay, Lucy Ella (1875-1963)
    Amer. librarian
    Women—Achieve. p133,por.

Fay, Lydia Mary (fl. 1850's)
    Amer. missionary
    Logan—Part p514

Faye, Alice (1915-   )
    Amer. actress
    CR '59 p250,por.
    CR '63 p203,por.
    Settel—Radio p150,por.

Fayerweather, Sarah Harris (1802-1868)
    Amer. social reformer
    Brown—Home p23-29,por.

Fayette, Marie-Madeleine, Comtesse de
        (1634-1692)
    Fr. novelist, social leader
    Adelman—Famous p63-64

Fayweather, Hannah.
    See Winthrop, Hannah

Fealey, Maude (1886-   )
    Amer. actress
    Logan—Part p780

Fearn, Anne Walter (1867/71-1939)
    Amer. physician
    Fabricant—Why p112-113
    Hazeltine—We p98-107

Fedde, Elizabeth, Sister (1850-1921)
    Nor.-Amer. nun, nurse
    Dolan—Goodnow's p209
    Pennock—Makers p43,por.

Fedorova, Nina (1895-)
Russ. author
Cur. Biog. '40 p288-290,por.

Fedorovitch, Sophie (d. 1953)
Russ. Brit. ballet designer
Haskell—Ballet p132-140

Feeney, Mary Ignatius, Sister (d. 1915)
Amer. pharmicist, nun, nurse
Pennock—Makers p36-37,por.

Fehrmann, Minny. See Brema, Marie

Feigenblatt, Ann (fl. 1930's)
Pol.-Amer. retailer, actress
Women—Achieve. p174,por.

Felch, Amanda Farnham (b. 183)
Amer. Civil war patriot

Feliciani, Lorenzo. See "Seraphina"

Felicie, Jacobe (fl. c. 1220)
Fr. physician
Mozans—Woman p289-290

Felicitas (1) (fl. 138-161)
Rom. saint
Blunt—Great p9-10
Wescott—Calen. p183-184

Felicitas (2) (d. 203)
Carth. slave, saint
Blunt—Great p16-18
Culver—Women p75-76
Englebert—Lives p91-92
Sharkey—Pop. p30-34

Felix Elisabeth Rachel. See Rachel

Fell, Margaret (1614-1702)
Eng. religious leader
Best—Rebel p51-73
Culver—Women p145-148
Lambert—Quiet p21-26
Stenton—English p176-180

Fell, Sarah (fl. 1670's)
Eng. religious leader
Stenton—English p177-178

Feller, Henrietta (1800-1868)
Swiss missionary
Schmidt—400 p383,por.

Fellows, Mary (1868-1941)
Eng. governess
Howe—Galaxy p193-196

"Felseck," Marie von (fl. 1940's)
Alsac. spy
Singer—World's p283-291

Felton, Rebecca Latimer (1835-1930)
Amer. senator, author, journalist,
lecturer
Paxton—Women p11-12,128

Felton, Verna (1890-1966)
Amer. actress
TV—Person. (3) p36,por.

Fêng Pao (fl. A.D. 590)
Chin. soldier
Ayscough—Chinese p222-223

Fenimore-Cooper, Susan de Lancey (1857-
1940)
Amer. educator
Cur. Biog. '40 p290

Fenn, Mrs. Curtis T. (fl. 1860's)
Amer. Civil war humanitarian
Brockett—Woman's p665-675

Fenn, Jean (1930-)
Amer. singer
Matz—Opera p115-116

Fenner, Beatrice (1904-)
Amer. composer, author, publisher
ASCAP p151

Fenollosa, Mary McNeill (Sidney McCall;
Mrs. Rolfs) (c. 1865-1954)
Amer. author
Maurice—Makers p6-7
Smith—Women's p64

Fensham, Florence Amanda (b. 1861)
Amer. religious educator
Logan—Part p718-719

Fenstock, Belle (1914-)
Amer. composer, pianist
ASCAP p152

Fenton, Beatrice (b. 1887)
Amer. sculptor
National—Contemp. p99

Fenton, Lavinia, Duchess of Bolton (1709-
1760)
Eng. actress
Hammerton p585
MacQueen—Pope p165-171,por.
Melville—Stage p33-50,por.
Wyndham—Chorus p33-36,por.

Fenwick, Ethel Gordon Manson (1857-1947)
Scot. nurse
Dolan—Goodnow's p298-299,por.
Hammerton p585
Pennock—Makers p131,por.

Fenwick, Lady (1639-1645)
Amer. pioneer gardener
Hollingsworth—Her p10-17

Ferber, Edna (1887-1968)
Amer. author
Burnett—Amer. p549,por.
Burnett—This p1136-1137

(Continued)

Ferber, Edna—*Continued*

*Cournos—Famous p69-73,por.
CR '59 p250-251,por.
CR '63 p204,por.
Dodd—Celeb. p141-145
Farrar—Literary p135-145,320,por.
Hammerton p585
Lawrence—School p187-193
Mantle—Amer. p218-219
Mantle—Contemp. 9-13,265
Maurice—Makers p9
Mersand—Amer. p161-162
*Millett—Amer. p348-351
Overton—Women p126-138
Rogers—Women p109,por.
Van Gelder—Writers p360-365
Warfel—Amer. p147-150,por.
Williams—Amer. p147-150,por.
*Witham—Pan. p277-278,por.

Fergus, Phyllis (fl. 1940's)
    Amer. composer
Elson—Woman's p255-256
McCoy—Portraits p47,por.

Ferguson, Catherine (c. 1749-1854)
    Amer. religious worker, welfare
        worker
Brown—Home. p3-4,por.
Robinson—Hist. p79-80,por.

Ferguson, Edna (fl. 1920's)
    Amer. journalist, parachute jumper
Ross—Ladies p293-296

Ferguson, Elizabeth Graeme (1739-1801)
    Amer. Rev. war heroine, colonial
        poet, social leader
Ellet—Women (1) p219-232,por.
Hanaford—Dau. p140
Leonard—Amer. p115
Logan—Part p179-181

Ferguson, Elsie (1883-1961)
    Amer. actress
Blum—Great p64,por.
Cur. Biog. '44 p200-201,por.
Cur. Biog. '62 p127
Izard—Heroines p364
Wagenknecht—Movies p169

Ferguson, Harriet Rankin (1888-1966)
    Amer. organization official
Cur. Biog. '47 p199-201,por.
Cur. Biog. '66 p464

Ferguson, Margaret Clay (b. 1863)
    Amer. botanist
Adelman—Famous p298

Ferguson, Miriam Amanda Wallace ("Ma")
        (1875-1961)
    Amer. politician, governor
Fairfax—Ladies p235
Jensen—Revolt p58,por.
Roosevelt—Ladies p115-118

Fergusson, Erna (1888-   )
    Amer. author
Cur. Biog. '55 p201-202,por.

Fermi, Laura Capon (1907-   )
    It.-Amer. author, wife of Enrico
        Fermi
CR '63 p205,por.
Cur. Biog. '58 p137-139,por.

Fern, Fanny, pseud. (Sara Payson Willis
        Parton) (1811-1846)
    Amer. author
Bruère—Laugh. p9-10
Dorland—Sum p32,172
Hanaford—Dau. p245
Papashvily—All p123-125
Pattee—Fem. p115-120,184-186,por.
Whitton—These p128-129

Fern, Fanny (fl. 1850's-1860's)
    Amer. journalist, club foundress,
        leader
Ross—Ladies p16,39,43,45

Fernald, M. E. (1839-1919)
    Amer. entomologist, author
Osborn—Fragments p178

Fernig, Félicité de (Madame Van de Walen)
        (1776-1831)
    Fr. soldier
Kavanagh—Woman (2) p248

Fernig, Theophile de (1779-1819)
    Fr. soldier
Kavanagh—Woman (2) p248

Feron, Madame (b. 1797)
    Amer. actress
Coad—Amer. p147,por.

Ferrabini, Esther (fl. 1910's)
    It. singer
Lahee—Grand p392

Ferrara, Duchess of. See Borgia, Lucrezia

Ferrari, Carlotta (1837-1907)
    It. composer
Elson—Woman's p212-213

Ferree, Mary Warenbuer (d. 1716)
    Amer. colonial property manager
Dexter—Colonial p101-102

Ferrens, Norah (m. 1923)
    Eng. actress
Wyndham—Chorus p170-171

Ferrero, Gina Lombroso (1872-1944)
    It. physician, psychologist, author,
        sociologist
Cur. Biog. '44 p205
Lovejoy—Women p203

Ferret, Monique (fl. 1960's)
Fr. airline hostess
*May—Women p241

Ferrier, Kathleen (1912-1953)
Eng. singer
Beaton—Persona p46-47,por.
Cur. Biog. '51 p197-199,por.
Cur. Biog. '53 p194
Davidson—Treas. p98-101,por.

Ferrier, Susan Edmonstone (1782-1854)
Scot. novelist
Adelman—Famous p119-120
Dorland—Sum p55
Hammerton p588,por.
Johnson—Women p131-140
MacCarthy—Later p229-234

Ferrin, Mary Upton (fl. 1840's-1850's)
Amer. feminist
Beard—Woman p161-162

Ferriol, Madame de (fl. 18th cent.)
Fr. social leader
Kavanagh—Woman (1) p74-76

Ferris, Helen Josephine (1890-   )
Amer. author, editor
Women—Achieve. p66,por.

Fethers, Frances Conkey (m. 1868)
Amer. club leader
Logan—Part p473

Fetherstone, Edith Hedges (fl. 1930's)
Amer. artist
Women—Achieve. p101,por.

Fetter, Ellen Cole (fl. 1930's)
Amer. teacher
Women—Achieve. p182,por.

Feucheres, Sophie, Baronne de.
See Dawes, Sophia

Feuillere, Edwige (n.d.)
Fr. actress
Beaton—Persona p40-41

Ffrangcon-Davies, Gwen (1896-   )
Brit. actress
Hammerton p589

Fibiger, Mathilde (1830-1871)
Dan. author, feminist
Schmidt—400 p98-99

Fickert, Augusta (1855-1910)
Aust. educator, feminist
Schmidt—400 p52-53,por.

Fickett, Mary (n.d.)
Amer. actress
CR '63 p206,por.

Field, Betty (1918-   )
Amer. actress
Blum—Great p130,por.
CR '59 p252,por.
CR '63 p206-207,por.
Cur. Biog. '59 p116-117,por.

Fief, Madame du (fl. 1790's)
Fr. soldier
Kavanagh—Woman (2) p198

Field, Catherine (fl. 1770's)
Amer. social leader
Hanaford—Dau. p143

Field, Delia Caton (d. 1937)
Amer. social leader
Tebbel—Inher. p233-236

Field, Kate (1838-1896)
Amer. actress, journalist
Hanaford—Dau. p590
Ross—Ladies p36-37,por.
Woodward—Bold p201-214

Field, Laura (fl. 1930's)
Amer. pianist, ballet dancer
Women—Achieve. p173,por.

Field, Mildred Fowler (fl. 1920's)
Amer. poet
Smith—Women's p68

Field, Nannie Douglas (fl. 1837-1896)
Amer. social leader
Tebbel—Inher. p226-232

Field, Pauline O. (fl. 1930's)
Amer. lawyer
Women—Achieve. p130,por.

Field, Rachel Lyman (1894-1942)
Amer. author
*Benet—Famous Poets p123-128,por.
Cur. Biog. '42 p264
Millett—Amer. p351-353

Field, Regina (fl. 1930's)
Hung. publisher
Women—Achieve. p108,por.

Fielding, Lola (1930-   )
Eng. illustrator
Ryder—Artists p71

Fielding, Sarah (1710-1768)
Eng. novelist
Hammerton p591
MacCarthy—Women p255-262

Fields, Annie Adams (1834-1915)
Amer. poet
Howe—Memories (see index),por.
Logan—Part p860

Fields, Dorothy (1905-   )
    Amer. lyricist, librettist
ASCAP p153-154
CR '59 p253,por.
Cur. Biog. p141-143,por.
Stambler—Ency. p79-80

Fields, Gracie (1898-   )
    Eng. actress, singer
CR '59 p253,por.
Cur. Biog. '41 p274-275,por.
Hammerton p591,por.
Winn—Queen's p190-207,por.

Fiennes, Celia (1662-1741)
    Eng. traveller, diarist
Dunaway—Treas. p178-180
Stenton—English p231

Fiersohn, Reba. See Gluck, Alma

Fife, Louise, Duchess of (m. 1889)
    Eng., dau. of Edward VII
Hammerton p591,por.

Fifield, Elaine (1931-   )
    Austral. ballet dancer
Atkinson—Dancers p52-54,por.

Figner, Vera Nikolayevna (1852-1942)
    Russ. revolutionist
Goldsmith—Seven p119-151,por.
Padover—Confess. p330-337

Figueredo, Candelaria (1852-1913)
    Cub. soldier
Schmidt—400 p85,por.

Figueroa, Ana (1907-   )
    Chile. U.N. representative
Cur. Biog. '52 p190-191,por.

Filaretova, Iordana Nikolaeva (1843-1915)
    Bulg. patriot, nurse
Schmidt—400 p65-66,por.

Fillmore, (Mary) Abigail (c. 1832-1854)
    Amer. social leader, dau. of Millard
    Fillmore
Hanaford—Dau. p134-135
Logan—Part p248-249

Fillmore, Abigail Powers (1798-1853)
    Amer., wife of Millard Fillmore
Farmer—What p84-85
Gerlinger—Mis. p44-45,por.
Hanaford—Dau. p88-90
Jensen—White p72
Logan—Ladies p72-76
Logan—Part p247-248
*MacConnell—Our p139-146,por.
Prindiville—First p120-125
*Ross—Know p29,por.
Smith—Romances p181-191,por.
Truett—First p36,por.
Whitton—First p235-249,por.

Fillmore, Caroline Carmichael McIntosh
    (d. 1881)
    Amer., 2d wife of Millard Fillmore
*Ross—Know p29

Fillmore, Phebe Millard (fl. 1700's)
    Amer., mother of Millard Fillmore
Hampton—Our p100-108

Fillmore, Myrtle (d. 1948)
    Amer. religious foundress, leader
Culver—Women p189

Finch, Anne, Countess of Winchelsea (1661-
    1720)
    Eng. poet
Dorland—Sum p30,178-179
Fifty—Famous p311
Hammerton p1409
Untermeyer—Lives p217-218

Finch, Flora (1869-1940)
    Amer. actress
Cur. Biog. '40 p290

Findlater, Jane Helen (1866-1946)
    Scot. novelist
Hammerton p592

Findlay, Jane (fl. 1840's)
    Amer., hostess for William Henry
    Harrison
Truett—First p28,por.

Fine, Sylvia (1893-   )
    Amer. composer, author
ASCAP p155

Fine, Vivian (1913-   )
    Amer. composer, pianist
Reis—Composers p120

Finkler, Rita V. (b. 1888)
    Russ. physician, endocrinologist
*Knapp—Women p165-184,por.

Finley, Lorraine Noel (1899-   )
    Can.-Amer. composer, author
ASCAP p156

Finley, Martha Farquharson (1828-1909)
    Amer. author
Dorland—Sum p29,188
Papashvily—All p170-178

Finney, Emily Jex (d. 1952)
    Amer. author
Erskine—Out p244-245

Finney, Gertrude Elva Bridgeman (1892-)
    Amer. author
Cur. Biog. '57 p189-190,por.

Finnie, Mrs. Haldeman. See Holt, Isabella

Finney, May Emily.
    See Cairns, May Emily Finney, Countess
    of

Finney, Ruth Ebright (1884-1955)
    Amer. journalist, editor, author,
      club leader
    Ross—Ladies p4, 7, 339-342,por.
    Women—Achieve. p75,por.

Firestone, Isabella Smith (1874-1954)
    Amer. composer, song-writer
    ASCAP p157

Fischer, Clara Elizabeth (b. 1856)
    Ger. painter
    Waters—Women p125

Fischer, Helene von (b. 1843)
    Ger. painter
    Waters—Women p125-126

Fischer, Ruth (1895-1961)
    Ger. spy
    Singer—World's p101-112

Fish, Marie Poland (1902-   )
    Amer. ichthyologist
    Cur. Biog. '41 p280-281,por.

Fish, Marion Graves Anthon (m. 1876)
    Amer. social leader
    Jensen—Revolt. p30-31,por.

Fish, Marjorie (fl. 1930's-1940's)
    Amer. occupational therapist
    Epstein—People p144-159

Fish, Mary. See Silliman, Mary Fish

Fishback, Margaret (1904-   )
    Amer. author, advertiser
    Cur. Biog. '41 p281-282,por.
    Women—Achieve. p87,por.

Fisher, Alice (1839-1888)
    Eng. pioneer nurse
    Cope—Six p57-74,por.

Fisher, Anne Benson (1898-   )
    Amer. author
    Warfel—Amer. p153,por.

Fisher, Bernice (b. 1889)
    Amer. singer
    Lahee—Grand p383,388-389,por.

Fisher, Clara (1811-1898)
    Eng. actress
    Coad—Amer. p98,por.
    Dexter—Career p85-86
    Dorland—Sum p45,69,79,167-168

Fisher, Desire. See Osborn, Desire Allen

Fisher, Doris (1915-   )
    Amer. composer, producer, singer,
      author
    ASCAP p157-158

Fisher, Dorothy Canfield (1879-1958)
    Amer. novelist, essayist
    Burnett—Amer. p549,por.
    Burnett—This p1137-1138
    Fisher—Amer. p147-148,por.
    *Kirkland—Writers p113-121
    Lawrence—School p218-222
    *Logie—Careers p343-353,por.
    Maurice—Makers p8,por.
    Mears—They p85-86
    *Millett—Amer. p77-79,285-288
    Overton—Women p61-74
    Van Doren—Amer. p173-175
    Warfel—Amer. p79-81,por.
    Williams—Our p41-54
    Witham—Pan. p259-260,por.
    Women—Achieve. p63,por.

Fisher, Emma Roderick (fl. 1940's)
    Amer. music patron
    McCoy—Portraits p49,por.

Fisher, Harriet White (m. 1898)
    Amer. business manager, author
    Logan—White p900-901

Fisher, Jane, Lady.
    See Lane, Jane, Lady Fisher

Fisher, Katharine.
    See Steel, Katharine Fisher

Fisher (Fischer), Kitty (c. 1738-1767)
    Eng. courtesan
    Bleakley—Ladies p51-97,299-302,por.

Fisher, Lettice Ilbert (gr. 1897)
    Eng. tutor
    Brittain—Women p96,197,200,244

Fisher, Mary (fl. 1652-1697)
    Amer. missionary, religious leader
    Best—Rebel p100-116
    Culver—Women p148-149
    Deen—Great p125-129
    Dexter—Colonial p146
    Jones—Quakers p3-4,26-29,41

Fisher, Mary Frances Kennedy (1908-   )
    Amer. author
    Cur. Biog. p208-209,por.

Fisher, Parnell. See Pease, Parnell Smith

Fisher, Rebecca J. (m. 1848)
    Amer. pioneer
    Logan—Part p96-98

Fisher, Susan. See Folger, Susan

Fitzhugh, Anne (1727-1793)
    Amer. Rev. war patriot
    Green—Pioneer (3) p373-378
    Hanaford—Dau. p52

Fitzu (Fitziu), Anna (c. 1886-1967)
    Amer. singer
    McCoy—Portraits p49,por.

Fitzwater, Fanny Fern (fl. 1930's)
    Amer. editor, fashion expert
    Women—Achieve. p119,por.

Fitzwilliam, Fanny Elizabeth Copeland
        (1801-1854)
    Eng. actress
    Bleakley—Ladies p215,por.
    Coad—Amer. p171-172,por.

Flaccilla, Aelia (d.c. 386)
    Rom. empress
    Dolan—Goodnow's p72
    McCabe—Empr. p317-318,por.

Flack, Marjorie (1897-1958)
    Amer. illustrator, author
    Mahony—Illus. p308

Flager, Alicia Mayre (fl. 1930's)
    Amer. nutritionist
    Women—Achieve. p120,por.

Flagg, Marion (fl. 1930's)
    Amer. music teacher
    Women—Achieve. p158,por.

Flagstad, Kirsten (1895-1962)
    Nor. singer
    Brook—Singers p85-89,por.
    CR '59 p257-258,por.
    Cur. Biog. '47 p204-206,por.
    Cur. Biog. '63 p139
    Davidson—Treas. p104-108,por.
    Ewen—Ency. p156-157
    Ewen—Living p119-121,por.
    Ewen—Men p5-21
    Gelatt—Music p111-120,por.
    McCoy—Portraits p49,por.
    O'Connell—Other p143-155
    Pleasants—Great p339-346,por.
    Rosenthal—Sopranos p41-43,por.
    Time Dec. 23,1935 p19,por.(Cover)
   *Ulrich—Famous p89-94,por.

Flahaut, Marianne (fl. 1900's)
    Belg. singer
    Lahee—Grand p279-280

Flaminia (fl. 1565)
    Rom. actress
    Gilder—Enter p57-58

Flanner, Janet (1892-   )
    Amer. journalist, author, lecturer
    CR '59 p258,por.
    CR '63 p211,por.
    Cur. Biog. '43 p204-206,por.

Flavacourt, Hortense Félicité, Marquise de
        (fl. 1740's)
    Fr., friend of Louis XV
    Haggard—Remark. p281-283

Flavia, Domitilla (fl. 1st cent.)
    Rom. saint
    Balsdon—Roman p248-249
    Blunt—Great p27-28
    Deen—Great p312-313

Flebbe, Beulah Marie Dix (b. 1876)
    Amer. playwright, novelist
    Logan—Part p791
    Mantle—Contemp. p299-300

Fleeson, Doris (m. 1930)
    Amer. journalist
    CR '63 p211,por.
    Cur. Biog. '59 p122-123,por.
    Ross—Ladies p350-352
    Women—Achieve. p110,por.

Fleischer, Editha (1898-   )
    Ger. singer
    McCoy—Portraits p49,por.

Fleming, Elizabeth (fl. 1750's)
    Amer. colonial author, Indian
        captive
    Dexter—Colonial p138

Fleming, Margaret (Marjory) (1803-1811)
    Scot. poet
    Dorland—Sum p71-72
    Dunaway—Treas. p181-185
    Hammerton p598,por.

Fleming, May Agnes (1840-1880)
    Can. author
    Dorland—Sum p48,195
    Papashvily—All p181

Fleming, Mina (fl. 1890's)
    Amer. astronomer
    Farmer—What p272,275-277,279-280

Fleming, Peggy Gale (1948-   )
    Amer. skater
    Cur. Biog. '68 p128-130,por.129

Fleming, Rhonda (1923-   )
    Amer. actress
    CR '59 p528,por.
    CR '63 p212,por.

Fleming, Williamina Paton Stevens (1857-
        1911)
    Amer. astronomer
    Adelman—Famous p245
    Armitage—Cent. p174-175,por.
    Dorland—Sum p53,142

Flemion, Florence (fl. 1930's)
    Amer. plant physiologist
    Women—Achieve. p180,por.

Flemming, Emily (fl. 1860's-1900's)
Eng. physician
Martindale—Some p61-69

Flesch-Brunnengen, Luma von (b. 1856)
Morav. painter
Waters—Women p126

Fletcher, Alice Cunningham (1838/45-1923)
Amer. ethnologist
Adelman—Famous p277
Dorland—Sum p143
Hanaford—Dau. p534
Howard—Our p616
Logan—Part p881
*Moore—When p90-96
Mozans—Woman p322-323
*Parkman—Heroines p211-231,por.

Fletcher, Evelyn (fl. 1930's)
Can. aviatrix, glider pilot
*May—Women p214

Fletcher, Inglis Clark (b. 1888)
Amer. author
Cur. Biog. '47 p206-207,por.
Hoyle—Tar p61-65,por.
Warfel—Amer. p157,por.

Fletcher-Copp, Evelyn (d. 1944)
Can. music teacher
McCoy—Portraits p49,por.

Flexner, Anne Crawford (1874-1955
Amer. playwright
Mantle—Contemp. p310

Flexner, Hortense (b. 1885)
Amer. poet
Cook—Our p321
Smith—Women's p71

Flexner, Jennie Maas (1882-1944)
Amer. librarian, author
Bul. of Bibl. Jan.-April 1940 p1-2,por.
Cur. Biog. '45 p195
Marshall—Amer. p452

Fliedner, Caroline (1811-1895)
Ger. nun
Schmidt—400 p395-396,por.

Fliedner, Frederica (1800-1841/42)
Ger. nurse, foundress, educator
Dolan—Goodnow's p208-209
Pennock—Nursing p12-13

Flikke, Julia Otteson (b.c. 1879)
Amer. army nurse
Cur. Biog. '42 p265-266,por.
Pennock—Makers p59,por.

Flinders, Annette (Ann) Chappelle (d. 1852)
Austral. pioneer
Prout—Petticoat p106-111

Flint, Annie Johnson (1866-1932)
Amer. poet
Miller—Handi. p14-19,por.

Flint, Eva Kay (1902-   )
Russ.-Amer. playwright
Mantle—Contemp. p310

Flintham, Lydia Stirling (fl. 1780's-1790's)
Amer. author, lecturer
Logan—Part p834-835

Flood, Frances M. (fl. 1910's)
Amer. physician
Lovejoy—Women p314-315

Flora of Cordova (d. 851)
Sp. saint
Englebert—Lives p447
Husslein—Heroines p118-127

Florence, Malvina Pray (1830-1906)
Amer. actress
Coad—Amer. p209,por.

Florentina (Florence) (d. 7th cent.)
Colom. saint
Englebert—Lives p236-237

Flores, Dona Francisca (fl. 1720's)
Mex. printer
Club—Printing p14

Florey, Mary Ethel Reed, Lady (n.d.)
Eng. physician, research worker
Lovejoy—Women p251

Floyd, Hannah Jones (d. 1781)
Amer. patriot
Green—Pioneer (3) p112-115,151

Floyd, Joanna Strong (fl. 1770's)
Amer. patriot
Green—Pioneer (3), p115

Floyd, Ruth. See Woodhull, Ruth Floyd

Floyd, Theodora A. (1896-   )
Amer. nurse
*Yost—Nursing p155-173

Flucker, Lucy. See Knox, Lucy Flucker

Flynn, Catherine (fl. 1930's)
Amer. radio broadcaster
Women—Achieve. p56,por.

Flynn, Elizabeth Gurley (1890-   )
Amer. political leader
Cur. Biog. '61 p160-163,por.
Cur. Biog. '64 p126
Holbrook—Dreamers p330-331
Irwin—Angels p323

Focca, Italia Zanardelli (b. 1872)
It. sculptor
Waters—Women p126-127

Foch, Nina (1924-   )
Nether.-Amer. actress
CR '59 p259,por.
CR '63 p213,por.

Foerster, Alma (fl. 1913-1918)
Amer. Red Cross nurse
DAR Mag. Nov.1921 p645-646,por.

Fogarty, Anne (1919-   )
Amer. fashion designer
CR '59 p259-260,por.
CR '63 p213,por.
Cur. Biog. '58 p143-145,por.
Epstein—Young p7-25

Fogg, Isabella (fl. 1860's)
Amer. Civil war nurse,
philanthropist
Brockett—Woman's p505-510
Moore—Women p113-126

Foldes, Peggy (fl. 1930's)
Amer. editor, journalist
Ross—Ladies p238-239

Foley, Edna (fl. 1920's)
Amer. nurse
Dolan—Goodnow's p271,316

Foley, Helen (1896-1938)
Eng. poet
Eustace—Infinity p29-52,por.

Foley, Margaret E. (d. 1877)
Amer. sculptor
Hanaford—Dau. p292,323,738
Tuckerman—Book p603
Waters—Women p127

Foley, Martha (m. 1930)
Amer. editor, author
Cur. Biog. '41 p293-294,por.
O'Brien—50 p861

Foley, Pearl (Paul De Mar, pseud.)
Can. author
Thomas—Canad. p47

Folger, Susan (m. 1831)
Amer. whaling voyager
Whiting—Whaling p25-32,42

Follansbee, Elizabeth A. (fl. 1880's)
Amer. physician
Lovejoy—Women p105-106,127

Follen, Eliza Lee Cabot (1787-1860)
Amer. author
Hanaford—Dau. p226-227
Papashvily—All p44-45

Folsom, Mariana Thompson (fl. 1870's)
Amer. clergyman
Hanaford—Dau. p450

Folville (Eugenie-Emilie) Juliette (1870-
1946)
Belg. composer, violonist, conductor
Elson—Woman's p218

Fonaroff, Vera (fl. 1890's-1930's)
Russ.-Amer. violinist
McCoy—Portraits p50,por.
Women—Achieve. p91,por.

Fonda, Jane (1937-   )
Amer. actress
CR '63 p214,por.
Cur. Biog. '64 p128-130,por.
Ross—Player p92-102,por.

Fonssagrives, Lisa (1911-   )
Swed. fashion model
CR '59 p260-261
Time Sept.19,1949 p89,por.,(Cover)

Fontanges, Magda (fl. 1940's)
It. spy
Singer—World's p178-181

Fontaine, Jenny (fl. 1890's-1900's)
Fr. painter
Waters—Women p127-128

Fontaine, Joan (1917-   )
Amer. actress
CR '59 p261,por.
CR '63 p215,por.
Cur. Biog. '44 p211-215,por.
Time Jan.8,1945 p39,por.(Cover)

Fontaine, Pat (n.d.)
Amer. T.V. personality
CR '63 p215,por.

Fontana, Lavinia (1552-1614)
It. painter
Dorland—Sum p55,156
Waters—Women p128-130

Fontana, Veronica (b. 1576)
It. wood-etcher, engraver
Waters—Women p130

Fontanne, Lynn (b. 1887-   )
Eng. actress
Beaton—Persona p43-44,por.
Blum—Great p94,por.
Brown—Upstage p110-114
Cocroft—Great p201-217,por.
CR '59 p261,por.
CR '63 p215,por.
Cur. Biog. '41 p532-535,por.
Eustis—Players p34-46,por.
Forsee—My p9-42
Funke—Actors p37-75,por.
Hammerton p602
Ormsbee—Back. p257-259,por.
Stern—And p93-103
Time Nov.8,1937 p25,por.(Cover)
*Wagner—Famous p115-120,por.

Fontenelle, Miss (Mrs. John Brown
        Williamson) (fl. 1790's)
        Amer. actress
    Coad—Amer. p40,por.

Fonteyn, Margot (1919-   )
        Eng. ballet dancer
    Atkinson—Dancers p55-60,por.
    Beaton—Persona p46,por.
    Clarke—Six p158-190,por.
    Crowle—Enter p92-113,por.
    CR '59 p261-262,por.
    CR '63 p215-216,por.
    Cur. Biog. '49 p206-207,por.
    Davidson—Ballet p85-91,por.
    Fisher—Ball. p12,por.
    Haskell—Ballet p45,75-76,197-200,por.
    Haskell—Vignet. p37-38,43-44,por.
    *McConnell—Famous p86-94,por.
    *Muir—Famous p135-145,por.
    Phelps—Men (2) p94-95
    Swinson—Great p10,por.
    *Terry—Star p194-202,por.
    Time Nov.14,1949 p70,por.(Cover)

Foord, J. (fl. 1900's)
        Eng. painter
    Waters—Women p130

Foote, Maria, Countess of Harrington
        (c. 1797-1867)
        Eng. actress
    MacQueen—Pope p264-266,por.
    Wyndham—Chorus p52-53,156-160

Foote, Mary Hallock (1847-1938)
        Amer. illustrator, author
    Waters—Women p130-131

Forbes, Arethusa L. (fl. 1860's)
        Amer. humanitarian
    Hanaford—Dau. p660

Forbes, Elizabeth Adela Armstrong (1859-
        1912)
        Can.-Eng. painter
    Waters—Women p131

Forbes, Esther (1894-1967)
        Amer. novelist
    Overton—Women p139-142
    Van Gelder—Writers p291-295
    Warfel—Amer. p158-159,por.

Forbes, Genevieve.
    See Herrick, Genevieve Forbes

Forbes, Grace Springer (fl. 1930's)
        Amer. teacher, zoologist
    Women—Achieve. p197

Forbes, Jessica L. (fl. 1930's)
        Amer. publisher
    Women—Achieve. p183,por.

Forbes, Katherine Frefusis (fl. 1940's)
        Brit., director WAAF
    *May—Women p160

Forbes, Kathryn (1909-1966)
        Amer. author
    Cur. Biog. '44 p215-216,por.
    Cur. Biog. '66, p465
    Warfel—Amer. p159,por.

Forbes, (Joan) Rosita (1893-   )
        Eng. traveller, author, lecturer
    *Bridges—Heroes p101-115,por.
    Cole—Women p291-311,por.
    Hammerton p603,por.

Forbes-Robertson, Gertrude Elliott, Lady
        Amer.-Eng. actress
    Hammerton p603,por.
    Logan—Part p777

Force, Juliana (c. 1888-1948)
        Amer. museum director
    Cur. Biog. '41 p294-296,por.
    Cur. Biog. '48 p218
    Women—Achieve. p197

Ford, Antonia (fl. 1860's)
        Amer. Civil war spy, heroine
    Harkness—Heroines p6
    Simkins—Women p78

Ford, Blanche Chapman.
    See Chapman, Blanche

Ford, Constance (n.d.)
        Amer. actress
    TV—Person (2) p139-140,por.

Ford, Eleanor Clay (gr. 1916)
        Amer. philanthropist
    CR '63 p216,por.

Ford, Florrie Flanagan (c. 1876-1940)
        Austral. singer
    Le Roy—Music p59

Ford, Gertrude H. (fl. 1930's)
        Can.-Amer. business executive,
            importer
    Women—Achieve. p161,por.

Ford, Harriet (1863/78-1949)
        Amer. playwright
    Logan—Part p792
    Mantle—Amer. p248-250
    Mantle—Contemp. p310-311

Ford, Irene De Pendall (fl. 1930's)
        Amer. artist
    Women—Achieve. p155,por.

Ford, Mrs. John S. (fl. 1910's)
        Amer. social leader
    Logan—Part p302-303

Ford, Kathryn (fl. 1930's)
    Amer. club leader, insurance agent
    Women—Achieve. p57,por.

Ford, Lauren (1891-   )
    Amer. painter
    Mahony—Illus. p308

Ford, Mary (n.d.)
    Amer. singer, guitarist
    CR '63 p482-483,por.
    Popular Record p101,por.

Ford, Ruth (n.d.)
    Amer. actress
    CR '63 p218,por.

Forde, Florrie (fl. 1890's-1920's)
    Amer. singer
    Felstead—Stars p103-104

Forestier, Auber, pseud.
    See Moore, Annie Aubertine Woodward

Forman, Mary Leavenworth (fl. 1870's)
    Amer. social leader
    Hanaford—Dau. p145

Forman, Mrs. R. R. (1855-1947)
    Amer. composer
    McCoy—Portraits p50,por.

Fornia-Labey, Rita (1878-1922)
    Amer. singer
    Lahee—Grand p58-60
    McCoy—Portraits p50,por.

For(r)ester, Fanny.
    See Judson, Emily Chubbuck

Forrester, Maureen (Kathleen Stewart)
    (1931-   )
    Can. singer
    Cur. Biog. '62 p139-141,por.

Forsee, Aylesa (fl. 1950's)
    Amer. author
    *Forsee—Amer. p253
    *Forsee—Women p203

Forster, Dorothy (1884-1950)
    Eng. composer, pianist
    ASCAP p162
    McCoy—Portraits p51,por.

Forsyth, Josephine (1940-   )
    Amer. singer
    McCoy—Portraits p51,por.

Fort, Cornelia (fl. 1940's)
    Amer. aviatrix
    *May—Women p150-151,por.

Fort, Eleanor H. (Hank) (c. 1914-   )
    Amer. composer, author
    ASCAP p162

Fortescue, Julia, Lady Gardner (m. 1862)
    Eng. actress
    Wyndham—Chorus p58-59,por.

Fortescue, May (c. 1862-1950)
    Eng. actress
    Furniss—Some p58,por.

Fortescue-Brickdale, Eleanor (d. 1945)
    Eng. illustrator, painter
    Mahony—Illus. p283

Fortin de Cool, Delfina (fl. 1860's)
    Fr. painter
    Waters—Woman p131-132

Fortnum, Peggy (1919-   )
    Eng. illustrator
    Ryder—Artists p73

Fortunata (fl. 1st cent. A.D.)
    Rom., wife of Trimalchio
    Balsdon—Roman p206,255,272

Fortune, Jennie (1895-   )
    Amer. politician, state official
    Binheim—Women p147,por.

Foss, Louise Woodworth (fl. 1870's-1880's)
    Amer. speaker
    Hanaford—Dau. p582,585-590,por.

Foster, Abigail Kelley (1810/11-1887)
    Amer. feminist, social reformer,
        lecturer
    Bruce—Woman p178-180
    Hanaford—Dau. p354-355
    Irwin—Angels p75,107-108
    O'Connor—Pioneer (see index)
    Riegel—Amer. p34-40

Foster, Annette Hotchkiss Dimsdale
    (c. 1836-1874)
    Amer. W. pioneer, vigilante
    Towle—Vigil. p152-162

Foster, Bertha M. (fl. 1940's)
    Amer. organist, educator,
        choirmaster, foundress
    McCoy—Portraits p51,por.

Foster, Edna Abigail (d. 1945)
    Amer. author
    Logan—Part p860

Foster, Fay (1886-1960)
    Amer. composer, pianist, educator
    ASCAP p163
    Howard—Our p566,656
    McCoy—Portraits p51,por.
    Women—Achieve. p92,por.

Foster, Hannah Webster (1759-1840)
    Amer. author
    Benson—Women p178,181,189-192
    Dexter—Career p99-100
    Papashvily—All p30-31

Foster, Harriet (fl. 1940's)
Amer. singer
McCoy—Portraits p51,por.

Foster, Mrs. John W. (fl. 1870's)
Amer. club leader
Logan—Part p454

Foster, Judith Horton (1840-1910)
Amer. lawyer, politician, foundress,
social reformer
Adams—Heroines p245-279,por.
Farmer—What p318,por.
Hanaford—Dau. p673-674,por.
Logan—Part p748-749

Foster, Mrs. Lawrence. See Godden, Rumer

Foster, Marcia Lane (1897-   )
Eng. illustrator, wood-engraver
Mahony—Illus. p308-309

Fothergill, Jessie (1851-1891)
Eng. novelist
Black—Notable p184-197,por.

Fouchard, Clairdinette (fl. 1960's)
Hait. beauty
Stiles—Postal p92

Foulques, Elisa ((fl. 1880's)
Russ. painter
Waters—Women p132

Fourmént, Helena (b. 1614)
Belg. model, wife of Peter Paul
Rubens
Phila.—Women, unp.,por.
Stiles—Postal p92

Foutekova, Raina Pop Georgieva (1856-
1917)
Bulg. teacher, patriot
Schmidt—400 p68-69,por.

Fowke, Frances. See Brown, Frances Fowke

Fowle, Elida B. Rumsey (fl. 1860's)
Amer. Civil War nurse
Logan—Part p338-340
Moore—Women p91-108
Young—Women p86,203-204

Fowler, Lydia Folger (1822-1879)
Amer. pioneer physician, lecturer,
author, astronomer
Hanaford—Dau. p287-288,559
Lovejoy—Women p8-21,por.
Mead—Medical p41-42

Fowler, Marie Louise (fl. 1930's)
Amer. author
Women—Achieve. p187,por.

Fowler, Mary F. ("Addie") (fl. 1900's)
Amer., mother of Robert Fowler
Planck—Women p44

Fowler, Sally. See Plumer, Sally Fowler

Fowler-Billings, Katharine (1902-   )
Amer. geologist, author, explorer
Cur. Biog. '40 p311

Fox, Delia (b. 1872)
Amer. singer
Strang—Prima p192-207,por.

Fox, Eliza P. (n.d.)
Amer. club leader
Brown—Home. p247-248

Fox, Elizabeth Gordon (1884-1958)
Amer. nurse
Pennock—Makers p126-127,por.

Fox, Genevieve May (b. 1888)
Amer. author
Cur. Biog. '49 p208-209,por.
Cur. Biog. '59 p27

Fox, Gertrude Elizabeth Wilbur (1878-
1947)
Amer. animal breeder
Women—Achieve. p57,por.

Fox, Hannah (fl. 1800's)
Amer. pioneer
Fowler—Women p70-73

Fox, Kate (b. 1839)
Amer. spiritualist
Pattee—Fem. p239-244,por.
Ross—Charmers p89-109,287-288,por.
Whitton—These, p181-182
Wright—Forgot. p220-226,248-249,por.

Fox, Margaret (1833-1893)
Amer. spiritualist
Pattee—Fem. p239-244
Ross—Charmers p89-109,287-288,por.
Whitton—These p181-182

Fox, Margaret Fell (1614-1702)
Amer. religious leader
Deen—Great p116-125

Fox, Mary Jane (fl. 1860's)
Amer. Civil war nurse
Logan—Part p369

Frackleton, Susan Stuart (b. 1848)
Amer. artist
Waters—Women p132-133

Frajoso de Rivera, Bernardina (1800-1863)
Urug. patriot, humanitarian
Schmidt—400 p411-412,por.

Frame, June. See Wetherell, June

Franca, Celia (1921-   )
 Eng. ballet dancer, choreographer
Cur. Biog. '56 p186-188,por.
Davidson—Ballet p91-94

France, Madame Anatole (fl. 1890's-1900's)
 Fr., wife of Anatole Francé
Skinner—Elegant p160-162

France, Marie de (fl. 1170's)
 Eng. novelist
MacCarthy—Women p12,21

Frances (1384-1440)
 Rom. saint
Blunt—Great p162-163
Englebert—Lives p94-95
Wescott—Celen. p35-36
*Windham—Sixty p317-321

Frances Teresa.
 See Richmond and Lennox, Frances
  Teresa, Duchess of

Frances Xavier Cabrini.
 See Cabrini, Frances Xavier

Francesca da Rimini (fl. 13th cent.)
 It., Dante's heroine
Davenport—Great p102-106
MacVeagh—Champlin p229

Francis, Arlene (1908/12-   )
 Amer. actress, TV personality
Blum—Television p171,259,por.
CR '59 p267,por.
CR '63 p221,por.
Cur. Biog. '56 p188-190,por.
Donaldson—Radio p13-14
TV—Person. (1) p134-135,por.
Wilson—NBC p85-97,por.

Francis, Connie (1938-   )
 Amer. singer
CR '63 p221,por.
Cur. Biog. '62 p142-143,por.
Kahn—Tops p89-95,por.

Francis, Kay (1899/1905-1968)
 Amer. actress
Hammerton p612
Hughes—Famous p180-200,por.

Francis, Lydia Maria.
 See Child, Lydia Maria

Francisco Josefa de la Concepcion (1671-
  1742)
 Colom. nun, author
Schmidt—400 p77,por.

Franco, Cannen Polo de (1898-   )
 Sp., wife of Francisco Franco
Frederick—Ten p78-94,por.

François, Luise von (1817-1893)
 Ger. author
Heller—Studies p258-259

Frank, Anne (1929-1945)
 Ger. heroine, diarist
Dunaway—Treas. p1-15
Fellowes—Heroes p264-276,por.
*Moderow—People p17-49,por.

Frank, Mary Hughes (1919-   )
 Irish-Amer. author, child guidance
  expert
Cur. Biog. '58 p146-148,por.

Frankau, Julia. See Danby, Frank, pseud.

Frankau, Pamela (1908-   )
 Eng. author
Stern—And p115-135

Franken, Rose (1898-   )
 Amer. author, playwright
Cur. Biog. '41 p303-305,por.
Cur. Biog. '47 p211-212,por.
Mantle—Contemp. p190-191
Warfel—Amer. p162-163

Frankenberg, Mrs. Lloyd.
 See MacIver, Loren Newman

Frankelstein, Beatrice (fl. 1960's)
 Amer. space nutrition expert
*May—Women p245-246

Frankenstein, Mrs. Joseph M.
 See Boyle, Kay

Frankenthaler, Helen (1928-   )
 Amer. artist
Cur. Biog. '66 p107-108,por.

Frankfurt, Elsie (1918-   )
 Amer. fashion designer
Epstein—Young p71-87

Franklin, Abiah Folger (fl. 1690's-1700's)
 Amer. mother of Benjamin Franklin
Donovan—Women p2-4

Franklin, Ann (1696-1763)
 Amer. colonial printer
Brigham—Journals p77
Club—Printing p12
Dexter—Colonial p168-169,212-214
Earle—Colon. p65
Hanaford—Dau. p708-709
Irwin—Angels p7-8
Leonard—Amer. p115

Franklin, Aretha (n.d.)
 Amer. singer
Cur. Biog. '68 p132-134,por.

Franklin, Blanche Ortha (1895-   )
 Amer. composer, author
ASCAP p164-165

Franklin, Christine Ladd (fl. 1890's)
Amer. scientist, author
Dorland—Sum p148

Franklin, Deborah Read Rogers (d. 1744)
Amer., wife of Benjamin Franklin
Donovan—Women p33-60,65-68,74-76, 83
Green—Pioneer (3) p174-179,por.
Hanaford—Dau. p48

Franklin, Eleanor Ann Porden (1795-1825)
Eng. author
Parton—Dau. p406-416,por.

Franklin, Elizabeth (fl. 1750's)
Amer. colonial merchant, manufacturer
Dexter—Colonial p52

Franklin, Mrs. Hugh.
See L'Engle, Madeleine

Franklin, Irene (c. 1876-1941)
Amer. actress
Cur. Biog. '41 p308

Franklin, Jane (fl. 1930's)
Amer. journalist
Ross—Ladies p298-301

Franklin, Jane Griffin, Lady (1792/94-1875)
Austral. traveller, author
Parton—Noted p406-416
Prout—Petticoat p144-163,por.

Franklin, Pearl (b.c. 1888-   )
Amer. playwright
Mantle—Amer. p285
Mantle—Contemp. p311

Franklin, Sarah.
See Bache, Sarah Franklin

Franks, Abigail Levy (1696-1756)
Amer. pioneer
Leonard—Amer. p115

Franks, Rebecca (d. 1823)
Amer. Rev. war heroine, social leader
Burt—Phila. p282-283
Ellet—Women (1) p207-218
Hanaford—Dau. p141
Simonhoff—Jew. p25-28,por.

Fraser, Mrs. Alexander (fl. 1890's)
Eng. author
Black—Notable p234-246,por.

Fraser, Anne Ermatinger (d. 1930)
Can. literary critic, author
Thomas—Canad. p47-48

Fraser, Gretchen Kunigh (1919-   )
Amer. skier
*Jacobs—Famous p31-37,por.
Jensen—Revolt p132,por.
*Meyers—Champ. p13-30
Stump—Champ. p214-221

Fraser, Laura Gardin (1889-   )
Amer. sculptor
Jackman—Amer. p448-449
National—Contemp. p109
Taft—Women, Mentor #4 (172) p9,por.

Fraser, Marjorie Kennedy (1857-1930)
Scot. singer
Hammerton p616
McKay—Portraits p53,por.

Fraser, Mary Crawford (b. 1851)
Amer. author
Adelman—Famous p317
Logan—Part p835

Fraser, Matilda (fl. 1750's)
Amer. teacher
Woodward—Way p112-120

Fraser, Moyra (fl. 1930's-1950's)
Eng. ballet dancer
Davidson—Ballet p98-102

Frazier, Brenda Diana Dudd (1921-   )
Amer. heiress, social leader
CR '59 p269,por.
New Yorker June 10,1939 p23-28,por.
(Profiles)
Tanner—Here p143-164

Frazier, Susan Elizabeth (1864-1924)
Amer. teacher
Brown—Home. p222-224,por.

Fredegunde (Fredegonde) (d. 597 A.D.)
Frankish queen
Hammerton p616
Muir—Women p102-103

Frederica of Meckenburg-Strelitz, Duchess of Cumberland (1778-1841)
Eng. hostess
Hasted—Unsuccess. p163-190,por.

Frederick, Christine McGaffey (fl. 1930's)
Amer. home economist, author
Women—Achieve. p85,por.

Frederick, Pauline (1885/86-1938)
Amer. actress
Hammerton p621
Stuart—Immort. p120-121,por.

Frederick, Pauline (n.d.)
Amer. radio & TV commentator
CR '63 p223,por.
*Clymer—Modern p141-149,por.
Cur. Biog. '54 p291-293,por.
Parshalle—Kash. p183-185,por.

Frederika (1917-   )
    Gr. queen, Ger. princess
    CR '59 p269,por.
    Cur. Biog. '55 p212-215,por.
    Phelps—Men '58 (1) p93-94
    Phila.—Women unp.,por.
    Stiles—Postal p95
    Time Oct. 26,1953 p35,por. (Cover)

Freedman (Lois-) Nancy Mars (1920-   )
    Amer. author
    Cur. Biog. '47 p218-220,por.
    Warfel—Amer. p164,por.

Freeman, Alice Elvira (b. 1855)
    Amer. educator
    Bonte—Amer. p155,por.
    Hanaford—Dau. p545-547

Freeman, Bettina (1889-   )
    Amer. singer
    Lahee—Grand p366-367

Freeman, Florence (1836-1883)
    Amer. sculptor
    Logan—Part p763
    Tuckerman—Book p604-605
    Waters—Women p133

Freeman, Lucy Greenbaum (1916-   )
    Amer. journalist
    Cur. Biog. '53 p204-206,por.
    Murrow—This (1) p57-58

Freeman, Margaret (1893-   )
    Amer. illustrator
    Mahony—Illus. p309

Freeman, Marilla Waite
    Amer. librarian, author
    Bul. of Bibl. Jan.-Apr.1947 p29-32,por.

Freeman, Mary Eleanor Wilkins (1852-
    1930)
    Amer. author
    Adelman—Famous p297
    Harkins—Famous p141-156
    Harkins—Little p141-156,por.
    Logan—Part p804
    Maurice—Makers p2-3
    Williams—Our p160-181
    *Witham—Pan. p179-180,por.

Freer, Agnes. See Lee, Agnes

Freer, Eleanor Everest (1864-1942)
    Amer. composer
    ASCAP p167
    Elson—Woman's p259
    Hipsher—Amer. p183-189,por.
    Howard—Our p361
    McCoy—Portraits p53,por.

Freemont, Jessie Benton (1824-1902)
    Amer. author, social leader

Farmer—What p125,182,por.
    Hanaford—Dau. p149-150
    Sargent—Pioneers p27
    Whitton—These p215-217,242-244,
    267-268

Fremstad, (Anna) Olive (1870/72-1951)
    Swed.-Amer. singer
    Adelman—Famous p311-312
    Ewen—Ency. p165-166
    Ewen—Living p123-124,por.
    Lahee—Grand p42-48,331-332,por.
    McCoy—Portraits p53,por.
    Wagner—Prima p24-37,83,110,241

French, Alice. See Thanet, Octave, pseud.

French, Anna Densmore (fl. 1870's-1880's)
    Amer. lecturer
    Hanaford—Dau. p343

French, Anne Warner.
    See Warner, Anne Richmond

French, Florence (d. 1941)
    Eng. music editor
    McCoy—Portraits p53,por.

French, Jane Kathleen (fl. 1900's)
    Irish painter
    Waters—Woman p133-134

French, Mary Adams (b. 1859)
    Amer., wife of Daniel Chester
    French
    Wagenknecht—When p161-166

French, Susannah.
    See Putney, Susannah French

Freudenthal, Elsbeth Estelle (c. 1902-1953)
    Amer. economist, aviation writer
    Planck—Women p240

Freyberg, Marie Electrine, Baronesse
    (1797-1847)
    Ger. painter
    Waters—Women p134

Frick, Helen Clay (fl. 1930's)
    Amer. art expert
    New Yorker July 15,1939,p21-25,por.;
    July 22,1939 p23-26 (Profiles)

Frick, Rebecca E. (fl. 1860's)
    Amer. Civil war nurse
    Logan—Part p365

Frideswide (d.c. 735)
    Eng. saint, abbess, foundress,
    princess
    Hammerton p623

Friedländer, Camilla (b. 1856)
    Aust. painter
    Waters—Women p134

Friedlander, Elizabeth (fl. 1950's)
    Ger. printer, type designer
    Club—Printing p17-18

Friedrich, Caroline Friederike (1749-1815)
    Ger. painter
    Waters—Women p134-135

Friedrichson, Ernestine (1824-1892)
    Pol. painter
    Waters—Women p135

Friend, Florence. See Mannering, Mary

Frier, Peg (fl. 1660's)
    Eng. actress
    Wilson—All p144-145

Fries, Anna (b. 1827)
    Swiss painter
    Waters—Women p135-136

Fries, Constance (fl. 1930's)
    Amer. physician, educator
    Women—Achieve. p197

Frietchie, Barbara (1766-1862/65)
    Ger.-Amer. Civil war patriot
    Brockett—Woman's p761-763,por.
    Dolin—World p40-47
    Dorland—Sum p96
    Horowitz—Treas. p59-65
    *Humphrey—Women p179-188
    Muir—Women p170-171
    Strong—Of p185-191

Frijsh, Povla (Povia) (c. 1875-1960)
    Dan. singer
    Ewen—Living p126-127,por.
    McCoy—Portraits p53,por.

Frings, Ketti Hartley (1915-   )
    Amer. author, screen writer
    CR '59 p271,por.
    Cur. Biog. '60 p151-153,por.

Frisby, Anne. See Fitzhugh, Anne

Frishmuth, Harriet Whitney (b. 1880)
    Amer. sculptor
    Jackman—Amer. p417-418
    Michigan—Biog. p123
    National—Contemp. p121
    Taft—Women, Mentor #4 (172) p10

Frissell, Toni (1907-   )
    Amer. photographer
    Cur. Biog. '47 p220-221,por.

Fritcher, Elizabeth L. (fl. 1860's)
    Amer. Civil war nurse
    Logan—Part p369

Fritze, Margarethe Auguste (b. 1845)
    Ger. painter
    Waters—Women p136

Frolich, Katherina (1800-1879)
    Aust., friend of Franz Grillparzer
    Schmidt—400 p47-48,por.

Froman, Jane (1917-   )
    Amer. singer
    CR '59 p271,por.
    Popular Record p55,por.
    TV—Person. (1) p97-98,por.

Frooks, Dorothy (fl. 1930's)
    Amer. lawyer
    Women—Achieve. p61,por.

Froriep, Bertha (b. 1833)
    Ger. painter
    Waters—Women p136

Frost, Elizabeth Hollister(c. 1886-1958)
    Amer. author
    Warfel—Amer. p166, por.

Frost, Frances Mary (1905-1959)
    Amer. poet, novelist
    Cur. Biog. '50 p157-158,por.
    Cur. Biog. '59 p135
    Warfel—Amer. p167,por.

Frost, Sarah Frances. See Marlowe, Julia

Frothingham, Ellen (1835-1902)
    Amer. translator, linguist
    Dorland—Sum p30,177

Frowne, Sadie (fl. 1900's)
    Pol. immigrant
    Cavanah—We p207-213

Frumerie, Agnes de (b. 1861-   )
    Swed. painter
    Waters—Women p136-137

Fry, Elizabeth Gurney (1780-1845)
    Eng. philanthropist, social reformer,
        religious leader
    *Adams—Heroines p1-29,por.
    Adelman—Famous p137-138
    *Borer—Women p73-91,por.
    Bottrall—Pers. p83-84,222
    Bowie—Women p54-70
    Carey—Twelve p109-154,por.
    Courtney—Adven. p169-193,por.
    Deen—Great p164-171
    De Morny—Best p117-123
    Dolan—Goodnow's p207,por.
    Dorland—Sum p20,124,129
    Fifty—Famous p275-278,por.
    Hammerton p625-626,por.
    Holroyd—Fifty p194-198
    *Horowitz—Treas. p132-138
    Hubbard—Little p251-288,por.

(Continued)

Fuller, Sarah R. (fl. 1880's-1890's)
Amer. club leader
Logan—Part p348

Fuller, Susanna.
See Winslow, Susanna Fuller White

Fuller, Tyra Lundberg (fl. 1930's)
Swed.-Amer. journalist
Women—Achieve. p159,por.

Fullerton, Georgiana Charlotte, Lady (1812-
1885)
Eng. novelist, philanthropist
Blunt—Great p341-366
Dorland—Sum p24,132-133
Oliphant—Women p195-203

Fulmer, Willa L. (b. 1884)
Amer. congresswoman
Paxton—Women p103-106,128,por.

Fulton, Mary (fl. 1910's)
Eng. novelist
Johnson—Some Contemp. p197-210

Fulton, Maud (1881-1950)
Amer. actress
Caffin—Vaud. p109

Fulton, Sarah Bradlee (1740-1835)
Amer. Rev. heroine
Green—Pioneer (2) p207,227-235

Fulvia (1) (d. 40 B.C.)
Rom., wife of Publius Clodius
Pulcher and Mark Antony
Balsdon—Roman p49-50,56,178
*MacVeagh—Champlin p240

Fulvia (2) (fl. c. 63 B.C.)
Rom. courtesan
Balsdon—Roman p42,99

Fundana, Galeria (fl. 20's-60's)
Rom. empress, wife of Vitellius
McCabe—Empr. p123-128
Serviez—Roman (1) p308-323

Funicello, Annette (1942-   )
Amer. actress, singer
*Kahn—Tops p19-27,por.

Funk, Mary Wallace (gr. 1958)
Amer. aviatrix, space woman
*May—Women p247,por.

Furbeck, Mary Elizabeth (fl. 1920's 1940's)
Amer. editor, librarian
Marshall—Amer. p102

Furman, Bess (1894-   )
Amer. journalist
Ross—Ladies p319-321,345-347

Furnas, Marthedith (1904-   )
Amer. novelist
Warfel—Amer. p168,por.

Furness, Betty (1916-   )
Amer. actress, TV personality,
govt. official
CR '59 p275-276,por.
CR '63 p226,por.
Cur. Biog. '68 (Feb.) p134-136,por.

Furness, Thelma Morgan Converse,
Viscountess (1904-   )
Amer.-Brit. social leader
Pearson—Marry. p221-230,por.

Furse, (Dame) Katharine Symonds (1875-
1952)
Eng. war nurse
Hammerton p627-628,por.

Furtseva, Eketerina (c. 1909-   )
Russ. political leader
Cur.Biog. '56 p196-197,por.

Fyan, Loleta Dawson (1894-   )
Amer. librarian, author, organiza-
tion official
Bul. of Bibl. Jan.-Apr.'61 p73-75,por.
Cur. Biog. '51 p221-223,por.

G

Gabor, Eva (n.d.)
Hung.-Amer. actress
CR '59 p277,por.
CR '63 p227,por.
Cur. Biog. '68 p136-138,por.

Gabor, Jolie (1896-   )
Hung.-Amer. business woman,
mother of Gabor sisters
CR '59 p277,por.
CR '63 p227,por.

Gabor, Magda (c. 1918-   )
Hung.-Amer. actress
CR '59 p277,por.
CR '63 p228,por.

Gabor, Zsa Zsa (c. 1920-   )
Hung-Amer. actress
CR '59 p278,por.
CR '63 p228,por.
Martin—Pete p286-299,por.
TV Guide—Roundup p37-40

Gabriel, Mary Ann Virginia (1825-1877)
Eng. composer
Dorland—Sum p33,71,160

Gabrielli, Catarina (1730-1796)
Ferris—Great p32-54
It. singer
Lahee—Famous p18-20
Wagner—Prima p176-178,241

Gadd, May (1894-   )
Amer. folk dance teacher, organizer
New Yorker Feb.7,1953,p36-38,por.
(Profiles)

Gaddis, Edith (fl. 1920's-1930's)
Amer. purchasing agent
Women—Achieve. p197-198

Gadsby, Mrs. James Eakin (fl. 1900's)
Amer. club leader, author
Logan—Part p478

Gadski, Johanna (1872-1932)
Ger. singer
Ewen—Ency. p167-168
McCoy—Portraits, p55,por.
Wagner Prima p82,241

Gág, Flavia (1907-   )
Amer. illustrator
Mahony—Illus. p309

Gág, Wanda Hazel (1893-1946)
Amer. illustrator, painter
Cur. Biog. '46 p200
Dunaway—Treas. p130-138
Kirkland—Artists p1-12
Mahony—Illus. p309-310

Gage, Frances Dana (1808-1884)
Amer. Civil war humanitarian,
social reformer, lecturer
Brockett—Woman's p683-690
Hanaford—Dau. p208-209,360-362
Logan—Part p313-314
O'Connor—Pioneer p91-93,152,168-
169

Gage, Gloria (fl. 1930's)
Amer. government official, musician
Women—Achieve. p73,por.

Gage, Matilda Joslyn (1826-1898)
Amer. author, feminist, lecturer
Hanaford—Dau. p641
O'Connor—Pioneer p88

Gage, Nina Diadamia (1883-1948)
Amer. nurse, bacteriologist
Pennock—Makers p137-138,por.

Gaggiotti-Richards, Emma (1825-1912)
It. painter
Waters—Women p137

Gahagan, Helen Mary.
See Douglas, Helen Mary Gahagan

Gaia Cyrilla (fl. c. 570 B.C.)
Rom., wife of Tarquinius Priscus
Boccaccio—Conc. p98

Gaidule, Paula (1848-1925)
Lat. teacher
Schmidt—400 p274

Gail-Garré, Edmee Sophia Garre (1775-
1819)
Fr. composer, singer
Dorland—Sum p159

Gaines, Myra Clark (1805-1885)
Amer. heiress, social leader
Hanaford—Dau. p146

Gaines, Ruth (fl. 1910's)
Amer. social worker, author
Bruce—Woman p279-281

Gainsborg, Lolita Cabrera (fl. 1910's)
Amer. composer, pianist
McCoy—Portraits p55,por.

Gaither, Frances (1889-1955)
Amer. author
Cur. Biog. '50 p161-162,por.
Cur. Biog. '56 p197
Warfel—Amer.p170,por.

Galajikian, Florence Grandland (1900-   )
Amer. composer, pianist, teacher
Howard—Our p536
McCoy—Portraits p55,por.
Reis—Somposers p133

Galard Terraube, Geneviève de (1925-   )
Fr. nurse
Cur. Biog. '54 p294-296,por.
Dolan—Goodnow's p338-340,por.
McKown—Heroic p267-290,por.

Gale, Zona (1874-1938)
Amer. author
Cook—Our p322
Dodd—Celeb. p226-231
Hammerton p630
Mantle—Amer. p55-59
Mantle—Contemp. p96,98-99
Maurice—Makers p6,por.
Millett—Amer. p366-367
Overton—Authors p138-143
Overton—Women p143-156
Prochnow—Great p336-342
Van Doren—Amer. p164-166

Galeria Fundana. See Fundana, Galeria

Galgani, Gemma (1878-1903)
It. saint
Husslein—Heroines p44-50

Gall, Yvonne Irma (b. 1885)
Fr. singer
McCoy—Portraits p55,por.

Galla (1) (d. before 350)
Rom. empress, wife of Constantius
McCabe—Empr. p288

Galla (2) (fl. 370-380)
Rom. empress, wife of Theodosius
McCabe—Empr. p317-321

Galla (3) (fl. 6th cent.)
    Rom. saint
    Blunt—Great p42
    Wescott—Calen. p155-156

Galla Placidia (338-450)
    Rom. empress
    McCabe—Empr. p341-345,por.

Galli, Emira (fl. 1880's)
    It. painter
    Waters—Women p138

Galli, Rosina (1896-1940)
    Amer. dancer
    Cur. Biog. '40 p319,por.

Galli-Campi, Amri (fl. 1920's-1930's)
    Amer. Singer
    Ewen—Living p128-129,por.
    McCoy—Portraits p55,por.

Galli-Curci, Amelita (1889-1963)
    It. singer
    Davidson—Treas. p108-111,por.
    Ewen—Ency. p168
    Ewen—Living p129-130,por.
    Hammerton p632,por.
    McCoy—Portraits p55,por.
    Pleasants—Great p289-292,por.
    *Ulrich—Famous p79-86,por.
    Wagnalls—Opera p1-13,por.
    Wagner—Prima p241-242

Galli-Marie, Marie Célestine De L'Isle
        (1840-1905)
    Fr. singer
    Ewen—Ency. p168-169
    Lahee—Famous p114-115

Galloway, Anne (fl.1700's)
    Amer. colonial religious worker
    Jones—Quakers p293-294,310

Galloway, Irene Otillia (1908-   )
    Amer. army officer
    Cur. Biog. '53 p214-215,por.
    Cur. Biog. '63 p144

Gallup, Anna Billings (1872-1956)
    Amer. museum curator
    Women—Achieve. p83,por.

Gam, Rita (1928-   )
    Amer. actress
    CR '59 p279,por.
    CR '63 p229,por.

Gamelin, Mother (1800-1851)
    Can. foundress
    Code—Great p329-357

Gammons, Ethel Thirza (fl. 1930's)
    Amer. banker
    Women—Achieve. p198

Gandhi, Indira Priyadarshini Nehru (1917-)
    Ind. government official
    Cur. Biog. '59 p144-145,por.
    Cur. Biog. '66 p114-116,por.
    Frederick—Ten p2-16,por.
    Phelps—Men (2) '59 p104-105
    Time Jan.28,1966 p24-26,31-32,por.
        (Cover)

Gandhi, Kasturbai Nakanji (c. 1869-1944)
    Ind., wife of Mahatma Gandhi
    Stern—Women (see index)
    Stiles—Postal p98

Gandhi, Putlibai (1841-1891)
    Ind., mother of Mahatma Gandhi
    Stern—Women p16-32,39-44

Gannett, Deborah. See Sampson, Deborah

Gannett, Mary Chase (m. 1874)
    Amer. club leader
    Logan—Part p478

Gannon, Margaret (1829-1868)
    Amer. actress
    Coad—Amer. p201,por.

Gans, Bird Stein (fl. 1930's)
    Amer. child study expert
    Women—Achieve. p159,por.

Gantt, L. Rosa H. (b. 1875)
    Amer. physician
    Lovejoy—Women p352-355
    Lovejoy—Women Phys. p205-209

Gaposchkin, Cecilia Payne.
    See Payne-Gaposchkin, Cecilia Helena

Garbo, Greta Gustaffson (1905-   )
    Swed.-Amer. actress
    Beaton—Persona p48-49,por.
    Cantor—As p94-97,por.
    Carnegie—Little p19-22,por.
    CR '59 p280-281,por.
    CR '63 p229-230,por.
    Cur. Biog. '55 p221-223,por.
    Hammerton p635,por.
    Herman—How p37,por.
    Hughes—Famous p201-221,por.
    New Yorker Mar.7,1831 p28-31,por.
        (Profiles)
    Ormsbee—Back. p219-222,por.
    *Richmond—Immig. p39-41
    Rivkin—Hello p245-253
    Rogers—Women p175,por.
    Schickel—Stars p79,82,85-87,por.

Garbousova, Raya (1909-   )
    Russ. cellist
    Ewen—Living p131-132,por.
    McCoy—Portraits p56,por.
    Saleski—Jewish p423-424,por.
    Saleski—Wander. p273,por.

Garcia, Maria-Felicita ("Malibran") (1808-
1836)
　　Fr. singer
　　Mayne—Enchant. p228-240,por.

Garcia Montes, Teresa (1880-1930)
　　Cub. musician, foundress
　　Stiles—Postal p99

Garden, Mary (1877-1967)
　　Scot.-Amer. singer
　　Adelman—Famous p317-318
　　CR '59 p281,por.
　　Davidson—Treas. p111-116
　　Downes—Olin p41-43
　　Ewen—Ency. p170-171
　　Ewen—Living p132-133,por.
　　Hammerton p635
　　Lahee—Grand (see index), por.
　　Logan—Part p779
　　McCoy—Portraits p56,por.
　　New Yorker Dec.11,1926 p31-33,por.
　　　(Profiles)
　　Pleasants—Great p308-313,por.
　　Time Dec.15,1930 p24,por. (Cover)
　*Ulrich—Famous p61-66,por.
　　Wagenknecht—Seven p161-179,por.
　　Wagnalls—Opera p110-118,por.
　　Wagner—Prima p86-89,242

Gardener, Helen Hamilton (1853-1925)
　　Amer. feminist, social reformer
　　Irwin—Angels p374

Gardiner, Deborah.
　　See Putnam, Deborah Lothrop

Gardner, Adaline (fl. 1860's)
　　Ger.-Amer. Civil war patriot
　　Logan—Part p498

Gardner, Anna (fl. 1770's-1780's)
　　Amer. lecturer, poet
　　Hanaford—Dau. p262,341

Gardner, Ava (1923-　　)
　　Amer. actress
　　CR '59 p282,por.
　　CR '63 p230,por.
　　Cur. Biog. '65 p153-155,por.
　　Schickel—Stars p231,por.
　　Time Sept.3,1951 p68,por.(Cover)

Gardner, Bertha (fl. 1860's)
　　Amer. Civil war patriot
　　Logan—Part p498

Gardner, Eliza Ann (1831-1922)
　　Amer. club leader
　　Brown—Home. p117-118

Gardner, Elizabeth Jane.
　　See Bouguereau, Elizabeth, Jane

Gardner, Elsa (fl. 1930's-1940's)
　　Amer. Navy aeronautical engineer
　　Planck—Women p218-220

Gardner, Helen (fl. 1910's)
　　Amer. actress
　　Wagenknecht—Movies p26-27,46-47,
　　por.

Gardner, Isabel Stewart (1840-1924)
　　Amer. social leader
　　Amory—Proper p129-138,182,243-244,
　　255
　　Ross—Charmers p137-172,290-292,por.

Gardner, Mary Fryer (fl. 1860's)
　　Amer. Civil war nurse
　　Logan—Part p366

Gardner, Mary Sewall (fl. 1900's-1930's)
　　Amer. public health nurse, author
　　Dolan—Goodnow's p316,por.
　　Pennock—Makers p70,por.

Gardner, Maude Elsa (1894-　　)
　　Amer. aeronautical engineer
　　Goff—Women p113-115

Gardner, Pearl (b. 1881)
　　Amer. religious worker, editor
　　Phillips—33 p168-172

Garfield, Eliza Ballou (fl. 1830's)
　　Amer., mother of James A. Garfield
　　Hampton—Our p155-163
　　Hanaford—Dau. p639-640,por.
　　Logan—Part p274
　　Peyton—Mothers p113-120

Garfield, Lucretia Rudolph (1833-1918)
　　Amer., wife of James A. Garfield
　　Farmer—What p96-98,por.
　　Gerlinger—Mis. p65-67,por.
　　Hanaford—Dau. p105-107,por.
　　Jensen—White p120-121,por.
　　Logan—Ladies p113-117
　　Logan—Part p272-274
　*McConnell—Our p205-212,por.
　　Prindiville—First p169-174
　*Ross—Know p43,por.
　　Smith—Romances p274-283,por.
　　Truett—First p50-51,por.

Garibaldi, Anita Riveira de Silva (1807/20-
1849)
　　It. heroine, soldier
　　Arsenius—Dict. p74
　　Phila.—Women, unp.,por.
　　Schmidt—400 p260-261,por.
　　Stiles—Postal p100

Garland, Judy (1922-1969)
　　Amer. singer, actress
　　Beaton—Persona p49-50,por.
　　Cantor—As p127-129,por.
　　CR '59 p283-284,por.
　　CR '63 p231-232,por.
　　Cur. Biog. '41 p317-318,por.
　　Cur. Biog. '52 p204-207,por.

(Continued)

Garland, Judy—*Continued*

Donaldson—Radio p14
Schickel—Stars p138,por.
Stambler—Ency. p86-87,por.
Zierold—Child p107-177,por.

Garms, Shirley Rudolph (1924-   )
Amer. bowler
*Jacobs—Famous p38-44,por.

Garner, Elvira Carter (1895-   )
Amer. illustrator, author
Mahony—Illus. p310

Garner, Florence (m. 1891)
Amer. heiress
Eliot—Heiresses p153-157,por.
Pearson—Pilgrim p221-224

Garnerin, Elisa (fl. 1790's)
Fr. pioneer ballonist, parachutist
Earhart—Fun p197-198
*Lauwick—Heroines p23-24
*May—Women p46-48
Planck—Women p5

Garnerin, Jeanne Genieve (fl. 1790's)
Fr. pioneer aeronaut
Earhart—Fun p194-195

Garnet, Sarah J. Smith Tompkins (1831-1911)
Amer. teacher
Brown—Home. p110-116,por.

Garnett, Eve (fl. 1940's)
Eng. illustrator, painter
Mahony—Illus. p310

Garnett, Mrs. James M. (fl. 1820's)
Amer. teacher
Dexter—Career p15-16

Garrett, Eliza Clark (1805-1855)
Amer. philanthropist
Deen—Great p391-392
Logan—Part p540-542
Schmidt—400 p9-10,por.

Garrett, Elizabeth.
See Anderson, Elizabeth Garrett

Garrett, Mary E. (d. 1915)
Amer. philanthropist
Adelman—Famous p249-250

Garrett, Millicent.
See Fawcett, Millicent Garrett

Garrido y Agudo, Maria de la Soledad (fl. 1870's)
Sp. painter
Waters—Women p138

Garrigues, Malvina (1825-1904)
Ger. singer
Peasants—Great p229-230,p232-233,por.

Garrison, Adele (fl. 1910's)
Amer. journalist
Ross—Ladies p467-468

Garrison, Helen Eliza Benson (1811-1876)
Amer., wife of William Lloyd Garrison
Hanaford—Dau. p375-376

Garrison, Jane Wilson (fl. 1930's)
Amer. museum curator
Women—Achieve. p122,por.

Garrison, Mabel (1886-1963)
Amer. singer
McCoy—Portraits p56,por.

Garrison, Theodosia (b. 1874)
Amer. poet
Cook—Our p219-220
Smith—Women's p74

Garson, Greer (1908-   )
Irish-Amer. actress
CR '59 p285,por.
CR'63 p233,por.
Cur. Biog. '42 p289-292,por.
Schickel—Stars p220,por.
Time Dec.20,1943 p54,por.(Cover)

Garst, Shannon (1899-   )
Amer. author
Cur. Biog. '47 p232-233,por.

Gartner, Louise Frankfurt (n.d.)
Amer. fashion designer
Epstein—Young p71-87

Gasaway, Alice Elizabeth (fl. 1930's)
Amer. lecturer
Women—Achieve p172,por.

Gasch, Marie Manning.
See Fairfax, Beatrice

Gaskell, Elizabeth Cleghorne Stevenson (1810-1865)
Eng. novelist
Adelman—Famous p152-153
Bald—Women p100-161
Dorland—Sum p16,195
*Green—Authors p27-32
Hammerton p639,por.
*Humphrey—Elizabeths p130-146
Johnson—Women p152-163
Love—Famous p16
*MacVeagh—Champlin p246
Oliphant—Women p117-145
Stebbins—Victorian p95-128,213

Gasparotti, Elizabeth. See Seifert, Elizabeth

Gasque, Bessie Hawley (fl. 1930's)
   Amer. congresswoman
   Paxton—Women p128

Gassion, Giovanna. See Piaf, Edith

Gasso y Vidal, Leopolda (fl. 1870's-1880's)
   Sp. painter
   Waters—Women p138-139

Gaston, Esther (fl. 1770's-1780's)
   Amer. Rev. war heroine, patriot
   Fowler—Woman p132
   Hanaford—Dau. p61-62

Gaston, Margaret (b. 1755)
   Amer. Rev. war patriot
   Ellet—Women (2) p159-165
   Green—Pioneer (3) p519-520
   Logan—Part p149-150

Gates, Edith Mildred (fl. 1930's)
   Amer. educator
   Women—Achieve. p109,por.

Gates, Lucy (c. 1880-1951)
   Amer. singer
   McCoy—Portraits p57,por.

Gates, Mary Valence (fl. 1800's)
   Eng.-Amer. pioneer
   Green—Pioneer (2) p178-181,203

Gates, Susa Young (b. 1856)
   Eng. author, feminist, genealogist
   Binheim—Women p174,por.

Gatti-Casazza, Frances Alda.
   See Alda, Frances

Gatty, Margaret ("Aunt Judy") (1807/09-
   1873)
   Eng. author
   Dorland—Sum p44,188
   *Green—Authors p76-77,80-81
   Hammerton p639-640

Gaunt, Mary (fl. 1930's)
   Brit. author
   Hammerton p640

Gauthier, Eva (1885/86-1958)
   Can. singer
   Ewen—Living p135
   McCoy—Portraits p57,por.

Gautier, Felisa Rincón de (1897-   )
   Puert. Ric. politician
   CR '59 p286,por.
   CR '63 p234,por.
   Cur. Biog. '56 p205-206,por.

Gautier, Madame (fl. 1850's)
   Amer. W. pioneer
   Sargent—Pioneers p15,18

Gaver, Mary Virginia (1906-   )
   Amer. librarian, educator,
   organization official
   Cur. Biog. '66 p122-124,por.

Gaw, Ethelean Tyson (fl. 1900's-1920's)
   Amer. poet, playwright
   Smith—Women's p80

Gay, Delphine (1804-1855)
   Fr. author
   Hammerton p659
   Watson—Some p149-179,por.

Gay, Maisie (b. 1883)
   Eng. actress
   Hammerton p642

Gay, Maria (1879-1943)
   Sp. singer
   Lahee—Grand p272-275,303,384,416,
   por.
   McCoy—Portraits p57,por.

Gay, Marie Françoise Sophie (1776-1852)
   Fr. author, musician
   Dorland—Sum p54,197

Gay, Mary Ann Harris (b. 1829)
   Amer. Civil war diarist
   Andrews—Women p303-335
   Jones—Heroines p329-335,345-348

Gay, Zhenya (1906-   )
   Amer. author, illustrator
   Mahony—Illus. p310

Gaylord, Katherine Cole (1745-1840)
   Amer. Rev. patriot, heroine
   Green—Pioneer (3) p409-415
   Root—Chapter p375-394

Gaylord, Sabra. See Bissell, Sabra Trumbull

Gaynor, Janet (1906-   )
   Amer. actress
   CR '59 p286-287,por.
   CR '63 p234-235,por.
   Hammerton p643
   Hughes—Famous p222-242,por.
   Newquist—Show. p123-133,por.
   Schickel—Stars p76-77,por.
   Wagenknecht—Movies p218-219

Gaynor, Jessie Lovel (1863-1921)
   Amer. composer, song-writer
   Elson—Woman's p208
   Howard—Our p564-565
   McCoy—Portraits p57,por.

Gaynor, Mitzi (1931-   )
   Amer. actress
   CR '59 p287,por.
   CR '63 p235,por.

Gazley, Martha (fl. 1730's)
Amer. colonial manufacturer,
teacher, needlewoman
Dexter—Colonial p92-93

Geddes, Barbara Bel (1922-   )
Amer. actress
Beaton—Persona p19,por.
Blum—Great p139,por.
CR '59 p63,por.
CR '63, p44,por.
Cur. Biog. '48 238-240,por.
Time April 9,1951 p78,por. (Cover)

Geddes, Janet (fl. 1630's-1660's)
Scot. covenanter
Anderson—Ladies p14
Hammerton p643

Geefs, Fanny Isabelle Marie (1814-1883)
Belg. painter
Waters—Women p139

Geer, Augusta Danforth (m. 1856)
Amer. club leader
Logan—Part p460-461

Geer, Charlotte Clark (fl. 1800's)
Amer. W. pioneer
Ellet—Pioneer p350-360

Geiger, Emily (fl. 1760's-1770's)
Amer. Rev. war heroine
Ellet—Women (2) p341-342
Fowler—Woman p138-139
Green—Pioneer (2) p256-265,343,por.
Hanaford—Dau. p60
Logan—Part p175-176

Geiringer, Hilda (fl. 1960's)
Amer. space scientist
*May—Women p243-244

Geistinger, Marie (1836-1904)
Aust. actress, singer
Schmidt—400 p49-50,por.

Gelder, Lucia van (1864-1899)
Ger. artist
Waters—Women p139-140

Gellhaus, Olga E. (fl. 1930's)
Amer. journalist
Ross—Ladies p453-454

Gellhorn, Martha (1908-   )
Amer. novelist
Warfel—Amer. p172-173,por.

Genauer, Emily (fl. 1930's)
Amer. journalist, art critic, editor
Women—Achieve. p93,por.

Genée (or Genée-Isitt), **Adeline** (b. 1878)
Dan. ballet dancer
Davidson—Ballet p102-108
Hammerton p644-645,por.

Genet, Cornelia (m. 1774)
Amer. pioneer
Green—Pioneer (3) p302

Genet, Marianne (fl. 1900's)
Amer. composer, organist
McCoy—Portraits p58,por.

Genevieve (Ginette Auger) (1930-   )
Fr. singer, restaurant manager
CR '59 p287,por.
CR '63 p236,por.

Genevieve (c422-c512)
Fr. saint
Adelman—Famous p29-30
Culver—Women p79
Deen—Great p318
Englebert—Lives p4-5
Hammerton p645
Muir—Women p60-62
Schmidt—400 p171,por.
Sharkey—Pop. p54
Wescott—Calen. p1-2

Genevieve of Brabant, Duchess of Brabant
(fl. 8th cent.)
Belg. saint, wife of Siegfried
Phila.—Women, unp.,por.

Genlis, Sephanie Felicité du Crest de Saint-
Aubin, Comtesse de (1746-1830)
Fr. author, educator
Adelman—Famous p113-114
Benson—Women p81-84
Dobson—Four p107-207
Kavanagh—Woman (2) p34-42,59-60,
91

Genth, Lillian Matilde (c. 1876-1953)
Amer. painter
Bryant—Amer. p215-216
Michigan—Biog. p130-131
Women—Achieve. p78,por.

Gentileschi, Artemisia (1590-1642)
It. painter
Waters—Women p140-141

Gentle, Alice (1888-1958)
Amer. singer
McCoy—Portraits p58,por.

Gentry, Helen (gr. 1922)
Amer. printer
Club—Printing p26-27

Gentry, Viola (1900-   )
Amer. aviatrix
Earhart—Fun p148
Heinmuller—Man's p328,por.
*May—Women p92,186,por.

Geoffrin, Marie Thérèse Rodet (1669-1757)
Fr. salonist, literature patron

(Continued)

Geoffrin, Marie—*Continued*

    Blei—Fasc. p154-158,por.
    Dorland—Sum p33,105-106
    Kavanagh—Women (1) p193-204
    Russell—Glit. p161
    Tallentyre—Women p40-61,por.

George, Anna E. (fl. 1920's)
    Amer. composer, pianist
    McCoy—Portraits p58,por.

George, Mrs. E. E. (fl. 1860's)
    Amer. Civil war humanitarian,
      nurse
    Brockett—Woman's p511-513
    Moore—Women p333-340

George, Grace (1878/80-1961)
    Amer. actress, playwright
    Blum—Great p26,por.
    Dodd—Celeb. p352-356
    Izard—Heroines p359-360
    Mantle—Contemp. p311

George, Zelma Watson (1903-   )
    Amer. sociologist, singer
    Cur. Biog. '61 p171-173,por.

Georges, Marguerite Josephine (1787-1867)
    Fr. actress
    Adelman—Famous p146
    Collins—Great p217-241,por.

Georgia (or Georgette)
    Fr. saint
    Englebert—Lives p64

Georgiana, Duchess of Devonshire (d. 1806)
    Eng., aunt of Caroline Lamb
    Iremonger—And p211-220,por.

Georgiou, Vilma (n.d.)
    Ger. singer
    Matz—Opera p8-11,por.

Geraldine (m. 1938)
    Alb. queen
    Phila.—Women unp.,por.
    Stiles—Postal p102

Gerberding, Elizabeth (b. 1857)
    Amer. social reformer, sociologist
    Logan—Part p599

Gere, Florence Parr (fl. 1940's)
    Amer. composer, pianist
    McCoy—Portraits p58,por.

Gerhardt, Elena (1883-1961)
    Ger. singer
    Ewen—Living p136,por.
    Hammerton p649-650
    McCoy—Portraits p58,por.

Germain, Sophie (1776-1831)
    Fr. mathematician
    Coolidge—Six p26-29
    Mozans—Woman p154-157

Germain (or German) sisters (fl. 1870's)
    Amer. Ind. captives
    Johnson—Some p22-34,por.

Gerould, Katharine Fullerton (1879-1944)
    Amer. author
    °Millett—Amer. p372-373
    O'Brien—50 p857

Gerrard, Miss (fl. 19th cent.)
    Eng. actress
    Furniss—Some p53

Gerrish-Jones, Abbie (1863-1929)
    Amer. composer, author, critic
    Hipsher—Amer. p242-247
    McCoy—Portraits p59,por.

Gerry, Ann Thompson (1763-1849)
    Irish-Amer. patriot, pioneer
    Green—Pioneer (3) p83-86

Gerson, Virginia (c. 1864-1951)
    Amer. illustrator, author
    Mahony—Illus. p312

Gerson-Kiwi, Edith (n.d.)
    Ger.-Israeli musicologist, pianist,
      harpsichordist, lecturer
    Saleski—Jewish p713-714

Gerster, Etelka (1855-1920)
    Hung. singer
    Adelman—Famous p267
    Ewen—Ency. p173
    Lahee—Famous p201-209
    McCoy—Portraits p59,por.
    Wagner—Prima p60,74-79,242

Gertrude of Nivelles (626-659)
    Belg. saint
    Englebert—Lives p106
    Hammerton p650
    Phila.—Women, unp.,por.
    Stiles—Postal p234

Gertrude the Great (1256-1301)
    Ger. saint
    Culver—Women p101
    Deen—Great p330-331
    Englebert—Lives p434-435
    Hammerton p650

Gertrude van der Oosten (d. 1358)
    Nether. mystic, saint
    Englebert—Lives p8

Gerville-Réache, Jeanne (1882-1915)
    Fr. singer
    Ewen—Ency. p173-174
    Lahee—Grand p190-196,por.
    McCoy—Portraits p59,por.

Gervis, Ruth Streatfield (1894-   )
Eng. illustrator, teacher
Mahony—Illus. p312-313

Gescheidt, Adelaide (fl. 1940's)
Amer. musician, vocal teacher
McCoy—Portraits p59,por.

Gesmerais, Marie.
See Youville, Marie Marguerite

Gessler de Lacroix, Alejandrena (Madame Anselma) (fl. 1880's)
Sp. painter
Waters—Women p141

Gest, Elizabeth (fl. 1940's)
Amer. composer, pianist
Howard—Our p582
McCoy—Portraits p59,por.

Gestefeld, Ursula Newell (fl. 1890's)
Amer. religious leader
Logan—Part p855

Getchell, Donnie Campbell (fl. 1930's)
Amer. educator
Women—Achieve. p198

Gethin, Grace Norton, Lady (1676-1697)
Eng. essayist, moralist
Stenton—English p234-235

Gheen, Celeste (1914-   )
Amer. fashion model
New Yorker Sept.14,1941 p24-28,por. (Profiles)

Ghika, Elena. See d'Istria, Dora, pseud.

Ghosal, Mrs. (1857-1932)
Ind. author
Hammerton p651

Giannini, Dusolina (1902-   )
Amer. singer
Ewen—Ency. p174-175
Ewen—Living p137-138,por.
McCoy—Portraits p59,por.
Women—Achieve. p198

Gibbes, Mary Ann (fl. 1770's)
Amer. Rev. war heroine, patriot
Farmer—What p155
Hanaford—Dau. p62

Gibbes, Sarah Reeve (1746-1825)
Amer. Rev. war heroine
Ellet—Women (1) p239-253
Logan—Part p169-172

Gibbons, Abigail Hopper (1801-1893)
Amer. Civil war philanthropist, nurse, feminist, journalist
Adelman—Famous p149
Brockett—Woman's p467-476
Dorland—Sum p37,83,124

Gibbons, Marie Raymond (m. 1871)
Amer. club leader
Logan—Part p478-479

Gibbs, Ann (fl. 1660's-1680's)
Brit. actress
MacQueen—Pope p43

Gibbs, Florence R. (fl. 1940's)
Amer. Congresswoman
Paxton—Women p129

Gibbs, Georgia (n.d.)
Amer. singer
CR '59 p288-289,por.
CR '63 p237,por.
Popular Record p56,por.
TV—Person (3) p101,por.

Gibbs, Mrs. (fl. 1670's)
Eng. actress, sister of Anne Shadwell (?)
Wilson—All p145

Gibbs, Willa (1917-   )
Amer. novelist
Warfel—Amer. p173-174,por.

Giberne, Agnes (b. 1845)
Brit. author
Hammerton p653

Gibson, Althea (1927-   )
Amer. tennis player
*Cherry—Portraits p170-173
CR '59 p289,por.
CR '63 p237, por.
Cur. Biog. '57 p203-204,por.
*Forsee—Women p56-80
Robinson—Hist. p194-195,por.
Time, Aug.26,1957 p44,por.(Cover)

Gibson, Anna L. (fl. 1940's)
Amer. nurse, author
Pennock—Makers p111,por.

Gibson, Mrs. E. O. (fl. 1860's)
Amer. Civil War nurse
Brockett—Woman's p396,399

Gibson, Margaret Dunlop (1843-1920)
Eng. archaeologist
Hammerton p654
Mozans—Woman p327-333

Gibson, Virginia (n.d.)
Amer. singer, actress
TV—Person. (3) p94-95,por.

Gideon, Miriam (1906-   )
Amer. composer
Ewen—American p103,por.
Reis—Composers p139-140

Giese, Lulu Gable (fl. 1930's)
Amer. poet
Women—Achieve. p141,por.

Giffin, Etta Josselyn (1863-1932)
Amer. librarian for blind
Logan—Part p698-699

Gifford, Chloe (n.d.)
Amer. educator, organization
official
Cur. Biog. '59 p149-150,por.

Gifford, Fannie Stearns Davis (b. 1884)
Amer. poet
Smith—Women's p83

Gifford, Susan A. (b. 1826)
Amer. social reformer
Hanaford—Dau. p386-387

Gilbert, Anne Hartley (1821-1904)
Amer. actress
Adelman—Famous p207
Dorland—Sum p40,80,165

Gilbert, Deborah. See Champion, Deborah

Gilbert, Florence (fl. 1930's)
Eng. ballad composer
Elson—Woman's p151

Gilbert, Mrs. G. H. ("Grandma") (1822-1904)
Amer. actress
Coad—Amer. p243,por.

Gilbert, Ina Claire.
See Claire, Ina Fagan

Gilbert, Linda (1847-1895)
Amer. philanthropist, prison
reformer
Dorland—Sum p32,124
Hanaford—Dau. p181
Holbrook—Dreamers p254-255

Gilbert, Marie Dolores Eliza Rosanna.
See Montez, Lola

Gilbreth, Lillian Evelyn Moller (1878-   )
Amer. engineer
*Boynick—Pioneers p150-177
*Clymer—Modern p1-11,por.
Cur. Biog. '40 p336-337,por.
Cur. Biog. '51 p233-235,por.
*Fleischman—Careers p166
Goff—Women p116-132
Jensen—Revolt p102,por.
*Logie—Careers p312-326
*Logie—Careers (2nd) p79-87
*Stoddard—Top. p88-99
*Watson—Engineers p139-142,por.
Women—Achieve. p54,por.
*Yost—Women Sci. p99-121

Gilchrist, Anne (1828-1885)
Amer. author
Winwar—Poor p200-202,306-309

Gilchrist, Constance (Connie), Countess of
Orkney (1865-1946)
Eng. actress, dancer
Wyndham—Chorus p88-92,por.

Gilder, Jeanette Leonard (fl. 1870's-1880's)
Amer. critic, editor, journalist,
author
Dorland—Sum p115-171
Logan—Part p867-868

Gilder, Rosamond (n.d.)
Amer. editor, author, drama critic
Cur. Biog. '45 p237-239,por.
Women—Achieve. p198

Gildersleeve, Virginia Crocheron (1877-1965)
Amer. educator
*Clymer—Modern p12-21
Cur. Biog. '40 p337-338,por.
Cur. Biog. '41 p319-320,por.
Cur. Biog. '65 p163
Fleming—Great p145-157
Logan—Part p732
Time Oct.8'34 p59,por.(Cover)
Women—Achieve. p53,por.

Gilead's wife (Biblical)
Deen—All p324-325

Giles, Hannah Kilty.
See Chase, Hannah Kilty

Giles, Janice Holt (1909-   )
Amer. author
Cur. Biog. '58 p162-163,por.

Giles, Miss (Mrs. Bernard Jenkin)
Eng. sculptor
Waters—Women p141

Gilfert, Mrs. Charles (fl. 1810's)
Amer. actress
Coad—Amer. p72,por.

Gill, Elizabeth Mary (fl. 1870's-1880's)
Amer. business woman
Hanaford—Dau. p615-616

Gill, Jocelyn R. (n.d.)
Amer. space scientist
Poole—Astronauts p29,33-34,38,40-43,
por.

Gill, Margery (1925-   )
Eng. illustrator
Ryder—Artists p77

Gillespie, Eliza Maria (1824-1887)
Amer. abbess, educator
Logan—Part p724

Gillespie, Jean (n.d.)
Amer. TV actress
TV—Person. (1) p13,por.

Gillespie, Marian (1) (fl. 1930's)
    Amer. explorer, photographer,
        editor, author
    Women—Achieve. p102,por.

Gillespie, Marian (2) (1889-1946)
    Amer. composer, pianist, author,
        actress, journalist
    ASCAP p182

Gillett, Fidelia Woolley (fl. 1780's-1880's)
    Amer. clergyman
    Hanaford—Dau. p451

Gillett sisters (fl. 1860's-1880's)
    Amer. farm managers, business
        women
    Logan—Part p894-896

Gillette, Martha Taylor (fl. 1930's)
    Amer. engineer, draftsman
    Women—Achieve. p189,por.

Gillham, Elizabeth. See Enright, Elizabeth

Gilian (1340 A.D.)
    It. saint
    *Windham—Sixty p293-294

Gillies, Betty Huyler (fl. 1920's-1930's)
    Amer. aviatrix
    Earhart—Fun p150
    *May—Women p149-150,167,185-186,
        por.
    *Peckham—Women p3

Gillies, Pat (fl. 1950's)
    Amer. aviatrix
    *May—Women p186

Gillis, Fay (fl. 1920's)
    Amer. aviatrix
    Planck—Women p117-118

Gillis, Pearl (n.d.)
    Amer. mother of 1949
    Davis—Mothers p100-104

Gilman, Caroline Howard (1794-1888)
    Amer. author, editor
    Hanaford—Dau. p227,256-257,696
    Jones—Heroines p16-17
    Papashvily—All p41-43

Gilman, Charlotte Perkins (1860-1935)
    Amer. author, lecturer, feminist,
        social reformer
    Adelman—Famous p295
    Beard—Women p26-28
    Bruère—Laugh. p204-205
    Logan—Part p873
    Love—Famous p10
    Riegel—Amer. p163-173,por.
    Rogers—Women p36-37,por.
    Smith—Women's p87
    Wellington—Women p113-131,por.

Gilman, Mabelle (or Mabella) (fl. 1890's)
    Amer. actress, singer
    Strang—Prima p56-66,por.

Gilman, Mary C. (fl. 1900's)
    Amer. club leader
    Logan—Part p355

Gilman, Mary L. (m. 1870)
    Amer. philanthropist
    Logan—Part p533-534

Gilman, Mary Rebecca Foster (b. 1859)
    Amer. author
    Logan—Part p850

Gilman, Mildred (fl. 1930's)
    Amer. journalist, author
    Ross—Ladies p246-251

Gilmer, Elizabeth Meriwether.
    See Dix, Dorothy, pseud.

Gilmer, Louisa Fredericka (fl. 1860's)
    Amer. Civil war diarist, wife of
        Jeremy F. Gilmer
    Jones—Heroines p93-94

Gilmer, Loulie (fl. 1860's)
    Amer. Civil war diarist, dau. of
        Jeremy F. Gilmer
    Jones—Heroines p93-94

Gilmore, Elizabeth McCabe (b. 1874)
    Amer. author, publisher, critic
    ASCAP p182

Gilmore, Florence MacGruder (b. 1881)
    Amer. philanthropist, author
    Logan—Part p534

Gilmore, Gladys Chase (fl. 1930's)
    Amer. teacher, business executive
    Women—Achieve. p84,por.

Gilmore, Marion Sprague (fl. 1930's)
    Amer. dietician
    *Ferris—Girls p153-163

Gilmour, Ellen (fl. 1960's)
    Amer. helicopter pilot
    *May—Women p209,por.

Gilmour, Sally (1921-   )
    Brit. ballet dancer
    Davidson—Ballet p109-111

Gilpin, Mrs. Henry D. (fl. 1900's)
    Amer. social leader
    Hanaford—Dau. p146-147
    Logan—Part p287

Gilson, Helen Louise (1835-c. 1868)
    Amer. Civil war nurse
    Brockett—Woman's p133-148

(Continued)

Gilson, Helen Louise—*Continued*

Bruce—Woman p209-212
Hanaford—Dau. p200-203
Logan—Part p331-333
Young—Women p179,213-214,372

Gilson, Mary Barnett (b. 1877)
Amer. economist
Hazeltine—We p26-33

Gimbel, Sophie (1902-   )
Amer. fashion designer
CR '63 p239,por.
Time Sept.15,1947 p87,por.(Cover)

Ginassi, Catterina (b. 1590)
It. painter
Waters—Women p141-142

Gingold, Hermione (1897-   )
Eng. actress
CR '59 p291,por.
CR '63 p240,por.
Cur. Biog. '58 p165-167,por.

Ginner, Ruby (b. 1886)
Eng. dancer
Hammerton p657

Ginster, Ria (1898-   )
Ger. singer
Ewen—Living p140-141,por.
McCoy—Portraits p61,por.

Gioconda, Lisa Gherardini (b. 1474)
It. beauty
Adelman—Famous p44-45

**Giovanna, Elisabetta Antonia Romana
    Maria (1907-   )**
Belg. queen
Arsenius—Dict. p77,por.
Phila.—Women, unp.por.
Stiles—Postal p103

Gipson, Elsie (fl. 1930's)
Amer. aviation instructor
Planck—Women p165

Girardet, Berthe (b. 1867)
Fr. sculptor
Waters—Women p142-143

Giradin, Delphine Gay de.
See Gay, Delphine

Gisela (or Gizella) (m. 995)
Hung. saint
Arsenius—Dict. p173
Phila.—Women, unp.,por.
Stiles—Postal p234

Gisela (or Isberge) (d.c. 807)
Fr. saint
Engelbert—Lives p197-198

Gish, Dorothy (c. 1898-1968)
Amer. actress
Blum—Great p113,por.
CR '59 p291,por.
CR '63 p240,por.
Cur. Biog. '68 p455
Cur. Biog. '44 p238-242,por.
Hammerton p659
Wagenknecht—Movies p224-225,por.

Gish, Lillian (c. 1896-   )
Amer. actress
Blum—Great p114,por.
Cocroft—Great p93-101,por.
CR '59 p291-292,por.
CR '63 p241,por.
Cur. Biog. '44 p238-242,por.
Hammerton p659-660
Talmey—Doug. p67-73,por.
Wagenknecht—Movies p116-117,126-
    128,246-256,por.

Gist, Malvina Black (b. 1842)
Amer. Civil war diarist
Jones—Heroines p356-360,375-383

Gitana, Gertie (fl. 1910's)
Eng. singer
Felstead—Stars p43,169-170

Giuliani, Veronica.
See Veronica Giuliani, Saint

Given, Thelma (1898-   )
Amer. violinist
McCoy—Portraits p61,por.

Glade, Coe (1906-   )
Amer. singer
McCoy—Portraits p61,por.

**Gladstone, Catherine Glynne (c. 1813-
    1900)**
Eng., wife of William Gladstone
Corkran—Romance p87-92,por.
Guedalla—Bonnet p41-65,por.
Iremonger—And p142-171,por.
Lee—Wives p156-217,por.

Gladwin, Mary E. (d. 1939)
Amer. World war I nurse
DAR Mag. Nov.1921 p646,por.
Pennock—Makers p67-68,por.

Gladys (fl. 5th cent.)
Welsh saint
*Windham—Sixty p137-143

Glantzberg, Pinckney L. (fl. 1920's-1930's)
Amer. lawyer
Women—Achieve. p135,por.

Glaser, Lulu (b. 1874)
Amer. actress
Caffin—Vaud. p78,por.
Strang—Prima p120-133,por.

Glasgow, Ellen Anderson Gholson (1874-
1945)
Amer. author
Adelman—Famous p315
Auchincloss—Pion. p56-91
Burnett—This p1138-1139
Clark—Innocence p55-69,por.
Cooper—Authors p23-27
*Cournos—Famous p172-173
Cur. Biog. '46 p212
Hammerton p662
Harkins—Famous p315-329,por.
Harkins—Little p315-329,por.
Jessup—Faith p34-53,122-125
Lawrence—School p290-293
Logan—Part p807
Loggins—Hear p188-194
Maurice—Makers p3,por.
*Millett—Amer. p42-43,374-376
Morgan—Writers p42-59
Overton—Women p157-166
Rogers—Women p108,por.
Scherman—Literary p123
Smith—Women's p93
Van Doren p132-134
Van Gelder—Writers p319-323
Wellington—Women p157-173

Glaspell, Susan (1882-1948)
Amer. author
Adelman—Famous p322
Gould—Modern p26-49,por.
Hammerton p662
Mantle—Amer. p285
Mantle—Contemp. p48-50
Millett—Amer. p376-377
Warfel—Amer. p174-175,por.

Glass, Mrs. (fl. 1780's)
Amer. W. pioneer
Ellet—Pioneer p118-120

Glaz, Herta (1914-   )
Aust. singer
Ewen—Ency. p180
Ewen—Living p141-142,por.
McCoy—Portraits p61,por.
Matz—Opera p177-179,por.
Peltz—Spot. p99
Saleski—Jewish p586,por.

Gleason, Rachel Brooks (1820-1905)
Amer. physician
Mead—Medical p44-45

Gleeson, Evelyn (fl. 1900's)
Irish printer
Club—Printing p16

Gleichen, Feodora Georgina Maud, Countess
(1861-1922)
Eng. sculptor
Waters—Women p144

Gleitze, Mercedes (1901-   )
Eng. swimmer
Hammerton p662

Glen, Katherine (fl. 1940's)
Amer. pianist
McCoy—Portraits p62,por.

Glendenning, Mrs. (fl. c. 1760's)
Amer. Ind. captive, pioneer
Fowler—Woman p87-88

Glenn, Carroll (c. 1922-   )
Amer. violinist
McCoy—Portraits p62,por.

Glenn, Mabelle (fl. 1940's)
Amer. music educator, author
McCoy—Portraits p62,por.

Glenn, Mary Wilcox (1869-1940)
Amer. social welfare leader
Cur. Biog. '40 p339

Glennon, Nan (fl. 1960's)
Amer. space scientist, mechanical
engineer, rocket designer
*May—Women p243

Glick, Virginia. See Kirkus, Virginia

Gloag, Isobel Lilian (fl. 1900's)
Eng. painter
Waters—Women p145-146

Glover, Anna (fl. 1870's)
Amer. genealogist, author
Hanaford—Dau. p530

Glover, Elizabeth (fl. 1630's)
Amer. pioneer printer
Club—Printing p11

Glover, Jean (1758-1801)
Scot. song-writer, poet
Findlay—Spindle p69-76

Glover, Julia (1779-1850)
Eng. actress
MacQueen—Pope p304-305,por.

Glover, Mildred S. (fl. 1930's)
Amer. club leader
Women—Achieve. p156,por.

Glover, Sarah Ann (1785-1867)
Eng. music teacher, inventor
Hammerton p663

Gluck, Alma (Reba Fiersohn) (1884-1938)
Rum. singer
Ewen—Ency. p181
Lahee—Grand p298-301,por.
McCoy—Portraits p62,por.
Saleski—Jewish p587-589,por.
Saleski—Wander. p404-405,por.

Gluck, Barbara Elisabeth (Betty Paoli,
pseud.) (1812/15-1894)
Aust. author, critic
Heller—Studies p248

Glueck, Eleanor Touroff (1898-   )
    Amer. research criminologist
Cur. Biog. '57 p208-210,por.

Glyn, Elinor Sutherland (1864-1943)
    Eng. novelist
Cur. Biog. '43 p233
Hammerton p663,por.
Jensen—Revolt p170-171,por.
Rogers—Women p40,por.
Schickel—Stars p40,57

Glyndon, Howard.
    See Searing, Laura Catherine Redden

Glynn, Elizabeth E. (d. 1904)
    Amer. W. pioneer
Sargent—Pioneers p69-70,por.

Glynne, Mary (1898-   )
    Welsh actress
Hammerton p663-664

Gnaea Seia (fl. c. 200 A.D.)
    Rom., wife of Alexander Severus
Balsdon—Roman p163

Goatley, Alma (fl. 1940's)
    Fr. composer
McCoy—Portraits p62,por.

Gober, Belle Biard (fl. 1940's)
    Amer. composer, pianist, music
        teacher
McCoy—Portraits p62,por.

Gobulkina, Anna Semenovna (1864-1927)
    Russ. sculptor
Stiles—Postal p104

Godby, Ann (fl. 1650's)
    Amer. religious leader
Jones—Quakers' p275

Goddard, Anna (fl. 1770's)
    Amer. printer, publisher
Earle—Colon. p61-62

Goddard, Arabella (1836/38-1922)
    Eng. pianist
Elson—Women's p146
Schonberg—Great p238-239,por.

Goddard, Hannah (fl. '1770's)
    Amer. patriot, pioneer
Green—Pioneer (3) p479-480

Goddard, Mary Katherine (1736-1816)
    Amer. colonial printer, publisher,
        merchant
Club—Printing p14
Dexter—Career' p103-104,145
Dexter—Colonial p172-173
Earle—Colon. p59-60
Hanaford—Dau. p647-710
Leonard—Amer. p116
Spruill—Women's p266-267

Woody—Hist. (1) p262-263
*Yost—Famous p29-37,por.

Goddard, Paulette (1911-   )
    Amer. actress
CR '59 p293,por.
CR' '63 p242,por.
Cur. Biog. '46 (Nov.) p13-15,por.
Lamparski—What p172-173,por.
Schickel—Stars p214,por.

Goddard, Sarah Updike (d. 1770)
    Amer. colonial editor, publisher,
        printer
Brigham—Journals p77
Club—Printing p14
Dexter—Colonial p171-172
Earle—Colon. p57-58
Hanaford—Dau. p709
Leonard—Amer. p116

Godden, Rumer, pseud. (Mrs. Laurence
        Foster) (1907-   )
    Eng. novelist
CR '59 p293,por.
Fitzgibbon—My' p263-270

Godelina (b. 1049-c. 1070)
    Fr. saint
Blunt—Great p152-154

Godewyck, Margaretta (1627-1677)
    Nether. painter, linguist
Waters—Women p146

Godfrey, Daisy May (m.'1911)
    Amer. seafarer
Snow—Women p233-244

Godfrey, Kathryn Morton (n.d.)
    Amer. TV personality
TV—Person (1) p51-52,por.

Godiva (or' Godgifu), Lady (fl. 11th cent.)
    Eng. philanthropist, social reformer
Adelman—Famous p32
Armour—It p50-59
Cuppy—Decline p86-95
Hammerton p665
*MacVeagh—Champlin p253
Muir—Women p75-76
Stenton—English p5

Godolphin, Margaret Blagge (1652-1678)
    Eng. Christian
Deen—Great p369-371
Stenton—English p198-199

Godowski, Dagmar (1897-   )
    Aust.-Amer. actress
Lamparski—What. p182-183,por.

Godoy Alcayaga, Lucila.
    See Mistral, Gabriela

Godwin, Frances Bryant (1892-   )
    Amer. sculptor
    National—Contemp. p126

Godwin, Mary Wollstonecraft (1759-1797)
    Eng. author
    Adelman—Famous p96-97
    Benson—Women p60-61,85-92,98-99,
        136,172-173
    *Borer—Women p32-35,por.
    Dorland—Sum p45,136
    Douglas—Remember p52
    Hammerton p665-666,por.
    Jensen—Revolt p42-43,por.
    Johnson—Women p143-145
    Lawrence—School p14-31,por.
    MacCarthy—Later p189-196
    *MacVeagh—Champlin p535
    Orr—Famous Affin. IV p38-40
    Riegel—Amer. p8-10
    Sherman—World's p99-105
    Sitwell—Women p21-22,por.
    Stenton—English (see index)
    Wellington—Women p9-15,por.
    Woody—Hist. (1) p31,34-35,por.

Goebeler, Elise (fl. 1880's-1890's)
    Ger. artist
    Waters—Women p378-379

Goelet, May Wilson, Duchess of Roxburgh
        (m. 1903)
    Amer. heiress, social leader
    Eliot—Heiresses p99-104,por.
    Pearson—Pilgrim p219-220

Goertz, Arthémise (1905-   )
    Amer. author
    Cur. Biog. '53 p221-222,por.
    Warfel—Amer. p176,por.

Goessmann, Helena Theresa (fl. 1890's-
        1900's)
    Amer. educator, lecturer
    Logan—Part p730

Goethe, Katherina Elizabeth Textor
        (1731-1808)
    Ger. salonist, mother of
        Johann Wolfgang Goethe
    Chandler—Famous p61-77
    Hargrave—Some p1-50,por.
    Peyton—Mothers,p24-32
    Schmidt—400 p191-192,por.
    Wallace—Mothers p30-35

Goetschius, Marjorie (1915-   )
    Amer. composer, author
    ASCAP p185

Goetz, Delia (1898-   )
    Amer. author
    Cur. Biog. '49 p228-229,por.

Goff, Anna Chandler (fl. 1940's)
    Amer. music educator
    McCoy—Portraits p63,por.

Goff, Hazel A. (fl. 1910's-1930's)
    Amer. nurse
    Pennock—Makers p129,por.

Golay, Mary (fl. 1890's-1900's)
    Swiss painter
    Waters—Women p146-147

Golden, Sylvia (1900-   )
    Amer. author, editor, song-writer
    ASCAP p187

Goldfield, Gladys.
    See Schmitt, Gladys Leonore

Goldman, Emma (1869-1940)
    Russ. political leader
    Cur. Biog. '40 p339,por.
    Goldsmith—Seven p153-182
    Jensen—Revolt p83,por.
    Madison—Critics p214-237
    Rogers—Women p68,por.
    Simonhoff—Saga p202-210,por.

Goldman, Olive Remington (n.d.)
    Amer. U.N. official
    Cur. Biog. '50 p175-177,por.

Goldmark, Pauline Dorothea (fl. 1890's-
        1930's)
    Amer., welfare worker, business
        research worker
    Women—Achieve. p62,por.

Goldsmith, C. Elizabeth (fl. 1930's)
    Amer. psychologist
    Women—Achieve. p178,por.

Goldsmith, Deborah (1808-1836)
    Amer. painter
    Lipman—Primitive p90-96,por.

Goldsmith, Margaret (1897-   )
    Amer. author, journalist
    Lawrence—School p272-276

Goldsmith, Sophia (b.c. 1847)
    Bohem.-Amer. author
    Marcus—Memoirs (2) p268-280

Goldstein, Ella (1927-   )
    Palest. pianist
    Saleski—Jewish p477-478,por.

Goldstein, Kate Arlene (fl. 930's)
    Amer. fashion expert
    Women—Achieve. p140,por.

Goldstone, Aline Lewis (b.c. 1868)
    Amer. poet
    Women—Achieve, p169,por.

Goldsworthy, Phillipia Vanbrugh (c. 1716-
1777)
Brit. wife of consul
Smith—Originals p13-75,por.

Goldthwaite, Anne (c. 1875-1944)
Amer. painter, etcher, lithographer
Cur. Biog. '44 p246

Golescu, Zinca (1790-1878)
Rum. patriot
Schmidt—400 p339,por.

Gollner, Nana (1920-   )
Amer. ballet dancer
Davidson—Ballet p113-115
Terry—Star p186-188,por.

Golovina, Anastasia (d. 1932)
Bulg. physician
Lovejoy—Women p210

Golson, Florence (fl. 1940's)
Amer. composer, singer
McCoy—Portraits p63,por.

Goltz, Christel (n.d.)
Ger. singer
Rosenthal—Sopranos p44-45,por.

Gomer (Biblical)
Deen—All p263-264
Lewis—Portraits p55-56
Nelson—Bible p61-63

Gomez, Doña Josefa Acevedole (1803-1861)
Colom. author
Schmidt—400 p80-81

Gonges, Olympe de (fl. 18th cent.)
Fr. author
Kavanagh—Women (2) p216-217,252

Gonne, Maud (Maude Gonne MacBride)
(1866-1953)
Irish patriot, philanthropist,
illustrator
Mahony—Illus. p336

Gonzalez, Inés (fl. 1840's)
Sp. painter
Waters—Women p147-148

Goodall, Jane.
See Van Lawick-Goodall, Jane, Baroness

Goodbar, Octavia Walton (fl. 1930's)
Amer. artist, journalist
Women—Achieve. p102,por.

Goodell, Lavina (fl. 1870's)
Amer. lawyer
Hanaford—Dau. p663
Irwin—Angels p174-175

Goodin, Peggy (1923-   )
Amer. novelist
Warfel—Amer. p176-177,por.

Goodman, Dody (n.d.)
Amer. dancer, actress
CR '59 p298,por.

Goodman, Lillian Rosedale (b. 1888)
Amer. composer, singer, pianist,
author, linguist, critic
ASCAP p190

Goodner, Carol (fl. 1920's-1930's)
Amer. actress
Hammerton p671

Goodnow, Minnie (d. 1952)
Amer. nurse, author, educator
Dolan—Goodnow's p261,por.
Pennock—Makers p100-101,por.

Goodrich, Abigail Whittlesey (fl. 1870's)
Amer. editor
Hanaford—Dau. p702

Goodrich, Ann. See Story, Ann

Goodrich, Annie Warburton (1866-1954)
Amer. nurse, educator
Dolan—Goodnow's p309,311,313,por.
Pennock—Makers p52-53,por.
Women—Achieve. p74,por.
*Yost—Nursing p42-60

Goodrich, Florence (fl. 1940's)
Amer. composer, organ teacher
McCoy—Portraits p64,por.

Goodrich, Frances (1890-   )
Amer. actress, playwright
Cur. Biog. '56 p216-218,por.
Mantle—Contemp. p237-238

Goodrich, Frances Louisa (b. 1856)
Amer. weaver, business executive,
author
*Kirkland—Achieved p127-132

Goodrich, Mary Ann (Mary Ann Wolcott)
(b. 1765)
Amer. patriot, pioneer
Green—Pioneer (3) p108,112,por.

Goodrich, Mrs. (fl. 1820's)
Amer. W. pioneer
Ellet—Pioneer p400

Goodrich, Nelle Chatburn (b. 1875)
Amer. religious worker, pioneer
Phillips—33 p159-163

Goodridge, Ellen (fl. 1860's)
Amer. Civil war soldier
Moore—Women p532-533

Goodsell, Willystine (b. 1870)
Amer. educator, author
Women—Achieve. p158,por.

Goodson, Katherine (1872-1958)
Eng. pianist
McCoy—Portraits p64,por.

Goodwin, Amina Beatrice (1867-1942)
Eng. composer, pianist
Elson—Woman's p146

Goodwin, Sarah (fl. 1740's)
Amer. colonial business woman
Dexter—Colonial p51

Goon, Toy Len Chin (n.d.)
Chin.-Amer. mother of 1952
Davis—Mothers p105-110

Goose, Mrs. (fl. 1640's)
Amer. colonial grocer
Dexter—Colonial p218

Gordimer, Nadine (1923-   )
S. Afric. author
Cur. Biog. '59 p152-153,por.

Gordon, Anna Adams (1853-1931)
Amer. social reformer
Logan—Part p658-660
Webb—Famous p225-233,por.

Gordon, Caroline (Caroline Tate) (1895-)
Amer. novelist
Warfel—Amer. p178-179,por.

Gordon, Cyrena Van (fl. 1930's)
Amer. singer
McCoy—Portraits p64,por.

Gordon, Dorothy (n.d.)
Russ.-Amer. radio, TV personality,
author
CR '63 p248,por.
Cur. Biog. '55 p236-239,por.

Gordon, Dorothy (fl. 1940's)
Amer. singer
McCoy—Portraits p64,por.

Gordon, Edith Frances (fl. 1930's)
Amer. business executive
Women—Achieve. p167,por.

Gordon, Gertrude G., pseud.
See **Kelley, Gertrude**

Gordon, Isabel.
See **Aberdeen and Temair, Ishbel Maria
Marjoribanks Gordon,** Marchioness

Gordon, Isabella.
See **Mercer, Isabella Gordon**

Gordon, Jane, Duchess of (1749-1812)
Scot. Amazon, politician, hostess,
art and literature patron
Graham—Group p27,231-256
Thomson—Queens p229-251

Gordon, Jeanne (1893-   )
Can. singer
McCoy—Portraits p64,por.

Gordon, Julia Swayne (fl. 1900's-1910's)
Amer. actress
Wagenknecht—Movies p47

Gordon, Laura DeForce (fl. 1870's)
Amer. lawyer, lecturer, feminist
Hanaford—Dau. p344
Irwin—Angels p175
Riegel—Amer. p135

Gordon, Mazie P. (b.c. 1895)
Amer. theater owner
New Yorker Dec.21,1940 p22-26,por.
(Profiles)

Gordon, Odetta Felious. See **Odetta**

Gordon, Ruth (1896-   )
Amer. actress
Blum—Great p108,por.
CR '59 p298-299,por.
CR '63 p249,por.
Cur. Biog. '43 p238-241,por.
Time Dec.21,1942,p45,por.(Cover)

Gordon, Sallie Chapman (b. 1805)
Amer. Civil war patriot
Logan—Part p490-491

Gordon-Cumming, Constance (fl. 1870's)
Amer. author
Sargent—Pioneers p30-31,41

Gordon-Cumming, Florence Garner, Lady
(d. 1922)
Amer. heiress
Pearson—Marry. p213-216

Gore, Ann Avery (fl. 1770's)
Amer. pioneer
Green—Pioneer (3) p450

Gore, Catherine Grace Frances Moody
(1799-1861)
Eng. novelist
Dorland—Sum p48,193
Stebbins—Victorian p25-29,196-197,
207

Gore, Hannah Park (fl. 1760's)
Amer. pioneer
Green—Pioneer (3) p450-451

Gore, Margot (fl. 1940's)
Amer. aviatrix
*May—Women p143

Gore, "Widow" (fl. 1790's)
  Amer. beauty, social leader
  Amory—Proper p119-120

Gorenko, Anna Andreevna (Anna
        Akhmatova, pseud.) (b. 1888)
  Russ. poet
  Yarmolinky—Treas. p283

Goretti, Maria (1890-1902)
  It. saint
  Burton—Valiant p38-55

Gorgo of Sparta (fl. 331 B.C.)
  Gr. patriot
  Schmidt—400 p215,por.

Gormé, Eydie (1931/32-   )
  Amer. singer, TV personality
  CR '59 p299,por.
  CR '63 p249,por.
  Cur. Biog. '65 p168-170,por.
  Popular Record p58,por.
  Stambler—Ency. p94,por.

Gormlaith (Gormflaith) (d. 947/948)
  Irish queen, heroine, poet
  Concannon—Dau. p232-235
  McCraith—Romance p26-41,42-50

Gosnell, Winifred (fl. 1660's)
  Eng. actress
  Wilson—All p145-146

Goss, Margaret (fl. 1920's)
  Amer. journalist, athlete
  Ross—Ladies p468-470

Gottchalk (Gottschalk), Laura Riding.
  See Riding, Laura

Goudge, Elizabeth (1900-   )
  Eng. author
  Cur. Biog. '40 p344-345,por.

Goudy, Bertha M. 1865-1935)
  Amer. printer
  Club—Printing p17,25-26

Gougar, Helen Mar Jackson (1843-1907)
  Amer. feminist, lecturer, author
  Logan—Part p583

Gough, Jane (1817-1834)
  Brit., mother of John B. Gough
  Wallace—Mothers p48-55

Gould, Anna.
  See Talleyrand-Perigord, Anna Gould,
    Duchesse de

Gould, Beatrice Blackmar (n.d.)
  Amer. editor
  Cur. Biog. '47 p250-252,por.
  Jensen—Revolt p103,por.
  Women—Achieve. p198

Gould, Edith M. Kingdom (d. 1921)
  Amer. wife of George Jay Gould
  Jensen—Revolt p29,por.
  Tebbel—Inher. p140,por.

Gould, Elizabeth (Eliza) Coxen (1804-
        1841)
  Austral. painter
  Prout—Petticoat p112-116,por.

Gould, Elizabeth Lincoln (d. 1914)
  Amer. author
  Logan—Part p860

Gould, Hannah Flagg (1789-1865)
  Amer. poet
  Dexter—Career p95
  Hanaford—Dau. p262

Gould, Helen Miller (b. 1868)
  Amer. philanthropist
  Adelman—Famous p309-310
  Logan—Part p537

Gould, Paula (fl. 1930's)
  Amer. publicist, radio personality
  Women—Achieve. p73,por.

Gourielli, Helena Rubinstein.
  See Rubinstein, Helena

Gournay, Marie le Jars de (1565-1645)
  Fr. author
  Benson—Women p13-15

Gousha, Mrs. Joseph R.
  See Powell, Dawn

Gouveia, Joana de (fl. 14th cent.)
  Port. patriot, heroine
  Arsenius—Stamp p79,por.
  Phila.—Women, unp.,por.
  Stiles—Postal p107

Gouverneur, Maria Hester Monroe (1802-
        1850)
  Amer., dau. of James Monroe
  Sweetser—Famous p85-99
  Truett—First p18-19,por.

Govan, Christine Noble (1898-   )
  Amer. author, critic
  Warfel—Amer. p181,por.

Gove, Mary
  See Nichols, Mary Sargeant Neal Gove

Gowan, M. Oliva, Sister (b. 1888)
  Amer. nurse
  Dolan—Goodnow's p333,por.
  *Yost—Nursing p77-95

Gower, Nancy (fl. 1770's-1780's)
  Amer. pioneer
  Green—Pioneer (3) p443-444

Gower, Pauline (Mary de Peauly) (1910-1947)
　　Eng. pioneer aviatrix
　　Cur. Biog. '43 p241-242,por.
　　Cur. Biog. '47 p252
　　Goff—Women p133-158
　　*Knapp—New p19-33,por.
　　*May—Women p139-142,por.

Goya, Carola (fl. 1930's)
　　Amer. dancer
　　Women—Achieve. p65,por.

Gozzadini, Bettisia (d. 1249)
　　It. lawyer, lecturer
　　Farmer—What p391-392

Grable, Betty (1916-　　)
　　Amer. actress
　　CR '59 p301,por.
　　CR '63 p251,por.
　　Schickel—Stars p217,por.
　　Time Aug.23,1948 p40,por. (Cover)
　　TV—Person (3) p33-35,por.

Grace (dates unknown)
　　Eng. saint
　　*Windham—Sixty p186-193

Gradova, Gitta (Gidda) (1904-　　)
　　Amer. pianist
　　Ewen—Living p150
　　McCoy—Portraits p65,por.
　　Saleski—Jewish p479-480
　　Saleski—Wander. p319-320,por.

Graff, Elfie R. (fl. 1920's)
　　Amer. physician
　　Lovejoy—Women p170,322,330,345
　　Lovejoy—Women Phys. p109-111,por.

Graffenrief, Mary Clare de (b. 1849)
　　Amer. statistician
　　Logan—Part p853

Graham, Aubry Lee (fl. 1930's)
　　Amer. librarian
　　Women—Achieve. p151,por.

Graham, Cecelia B. (fl. 1920's)
　　Amer. sculptor
　　National—Contemp. p130

Graham, Clementina Stirling (1782-1877)
　　Scot. salonist, author,
　　　philanthropist
　　Graham—Group p316-331,por.

Graham, Dorothy.
　　See Bennett, Dorothy Graham

Graham, Elinor Mish (1906-　　)
　　Amer. author
　　Cur. Biog. '52 p219-220,por.

Graham, Elizabeth Nightingale.
　　See Arden, Elizabeth

Graham, Ennis, pseud.
　　See Molesworth, Mary Louisa Stewart

Graham, Florence Nightingale.
　　See Arden, Elizabeth

Graham, Gwethalyn (1913-1965)
　　Can. novelist
　　Cur. biog. '45 p246-247,por.
　　Cur. Biog. '66 p465
　　Thomas—Canad. p54-55

Graham, Isabella (1742-1814)
　　Amer. philanthropist
　　Adelman—Famous p101
　　Hanaford—Dau. p162-164

Graham, Margaret (fl. 1850's)
　　Eng. balloonist, parachutist
　　Earhart—Fun p198-201
　　*May—Women p15,48-49

Graham, Maria
　　See Callcott, Maria, Lady

Graham, Martha (c. 1894-　　)
　　Amer. dancer
　　CR '59 p302-303,por.
　　CR '63 p252,por.
　　Cur. Biog. '44 p251-253,por.
　　Cur. Biog. '61 p182-185,por.
　　Haskell—Ballet p84-85
　　*Maynard—Amer. p105-125,por.
　　Muir—Famous p89-97,por.
　　Murrow—This (2) p58-59

Graham, Rose (gr. 1898)
　　Eng. historical, archaeological
　　　author
　　Brittain—Women p96,176,188,223,249

Graham, Sheilah (1910-　　)
　　Eng. journalist
　　CR '59 p303,por.
　　CR '63 p252-253,por.

Graham, Shirley (1907-　　)
　　Amer. author, composer
　　Cur. Biog. '46 p221-222,por.

Graham, Virginia (1912-　　)
　　Amer. radio, TV personality
　　CR '63 p253,por.
　　Cur. Biog. '56 p221-223,por.

Graham, Winifred c. 1873-1950)
　　Eng. author
　　Hammerton p680

Grahme, Dorothy (fl. 1600's)
　　Eng. hostess
　　Stenton—English p198-199,235-236

Grahn, Lucile (1821-1907)
　　Dan. ballet dancer
　　*Terry—Star p83-86,por.

Grammont (or Gramont), Charlotte de
(1619-1673)
Mon. wife of Louis I.
Phila.—Women, unp.,por.
Stiles—Postal p54

Grammont, Duchess of (fl. 18th cent.)
Fr. accused criminal
Kavanagh—Women (2) p223

Grammont, Elizabeth, Countess of (1641-
1708)
Fr. author
Melville—Windsor p111-128,por.
Skinner—Elegant p3,65,67-69

Granahan, Kathryn Elizabeth (n.d.)
Amer. congresswoman
Cur. Biog. '59 p157-158,por.
U.S.—Women (87th) p17,por.

Granby, Marchioness of (fl. 1900's)
Eng. artist
Waters—Women p148

Grand, Sarah, pseud. (Frances Elizabeth
Clarke M'Fall) (1855/62-1943)
Irish novelist, feminist
Black—Notable p320-328,por.
Cur. Biog. '43 p244
Hammerton p681,por.

Grandfield, Jennie McKee (m. 1885)
Amer. social reformer
Logan—Part p663

Grandi, Marghuerita (1909-   )
Tas. singer
Davidson—Treas. p124-126,por.

"Grandma" (d. 1946)
Amer. spy
Singer—World's p40-50

Grandma Moses.
See Moses, Anna Mary Robertson
(Grandma)

Grandstaff, Grace M. (fl. 1930's)
Amer. personnel worker
Women—Achieve. p184,por.

Grandval, Marie Felicie Clemence de Reiset,
Viscountess de (1830-1907)
Fr. composer
Elson—Woman's p180-181

Granger, Euphrasia Smith (fl. 1900's)
Amer. patriot
Logan—Part p437

Granger, Nellie (fl. 1930's)
Amer. airline hostess
Planck—Women p204-205

Granier, Jeanne (fl. 1900's)
Fr. actress
Skinner—Elegeant p125

Grant, Anne MacVicar (1755-1838)
Scot. author
Dorland—Sum p19,173
Graham—Group p279-293
Leonard—Amer. p116

Grant, Blanche C. (fl. 1920's)
Amer. artist, author
Binheim—Women p148,por.

Grant, Bridget (1831-1923)
Irish-Amer. pioneer, inn-keeper
Aikman—Calamity p328-347

Grant, Dorothy Fremont (1900-   )
Warfel—Amer. p182-183,por.

Grant, Ethel Watts Mumford.
See Mumford, Ethel Watts

Grant, Frances R. (fl. 1920's-1930's)
Amer. museum director, editor
Women—Achieve. p90,por.

Grant, Hannah Simpson (fl. 1800's)
Amer., mother of Ulysses S. Grant
Hampton—Our p139-146

Grant, Hannah Tracy (fl. 1700's)
Amer. patriot
Green—Pioneer (3) p498-500

Grant, Jane (fl. 1930's)
Amer. journalist
Ross—Ladies p149-152

Grant, Julia Dent (1826-1902)
Amer., wife of Ulysses S. Grant
Farmer—What p58-59,87-90
Gerlinger—Mis. p57-60,por.
Hanaford—Dau. p97-101,por.
Harkness—Heroines p9
Jensen—White p104-106,por.
Logan—Ladies p102-107
Logan—Part p267-269
*McConnell—Our p181-193
Prindiville—First p157
*Ross—Know p39,por.
Smith—Romances p244-256,por.
Truett—First p46,por.
Young—Women p257-258,332-334

Grant, Kathryn (Kathy) (1933-   )
Amer. actress
CR '59 p304-305,por.
CR '63 p253-254,por.

Grant, Mary (   )
Bolitho—Biog. p158-161

Grant, Mary R. (1831-1908)
Scot. sculptor
Waters—Women p148

Grant, Nellie (m. 1874)
Amer., dau. of Ulysses S. Grant
Jensen—White p108,por.
Smith—White p81-89,por.

Grant, Mrs. Sueton (fl. 1740's)
Amer. colonial merchant, importer
Dexter—Colonial p33-34

Grant, Sybil, Lady (b. 1879)
Eng. author, artist
Hammerton p681

Grant, Zilpah P. (1794-1874)
Amer. educator
Farmer—What p247-263
Irwin—Angels p29-31
Woody—Hist. (1) p349-351

Granuaile (fl. 16th cent.)
Irish, sea queen of Connaught
*O'Clery—Queens p102-114

Granville, Christine.
See Skarbek, Krystyna Gizycka Granville

Granville, Mary.
See Delany, Mary Granville

Granville-Barker, Helen Gates (d. 1950)
Amer. author
Pearson—Marry. p288-303,por.

Gras, Louise de (1591-1660)
Fr. nurse, social worker
Pennock—Makers p8,142,por.
Schmidt—400 p392-393,por.

Grass, Elizabeth (fl. 1860's)
Amer. Civil war nurse
Logan—Part p368

Grassini, Josephina (Giuseppini) (1773-1850)
It. singer
Ewen—Ency. p188
Ferris—Great p120-129
Wagner—Prima p242

Grasso, Ella Tambussi (n.d.)
Amer. politician
Lamson—Few p215-228

Gratz, Marie (b. 1839)
Ger. painter
Waters—Women p148-149

Gratz, Rebecca (1781/82-1869)
Amer. educator, philanthropist, humanitarian
Dorland—Sum p16,80,109
*Levinger—Great p131-135
Logan—Part p647-648
Marcus—Memoirs (1) p272-280
Simonhoff—Jew. p172-173,por.

Grau, Shirley Ann (1929-   )
Amer. author
Cur. Biog. '59 p158-160,por.

Graudan, Joanna Freudberg (n.d.)
Russ.-Amer. pianist
Saleski—Jewish p645-646,por.

Grauer, Melanie. See Kahane, Melanie

Graves, Clotilde Inez (1863-1932)
Irish author
Hammerton p683

Graves, Dixie Bibb (fl. 1930's)
Amer. senator
Paxton—Women p129

Graves, Lulu Grace (1874/78-1949)
Amer. dietician, home economist
Women—Achieve. p106,por.

Graves, Mary H. (fl. 1870's-1880's)
Amer. clergyman, lecturer
Hanaford—Dau. p489-490

Gray, Adeline (fl. 1940's)
Amer. parachutist
*May—Women p58-59,por.
Peckham—Women p84-85

Gray, Mrs. Carl (fl. 1940's)
Amer. mother of the year
Davis—Mothers p177,179

Gray, Caroline E. (d. 1938)
Amer. author, nurse
Brockett—Woman's p789
Dolan—Goodnow's p262,313,por.

Gray, Coleen (1922-   )
Amer. actress
TV—Person (2), p89,por.

Gray, Dolores (1930-   )
Amer. singer, actress
CR '59 p305,por.
CR '63 p254,por.

Gray, Elizabeth Janet (1902-   )
Amer. author, librarian, teacher
Cur. Biog. '43 p249-251,por.

Gray, Etta (b. 1880)
Amer. physician
Lovejoy—Women p317-321,333
Lovejoy—Women Phys. p73-83,por.

Gray, Euphemia Chalmers (fl. 19th cent.)
Eng. model
Winwar—Pope p49,67-69,271-272

Gray, Gilda (1901-   )
Pol.-Amer. dancer
CR '59 p305-306,por.
Talmey—Doug. p83-90,por.

Gray, Hannah.
    See Bartlett, Hannah Gray

Gray, Mary Augusta Fox (1810-1881)
    Amer. pioneer
    Drury—First (1) p237-269,por.

Gray, Maxwell (1847-1923)
    Eng. novelist
    Hammerton p683,por.

Gray, Nicolette Mary Binyon (gr. 1932)
    Brit. author of art and archaeology
    Brittain—Women p177,253

Gray, Phyllis (fl. 1950's)
    Amer. aviatrix
    *May—Women p191,por.

Gray, Sophie de Butts (fl. 1890's)
    Amer. artist
    Waters—Women p149

Gray-Lhevinne, Estelle (1892-1933)
    Amer. violinist
    McCoy—Portraits p66,por.

Grayco, Helen (n.d.)
    Amer. singer
    TV—Person (3) p77-78,por.

Graydon, Mrs. (fl. 1770's)
    Amer. Rev. war patriot
    Ellet—Women (2) p274-280

Grayson, Ethel Vaughan Kirk (n.d.)
    Can. author, club leader
    Thomas—Canad. p56-57

Grayson, Francis W. (fl. 1920's)
    Amer. aviatrix
    Planck—Women p69

Grayson, Kathryn (1921-   )
    Amer. singer, actress
    CR '63 p255,por.
    Popular Record p60,por.

Grazie, Marie Eugenie Delle (1864-1931)
    Aust. poet, playwright
    Heller—Studies p282-283

Greaney, Helen F. (gr. 1883)
    Amer. nurse
    Pennock—Makers p81,por.

Greatorex, Eliza (1820-1897)
    Irish-Amer. painter
    Adelman—Famous p185
    Hanaford—Dau. p296-298
    Michigan—Biog. p135
    Waters—Women p149

Greble, Susan Virginia (fl. 1860's)
    Amer. Civil war humanitarian
    Brockett—Woman's p503-504

Greeley, Mary Y. C. (fl. 1870's)
    Amer. social reformer
    Hanaford—Dau. p433

Greeley-Smith, Nixola (b. 1880)
    Amer. journalist
    Fairfax—Ladies p57,73,106-112
    Ross—Ladies p22,86-95,por.

Green, Alice Kollock (d. 1832)
    Amer. Rev. war patriot
    Green—Pioneer (3) p361-367

Green, Anna Katharine (Mrs. Charles Rohlfs)
        (1846-1935)
    Amer. novelist
    Harkins—Famous p91-106,por.
    Harkins—Little p91-106,por.
    Logan—Part p803
    Maurice—Makers p6
    Overton—Women p167-173

Green, Anne (1899-   )
    Amer. novelist
    *Millett—Amer. p377-378
    Warfel—Amer. p184,por.

Green, Ann(e), Catharine (d. 1775)
    Amer. colonial printer, publisher
    Brigham—Journals p77-78
    Club—Printing p14,22-24,29,31,33
    Dexter—Colonial p174-176,178
    Earle—Colon. p62-63
    Hanaford—Dau. p710
    Spruill—Women's p264-265
    Woody—Hist. (1) p262

Green, Blanche Tucker (1903-1949)
    Amer. religious worker
    Phillips—33 p191-196

Green, Charlotte Byron (d. 1929)
    Eng. council member
    Brittain—Women (see index)

Green, Charlotte Hilton (b. 1889)
    Amer. naturalist, author
    Hoyle—Tar p67-71,por.

Green, Constance Winsor McLaughlin
        (1897-   )
    Amer. historian
    Cur. Biog. '63 p156-157,por.

Green, Cordelia A. (b. 1831)
    Amer. physician
    Mead—Medical p47

Green, Edith Starrett (1910-   )
    Amer. Congresswoman
    Cur. Biog. '56 p225-277,por.
    U.S.—Women (87th) p19,por.
    U.S.—Women (88th) p9,por.

Green, Eleanor (1911-   )
    Amer. novelist
    Warfel—Amer. p185,por.

Green, Elizabeth Shippen (Elizabeth Elliott)
    (c. 1871-1954)
    Amer. illustrator
    Mahony—Illus. p306
    Michigan—Biog. p135

Green, Ethel (fl. 1910's)
    Amer. singer, actress
    Caffin—Vaud. p74,por.

Green, Florence Topping (c. 1882-1945)
    Brit.-Amer. painter
    Cur. Biog. '45 p248

Green, Henrietta Howland Robinson (Hetty)
    (1834/35-1916)
    Amer. financier, millionnaire
    Carnegie—Five p157-160
    Fairfax—Ladies p85-88
    Muir—Women p209-210
    Rogers—Women p57,por.
    Ross—Charmers p26-60,284-285,por.
    Sickels—Twelve p34-50,252

Green, Lucille H. (d. 1878)
    Amer. physician
    Lovejoy—Women p221-222

Green, Mary (fl. 1750's)
    Amer. colonial teacher
    Dexter—Colonial p81

Greenaway, Kate (Catherine) (1846-1901)
    Eng. painter, illustrator
    Adelman—Famous p233
    Dorland—Sum p21,155
    Furniss—Some p85-87,por.
    Hammerton p685-686,por.
    Waters—Women p150-151

Greenbaum, Lucy.
    See Freeman, Lucy Greenbaum

Greene, Catherine (1731-c.1794)
    Amer. inventor, landholder,
        friend of Eli Whitney
    Dexter—Career p187-188
    Mozans—Woman p351-352
    Whitton—These p48-49

Greene, Catharine Littlefield (1753-1814)
    Amer. Rev. war heroine, patriot
    Ellet—Women (1) p77-89
    Green—Pioneer (2) p112-124
    Hanaford—Dau. p139
    Logan—Part p112-115

Greene, Eleanore D. (fl. 1930's)
    Can.-Amer. author
    Women—Achieve. p69,por.

Greene, Mabel (fl. 1920's)
    Amer. journalist
    Ross—Ladies p233-235

Greene, Marie Louise (gr. 1891)
    Amer. author
    Logan—Part p841

Greene, Mary Anne (fl. 1890's)
    Amer. pioneer lawyer
    Irwin—Angels p177

Greene, Mary Shepard (fl .1900's)
    Amer. painter
    Waters—Women p151-152

Greene, Rosaline (fl. 1930's)
    Amer. radio actress
    Women—Achieve. p84,por.

Greene, Ruhama (m. 1785)
    Amer. W. pioneer
    Ellet—Pioneer p196-198
    Logan—Part p60

Greene, Sarah Pratt McLean (1856-1935)
    Amer. author
    Logan—Part p850

Greene, Sigrid. See deLima, Sigrid

Greene, Zula Bennington (fl. 1930's)
    Amer. journalist
    Ross—Ladies p461

Greenfield, Elizabeth Taylor (1808/09-1876)
    Amer. singer
    Cuney-Hare—Negro p202-204,por.
    Robinson—Hist. p84-85,por.

Greenglass, Ruth (fl. 1940's)
    Russ. spy
    Singer—World's p83-84

Greenhow, Rose O'Neal (d. 1864)
    Amer. Civil war patriot, spy,
        heroine
    *Foley—Famous p75-83
    Harkness—Heroines p4-5
    Hoehling—Women p21-24
    Horan—Desperate p3-55,por.
    Jones—Heroines p61-66,74-75,249-254
    Kane—Spies p17-67
    *Komroff—True p85-108
    Leetch—Reveille p10-20,94-96,106,299,
        441
    *Nolen—Spies p33-47
    Simkins—Women p12,78-79,por.
    Whitton—These p161-162
    Young—Women p29,51,108,110-111

Greenleaf, Ann (fl. 1790's, 1800's)
    Dexter—Career p108

Greenwalt, Mary Elizabeth Hallock (1871-
    1950)
    Amer. pianist, lecturer
    Hanaford—Dau. p302

Greenway, Isabella (fl. 1930's)
Amer. Congresswoman
Paxton—Women p7-8,129

Greenwell, Dora (1821-1882)
Eng. author
Hammerton p686

Greenwood, Charlotte (1893-   )
Amer. actress
Blum—Great p78,por.
Hammerton p686

Greenwood, Gertrude B. (fl. 1920's)
Amer. sculptor
National—Contemp. p130

Greenwood, Grace, pseud. (Sarah Jane
Clark Lippincott) (1823-1904)
Amer. author, editor, journalist,
feminist, lecturer
Dorland—Sum p40,188
Hanaford—Dau. p223-224
Logan—Part p841
Pattee—Fem. p277-282,por.
Ross—Ladies p16,39,327-329,por.
Sargent—Pioneers p28-29
Thorp—Female p143-178,por.

Greenwood, Joan (1921-   )
Eng. actress
Cur. Biog. '54 p309-310,por.

Greenwood, Marion (1909-   )
Amer. artist
Ency. Brit.—Amer. p47,por.

Greer, Frances (n.d.)
Amer. singer
Peltz—Spot. p101,por.

Greffulhe, Elisabeth (de Caraman-
Chimay) (d. 1952)
Fr. philanthropist, art patron
Skinner—Elegant p52-54,por.

Gregg, Elinor D. (fl. 1920's)
Amer. nurse
Pennock—Makers p65,por.

Gregory, Angela (1903-   )
Amer. sculptor
National—Contemp. p131

Gregory, Augusta Persse, Lady (1860-1932)
Irish playwright
Adelman—Famous p294
Hammerton p689,por.
MacVeagh—Champlin p262
Millett—Brit. p257-259
Schmidt—400 p242-243,por.

Grenfell, Anne MacClanahan, Lady
(d. 1938)
Amer., wife of Dr. Grenfell
*Kirkland—Achieved p74-83

Grenfell, Helen Loring (b. 1868)
Amer. educator, penologist
Adelman—Famous p309

Grenfell, Joyce Irene (1910-   )
Eng. actress, author
CR '59 p310-311,por.
Cur. Biog. '58 p175-177,por.
Murrow—This (1) p63-64

Grenville, Lillian Goertner (fl. 1900's)
Can.-Amer. singer
Lahee—Grand p111,433-434

Grese, Irma (1923-1945)
Ger. accused criminal
Ewart—World's p262-278

Gretter, Lystra E. (fl. 1920's)
Amer. nurse
Pennock—Makers p71,por.

Grever, Maria (1894-1951)
Mex.-Amer. composer, singer,
pianist
ASCAP p199
Howard—Our p567

Greville, Henry.
See Durand, Alice Celeste Fleury

Greville, Ursula (fl. 1940's)
Eng. singer, editor, composer
McCoy—Portraits p67,por.

Grew, Agnes Mengel (fl. 1930's)
Amer. motion picture executive
Women—Achieve. p28,por.

Grew, Mary (fl. 1840's)
Amer. feminist, social reformer,
lecturer
Hanaford—Dau. p355-356
O'Connor—Pioneer p73-74,152

Grey, Beryl (1927-   )
Eng. ballet dancer
Atkinson—Dancers p65-68,por.
Davidson—Ballet p122-124
Fisher—Ball. p18,por.
Haskell—Vignet. p50-51,por.
Swinson—Dancers p33-38,por.

Grey, Edith F. (fl. 1890's-1900's)
Eng. artist
Waters—Women p152-153

Grey, Elizabeth, Lady (Elizabeth
Woodeville) (1428-1495)
Eng., friend of Richard III
Leary—Golden p277-279,285-287,292-
295

Grey, Jane, Lady (Lady Jane Dudley)
(1537-1554)
Eng. martyr, queen
Abbot—Notable p87-92
Adelman—Famous p50-52
Dorland—Sum p15,76
Fifty—Famous p66-73,por.
Hammerton p692,por.
Humphrey—Janes p126-148
*MacVeagh—Champlin p264
Nisenson—More Minute p63,por.
Sanders—Intimate p36-41,por.

Grey, Jane Cannon (b.c. 1816)
Amer. teacher,feminist, social
reformer
Woodward—Bold p53-89

Grey, Sylvia (1865-1958)
Eng. dancer
MacQueen—Pope p362-363

Gridley, Ann Eliza (d. 1909)
Amer. Civil war nurse
Logan—Part p370

Grieder, Naomi Lane Babson.
See Babson, Naomi Lane

Grier, Maria C. (fl. 1860's)
Amer. Civil war humanitarian
Brockett—Woman's p597-599,600-601

Grier, Mary Lynda Dorothy (fl. 1940's)
Eng. educator, author
Brittain—Women p161,172,190,201-
206,208,216

Grierson, Cecilia (gr. 1882)
Argent. physician
Lovejoy—Women p267

Griffies, Ethel (b. 1878)
Eng. actress
Cur. Biog. '68 p169-171,por.

Griffin, Josephine R. (fl. 1860's)
Amer. Civil war humanitarian,
heroine, philanthropist
Brockett—Woman's p707-709
Hanaford—Dau. p210,373-375
Logan—Part p314-315

Griffin, Mrs. William Preston (fl. 1860's)
Amer. Civil war patriot
Brockett—Woman's p316-534
Young—Women p176-178

Griffing, Josephine Sophie White (1814-
1872)
Amer. social reformer
Beard—Amer. p232-234

Griffith, Corrine (fl. 1920's-1930's)
Amer. actress, author
ASCAP p201
Herman—How p97,por.

Griffith, Elizabeth (c. 1730-1793)
Eng. novelist, playwright
Benson—Women p93-94
MacCarthy—Later p74-79

Griffiths, Martha (1912-   )
Amer. Congresswoman
CR '63 p259,por.
Cur. Biog. '55 p244-245,por.
Lamson—Few p87-98,por.
U.S.—Women (87th) p21,por.
U.S.—Women (88th) p11,por.

Grignan, Francoise Margaret de Sevigné,
Countess of (1648-1705)
Fr. letter-writer
Ravenel—Women p181-189

Grigsby, Sarah Lincoln (b. 1807)
Amer., sister of Abraham Lincoln
Barton—Women p109-113

Grimaldi, Charlotte (fl. c. 1730's)
Mon. princess
Phila.—Women, unp.,por.

Grimaldi, Jeanne (1596-1620)
Mon. princess, patron of arts, letters
Phila.—Women, unp.,por.
Stiles—Postal p130

Grimes, Frances (b. 1869)
Amer. sculptor
Jackman—Amer. p427-428
National—Contemp. p134
Women—Achieve. p151,por.

Grimes, Tammy Lee (1934-   )
Amer. actress, singer, dancer
CR '63 p259,por.
Cur. Biog. '62 p170-172,por.

Grimké, Angelina Emily (1805-1879)
Amer. lecturer, social reformer
Adelman—Famous p131
Bruce—Woman p163-173
Culver—Women p176-177
Douglas—Remember p114-120
Hanaford—Dau. p345,355
Irwin—Angels p74-75,107,240
Johnson—Lunatic p33-56
Lader—Bold p61-69,106
O'Connor—Pioneer p22,32,43,56-57,
137-138,178-179
Riegel—Amer. p26-34
Whitton—These p126-128

Grimké, Charlotte L Forten (1838-1915)
Amer. social reformer, teacher
Robinson—Hist. p86,por.

Grimké, Elizabeth.
See Ross, Betsy Griscom

Grimké, Sarah Moore (1792-1873)
    Amer. philanthropist, social
      reformer, feminist, lecturer,
      author
    Adelman—Famous p130-131
    Bruce—Woman p163-173
    Culver—Women p176-177
    Dorland—Sum p51,79,136
    Douglas—Remember p114-120
    Hammerton p694
    Hanaford—Dau. p345,355
    Irwin—Angels p75,82
    Johnson—Lunatic p33-56
    Lader—Bold p61-69
    Riegel—Amer. p26-30,33-34
    Whitton—These p126-128

Grimm, Katherine (fl. 1940's)
    Amer. secretary
    Taves—Success p202-211,por.

Grimshaw, Beatrice Ethel (c. 1871-1953)
    Irish traveler, author
    Hammerton p694

Gripenberg, Alexandra (1856-1911)
    Fin. author, feminist
    Schmidt—400 p167,por.

Grippon, Eva (d. 1956)
    Fr.-Amer. singer
    Lahee—Grand p314

Grisi, Carlotta (1819-1899)
    It. ballet dancer
    *Terry—Star p75-79

Grisi, Guilia (c. 1811-1869)
    It. singer
    Adelman—Famous p158
    Coad—Amer. p199,por.
    Davidson—Treas. p126-127
    Ewen—Ency. p191
    Hammerton p694
    Lahee—Famous p58-63
    McCoy—Portraits p67,por.
    Marks—Glamour p103-111,por.
    Mayne—Enchant. p241-251,por.
    Pleasants—Great p178-180,por.
    Wagner—Prima p180,242

Grissom, Irene Welch (fl. 1920's)
    Amer. poet
    Binheim—Women p122,por.

Griswold, Henrietta Dippman (fl. 1940's)
    Amer. composer, pianist
    McCoy—Portraits p67

Griswold, Ursula Wolcott (fl. 1770's)
    Amer. Rev. war patriot
    Ellet—Women (2) p342-344
    Green—Pioneer (1) p339

Grizodubova, Valentina Stepanova (c. 1910-)
    Russ. aviatrix, aeronautical
      pioneer
    Cur. Biog. '41 p347-348,por.
    *Knapp—New p129-139,por.
    Phila.—Women, unp.,por.
    Stiles—Postal p109

Grondahl, Agathe Backer (1847-1907)
    Nor. composer, music teacher
    Schmidt—400 p310,por.

Grose, Helen Mason (b. 1880-   )
    Amer. illustrator
    Mahony—Illus. p314

Gross, Elizabeth West (b. 1817)
    Amer. pioneer
    Brown—Home. p69-70,por.

Gross, Miriam Zeller (fl. 1930's)
    Amer. teacher, public relations
      worker
    Women—Achieve. p139,por.

Grossinger, Jennie (1892-   )
    Aust.-Amer. hotel owner, manager
    Cantor—As p59-63,por.
    CR '59 p313,por.
    CR '63 p260,por.
    Cur. Biog. '56 p235-237,por.

Grouitch, Madame Slavko (fl. 1900's)
    Amer. philanthropist
    Logan—Part p542-543

Grove, Betty Ann (n.d.)
    Amer. dancer, singer
    TV—Person (1) p58-59,por.

Grove, Mary (fl. 1830's)
    Amer. lecturer, physiologist
    Dexter—Career p44

Groves, Gladys Hoagland (1894-   )
    Amer. author, educator
    Cur. Biog. '43 p257-259,por.

Groves, May Showler (b. 1888)
    Amer. author
    Binheim—Women p50,por.

Gruenberg, Sidonie Matsner (b. 1881)
    Aust.-Amer. educator, organization
      official, author, lecturer
    Cur. Biog. '40 p352-353,por.
    Women—Achieve. p96,por.

Grümmer, Elizabeth (n.d.)
    Ger. singer
    Rosenthal—Sopranos p46-47,por.

Grummond, Frances (fl. 1860's)
    Amer. W. pioneer
    Brown—Gentle p12-13,39,49-59,por.

Grymes, Lucy. See Lee, Lucy Grymes

Gscheidle, Gertrude E. (1905-   )
Amer. librarian
Bul. of Bibl. Sept.-Dec.1954 p97-99,por.

Güden (Gueden), Hilde (1923-   )
Aust. singer
Brook—Singers p100-103,por.
CR '59 p315,por.
Cur. Biog. '55 p247-248,por.
Ewen—Ency. p192
Matz—Opera p116-119,por.
Rosenthal—Sopranos p48-57,por.

Gudzin, Margaret S.
Amer. aviatrix
*Peckham—Women p35

Guérin, Eugénie de (1805-1848)
Fr. author
Bradford—Women p177-202
Corkran—Romance p234-240
Dorland—Sum p51

Guérin, Theodore, Mother (1798-1856)
Fr. foundress
Code—Great p292-328

Guerrier, Edith (b. 1870)
Amer. librarian
Bul. of Bibl. May-Aug. '43 p1-3,por.
Logan—Part p860

Guest, Charlotte Elizabeth Bertie, Lady
Schreiber (1812-1895)
Welsh diarist, social reformer
Dorland—Sum p47
Dunaway—Treas. p468-476
Hammerton p697
Iremonger—And p74-100,por.

Guest, Lucy Douglas Cochrane (1920-   )
Amer. fashion model
CR '59 p315,por.
CR '63 p262,por.
Time June 20, 1962 p45,por.(Cover)

Guggenheim, Florence Shloss (1863-1944)
Amer. philanthropist, organization
official
Cur. Biog. '44 p262
Women—Achieve. p60,por.

Guggenheim, Alicia.
See Patterson, Alicia

Guggenheim, Minnie (1882-1966)
Amer. music patron, philanthropist
Cur. Biog. '62 p174-177,por.
Cur. Biog. '66 p465
Phelps—Men (2) '59 p122-123

Guggenheim, Peggy (1898-   )
Amer. music, art patron, collector,
author
CR '63 p262,por.
Cur. Biog. '62 p172-174,por.

Guiccioli, Teresa Gamba, Countess (1801/
02-1873)
It., friend of Lord Byron
Hammerton p697
Mayne—Enchant. p279-297,por.
Orr—Famous Affin. III p85-95

Guilbert, Yvette (c. 1865-1944)
Fr. singer, actress
Caffin—Vaud. p57-60,por.
Dorland—Sum p169
Ewen—Living p153-154,por.
Hammerton p697-698,por.

Guild, Emma Cadwalader (b. 1843)
Amer. sculptor
Waters—Women p153-154

Guilford, Nanette (1906-   )
Amer. singer
McCoy—Portraits p69,por.
Saleski—Wander. p402-403,por.

Guillard, Charlotte (fl. 1500's)
Fr. pioneer printer
Club—Printing p10

Guimard, Marie Madeleine (1743-1816)
Fr. ballet dancer
Ferris—Great p78-79
Hammerton p698
*Terry—Star p47-55,por.

Guinan, Mary Louise Cecelia ("Texas")
Amer. actress, circus performer
Jensen—Revolt p167,por.
Rogers—Women p116,por.

Guion, Connie Myers (b. 1882)
Amer. physician
Cur. Biog. '62 p177-178,por.
*Fleming—Doctors p144-159
Taves—Success p226-239,por.
Women—Achieve. p151,por.

Gulesian, Grace Warner (b. 1884)
Amer. composer, pianist, music
teacher, choral director
ASCAP p206
McCoy—Portraits p69,por.

Gullen, Augusta Stow (1856-1943)
Can. physician
Lovejoy—Women p112-113
Sanders—Canadian p85-110,por.

Gullett, Lucy E. (fl. 1920's)
Austral. physician, foundress
Lovejoy—Women p249-250,por.

Gunderson, Barbara Bates (m. 1941)
      Amer. government official
      Phelps—Men (1) '58 p106-107

Gungabehn Majmundar (fl. 1930's-1940's)
      Ind. spinner, co-worker of Gandhi
      Stern—Women p122-124

Gunning, Elizabeth (1734-1790)
      Irish beauty
      Hammerton p699,por.

Gunning, Maria (1733-1760)
      Irish beauty
      Hammerton p699,por.

Gunning, Susannah Minifie (c. 1740-1800)
      Eng. novelist
      MacCarthy—Later p58-63

Gunterman, Bertha Lisette (fl. 1910's-1930's)
      Amer. librarian, editor
      Women—Achieve. p198

Günther, Irene von.
      See Ivogün, Maria

Gunther-Amberg, Julie (b. 1855)
      Ger. painter
      Waters—Women p154

Gurney, Elizabeth.
      See Fry, Elizabeth Gurney

Gustin, Ellen G. (fl. 1870's)
      Amer. clergyman
      Hanaford—Dau. p488

Gutheil-Schoder, Marie (1874-1935)
      Ger. singer
      Ewen—Ency. p193-194

Guthrie, Mrs. James (fl. 1660's)
      Scot. covenanter
      Anderson—Ladies p111-118

Guyart, Marie de l'Incarnation (1599-1672)
      Can. nun
      Innis—Clear p25-41 (in French), por.

Guyon, Jean Marie de la Motte-Guyon
            Bouvier (1648-1717)
      Fr. mystic, author
      Adelman—Famous p64-65
      Bradford—Daughters p75-114,por.
      Corkran—Romance p294-325,por.
      Culver—Women p105-106
      Deen—Great p130-140
      Dorland—Sum p27,133
      Haggard—Remark. p166-175,177-179
      Hammerton p702,por.
      Hubbard—Little p41-78,por.

Guyon, Marie Thérèse.
      See Cadillac, Marie Thérèse Guyon

Guyon, Maximiliènne Goepp (1868-1903)
      Fr. painter
      Waters—Women p154-155

Gwen (fl. 587 A.D.)
      Fr. saint
      *Windham—Sixty p158-165

Gwinnett, Mrs. Button (m.c. 1760)
      Amer. patriot
      Green—Pioneer (3) p273-275

Gwyer, Barbara Elizabeth (fl. 1930's)
      Eng. educator
      Brittain—Women (see index)

Gwyn (Gwynn or Gwynne), Eleanor "Nell"
            (1653-1691)
      Eng. actress
      Abbot—Notable p328-331,por.
      Adelman—Famous p67-68
      Collins—Great p1-26,por.
      Coryn—Enchant. p97-126
      Dark—More p155-176
      Dorland—Sum p22,70,165
      Hammerton p702-703,por.
      MacQueen—Pope p75-91,por.
      Melville—Windsor p242-275
      Orr—Famous p91-105
      Orr—Famous Affin. I p121-140
      Wilson—All p146-148

Gwynne, Rose (b. 1650)
      Eng. actress
      MacQueen—Pope p78-79

Gwynne-Vaughan, Helen Charlotte Isabella,
            Dame (b. 1879)
      Eng. botanist
      Hammerton p703

Gye, Madame Albani b. 1847)
      Can. singer
      Schmidt—400 p74-75,por.

Gyp (Sybille Gabrielle Marie Antoinette de
            Riquetti de Mirabeau) (1850-
            1932)
      Fr. author
      Hammerton p703,por.

H

Haake, Gail Martin (b. 1884)
      Amer. pianist, music teacher
      McCoy—Portraits p69,por.

Haanen, Elizabeth Alida (1809-1845)
      Nether. painter
      Waters—Women p155

Hachard, Marie-Madeleine Sister (fl. 1710's)
      Amer. pioneer, nun
      *Sickels—Calico p57-71

Hackett, Frances. See Goodrich, Frances

Hackley, Emma Azalia (1867-1922)
Amer. musician, humanitarian
Brown—Home. p231-236,por.
Cuney-Hare—Negro p241-242,por.

Hadad's wife (Biblical)
Deen—All p331

Hadakin, Helen (fl. 1920's)
Amer. journalist
Ross—Ladies p302-303

Hadassah (Biblical)
Deen—All p264

Haddock, Emma (fl. 1870's-1880's)
Amer. lawyer
Hanaford—Dau. p661-662

Haddon, Elizabeth.
See Estaugh, Elizabeth Haddon

Hader, Berta Hoerner (fl. 1920's-1940's)
Amer. illustrator
Mahony—Illus. p314

Hading, Jane (1859-1941)
(Jeanne Alfrédine Trefouret)
Fr. actress
Hammerton p704
Marks—Glamour p305-306

Hadley, Piety Lucretia (fl. 1860's)
Amer. Civil war philanthropist
Andrews—Women p416-420
Irwin—Angels p154-155
Logan—Part p101

Hadow, Grace Eleanor (1875-1940)
Eng. educator
Brittain—Women (see index)

Hagan, Helen E. (1893-   )
Amer. pianist, educator
Cuney-Hare—Negro p375-376

Hagar (Biblical)
Buchanan—Women p16-17
Chappell—Fem. p23-35
Culver—Women p19
Deen—All p264-266
Lewis—Portraits p34-36
Lofts—Women p6-22
MacVeagh—Champlin p269
Marble—Women p121-122
Mead—250 p21
Nelson—Bible p14-16
Spurgeon—Sermons p7-32
Van der Velde—She p36-43

Hagar, Emily Stokes (fl. 1940's)
Amer. singer
McCoy—Portraits p70,por.

Hagar, Sarah J. (d. 1864)
Amer. Civil war nurse
Brockett—Woman's p704-706
Hanaford—Dau. p210

Hagen, Uta (1919-   )
Ger. actress
Blum—Great p132,por.
CR '59 p317,por.
CR '63 p265,por.
Cur. Biog. '44 p202-205,por.
Cur. Biog. '63 p173-175,por.
Murrow—This (2) p62-63
TV—Person (1) p22

Hager, Alice Mayre (fl. 1930's)
Amer. dietician
Women—Achieve. p198

Hager, Alice Rogers (1894-   )
Amer. aviation author
Planck—Women p231-234,por.

Hager, Carol (fl. 1930's)
Amer. aviation instructor
Planck—Women p160

Hager, Elizabeth.
See Pratt, Elizabeth ("Betsy")

Hager, Mina (fl. 1940's)
Amer. singer
McCoy—Portraits p70,por.

Haggith (Biblical)
Deen—All p266-267

Hagidorn, Mary (fl. 1770's)
Amer. Rev. war patriot
Hanaford—Dau. p51

Hague, Parthenia Antoinette (fl. 1860's)
Amer. Civil war diarist
Jones—Heroines p260-265

Hagy, Ruth Geri (1911-   )
Amer. TV personality, journalist
Cur. Biog. '57 p227-229,por.

Hahn, Anna (fl. 1860's)
Amer. Civil war nurse
Logan—Part p368

Hahn, Emily (1905-   )
Amer. geologist, author
CR '59 p318,por.
CR '63 p266,por.
Cur. Biog. '42 p324-325,por.

Hahn, Helen (n.d.)
Amer. radio personality
Settel—Radio p50,por.

Hahn-Hahn, Ida, Countess (1805-1880)
Ger. author
Blunt—Great p417-419
Heller—Studies p241-245

Haia, Nichola de (fl. 1190's)
Eng. heroine
Stenton—English p37

Haines, Connie (1923-   )
Amer. singer
TV—Person (2) p78,por.

Haines, Edith Key (fl. 1930's)
Amer. cookery author
Women—Achieve. p170,por.

Haines, Frances E. (fl. 1910's)
Amer. pioneer physician, surgeon
Lovejoy—Women p303-304

Haines, Helen Colby (fl. 1900's)
Amer. author
Logan—Part p835

Haines, Helen Elizabeth (1872-1961)
Amer. librarian, author, editor,
educator
Bul. of Bibl. Sept.-Dec."51 p129-131,
por.

Haines, Sarah Platt (b. 1842)
Amer. missionary
Logan—Part p519

Haizlip, Mae (fl. 1930's-1940's)
Amer. aviatrix
*Adams—Sky p137-153,por.
*May—Women p99,125
Planck—Women p48,86-88

Halban, Desi (n.d.)
Aust. singer
Saleski—Jewish p591-592,por.

Haldane, Elizabeth Sanderson (1862-1937)
Scot. author, social welfare worker
Hammerton p707

Hale, Ellen Day (b. 1855)
Amer. painter
Hanaford—Dau. p299
Waters—Women p155-156

Hale, Evelyn Wickham (fl. 1930's)
Amer. astronomer
Women—Achieve. p173,por.

Hale, Lilian Westcott (b. 1881)
Amer. artist
Jackman—Amer. p255

Hale, Louise Closser (1872-1933)
Amer. actress
Hammerton p708
Maurice—Makers p11,por.

Hale, Lucretia Peabody (1820-1900)
Amer. author
Benét—Humorists p17-20,por.
Dorland—Sum p33,83,189

Hale, Mary (1920-   )
Amer. musician
Parshalle—Kash. p13-17,por.

Hale, Mary W. (b. 1810)
Amer. poet
Hanaford—Dau. p258

Hale, Nancy (1908-   )
Amer. author
CR '63 p266-267,por.
Van Gelder—Writers p330-333

Hale, Sarah Josepha (1788-1879)
Amer. editor, author
Adelman—Famous p164
Culver—Women p182
Davenport—Ladies p51-79,por.
Dorland—Sum p28,111,116-117
131,173
Douglas—Remember p57-58,180
Fairfax—Ladies p155-156
Hanaford—Dau. p227-229,702
Irwin—Angels p9,54
*Kirkland—Writers p68-79
Love—Famous p8
Lownsbery—Saints p223-240
Papashvily—All p41,46,76
Pattee—Fem. p103-105,por.
Schmidt—400 p8,por.
Whitton—These p101-103
Woodward—Bold p181-200
Wright—Forgot. p187-217,por.

Hale, Susan (1834-1910)
Amer. artist
Logan—Part p754

Halkett, Anne Murray (1622-1699)
Eng. author
Bottrall—Pers. p112-113,223
Stenton—English p158-164

Hall, Abigail Burr (d. 1753)
Amer. pioneer, wife of Lyman Hall
Green—Pioneer (3) p275-278

Hall, Addye Yeargain (fl. 1940's)
Amer. musician, lecturer, author
McCoy—Portraits p71,por.

Hall, Adelaide S. (b. 1857)
Amer. art lecturer, author
Logan—Part p858

Hall, Amanda Benjamin (1890-   )
Amer. poet
Smith—Women's p96

Hall, Anna Maria Fielding (1800-1881)
Brit. novelist, philanthropist
Dorland—Sum p34,79,128,199
Stebbins—Victorian p40-41,197,208-
209

Hall, Anne (or Ann) (1792-1863)
Amer. artist
Hanaford—Dau. p294

Hall, Carrie M. (fl. 1920's-1930's)
Amer. nurse
Pennock—Makers p123-124,por.

Hall, Mrs. Daniel (fl. 1770's)
Amer. Rev. war patriot
Ellet—Women (2) p355-356

Hall, Mrs. Dorian (fl. 1860's)
Amer. Civil war diarist
Jones—Heroines p71-72

Hall, Elaine Goodale (b. 1863)
Amer. teacher, Ind. authority
Logan—Part p858

Hall, Elizabeth (fl. 1660's)
Eng. actress
Wilson—All p148-149

Hall, Elizabeth (n.d.)
Amer. aviation instructor
*Peckham—Women p163,por.

Hall, Florence Louise (1888-   )
Amer. director, Women's Land
Army
Cur. Biog. '43 p270-272,por.

Hall, Frances M. (fl. 1880's)
Amer. W. pioneer, teacher
Sargent—Pioneers p42,44,por.

Hall, Gertrude.
See Brownell, Gertrude Hall

Hall, Hazel (1886-1924)
Amer. poet
Cook—Our p196-200
Smith—Women's p103

Hall, Helen (fl. 1910's-1930's)
Amer. social worker
Women—Achieve. p176,por.

Hall, Mrs. Herman J. (fl. 1880's)
Amer. club leader
Logan—Part p411

Hall, Josephine (fl. 1890's)
Amer. actress, singer
Strang—Prima p46-55,por.

Hall, Juanita (c. 1913-1968)
Amer. singer, actress
CR '59 p319,por.
CR '63 p267,por.

Hall, Kay (fl. 1930's)
Amer. journalist
Ross—Ladies p544,547

Hall, Louisa Jane (1802-1892)
Amer. poet
Hanaford—Dau. p257

Hall, Lydia S. (fl. 1870's)
Amer. lawyer
Hanaford—Dau. p668

Hall, Maria M. C. (fl. 1860's)
Amer. Civil war nurse
Brockett—Woman's p448-454
Moore—Women p397-408

Hall, Marian Wells (fl. 1930's)
Amer. interior decorator
Women—Achieve. p166,por.

Hall, Marie (1884-1956)
Eng. violinist
McCoy—Portraits p71,por.

Hall, Marjory (1908-   )
Amer. author, businesswoman
Cur. Biog. '57 p230-232,por.

Hall, Mary (fl. (1660's)
Amer. accused witch
Green—Pioneer (1) p238

Hall, Mary (fl. 1750's)
Amer. pioneer, 2nd wife of Lyman
Hall
Green—Pioneer (3) p275-278

Hall, Pauline (fl. 1870's-1880's)
Amer. singer, actress
Strang—Prima p239-252,por.

Hall, Radclyffe (c. 1886-1943)
Eng. novelist, poet
Cur. Biog. '43 p272
Hammerton p710
Lawrence—School p323-331

Hall, Rosetta Sherwood (1865-1951)
Amer. physician, missionary
Lovejoy—Women p239-241
Mead—Medical p70-71

Hall, Ruth Julia (fl. 1920's)
Eng. pianist, organist, lecturer
McCoy—Portraits p71,por.

Hall, Sarah Ewing (1761-1830)
Amer. essayist
Hanaford—Dau. p.243-244

Hall, Sharlott Mabridth (1870-1943)
Amer. poet
Smith—Women's p105

Hall, Susan E. (fl. 1860's)
Amer. Civil war nurse
Brockett—Woman's p431-439

Hall, Sylvia and Rachel (fl. 1830's)
    Amer. Ind. captives
    Schmidt—400 p536

Hallady, Bessie G. (fl. 1930's)
    Amer. aviation instructor
    Planck—Women p164

Hallam, Mrs. Lewis (m.c. 1793/94)
    Amer. actress
    Coad—Amer. p44,por.
    Dexter—Career p80-81

Hallam, Nancy (fl. 1759-1775)
    Amer. colonial actress
    Dexter—Colonial p161-163,212

Hallam, Sarah (fl. 1760's-1770's)
    Amer. actress, dancer, niece of
      Sarah Hallam Douglass
    Spruill—Women's p97,204,262-263

Hallaren, Mary Agnes (1907-   )
    Amer. army officer, director of
      WAC
    Cur. Biog. '49 p238-239,por.

Hallé, Wilhelmina (Wilma) Maria Franziska
      Neruda, Lady (1838/39-1911)
    Aust.
    Adelman—Famous p243-244
    Ehrlich—Celeb. p218-220,por.
    Hammerton p710,por.
    McCoy—Portraits p140,por.

Hallock, Mary Elizabeth.
    See Greenwalt, Mary Elizabeth Hallock

Hallowell, Mrs. M. M. (fl. 1860's)
    Amer. Civil War humanitarian
    Brockett—Woman's p710-712

Hallowell, May.
    See Loud, May Hallowell

Hallowell, R. C. (fl. 1870's-1880's)
    Amer. editor
    Hanaford—Dau. p703

Hal-Mehi (fl. 1800's)
    Pers. heroine
    *Deakin—True p281-296

Halop, Florence (n.d.)
    Amer. actress
    TV—Person (2) p43-44,por.

Halpert, Edith Gregor (1900-   )
    Russ.-Amer. art dealer, collector
    Cur. Biog. '55 p254-256,por.

Halpir, Salomee (fl. 18th cent.)
    Pol. physician, surgeon
    Lovejoy—Women p172

Halprin, Rose Luria (n.d.)
    Amer. organization official
    Cur. Biog. '50 p217-218,por.

Halse, Emmeline (c. 1878-1929)
    Eng. sculptor
    Waters—Women p156

Halse, Margaret Frances (1910-   )
    Amer. author
    Cur. Biog. '44 p262-264,por.

Halstead, Margaret (fl. 1930's)
    Amer. singer
    Ewen—Living p156,por.
    McCoy—Portraits p71,por.

Halverson, Frances Ridley (fl. 1870's)
    Eng. religious author, hymn-writer
    Edman—They p72-77

Halvey, Margaret Mary Brophy (fl. 1880's)
    Irish-Amer. club leader, educator,
      poet
    Logan—Part p862-863

Hamblet, Julia E. (1916-   )
    Amer. Marine Corps officer
    Cur. Biog. '53 p240-241,por.

Hambly, Loveday Billing (c. 1604-1682)
    Eng. clergyman
    Lambert—Quiet p50-54

Hamblyn, Mistress (fl. 1576)
    Eng. governess
    Howe—Galaxy p33-35

Hamburger, Bessie Snow (1880-1952)
    Amer. lawyer
    Women—Achieve. p77,por.

Hamill, Virginia (fl. 1930's)
    Amer. interior decorator
    Women—Achieve. p110,por.

Hamilton, Alice (1869-   )
    Amer. pioneer industrial physician
    *Boynick—Pioneers p121-149
    Chandler—Medicine p117-122,por.
    Cur. Biog. '46 p234-236,por.
    Douglas—Remember p204-205
    Fabricant—Why p135-136
    *Fleming—Doctors p70-85
    Hume—Great p252-256,por.
    Lovejoy—Women p123-124,por.
    Rosen—Four p42-44,130-132,211-214
    *Yost—Women Sci. p44-61

Hamilton, Anna (d. 1936)
    It. nurse
    Pennock—Makers p132-133,por.

Hamilton, Anna Havermann (fl. 1940's)
    Amer. piano teacher
    McCoy—Portraits p72,por.

Hamilton, Anne, Lady (1776-1846)
Eng. lady-in-waiting
Melville—Regency p117-119

Hamilton, Anne, Marchioness (1636-1716)
Scot. convenanter
Anderson—Ladies p129-159
Graham—Group p80,por.

Hamilton, Anne Kennedy (c. 1760-1836)
Amer. Rev. heroine
Green—Pioneer (3) p415-419

Hamilton, Catharine, Lady, Duchess of
Athol (1662-1707)
Scot. covenanter
Anderson—Ladies p459-472

Hamilton, Cecile (fl. 1930's-1940's)
Amer. aviatrix
*May—Women p164-165
Planck—Women p228

Hamilton, Cicely (1872-1952)
Eng. author, actress
Hammerton p712

Hamilton, Edith (1867-1963)
Amer. author, educator, scholar
CR '59 p320,por.
Cur. Biog. '63 p175-178,por.
Murrow—This (2) p64-65

Hamilton, Elizabeth (1758-1816)
Scot. author, philanthropist,
song-writer
Dorland—Sum p45,172,182-183
Findlay—Spindle p76-84
Hammerton p712,por.
MacCarthy—Later p199-202

Hamilton, Elizabeth Schuyler (1757-1854)
Amer. Rev. war patriot, belle, wife
of Alexander Hamilton
Brooks—Colonial p215-244
Donovan—Women p258-270,279-288,
por.
Green—Pioneer (2) p94-100,por.
*Humphrey—Elizabeths p56-75
Logan—Part p117-120
Sale—Old p145-151,por.

Hamilton, Emma Lyon, Lady (c. 1761-1815)
Eng., mistress of Lord Nelson
Adelman—Famous p107-108
Blei—Fasc. p185-191,por.
Collins—Biog. p302-306,por.
Davenport—Great p129-137
Hahn—Love p211-233
Hammerton p712-713,por.
Kemble—Idols p129-135
Mozans—Woman p382-383
Terhune—Super. p250-271

Hamilton, Florence (fl. 1930's)
Amer. editor, poet
Women—Achieve. p80,por.

Hamilton, Gail. See Dodge, Mary Abigail

Hamilton, Janet (c. 1795-1873)
Scot. poet, song-writer
Findlay—Spindle p183-197
Hammerton p713

Hamilton, Margaret (b. 1840)
Amer. Civil war nurse
Logan—Part p362

Hamilton, Mary Agnes Adamson (b. 1883/
84)
Eng. author, politician
Hammerton p713

Hamilton, Nancy (1908-   )
Amer. author, singer
ASCAP p211

Hamilton, Narcissa (fl. 1830's-1850's)
Amer., cousin of Sam Houston
Turner—Sam p57-61

Hamilton, Rachel Faucett (b.c. 1729-   )
Amer., wife of Alexander Hamilton
Donovan—Women p23-26

Hamlin, Frances Bacon (m. 1873)
Amer. club leader
Logan—Part p476

Hamlin, Genevieve Karr (1896-   )
Amer. sculptor
National—Contemp. p140
Women—Achieve. p139,por.

Hammersley, Lily Warren.
See Marlborough, Lily Hammersley,
Duchess of

Hammoleketh (Biblical)
Deen—All p267

Hammond, Barbara Bradby (gr. 1895)
Brit. historian, economist
Brittain—Women p93,96,249

Hammond, Fanny Reed (fl. 1940's)
Amer. composer, pianist, music
teacher
McCoy—Portraits p72,por.

Hammond, Gertrude Demain (1880's-1900's)
Eng. illustrator, designer
Waters—Women p156-157

Hammond, Joan (1912-   )
New Z. singer
Brook—Singers p104-109,por.
Davidson—Treas. p128-130
Rosenthal—Sopranos p58-59,por.

Hammond, Natalie Harris (m. 1881)
Amer. philanthropist, social leader
Logan—Part p289

Hampton, Emma Stark (fl. 1900's)
  Logan—Part p348-349

Hampton, Hope (1901-   )
  Amer. social leader
  CR '63 p269,por.

Hampton, Hope (fl. 1920's-1930's)
  Amer. singer
  McCoy—Portraits p73,por.

Hampton, Isabel. See Robb, Isabel Hampton

Hampton, Louise (c. 1877-1954)
  Eng. actress
  Hammerton p715

Hamutal (Biblical)
  Deen—All p267

Hanaford, Phoebe A. Coffin (b. 1829)
  Amer. clergyman, social reformer,
    author, journalist, historian,
    lecturer
  Dexter—Career p61
  Hanaford—Dau. (see index),por.

Hanbury, Felicity (fl. 1940's)
  Eng. air chief commandant WRAF
  *May—Women p189

Hancock, Cornelia (1839/40-1926)
  Amer. Civil war nurse
  Brockett—Woman's p284-286
  Logan—Part p366
  Young—Women (see index)

Hancock, Dorothy Quincy (1750-1828)
  Amer. Rev. war patriot, wife of
    John Hancock
  Brooks—Young p243-268
  Ellet—Women (1) p167-170
  Green—Pioneer (3) p18-32,por.
  Hanaford—Dau. p138
  Logan—Part p123-124
  Whitton—These p2,11-13

Hancock, Florence (1893-   )
  Eng. labor union official
  Cur. Biog. '48 p268-269,por.

Hancock, Joy Bright (1898-   )
  Amer. aviatrix, naval officer,
    Director, WAVES
  Cur. Biog. '49 p241-243,por.
  *May—Women p191,193
  Planck—Women p231,237

Hancock, Lydia (fl. 1770's)
  Amer., aunt of John Hancock
  Green—Pioneer (3) p25,27-29

Haney, Carol (1924-   )
  Amer. dancer
  CR '59 p323,por.
  CR '63 p270,por.

Hanks, Lucy (d. 1825/26)
  Amer., mother of Lucy Hanks
  Barton—Women p1-97

Hanks, Nancy (1).
  See Lincoln, Nancy Hanks

Hanks, Nancy (2).
  See Bowles, Mrs. A. Lincoln

Hanna, Rebecca (fl. 1870's)
  Amer. physician
  Hanaford—Dau. p557

Hannah (1) (Biblical)
  Mother of Samuel
  Buchanan—Women p46-48
  Culver—Women p31
  Deen—All p87-92
  Hughes—Mothers p110-115
  *Levinger—Great p50-53
  Lewis—Portraits p78-82
  *MacVeagh—Champlin p273-274
  Marble—Women, Bible p136-139
  Mead—250 p77
  Nelson—Bible p37-40
  Ockenga—Women p90-100
  Spurgeon—Sermons p147-159
  Van der Velde—She p115-121

Hannah (2) (Biblical)
  mother of 7 martyrs
  Levinger—Great p75-78

Hannah, Persis Dwight (fl. 1900's)
  Amer. journalist
  Ross—Ladies p386-387

Hannum, Alberta Pierson (1906-   )
  Amer. novelist
  Warfel—Amer. p192-193,por.

Hansberry, Lorraine (1930-1965)
  Amer. playwright
  Cherry—Portraits p148-152
  CR '63 p270,por.
  Cur. Biog. '59 p165-167
  Cur. Biog. '65 p184
  Phelps—Men (2) '59 p127-128

Hanschman, Nancy Conners (c. 1929-   )
  Amer. journalist
  Cur. Biog. '62 p183-185,por.

Hansen, Cecilia (1898-   )
  Russ.-Dan. violinist
  McCoy—Portraits p73,por.

Hansen, Julia Butler (1907-   )
  Amer. Congresswoman, politician
  U.S.—Women (87th) p23,por.
  U.S.—Women (88th) p13,por.

Hanska, Evelina von (1804/04-1882)
  Fr., wife of Honoré de Balzac

(Continued)

Hanska, Evelina von—*Continued*

> Blei—Fasc. p195-199,por.
> Mayne—Enchant. p298-311,por.
> Orr—Famous Affin. IV p155-166

Hansl, Eva Von Baur (fl. 1930's)
> Amer. journalist, editor
> Women—Achieve. p163,por.

Hanssen, Hertha I. (fl 1930's)
> Amer. business executive
> Women—Achieve. p147,por.

Han Suyin (Elizabeth Comber) (1917-   )
> Chin. author, physician
> Cur. Biog. '57 p237-238,por.

Harazthy, Mrs. (fl. 1840's)
> Aust.-Amer. W. pioneer
> Ellet—Pioneer p374-375

Harbert, Lizzie Boynton (m. 1870)
> Amer. lecturer
> Hanaford—Dau. p344-345

Harbeson, Georgiana Brown (1894-   )
> Amer. industrial artist, designer
> Women—Achieve. p115,por.

Harbord, Mrs. Assheton (fl. 1900's)
> Eng. balloonist
> *May—Women p30-31

Harcourt, Elizabeth Cabot Motley, Lady
> (d. 1928)
> Amer., daughter of John Lothrop
> Motley
> Pearson—Many p217-220

Hard, Darlene (1936-   )
> Amer. tennis player
> CR '63 p270-271
> Cur. Biog. '64 p176-179,por.

Hard, Eliza (fl. 1660's-1680's)
> Amer. pioneer
> Green—Pioneer (1) p371-373

Hardelot, Guy D' (Mrs. W. I. Rhodes)
> (1858-1936)
> Fr. singer
> McCoy—Portraits p73,por.

Harden, Mrs. Cecil Murray (1894-   )
> Amer. Congresswoman
> Cur. Biog. '49 p243-245,por.

Hardenbroeck, Margaret.
> See Philipse, Margaret Harden-Broeck
> De Vries

Hardey, Mary (Mother Mary Aloysia
> Hawley) (1810-1886)
> Amer. nun
> Logan—Part p625-630

Hardin, Julia Carlin (fl. 1870's)
> Amer. religious worker
> Logan—Part p620

Harding, Ann (1902-   )
> Amer. actress
> Hughes—Famous p243-262,por.

Harding, Caroline (fl. 1900's)
> Amer. journalist
> Ross—Ladies p448-449

Harding, Charlotte (b. 1873)
> Amer. illustrator
> Mahony—Illus. p316
> Waters—Women p157

Harding, Elizabeth McGavock (b.c. 1818)
> Amer. Civil war diarist
> Jones—Heroines p155-165

Harding, Florence King (1860-1924)
> Amer., wife of Warren G. Harding
> Fairfax—Ladies p204-205
> Gerlinger—Mis. p92-94,por.
> Jensen—White p215-218,por.
> Logan—Ladies p166-173
> *McConnell—Our p277-284,por.
> Means—Woman p165-188
> Prindiville—First p221-228
> *Ross—Know p59,por.
> Smith—Romances p369-375,por.
> Truett—First p70,por.

Harding, Jane (m. 1852)
> Amer. whaling voyager
> Whiting—Whaling p99-114,178-182,
> por.

Harding, Margaret Snodgrass (1885-   )
> Amer. editor, publisher
> Cur. Biog. '47 p274-275,por.

Harding, Phoebe Elizabeth Dickerson
> (fl. 1850's-1970's)
> Amer., mother of Warren G.
> Harding
> Hampton—Our p240-255

Hardwick, Bess of.
> See Talbot, Countess of Shrewsbury

Hardy, Duffus, Lady (fl. 1870's-1890's)
> Eng. author
> Black—Notable p198-204,por.

Hardy, Iza Duffus (fl. 1890's-1900's)
> Eng. author, daughter of Lady
> Duffus Hardy
> Black—Notable p204-209,por.

Hardy, Kay (1902-   )
> Amer. artist, lecturer, teacher
> Women—Achieve. p142,por.

Hare, Amory (1885-1964)
Amer. poet, horse breeder
Cook—Our p307-310
Smith—Women's p108

Hare, Jeannette R. (1898-   )
Belg.-Amer. sculptor
National—Contemp. p141

Hargreaves, Sheba (b. 1882)
Amer. author
Binheim—Women p160,por.

Hari, Mata (Gertrude Margarete Zelle
(1876-1917)
Neth.-Ger. spy
Armour—It p126-134
Barton—Celeb. p201-212,por.
Blei—Fasc. p217-225,por.
Rogers—Gallant p15-51
Singer—3000 p236-244
Singer—World's p140-161,por.

Harker, Lizzie Allen Watson (1863-1933)
Eng. novelist
Hammerton p723

Harkness, Georgia Elma (1891-   )
Amer. teacher clergyman, author
Cur. Biog. '60 p178-180,por.

Harkness, Mary Stillman (fl. 1930's)
Eng. philanthropist
Brittain—Women p186,216,260

Harkness, Mrs. William (fl. 1930's)
Amer. explorer
Rogers—Women p141,por.

Harlan, Mrs. James (m. 1845/46)
Amer. Civil war humanitarian
Brockett—Woman's p676-678

Harland, Elizabeh Carraway (fl. 1860's)
Amer. spy
Simkins—Women p78

Harland, Lizzie (fl. 1880's)
Eng. composer, conductor
Elson—Woman's p143

Harland, Marion, pseud.
See Terhune, Mary Virginia Hawes

Harley, Brilliana Conway, Lady (c. 1600-
1643)
Eng. letter-writer
Stenton—English p170-171

Harlow, Jean (1911-1937)
Amer. actress
Hammerton p733
Schickel—Satrs p125,por.
Time Aug.19,1935 p26,por.(Cover)

Harman, Catharine Maria (d. 1775)
Amer. Colonial actress
Dexter—Colonial p159-162-164

Harman, Elizabeth, Lady Pakenham
(gr. 1930)
Eng. lecturer, politician
Brittain—Women p176,224,253

Harmer, Bertha (d. 1934)
Can. nurse, educator
Dolan—Goodnow's p262,por.
Pennock—Makers p114-115,por.

Harmon, Amelia (fl. 1860's)
Amer. Civil war heroine, patriot
Brockett—Woman's p777-778
Hanaford—Dau. p212

Harmon, Lily (1913-   )
Amer. artist
Ency. Brit.-Amer. p52,por.

Harmon, Ruth J. (fl. 1930's)
Amer. aviation instructor
Planck—Women p167

Harmonia (fl. 470's B.C.)
Sic., dau. of Gelon
Boccaccio—Conc. p148-149

Harnack, Mildred (1902-1943)
Ger. politician
Stiles—Postal p115

Harned, Virginia (c. 1868-1946)
Amer. actress
Coad—Amer. p277,por.
Moses—Famous p111,por.
Strang—Actresses p125-133,por.

Harnet, Mary (d. 1792)
Amer. colonial plantation manager
Dexter—Colonial p116-117

Harper, Elizabeth (d. 1833)
Amer. W. pioneer
Ellet—Pioneer p254-266

Harper, Frances Allen Watkins (1825-1911)
Amer. poet, social reformer, lecturer
Brown—Home p97-103,por.
Hanaford—Dau. p346
O'Connor—Pioneer p93-94,197
Robinson—Hist. p88,por.
*Rollins—Famous p21-27,por.

Harper, Ida Husted (1851-1931)
Amer. feminist, journalist
Rogers—Women p63,por.

Harper, Lee. See Lee, (Nelle) Harper

Harpman, Julia (fl. 1920's)
Amer. journalist
Ross—Ladies p261-270,291,por.

Harraden, Beatrice (1864-1936)
Eng. novelist
Hammerton p725,por.

Harriman, Florence Jaffray (1870-1967)
Amer. diplomat, journalist,
politician, govt. official
Cur. Biog. '40 p365-366
Cur. Biog. '67 p477
Fairfax—Ladies p211
Rogers—Women p66,por.
Roosevelt—Ladies p206-209
Women—Achieve. p50,por.

Harriman, Grace Carley (1873-1950)
Amer. humanitarian
Women—Achieve. p40,por.

Harriman, Mary Williamson Averill (1851-
1932)
Amer. philanthropist, business
woman
Logan—Part p893

Harrington, Cornelia (fl. 1860's)
Amer. Civil war nurse
Logan—Part p368

Harrington, Helen (fl. 1930's)
Amer. physician, pediatrician
Women—Achieve. p123,por.

Harrington, Maria, Countess of.
See **Foote, Maria,** Countess of
Harrington

Harris, Arlene (1898-   )
Can. monologist, radio personality
Donaldson—Radio p15

Harris, Barbara (1935/37-   )
Amer. actress
CR '63 p272,por.
Cur. Biog. '68 p173-176,por.

Harris, Belle C. (fl. 1890's-1900's)
Amer. club leader
Logan—Part p356

Harris, Bernice Kelly (1894-   )
Amer. author
Cur. Biog. '49 p250-251,por.
Hoyle—Tar p93-96,por.
Warfel—Amer. p194-195,por.

Harris, Corra May White (1869-1935)
Amer. author
Bruère—Laugh p45
Maurice—Makers p7-8,por.
Overton—Women p174-177

Harris, Eliza (fl. 1860's)
Amer. Civil war humanitarian,
author
Dannett—Noble p101-102,184-187,214-
215

Harris, Elizabeth (fl. 1650's)
Eng.-Amer. religious worker
Jones—Quakers p265-268,276

Harris, Hettie (fl. 1930's)
Amer. secretary, singer
Women—Achieve. p67,por.

Harris, Mrs. Irving Drought.
See **McCardell, Claire**

Harris, Jane Davenport (fl. 1930's)
Fr.-Amer. sculptor, explorer
Women—Achieve. p124,por.

Harris, Mrs. John (fl. 1860's)
Amer. Civil war nurse,
humanitarian
Brockett—Woman's p149-160,643-645
Logan—Part p311
Moore—Women p176-212
Young—Women p185-186,213

Harris, Julie (1925-   )
Amer. actress
Beaton—Persona p58-59
Blum—Great p138,por.
CR '59 p326,por.
CR '63 p272-273,por.
Cur. Biog. '56 p250-252,por.
Newquist—Show p181-193,por.
*Seventeen—In p5-8,por.
Time Nov.28,1955 p76,por. (Cover)
*Wagner—Famous p143-147

Harris, Letitia Radcliffe (fl. 1940's)
Amer. composer
McCoy—Portraits p74,por.

Harris, Patricia Roberts (1924-   )
Amer. ambassador, lawyer,
educator
Cur. Biog. '65 p189-191,por.

Harris, Rosemary (1930-   )
Brit. actress
Cur. Biog. '67 p162-164,por.

Harris, Sarah (fl. 1830's)
Amer. pupil of Prudence Crandall
Douglas—Remember p106-108,112

Harris, Ula Moulton (m. 1946)
Amer. missionary
They—Went p121-122

Harris, Miss W. F. (fl. 1860's)
Amer. Civil war nurse
Brockett—Woman's p742-743

Harrison, Anna Symmes (1775-1864)
Amer., wife of William Henry
Harrison
DAR Mag. July 1921 p390,por.
Gerlinger—Mis. p32-34,por.

(Continued)

Harrison, Anna Symmes—*Continued*

    Green—Pioneer (3) p250,310,313
    Hanaford—Dau. p82-85
    Logan—Ladies p50-54
    Logan—Part p238-240
    *McConnell—Our p103-111,por.
    Prindiville—First p83-93
    *Ross—Know p21,por.
    Smith—Romances p127-136,por.
    Whitton—First p152-176

Harrison, Anne (1).
    See Fanshawe, Anne Harrison, Lady

Harrison, Anne (2).
    See Paca, Anne

Harrison, Beatrice (1892-   )
    Brit. cellist
    McCoy—Portraits p74,por.

Harrison, Caroline Lavinia Scott (1832-
    1892)
    Amer., wife of Benjamin Harrison
    Farmer—What p99-100,145-146
    Gerlinger—Mis. p73-74,por.
    Hanaford—Dau. p118-128,por.
    Jensen—White p138-143,por.
    Logan—Ladies p121-125
    Logan—Part p279-281,430-431
    *McConnell—Our p229-234,por.
    Prindiville—First p185-189
    *Ross—Know p49,por.
    Smith—Romances p307-314,por.
    Truett—First p56,por.

Harrison, Constance Cary (Mrs. Burton
    Harrison) (1843-1920)
    Amer. author
    Harkins—Famous p59-74,por.
    Harkins—Little p59-74,por.
    Logan—Part p801-802

Harrison, Dorothy Ann (fl. 1930's)
    Amer. journalist
    Ross—Ladies p518-520

Harrison, Edith Ogden (   )
    Amer. author
    Logan—Part p835

Harrison, Elizabeth Bassett (b. 1741/42)
    Amer. patriot, mother of William
    Henry Harrison
    Green—Pioneer (3) p247-250
    Hampton—Our p73-80

Harrison, Elizabeth F. Irwin (fl. 18th cent.)
    Amer., mother of Benjamin Harrison
    Hampton—Our p183-192

Harrison, Hazel (gr. 1903)
    Amer. pianist
    Cuney-Hare—Negro p373-375

Harrison, Helen (fl. 1930's-1940's)
    Can. aviatrix
    *Knapp—New p86-99,por.
    *May—Women p144-145

Harrison, Jane Ellen (1850-1928)
    Eng. archaeologist
    Dorland—Sum p143
    Mozans—Woman p332-333

Harrison, Joan Mary (c. 1908-   )
    Eng.-Amer. producer, scenarist
    Cur. Biog. '44 p272-274,por.

Harrison, Margaret (fl. 1800's)
    Amer. printer
    Club—Printing p21
    Dexter—Career p108

Harrison, Margaritta Willetts (1870's-
    1880's)
    Amer. artist
    Hanaford—Dau. p320

Harrison, Marjorie (fl. 1920's-1930's)
    Amer. journalist
    Women—Achieve. p98,por.

Harrison, Mary Scott Lord Dimmick (1858-
    1948)
    Amer., 2nd wife of William Henry
    Harrison
    Gerlinger—Mis. p75-77
    Ross—Know p49
    Women—Achieve. p122,por.

Harrison, Mary St. Leger (Lucas Malet,
    pseud.)
    Eng. author, daughter of Charles
    Kingsley
    Furniss—Some p18-20,por.

Harron, Marion Janet (1903-   )
    Amer. judge
    Cur. Biog. '49 p256-258,por.
    Women—Achieve. p64,por.

Harrower, Elizabeth (1928-   )
    Austral. author
    Hetherington—42 p237-241,por.

Harshaw, Margaret (c. 1912-   )
    Amer. singer
    Matz—Opera p179-183,por.
    Peltz—Spot. p101,por.

Hart, Deborah Scudder (m. 1740)
    Amer. pioneer, patriot
    Green—Pioneer (3) p144-147

Hart, Dorothy (c. 1923-   )
    Amer. actress
    TV—Person. (2) p22-23

Hart, Emma. See Willard, Emma Hart

Hart, Fanchon (fl. 1930's)
     Amer. bacteriologist
     Women—Achieve. p141,por.

Hart, Janey (fl. 1960's)
     Amer. aviatrix, helicopter pilot,
       "space woman"
     *May—Women p247-248,por.

Hart, Letitia Bennet (b. 1867)
     Amer. painter
     Waters—Women p157

Hart, Marion Rice (1891-   )
     Amer. aviatrix
     *May—Women p199

Hart, Nancy Morgan (c. 1755-c. 1840)
     Amer. Rev. war heroine
     Ellet—Women (2) p263-269
     Green—Pioneer (2) p247-256,por.
     Leonard—Amer. p116
     *Nida—Pilots p200-202
     Whitton—These p26-27

Hart, Pearl (b.c. 1872)
     Amer. W. bandit
     Aikman—Calamity p253-279,por.
     Horan—Desperate p287-304,por.

Hart, Ruth Cole (1742-1844)
     Amer. Rev. war patriot
     Green—Pioneer (3) p518-519
     Root—Chapter p187-208

Hart, Susannah.
     See Shelby, Susanna Hart

Hartigan, Grace (1922-   )
     Amer. painter
     Cur. Biog. '62 p192-194,por.

Hartline, Mary (1926-   )
     Amer. TV performer, orchestra
       leader
     TV—Person. (1) p151-152,por.

Hartman, Grace (1907-1955)
     Amer. dancer, comedienne
     Cur. Biog. '42 p338-340,por.
     Cur. Biog. '55 p263

Hartman, Mrs. Gustave (1900-   )
     Amer. philanthropist, author
     Ribalow—Auto. p352-357

Hartman, May Weisser (c. 1900-   )
     Amer. humanitarian, social welfare
       leader
     Women—Achieve. p139,por.

Hartman, Regina (fl. 1750's)
     Amer. pioneer, Ind. captive
     *Elson—Side p15-20

Hartt, Mary Bronson (b. 1873)
     Amer. author
     Logan—Part p860-861

Hartwell, Elizabeth.
     See Sherman, Elizabeth Hartwell

Harvard, Sue (fl. 1920's-1940's)
     Welsh singer
     McCoy—Portraits p75,por.

Harvey, Cordelia Adelaide Perrine (1824-
       1895)
     Amer. Civil war nurse,
       humanitarian, social welfare
       leader
     Brockett—Woman's p260-268
     Moore—Women p409-414

Harvey, Jenny Dow (fl. 1890's-1920's)
     Amer. social worker
     Addams—Excellent p17-25

Harvey, Marion (d. 1681)
     Scot. covenanter
     Anderson—Ladies p288-299

Harvey, Maud Clark (b. 1865)
     Amer. religious worker
     Logan—Part p664

Harvey, Mrs. (fl. 1770's)
     Amer. Rev. war patriot
     Ellet—Women (2) p309-310

Harvitt, Helene (fl. 1930's)
     Amer. editor, educator
     Women—Achieve. p95,por.

Hasdew, Julia (1869-1888)
     Rum. scholar, lecturer, author
     Schmidt—400 p342,por.

Haseley, Julia.
     See Tester, Dorothy Julia

Hashop (Ancient)
     Egypt. architect, queen
     Waters—Women p xii

Haskell, Helen Eggleston (m. 1903)
     Amer. author
     Women—Achieve. p167,por.

Haskell, Parola (fl. 1870's)
     Amer. librarian
     Hanaford—Dau. p719

Haskil, Clara (1895-1960)
     Hung. pianist
     Schonberg—Great p424

Haslett, Caroline, Dame (1895-1957)
Brit. engineer, feminist
Asquith—Myself p97-116,por.
Cur. Biog. '50 p223-225,por.
Cur. Biog. '57 p244

Hasse, Faustina. See Bordoni, Faustina

Hassel, Miss (fl. 1800's)
Amer. friend of Aaron Burr
Burt—Phila. p308,315-317

Hasselaer, Kenau (1526-1589)
Nether. patriot, heroine
Schmidt—400 p296-297,por.

Hasselriis, Else (n.d.)
Dan. illustrator.
Mahony—Illus. p316

Hasseltine, Ann.
See Judson, Ann Hasseltine

Hasson, Esther Vorhees (fl. 1900's)
Amer. nurse
Pennock—Makers p60

Haste, Gwendolen (fl. 1920's-1930's)
Amer. poet
Women—Achieve. p187,por.

Hastings, Anna Maria Apollonia (1747-1837)
Brit., wife of Warren Hastings
Hahn—Love p237-279

Hastings, Caroline E. (fl. 1870's)
Amer. lecturer
Hanaford—Dau. p343

Hastings, Elizabeth, Lady (1682-1739)
Eng. philanthropist, beauty
Stenton—English p224-227,283,304

Hastings, Flora Elizabeth, Lady (1806-1839)
Eng. lady-in-waiting
Hahn—Love p287-310
Hammerton p730

Hastings, Margaret (fl. 1960's)
Amer. glider pilot
*May—Women p217-218,por.

Hastings, Selina, Countess of Huntingdon (1707-1791)
Eng. foundress
Dorland—Sum p35,133

Haswell, Susanna Haswell (c. 1763-1824)
Amer. seafarer
Snow—Women p1-13,por.

Hatasu. See Hatshepsut

Hatch, Edith (b. 1884)
Amer. organist, composer, piano teacher
McCoy—Portraits p75,por.

Hatcher, Georgia H. Stockton (b. 1864)
Amer. club leader
Logan—Part p468

Hatfield, Sarah.
See Clark, Sarah Hatfield

Hathaway, Ann (fl. 1940's)
Amer. violinist, author, teacher
McCoy—Portraits p76,por.

Hathaway, Anne (c. 1557-1623)
Eng., wife of William Shakespeare
Brown—Dark p293-294
Hammerton p730

Hathaway, Katherine Butler (1890-1942)
Amer. author
*Eby—Marked p105-109
Stone—We p231-237

Hathaway, Maggie Smith (b. 1867)
Amer. educator, welfare worker, politician
Binheim—Women p132,por.

Hathaway, Mrs. P. V. (fl. 1870's-1880's)
Amer. botanist
Hanaford—Dau. p288-289

Hathaway, Sibyl Mary Collings, Dame of Sark (fl. 1920's)
Parkinson—Law p197-218,por.

Hathaway, Winifred Phillips (c. 1870-1954)
Amer. educator
Women—Achieve. p61,por.

Hathorne, Mary (d. 1802)
Amer. merchant
Dexter—Career p150-151

Hatshepsut (d. 1479/80 B.C.)
Egypt. queen
*Boyd—Rules p15-24,por.
Cuppy—Decline p17-25
D'Humy—Women p53-94
Hammerton p731,por.
*Holmes—She p9-46
Koven—Women p2-3
Muir—Women p16-18
Schmidt—400 p110-111,por.

Hatton, Elizabeth, Lady (fl.c. 1617)
Eng., wife of Sir Edward Coke
Stenton—English p66-67

Hatton, Fanny Cottinet Locke (1869-1939)
Amer. playwright
Mantle—Amer. p288
Mantle—Contemp. p235-**236**

Hauck, Louise Platt (1883-1943)
Amer. author
Cur. Biog. '44 p281-282

Haughery, Margaret (1814-1882)
Amer. baker, social worker,
philanthropist
Blunt—Great p367-379
DAR Mag. July 1921 p394,por.
Logan—Part p303-304

Haugland, Brynhild (1905-   )
Amer. agriculturist, politician
Roosevelt—Ladies p140-143

Hauk (Hauck), Minnie (1851/52-1929)
Amer. singer
Ewen—Ency. p202-203
Lahee—Famous p181-185
McCoy—Portraits p76,por.
Marks—Glamour p218-223,por.
Wagner—Prima p51-52,59-60,102-
104,243

Haupt, Enid (1906-   )
Amer. editor
CR '63 p276,por.

Havener, Helen (fl. 1900's-1920's)
Amer. journalist, editor
Ross—Ladies p527-531

Havens, Belle (fl. 1900's)
Amer. painter
Waters—Women p157-158

Havens, Mary Sue McDonald (fl. 1920's-
1950's)
Amer. missionary
They—Went p78-80

Haver, Phyllis (1926-   )
Amer. actress
Herman—How p45,por.

Haverfield, Evelina (1867-1920)
Eng. feminist
Hammerton p732

Havergal, Frances Ridley (1836-1879)
Eng. poet, hymn-writer
Carey—Twelve p351-380,por.
Deen—Great p307
Dorland—Sum p29,72,186
Foster—Religion p179-195,por.
Hammerton p732
Miller—Ten p67-72

Havers, Alice (fl. 19th cent.)
Eng. artist
Furniss—Some p87-88

Havoc, June (1916-   )
Amer. actress
CR '59 p329,por.
CR '63 p277,por.
TV—Person. (1) p123-124,por.

Hawes, Elizabeth (1903-   )
Amer. designer, author
Cur. Biog. '40 p370-372,por.
Rogers—Women p115,por.

Hawes, Frances Anne, Viscountess Vane
(1713-1788)
Eng. maid-of-honor
Melville—Maids p254-266

Hawes, Harriet Boyd (b. 1871)
Eng. archaeologist, anthropologist,
nurse, author
Logan—Part p882
Mozans—Woman p321-322

Hawes, Mary. See Holmes, Mary Jane Hawes

Hawes, Mary Virginia.
See Terhune, Mary Virginia Hawes

Hawkes, Anna Lorette Rose (1890-   )
Amer. educator, organization
official
Cur. Biog. '56 p256-258,por.

Hawkes, Sylvia (fl. 1920's-1940's)
Eng. actress
Wyndham—Chorus p139

Hawkins, Jane (fl. 17th cent.)
Amer. pioneer, midwife
Bell—Women p266-269
Douglas—Remember p17-18,96

Hawkins, Sheila (1905-   )
Austral. illustrator
Mahony—Illus. p316-317

Hawkinson, Nellie X. (fl. 1920's-1930's)
Amer. nurse, educator
Pennock—Makers p84,por.

Hawks, Annie S. (1835-1918)
Amer. hymn-writer
Deen—Great p308

Hawks, Rachel Marshall (b. 1879)
Amer. sculptor
National—Contemp. p144

Hawley, Adelaide (fl. 1930's)
Amer. radio personality
Women—Achieve. p64,por.

Hawley, Gertrude (fl. 1920's)
Amer. athlete, coach
*Ferris—Girls p3-17

Hawley, Harriet Foote (fl. 1860's)
Amer. Civil war nurse
Brockett—Woman's p416-419
Dannett—Noble p302-304,316-320
Moore—Women p387-396

Hawley, Laura M. (1812-1842)
Amer. poet
Hanaford—Dau. p265

Hawley, Margaret Foote (1810-1963)
Amer. painter
Michigan—Biog. p144-145

Hawley, Maria (fl. 1870's)
Amer. publisher
Hanaford—Dau. p704

Hawthorne, Mrs. (fl. 1880's)
Amer. painter, sculptor
Hanaford—Dau. p295-296

Hawthorne, Rose.
See Lathrop, Rose Hawthorne

Hay, Eliza Monroe (b.c. 1787)
Amer., dau. of James Monroe
Jensen—White p36-38,por.
*Sweetser—Famous p85-99

Hay, Helen Scott (d. 1932)
Amer. Red Cross nurse
DAR Mag. Nov.1921 p642-644,por.
Pennock—Makers p48-49,por.

Hay, Mary Garrett (d. 1928)
Amer. feminist
Irwin—Angels p342-343,349

Hay, Regina Deem (1890-   )
Amer. politician, club leader
Cur. Biog. '48 p271-272,por.

Hay, Sarah (fl. 1770's)
Amer. educator
Dexter—Colonial p91-92

Hayden, Ethyl (fl. 1940's)
Amer. singer
McCoy—Portraits p77,por.

Hayden, Mary F. Strahan (fl. 1860's)
Amer. Civil war nurse
Logan—Part p369

Hayden, Melissa (1928-   )
Can. ballet dancer
CR '59 p330-331,por.
CR '63 p278,por.
Cur. Biog. '55 p271-272,por.
*Terry—Star p193

Hayden, Sophia G. (c. 1868-1953)
Amer. architect
Stern—We p67-76

Hayes, Anna Hansen (b. 1886)
Amer. organization official
Cur. Biog. '49 p261-263

Hayes, Dorsha (fl. 1930's-1940's)
Amer. novelist
Warfel—Amer. p199,por.

Hayes, Ellen (b. 1851)
Amer. author, educator
Logan—Part p720-721

Hayes, Evelyn Carroll (fl. 1930's)
Amer. educator
Women—Achieve. p198

Hayes, Helen (1900-   )
Amer. actress
Blum—Great p107,por.
*Clymer—Modern p109-119,por.
Coad—Amer. p324,por.
Cocroft—Great p179-191,por.
CR '59 p331,por.
CR '63 p278-279,por.
Cur. Biog. '42 p348-352,por.
Cur. Biog. '56 p258-260,por.
Dodd—Celeb. p111-115
Eichberg—Radio p80-81,por.
Eustis—Players p15-28,por.
Fisher—Amer. p303-304,por.
Funke—Actors p77-112,por.
Martin—Pete p428-437
Murrow—This (1) p65-66
New Yorker May 20,1939 p24-30,por.;
    May 27, 1939 p28-38 (Profiles)
Newquist—Show. p195-209,por.
Ormsbee—Back. p228,244-248,279,por.
Taves—Success. p50-59,por
Thomas—Modern p451-465
Time Dec.30,1935,p22,por. (Cover)
*Wagner—Famous p133-140
Women—Achieve. p71,por.

Hayes, Irene (fl. 1930's)
Amer. florist
Women—Achieve. p57,por.

Hayes, Lucy Webb (1831-1889)
Amer., wife of Rutherford B. Hayes
Deen—Great p245-248
Fairfax—Ladies p201-202
Farmer—What p90-96,144-145,por.
Gerlinger—Mis. p61-64,por.
Hanaford—Dau. p101-105,por.
Jensen—White p111-119,por.
Logan—Ladies p108-112
Logan—Part p269-272
*McConnell—Our p195-203,por.
Prindiville—First p164-168
*Ross—Know p41,por.
Smith—Romances p262-269,por.
Truett—First p48,por.

Hayes, Margaret Meserolle (fl. 1860's)
Amer. Civil war nurse
Logan—Part p369,334

Hayes, Sophia Birchard (fl. 1810's-1830's)
Amer., mother of Rutherford B.
Hayes
Hampton—Our p147-154

Hayman, Charlotte Law (1906-   )
Amer. social worker
Epstein—People p18-37

Hayman, Laure (b.c. 1851)
    Fr. courtesan
    Skinner—Elegant p230-231

Haynes, Ann (d. 1790)
    Amer. W. pioneer
    Ellet—Pioneer p145-152

Haynes, Elizabeth A. Ross (fl. 1930's)
    Amer. business woman, author,
        social worker
    Women—Achieve. p158,por.

Haynes, Lorenza (b. 1820)
    Amer. clergyman
    Hanaford—Dau. p450,719
    Irwin—Angels p121,164-165

Hays, Mary (1760-1843)
    Brit. novelist
    MacCarthy—Later p196-198

Hays, Mary Ludwig.
    See Pitcher, Molly

Hayward, Ruth Rutter (d. 1761)
    Amer. pioneer, foundress
    Green—Pioneer (3) p427-431

Hayward, Susan (1917/19-   )
    Amer. actress
    CR '59 p333,por.
    CR '63 p280,por.
    Cur. Biog. '53 p258-259,por.
    Phelps (2) '59 p129-130

Haywood, Eliza (c. 1693-1756)
    Eng. author
    Benson—Women p41-45
    Hammerton p735
    MacCarthy—Later p18-21
    MacCarthy—Women p233-251

Haywood, Rosemary (fl. 1930's)
    Amer. editor, publisher
    Women—Achieve. p183,por.

Hayworth, Rita (1919-   )
    Amer. actress
    CR '59 p333-334,por.
    CR '63 p280-281,por.
    Cur. Biog. '60 p184-185,por.
    Schickel—Stars p142,218,por.
    Time Nov. 10,1941 p90,por. (Cover)

Hazard, Caroline (1856-1945)
    Amer. educator
    Adelman—Famous p286-287
    Logan—Part p715-716

Hazard, Mary (c. 1639-1739)
    Amer. colonial nurse
    Dexter—Colonial p58-59

Hazeleponi (Biblical)
    Deen—All p268

Hazeltine, Mary E. (1868-1949)
    Amer. pioneer librarian
    Marshall—Amer. p454

Hazen, Fanny Titus (b. 1840)
    Amer. Civil war nurse
    Logan—Part p362

Hazleton, Mary Brewster (1890's-1900's)
    Amer. artist
    Waters—Women p158

H. D., pseud. See Doolittle, Hilda

Head, Edith (n.d.)
    Amer. fashion designer
    CR '59 p334,por.
    CR '63 p281,por.
    Cur. Biog. '45 p276-278,por.
    *Forsee—Women p152-177

Headfort, Marchioness of.
    See Boote, Rose

Headlam-Morley, Agnes (gr. 1924)
    Eng. educator
    Brittain—Women p222,235,246

Headley, Elizabeth Cavanna.
    See Cavanna, Betty

Heald, Rebecca (fl. 1800's)
    Amer. W. pioneer
    Ellet—Pioneer p281-302
    Logan—Part p85-89

Healy, Mary (1918-   )
    Amer. actress
    Blum—Television p57,por.
    CR '59 p331-332,por.
    CR '63 p279,por.
    TV—Person. (3) p61-62,por.

Heard, Marie Bartlett (b. 1868)
    Amer. club leader
    Binheim—Women p7,por.

Heard, Marilyn Grover (fl. 1940's-1950's)
    Amer. aviatrix, helicopter pilot
    *May—Women p197,204-205

Heard, Mrs. (fl. c. 1680's)
    Amer. pioneer, Ind. captive
    Fowler—Woman p83

Hearst, Millicent W. (m. 1903)
    Amer., wife of William Randolph
        Hearst
    Tebbel—Inher. p167-169

Hearst, Phoebe Apperson (1842-1919)
    Amer. philanthropist
    Adelman—Famous p256-257
    *Curtin—Gallery p42,por.
    Logan—Part p530-531
    Tebbel—Inher. p161,163-164,166-167

Heath, Mary, Lady (fl. 1920's)
    Eng. aviatrix
    *May—Women p101-102

Hebard, Grace Raymond (b. 1861)
    Amer. educator
    Binheim—Women p214,por.

Hebden, Katharine (fl. 1640's)
    Amer. colonial physician
    Spruill—Women's p267,351-352

Heberding, Dolly (fl. 1940's)
    Amer. aviatrix
    *May—Women p165-166

Heck, Barbara Ruckle (1734-1804)
    Irish-Amer. religious foundress,
      missionary
    Culver—Women p152-153
    Deen—Great p371-373
    Dexter—Career p57-58
    Dexter—Colonial p149-150
    Irwin—Angels p56
    Leonard—Amer. p44,116
    Logan—Part p509-510
    Spruill—Women's p248

Heckart, Eileen (1919-   )
    Amer. actress
    Cur. Biog. '58 p188-189,por.
    Ross—Players p132-137

Heckewelder, Mary (b. 1781)
    Amer. W. pioneer
    Ellet—Pioneer p193-196

Heckler, Margaret M. (n.d.)
    Amer. Congresswoman
    Lamson—Few p109-123,por.

Heckscher, Celeste de Longpré (1860-
      1928)
    Amer. composer
    Elson—Woman's p254-255
    Hipsher—Amer. p225-226
    McCoy—Portraits p77,por.

Hector, Annie Alexander (1825-1902)
    Irish novelist
    Black—Notable p58-67,por.
    Dorland—Sum p55
    Hammerton p737

Hedden, Worth Tuttle (1896-   )
    Amer. author
    Cur. Biog. '57 p247-248,por.
    Warfel—Amer. p200,por.

Hedges, Lillie Bowyer (fl. 1910's-1940's)
    Amer. missionary
    They—Went p29-30

Hedinger, Elise Neumann (b. 1854)
    Ger. painter
    Waters—Women p158

Hedwig, Queen. See Jadwiga (Jodwiga)

Hedwig (1174-1243)
    Siles. duchess, saint
    Blunt—Great p157-159
    Englebert—Lives p394-395
    Stiles—Postal p234
    Wescott—Calen. p163

Hedyle (fl. 260's-240's B.C.)
    Gr. poet, mother of Hedylus
    Anthologia—Poets p97

Heed, Ruth. See Byers, Ruth

Heer, Anna (d. 1918)
    Swiss. physician
    Lovejoy—Women p166-167
    Stiles—Postal p117

Heeren, Minna (fl. 1813-1870's)
    Ger. painter
    Waters—Women p158

Hegan, Alice Caldwell.
    See Rice, Alice Caldwell Hegan

Heiberg, Johanne Louise Patges (1812-
      1890)
    Dan. actress, author
    Schmidt—400 p95-97,por.

Heikel, Rosina (gr. 1878)
    Fin. pioneer physician
    Lovejoy—Women p174-175

Heilein, Mrs. Matheis (fl. 1750's)
    Amer. pioneer
    Green—Pioneer (2) p202

Heilein, Sarah. See Morgan, Sarah

Heiman, Gertrude (fl. 1930's)
    Amer. hotel executive
    Women—Achieve. p109,por.

Heimer, Ruth Loretta Duggins (m. 1948)
    Amer. missionary
    They—Went p130-131

Heim-Vogtlin, Marie (1846-1916)
    Swiss pioneer physician
    Lovejoy—Women p165-167
    Schmidt—400 p385-386

Heine, Madame. See Mirat, Mathilde

Heinkel, Susan (c. 1944-   )
    Amer. actress
    TV—Person. (3) p89-91,por.

Heiss, Carol (1940-   )
    Amer. skater
    CR '59 p337,por.
    CR '63 p284,por.
    Cur. Biog. '59 p181-183,por.

Heitz, Margaret (fl. 1960's)
    Amer. airline hostess
*May—Women p237

Hekking, Avis (fl. 1900's)
    Amer. artist
    Logan—Part p764

Helah (Biblical)
    Deen—All p268

Helburn, Theresa (c. 1887-1959)
    Amer. playwright, theatrical
        producer and director
    Cur. Biog. '44 p381-385,por.
    Cur. Biog. '59 p183
    New Yorker Dec.6,1930 p31-34,por.
        (Profiles)

Held, Anna (c. 1873-1918)
    Fr. actress, comedienne
    Blum—Great p38,por.

Helen (fl. 1500's A.D.)
    Ethiop. empress
    Stiles—Postal p117

Helen (1896-   )
    Rum. queen
    Phila.—Women unp.,por.
    Stiles—Postal p117

Helen of Skofde (fl. 12th cent.)
    Swed. saint
    Blunt—Great p157

Helen, Sister (d. 1876)
    Eng. nun, nurse
    Pennock—Makers p20,por.

Helen of Troy (fl. c. 1100 B.C.)
    Gr. beauty
    Adelman—Famous p17-18
    Armour—It p25-35
    Brown—Dark p11-90
    Davenport—Great p29-33
    Hahn—Love p15-26
    Terhune—Super. p62-88

Helena (fl. 4th cent. B.C.)
    Gr. painter
    Waters—Women p158

Helena (1846-1923)
    Eng. princess, daughter of Queen
        Victoria
    Benson—Queen (see index)
    Hammerton p740

Helena, Flavia Julia (c. 247-328/330)
    Rom. empress, saint, philanthropist,
        mother of Constantine the Great
    Adelman—Famous p27
    Balsdon—Roman p166,169,233,249,por.
*Beebe—Saints p78-84
    Blunt—Great p72-75
    Deen—Great p7-10

Dolan—Goodnow's p72,por.
    Englebert—Lives p316-317
    Hammerton p740
    McCabe—Empr. (see index), por.
*MacVeagh—Champlin p281
    Sharkey—Pop. p52-53
    Stiles—Postal p234
    Wescott—Calen. p123
*Windham—Sixty p104-109

Hellen, Mary Catherine (d. 1870)
    Amer., wife of John Adams, II.
    Smith—White p31-39,por.

Hellman, Lillian (1905-   )
    Amer. playwright
    Burnett—This p1140
    CR '59 p337,por.
    CR '63 p285,por.
    Cur. Biog. '41 p375-376,por.
    Cur. Biog. '60 p186-187,por.
    Gould—Modern p168-185,por.
    Mantle—Contemp. p180-181
    New Yorker Nov.8,1941 p22-26,por.
        (Profiles)

Helm, Emilie (fl. c. 1850's-1860's)
    Amer., half-sister of Mary Todd
        Lincoln
    Leetch—Reveille p306-307

Helm, Lina J. Helm McKillip (d. 1844)
    Amer. W. pioneer
    Ellet—Pioneer p302-303

Helmer, Bessie Bradwell (b. 1858)
    Amer. editor, lawyer, publisher
    Irwin—Angels p176,179,224

Héloïse (c. 1101-1164)
    Fr. abbess, scholar
    Adelman—Famous p34-35
    Davenport—Great p93-101,
    Hammerton p740
    Orr—Famous p19-35
    Orr—Famous Affin. I p25-48
    Watson—Some p1-21

Heloise (1919-   )
    Amer. journalist
    CR '63 p285,por.

Helvarg, Sue (fl. 1930's)
    Russ.-Amer. model, photographer's
        agent
    Women—Achieve. p113,por.

Helvetius, Madame (fl. 1740's-1750's)
    Amer., friend of Benjamin Franklin
    Donovan—Women p89-92

Helvia (fl. c. 50 B.C.-80 B.C.)
    Rom., mother of Seneca
    Beard—Woman p319-320

Hemans, Felicia Dorothea Browne (1793-
1835)
Eng. poet
Adelman—Famous p120
Courtney—Adven. p19-33,por.
Dorland—Sum p51,72,178
Fifty—Famous p279-281,por.
Hammerton p741,por.
MacVeagh—Champlin p281-282

Hemenway, Mary Tileston (1822-1894)
Amer. philanthropist
Logan—Part p525-526

Hemingway, Clara Edwards (fl. 1940's)
Amer. composer, singer, voice
teacher, author
McCoy—Portraits p79,por.

Hemingway, Mary Welsh (1908-   )
Amer. author, journalist, wife of
Ernest Hemingway
Cur. Biog. '68 p182-185,por.

Hempel, Frieda (1885-1955)
Ger. singer
Ewen—Ency. p204
Ewen—Living p164-165,por.
Hammerton p741
McCoy—Portraits p79,por.
Wagnalls—Opera p150-156,por.

Hemsley, Josephine (b. 1880)
Amer. author, song-writer
ASCAP p225

Henders, Harriet (fl. 1920's-1930's)
Amer. singer
Ewen—Living p165

Henderson, Allison Jamison (m. 1939)
Amer. missionary
They—Went p108-109

Henderson, Florence (1934-   )
Amer. actress, singer
CR '63 p285,por.

Henderson, Marcia (1930-   )
Amer. actress
TV—Person (1) p122-123,por.

Henderson, Miriam.
See Richardson, Dorothy M.

Henderson, Rise (fl. 1920's)
Amer. poet
Smith—Women's p111

Hendrikson, Blanche (fl. 1930's)
Amer. club leader
Women—Achieve. p96,por.

Henie, Sonja (1913-   )
Nor. skater
CR '59 p339,por.
CR '63 p286,por.
Cur. Biog. '40 p380-382,por.

Cur. Biog. '52 p258-259,por.
Davis—100 p52,por.
*Deakin—True p248-263
*Gelman—Young p114-123,por.
Lamparski—What. p112-113,por.
Time July 17,1939 p51,por.(Cover)

Henkle, Henrietta.
See Buckmaster, Henrietta

Hennock, Frieda Barkin (1904-1960)
Pol.-Amer. government official,
lawyer
Cur. Biog. '48 p278-280,por.
Cur. Biog. '60 p188
Phelps—Men (1) '58 p113-114

Henrietta, Countess of Rochester (Lady
Boyle) (c. 1643-1687)
Eng. beauty
Melville—Windsor p142-146,por.

Henrietta, Anne, Duchess of Orlèans.
See Orlèans, Henrietta Anne, Duchess d'

Henrietta Maria (1609-1669)
Eng., queen of Charles I
Dark—Royal p137-151,por.
Fifty—Famous p262-264,por.
Hammerton p742,por.
Sanders—Intimate p94-109,por.

Henriette, Madame (fl. 1760's)
Fr., sister of Louis the Dauphin
Haggard—Remark. p325,329-333,337-
338

Henriquez, Salomé Ureña de (1851-1899)
Dom.R. educator, poet
Schmidt—400 p104-105,por.

Henrotin, Ellen M. Martin (b. 1847)
Amer. philanthropist
Farmer—What p370,por.
Logan—Part p532

Henry, Anne Wood (1732-1799)
Amer. colonial county treasurer
Leonard—Amer. p116

Henry, Charlotte V. (b.c. 1916)
Amer. actress
Time Dec.25,1933 p20,por.(Cover)

Henry, Dorothea Dandridge (m. 1776)
Amer., 2nd wife of Patrick Henry
Green—Pioneer (3) p317-318

Henry, Marguerite (1902-   )
Amer. author
Cur. Biog. '47 p294-295,por.

Henry, Sarah Shelton (d. 1775)
Amer., 1st wife of Patrick Henry
Green—Pioneer (3) p315-317

Henschel, Lillian June (1860-1901)
Amer. singer
McCoy—Portraits p79,por.

Hensel, Fanny Cécile Mendelssohn (1805-1847)
Ger. composer, pianist
Elson—Woman's p125-128
McCoy—Portraits p79,por.,130,por.
Parton—Dau. p124-142
Parton—Noted p124-142

Hensey, Alice Ferrin (d. 1950)
Amer. missionary
They—Went p24-25

Hensel, Ruth (fl. 1930's)
Amer. teacher
Women—Achieve. p123,por.

Hentz, Caroline Lee (1800-1856)
Amer. author, teacher
Hanaford—Dau. p229
Papashvily—All p63-64,77-94,135,180

Hentz, Eta (fl. 1930's)
Hung.-Amer. business executive
Women—Achieve. p183,por.

Hepburn, Audrey (1929-   )
Belg.-Amer. actress
CR '59 p340,por.
CR '63 p286-287,por.
Cur. Biog. '54 p331-333,por.
°Forsee—Women p9-35
Schickel—Stars p263,por.
Time Sept.7,1953 p60,por.(Cover)

Hepburn, Emily Eaton (1865-1956)
Amer. club leader
Women—Achieve. p104,por.

Hepburn, Katharine (1909-   )
Amer. actress
Beaton—Persona p57-58,por.
Blum—Great p127,por.
Cocroft—Great p119-136,por.
CR '59 p340,por.
CR '63 p340,por.
Cur. Biog. '42 p362-364,por.
Hammerton p750
°Logie—Careers (2nd) p179-185
Schickel—Stars p168-169,por.
Time Sept.1,1952 p60,por. (Cover)

Heph-Zibah (Biblical)
Deen—All p268

Hepworth, Barbara (1903-   )
Brit. sculptor
Cur. Biog. '57 p250-252,por.

Hepworth, Jocelyn Barbara (1903-   )
Eng. sculptor
Hammerton p750

Herbelin, Jeanne Mathilde Habert (1820-1904)
Fr. painter
Waters—Women p159,379-380

Herbert, Elizabeth A'Court, Lady of Lea (1822-1911)
Eng. author
Blunt—Great p419-421

Herbert, Elizabeth Sweeney (1899-   )
Amer. organization official, editor, home economist
Cur. Biog. '54 p333-334,por.

Herbert, Mary.
See Pembroke, Mary Herbert Sidney, Countess of

Herbeson, Massy (fl. 1780's-1790's)
Amer. heroine, Ind. captive
Fowler—Woman p112-113

Herbst, Josephine Frey (1897-   )
Amer. author
°Millett—Amer. p388-390
Warfel—Amer. p202-203,por.

Herdman, Ramona (fl. 1920's-1930's)
Amer. journalist
Ross—Ladies p526-527
Women—Achieve. p75,por.

Hereford, Laura 1831-1870)
Eng. painter
Waters—Women p159

Herennia Etruscilla (fl. 230's-240's)
Rom. empress
Serviez—Roman (2) p308-310

Hereswitha (d.c. 690)
Eng. saint
Englebert—Lives p363

Herford, Beatrice (1868-1952)
Eng. actress
Dodd—Celeb. p191-195

Hering, Elsie Ward (1871-1923)
Amer. artist
Jackman—Amer. p30

Herman, Hermine von (b. 1857)
Hung. painter
Waters—Women p159

Herman, Mollie C. (fl. 1930's)
Amer. advertising executive
Women—Achieve. p113,por.

Herne, Katherine Corcoran (m. 1878)
Amer. actress
Coad—Amer. p286

Herodias (Biblical)
  Deen—All p184-188
  Lewis—Portraits p141-142
  MacVeagh—Champlin p289
  Marble—Women p157-161
  Morton—Women p167-173
  Van Der Velde—She p182-188

Herodias' daughter (Biblical)
  Deen—All p319-320

Heron, Matilda (1830/31-1877)
  Amer. actress
  Adelman—Famous p187-188
  Bodeen—Ladies p96-99
  Coad—Amer. p203,por.
  Ormsbee—Back. p145-152,154,por.

Herrad of Lansberg (d. 1195)
  Alsac. abbess, artist, poet,
    encyclopedist
  Drinker—Music p198-199
  Mozans—Woman p48-49

Herrick, Christian Terhune (1859-1944)
  Amer. author, home economist
  Dorland—Sum p150-151

Herrick, Elinore Morehouse (1895-1964)
  Amer. labor, personnel expert
  Cur. Biog. '47 p295-297,por.
  Cur. Biog. '65 p198
  Epstein—People p74-92

Herrick, Genevieve Forbes (m. 1924)
  Amer. journalist
  Ross—Ladies p7,539-543,por.

Herrick, Mary Elizabeth (fl. 1870's-1880's)
  Amer. lawyer, social reformer
  Hanaford—Dau. p679-680

Herring, Mary.
  See Middleton, Mary Williams

Herrmann, Josephine.
  See Herbst, Josephine Frey

Hersch, Virginia Davis (1896-   )
  Amer. novelist
  Warfel—Amer. p203-204,por.

Herschel, Caroline Lucretia (1750-1848)
  Ger.-Eng. astronomer
  Adelman—Famous p114
  Corkran—Romance p141-184,por.
  *Darrow—Thinkers p121-123
  Dorland—Sum p56,84,141
  Hammerton p754,por.
  Law—Civiliz. p179-182
  Mozans—Woman p182-190
  Parton—Dau. p302-308
  Parton—Noted p302-308,por.
  Schmidt—400 p195,por.
  Stenton—English p330
  Williams—Great p254-255,por.

Hershman, Aleene (fl. 1950's)
  Amer. business woman
  Fortune—100 p104-105

Hertford, Lady (1760-1834)
  Eng. social leader, friend of
    George, Prince of Wales
  Melville—Regency p148-154

Hertz, Laura B. (b. 1869)
  Amer. social reformer, sociologist
  Logan—Part p594-595

Herveu, Jeanne (fl. 1910's)
  Fr. pioneer aviatrix
  Planck—Women p25-26

Hervey, Mary Lepell (1700-1768)
  Eng. social leader
  Stenton—English p257,266,291
  Thomson—Queens p287-306

Herwig, Kathleen. See Winsor, Kathleen

Herz, Henriette (1764-1847)
  Ger. salonist
  Hargrave—Some p59-94,por.
  *Levinger—Great p114-116
  Schmidt—400 p196-197

Herzog, Beatrice (d. 1934)
  Amer. recluse
  Erskine—Out p125-135

Herzog, Helene (d. 1945)
  Amer. recluse
  Erskine—Out p125-135

Hess, Myra, Dame (1890-1965)
  Eng. pianist
  Brooks—Masters p164-166,por.
  CR '59 p342-343,por.
  Cur. Biog. '43 p289-291,por.
  Cur. Biog. '66 p466
  Dodd—Celeb. p232-236
  Downes—Olin p104-105,343-345
  Ewen—Living p166-167,por.
  Ewen—Men p146-150
  Gelatt—Music p223-231,por.
  Hammerton p756
  McCoy—Portraits p80,por.
  Saleski—Jewish p482-485,por.
  Saleski—Wander. p324-325,por.
  Schonberg—Great p422

Hesse-Darmstadt, Alice Maud, Grand
    duchess of (1843-1878)
  Eng. princess
  Hammerton p756

Hesselgren, Kerstin (1872-1962)
  Swed. feminist, sociologist
  Cur. Biog. '41 p383-384,por.
  Cur. Biog. '62 p205

Hester, Dorothy (fl. 1930's)
    Amer. aviatrix
    Earhart—Fun p150

Hetepheres (fl. 3000 B.C.)
    Egypt. queen
    Hammerton p756

Heustis, Louise Lyons (fl. 1900's)
    Amer. painter, illustrator
    Waters—Women p159-160

Hewett, Mary (d. 1853)
    Eng. clergyman
    Lambert—Quiet p87-91

Hewins, Caroline Maria (1846-1926)
    Amer. librarian, author
    Bul. of Bibl. Sept.-Dec.1920 p42,por.
    Marshall—Amer. p300-454

Hewlett, Hilda R. (fl. 1910's)
    Eng. pioneer aviatrix
    Dorland—Sum p102
    *May—Women p85,por.

Hewson, Mary Stevenson.
    See Stevenson, Mary (Polly)

Heylyn (Heylin), Mrs. Peter (fl. 17th cent.)
    Eng. clergyman
    Stenton—English p152-153,158

Heyman, Katherine Ruth Willoughby (1877-
    1944)
    Amer. composer, pianist
    Elson—Woman's p257-258

Heyman, Mrs. Marcus A.
    See Komarovsky, Mirra

Heymann, Lida Gustava (1868-1943)
    Ger, feminist
    Cur. Biog. '43 p294

Heyneman, Anne (1910-   )
    Amer. illustrator
    Mahony—Illus. p318

Heyrick, Elizabeth (fl. 19th cent.)
    Eng. social reformer
    Hanaford—Dau. p352

Heyward, Dorothy Hartzell Kuhns (1890-
    1961)
    Amer. playwright
    Mantle—Contemp. p231-232

Heyward, Elizabeth Mathews (m.c. 1767/
    68)
    Amer. Rev. war patriot
    Ellet—Pioneer (2) p353-354
    Green—Pioneer (3) p266-268

Heywood, Anne (c. 1913-1961)
    Amer. business woman, vocational
    counsellor
    Murrow—This (1) p69-70

Heywood, Mrs. (fl. 17th cent.)
    Eng., mother of Oliver Heywood
    Stenton—English p171

H.H., pseud.
    See Jackson, Helen Maria Hunt Fiske

Hibbard, Edna (c. 1895-1942)
    Amer. actress, comedienne
    Cur. Biog. '43 p294

Hibbard, Julia A. (fl. 1860's)
    Amer. Civil war nurse
    Logan—Part p366

Hibbins (Hibbens), Ann (fl. 1680's)
    Amer., accused witch
    Earle—Colon. p122-123
    Green—Pioneer (1) p225,294

Hichborn, Jennie Franklin (fl. 1890's)
    Amer. club leader
    Logan—Part p474-475

Hickenlooper, Olga. See Samaroff, Olga

Hickey, Margaret A. (1902-   )
    Amer. editor, govt. employee,
    personnel worker
    Cur. Biog. '44 p291-293,por.
    Parshalle—Kash. p93,por.

Hickey, Mary A. (c. 1873-1954)
    Amer. nurse
    Pennock—Makers p64,por.

Hickman, Emily Gregory (1880-1947)
    Amer. educator
    Cur. Biog. '45 p281-283,por.
    Cur. Biog. '47 p304

Hickok, Lorena A. (fl. 1910's)
    Amer. journalist, author
    Ross—Ladies p7,203-209,por.

Hicks, Ami Mali (fl. 1890's-1930's)
    Amer. fashion designer
    Women—Achieve. p174,por.

Hicks, Beatrice A. (1919-   )
    Amer. engineer
    Cur. Biog. '57 p255-257,por.

Hicks, Betty (fl. 1960's)
    Amer. aviatrix
    *May—Women p197

Hicks, Mrs. H. W. See Baer, Leone Cass

Hicks, Leone. See Baer, Leone Cass

Hicks, Margaret (fl. 1600's)
 Amer. pioneer, colonial teacher
 Bell—Women p94

Hicks, Margaret (fl. 1870's-1880's)
 Amer. pioneer architect
 Hanaford—Dau. p306

Hidalgo, Elvira de (fl. 1910's)
 Sp. singer
 Lahee—Grand p313-314

Hier, Ethel Glenn (b. 1889)
 Amer. pianist, composer, teacher
 Howard—Our p438
 McCoy—Portraits p81,por.
 Reis—Composers p181-182
 Women—Achieve. p154,por.

Higginbotham, Irene (1918-   )
 Amer. composer, pianist
 ASCAP p232

Higgins, Alma Margaret (n.d.)
 Amer. club leader
 Binheim—Women p133,por.

Higgins, Marguerite (1920-1966)
 Amer. journalist, foreign
  correspondent
 CR '59 p344,por.
 CR '63 p290,por.
 Cur. Biog. '51 p274-276,por.
 Cur. Biog. '66 p466
 *Forsee—Amer. p205-229
 Kelly—Reporters p209-218
 Parshalle—Kash. p31-32,por.

Highet, Helen Clark.
 See MacInnes, Helen Clark

Hightower, Rosella (1920-   )
 Amer. ballet dancer,
  choreographer
 Atkinson—Dancers p74-76,por.
 Davidson—Ballet p139-142,por.
 Swinson—Great p12,por.
 *Terry—Star p190

Higlsee, Lenah S. (fl. 1910's-1920's)
 Amer. Navy nurse
 Pennock—Makers p60,por.

Higuchi, Ichiyo (1872-1896)
 Japan. poet
 Phila.—Women, unp.,por.
 Stiles—Postal p120

Hikes, Julia. See Yenni, Julia Truitt

Hilaria (d. 283)
 Rom. saint
 Blunt—Great p21

Hilda (Hild) (614-680)
 Eng. abbess, saint, scholar, nurse,
  teacher
 Deen—Great p34-37
 Dolan—Goodnow's p89-90,por.
 Mozans—Woman p36-39
 Stenton—English p13
 *Unstead—People p74-82
 Wescott—Calen. p180
 *Windham—Sixty p178-186

Hildeck, Leo, pseud. (Leonie Meyerhof)
  (fl. 19th cent.)
 Ger. author
 Heller—Studies p283

Hildegarde (Hildegarde Loretta Sell)
 Amer. singer
 Bakeless—In. p133-152,por.
 CR '59 p345,por.
 CR '63 p290-291,por.
 Cur. Biog. '44 p293-296,por.
 Donaldson—Radio p16

Hildegarde of Bingen (c. 1098-1179)
 Ger. saint, abbess, mystic,
  foundress, scholar, nurse
 Adelman—Famous p34
 Culver—Women p101
 Deen—Great p328-329
 Dolan—Goodnow's p115-116,por.
 Drinker—Music p200-203
 Englebert—Lives p355
 Mozans—Woman p45-48,169-170,233-
  235,277-281
 Schmidt—400 p389,por.

Hilder, Vera Gertrude (fl. 1930's)
 Eng.-Amer. actress, business
  executive
 Women—Achieve. p167,por.

Hilger, Elsa (fl. 1940's)
 Aust. violoncellist
 McCoy—Portraits p82,por.

Hill, Agnes Leonard (1842-1917)
 Amer. religious author
 Logan—Part p828

Hill, Amelia Leavitt (fl. 1930's)
 Amer. editor, author
 Women—Achieve. p180,por.

Hill, Amelia R. (fl. 1870's)
 Scot. sculptor
 Waters—Women p160

Hill, Carol (fl. 1930's)
 Amer. author, literary agent
 Women—Achieve. p163,por.

Hill, Caroline Sherman Andrews (1829-
  1914)
 Amer. race leader
 Brown—Home p104-107,por.

Hill, Carolyn. See Bailey, Carolyn Sherwin

Hill, Dedette Lee (1900-1950)
Amer. author, song-writer
ASCAP p233

Hill, Dorothy Lampe (fl. 1930's)
Amer. advertising manager
Women—Achieve. p178,por.

Hill, Edith Knight (fl. 1920's)
Amer. journalist
Binheim—Women p161,por.

Hill, Ernestine Hemmings (fl. 1930's-1940's)
Austral. author
Roderick—20 p295-304

Hill, Florence Davenport (1829-1919)
Eng. social reformer, philanthropist
Hammerton p758,por.

Hill, Frances Mulligan 1807-1884)
Amer. missionary
Hanaford—Dau. p509-510

Hill, Helen (d. 1942)
Amer. author
Cur. Biog. '42 p371

Hill, Mrs. Iley Lawson (b. 1808)
Amer. patriot
Logan—Part p436-437

Hill, Jenny (c. 1850-1896)
Eng. actress, comedienne, singer
Felstead—Stars p83-84,por.
Leroy—Music p31-32,por.

Hill, Justina Hamilton (1893-   )
Amer. bacteriologist
Cur. Biog. '41 p384-385,por.

Hill, Mabel Wood (1891-   )
Amer. composer
McCoy—Portraits p82,por.
Reis—Composers p183-184
Women—Achieve. p52,por.

Hill, Mildred J. (1859-1916)
Amer. composer
ASCAP p233
McCoy—Portraits p82,por.

Hill, Nancy M. (fl. 1860's)
Amer. Civil war nurse
Logan—Part p334-335,374

Hill, "Nurse" (fl. 1680's-1700's)
Amer. colonial nurse
Dexter—Colonial p63-65

Hill, Octavia (1836/38-1912)
Eng. social reformer, author
Adelman—Famous p245
Dorland—Sum p57,78,120
Hammerton p758,por.

Hill, Patty Smith (1868-1946)
Amer. educator
Cur. Biog. '46 p259
Women—Achieve. p62,por.

Hill, Sarah Althea (d. 1937)
Amer. heiress
Eliot—Heiresses p229-253

Hill, Wiletta ("Lettie") (fl. 1890's)
Amer. W. pioneer
Sargent—Pioneers p61,por.

Hiller, Alma Elizabeth (1892-1958)
Amer. chemist
Women—Achieve. p198

Hiller, Margaret (fl. 1930's)
Amer. editor, author
Women—Achieve. p78,por.

Hiller (Hillyer), Mrs. (fl. 1740's)
Amer. colonial teacher
Dexter—Colonial p93,155

Hiller, Wendy (1912-   )
Eng. actress
CR '59 p346,por.
Cur. Biog. '41 p386-387,por.

Hillhouse, Sarah Porter (b. 1763)
Amer. colonial editor, publisher
Dexter—Career p103
Leonard—Amer. p116

Hilliard, Harriet. See Nelson, Harriet

Hillis, Margaret Eleanor (1921-   )
Amer. conductor
Cur. Biog. '56 p272-274,por.

Hillis, Marjorie (fl. 1930's)
Amer. editor, author
Women—Achieve. p100,por.

Hillman, Charlotte (fl. 1886-1897)
Amer. whaling voyager
Whiting—Whaling p274-275

Hills, Laura Coombs (1859-1952)
Amer. painter
Michigan—Biog.. p149-150
Waters—Women p160-162

Hills, Mrs. (fl. 1860's)
Amer. social leader
Logan—Part p261

Hilsz, Maryse (d. 1946)
Fr. aviatrix, athlete
*Lauwick—Heroines p97-103,por.
*May—Women p127-128,por.

Hiltrude (fl. 8th cent.)
Fr. saint
Englebert—Lives p367

Hilyer, Mrs. Andrew F. (d. 1916)
  Amer. musician, foundress
  Cuney-Hare—Negro p244-246

Hind, Ella Cora (1861-1942)
  Amer. agriculturist, editor,
    journalist
  Innis—Clear p120-141,por.
  Sanders—Canadian p47-81

Hind al-Hunud (fl. 5th cent. A.D.)
  Arab. religious leader
  Beard—Woman p284-285

Hines, Eleanor Culton (fl. 1930's)
  Amer. business executive, realtor
  Women—Achieve. p146,por.

Hinestrosa, Francsica (d. 1534)
  Amer. pioneer
  Leonard—Amer. p116

Hinkle, Florence (1885-1933)
  Amer. singer
  McCoy—Portraits p83,por.

Hinkson, Katherine Tynan.
  See Tynan, Katherine

Hinman, Edna J. (n.d.)
  Amer. legal secretary
  Parshalle—Kash. p99,por.

Hinman, Mrs. (fl. 1840's)
  Amer. pioneer
  Fowler—Woman p435-443

Hippius, pseud.
  See Merezhkovskava, Zinaida Nikola

Hippo (Hippon) (5th cent. B.C.)
  Gr. philosopher
  Boccaccio—Conc. p116

Hippolyte, Louise (m. 1715)
  Mon., daughter of Anthony I
    (Grimaldi)
  Phila.—Women unp.,por.

Hiram's mother (Biblical)
  Deen—All p343
  Lewis—Portraits p161

Hirsch, Clara de, Baroness (1833-1899)
  Belg. philanthropist, humanitarian
  *Levinger—Great p145-147

Hirst, Anne (fl. 1930's)
  Amer. journalist
  Ross—Ladies p84-85

Hirszfield, Hanna (n.d.)
  Pol. physician, pediatrician
  Knapp—Women p137-150,por.

Hispala Fecencia (fl.c. 186 B.C.)
  Rom. cortesan
  Balsdon—Roman p37-43,227

Hitchcock, Nevada Davis.
  See Davis, Nevada Victoria

Hitchcock, Mrs. Thomas, Sr. (fl. 1930's)
  Amer. wife of Thomas Hitchcock,
    Sr.
  Time Aug.18,1930 p24,por.(Cover)

Hitt, Agnes (fl. 1890's-1900's)
  Amer. club leader
  Logan—Part p351

Hitz, Ann (fl. 1860's)
  Swiss, Civil war humanitarian
  Moore—Women p472-477

Hitz, Dora (b. 1856)
  Ger. artist
  Waters—Women p162-163

Hixon, Evalyn Willard (fl. 1930's-1950's)
  Amer. missionary
  They—Went p103-104

Hixson, Jean (fl. 1950's)
  Amer. teacher, aviatrix
  *May—Women

Hobart, Alice Tisdale Nourse (1882-1967)
  Amer. author
  *Stoddard—Top. p123-130
  Warfel—Amer. p210-212,por.

Hobart, Lucy M. P. (Lucy Osborn)
    (fl. 1870's)
  Amer. whaling voyager
  Furniss—Some p217-218,por.
  Whiting—Whaling p237-239

Hobart, Miss (fl. 17th cent.)
  Eng. maid-of-honor
  Melville—Windsor p134

Hobbes, Deliverance (fl. 1680's-1690's)
  Amer., accused witch
  Green—Pioneer (1) p231

Hobbes, John Oliver, pseud.
  See Craigie, Pearl Mary Teresa
    Richards

Hobbs, Amelia (fl. 1870's)
  Amer. pioneer justice of peace
  Hanaford—Dau. p669

Hobby, Oveta Culp (1905-   )
  Amer. government official, Director
    WAAC, editor, politician
  CR '59 p348-349,por.
  CR '63 p293,por.
  Cur. Biog. '42 p386-388,por.
  Cur. Biog. '53 p267-269,por.
  *Heath—Women p32.por.
  Roosevelt—Ladies p222-230
  Time Jan.17,1944 p57,por.(Cover)
  Time May 4,1953 p24,por.(Cover)

Hobdy, Ann F. (fl. 1930's)
    Amer. needlework designer
    Women—Achieve. p70,por.

Hobgood, Tabitha Aldersen (m. 1916)
    Amer. missionary
    They—Went p40-42

Hobson, Laura Kean Zametkin (n.d.)
    Amer. author
    Cur. Biog. '47 p311-313,por.
    Warfel—Amer. p212-213,por.

Hoby, Elizabeth Cooke (m. 1558)
    Eng., wife of Sir Thomas Cooke
    Stenton—English p131,133-134

Hodesh (Biblical)
    Deen—All p268

Hodge, Lydia Herrick (b. 1889)
    Amer. sculptor
    National—Contemp. p151

Hodges, Florrie (n.d.)
    Austral. heroine
    *Deakin—True p122-135

Hodgkin, Dorothy Mary Crowfoot (1910-)
    Eng. chemist
    Calder—Science p92

Hodgkins, Frances (1870-1947)
    New Z. artist
    De Morny—Best p204-209

Hodgkinson, Mrs. John (d. 1803)
    Amer. actress, singer
    Coad—Amer. p35,por.

Hodgson, M. J. (gr. 1941)
    Eng. radio editor
    Brittain—Women p254

Hodiah (Biblical)
    Deen—All p268

Hoechstetter, Sophie (fl. 19th cent.)
    Ger. author
    Heller—Studies p283-284

Hoederlin, Lillina Ottilie (fl. 1930's)
    Amer. business executive
    Women—Achieve. p72,por.

Hoerle, Helen (fl. 1930's)
    Amer. author
    Women—Achieve. p76,por.

Hoey, Iris (b. 1885)
    Eng. actress
    Hammerton p765

Hoey, Jane Margueretta (1892-   )
    Amer. government official, social
        worker
    Cur. Biog. '50 p244-246,por.

Hoff, Madeline (fl. 1930's)
    Amer. engineer, aviatrix
    Planck—Women p221-222

Hoffa, Portland (1910-   )
    Amer. radio actress, wife of Fred
        Allen
    Donaldson—Radio p4
    Settel—Radio p82-83,por.

Hoffman, Malvina (1887-1966)
    Amer. sculptor
    Ames—These p457-463
    *Clymer—Modern p48-60,por.
    *Cooper—Twenty p219-234,por.
    CR '63 p295
    Cur. Biog. '40 p393-395,por.
    Cur. Biog. '66 p466
    Dodd—Celeb. p285-289
    Hammerton p766
    *Heath—Women (4) p28,por.
    Jackman—Amer. p424-426
    *Kirkland—Artists p110-115
    Michigan—Biog. p152-153
    National—Contemp. p152
    Taft—Women, Mentor #4, #6 (172)
    Women—Achieve. p107,por.

Hoffman, Myn M. (fl. 1930's-1940's)
    Amer. Army nurse
    Pennock—Makers p60,por.

Hoffman, Sarah C. (b. 1742)
    Amer. philanthropist
    Hanaford—Dau. p164

Hoffman, Sophia C. (fl. 1860's)
    Amer. philanthropist
    Hanaford—Dau. p164-166

Hoffmann, Emma (fl. 1910's)
    Amer. singer
    Lahee—Grand p367-368

Hoffmann, Felicitas (d. 1760)
    It. painter
    Waters—Women p163

Hoffman, Gertrude (fl. 1910's)
    Russ. dancer
    Caffin—Vaud. p102-103,por.

Hoffman-Tedesco, Giulia (b. 1850)
    Ger. painter
    Waters—Women p163

Hofmanova, Klentyna Tanska (1798-1845)
    Pol. author
    Schmidt—400 p322-323,por.

Hogan, Inez (1900-   )
    Amer. illustrator
    Mahony—Illus. p319

Hogarth, Mary (fl. 1900's)
    Eng. painter
    Waters—Women p163-164

Hoge, Mrs. A. H. (1811-1890)
Amer. Civil war humanitarian
Brockett—Woman's p562-576
Hanaford—Dau. p205-206
Logan—Part p336-338
Moore—Women p347-372,por.
Young—Women (see index),por.

Hoge, Jane C. (fl. 1860's)
Amer. Civil war author, sanitary
commission worker
Dannett—Noble p220-223,334-340,por.

Hogg, Helen Swayer (1905-   )
Can. astronomer
*Yost—Women Mod. p31-47,por.

Högquist, Emilie (1812-1846)
Swed. actress
Schmidt—400 p371,por.

Hohenburg, Sophie Chotek, Duchess of
(1868-1914)
Aust. princess
Hammerton p767

Hohenlohe-Waldenburg, Stefanie Richter,
Princess (1896-   )
Aust. politician
Cur. Biog. '40 p395-396,por.

Hoisington, Lauretta H. Cutler (fl. 1860's)
Amer., Civil war nurse
Logan—Part p369

Hoisington, May Folwell (b. 1894)
Amer. poet, teacher
Smith—Women's p116

Hoit, Mary (fl. 1770's)
Amer. publisher
Hanaford—Dau. p710

Hokanson, Margrethe (1893-   )
Amer. composer
ASCAP p236

Hokinson, Helen (1893-1949)
Amer. artist
Taves—Success. p261-270,por.

Holberg, Ruth Langland (1891-   )
Amer. author
Cur. Biog. '49 p278-279,por.

Holborn, Helen. See Dubrow, Angelica

Holbrook, Sabra Rollins (1912-   )
Amer. educator, youth worker.
Cur. Biog. '48 p290-291,por.

Holden, Anne Stratton (b. 1887)
Amer. composer
ASCAP p236-237

Holden, Miriam Young (fl. 1930's)
Amer. humanitarian, club leader
Women—Achieve. p146,por.

Holder, Myrtle Avery (fl. 1910's-1950's)
Amer. missionary
They—Went p42-43

Holderman, Dorothy (fl. 1930's)
Amer. glider pilot
*May—Women p216-217

Holiday, Billie (1915-1959)
Amer. singer
*Cherry—Portraits p27-29
Jazz—Panorama p145-153
Shapiro—Jazz p276-287,por.
*Terkel—Giants p134-146,por.

Holland, Clara Helena (fl. 1930's)
Can.-Amer. personnel director
Women—Achieve. p85,por.

Holland, Claudia (1903-   )
Amer. novelist
Warfel—Amer. p213,por.

Holland, Elizabeth Vassall (1770/71-1845)
Eng. salonist
Bradford—Women p23-44,por.
Courtney—Adven. p233-248,por.
Pearson—Marry. p18-27
Pearson—Pilgrim p7-17,por.

Holland, Mary E. (fl. 1910's)
Amer. finger-print expert
Dorland—Sum p148

Holley, Bertha Delbert (fl. 1930's)
Amer. artist, fashion designer
Women—Achieve. p124,por.

Holley, Marietta (1836/44-1926)
Amer. feminist, humorist
Beard—Amer. p252-258
Bruère—Laugh. p52
Logan—Part p873

Holley (Hollie), Sallie (b. 1818)
Amer. feminist, lecturer
Bruce—Woman p179-180
O'Connor—Pioneer p96-97

Holliday, Judy (1922-1965)
Amer. actress
CR '59 p351,por.
CR '63 p297,por.
Cur. Biog. '51 p279-281
Cur. Biog. '65 p203
Stuart—Immort. p140-141,por.

Hollingsworth, Mildred Harvey (fl. 1930's)
Amer. political scientist
Women—Achieve. p134,por.

Hollingsworth, Thekla (fl. 1930's)
    Amer. composer, author
ASCAP p237-238
Women—Achieve. p162,por.

Hollister, Antoinette B. (b. 1873)
    Amer. sculptor
National—Contemp. p158

Holm, Celeste (1918-   )
    Amer. actress
CR '59 p351-352,por.
CR '63 p298,por.
Cur. Biog. '44 p299-302,por.
TV—Person. (1) p42-43,por.

Holm, Eleanor (n.d.)
    Amer. swimmer
Time Aug.21,1939 p31,por.(Cover)

Holm, Hanya Eckert (n.d.)
    Ger.-Amer. dancer
CR '63 p298,por.
Cur. Biog. '54 p340-342,por.
*Maynard—Amer. p151-156,por.

Holman, Libby (1905-   )
    Amer. singer, actress
CR '59 p352,por.
CR '63 p298,por.
Jensen—Revolt p166
Lamparski—What. p42-43,por.

Holmès, Augusta Mary Anne (1847-1903)
    Fr. composer, pianist, song-writer
Adelman—Famous p233-234
Dorland—Sum p23,161
Elson—Woman's p178-180,por.
McCoy—Portraits p85,por.

Holmes, Emma E. (fl. 1860's)
    Amer. Civil war heroine
Jones—Heroines p4,17-22

Holmes, Margaret.
See Wyman, Margaret Holmes

Holmes, Marjorie (1910-   )
    Amer. novelist
Warfel—Amer. p213-214,por.

Holmes, Mary Jane Hawes (1825-1907)
    Amer. novelist
Dorland—Sum p41,197
Papashvily—All p62,145-151

Holst, Marie Seuel (fl. 1940's)
    Amer. composer, pianist, music
    teacher
McCoy—Portraits p85,por.

Holstein, Anna (1824-1890)
    Amer. author, Civil war nurse
Brockett—Woman's p251-259
Dannett—Noble (see index)
Young—Women p210,373

Holt, Elizabeth Hunter (1784-1785)
    Amer. printer, publisher
Club—Printing p22
Dexter—Career p107

Holt, Isabella (1892-1962)
    Amer. author
Cur. Biog. '56 p282-283,por.
Cur. Biog. '62 p214

Holt, Maggie Winifred Mair (m. 1927)
    Eng. missionary
They—Went p146-147

Holt, Rackham (1899-   )
    Amer. author
Cur. Biog. '44 p304-305,por.

Holt, Winifred (d. 1945)
    Amer. sculptor, philanthropist
Adelman—Famous p324

Holtby, Winifred (1898-1935)
    Eng. author
Britain—Women (see index)

Holton, Susan May (c. 1875-1951)
    Amer. business executive, author,
    teacher
Women—Achieve. p198

Holtzmann, Fanny (fl. 1920's-1930's)
    Amer. lawyer
New York. p381-400
New Yorker Jan.30,1937 p21-25,por.;
    Feb.6,1937 p22-25 (Profiles)

Homans, Amy Morris (1848-1933)
    Amer. educator, physical director
Logan—Part p720

Home, Jessie (fl. 1860's)
    Scot. Civil war nurse
Brockett—Woman's p427-428

Homer, Ella (fl. 1870's-1880's)
    Amer. mineralogist
Hanaford—Dau. p279

Homer, Mrs. Francis T. (m. 1902)
    Amer. religious worker
Logan—Part p620

Homer, Louise Dilworth Beatty (1871-
    1947)
    Amer. singer
Ewen—Ency. p211-212
Ewen—Living p170-171,por.
McCoy—Portraits p85,por.
*Moore—When p97-102

Honer, Mary (n.d.)
    Eng. dancer
Fisher—Ball. p14,por.

Honeyman, Mary Henry (fl. 1770's)
Amer. Rev. war patriot
Green—Pioneer (3) p423-427

Honeyman, Nan Wood (fl. 1930's)
Amer. congresswoman
Paxton—Women p129

Honeywell, Annette (1904-   )
Amer. commercial artist, designer
Cur. Biog. '53 p271-272,por.

Honeywell, Martha Ann (b.c. 1787)
Amer. artist
Dexter—Career p75-76

Honore, Ida Marie (m. 1874)
Amer., wife of Frederick Dent
Grant
Smith—White p91-97,por.

Honoria, Justa Grata (fl. 5th cent., A.D.)
Rom. princess
Hammerton p774
McCabe—Empr. p335,342,344-345,por.

Hood, Helen (b. 1863)
Amer. composer
Elson—Woman's p207
McCoy—Portraits p85,por.

Hood, Marguerite Vivian (fl. 1940's)
Amer. pianist, editor, educator,
author
McCoy—Portraits p85,por.

Hoodless, Adelaide Hunter (1857-1910)
Can. educator, home economist
Innis—Clear p103-119,por.

Hooker, Elizabeth (fl. 1940's)
Amer. aviatrix
*May—Women p167-168

Hooker, Isabella Beecher (1822-1907)
Amer. feminist
Holbrook—Dreamers p198-200
Irwin—Angels p32
Logan—Part p573-575
Riegel—Amer. p141-144,por.

Hooks, Mary.
See Slocumb, Mary Hooks

Hoon, Pierra.
See Vejjabul, Pierra Hoon

Hooper, Anne Clark (m. 1767)
Amer. patriot
Green—Pioneer (3) p258-262

Hooper, Lucy (1816-1841)
Amer. poet
Hanaford—Dau. p267-268

Hooper, Rebecca Lane (fl. 1890's-1900's)
Amer. playwright
Logan—Part p791

Hooper, Virginia Fite (1917-   )
Amer. politician, club leader
Parshalle—Kash. p77-78,por.

Hooten, Elizabeth
See Warren, Elizabeth Hooten

Hooten, Elvira (fl. 1930's-1940's)
Amer. journalist, editor
Fairfax—Ladies p106-110

Hoover, Lou Henry (c. 1875-1944)
Amer., wife of Herbert Hoover
Cur. Biog. '44 p305
Gerlinger—Mis. p97-100,por.
Jensen—White p229-233
Logan—Ladies p183-192
*McConnell—Our p295-304,por.
Prindiville—First p236-244
*Ross—Know p63,por.
Smith—Romances p390-400,por.
Time Apr.21,1924 p5,por.;May 13,1929
p9 (Cover)
Ind. Maharani of Sikkim

Hope Namgyal (Hope Cooke) (1940-   )
Ind., Maharani of Sikkim
Cur. Biog. '67 p174-177,por.

Hopekirk, Helen (1856-1945)
Scot. composer, pianist
McCoy—Portraits p86,por.
Schonberg—Great p337

Hopkins, Anne Smith (d.c. 1783)
Amer. patriot
Dexter—Colonial p30
Green—Pioneer (3) p88-89

Hopkins, Mrs. Archibald (b. 1857)
Amer. sociologist, social reformer
Logan—Part p598

Hopkins, Constantia.
See Snow, Constantia

Hopkins, Damaris.
See Cooke, Damaris Hopkins

Hopkins, Edna Boies (b. 1878)
Amer. painter, etcher
Michigan—Biog. p155-156

Hopkins, Elizabeth (fl. 1600's)
Amer. Pilgrim
Bell—Women p18-19
Green—Pioneer (1) p140-141
Logan—Part p33
Marble—Women p68-69

Hopkins, Jenny Lind (d. 1925)
    Amer. journalist
    Ross—Ladies p569-570

Hopkins, Julia B. (n.d.)
    Amer. lawyer, airline adviser, tax
        consultant
    Peckham—Women p93

Hopkins, Miriam (1902-   )
    Amer. actress
    CR '59 p354,por.
    Time May 27,1935 p28,por. (Cover)

Hopkins, Pauline Bradford.
    See Mackie, Pauline Bradford

Hopkins, Sarah Scott (m. 1726)
    Amer. patriot
    Green—Pioneer (3) p86-88

Hopkinson, Ann Borden McKean (d. 1827)
    Amer. patriot
    Green—Pioneer (3) p141-144,215

Hopper, Anna M. (fl. 1870's)
    Amer. educator
    Hanaford—Dau. p633

Hopper, Edna Wallace (b. 1864)
    Amer. actress
    Strang—Prima p104-112,por.

Hopper, Hedda (1890-1966)
    Amer. journalist, columnist,
        actress
    CR '59 p355,por.
    CR '63 p301,por.
    Cur. Biog. '42 p391-392,por.
    Cur. Biog. '66 p466
    Jensen—Revolt p99,por.
    Time July 28, 1947 p60,por. (Cover)

Hopson, Elizabeth Louise (fl. 1915-1927)
    Can. music teacher
    McCoy—Portraits p86,por.

Hopton, Sarah (fl. 1770's)
    Amer. Rev. war patriot
    Ellet—Women (2) p108-109

Hopton, Susanna Harvey (1627-1709)
    Eng. religious author
    Stenton—English p236

Horakova, Milada (d. 1950)
    Czech. spy
    Hoehling—Women p164-192,por.

Horan, Mrs. Kenneth (1890-   )
    Amer. novelist
    Warfel—Amer. p214,por.

Horatia (fl. 7th cent.)
    Rom., sister of the Haratii
    Balsdon—Roman p26

Hormel, Olive Deane (fl. 1930's)
    Amer. author
    Women—Achieve. p145,por.

Hormuth-Kallmorgen (Kollmorgen),
        Margarete (1858-1916)
    Ger. painter
    Waters—Women p164

Horn, Berta (fl. 1930's)
    Amer. business executive
    Women—Achieve. p198-199

Hornaday, Mary F. (fl. 1920's)
    Amer. journalist
    Ross—Ladies p334-335

Hornby, Leslie. See "Twiggy"

Horne, Lena (c. 1917-   )
    Amer. singer, actress
    *Cherry—Portraits p117-118
    CR '59 p355-356,por.
    CR '63 p301,por.
    Cur. Biog. '44 p310-312,por.
    *Hughes—First p64,por.
    *Hughes—Music p155-160,por.
    New Yorker Feb.21,1957 p95,por.
        (Profiles)
    Popular Record p67,por.
    Robinson—Hist. p205-206,por.
    *Rollins—Enter. p69-73
    Stambler—Ency. p113

Horne, Marilyn (1934-   )
    Amer. singer
    Cur. Biog. '67 p180-183,por.
    Pleasants—Great p351-353,por.

Horne, Mrs. William Henry (fl. 1900's-
        1910's)
    Amer. artist
    Logan—Part p573

Horner, Marjorie Crittenden (m. 1938)
    Amer. missionary, physician
    They—Went p106-107

Horney, Karen Danielson (1885-1952)
    Ger.-Amer. psychiatrist, physician,
        psychoanalyst
    Cur. Biog. '41 p409-410,por.
    Cur. Biog. '53 p279
    *Fleming—Doctors p116-129
    Women—Achieve. p199

Horniman, Annie Elizabeth Fredericka
        (1860-1937)
    Eng. theatre manager, producer
    Adelman—Famous p294
    Hammerton p780

Hornsby-Smith (Margaret) Patricia (1914-)
    Eng. member of Parliament
    Winn—Queen's p32-48,por.

Horrocks, Amy Elsie (fl. 1890's)
  Brazil.-Anglo composer, pianist
  Elson—Woman's p138

Horsbrugh, Florence (1889-1969)
  Scot. educator
  Cur. Biog. '52 p276-278,por.

Horsford, Cornelia (b. 1861)
  Amer. archaeologist
  Dorland—Sum p143

Horstmann, Dorothy M. (1911-   )
  Amer. physician
  Lovejoy—Women p377

Hortense Bonaparte (1783-1837)
  Nether. queen
  Abbot—Notable p170-174

Hortensia (fl.c. 50 B.C.)
  Rom., dau. of Quintus Hortensius
  Balsdon—Roman p56
  Boccaccio—Conc. p185

Hortensia, Mazarin, Duchess (1646-1699)
  Eng. beauty
  Melville—Windsor p166-182

Horthy, Magdalene (fl. 1920's-1940's)
  Hung., wife of Admiral Stephen
    Horthy
  Phila.—Women unp.,por.
  Stiles—Postal p122

Horthy de Nagbanya, Magdalene Purgly de
    Joszahely (m. 1901)
  Hung., wife of Nicholas Horthy
    de Nagbanya
  Stiles—Postal p122

Horton, Abbie Augusta Wingate (1836-
    1925)
  Amer. pioneer, religious worker
  Phillips—33 p39-43

Horton, Constance Smith (fl. 1930's-1950's)
  Amer. missionary
  They—Went p100-101

Horton, Mrs. John Miller (fl. 1880's-1900's)
  Amer. philanthropist, clubleader,
    educator
  Logan—Part p481-484

Horton, Mildred Helen McAfee (1900-   )
  Amer. educator
  *Stoddard—Top p69-85

Hortulana (fl. 13th cent.)
  It. saint
  Blunt—Great p154-155

Horwich, Frances Rappaport (1908-   )
  Amer. educator, TV personality
  Cur. Biog. '53 p279-280,por.
  TV—Person. (1) p89-90

Hosea, wife of (Biblical)
  Horton—Women p259-263

Hoskens, Jane (1694-   )
  Amer. colonial clergyman,
    teacher
  Benson—Women p266
  Dexter—Colonial p96-97,147-148

Hosmer, Harriet Goodhue (1830-1908)
  Amer. sculptor
  Adelman—Famous p218-219
  Dorland—Sum p50,158
  Hanaford—Dau. p320-323
  Jackman—Amer. p308
  Logan—Part p761-763
  McSpadden—Sculptors p329-340
  *McVeagh—Champlin p296-297
  Michigan—Biog. p157-158
  *Moore—When p103-110
  Taft—Women, Mentor (172) #1, por.
  Tuckerman—Book p601-602
  Waters—Women p164-165
  Whitton—These p194-196,206

Hosmer, Mrs. O. E. (fl. 1860's)
  Amer. Civil war humanitarian
  Brockett—Woman's p719-724

Hostia. See Cynthia of Propertius

Hostilia Severa (fl. 230's)
  Rom. empress, wife of Gallus
  Serviez—Roman (2) p311

Hottel, Althea Hallowell Kratz (1907-   )
  Amer. educator
  Cur. Biog. '48 p294-295,por.

Hotz, Mae Ebrey (fl. 1940's)
  Amer. singer
  McCoy—Portraits p87,por.

Hough, Maude Clark (fl. 1930's)
  Amer. poet, telegraph operator
  Women—Achieve. p47,por.

Houghton, Dorothy Deemer (1890-   )
  Amer. organization official
  Cur. Biog. '50 p260-261,por.

Hoult, Norah (1901-   )
  Irish author
  Millet—Brit. p276-277

Hours-Miedan, Magdeleine (1915-   )
  Fr. art expert, historian
  Cur. Biog. '61 p209-211,por.

Housman, Rosalie Louise (c. 1888-1949)
  Amer. composer, pianist, lecturer,
    musicologist
  McCoy—Portraits p87,por.

Houston, Eliza Allen (d. 1862)
>Amer., wife of Sam Houston
Orr—Famous p295-300
Orr—Famous Affin. III. p8-15
Turner—Sam p12-20

Houston, Elizabeth Paxton (c. 1765-1831)
>Amer., mother of Sam Houston
Bruce—Woman p153-155
Turner—Sam p1-4

Houston, Fanny Lucy Radmall, Lady
>(1857-1936)
>Eng. feminist
Hammerton p782,por.

Houston, Frances C. Lyons (1867-1906)
>Amer. painter
Michigan—Biog. p158
Waters—Women p165

Houston, Margaret Moffette Lea (c. 1819-
>1867)
>Amer., Civil war diarist, wife of
>General Houston
Jones—Heroines p106-107

Houstoun, Mrs. (fl. 1890's)
>Eng. author
Black—Notable p223-233,por.

Hovey, Augusta M. (fl. 1870's1880's)
>Amer. religious worker
Hanaford—Dau. p493

Hovick, Rose Louise.
>See Lee, Gypsy Rose

Howard, Alice Sturtevant (1878-1945)
>Amer. foundress, author
Cur. Biog. '45 p295

Howard, Andree (1910-   )
>Brit. ballet dancer
Davidson—Ballet p142-145,por.

Howard, Catherine (1520/22-1542)
>Eng. queen
Hammerton p782,por.
Sanders—Intimate p27-28,por.

Howard, Cordelia.
>See MacDonald, Cordelia Howard

Howard, Elizabeth (1907-   )
>Amer. author
Cur. Biog. '51 p282-283,por.
Warfel—Amer. p216,por.

Howard, Florence Ruth (1902-   )
>Amer. author
Warfel—Amer. p216-217,por.

Howard, Floretta (n.d.)
>Amer. poet, playwright, teacher
Dreer—Amer. p52

Howard, Frances.
>See Somerset, Frances Howard Carr,
>Countess

Howard, Harriet (1823-1865)
>Fr., mistress of Napoleon III
Kelen—Mist. p82-85,330,por.

Howard, Henrietta Hobart, Countess of
>Suffolk (1681-1767)
>Eng. letter-writer
Melville—Maids p61-115,por.
Sherman—World's p48-51

Howard, Ida Tinsley (fl. 1870's)
>Amer. pioneer, teacher
Sargent—Pioneers p41-42

Howard, Jane, Lady (fl.c. 1547)
>Eng., daughter of Earl of Surrey
Stenton—English p129-130

Howard, Jean Ross (fl. 1950's)
>Amer. aviatrix, helicopter pilot
*May—Women p204-206,por.

Howard, Katherine Montague Graham
>(1898-   )
>Amer. government official,
>politician
Cur. Biog. '53 p280-282,por.
Roosevelt—Ladies p39-46

Howard, Katheryn. See Catherine of Aragon

Howard, Kathleen (fl. 1900's-1940's)
>Can. singer, author
McCoy—Portraits p87,por.

Howard, (King) Lenora (fl. 1870's)
>Amer. physician
Lovejoy—Women p231

Howard, Lulu Smih (fl. 1930's)
>Amer. investment analyst
Women—Achieve. p115,por.

Howard, Maxine ("Mike") (fl. 1940's)
>Amer. aviatrix
Planck—Women p77

Howard, Minnie F. (b. 1872)
>Amer. author, historian, public
>welfare worker
Binheim—Women p123,por.

Howard, Sarah (fl. 1800's-1820's)
>Amer., grandmother of William
>Howard Taft
Green—Pioneer (3) p452

Howard, Sylvia. See Taft, Sylvia Howard

Howard, Victorine. See Mears, Marjorie

Howe, Abbie J. (fl. 1860's)
>Amer. Civil war nurse
Brockett—Woman's p465-466

Howe, Harriet M.
    See Wilson, Harriet M. Howe

Howe, Helen (Helen Allen) (1905-   )
    Amer. author
    Cur. Biog. '54 p347-348,por.

Howe, Helen (fl. 1940's)
    Amer. music educator
    McCoy—Portraits p87,por.

Howe, Janet (fl. 1940's)
    Scot. singer
    Brook—Singers p121-124,por.

Howe, Jemima (fl. 1750's)
    Amer. pioneer, Ind. captive
    Green—Pioneer (1) p435-442
    Peckham—Capt. p50-61

Howe, Julia Ward (1819-1910)
    Amer. song-writer, feminist, social
        reformer, lecturer, traveller,
        humanitarian, Civil war patriot
    Abbot—Notable p284-288,por.
    *Adams—Heroines p178-214,por.
    Adelman—Famous p174-176
    America's 12 p28-30
    Beard—Amer. p170-171,195-197
    *Bolton—Famous Leaders p272-303,por.
    *Bolton—Lives p179-192,por.
    Bonte—Amer. p119,por.
    Bruce—Woman p213-216,241-242
    *Carmer—Caval. p138-141,por.
    *Daugherty—Ten p95-107,por.
    Deen—Great p305
    Dorland—Sum p45-46,83,127,137,180
    Douglas—Remember p127-129
    Farmer—What p16,189,por.
    Hammerton p784,por.
    Hanaford—Dau. (see index),por.
    Harkness—Heroines p12
    *Heath—Women (4) p12,por.
    Howard—Our p259,por.
    *Humphrey—Women p154-163
    Irwin—Angels p106,169,217,220
    Jensen—Revolt p56,por.
    Ladies'—Amer. 12 p28-30,por.
    Logan—Part p798
    McCoy—Portraits p87,por.
    *MacVeagh—Champlin p298
    *Moore—When p111-117
    *Nisenson—Minute p86,por.
    O'Higgins—Amer. p251-276
    Orcutt—Celeb. p134-140,por.
    *Parkman—Heroines p119-147,por.
    Rogers—Women p39,por.
    Sturges—Celeb. p134-140,por.
    Tappan—Heroes p91-96,por.
    Whitton—These p151
    Young—Women (see index)

Howe, Mary (b. 1881/82)
    Amer. composer, pianist
    Goss—Modern p71-80,por.

Howard—Our p434
    McCoy—Portraits p87,por.
    Reis—Composers p187-188

Howe, Sophia (d. 1726)
    Eng. maid-of-honor
    Melville—Maids p208-211

Howell, Dorothy (1898-   )
    Eng. composer, pianist
    McCoy—Portraits p87,por.

Howell, Elizabeth Lloyd (fl. 1870's-1880's)
    Amer. poet
    Hanaford—Dau. p259-260

Howes, Sally Ann (1930-   )
    Eng. actress
    CR '63 p304,por.

Howey, Ella Mae (fl. 1950's)
    Amer. deaf lecturer
    Murrow—This (2) p74-75

Howitt, Mary Botham (1799-1888)
    Eng. author
    Adelman—Famous p110
    Furniss—Some p142-144,por.
    Stebbins—Victorian p41,197,209

Howland, Edith (c. 1863-1949)
    Amer. sculptor
    National—Contemp. p158

Howland, Eliza W. (fl. 1860's)
    Amer. Civil war nurse, author
    Brockett—Woman's p301,324,326
    Dannett—Noble (see index)

Howland, Elizabeth Tilley (b. 1608-1687)
    Amer. Pilgrim, wife of John
        Howland
    Bell—Women p21
    Green—Pioneer (1) p146-147
    Logan—Part p34
    Marble—Women p85-89

Howland, Mary Woolsey (d. 1864)
    Amer. Civil war nurse
    Dannett—Noble p75-76,385-386

Howland, Ruth B. (fl. 1930's)
    Amer. biologist
    Women—Achieve. p199

Howley, Christine Wetherill.
    See Leser, Tina

Howorth, Lucy Somerville (1895-   )
    Amer. government official, club
        leader
    Cur. Biog. '51 p283-285,por.

Hoxie, Vinnie Ream (1847-1914)
　　Amer. sculptor
　　Adelman—Famous p247-248
　　Dorland—Sum p159
　　Hanaford—Dau. p320
　　Logan—Part p761
　　Muir—Women p185-189
　　Schmidt—400 p22-23,por.
　　Taft—Women, Mentor (172) #1
　　Tuckerman—Book p605
　　Waters—Women p165-166

Hoyle, Ethel (fl. 1950's)
　　Amer. printer, type designer
　　Club—Printing p18

Hoyt, Alva (fl. 1950's)
　　Brit. novelist
　　Shapiro—Contemp. p125-143

Hoyt, Lucy (fl. 1870's-1880's)
　　Amer. religious worker
　　Hanaford—Dau. p618

Hoyt, Mrs. (fl. 1660's)
　　Amer. pioneer, heroine
　　Green—Pioneer (1) p258

Hoyt, Peggy (fl. 1930's)
　　Amer. designer
　　*Ferris—Girls p167-177

Hrotsvitha (or Hrotswitha).
　　See Roswitha

Hsiang Fei (fl. 1750's)
　　Chin. concubine
　　Llewellyn—China's p164-170

Hsi Ching Yih (fl.c. 1800's)
　　Chin. pirate, seafarer
　　Snow—Women p34-46

Hsieh-Ping-Ying (fl. 1920's)
　　Chin. warrior
　　Ayscough—Chinese p223-226,

Hsi Shih (f.c. 485 B.C.)
　　Chin. beauty, consort of King Wu
　　Llewellyn—China's p13-22

Hsi Wang Mu (fl. 110 B.C.)
　　Chin. beauty
　　Llewellyn—China's p45-46

Hsü, Lydia (fl. 1930's)
　　Chin. physician
　　Lovejoy—Women Phys. p113,por.

Hua Mu-Lan (fl. 5th cent.)
　　Chin. warrior
　　Ayscough—Chinese p214-222

Hubbard, Ann (Anna) (n.d.)
　　Amer. recluse
　　Erskine—Out p248-254

Hubbard, Emma (fl. 1870's-1880's)
　　Amer. lawyer, teacher
　　Hanaford—Dau. p668

Hubbard, Mabel Gardiner (m. 1877)
　　Amer., wife of Alexander Graham
　　　　Bell
　　Holbrook—Dreamers p265-266

Hubbard, Margaret Ann (1909-　　　)
　　Amer. author
　　Cur. Biog. '58 p207-208,por.

Hubbard, Margaret E. (gr. 1953)
　　Eng. educator
　　Brittain—Women p224,247

Huber, Alice (fl. 1890's)
　　Amer. nurse, artist
　　Dolan—Goodnow's p276-277

Hubou, Marie Hebert (fl. 1610's)
　　Fr. colonial nurse
　　Dolan—Goodnow's p152

Huch, Ricarda (1864-1947)
　　Ger. author
　　Hammerton p785,por.
　　Heller—Studies p285-287-291

Huck, Winifred Sprague Mason (fl. 1920's)
　　Amer. congresswoman
　　Paxton—Women p129

Hudavent (fl. 13th-14th cent.)
　　Turk. noblewoman
　　Stiles—Postal p123

Hudlun, Ann Elizabeth (1840-1914)
　　Amer. social welfare worker
　　Brown—Home. p141-144,por.

Hudson, Grace (fl. 1900's)
　　Amer. painter
　　Waters—Women p166-167

Hudson, Henrietta (d. 1942)
　　Amer. photographer
　　Cur. Biog. '42 p396

Hudson, Hester (d.c. 1796)
　　Amer. inn-keeper
　　Dexter—Career p120,122

Hudson, Hortense Imboden (fl. 1930's)
　　Amer. personnel worker
　　Women—Achieve. p131,por.

Hudson, Octavia (fl. 1940's)
　　Amer. composer, pianist, music
　　　　teacher, author
　　McCoy—Portraits p88,por.

Hudson, Rochelle (n.d.)
　　Amer. actress
　　TV—Person (1) p130

Huebner, Ilse (fl. 1940's)
Aust. composer, pianist, music
teacher
McCoy—Portraits p88,por.

Hueston, Ethel Powelson (b. 1887)
Amer. author
Warfel—Amer. p218-219,por.

Huggins, Margaret Lindsay, Lady (1848-
1915)
Eng. astronomer, wife of Sir
William Huggins
Cockran—Romance p83-84

Hughan, Jessie Wallace (1875-1955)
Amer. author, politician
Women—Achieve. p135,por.

Hughes, Alice (fl. 1930's)
Amer. journalist
Ross—Ladies p393-396,por.

Hughes, Anne. See Fitzhugh, Anne

Hughes, Annie (1869-1931)
Eng. actress
Hammerton p787

Hughes, Bernice Gaines (1904-   )
Amer. military officer
Robinson—Hist. p207

Hughes, Margaret (d. 1719)
Eng. actress
Gilder—Enter p142-144,168-169,por.
MacQueen—Pope p35-36,por.
Wilson—All p149-151

Hughes, Toni (Martha Groomas) (n.d.)
Amer. artist
Cur. Biog. '41 p422-423

Hughes, Sarah Tilghman (1896-   )
Amer. judge, organization official
Cur. Biog. '50 p267-269,por.

Hugo, Adèle Foucher (1806-1868)
Fr., wife of Victor Hugo
Orr—Famous Affin. IV p78-92

Hugo, Mrs. Ian. See Nin, Anais

Hugo, Sophie Trébuchet (d.c. 1821)
Fr., mother of Victor Hugo
Peyton—Mothers p33-35
Parton—Dau. p225-242,por.
Parton—Noted p225-240

Hugonay, Vilma, Countess (fl. 1920's)
Hung. physician
Lovejoy—Women p200

Hü King Eng (b. 1865)
Chin. physician
Burton—Notable p15-70,por.

Hulbert, Katherine Allmond (fl. 1900's)
Amer. painter, illustrator, designer
Warers—Women p167

Huldah (Biblical)
Culver—Women p34-36
Deen—All p143-145
Horton—Women p243-257
*Levinger—Great p59-61
Lewis—Portraits p176-177
Marble—Women, Bible p205-209
Nelson—Bible p66-68

Hulett, Alta M. (1854-1877)
Amer. lawyer
Farmer—What p395,403
Hanaford—Dau. p663-667

Hull, Eleanor H. (b. 1860)
Eng. author
Hammerton p789

Hull, Elizabeth Clarke (1732-1826)
Amer. Rev. war patriot
Root—Chapter p224-237

Hull, Helen Rose (fl. 1930's-1940's)
Amer. novelist, educator
Cur. Biog. '40 p415-417,por.
Overton—Women p178-179
Warfel—Amer. p220,por.
Women—Achieve. p74,por.

Hull, Josephine Sherwood (1886-1957)
Amer. actress
Blum—Great p111,por.
Cur. Biog. '53 p283-286,por.
Cur. Biog. '57 p271

Hull, Peggy (fl. 1930's-1940's)
Amer. journalist
Ross—Ladies p230,377

Hull, Rose Mitchell (fl. 1860's)
Amer. W. pioneer
*Miller—West. p184-192

Hull, Sarah (c. 1755-1826)
Amer. Rev. war patriot
Logan—Part p120-121

Hulse, Anne Elizabeth (fl. 1930's)
Amer. teacher, economist
Women—Achieve. p136,por.

Hulshoff, Annette Von Droste (1797-1848)
Ger. poet, song-writer
Schmidt—400 p198-199,por.

Hulton, Ann (fl. 1760's)
Amer. letter-writer
Benson—Women p292-293,298

Humaston, Abi (c. 1759-1847)
Amer. Rev. war heroine
Root—Chapter p395-402

Humbeline (fl. 12th cent.)
　　Fr. saint
　　Wescott—Calen. p125

Humby, Betty, Lady Beecham (fl. 1940's)
　　Eng. pianist
　　McCoy—Portraits p88,por.

Hume, Grisell, Lady (1665-1746)
　　Scot. poet, song-writer, covenanter
　　Anderson—Ladies p428-459
　　Findlay—Spindle p7-25

Hume, Sophie Wiginton (1702-1774)
　　Amer. colonial clergyman
　　Leonard—Amer. p117
　　Spruill—Women's p252-253

Hummel, Lisl (fl. 1940's)
　　Aust. illustrator
　　Mahony—Illus. p322

Hummert, Anne Schumacher (fl. 1930's-
　　　　1940's)
　　Amer. advertising executive, radio
　　　　producer
　　Taves—Success. p96-105,por.
　　Women—Achieve. p199

Humphrey, Doris (1895-1958)
　　Amer. dancer, choreographer
　　Cur. Biog. '42 p398-400,por.
　　Cur. Biog. '59 p196
　　*Maynard—Amer. p125-151,por.

Humphrey, Grace (b. 1882)
　　Amer. author
　　Women—Achieve. p199

Humphrey, Helen Florence (1909-1963)
　　Amer. lawyer, government official
　　Cur. Biog. '52 p280-281,por.
　　Cur. Biog. '63 p201

Humphrey, Mary (fl. 1920's)
　　Amer. journalist, public relations
　　　　expert
　　Ross—Ladies p535-536

Humphreys, Marie Champney (1867-1906)
　　Amer. painter
　　Michigan—Biog. p160

Humphreys, Sarah Riggs (1711-1787)
　　Amer. Rev. war patriot
　　Green—Pioneer (3) p490-492
　　Root—Chapter p209-223

Hungerford, Margaret Hamilton (1855-
　　　　1897)
　　Irish novelist
　　Black—Notable p107-119,por.
　　Dorland—Sum p24,198

Hunt, Arabella (d. 1705)
　　Eng. singer, lutenist, music teacher
　　McCoy—Portraits p89,por.

Hunt, Elizabeth Pickard (fl. 1860's)
　　Amer. Civil war nurse
　　Logan—Part p369

Hunt, Harriet Kezia (1805-1875)
　　Amer. pioneer physician
　　Dexter—Career p40-41,44-45,177
　　Irwin—Angels p44-46,218
　　Lovejoy—Women p78-80
　　Mead—Medical p20-21
　　O'Connor—Pioneer p86,139-140,184,
　　　　213-214
　　Riegel—Amer. p122-124
　　Whitton—These p119-120

Hunt, Helen Fiske (b. 1831)
　　Amer. author
　　Hanaford—Dau. p246

Hunt, Louise Frances (b. 1837)
　　Fr.-Amer. religious worker
　　Logan—Part p620

Hunt, Mabel Leigh (1892-　　)
　　Amer. author
　　Cur. Biog. '51 p290-291,por.

Hunt, Sarah (b. 1808)
　　Amer. midwife, physician
　　Dexter—Career p40-41
　　Hanaford—Dau. p556-557
　　Mead—Medical p20-21

Hunt, Violet (1866-1942)
　　Eng. author
　　Hammerton p792

Hunter, Jane Edna Harris (b. 1882)
　　Amer. nurse, social worker,
　　　　educator, club leader
　　Daniel—Women p164-187

Hunter, Kim (1922-　　)
　　Amer. actress
　　CR '59 p361,por.
　　CR '63 p308,por.
　　Cur. Biog. '52 p281-283,por.
　　Ross—Player p316-325,por.

Hunter, Lady (fl. 19th cent.)
　　Eng. hostess
　　Furniss—Some p198

Hunter, Louise (fl. 1940's)
　　Amer. singer
　　McCoy—Portraits p89,por.

Hunter, Mrs. M. A. (fl. 1810's)
　　Amer. philanthropist
　　Logan—Part p544

Hunter, Mary.
　　See Sutherland-Hunter, Mary

Hunter, Nancy. See Linn, Nancy Hunter

Huntingdon, Helen (1950-   )
    Amer. heiress
    Pearson—Pilgrim p310-319,por.

Huntingdon, Selina, Countess (1707-1791)
    Eng. religious worker
    Adelman—Famous p80
    Deen—Great p149-156
    Hammerton p793-794,por.
    Stenton—English p283-285

Huntington, Anna Vaughn Hyatt (1876-   )
    Amer. sculptor
    Adelman—Famous p316
    Cur. Biog. '53 p288-290,por.
    Jackman—Amer. p403-406
    *Kirkland—Artists p98-109
    McSpadden—Sculptors p340-351
    Michigan—Biog. p161-163
    National—Contemp. p162
    Taft—Women, Mentor p8, #3,por.
    Waters—Women p170-171

Huntington, Clara (b. 1878)
    Amer. sculptor
    National—Contemp. p165

Huntington, Faith Trumbull (fl. 1770's)
    Amer., daughter of Faith Robinson
        Trumbull
    Green—Pioneer (3) p295-296

Huntington, Grace (fl. 1930's)
    Amer. aviatrix
    *May—Women p136
    Planck—Women p177-178

Huntington, Martha Devotion (d. 1794)
    Amer. Rev. war patriot
    Green—Pioneer (3) p98-100

Huntington, Mrs. Rudd (fl. 1900's)
    Amer. social leader
    Logan—Part p261

Huntington, Susan (b. 1791)
    Amer. philanthropist
    Hanaford—Dau. p152-153

Huntley, Amelia Elmore (b. 1844)
    Amer. missionary
    Logan—Part p519-520

Huntley, Elizabeth Maddox (n.d.)
    Amer. playwright, musician,
        teacher
    Dreer—Amer. p306

Huntley, Florence (d. 1912)
    Amer. author
    Logan—Part p855

Huntley, Frances E.
    See Mayne, Ethel Colburn

Huntley, Lydia.
    See Sigourney, Lydia Howard Huntley

Hunton, Hazel (fl. 1930's)
    Amer. patriot, humanitarian
    Women—Achieve. p106,por.

Hurd, Kate Campbell (fl. 1890's)
    Amer. physician
    Irwin—Angels p141-142

Hurd, Mrs. P. B. (m. 1857)
    Amer. Civil war heroine
    Moore—Women p65-74

Hurdon, Elizabeth (1868-1941)
    Eng.-Can. physician
    *Lovejoy—Women p117-118

Huré, Anne (1918-   )
    Fr. novelist
    Peyre—French p420

Hurlburt, Margaret (c. 1915-1947)
    Amer. aviatrix, teacher
    *May—Women p198

Hurley, Catherine (fl. 1800's-1810's)
    Amer. teacher
    Dexter—Career p12-14

Hurley, Laurel (1927-   )
    Amer. singer
    Cur. Biog. '57 p273-274,por.
    Matz—Opera p14-18,por.

Hurley, Marie Louise (fl. 1950's)
    Amer. airline hostess
    *May—Women p233-234

Hurll, Estelle May (b. 1863)
    Amer. teacher, author
    Logan—Part p843

Hurst, Fannie (1889-1968)
    Amer. author
    CR '59 p362-363,por.
    CR '63 p310,por.
    Dodd—Celeb. p248-252
    Farrar—Literary p268-276,326,por.
    Fitzgibbon—My p137-142
    Hammerton p794
    Lawrence—School p193-198
    Loggins—Hear p344-348
    Lotz—Jews p48-55
    Mantle—Amer. p219-220
    Mantle—Contemp. p270-271
    *Millett—Amer. p404-406
    Overton—Women p180-186
    Saturday Rev. p220-224
    Warfel—Amer. p221-223,por.
    Williams—Our p237-255
    Women—Achieve. p50,por.

Hurston, Zora Neale (1903-1960)
   Amer. anthropologist, author
   Burnett—Amer. p550,por.
  *Cherry—Portraits p24-26
   Cur. Biog. '42 p402-404,por.
   Cur. Biog. '60 p195
   Dreer—Amer. p10,132-136
   Robinson—Hist. p208-209,por.
   Warfel—Amer. p223,por.

Hurt, Ambra Halsey (m. 1916)
   Amer. missionary
   They—Went p65-66

Husband, Mary Morris (fl. 1860's)
   Amer. Civil war nurse
   Brockett—Woman's p287-298,por.
   Moore—Women p313-332,por

Hushim (Biblical)
   Deen—All p269

Huss, Hildegarde Hoffman (fl. 1940's)
   Amer. singer, music teacher,
    lecturer
   McCoy—Portraits p89,por.

Husted, Marjorie Child (n.d.)
   Amer. home economist, business
    executive
   Cur. Biog. '49 p286-287

Hutchings, Augusta Ladd Sweetland
   (d. 1881)
   Amer. W. pioneer
   Sargent—Pioneers p37-38

Hutchings, Elvira Bonney Sproat (b. 1842)
   Amer. W. pioneer
   Sargent—Pioneers p34-36,por.

Hutchings, Florence (1864-1881)
   Amer. W. pioneers
   Sargent—Pioneers p34-37,por.

Hutchings, Gertrude ("Cosie") (1867-1956)
   Amer. W. pioneer
   Sargent—Pioneers p35-40,por.

Hutchinson, Abigail ("Abby") Jemima
   (fl. 1820's-1830's)
   Amer. singer, hymn-writer, social
    reformer
  *Carmer—Young p169-177
   Hanaford—Dau. p591
   Whitton—These p204

Hutchinson, Alice (fl. 1910's)
   Amer. physician
   Lovejoy—Women p283,285,288

Hutchinson, Anne Marbury (1590/91-1643)
   Eng.-Amer. religious leader
   Abbott—Notable p303-307
   Abramowitz—Great p307-340
   Bell—Women p222-238,247-253,347-
    353

   Bonte—Amer. p36,por.
   Brooks—Colonial p1-29
   Bruce—Woman p28-33
  *Daugherty—Ten p1-16,por.
   Deen—Great p108-116
   Dexter—Colonial p60,102,142-146
  *Dolin—World p12-21
   Dorland—Sum p37,132
   Douglas—Remember p13-32,por.
   Earle—Colon. p111-119
   Green—Pioneer (1) p201-237,284,294,
    300
   Hammerton P795
  *Humphrey—Women p18-29
   Irwin—Angels p60-61
   Jones—Quakers p4-11,16-21,25
   Leonard—Amer. p26,117
   Logan—Part p37-43
   Longwell—Amer. p31-55
  *McCallum—Women p13-32
  *MacVeagh—Champlin p302
   Morris—400 p138-139
   Muir—Women p107-109
   Papashvily—All p103-104
  *Sickels—Calico p17-29
  *Yost—Famous p17-28,por.

Hutchinson, Elizabeth (fl. 1750's-1770's)
   Amer., mother of Andrew Jackson
   Bartlett—Mothers p75-79

Hutchinson, Elizabeth Chase (fl. 1870's-
   1880's)
   Amer. social reformer, singer
   Hanaford—Dau. p363-591

Hutchinson, Lucy Apsley (1620-1671)
   Amer. colonial author
   Bottrall—Pers. p26-27,225
   Deen—Great p360-362
   Fifty—Famous p118-120,por.
   Hammerton p795,por.
   MacCarthy—Women p93-107
   Stenton—English p164-166·

Hutchinson, Viola (fl. 19th cent.)
   Amer. social reformer, singer
   Hanaford—Dau. p591

Hutchison, Ida Jones Seymour (1877-1950)
   Amer. educator, philanthropist
   Women—Achieve. p182,por.

Hutten, Bettina, Baroness von (m. 1897)
   Amer. author
   Asquith—Myself p117-129,por.
   Hammerton p796

Hutton, Barbara (1912-   )
   Amer. heiress
   CR '59 p364-365,por.
   CR '63 p311
   Jensen—Revolt p167,por.
   Tanner—Here p121-142

Hutton, Betty (1921-   )
 Amer. singer
 CR '59 p365-366,por.
 CR '63 p311,por.
 Cur. Biog. '50 p269-271,por.
 Tebbel—Inher. p98-100-102,por.
 Time Apr.24,1950 p66,por.(Cover)

Hutton, Mrs. Lee William (1899-   )
 Amer. organization official
 Cur. Biog. '48 p299-301,por.

Huxley, Julia F. Arnold (1862-1908)
 Eng. educator, foundress
 Brittain—Women p62,83,248

Hyacintha Mariscotti (1585-1640)
 It. saint
 Englebert—Lives p42
 Wescott—Calen. p17

Hyatt, Anna.
 See Huntington, Anne Vaughn Hyatt

Hyatt, Harriet Randolph.
 See Mayor, Harriet Hyatt

Hyde, Catherine, Duchess of Queensberry
    (d. 1777)
 Eng. maid of honor
 Melville—Maids p226-245,por.

Hyde, Edith (fl. 1910's)
 Amer. beauty, fortune-teller
 Lamparski—What p20-21,por.

Hyde, Helen (1868-1919)
 Amer. etcher, engraver, painter
 Dorland—Sum p155
 Michigan—Biog. p164-165
 Waters—Women p171

Hyde, Helen Smith (fl. 1930's)
 Amer. business woman,
    employment manager
 Women—Achieve. p187,por.

Hyde, Madeline (1907-   )
 Amer. composer, author
 ASCAP p246-247

Hyde, Violet McDougall Buel (m. 1899)
 Amer. religious worker
 Logan—Part p620

Hyers, Anna Madah (fl. 1860's-1870's)
 Amer. singer
 Cuney-Hare—Negro p215-218

Hyers, Emma Louise (fl. 1860's-1870's)
 Amer. singer
 Cuney-Hare—Negro p215-218

Hyman, Libbie Henrietta (b. 1888)
 Amer. zoologist, author
 Women—Achieve. p75,por.
 *Yost—Women Sci. p122-138

Hypatia of Alexandria (c. 380-415)
 Gr. philosopher, mathematician,
    teacher, beauty
 Abbot—Notable p35-38
 Adelman—Famous p27-29
 Beard—Woman p299-300
 Cajori—Hist. p50-51
 Coolidge—Six p20-21
 Culver—Women p81
 Hammerton p799
 Koven—Women p6
 MacVeagh—Champlin p302
 Mozans—Woman p137-141,168,199-
    201
 Muir—Women p57-58
 Schmidt—400 p211,por.
 Smith—Hist. (1) p137

Hypsicratea (fl. B.C. 130's-160's)
 Pontus queen, wife of Methridates
    the Great
 Boccaccio—Conc. p170-172

I

Iantha (or Ianthe).
 See Digby, Jane Elizabeth

Ibarbourou, Juana de (1895-   )
 Urug. poet
 Rosenbaum—Modern p229-256

Ibarruri, Dolores Gomez (1895-   )
 Span. politician
 Cur. Biog. '67 p194-196,por.

Ibbotson, Mrs. (fl. 19th cent.)
 Eng. belle
 Furniss—Some p154-156

Ichabod's mother (Biblical)
 Deen—All p93-95

Iconoclast, pseud.
 See Hamilton, Mary Agnes Adamson

Ida (1040-1113)
 It. saint
 Englebert—Lives p144
 *Windham—Sixty p268-275

Ida (760's-800's)
 Fr. saint
 Blunt—Great p152

Idelette de Bures (d. 1549)
 Fr. religious worker
 Deen—Great p340-342

Ighino, Mary (fl. 1880's)
 It. sculptor
 Waters—Women p171-172

Ijkens, Catherine.
See Yjkens (Laurence) Catherine

Ileana, Princess (fl. 1940's)
Rom. philanthropist, princess
Cavanah—We p215-225
Wright—Great p100-117

Ilg, Frances Lillian (1902-   )
Amer. physician
Cur. Biog. '56 p299-301,por.

Illington, Margaret (1881-1934)
Amer. actress
Izard—Heroines p363-364

Ilona, Zrini (d. 1703)
Hung. patriot
Schmitt—400 p224-225,por.

Ima Shalom (fl. 70 A.D.)
Israeli religious scholar
*Levinger—Great p87-89

Imelda (fl. c. 1330's)
It. saint
*Beebe—Saints p85-88
Wescott—Calen. p69

Inchbald, Elizabeth Simpson (1753-1821)
Eng. actress, author
Dorland—Sum p26,194
Hammerton p801
Jenkins—Ten p101-119,por.
Johnson—Women p59-60
MacCarthy—Later p202-210
Stebbins—London p29-58

Inez de Castro (d. 1355)
Port. queen
Muir—Women p83-84

Ingalls, Laura (fl. 1920's-1940's)
Amer. pioneer aviatrix
Adams—Sky p197-211
Dwiggins—They p75,80,82-83,89-91,
93,por.
Earhart—Fun p179
*May—Women p95,131-134,por.
Planck—Women p76-77

Ingalls, Mildred Dodge Jeremy (1911-   )
Amer. poet, teacher
Cur. Biog. '54 p358-359,por.

Ingalls, Murilla Baker (m. 1850)
Amer. missionary
Logan—Part p516

Ingeborg (c. 1176-c. 1237)
Fr. queen
Hammerton p802

Ingelow, Jean (1820-1897)
Eng. poet, novelist
Adelman—Famous p180
Black—Notable p299-312,por.
Dorland—Sum p20,72,181,195
Hammerton p802,por.
*MacVeagh—Champlin p303

Ingels, Margaret (gr. 1916)
Amer. mechanical engineer
Goff—Women p66-76

Ingersoll, Marion Crary (fl. 1930's)
Amer. humanitarian
Women—Achieve. p110,por.

Inghin Dubh (fl. 1500's)
Irish patriot
Concannon—Dau. p75-77

Ingles, Mary Draper (c. 1718-1810)
Amer. pioneer
Green—Pioneer (1) p425-435,485

Inglesby, Mona (1918-   )
Eng. ballet dancer, choreographer
Davidson—Ballet p146-152,por.
Haskell—Ballet p182-186,por.

Inglis, Elsie Maud (1864-1917)
Scot. nurse, physician, surgeon
Bell—Storm. p152-159
Hammerton p803
Holroyd—Fifty p203-206
Lovejoy—Women p282-283,287-291

Inglis, Hester. See Kello, Esther English

Ingram, Frances (b. 1888)
Eng. singer
McCoy—Portraits p90,por.

Ingram, Marie Louise Augusta (fl. 1940's)
Ger. spy
Singer—World's p251-254

Ingrid (1910-   )
Dan. queen
Phila.—Women unp.,por.
Stiles—Postal p126

Innis, Anna (d. 1851)
Amer. W. pioneer
Ellet—Pioneer p61
Logan—Part p75

Innis, Mary Quayle (n.d.)
Amer.-Can. author
Thomas—Canad. p67

Inskeep, Alice Carey (fl. 1940's)
Amer. musical educator, director,
supervisor
McCoy—Portraits p90,por.

Inverness, Cecilia Laetitia Underwood,
Duchess of (c. 1788-1873)
Eng. hostess
Hasted—Unsuccess. p212-221,por.

Io. See Isis

Ioannovna. See Anna Ivanovna

Iredel, Hannah (fl. 1779)
Amer. pioneer
Green—Pioneer (3) p283

Ireland, Norma Olin (1907-   )
Amer. author, technical indexer,
librarian
Bul. of Bibl. My.-Aug.1948 p141-143,
por.

Iremonger, Lucille Parks (gr. 1937)
Eng. author
Brittain—Women p115,164,192,254
Iremonger—And p9-50,por.

Irene (1) (fl. 7th cent.)
Sp. saint
Englebert—Lives p398-399

Irene (2) (fl. A.D. 1124)
Hung. saint, princess
*Windham—Sixty p258-263

Irene (3) (752-803)
Byzant. empress, daughter of
Constantine V
Boccaccio—Conc. p234-236
Diehl—Byzant. p65-93
Diehl—Portraits p73-104
Hammerton p805,por.
*MacVeagh—Champlin p305

Irene (4) (d. 1160)
Byzant. empress, wife of
Manuel Commenus
Diehl—Byzant. p226-243

Irene (5) (Yolanda).
See Yolanda of Montferrat

Irene (6) (1907-1962)
Amer. fashion designer
Cur. Biog. '46 p276-277,por.
Cur. Biog. '63 p206

Irene Emma Elizabeth (1939-   )
Nether. princess
Stiles—Postal p127

Irion, Anna Raguet (c. 1819-1883)
Amer., friend of Sam Houston
Turner—Sam p28-50,por.

Irmina (d. 708/716)
Luxem. saint
Englebert—Lives p487
Stiles—Postal p234

Iron, Ralph, pseud.
See Schreiner, Olive

Irons, Evelyn (gr. 1921)
Eng. journalist
Brittain—Women p144,251

Irvine, Theodora Ursula (fl. 1930's)
Can.-Amer. teacher
Women—Achieve. p107,por.

Irving, Isabel (1871-1944)
Amer. actress
Strang—Actresses p98-103,por.

Irwin, Elizabeth Antoinette (d. 1942)
Amer. educator
Cur. Biog. '42 p409

Irwin, Flora (fl. 1870's)
Amer. actress
Marks—Glamour p308

Irwin, Harriet (d. 1897)
Amer. architect
Stern—We p55-61

Irwin, Helen (fl. 1950's-1960's)
Amer. librarian, club leader
Parshalle—Kash. p49-50,por.

Irwin, Helen Gould (n.d.)
Amer., organization official
Cur. Biog. '52 p285-287,por.

Irwin, Inez Haynes (b. 1873)
Amer. author
*Ferris—Girls p77-90
Overton—Women p187-188

Irwin, Laetitia McDonald (fl. 1930's)
Amer. author
Women—Achieve. p199

Irwin, Margaret (n.d.)
Eng. author
Cur. Biog. '46 p277-278,por.

Irwin, May (Ada Campbell) (1862-1938)
Can. actress
Blum—Great p22,por.
Cahn—Laugh. p48-49,por.
Strang—Actresses p174-186

Isaacs, Adah (Isaac Menken, pseud.) 1835-
1868)
Amer. Eng. actress, author
Pattee—Fem. p128-129

Isabel (Saint).
See Elizabeth of Portugal (Elizabeth
of Aragon)

Isabel (queen).
See Elizabeth (Sp. queen)

Isabel, Blessed (1225-1270)
    Fr. religious worker
    Englebert—Lives p73-74

Isabel d'Orleans (1846-1921)
    Brazil. princess
    Stiles—Postal p127

Isabella I, of Castile (1451-1504)
    Sp. queen
    Abbott—Notable p127-136
    Adelman—Famous p43-44,por.
    Arsenius—Dict. p93,por.
    Beard—Woman p258,304
    Blunt—Great p176-196
    Boyd—Rulers p79-88,por.
    *Cather—Girlhood p165-184
    Club—Printing p8
    Deen—Great p67-74
    Dolan—Goodnow's p117
    Dorland—Sum p56-57
    *Farmer—Book p42-56
    Farmer—What p19-22
    Fifty—Famous p236-241,por.
    Fitzhugh—Concise p205-206
    Hammerton p807,por.
    Jenkins—Heroines p53-136,por.
    *MacVeagh—Champlin p306
    Muir—Women p91-93
    *Nisenson—More Minute p76,por.
    Phila.—Women, unp.,por.
    Schmidt—400 p353-354,por.
    Stiles—Postal p127
    Thomas—Vital p194-198

Isabella II, Maria Isabella Louise (1830-
        1904)
    Sp. queen
    Arsenius—Dict. p93,por.
    Hammerton p807
    Phila.—Women, unp.,por.
    Stiles—Postal p127

Isabella, Countess of Castile (c. 1722-1795)
    Eng., friend of "Baron de
        Wenheim"
    Smith—Originals p97-112

Isabella of Austria, Clara E. (1566-1633)
    Sp. infanta
    Arsenius—Dict. p93,por.
    Phila.—Women, unp.,por.
    Stiles—Postal p127

Isabella of Bavaria (1370-1435)
    Fr. queen
    Hammerton p807

Isabella of Brazil (1846-1921)
    Brazil. princess
    Muir—Women p210-211

Isabella of France (c. 1292-1358)
    Eng. queen
    Hammerton p807

Isaiah's wife (Biblical)
    Deen—All p334
    Horton—Women p263-269

Isberge. See Gisela (Fr. saint)

Iscah (Biblical)
    Deen—All p269

Isely, Elise Dubach (b.c. 1843)
    Swiss-Amer. pioneer
    Cavanah—We p261-272

Isis (fl. c. 1700-1100 B.C.)
    Egypt. queen
    Boccaccio—Conc. p18-19
    *O'Clery—Queens p3-10

Isobel. See Isabella

Isoltseva, Apollovna (fl. 1910's)
    Russ. soldier, war heroine
    Dorland—Sum p99

Isom, Mary Frances (1865-1920)
    Amer. librarian
    Marshall—Amer. p257-269

Israel, Hannah Erwin (c. 1743-1821)
    Amer. Rev. war heroine
    Ellet—Women (1) p181-196
    Hanaford—Dau. p59

Ita (d.c. 570)
    Irish saint
    Concannon—Dau. p38-40

Itasse, Jeanne (fl. 1880's-1900's)
    Fr. sculptor
    Waters—Women p172-173

Iturbi, Amparo (1898-   )
    Sp. pianist
    Ewen—Living p176-177,por.
    McCoy—Portraits p91,por.

Ivanovsky, Elizabeth (1910-   )
    Russ. illustrator
    Mahoney—Illus. p323

Ivans, Martha (fl. 1780's)
    Amer., W. pioneer
    Ellet—Pioneer p132

Ivers, Alice (1851-1930)
    Eng.-Amer. pioneer
    Horan—Desperate p315-321,por.

Iverson, Caroline (n.d.)
    Amer. aviatrix
    *Knapp—New p100-116,por.

Ives, Alice (fl. 1900's)
    Amer. playwright
    Logan—Part p790

Jackson, Rachel Donelson Robards (1767-1828)
    Amer., wife of Andrew Jackson
Brooks—Young p216-242
Gerlinger—Mis. p24-26,por.
Green—Pioneer (3) p443
Hanaford—Dau. p80-82
Logan—Ladies p41-45
Logan—Part p234-237
*McConnell—Our p83-94,por.
Minnigerode—Some p183-193,por.
Prindiville—First p66-76
Ross—Know p17,por.
Smith—Romances p98-111,por.
Turner—Sam p4-8,por.
Whitton—iFrst p116-135,por.

Jackson, Rowena (1926-   )
    New Z. dancer
Fisher—Ball. p28-29,por.

Jackson, Sherry (n.d.)
    Amer. TV actress
TV—Person (1) p153-154,por.

Jackson, Shirley (1919-   )
    Amer. author
CR '63 p316,por.

Jacob, Mrs. Arthur Violet (fl. 1900's-1920's)
    Scot. poet
Hammerton p810

Jacoba (Jacqueline) (d.c. 1273)
    It. saint
Englebert—Lives p55-56

Jacobi, Lotte J. (fl. 1930's)
    Ger.-Amer. photographer
Women—Achievement p199

Jacobi, Mary Putnam (1842-1906)
    Amer. pioneer physician, feminist
Adelman—Famous p236
Beard—Amer. p367-376
Dorland—Sum p27,148
*Fleming—Doctors p23-38
Hammerton p810
Hanaford—Dau. p572
Hume—Great p173-217,por.
Irwin—Angels p49,139,144,180
Logan—Part p741
Lovejoy—Women p73-75,158-160,por.
Mead—Medical p37-40,por.
Riegel—Amer. p124-125

Jacob-Loewenson, Alice (n.d.)
    Ger.Israeli musicologist, composer, pianist
Saleski—Jewish p714

Jacobs, Aletta H. (1849-1929)
    Nether. pioneer physician, feminist
Lovejoy—Women p183-184

Jacobs, Helen Hull (1908-   )
    Amer. tennis player
Hammerton p810
Lamparski—What. p206-207
Time Sept.14,1936 p36,por. (Cover)

Jacobs, Leonebel (fl. 1930's)
    Amer. painter
Women—Achieve. p113,por.

Jacobson, Pauline (fl. 1920's-1930's)
    Amer. journalist
Ross—Ladies p586-588

Jacqueline (saint). See **Jacoba**

Jacqueline, Mary Frances.
    See Latour, Frances Mary Jacqueline

Jacqueline of Bavaria, Countess of Holland (fl. 15th cent.)
    Nether. princess
*Cather—Girlhood p121-138

Jacquemart, Nélie (fl. 1860's-1870's)
    Fr. painter
Waters—Women p173-174

Jadwiga (Jodwiga; Hedwig) (1370/73-1399)
    Pol. queen
Arsenius—Dict. p95,por.
Mizwa—Great p24-36,por.
Phila.—Women unp.,por.
Schmidt—400 p316,por.
Stiles—Postal p117

Jael (Biblical)
Deen—All p269-270
Horton—Women p119-133
Lewis—Portraits p216-217
Lofts—Women p66-76
Mead—250 p62
Muir—Women p22-24

Jaffe, Rona (1932-   )
    Amer. author
CR '59 p370-371,por.
CR '63 p317,por.

Jaggard, Annella (d. 1918)
    Amer. missionary
They—Went p30

Jaggard, Wilhelmina Zoe Smith (fl. 1910's-1950's)
    Amer. missionary
They—Went p30-32

Jahangir. See **Nur Jahan** (Nur Mahal)

Jaipur, Maharani of (1919-   )
    E. Ind. politician
Cur. Biog. '68 p196-198

Jairus' daughter (Biblical)
Deen—All p318-319
Lewis—Portraits p190-191

Jaissle, Louise (n.d.)
Amer. nurse
Wright—Great p48-55

James, Alice Archer Sewall (b. 1870)
Amer. artist
Logan—Part p811

James, Annie Laurie Wilson (b. 1862)
Amer. editor, horse authority
Logan—Part p863

James, Annie P. (b. 1825)
Amer. missionary
Hanaford—Dau. p510

James, Belle Robinson (1868-1935)
Can.-Amer. religious worker, author
Phillips—33 p102-107

James, Bessie (fl. 1910's)
Amer. journalist
Ross—Ladies p592-594

James, Dorothy (1901-   )
Amer. composer
Howard—Our p537
Reis—Composers p194-195

James, Elizabeth (fl. 1660's-1670's)
Eng. actress
Wilson—All p151-152

James, Hannah Packard (1835-1903)
Amer. librarian
Bul. of Bibl. Oct.1914 p89,91-92,por.

James, Inez Eleanor (n.d.)
Amer. composer
ASCAP p250

James, Joni (1930-   )
Amer. singer
CR '59 p371,por.
CR '63 p317-318,por.
Popular Record p71,por.

James, Mary Robertson (1810-1881)
Amer., mother of Henry James,
William James
Davis—Mothers p45-53

James, Winifred Lewellin (1876-1941)
Austral. author, journalist
Hammerton p813

Jameson, Anna Brownell Murphy (1794-
1860)
Irish archaeologist, iconographer,
art critic, author
Adelman—Famous p134-135
Dorland—Sum p41,171-172
Mozans—Woman p313-316

Jameson, Mrs. Edward (fl. 1780's)
Amer. pioneer
Fowler—Woman p158-166

Jameson (Jamison), Hannah Taggart
(d. 1830)
Amer. pioneer
Green—Pioneer (3) p521-522

Jameson, Margaret Storm (1897-   )
Eng. novelist
Hammerton p814
Lawrence—School p227-230
Millett—Brit. p295-296

Jamieson, Nina Moore (1885-1932)
Can. author
Thomas—Canad. p68

Jamison, Evelyn Mary (gr. 1901)
Eng. librarian, educator
Brittain—Women (see index)

Jammé, Anne C. (f. 1939)
Amer. nurse
Pennock—Makers p39,por.

Janauschek, Fanny (1830-1904)
Bohem. actress
Adelman—Famous p208-209
Coad—Amer. p231,por.
Dorland—Sum p41,70,166-167

Janda, Herminie von (b. 1854)
Aust. painter
Waters—Women p174

"Jane." See Silcott, Jane

Jane, Calamity. See "Calamity Jane"

Jane, Seymour (c. 1509-1537)
Eng. queen
Hammerton p1206,por.
*Humphrey—Janes p190-208
Sanders—Intimate p20-21,por.
Stenton—English p130

Jane de Chantal (1572-1641)
Fr. saint
Elgin—Nun p40-43,por.
Englebert—Lives p320-321
*Windham—Sixty p355-362

Janes, Martha Waldron (b. 1832)
Amer. clergyman
Logan—Part p736

Janeway, Elizabeth Hall (1913-   )
Amer. author
CR '59 p371,por.
CR '63 p318,por.
Cur. Biog. '44 p327-328,por.
Lovejoy—Women p366-367
Warfel—Amer. p227,por.

Janis, Elsie (1889-1956)
Amer. actress, author song-writer
ASCAP p251

(Continued)

Janis, Elsie—*Continued*

    Blum—Great p69,por.
    Caffin—Vaud. p140
    Settel—Radio p64,por.

Janitschek, Maria (fl. 19th cent.)
    Gr. author
    Heller—Studies p266-267

Janotha, (Maria Cecilia) Nathalie (1856-
    1932)
    Pol. pianist
    Hammerton p814
    Schonberg—Great p335-336

Janowszky, Bela (1900-   )
    Hung.-Amer. sculptor
    National—Contemp. p168

Jans (Janssen), Annetje.
    See Bogardus, Annetje Jans

Jarboe, Elizabeth.
    See Kenton, Elizabeth Jarboe

Jarboe, Elizabeth (2) (fl. 1770's)
    Amer. pioneer
    Green—Pioneer (3) p492-493

Jarboro, Caterina (1903-   )
    Amer. singer
    Cuney-Hare—Negro p362-364,por.
    Robinson—Hist. p210-211,por.

Jardine, Mrs. John Alexander (fl. 1930's)
    Amer. musician, organization
      official
    McCoy—Portraits p92,por.

Jaricot, Pauline (1799-1862)
    It. foundress
    Stiles—Postal p129

Jarius, daughter of.
    See Jaruis' daughter

Jasmyn, Joan (1898-   )
    Amer. composer, author
    ASCAP p251

Jay, Harriet (1863-1932)
    Scot. author
    Hammerton p815

Jay, Sarah Van Brugh Livingston (1757-
    1802)
    Amer., wife of John Jay, social
      leader
    Brooks—Young p43-83
    Ellet—Women (2) p140-142
    Green—Pioneer (2) p152-158
    Green—Pioneer (3) p305,por.
    Hanaford—Dau. p137
    Sale—Old p134-138,por.

Jayne, Barbara (fl. 1940's)
    Amer. aviatrix, test pilot
    *May—Women p167

Jaynes, Clare, pseud.
    See Mayer, Jane Rothschild; Spiegel,
      Clara Gatzert

Jean, Elsie (1907-   )
    Amer. composer, author
    ASCAP p252

Jean, Sally Lucas (b. 1878)
    Amer. nurse, educator
    Pennock—Makers p89,por.

Jeanmaire, Renée (1924-   )
    Fr. ballet dancer
    Atkinson—Dancers p77-79,por.
    CR '59 p372,por.
    Cur. Biog. '52 p289-290,por.
    Davidson—Ballet p152-155
    Haskell—Vignet. p77
    *McConnell—Famous p150-156,por.

Jeanne d'Arc. See Joan of Arc

Jeanne de Bourbon (m. 1350)
    Fr. queen, wife of Charles V
    Koven—Women p64-66

Jeanne de Lestonac (1556-1640)
    Fr. saint
    Elgin—Nun p36-39,por.
    Englebert—Saints p48

Jeanne de Valois (1464-1505)
    Fr. saint, queen
    Blunt—Great p95-96
    Englebert—Lives p51

Jeanne-Francoise de Chantal (1575-1643)
    Fr. saint
    Wescott—Calen. p126

Jeanne Grimaldi. See Grimaldi, Jeanne

Jeanne Marie de Maillé (1332-1414)
    Fr. saint
    Englebert—Lives p121

Jeans, Isabel (1891-   )
    Eng. actress
    Hammerton p815

Jeans, Ursula (1906-   )
    Eng. actress
    Hammerton p816

Jebb, Caroline Lane Reynolds Slemmer
    (1840-1930)
    Amer. hostess, author
    Pearson—Marry. p231-246

Jebb, Eglantyne Mary (b. 1889)
    Eng. educator, social welfare
      worker
    Brittain—Women p126-179-250

Jecholiah (Biblical)
Deen—All p270

Jecks, Clara (fl. 19th cent.)
Eng. actress
Furniss—Some p54

Jedidah (Biblical)
Deen—All p270-271

Jefferis, Marea Wood (fl. 1900's)
Amer. poet
Logan—Part p820

Jefferson, Cornelia Burke (fl. 1830's-1840's)
Amer. actress
Coad—Amer. p72,169,por.

Jefferson, Jane Randolph (fl. 1730's-1740's)
Amer., mother of Thomas Jefferson
Donovan—Women p18-22
Hampton—Our p25-31

Jefferson, Martha.
See Randolph, Martha Jefferson

Jefferson, Martha Wayles (1748--1782)
Amer., wife of Thomas Jefferson
Donovan—Women p212-223
Gerlinger—Mis. p11-14
Green—Pioneer (3) p240-247
Hanaford—Dau. p75
Logan—Ladies p22-23
Logan—Part p217
*McConnell—Our p33-41
Ross—Know p9
Smith—Romances p47-51
Whitton—First p39-53,por.

Jefferson, Mary (Polly) (fl. 1770's-1800's)
Amer., dau. of Thomas Jefferson
Donovan—Women p223,228-230,244,
246-248
*Sweetser—Famous p50-84

Jefferson, Mary Anne (fl. 1820's)
Amer. actress
Moses—Famous p68-69

Jeffreys, Anne (1923-   )
Amer. actress
TV—Person (1) p157-158,por.

Jeffreys, Ellis (1868/73-1943)
Eng. actress
Marks—Glamour p309

Jeffreys, Henrietta Louisa, Countess of
Pomfret (d. 1761)
Eng. maid of honor
Melville—Maids p212-222,por.

Jeffries, Lila F. S. (fl. 1930's)
Amer. editor, publicist
Women—Achieve. p168,por.

Jehoaddan(Biblical)
Deen—All p271

Jehosheba(Biblical)
Deen—All p271-272
Hughes—Mothers p127-128

Jehudijah (Biblical)
Deen—All p272

Jekyll, Gertrude (1843-1932)
Eng. author, landscape gardener
Hammerton p817
Hollingsworth—Her p121-125

Jemima (Biblical)
Deen—All p272-273

Jemison, Mary Dehewamis (c. 1742-1833)
Amer. pioneer, Ind. captive
Peckham—Capt. p62-79
Whitton—These p23-25

Jemne, Elsa Laubach (b. 1888)
Amer. painter
Mahony—Illus. p323

Jencks, Virginia Ellis (fl. 1930's)
Amer. Congresswoman
Paxton—Women p11,129

Jenkin, Mrs. Bernard. See Giles, Miss

Jenkins, Carol Heiss (1940-   )
Amer. skater
*Jacobs—Famous p45-58,por.

Jenkins, Cora W. (c. 1870-1947)
Amer. composer, music teacher
McCoy—Portraits p93,por.

Jenkins, Elizabeth (1907-   )
Eng. author
Brittain—Women p253

Jenkins, Florence F. (fl. 1930's)
Amer. singer
Women—Achieve. p88,por.

Jenkins, Helen Hartley (d. 1934)
Amer. nurse
Pennock—Makers p40-41,por.

Jenkins, Helen P. (fl. 1880's)
Amer. lecturer
Hanaford—Dau. p341

Jenkins, Lydia A. (fl. 1850's)
Amer. clergyman, feminist, lecturer
Hanaford—Dau. p445,563
O'Connor—Pioneer p88

Jenkins, Sara (1904-   )
Amer. author
Cur. Biog. '53 p296-298,por.

Jenks, Phoebe A. Pickering Hoyt (1847-
    1907)
    Amer. painter
    Waters—Women p174

Jennifer (fl. A.D. 512)
    Fr. saint
    *Windham—Sixty p150-156

Jennings, Anne. See Johnson, Anne Jennings

Jennings, Gertrude E. (c. 1877-1958)
    Eng. playwright
    Hammerton p818

Jennings, Mrs. (fl. 1770's)
    Amer. pioneer
    Green—Pioneer (3) p444-445

Jennings, Mrs. (fl. 1720's)
    Eng., wife of tutor
    Stenton—English p281-282

Jennings, Sarah, Duchess of Marlborough
    (1660-1744)
    Eng. society leader, builder
    Abbot—Notable p253-257,por.
    Dorland—Sum p30
    Fifty—Famous p112-117
    Hammerton p965,por.
    Schmidt—400 p135-136,por.
    Sitwell—Women p12-14,por.
    Stenton—English (see index)
    Thomson—Queens p13-47

Jennison, Eunice.
    See Baldwin, Euice Jennison

Jennison, Mary (d.c. 1825/30)
    Amer. landholder, Ind. captive
    Dexter—Career p196-197

Jensen, Mrs. Clyde Reynolds.
    See Bard, Mary Ten Eyck

Jensen, Mrs. Oliver. See Stafford, Jean

Jepson, Helen (1906-   )
    Amer. singer
    Ewen—Ency. p225-226
    Ewen—Living p182-183,por.
    McCoy—Portraits p93,por.
    Peltz—Spot. p39,por.
    Women—Achieve. p56,por.

Jepthah's daughter (Biblical)
    Buchanan—Women p41-42
    Culver—Women p26
    Deen—All p74-78
    Faulhaber—Women p120-126
    Hastings—Greater p458-494
    Lewis—Portraits p106-107
    Lofts—Women p57-65
    Marble—Women, Bible p178-183
    Muir—Women p20-22
    Schmidt—400 p270-27-,por.

Jeremiah's mother (Biblical)
    Deen—All p345

Jerichau-Baumann, Elizabeth (1817-1881)
    Pol. painter
    Waters—Women p175-176

Jerioth (Biblical)
    Deen—All p273

Jeritza, Maria, Baroness Von Popper (1891-)
    Aust. singer
    Collins—Biog. p221-222
    Davidson—Treas. p136-139
    Downes—Olin p91-92,139-141
    Ewen—Ency. p226
    Ewen—Living p183-184,por.
    *Ferris—Girls p273-285
    Hammerton p818
    *Kirkland—Achieved p52-58
    McCoy—Portraits p93,por.
    New Yorker Jan.24,1931,p21-24,por.
        (Profiles)
    Time Nov.12,1928 p40,por.(Cover)
    Wagnalls—Opera p54-66,por.
    Wagner—Prima p96-97,243

Jernegan, Abigail S. See Vincent, Abigail S.

Jernegan, Amy Chase (b. 1863)
    Amer. whaling voyager
    Whiting—Whaling p256-258,por.

Jernegan, Charlotte.
    See Dunham, Charlotte Corday

Jernegan, Helen. See Clark, Helen

Jernegan, Laura (fl. 1860's-1870's)
    Amer. whaling voyager child
    Whiting—Whaling p126-133,277

Jeroboam, wife of (Biblical)
    Buchanan—Women p58-59
    Deen—All p331-332
    Lewis—Portraits p88-90

Jerome, Albertina P. (n.d.)
    Amer. nurse
    *Wright—Great p179-200

Jerome, Jennie.
    See Churchill, Jeanette Jerome, Lady
    Randolph

Jerome, Maude Nugent (1877-1958)
    Amer. author, composer, actress
    ASCAP p252

Jerusalem, woman of (Biblical)
    Nelson—Bible p69-73

Jerusha (Biblical)
    Deen—All p273

Jesse, Frynwid Tennyson (d. 1958)
　　Eng. novelist, playwright
　　Hammerton p819

Jessey, Cornelia (1910-   )
　　Amer. novelist
　　Warfel—Amer. p229-230,por.

Jessner, Irene (1910-   )
　　Aust. singer
　　Ewen—Ency. p226-227
　　Ewen—Living p184,por.
　　Peltz—Spot. p98

Jessye, Eva (fl. 1930's)
　　Amer. conductor, author, editor
　　Cuney-Hare—Negro p258
　　McCoy—Portraits p93,por.

Jeune, Lady (Lady St. Helier) (fl. 19th
　　cent.)
　　Eng. hostess
　　Furniss—Some p186-193,por.

Jewell, Catherine Underwood (d. 1873)
　　Amer. physician
　　Hanaford—Dau. p557-558

Jewett, Alice L. (fl. 1920's)
　　Amer. editor, librarian
　　Marshall—Amer. p101-102

Jewett, Maude Sherwood (b. 1873)
　　Amer .sculptor
　　National—Contemp. p171

Jewett, Mildred ("Madaket Millie")
　　Amer. dog-trainer
　　Snow—Women p113-123,por.

Jewett, Sarah Orne (1849-1909)
　　Amer. author
　　Adelman—Famous p239
　　Auchincloss—Pion. p6-19
　　Dorland—Sum p51
　　Harkins—Famous p43-58,por.
　　Harkins—Little p43-58,por.
　　Howe—Memories p281-303,por.
　　Logan—Part p801
　　Scherman—Literary p86-87
　　*Witham—Pan. p176-177,por.

Jewitt, Jessie Mae (fl. 1940's)
　　Amer. composer, organist, pianist
　　McCoy—Portraits p93,por.

Jewsbury, Geraldine Endsor (1812-1880)
　　Eng. author
　　Dorland—Sum p44,118
　　Hammerton p821

Jewsbury, Maria Jane (1800-1833)
　　Eng. author
　　Courtney—Adven. p94-95

Jex-Blake, Henrietta (c. 1863-c. 1953)
　　Eng. educator
　　Brittain—Women (see index)

Jex-Blake, Sophia Louisa (1840-1912)
　　Eng. pioneer physician
　　Adelman—Famous p246
　　Bell—Storm p62-83,por.
　　Dorland—Sum p146
　　Hume—Great p124-172,por.
　　Lovejoy—Women p144-157,por.
　　Mozans—Woman p305-307

Jezebel (Biblical)
　　Buchanan—Women p59-62
　　Deen—All p125-131
　　Ewart—World's p19-21
　　Hammerton p821
　　Lewis—Portraits p124-127
　　Lofts—Women p140-156
　　Lord—Great p59-70
　　Marble—Women, Bible p195-201
　　Mead—250 p121
　　Morton—Women p135-142
　　Muir—Women p98-99
　　Nelson—Bible p55-57

Jingo Kogo (fl.c. 200-270)
　　Japan. empress
　　Arsenius—Dict. p97,por.
　　Phila.—Women unp.,por.
　　Stiles—Postal p131

Jmelda. See Imelda.

Joan ("Fair Maid of Kent") (1328-1385)
　　Eng. princess
　　Hammerton p821

Joan (fl. 853-855)
　　Rom. pope, avowed
　　Boccaccio—Conc. p231-233
　　Ewart—World's p97-98

Joan (Joanna) (1452-1490)
　　Port. princess, acting regent
　　Stiles—Postal p131

Joan, Elsa (fl. 1900's-1910's)
　　Eng. singer
　　Felstead—Stars p102,por.

Joan of Arc (Jeanne d'Arc) (1412-1431)
　　Fr. saint, heroine, martyr, patriot
　　Abbot—Notable p439-448,por.
　　Abramowitz—Great p75-98
　　Adelman—Famous p41-43,por.
　　Arsenius—Dict. p96,por.
　　Bowie—Women p24-41
　　Clark—Great p316-326
　　Culver—Women p125-126
　　Deen—Great p60-66
　　Dorland—Sum p20
　　Dunaway—Turn. p408-428
　　Englebert—Lives p208

(Continued)

Johnson, Betsey.
  See Payne, Betsey Johnson

Johnson, Christine (fl. 1940's)
    Amer. singer
    Peltz—Spot. p105,por.

Johnson, Claudia Alta Taylor.
  See Johnson, Lady Bird

Johnson, Corinne (fl. 1930's)
    Amer. botanist
    Women—Achieve. p165,por.

Johnson, Dorothy B. (fl. 1930's)
    Amer. entomologist
    Osborn—Fragments p268,por.

Johnson, Electa Amanda (b. 1838)
    Amer. philanthropist
    Logan—Part p539

Johnson, Eliza McCardle (1810-1876)
    Amer., wife of Andrew Johnson
    Farmer—What p87
    Gerlinger—Mis. p54-56,por.
    Hanaford—Dau. p93-97
    Jensen—White p96,por.
    Logan—Ladies p94-101
    Logan—Part p265-267
    *McConnell—Our p171-179,por.
    Prindiville—First p150-156
    *Ross—Know p37,por.
    Smith—Romances p233-241,por.

Johnson, Emily Pauline (1861-1913)
    Can. poet, Mohawk princess
    Innis—Clear p74-90,por.
    Logan—Part p826
    Schmidt—400 p75,por.
    Stiles—Postal p132

Johnson, Esther (Stella) (1681-1728)
    Eng., friend of Jonathan Swift
    Cockran—Romance p340-348
    Fifty—Famous p46-52,por.
    Orr—Famous Affin. IV p5-15
    Sitwell—Women p15-16,por.

Johnson, Eva Marie (fl. 1940's-1950's)
    Amer. missionary
    They—Went p127-128

Johnson, Florence Merriam (fl. 1910's)
    Amer. Red Cross nurse
    DAR Mag. Nov.1921 p646-647,por.

Johnson, Georgia Douglas (fl. 1920's)
    Amer. poet
    Dreer—Amer. p73

Johnson, Grace Mott (b. 1882)
    Amer. sculptor
    Jackman—Amer. p407
    National—Contemp. p174

Johnson, Isabella (fl. 1770's)
    Amer. pioneer
    Green—Pioneer (3) p283

Johnson, Jemima Suggett (1753-1814)
    Amer. heroine
    Bruce—Woman p145-148
    Green—Pioneer (3) p402-405
    *Humphrey—Woman p72-79

Johnson, Mrs. John (fl. 1790's)
    Amer. actress
    Coad—Amer. p43,52-54

Johnson, Josephine Winslow (Josephine
       Cannon) (1910-   )
    Amer. novelist
    *Millett—Amer. p411-412
    Warfel—Amer. p230,por.

Johnson, Judy (1928-   )
    Amer. singer
    TV—Person (3) p156,por.

Johnson, Lady Bird (Claudia Alta Taylor
       Johnson) (1912-   )
    Amer., wife of Lyndon B. Johnson
    CR '63 p320,por.
    Cur. Biog. '64 p212-215,por.
    Frederick—Ten p19-37,por.
    Time Aug.28,1964 p20-23,por.(Cover)

Johnson, Louisa Catherine.
  See Adams, Louisa Catherine Johnson

Johnson, Luci Baines.
  See Nugent, Luci Baines Johnson

Johnson, Lucy (c. 1789-1867)
    Amer. inventor
    Hanaford—Dau. p653
    Logan—Part p883-884

Johnson, Lucy Ann Taylor (b. 1855)
    Amer., grandmother of Ralph
       Bunche
    Davis—Mother p131-144

Johnson, Lydia S. (fl. 1860's)
    Amer. Civil war nurse
    Logan—Part p366

Johnson, Mary (b. 1870)
    Amer. novelist
    Farrar—Literary p43-50,329-330,por.

Johnson, Mary C. (fl. 1870's)
    Amer. social reformer
    Hanaford—Dau. p420-423,por.

Johnson, Mary Katharine (fl. 1900's)
    Amer. club leader
    Logan—Part p461-462

Johnson, Mary McDonough (fl. 1790's-
        1820's)
    Amer., mother of Andrew Johnson
    Hampton—Our p132-138

Johnson, Mrs. (fl. 1660's-1670's)
    Eng. actress
    Wilson—All p152-153

Johnson, Nancy Cummings (Minnie Myrtle)
        (1818-1892)
    Amer. journalist
    Ross—Ladies p46-47,por.

Johnson, Olivia (fl. 1950's-1960's)
    Amer. club leader
    Parshalle—Kash. p73-75,por.

Johnson, Osa Helen Leighty (1894-1953)
    Amer. author, explorer, motion
        picture producer
    Cur. Biog. '40 p434-435,por.
    Cur. Biog. '53 p298
    Forsee—My p137-171
    *Kirkland—Achieved p28-35

Johnson, Pamela Hansford (1912-   )
    Eng. author
    Cur. Biog. '48 p322-323,por.

Johnson, Rebecca Franks, Lady.
    See Franks, Rebecca

Johnson, Sonya Bortin (fl. 1930's)
    Amer. business woman, advertising
        executive
    Women—Achieve. p166,por.

Johnson, Thomasina Walker (1911-   )
    Amer. government official, lobbyist
    Cur. Biog. '47 p335-337,por.

Johnston, Agnes M. (fl. 1930's)
    Amer. educator
    Women—Achieve. p160,por.

Johnston, Edith Constance Farrington
        1890-   )
    Amer. painter, illustrator
    Mahony—Illus. p325

Johnston, Elizabeth (m. 1821)
    Amer., wife of Dennis Hanks
    Barton—Women p114-116

Johnston, Frances Benjamin (1864-1952)
    Amer. photographer, lecturer
    Logan—Part p788-789

Johnston, Harriet Lane (1833-1903)
    Amer., niece of James Buchanan
    Gerlinger—Mis. p48-50
    Prindiville—First p134-139

Johnston, Helen, Lady Graden (d. 1707)
    Scot. covenanter
    Anderson—Ladies p300-313

Johnston, Henrietta (d.c. 1728/29)
    Amer. pioneer painter
    Leonard—Amer. p107-117

Johnston, Mrs. John T. (fl. 1860's)
    Amer. Civil war patriot
    Simkins—Women p21

Johnston, Lillian Proefrock (d. 1946)
    Amer. missionary
    They—Went p43-45

Johnston, Maria I. (b. 1835)
    Amer. author
    Logan—Part p819

Johnston, Marjane (n.d.)
    Amer. airline worker
    *Peckham—Women p106-107

Johnston, Mary (1870-1936)
    Amer. novelist
    Adelman—Famous p311
    Hammerton p828
    Harkins—Famous p299-313
    Harkins—Little p299-313,por.
    Logan—Part p807
    Maurice—Makers p4-5,por.
    Overton—Women p189-201
    Rogers—Women p39,por.

Johnston, Mary, Lady, Countess of Crawford
        (m. 1670)
    Scot. covenanter
    Anderson—Ladies p213-220

Johnston, Mary Yellott (b. 1806)
    Amer. pioneer
    Logan—Part p69

Johnston, Matilda (fl. 1840's-1850's)
    Amer., stepmistress of Abraham
        Lincoln
    Barton—Women p144-146

Johnston, Patricia (1922-   )
    Amer. author, song-writer
    ASCAP p257-258

Johnston, Sarah R. (fl. 1860's)
    Amer. Civil war humanitarian
    Brockett—Woman's p269-272

Johnston, Velma B. ("Wild Horse Annie")
        (fl. 1950's-1960's)
    Amer. secretary, animal
        humanitarian
    Parshalle—Kash. p112-115,por.

Johnstone, Lady (fl. 14th cent.)
    Scot. fighter, "Amazon"
    Graham—Group p24-25

Johnstone, Margaret Blair (1913-   )
    Amer. clergyman, author, lecturer
    Cur. Biog. '55 p306-308,por.

Johnstone, Mary H. (fl. 1860's)
    Amer. Civil war diarist
    Jones—Heroines p75-77

Joliot-Curie, Irène (1897-1956)
    Fr. physicist
    Calder—Science p70-71
    Chambers—Dict. col. 242-243
    Cur. Biog. '40 p435-436,por.
    Cur. Biog. '56 p314
    Farber—Nobel p142-144,por.
    Nobel—Man p355-356,462,466
    Progress—Science '40 p213
    *Riedman—Men p130-136,por.
    Weeks—Discovery p830-838,por.
    Year—Pic p212,por.

Jonas, Ānnetje.
    See Bogardus, Annetje Jans

Jonas, Marrietje.
    See Lockermans, Marrietje

Jonas, Maryla (1911-   )
    Pol. pianist
    Saleski—Jewish p494-495,por.

Jonas, Mrs. Tryntje (fl. 1630's)
    Amer. pioneer midwife
    Green—Pioneer (1) p154-158,196

Jones, Abbie Gerrish (fl. 1930's)
    Amer. composer
    Elson—Woman's p257

Jones, Agnes Elizabeth (1832-1868)
    Eng. pioneer nurse
    Cope—Six p1-9,por.

Jones, Anne Scotton (fl. 1750's)
    Amer. colonial needlewoman
    Dexter—Colonial p44

Jones, Avonia (1839-1867)
    Amer. actress
    Coad—Amer. p224,por.

Jones, Betty. See Smith, Betty Wehner

Jones, Calista Robinson (fl. 1860's)
    Amer. Civil war patriot
    Logan—Part p353

Jones, Candy (1925-   )
    Amer. model, business woman
    Cur. Biog. '61 p224-225,por.

Jones, Carolyn (1933-   )
    Amer. actress
    Cur. Biog. '67 p208-210,por.

Jones, Eleanor Dwight (c. 1881-1965)
    Amer. humanitarian
    Women—Achieve. p199

Jones, Elizabeth Dickson (b. 1862)
    Amer. philanthropist
    Logan—Part p529

Jones, Elizabeth Orton (1910-   )
    Amer. illustrator
    Mahony—Illus. p325

Jones, Emily Beatrix Coursolles (1893-   )
    Brit. author, journalist
    Millett—Brit. p297-298

Jones, Flora MacDonald (fl. 1860's)
    Amer. Civil war patriot
    Simkins—Women p17-18

Jones, Gail (n.d.)
    Amer. actress
    *Cherry—Portraits p198

Jones, Hannah. See Floyd, Hannah Jones

Jones, Harriet B. (b. 1856)
    Amer. physician
    Logan—Part p742

Jones, Helen Swift (fl. 1930's)
    Amer. landscape architect
    Women—Achieve. p159,por.

Jones, Hetty A. (fl. 1860's)
    Amer. Civil war nurse
    Brockett—Women's p783-786

Jones, Irma Theoda (b. 1845)
    Amer. philanthropist
    Logan—Part p539-540

Jones, Jane Elizabeth Hitchcock (fl. 1840's-
        1860's)
    Amer. feminist, lecturer
    O'Connor—Pioneer p20,65-69,147,152,
        168,197-198,216,226

Jones, Jennifer (1919-   )
    Amer. actress
    CR '59 p379,por.
    CR '63 p323,por.
    Cur. Biog. '44 p328-331,por.
    Time Jan.8,1945 p39,por.

Jones, Julia L. (fl. 1890's)
    Amer. W. pioneer, teacher
    Sargent—Pioneers p44

Jones, Kate E. (fl. 1900's)
    Amer. poet, club leader
    Logan—Part p355

Jones, Katherine Black (fl. 1930's)
    Amer. club leader
    Women—Achieve. p199

Jones, Lois Mailou (1905-   )
    Amer. artist, educator
    Robinson—Hist. p217

Jones, Margaret (fl. 1650's)
 Amer. accused witch
 Green—Pioneer (1) p225

Jones, Mary (fl. 18th cent.)
 Eng. author
 Stenton—English p298

Jones, Mary (1784-1866)
 Welsh religious worker
 Miller—Handi. p7-13,por.

Jones, Mary ("Molly") (1762-1833)
 Scot., Austral. pioneer
 Prout—Petticoat p25-29

Jones, Mary C. (b. 1842)
 Amer. clergyman, evangelist
 Logan—Part p736

Jones, Mary Harris ("Mother") (1830-1930)
 Irish-Amer. labor leader
 *Gersh—Women p97-117,por.
 *Kirkland—Achieved p9-16
 Rogers—Women p68,por.
 Sickels—Twelve p52-69,252
 Stone—We p326-331

Jones, Mary M. (fl. 1930's)
 Amer. author
 Women—Achieve. p189,por.

Jones, Minona Stearns Fitts (b. 1855)
 Amer. politician, feminist, social
  reformer
 Logan—Part p411-412

Jones, Mrs. (fl. 1820's)
 Amer. missionary, seafarer
 Snow—Women p58-70

Jones, Polly (fl. 1770's)
 Eng., mistress of Lord Bolingbroke
 Bleackley—Ladies p152-153,181,por.

Jones, Rebecca (1739-1818)
 Amer. clergyman
 Dexter—Career p56

Jones, Ruth E. (fl. 1930's)
 Amer. journalist
 Ross—Ladies p445-446

Jones, Sarah G. (fl. 1860's)
 Amer. poet, physician
 Brown—Home. p247,por.

Jones, Shirley (1934-)
 Amer .actress
 CR '63 p323,por.
 Cur. Biog. '61 p225-227,por.

Jones, Siseretta (d. 1933
 Amer. singer
 Cuney-Hare—Negro p230-231

Jones, Sybil (1813-1873)
 Amer. clergyman
 Hanaford—Dau. p438-441

Jones, Virginia Lacy (1914-)
 Amer. librarian, educator
 *Cherry—Portraits p54-56
 Robinson—Hist. p217-218

Jones, Mrs. Willie (d. 1828)
 Amer. Rev. war heroine
 Ellet—Women (2) p188-190

Jopling-Rowe, Louise (1843-1923)
 Eng. painter
 Hammerton p830
 Waters—Women p176-178

Jordan, Alice Boyer (fl. 1930's)
 Amer. nurse, business executive
 Women—Achieve. p95,por.

Jordan, Cornelia Jane Matthews (1830-
  1898)
 Amer. poet
 Logan—Part p819-820

Jordan, Dorothea (Dora, Dorothy) **Bland**
  (1762-1816)
 Irish actress
 Adelman—Famous p105-106
 Collins—Great p265-290
 Dorland—Sum p46
 Hammerton p831,por.
 Hasted—Unsuccess p80-111,por.
 *MacVeagh—Champlin p323
 MacQueen—Pope p279-287,por.
 Melville—More p197-279,por.
 Melville—Regency p245-255,por.
 Wyndham—Chorus p25-30,por.

Jordan, Elizabeth (b. 1867)
 Amer. journalist, editor, author
 Hammerton p831
 Logan—Part p835
 Ross—Ladies p9,176-179

Jordan, Mrs. Jesse (fl. 1940's)
 Eng. eccentric
 Hoehling—Women p145-146

Jordan, Jessie Knight (b. 1866)
 Amer. club leader, wife of David
  Starr Jordan
 Binheim—Women p57,por.

Jordan, Louise (1908-)
 Amer. paleontologist, geologist
 Goff—Women p161-167

Jordan, Marian Driscoll (1898-1961)
 ("Molly McGee")
 Amer. radio actress, comedienne
 Cahn—Laugh p162,por.

(Continued)

Jordan, Marion—*Continued*

    Cur. Biog. '41 p543-545,por.
    Cur. Biog. '61 p229
    Donaldson—Radio p13
    Settel—Radio p100,por.

Jordan, Mary (1879-1961)
    Welsh-Amer. singer
    McCoy—Portraits p94,por.

Jordan, Mildred (1901-)
    Amer. author
    Cur. Biog. '51 p316-317,por.
    Warfel—Amer. p233,por.

Jordan, Sara Murray (1884-1959)
    Amer. physician, gastroenterologist
    CR '59 p379-380,por.
    Cur. Biog. '54 p367-369,por.
    Cur. Biog. '60 p208
    Fleming—Doctors p100-115

Jorgensen, Christine (1926-)
    Amer. actress
    CR '59 p380,por.
    Lamparski—What p56-57,por.

Jorgensen, Evelyn (n.d.)
    Amer. aircraft instructor
    *Peckham—Women p138

Jorgensen-Krogh, Marie (gr. 1907)
    Dan. physician
    Lovejoy—Women p181-182

Joris, Agnese (Altissimi, pseud.)
    It. painter
    Waters—Women p178-179

Jorzick, Mary Louise (fl. 1930's)
    Amer. secretary
    Women—Achieve. p164,por.

Joseph, Dola. See De Jong, Dola

Joseph, Mary, Sister (b. 1883)
    Amer. nun, educator
    Cur. Biog. '42 p426-427,por.

Joseph, Nannine (fl. 1930's)
    Amer. business executive
    Women—Achieve. p139,por.

Joseph Calasanctius, Sister (1860-1946)
    Belg. missionary, nun
    Burton—Valiant p56-75

Josephine (Josephine de Beauharnais)
    (1763-1814)
    Fr. empress, wife of Napoleon
    Abbott—Notable p160-169,por.
    Adelman—Famous p102-103
    Armour—It p107-116
    Carnegie—Little p37-40,por.
    Dark—Royal p293-313,por.
    Davenport—Great p138-146

    De Morny—Best p34-42
    Dorland—Sum p16
    *Farmer—Book p140-152
    Fifty—Famous p22-32,por.
    Guerber—Empresses p1-144,por.
    Hammerton p831-832,por.
    Hubbard—Little p355-391,por.
    Jenkins—Heroines p221-268,por.
    *MacVeagh—Champlin p324,por.
    Parton—Dau. p372-373,por.
    Parton—Noted p435-439
    Schmidt—400 p180-181,por.

Josephine, Charlotte (1927-)
    Belg. princess
    Stiles—Postal p133

Josephine O. S. D. Meagher (b. 1841)
    Irish-Amer. nun
    Logan—Part p621

Joshee, Anandibai (1865-1887)
    Ind. pioneer physician
    Lovejoy—Women p223-224

Joteyko, Josephine (gr. 1896)
    Pol. physician, psychologist
    Lovejoy—Women p173,188

Jourdain, Eleanor Frances (1863-1929)
    Eng. educator
    Brittain—Women (see index)

Jourdaine, Clare Melicent (Joan Arden,
    pseud) (c. 1875-1925)
    Eng. author
    Wagenknecht—When p466-477

Jourjon, Yvonne (fl. 1930's)
    Fr. pioneer aviatrix, parachutist
    *Lauwick—Heroines p29,101,134-135,
    140

Jovane, Josefa Jacoba (1860-1929)
    Pan. humanitarian, philanthropist
    Schmidt—400 p313-314,por.

Joy, Charlotte Austin (fl. 1880's)
    Amer. social reformer
    Hanaford—Dau. p371-372

Joy, Helen N. (fl. 1920's-1930's)
    Amer. nurse
    Pennock—Makers p76,por.

Joy, Josephine (b. 1869)
    Amer. artist
    Janis—They p201-203,por.

Joy, Leatrice (fl. 1910's-1920's)
    Amer. actress
    Herman—How p81,por.
    Lamparski—What. p148-149,por.

Joy, Sally (fl. 1870's)
    Amer. journalist
    Ross—Ladies p1-2

Joyce, Alice (1890-1955)
    Amer. actress
    Wagenknecht—Movies p56

Joyce, Eileen (1912-   )
    Austral. pianist
    Brook—Masters p167-171,por.

Joyce, Eliza Le Brun Miller (b. 1840)
    Amer. religious worker
    Logan—Part p620

Joyce, Margaret (fl. 1500's)
    Irish bridge-builder
    Concannon—Dau. p88-89

Joyce, Peggy Hopkins (1893-1957)
    Amer. actress
    Jensen—Revolt p166,por.

Juch, Emma Antonia Joanna (1863-1939)
    Aust. singer
    Ewen—Ency. p231-232
    McCoy—Portraits p95,por.

Judah's wife (Biblical)
    Deen—All p324

Judith (Biblical)
    Culver—Women p46-47
    Deen—All p275
    Faulhaber—Women p93-98
    *Levinger—Great p62-66
    *MacVeagh—Champlin p326,por.
    Marble—Women, Bible p213-219
    Muir—Women p24-27

Judith (fl. 9th cent.)
    Eng.-Ger. saint
    *Windham—Sixty p214-220

Judith (Jutta) (d. 1260)
    Ger. saint
    Englebert—Lives p176

Judith, the Merry Heart (fl. 860's-880's
        A.D.)
    Fr., daughter of Charles the Bald
    *Cather—Girlhood p27-51

Judson, Ann Hasseltine (1789-1826)
    Amer. missionary, pioneer
    Culver—Women p155-156
    Deen—Great p171-178
    Dexter—Career p64-65,67
    Hanaford—Dau. p502
    Logan—Part p507-508
    *Matthews—Daunt. p4-29
    Miller—Ten p14-19
    Thomas—Crusaders p82-117

Judson, Clara Ingram (b. 1879)
    Amer. author
    Cur. Biog. '48 p331-332,por.

Judson, Emily Chubbuck (Fanny Forrester,
        pseud.) (1817-1854)
    Amer. author
    Deen—Great p392-394
    Hanaford—Dau. p219-221,266,505
    Papashvily—All p47-49
    Pattee—Fem. p282-283

Judson, Sarah Hall (1803-1845)
    Amer. missionary, hymn-writer,
        translator
    Deen—Great p390-391
    Hanaford—Dau. p503-505

Juggins, Elizabeth (fl. 1780's)
    Amer. W. pioneer
    Ellet—Pioneer p115

Julia (1) (Biblical)
    Deen—All p276

Julia (2) (fl. 6th or 7th cent.)
    Carthaginian saint
    Englebert—Lives p197
    *Windham—Sixty p143-150

Julia (3) (fl. c. 63 B.C.)
    Rom., mother of M. Antonius
    Balsdon—Roman p52-53

Julia (4) (fl. c. 13 B.C.)
    Rom. empress, daughter of
        Octavian
    McCabe—Empr. p23-30,por.

Julia (5) (39 B.C.-14 A.D.)
    Rom. empress, daughter of
        Augustus
    Balsdon—Roman (see index)
    Ewart—World's p44-48
    Ferrero—Women p73-85,99-107
    Serviez—Roman (1) p89-116

Julia (6) (c. 83-54 B.C.)
    Rom., daughter of Caesar
    Balsdon—Roman p47,178,195
    Boccaccio—Conc. p179-180

Julia (7) (d.c. 28 A.D.)
    Rom., granddaughter of Augustus
    Balsdon—Roman p75,80,88,95,196

Julia (8) (d. 68 B.C.)
    Rom., wife of C. Marius
    Balsdon—Roman p46

Julia Aquilia Severa.
    See Severa, Julia Aquilia

Julia, Augusta. See Livia Drusilla

Julia Berenice. See Berenice

Julia Billiart.
    See Billiart, Julie, Blessed

Julia Cornelia Paula (fl. 200-220's)
    Rom. empress, 2nd wife of
        Heliogabalus
    Serviez—Roman (2) p237-239

Julia Domna (c. 157-217)
    Rom. empress, wife of Severus
    Balsdon—Roman p150-155,160,257,por.
    McCabe—Emp. p194-209,por.
    Serviez—Roman (2) p146-208

Julia (Flavia) (fl. 82)
    Rom., daughter of Titus
    Balsdon—Roman p133,193,256,por.

Julia Livilla (fl. 39/40-47 A.D.)
    Rom., sister of Gaius Galigula
    Balsdon—Roman p103-117

Julia Maesa (fl. c. 217 A.D.)
    Rom. empress, patriot, head of
        army, mother of Julia Mamaea
    Balsdon—Roman p156-162,282
    Beard—Woman p297-298
    McCabe—Empr. p194-209,211-219,por.
    Serviez—Roman (2) p226-232,246-247,
        258

Julia Mamaea (d. 235 A.D.)
    Rom. empress, mother of Alexander
        Severus
    Balsdon—Roman p156,158,161-164
    Beard—Woman p298-299
    McCabe—Empr. p219-231,por.
    Serviez—Roman (2) p248-250,256-277

Julia of Rena (d. 1367)
    It. saint
    Englebert—Lives p482
    Wescott—Calen. p200

Julia Soemias (Soemis) (fl. 200's A.D.)
    Rom., daughter of Julia Maesa
    Balsdon—Roman p156-162,por.
    Beard—Woman p298

Juliana (d.c. 305)
    It. saint
    Englebert—Lives p66
    Stiles—Postal p236
    Wescott—Calen. p25-26

Juliana, Louise Emma Marie Wilhelmina
        (1909-   )
    Nether. queen
    Arsenius—Dict. p100,por.
    *Boyd—Rulers p201-205
    CR '59 p381,por.
    Cur. Biog. '44 p333-336,por.
    Cur. Biog. '55 p312-314,por.
    *Farmer—Book p201-218
    *O'Clery—Queens p175-184
    Phila.—Women, unp.,por.
    Schmidt—400 p131,por.
    Stiles—Postal p134
    Time Sept.6,1948 p23,por.(Cover)

Juliana Falconieri (1270-1340/41)
    It. saint
    Englebert—Lives p236
    Wescott—Calen. p89-90

Juliana of Norwich (1342-c. 1413)
    Eng. mystic, author
    Culver—Women p103
    Deen—Great p333-334

Julitta (d.c. 305)
    Palest. saint
    Blunt—Great p20-21
    Englebert—Lives p291-292

Jumel, Elizabeth (Eliza, Betty, Betsy)
        Bowen (1769/75-1865)
    Amer., wife of Aaron Burr
    Ross—Charmers p1-25,283-284,por.
    Terhune—Super. p89-114
    Whitton—These p89-92

June (June Howard Tripp) (1901-   )
    Eng. actress
    Hammerton p834

June, Jane (Jennie).
    See Croly, Jane Cunningham

"June, Miss" (fl. 1910's)
    Eng. parachutist
    *May—Women p52-53

Junia Calvina (fl. c. A.D. 48)
    Rom., wife of L. Vitellius
    Balsdon—Roman p114,129-130

Junia Silana (d. 59)
    Rom., wife of C. Silius
    Balsdon—Roman p114,120-121

Junot, Laure Permon, Duchess of Abrantès
        (1784-1838)
    Fr., wife of General Junot
    *MacVeagh—Champlin p328

Jurinac, Sena (1921-   )
    Yugoslav. singer
    Davidson—Treas. p149-151
    Ewen—Ency. p234
    Rosenthal—Sopranos p60-61,por.

Justa (1). See Syro-Pheonician woman

Justa (2) (d. 287)
    Sp. saint
    Wescott—Calen. p105-106

Justina of Padua (cl. 1st. cent.)
    It. saint
    Wescott—Calen. p157

Justis, Anne. See Morton, Anne Justis

Jutta. See Judith (saint)

K

Kablick, Josephine (b. 1787)
    Bohem. paleontologist
    Mozans—Woman p242-243

Kaerling, Henriette (b. 1832)
    Hung. painter
    Waters—Women p179

Kagan, Helen (fl. 1910's-1950's)
    Israeli physician
    Lovejoy—Women p217-218

Kaghan, Leonora (fl. 1930's)
    Amer. playwright
    Mantle—Contemp. p209

Kahane, Melanie (1910-   )
    Amer. interior decorator, industrial
        engineer
    CR '63 p325,por.
    Cur. Biog. '59 p218-220,por.

Kahlenberg, Hans von, pseud. (Helene von
        Montbart) (fl. 19th cent.)
    Ger. author
    Heller—Studies p284-285

Kahlo, Frida (1910-   )
    Mex. painter
    Stewart—45 p120-121,por.

Kahmann (Mable) Chesley (1901-   )
    Amer. author
    Cur. Biog. '52 p293-294,por.
    Women—Achieve. p133,por.

Kahn, Florence Prag (1868-1948)
    Amer. Congresswoman
    Paxton—Women p3-4,129

Kahn, Grace LeBoy (1891-   )
    Amer. composer
    ASCAP p263

Kahn, Ida (fl. 1890's-1900's)
    Chin. physician
    Burton—Notable p115-158,por.

Kahn, Ruth Ward (b. 1870)
    Amer. author
    Logan—Part p820

Kainen, Greta (fl. 1940's)
    Ger. nurse, spy
    Singer—World p31-41

Kaiser, Lucy L. Campbell (fl. 1860's)
    Amer. Civil war nurse
    Logan—Part p366
    Young—Women p168-170

Kalapothakis, Minnie (gr. 1894)
    Gr. physician
    Lovejoy—Women p212,por.

Kalckreuth, Maria, Countess (1857-1897)
    Ger. painter
    Waters—Women p179

Kaldikhina, Fatiana (fl. 1910's)
    Russ. war heroine
    Dorland—Sum p99

Kaleleonalani, Emma (1835-c. 1875)
    Haw. Isl. queen
    Stiles—Postal p135

Kalep, Elvy (n.d.)
    Est. pioneer aviatrix, business
        executive
    *Peckham—Women p86

Kalich, Mrs. Jacob. See **Picon, Molly**

Kallio, Elin Waenerberg (1859-1927)
    Fin. pioneer gymnast
    Schmidt—400 p169,por.

"Kalogréza."
    See **Benizelos, Philothéy**

Kamanalu, Victoria (d.c. 1824)
    Haw. Isl. queen, wife of King
        Kamehameha II
    Arsenius—Dict. p101,por.
    Phila.—Women unp.,por.
    Stiles—Postal p135

Kamanalu, Victoria (1839-1866)
    Haw. Isl. princess, prime minister,
        sister of Kamehameha IV, V
    Stiles—Postal p135

Kander, Lizzie Black (1858-1940)
    Amer. author, social worker
    Cur. Biog. '40 p448,por.

Kanizsai, Dorothy (fl. 15th cent.)
    Hung. patriot, philanthropist,
        humanitarian
    Phila.—Women unp.,por.
    Schmidt—400 p227-228,por.
    Stiles—Postal p135

Kapiolani (1834-1899)
    Haw. Isl. queen
    Arsenius—Dict. p102,por.
    Phila.—Women unp.,por.
    Stiles p136

Kappel, Gertrude (1895-   )
    Ger. singer
    Ewen—Ency. p236
    Ewen—Living p185-186,por.
    McCoy—Portraits p96,por.

Karll, Agnes, Sister (1872-1927)
    Ger. nurse
    Dolan—Goodnow's p300,por.
    Schmidt—400 p408-409,por.

Karnes, Matilda Theresa (fl. 1900's)
    Amer. teacher, club leader
    Logan—Part p723

Karpeles, Kate B. (fl. 1930's)
    Amer. physician
    Mead—Medical p67

Karsavina, Tamara (b. 1885)
    Russ. dancer
    Clarke—Six p95-126,por.
    Davidson—Ballet p160-168,por.
    Hammerton p839,por.
    Haskell—Vignet. p13-15
    Love—Famous p34
    *McConnell—Famous p14-26,por.
    *Terry—Star p123-125,por.

Kartini, Raden Adjeng (1879-1904)
    Jav. teacher
    Schmidt—400 p305-306,por.

Kaschowska, Felicie (fl. 1890's-1900's)
    Pol. singer
    Lahee—Grand p278-279

Kaskas, Anna (1910-   )
    Amer. singer
    Ewen—Living p186-187,por.
    McCoy—Portraits p96,por.
    Peltz—Spot. p100,por.

Kasper, Catharine (fl. 1810's)
    Ger. nurse, nun, foundress
    Pennock—Makers p23

Kasturbai (Kasturba).
    See Gandhi, Kasturbai Nakanji

Kate, Elinor (fl. 1910's)
    Amer. actress
    Caffin—Vaud. p213,por.

Kate, Maxwell. See Watson, Ella

Katherine (fl. A.D. 1378)
    Swed. saint
    *Windham—Sixty p298-304

Katherine.
    See also Catherine

Katheryn Howard. See Catherine of Aragon

Kauffman, (Maria) Angelica (1741-1807)
    Swiss painter
    Adelman—Famous p88-89
    *Borer—Women p36-53,por.
    De Morny—Best p195-204,por.
    Dorland—Sum p38,75-76,155
    Hammerton p839,por.

*Kirkland—Artists p79-85
*MacVeagh—Champlin p329
Parton—Dau. p143-148
Parton—Noted p143-148
Schmidt—400 p380-382,por.
Waters—Women p179-190,por.

Kauffman, Mildred (fl. 1930's)
    Amer. aviatrix
    Planck—Women p117

Kaufman, Beatrice Bakrow (fl. 1920's-1930's)
    Amer. journalist, editor, playwright
    Mantle—Contemp. p201-202
    New Yorker July 7,1928 p16-17,por.
    (Profiles)

Kaula, Lee Lufkin (fl. 1900's)
    Amer. painter
    Waters—Women p190

Kaup, Elizabeth Bartol Dewing (b. 1885)
    Amer. author
    Warfel—Amer. p240-241,por.

Kaur, (Raj)kumari Amrit (b. 1889)
    Ind. government official, social
        worker
    Cur. Biog. '55 p319-321,por.
    Lovejoy—Women p226,230,379-380
    Stern—Women p221-232,por.

Kavanagh, Eibhlin (   )
    Irish "woman of the castle"
    Concannon—Dau. p77-78

Kavanagh, Frances Leathley (fl. 1850's-
        1860's)
    Eng. hostess
    Iremonger—And p230-236,por.

Kavanagh, Julia (1824-1877)
    Irish novelist
    Dorland—Sum p56,193
    Oliphant—Women p251-262

Kay, Beatrice (n.d.)
    Amer. singer, comedienne
    Cur. Biog. '42 p440-441,por.

Kay, Katherine (Katherine Cameron)
        (fl. 1900's)
    Scot. painter, illustrator
    Waters—Women p70-71

Kaye, Nora (1920-   )
    Amer. ballet dancer
    Atkinson—Dancers p80-83,por.
    CR '59 p386-387,por.
    CR '63 p328,por.
    Cur. Biog. '53 p308-310,por.
    Davidson—Ballet p169-171
    Haskell—Vignet. p66-74,por.
    Swinson—Dancers p67-70,por.
    Swinson—Great p14,por.
    *Terry—Star p166-176,por.

Kaye-Smith, Sheila (1887-1956)
    Eng. novelist
    Hammerton p840,por.
    Johnson—Some Contemp. p81-93
    Lawrence—School p236-240
    Millett—Brit. p303-304
    Stern—And p74-92

Kayne, Hilde (1903-   )
    Aust.-Amer. artist
    Ency. Brit.-Amer. p66,por.

Kayser, Ebba (b. 1846)
    Swed. painter
    Waters—Women p190

Kayshus, Effie (fl. 1930's)
    Amer. business woman
    New Yorker Jan.16,1937 p20-25,por.
    (Profiles)

Kchessinska, Mathilde (b. 1872)
    Russ. ballet dancer
    *Muir—Famous p31-39,por.
    *Terry—Star p107-111,por.

Kean, Ellen Tree (1805-1880)
    Eng. actress
    Adelman—Famous p160
    Coad—Amer. p99,175,por.

Keane, Doris (1885-1945)
    Amer. actress
    Blum—Great p67,por.
    Cur. Biog. '46 p300
    Hammerton p840,por.

Kearney, Martha Eleanor (1842-1930)
    Amer. religious worker, author
    Phillips—33 p53-57

Kearns, Nora Lynch (1902-   )
    Amer. organization official
    Cur. Biog. '56 p326-327,por.

Keary, Annie (1825-1879)
    Eng. novelist
    Dorland—Sum p42,193

Keating, Isabelle (fl. 1930's)
    Amer. journalist
    Ross—Ladies p236-237

Keating, Micheline (fl. 1920's-1930's)
    Amer. journalist
    Ross—Ladies p304-305

Keator, Harriet Scudder (d. 1932)
    Brit. singer
    McCoy—Portraits p97,por.

Keck, Lucile Liebermann (1898-   )
    Amer. organization official,
        librarian
    Cur. Biog. '54 p369-370,por.

Keckley, Elizabeth Hobbs (1840-1900)
    Amer. dressmaker, author
    Brown—Home. p147,por.
    Leetch—Reveille p287,310

Kee, Elizabeth Frazier (1899-   )
    Amer. Congresswoman, politician
    Cur. Biog. '54 p370-371,por.
    U.S.—Women (87th) p25,por.
    U.S.—Women (88th) p15,por.

Keeler, Ruby (1909-   )
    Can.-Amer. dancer
    Lamparski—What. p76-77,por.
    Schickel—Stars p118,por.

Keeley, Mary Anne (1806-1899)
    Eng. actress
    Adelman—Famous p163-164
    Furniss—Some p137-139,por.
    Wyndham—Chorus p60-61

Keen, Dora (b. 1871)
    Amer. traveler, author
    Adelman—Famous p312

Keene, Laura (1820/26-1873)
    Eng.-Amer. actress, manager
    Adelman—Famous p186-187
    Bodeen—Ladies p67-70
    Coad—Amer. p203-204,por.
    Dorland—Sum p42,168

Keene, Mona (fl. 1930's)
    Amer. airline hostess
    Planck—Women p191

Keeney, Ana (1898-   )
    Amer. sculptor
    National—Contemp. p176

Keep, Mabel Hazlett (fl. 1930's)
    Amer. philanthropist, editor
    Women—Achieve. p139,por.

Keim, Jane Sumner Owen (gr. 1862)
    Amer. social reformer,
        humanitarian
    Logan—Part p433-434

Keister, Lillie Resler (b. 1851)
    Amer. missionary
    Logan—Part p521

Keith, Dora Wheeler (1857-1940)
    Amer. artist
    Cur. Biog. '41 p461

Keith, Mrs. Franklin (fl. 1770's-1780's)
    Amer. theater operator
    Cahn—Laugh. p41,58

Keith, Marion (b. 1876)
    Can. novelist
    Thomas—Canad. p69-70

Keith, Mary Isham (b. 1737)
    Amer. Rev. war patriot
    Green—Pioneer (3) p473

Keldysh, Lyudmila Vseyolodovna (1904-   )
    Russ. mathematician
    U.S.—Biog. Soviet p290

Kellas, Eliza (1864-1943)
    Amer. educator
    Cur. Biog. '43 p370

Kellems, Vivien (1896-   )
    Amer. industrialist, engineer
    Cur. Biog. '48 p340-342,por.
    Goff—Women p215-227
    Logie—Careers (2nd) p117-124

Keller, Elizabeth C. (b. 1873)
    Amer. physician
    Hanaford—Dau. p572-573

Keller, Helen Adams (1880-1968)
    Amer. blind, deaf, author, lecturer,
        educator
    Adelman—Famous p320
    America's 12 p31-33por.
    Ames—These p349-366
    Bartlett—They p76-80
    *Bolton—Lives p195-207,por.
    Bowie—Women p160-175
    Canning—100 p434-439
    *Carmer—Young p239-246
    Carnegie—Five p73-76
    CR '59 p389,por.
    CR '63 p330,por.
    Cur. Biog. '42 p441-444,por.
    Cur. Biog. '68 p457
    *Dolin—World p181-191,por.
    Douglas—Remember p237-238,por.
    Dunaway—Turn. p105-108
    *Eby—Marked p67-72
    Fellowes—Heroes p107-117
    Fitzhugh—Concise p371-372
    Galloway—Roads p15-37,por.
    Hammerton p843,por.
    *Heath—Woman (4) p26,por.
    Holbrook—Dreamers p274-276
    *Horowitz—Treas. p92-99
    *Kirkland—Achieved p36-44
    Ladies'—Amer. p31-33,por.
    Logan—Part p699-700
    Lotz—Women p48-56
    *MacVeagh—Champlin p330
    *Moderow—People p99-109,por.
    *Moore—When p118-124
    Muir—Women p215-216
    Murrow—This (1) p89-90
    New Yorker Jan. 25,1930 p24-26
      (Profiles)
    Padover—Confess. p312-314
    Parshalle—Kash. p3-10,por.
    *Pringle—When p193-208,por.
    Reader's—Great p34-42,por.
    *Stevens—Human. p29-30,por.
    Stone—We p218-223
    *Strong—Of p276-283

Thomas—50 p414-420
Thomas—Living Women p289-298,por.
Webb—Famous p277-286,por.

Keller, Manelva Wylie (fl. 1900's)
    Amer. nurse
    Pennock—Makers p120,por.

Kellerman, Annette (b.c. 1888)
    Austral. swimmer, actress
    Caffin—Vaud. p183-184,por.
    Rogers—Women p130,por.

Kelley, Abigail.
    See Foster, Abigail Kelley

Kelley, Catherine Bishop (1853-1944)
    Amer. teacher, religious worker
    Phillips—33 p79-84

Kellet, Charlotte (n.d.)
    Amer. teacher, aviatrix, airline
        hostess
    *May—Women p178-180,210,232,por.

Kelley, Mrs. Edgar Stillman (fl. 1910's-
        1930's)
    Amer. pianist, music teacher
    McCoy—Portraits p97,por.

Kelley, Florence (1859-1932)
    Amer. social worker
    Douglas—Remember p201-205

Kelley, Gertrude (Gertrude B. Gordon,
        pseud.) (c. 1882-1955)
    Amer. journalist
    Ross—Ladies p560-561

Kelley, Marion Booth (fl. 1930's)
    Amer. lecturer
    Women—Achieve. p187,por.

Kello, Esther English (Hester Inglis) (1571-
        1624)
    Fr.-Eng. calligrapher, artist
    Waters—Women p172

Kellogg, Clara Louise (1842-1916)
    Amer. singer
    Adelman—Famous p250
    Beard—Amer. p268-274
    Coad—Amer. p232,por.
    Ewen—Ency. p237-238
    Lahee—Famous p147-150
    Logan—Part p767
    McCoy—Portraits p97,por.
    Marks—Glamour p209-217,por.
    Wagner—Prima p99, 205,243
    Whitton—These p197-199

Kellogg, Elenore (d. 1935)
    Amer. journalist
    Ross—Ladies p7,24,165-169,por.

Kellogg, Paulina.
    See Davis, Paulina Kellogg Wright

Kellor, Frances Alice (1873-1952)
    Amer. economist, social worker
    Bennett—Amer. p161-179,por.

Kelly, Amie (fl. 1860's)
    Amer. Civil war diarist
    Jones—Heroines p153-155

Kelly, Edna Flannery (1906-   )
    Amer. Congresswoman
    Cur. Biog. '50 p289-291,por.
    U.S.—Women (87th) p27,por.
    U.S.—Women (88th) p17,por.

Kelly, Eleanor Mercein (b. 1880)
    Amer. author
    Overton—Women p205

Kelly, Elizabeth (1910's-1920's)
    Amer. journalist
    Ross—Ladies p566-569

Kelly, Ella Maynard (b. 1857)
    Amer. railroad operator, telegrapher
    Logan—Part p900

Kelly, Fanny (fl. 19th cent.)
    Eng. pioneer theatre builder,
        manager
    MacQueen—Pope p301,por.

Kelly, Fanny Wiggins (c. 1845-1904)
    Amer. pioneer, Ind. captive
    *Johnson—Some p8-21,por.
    Peckham—Capt. p215-234

Kelly, Florence Finch (1858-1939)
    Amer. journalist, author
    Cur. Biog. '40 p450

"Kelly, Glenn."
    See McNeilly, Mildred Masterson

Kelly, Grace Patricia (1929-   )
    Mon. princess, Amer. actress
    CR '59 p390-391,por.
    CR '63 p331,por.
    Cur. Biog. '55 p324-325,por.
    Martin—Pete p252-276,por.,jacket
    Schickel—Stars p260,por.
    Stiles—Postal p137
    Time Jan.31,1955 p46,por.(Cover)

Kelly, Joanna Beadon (fl. 1950's)
    Eng. prison governor
    Winn—Queen's p114-115,118-125,por.

Kelly, Judith (1908-1957)
    Can. author
    Cur. Biog. '41 p461-463,por.
    Cur. Biog. '57 p294
    Warfel—Amer. p242-243,por.

Kelly, Margaret V. (fl. 1900's)
    Amer. government employee
    Logan—Part p901

Kelly, Myra (1875-1910)
    Amer. author, social reformer,
        educator
    Dorland—Sum p16,120,173
    Maurice—Makers p11,por.

Kelly, Nancy (1921-   )
    Amer. actress
    CR '59 p391,por.
    CR '63 p331,por.
    Cur. Biog. '55 p325-327,por.

Kelly, Patsy (fl. 1930's-1940's)
    Amer. actress, comedienne
    Lamparski—What. p104-105,por.

Kelly, Patsy (fl. 1930's)
    Amer. aircraft librarian
    Planck—Women p216

Kelly, Regina Zimmerman (1898-   )
    Amer. author, educator
    Cur. Biog. '56 p331-332,por.

Kelner, Sophie (fl. 1930's)
    Aust.-Amer. dentist
    Women—Achieve. p142,por.

Kelsey, Frances (1914-   )
    Amer. physician, government
        employee
    CR '63 p332,por.
    Cur. Biog. '65 p218-220,por.
    Dolan—Goodnow's p291-292
    Parshalle—Kash. p27-28,por.

Kemble, Adelaide (1814-1879)
    Eng. singer, author
    Adelman—Famous p160-161
    Hammerton p844,por.

Kemble, Elizabeth (Eliza Kemble Whitlock)
    (1761/62-1836)
    Amer. actress
    Coad—Amer. p38,por.

Kemble, Fanny (Fanny Butler) (fl. 1880's)
    Eng. physician
    Lovejoy—Women p222

Kemble, Frances Anne ("Fanny") (1809-
    1893)
    Eng. actress, author
    Adelman—Famous p161-162
    Bottrall—Pers. p139-141,226
    Coad—Amer. p103,por.
    Dorland—Sum p43,81,166
    Douglas—Remember p64-65,124
    Hammerton p844,por.
    *MacVeagh—Champlin p330-331
    Prochnow—Great p70-81
    Whitton—These p165-166,182

Kemble, Sarah.
  See Knight, Sarah Kemble

Kemp, Barbara (1883-1959)
  Ger. singer
  McCoy—Portraits p97,por.

Kempe, Margery (1373-c. 1438)
  Eng. religious worker, evangelist,
    author
  Bennett—Six p124-150
  Bottrall—Pers. p184-187,226
  Deen—Great p334-336
  Stenton—English p120-121

Kemper, Ruth (fl. 1920's)
  Amer. violinist
  McCoy—Portraits p97,por.

Kempin, Emile (fl. 1880's-1890's)
  Swiss-Amer. lawyer, teacher
  Farmer—What p400-401

Kempner, Mary Jean (n.d.)
  Amer. nurse
  *Wright—Great p275-285

Kempthorne, Edith M. (fl. 1910's-1930's)
  New Z. organization official
  Women—Achieve. p148,por.

Kemp-Welch, Lucy Elizabeth (1869-1958)
  Eng. painter
  Furniss—Some p78-79,por.
  Hammerton p845,por.
  Waters—Women p191

Kendal, Duchess of.
  See Schulenburg, Ehrengarde Melusina
    von der, (Duchess of Kendal)

Kendal, Margaret Robertson, Dame (c. 1849-
    1917)
  Eng. actress
  Coad—Amer. p293,por.
  Hammerton p845,por.
  MacQueen—Pope p349-350,por.
  Marks—Glamour p309

Kendall, Margaret Stickney (b. 1871)
  Amer. painter
  Michigan—Biog. p175

Kendell, Marie von (b. 1838)
  Ger. painter
  Waters—Women p191-192

Kenealy, Arabella (fl. 1890's-1900's)
  Eng. author, physician
  Hammerton p845

Kennard, Mrs. Edward (fl. 1890's)
  Brit. author
  Black—Notable p172-183,por.

Kennedy, Anne.
  See Hamilton, Anne Kennedy

Kennedy, Ethel Skakel (n.d.)
  Amer., wife of Robert Kennedy
  CR '63 p333,por.

Kennedy, Jacqueline Lee Bouvier (1929-   )
  Amer., wife of John F. Kennedy,
    later Mrs. Onassis
  CR '63 p333,por.
  Cur. Biog. '61 p237-239,por.
  Logan—Ladies p194
  *McConnell—Our p335-347,por.
  Means—Woman p264-299,por.,cover
  *Ross—Know p71,por.
  Time July 11,1960 p19,por.(Cover)
  Time Jan.20,1961 p18,por.(Cover)

Kennedy, Kitty (c. 1751-1781)
  Eng. courtesan
  Bleackley—Ladies p147-188,304-305,
    por.

Kennedy, Margaret (1896-   )
  Eng. novelist, playwright
  Brittain—Women p144,251
  Hammerton p846,por.
  Lawrence—School p296-298
  Millett—Brit. p304-305

Kennedy, Mary (fl. 1920's-1930's)
  Amer. playwright, wife of Deems
    Taylor
  Mantle—Amer. p290-291
  Mantle—Contemp. p314-315

Kennedy, Rose Fitzgerald (1890-   )
  Amer., mother of John F. Kennedy
    Robert Kennedy
  CR '63 p335,por.
  Time July 11, 1960 p19,por.(Cover)

Kennedy-Fraser, Marjorie (1857-1930)
  Brit. singer
  Gammond—Dict. p120,por.

Kennelly, Ardyth (1912-   )
  Amer. author
  Cur. Biog. '53 p310-311,por.

Kenny, Elizabeth (1886-1952)
  Austral. nurse
  *Bolton—Lives p209-221,por.
  Cur. Biog. '42 p444-446,por.
  Cur. Biog. '53 p311
  *McKown—Heroic p189-211,por.
  Thomas—Modern p430-438
  Wright—Great p90-99

Kent, Elizabeth, Countess of (fl. 1630's)
  Eng. hostess
  Stenton—English p60-61

Kent, Louise Andrews ("Therea Tempest")
    (b. 1886)
        Amer. author
    Warfel—Amer. p243-244,por.

Kent, Marina, Duchess of (1906-   )
        Eng. princess
    CR '59 p394,por.

Kent, Rachel Fitch (1898-   )
        Amer. educator
    Binheim—Women p140,por.

Kent, Sibbil Dwight (1744-1822)
        Amer., wife of Elihu Kent
    Root—Chapter p298-302

Kentigerna (fl. 8th cent.)
        Irish saint
    Blunt—Great p159

Kenton, Elizabeth Jarboe (d. 1842)
        Amer. W. pioneer
    Ellet—Pioneer p428-434
    Green—Pioneer (3) p492-493
    Logan—Part p82-84

Kenyon, Bernice (1897-   )
        Amer. poet
    Smith—Women's p120

Kenyon, Cecil ("Teddy") MacGlashan
    (fl. 1930's-1940's)
        Amer. pioneer aviatrix, test pilot,
        helicopter pilot
    °Knapp—New p1-18,por.
    °May—Women p166-168,208-209,por.

Kenyon, Dorothy (b. 1888)
        Amer. lawyer, judge, U.N. official
    Cur. Biog. '47 p348-350,por.
    Taves—Success. p212-225,por.
    Women—Achieve. p43,por.

Kenyon, Helen (b. 1884)
        Amer. relig. worker
    Cur. Biog. '48 p342-343,por.

Kenyon, "Teddy."
    See Kenyon, Cecil MacGlashan

Kenyon, Theda (fl. 1930's)
        Amer. novelist
    Warfel—Amer. p244,por.
    Women—Achieve. p144,por.

Kepeas, Dorothy (d.c. 1534)
        Eng. hostess
    Stenton—English p88-89

Kepley, Ada H. (gr. 1870)
        Amer. pioneer lawyer
    Farmer—What p394-395

"Kera." See Benizélos, Philothéy

Keren-Happuch (Biblical)
    Deen—All p276

Kerfoot, Annie Warfield (b. 1829)
        Amer. club leader
    Logan—Part p467-468

Kernahan, Mrs. Coulson (1858-1943)
        Eng. author
    Furniss—Some p32-34

Kéroualle, Louise Renée de, Duchess of
        Portsmouth and Cubigny (1649-
        1734)
        Fr., mistress of Charles II
    Haggard—Remark. p116-117
    Hammerton p848, 1110,por.
    MacQueen—Pope p123-124

Kerr, Adelaide (fl. 1930's)
        Amer. journalist
    Ross—Ladies p375-376,436

Kerr, Deborah (1921-   )
        Scot.-Amer. actress
    CR '59 p395-396,por.
    CR '63 p337,por.
    Cur. Biog. '47 p350-352,por.
    Schickel—Stars p260,por.
    Time Feb.10,1947 p95,por.(Cover)

Kerr, Jean Collins (1923/1924-   )
        Amer. playwright, humorist
    CR '59 p396,por.
    CR '63 p337,por.
    Cur. Biog. '58 p222-224,por.
    Time Apr. 14,1961 p82,por.(Cover)

Kerr, Joyce (m. 1924)
        Eng. actress
    Wyndham—Chorus p138

Kerr, Muriel (1911-   )
        Can. pianist
    Ewen—Living p188-189,por.
    McCoy—Portraits p98,por.

Kerr, Sophie (1880-1965)
        Amer. author
    Maurice—Makers p9,por.
    Overton—Women p202
    Warfel—Amer. p245-246,por.

Kessel, Mary Hickman (fl. 1950's-1960's)
        teacher, social worker
    °Gelfand—They p50-52

Keturah (Biblical)
    Deen—All p276-277
    Lewis—Portraits p57-58

Key, Ellen Karoline Sofia (1849-1926)
　　　Swed. feminist, author
　　Adelman—Famous p282-283
　　*MacVeagh—Champlin p331
　　Schmidt—400 p374-376,por.

Keyes, Frances Parkinson Wheeler
　　　　(1885-　　)
　　　Amer. novelist
　　Breit—Writer p151-153
　　CR '59 p397,por.
　　CR '63 p338,por.
　　Fitzgibbon—My p99-105
　　O'Brien—Road p56-72
　　Warfel—Amer. p246-247,por.

Keyes, Regina Flood (b. 1870)
　　　Amer. physician
　　Lovejoy—Women p314-315
　　Lovejoy—Women Phys. p69-70

Keyser, Agnes (b. 1853)
　　　Eng. philanthropist
　　Hammerton p1450

Kezia (Biblical)
　　Deen—All p277

Khadija (556-619)
　　　Arab., wife of Mahomet
　　　　(Mohammed)
　　Cockran—Romance p84
　　De Morny—Best p219-224
　　Hammerton p849
　　Muir—Women p68-69

Khan, Begum Liaquat Ali (n.d.)
　　　Fr. beauty, wife of Aga Khan,
　　　　Pak. club leader
　　CR '59 p399,por.
　　Cur. Biog. '50 p301-303,por.

Khan, Noor Inayat (1914-　　)
　　　Ind. spy
　　Hoehling—Women p123-130

Khrushchev, Nina Petrovna (b.c. 1900)
　　　Russ., wife of N. Khrushchev
　　Phelps—Men (2) '59 p154-155

Khuwyt (fl.c. 1950 B.C.)
　　　Egypt. singer, harpist
　　Schmidt—400 p122,por.

Kidd, Edna Gardner fl. 1930's)
　　　Amer. aviatrix
　　Planck—Women p187-188,por.

Kidd, Lucy Ann (b. 1839)
　　　Amer. educator
　　Logan—Part p731

Kidder, Kathryn (c. 1868-1939)
　　　Amer. actress
　　Caffin—Vaud. p124-126
　　Marks—Glamour p310
　　Strang—Actresses p299-305

Kielland, Kitty (1843-1914)
　　　Nor. painter
　　Schmidt—400 p309,por.
　　Waters—Women p192

Kielmansegg, Baroness von, Countess of
　　　　Darlington (fl. 1680's-1720's)
　　　Ger. courtesan
　　Trowbridge—Seven p71-72,por.

Kiernan, Barbara (fl. 1950's)
　　　Amer. helicopter test pilot
　　*May—Women p208, por.

Kies, Mary (fl. 1800's)
　　　Amer. pioneer inventor
　　Dexter—Career p172-173
　　Mozans—Woman p344-346

Kildare, Brigid of (453-523)
　　　Irish nun, nurse
　　*McKown—Heroic p16

Kilgallen, Dorothy (1913-1965)
　　　Amer. journalist, TV personality
　　Blum—Television p259,por.
　　CR '59 p401,por.
　　CR '63 p340,por.
　　Cur. Biog. '52 p303-305,por.
　　Cur. Biog. '66 p467
　　Ross—Ladies p240-245,por.,cover
　　Settel—Radio p168,por.
　　TV—Person (1) p47-48,por.
　　Women—Achieve. p88,por.

Kilgore, Carrie Burnham (1836-1908)
　　　Amer. pioneer lawyer
　　Adelman—Famous p213
　　Farmer—What p397-398
　　Irwin—Angels p176

Kilgore, Evelyn (fl. 1930's)
　　　Amer. aviatrix, head training school
　　*May—Women p162
　　Planck—Women p161-162,por.

Killegrew, Anne (1660-1685)
　　　Eng. painter, poet, maid of honor
　　Waters—Women p192-193

Kilmer, Aline (1888-1941)
　　　Amer. poet, lecturer, wife of
　　　　Joyce Kilmer
　　Cook—Our p302-304
　　Cur. Biog. '41 p469
　　Smith—Women's p123

Kilroy, Alix, Dame (gr. 1925)
    Eng., member Board of Trade
    Brittain—Women p177,252

Kimball, Corinne (b. 1873)
    Amer. actress
    Logan—Part p780

Kimball, Grace (b. 1887)
    Amer. actress
    Logan—Part p780

Kimball, Grace N. (fl. 1920's)
    Amer. physician
    Lovejoy—Women p97-98,333,360

Kimball, Jennie (b. 1851)
    Amer. actress
    Logan—Part p780-781

Kimball, Josephine (fl. 1930's)
    Amer. bookseller, business
        executive
    Women—Achieve. p166,por.

Kimball, Kate Fisher (b. 1860)
    Amer. editor
    Logan—Part p855

Kimball, Martha Gertrude (1840-1894)
    Amer. philanthropist, nurse
    Adelman p185-186

Kimber, Diana Clifford (d. 1928)
    Can. nurse, author
    Dolan—Goodnow's p260-261,por.
    Pennock—Makers p109,por.

Kimbrough, Emily (1899-   )
    Amer. author, editor
    CR '59 p402,por.
    CR '63 p341,por.
    Cur. Biog. '44 p340-342,por.

Kinder, Katharine Louise (1912-   )
    Amer. librarian, organization official
    Cur. Biog. '57 p298-299,por.

Kindt, Adele (b. 1805)
    Belg. artist
    Waters—Women p193-194

King, Anna Page (1798-1859)
    Amer. pioneer gardener
    Hollingsworth—Her p71-85

King, Billie Jean (1943-   )
    Amer. tennis player
    Cur. Biog. '67 p225-227,por.
    Cur. Biog. '68 p46,por.

King, Carol Weiss (fl. 1930's)
    Amer. lawyer
    Women—Achieve. p199

King, E. M. (fl. 1860's)
    Amer. Civil war nurse
    Brockett—Woman's p789

King, Fay (fl. 1910's)
    Amer. journalist
    Ross—Ladies p420-424

King, Frances (1863-1948)
    Amer. author, landscape gardener
    Hollingsworth—Her p143-154

King, Frances Rockefeller (fl. 1930's)
    Amer. press agent, radio agent
    Women—Achieve. p41,por.

King, Grace Elizabeth (b. 1852)
    Amer. author
    Bruère—Laugh. p31-32
    Logan—Part p380,817

King, Hetty (fl. 1920's-1930's)
    dancer
    Felstead—Stars p41-42,100-101

King, Jessie M. (fl. 1900's)
    Scot. illustrator, book-cover
        designer
    Waters—Women p194-195

King, Julie Rive (b. 1857)
    Amer. musician, teacher
    Logan—Part p764

King, Loretta. See Cameron, Kate

King, Marion P. (1894-   )
    Amer. sculptor
    National—Contemp. p183

King, Mary (fl. 1920's-1930's)
    Amer. journalist
    Ross—Ladies p413-414,427-428,542

King, Mary Alsop (fl. 1770's)
    Amer. social leader
    Hanaford—Dau. p141

King, Muriel (n.d.)
    Amer. fashion designer
    Cur. Biog. '43 p379-380,por.

King, Peggy (1931-   )
    Amer. singer
    TV—Person (2) p12-13

King, Susan (fl. 1880's)
    Amer. business woman
    Hanaford—Dau. p611

King, Violet (fl. 1940's)
    Can. author
    Thomas—Canad. p74

Kinga (saint). See Cunegund(es)

Kingsbury, Elizabeth A. (fl. 1880's)
   Amer. lecturer, poet
   Hanaford—Dau. p343

Kingsbury, Emeline D. (fl. 1860's)
   Amer., Civil war nurse
   Logan—Part p367

Kingsley, Mary Henrietta (1862-1900)
   Eng. explorer, ethnologist. nurse,
   author
   Adelman—Famous p228-229
   *Borer—Women p132-150,por.
   Dorland—Sum p44,114
   Holmes—Seven p136-154
   Mozans—Woman p256-258

Kingsley, Mary St. Leger.
   See Harrison, Mary St. Leger

Kingsley, Myra (1897-   )
   Amer. astrologer
   Cur. Biog. '43 p380-382,por.
   Women—Achieve. p123,por.

Kingston, Gertrude (fl. 1900's)
   Eng. actress, author
   Hammerton p852

Kinkead, Elizabeth Shelby (fl. 1900's)
   Amer. lecturer, author
   Logan—Part p786

Kinne, Elizabeth D'Arcy (fl. 1860's-1900's)
   Amer. club leader
   Logan—Part p348

Kinnear, Helen Alice (1894-   )
   Can. judge
   Cur. Biog. '57 p301-302,por.

Kinney, Belle (n.d.)
   Amer. sculptor
   Taft—Women, Mentor (172) #2

Kinney, Dita H. (fl. 1900's)
   Amer. army nurse
   Dolan—Goodnow's p305

Kinney, Margaret West (1872-1952)
   Amer. illustrator
   Michigan—Biog. p177

Kinscella, Hazel Gertrude (fl. 1940's)
   Amer. musician, composer,
   educator
   ASCAP p276-277
   McCoy—Portraits p99,por.

Kinsky, Countess.
   See Suttner, Bertha, Baroness von

Kintore, Helena Zimmerman Keith-Falconer,
   Countess of.
   See Zimmerman, Helena, Duchess of
   Manchester

Kipling, Caroline Starr Balestier (1865-
   1939)
   Eng., wife of Rudyard Kipling
   Cur. Biog. '40 p459
   Pearson—Marry. p264-287,por.
   Pearson—Pilgrim p285-301

Kipnis, Hanna (1910-   )
   Israeli singer
   Saleski—Jewish p707,por.

Kirby, Mrs. William (fl. 1860's)
   Amer. Civil war heroine
   Andrews—Women p116-119
   Simkins—Women p135-136

Kirch, Maria (1670-1720)
   Ger. astronomer
   Mozans—Woman p173-174

Kirchsberg, Ernestine von (b. 1867)
   It. painter
   Waters—Women p195

Kirchwey, Freda (1893-   )
   Amer. editor, publisher
   Cur. Biog. '42 p460-462,por.
   Women—Achieve. p180,por.

Kirk, Ellen Warner Olney (b. 1842)
   Amer. author
   Farmer—What p185-186,194,por.
   Logan—Part p827

Kirk, Henrietta (fl. 1920's)
   Amer. swimmer, heroine
   *Deakin—True p66-76

Kirk, Lisa (1925-   )
   Amer. singer
   CR '59 p405,por.
   CR '63 p344,por.
   TV—Person (2) p61-62,por.

Kirk, Maria Louise (fl. 1890's)
   Amer. painter, illustrator
   Michigan—Biog. p177

Kirk, Phyllis (1930-   )
   Amer. actress
   CR '59 p405,por.

Kirkby, Louise. See Lun, Louise Kirkby

Kirkland, Caroline Matilda Stansbury
   (1801-1864)
   Amer. author, editor, journalist
   Bruère—Laugh. p5-6
   Hanaford—Dau. p229,792
   Ross—Ladies p454-455

Kirkland, Jerusha (Jemima) Bingham
   (m. 1769)
   Amer. pioneer missionary
   Fowler—Woman p363-365
   Logan—Part p516-517

Kirkland, Winifred Margaretta (1872-
1943)
Amer. author
Cur. Biog. '43 p389

Kirkpatrick, Helen Paull (1909-   )
Amer. journalist
Cur. Biog. '41 p469-470,por.

Kirkus,Virginia (1893-   )
Amer. literary critic, author
Cur. Biog. '41 p470-471,por.
Cur. Biog. '54 p382-384,por.
Women—Achieve. p70,por.

Kirmse, Marguerite (1885-1954)
Anglo-Amer. illustrator, etcher
Kirkland—Artists p23-33
Mahoney—Illus. p328

Kirschner, Lola. See Schubin, Ossip

Kirschner, Marie (b. 1852)
Czech. painter
Waters—Women p195

Kirsten, Dorothy (1917/19-   )
Amer. singer
CR '59 p405-406,por.
CR '63 p345,por.
Cur. Biog. '48 p352-355,por.
Ewen—Ency. p241-242
Matz—Opera p121-124,por.
Ulrich—Famous p119-123,por.

Kisich, Margaret. See Shedd, Margaret

Kissling, Dorothy. See Langley, Dorothy

Kitchell, Iva (1912-   )
Amer. dancer, comedienne
Cur. Biog. '51 p346-348,por.
Dodd—Celeb. p337-341

Kitchin, Hannah Chapman (m. 1751)
Amer. colonial manufacturer
Dexter—Colonial p72

Kitson, Theo Alice Ruggles (1871-1932)
Amer. sculptor
Adelman—Famous p313
Taft—Women, Mentor (172) p10
Waters—Women p196

Kitt, Eartha (1928-   )
Amer. singer, dancer, actress
Beaton—Persona p63
°Cherry—Portraits p98-104,por.
CR '59 p407,por.
CR '63 p345,por.
Cur. Biog. '55 p327-329,por.
Popular Record p79,por.
°Rollins—Enter. p75-80,por.

Kitt, Edith O. (b. 1878)
Amer. club leader
Binheim—Women p7,por.

"Kitty the Schemer" (fl. 1870's)
Amer. W. pioneer
Aikman—Calamity p311-312

Klafsky, Katharina (1855-1896)
Hung. singer
Ewen—Ency. p242
Klein—Great p224-229,por.
McCoy—Portraits p100,por.

Klahre, Ethel Susan (1905-   )
Amer. librarian
Cur. Biog. '62 p239-240,por.

Kleeberg, Clotilde(1866-1909)
Fr. pianist
McCoy—Portraits p100,por.

Kleegman, Sophia J. fl. 1930's)
Russ.-Amer. physician, obstetrician
gynecologist
Women—Achieve. p140,por.

Kleeman, Rita Halle (b. 1887)
Amer. author
Women—Achieve. p94,por.

Kline, Clarice Lenore (1912-   )
Amer. educator, organization
official
Cur. Biog. '61 p248-249,por.

Klink, Gertrud Scholtz (b. 1874)
Ger. feminist, poet, playwright
Beard—Woman p11-12

Klous, Augusta Doria. See Doria, Augusta

Kluegel, Anne Jennings (b. 1880)
Amer. author, educator
Binheim—Women p59,por.

Klumpke, Anna Elizabeth (b. 1856)
Amer. painter
Waters—Women p196-198

Klumpke, Dorothea (fl. 1900's)
Amer. astronomer
Mozans—Woman p193-195

Klumpp, Margaret M. (fl. 1930's)
Amer. physician
Women—Achieve. p79,por.

Kmetz, Annette L. (fl. 1930's)
Amer. nurse, public health worker
Women—Achieve. p199

Knapp, Hazel (1908-   )
Amer. artist
Janis—They p178-181,por.

Knep (Knipp), Mary (fl. 1670's)
Eng. actress
MacQueen—Pope p66-72
Wilson—All p154-156

Knight, Ellis Cornelia (1758-1838)
Eng., preceptress to Princess
Charlotte
MacCarthy—Later p25-28

Knight, Frances Gladys (1905-   )
Amer. government official
CR '63 p346,por.
Cur. Biog. '55 p329-331,por.

Knight, Frances Maria (fl. 1676-1719)
Eng. actress
Wilson—All p156-159

Knight, Laura Johnson, Dame (b. 1877)
Eng. painter
Cole—Women p161-189,por.
Hammerton p857
Murrow—This (2) p76-77

Knight, Margaret (fl. 1870's)
Amer. inventor
Hanaford—Dau. p652-653
Mozans—Woman p350-351

Knight, Mary Worrell (c. 1759-1849)
Amer. Rev. war heroine
Green—Pioneer (2) p405-406
Hanaford—Dau. p63

Knight, Peggy (fl. 1940's)
Eng. war heroine, spy
*Deakin—True p77-100

Knight, Ruth Adams Yingling (1898-   )
Amer. author
Cur. Biog. '43 p393-395,por.
Cur. Biog. '55 p333-334,por.

Knight, Sarah Kemble (1666-1727)
Amer. colonial diarist, hotel-keeper,
teacher, traveller, business
woman
Benson—Women p279-280,304-305
Brooks—Colonial p75-101
Dexter—Colonial p3-6,83-84,133-134
Dunaway—Treas. p52-55
Earle—Colon. p135-159
Green—Pioneer (1) p397,442-455
Keyes—Lives p123-131
Leonard—Amer. p117
MacQueen—Pope p317-319
Woodward—Way p67-68

Knipp, Mary. See **Knep, Mary**

Knobloch, Gertrude (b. 1867)
Ger. painter, sculptor
Waters—Women p198

Knopf, Amy. See **Vanderbilt, Amy**

Knopf, Blanche Wolf (c. 1894-1966)
Amer. publisher
Cur. Biog. '57 p308-310,por.
Cur. Biog. '66 p467

Knott, Mrs. A.Leo (fl. 1890's)
Amer. club leader
Logan—Part p455-456

Knott, Sarah Gertrude (n.d.)
Amer. folk dance director
Cur. Biog. '47 p357-359,por.

Knouss, Isabelle G. (fl. 1940's)
Amer. composer, pianist, music
teacher
McCoy—Portraits p101,por.

Knowles, Ella (b. 1870)
Amer. lawyer
Logan—Part p746

Knowlton, Fanny Snow (1859-1926)
Amer. composer
McCoy—Portraits p101,por.

Knox, Adeline Grafton ,b. 1845)
Amer. author
Logan—Part p827-828

Knox, Helen (fl. 1930's)
Amer. banker
Women—Achieve. p150,por.

Knox, Helen Boardman (1870-1947)
Amer. author
ASCAP p280-281

Knox, Jane (fl. 1780's-1800's)
Amer., mother of James K. Polk
Hampton—Our p86-91

Knox, Jean, Lady Swaythling (1908-   )
Brit. military director
Cur. Biog. '42 p467-469,por.

Knox, Louise Chambers (c. 1860-1942)
Amer. religious worker
Cur. Biog. '42 p469

Knox, Lucy Flucker (c. 1756-1824)
Amer. Rev. war heroine, patriot
Ellet—Women (1) p127-133
Green—Pioneer (2) p13,79,100-112,
117-118,120
Hanaford—Dau. p138

Knox, Margaret Stuart (c. 1547-1612)
Scot. religious worker
Deen—Great p349-350

Knox, Marjory Bowes (c. 1538-1560)
Scot. religious worker
Deen—Great p349-350

Knox, Rose Markward (1857-1950)
Amer. industrialist
Cur. Biog. '49 p330-332,por.
Cur. Biog. '50 p310

Knox, Susan Ricker (n.d.)
Amer. painter
Michigan—Biog. p178-179

Knurr, Palne (fl. 1940's)
Hung. martyr
Stiles—Postal p140

Knutson, Coya (1912-   )
Amer. Congresswoman
Cur. Biog. '56 p340-342,por.

K'o, Lady (fl. 1620's)
Chin., foster mother of Hsi Tsung
Llewellyn—China's p150-152,154-158

Kobyljanska, Olga (1863-1942)
Russ. novelist
Stiles—Postal p140

Koch, Ilse (1907-1967)
Ger. criminal
Ewart—World's p279-283

Koch, Marion (fl. 1930's)
Amer. retail buyer
Women—Achieve. p155,por.

Kochanksa, Praxede Marcelline.
See Sembrich, Marcella

Kochina (Palubarinova-Kochina), Pelageya
Yakovlevna (1899-   )
Russ. scientist
U.S.—Biog., Soviet p327-328

Kock, Karin (1891-   )
Swed. government official, author
Cur. Biog. '48 p359-360,por.

Koegel, Linda (fl. 1890's)
Nether. painter
Waters—Women p381

Koenen, Tilly (1873-1941)
Nether. singer
McCoy—Portraits p102,por.

Koernig, Anna Mabel (fl. 1930's)
Amer. business executive
Women—Achieve. p164,por.

Kohlhepp, Evelyn Marie (fl. 1930's)
Amer. dentist
Women—Achieve. p117,por.

Kohn, Estelle Rumbold (fl. 1920's)
Amer. sculptor
National—Contemp. p183

Kohut, Rebekah (1864-1951)
Hung.-Amer. lecturer, teacher,
author
Collins—Biog. p323-326
Ribalow—Auto. p181-200

Koker, Anna Maria de (fl. 17th cent.)
Nether. etcher, engraver
Waters—Women p199

Kokovtseva, Mlle. (fl. 1910's)
Russ. military heroine
Dorland—Sum p99

Kolb-Danvin, Mrs. Charles Louis.
See Radziwill, Catherine, Princess

Kollmar, Dorothy. See Kilgallen, Dorothy

Kollock, Alice. See Green, Alice Kollock

Kollock, Augusta J. (fl. 1860's)
Amer. Civil war heroine
Jones—Heroines p11-12

Kollock, Florence E. (b. 1848)
Amer. missionary
Logan—Part p737

Kollock, Mary (1840-1911)
Amer. painter
Waters—Women p198-199

Kollontay, Alexandra Mikhailovna (1872-
1952)
Russ. diplomat
Cur. Biog. '43 p401-403,por.
Cur. Biog. '52 p315

Kollwitz, Kaethe Schmidt (1867-1945)
Ger. artist, sculptor
Stiles—Postal p141

Koltoi, Anna (fl. 1940's)
Hung. martyr
Stiles—Postal p142

Komarovsky, Mirra (1906-   )
Russ.-Amer. educator, sociologist
Cur. Biog. '53 p325-327,por.

Komisarjevskava, Vera (1864-1910)
Russ. actress, producer
Stiles—Postal p142

Komlosi, Irma (b. 1850)
Czech. painter
Waters—Women p199

Kommer, Jayne (fl. 1950's)
Amer. airline hostess
*May—Women p233

Komroff, Elinor M. See Barnard, Elinor M.

Kondelka, Pauline von, Baroness
(1806-1840)
It. painter
Waters—Women p199

Konek, Ida (b. 1856)
Hung. painter
Waters—Women p200

Koner, Pauline (c. 1912-   )
Amer. dancer, choreographer
Cur. Biog. '64 p237-239,por.

Ko-Ngai (fl. 15th cent.)
Chin. heroine
Muir—Wome p81-83

Konigsmark, Sophia Dorothea (d. 1726)
Ger. princess
Hahn—Love p140-171

Konopnicka, Maria Wasilowska (1840/46-
1910/16)
Pol. author
Schmidt—400 p328-329,por.
Stiles—Postal p142

Konstaninu, Eugenie. See Clark, Eugenie

Koontz, Elizabeth Duncan (1919-   )
Amer. educator
Robinson—Hist. p220

Kops, Margot De Bruyn (fl. 1930's)
Amer. fashion designer
Women—Achieve. p165,por.

Kora (Callirhoë) (fl. 7th cent. B.C.)
Greek pioneer artist
Waters—Women p200-201

Korn, Clara Ann (fl. 1940's)
Ger. composer, pianist
McCoy—Portraits p102,por.

Korolowicz, Jeanne (fl. 1900's-1910's)
Pol. singer
Lahee—Grand p383,427

Korumdevi, Princess (fl. 1407 A.D.)
E. Ind., daughter of Manik Rao
Pool—Famous p59-63

Korzhenko, Nora (1919-   )
Russ. spy
Singer—World's p317-318

Korzybska, Countess. See Edgerley,Mira

K.O.S., pseud.
See Dombroski zu Papros und Krusvic,
Kathe Schönberger von

Koshetz, Nina (1894-   )
Russ. singer
Ewen—Living p197,por.
McCoy—Portraits p103,por.

Kosmodemyanskaia, Zoya Anatolyevna
(1923-1941)
Russ. heroine, martyr
Stiles—Postal p143

Kossak-Szcuka, Zofia (1890-1968)
Pol. author
Cur. Biog. '44 p357-358,por.
Cur. Biog. '68 p457

Kossamak Nearirat Serey Vathana
(fl. 1950's-1960's)
Camb. queen, wife of Norodom
Suramarit
Stiles—Postal p143

Kottauer, Helene (1410-1470)
Aust. diplomat
Schmidt—400 p41-42,por.

Kotzschmar, Mrs. Hermann (b. 1853)
Amer. music teacher, pianist
McCoy—Portraits p103,por.

Koussevitzky, Olga Naumoff (Natalya)
(c 1881-1942)
Russ. sculptor, wife of Serge
Koussevitzky
Cur. Biog. '42 p472
Murrow—This (1) p93-94

Kovalevsky, Sonya (Sofie) (1850-1891)
Russ. mathematician, author
Adelman—Famous p224-225
Cajori—Hist. p456
Coolidge—Six p29-31
Hammerton p861
Mozans—Woman p161-166
Ravenel—Women p56-60
Schmidt—400 p346,por.
Smith—Hist. (1) p530
Stiles—Postal p143

Kovovtseva, Mlle.

Kovriga, Mariai Dmitrievna (fl. 1950's)
Russ. physician, government
official,
Lovejoy—Women p171,por.

Kovshova, N. V. (fl. 1940's)
Russ. soldier, heroine
Stiles—Postal p143

Koyke, Hitzi (1926-   )
Jap. singer
McCoy—Portraits p103,por.

Kraeuter, Phyllis Marie (fl. 1930's)
Amer. cellist
Women—Achieve. p67,por.

Krafft, Anna Barbara (1764-1825)
Aust. painter
Waters—Women p201

Kraft, Lucile L. (fl. 1930's)
Amer. secretary, humanitarian
Women—Achieve. p129,por.

Krakower, Kathleen.
See Winsor, Kathleen

Krall, Heidi (fl. 1950's)
Swiss-Amer. singer
Matz—Opera p188-190,por.

Kramer, Maria (fl. 1930's)
Amer. hotel owner, operator
Women—Achieve. p46,por.

Krasinska, Françoise (1742-1795)
It., wife of Duke Charles
Stirling—Odd p13-66

Krasnohorska, Elisa, pseud. (Eliska
Pechova) (b. 1847)
Czech. poet, translator
Schmidt—400 p87,por.

Krasnow, Frances (fl. 1930's)
Amer. biochemist
Women—Achieve. p78,por.

Kratz, Althea Hallowell.
See Hottel, Althea Hallowell Kratz

Krauss, Gabrielle (1842-1906)
Aust. singer
Ewen—Ency. p247

Krautter, Elisa Bialk. See Bialk, Elisa

Kremer, Isa (c. 1887-1956)
Russ. singer
McCoy—Portraits p104,por.
Saleski—Jewish p595
Saleski—Wander. p411-412,por.

Kretschmar, Alice Anne (fl. 1930's)
Amer. personnel director
Women—Achieve. p161,por.

Kripps, Susanna (fl. 1860's)
Amer. Civil war nurse
Logan—Part p363

Kristiansen, Mrs. Erling.
See Selinko, Annemarie

Kristina, Beatrice. See Beatrice Kristina

Kristina, Maria. See Maria Cristina

Kroeger, Alice Bertha (d. 1909)
Amer. pioneer librarian
Marshall—Amer. p455

Kroener, Magda (fl. 1890's)
Ger. painter
Waters—Women p381-382

Krog, Gina (1847-1961)
Nor. feminist
Schmidt—400 p310-311,por.

Krogman, Mrs. C. W. (d. 1943)
Amer. composer
McCoy—Portraits p105,por.

Kronold, Selma (1866-1920)
Pol. singer
Ewen—Ency. p248
Logan—Part p767

Kross, Anna Moscowitz (1891-   )
Russ.-Amer. judge, feminist
Cur. Biog. '45 p328-329,por.
Phelps—Men (1) '58 p143-144
Women—Achieve. p51,por.

Krout, Mary Hannah (1857-1927)
Amer. journalist, author
Logan—Part p828

Krüdener, Barbara Juliane von Vietinghoff,
Baroness (1764-1824)
Russ. novelist, mystic
Adelman—Famous p116-117
Dorland—Sum p34,132
Kelen—Mist. p13-47,329,por.

Krupskaya, Nadezhda Konstantinovna
(1869-1939)
Russ. social worker, politician,
wife of Lenin
Beard—Woman p2-3

Kuan Fu-Jên (fl. 1310's-1320's)
Chin. painter
Ayscough—Chinese p202-210

Kubie, Matilda Steinam (fl. 1930's)
Amer. humanitarian, philanthropist,
club leader
Women—Achieve. p37,por.

Kuehn, Friedel (fl. 1936-1941)
Ger. spy
*Komroff—True p186-196
Singer—World's p202-208

Kuehn, Ruth (fl. 1940's)
Ger. spy
Komroff—True p186-196
Singer—World (II) p89-97
Singer—World's p198-208

Kugler, Annie (fl. 1880's)
Amer. physician
Irwin—Angels p141

Kuhn, Irene Corbally (1900-   )
Amer. journalist, editor, radio
executive, lecturer
Cur. Biog. '46 p312-315,por.
Ross—Ladies p197,228-233,por.,cover
Women—Achieve. p153,por.

Kuhn, Rene Leilani (1923-   )
    Amer. novelist
    Warfel—Amer. p253,por.

Kuhns, Dorothy Hartzell.
    See Heyward, Dorothy Hartzell Kuhns

Kuitka, Larissa Kossach.
    See Ukrainka, Lesya, pseud.

Kulka, Leopoldine (1872-1920)
    Aust. feminist, author, social
        reformer
    Schmidt—400 p53-54,por.

Kullmer, Ann (1917-   )
    Amer. orchestra conductor
    Cur. Biog. '49 p336-337,por.

Kumler, Mrs. Charles H. (fl. 1900's)
    Amer. club leader
    Logan—Part p403

Kummer, Clare Rodman Beecher (b. 1888)
    Amer. composer, song-writer,
        playwright
    ASCAP p287-288
    Mantle—Contemp. p292-293
    Millett—Amer. p427-428

Kung, Eling Soong Hsiang-Hsi (fl. 1900's-
        1930's)
    Chin., wife of H. H. Kung
    Clark—Chiangs p40-57,por.

Kunigunde (d. 1037)
    Ger. saint
    Hammerton p863

Kuntze, Martha (b. 1849)
    Ger. painter
    Waters—Women p201-202

Kurenko, Maria (fl. 1920's-1940's)
    Russ.-Amer. singer
    Cur. Biog. '44 p366-368,por.
    Ewen—Living p205,por.
    McCoy—Portraits p106,por.

Kurnarath (fl. 16th cent.)
    E. Ind. queen, wife of Rana Sanga
    Pool—Famous p69-74

Kurner, Mae. See Tinee, Mae

Kurt, Melanie (1880-1941)
    Aust. singer
    Ewen—Ency. p249

Kurz, Isolde (b.c. 1853)
    Ger. author
    Heller—Studies p285-287

Kurz, Selma (1875-1933)
    Aust. singer
    Ewen—Ency. p249
    Saleski—Wander. p401
    Wagner—Prima p61,243

Küssner, Amalia.
    See Coudert, Amalia Küssner

Kutz, Sally (fl. 1930's)
    Amer. public health worker
    Women—Achieve. p97,por.

Kuusinen, Hertta Elina (1904-   )
    Fin. government official, journalist
    Cur. Biog. '49 p337-339,por.

Kuyper, Elizabeth (b. 1877)
    Nether. composer, conductor,
        violinist
    McCoy—Portraits p107,por.

Kvapilova, Hana (1860-1906)
    Czech. actress
    Stiles—Postal p145

Kwan, Nancy (1939-   )
    Jap. actress
    CR '63 p352,por.

Kyasht, Lydia (b. 1886)
    Russ. ballet dancer
    Davidson—Ballet p171-174
    Hammerton p863-864,por.

Kyneburge (fl. 7th cent.)
    Eng. queen, saint
    Blunt—Great p81-82

L

Labé, Louise Charlin Perrin (La Bella
        Cordière)
    Fr. poet
    Adelman—Famous p47-48
    Hammerton p864
    Koven—Women p157-174,por.

La Belle Otèro.
    See Otèro, Caroline

Labia, Maria (b. 1885)
    It. singer
    Lahee—Grand p211-213

Labille, Adelaide Vertus (1749-1803)
    Fr. painter
    Waters—Women p202-203

Labouré, Catherine (1806-1876)
    Fr. saint
    Husslein—Heroines p128-141

La Camargo (1710-1770)
    Fr. singer, dancer
    Blei—Fasc. p144-148,por.
    Schmidt—400 p177,por.

La Carmencita (fl. 1870's-1880's)
    Sp. dancer
    Schmidt—400 p361,por.

Lacey, Margaret E. (fl. 1900's-1930's)
Amer. teacher, song-writer
Women—Achieve. p105,por.

Lacey, Mary Roby (fl. 1860's)
Amer. Civil war nurse
Logan—Part p360

La Chapelle, Marie Louise Dugès (1769-
1822)
Fr. physician
Mozans—Women p293-294

LaGrange, Anna De (1825-1905)
Aust. illustrator
Mahony—Illus. p330

Lachmann, Theresa (m. 1836)
Pol.-Russ. courtesan
Blei—Fasc. p210-213

Lacoste, Josette (fl. 1930's)
Fr. literary critic, editor
Women—Achieve, p149,por.

La Croix, Aurore (fl. 1910's)
Amer. pianist
McCoy—Portraits p107,por.

Lacy, Harriette Deborah Lacy (1807-1874)
Eng. actress
Dorland—Sum p47,167

Lacy, Mary Goodwin (1875-1962)
Amer. librarian, author, government
employee
Bul. of Bibl. May-Aug.1940 p21-22,por.

Ladd, Anna Coleman (1878-1939)
Amer. sculptor
Bruce—Woman p286-287
Jackman—Amer. p344-346
Michigan—Biog. p181-182
National—Contemp. p192
Taft—Women, Mentor (172) #4,
#6 p10,por.

"Lady Olga." See Barnell, Jan

Lafayette, Anastasie de Noailles (d. 1807)
Parton—Noted p494-506

Lafayette, Louise Emile, Madame de
(c. 1616-1665)
Fr. heroine, nun, beauty, wit
Fifty—Famous p5-13,por.

Lafayette, Marie Madeleine Pioche de la
Vergne, Comtesse de (1634-1693)
Fr. author
Farmer—What p22-29,76-78
Hammerton p866,por.
Koven—Women p252-259,282-300
Parton—Dau. p494-506
Ravenel—Women p146-177,por.
Schmidt—400 p175-176,por.

La Fetra, Sarah Doan (b. 1843)
Amer. social reformer
Logan—Part p661-662

LaFollette, Belle Case (b. 1859-   )
Amer. social leader
Logan—Part p290-291

Lafontaine, Mlle. (c. 1665-1738)
Fr. pioneer ballet dancer
*Terry—Star p17-20,por.

Lagerlöf, Selma Ottiliana Louisa (1858-
1940)
Swed. novelist, poet
Adelman—Famous p291-292
*Cather—Younger p257-285
Cooper—Authors p81-97
Cur. Biog. '40 p471-473,por.
Dunaway—Treas. p350-352
Ewen—Ency. p251
Hammerton p867,por.
*Kirkland—Writers p13-25
McClintock—Nobel p606
*MacVeagh—Champlin p339
Phila.—Women unp.,por.
Stiles—Postal p146

LaGrange, Anna De (1825-1905)
Fr. singer
McCoy—Portraits p107,por.

Laidlaw, Harriet Burton (1873-1949)
Amer. author, teacher, lecturer,
club leader
Women—Achieve. p83,por.

Laing, Mrs. J. G. (fl. 1900's)
Scot. painter
Waters—Women p203

Laïs, the elder (fl. 5th cent. B.C.)
Gr. courtesan
Hammerton p868

Laïs, the younger (fl. 4th cent. B.C.)
Gr. courtesan
Hammerton p868

Lajeunnesse, Emma.
See Albani (Madame Marie Louise
Cecily) Emma Lajeunesse

Lake, Mrs. Andrew (fl. 1780's)
Amer. W. pioneer, religious worker
Ellet—Pioneer p185-186
Fowler—Woman p365-366

Lake, Veronica (1919-   )
Amer. actress
Lamparski—What. p142-143,por.

Lakey, Emily Jane (1837-1896)
Amer. artist
Dorland—Sum p28

Lakshmi, Bai. See Ranee of Jhansi

Lakshmi, Vijaya (fl. 1930's-1940's)
   Ind., co-worker of Gandhi
   Stern—Women p149,176

LaLaing, Marie-Christine de (1545-1582)
   Belg. princess, patriot
   Schmidt—400 p57-58,por.

L'Allemande, Pauline (b. 1862)
   Amer. singer
   McCoy—Portraits p108,por.

Lally, Grace (n.d.)
   Amer. nurse
   *Wright—Great p263-274

Lalor, Teresa, Mother (1769-1846)
   Irish foundress, nun
   Code—Great p180-205

La Malinche, O Dona Marina (b. 1519)
   Mex. Ind. patriot, translator
   Schmidt—400 p287,por.

Lamar, Mirebean B. (d. 1871)
   Amer. pioneer
   Logan—Part p101-102

La Mara. See Lipsius, Marie

La Marr, Hedy (1915-   )
   Aust.-Amer. actress
   CR '59 p419,por.
   CR '63 p353-354
   Martin—Pete p470-482
   Schickel—Stars p212,por.

Lamarsh, Judy (1924-   )
   Can. government official, lawyer
   Cur. Biog. '68 p214-216,por.

Lamartine, Alix de Roys de (d.c. 1829)
   Fr. diarist, mother of Lamartine
   Peyton—Mothers p49-52

La Maupin, Mlle. (Mlle. D'Aubigny)
        (fl. 1700's)
   Fr. singer, swordsman
   Rogers—Gallant p175-206

Lamb, Caroline, Caroline, Lady (1785-
        1828)
   Eng. essayist, critic
   Hammerton p869
   Iremonger—And p51-73,por.
   Lee—Wives p1-43,por.
   Thomson—Queens p369-381

Lamb, Ella Condie (fl. 1890's-1900's)
   Amer. sculptor, illustrator, painter
   Michigan—Biog. p183
   Waters—Women p204-205

Lamb, Martha Joan Reade Nash (1829-
        1893)
   Amer. historian, editor
   Adelman—Famous p216
   Dorland—Sum p48,117,175
   Hanaford—Dau. p730-733
   Logan—Part p812-813

Lamb, Mary Anne (1764/65-1841)
   Abbot—Notable p416-420
   Adelman—Famous p117-118
   Hammerton p870,por.
   Hubbard—Little p289-321,por.
   *Humphrey—Marys p93-109
   Pomeroy—Little p45-72,por.

Lamb, Rose (fl. 1870's-1880's)
   Amer. painter
   Waters—Women p204-205

Lamb, Mrs. William (fl. 1860's)
   Amer. Civil war diarist
   Jones—Heroines p352-355

Lamballe, Marie Therese Louise De Savoie
        (1749-1792)
   It.-Fr. princess
   Dobson—Four p63-104
   Hammerton p870-871
   Schmidt—400 p253-254,por.

Lamber, Juliette.
   See Adam, Juliette Lamber

Lambert, Janet Snyder (1894-   )
   Amer. author
   Cur. Biog. '54 p395-396,por.

Lambert, Marquise de (1647-1733)
   Fr. author
   Benson—Women p23-24
   Kavanagh—Woman (1) p61-62

La Meri (fl. 1930's)
   Amer. dancer
   Women—Achieve. p107,por.

La Messine, pseud.
   See Adam, Juliette Lamber

La Motte, Ellen Newbold (1873-1961)
   Amer. nurse, author
   Pennock—Makers p136-137,por.

La Motte, Jeanne de Saint-Rémy de Valois
        (Mlle. D'Olisva; Jeanne de
        Valois) (1756-1791)
   Fr. adventuress
   Hammerton p871
   Kavanagh—Woman (2) p64-69
   Rogers—Gallant p207-256
   Trowbridge—Seven p196-248,por.

Lamour, Dorothy (1914-   )
   Amer. actress, singer

(Continued)

Lamour, Dorothy—*Continued*

    CR '59 p420,por.
    CR '63 p354,por.
    Cur. Biog. '46 (May) p33-34
    Schickel—Stars p217,por.

Lamson, Lucy Stedman (b. 1857)
    Amer. educator, business woman
    Logan—Part p905-906

Lancaster, Duchess of.
    See Swynford, Catherine, Duchess of
    Lancaster

Lancaster, G. B., pseud.
    See Lyttleton, Doris Jean

Lancaster, Sarah (fl. 1730's)
    Amer. colonial needlewoman
    Dexter—Colonial p54

Lanchester, Ella (1902-   )
    Eng. actress
    CR '59 p420,por.
    CR '63 p355,por.
    Cur. Biog. '50 p316-318,por.
    Hammerton p872

Lanciania, Marcella (fl. 1900's)
    It. artist
    Waters—Women p205

Lander, Hilda Cowham (n.d.)
    Eng. artist
    Hammerton p451

Lander, Jean Margaret Davenport (1829-
    1903)
    Amer. actress
    Coad—Amer. p172,por.
    Dorland—Sum p31
    Eaton—Actor's p103-104,por.
    Leetch—Reveille p446

Lander, Louisa (b. 1826)
    Amer. sculptor
    Hanaford—Dau. p304-306
    Waters—Women p205-206
    Whitton—These p194,206

Landers, Ann (1918-   )
    Amer. journalist, columnist
    CR '59 p421,por.
    CR '63 p355,por.
    Cur. Biog. '57 p315-317,por.

Landers, Olive Richards (fl. 1930's)
    Amer. editor, author
    Women—Achieve. p117,por.

Landes, Bertha Knight (1868-1943)
    Amer. politician, mayor
    Binheim—Women p196,por.
    Cur. Biog. '44 p372

Landi, Elissa (1904-1948)
    It. actress
    Stuart—Immort. p148-149,por.

Landon, Letitia Elizabeth ("L.E.L.")
    (1802-1838)
    Eng. poet
    Courtney—Advent. p44-72
    Dorland—Sum p49,74,181
    Thomson—Queens p145-179,por.

Landon, Margaret Dorthea Mortenson
    (1903-   )
    Amer. author
    Cur. Biog. '45 p332-333,por.

Landowska, Wanda (1877-1959)
    Pol. pianist, harpsichordist
    Beaton—Persona p68
    Cur. Biog. '45 p333-334,por.
    Cur. Biog. '59 p245
    Ewen—Living p207-208,por.
    *Forsee—Women p81-100
    Gelatt—Music p254-286,por.
    Hammerton p873
    McCoy—Portraits p108,por.
    Saleski—Jewish p505-506,por.
    Saleski—Wander. p335,por.
    Schonberg—Great p397-399,por.

Lane, Abbe (1932/35-   )
    Amer. singer
    CR '59 p421,por.
    CR '63 p356,por.
    TV—Person (3) p145,por.

Lane, Adeline A. (fl. 1860's)
    Amer. Civil war nurse
    Brockett—Woman's p789

Lane, Amanda (m. 1876)
    Amer. social reformer
    Hanaford—Dau. p428,431-432

Lane, Columbia (fl. 1880's)
    Amer. business woman
    Hanaford—Dau. p609-610

Lane, Gertrude Battles (d. 1941)
    Amer. editor, journalist
    Cur. Biog. '41 p490

Lane, Harriet (1833-1903)
    Amer. social leader, niece of
    James Buchanan
    Hanaford—Dau. p135
    Jensen—White p76-79,por.
    Logan—Ladies p80-85
    Logan—Part p249-251
    Ross—Know p33,por.
    *Stevens—Women p67-72,por.
    *Sweetser—Famous p178-211,por.
    Truett—First p40-41,por.
    Whitton—First p266-283

Lane, Jane, Lady Fisher (d. 1689)
  Eng. heroine
  Stenton—English p164

Lane, Kate B. See Burr, Kate

Lane, Katherine Ward (1899-   )
  Amer. sculptor
  National—Contemp. p196

Lane, Louisa (1820-1897)
  Amer. actress
  Moses—Famous p169-183,por.

Lane, Margaret, Countess of Huntingdon
  (1907-   )
  Eng. journalist, author
  Brittain—Women p177,253

Lane, Rose Wilder (b. 1887)
  Amer. journalist, author
  Ross—Ladies p580-581

Lane, Sara (fl. 1890's)
  Eng. actress
  Felstead—Stars p62-63

Laney, Lucy Craft (b. 1854)
  Amer. educator
  Beard—Amer. p244-249
  Daniel—Women p1-27,por.
  Ovington—Por. p53-63

Lang, Edith (fl. 1940's)
  Amer. organist, music teacher
  McCoy—Portraits p108,por.

Lang, Margaret Ruthven (b. 1867)
  Amer. composer
  Elson—Woman's p201-202,243-244
  Howard—Our p565
  Logan—Part p770
  McCoy—Portraits p108,por.

Lange, Helene (1848-1930)
  Ger. educator, feminist
  Hammerton p875
  Schmidt—400 p204,por.

Lange, Hope (1933-   )
  Amer. actress
  CR '63 p356-357,por.

Langendorff, Frida (fl. 1900's)
  Ger. singer
  Lahee—Grand p61

Langer, Susanne Katherina Knauth (1895-)
  Amer. philosopher, author,
    educator
  Cur. Biog. '63 p233-235,por.
  New Yorker Dec.3,1960 p67,por.
  (Profiles)

"L'Angevin." See Bordereau, Jeanne

Langford, Frances (1914-   )
  Amer. singer
  Donaldson—Radio p19

Langles, Angele Marie (fl. 1830's)
  Fr. seafarer
  Snow—Women p212-220

Langley, Adria Locke (n.d.)
  Amer. author
  Cur. Biog. '45 p335-336,por.

Langley, Dorothy (1904-   )
  Amer. novelist
  Warfel—Amer. p257-258,por.

Langley, Katherine (1888-1948)
  Amer. congresswoman
  Paxton—Women p129

Langner, Armina Marshall (Isabelle Louden,
    pseud.) (1898-   )
  Amer. playwright, producer
  Mantle—Contemp. p227-229

Langston, Dicey.
  See Springfield, Laodicea (Dicey)
  Langston

Langston, Marie Stone (fl. 1940's)
  Amer. singer
  McCoy—Portraits p109,por.

Langtry, Lillie Emilie Charlotte Le Breton
    (1852-1929)
  Eng. actress
  Adelman—Famous p284
  Bodeen—Ladies p57-62,por.
  Coad—Amer. p295
  Hammerton p876,por.

Langtry, Lady de Bathe (m. 1899)
  Eng. society leader, belle
  Furniss—Some p149-153,por.
  Wyndham—Chorus p153-154

Langworthy, Elizabeth (b. 1837)
  Amer. club leader
  Logan—Part p410

Lansbury, Angela (1925-   )
  Eng.-Amer. actress
  CR '63 p357,por.
  Cur. Biog. '67 p237-240,por.
  Ross—Player p364-372,por.

Lantz, Emily Emerson (fl. 1900's)
  Amer. journalist, genealogist
  Ross—Ladies p496-497

Lanvin, Jeanne (c. 1867-1946)
  Fr. dressmaker
  Cur. Biog. '46 p325

Lanza, Clara (b. 1859)
  Amer. author
  Farmer—What p444,por.

Lape, Esther Everett (fl. 1930's)
Amer. educator, editor
Women—Achieve. p121,por.

La Peregrina.
See Avellaneda y Arteaga, Gertrudis
Gomez

La Planche, Rosemary (fl. 1940's)
Amer. actress, beauty
Lamparski—What. p198-199,por.

La Plante, Laura (fl. 1920's)
Amer. actress
Herman—How p21,por.

La Pola. See Salavarrieta, Policarpa

Laporte, Marie Vernier (fl. 1610's)
Fr. actress
Gilder—Enter p91-92

Lara, Adelina de (b. 1872)
Eng. pianist
Schonberg—Great p336

Laraguais, Duchess de (fl. 1740's)
Fr. social leader
Haggard—Remark. p290-295

Laramore, Vivian Yeiser (1895-   )
Amer. poet, song-writer
ASCAP p293

Larcom, Lucy (1824/26-1893)
Amer. author, educator, poet
Adelman—Famous p199-200
Dorland—Sum p47,180
Douglas—Remember p62-63
Farmer—What p40,189,192-193,por.
Hanaford—Dau. p254-255
*Kirkland—Good p69-84
Logan—Part p820-821
*Sickels—Calico p189-204

Laroche, Baronne Raymond de (1886-1919)
Fr. pioneer aviatrix
Heinmuller—Man's p276,por.

La Roe, Else K. (fl. 1930's)
Amer. physician
Women—Achieve. p36,por.

Larrocha, Alicia de (1923-   )
Sp. pianist
Cur. Biog. '68 p219-221,por.

Larrimore, Francine (1898-
Fr.-Amer. actress
Blum—Great p82,por.

Larrimore, Lida, pseud.
See Turner, Lida Larrimore

Larsen-Todsen, Nanny (b. 1884)
Swed. singer
Ewen—Ency. p253
Ewen—Living p209
McCoy—Portraits p110,por.

La Sablière, Marguerite de (1636-1693)
Fr. astronomer
Mozans—Woman p171-173

Lascari, Hilda Kristina (b. 1886)
Swed. sculptor
National—Contemp. p197

Lascelles, Mary Madge (g. 1922)
Eng. teacher
Brittain—Women p183,246

Lashanska, Hulda (1893-   )
Amer. singer
Ewen—Living p209-210,por.
McCoy—Portraits p110,por.
Saleski—Wander. p412-413,por.

Lasker, Mary Woodward (1900-   )
Amer. philanthropist, organization
official
CR '63 p358,por.
Cur. Biog. '59 p245-247,por.

Laski, Marghanita (1915-   )
Eng. author
Cur. Biog. '51 p364-365,por.

Laslett, Dixie L. (fl. 1930's)
Amer. personnel executive
Women—Achieve. p156,por.

Lasswell, Mary (1905-   )
Amer. novelist
Warfel—Amer. p260-261,por.

Latham, Barbara (1896-   )
Amer. illustrator, painter
Mahony—Illus. p331

Latham, Eunice Forsythe (fl. 1780's)
Amer. patriot
Green—Pioneer (3) p419-422

Latham, Jean Lee (1902-   )
Amer. author
Cur. Biog. '56 p360-362,por.

Latham, Natalie Wales (b. 1911)
Amer. foundress, humanitarian
New Yorker Apr.19,1941 p21,por.
(Profiles)

Lathrop, Clarissa Cladwell (1892-   )
Amer. social reformer
Logan—Part p598

Lathrop, Dorothy Pulis (1891-   )
Amer. illustrator, author
Mahony—Illus. p331
*Stoddard—Top p45-53

Lathrop, Gertrude K. (1896-   )
Amer. sculptor
National—Contemp. p200

Lathrop, Julia Clifford (1858-1932)
Amer. government official,
humanitarian, social welfare
worker
Adelman—Famous p291
Bruce—Woman p295-296
Douglas—Remember p199-201
Rogers—Women p71,por.

Lathrop, Mary Florence (1865-1951)
Amer. pioneer lawyer
Irwin—Angels p300
Parkhill—Wildest p82-84

Lathrop, Rose Hawthorne (Mother Mary
Alphonsa) (1851-1926)
Amer. philanthropist, foundress
nurse, poet, nun
Adelman—Famous p283
Code—Great p472-498
Deen—Great p274-277
Dolan—Goodnow's p275-277
Dorland—Sum p49,129
Elgin—Nun p116-119,por.
Logan—Part p532-533
*McKown—Heroic p121-143
Maynard—Great p223-233
Wright—Great p157-161
*Yost—Famous p109-119,por.

Latimer, Elizabeth Wormeley (1822-1904)
Eng.-Amer. author
Logan—Part p817

Latouche, Mrs.fl. 19th cent.)
Eng., mother of Rose Latouche
Winwar—Poor p225-232,293-295

Latouche, Rose (d. 1875)
Eng., friend of John Ruskin
Winwar—Poor p226-234,292-301,por.

Latour, Frances Mary Jacqueline (1600-
1645)
Fr.-Can. heroine, colonial
landowner
Brooks—Colonial p31-58
Earle—Colon. p129-134
Green—Pioneer (1) p283,295,311-328
Leonard—Amer. p117

Lattimore, Eleanor Frances (1904-   )
Amer. illustrator
Mahony—Illus. p331

Laubach, Harriet Derr (fl. 1930's-1950's)
mother of Dr. Frank Laubach
Davis—Mothers p155-165

Lauderdale, Elizabeth Murray, Duchess of
Maitland (d. 1697)
Scot. patriot
Graham—Group p57-76
Jenkins—Ten p179-191,por.

Lauenstein, Henriette Sontag von.
See Sontag, Henriette, Countess Rossi

Laufer, Beatrice (1916-   )
Amer. composer
Reis—Composers p221

Lauferty, Lilian (1887-1958)
Amer. journalist, author
Ross—Ladies p83-84
Warfel—Amer. p261,por.

Laughlin, Clara Elizabeth (1873-1941)
Amer. author
Cur. Biog. '41 p495
Wagenknecht—When p180-192

Laukota, Herminie (b. 1853)
Czech. painter
Waters—Women p206

Launay, Marguerite.
See Staal, Marguerite Jeanne Cordier,
Baroness

Laura (c. 1308-1348)
Fr., friend of Petrarch
Cockran—Romance p361-369

Laurence, Katie (fl. 1890's)
Eng. singer
Felstead—Stars p39-40

Laurens, Martha.
See Ramsay, Martha Laurens

Laurie, Annie (1682-1764)
Scot. heroine
Hammerton p883

Laurie, Annie.
See Black, Winifred

Laurie, Piper (1932-   )
Amer. actress
CR '63 p359,por.

Laut, Agnes Christina (1871/72-1936)
Can.-Amer. journalist, author
Thomas—Canad. p77-78
Maurice—Makers p9,por.

Lautz, Katherine Bardol (b. 1842)
Amer. philanthropist
Logan—Part p534

Lavallière, Eve (1866-1929)
Fr. actress
Burton—Valiant p20-37

La Valliere, Louise Baume Le Blanc
(1644-1710)
Fr., mistress of Louis XIV
Abbot—Notable p258-262,por.
Adelman—Famous p60

(Continued)

La Valliere, Louise—*Continued*

    Dark—Royal p201-228,por.
    Dorland—Sum p16
    Haggard—Remark. p100-103,105-107
      120-121,123-126,128,131
    Hall—Moths p158-189,por.
    Hammerton p883,por.

Laverty, Maura (1907-   )
    Irish author
    Cur. Biog. '47 p377-378,por.

La Villette, Elodie (f. 1870's 1880's)
    Fr. painter
    Waters—Women p206-207

La Villiers (Devilliers), Mlle. (fl. 1620's)
    Fr. actress
    Gilder—Enter p92-94,101

Lavoisier, Marie.
    See Rumford, Marie Anne Pierrette
    Paulze Lavoisier, Countess

Law, Helen Lynch (fl. 1930's)
    Amer. radio advertising executive
    Women—Achieve. p167,por.

Law, Ruth Bancroft (b. 1887)
    Amer. pioneer aviatrix
    *Adams—Sky p49-65,por.
    Dorland—Sum p102
    Earhart—Fun p185-189,por.
    Heinmuller—Man's p294,por.
    Maitland—Knights p161-163
    *May—Women p73,76-81,100,212,por.
    Planck—Women p33-35,por.

Law, Sallie Chapman Gordon ("Mother of
    the Confederacy") (1805-1894)
    Amer. Civil war nurse
    Bruce—Woman p222

Lawler, Anne.　See Ross, Anne Lawler

Lawler, Elsie M. (fl. 1900's)
    Amer. nurse
    Pennock—Makers p119,por.

Lawless, Emily(1845-1913)
    Irish novelist
    Stebbins—Victorian p41-42,209

Lawless, Margaret H. Wynne (b. 1847)
    Amer. religious worker, author,
      club leader
    Logan—Part p836

Lawnhurst, Vee (1905-   )
    Amer. composer, pianist, singer
    ASCAP p295

Lawrence, Andrea Mead (b. 1933)
    Amer. skier
    Time Jan.21,1952 p64,por.(Cover)

Lawrence, Arabella Susan (1871-1947)
    Brit. politician, Parliamentary
      member
    Hammerton p885

Lawrence, Carol (1934-   )
    Amer. actress, dancer, singer
    CR '63 p360,por.
    Cur. Biog. '61 p257-258,por.

Lawrence, Charlotte Louise (fl. 1910's)
    Amer. club leader
    Logan—Part p459

Lawrence, Florence (d. 1938)
    Amer. actress
    Wagenknecht—Movies p52-53,por.

Lawrence, Gertrude (1898/1901-1952)
    Eng. actress
    Blum—Great p118,por.
    Cur. Biog. '40 p485-487,por.
    Cur. Biog. '52 p332-334,por.
    Hammerton p1450,por.
    Marinacci—Lead p269-291,por.
    Time—Feb.3,1941 p53,por.(Cover)

Lawrence, Hilda (n.d.)
    Amer. author
    Cur. Biog. '47 p381-382

Lawrence, Jeanette (fl. 1930's)
    Amer. author, lecturer
    Binheim—Women p61,por.

Lawrence, Josephine(n.d.)
    Amer. novelist
    Van Gelder—Writers p156-158
    Warfel—Amer. p261-262,por.

Lawrence, Lillian (fl. 1890's)
    Amer. actress
    Strang—Actresses p232-242,por.

Lawrence, Margery (b.c. 1880-   )
    Eng. author
    Hammerton p886

Lawrence, Marjorie (1908-   )
    Austral. singer
    Cur. Biog. '40 p487-488,por.
    Davidson—Treas. p158-160
    Ewen—Ency. p255
    Ewen—Living p211-212,por.
    Ewen—Men p67-72
    McCoy—Portraits p111,por.
    Peltz—Spot. p47,por.
    Wagner—Prima p155,244

Lawrence, Mary Viola Tingley (d. 1931)
    Amer. journalist
    Sargent—Pioneers p16,18,27-28,por.

Lawrence, Mildred (1907-   )
    Amer. author
    Cur. Biog. '53 p345-347,por.

Lawson, Deborah (fl. 1770's)
Amer. soldier
Farmer—What p38

Lawson, Katherine Stewart (b. 1885)
Amer. sculptor
National—Contemp. p203

Lawson, Mary (1910-1941)
Brit. actress
Cur. Biog. '41 p498

Lawton, Elizabeth Tillinghast (1832-1904)
Amer. educator
Logan—Part p292

Lawton, Hattie (fl. 1860's)
Amer. Civil war spy
Kane—Spies p100-108

Lawton, Sarah Alexander (fl. 1860's)
Amer. Civil war diarist
Jones—Heroines p298-302

Laxmibai (d. 1857)
Ind. (Jhansi) queen
Stiles—Postal p150

Lay, Julia (fl. 1860's)
Amer. Civil war patriot, author,
social leader
Dannett—Noble p266-267

Lay, Margaret Rebecca (1905-   )
Amer. author
Warfel—Amer. p262-263,por.

Laya (fl. 100 B.C.)
Gr.-Rom. painter
Hanford—Dau. p291
Waters—Women p xii

Laydon, Annie Burras (fl. 17th cent.)
Amer. pioneer
*Sickels—Calico p1-15

Laye, Evelyn (1900-   )
Eng. actress
Hammerton p887

Layton, Jessie Trunkey (d. 1934)
Amer. missionary
They—Went p20-21

Layton, Olivia Cameron Higgins (n.d.)
Amer. organization official
Cur. Biog. '52 p334-336,por.

Lazarenko, Natalita Iosafovna (1911-   )
Russ. inventor
U.S.—Biog., Soviet p360

Lazarovich, Eleanor.
See Calhoun, Eleanor, Princess
Lazarovich-Hrebelianovich

Lazarus, Emma (1849-1887)
Amer. poet, essayist, philanthropist
Adelman—Famous p226-227
*Dolin—World p132-143,por.
Dorland—Sum p24,179-180
*Horowitz—Treas. p82-91
*Levinger—Great p140-144
Logan—Part p852-853
Longwell—Amer. p150-184
Ribalow—Auto. p27-37
Simonhoff—Saga p130-136,por.
*Strong—Of p224-233

Lazarus, Hilda (fl. 1940's)
E. Ind. physician
Lovejoy—Women p227-228,por.

Lazzari, Carolina Antoinette (1891-1946)
Amer. singer
McCoy—Portraits p111,por.
Women—Achieve. p184,por.

Lea (d.c. 383)
Rom. saint
Englebert—Lives p113
Wescott—Calen. p42

Lea, Anna M. (fl. 1880's)
Amer. artist
Hanaford—Dau. p299-300

Lea, Mrs. Frank T. (m. 1896)
Amer. missionary
They—Went p19-20

Lea, Margaret Moffette (d. 1867)
Amer., 3d wife of Sam Houston
Turner—Sam p61-78,por.

Leach, Agnes Brown (fl. 1930's)
Amer. humanitarian, club leader
Women—Achieve. p119,por.

Leach, Ruth Marian (1916-   )
Amer. business executive
Cur. Biog. '48 p373-374,por.

Leade, Jane (1623-1704)
Ger. religious author
Culver—Women p150

Leaena (fl. 500's B.C.)
Gr. courtesan
Boccaccio—Conc. p107-109

Leaf, Freydia (fl. 1950's-1960's)
Eng. aviatrix
*May—Women p198

Leah (Biblical)
Buchanan—Women p20-23
Deen—All p28-36
Harrison—Little p11-22
*Levinger—Great p20-25
Lewis—Portraits p71-74

(Continued)

Leah (Biblical)—*Continued*

Lofts—Women p32-41
*MacVeagh—Champlin p346
Marble—Women p130-133
Mead—250 p30
Nelson—Bible p24-26
Van Der Velde—She p59-63

Leahy, Agnes Berkeley (fl. 1930's)
Amer. personnel worker
Women—Achieve. p117,por.

Learned, Grace Utter (fl. 1920's-1950's)
Amer. missionary
They—Went p72-73

Leary, Anna (n.d.)
Amer. recluse
Erskine—Out p100-113

Leary, Anne (fl. 1910's)
Amer. social leader
Logan—Part p620-621

Leary, Louise(n.d.)
Amer. recluse
Erskine—Out p100-103

Lease, Mary Elizabeth Clyens (1853-1933)
Amer. W. pioneer, feminist, lecturer
Brown—Gentle p279-283
Holbrook—Dreamers p158-159
Johnson—Lunatic p152-170

Leavenworth, Harriet (fl. 1800's)
Amer. patriot
DAR Mag. July 1921 p389,por.

Leavenworth, Mary(fl. 1880's)
Amer. social leader
Hanaford—Dau. p145

Leavitt, Adelia (fl. 1860's)
Amer. Civil war nurse
Logan—Part p375

Leavitt, Henrietta (1868-1921)
Amer. astronomer
Armitage—Cent. p180-181
Williams—Great p455-460,por.

Leavitt, Martha (fl. 1930's)
Amer. editor
Women—Achieve. p168,por.

Lebeau, Louise Adolpha(1850-1927)
Ger. composer, pianist
Elson—Woman's p164-165,por.

Lebedeva, Vera Pavlovna (b. 1881)
Russ. physician, public health
worker
U.S.—Biog. Soviet p367-368

LeBlanc, Georgette (Georgietta Maeterlinck)
(c. 1875-1941)
Fr. singer, actress
Cur. Biog. '41 p503
Lahee—Grand p399-404
Wagner—Prima p244

Leblanc, Léonide (fl. 1860's-1870's)
Fr. actress
Skinner—Elegant p78-80,por.

Le Blonde, Elizabeth Frances (d. 1934)
Eng. author
Hammerton p888

Le Brun, Adele (fl. 1880's-1890's)
Amer. religious worker
Logan—Part p621

Lebrun, Marie Louise Elizabeth Vigée
(1755-1842)
Fr. painter
Adelman—Famous p116
*Bolton—Famous Leaders p92-122,por.
*Cather—Girlhood p291-307
Dorland—Sum p32,75
Douglas—Remember p181
Hammerton p888,por.
*Kirkland—Artists p69-78
*MacVeagh—Champlin p347,por.
Schmidt—400 p178,por.
Stiles—Postal p280
Tallentyre—Women p223-235,por.
Waters—Women p340-350

Le Clercq, Tanaquil (1929-   )
Fr. ballet dancer
Atkinson—Dancers p92-95,por.
Beaton—Persona p67-68,por.
CR '59 p427,por.
Cur. Biog. '53 p349-350,por.
*Terry—Star p193

Le Conte, Emma Florence(fl. 1860's)
Amer. Civil war diarist
Jones—Heroines p360-370

Lecouvreur, Adrienne (1692-1726/30)
Fr. actress
Adelman—Famous p73-74
Collins—Great p111-137,por.
Haggard—Remark. p304-310
Mayne—Enchant. p215-227,por.
Orr—Famous p109-125
Orr—Famous Affin. I p143-166
Rogers—Gallant p257-295
Schmidt—400 p176,por.
Terhune—Super. p115-134

Le Cron, Helen Cowles (fl. 1920's)
Amer. poet
Smith—Women's p125

Leczinska, Marie.
See **Lesczczynska, Marie**

Lederer, Esther Friedman.
　　See Landers, Ann

Leduc, Violette (1910-　　)
　　Fr. novelist
　　Peyre—French p423-456

Ledyard, Fannie.
　　See Peters, Fannie Ledyard

Ledyard, Mary (fl. 1770's)
　　Amer. Rev. war heroine,
　　　philanthropist
　　Fowler—Woman p131
　　Hanaford—Dau. p155

Lee, Agnes, pseud. (Mrs. Otto Freer)
　　Amer. poet
　　Cook—Our p215-217
　　Smith—Women's p128

Lee, Ann ("Mother Ann," Ann Lee
　　　Standerin) (1736-1784)
　　Eng.-Amer. religious mystic,
　　　foundress
　　Benson—Women p272-273
　　Deen—Great p159-164
　　Dexter—Career p53
　　Dexter—Colonial p102,150-153
　　Hammerton p889
　　Leonard—Amer. p46,122
　　Logan—Part p509
　　*MacVeagh—Champlin p347-348

Lee, Anne Aylett (d. 1767)
　　Amer. patriot
　　Green—Pioneer (3) p235-240

Lee, Auriol (c. 1880-1941)
　　Eng. actress, director, producer
　　Cur. Biog. '41 p503-504

Lee, Brenda (1944-　　)
　　Amer. singer
　　CR '63 p362, por.
　　Kahn—Tops p95-100,por,cover
　　Stambler—Ency. p135-136
　　TV—Person (3) p63-65,por.

Lee, Bridget.
　　See Fuller, Bridget Lee

Lee, Doris Emrick (1905-　　)
　　Amer. artist
　　Cur. Biog. '54 p401-403,por.
　　Ency. Brit.—Amer. p72,por.

Lee, Dorothy McCullough (1901-　　)
　　Amer. mayor, lawyer
　　Cur. Biog. '49 p346-347,por.
　　Roosevelt—Ladies p77-84

Lee, Eliza Buckminster (1794-1864)
　　Amer. novelist, translator
　　Dorland—Sum p32

Lee, Frances Marron (fl. 1950's-1960's)
　　Amer. rancher, politician
　　Parshalle—Kash. p119-120,por.

Lee, Gypsy Rose (1914-1970)
　　Amer. actress, author
　　CR '59 p428,por.
　　CR '63 p362,por.
　　Cur. Biog. '43 p434-436,por.
　　Rogers—Women p192,por.

Lee, Hannah Farnham Sawyer (1780-1865)
　　Amer. author
　　Hanaford—Dau. p229-230
　　Papashvily—All p44,47

Lee, Hannah Ludwell (fl. 1770's)
　　Amer. pioneer
　　Green—Pioneer (3) p237,282

Lee, Harriet (1757-1851)
　　Eng. novelist
　　MacCarthy—Later p146-153

Lee, Helen (n.d.)
　　Amer. fashion designer
　　Epstein—Young p89-106

Lee, Henrietta Bedinger (fl. 1860's)
　　Amer. Civil war letter-writer
　　Andrews—Women p201-204
　　Jones—Heroines p309-312

Lee, Jennette Barbour Perry (1860-1951)
　　Amer. teacher, author
　　Logan—Part p843

Lee, Jennie(1904-　　)
　　Eng. Parliamentary member,
　　　politician
　　Cur. Biog. '46 p337-340,por.
　　Hammerton p889-890,1450

Lee, Mrs. John G. (1906-　　)
　　Amer. organization official
　　Cur. Biog. '50 p331-333
　　Murrow—This (1) p97-98

Lee, Lila (1901-　　)
　　Amer. actress
　　Lamparski—What. p108-109,por.

Lee, Lillie (fl. 1850's)
　　Amer. W. pioneer
　　Brown—Gentle p87-88

Lee, Lucy Grymes (fl. 1780's)
　　Amer. pioneer
　　Green—Pioneer (3) p282

Lee, Mary Aldridge.
　　See Slingsby, Mary Aldridge, Lady

Lee, Mary Ann (1826-1899)
　　Amer. pioneer ballet dancer
　　Stern—We p5-28,por.
　　*Terry—Star p92-95,por.

Lee, Mary E. (d. 1849)
    Amer. author
    Hanaford—Dau. p244

Lee, Mary Randolph Custis (1806-1873)
    Amer. Civil war heroine, wife of
        General Lee
    Harkness—Heroines p2
    Jones—Heroines p23-24,26-27,403-404

Lee, Mary W. (fl. 1860's)
    Irish-Amer. Civil war nurse,
        patriot, philanthropist
    Brockett—Woman's p480-488
    Moore—Women p148-169

Lee, Nelle Harper (Lee Harper) (1926-   )
    Amer. author
    CR '63 p362-363,por.
    Cur. Biog. '61 p260-262,por.

Lee, Norah (1898-1941)
    Amer. composer
    ASCAP p298

Lee, Peggy (Peggy Lee Barbour) (1920-   )
    Amer. singer, composer, actress,
        business woman
    ASCAP p22
    CR '59 p428,por.
    CR '63 p363,por.
    Cur. Biog. '63 p237-239,por.
    Popular Record p83,por.
    Stambler—Ency. p136-137,por.
    TV—Person (2) p18-19,por.

Lee, Rebecca (gr. 1864)
    Amer. pioneer physician
    Lovejoy—Women p82,121

Lee, Rebecca Tayloe (d. 1797)
    Amer. Rev. war patriot
    Green—Pioneer (3) p254-256

Lee, Rosamond (fl. 1930's)
    Amer. business executive
        journalist, advertising director
    Women—Achieve. p124,por.

Lee, Sarah Gould (1821-1905)
    Amer. pioneer
    Brown—Home. p86-89

Lee, Sophia (1750-1824)
    Eng. playwright, novelist
    MacCarthy—Later p142-146

Lee, Vernon, pseud. (Violet Paget) (1856-
        1935)
    Brit. author
    Millett—Brit. p326-328

Leech, Lida Shivers (b. 1873)
    Amer. composer, author
    ASCAP p298

Leech, Margaret Kernochan (1893-   )
    Amer. author, historian
    Cur. Biog. '42 p492-494,por.
    Cur. Biog. '60 p230-232,por.
    Mantle—Contemp. p201-202
    Van Gelder—Writers p212-215

Lees, Dacre (fl. 1870's)
    Eng. nurse
    Dolan—Goodnow's p268-269

Leese, Mary Elizabeth (b. 1853)
    Amer. politican
    Logan—Part p292

Leete, Harriet L. (d. 1927)
    Amer. nurse
    Pennock—Makers p99,por.

Lefaucheux, Marie-Hélène(1904-1964)
    Fr. U.N. representative
    Cur. Biog. '47 p385-386,por.
    Cur. Biog. '64 p253

Lefebre, Madame (fl.c. 1850's)
    Fr. inventor
    Mozans—Woman p353-354

Leffler-Burkhardt, Madame (fl. 1890's-
        1900's)
    Ger. singer
    Lahee—Grand p60-61,278

Le Gallienne, Eva (1899-   )
    Eng. actress
    Blum—Great p90,por.
    Brown—Upstage p129-135
    Coad—Amer. p323,por.
    CR '59 p428,por.
    CR '63 p363,por.
    Cur. Biog. '42 p494-497,por.
    Cur. Biog. '55 p349-352,por.
    *Logie—Careers p278-287,por.
    New Yorker April 6,1929 p29-32,por.
        (Profiles)
    Ormsbee—Back. p250-253,por.
    Stone—We p136-143
    Time Nov. 25,1929 p32,por.(Cover)

Legaré, Mary Swinton (fl. 1840's)
    Amer. artist
    Hanaford—Dau. p295

Leger, Elizabeth Saint (b. 1693)
    Irish Mason
    Muir—Women p113-115

Leggett, Mary Lydia (b. 1852)
    Amer. clergyman
    Logan—Part p737

Leginska, Ethel Liggins (1890-   )
    Eng. pianist, conductor, composer
    Elson—Woman's p244-246,por.
    McCoy—Portraits p112,por.

Legnani, Pierina (1863-1923)
    It. ballet dancer
*Terry—Star p106-107,por.

Le Grand, Julia (fl. 1860's)
    Amer. Civil war diarist
Jones—Heroines p124-128,193-195

Le Grange, Ann (fl. 1930's)
    Amer. fashion designer
Women—Achieve. p175,por.

Le Gras, Louise, Madame (Louise de
        Marrilac, Saint) (1591-1660)
    Fr. saint, nurse, philanthropist
Blunt—Great p166-168
Dolan—Goodnow's p144-145
Englebert—Lives p103
McKown—Heroic p17-23
Stiles—Postal p236

Le Hand, Marguerite (fl. 1920's)
    Amer. secretary, government
        employee
Time Dec.17,1934 p11,por.(Cover)

Lehman, Edith (fl. 1930's)
    Amer. humanitarian
Women—Achieve. p39,por.

Lehman, Evangeline (fl. 1940's)
    Amer. composer, singer
McCoy—Portraits p12,por.

Lehmann, Charlotte (b. 1860)
    Aust. painter
Waters—Women p207

Lehmann, Elizabetta Nina Mary Frederika.
See Lehmann, Liza

Lehmann, Inge (b. 1888)
    Dan. seismologist, geodesist
Cur. Biog. '62 p250-252,por.

Lehmann, Lilli (1848-1929)
    Ger. singer
Adelman—Famous p280
Davidson—Treas. p160-163
Ewen—Ency. p256-257
Hammerton p892
Klein—Great p215-223,por.
Lahee—Famous p178-181
McCoy—Portraits p112,por.
Pleasants—Great p233-242,por.
Saleski—Jewish p598-600,por.
Saleski—Wander. p414-417,por.
Wagnalls—Opera p372-378,por.
Wagner—Prima p93-94,129,244

Lehmann, Liza (1862-1918)
    Eng. singer
Adelman—Famous p296
Elson—Woman's p146-148
Hammerton p892
McCoy—Portraits p112,por.

Lehmann, Lotte (b. 1888)
    Ger. singer
CR '59 p429,por.
CR '63 p364,por.
Cur. Biog. '41 p504-506,por.
Davidson—Treas. p164-166
Downes—Olin p173-176
Eustis—Players p118-127,por.
Ewen—Ency. p257-258
Ewen—Living p212-214,por.
Ewen—Men p54-66,por.
Gelatt—Music p121-132,por.
Hammerton p892
McCoy—Portraits p112,por.
New Yorker Feb. 23,1935 p20-24,por.
    (Profiles)
Peltz—Spot. p49,por.
Time Feb.18,1935 p48,por.(Cover)
Wagner—Prima p80-82,184,244
Women—Achieve. p45,por.

Lehmann, Rosamond (c. 1904-   )
    Eng. novelist
Millett—Brit. p328

Leider, Frida (b. 1888)
    Ger. singer
Ewen—Ency. p258
Ewen—Living p214,por.
McCoy—Portraits p112,por.

Leidig, Isabela ("Belle") Dobie (fl. 1880's)
    Amer. W. pioneer
Sargent—Pioneers p20-22,por.

Leigh, Adèle (1928-   )
    Eng. singer
Davidson—Treas. p167-168
Rosenthal—Sopranos p62-63,por.

Leigh, Dorian (1919-   )
    Amer. model, business executive
CR '59 p429-430,por.
CR '63 p364-365,por.

Leigh, Elinor (fl. 1672-1709)
    Eng. actress
MacQueen—Pope p119
Wilson—All p162-165

Leigh, Ethel. See Traphagen, Ethel

Leigh, Janet (1927-   )
    Amer. actress
CR '59 p430,por.
CR '63 p365,por.

Leigh, Vera (fl. 1940's)
    Eng. spy
Hoehling—Women p128-129,por.

Leigh, Vivien (1913-1967)
    Brit. actress
Blum—Great p136,por.
Cocroft—Great p238-264,por.

(Continued)

Leigh, Vivien—*Continued*

> CR '59 p430-431,por.
> CR '63 p365,por.
> Cur. Biog. '46 p340-342,por.
> Cur. Biog. '67 p479
> Funke—Actors p235-256,por.,end-paper
> Time Dec.25,1939 p30,por.(Cover)

Leigh-Smith, Barbara.
> See Bodichon, Barbara Leigh-Smith

Leighton, Margaret (1922-   )
> Eng. actress
> CR '59 p431,por.
> CR '63 p365-366,por.
> Cur. Biog. '57 p319-321,por.
> Ross—Player p386-393,por.

Leighton, Margaret Carver (1896-   )
> Amer. author
> Cur. Biog. '52 p340-342,por.

Leinster, Jessie Smither Fitzgerald, Duchess
> of (Denise Orme) (1874-1960)
> Eng. dancer
> Wyndham—Chorus p117-118,por.

Leis, B. Eugenia (fl. 1930's)
> Amer. retailer
> Women—Achieve. p124,por.

Leitch, Charlotte Cecilia Pitcairn (1890-   )
> Eng. golfer
> Hammerton p893

Leitch, Mary Sinton Lewis (b. 1876)
> Amer. poet
> Smith—Women's p132

Leiter, Fannie W. (b. 1844)
> Amer. social reformer
> Hanaford—Dau. p399-402

Leiter, Mary Victoria, Lady Curzon
> (d. 1906)
> Amer. heiress
> Pearson—Pilgrim p99-112,por.

Leitzel, Lillian (1891-1931)
> Ger. aerialist
> New Yorker, Apr.21,1956 p45,por.
> Apr.28,1956 p47 (Profiles)

"L.E.L." See Landon, Letitia Elizabeth

Lelash, Ethelyn L. (fl. 1930's)
> Amer. business school executive
> Women—Achieve. p66,por.

Le Mair, Henriette Willebeek (Saida,
> pseud.) (b. 1889)
> Nether. illustrator
> Mahony—Illus. p332

Lemaire, Madeleine Jeane (1845/46-1928)
> Fr. painter
> Waters—Women p207-209

Lemmon, Sarah A. Plummer (fl. 1860's)
> Amer. Civil war nurse
> Logan—Part p367

Lemnitz, Tiana (1897-   )
> Ger. singer
> Ewen—Living p215

Lemon, Catharine (fl.c. 1786)
> Amer. W. pioneer
> Ellet—Pioneer p304

Lemon, Dot (fl. 1920's-1930's)
> Amer. aviatrix
> Planck—Women p179-181

Lemond, Margaret ("Maggie") (fl. 1950's)
> Eng. camp director
> Winn—Queen's p85,89-97,por.

LeMoyne, Sarah Cowell (fl. 1890's)
> Amer. actress
> Strang—Actresses p39-49,por.

Lenanton, Carola.
> See Oman, Carola Mary Anima

Lenart, Marian F. (fl. 1930's)
> Amer. business executive
> Women—Achieve. p161,por.

L'Enclos, Ninon (Anne) **de** (1616/20-
> 1705/06)
> Fr. courtesan
> Abbot—Notable p227-231
> Adelman—Famous p58
> Blei—Fasc. p65-78,por.
> Bradford—Dau. p1-32,por.
> Gade—Under p154-181,por.
> Hall—Moths p211-229,por.
> Hammerton p894
> Kavanagh—Woman p16-17
> Koven—Women p272-273,por.
> Mayne—Enchant. p95-108,por.
> Terhune—Super. p19-40

L'Engle, Madeleine (1918-   )
> Amer. novelist
> Warfel—Amer. p263,por.

Lenglen, Suzanne (1899-1938)
> Fr. tennis player
> Davis—100 p68,por.
> Gardiner—Por. p129-137
> Hammerton p894
> New Yorker Feb.27,1926 p15-17,por.
> (Profiles)

Lenihan, Winifred (1898-   )
> Amer. actress
> Coad—Amer. p324,por.

Lennox, Charlotte Ramsay (1720-1804)
Amer. novelist
Coad—Amer. p21,por.
Dorland—Sum p52,193
MacCarthy—Later p44-57

Lennox, Mary Anne Paton, Lady Pitt
(d. 1864)
Eng. singer, actress
Wyndham—Chorus p55-58,por.

Lennox, Peggy (fl. 1930's-1940's)
Amer. aviatrix, flying instructor
*May—Women p185
Planck—Women p157

Lennox, Sarah, Lady.
See Napier, Sarah Lennox Bunbury,
Lady

Lenroot, Katharine Fredrica (1891-   )
Amer. government official, social
worker
*Clymer—Modern p61-71,por.
Cur. Biog. '40 p493-495,por.
Cur. Biog. '50 p338-340,por.
Rogers—Women p71
Women—Achieve. p53,por.

Lenski, Lois (1893-   )
Amer. illustrator, author
Mahony—Illus. p333

Lent, Sylvia (1923-   )
Amer. violinist
McCoy—Portraits p113,por.

Lenya, Lotte (1905-   )
Aust. actress
CR '59 p432,por.
CR '63 p367,por.
Cur. Biog. '59 p254-256,por.

Leoba. See Lioba

Leocadia (d.c. 303)
Sp. saint
Englebert—Lives p467
Phila. —Women unp.
Stiles—Postal p236
Wescott—Calen. p59

Leofgyth. See Lioba

Lenngren, Anna Malmstedt (1754-1817)
Swed. poet
Hammerton p896
Schmidt—400 p367-368,por.
Stiles—Postal p152

Léon, Léonie (d. 1906)
Orr—Famous p317-333
Orr—Famous Affin. III p37-57

Leonard, Anita 1922-   )
Amer. composer, author
ASCAP p300-301

Leonard, Anna Byford (b. 1843)
Amer. sociologist, social reformer,
social leader
Logan—Part p596

Leonard, Cynthia H. Van Name (b. 1828)
Amer. philanthropist
Logan—Part p527-528

Leonard, Florence (fl. 1940's)
Amer. musician, pianist, music
teacher, author
McCoy—Portraits p113,por.

Leonard, Helen Louise.
See Russell, Lillian

Leonard, Lucille Putnam (1895-   )
Amer. organization official
Cur. Biog. '53 p355-356,por.

Leonard, Lydia. See Cobb, Lydia

Leonard, Myrtle (fl. 1930's)
Amer. singer
McCoy—Portraits p113,por.

Leonard, Mrs. Willard A. (fl. 1860's)
Amer. government employee,
money specialist
Logan—Part p901

Leone, Lucile Petry. See Petry, Lucile

Leone, Maria (n.d.)
It.-Amer. singer
Matz—Opera p272-274

Leonor (1458-1526)
Port. queen
Stiles—Postal p152

Leonora, Ulrica (fl. 1740's-1760's)
Ger., sister of Frederick the Great
Russell—Glit. p277-278

Leonowens, Anna Harriette Crawford
(d. 1915)
Welsh governess (in Siam)
Holmes—Seven p79-111
Howe—Galaxy p162-167,por.

Leontium (340's-270's B.C.)
Gr. courtesan, mistress of Epicurus,
philosopher
Boccaccio—Conc. p132

Leopold, Alice Koller (1909-   )
Amer. government official, politician
Cur. Biog. '55 p359-361,por.
Roosevelt—Ladies p119-130

Leopoldina, D. Maria (fl. 1797-1826)
Brazil. empress
Stiles—Postal p153

Lepaute, Hortense (fl.c. 1750's)
Fr. astronomer
Mozans—Woman p178-181

Lepaute, Nicole R. (1723-1788)
Fr. Mathematician
Adelman—Famous p82

Lepell, Mary, Lady Hervey (1700-1768)
Eng. maid-of-honor
Melville—Maids p176-198

Lepeshinskaya, Ol'ga Borisovna (1871-
1963)
Russ. biologist
U.S.—Biog., Soviet p373-374

Lepida, Domitia. See **Domitia Lepida**

Lepi'n (Liyzpinya), Lidiya Karlovna
(1891-   )
Russ. physico-chemist
U.S.—Biog. Soviet p374-375

Leporin-Erxleben, Dorothea Christin (1715-
1762)
Ger. pioneer physician
Lovejoy—Women p189-190
Mozans—Woman p293

Lepsius, Sabina (fl. 1900's)
Ger. painter
Waters—Women p382

Lerch, Louise (c. 1895-1967)
Amer. singer
McCoy—Portraits p113,por.

Leris, Claire Josephe.
See **Clairon, Mademoiselle**

Lerner, Tina (1889/1900-   )
Russ. pianist
McCoy—Portraits p113,por.
Saleski—Wander. p336-338

Le Roux, Yvonne (1882-1945)
Fr. heroine, patriot
Stiles—Postal p153

Leroy, Anita (n.d.)
Amer. painter, illustrator
Michigan—Biog. p187

Le Roy, Kitty (fl. 1870's)
Amer. W. pioneer
Brown—Gentle p85-86

Lert, Mrs. Richard. See **Baum, Vicki**

"Lesbia." See **Clodia**

Lesczczynska, Marie (1703-1768)
Fr. queen, wife of Louis XV
Haggard—Remark. p233-236,240-252,
339-341
Kemble—Idols p63-64
Schmidt—400 p317-318,por.

Leser, Tina (1901-   )
Amer. fashion designer
CR '59 p434,por.
CR '63 p368-369,por.
Cur. Biog. '57 p321-323

Le Seur, Elizabeth Arrighi (1866-1914)
Fr. mystic
Eustace—Infinity p96-117,por.
Graef—Mystics p107-126

Leslie, Amy (fl. 1920's)
Amer. journalist, dramatic critic
Ross—Ladies p408-409

Leslie, Ann (fl. 1880's)
Amer. artist
Hanaford—Dau. p293

Leslie, Eliza (1787-1858)
Amer. author, editor, humorist,
cookery expert
Bruère—Laugh. p12-13
Dorland—Sum p19,119
Hanaford—Dau. p230-233

Leslie, Joan (1925-   )
Amer. actress
Lamparski—What. p200-201,por.

Leslie, Mabel (fl. 1930's)
Amer. club leader
Women—Achieve. p171,por.

Leslie, Miriam Florence Folline (c. 1836-
1914)
Amer. publisher, editor, feminist,
philanthropist, social leader
Adelman—Famous p247
Brown—Gentle p185-186
Davenport—Ladies p43-49
Farmer—What p147,430-434,por.
Holbrook—Dreamers p219-221
Logan—Part p873-874
Pearson—Pilgrim p177-187
Ross—Charmers p61-88,285-287,por.
Schmidt—400 p14,por.

Leslie, Nan (1926-   )
Amer. actress
TV—Person (2) p17-18,por.

L'Esperance, Elise Depew Strang (c. 1879-
1959)
Amer. physician, foundress
Cur. Biog. '50 p340-341,por.
Cur. Biog. '59 p256
Lovejoy—Women p76,97,127-128,por.
1776)

Lespinasse, Julie Jeanne Éléonore de (1732-
1776)
Fr. salonist, author
Adelman—Famous p84
Bradford—Dau. p115-153,por.

(Continued)

Lespinasse, Julie—*Continued*

    De Morny—Best p60-68
    Dorland—Sum p104
    Hammerton p900,por.
    Herold—Love p193-257,por.
    Kavanagh—Woman (1) p177-192
    Mozans—Woman p89-91
    Tallentyre—Women p22-39,por.

Lesser, Margaret Helen (fl. 1930's)
    Amer. editor
    Women—Achieve. p189,por.

Lessing, Doris (1919-   )
    Brit. novelist
    Shapiro—Contemp. p48-61

Lessing, Madge (fl. 1890's)
    Eng.-Amer. singer
    Strang—Prima p81-87,por.

Lester, Muriel (b. 1883)
    Eng. social worker, Gandhi
        co-worker
    Bartlett—They p105-108
    Lotz—Women p57-65
    Stern—Women p146-148,por.

Lev, Ray (1912-   )
    Russ.-Amer. pianist
    Cur. Biog. '49 p353-354,por.
    Ewen—Living p216-217,por.
    McCoy—Portraits p114,por.
    Saleski—Jewish p508-509,por.

Leveroni, Elvira (fl. 1900's)
    Amer. singer
    Lahee—Grand p371-372

Leverson, Sarah Rachel (1806-1888)
    Eng. accused criminal
    Jenkins—Six p1-30

Le Vert, Octavia Walton (1810-1877)
    Amer. author
    Hanaford—Dau. p147-148

Levett, Ada Elizabeth (gr. 1910)
    Eng. author, educator
    Brittain—Women p55,124,142, 185,
        206,245

Levey, Ethel (c. 1881-1955)
    Eng. actress, philanthropist
    Asquith—Myself p157-171,por.
    Felstead—Stars p103

Levick, Ruby Winifred (fl. 1890's)
    Welsh sculptor
    Waters—Women p209-210

Levis, Elizabeth (fl. 1750's)
    Amer. colonial clergyman
    Dexter—Colonial p148

Levi-Tanai, Sara (n.d.)
    Israeli director, composer,
        choreographer
    Cur. Biog. '58 p246-247,por.

Lewald, Fanny (1811-1889)
    Ger. author
    Hammerton p902
    Heller—Studies p241,245-246

Lewars, Mrs. Harold.
    See **Singmaster, Elsie**

Lewing, Adele (1866-1943)
    Ger. pianist, composer, music
        teacher
    Cur. Biog. '43 p445
    McCoy—Portraits p115,por.

Lewinson, Ruth (fl.1920's-1930's)
    Amer. lawyer
    Women—Achieve. p93,por.

Lewinson, Thea Stein (fl. 1930's)
    Ger.-Amer. graphologist
    Women—Achieve. p199-200

Lewis, Agnes Smith (1843-1926)
    Scot. archaeologist, Orientalist
    Adelman—Famous p306-307
    Mozans—Woman p327-333

Lewis, Ann. See Robertson, Ann Lewis

Lewis, Mrs. Arthur (fl. 19th cent.)
    Eng. hostess
    Furniss—Some p199-200

Lewis, Brenda (1921-   )
    Amer. singer
    Matz—Opera p190-192
    Saleski—Jewish p600-601,por.

Lewis, Delecta Barbour (fl. 1850's)
    Amer. social reformer
    Irwin—Angels p70,193

Lewis, Edmonia (1845-1890)
    Amer. pioneer sculptor
    Adams—Great p158,por.
    Adelman—Famous p277-278
    Hanaford—Dau. p316-318
    Michigan—Biog. p188-189
    Robinson—Hist. p95-96,por.
    Tuckerman—Book p603-604
    Waters—Women p210-211

Lewis, Eleanor Parke Custis ("Nellie"
    Custis) (c. 1779-1852)
    Amer. social leader, granddaughter
        of George Washington
    Green—Pioneer (2) p75,por.
    Hanaford—Dau. p144
    Sale—Old p234-246,por.
    Sweetser—Famous p1-22,por.

Lewis, Elizabeth Annesley (m. 1745)
    Amer. patriot
    Green—Pioneer (3) p119-126

Lewis, Elizabeth ("Betty") Washington
    (d. 1797)
    Amer. Rev. war patriot
    Green—Pioneer (1) p474-482
    Green—Pioneer (2) p72-78

Lewis, Estelle Anna Blanche (1824-1880)
    Amer. playwright, poet
    Adelman—Famous p181-182
    Dorland—Sum p25,72,179
    Hanaford—Dau. p266-267

Lewis, Ethel (fl. 1930's)
    Amer. interior decorator
    Women—Achieve. p79,por.

Lewis, Ethelinda. See Claghorn,Ethelinda

Lewis,Ethelreda (189?-1946)
    S. Afr. novelist
    Cur. Biog. '46 p342

Lewis, Flora (1903-   )
    Amer. painter
    Janis—They p208-212,por.

Lewis, Grace Anna (b.1821)
    Amer. ornithologist
    Hanaford—Dau. p279-282
    Logan—Part p877-878

Lewis, Ida. See Arthur, Julia (actress)

Lewis, Idawalley (1814-c. 1910)
    Amer. lighthouse heroine
    Carmer—Young p195-201
    Dolin—World p92-97
    Hanaford—Dau. p156-162,por.
    *Horowitz—Treas. p71-75
    Logan—Dau. p156-162,por.
    *Strong—Of p197-201

Lewis, Jane Mary Dealy, Lady (fl. 1900's)
    Eng. etcher, painter
    Waters—Women p101-102

Lewis, Janet (1899-   )
    Amer. novelist, poet
    Warfel—Amer. p265

Lewis, Jean Satterlee (fl. 1930's)
    Amer. meteorologist
    Planck—Women p222-223,por.

Lewis, Mrs. Lawrence (fl. 1910's)
    Amer. feminist
    Irwin—Angels p382-387

Lewis, Lillian Callis (fl. 1940's-1950's)
    Amer. missionary
    They—Went p118-119

Lewis, Louise Hills (1887-1948)
    Amer. composer, religious worker,
        hymn-writer
    Phillips—33 p182-185

Lewis, Margaret (fl. 1732-1776)
    Amer. pioneer
    *Stevens—Women p15-19

Lewis, Margaret (b. 1881)
    Amer. medical research worker,
        cytologist
    Castiglioni—Hist. p1127

Lewis, Mary (1897-   )
    Amer. fashion designer
    Cur. Biog. '40 p498-500,por.
    *Stoddard—Top. p102-108

Lewis, Mary Anne (d. 1866)
    Amer., dau. of Major William Lewis
    Smith—White p48-49

Lewis, Mary Carlile (fl. 1930's)
    Amer. business executive
    Women—Achieve. p181,por.

Lewis, Mary Sybil (1900-1941)
    Amer. singer
    Cur. Biog. '42 p515
    McCoy—Portraits p115,por.

Lewis, Millicent Porter.
    See Camp, Milicent Baldwin Porter

Lewis, Rosa Ovenden (fl. 1930's)
    Amer. hotel manager
    New Yorker Sept.16,1933 p25-28,por.
    (Profiles)

Lewis, Sarah Anna.
    See Lewis, Estelle Anna Blanche

Lewis, Sarah Masten (d. 1931)
    Amer. singer
    Cuney-Hare—Negro p221

Lewis, Shari (1934-   )
    Amer. TV personality, puppeteer,
        ventriloquist
    CR '63 p372,por.
    Cur. Biog. '58 p247-249,por.

Lewis, Mrs. Wyndham.
    See Beaconsfield, Mary Anne Evans
    Disraeli, Viscountess

Lewisohn, Alice Irene (fl. 1910's)
    Amer. theatrical founder
    Coad—Amer. p318

Lewisohn, Irene (fl. 1910's-1930's)
    Amer. social worker, humanitarian
    Women—Achieve. p117,por.

Lewisohn, Margaret S. (1895-1954)
    Amer. art. sponsor, club leader,
        educator
    Women—Achieve. p75,por.

Lewyn, Helena (fl. 1940's)
    Amer. pianist, teacher
    McCoy—Portraits p115,por.

Ley, Sophie (b. 1859)
    Aust. painter
    Waters—Women p211-212

Leyster, Judith Molenaer (1600-1660)
    Nether. painter
    Waters—Women p382-383

Lhevinne, Rosina (b. 1880)
    Russ.-Amer. pianist, music teacher
    CR '63 p373,por.
    Cur. Biog. '61 p269-271,por.
    Ewen—Living p220,por.
    McCoy—Portraits p115,por.
    New Yorker Jan. 12,1963 p37,por.
        (Profiles)

Li, Katherine Yuch-Yuin (1911-   )
    Chin. physician, surgeon
    Knapp—Women p1-15,por.

Li, Mistress (fl. 17th cent.)
    Chin. concubine
    Llewellyn—China's p148,150-151

Liadain (fl. 9th cent.)
    Irish poet
    Concannon—Dau. p230-231

Libbey, Laura Jean (1862-1924)
    Amer. author
    Papashvily—All p199-200,202-204
    Pattee—Fem. p125-126

Licata-Faccioli, Orsola (b. 1826)
    It. painter
    Waters—Women p212

Li Ch'ing-Chao (b. 1081)
    Chin. poet
    Ayscough—Chinese p178-195

Lichtmann, Sina (fl. 1930's)
    Russ.-Amer. pianist
    Women—Achieve. p111,por.

Liddell, Mary (1891-   )
    Amer. illustrator
    Mahony—Illus. p33

Lidwina (d. 1433)
    Nether. saint
    Wescott—Calen. p53-54

Liebling, Estelle (b. 1884/86)
    Amer. composer, singer, teacher,
        editor
    ASCAP p306
    McCoy—Portraits p115,por.

Liebes, Dorothy Wright (1899-   )
    Amer. weaver, textile designer
    Cur. Biog. '48 p376-378,por.

Liedloff, Helen (fl. 1930's)
    Amer. sculptor
    Women—Achieve. p129,por.

Lieven, Dorothea (1785-1857)
    Russ. diplomat, princess
    Adelman—Famous p109
    De Morny—Best p53-59
    Stebbins—London p117-158

Lifelike, Miriam (1851-1887)
    Haw. Isl. princess
    Arsenius—Dict. p116,por.
    Phila.—Women, unp.,por.
    Stiles—Postal p154

Light, Mary (fl. 1930's)
    Amer. aeronautical photographer
    Planck—Women p240-241

Lightfoot, Hannah (b. 1730)
    Eng. maid-of-honor
    Melville—Maids p284-303,por.

Lightstone, Pauline.
    See Donalda, Pauline Mischa Léon

Lilioukolani, Lydia Kamekeha (1838-1917)
    Haw. Isl. queen
    Arsenius—Hist. p117,por.
    Hammerton p905
    Phila.—Women, unp.,por.
    Stiles—Postal p155

Lilith (Biblical)
    Ewart—World's p18-19

Lillenas, Bertha Mae (1889-1945)
    Amer. composer, author
    ASCAP p308

"Lilliard" (fl. 1540's)
    Scot. soldier, "Amazon"
    Graham—Group p26

Lillie, Beatrice, Lady Peel (1898-   )
    Can. actress
    Beaton—Persona p66-67,por.
    Blum—Great p116,por.
    Cantor—As p124-126,por.
    CR '59 p440-441,por.
    CR '63 p374-375,por.
    Cur. Biog. '45 p347-350
    Cur. Biog. '64 p255-258,por.
    New Yorker Sept.19,1931 p22-25,por.
        (Profiles)

Lilly, Doris (1926-   )
    Amer. author, journalist
    CR '63 p375,por.

Lily of the Merovingians. See Clotilda

Lima, Sigrid de. See De Lima, Sigrid

Limardo, Mercedes Emilia (1855-1906)
  Venez. educator, translator
  Schmidt—400 p418,por.

Lincoln, Bathsheba (m. 1770)
  Amer., grandmother of Abraham
    Lincoln
  Barton—Women p51-59

Lincoln, Jennie Gould (fl. 1910's)
  Amer. author, social leader
  Logan—Part p854

Lincoln, Margaret, Countess of (d. 1266)
  Eng. hostess
  Stenton—English p52,56

Lincoln, Mary Johnson Bailey (1844-1921)
  Amer. educator, author, lecturer,
    home economist
  Logan—Part p830

Lincoln, Mary Todd (1818-1882)
  Amer., wife of Abraham Lincoln
  Balch—Modern p154-175,por.
  Barton—Women p210-368,por.
  Beckwith—Contemp. p95-117
  Bradford—Wives p15-52,por.
  Carnegie—Little p133-137,por.
  Gerlinger—Mis. p51-53,por.
  Hanaford—Dau. p91-93
  Jensen—White p83-94,por.
  Leetch—Reveille p285-310,447
  Logan—Ladies p86-93
  Logan—Part 263-265
  Love—Famous p21-22
  *McConnell—Our p157-169,por.
  Means—Women p74-115,por.
  Prindiville—First p140-149
  *Ross—Know p35,por.
  Schmidt—400 p13-14,por.
  Smith—Romances p225-229,por.
  Truett—First p42-43,por.
  Whitton—First p284-302,por.
  Young—Women p331-335,338

Lincoln, Nancy Hanks (1783/84-1818)
  Amer., mother of Abraham Lincoln
  Adelman—Famous p113
  Bartlett—Mothers p60-64
  Barton—Women p60-97
  Farmer—What p61-62
  Hampton—Our p121-131
  Hughes—Mothers p131-138
  Peyton—Mothers p75-81
  Wallace—Mothers p56-62

Lincoln, Sarah Bush Johnston (1788-1869)
  Amer., step-mother of Abraham
    Lincoln
  Barton—Women p98-108
  *Chandler—Famous p199-208
  Parton—Noted p19-25,por.
  Wallace—Mothers p63-68

Lincoln, Victoria (1904-   )
  Amer. novelist
  Warfel—Amer. p269-270,por.

Lind, Jenny (Johanna Maria Lind-
    Goldschmidt) (1820/21-1887)
  Swed. singer
  Abbot—Notable p332-336
  Adelman—Famous p162-163,por.
  *Bolton—Lives p223-235,por.
  Coad—Amer. p193,por.
  Davidson—Treas. p169-172
  Dorland—Sum p16, 162
  *Elson—Side (1) p257-261
  Ewen—Ency. p265
  Hammerton p907,por.
  Holroyd—Fifty p199-202
  Howard—Our p199, 202-204, 233
  *Humphrey—Janes p15-42
  Lahee—Famous p81-88,por.
  Lotz—Women p66-76
  McCoy—Portraits p116,por.
  *MacVeagh—Champlin p355
  Marks—Glamour p127-137,por.
  Mayne—Enchant. p263-275,por.
  Muir—Women p166-167
  Pattee—Fem. p148-156,por.
  Pleasants—Great p197-204,por.
  *Pringle—When p103-116
  Schmidt—400 p371-372,por.
  *Steedman—When p309-323
  *Trease—Seven stages p109-139,por.
  Ulrich—Famous p3-7,por.
  Wagenknecht—Seven p3-49,por.
  Wagner—Prima p114-115, 244

Lind, Paula (fl. 1940's)
  Amer. aviatrix
  *Peckham—Women p144

Lind-af-Hageby, Emelie Augusta Louise
    (b. 1878)
  Anglo-Swed. author
  Hammerton p907

Lindbergh, Anne Spencer Morrow
    (1906-   )
  Amer. pioneer aviatrix, author, poet
  *Adams—Sky p215-236,por.
  CR'59 p442,por.
  CR'63 p376,por.
  Cur. Biog. '40 p505-508,por.
  Earhart—Fun p170-175,por.
  Forsee—My p75-108
  *Fraser—Heroes p609-614, 665-676
  *Lauwick—Heroines p147-159,por.
  Love—Famous p43
  *May—Women p123,128-131,209,215-
    216
  Planck—Women p103,108,230-231
  Rogers—Women p140,por.

Lindegren, Amalia (1814-1891)
  Swed. painter
  Waters—Women p212-213

Lindem, Selma Marie (fl. 1930's)
Amer. librarian
Women—Achieve. p114,por.

Lindfors, Elsa Viveca Torstensdotter
(1920-   )
Swed.-Amer. actress
CR '59 p443,por.
Cur. Biog. '55 p363-364,por.

Lind-Goldschmidt, Johanna Maria.
See Lind, Jenny

Lindheim, Irma (b. 1886)
Amer. club-leader, author
Ribalow—Auto. p420-445

Lindsay, Anne, Lady (d. 1700)
Scot. covenanter
Anderson—Ladies p199-212

Lindsay, Anne Barnard, Lady (1750-1825)
Scot. song-writer, poet
Findlay—Spindle p85-113,por.

Lindsay, Charlotte, Lady (b. 1770)
Eng. lady-in-waiting
Melville—Regency p119-120

Lindsay, Dorothy. See Stickney, Dorothy

Lindsay, Henrietta, Lady Campbell
(1657/58-c.1721)
Scot. covenanter
Anderson—Ladies p395-427

Lindsay, Malvina (fl. 1930's)
Amer. journalist
Ross—Ladies p84,505-507

Line, Anne (d. 1601)
Eng. religious martyr
Blunt—Great p248-249

Linley, Elizabeth (1754-1792)
Eng. singer
Adelman—Famous p89-90
Sitwell—Women p16,por.

Linn, Bambi (1926-   )
Amer. ballet dancer
CR '63 p377,por.

Linn, Nancy Hunter (fl. 18th cent.)
Amer. pioneer
Green—Pioneer (3) p327,385-388

Linton, Elizabeth (Eliza) Lynn (1822-
1898)
Eng. novelist
Black—Notable p1-10,por.
Dorland—Sum p19,79,196
Stebbins—Victorian p7-12,197,204-
205

Linton, Laura A. (b. 1853)
Amer. scientist
Logan—Part p878

Linwood, Mary (1755-1845)
Eng. composer, needlework artist
Elson—Women's p133

Lioba (Leoba, Leofgyth) (d. 779/780)
Ger. saint, abbess, poet
Deen—Great p324-325
Stenton—English p14-17
Wescott—Calen. p147

Lion, Elisabeth (fl. 1910's)
Fr. pioneer aviatrix
*Lauwick—Heroines p28-29

Lipei Naij (Elizabeth Worth) (m. 1880)
Amer. whaling voyager
Whiting—Whaling p226-228

Lipkovska, Lydia (1887-1955)
Russ. singer
Lahee—Grand p362-365,por.
McCoy—Portraits p116,por.

Lipman, Clara (b. 1869)
Amer. actress, playwright
Mantle—Amer. p294
Mantle—Contemp. p316-317

Lipman, Miriam Hillman (fl. 1930's)
Amer. teacher
Women—Achieve. p200

Lippincott, C. H. (b. 1860)
Amer. business woman
Logan—Part p898

Lippincott, Margarette (1862-1910)
Amer. painter
Waters—Women p213

Lippincott, Sarah Jane.
See Greenwood, Grace, pseud.

Lippmann, Julie Mathilde (d. 1952)
Amer. playwright, author, critic
Women—Achieve. p72,por.

Lippner, Sally Nemerover (fl. 1930's)
Amer. lawyer
Women—Achieve. p172,por.

Lipschitz, Sylvia Steinberg (fl. 1930's)
Amer. lawyer
Women—Achieve. p141,por.

Lipsius, Marie (La Mara, pseud.)
Ger. musician, author
McCoy—Portraits p116,por.

Lipton, Martha (n.d.)
Amer. singer
Matz—Opera p192-195,por.
Saleski—Jewish p601-602,por.

Liselotte of the Palatine (Elizabeth
　　Charlotte of Orleans) (c. 1652-
　　1722)
　　Ger. courtesan
　　Blei—Fasc. p81-102

Lisle, Alice, Lady (c. 1614-1685)
　　Eng., wife of John Lisle
　　Hammerton p910

Liszewska, Anna Dorothea (1722-1782)
　　Ger. painter
　　Waters—Women p213-214

Liszewska, Anna Rosina (1716-1783)
　　Ger. painter
　　Waters—Women p214

Liszniewska, Marguerite Melville (fl. 1940's)
　　Amer. pianist, music teacher,
　　　composer
　　McCoy—Portraits p116,por.

Litchfield, Mary Elizabeth (b. 1854)
　　Amer. author
　　Logan—Part p719

Little, Mrs. Archibald (fl. 19th cent.)
　　Eng. author
　　Furniss—Some p13-14

Little, Ethel Holland (fl. 1920's-1930's)
　　Amer. fashion editor
　　Women—Achieve. p97,por.

Little, Frances, pseud.
　　See Macaulay, Fannie Caldwell

Little, Sarah F. Coles (b. 1838)
　　Amer. educator for blind
　　Logan—Part p729

Littledale, Clara Savage (1891-1956)
　　Amer. editor, author, journalist
　　Cur. Biog. '46 p349-350,por.
　　Cur. Biog. '56 p381
　　Women—Achieve. p92,por.

Litton, Marie (d. 1884)
　　Eng. actress
　　Furniss—Some p52-53,por.

Litvinne, Félia (1860-1936)
　　Russ. singer
　　Ewen—Ency. p266

Liu Tsui (fl. 1930's)
　　Chin. warrior
　　Ayscough—Chinese p226-227

Livermore, Harriet (d. 1868)
　　Amer. clergyman
　　Dexter—Career p53-54

Livermore, Mary Ashton Rice (1820/21-
　　1905)
　　Amer. Civil war patriot, social
　　　reformer, humanitarian, lecturer
　　Adelman—Famous p203-204
　　Brockett—Woman's p577-589,por.
　　Dannett—Noble p35-40,223-226
　　Dolan—Goodnow's p240,por.
　　Dorland—Sum p24,79,117,125,127,136
　　Douglas—Remember p145-146
　　Farmer—What p161,289,por.
　　Hanaford—Dau. p205-206,325-337,por.
　　Harkness—Heroines p13
　*Humphrey—Marys p158-186
　*Humphrey—Women p164-178
　　Irwin—Angels p121,259
　　Logan—Part p325-326,591-593,por.
　　Riegel—Amer. p92-93,por.
　　Young—Women p375,por.

Livermore, Sarah White (1789-1874)
　　Amer. poet
　　Hanaford—Dau. p256

Livesay, Florence Hamilton Randal (m.
　　1908)
　　Can. author
　　Thomas—Canad. p78

Livia (fl. 91 B.C.)
　　Rom., sister of Livius Drusus
　　Balsdon—Roman p216

Livia Drusilla (Julia Augusta) (c. 56 B.C.-
　　29 A.D.)
　　Rom., wife of Augustus
　　Balsdon—Roman (see index),por.
　　Beard—Woman p292-294
　　Ferrero—Women p46-95,99-101,127-
　　　128,por.
　　Hammerton p912,por.
　　Koven—Women p5
　　McCabe—Empr. p8-10,15-20,22-44,
　　　por.
　　Serviez—Roman (1) p28-88

Livia Orestilla (fl. c. 12-41)
　　Rom. empress, wife of Caius
　　　Caesar
　　McCabe—Empr. p52
　　Serviez—Roman (1) p126-128

Livingston, Christina Ten Broeck
　　(fl. 1770's)
　　Amer. Rev. war patriot
　　Green—Pioneer (3) p115-119

Livingston, Clara E. (fl. 1930's-1960's)
　　Amer. aviatrix
　*May—Women p193-194,205,por.

Livingston, Joanna.
　　See Van Courtlandt, Joanna Livingston

Livingston, Mrs. Leon J. See Parnis, Mollie

Livingston, Margaret Beekman (m. 1742)
Amer. Rev. war patriot
Green—Pioneer (3) p125,por.

Livingston, Nora Gertrude (1847-1927)
Amer. nurse
Dolan—Goodnow's p255,por.
Schmidt—400 p401,por.

Livingston, Sarah.
See **Jay, Sarah Van Brugh Livingston**

Livingston, Susan (fl. 1770's)
Amer. Rev. war heroine
DAR Mag. July 1921 p374-375,
portrayal
Ellet—Women (2) p135-136

Livingston, Susannah.
See **Symmes, Susannah**

Livingston, Susannah French (d. 1789)
Amer. Rev. war patriot
Ellet—Women (2) p138-140
Green—Pioneer (3) p302-313

Livingstone, Janet Fleming (m. 1635)
Scot. covenanter
Anderson—Ladies p181-199

Livingstone, Mabel (1926-   )
Amer. author, poet
ASCAP—310

Livingstone, Mary (1909-   )
Amer. comedienne, radio actress,
wife of Jack Benny
Donaldson—Radio p20

Livingstone, Mary Moffat (1820-1862)
Brit.-Amer. missionary
Deen—Great p185-197
*Matthews—Daunt. p50-72

Ljotchitch-Milochevitch, Draga (d. 1927)
Yugoslav. pioneer physician
Lovejoy—Women p209

Ljungberg, Gota (1893-1955)
Swed. singer
Ewen—Ency. p266
Ewen—Living p222,por.
Hammerton p913
McCoy—Portraits p117,por.

Lloyd, Alice (c. 1873-1949)
Scot. actress
Caffin—Vaud. p156,por.

Lloyd, Elizabeth.
See **Cadwalader, Elizabeth Lloyd**

Lloyd, Marie (1870-1922)
Eng. actress, comedienne
Caffin—Vaud. p152-156,por.
Felstead—Stars p42,61,91-94,por.

Hammerton p914,por.
LeRoy—Music p11-12,por.

Lobdell, Avis (fl. 1930's)
Amer. railroad public relations
expert, editor
Women—Achieve. p86,por.

Locatelli (Lucatelli), Maria Caterina
(d. 1723)
It. painter
Waters—Women p214

Locatelli, Piera (gr. 1924)
It. physician
Lovejoy—Women p203-204,por.

Locke, Bessie (d. 1952)
Amer. educator
Women—Achieve. p76,por.

Lockermans, Annetje.
See **Van Cortland, Annetje Lockermans**

Lockett, Alice (fl. 1880's)
Eng., friend of George Bernard
Shaw
Du Cann—Loves p28-56

Lockhart, June (1925-   )
Amer. actress
CR '63 p379,por.
TV—Person (1) p111,por.

Lockwood, Belva Ann Bennett (1830-1917)
Amer. pioneer lawyer
Adelman—Famous p252
*Boynick—Pioneers p59-89
Douglas—Remember p101-104,148,por.
Farmer—What p395-396,398
Hanaford—Dau. p670-673
Irwin—Angels p178-179
Logan—Part p583-585
Riegel—Amer. p135-136
Stern—We p205-234,por.

Lockwood, Charlotte (fl. 1940's)
Amer. organist, teacher
McCoy—Portraits p117,por.

Lockwood, Margaret (1916-   )
Eng. actress
Cur. Biog. '48 p382-383,por.

Lockwood, Mary Smith (b. 1831)
Amer. editor, club leader, author,
foundress, patriot
Logan—Part p477-478,854

Lodge, Eleanor Constance (1869-1936)
Eng. historian, librarian, educator
Brittain—Women (see index)
Hammerton p916

Loeb, Sophie Irene (1876-1929)
   Russ.-Amer. journalist, social
      worker, humanitarian
   °Levinger—Great p153-155
   Ross—Ladies p117-118
   Sickels—Twelve p210-225,255

Loeber, L. Elsa (fl. 1930's)
   Amer. teacher, librarian
   Women—Achiev. p171,por.

Loewenthal, Anka, Baroness (b. 1853)
   Yugoslav. painter
   Waters—Women p214-215

Loftus, Cecilia ("Cissy"; Marie Cecilia
      M'Carthy) (1876-1943)
   Scot. actress
   Blum—Great p40,por.
   Caffin—Vaud. p137-139,por.
   Cur. Biog. '40 p515-516,por.
   Cur. Biog. '43 p453
   Dodd—Celeb. p76-80
   Felstead—Stars p145,180,por.
   Hammerton p917
   Marks—Glamour p313

Logan, Celia (1840-1904)
   Amer. author
   Logan—Part p824

Logan, Charlotte (fl. 1930's)
   Amer. commercial artist, fashion
      designer, inventor
   Women—Achieve. p173,por.

Logan, Deborah Norris (1761-1839)
   Amer. colonial social leader
   Leonard—Amer. p117

Logan, Ella (1913-   )
   Scot. actress
   Lamparski—What p88-89,por.

Logan, Jacqueline (fl. 1920's)
   Amer. actress
   Herman—How p77,por.

Logan, Mrs. John A. (fl. 1890's)
   Amer. editor, author
   Farmer—What p182,por.
   Logan—Part p1-17

Logan, Laura R. (fl. 1920's-1930's)
   Amer. nurse, educator
   Pennock—Makers p90-91,por.

Logan, Martha Daniel (1702/04-1779)
   Amer. colonial botanist, florist,
      horticulturist
   Earle—Colon. p85-86
   Hollingsworth—Her p18-22
   Leonard—Amer. p118
   Spruill—Women's p257,278

Logan, Olive (1839-1909)
   Amer. actress
   Coad—Amer. p230,por.
   Easton—Actor's p272-281,285-286

Logan, Sallie (b. 1853)
   Amer. club leader
   Logan—Part p303

Logan, Virginia Knight (1850-1940)
   Amer. composer, author
   ASCAP p312-313

Logasa, Hannah (b. 1879)
   Amer. librarian, author
   Bul. of Bibl. Sept.-Dec.1956 p1-3,por.

Lohorra, Cora (n.d.)
   Phil. airline hostess
   °May—Women p239-240

Lohr, Marie (1890-   )
   Brit. actress
   Hammerton p917,por.

Loines, Hilda (fl. 1930's)
   Amer. horticulturist
   Women—Achieve. p150,por.

Lois (Biblical)
   Buchanan—Women p107-110
   Deen—All p238-241
   Lewis—Portraits p96-97
   Van Der Velde—She p251-257

Lokhvitsky, Mirra A. (b. 1871)
   Russ. poet
   Schmidt—400 p348,por.

Lollia, Paulina (d. 49 A.D.)
   Rom. empress, wife of Caligula
   Balsdon—Roman p107,114,264
   McCabe—Empr. p52-53,80,83-84
   Serviez—Roman (1) p129-137

Lollini, Clelia (fl. 1910's)
   It. physician
   Lovejoy—Women p203,205

Lollobrigida, Gina (1928-   )
   It. actress
   CR '59 p450,por.
   CR '63 p382,por.
   Cur. Biog. '60 p235-237,por.
   Time Aug.16,1954 p54,por.(Cover)

Lombard, Carole (1908-1942)
   Amer. actress, wife of Clark Gable
   Cur. Biog. '42 p526-527
   Schickel—Stars p154,por.
   Stuart—Immort. p158-159,por.

Lombard, Helen Carusi (1905-   )
   Amer. author, journalist
   Cur. Biog. '43 p453-454,por.

Lombroso-Ferrero, Gina (fl. 1900's)
It. physician
Lovejoy—Women p203

Lon, Alice (n.d.)
Amer. TV singer
TV—Person (2) p32-33,por.

London, Julie (1926-   )
Amer. singer
CR '59 p451,por.
CR '63 p383,por.
Cur. Biog. '60 p237-239,por.
Martin—Pete p299-308
Popular Record p87,por.
Stambler—Ency. p143

Londonderry, Edith Helen Chaplin Vane-
Tempest-Stewart, Marchioness of
(1878-1959)
Eng. social leader
Asquith—Myself p173-213,por.

Lonergan, Anna (fl. 1930's)
Amer. labor leader
New York p3-21
New Yorker Oct.5,1935 p28-32,por.;
Oct.12,1935 p25-29 (Profiles)

Long, Elsie (1880-1946)
Amer. composer, author
ASCAP p313

Long, Gabrielle Margaret Vere Campbell
(Majorie Bowen, pseud) (1888-
1952)
Eng. novelist, playwright
Hammerton p287,918
Wagenknecht—When p220-242

Long, Jane (fl. 1660's-1670's)
Eng. actress
MacQueen—Pope p41-42
Wilson—All p165-167

Long, Mary M'Kinney (fl. 1770's)
Amer. Rev. war patriot
Ellet—Women (2) p186-188

Long, Rose McConnell (fl. 1930's)
Amer. senator
Paxton—Women p129

Long, Tania (1913-   )
Ger.-Anglo-Amer. journalist
Cur. Biog. '46 p357-358,por.

Longfellow, Margaret Bigelow (1747-1842)
Amer. seafarer
Snow—Women p29-33,por.

Longhi, Barbara (1552-c. 1619)
It. painter
Waters—Women p215

Longman, (Mary) Evelyn Beatrice (Mary
Batchelder) (c. 1874-1954)
Amer. sculptor
Adelman—Famous p316
Jackman—Amer. p437-439
Logan—Part p759
Michigan—Biog. p35
National—Contemp. p209
Taft—Women, Mentor (172) p2-4,
#2,4,6,por.
Waters—Women p215

Longmire, Mrs. (fl. 1850's)
Amer. W. pioneer
*Ross—Heroines p20-22

Longshore, Hannah E. (1819-1902)
Amer. physician
Hanaford—Dau. p559
Logan—Part p739
Irwin—Angels p43-44
Lovejoy—Women p28-30

Longueville, Anne Geneviève de
Bourbon-Condé (1619-1679)
Fr. patriot
Dorland—Sum p47
Haggard—Remark. p56-57,66-68
Hall—Moths p1-12,por.
Hammerton p919,por.

Longworth, Alice Roosevelt (1884-   )
Amer. social leader, daughter of
Theodore Roosevelt
CR '59 p452-453,por.
CR '63 p384,por.
Cur. Biog. '43 p457-459,por.
Fairfax—Ladies p51,99
Jensen—White p183-184,188-189,por.
New Yorker Feb.28,1925 p9-10,por.
(Profiles)
Rogers—Women p67,por.
Ross—Know p53
Smith—Romances p330-334,por.
Smith—White p119-131,por.
*Sweetser—Famous p238-253,por.
Time Feb.7,1927 p12,por (Cover)

Look, Lilly Chin (b. 1873)
Amer.-Chin., W. pioneer
Parkhill—Wildest p108-109

Loomis, Mary A. (fl. 1860's)
Amer. Civil war nurse
Logan—Part p334

Loop, Mrs. Henry Augusta (1840-1909)
Amer. painter
Waters—Women p215-216

Loos, Aita (1893-   )
Amer. playwright, humorist
Bruère—Laugh. p191-192
CR '59 p453,por.
CR '63 p384,por.

(Continued)

Loos, Anita—*Continued*

Fitzgibbon—My p159-166
Jensen—Revolt p171,por.
Lawrence—School p166-172
Mantle—Amer. p252-255
Mantle—Contemp. p238-239
New Yorker Nov.6,1926 p25-28,por.
(Profiles)

Lopez, Encaracion. See **Argentinita**

Lopez, Pilar (fl. 1950's)
Sp. ballet choreographer
Haskell—Ballet p82

Lopez, Rita Lobato Velho (b. 1866)
Brazil. physician
Lovejoy—Women p262-263,por.

Lopokova, Lydia, Lady Keynes (1891/92-)
Anglo.-Russ. ballet dancer, actress
Davidson—Ballet p187-191
Hammerton p919-920,por.
Wyndham—Chorus p128-130,por.

Lopp, Clara Washington (fl. 1910's)
Fr. philanthropist
Dorland—Sum p126

Lor, Denise (n.d.)
Amer. singer
TV—Person (1) p153,por.

Lorantffy, Susanna (1600-1660)
Hung. religious worker, educator
Phila.—Women unp.,por.
Schmidt—400 p228-229,por.
Stiles—Postal p157

Lord, Eleanor Louise (fl. 1890's-1900's)
Amer. educator
Logan—Part p727

Lord, Elizabeth W. Russell (b. 1819)
Amer. teacher of blind
Logan—Part p731

Lord, Isabel Ely (fl. 1930's)
Amer. librarian, home economist
Women—Achieve. p114,por.

Lord, Marjorie (n.d.)
Amer. TV actress
TV—Person (3) p155-156,por.

Lord, Mary Stimson Pillsbury (1904-)
Amer. organization official, social
welfare worker, U.N.
representative, humanitarian
Cur. Biog. '52 p359-361,por.
New Yorker May 16,1953 p37,por.,
(Profiles)
Roosevelt—Ladies p238-247
Women—Achieve. p147,por.

Lord, Pauline (1890-1950)
Amer. actress
Blum—Great p88,por.
Brown—Upstage p115-119
Coad—Amer. p328,por.
Ormsbee—Back. p238,242-244,por.

Loren, Sophia (b. 1934)
It. actress
CR '59 p454,por.
CR '63 p385-386,por.
Cur. Biog. '59 p266-267,por.
Ross—Player p50-54,por.
Schickel—Stars p275,por.
Time Apr.6,1962 p78,por.(Cover)

Lorentowicz, Irena (1910-   )
Pol. illustrator
Mahony—Illus. p335

Lorenz, Ellen Jane (1907-   )
Amer. composer, editor, educator
ASCAP p315

Loreto, Our Lady of (fl. 13th cent.)
It. saint
Stiles—Postal p158

Lorimer, Emily M. Overend (gr. 1906)
Eng. editor, teacher
Brittain—Women p117-118,245

Lorimer, Hilda Lockhart (gr. 1896)
Eng. teacher
Brittain—Women (see index)

Lorimer, Norma Octavia (fl. 1900's-1930's)
Scot. author
Hammerton p920

Loring, Emilie Baker (Josephine Story,
pseud.) (d. 1951)
Amer. author
Warfel—Amer. p270-271,por.

Loring, Joan (n.d.)
Amer. actress
TV—Person (1) p148,por.

Lorne, Marion (1888-1968)
Amer. actress, comedienne
Hammerton p920
TV—Person (3) p118-119,por.

Lorraine. See **Marie de Lorraine-Armagnac**

Lo-Ruhamah (Biblical)
Deen—All p277

Los Angeles, Victoria.
See **Angeles, Victoria de Los**

Losch, Tilly (Ottilie Ethel), Countess of
Carnarvon (1907-   )
Aust.-Eng. dancer

(Continued)

Losch, Tilly—*Continued*

    Cur. Biog. '44 p424-426,por.
    Hammerton p920
    Wyndham—Chorus p142-145

Lothrop, Amy, pseud.
    See Warner, Anna Bartlett

Lothrop, Deborah.
    See Putnam, Deborah Lothrop

Lothrop, Harriet Mulford Stone (1844-1924)
    Amer. author
    Farmer—What p183,por.
    Logan—Part p824

Lot's wife (Biblical)
    Chappell—Fem. p9-22
    Deen—All p17-20
    Lewis—Portraits p165-166
    Macartney—Great p60-72
    Marble—Women, Bible p47-50
    Morton—Women p29-34
    Nelson—Bible p11-13
    Van Der Velde—She p30-35

Lott, Emmeline (fl. 1890's)
    Eng. governess
    Howe—Galaxy p167-178,por.

Lotz, Matilda (fl. 1900's)
    Amer. painter
    Waters—Women p216

Loubet, Mrs. (fl. 1820's-1860's)
    Fr., mother of Emile Loubet
    Cockran—Romance p21

Louchheim, Aline.
    See Saarinen, Aline Berstein Louchheim

Louchheim, Katie Scofield (1903-   )
    Amer. government official,
        politician
    CR '63 p386,por.
    Cur. Biog. '56 p385-386,por.

Loud, Hulda Barker (b. 1844)
    Amer. publisher, editor, lecturer
    Hanaford—Dau. p344
    Logan—Part p874

Loud, May Hallowell (b. 1860)
    Amer. painter
    Waters—Women p216-217

Louden, Isabelle, pseud.
    See Langner, Armina Marshall

Loudon, Jane Webb (1807-1858)
    Eng. author, gardener
    Hollingsworth—Her p86-90

Loufek, Betty (fl. 1940's)
    Amer. glider pilot
    °May—Women p219-220

Lough, Orpha Maust (1902-   )
    Amer. psychologist
    Women—Achieve. p55,por.

Loughborough, Mary Ann Webster
    (fl. 1860's)
    Amer. Civil war diarist
    Jones—Heroines p224-237

Loughlin, Anne, Dame (1894-   )
    Eng. labor leader
    Cur. Biog. '50 p352-354

Loughlin, Mary (fl. 1930's)
    Amer. advertising executive
    Women—Achieve. p188,por.

Louisa, Countess of Craven
    See Brunton, Louisa, Countess of
    Craven

Louise, Caroline Alberta, Duchess of Argylle
    (1849-1939)
    Eng. sculptor, painter, daughter of
        Queen Victoria
    Benson—Queen (see index),por.
    Cur. Biog. '40 p525
    Parton—Dau. p115-123,por.
    Parton—Noted p115-123,por.
    Waters—Women p18-19

Louise, Duchess of Portsmouth (1649-1734)
    Eng. beauty
    Melville—Windsor p223-241

Louise, Duchess of Saxe-Coburg-Gotha
    (1800-1831)
    Eng., consort of Ernest I
    Bolitho—Biog. p106-127,por.

Louise, Madame (fl. 1700's)
    Fr., daughter of Louis XV
    Concannon—Dau. p220-225

Louise, Tina (1934-   )
    Amer. actress
    CR '59 p455-456,por.
    CR '63 p386,por.

Louise de Marillac, Saint.
    See Le Gras, Louise, Madame

Louise de Vaudémont (1553-1602)
    Fr. queen, wife of Henry III
    Imbert—Valois p299-303,340

Louise-Hippolyte (1697-1731)
    Mon. ruler
    Stiles—Postal p158

Louise Marie (fl. 1720-1788)
    Ger., wife of Prince Charles
        Edward Stuart
    Orr—Famous Affin. I p184-186

Louise of Prussia (1776-c.1810)
    Ger. (Prussian) queen
    Abbott—Notable p175-179
    Adelman—Famous p101
    Fifty—Famous p188-198,por.
    Hammerton p925
    Hargrave—Some p205-245,por.
    *MacVeagh—Champlin p366
    Schmidt—400 p197-198,por.

Louise of Savoy (1461-1503)
    Fr., mother of Francis I.
    Englebert—Lives p285
    Hammerton p925

Louise of Stolberg, Countess of Albany
    (1753-1824)
    Eng. salonist
    Mayne—Enchant. p198-212,por.

Love, Mary (fl. 1860's)
    Amer. Civil war heroine
    Harkness—Heroines p14

Love, Nancy (1914-   )
    Amer. aviatrix
    *Knapp—New p47-60,por.
    *May—Women p147-149,163,por.
    Peckham—Women p3,10

Lovejoy, Esther Clayson Pohl (1870-1967)
    Amer. physician
    Lovejoy—Women p192-309,por.
    Lovejoy—Women Phys. p34-35,por.
    Mead—Medical p75-77,por.

Lovejoy, Julia (fl. 1800's)
    Amer. W. pioneer
    Brown—Gentle p11,131-132,285-286
    Ellet—Pioneer p368-369

Loveman, Amy (1881-1955)
    Amer. editor, author
    Cur. Biog. '43 p459-461,por.
    Cur. Biog. '56 p386
    Saturday Rev. p403-412
    Women—Achieve. p200

Loveridge, Emily L. (b. 1860)
    Amer. nurse, hospital administrator
    Pennock—Makers p78,por.

Low, Esther (fl. 1810's)
    Amer. printer, bookseller
    Club—Printing p22

Low, Juliette Gordon (1860-1927)
    Amer. foundress, club leader
    *Dolin—World p144-153
    *Forsee—Amer. p230-251
    *Heath—Women (4) p23,por.
    Phila.—Women unp.,por.
    Stiles—Postal p158

Low, Mary Fairchild (1858-1946)
    Amer. painter
    Adelman—Famous p305
    Women—Achieve. p200

Lowden, Florence Pullman (b. 1868)
    Amer. social leader, philanthropist
    Logan—Part p301-302

Lowe, Corinne Martin (1882-1952)
    Amer. journalist, fashion editor,
        author
    Ross—Ladies p437

Lowe, Lucy (fl. 1860's)
    Amer. Civil war diarist
    Jones—Heroines p149-150

Lowe, Marie (fl. 1840's-1900's)
    Ger. harpist, singer, mother of
        Lilli Lehmann
    Wagner—Prima p154,244

Lowe, Martha Perry (1829-1902)
    Amer. author, poet
    Hanaford—Dau. p259

Lowe, Ruth (1914-   )
    Can.-Amer. composer, pianist,
        author
    ASCAP p316

Lowell, Amy (1874-1925)
    Amer. poet, critic
    Adelman—Famous p273
    Boynton—Some p72-88
    *Brenner—Ten p29-60,por.
    Cook—Our p1-18
    Dodd—Celeb. p7-14
    Farrar—Literary p51-64,333,por.
    Hammerton p926
    Jensen—Revolt p100,por.
    Loggins—Hear p77-84
    *MacVeagh—Champlin p367
    *Millett—Amer. p141-142,452-457
    *Muir—Writers p73-84,por.
    Rogers—Women p109,por.
    Saturday Rev. p190-192
    Time Mar.2,1925 p15,por.(Cover)
    Witham—Pan. p228-230,por.

Lowell, Anna (fl. 1860's)
    Amer. Civil war patriot
    Brockett—Woman's p792-793

Lowell, Josephine Shaw (1843-1905)
    Amer. philanthropist, social worker
    Adelman—Famous p235
    Hanaford—Dau. p667
    Irwin—Angels p188-190

Lowell, Susan R. (fl. 1860's)
    Amer. Civil war nurse
    Logan—Part p375

Lowitz, Sadyebeth Heath (fl. 1930's)
Amer. author
Women—Achieve. p200

Lowman, Mary D. (b. 1842)
Amer. mayor, politician
Logan—Part p898

Lowndes, Mrs. Belloc, pseud.
See Belloc, Marie Adelaide

Lownsbery, Eloise (b. 1888)
Amer. author
Cur. Biog. '47 p396-397,por.

Lowrey, Esther Fleming (1739-1814)
Amer. patriot
Green—Pioneer (3) p511-512,por.

Lowrie, Mrs. (fl. 1880's)
Amer. actress, clergyman
Hanaford—Dau. p475

Lowry, Ellen J. (fl. 1860's)
Amer. Civil war nurse
Brockett—Women's p736

Loy, Myrna (1905-   )
Amer. actress
CR '59 p457,por.
CR '63 p387-388,por.
Cur. Biog. '50 p356-358,por.
Schickel—Stars p127,por.

Loynes, Jeanne Detourbey, Countess de
(d. 1908)
Fr. salonist
Skinner—Elegant p184-217,por.

Loyola, Sister (fl. 1840's)
Amer. W. pioneer
Ross—Heroines p126-155

Lozier, Clemence Sophia (1812-1888)
Amer. physician
Adelman—Famous p184
Hanaford—Dau. p558-559
Irwin—Angels p143-144
Lovejoy—Women p63-67
Whitton—These p134-138,150

Lozier, Jennie de la (m. 1872)
Amer. physician, club leader
lecturer,
Logan—Part p739-740

Luban, Francia (1914-   )
Russ.-Amer. musician, song-writer,
author
ASCAP p316

Lubbetse, Cornelia.
See De Peyster, Cornelia Lubbetse

Lubin, Germaine (1890-   )
Fr. singer
Ewen—Ency. p273

Luboschutz, Lea (1889-1965)
Russ. violinist, music teacher
Ewen—Living p223-224,por.
McCoy—Portraits p119,por.
Saleski—Jewish p369-370,por.
Saleski—Wander. p218-219,por.

Lucar, Elizabeth (d. 1537)
Eng. needlewoman
Stenton—English p123-124

Lucas, Mrs. Dione Narona Margaris Wilson
(1909-   )
It. cookery expert
New Yorker May 28,1949,p34,por.
(Profiles)

Lucas, Eliza.
See Pinckney, Elizabeth Lucas

Lucas, Margaret Duchess of Newcastle
(b.c. 1623)
Eng. poet
Untermeyer—Lives p215-216

Lucas, Martha B. (1912-   )
Amer. educator
Cur. Biog. '47 p398-399,por.

Lucatelli, Maria.
See Locatelli, Maria Caterina

Lucca, Pauline (1841-1908)
Aust. singer
Ewen—Ency. p273
Klein—Great p50-65,por.
Lahee—Famous p116-128
McCoy—Portraits p119,por.
Marks—Glamour p203-208,por.
Saleski—Wander. p413-414

Lucchese, Josephine (fl. 1920's)
Amer. singer
McCoy—Portraits p119,por.

Luce, Almira E. (b.c. 1832)
Amer. whaling voyager
Whiting—Whaling p148-158

Luce, Clare Boothe (1903-   )
Amer. playwright, author,
politician, ambassador, journalist
*Clymer—Modern p129-140,por.
CR '59 p457-458,por.
CR '63 p388,por.
Cur. Biog. '42 p97-100,por.
Cur. Biog. '53 p375-378,por.
Fairfax—Ladies p240-241
*Heath—Women (4) p32,por.
Jensen—Revolt p103,por.
Mantle—Connemp. p170-172
Mersand—Amer. p47-59
New Yorker Jan.4,1941,p21,por.;Jan.11,
1941,p22 (Profiles)
O'Brien—Road p213-230

(Continued)

Luce, Clare Boothe—*Continued*

    Paxton—Women p81-91,129,por.
    Phelps—Men (2) '59 p179-180
    Rogers—Women p65,por.
    Roosevelt—Ladies p230-238
    Stewart—Makers p438-439

Luce, Sarah Reynolds (fl. 1860's-1870's)
    Amer. whaling voyager
    Whiting—Whaling p97-99,182-189,por.

Luceja (fl. 3rd cent.)
    Rom. saint
    Wescott—Calen. p92

Lucia Filippini (1672-1732)
    It. saint
    Englebert—Lives p117

Lucilla. See Annia Lucilla

Lucretia (fl.c. 510 B.C.)
    Rom. heroine
    Adelman—Famous p20-21
    Balsdon—Roman p27
    Boccaccio—Conc. p101-103
    Hammerton p928
    Muir—Women p39-40

Lucy (d.c. 303/304)
    It. saint
    Eglebert—Lives p472
    Husslein—Heroines p151-156
    Sharkey—Pop. p35-36
    Wescott—Calen. p197
    *Windham—Sixty p92-97

Lucy of Scotland (d. 1090)
    Scot. saint
    Englebert—Lives p358

Ludington, Flora Belle (1898-   )
    Amer. librarian, organization
      official
    Bul. of Bibl. Jan.-Apr.1956 p193-195,
      por.
    Cur. Biog. '53 p378-379,por.

Ludington, Sybil (1761-1839)
    Amer. Rev. heroine
    *Carmer—Young p68-74

Ludlow, Sarah (d. 1773)
    Amer. Rev. war patriot
    Root—Chapter p342

Ludmilla (d. 927)
    Bohem. saint
    Culver—Women p79
    Englebert—Lives p254
    Wescott—Calen. p140

Ludwell, Frances Culpeper Stephens
      Berkeley, Lady (fl. 17th cent.)
    Amer. colonial patriot
    Leonard—Amer. p118

Ludwig, Josephie. See Noria, Jana

Ludwig, Mary. See Pitcher, Molly

Luhan, Mabel Dodge (1879-1962)
    Amer. author, patron
    Cur. Biog. '40 p526-527,por.
    Cur. Biog. '62 p270
    *Millet—Amer. p175-176,457-458

Luisi, Paulina (gr. 1908)
    Urug. physician
    Lovejoy—Women p269

Luke, Jemima (1813-1906)
    Eng. hymn-writer
    Deen—Great p307-308

Lukens, Anna (b. 1844)
    Amer. physician
    Logan—Part p740-741

Lukens, Rebecca W. (1794-1854)
    Amer. pioneer ironmaster,
      shipwright
    Burt—Phila. p251
    Stern—We p237-250,por.

Lulham, Rosalie Blanche Jermaine (1872-
      1934)
    Eng. naturalist, zoologist
    Martindale—Some p87-97,por.

Lum, Mary (d. 1815)
    Amer. philanthropist
    Burt—Phila. p327,330-331

Lummis, Dorothea (b. 1860)
    Amer. physician, author
    Logan—Part p741

Lummis, Eliza O'Brien (fl. 1910's
    Amer. editor, publisher, author,
      religious worker
    Logan—Part p836

Lumpkin, Alva Moore (1886-1941)
    Amer. senator
    Cur. Biog. '41 p531

Lumpkin, Grace (n.d.)
    Amer. author
    *Millett—Amer. p458-459

Lund, Charlotte (1870-1951)
    Amer. musical director, lecturer
    McCoy—Portraits p119,por.

Lund, Signe (b. 1868)
    Nor. composer
    McCoy—Portraits p120,por.

Lundborg, Florence (fl. 1910's-1930's)
    Amer. painter
    Women—Achieve. p127,por.

Lunn, Katharine Fowler.
See **Fowler-Billings, Katharine**

Lunn, Louise Kirkby (1873-1930)
Eng. singer
Davidson—Treas. p172-174
Hammerton p930,por.
Lahee—Grand p12,94
McCoy—Portraits p120,por.

Lunt, Dolly Sumner.
See **Burge, Dolly Sumner Lunt**

Lupescu, Magda (1896/04-   )
Rum., friend of Prince Carol
CR '59 p459-460,por.
Cur. Biog. '40 p527-529,por.
Lamparski—What. p96-97,por.

Lupino, Ida (1918-   )
Eng.-Amer. actress
Blum—Television p111,por.
CR '59 p460,por.
CR '63 p390,por.
Cur. Biog. '43 p467-469,por.
TV—Person (3) p16-17,por.

Lupton, Mary Josephine (fl. 1910's)
Amer. editor, translator, author
Logan—Part p836

Lusk, Georgia Lee (1893-   )
Amer. Congresswoman, educator
Cur. Biog. '47 p405-406,por.
Roosevelt—Ladies p130-136

Lussan, Zélie de (1863-1949)
Amer. singer
Davidson—Treas. p174-176
Lahee—Famous p258-259,por.

Lussi, Marie (Mari Mitale) (1892-   )
Amer. song-writer, author
ASCAP p317

Lutes, Della Thompson (d. 1942)
Amer. author
Cur. Biog. '42 p538

Lutgard (1182-1246)
Flem. saint, mystic
Englebert—Lives p232

Lutmer, Emmy (b. 1859)
Ger. painter (enamel)
Waters—Women p217

Luxembourg, Marechale de (1707-1787)
Fr., granddaughter of Marshal
Villeroi
Kavanagh—Woman (2) p19-23

Luxemburg, Rose (1870-1919)
Pol.-Ger. revolutionary, editor,
author
Abramowitz—Great p726-752

Goldsmith—Seven p183-216
Hammerton p932,por.
Phila.—Women, unp.,por.
Stiles—Postal p160

Luynes, Madame de (fl. 1870's)
Fr. Beauty
Skinner—Elegant p75-76

Lyall, Beatrix Margaret, Dame (fl. 1890's-
1930's) Eng. politician
Hammerton p932

Lyall, Edna, pseud.
See **Bayly, Ada Ellen**

Lydia (Biblical)
Barker—Saints p53-60
Buchanan—Women p101-103
Culver—Women p56-57
Deen—All p221-226
Englebert—Lives p298
Falhaber—Women p195-198
Harrison—Little p124-133
Lewis—Portraits p207-208
Lord—Great p173-184
Marble—Women, Bible p288-291
Mead—250 p237
Nelson—Bible p108-110
Ockenga—Women p231-239
Schmidt—400 p271-272,por.
Van Der Velde—She p234-241

Lydig, Rita de Alba de Acosto (fl. 1920's)
Amer. society leader
New Yorker Nov. 19, 1927 p28-30,por
(Profiles)

Lyford, Sarah (fl. 1620's)
Amer. pioneer
Bell—Women p127-129,138-139,153-
154

Lyman, Amy Brown (b.1872)
Amer. social worker
Binheim—Women p177,por.

Lyman, Esther (fl. 1930's)
Amer. fashion editor, advertising
manager
Women—Achieve. p185,por.

Lyman, Laura Elizabeth (fl. 1930's)
Amer. business executive
Women—Achieve. p184,por.

Lyman, Mrs. Walter C. (fl. 1880's)
Amer. lecturer
Hanaford—Dau. p343

Lyme, Susan.
See **Penn, Susan Lyme**

Lynahan, Gertrude (fl. 1920's)
Amer. journalist
Ross—Ladies p175-176

Lynch, Elizabeth Shubrick (m. 1773)
Amer. pioneer
Green—Pioneer (3) p268-270

Lynch, Joseph, Mother (fl. 1860's)
Irish-Amer. nurse
Pennock—Makers p24,por.

Lynch, Maude Dutton (fl. 1930's)
Amer. author
Women—Achieve. p185,por.

Lynch, Peg. (n.d.)
Amer. radio-TV. actress, author
Cur. Biog. '56 p389-390,por.
TV—Person (1) p88,por.

Lynde, Mary Elizabeth Blanchard (b. 1819)
Amer. philanthropist
Logan—Part p544

Lyne, Felice (1891-1935)
Amer. singer
Lahee—Grand p256-259
McCoy—Portraits p120,por.

Lynley, Carol (1943-   )
Amer. actress
CR '63 p391,por.
Ross—Player p268-274,por.

Lynn, Diana (1926-   )
Amer. actress
CR '63 p391,por.
Cur. Biog. '53 p379-381,por.

Lynn, Meda C. (fl. 1930's)
Amer. teacher, humanitarian
Women—Achieve. p147,por.

Lyon, Mary (1797-1849)
Amer. educator
*Adams—Heroines p30-57
Adelman—Famous p128
America's 12 p34-36,por.
*Bolton—Lives p237-248,por.
*Boynick—Pioneers p1-26
Bradford—Portraits p65-97,por.
*Carmer—Caval. p297,por.
*Commager—Crus. p163-165
*Curtin—Gallery p60,por.
*Daugherty—Ten p63-79,por.
Dexter—Career p26-28
*Dolin—World p68-73,por.
Dorland—Sum p39,108
Douglas—Remember p90-91
Farmer—What p226-227,258
*Fleming—Great p27-41
Goodsell—Pioneers p227-303,por.
Hanaford—Dau. p519-524
*Heath—Woman p6,por.
Horowitz—Treas. p24-28
*Humphrey—Marys p129-145
Irwin—Angels p29-31
Ladies'—Amer. 12 p34-36,por.
*Lamm—Biog. p104

Logan—Part p511-512,708-711
*McCallum—Women p81-90
Melikov—Immort. p67,149,por.
Morello—Hall p48,por.
Morris—400 p164
Muir—Women p159-161
*Parkman—Heroines p3-30,por.
Schmidt—400 p9,por.
*Strong—Of p145-149
*Vance—Lamp p42-65,por.
Whitton—These p107-108
Woody—Hist.(1) p357-362,por.

Lyon, Sue (1946-   )
Amer. actress
CR '63 p391-392,por.

Lyons, Ruth (n.d.)
Amer. TV personality
CR '63 p392,por.

Lyster, Annette (fl. 19th cent.)
Eng. author
Furniss—Some p23-24

Lyth, Mrs. R. B. (d. 1890)
Amer. missionary
Logan—Part p513

Lyttleton, Doris Jean (1873-1945)
(G. B. Lancaster, pseud.), Tas.
novelist
Roderick—20 p155-176

Lytton, Rosina Doyle Bulwer-Lytton, Lady
(1809-1882) Brit. author
Hammerton p934

M

Maachah (1) (Biblical)
daughter of Nahor
Deen—All p278

Maachah (2) (Biblical)
daughter of Talmai
Deen—All p278

Maachah (3) (Biblical)
daughter or granddaughter of
Absalom
Deen—All p278-279

Maachah (4) (Biblical)
mother of Asa (may be same as
#3)
Deen—All p279-280

Maachah (5) (Biblical)
Caleb's concubine
Deen—All p280

Maachah (6) (Biblical)
wife of Machir
Deen—All p280

Maachah (7) (Biblical)
    wife of Jehiel
    Deen—All p280

Maass, Clara Louise (1876/79-1901)
    Amer. nurse
    Dolan—Goodnow's p266-267
    Phila—Women unp.,por.
    Stiles—Postal p160

Mabry, Beatrice (fl. 1930's)
    Amer. advertising executive
    Women—Achieve. p99,por.

McAfee, Mildred Helen (1900-   )
    Amer. military officer (WAVES)
    Cur. Biog. '42 p539-541
    Time Mar. 12, 1945 p20,por.(Cover)
    Women—Achieve. p200-201

MacAlindon, Mary (fl. 18th cent.)
    Irish harpist
    Concannon—Dau. p241-242

McAndrew, Helen Walker (fl. 1860's)
    Amer. physician
    Lovejoy—Women p100-101

MacArthur, Mrs. Charles G.
    See Hayes, Helen

MacArthur, Elizabeth Veale (1786-1850)
    Eng. Austral. pioneer
    Prout—Petticoat p30-52,por.

MacArthur, Mary.
    See Anderson, Mary Reid MacArthur

Macaulay, Catharine Sawbridge (1731-1791)
    Eng. historian
    Stenton—English p267,306-311,313-
    315

Macaulay, Emily Rose (1881-1958)
    Eng. novelist
    Brittain—Women p118-119,223,249
    Hammerton p936,por.
    Johnson—Some Contemp. p63-79
    Lawrence—School p203-209
    Millett—Brit. p341-342

Macaulay, Fannie Caldwell (1863-1941)
    (Frances Little, pseud.) Amer.
        author
    Maurice—Makers p10

Macaulay, Hanna, Lady Trevelyan
    (d. 1873) Eng., sister of Lord
        Macaulay
    Pomeroy—Little p181-221

Macaulay, May (fl. 1900's-1920's)
    Johnson—Some Contemp. p63-74

MacAuley, Catherine, Mother (1787-1841)
    Irish foundress, philanthropist,
        nurse, nun
    Adelman—Famous p121-122
    Burton—Loveliest p39-57
    Dorland—Sum p24
    Pennock—Makers p14-17,por.
    Schmidt—400 p244,por.

McAvoy, May (fl. 1920's)
    Amer. actress
    Herman—How p69,por.
    Wagenknecht—Movies p229-232,por.

Macbeth, Florence (b.c. 1891-   )
    Amer. singer
    McCoy—Portraits p120,por.

Macbeth, Madge Hamilton Lyons
    (1878/1883-1965) Can. author
    Thomas—Canad. p79-80

McBride, Elizabeth Craig (fl. 1890's-1900's)
    Amer., mother of Mary Margaret
        McBride
    Davis—Mothers p111-123

McBride, Helen (fl. 1940's)
    Amer. aviatrix
    *May—Women p185

McBride, Katharine Elizabeth (1904-   )
    Amer. psychologist, educator
    Cur. Biog. '42 p541-542,por.

McBride, Mary Margaret (1899-   )
    Amer. journalist, radio personality
    CR '59 p463,por.
    CR '63 p411-412,por.
    Cur. Biog. '41 p540-542,por.
    Cur. Biog. '54 p420-422,por.
    New Yorker Dec. 19, 1942 p27,por.
        (Profiles)
    Rogers—Women p174,por.
    Ross—Ladies p254-256,por.,cover
    Settel—Radio p105,por.
    Taves—Success p17-31,por.

McBride, Maude Gonne.
    See Gonne, Maud

McBride, Patricia (1942-   )
    Amer. ballet dancer
    Cur. Biog. '66 p248-251,por.

McCabe, Harriet (1827-1919)
    Amer. social former, religious
        worker
    Hanaford—Dau. p402-412,por.

McCabe, Lida Rose (1865-1938)
    Amer. author, lecturer
    Logan—Part p730

MaCabe, Margaret (b. 1846)
Amer. religious worker
Logan—Part p621

McCall, Annie (1859-1949)
Eng. physician
Bell—Storm. p145-147

McCall, Sidney.
See Fenollosa, Mary McNeill

McCalla, Mrs. (fl. 1770's)
Amer. Rev. war heroine
Fowler—Woman p142-143

McCambridge, Mercedes (1918-   )
Amer. actress
Cur. Biog. '64 p262-264,por.
TV—Person (3) p48-49,por.

McCardell, Claire (1905-1958)
Amer. fashion designer
Cur. Biog. '54 p422-424,por.
Cur. Biog. '58 p255
Time May 2, 1955 p85,por.(Cover)

McCarthy, Julia (fl. 1920's)
(Margery Rex) Amer. journalist
Ross—Ladies p194-202,por.,cover

MaCarthy, Kathryn O'Loughlin (1894-1952)
Amer. Congresswoman
Paxton—Women p130

McCarthy, Mary Therese (1912-   )
Amer. author, educator
Auchincloss—Pion. p170-186
CR '59 p464-465,por.
CR '63 p412-413,por.
Cur. Biog. '55 p378-379,por.
Writers—Paris p283-315,por.

McCartney, Katharine Searle (fl. 1910's)
Amer. club leader
Logan—Part p431-432

McCauley, Barbara (fl. 1870's)
Ger.-Amer. W. pioneer
Sargent—Pioneers p20,24-25

McCauley, Jane Hamilton (1916-   )
Amer. politician
Cur. Biog. '49 p364-366,por.

McCauley, Mary Ludwig Hays.
See Pitcher, Molly

MacChesney, Clara Taggart (fl. 1890's-
1900's) Amer. painter
Waters—Women p217-218

MacChesney, Norma Gertrude (b. 1876)
Amer. music teacher
Logan—Part p837

Maccio of Campisteguy, Aurelia (1871-1931)
Urug. humanitarian
Schmidt—400 p414,por.

Ma Ch'üan (fl. 17th-18th cent.)
Chin. painter
Ayscough—Chinese p210-213

M'Cleary, Dorothy (1894-   )
Amer. author
O'Brien—50 p864

McClellan, Aurora Pryor (fl. 1910's)
Amer. club leader
Logan—Part p479-480

McClendon, Sarah (1913-   )
Amer. journalist
CR '63 p413,por.

McClintock, Katharine Morrison (1899-   )
Amer. author
Cur. Biog. '58 p255-256,por.

McCloskey, Helen (fl. 1930's)
Amer. aviatrix
*May—Women p98
Planck—Women p75,por.

McClung, Mary J. (fl. 1930's)
Amer journalist, personnel director,
advertising executive
Women—Achieve. p60,por.

McClung, Nellie Mooney (1874-1951)
Can. author, feminist, social
reformer, politician
Innis—Clear p165-170,por.
Thomas—Canad. p80-81

McClure, Mary (fl. 1770's)
Amer. pioneer heroine
Green—Pioneer (2) p395-399

McClurg, Virginia Donaghé (fl. 1920's)
Amer. author, lecturer
Binheim—Women p109-110,por.

McCluskey, Ellen (n.d.)
Amer. interior decorator
CR '63 p414,por.

McCollin, Frances (1892-1960)
Amer. blind composer, teacher,
lecturer
ASCAP p319-320
Elson—Woman's p261
Howard—Our p494-495
McCoy—Portraits p128,por.
Reis—Composers p247-248

McCord, Louisa Susannah (1810-1879/80)
Amer. Civil war patriot, feminist,
poet, plantation manager
*Sickels—Calico p205-220

(Continued)

McCord, Louisa Susannah—*Continued*

Simkins—Women p87-88
Thorp—Female p179-214,por.
Whitton—These p164-165

McCormic,Mary (fl. 1940's)
Amer. singer
McCoy—Portraits p128,por.

McCormick, Anne O'Hare (1881/82-1954)
Amer. journalist, foreign
correspondent
*Clymer—Modern p31-40,por.
Cur. Biog. '40 p530-531,por.
Cur. Biog. '54 p426
Jensen—Revolt p103,por.
Ross—Ladies p150,163,360,366-369,
por., cover

McCormick, Edith Rockefeller (1872-1932)
Amer. music patron
McCoy—Portraits p128,por.
Tebbel—Inher. p220-222

McCormick, Elsie (1894-1962)
Amer. journalist
Bruère—Laugh. p224
Ross—Ladies p381-384

McCormick, Mary Ann Hall ("Polly")
Amer. heiress
Tebbel—Inher. p210-212

McCormick, Nettie Fowler (1835-1923)
Amer. philanthropist
Deen—Great p248-251

McCormick, Pat Keller (fl. 1950's)
Amer. swimmer
Stump—Champ. p149-164

McCormick, Ruth Hanna.
See **Simms, Ruth Hanna McCormick**

McCoy, Iola.
See **Fuller, Iola**

McCracken, Faith A. (fl. 1920's-1950's)
Amer. missionary
They—Went p91-92

McCracken, Joan (1922-1961)
Amer. actress, dancer
Blum—Great p150,por.
Cur. Biog. '45 p360-362,por.
Cur. Biog. '62 p278

McCracken, Mary Isabel (fl. 1930's)
Amer. entomologist
Osborn—Fragments p270

McCrackin, Josephine (b. 1846)
Ger.-Amer. journalist, club leader
Logan—Part p844-845

McCrary, Jinx.
See **Falkenburg, Jinx**

M'Crea, Jane (1753-1777)
Amer., Ind. captive
Ellet—Women (2) p255-261

McCrea, Vera T. (fl. 1930's)
Amer. business woman
Women—Achieve. p72,por.

McCrossan, Mary (fl. 1900's)
Eng. painter
Waters—Women p232-233

McCue, Lillian,
See **De La Torre** (Bueno), **Lillian**

McCullers, Carson Smith (1917-   )
Amer. novelist
Auchincloss—Pion. p161-169
CR '59 p467-468,por.
CR '63 p415,por.
Cur. Biog. '40 p535-536,por.
Warfel—Amer. p292,por.

McCulloch, Rhoda E. (fl. 1930's)
Amer. editor
Women—Achieve. p163,por.

McCullough, Esther Morgan (fl. 1930's)
Amer. artist, author
Women—Achieve, p143,por.

McCune, Vesta Marie (d. 1938)
Amer. missionary
They—Went p101-102

McCutcheon, Floretta Doty (b. 1888)
Amer. bowler
Davis—100 p77,por.
*Jacobs—Famous p59-64,por.

McDaniel, Eugenia I. (b. 1884)
Amer. entomologist
Osborn—Fragments p270

McDaniel, Hattie (1898-1952)
Amer. actress
*Cherry—Portraits p132-134
Cur. Biog. '40 p536-537,por.
Cur. Biog. '52 p370-371
Robinson—Hist. p224-225,por.

McDaniel, Mildred (fl. 1950's)
Amer. track woman
Stiles—Postal p171

McDannel, Lucy C. (fl. 1930's)
Amer. lawyer
Women—Achieve. p149,por.

MacDermott, Una (fl. 16th cent.)
Irish
Concannon—Dau. p78-81,247-248

Macdonald, Ada (fl. 1890's)
　　Brit. parachutist
　*May—Women p49-51

MacDonald, Betty (1908-1958)
　　Amer. author
　　Cur. Biog. '46 p362-363,por.
　　Cur. Biog. '58 p260

MacDonald, Christie (c. 1875-1962)
　　Can.-Amer. actress
　　Blum—Great p42,por.
　　Strang—Prima p172-180,por.

MacDonald, Cordelia (1848-1941)
　　Amer. actress
　　Carmer—Young p187-194
　　Coad—Amer. p196,por.
　　Cur. Biog. '41 p543
　　Jones—Heroines p94-106,140-145,
　　　304-309

MacDonald, Flora (1722-1790)
　　Scot. heroine
　　Ellet—Women (2) p167-175,por.
　　Hammerton p938,por.
　*MacVeagh—Champlin p374
　　Muir—Women p126-127
　　Orr Famous p139-141
　　Orr—Famous Affin. I p182-184
　　Schmidt—400 p138-139,por.

MacDonald, Florence.
　　See Howard, Florence Ruth

McDonald, Hannah ("Aunt Mac") (b. 1810)
　　Amer. pioneer
　　Brown—Home. p50-54,por.

MacDonald, Isabella.
　　See Alden, Isabella MacDonald

MacDonald, Jeanette (1907-1965)
　　Amer. singer, dancer
　　CR '59 p468,por.
　　CR '63 p394-395,por.
　　Stuart—Immort. p168-169,por.

McDonald, Lucile Saunders (1898-   )
　　Amer. author, journalist
　　Ross—Ladies p370-372

MacDonald, Lucy Maude Montgomery
　　(1874-1942) Can. novelist
　　Thomas—Canad. p83-84

MacDonald, Margaret (1870-1910)
　　Brit. social reformer, wife of James
　　　Ramsay MacDonald
　*Kirkland—Girls p84-92

McDonald, Marie Frye (1920/23-1965)
　　Amer. actress
　　CR '59 p468-469,por.
　　CR '63 p416,por.

MacDonald, V. May (fl. 1920's)
　　Can. nurse
　　Pennock—Makers p104,por.

MacDougal, Violet (fl. 1920's)
　　Amer. poet
　　Smith—Women's p135

MacDougall, Alice Foote (1867-1945)
　　Amer. business woman, restaurant
　　　manager
　*Ferris—Girls p239-250
　*Kirkland—Good p102—110
　*Logie—Careers p138-158
　　New Yorker Feb.4,1928 p21-23,por.
　　(Profiles)

McDougall, Irene G. (fl. 1930's)
　　Amer. club leader, philanthropist
　　Women—Achieve. p113,por.

MacDougall, Sally (fl. 1930's)
　　Ross—Ladies p434-435

MacDowell, Annie A. E. (fl. 1870's)
　　Amer. editor, publisher
　　Hanaford—Dau. p702

MacDowell, Katherine Sherwood Bonner
　　(1849-1883) Amer. author
　　Sickels—Twelve p14-32,251-252

MacDowell, Marian Griswold Nevins (1857-
　　1956) Amer. pianist, lecturer,
　　　wife of Edward MacDowell
　　McCoy—Portraits p121,por.

McDowell, Mary Eliza (1854-1936)
　　Amer. social worker
　*Logie—Careers p40-58

McDowell, Rachel Kollock (1880-1949)
　　Amer. journalist
　　Ross—Ladies p152-161,por.,cover
　　Women—Achieve. p54,por.

Mace, Frances Lawton (b. 1836)
　　Amer. poet
　　Logan—Part p825

McElliott, Martha (fl. 1920's)
　　Amer. journalist
　　Ross—Ladies p542-543

McElroy, Lenore (fl. 1930's)
　　Amer. aviation instructor
　　Planck—Women p164-165

McElroy, Mary Arthur (fl. 1880's)
　　Amer. sister of Chester Alan Arthur
　　Gerlinger—Mis. p68-69
　　Logan—Part p274-275
　　Truett—First p52,por.

McEwen, Hettie M. (fl. 1860's)
 Amer. Civil war heroine, patriot
 Brockett—Woman's p764-766
 Hanaford—Dau. p212

McFadden, Dorothy L. (fl. 1930's)
 Ger.-Amer. business executive
 Women—Achieve. p201

McFadden, Margaret Bischell (m. 1890)
 Amer. philanthropist
 Logan—Part p534

M'Fall, Frances Elizabeth Clarke.
 See Grand, Sarah, pseud.

McFarland, Amanda (c. 1837-c.1898)
 Amer. missionary
 Deen—Great p400-401

MacFarland, Irene (fl. 1920's)
 Amer. parachutist
 *May—Women p56

MacFarlane, Irene (fl. 1920's)
 Eng. aviatrix
 Planck—Women p116

McGarvah, Eleanor (fl. 1930's)
 Amer. public health nurse
 Pennock—Makers p69,por.

McGauley, Minna Hoppe (fl. 1920's)
 Amer. author, dramatic coach
 Binheim—Women p65,por.

McGeachy, Mary Agnes Craig (1904-   )
 Amer. social worker, administrator
 Cur. Biog. '44 p430-432,por.

McGee, Anita Newcomb (b. 1864)
 Amer. physician, surgeon, army
  officer
 Adelman—Famous p300
 Dolan—Goodnow's p265,305,por.
 Dorland—Sum p148,130
 Mead—Medical p66

McGee, Molly.
 See Jordan, Marian Driscoll

McGill, Elizabeth Gregory (gr. 1929)
 Amer. aeronautical engineer
 Planck—Women p220

McGill, Josephine (1877-1919)
 Amer. composer
 Howard—Our p589,635

McGill, Sarah (fl. 1910's)
 Amer. linguist, translator,
  philanthropist
 Logan—Part p534-535

McGinley, Phyllis (1905-   )
 Can.-Amer. poet
 Breit—Writer p211-213
 CR '59 p470,por.
 CR '63 p417-418,por.
 Cur. Biog. '41 p545-546,por.
 Cur. Biog. '61 p284-285,por.
 Dodd—Celeb. p274-278
 Time June 18, 1965 p74,por.(Cover)

McGowan, Alice (b. 1858)
 Amer. author
 Logan—Part p847

McGowan, Elizabeth Blaney (fl. 1910's)
 Amer. teacher
 Logan—Part p723

MacGrath, Leueen (1914-   )
 Eng.-Amer. actress, playwright
 CR '63 p395,por.

McGraw, Eloise Jarvis (1915-   )
 Amer. author
 Cur. Biog. '55 p389-390,por.

McGreal, Elizabeth.
 See Yates, Elizabeth

MacGregor, Ellen (1906-   )
 Amer. author, librarian
 Cur. Biog. '54 p430-431,por.

MacGregor, Jessie (fl. 1900's)
 Eng. painter
 Waters—Women p218-219

MacGuffie, Martha (fl. 1950's)
 Amer. physician
 Jensen—Revolt p211,por.

McGuire, Dorothy (1918-   )
 Amer. actress, singer
 CR '59 p470-471,por.
 CR '63 p418,por.
 Cur. Biog. '41 p546-547,por.
 Popular Record p96,por.
 Time Jan. 8, 1945 p39,por.(Cover)
 TV—Person (1) p112-113,por.

McGuire sisters.
 See also McGuire, Dorothy
 Amer. singers
 CR '59 p471,por.
 CR '63 p418,por.
 Popular Record p96,por.
 TV—Person (1) p112-113,por.

McGuire, Judith Brockenbrough (b. 1813)
 Amer. Civil war diarist, patriot
 Andrews—Women p71-103,155-189,
  372-412
 Jones—Heroines (see index)
 Simkins p60-61,183

Mach, Hildegarde von (fl. 1900's)
Ger. painter
Waters—Women p383-384

Macha, Mong Ruadh (fl. 330 B.C.)
Irish, queen, heroine, builder
McCraith—Romance p1-6

Machabees, mother of (Biblical)
Faulhaber—Women p132-140

Machado, Lena (n.d.)
Amer. singer
Parshalle—Kash. p43,por.

McHale, Kathryn (1890-1956)
Amer educator, psychologist
Cur. Biog. '47 p415-416,por.
Cur. Biog. '57 p341
Women—Achieve. p90,por.

Machat, Rivka (fl. 1920's)
Russ.-Israeli singer
Saleski—Jewish p707-708

McHenry, Mary Sears (fl. 1910's)
Amer. club leader
Logan—Part p349

McHugh, Mrs. Bernard (1894-   )
Amer. club leader
Binheim—Women p125,por.

McIlweane, Mary
See Caswell, Mary McIlweane

MacInnes, Helen Clark (Helen Gilbert
Highet (1907-   )
Scot.-Amer. author
Breit—Writer p187-189
Cur. Biog. '67 p268-270
Van Gelder—Writers p304-307

McInnis, Clara Ogilvie (fl. 1930's)
Amer. cosmetic executive
Women—Achieve. p31,33,por.

MacIntosh, Anne (fl. 1740's)
Scot. soldier
Graham—Group p26-27

McIntosh, Hannah.
See Cady, Hannah McIntosh

McIntosh, Maria Jane (1803-1878)
Amer. author
Hanaford—Dau. p233

McIntosh, (Margaret) Millicent (1898-   )
Amer. educator, dean
CR '59 p471,por.
CR '63 p418,por.
Cur. Biog. '47 p416-418,por.

McIntosh, Sarah Swinton (fl. 1770's)
Amer. Rev. war patriot
Green—Pioneer (3) p391-394

MacIntyre, Elizabeth (n.d.)
Austral. illustrator
Mahony—Illus. p337

Macironi, Clara Angela (1821-1895)
Eng. composer, song-writer, teacher
Dorland—Sum p48,160
Elson—Woman's p151-152
McCoy—Portraits p121,por.

McInsaac, Isabel 1858-1914)
Amer. nurse
Schmidt—400 p403,por.

MacIver, Loren Newman (1909-   )
Amer. painter
Cur. Biog. '53 p399-401,por.

McIver, Pearl (1893-   )
Amer. public health worker,
government official, nurse
Cur. Biog. '49 p378-380,por.

Mack, Mrs. (fl. 17th cent.)
Amer. pioneer heroine
Fowler—Woman p100-104

Mack, Nila (d. 1953)
Amer. radio director, producer,
author
Cur. Biog. '52 p373-375,por.
Cur. Biog. '53 p401

Mack, Pauline Beery (1891-   )
Amer. chemist
Cur. Biog. '50 p373-374,por.

Mackall, Lillie (fl. 1860's)
Amer. Civil war spy
Kane—Spies p47-48,52-53,57

Mackarel, Betty (fl. 1670's)
Eng. actress
Wilson—All p167-168

McKay, Charlotte E. (fl. 1860's)
Amer., Civil war nurse
Brockett—Woman's p514-516
Dannett—Noble (see index)
Moore—Women p278-306
Young—Women p345-346

Mackay, Dorothy A. (fl. 1930's)
Amer. aviatrix
Planck—Women p226-227

Mackay, Frances I. (1906-   )
Amer. sculptor
National—Contemp. p215

Mackay, Helen Marion MacPherson (1891-)
Scot. physician
Hammerton p942

McKay, Isabel (fl. 1930's)
Amer. fashion executive
Women—Achieve. p120,por.

Mackay, Isabel Ecclestone Macpherson
(1875-1928)
Can. novelist
Thomas—Canad. p85-86

Mackay, Margaret (1907-   )
Amer. novelist
Warfel—Amer. p274-275,por.

Mackay, Mary. See Corelli, Marie, pseud.

MacKaye, Julia Josephine Gunther
(fl. 1890's)
Amer. author, librarian
Cur. Biog. '49 p382-383,por.

McKean, Mary (Maria) Borden (d.c. 1773)
Amer. patriot
Green—Pioneer (3) p142-143,215-217

McKean, Sarah. See Yrujo, Sarah McKean

McKee, Mary Harrison (1858-1930)
Amer., daughter of Benjamin
Harrison
Gerlinger—Mis. p74-75
Truett—First p58,por.

McKee, Ruth Eleanor (1903-   )
Amer. novelist
Warfel—Amer. p294,por.

McKee, Ruth Karr (1874-1951)
Amer. club leader
Binheim—Women p198,por.

McKenna, Siobhan (1923-   )
Irish actress
CR '59 p472,por.
CR '63 p420,por.
Cur. Biog. '56 p392-394,por.

McKenna, Virginia (1931-   )
Eng. actress
Winn—Queen's p127-137,por.

McKenney, Eileen (d. 1940)
Amer. author
Cur. Biog. '41 p912

McKenney, Ruth (1911-   )
Amer. author
Cur. Biog. '42 p549-551,por.

MacKenzie, Agnes Mure (1891-   )
Scot. author
Hammerton p942

Mackenzie, Anne, Lady, Countess of
Balcarres, Argyll (d., after 1706)
Scot. covenanter
Anderson—Ladies p356-394

MacKenzie, Constance, Lady (m. 1904)
Eng. dancer
Wyndham—Chorus p151-152

MacKenzie, Gisele (1927-   )
Can.-Amer. actress, singer, violinist,
TV personality
CR '59 p472,por.
CR '63 p395,por.
Cur. Biog. '55 p390-391,por.
Popular Record p89,por.
TV—Person (1) p156-157,por.
Wilson—NBC p15-25,por.

MacKenzie, Winifred (fl. 1940's)
Austral. army officer, physician
Lovejoy—Women p249,363-364

McKernan, Maureen (fl. 1920's)
Amer. journalist
Ross—Ladies p543-544

Mackie, Pauline Bradford (b. 1873/74-   )
Amer. author
Harkins—Famous p283-298,por.
Harkins—Little p283-298,por.
Logan—Part p807

Mackin, Sarah Maria Spottiswood, Countess
(b. 1850)
Amer. author
Logan—Part p836

McKinlay, Katherine (fl. 1940's)
Brit. WAAF, ambulance driver
*May—Women p161

McKinley, Ida Saxton (1844-1907)
Amer., wife of William McKinley
Gerlinger—Mis. p78-80,por.
Jensen—White p176,por.
Logan—Ladies p134-138
Logan—Part p281-282
*McConnell—Our p235-241,por.
Prindiville—First p190-194
*Ross—Know p51,por.
Smith—Romances p319-327,por.
Truett—First p60,per.

McKinley, Nancy Allison (fl. 1840's-1860's)
Amer., mother of William McKinley
Hampton—Our p193-202

McKinney, Louise (1868-1933)
Can. social reformer, politician
Innis—Clear p170-171

McKinnon, Emily H. S. (gr. 1896)
New Z. physician
Lovejoy—Women p252-253

MacKinstry, Elizabeth (d. 1956)
Amer. illustrator, sculptor,
violinist
Cooper—Authors p33-51
Mahony—Illus. p337

MacKintosh, Elizabeth (1896-1952)
Scot. novelist, playwright
Hammerton p943

McKisack, May (gr. 1923)
  Eng. educator
  Brittain—Women p191,206,246

McKissick, Margaret Smith (fl. 1910's)
  Amer. sociologist, social reformer
  Logan—Part p595

Macklewain, Margaret (fl. 1730's)
  Amer. educator, business woman
  Dexter—Colonial p94

Macklin, Miss (fl. 18th cent.)
  Eng. actress
  MacQueen—Pope p250-251

MacKown, Marjorie T. (1896-   )
  Amer. composer
  Howard—Our p511

McKown, Robin (fl. 1960's)
  Amer. author
  *McKown—Heroic p320

Mackubin, Florence (1861-1918)
  It.-Amer. painter
  Logan—Part p754
  Waters—Women p219-220

MacLaine, Shirley (1934-   )
  Amer. actress, dancer
  CR '59 p473,por.
  CR '63 p395,por.
  Cur. Biog. '59 p277-279,por.
  Martin—Pete p276-286,por.,jacket
  Rivkin—Hello p234-239
  Schickel—Stars p271,por.
  Time June 22,1959 p66,por.

MacLane, Jean (1878-1964)
  Amer. painter
  Jackman—Amer. p254-255

McLaren, Agnes (1837-1913)
  Scot. physician, religious worker
  Burton—Valiant p147-165

MacLauchlan, Margaret (d. 1685)
  Scot. covenanter
  Anderson—Ladies p340,343,352
  Graham—Group p82-84
  Muir—Women p112

McLaughlin, Kathleen (fl. 1920's-1930's)
  Amer. journalist
  Ross—Ladies p161-163,543-544

McLaughlin, Mary Louise M. (fl. 1870's-
        1900's)
  Amer. artist
  Waters—Women p233-234

McLaughlin, Sara, Marchioness (fl. 1900's)
  Amer. religious worker
  Logan—Part p621

McLaurin, Kate (n.d.)
  Amer. actress, playwright
  Mantle—Amer. p300-301

McLean, Alice Throckmorton (1886-1968)
  Amer. organization official
  Cur. Biog. '45 p370-372,por.
  Cur. Biog. '68 p458
  New Yorker July 4,1942 p21,por.
    (Profiles)

McLean, Emily Nelson Ritchie (1859-1916)
  Amer. patriot
  Logan—Part p438-441

McLean, Evalyn Walsh (1886-1947)
  Amer. hostess
  Cur. Biog. '43 p480-482,por.
  Cur. Biog. '47 p419
  Stewart—Makers p451

McLean, Jean (fl. 1920's)
  Amer. painter
  Bryant—Amer. p233

McLean, Mrs. Louis (m. 1812)
  Amer. social leader
  Logan—Part p254-255

McLean, Margaret (fl. 1930's)
  Amer. dramatic, speech teacher
  Women—Achieve. p97,por.

MacLeary, Bonnie (1892-   )
  Amer. sculptor
  National—Contemp. p215
  Women—Achieve. p117,por.

MacLeod, Charlotte (gr. 1891)
  Can. nurse
  Dolan—Goodnow's p275
  Pennock—Makers p72,por.

MacLeod, Dorothy Shaw (1900-   )
  Amer. religious leader, social
      worker
  Cur. Biog. '49 p383-384,por.

McLeod, Edyth Thornton (fl. 1930's)
  Amer. cosmetician
  Women—Achieve. p146,por.

MacLeod, Grace (c. 1878-1962)
  Scot.-Amer. teacher, editor,
      nutritionist
  Women—Achieve. p200

McLure, Margaret A. E. (fl. 1860's)
  Amer. Civil war patriot
  Andrews—Women p336-343

MacMahon, Aline (1899-   )
  Amer. actress
  Coad—Amer. p329,por.

MacMahon, Ella (fl. 1910's)
    Irish novelist, translator
    Hammerton p945
    Logan—Part p837

MacManus Mansfield, Blanche (fl. 1900's)
    Amer. illustrator
    Waters—Women p234-237

McMeekin, Clark, pseud.
    See Clark, Dorothy Park; McMeekin,
    Isabel McLennan

McMeekin, Isabel McLenan (1895/99-   )
    Amer. author
    Cur. Biog. '42 p551-552,por.
    Cur. Biog. '57 p347-349,por.
    Warfel—Amer. p295-296,por.

McMeens, Anna C. (fl. 1860's)
    Amer. Civil war nurse
    Brockett—Woman's p491-492

McMein, Neysa (1890-1949)
    Amer. painter, illustrator
    Cur. Biog. '41 p548-549,por.
    Cur. Biog. '49 p386
    *Ferris—Girls p107-116
    Women—Achieve. p72,por.

McMichael, Margaret T. (fl. 1860's)
    Amer. Civil war patriot
    Simkins—Women p20-21

McMillan, Clara G. (fl. 1930's)
    Amer. Congresswoman
    Paxton—Women p130

McMillan, Hazel Fern (fl. 1940's-1950's)
    Amer. missionary
    They—Went p119-120

McMillan, Lida (fl. 1880's-1930's)
    Amer. actress
    Marks—Glamour p316

McMillan, Lucile Short (m. 1946)
    Amer. missionary
    They—Went p133-134

McMillan, Margaret (1860-1931)
    Scot. educator
    Hammerton p945

McMillan, Mary (fl. 1800's)
    Amer. W. pioneer
    Ellet—Pioneer p338-349
    Logan—Part p93-94

McMillin, Lucille Foster (d. 1949)
    Amer. politician, government
        official
    Women—Achieve. p53,por.

McMinnies, Mary Jackson (1920-   )
    Brit. author
    Cur. Biog. '59 p281-282,por.

MacMonnies, Mary Fairchild (b.c. 1860)
    Amer. painter
    Waters—Women p220

MacMullen, Frances A. (fl. 1930's)
    Can.-Amer. cosmetician
    Women—Achieve. p140,por.

McMurchy, Helen (1862-1953)
    Can. physician
    Lovejoy—Women p116-117

McNabb, Ann (fl. 1860's)
    Irish-Amer. immigrant
    Cavanah—We p138-143

McNall, Mrs. B. A. (fl. 1860's)
    Amer. educator, lawyer
    Hanaford—Dau. p671-673

McNally, Margaret (fl. 1930's)
    Amer. civil engineer
    Goff—Women p168-172

MacNaughton, Sarah (d. 1916)
    Eng. novelist
    Hammerton p945-946

MacNeil, Carol Brooks (b. 1871)
    Amer. artist, sculptor
    Jackman—Amer. p380
    Michigan—Biog. p202
    National—Contemp. p216
    Taft—Women, Mentor (172) #4 p10

McNeil, Claudia (n.d.)
    Amer. inger, actress
    CR '63 p421,por.

McNeilly, Mildred Masterson (James Dewey;
        Glenn Kelly) (1910-   )
    Amer. novelist
    Warfel—Amer. p296,por.

McNellis, Maggi (1917-   )
    Amer. radio, TV personality
    CR '63 p422,por.
    Cur. Biog. '55 p400-401,por.

Macomber, Eleanor (1801-1840)
    Amer. missionary
    Hanaford—Dau. p511-512

Macomber, Mary L. (1861-1916)
    Amer. painter
    Logan—Part p758
    Michigan—Biog. p203-204
    Waters—Women p220-221

"Maconaquah." See Slocum, Frances

McPeek, Allie (fl. 1860's)
    Amer. Civil war nurse, patriot
    Andrews—Women p284-285
    Bruce—Woman p219-221

Macphail, Agnes (1890-1954)
    Can. politician
    Innis—Clear p179-197,por.

McPherson, Aimee Semple (1890-1944)
        Amer. religious leader, evangelist
    Carnegie—Little p113-116,por.
    Cur. Biog. '44 p442
    Jensen—Revolt p89,por.
    Ross—Charmers p252-282,295,por.

MacQuoid, Katharine Sarah (1824-1917)
        Eng. author
    Hammerton p946

MacRae, Sheila Stevens (n.d.)
        Austral.-Amer. actress
    CR '63 p396,por.

Macrina (fl. 3rd cent.)
        Turk. saint
    Blunt—Great p32-34

Macrina the Younger (327-379)
        Turk. saint
    Deen—Great p11-14

Macrum, Adeline (fl. 1930's)
        Amer. librarian
    Women—Achieve. p81,por.

McShane, Agnes (fl. 1910's)
        Amer. philanthropist
    Logan—Part p535

McSherry, Virginia Faulkner (fl. 1860's)
        Amer. Civil war patriot
    Logan—Part p499-500

McSweeney, Mattie (fl. 1860's)
        Amer. Civil war patriot
    Simkins—Amer. p135

McSwigan, Marie (1907-1962)
        Amer. author
    Cur. Biog. '53 p404-405,por.
    Cur. Biog. '62 p280

MacVay, Anna Pearl (fl. 1930's)
        Amer. teacher
    Women—Achieve. p108,por.

MacVeigh, Sue.
    See Nearing, Elizabeth Custer

McWilliams, Margaret (1875-1952)
        Can. journalist, author
    Innis—Clear p279-297,por.

Macy, Anne Sullivan.
    See Sullivan, Anne Mansfield

Macy, Edith Downing (d. 1967)
        Eng.-Amer. organization official
    Cur. Biog. '52 p387-388,por.
    Cur. Biog. '67 p479

Macy, Margaret (fl. 1930's)
        Amer. advertising executive
    Women—Achieve. p200

Maddalena of Canossa (1774-1833)
        It. saint
    Englebert—Lives p141

Madden, Lotta (fl. 1940's)
        Amer. singer
    McCoy—Portrait p122,por.

Maddern, Minnie.
    See Fiske, Minnie Maddern

Madeira, Jean Browning (1924-   )
        Amer. singer
    Cur. Biog. '63 p258-260,por.
    Matz—Opera p124-126,por.

Madeleva, Mary, Sister (1887-1964)
        Amer. educator, poet, essayist, nun
    Cur. Biog. '42 p556-557,por.
    Cur. Biog. '64 p269
    Elgin—Nun p96-97,por.

Madison, Dorothy ("Dolley") Payne Todd
        (1768-1849)
        Amer. social leader, wife of
            James Madison
    Abbott—Notable p434-438
    Adelman—Famous p103-104,por.
    *Bolton—Famous Leaders p123-158,por.
    Bradford—Wives p125-160,por.
    Brooks—Young p1-42,
    *Daugherty—Ten p32-47,por.
    *Dolin—World p48-58,por.
    Donovan—Women p294-329,por.
    *Elson—Side (1) p163-166
    Farmer—What p71-75,por.
    Gerlinger—Mis. p15-17,por.
    Green—Pioneer (3) p485-486,por.
    Hanaford—Dau. p75-76
    *Horowitz—Treas. p21-23
    *Humphrey—Women p101-114
    Jensen—White p16-31,por.
    Logan—Ladies p24-30
    Logan—Part p221-226
    Love—Famous p21
    *McCallum—Women p67-68
    *McConnell—Our p43-59,por.
    Means—Woman p52-73,por.,cover
    Minnigerode—Some p89-132,por.
    Prindiville—First p36-46
    *Ross—Know p11,por.
    Sale—Old p186-199,por.
    Smith—Romances p54-66,por.
    *Stevens—Women p53-58,por.
    *Strong—Of p135-137
    Sweetser—Famous p23-49,por.
    Truett—First p14,por.
    Whitton—First p54-70,por.

Madison, Martha (fl. 1930's)
        Amer. playwright
    Mantle—Contemp. p317

Madison, Nelly Conway (fl. 1750's-1770's)
Amer., mother of James Madison
Donovan—Women p27-30
Hampton—Our p32-37

Madonna. See Mary (Biblical)

Maeder, Clara. See Fisher, Clara

Maertz, Louisa (fl. 1860's)
Amer. Civil war nurse
Brockett—Woman's p390-394

Maesa, Julia. See Julia Maesa

Maeterlinck, Georgietta Leblanc.
See LeBlanc, Georgette

Magdalen Taylor, Mother (1832-1900)
Eng. foundress
Burton—Loveliest p114-131

Magdalene. See Mary Magdalene (Biblical)

Magee, Elizabeth Stewart (1889-   )
Amer. social worker, labor leader
Cur. Biog. '50 p375-376,por.

Magill, Eileen (fl. 1920's)
Can. pioneer aviatrix
*May—Women p100

Magliani, Francesca (b. 1845)
It. painter
Waters—Women p221

Magliore, Yolette, Madame (fl. 1940's-
1950's)
Hait. social welfare leader
Stiles—Postal p162

Magnani, Anna (1908-   )
It. actress
CR '59 p476,por.
Cur. Biog. '56 p400-402,por.

Magnes, Frances (1922-   )
Amer. violinist
Saleski—Jewish p370-371,por.

Magnia Urbica (fl.c. 230-270)
Rom. empress, wife of Carus
Serviez—Roman (2) p365-366

Magnus, Lady (fl. 19th cent.)
Eng. author
Furniss—Some p29-32

Magoffin, Susan Shelby (m. 1845)
Amer. W. pioneer
Brown—Gentle p14,38,103,105,108,
122,por.
*Miller—West. p14-29

Magoon, Mary E. (1. 1860's)
Amer. pioneer lawyer
Farmer—What p394

Magri, Lavinia.
See Stratton, Lavinia Warren, Countess

Magruder, Julia (1854-1907)
Amer. novelist
Dorland—Sum p 48,198

Mahal, Mumtaz (b.c. 1593-1630)
E. Ind. queen, wife of Shah Jahan
Muir—Women p104-107
Schmidt—400 p236-237,por.

Mahalah (Biblical)
Deen—All p280
Nelson—Bible p30-32

Mahalath (1) (Biblical)
wife of Esau
Deen—All p280

Mahalath (2) (Biblical)
David's granddaughter
Deen—All p281

Mahaut, Countess of Artois and of Burgundy
(d. 1329)
Fr. art patron, philanthropist
Welch—Six p83-115,por.

Mahlah. See Mahalah

Mahnkey, Mary Elizabeth (fl. 1930's)
Amer. journalist
Ross—Ladies p462-463

Mahon, Gertrude (b. 1752)
Eng. courtesan
Bleackley—Ladies p245-294,308-309,
por.

Mahoney, Elizabeth Ann Katherine.
See Bellwood, Bessie

Mahoney, Mary (fl. 1920's)
Amer. journalist
Ross—Ladies p486-489

Mahoney, Mary Eliza (1845/53-1923/26)
Amer. nurse
Dolan—Goodnow's p249-251
Schmidt—400 p402-403,por.

Maichlé, Lidiana (m. 1893)
Russ. dancer
Wyndham—Chorus p147

Mailly, Louise Julie, Countess of (1710-1751)
Fr., mistress of Louis XV
Haggard—Remark. p253-264,268-271
Kavanagh—Woman (1) p107-110
Trowbridge—Seven p28-42,por.

Mailly-Nèsle, Marie Anne, Duchess of
Chateăuroux (1717-1744)
Fr. courtesan
Trowbridge—Seven p1-60,por.

Main, Charlotte Emerson (fl. 1890's-1910's)
Amer. club leader
Logan—Part p462-463

Main, Marjorie (1890-   )
Amer. actress
Cur. Biog. '51 p397-399,por.

Maime, Anne Louise Benedicte de Bourbon,
Duchess of (1676-1753)
Fr. salonist, politician
Kavanagh—Woman (1) p39-58,por.

Maintenon, Françoise D'Aubigné, Marquise
de (1635-1719)
Fr., mistress, wife of Louis XIV
Abbot—Notable p243-247
Adelman—Famous p61-62
*Bolton—Famous Leaders p54,por.
Bradford—Daughters p33-73,por.
Dark—More p131-154
De Morny—Best p22-34,por.
Dorland—Sum p28,108
Fifty—Famous p162-168,por.
Haggard—Remark. p158-165,167,189-
192,198-202
Hall—Moths p319-356,por.
Hammerton p950,por.
Kavanagh—Woman (1) p19-22
*MacVeagh—Champlin p380,por.
Mozans—Woman p83-85
Muir—Women p115-118
Russell—Glit. p49-58
Thomas—Living Women p81-93,por.
Thomson—Queens p473-488

Maish, Jennie Gauslin (fl. 1860's)
Amer. Civil war nurse
Logan—Part p367

Maitland, Agnes Catherine (1850-1906)
Eng. educator
Brittain—Women (see index)

Maitland, Duchess of.
See Lauderdale, Elizabeth Murray,
Duchess of Maitland

Majewska, Pelagie (fl. 1960's)
Pol. glider pilot
*May—Women p223

Major, Kathleen (gr. 1928)
Eng. librarian, educator
Brittain—Women p178,208-209,226

Makea, Takau Ariki (fl. 1890's)
Cook Isl. queen
Arsenius—Dict. p123,por.
Phila.—Women unp.,por.

Makeba, Miriam (1932-   )
S. Afr. singer
Cur. Biog. '65 p275-277,por.

Makemsen, Maud Worcester (1891-   )
Amer. astronomer
Cur. Biog. '41 p552-554,por.

Makin, Bathsua (or Bathshua) (fl. 1670's)
Eng. scholar, governess, author,
teacher
Howe—Galaxy p38-39,por.
Stenton—English p183-188,191-193,
200,214

Malahlele, Mary Susan (gr. 1947)
S. Afr. physician
Lovejoy—Women p258

Malatesta, Parisina (d. 1424)
It., wife of Nicolo III
Blei—Fasc. p19-21

Malbin, Elaine (1932-   )
Amer. singer
Cur. Biog. '59 p284-285,por.

Malessy, Madame (fl. 18th cent.)
Fr. Rev. war heroine
Kavanagh—Woman (2) p233-234

Malet, Lucas, pseud.
See Harrison, Mary St. Leger

Maley, Florence Turner (1927-   )
Amer. composer, singer, vocal
teacher
ASCAP p331-332

Malibran, Maria Felicia Garcia (1808-
1836)
Sp. singer
Adelman—Famous p120-121,por.
Coad—Amer. p86,por.
Derwent—Rossini p140,147-148,286-
287
Dorland—Sum p31,162
Ewen—Ency. p286
Hammerton p952
Howard—Our p204
Lahee—Famous p49-53
McCoy—Portraits p123,por.
*MacVeagh—Champlin p381
Marks—Glamous p93-102,por.
Pleasants—Great p146-151,por.
Wagner—Prima p244

Malkhazounie, Irma de (m. 1933)
Russ.-Fr. actress
Wyndham—Chorus p147

Malko, Marfa (fl. 1910's)
Russ. soldier
Dorland—Sum p99

Mallet, Elizabeth (fl. 1700's)
Eng. printer
Club—Printing p14-15

Mallet-Joris, Françoise (1930-   )
  Belg.-Fr. novelist
  Peyre—French p424-425,457

Mallette, Dorothy (n.d.)
  Amer. aircraft instructor
  *Peckham—Women p139

Mallette, Gertrude Ethel (b. 1887)
  Can. author
  Cur. Biog. '50 p379-380

Mallinger, Mathilde Lichtenegger (1847-
      1920)
  Yugoslav. singer
  Ewen—Ency. p287

Malloch, Elizabeth (fl. 1930's)
  Amer. actress
  Women—Achieve. p175,por.

Mallon, Mary (fl. 1930's)
  Amer. typhoid fever carrier
  New Yorker Jan.26,1935 p21-25,por.
    (Profiles)

Mallon, Winifred (1879-1954)
  Amer. journalist
  Ross—Ladies p342-345

Mallory, Lucy A. (b. 1846)
  Amer. publisher, editor, social
    reformer
  Logan—Part p874

Malloy, (Marie) Louise ("Josh Wink")
      (d. 1947)
  Amer. journalist, columnist
  Logan—Part p858
  Ross—Ladies p496

Malone, Leah Kay (gr. 1907)
  Eng. alderman
  Brittain—Women p250

Malsin, Lane Bryant (fl. 1930's)
  Lith.-Amer. fashion designer,
    business executive
  Women—Achieve. p53,por.

Maltby, Esther Stark (fl. 1920's)
  Amer. park board member
  Binheim—Women p196-197,por.

Maltby, Margaret E. (b. 1860)
  Amer. physicist
  *Ferris—Girls p213-226
  Women—Achieve. p91,por.

Malten, Thérèse (Thérèse Muller) (1855-
      1930)
  Ger. singer
  Klein—Great p211-214
  Lahee—Famous p199-200

Mamaea, Julia. See Julia Mamaea

"Mammy Kate" (fl. 1770's)
  Amer. Rev. war heroine
  Andrews—Women p334-335

Mana (Manna)-Zucca, Madame, pseud.
      (1894-   )
  Amer. composer, pianist, actress,
    singer
  ASCAP p333
  Howard—Our p565-566
  McCoy—Portraits p123,por.
  Saleski—Jewish p193,por.

Mance, Jeanne (1606-1673)
  Fr.-Can. foundress, pioneer nurse,
    philanthropist
  Burton—Loveliest p1-19
  Deakin—True p44-65
  Dolan—Goodow's p152-153
  *McKown—Heroic p25-49,por.
  Pennock—Makers p9,por.
  Schmidt—400 p393-394,por.

Manchester, Consuelo Yznaga, Duchess of
      (c. 1888-1909)
  Amer. heiress
  Pearson—Marry. p144-148,por.

Manchester, Helena Zimmerman, Duchess of
      (fl. 1930's)
  Amer. heiress
  Pearson—Marry. p149-152

Manchester, Kathleen, Duchess of.
  See Dawes, Kathleen, Duchess of
    Manchester

Manchester, Virginia (fl. 1880's)
  Amer. whaling voyager
  Whiting—Whaling p239

Mancini, Hortense, Duchess of Mazarin
      (c. 1646-1699)
  Fr. social leader
  Kavanagh—Woman (2) p18-19

Mancini, Maria (Marie) (1639-1715)
  It.-Fr., wife of Colonna
  Haggard—Remark. p80-93
  Mayne—Enchant. p52-66,por.
  Ravenel—Women p45,por.

Mandel, Carola Panerai (n.d.)
  Cub.-Amer. sportswoman
  CR '63 p399,por.

Mander, Rosalie Glynn Grylls (gr. 1927)
  Eng. author
  Brittain—Women p176,252

Mandigo, Pauline Eggleston (1892-1956)
  Amer. journalist, public relations
    counsel
  Ross—Ladies p524-525
  Women—Achieve. p184,por.

Mandola, Carol M. (fl. 1930's)
    Amer. metaphysicist, lecturer, poet
Women—Achieve. p106,por.

Maneck, Margaret Brown (fl. 1930's)
    Amer. business executive
Women—Achieve. p137,por.

Mangilla, Ada, Countess of Francessetti de
        Mersenile (b. 1863)
    It. artist
Waters—Women p221-222

Mangnall, Richmal (1769-1820)
    Eng. educator, author, governess
Howe—Galaxy p121,por.

Manicatide, Elena (gr. 1900)
    Rum. physician
Lovejoy—Women p208

Manigault, Ann (fl. 1750's-1780's)
    Amer. diarist, letter-writer
Spruill—Women's p99

Manigault, Judith Giton Royer (d. 1711)
    Amer. colonial agronomist, pioneer
 • Leonard—Amer. p118
Spruill—Women's p13-14

Mankiewicz, Henriette (fl. 1890's)
    Ger. artist
Waters—Women p222-223

Mankin, Helen Douglas (1896-   )
    Amer. Congresswoman, lawyer
Cur. Biog. '46 p379-381,por.

Mankin, "Widow" (fl. 1730's)
    Amer. colonial druggist
Dexter—Colonial p29-30

Manley, Marian C. (1892-   )
    Amer. librarian
Marshall—Amer. p94-150

Manley, Mary de la Rivière (1663/72-1724)
    Eng. playwright
MacCarthy—Women p34-35,214-233
MacQueen—Pope p128-131

Manlia Scantilla (fl. 130's-190's A.D.)
    Rom. empress, wife of Didius
        Severus Julianus
Serviez—Roman (2) p124-125

Manly, Alice Elfrida (fl. 1900's)
    Eng. painter, illustrator
Waters—Women p223-224

Mann, Elizabeth (d. 1954)
    Amer. printer
Club—Printing p27-28

Mann, Erika (1905-1969)
    Ger.-Amer. author, actress
        lecturer
Cur. Biog. '40 p550-552,por.

Mann, Helen (fl. 1960's)
    Amer. tracking engineer
*May—Women p242

Mann, Julia de Lacy (fl. 1910's)
    Eng. educator
Brittain—Women (see index)

Mann, Marguerite. See Sylva, Marguerite

Mann, Maria R. (fl. 1860's)
    Amer. Civil war philanthropist,
        teacher
Brockett—Woman's p697-703

Mann, Mrs. Marty (1904-   )
    Amer. organization official
Cur. Biog. '49 p398-399,por.
Murrow—This (1) p111-112

Mann, Mary Elizabeth (1848-1929)
    Brit. novelist
Hammerton p955

Mann, Pamela (d. 1840)
    Amer. pioneer
Turner—Sam p50-54

Manner, Jane (Jennie Mannheimer)
        (d. 1943)
    Amer. dramatic coach
Women—Achieve. p126,por.

Mannerheim, Sophie (1863-1928)
    Fin. nurse, educator
Dolan—Goodnow's p330,por.
Schmidt—400 p167-168,por.

Mannering, Mary (Florence Friend) (1876-
        1953)
    Eng. actress
Blum—Great p9,por.
*Kobbé—Homes p219-226,por.
Moses—Famous p164-165,por.
Strang—Actresses p156-160,por.

Manners, Diana, Lady (c. 1892-   )
    Brit. actress
Time Feb.15,1926 p17,por.(Cover)

Mannes, Clara Damrosch (1869-1948)
    Ger.-Amer. pianist
McCoy—Portraits p123,por.
Women—Achieve. p114,por.

Mannes, Marya (1904-   )
    Amer. author, critic, journalist
CR '59 p480,por.
CR '63 p399-400,por.
Cur. Biog. '59 p291-292,por.

Mannin, Ethel (1900-   )
    Eng. novelist, journalist
    Hammerton p955

Manning, Anne (1807-1879)
    Eng. author
    Oliphant—Woman p211-216

Manning, Mrs. Bruce. See Bristow, Gwen

Manning, Jessie Wilson (b. 1855)
    Amer. social reformer
    Logan—Part p670

Manning, Kathleen Lockhart (1890-1951)
    Amer. composer, pianist, singer
    ASCAP p334
    Howard—Our p567
    McCoy—Portraits p123,por.

Manning, Marie. See Fairfax, Beatrice

Manning, Mary Margaret Fryer (m. 1884)
    Amer. club leader
    Logan—Part p471-472

Manning, Mrs. (1821-1849)
    Eng. accused criminal
    Furniss—Some p218-219

Manning, Rosalie H. (fl. 1910's-1920's)
    Amer. sculptor
    National—Contemp. p220

Mannion, Madeleine Gosman (fl. 1930's)
    Amer. manager, teacher's agency
    Women—Achieve. p148,por.

Mannix, Mary Ellen Walsh (1846-1938)
    Amer. author, poet
    Logan—Part p837

Mannon, Mary L. (b. 1843)
    Amer. Civil war nurse
    Logan—Part p367

Manoah's wife (Biblical)
    Deen—All p325-326
    Lewis—Portraits p41-43
    Spurgeon—Sermons p69-80

Mansfield, Arabella A. (d. 1911)
    Amer. pioneer lawyer
    Farmer—What p394
    Hanaford—Dau. p662
    Irwin—Angels p171-172
    Logan—Part p749

Mansfield, Jayne (1933-1967)
    Amer. actress
    CR '59 p480-481,por.
    CR '63 p400,por.

Mansfield, Katherine, pseud. (Kathleen
    Beauchamp Murry) (1888-1923)
    New Z. author
    Church—British p104-106,por.
    Collins—Literature p151-169,por.
    Dunaway—Treas. p419-422
    Eustace—Infinity p53-78,por.
    Hammerton p956
    Lawrence—School p348-355
    Millett—Brit. p349-351
    Moore—Disting. p235-253

Manski, Dorothee (b.c. 1895)
    Ger.-Amer. singer
    Ewen—Living p230-231,por.
    McCoy—Portraits p123,por.
    Saleski—Jewish p603-605,por.

Manski, Inge (b.c. 1913)
    Ger.-Amer. singer
    Saleski—Jewish p605-606,por.

Mantell, Lynda, Baroness (m. 1925)
    Eng. actress
    Wyndham—Chorus p138

Manter, Parnel (fl. 1770's)
    Amer. Rev. war heroine
    *Carmer—Young p62-67

Manzolini, Anna Morandi (1716-c. 1774)
    It. anatomist
    Lovejoy—Women p202
    Mozans—Woman p236-237

Mara (Biblical)
    Deen—All p281

Mara, (Gertrude) Elizabeth Schmeling
    (1749-1833)
    Ger. singer
    Dorland—Sum p29,68,81,162
    Ferris—Great (1) p102-120
    Lahee—Famous p25-28
    McCoy—Portraits p123,por.
    Pleasants—Great p102-105,por.

Maracci, Carmelia (b.c. 1912)
    Amer. dancer
    *Maynard—Amer. p205

Maraini, Adelaide (b. 1843)
    It. sculptor
    Waters—Women p224

Marais, Miranda (1912-   )
    Nether. singer
    CR '63 p400,por.

Marble, Alice (1913-   )
    Amer. tennis player
    Cur. Biog. '40 p557-558,por.
    Hazeltine—We p185-195
    *Jacobs—Famous p65-72,por.

Marble, Anna (fl. 1900's)
Amer. journalist, wife of Channing
Pollock
Ross—Ladies p259

Marble, Annie Russell (b. 1864)
Amer. author, lecturer
Logan—Part p844

Marble, Callie Bonney (fl. 1910's)
Amer. author
Logan—Part p825

Marbury, Anne.
See Hutchinson, Anne Marbury

Marbury, Catharine.
See Scott, Catharine Marbury

Marbury, Elizabeth (1856-1933)
Amer. theatrical manager, author's
representative
Adelman—Famous p286
*Ferris—Five p137-184,por.
New Yorker Dec.24,1927 p19,por.
(Profiles)

Marcel, Lucille Wasself (1887-1921)
Amer. singer
Lahee—Grand p406-411,por.
McCoy—Portraits p124,por.

Marcel, Madame (1830-1875)
Fr., mother of inventor
Schmidtt—400 p187,por.

Marcella (325-410)
Rom. saint, nurse, educator
Blunt—Great p35-36
Culver—Women p84-85
Deen—Great p17-21
Dolan—Goodnow's p72-73
Englebert—Lives p42-43

Marcella Claudia, the younger (m. 28 B.C.)
Rom., wife of M. Agrippa,
Jullus Antonius
Balsdon—Roman p49,71,73-74

Marcelle, Adèle D'Affry, Duchess of
Castiglioni-Colonna (1837-
1879)
Swiss sculptor
Waters—Women p224-225

Marcellina (fl. 4th cent.)
Rom. saint
Englebert—Lives p275

Marcet, Jane (1785-1858)
Eng. physician, chemist, scientific
author
Smith—Torch. p164,por.
Stenton—English p324,329

Marchais, Madame du (Madame
d'Anglivilliers) (fl. 18th cent.)
Fr. politician
Kavanagh—Woman (1) p222-224

Marchand, Colette (1925-   )
Fr. ballet dancer
Atkinson—Dancers p105-107,por.
Haskell—Vignet. p78

Marchand, Marie Françoise.
See Dumesnil, Marie Françoise

Marchant, Mabel (fl. 1890's)
Amer. whaling voyager
Whiting—Whaling p253-255,por.

Marchesi, Blanche (1864-1940)
Fr. singer
McCoy—Portraits p124,por.

Marchesi, Mathilde (1826-1913)
Ger. singer, vocal teacher
Adelman—Famous p246
Ewen—Ency. p293
Hammerton p958
McCoy—Portraits p124,por.
Pleasants—Great p271-274,por.
Wagner—Prima p66-68,244

Marcia (fl. 180's-190's)
Rom. concubine of Commodus
Balsdon—Roman p147-150,232,249
McCabe—Empr. p185-189,193
Serviez—Roman (2) p101-110,142

Marcia (fl. 40's-50's B.C.)
Rom., wife of younger Cato,
Hortensius
Balsdon—Roman p185,190

Marcia Furnilla (fl. 50's-70's)
Rom. empress, wife of Titus
Serviez—Roman (1) p336-342

Marcia Otacilia Severa (fl. 200's-240's A.D.)
Rom. empress, wife of Julius
Phillipus
Serviez—Roman (2) p299-307

Marcial-Dorado, Caroline (1889-1941)
Span.-Amer. educator
Cur. Biog. '41 p557
Women—Achieve. p200

Marciana, Ulpia (d. 112)
Rom., sister of Trajan
Balsdon—Roman p133,135-136,138

Marcos, Imelda Romualdez (1931-   )
Phil., wife of president
Frederick—Ten p159-174,por.

Marcovigi, Clementina (fl. 1880's)
It. painter
Waters—Women p225

Mardyn, Mrs. (b. 1789)
    Irish actress
    MacQueen—Pope p305-306,por.

Margaret (1045/46-1093)
    Scot. saint, queen, wife of King
      Malcolm
    Blunt—Great p88-93
    Dolan—Goodnow's p91
    Hammerton p960
    *MacVeagh—Champlin p385
    Muir—Women p73-75
    *Unstead—People p117-126
    *Windham—Sixty p253-257

Margaret (1353-1412)
    Scand. queen
    *Boyd—Rulers p71-77,por.
    Hammerton p960
    Schmidt—400

Margaret (1283-1290)
    Scot. queen
    Hammerton p960

Margaret (1489-1541)
    Scot. queen
    Hammerton p960-961

Margaret, Duchess of Burgundy (1446-1503)
    Eng., daughter of Richard, Duke of
      York
    Hammerton p961

Margaret Beaufort (1443-1509)
    Eng., mother of Henry VII
    Culver—Women p110

Margaret Mary, Sister (b. 1884)
    Amer. nun
    Elgin—Nun p28-29,por.

Margaret Mary Alacoque (1645/47-1690)
    Fr. saint
    Englebert—Lives p395
    Sharkey—Pop. p168-173
    Stiles—Postal p236

Margaret of Anjou (1430-1482)
    Eng. queen, military heroine,
      wife of Henry VI
    Fifty—Famous p33-45,por.
    Hammerton p960
    Muir—Women p84-86

Margaret of Antioch (fl. 3rd cent.)
    Gr. saint
    Englebert—Lives p278-279
    Wescott—Calen. p106-107

Margaret of Austria (1480-1530)
    Aust. regent, daughter of Emperor
      Maximillian
    Culver—Women p110
    Phila.—Women unp.,por.
    Stiles—Postal p165

Margaret of Cortona (1247-1297)
    It. saint
    Englebert—Lives p74
    Wescott—Calen. p28-29

Margaret of Hungary (1242-1271)
    Hung. saint
    Phila.—Women, unp.,por.
    Schmidt—400 p227,por.
    Stiles—Postal p236

Margaret of Lorraine (1463-1521)
    Fr. saint
    Blunt—Great p166
    Englebert—Lives p417

Margaret of Meteola ("Mantellate") (1287-
    1320)
    It. nurse
    Dolan—Goodnow's p110

Margaret of Navarre (1492-1549)
    Fr. politician, poet, scholar,
      religious reformer
    Adelman—Famous p46-47
    Culver—Women p115-116
    Deen—Great p82-90
    Dorland—Sum p42,104
    Imbert—Valois p3-119,por.
    Koven—Women p122-156,por.
    Love—Famous p23
    *MacVeagh—Champlin p385-386
    Maurice—Makers p12

Margaret of Parma, Duchess (1522-1586)
    Neth. regent
    Hammerton p961,por.
    Phila.—Women unp.,por.
    Stiles—Postal p165

Margaret of Savoy (fl. 15th cent.)
    Fr. saint
    Blunt—Great p163-164
    Wescott—Calen. p186

Margaret of Savoy (1851-1926)
    It. queen
    Schmidt—400 p256-257,por.

Margaret of Valois (1553-1615)
    Fr. queen
    Haggard—Remark. p18-21
    Hammerton p960
    Imbert—Valois (see index)

Margaret of Valois—Angoulême.
    See Margaret of Navarre

Margaret of Verona (d. 1395)
    It. saint
    Wescott—Calen. p128

Margaret Rose (1930-   )
    Eng. princess
    CR '59 p485-486,por.

(Continued)

Margaret Rose—Continued

> Crawford—Little p1-314,por.
> Cur. Biog. '53 p413-415,por.
> Phila.—Women, unp.,por.
> Stiles—Postal p165
> Time June 13,1949 p36,por.(Cover);
> Nov.7,1955 p35,por.(Cover)

Margaretha Antonia Marie Felicite (1957)
> Luxem. princess
> Stiles—Postal p165

Margarita. See Rita, Saint

Marge. See Damerel, Donna

Margot. See Margaret of Valois

Margrethe (or Margaret) (1940-   )
> Dan. princess
> Stiles—Postal p166

Margriet Francesca (1943-   )
> Nether. princess
> Stiles—Postal p166

Marguerite, Marie.
> See Alacoque, Marguerite Marie,
> Saint

Marguerite of Valois.
> See Margaret of Valois

Maria (fl. 1920's)
> Rum. queen, consort of
> Ferdinand I
> New Yorker Oct.23,1926 p26,por.
> (Profiles)

Maria II (Maria da Gloria) (1819-1853)
> Port. queen
> Arsenius—Dict. p124,por.
> Phila.—Women, unp.,por.
> Stiles—Postal p166

Maria Alvarez, Mother (fl. 1900's)
> Fr. missionary nun
> Elgin—Nun p66-67

Maria Antonia Walpurgis (1724-1780)
> Ger. electress of Saxony, art,
> music patroness
> McCoy—Portraits p124,por.

Maria Feodorovna (b. 1759)
> Russ., wife of Czar Peter I
> Waters—Women p225

Maria Goretti (1890-1902)
> It. saint
> Sharkey—Pop. p215-217
> Stiles—Postal p237

Maria Gratia, Mother (fl. 1920's)
> Amer. missionary nurse
> Elgin—Nun p88-89,por.

Maria Josepha Rosello (c. 1811-1880)
> It. saint
> Englebert—Lives p466

Maria Kristina (or Cristina) (1911-   )
> Sp. princess, Red Cross nurse
> Arsenius—Dict. p124-125,por.
> Phila.—Women unp.,por.
> Stiles—Postal p166

Maria of Cordova (d. 851)
> Sp. saint
> Englebert—Lives p447

Maria of Victorica (d. 1920)
> Ger. spy
> Hoehling—Women p75-98

Maria Soledad, Sister (b. 1826)
> Sp. nun
> Elgin—Nun p108-109,por.

Maria Theresa (1717-1780)
> Aust. empress, Hung. queen
> Abbott—Notable p137-145
> Arsenius—Dict. p125,por.
> Dorland—Sum p52
> °Farmer—Book p102-112
> Fifty—Famous p180-187,por.
> Fitzhugh—Concise p444-445
> Haggard—Remark. p88-91,120-127
> Hammerton p961,por.
> Jenkins—Heroines p183-218,por.
> MacVeagh—Champlin p386,por.
> Muir—Women p131-135
> °Nisenson—More Minute, p94,por.
> Parton—Dau. p399-405,por.
> Parton—Noted p399-405,por.
> Phila.—Women, unp.,por.
> Russell—Glit. p128,136,161,184-185,
>   227,por.
> Schmidt—400 p43,por.
> Stiles—Postal p166

Maria Theresa (1855-1944)
> Aust. arch duchess
> Cur. Biog. '44 p447

Maria Victoria Fornari (1562-1617)
> It. saint
> Englebert—Lives p348-349

Mariamne (Biblical) (c. 60-c. 29 B.C.)
> Judaean queen, wife of Herod the
> Great
> Boccaccio—Conc. p189-191
> °Levinger—Great p81-84
> °MacVeagh—Champlin p386
> Marble—Women, Bible p94-97

Mariana, Sister (fl. 1660's)
> Port. nun, friend of Marquis de
> Chanilly
> Blei—Fasc. p59-62

Mariana de Jesus.
See Parades y Flores, Mariana de Jesus

Mariani, Virginia (b. 1824)
It. painter
Waters—Women p225

Marianne, Sister (fl. 1900's)
Amer. nurse, foundress, nun
Pennock—Makers p23-24

Marie (fl. 1910's)
Belg. child spy
*Nolen—Spies p100-105

Marie (1890-1958)
Russ. grand duchess
Carnegie—Little p147-150,por.
*Ferris—Five p185-269,por.

Marie (1899-   )
Rum. princess
Arsenius—Dict. p126

Marie Adelaide (1894-1924)
Luxem. grand duchess
Arsenius—Dict. p125,por.
Phila.—Women, unp.,por.
Stiles—Postal p166

Marie Adelaide (1924-   )
Luxem. princess
Arsenius—Dict. p125,por.
Hammerton p961-962
Stiles—Postal p167

Marie Alexandria Victoria (1875-1938)
Rum. queen, consort of Ferdinand I
Arsenius—Dict. p125,por.
Bolitho—Biog. p8-66,por.
New Yorker Oct.23,1926 p26-27,por.
Phila.—Women, unp.,por.
Stiles—Postal p166
Time Aug.4,1924 p9,por.(Cover)

Marie Alicia, Sister (fl. 1960's)
Belg. nun, social worker
Elgin—Nun p114-115,por.

Marie-Amélie de Bourbon (1782-1866)
Fr. queen
Schmidt—400 p182-183,por.

Marie Anne (1861-1942)
Luxem. regent
Stiles—Postal p166

Marie Antoinette (1755-1793)
Fr. queen
Abbott—Notable p146-155,por.
Adelman—Famous p91-93,por.
Armour—It p87-96
Blei—Fasc. p161-164,por.
*Cather—Girlhood p271-288
Chandler—Famous p117-142
Coffman—Kings p117-120,por.

Dark—Royal p275-290,por.
Dorland—Sum p27
Elson—Woman's p114-116,por.
*Farmer—Book p127-130
Fifty—Famous p242-248,por.
Fitzhugh—Concise p445-446
Hammerton p962,por.
*Hayward—Book p167-184
*Humphrey—Marys p66-92
Hyde—Modern p231-256
Jenkins—Heroines p445-469
*Jones—Modern p33-45,por.
Kavanagh—Woman (2) (see index),
por.
*MacVeagh—Champlin p386-387,por.
Mayne—Enchant. p154-165,por.
Nisenson—Minute p108,por.
*O'Clery—Queens p115-122
Orr—Famous p163-177
Orr—Famous Affin. II p25-44
Russell—Glit. p260-262,271-275
Schmidt—400 p177-178,por.
Sewell—Brief p96-97
Thomas—Vital p369-372

Marie-Astrid (1954-   )
Luxem. princess
Stiles—Postal p166

Marie-Caroline Ferdinande Louise, Duchess
de Berry (1798-1870)
Fr., wife of Charles Ferdinande
de Bourbon
Mayne—Enchant. p166-178,por.

Marie Christine of Savoy (b. 1812)
Fr. saint
Blunt—Great p96-97

Marie Christine de Lalaing, Princess of
Espinoy (1545-1582)
Belg. princess
Phila.—Women unp.,por.

Marie Clotilde (d. 1794)
Belg. saint
Englebert—Lives p402

Marie D'Aubray, Marquise de Brinvilliers
(d. 1676)
Fr., mistress of Gaudin de Sainte-
Croix
Ewart—World's p177-185

Marie de France (fl. 12th cent.)
Fr. poet
*MacVeagh—Champlin p388
Welch—Six p29-56

Marie de L'Incarnation (1599-1672)
Fr.-Can. educator, religious worker
Deen—Great p358-360
Englebert—Lives p151

Marie de Lorraine-Armagnac (1688-1724)
    Mon. princess, daughter of Louis I
    Phila.—Women unp.,por.
    Stiles—Postal p166

Marie de Medici (1573-1642)
    Fr., queen of Henry IV
    Beard—Woman p305-306
    Fifty—Famous p257-261,por.
    Haggard—Remark. p20,22-30
    Hammerton p981,por.
    Waters—Women p237

Marie Feodorovna (1847-1928)
    Russ. empress
    Hammerton p962

Marie Françoise (1646-1683)
    Port. queen
    Hahn—Love p89-119

Marie Gabrielle, Alegonda Wilhelmina
        Louise (1925-   )
    Luxem. princess
    Arsenius—Dict. p125,por.
    Stiles—Postal p166

Marie José, Charlotte Sophie Henriette
        Gabrielle (1906-   )
    Belg. princess, It. queen
    Arsenius—Dict. p126,por.
    Phila.—Women unp.,por.
    Stiles—Postal p166

Marie Leszczynska (1703-1768)
    Fr. queen
    Hammerton p962

Marie Louise (1791-1847)
    Fr. empress, wife of Napoleon
    Guerber—Empresses p145-249,por.
    Hammerton p962,por.
    *MacVeagh—Champlin p387-388,por.
    Orr—Famous p267-288
    Orr—Famous Affin. II p155-185
    Stiles—Postal p166
    Waters—Women p226

Marie Louise, Sister, D. W. (fl. 1700's)
    Fr. nun
    Elgin—Nun p60-61,por.

Marie Maddalena Pasini, Sister (b. 1731)
    It. nun
    Ewart—World's p125-128

Marie Madeleine Postel (1746-c. 1836)
    Fr. saint
    Englebert—Lives p274

Marie of Rohan, Duchess of Chevreuse
        (d. 1679)
    Fr. politician
    Rogers—Gallant p297-343

Marie of Würtemberg, Duchess
        (1813-1839)
    It. sculptor, artist
    Waters—Women p226

Marie (or Maria) of Yugoslavia (1899-
        1961)
    Yugoslav. queen
    Phila.—Women, unp.,por.
    Stiles—Postal p166

Marie Suzanne, Sister (fl. 1900's)
    Fr. missionary, nun, microbiologist
    *Moore—Modern p93-99

Marie Thérèse de Soubiran (1834-1889)
    Fr. saint
    Englebert—Lives p220-221

Marie Victoire (Mary Victoria) (1850-1922)
    Mon., wife of Albert I
    Phila.—Women, unp.,por.
    Stiles—Postal p166

Mariemma (fl. 1940's)
    Sp. ballet dancer
    Haskell—Ballet p46

Marietta, Sister, M.S.V. (n.d.)
    It. missionary, nun
    Elgin—Nun p110-111,por.

Marillac, Louise de, Saint.
    See Le Gras, Louise

Marina (1906-1968)
    Brit. princess
    Hammerton p1451

Mariniana (fl. 260's A.D.)
    Rom. empress, wife of Valerianus
    Serviez—Roman (2) p314-319

Mario, Queen Tillotson (1896-1951)
    Amer. singer
    Ewen—Ency. p295
    Ewen—Living p231-232,por.
    McCoy—Portraits p124,por.
    Women—Achieve. p89,por.

Marion, Elizabeth (1916-   )
    Amer. novelist
    Warfel—Amer. p279-280,por.

Marion, Frances (1900-   )
    Amer. playwright, novelist
    Warfel—Amer. p280

Marion, Mary Videau (m. 1784)
    Amer. pioneer
    Green—Pioneer (2) p192-193

Mariquita (183?-1922)
    Fr. ballet dancer
    Beaumont—Complete p533-536

Marisol (Escobar) (1930-   )
Venez.-Amer. sculptor, painter
Cur. Biog. '68 p241-244,por.

Mark, Joyce (n.d.)
Amer. pioneer airline radio operator
°Peckham—Women p120

Markan, Maria (fl. 1930's)
Ice. singer
McCoy—Portraits p125,por.

Markham, Beryl (1902-   )
Eng. aviatrix
Cur. Biog. '42 p570-572,por.
°Fraser—Heroes p755-761,781-784,por.
°May—Women p124-125

Markham, Daisy (b. 1886)
Eng. actress
Wyndham—Chorus p165-168

Markham, Elizabeth (1780-1837)
Brit. author
Hammerton p963

Markham, Violet Rosa (c. 1872-1959)
Eng. social welfare worker
Hammerton p963

Markidis, Mae (fl. 1950's)
Amer. hostess
°May—Women p235

Markievicz, Constance Gore-Booth, Countess
de (1876-1927)
Irish politician
Abramowitz—Great p531-546
Hammerton p963,por.
Stiles—Postal p167

Markova, Alicia (1910-   )
Eng. ballet dancer
Atkinson—Dancers p108-114,por.
Beaton—Persona p71,por.
CR '59 p486-487,por.
Crowle—Enter p65-91,por.
Cur. Biog. '43 p497-500,por.
Davidson—Ballet p191-198,por.
Fisher—Ball. p8,por.
Haskell—Ballet p38-39,200-201,por.
Haskell—Vignet. p20-21,por.
°McConnell—Famous p62-75,por.
°Muir—Famous p101-111,por.
New Yorker Apr.15,1944 p23,por.
(Profiles)
°Seventeen—In p109-112,por.
Swinson—Dancers p39-43,por.
Swinson—Great p16,por.
°Terry—Star p154-165,por.

Marks, Jane (n.d.)
Amer. pioneer scout
°Deakin—True p173-189

Marks, Jeannette Augustus (1875-1964)
Amer. poet, playwright
Cook—Our p311-312

Marlatt, Frances Knoche (fl. 1930's)
Amer. lawyer, editor
Women—Achieve. p103,por.

Marlatt, Jean Steele (fl. 1930's)
Amer. poet
Women—Achieve. p175,por.

Marlborough, Consuelo Vanderbilt, Duchess
of (b.c. 1877)
Amer. heiress
Pearson—Marry. p90-100,por.

Marlborough, Lily Hammersley, Duchess of
d. 1909)
Amer. heiress
Pearson—Marry p86-88
Pearson—Pilgrim p80-95,por.

Marlborough, Sarah, Duchess of.
See Jennings, Sarah

Marlef, Claude Lefebure (fl. 1890's-1900's)
Fr. painter
Waters—Women p226-227

Marlett, Melba Balmat Grimes (1909-   )
Amer. author
Warfel—Amer. p281-282,por.

Marlowe, Julia (1865/10-1950)
Eng.-Amer. actress
Adelman—Famous p310
Blum—Great p13,por.
Bodeen—Ladies p101-106,por.
Coad—Amer. p298,por.
Dodd—Celeb. p244-247
Hammerton p965
Izard—Heroines p299-323,por.
Kobbé—Homes p67-94,por.
Logan—Part p778
°MacVeagh—Champlin p390
Marks—Glamour p317
Strang—Actresses p27-38,por.
Vance—Hear p101-130,por.
Wagenknecht—Seven p119-136,por.
°Wagner—Famous p80-86,por.

Marlowe, Marion (n.d.)
Amer. singer
TV—Person. (1) p117,por.

Marlowe, Sylvia (1908-   )
Amer. harpsichordist
Saleski—Jewish p522-523

Marmorston, Jessie (fl. 1930's)
Russ.-Amer. physician, pathologist
Women—Achieve. p99,por.

Marohn, Irma Elaine (fl. 1930's)
Amer. artist
Women—Achieve. p185,por.

Marot, Helen (b. 1865)
    Amer. labor leader
    Adelman—Famous p301-302
    Logan—Part p600-601

Marquardt, Alexandria (c. 1866-1943)
    Russ.-Amer. harpist
    Cur. Biog. '43 p550

Marriot, Emil, pseud. (Emilie Mataja)
        (fl. 1900's)
    Ger. author
    Heller—Studies p282

Marriott, Alice Lee (1910-   )
    Amer. ethnologist
    Cur. Biog. '50 p382-383,por.

Marriott, Elizabeth (d. 1755)
    Amer. colonial merchant, innkeeper
    Spruill—Women's p277,297-298

Marryat, Florence (1838-1899)
    Eng. novelist, lecturer, singer,
        comedienne
    Black—Notable p81-95,por.
    Dorland—Sum p34,198
    Furniss—Some p7-12,por.

Mars, Anne Françoise Hippolyte Boutet
        (1779-1847)
    Fr. actress, comedienne
    Adelman—Famous p132-133
    Dorland—Sum p18,164
    Hammerton p966

Marsalis, Frances Harrell (fl. 1930's-1940's)
    Amer. aviatrix
    *Adams—Sky p185-193, por.
    Earhart—Fun p177
    *May—Women p94-96,134,137

Marschal-Loepke, Grace (fl. 1940's)
    Amer. composer, pianist
    McCoy—Portraits p125,por.

Marsh, Alice Randall (fl. 1930's)
    Amer. painter
    Michigan—Biog. p207

Marsh, Clara Jo (fl. 1940's)
    Amer. WASP
    *May—Women p184

Marsh, Ellen (1922-   )
    Amer. novelist
    Warfel—Amer. p285,por.

Marsh, Lucille (fl. 1930's)
    Amer. teacher, dancer
    Women—Achieve. p85,por.

Marsh, Lucille Crews (b. 1888)
    Amer. composer
    Hipsher—Amer. p271-272

Marsh, Mrs. M. M. (fl. 1860's)
    Amer. Civil war humanitarian
    Brockett—Woman's p621-629

Marsh, Ngaio (1899-   )
    New Z. author, actress
    CR '59 p487,por.

Marsh, Susan Ellen (fl. 1860's)
    Amer. Civil war nurse
    Logan—Part p370

Marshall, Ann (1661-1682)
    Eng. actress
    MacQueen—Pope p57-58,62
    Wilson—All p168-170

Marshall, Armina.
    See Langner, Armina Marshall

Marshall, Bernice C. (fl. 1920's-1930's)
    Amer. club leader
    Women—Achieve. p162,por.

Marshall, (Sarah) Catharine (1914-   )
    Amer. author, wife of Peter
        Marshall
    CR '59 p487-488,por.
    Cur. Biog. '55 p403-405,por.
    Fitzgibbon—My p33-39

Marshall, Mrs. Christopher (fl. 1770's)
    Amer. pioneer, Rev. war patriot
    Earle—Colonial p258-275

Marshall, Clara (1848-1931)
    Amer. physician
    Mead—Medical p30

Marshall, Elizabeth (fl. 1800's)
    Amer. pioneer pharmacist
    Dolan—Goodnow's p176

Marshall, Emily. See Otis, Emily Marshall

Marshall, Florence M. (fl. 1900's-1930's)
    Amer. vocational educator
    Women—Achieve. p200

Marshall, Harriet Gibbs (fl. 1900's)
    Amer. music teacher
    Cuney-Hare—Negro p255,por.

Marshall, Lois (1924-   )
    Can. singer
    Cur. Biog. '60 p263-264,por.

Marshall, Marguerite Moers (1887-1964)
    Amer. journalist, author
    Ross—Ladies p94-96,485,por.,cover
    Women—Achieve. p86,por.

Marshall, Mary Isham (1737-1809)
    Amer. pioneer
    Green—Pioneer (3) p473

Marshall, Nancy Stinnett (d. 1831)
  Amer. pioneer
  DAR Mag. p388-389 July 1921,portrayal

Marshall, Rebecca ("Becky") (1663-1677)
  Eng. actress
  MacQueen—Pope p58-62,86
  Wilson—All p170-172

Marshall, Rosamond Van der Zee (1900/02-
    1957)
  Amer. author
  Cur. Biog. '42 p575,por.
  Cur. Biog. '58 p273
  Warfel—Amer. p287,por.

Marshman, Hannah (1767-1847)
  Eng. missionary
  Deen—Great p378-380

Martesia. See Marpesia

Martha (Biblical)
  Buchanan—Women p91-93
  Chappell—Fem. p167-180
  Culver—Women p53-54
  Deen—All p176-181
  Englebert—Lives p290
  Faluhaber—Women p175-179
  Lewis—Portraits p116-119
  Lord—Great p160-172
  McCartney—Great p73-85
  *MacVeagh—Champlin p391
  Marble—Women, Bible p270-281
  Mead—250 p212
  Morton—Women p159-165
  Ockenga—Women p183-196
  Sharkey—Pop. p26-29
  Van der Velde—She p165-171
  Wescott—Calen. p112
  *Windham—Sixty p14-18

Martha (d. 270)
  Pers. saint
  Blunt—Great p19-20
  Englebert—Lives p24-25

Martha (fl.c. 1400)
  Fr. saint
  Schmidt—400 p392,por.

Martha (1901-1954)
  Nor. princess
  Fairfax—Ladies p213-214

Martha (m. 1929)
  Swed. princess
  Time Mar.25,1929 p24,por.

Martia. See Proba, Anicia Faltonia

Martin, Elizabeth ("Betty").
  See Smith, Elizabeth ("Betty") Martin

Martin, Elizabeth Gilbert (b. 1837)
  Amer. author and translator
  Logan—Part p837

Martin, Elizabeth Marshall (fl. 1770's)
  Amer. Rev. war patriot, heroine
  Ellet—Women (1) p311-318
  Hanaford—Dau. p48-49
  Logan—Part p156-157
  *Sickels—Calico p41-55

Martin, Gertrude (fl. 1910's)
  Amer. educator
  Logan—Part p725-726

Martin, Grace (fl. 1770's)
  Amer. Rev. war heroine, patriot
  Ellet—Women (1) p311-318
  Green—Pioneer (2) p336-343,por.
  Hanaford—Dau. p49
  Logan p157

Martin, Helen. See Rood, Helen Martin

Martin, Helen Frances Theresa (1912-   )
  Amer., animal keeper
  Cur. Biog. '55 p405-407,por.

Martin, Helen Reimensnyder (1868-1939)
  Amer. novelist
  Overton—Women p203-204

Martin, Jackie (Cecilia) (1903-   )
  Amer. photographer
  Cur. Biog. '43 p505-506,por.

Martin, Lillien Jane (1851-1943)
  Amer. psychologist
  Cur. Biog. '42 p575-577,por.
  Cur. Biog. '43 p506

Martin, Lily Irvine (fl. 1910's)
  Eng. pioneer aviatrix
  Planck—Women p15

Martin, Maria (1796-1863)
  Amer. botanical artist, friend of
    Audubon
  Hollingsworth—Her p54-66

Martin, Marie Celeste. See Celeste, Marie

Martin, Martha (fl. 1930's)
  Ger. poet, musician
  Women—Achieve. p116,por.

Martin, Mary (1913-   )
  Amer. actress, singer
  Beaton—Persona p72
  Blum—Great p123,por.
  Blum—Television p188-189,por.
  CR '59 p489-490,por.
  CR '63 p404,por.
  Cur. Biog. '44 p447-449,por.
  Martin—Pete p437-488,por, jacket
  Murrow—This (2) p84-85
  Stambler—Ency. p148,150,por.

Martin, Mary, Mother (1892-   )
    Irish foundress, nun
    Burton—Loveliest p169-186

Martin, Minta (fl. 1900's)
    Amer. mother of Glenn Martin
    Planck—Women p43-44

Martin, Mrs. (fl. 1900's-1910's)
    Eng.-Amer. aviatrix
    Logan—Part p300-301

Martin, Rachel (Rachel Clay) (fl. 1770's)
    Amer. Rev. war heroine
    Ellet—Women (1) p311-318
    Green—Pioneer (2) p336-342,343,por.
    Hanaford—Dau. p49
    Logan—Part p157

Martin, Sarah J. (1840-1900)
    Amer. club leader
    Logan—Part p352

Martin, Victoria Claflin Woodhull
    See Woodhull, Victoria Claflin

Martin, Violet Florence (1862-1915)
    (Martin Ross)
    Irish novelist
    Hammerton p967

Martin de Campo, Victoria (fl. 1840's)
    Sp. painter
    Waters—Women p227-228

Martindale, Elizabeth Hall fl. (1660's-1670's)
    Eng. Puritan
    Stenton—English p111-113

Martindale, Louisa (1839-1914)
    Eng., mother of Hilda Martindale
    Marindale—Some p15-16

Martineau, Edith (fl. 1900's)
    Eng. painter
    Waters—Women p228

Martineau, Harriet (1802-1876)
    Eng. author, translator, social re-
      former, economist, philanthropist
    Abbott—Notable p318-322,por.
    Adelman—Famous p153-154
    Bottrall—Pers. p116-119,227
    Courtney—Adven. p137-157,193-207,
      por.
    Dexter—Career p124,129-133,136
    Dorland—Sum p44,171,189
    Hammerton p967
    Hubbard—Little p79-114,por.
    Johnson—Women p148-152
    MacCarthy—Women p39-40
    Padover—Confess. p176-180
    Parton—Dau. p483-493,por.
    Parton—Noted p555-563,por.
    Stebbins—Victorian p15-20,197,205
    Stenton—English p277,324,326,338-
      343,345

Martinelli, Angelica (f.c. 1579)
    It. actress
    Gilder—Enter p60-61

Martinez, Marianne (b. 1744)
    Aust. pianist, singer, composer
    Elson—Woman's p158-159

Martyn, Marguerite (fl. 1930's)
    Amer. journalist
    Ross—Ladies p555-556

Marusia (1918-   )
    Pol. fashion designer
    CR '63 p405,por.

Marvel, Elizabeth Newell (1904-   )
    Amer. organization official
    Cur. Biog. '62 p292-294,por.

Marvel, Louise ("Cattle Lady") (fl. 1960's)
    Amer. rancher
    Parshalle—Kash. p117,por.

Marvingt, Marie (c. 1874-1963)
    Fr. pioneer, aviatrix, adventurer
    *Lauwick—Heroines p25,28

Marx, Elizabeth Lisl Weil
    See Weil, Lisl

Marx, Jenny von Westphalen (m. 1843)
    Ger. wife of Karl Marx
    Orr—Famous Affin. III p128-144
    Stiles—Postal p168

Marx-Aveling, Eleanor (b. 1856)
    Ger., daughter of Karl Marx, friend
      of G. B. Shaw
    DuCann—Loves p136-151

Mary (Biblical) Virgin, mother of Jesus
    Adelman—Famous p25-26
    Arsenius—Dict. p173,portrayal
    Beebe—Saints p143-147
    Bowie—Women p8-12
    Buchanan—Women p75-77
    Deen—All p156-167
    D'Humy—Women p1-51
    Drinker—Music p144-164
    Faulhaber—Women p205-248
    Hammerton p969
    Heaps—Five p17-34
    *Humphrey—Marys p187-203
    Lewis—Portraits p22-32
    Lord—Great p109-122
    *MacVeagh—Champlin p391-392
    Marble—Women, Bible p145-153
    Mead—250 p190
    Muir—Women p49-53
    Nelson—Bible p119-122
    Ockenga—Women p171-181
    Phila.—Women, unp.,por.
    Schmidt—400 p269,portrayal
    Stiles—Postal p168
    Van Der Velde—She p133-147

Mary (Biblical), mother of James, Joses
    Buchanan—Women p82-83
    Deen—All p209-213

Mary (Biblical), wife of Cleophas,
    sister-in-law of Joseph
    Heaps—Five p39-49

Mary (Biblical), mentioned by Paul
    Deen—All p281-282

Mary I (1516-1558) (or Mary Tudor,
    "Bloody Mary")
    Brit. queen
    Abbott—Notable p65-75
    *Boyd—Rulers p103-113,por.
    Dark—Royal p57-82,por.
    Dorland—Sum p19
    Ewart—World's p129-155
    *Farjeon—Kings p50,por.
    Hammerton p969,por.
    MacVeagh—Champlin p392,por.
    Sanders—Intimate p42-58,por.
    Thornton-Cook—Royal p62-118,por.
    Trease—Seven p39-75

Mary II (1662-1692)
    Brit. queen
    Farjeon—Kings p64,por.
    Fifty—Famous p217-227
    Parton—Dau. p354-361
    Parton—Noted p355-361
    Sanders—Intimate p121-137,por.
    Stenton—Eng. p191,198,209-212,216
    Thornton—Cook—Royal p166-191,por.
    Trease—Seven p117-146

Mary (1542-1587) (Mary Stuart,
    queen of Scots)
    Scot. queen
    Abbott—Notable p76-86,por.
    Adelman—Famous p53-55,por.
    *Boyd—Rulers p129-139,por.
    *Cather—Girlhood p243-267
    Clark—Great p516-533
    Dark—Royal p85-134,por.
    Dorland—Sum p19
    *Farmer—Book p89-101
    Fifty—Famous p177-179,por.
    Fitzhugh—Concise p451-452
    Golding—Great p84-89
    Hammerton p970-971,por.
    *Hayward—Book p146-166
    *Humphrey—Marys p11-26,por.
    Imbert—Valois p190-205,339,por.
    Jenkins—Heroines p325-390,por.
    Kemble—Idols p173-195
    Koven—Women p212-230,por.
    Love—Famous p25
    *MacVeagh—Champlin p392-393,por.
    *Nisenson—Minute p105,por.
    *O'Clery—Queens p86-101
    Orr—Famous p55-70
    Orr—Famous Affin. I p73-94
    *Power—More p14-34,por.
    Sanders—Intimate p223-226

    Schmidt—400 p132-134,por.
    Sewell—Brief p52-53
    Snyder—Treas. p84-92
    *Steedman—When p52-61
    Thomas—Living Women p53-63,por.
    Thomas—Vital p271-275,por.

Mary (1867-1953)
    Brit. queen, consort of George V.
    Arsenius—Dict. p126,por.
    Hammerton p969-970,por.
    New York p247-267
    New Yorker May 4,1935 p20-24,por.;
      May 11, 1935 p28-32 (Profiles)
    Phila.—Women, unp.,por.
    Time May 30,1927 p14,por.; Mar. 17,
      1930 p22,por.; Oct. 27,1930 por.
    (Covers)

Mary, Lady (fl. c. 1720's)
    Eng. author, social reformer
    Stenton—Eng. p261-263

Mary, Princess, Duchess of **Gloucester**
    (1776-1857)
    Eng. daughter of George III.
    Thornton-Cook—Royal p208-221,por.

Mary, Princess **Langravine of Hesse Cassel**
    (1723-1772)
    Eng. daughter of George II.
    Thornton-Cook—Royal p194-205,por.

Mary Alma, Sister (fl. 1960's)
    Amer. biochemist, nun
    Elgin—Nun p34-35,por.

Mary Alphonsa, Mother
    See **Lathrop, Rose Hawthorne**

Mary Ann Ida, Sister (fl. 1950's)
    Amer. nun
    Elgin—Nun p82-83,por.

Mary Aquinas, Sister (fl. 1950's)
    Amer. nun, aviatrix, jet pilot
    *May—Women p182,por.

Mary Bartholomew of Bagnesi (d. 1577)
    It. saint
    Wescott—Calen. p77

Mary Beatrice ("Mary of Modena")
    (1658-1718)
    Brit. queen
    Hammerton p969
    Sanders—Intimate p112-120,por.

Mary Benedict (fl. 1960's)
    Amer. nun, surgeon
    Elgin—Nun p132-133,por.

Mary Bernard Soubirous (1844-1879)
    Fr. saint
    Maynard—Saints p249-263

Mary Carmelita, Mother (fl. 1920's)
    Amer. nun
    Elgin—Nun p92-95,por.

Mary Columba, Mother (1892-   )
    Amer. nun
    Time Apr.11,1955 p76,por.(Cover)

Mary de Sales, Mother (Wilhelmina
        Tredow) (fl. 1910's)
    Amer. educator
    Logan—Part p622

Mary Frances (1715-1791)
    It. saint
    Wescott—Calen. p156

Mary Julia, Sister (Elizabeth Ann Dullea)
    (b. 1886)
    Amer. teacher
    Logan—Part p723

Mary Lange, Mother (fl. 1820's)
    Fr.-Amer. nun
    Elgin—Nun p80-81,por.

Mary Liliane, Princess of Rethy (m.c. 1940)
    Belg. 2nd wife of Leopold III
    Time July18,1949 p23,por.(Cover)

Mary Loyola, Sister (fl. 1840's)
    Amer. nun, W. pioneer
    Ross—Westward p77-92

Mary Madeleva.
    See Madeleva, Mary Evaline, Sister

Mary Magdalene (Biblical)
    Buchanan—Women p87-89
    Deen—All p200-205
    Englebert—Lives p281-282
    Faulhaber—Women p169-175
    Hammerton p971
    Heaps—Five p73-82
    Lewis—Portraits p192-195
    Lord—Great p135-147
   *MacVeagh—Champlin p392
    Marble—Women, Bible p266-270
    Mead—250 p207
    Morton—Women p193-199
    Nelson—Bible p103-105
    Ockenga—Women p197-210
    Phila.—Women, unp.,por.
    Stiles—Postal p236
    Van Der Velde—She p212-219
    Wescott—Calen. p107

Mary Magdalene, Sister (fl. 1910's)
    (Sarah C. Cox)
    Amer. translator
    Logan—Part p837

Mary Magdalene de' Pazzi (1566-1607)
    It. saint
    Dingwall—Very p119-144,por.

Mary, Mother Mary of Jesus (1818-1878)
    Belg. foundress
    Burton—Loveliest p77-95

Mary, Mother of Providence (1825-1871)
    Fr. foundress
    Burton—Loveliest p96-113

Mary of Atholl (b. 1085)
    Scot. daughter of King Malcolm
    Thornton-Cook—Royal p2,4

Mary of Bethany (Biblical) sister of
       Martha and Lazarus
    Buchanan—Women p91-93
    Chappell—Fem. p181-194
    Culver—Women p53-54
    Deen—All p176-181
    Heaps—Five p55-67
    Lewis—Portraits p116-119
    Lord—Great p160-172
    Macartney—Great p73-85
   *MacVeagh—Champlin p392
    Marble—Women, Bible p270-281
    Mead—250 p213
    Morton—Women p159-165
    Van Der Velde—She p173-180

Mary of Boulogne (1136-1181)
    Eng. daughter of King Stephen
    Thornton-Cook—Royal p3,5-7

Mary of Burgundy (Marie de Bourgogne)
    Duchess of Burgundy
    (1457-1482)
    Fr. daughter of Charles the Bold
    Hammerton p971

Mary of Champagne (1145-c 1198)
    Beard—Woman p214,217

Mary of Egypt (d. 430)
    Egypt saint
    Englebert—Lives p129
    Wescott—Calen. p48

Mary of France (1496-1533)
    Fr. queen of Louis XIII
    Hammerton p971
    Thornton-Cook—Royal p26-60,por.

Mary of Guise (Mary of Lorraine)
    (1515-1560)
    Scot., queen of James V
    Hammerton p971

Mary of Jerusalem (Biblical) mother of Mark
    Buchanan—Women p96-98
    Deen—All p209-213
    Heaps—Five p87-101
    Hughes—Mothers p139-143
    Marble—Women, Bible p247-249

Mary of Lorraine.
    See Mary of Guise

Mary of Modena.
See **Mary Beatrice**

Mary of Oignies, Blessed (d. 1213)
Belg. mystic
Englebert—Lives p241-242

Mary of Orange (1631-1660)
Eng. princess, daughter of Charles I
Hammerton p971
Thornton-Cook—Royal p128-164,por.

Mary of Rome (d. 120)
Rom. saint
Wescott—Calen. p171

Mary of St. Euphrasia, Sister.
See **Pelletier, Marie de Saint Euphrasia,**
Saint

Mary of the Infant Jesus, Sister (c. 1830-1917)
Amer. nun, W. pioneer
*Johnson—Some p48-52,por.

Mary of Waltham, Duchess of Brittany
(1344-1361)
Eng. daughter of Edward III
Thornton-Cook—Royal p9,19-21

Mary of York (1466-1482)
Eng. princess
Thornton—Cook—Royal p9,22-24

Mary Plantaganet (1279-1333)
Eng. princess, daughter of Edward I
Thornton-Cook—Royal p9,11-17

Mary Stuart.
See **Mary** (1542-1587)

Mary Theodore, Sister (fl. 1930's)
Amer. nun
Elgin—Nun p106-107,por.

Mary Victoria Alexandra Alice (1897-1965)
Eng. princess
Arsenius—Dict. p127,por.
Hammerton p971,por.
Stiles—Postal p168
Thornton-Cook—Royal p224-233,por.

Mary Victoria Mary Augusta Louise Olga
(1867-1953)
Eng. wife of George V
Stiles—Postal p169

Masaryk, Charlotte Garrigue (1850-1923)
Czech. labor leader
Schmidt—400 p88,por.

Masha, pseud.
See **Stern, Marie Simchow**

Masham, Abigail Hill, Lady (d. 1734)
Eng. friend of Queen Anne
Hammerton p972
Stenton—English p247-249

Masham, Damaris Cudworth, Lady
(1658-1708)
Eng. scholar, writer
Stenton—English p219-221,223,233

Masina, Giulietta (1927-   )
It. actress
CR '59 p493,por.
Cur. Biog. '58 p275-276,por.

Masland, Mary Elizabeth (fl. 1910's-1930's)
Amer. educator
Women—Achieve. p121,por.

Mason, Amelia Gere (d. 1923)
Amer. author
Logan—Part p855

Mason, Biddy (fl. 1850's)
Amer. pioneer nurse
Brown—Home. p242-244

Mason, Clara (fl. 1930's)
Amer. industrial artist
Women—Achieve. p154,por.

Mason, Edith Barnes (1893-   )
Amer. singer
McCoy—Portraits p126,por.

Mason, Emily Virginia (1815-1909)
Amer. humanitarian
Logan—Part p380

Mason, Mary Hewett.
See **Hewett, Mary**

Mason, Mary Knight (1857-1944)
Amer. song writer, pianist
McCoy—Portraits p234,por.

Mason, Maud M. (1867-1956)
Amer. artist
Women—Achiev. p98,por.

Mason, Mrs. (fl. 1790's)
Amer. pioneer
Ellet—Pioneer p58-59

Massari, Luigia (b. 1810)
It. painter, needlewoman
Waters—Women p228

Massevitch, Alla Genrikhovna (1918-   )
Russ. astrophysicist, educator
Cur. Biog. '64 p283-284,por.

Massey, Gertrude (b. 1868)
Eng. painter
Waters—Women p228-229

Massey, Ilona (1912-   )
    Hung.-Amer. actress
    Lamparski—What. p180-181,por.

Massip, Marguerite (fl. 1900's)
    Swiss painter
    Waters—Women p229-230

Massolien, Ann (b. 1848)
    Ger. painter
    Waters—Women p230

Masters, Sybilla (fl.c. 1710's)
    Amer. colonial inventor
    Leonard—Amer. p118

Mata Hari.
    See Hari, Mata

Mataja, Emilie.
    See Marriot, Emil, pseud.

Materna, Amelie (c. 1845-1918)
    Aust. singer
    Adelman—Famous p254
    Ewen—Ency. p304
    Klein—Great p190-193
    Lahee—Famous p168-175
    McCoy—Portraits p127,por.
    Wagner—Prima p245

Mather, Eunice.
    See Williams, Eunice

Mather, Margaret (b. 1862)
    Can.-Amer. actress
    Logan—Part p777-778

Mather, Sarah Ann (b. 1820)
    Amer. philanthropist, author
    Logan—Part p545

Mathers, Diana, pseud.
    See Cooper, Diana, Lady

Mathers, Helen (fl. 1890's)
    Eng. author
    Black—Notable p68-80,por.

Mathews, Blanche Dingley (d. 1932)
    Amer. composer, author, music
        teacher
    McCoy—Portraits p127,por.

Mathews, Lucia Elizabeth.
    See Vestris, Lucia Elizabeth

Mathias, Mildred E. (1906-   ,)
    Amer. botanist
    Parshalle—Kash. p95-97,por.

Mathilde (1046-1115)
    It. countess, religious leader, abbess,
        daughter of Duke Bonefacius of
        Toscana
    Arsenius—Dict. p127,por.
    Culver—Women p87

Hammerton p973
Phila.—Women, unp.,por.
Schmidt—400 p246,por.
Stiles—Postal p170

Mathilde (1820-1904)
    It. princess, painter
    Waters—Women p230-231

Mathilde (1820-1902)
    Fr. princess, salonist
    Skinner—Elegant p171-183,por.

Mathilde Caroline (1813-1863)
    Grand duchess of Hesse
    Ger. painter
    Waters—Women p231

Mathilde of Canossa.
    See Mathilde (1046-1115)

Mathilde.
    See also Matilda

Matidia, Vibia (fl.c. 113)
    Rom., wife of L. Vibius Sabinius
    Balsdon—Roman p133,136-138,251

Matienzo, Carlota (1881-1926)
    Puert.Ric. teacher, feminist
    Schmidt—400 p336-337,por.

Matilda (Maude) (c. 895-c. 968)
    Ger. queen, saint, mother of Otto I
    Blunt—Great p84-86
    Deen—Great p325-326
    Engelbert—Lives p101-102
    Sharkey—Pop. p123-124
    Wescott—Calen. p38
    *Windham—Sixty p221-226

Matilda (Maude) (1102-1167)
    Eng. queen, wife of Henry V
    Fifty—Famous p74-82
    Hammerton p973
    Stenton—English p37
    Trease—Seven p14-35

Matilda of Flanders (d. 1083)
    Eng., wife of William the Conqueror
    Hammerton p973
    Muir—Women p72-73

Matilda of Tuscany.
    See Mathilde (1046-1115)

Matoaka.
    See Pocahontas

Matred (Biblical)
    Deen—All p282

Mattfeld, Marie (1870-1927)
    Ger. singer
    McCoy—Portraits p127,por.

Matthews, Adelaide b. 1886)
Amer. playwright
Mantle—Amer. p297
Mantle—Contemp. p318

Matthews, Anne (fl. 1750's)
Amer. merchant
Spruill—Women's p280,283

Matthews, Burnita Shelton (1894-   )
Amer. judge
Cur. Biog. '50 p385-387,por.

Matthews, Frances Aymar (fl. 1910's)
Amer. playwright, poet
Logan—Part p793

Matthews, Honor (fl. 1890's-1900's)
Amer. whaling voyager
Whiting—Whaling p259-262

Matthews, Jessie (1907-   )
Eng. actress
Hammerton p974

Matthews, Rebecca (fl. 1870's-1880's)
Amer. whaling voyager
Whiting—Whaling p240

Matthews, Victoria Earle (1861-1898)
Amer. club leader
Brown—Home p208-216,por.

Matthison, Edith Wynne (1875-1955)
Anglo-Amer. actress
Izard—Heroines p358-359

Mattingly, Marie.
See Meloney, Marie Mattingly

Mattocks, Isabella (1746-1826)
Eng. actress
MacQueen—Pope p294-295,por.

Matton, Ida (b. 1863)
Swed. sculptor
Waters—Women p231

Mattoon, Mary Dickinson (1758-1835)
Amer. Rev. war patriot
Green—Pioneer (3) p474-477,por.

Matveyeva, Novella (1935-   )
Russ. poet
Reavey—Nea p223

Matzenauer, Margarete (1881-1963)
Hung. singer
Ewen—Ency. p305
Ewen—Living p236,por.
Lahee—Grand p330-333,350,por.
McCoy—Portraits p127,por.

Maubourg, Jeanne (b. 1875)
Fr. singer
Lahee—Grand p280-281,371

Maud, Charlotte Mary Victoria (1869-1938)
Nor. queen
Hammerton p974
Phila.—Women unp.,por.
Stiles—Postal p170

Maude. See Matilda

Mauduit, Roberta, Countess de (fl. 1940's)
Eng. spy
Hoehling—Women p141

Maule, Frances (fl. 1930's)
Amer. journalist, advertising writer
Women—Achieve. p96,por.

Maura (period unknown)
Gr. saint
Englebert—Lives p456

Maurice, Mrs. (fl. 1840's)
Amer. "healer"
Fowler—Woman p476-479

Maurier, Daphne du.
See Du Maurier, Daphne

Maury, Antonia Caetana de Palva Pereira (b. 1886)
Amer. astronomer
Dorland—Sum p142

Maury, Betty Herndon (fl. 1860's)
Amer. Civil war diarist
Jones—Heroines p117-121,150-153,197-198,207-209
Simkins—Women p222-223

Maury, Cornelia Field (b. 1866)
Amer. painter
Waters—Women p231-232

Maverick, Amias Thomson (fl. 17th cent.)
Amer. pioneer
Bell—Women p147-149

Maxfield, Kathryn Erroll (fl. 1930's)
Amer. humanitarian
Women—Achieve. p110,por.

Maxfield, Mary B. (fl. 1860's)
Amer. Civil war nurse
Logan—Part p367

Maxfield, Winifred Hill (fl. 1930's)
Amer. club leader
Women—Achieve. p167,por.

Maxon, Hannah W. (d. 1910)
Amer. Civil war nurse
Logan—Part p361

Maxtone Graham, Joyce.
See Struther, Jan

Maxwell, Anna Caroline (1851-1929)
Amer. nurse
Pennock—Makers p42,por.
Schmidt—400 p401-402,por.

Maxwell, Coralie DeLong (b. 1898)
Amer. sculptor
National—Contemp. p224

Maxwell, Ellen Blackmar.
See Barker, Ellen Blackmar

Maxwell, Elsa (1883-1963)
Amer. hostess
CR '59 p498-499,por.
CR '63 p409,por.
Cur. Biog. '43 p518-521,por.
Cur. Biog. '64 p287
New Yorker Nov.25,1933 p24-27,por.
(Profiles)

Maxwell, Kate ("Cattle Kate") (fl. 1880's-
1890's)
Amer. W. rancher, cattlewoman
Horan—Desperate p227-241,por.

Maxwell, Mrs. Lawrence (fl. 1910's)
Amer. club leader
Logan—Part p402

Maxwell, Margery (fl. 1910's)
Amer. singer
McCoy—Portraits p128,por.

Maxwell, Marilyn (1922-   )
Amer. actress
CR '59 p499,por.
CR '63 p409-410,por.

Maxwell, Mrs. pseud.
See Payne, Winona Wilcox

May, Abbie W. (b. 1829)
Amer. Civil war humanitarian
Brockett—Woman's p554-557
Hanaford—Dau. p205-207,295

May, Catherine Dean (1914-   )
Amer. congresswoman, radio
commentator, producer
Cur. Biog. '60 p269-271,por.
Parshalle—Kash. p213-217,por.
U.S.—Women (87th) p29,por.
U.S.—Women (88th) p19,por.

May, Dorothy.
See Bradford, Dorothy

May, Edna (1878-1948)
Amer. actress, singer
Blum—Great p39,por.
Hammerton p978
Strang—Prima p147-155,por.

May, Elaine (1932-   )
Amer. actress
CR '63 p410,por.
Cur. Biog. '61 p300-302,por.

May, Geraldine Pratt (1895-   )
Amer. military officer, WAC, WAF
Cur. Biog. '49 p416-417,por.
*May—Women p190-191

May, Marjorie Merriweather Post Close
Hutton Davies (b. 1887)
Amer. financier
CR '63 p410,por.

May, Miss (fl. 1890's)
Eng. governess
Howe—Galaxy p154-161,por.

May, Olive.
See Drogheda, Olive Mary Meatyard
Moore, Countess of

May, Pamela (1917-   )
Brit. ballet dancer
Davidson—Ballet p205-208
Fisher—Ball. p16,por.
Haskell—Vignet. p49-50,por.

Mayer, Emilie (1812-1883)
Ger. composer
Elson—Woman's p161-162

Mayer, Harriet Wilbur (fl. 1910's-1930's)
Amer. organization official, public
welfare worker, translator
Women—Achieve. p200

Mayer, Jane Rothschild (Clare Jaynes,
pseud.) (n.d.)
Amer. author
Cur. Biog. '54 p364-365,por.
Warfel—Amer. p228-229,por.

Mayer, Maria Goeppert (1906-   )
Ger.-Amer. physicist, educator,
author
Cur. Biog. '64 p287-289,por.

Mayer, Marie Françoise Constance
(1775-1821)
Fr. artist
Waters—Women p384-386

Mayes, Rose Gorr (1898-   )
Amer. politician
Cur. Biog. '50 p388-390,por.

Mayhew, Adelaide (fl. 1900's-1910's)
Amer. Whaling voyager
Whiting—Whaling p270-274,por.

Mayhew, Caroline (m. 1834)
Amer. whaling voyager
Whiting—Whaling p10-20,233-236,por.

Mayhew, Eliza (m. 1851)
Amer. whaling voyager
Whiting—Whaling p196-199,236-237,
por.

Mayne, Clarice (fl. 1910's)
Eng. actress
Felstead—Stars p156-157,171,179,por.

Mayne, Ethel Colburn (d. 1941)
Irish author
Cur. Biog. '41 p566
Millett—Brit. p357-358

Maynor (Mainor) Dorothy (1910-   )
Amer. singer
*Cherry—Portraits p85-88
Cuney-Hare—Negro p385,por.
Cur. Biog. '40 p568-569,por.
Cur. Biog. '51 p419-421,por.
Ewen—Living p236-237,por.
McCoy—Portraits p128,por.

Mayo, Edith Graham (fl. 1930's-1940's)
Amer. mother of year
Davis—Mothers p178-179

Mayo, Eleanor R. (1920-   )
Amer. novelist
Warfel—Amer. p290,por.

Mayo, Katherine (1867-1940)
Amer. author
Cur. Biog. '40 p569,por.
Hammerton p979

Mayo, Louise Abigail Wright (1825-1915)
Amer., mother of Mayo brothers
Davis—Mothers p88-89

Mayo, Margaret (1882-1951)
Amer. playwright
Logan—Part p789
Mantle—Amer. p298
Mantle—Contemp. p318

Mayo, Sarah Edgarton (d. 1848)
Amer. poet
Hanaford—Dau. p268

Mayor, Harriet Hyatt (1868-1934)
Amer. sculptor
National—Contemp. p224
Waters—Women p170

Mayreder-Obermayer, Rose (b. 1858)
Aust. painter
Waters—Women p232

Maywood, Augusta (b. 1825)
Amer. ballet dancer
*Terry—Star p87-92,por.

Mazarin, Duchess of.
See **Mancini, Hortense**, Duchess of
Mazarin

Mazarin, Mariette (1874-1953)
Fr. singer, actress
Lahee—Grand p218,222-223,229-231

Mc.   See Mac

Mead, Kate Campbell (1867-1941)
Amer. physician
Cur. Biog. '41 p568
Lovejoy—Women Phys. p19,21,por.

Mead, Marcia (b. 1879)
Amer. architect
Women—Achieve. p201

Mead, Margaret (Margaret Bateson)
(1901/1902-   )
Amer. anthropologist
*Clymer—Modern p120-128,por.
CR '59 p500,por.
CR '63 p422,por.
Cur. Biog. '40 p569-570,por.
Cur. Biog. '51 p421-423,por.
Murrow—This (1) p115-116
*Nathan—Women p147-175
New Yorker Dec.30,1961 p31,por.
(Profiles)
Parshalle—Kash. p187-190,por.
*Poole—Outdoors p161-173,por.
Progress—Science p226,por.
*Yost—Women Sci. p214-232

Mead, Olive (fl. 1940's)
Amer. violinist
McCoy—Portraits p129,por.

Meade, Elizabeth Thomasina (d. 1914)
Irish novelist
Hammerton p980

Meade, Julia (1930-   )
Amer. actress, TV personality
CR '63 p423,por.

Meadowcroft, Enid La Monte (1898-1966)
Amer. author
Cur. Biog. '49 p421-422,por.

Meadows, Audrey (1922/29-   )
Amer. actress, TV personality
CR '59 p500-501,por.
CR '63 p423,por.
Cur. Biog. '58 p278-280,por.
TV—Person. (2) p11-12,por.

Meadows, Jayne Cotter (1925-   )
Amer. actress
CR '59 p501,por.
CR '63 p423-424,por.
Cur. Biog. '58 p280-281,por.
TV—Person (2) p93-94,por.

Meadows, Margaret (fl. 1720's)
Eng. maid of honor
Melville—Maids p206-208

Meagher, Katherine Kelly (m. 1907)
    Amer. philanthropist
    Logan—Part p535

Meagher, Mary (b.c. 1855)
    Amer. W. pioneer, agriculturist
    Brown—Gentle p255

Means, Helen Hotchkin (1897-   )
    Amer. organization official
    Cur. Biog. '46 p386-387

Mears, Helen (1900-   )
    Amer. author, lecturer
    Cur. Biog. '43 p527-528,por.

Mears, Helen Farnsworth (1876-1916)
    Amer. sculptor
    Dorland—Sum p158-159
    Jackman—Amer. p411-412
    Michigan—Biog. p210
    Taft—Women, Mentor (172) #2 p11

Mears, Marjorie (fl. 1920's)
    Amer. journalist
    Ross—Ladies p430-431

Mears, Virginia (fl. 1930's)
    Amer. advertising executive
    Women—Achieve. p155,por.

Meave (d. 70 A.D.)
    Irish queen, heroine
    McCraith—Romance p7-17

Mechthild of Magdeburg (1210-1280)
    Ger. religious leader, poet, mystic
    Deen—Great p329-330
    Drinker—Music p199-200
    Welch—Six p57-82

Mechtold, Mary Rider (fl. 1910's)
    Amer. playwright
    Logan—Part p791

Medhavi, Ramabai Dongre (b. 1858)
    Ind. religious leader, author,
        humanitarian, educator
    Foster—Religion p196-221,por.

Medicis, Catherine de.
    See Catherine de Medicis

Medicis, Marie de.
    See Marie de Medicis

Mee, Cassis Ward (b. 1848)
    Can.-Amer. lecturer, labor leader
    Logan—Part p903-904

Meech, Jeannette du Bois (b. 1835)
    Amer. evangelist, industrial
        educator, social reformer
    Logan—Part p905

Meeker, Caroline (d. 1835)
    Amer., friend of Abraham Lincoln
    Barton—Women p141-156

Meeker, Eleanor Richardson (fl. 1830's-1850's)
    Amer. missionary, teacher
    Whitton—These p214-215

Meeker, Josephine (g. 1878)
    Amer. W. pioneer
    Brown—Gentle p12,21-22,24-35,por.

Meekins, Mrs. A. M. (fl. 1860's)
    Amer. spy
    Simkins—Women p78

Meggers, Betty Jane (1921-   )
    Amer. cultural anthropologist
    *Poole—Outdoors p146-160,por.

Meggs, Mary (fl. 1660's) (Orange Moll)
    Eng. theatre contractor
    MacQueen—Pope p76

Megolastrata of Sparta (fl. 7th cent. B.C.)
    Gr. artist, singer
    Drinker—Music p103

Meherin, Elenore (fl. 1910's-1920's)
    Amer. journalist
    Ross—Ladies p465-467

Mehetabel (Biblical)
    Deen—All p282

Mehle, Aileen (Suzy, pseud.), (n.d.)
    Amer. journalist, columnist
    CR '63 p602-603,por.

Mehta, Hansa (1897-   )
    Ind. U.N. delegate
    Cur. Biog. '47 p432-433,por.

Mei Ying (fl. 1800's)
    Chin. seafarer
    Snow—Women p34,45-46

Meiere, M. Hildreth (fl. 1910's-1930's)
    Amer. painter
    Women—Achieve. p79,por.

Meigs, Elizabeth.
    See Chittenden, Elizabeth Meigs

Meigs, Mary Noel (fl. 1840's)
    Amer. poet
    Hanaford—Dau. p267

Meiner, Annamarie (fl. 1930's)
    Ger. printer
    Club—Printing p9-10

Meir, Golda (1898-   )
    Israeli diplomat
    CR '59 p502-503,por.
    Cur. Biog. '50 p395-397,por.

Meirs, Linda (fl. 1910's)
Amer. war nurse
DAR Mag. Nov.1921 p647-648,por.

Meisle, Kathryn (1898-   )
Amer. singer
Ewen—Living p238-239,por.
McCoy—Portraits p129,por.

Meitner, Lise (1878-1968)
Aust. physicist
Chambers—Dict. col.309
Cur. Biog. '45 p393-395,por.
Cur. Biog. '68 p459
*Larsen—Scrap. p148-149,152,por.
Muir—Women p200-202
*Riedman—Men p119-121,123
*Shippen—Design p126-128
Weeks—Discovery p812,820,868
Year—Pic. p213,por.
*Yost—Women Mod. p17-30,por.

Meitschik, Anna (1875/78)-1943)
Russ. singer
Lahee—Grand p370-371
Saleski—Wander p417-418

Meixell, Louise Granville (fl. 1930's)
Amer. librarian, editor
Women—Achieve. p138,por.

Melania the Elder (d. 410)
Rom. saint
Blunt—Great p28-30

Melania the Younger (383-439)
Rom. saint
Englebert—Lives p497

Melba, Nellie (Helen Porter Mitchell)
(1859-61/1931)
Austral. singer
Adelman—Famous p295-296
Davidson—Treas. p189-196,por.
Ewen—Ency. p311
Hammerton p982,por.
Klein—Great p141-148
Lahee—Famous p243-248,por.
Lahee—Grand p134-137
McCoy—Portraits p129,por.
*MacVeagh—Champlin p400
Pleasants—Great p270-278,por.
Schmidt—400 p40,por.
Stiles—Postal p172
Time Apr.18,1927 p16,por.(Cover)
*Ulrich—Famous p45-49,por.
Wagnalls—Opera p225-230,por.
Wagner—Prima (see index)

Mélesville, pseud.
See Duveyrier, Anne Honoré Joseph

Melis, Carmen (fl. 1910's)
It. singer
Lahee—Grand p237-238,382-383,por.
McCoy—Portraits p130,por.

Melius, Luella (fl. 1940's)
Amer. singer
McCoy—Portraits p130,por.

Mellen, Kate.
See Courtney, Kate

Mellen, Laura (fl. 1870's)
Amer. whaling voyager
Whiting—Whaling p209-212,278

Mellen, Mary B. (fl. 1880's)
Amer. artist
Hanaford—Dau. p309-310

Meller, Raquel (c. 1888-1962)
Sp. singer, actress
Time Apr.26,1926 p18,por.(Cover)

Mellichamp, Julia St. Lo (d. 1939)
Amer. nurse
Pennock—Makers p96-97,por.

Mellon, Eleanor M. (1894-   )
Amer. sculptor
National—Contemp. p230

Mellon, Harriot (c. 1777-1837)
Duchess of St. Albans
Eng. actress
McQueen—Pope p307-315,por.
Melville—More p208-209,por.
Wyndham—Chorus p41,49-51,por.

Melmoth, Charlotte (1749-1823)
Eng. actress
Coad—Amer. p36,por.
Dexter—Career p69-70,81

Melnik, Marite (n.d.)
Russ. patriot
Phila.—Women, unp.
Stiles—Postal p172

Meloney, Marie Mattingly (d. 1943)
Amer. editor
Cur. Biog. '43 p528
Ross—Ladies p139,141-144,332
Women—Achieve. p60,por.

Meloney, Rose Franken.
See Franken, Rose

Melton, Joanna (fl. 1860's)
Amer. Civil war nurse
Logan—Part p366

Melvill, Elizabeth, Lady Culross (fl. 1600's)
Scot. covenanter, poet
Anderson—Ladies p49-62

Melville, Velma (b. 1858)
Amer. editor, author
Logan—Part p825

Memmia (fl.c. 200's-230's A.D.)
Rom. empress, wife of Alexander
Severus
Serviez—Roman (2) p277

Mendelieva, Marie D. (b. 1815)
Russ., mother of Dmitri I. Mendeliev
Schmidt—400 p345,por.

Mendelsohn, Celia (fl. 1930's)
Amer. artist, business executive
Women—Achieve. p174,por.

Mendelssohn, Fanny.
See Hensel, Fanny Cécile Mendelssohn

Mendelssohn, Leah Salomon (1777-1842)
Ger. mother of Felix Mendelssohn
°Chandler—Famous p169-187
Peyton—Mothers p53-59

Mendenhall, Elizabeth S. (fl. 1860's)
Amer. Civil war humanitarian,
nurse, philanthropist
Brockett—Woman's p617-620
Moore—Women p491-497

Mendes, Grace P. (fl. 1890's-1910's)
Amer. club leader
Logan—Part p651

Mendesa, Gracia (Beatrice de Luna)
(c. 1510-1569)
Port. philanthropist
°Levinger—Great p107-109

Mendl, Lady (Elsie de Wolfe) (m. 1926)
Amer. actress, interior decorator
New Yorker Jan.15,1938, p25-29,por.
(Profiles)

Mendoza, Dona Ana de Zaldivar y
(fl. 16th cent.)
Amer. colonial pioneer
Leonard—Amer. p118

Mendoz-Gauzon, Marie Paz (gr. 1912)
Phil. pioneer physician
Lovejoy—Women p244

Menen (Manin), Waizaro (Waizero)
(1891-1962)
Ethiop. empress
Arsenius—Dict. p198,por.
Phila.—Women, unp.,por.
Stiles—Postal p173

Menges, Isolde (1893/94-   )
Eng. violonist
Ewin—Living p244
McCoy—Portraits p130,por.

Mengs, Anna Maria (1751-1790)
Ger. painter
Waters—Women p237-238

Menken, Adah Isaacs (1835/37-1868)
Amer. actress
Adelman—Famous p188
Bodeen—Ladies p12-17
Brown—Gentle p83,178-181,por.
Coad—Amer. p229,por.
Eaton—Actor's p273-274
Marks—Glamour p241-258,por.
Mayne—Enchant. p328-343
Whitton—These p206
Woodward—Bold p268-280

Menken, Helen (1901-   )
Amer. actress, humanitarian
CR '63 p426,por.

Menken, Isaac, pseud.
See Isaacs, Adah

Menken, La Belle (fl. 1860's)
Amer. actress
Simonhoff—Jew. p374-377,por.

Menter, Sophie (1846/48-1918)
Ger. pianist
McCoy—Portraits p130,por.
Schonberg—Great p246-247,por.

Mentuvat (fl. 1730 A.D.)
Ethiop. empress
Stiles—Postal p174

Merab (Biblical)
Buchanan—Women p51-52
Deen—All p282-283
Mead—250 p84

Mercedes, Mary Antonio Gallagher
(fl. 1910's)
Amer. author, religious worker
Logan—Part p837-838

Mercein, Eleanor.
See Kelly, Eleanor Mercein

Mercer, Beryl (fl. 1900's-1930's)
Amer. actress
Marks—Glamour p318

Mercer, Isabella Gordon (m. 1767)
Amer. pioneer
Green—Pioneer (2) p201

Mercer, Margaret (1792-1846)
Amer. philanthropist
Whitton—These p163

Mercereau, Ethel F. (fl. 1930's)
Amer. business executive
Women—Achieve. p165,por.

Merchant, Jane (1919-   )
    Amer. poet
    *Plumb—Lives p213-219

Mercouri, Melina (1925-   )
    Gr. actress
    Cur. Biog. '65 p289-291,por.

Meredith, Elizabeth.
    See Clymer, Elizabeth

Meredith, Louisa Anne Twamly (1812-1895)
    Tas. author
    Dorland—Sum p28,82,173

Meresankh III (2877 B.C.-2822 B.C.)
    Egypt. queen
    Schmidt—400 p107-108,por.

Merezhkovskava, Zinaida Nikola (Zinaida
    Nikolajewna Hippius) (b. 1869)
    Russ. author
    Hammerton p761

Mergler, Marie Josepha (gr. 1879)
    Amer. physician, educator
    Lovejoy—Women p92

Merian, Maria Sibylla (1647-1717)
    Swiss naturalist, painter, engraver
    Mozans—Woman p240-242
    Schmidt—400 p377,por.
    Waters—Women p238-240

Merian, Valeria Bachofen (1796-1856)
    Swiss, mother of Johann Jakob
    Bachofen
    Schmidt—400 p382-383,por.

Merici. See Angela Merici

Méricourt, Théroigne de.
    See Théroigne de Méricourt

Merki, Nancy Lees (1926-   )
    Amer. swimmer
    *Eby—Marked p38-40
    Stump—Champ. p75-82

Merman, Ethel Agnes Zimmerman
    (1908-   )
    Amer. actress
    Blum—Great p121,por.
    CR '59 p509,por.
    CR '63 p429,por.
    Cur. Biog. '41 p573-575,por.
    Cur. Biog. '55 p412-414,por.
    Stambler—Ency. p154-155
    Time Oct.28,1940 p54,por.(Cover)

Merö-Irion, Yolanda (c. 1877/87-1963)
    Hung.-Amer. pianist
    McCoy—Portraits p130,por.
    Saleski—Jewish p523-524,por.
    Saleski—Wander. p349-351,por.
    Women—Achieve. p170,por.

Mérode, Cléo de (b.c. 1873)
    Fr. dancer, mistress of Leopold II
    Kelen—Mist. p166-168

Merrick, Mary Virginia (1866-1955)
    Amer. social worker, philanthropist
    Logan—Part p535

Merrick, Mrs. C. (Edgar Thorn, pseud.)
    (fl. 1930's)
    Amer. composer
    Elson—Woman's p209

Merrick, Mrs. Wickliffe (fl. 1910's)
    Amer. social leader
    Logan—Part p356

Merrill, Blanche (1895-   )
    Amer. song-writer
    ASCAP p346

Merrill, Dina (1925-   )
    Amer. heiress, actress
    CR '59 p510,por.
    CR '63 p429,por.

Merrill, Eleanor Brown (fl. 1920's-1930's)
    Amer. humanitarian, worker with
    blind
    Women—Achieve. p126,por.

Merrill, Mrs. John (fl. 1770's-1780's)
    Amer. Rev. war heroine, pioneer
    Bruce—Woman p136-137
    Ellet—Women (2) p316-317
    Fowler—Woman p94-95
    Hanaford—Dau. p56-57

Merriman, Helen Biglow (b. 1844)
    Amer. author, artist
    Logan—Part p848

Merriman, Nan (n.d.)
    Amer. singer
    O'Connell—Other p328

Merritt, Anna Lea (1844-1930)
    Amer. artist, etcher
    Logan—Part p756-757
    Michigan—Biog. p212
    Waters—Women p240-241

Merry, Anne (1769-1808)
    Amer. actress
    Coad—Amer. p45,50,57,60,65,por.
    Dexter—Career p84-85,87

Mersereau, Charity (fl. 1770's)
    Amer. Rev. war patriot
    Green—Pioneer (3) p435-440

Merz-Tunner, Amelia (fl. 1920's)
    Aust. singer
    McCoy—Portraits p131,por.

Merzon, Ruth (fl. 1930's)
    Pol.-Amer. business woman
    Women—Achieve. p134,por.

Mesdag, Madame Sientje Van Houten
    (1834-1909)
    Nether. painter
    Waters—Women p386-387

Meshullemeth (Biblical)
    Deen—All p283

Messalina, Valeria (d. 48 A.D.)
    Rom. empress
    Balsdon—Roman (see index),por.
    Ewart—World's p48-60
    Ferrero—Women p251-275,por.
    Hammerton p987-988,por.
    McCabe—Empr. p60-78,por.
    Muir—Women p99-100
    Serviez—Roman (1) p283-298

Messick, Dale (c. 1906-   )
    Amer. cartoonist
    Cur. Biog. '61 p311-312,por.

Mesta, Perle (c. 1891-   )
    Amer. hostess
    CR '59 p511,por.
    CR '63 p430,por.
    Cur. Biog. '49 p424-425,por.
    Roosevelt—Ladies p209-213
    Time Mr.14,1949 p24,por.(Cover)

Metalious, Grace (1924-1964)
    Amer. author
    CR '59 p511,por.
    CR '63 p430,por.

Metcalf, Jean (fl. 1950's)
    Eng. TV personality
    Winn—Queen's p160-161,163,por.

Methven, Ann Keith, Lady (fl. 1670's)
    Scot. covenanter
    Anderson—Ladies p24-26
    Graham—Group p81

Metzelthin, Pearl Violetta (1894-1947)
    Amer. dietician, editor, author,
        health worker
    Cur. Biog. '42 p578-588,por.
    Cur. Biog. '48 p446
    Planck—Women p200-202

Metzger-Latterman, Ottilie (fl. 1940's)
    Ger. singer
    McCoy—Portraits p131,por.

Mew, Charlotte Mary (1870-1928)
    Eng. poet
    Millett—Brit. p360
    Moore—Disting. p189-202
    Untermeyer—Lives p655-657

Meyer, Agnes Elizabeth Ernst (b. 1887)
    Amer. publisher, journalist, social
        worker
    Cur. Biog. '49 p425-427,por.
    Murrow—This (2) p94-95
    Stewart—Makers p453

Meyer, Annie Nathan (1867-1951)
    Amer. author, feminist, educator,
        club leader
    Adelman—Famous p307
    Logan—Part p649
    New Yorker Oct.23,1943 p27-32,por.;
        Oct.30,1943 p32(Profiles)
    Women—Achieve. p162,por.

Meyer, Editha Paula Chartkoff (1903-   )
    Amer. engineer
    Goff—Women p19-44

Meyer, Elizabeth Stuart McCauley (1866-
    1952)
    Eng.-Amer. W. pioneer
    Sargent—Pioneers p63-68,por.

Meyerhof, Leonie.
    See Hildeck, Leo, pseud.

Meyerson, Golda. See Meir, Golda

Meynell, Alice Christina Gertrude Thompson
    (1850-1922)
    Eng. poet, essayist, critic
    Adelman—Famous p266-267
    Hammerton p989-990
    *MacVeagh—Champlin p403
    Millett—Brit. p361-362
    Moore—Disting. p161-174
    Saturday Rev. p161

Meynell, Viola (b. 1886)
    Eng. novelist
    Johnson—Some Contemp. p117-130
    Millett—Brit. p362-363

Meysenbug, Malwida von (1816-1903)
    Ger. author, social reformer
    Heller—Studies p258-259
    Lownsbery—Saints p80-110

Meysenheym, Cornelie (1849-1923)
    Nether. singer
    McCoy—Portraits p131,por.

(Ni) Mhaille, Gráinne. See O'Malley, Grace

Micah's mother (Biblical)
    Buchanan—Women p43-44
    Culver—Women p27-28
    Deen—All p340-341
    Lewis—Portraits p77-78

Michael, Moina ("Poppy Lady") (c. 1870-
    1944)
    Amer. educator
    Cur. Biog. '44 p469
    Phila.—Women, unp.,por.
    Stiles—Postal p175

Michael, Susie (n.d.)
Amer. pianist
Saleski—Jewish p641,por.

Michaela, Mary Michael Dermaisieres (1809-1865)
Sp. saint
Stiles—Postal p237-238

Michaelis, Karin (1872-1950)
Dan. author
Hammerton p990,por.

Michaiah. See Maachah (3)

Michal (Biblical)
Buchanan—Women p52-53
Culver—Women p32
Deen—All p96-100
Harrison—Little p53-67
Horton—Women p161-174
Lewis—Portraits p45-48
Lofts—Women p97-110
*MacVeagh—Champlin p404
Marble—Women, Bible p60-64
Mead—250 p85
Morton—Women p109-117
Nelson—Bible p46-48

Michallet, Françoise (fl. 18th cent.)
Fr. philanthropist
Kavanagh—Woman (2) p190

Michel, (Clémence) Louise (1830-1905)
Fr. revolutionist
Adelman—Famous p212
Goldsmith—Seven p91-117

Michel-Levy, Simone (c. 1904-1945)
Fr. patriot, heroine
Stiles—Postal p175

Michelina, Blessed, of Pesaro (1300-1357)
It. saint
Englebert—Lives p235-236

Michis, Maria. See Cattaneo, Maria

Micle, Veronica (b. 1850)
Rum. poet
Schmidt—400 p341,por.

Middlemass, Jean (fl. 1890's)
Eng. author
Black—Notable p260-270,por.

Middleton, Henrietta.
See Rutledge, Henrietta Middleton

Middleton, Jane.
See Myddleton, Jane Needham

Middleton, Mary Izard (d. 1814
Amer. patriot
Green—Pioneer (3) p270-273

Middleton, Mary Williams (d. 1761)
Amer. pioneer
Green—Pioneer (3) p264-265

Midwinter, Mrs. (fl. 1710's)
Eng., wife of printer
Stenton—English p218-219

Mieczyslawska, Makrena (1797-1864)
Pol. nun, martyr
Schmidt—400 p321-322,por.

Miele, Elizabeth (1900-   )
Amer. playwright
Mantle—Contemp. p319

Mighell, Marjorie. See Holmes, Marjorie

Mikeladze, Ketto (fl. 1920's-1930's)
Russ.-Amer. dancer, fashion designer
Women—Achieve. p159,por.

Milanollo, Marie (1832-1848)
It. violonist
Ehrlich—Celeb. p171-172

Milanollo, Therese (b. 1827-1904)
It. violinist, composer
Ehrlich—Celeb. p171-172,por.
McCoy—Portraits p132,por.

Milanov, Zinka Kunc (1906-   )
Yugoslav. singer
Brook—Singers p145-147,por.
CR '59 p514,por.
Cur. Biog. '44 p474-476,por.
Ewen—Ency. p323
Ewen—Living p246-247,por.
McCoy—Portraits p132,por.
Matz—Opera p130-133,por.
Peltz—Spot. p61,por.
Rosenthal—Sopranos p64,73,por.

Milbacher, Louise von (b. 1845)
Ger. painter
Waters—Women p241

Milcah (Biblical)
Buchanan—Women p13-16
Deen—All p283
Lewis—Portraits p64

Mildenburg, Anna von (1872-1947)
Aust. singer
Ewen—Ency. p323-324
McCoy—Portraits p132,por.

Milder-Hauptmann, Pauline Anna (1785-1838)
Turk. singer
Ewen—Ency. p324
McCoy—Portraits p132,por.

Mildner, Poldi Leopoldine (1916-   )
Aust. pianist
Ewen—Living p247-248,por.

Mildred (d.c. 700/725 A.D.)
Eng. saint
*Windham—Sixty p206-214

Milena Vucotic (1847-1923)
Monte. queen
Stiles—Postal p176

Miles, Allie Lowe (fl. 1930's)
Amer. cosmetician, radio personality,
advertising writer
Women—Achieve. p73,por.

Miles, Anne (b. 1803)
Amer. poet
Hanaford—Dau. p257-258

Miles, Ellen E. (b. 1835)
Amer. poet, teacher
Hanaford—Dau. p240,258

Miles, Emily Winthrop (fl. 1920's)
Amer. sculptor
National—Contemp. p230

Miles, (Maxine Frances) Mary Forbes-
Robertson (1900/01-   )
Eng. aircraft designer, aeronautical
engineer
Cur. Biog. '42 p596-597,por.
*Knapp—New p61-72,por.
*May—Women p169-170

Miles, Sarah E. (b. 1807)
Amer. poet
Hanaford—Dau. p257

Milgrim, Sally (fl. 1940's)
Amer. fashion designer
Taves—Success p128-132,por.

Milhous, Katherine (1894-   )
Amer. illustrator
Mahony—Illus. p338

Miliken, Mrs. D. A. (fl. 1910's)
Amer. philanthropist
Logan—Part p544

Mill, Harriet Hardy Taylor (1807-1858)
Eng. feminist, author, wife of
John Stuart Mill
Beard—Woman p100-103
Corchran—Romance p97-102
Douglas—Remember p154

Millais, Emily (fl. 19th cent.)
Eng., mother of John Millais
Winwar—Poor p3-7

Millar, Gertie (Gertrude Millar Monckton
Ward Dudley, Countess of)
(1879-1952)
Eng. actress
Wyndham—Chorus p136-138,por.

Millar, Margaret Storm (1915-   )
Can. author
Cur. Biog. '46 p396-397,por.
Warfel—Amer. p301,por.

Millar, Marjie (1930-   )
Amer. actress
TV—Person (1) p19-20,por.

Millard, Evelyn (b. 1873)
Eng. actress
Hammerton p995

Millay, Edna St. Vincent (1892-1950)
Amer. poet
ASCAP p349-350
*Brenner—Ten p61-81,por.
Bruère—Laugh. p99
Burnett—Amer. p552,por.
Burnett—This p1147
Cook—Our p245-249
Dodd—Celeb. p66-70
Farrar—Literary p77-90,345,por.
*Freedman—Teen p239-269,por.
*Heath—Woman (4) p29,por.
Jensen—Revolt p170,por.
*Kirkland—Writers p26-38
Loggins—Hear p84-90
*Millett—Amer. p133-134,487-491
Morris—400 p179-180
*Muir—Writers p87-100,por.
New Yorker Feb.12,1927,p25-27,por.
(Profiles)
Rogers—Women p109,por.
Saturday Rev. p200-206
Scherman—Literary p128-129
Smith—Women's p137
Tanner—Here p50-74
Untermeyer—Lives p645-647
*Witham—Pan. p304-306,por.

Mille, Agnes George de.
See De Mille, Agnes George

Millenchamps, Mrs. Henry (fl. 1890's)
Amer. whaling voyager
Whiting—Whaling p254-255

Miller, Adaline (fl. 1860's)
Amer. Civil war nurse
Logan—Part p367

Miller, Alice Duer (1874-1942)
Amer. author
Bruère—Laugh p221
Cur. Biog. '41 p580-581,por.
Cur. Biog. '42 p597
New Yorker Feb.19,1927 p25-27,por.
(Profiles)
Overton—Women p206-213
Smith—Women's p139

Miller, Ann (Lucille Ann Collier) (1919-   )
Amer. dancer
CR '59 p515,por.
CR '63 p432,por.

Miller, Anna Jenness (b. 1884)
    Amer. author, lecturer, fashion
      designer
Adelman—Famous p305
Farmer—What p151,por.
Logan—Part p845

Miller, August A. (fl. 1870's)
    Amer. printer
Hanaford—Dau. p714

Miller, Bernetta (fl. 1910's)
    Amer. pioneer aviatrix
*May—Women p83-84

Miller, Caroline (1903-   )
    Amer. novelist
Warfel—Amer. p302,por.

Miller, Daisy Orr (fl. 1930's)
    Amer. editor, dog specialist
Women—Achieve. p176,por.

Miller, Dora Richards (m. 1862)
    Amer. author
Logan—Part p825-826

Miller, Elizabeth (d. 1940)
    Amer. nurse
Pennock—Makers p86,por.

Miller, Elizabeth Smith (fl. 1850's)
    Amer. feminist
Riegel—Amer. p50-51

Miller, Emily Clark Huntington (1833-
    1913)
    Amer. journalist, author, editor,
      social reformer
Hanaford—Dau. p704,por.
Logan—Part p871

Miller, Emma Guffey (b.c. 1874)
    Amer. feminist, politician
Parshalle—Kash. p163-166,por.

Miller, Flo Jamison (fl. 1910's)
    Amer. club leader
Logan—Part p352

Miller, Frieda Segelke (1890-   )
    Amer. government official
Cur. Biog. '45 p405-407,por.
Women—Achieve. p50,por.

Miller, Gladys (fl. 1930's)
    Amer. interior decorator; retail
      executive
Women—Achieve. p144,por.

Miller, Harriet Granger (fl. 1870's)
    Amer. printer
Club—Printing p16
Hanaford—Dau. p714

Miller, Harriet Mann (Olive Thorne Miller,
    pseud.) (1831-1918)
    Amer. ornithologist, lecturer
Logan—Part p847-848

Miller, Helen Topping (1884-1960)
    Amer. novelist
Warfel—Amer. p302-303,por.

Miller, Hope Ridings (c. 190?-   )
    Amer. journalist
CR '63 p433-434,por.

Miller, Mrs. Keith (fl. 1920's-1930's)
    Eng. aviatrix
*May—Women p106

Miller, Louise Klein (1854-1943)
    Amer. horticulturist, landscape
      architect, educator
Logan—Part p716-717

Miller, Maria (fl. 1860's)
    Amer. Civil war nurse
Logan—Part p367

Miller, Marie (fl. 1910's-1920's)
    Amer. harpist
McCoy—Portraits p132,por.

Miller, Marilyn (1898-1936)
    Amer. actress
Blum—Great p86,por.

Miller, Marion M. (b. 1864)
    Amer. editor, author
Women—Achieve. p182,por.

Miller, Mary Britton (Isabel Bolton, pseud.)
Warfel—Amer. p41,por.

Miller, Mary E. (b. 1864)
    Amer. lawyer
Logan—Part p747-748

Miller, Mary P. (fl. 1900's)
    Amer. airship pilot
*May—Women p43

Miller, Mildred (1924-   )
    Amer. singer
Cur. Biog. '57 p364-366,por.
Matz—Opera p133-135,por.

Miller, Nellie Burget (b. 1875)
    Amer. poet, lecturer
Smith—Women's p141

Miller, Olive Thorne, pseud.
    See Miller, Harriet Mann

Miller, Patsy Ruth (1905-   )
    Amer. actress
Lamparski—What. p160-161,por.

Miller, Rose (fl. 1930's)
    Amer. humanitarian
    Women—Achieve. p95,por.

Miller, Sadie Kneller (d. 1920)
    Amer. journalist, photographer
    Ross—Ladies p497-498

Miller, Mrs. Walter McNab (fl. 1910's)
    Amer. feminist
    Irwin—Angels p373-374

Miller sisters (fl. 1940's)
    Amer. dancers
    Rogers—Women p46,por.

Millett, Deborah D. (1797-1869)
    Amer. religious worker
    Hanaford—Dau. p625-626,por.

Milligan, Mary Louise (1911-   )
    Amer. military officer, WAAC
    Cur. Biog. '57 p366-367,por.

Millin, Sarah Gertrude Liebson (1889-1968)
    S. Afr. novelist, historian
    Millett—Brit. p363-364

Mills, Dorothy Rachel Melissa, Lady
        (b. 1889)
    Brit. traveler
    Hammerton p996

Mills, Florence (1895-1927)
    Amer. singer, comedienne, dancer
    Cuney-Hare—Negro p136,163,170

Mills, Hayley (1946-   )
    Eng. actress
    CR '63 p435,por.
    Cur. Biog. '63 p268-270,por.

Mills, Juliet (1941-   )
    Eng. actress
    Ross—Player p113-116,por.

Mills, Marjorie (1891-   )
    Amer. editor
    CR '63 p435,por.

Mills, Mary Gills (fl. 1770's)
    Amer. Rev. war patriot
    Green—Pioneer (3) p457

Mills, Susan (1826-1912)
    Amer. teacher, missionary
    Whitton—These p258

Mills, Susan Carrie (fl. 1860's)
    Amer. Civil war nurse
    Logan—Part p366

Mills, Susan Lincoln Tolman (1826-1912)
    Amer. educator, missionary .
    Logan—Part p724-725

Mills, Vicki (1934-   )
    Amer. singer
    TV—Person (2) p27-28,por.

Millsap, Willa. See Gibbs, Willa

Mimieux, Yvette (1941-   )
    Amer. actress
    CR '63 p436,por.

Mims, Sue Harper (m. 1866)
    Amer. religious leader
    Logan—Part p705

Mingotti, Regina Valentini (1721/22-1808)
    It. singer
    McCoy—Portraits p133,por.

Minijima, Mrs. Kiyo (1833-1919)
    Jap. business woman, philanthropist
    Adelman—Famous p256

Minis, Abigail (1701-1794)
    Amer. planter
    Simonhoff—Jew. p17-20

Miniter, Edith Dowe (b. 1869)
    Amer. editor
    Logan—Part p830

Mink, Patsy Takemoto (1927-   )
    Amer. Congresswoman
    Cur. Biog. '68 p253-256,por.
    Lamson—Few p98-109,por.

Mink, Sarah C. (d. 1896)
    Amer. club leader
    Logan—Part p350

"Minnie" (fl. 1900's)
    Amer. frontier woman
    Aikman—Calamity p308-310

Minnigerode, Lucy (1871-1935)
    Amer. public health nurse
    Pennock—Makers p62-63,por.

Minot, Fannie E. (m. 1874)
    Amer. club leader
    Logan—Part p354

Minter, Desire (fl. 1600's)
    Amer. Pilgrim
    Logan—Part p31
    Marble—Women p58-59

Minter, Mary Miles (1902-   )
    Amer. actress
    Wagenknecht—Movies p232-238,por.

Minto, Mary, Countess of (m. 1883)
    Eng. lady-in-waiting
    Asquith—Myself p215-258

Mira Bai (fl. 15th-16th cent.)
 Ind. princess, poet, musician
 Phila.—Women unp.,por.
 Stiles—Postal p176

Miraben (Mira.)
 See Slade, Madeleine

Miramion, Marie Bonneau, Madame de
 (1629-1694)
 Fr. humanitarian, philanthropist
 Parton—Noted p417-422

Miranda, Carmen (1913-1955)
 Brazil. singer, dancer, actress
 Cur. Biog. '41 p586-588,por.
 Cur. Biog. '55 p421

Miranda, Salla (fl. 1900's)
 Austral. singer
 Lahee—Grand p235

Mirat, Mathilde (Madame Heine) (1818-
 1883)
 Belg., mistress of Heine
 Mayne—Enchant. p312-327

Mirenburg, Mary (fl. 1930's)
 Amer. lawyer
 Women—Achieve. p187,por.

Miriam (1) (Biblical)
 sister of Moses
 Chappell—Fem. p49-62
 Culver—Women p21-23
 Deen—All p57-61
 Faulhaber—Women p45-51
 Harrison—Little p23-37
 Hastings—Greater p327-339
 *Levinger—Great p31-34
 Lewis—Portraits p113-115
 *MacVeagh—Champlin p410
 Marble—Women, Bible p165-170
 Mead—250 p48
 Nelson—Bible p27-29
 Ockenga—Women p43-52
 Schmidt—400 p265,por.
 Van der Velde—She p78-84

Miriam (2) (Biblical)
 daughter of Ezra?
 Deen—All p283

Miriam Michael, Sister (fl. 1940's-1960's)
 Amer. nun, scientist
 Elgin—Nun p22-25,por.

Mirrlees, Hope (fl. 1910's)
 Eng. novelist
 Johnson—Some Contemp. p211-220

Misch, Mrs. Ceasar (fl. 1910's)
 Amer. religious worker, lecturer,
 author
 Logan—Part p650

Misset, Madame (fl. 1710's)
 Irish patriot
 Concannon—Dau. p217-220

Mistral, Gabriela (Lucila Godoy Alcayaga)
 (1889-1957)
 Chile. poet
 Cur. Biog. '46 p397-400,por.
 Cur. Biog. '57 p370-371
 McClintock—Nobel p607-708
 Nobel—Man p129-130
 Rosenbaum—Modern p171-203
 Stiles—Postal p177

Mistrot, Ethel Reed (fl. 1930's)
 Amer. business woman
 Women—Achieve. p185,por.

Mitchell, Abbie (1884-1960)
 Amer. actress, singer
 Cuney-Hare—Negro p369-371,por.
 Robinson—Hist. p229-230,por.

Mitchell, Ellen E. (fl. 1860's)
 Amer. Civil war nurse
 Brockett—Woman's p420-426

Mitchell, Elsie R. (fl. 1920's)
 Amer. physician
 Lovejoy—Woman p323-324
 Lovejoy—Women Phys. p87-91,por.

Mitchell, Hattie Poley (fl. 1920's-1950's)
 Amer. missionary
 They—Went p66-67

Mitchell, Helen Porter. See Melba, Nellie

Mitchell, Mae (n.d.)
 Amer. composer, author
 ASCAP p353

Mitchell, Margaret (1900-1949)
 Amer. novelist
 *Cournos—Famous p139-142
 Scherman—Literary p170
 Taves—Success p89-91,por.

Mitchell, Margaret Julia (1832/37-1918)
 Amer. actress
 Adelman—Famous p209
 Coad—Amer. p191,por.
 Dorland—Sum p168
 Hanaford—Dau. p590

Mitchell, Maria (1818-1889)
 Amer. pioneer astronomer,
 educator, novelist, poet
 Adelman—Famous p181
 *Carmer—Caval. p207-209,por.
 *Carmer—Young p133-139
 *Dolin—World p98-104,por.
 Dorland—Sum p21,142-143
 Douglas—Remember p95
 Farmer—What p264-270

(Continued)

Mitchell, Maria—*Continued*

    *Gersh—Women p13-31,por.
    Hanaford—Dau. p262-272,275-276,279,
      346,718-719
    *Heath—Woman (4) p11,por.
    Irwin—Angels p106,122
    Jensen—Revolt p108,por.
    Law—Civiliz. p183-184
    Logan—Part p876-877
    Melikov—Immort. p74,154,por.
    *Moore—When p125-132
    Morello—Hall p73,por.
    Mozans—Woman p190-192
    Parton—Dau. p322-331,por.
    Parton—Noted p322-331,por.
    Schmidt—400 p10-11,por.
    Snow—Women p106
    *Stevens—Women p105-108,por.
    Tappan—Heroes p54-60,por.
    *Vance—Lamp p128-154,por.
    Whitton—These p157
    *Yost—Famous p69-77,por.

Mitchell, Martha Reed (b. 1818)
    Amer. philanthropist
    Logan—Part p526-527

Mitchell, Mary (Josephine Plain, pseud.)
    (1892-   )
    Austral. author
    Hetherington—42 p30-35,por.

Mitchell, Milly Benett (fl. 1920's)
    Amer. journalist
    Ross—Ladies p588

Mitchell, Nellie Brown (fl. 1860's-1874's)
    Amer. singer
    Cuney-Hare—Negro p209,218-219

Mitchell, Norma.
    See Steele, Norma Mitchell Talbot

Mitchell, Ruth Comfort (fl. 1900's-1920's)
    Amer. poet
    Smith—Women's p146

Mitchell, Viola (1911-   )
    Amer. violinist
    Ewen—Living p249-250,por.

Mitchison, Naomi Margaret Haldane
    (1897-   )
    Irish author
    Hammerton p999
    Millett—Brit. p366-368

Mitford, Mary Russell (1787-1855)
    Eng. novelist, playwright
    Adelman—Famous p135-136
    Dorland—Sum p41,172-173
    Hammerton p999,por.
    Johnson—Women p140-143
    MacVeagh—Champlin p410

Mitford, Nancy (1904-   )
    Eng. author
    Beaton—Persona p70-71,por.
    CR '59 p520-521,por.

Mitre, Delfina Vedia de (1821-1882)
    Argent. author, translator
    Schmidt—400 p34,por.

Mitton, Geraldine Edith (fl. 1900's)
    Brit. author
    Hammerton p1000

Miura, Tamaki (fl. 1910's)
    Japan. singer
    McCoy—Portraits p133,por.

Mix, Josephine B. Dexter (b. 1837)
    Amer. physician
    Hanaford—Dau. p570-571

Miyakawa, Kikuko (fl. 1930's)
    Amer. poet, artist
    Women—Achieve. p105,por.

Mizner, Elizabeth Howard.
    See Howard, Elizabeth

Moats, Alice-Leone (1910/11-   )
    Amer. journalist, author
    Beckwith—Contemp. p317
    Cur. Biog. '43 p531-534,por.

Moberly, Charlotte Anne Elizabeth (1846-
    1937)
    Eng. educator
    Brittain—Women (see index),por.

Moberly, Winifred H. (fl. 1910's)
    Eng. teacher
    Brittain—Women p98,124-125,142,178

Mock, Alice (fl. 1920's-1930's)
    Amer. singer
    McCoy—Portraits p133,por.

Modave, Jeanne (c. 1873-1953)
    Belg. violoncellist
    McCoy—Portraits p133,por.

Modell, Merriam (Evelyn Piper, pseud.)
    (1908-   )
    Amer. author
    Warfel—Amer. p306,por.

Modersohn, Paula Becker (1876-1907)
    Ger. artist
    Schmidt—400 p206-207,por.

Modigliani, Corinna (fl. 1890's)
    It. painter
    Waters—Women p241-242

Modjeska, Helena (1840/44-1909)
Pol. actress
Adelman—Famous p240-241
Bodeen—Ladies p37-42,por.
Coad—Amer. p250,por.
Dorland—Sum p46,70,168
Hammerton p1000
Izard—Heroines p52-92,por.
*MacVeagh—Champlin p411
Mizwa—Great p250-262,por.
Phila.—Women, unp.,por.
Schmidt—400 p327,por.
Stiles—Postal p177
Strang—Actresses p306-322

Mödl, Martha (1912-   )
Ger. singer
Rosenthal—Sopranos p74-75,por.

Modlibowska, Wanda (fl. 1930's)
Pol. glider pilot
*May—Women p223

Mody, Perin (fl. 1960's)
E. Ind. airline hostess
*May—Women p239

Moero of Byzantium (fl. 5th cent. B.C.)
Gr. poet
Anthologia—Poets p93-94

Moeschlin-Hammar, Elsa (b. 1879)
Swed. illustrator
Mahony—Illus. p338

Moffat, Katharine.
See Whipple, Katharine Moffat

Moffat, Mary Smith (1795-1871)
Scot. missionary
Deen—Great p185-197
*Matthews—Daunt. p30-49

Moffo, Anna (c. 1935-   )
Amer. singer
CR '63 p438-439,por.
Cur. Biog. '61 p321-323,por.

Moggridge, Dolores Theresa (fl. 1950's)
Eng. aviatrix
*May—Women p177-178

Moir, Phyllis (fl. 1930's-1940's)
Eng.-Amer. author, lecturer, editor
Cur. Biog. '42 p600-601,por.
Women—Achieve. p188,por.

Moisant, Mathilde (Matilde) (c. 1878-1964)
Amer. pioneer aviatrix
*Adams—Sky p3-26,por.
Earhart—Fun p184-185
Heinmuller—Man's p290,por.
*May—Women p69-72,por.
Planck—Women p22-23,por.

Moise, Penina (1797-1880)
Amer. poet, hymn writer
*Levinger—Great p136-139
Simonhoff—Jew. p251-254,por.

Moiseiwitsch, Tanya (1914-   )
Eng. theatrical, fashion designer
Cur. Biog. '55 p423-425,por.
Newquist—Show. p277-286,por.

Moldura, Lilla (fl. 1900's)
It. painter
Waters—Women p242

Molesworth, Mary Louisa Stewart (Ennis
Graham, pseud.) (1839-1921)
Nether. author
Green—Authors p33-36,174
Hammerton p1001,por.

Molina, Julia (b. 1865)
Dom.R., wife of Jose Trujillo Valdez
Phila.—Women, unp.,por.

Molina, Marie De (d. 1321)
Sp. queen
Schmidt—400 p351-353,por.

Moll, Orange. See Meggs, Mary

Möller, Agnes Slott (b. 1862)
Dan. illustrator
Waters—Women p242,387-388

Mollison, Amy Johnson (1903/04-1941)
Austral. pioneer aviatrix
Asquith—Myself p131-156,por.
Burge—Ency. p636
Cur. Biog. '41 p439
*Deakin—True p101-121
*Fraser—Heroes p563-567,655-659
Hammerton p1002,por.
Heinmuller—Man's p346,183-192,por.
Holmes—Seven p177-204
*Kirkland—Achieved p107-114
*Lauwick—Heroines p180-185,por.
*May—Women p107-111,143-144,por.
*Shippen—Bridle p133-139

Molloy, Emma (b. 1839)
Amer. social reformer, editor,
printer
Hanaford—Dau. p427,693-695,711

Molloy, Mary Aloysius, Sister (b. 1880)
Logan—Part p838

Molza, Tarquinia (1542-1617)
It. translator, poet
Deinker—Music p220-222

Monaco, Princess of (fl. 18th cent.)
Fr. rev. patriot
Kavanagh—Woman (2) p235

Monasterio, Lillian (fl. 1930's)
Amer. aviation instructor
Planck—Women p167,281,por.

Monath, Hortense (c. 1903-1956)
Amer. pianist
Ewen—Living p252,por.
McCoy—Portraits p134,por.
Saleski—Jewish p529,por.

**Monckton, Mary, Countess of Cork and
Orrery** (1746-1840)
Eng. hostess
Hammerton p443

Moncrieffe, Margaret (fl. 1780's-1800's)
Amer., friend of Aaron Burr
Orr—Famous p186

Monica (or **Monnica**) (c. 333-387)
Rom. saint, mother of St.
Augustine
Blunt—Great p44-68
Corkran—Romance p19,25-77,por.
Culver—Women p76-78
Deen—Great p21-25
Englebert—Lives p174
Hammerton p1004
Sharkey—Pop. p41-44
Wallace—Mothers p1-6
Wescott—Calen. p64-65
*Windham—Sixty p109-117

Monk, Maria (c. 1817-1849/50)
Can. author, impostor
Whitton—These p92-93
Wright—Forgot. p121-155,por.

Monks, Victoria (c. 1894-1927)
Eng. singer
LeRoy—Music p59-60,por.

Monmouth, Duchess of.
See Buccleuch and Monmouth, Anne,
Duchess of

Monmouth, Mrs. L. N. (fl. 1880's)
Amer. business woman
Parton—Dau. p430-439
Parton—Noted p614-623

Monoghan, Josephine ("Little Jo")
(d. 1903)
Amer. pioneer, rancher
Horan—Desperate p305-310,por.

Monroe, Anne Shannon (1877-1942)
Amer. essayist, lecturer
Binheim—Women p162,por.
Cur. Biog. '42 p603
*Kirkland—Writers p80-91

Monroe, Eliza (1).
See Hay, Eliza Monroe

Monroe, Eliza (2) (Elizabeth) (1768-1830)
Amer. wife of James Monroe
Farmer—What p76-78,140
Gerlinger—Mis. p18-20,por.
Hampton—Our p38-41
Hanaford—Dau. p77-78
Jensen—White p33-38,por.
Logan—Ladies p31-34
Logan—Part p227-229
*McConnell—Our p61-70,por.
Minnigerode—Some p133-181,por.
Prindiville—First p47-53
*Ross—Know p13,por.
Smith—Romances p72-78,por.
Truett—First p16-17,por.
Whitton—First p71-90,por.

Monroe, Harriet (1860/61-1936)
Amer. poet, editor
Cook—Our p145-146
Logan—Part p841

Monroe, Lucy (1907-   )
Amer. singer
CR '59 p523,por.
CR '63 p440,por.
Cur. Biog. '42 p603-604,por.
Donaldson—Radio p21
McCoy—Portraits p134,por.
O'Connell—Other p330-331

Monroe, Maria Hester (m. 1820)
Amer., daughter of James Monroe
Smith—White p19-29,por.

Monroe, Marilyn (1926-1962)
Amer. actress
CR '59 p523-524,por.
Cur. Biog. '59 p303-305,por.
Cur. Biog. '62 p302
Ewen—Living p252-253,por.
Martin—Pete p157-191
Rivkin—Hello p218-234
Schickel—Stars p265,por.
Settel—Radio p136,por.
Stuart—Immort. p177-179,por.
Time May 14,1956 p74,por.(Cover)
Wagenknecht—Movies p241-243
Wagenknecht—Seven p183-215,por.

Montagu, Elizabeth Robinson (1720-1800)
Eng. author, wit, beauty
*Borer—Women p28-31
Hammerton p1005,por.
Thomson—Queens p433-454

Montagu, Mary Wortley, Lady (1689-1762)
Eng. poet, letter-writer, medical
pioneer
Adelman—Famous p74-75
*Borer—Women p21-28,por.
Bottrall—Pers. p122-124,234
Bradford—Women p1-22,por.
Dolan—Goodnow's p165
Dorland—Sum p17,73,130,171

(Continued)

Montagu, Mary Wortley—*Continued*

Hammerton p1005-1006,por.
Holmes—Seven p13-33
Melville—Maids p157-175,por.
Muir—Women p152-153
*Pringle—When p9-31,por.
Schmidt—400 p136-138,por.
Stenton—English p258-267,283,288
Thomson—Queens p87-124

Montagu-Douglas-Scott, Alice, Lady,
    Duchess of Gloucester (1901-)
    Eng. painter, horsewoman
Phila.—Women unp.,por.
Stiles—Postal p179

Montague, Mrs. Edward (fl. 18th cent.)
    Fr. literary patron
Kavanagh—Woman (1) p151-152

Montalba, Clara (1842-1929)
    Eng. painter
Waters—Women p242-243

Montana, Patsy (1914-   )
    Amer. composer, author, musician
ASCAP p355

Montansier, Marguerite Brunet, La
    Demoiselle de (b. 1730)
    Fr. actress
Gilder—Enter p227-257

Montbart, Helene von.
See Kahlenberg, Hans von, pseud.

Montefiore, Judith Cohen (fl. 19th cent.)
    Eng. traveler
Levinger—Great p126-130

Monterrosso de Lavalleja, Ana (1791-1853)
    Urug. patriot
Schmidt—400 p411,por.

Montespan, Françoise Athénais Rochechou-
    art, Marquise de (1641-1707)
    Fr. maid of honor
Adelman—Famous p60-61
Coryn—Enchant. p71-96
Dorland—Sum p24
Haggard—Remarkable p120-128,131-
    134,136-137
Hall—Moths p230-266,por.
Hammerton p1007,por.
Padover—Confess. p96-99

Montesson, Charlotte Jeane Béraud de la
    Haye de Riou, Marchioness of
    (1737-1805)
    Fr. author
Kavanagh—Woman (2) p38-41

Montessori, Maria (1870-1952)
Adelman—Famous p310-311
Cur. Biog. '40 p591-592,por.
Cur. Biog. '52 p434
Dorland—Sum p109
Fitzhugh—Concise p480-481
Hammerton p1007,por.
*Horowitz—Treas. p164-170
Lovejoy—Women p203
*Strong—Heroes p157-165
*Strong—Of p293-299
Time Feb.3,1930 p36,por.(Cover)

Montez, Lola (Marie Dolores Elsa Rosanna
    Gilbert) (c. 1818-1861)
    Irish dancer, W. pioneer
Aikman—Calamity p207-252,por.
Bodeen—Ladies p3-11,por.
Bolitho—Twelve p143-170,por.
Brown—Gentle p171-178,por.
Coad—Amer. p191,por.
Coryn—Enchant. p203-224
Hammerton p655,1007,por.
Kelen—Mist. p49-78,330,por.
Marks—Glamour p227-240,por.
Mayne—Enchant. p67-78,por.
Orr—Famous p307-314
Orr—Famous Affin. III p23-33
Prout—Petticoat p190-207,por.
Rogers—Gallant p85-114
Terhune—Super. p1-18
Trowbridge—Seven p280-320,por.

Montgomery, Carrie Frances Judd (b. 1858)
    Amer. social worker, author
Logan—Part p520-521

Montgomery, Elizabeth (1933-   )
    Amer. actress
TV—Person (1) p99

Montgomery, Elizabeth.
See Witherspoon, Elizabeth
    Montgomery

Montgomery, Elizabeth Rider (1902-   )
    Amer. author
Cur. Biog. '52 p434-435,por.

Montgomery, Helen Barrett (1861-1934)
    Amer. translator
Deen—Great p287-293

Montgomery, Helen Marie (1911-   )
    Amer. aviatrix, glider pilot
Knapp—New p140-156,por.
May—Women p217
Planck—Women p103

Montgomery, Janet Livingston (d. 1828)
    Amer. pioneer
Green—Pioneer (2) p165-172

Montgomery, Katherine.
See Bledsoe, Katherine Montgomery

Montgomery, Lucy Maud (1874-1942)
Can.-Amer. novelist
Cur. Biog. '42 p608
Innis—Clear p198-220,por.

Montgomery, Peggy ("Baby Peggy")
(1919-   )
Amer. actress
Lamparski—What. p116-117,por.

Montgomery, Roselle Mercier (d. 1933)
Amer. poet
Smith—Women's p150

Montgomery, Ruth Shick (1912-   )
Amer. journalist
Cur. Biog. '57 p374-375,por.

Monti-Gorsey, Lola (fl. 1930's)
It.-Amer. singer
Women—Achieve. p65,por.

Montour, Catherine (c. 1684-1752)
Amer. colonial negotiator
Leonard—Amer. p118

Montoya, Matilde (gr. 1887)
Mex. physician
Lovejoy—Women p264-265

Montpensier, Anne Marie Louise, Duchess
d'Orleans ("Le Grand
Mademoiselle") (1627-1693)
Fr. author, military heroine
Dorland—Sum p49,95-96
Haggard—Remark. p71-80
Hall—Moths p92-128,267-290
Imbert—Valois p124,126,336-338
Ravenel—Women p45-46

Montross, Lois Seyster (1897-1961)
Amer. novelist
Overton—Women p214-215

Montserrat, Caballé (1933-   )
Sp. singer
Cur. Biog. June 1967 p10-13,por.

Moodie, Alma (1900-1943)
Austral. violinist
McCoy—Portraits p135,por.

Moody, Deborah, Lady (fl. 1650's)
Amer. colonial leader, politician
Dexter—Colonial p189
Douglas—Remember p39
Earle—Colon. p51-52
Green—Pioneer (1) p221-223
Jones—Quakers p65,216-217,222
Leonard—Amer. p42,119

Moody, Emma Revell (1842-1902)
Amer. religious worker
Deen—Great p403-404

Moody, Helen Waterson (b. 1860)
Amer. journalist, educator
Logan—Part p829

Moody, Helen Wills.
See Wills, Helen Newington

Moon, Bessie Huntington (fl. 1900's-1940's)
Amer. missionary
They—Went p32-34

Moon, Charlotte (1829-1912)
Amer. Civil war heroine, spy
Harkness—Heroines p5

Moon, Lottie (Lottie Clark) (1840-1912)
Amer. missionary
Deen—Great p259-265
Kane—Spies p263-280

Moon, Virginia (1845-1926)
Amer. Civil War heroine, spy
Harkness—Heroines p5
Kane—Spies p263-267,271-281

Mooney, Hannah Gaunt (fl. 1770's)
Amer. Rev. War patriot
Ellet—Women (2) p344-345

Mooney, Loretta.
See Douglas, Loretta Mooney, Lady

Mooney, Rose (fl. 18th cent.)
Irish blind harpist
Concannon—Dau. p242

Moor, Eunice Farnsworth (1735-1822)
Amer. pioneer
Green—Pioneer (3) p469

Moore, Alma Chesnut (fl. 1930's)
Amer. editor
Women—Achieve. p172,por.

Moore, Anne (fl. 1930's)
Amer. physiologist, dramatic
teacher
Women—Achieve. p168,por.

Moore, Anne Carroll (1871-1961)
Amer. librarian, author
Bul. of Bibl. May-Aug.1946 p221-223,
por.
*Ferris—Girls p35-46
*Forsee—Women p36-55

Moore, Annie Aubertine Woodward (Auber
Forestier, pseud.) (1841-1929)
Amer. musician, translator, lecturer
Dorland—Sum p161
Logan—Part p864-865

Moore, Carrie (d. 1926)
Austral. singer
Schmidt—400 p39,por.

Moore, Charlotte.
See Sitterly, Charlotte Moore

Moore, Clara Jessup (fl. 1860's)
Amer. Civil war humanitarian
Brockett—Woman's p599
Logan—Part p826

Moore, Colleen (1902-   )
Amer. actress
Herman—How p17,por.

Moore, Elisabeth Luce (1903-   )
Amer. social worker, organization
official
Cur. Biog. '60 p282-284,por.

Moore, Elizabeth Evelyn (1891-   )
Amer. author, song-writer
ASCAP p356

Moore, Ella Maude (b. 1849)
Amer. hymn writer
Logan—Part p858

Moore, Eva (1870-1955)
Eng. actress
Hammerton p1009

Moore, Eva Perry (fl. 1900's)
Amer. club leader
Logan—Part p401-402

Moore, Grace (1901-1947)
Amer. singer
Cur. Biog. '44 p480-482,por.
Cur. Biog. '47 p451
Davidson—Treas. p202-204
Ewen—Living p254-255,por.
McCoy—Portraits p135,por.
O'Connell—Other p3-14
Peltz—Spot. p63,por.
Wagner—Prima p98,245
Women—Achieve. p51-por.

Moore, Huldah Traxler (fl. 1870's)
Amer. W. pioneer
Sargent—Pioneers p59

Moore, Idora McClellan Plowman (1843-
1929)
Amer. author
Logan—Part p827

Moore, Jane Boswell (fl. 1860's)
Amer. Civil war philanthropist
Moore—Women p554-570

Moore, Jeanne W. G. (fl. 1930's)
Amer. hymn writer
Women—Achieve. p106,por.

Moore, Kate (fl. 1850's)
Amer. philanthropist, pioneer
Hanaford—Dau. p155-156
Logan—Part p104

Moore, Kate (fl. 1890's)
Amer. hostess
Skinner—Elegant p46-47

Moore, Lizzie (1843-1915)
Amer. teacher
Peterson—Great p43-51

Moore, Luella Lockwood (fl. 1940's)
Amer. composer, pianist, teacher
McCoy—Portraits p135,por.

Moore, Marianne Craig (b. 1887)
Amer. poet
Burnett—This p1147-1148
CR '59 p528-529,por.
CR '63 p442,por.
Cur. Biog. '52 p435-437,por.
Cur. Biog. '68 p265-268,por.
Jensen—Revolt p101,por.
Millett—Amer. p144-145,491-492
New Yorker Feb. 16,1957 p38,por.
(Profiles)
*Seventeen—On p187-192,por.
Untermeyer—Lives p700-702
Women—Achieve. p182,por.
Writers—Paris p61-87,por.

Moore, Mary (1777-1790)
Amer. W. pioneer
Ellet—Pioneer p121-132
Logan—Part p50-54

Moore, Mary (1861-1931)
Eng. actress
Hammerton p1009-1010

Moore, Mary (fl. 1930's)
Amer. singer
McCoy—Portraits p135,por.

Moore, Mary Carr (1873-1957)
Amer. composer, singer
ASCAP p357
Hipsher—Amer. p287-291
Howard—Our p401
McCoy—Portraits p135,por.

Moore, Mary E. (fl. 1920's)
Amer. sculptor
National—Contemp. p231

Moore, Mary Tyler (1937-   )
Amer. actress
CR '63 p442-443,por.

Moore, Mona (1917-   )
Eng. illustrator
Ryder—Artists p103

Moore, Olive Mary.
See Drogheda, Olive Mary Meatyard
Moore

Moore, Ruth (1903-　)
　　　Amer. author
　　Cur. Biog. '54 p474-475,por.
　　Warfel—Amer. p307

Moore, Sarah (fl. 1910's)
　　　Amer. journalist, artist
　　Logan—Part p863

Moore, Mrs. Terris (fl. 1930's)
　　　Amer. aviatrix
　　*May—Women p210

Moore, Terry (1929-　)
　　　Amer. actress
　　CR '59 p529,por.
　　CR '63 p443,por.

Moore-Guggisberg, Decima, Lady (m. 1905)
　　　Eng. foundress
　　Hammerton p1010

Moorehead, Agnes (1906-　)
　　　Amer. actress
　　CR '59 p529-530,por.
　　CR '63 p443,por.
　　Cur. Biog. '52 p437-439,por.
　　Murrow—This (2) p100-101
　　Settel—Radio p102,por.

Moorland (Morland), Jane (fl,. 1760's)
　　　Amer. colonial caterer, grocer
　　Dexter—Colonial p46-47

Moos, Hortensia Gugelberg von (1659-
　　　1715)
　　　Swiss feminist, author
　　Schmidt—400 p377-378,por.

Moran, Lois (1907-　)
　　　Amer. actress
　　TV—Person. (1) p139-140,por.

Moran, Mary Nimmo (b. 1842)
　　　Scot.-Amer. etcher, painter
　　Michigan—Biog. p219-220

Morandi, Rosa (fl. 1810's)
　　　It. singer
　　Derwent—Rossini p60-61

Morant, Fanny (fl. 1870's)
　　　Amer. actress
　　Coad—Amer. p254,por.

Morazan, Tula Serra (fl. 1920's)
　　　Salv. beauty
　　Arsenius—Dict. p138,por.
　　Phila.—Women, unp.
　　Stiles—Postal p180

Morcomb, Mary (fl. 1760's)
　　　Amer. colonial dressmaker
　　Dexter—Colonial p42

Mordan, Clara Evelyn (fl. 1910's)
　　　Eng. feminist, philanthropist
　　Brittain—Women p140-141,173,190,
　　　259

Mordaunt, Elinor (Evelyn May Clowes)
　　　(1877-1942)
　　　Eng. traveler, author
　　Hammerton p1010
　　Johnson—Some Contemp. p45-61

Mordecai, Ellen (b. 1820)
　　　Amer. author
　　Marcus—Memoirs (1) p232-238

Mordecai, Rose (b. 1839)
　　　Amer. author, religious leader
　　Logan—Part p650
　　Marcus—Memoirs (1) p281-288

More, Ellen (fl. 1600's)
　　　Amer. pioneer
　　Logan—Part p32

More, Hannah (1745-1833)
　　　Eng. religious author,
　　　　humanitarian, social reformer
　　Adelman—Famous p100
　　Benson—Women p80-83,101
　　Deen—Great p373-375
　　Dorland—Sum p53,81,172,179,193
　　Hammerton p1010-1011,por.
　　Johnson—Women p63-65
　　Lownsbery—Saints p171-206
　　MacCarthy—Later p215-216
　　MacVeagh—Champlin p418
　　Muir—Women p135-139
　　Schmidt—400 p139-142,por.
　　Stenton—English p271,296,303,306,
　　　312-314
　　Woody—Hist. (1) p31-33

Moreau, Emilienne (fl. 1910's)
　　　Fr. heroine
　　Dorland—Sum p97-98

Moreau, Jean(ne) (1928-　)
　　　Fr. actress
　　Cur. Biog. '66 p283-285,por.
　　Time Mr.5,1965 p78-83,por.(Cover)

Morell, Imogene Robinson (d. 1908)
　　　Amer. artist
　　Hanaford—Dau. p302-304

Morena, Berta (1878-1952)
　　　Ger. singer
　　Lahee—Grand p99-111,por.
　　McCoy—Portraits p136,por.

Moreno, Rita (1931-　)
　　　Puert. Ric. actress
　　CR '63 p443-444,por.

Moresby, Louis, pseud.
　　See Beck, Lily Adams

Moretto, Emma (fl. 1870's-1880's)
It. painter
Waters—Women p243

Morgan, Abigail (Abbie) Bailey (1736-
1802)
Amer. pioneer, patriot
Green—Pioneer (2) p137-144

Morgan, Agnes (fl. 1910's)
Amer. playwright
Logan—Part p791

Morgan, Agnes Fay (1884-1968)
Amer. chemist, nutritionist
Progress—Science p260,por.

Morgan, Angela (d. 1957)
Amer. poet
Cook—Our p316-318
Smith—Women's p153

Morgan, Anne Eugenia Felicia (1845-1909)
Amer. educator, author
Farmer—What p240,por.
Logan—Part p728

Morgan, Anne Tracy (1873-1952)
Amer. philanthropist, social
worker
Adelman—Famous p312
Cur. Biog. '46 p412-414,por.
Cur. Biog. '52 p441
New Yorker Oct.22,1927 p21,por.
(Profiles)

Morgan, Charlotte E. (fl. 1930's)
Amer. educator, author
Women—Achieve. p168,por.

Morgan, Henrietta Hunt (1805-1891)
Amer. Civil war diarist, pioneer
Jones—Heroines p341-343
Logan—Part p69

Morgan, Jane (n.d.)
Amer. singer
CR '59 p531,por.
CR '63 p444,por.

Morgan, Jaye P. (1932-   )
Amer. singer
Popular Record p98,por.
TV—Person (2) p50-51,por.

Morgan, Lucy Calista (1889-   )
Amer. educator
Cur. Biog. '59 p307-308,por.

Morgan, Maria ("Middy," Midy or Marie)
(1828-1892)
Amer. author, horse authority
Logan—Part p864
Ross—Ladies p145-149

Morgan, Martha Ready (fl. 1860's)
Amer. Civil war diarist
Jones—Heroines p198-200

Morgan, Maud (1864-1941)
Amer. harpist, author
McCoy—Portraits p136,por.

Morgan, Michele (1920-   )
Fr. actress
CR '59 p531,por.

Morgan, Nancy. See Hart, Nancy Morgan

Morgan, Rose Meta (n.d.)
Amer. business woman, beautician
*Cherry—Portraits p190-191

Morgan, Sarah (b. 1841)
Amer. Civil war diarist
Green—Pioneer (2) p201-202
Jones—Heroines p121-123,128-138,
168-171
Simkins—Women p56-57,65-67

Morgan, Sarah Berrien Casey (fl. 1910's)
Amer. club leader
Logan—Part p432-433

Morgan, Sydney Oweson, Lady (1780-
1859)
Irish novelist
Adelman—Famous p119
Parton—Dau. p377-396
Parton—Noted p377-396
Thomson—Queens p207-228

Morgan, Therese E. (fl. 1930's)
Amer. retailer
Women—Achieve. p141,por.

Morgana, Nina (fl. 1920's-1930's)
Amer. singer
McCoy—Portraits p136,por.

Morgenstern, Lina Bauer (1830-1909)
Ger. social reformer
Adelman—Famous p222

Morini, Erica (Erika) (1906/10-   )
Aust. violinist
CR '59 p531,por.
Cur. Biog. '46 p418-420,por.
Ewen—Living p255-256,por.
McCoy—Portraits p136,por.
Saleski—Jewish p380-382,por.
Saleski—Wander. p224-227,por.

Morison, Elsie (1924-   )
Austral. singer
Brook—Singers p148-151,por.
Rosenthal—Sopranos p76-77,por.

Morison, Patricia (1919-   )
Amer. actress
CR '59 p531-532,por.

Morison, Rebecca Newell (fl. 1910's)
    Amer. religious worker
    Logan—Part p621

Morisot (Morizot), Berthe Manet (1840-
        1895)
    Fr. painter
    Waters—Women p388-389

Morlan, Jane. See Moorland, Jane

Morlay (Morlaix) Gaby (fl. 1910's)
    Fr. pioneer aviatrix
    Lauwick—Heroines p26-27

Morner, Countess. See Fitch, Geraldine

Moron, Theresa Concordia (1725-1806)
    Ger. enamelist, painter
    Waters—Women p243-244

Morouges, Marie Bigot de (1786-1820)
    Fr. pianist
    Schonberg—Great p86

Morris, Alice V. Shepard (fl. 1920's-1930's)
    Amer. foundress, club leader
    Women—Achieve. p66,por.

Morris, Ann Elliott (d. 1848)
    Amer. Rev. war patriot,
        humanitarian
    Ellet—Women (2) p100-102

Morris, Clara (1846/48-1925)
    Can.-Amer. actress
    Adelman—Famous p273-274
    Bodeen—Ladies p107-110
    Coad—Amer. p240,por.
    Dorland—Sum p168
    Farmer—What p414-415
    Logan—Part p779
    *Richmond—Immig. p77-79
    *Stevens—Women p129-133,por.

Morris, Constance Lily (d. 1954)
    Amer. club leader, author
    Women—Achieve. p138,por.

Morris, Deborah (d. 1800)
    Amer. pioneer
    Green—Pioneer (3) p126-132

Morris, Edita (1902-   )
    Swed.-Amer. author
    Warfel—Amer. p311,por.

Morris, Elizabeth (fl. 1770's)
    Amer. actress
    Dexter—Career p80

Morris, Esther Hobart McQuigg (1814-
        1902)
    Amer. feminist, W. pioneer
    Brown—Gentle p13,238-241,243-244,
        por.
    Bruce—Woman p230-231
    *Miller—West p166-181

Morris, Margaret (d. 1816)
    Amer. Rev. war patriot, author
    Ellet—Women (2) p325-332,por.

Morris, Margaret (1891-   )
    Eng. educator
    Hammerton p1013-1014

Morris, Mary Philipse ("Polly") (1730-
        1825)
    Amer. pioneer, friend of George
        Washington
    Donovan—Women p103-104,108,por.
    Green—Pioneer (2) p9,155-169

Morris, Matilda E. (fl. 1860's)
    Amer. Civil war nurse
    Brockett—Woman's p496
    Dannett—Nobel p313-315,343,361
    Logan—Part p367

Morris, May (1862-1938)
    Eng., friend of George Bernard
        Shaw, dau. of William Morris
    DuCann—Loves p118-131,por.

Morris, Mildred (fl. 1930's)
    Amer. journalist
    Ross—Ladies p214

Morris, Mrs. (d. 1767)
    Amer. colonial actress
    Dexter—Colonial p159,163

Morris, Myra (fl. 1930's-1940's)
    Austral. author
    Roderick—20 p281-294

Morris, Mrs. Owen (d.c. 1825)
    Amer. actress
    Coad—Amer. p32,por.

Morrisey, Marie (fl. 1940's)
    Amer. singer
    McCoy—Portraits p136,por.

Morrison, Adrienne (1889-1940)
    Amer. actress, literary agent
    Cur. Biog. '41 p595

Morrison, Anne (fl. 1920's)
    Amer. playwright
    Mantle—Amer. p301

Morrison, Margaret (fl. 1820's-1860's)
    Scot., mother of Andrew Carnegie
    Bartlett—Mothers p95-100

Morrison, Margaret Mackie.
    See Cost, March

Morrison, Mary Anna (fl. 1860's)
    Amer. Civil war heroine
    Harkness—Heroines p2

Morrow, Anne.
    See Lindbergh, Anne Spencer Morrow

Morrow, Elizabeth Cutter (1873-1955)
Amer. author, educator
Cur. Biog. '43 p538-540,por.
Cur. Biog. '55 p428

Morrow, Honoré Willsie (c. 1880-1940)
Amer. novelist
Cur. Biog. '40 p598,por.
Overton p216-218

Morsch, Lucile M. (1906-   )
Amer. librarian, organization
official
Cur. Biog. '57 p377-379,por.

Morse, Alice Cordelia (b. 1862)
Amer. artist
Logan—Part p751

Morse, Carol. See Hall, Marjory

Morse, Fanny (fl. 1930's)
Amer. business woman
Women—Achieve. p121,por.

Morse, Louisa Spruance (fl. 1950's)
Amer. aviatrix
*May—Women p193

Morse, Rebecca A. (fl. 1880's)
Amer. art patron
Hanaford—Dau. p306-307

Morse, Ruth V. (fl. 1930's)
Amer. travel specialist
Women—Achieve. p177,por.

Morse, Theodora (1883/90-1953)
Amer. song-writer, music publisher
ASCAP p361

Mortimer, Mary (1816-1877)
Amer. teacher, educator
Logan—Part p732

Morton, Anne Justis (m. 1745/46)
Amer. patriot, pioneer
Green—Pioneer (3) p192-195

Morton, Eleanor.
See Stern, Elizabeth Gertrude Levin

Morton, Eliza Happy (1852-1916)
Amer. author, song-writer
Logan—Part p857-858

Morton, Elizabeth Homer (1903-   )
Can. librarian, organization
official, editor
Cur. Biog. '61 p323-325,por.

Morton, Florrinell Francis (1904-   )
Amer. librarian, educator,
organization official
Cur. Biog. '61 p325-327,por.

Morton, Jane M. (fl. 1860's)
Amer. Civil war nurse
Logan—Part p367

Morton, Martha (fl. 1910's)
Amer. playwright
Logan—Part p790-791

Morton, Rosalie Slaughter (b. 1876)
Amer. physician, surgeon
Fabricant—Why p9-12
Irwin—Angels p284-285
Mead—Medical p67
Rosen—Four p124-127,317-320

Morton, Sarah Wentworth (Philenia,
pseud.) (1759-1846)
Amer. colonial poet
Dexter—Career p94-95,97
Douglas—Remember p46-47
Leonard—Amer. p119

Morton-Sale, Isobel (1904-   )
Eng. illustrator
Mahony—Illus. p340

Moseley, Mrs. (fl. 1890's-1900's)
Amer. pioneer
Logan—Part p96

Moser, Edwa Robert (1899-   )
Amer. author
Warfel—Amer. p313-314,por.

Moser, Mary (d. 1819)
Eng. painter
Waters—Women p244

Moses, mother of (Biblical)
Hughes—Mothers p75-103

Moses, wife of (Biblical)
Deen—All p324

Moses, Anna Mary Robertson ("Grandma")
(1860-1961)
Amer. artist
CR '59 p533,por.
Cur. Biog. '49 p441-443,por.
Cur. Biog. '62 p306
*Curtin—Gallery p69,por.
De Morny—Best, p209-213
Hazeltine—We p18-25
Janis—They p128-136,por.
Time Dec.28,1953 p38,por.(Cover)

Moses, Clara Lowenburg (1865-1951)
Amer. author
Marcus—Memoirs (1) p261-271

Mosher, Clelia (b. 1863)
Amer. physician, educator
Binheim—Women p70,por.

Mosher, Edith Apperson (fl. 1910's-1940's)
Amer. missionary
They—Went p46-48

Mosher, Edith R. (fl. 1900's-1910's)
Amer. teacher, author
Logan—Part p866-867

Mosher, Edna (fl. 1930's)
Can.-Amer. biologist, entomologist
Women—Achieve. p129,por.

Mosher, Eliza M. (1846-1928)
Amer. physician
Lovejoy—Women p87,97,102,304,308,
333,360
Lovejoy—Women Phys. p50-52,por.
Mead—Medical p49,por.

Moskowitz, Belle Iraels (1877-1933)
Amer. social worker, club leader
New Yorker Oct.9,1926,p26-28,por.
(Profiles)

Moss, Mary Hissem de (fl. 1940's)
Amer. singer
McCoy—Portraits p136,por.

Mossell, Mary Ella (1853-1886)
Amer. missionary
Brown—Home. p194-199,por.

Moten, Etta (fl. 1930's)
Amer. actress, singer
Cuney-Hare—Negro p385,por.

Mothe, Jeanne Bouvières de la.
See Guyon, Jean Marie de la Motte-
Guyon Bouvier

Motley, Constance Baker (1921-   )
Amer. lawyer, organization official,
state senator, judge
Cur. Biog. '64 p305-308,por.
Robinson—Hist. p230-231,por.
Lamson—Few p127-161,por.

Mott, Alice (fl. 1900's)
Eng. painter
Waters—Women p245

Mott, Lucreta Coffin (1793-1880)
Amer. feminist, social reformer
Abbot—Notable p308-312,por.
Adelman—Famous p167-168
Beard—Amer. p181-187
Bruce—Woman p178-179,225
Burnett—Five p13-48
*Commager—Crus. p155-157
Culver—Women p178-179
Dexter—Career p56
Dorland—Sum p19,74,80,127,137
Douglas—Remember p116,150-154,por.
Foster—Religion p88-114
Hanaford—Dau. p170-174,184,357-
359,437-438,por.
Heath—Woman (4) p5,por.
*Humphrey—Women p115-131
Irwin—Angels p56-59,70-81,91-95,98,
163

Jensen—Revolt p41-43,por.
*Lamm—Biog. p98
Logan—Part p590-591
O'Connor—Pioneer p57-59,138-139,
152-153,184,199,204-205,213
Phila.—Women unp.,por.
Riegel—Amer. p19-23,54-55,por.
Snow—Women p105-106
*Stevens—Women p85-86,por.
Stiles—Postal p181
Whitton—These p104-106,145
*Yost—Famous p49-58,por.

Mott, Mollie C. (fl. 1860's)
Amer. Civil war nurse
Logan—Part p367

Motte, Rebecca Brewton (1738-1815)
Amer. Rev. heroine, patriot
DAR Mag. July 1921 p372-373,portrayal
Dexter—Career p187
Ellet—Women (2) p79-89,92,por.
Green—Pioneer (2) p291-301,343,por.
Hanaford—Dau. p57-58,602
Leonard—Amer. p119
Logan—Part p136-140
Whitton—These p21

Motte-Guyon, Madame.
See Guyon, Jean Marie de la Moote-
Guyon Bouvier

Motteville, Dame Langlois de Françoise
Bertaut (1615/21-1689)
Fr. author
Dorland—Sum p53,104
Hall—Moths p53-91,por.

Moulton, Hannah Lynch (m. 1779)
Amer. pioneer
Green—Pioneer (2) p196

Moulton, Louise Chandler (1835-1908)
Amer. author
Hanaford—Dau. p246
Logan—Part p840

Moultrie, Elizabeth St. Julien (fl. 1770's)
Amer. pioneer
Green—Pioneer (2) p195-196

Mounsey, Ann Shepard (1811-1891)
Eng. composer
Elson—Woman's p134-135

Mountbatten of Burma, Edwina Cynthia
Annette Ashley, Countess
Eng. social welfare worker, friend
of Gandhi
Stern—Women p289-296
Winn—Queen's p64-81,por.

Mountfort, Susanna.
See Verbruggen, Susanna Percival

"Mouse, The" ("La Souris") (fl. 1940's)
Fr. spy
Singer—World's p229-231

"Moustache, Madame."
See Dumont, Eleanore

Mowat, Angus (1892-   )
Can. author, librarian
Thomas—Canad. p91-92

Mowat, Vivia A. (fl. 1910's)
Amer. agriculturist, business
woman
Logan—Part p907

Mowatt, Anna Cora Ogden (1819-1870)
Fr. actress, playwright
Coad—Amer. p117-118,por.
Ormsbee—Back. p137-140
Whitton—These p189-190

Mowrer, Lilian Thomson (n.d.)
Amer. journalist, lecturer
Cur. Biog. '40 p603-604,por.

Mowrey, Corma Alice (1907-   )
Amer. organization official
Cur. Biog. '50 p413-414,por.

Mowry, Crystal (fl. 1960's)
Amer. aviatrix
*May—Women p211

Moylan, Marianne (1932-   )
Amer. singer
Donaldson—Radio p21-22

Moylan, Mary Ellen (1926-   )
Amer. ballet dancer
Atkinson—Dancers p115-118,por.
Cur. Biog. '57 p386-388,por.
*Terry—Star p191-192

Moylan, Peggy Joan (1934-   )
Amer. singer
Donaldson—Radio p21-22

Mozart, Anna Maria (1720-1778)
Aust., mother of Mozart
Schmidt—400 p43-44,por.

Mozart, Maria Anna (1751-1829)
Aust., pianist, teacher, dau. of
Mozart
McCoy—Portraits p137,por.

Mozee, Phoebe Anne Oakley.
See Oakley, Annie

Mucia (fl. 62 B.C.)
Rom., wife of Scaurus, Pompey,
mother of Sextus Pompeius
Balsdon—Roman p53,59,220

Mudd, Emily Hatshore (1898-   )
Amer. educator, author, marriage
counselor
Cur. Biog. '56 p453-455,por.

Mudie, Rosemary (fl. 1950's)
Eng. balloonist
*May—Women p36-37

Muelbach, Louise.
See Mundt, Klara Müller

Mueller, Maria (1898-   )
Czech. singer
Ewen—Ency. p335-336
McCoy—Portraits p137,por.

Mugglebee, Ruth (fl. 1930's)
Amer. journalist
Ross—Ladies p491-492

Mühlbach, Louise, pseud.
See Mundt, Klara Müller

Muilman, Teresia Constantia (fl. 1750's)
Eng. author
Benson—Women p55-56

Muir, Florence Roma (Romer Wilson,
pseud.) (1891-1930)
Brit. author
Millett—Brit. p512-513

Mülinen, Helene Von (1850-1924)
Swiss feminist, humanitarian
Schmidt—400 p386,por.

Mullens, Alice (fl. 1600's)
Amer. pioneer
Logan—Part p33

Müller, Maria. See Mueller, Maria

Müller, Therese. See Malten, Therese

Mulliner, Gabrielle (fl. 1920's)
Amer. lawyer, social reformer,
sociologist
Logan—Part p593

Mullins, Edith (fl. 1930's)
Amer. poet
Women—Achieve. p201

Mullins, Priscilla.
See Alden, Priscilla Mullins

Mulock, Dinah Maria.
See Craik, Dinah Maria Mulock

Mulroney, Regina Winifred (fl. 1920's)
Amer. sculptor
National—Contemp. p233

Mumford, Ethel Watts (d. 1940)
        Amer. playwright, poet, novelist
    Cur. Biog. '40 p606

Mumtaz-Mahal (Mumtaza Zemani) (1592-
        1631)
        Ind., wife of Shah Jahan,
            inspiration for Taj Mahal
    Mozans—Woman p337
    Pool—Famous p106-112

Mundeville, Maude de (fl.c. 1140's)
        Eng. heiress
    Stenton—English p40-41

Mundt, Klara Müller (Louise Mühlbach,
        pseud.) (1814-1873)
        Ger. novelist
    Adelman—Famous p180-181
    Dorland—Sum p17,196
    Heller—Studies p249-250

Mundy, Ethel Frances (n.d.)
        Amer. wax sculptor
    Jackman—Amer. p442

Munford, Mary-Cooke Branch (1865-
        1938)
        Amer. educator
    Bowie—Women p140-159

Munro, Beatrice Lounsbery (fl. 1930's)
        Amer. business executive
    Women—Achieve. p164,por.

Munro, Mary Isobel (g. 1929)
        Eng. teacher
    Brittain—Women p176,246

Munro, Mrs. (fl. 1770's)
        Amer. Rev. war patriot
    Ellet—Women (2) p351-352

Munsel, Patricia (1925-   )
        Amer. singer
    Bakeless—In p167-176,por.
    CR '59 p537-538,por.
    CR '63 p451,por.
    Cur. Biog. '45 p412-413,por.
    Ewen—Ency. p336
    Hurok—Impres. p288-289,por.
    Matz—Opera p200-202,por.
    Peltz—Spot. p105,por.
    Time Dec.3,1951 p50,por.(Cover)

Munsell, Jane R. (fl. 1860's)
        Amer. Civil war nurse
    Brockett—Woman's p522-523

Murat, Carolina.
    See Bonaparte, Maria Annunciata

Murdoch, (Jean) Iris (1919-   )
        Irish author, educator
    Cur. Biog. '58 p293-294,por.
    Shapiro—Contemp. p62-80

Murdoch, Katharine (fl. 1920's-1930's)
        Amer. psychologist
    Women—Achieve. p146,por.

Murdock, Ellen E. (fl. 1860's)
        Amer. Civil war patriot
    Brockett—Woman's p616,633

Murdock, Marian (b. 1849)
        Amer. clergyman
    Logan—Part p738

Murfee, Mary Noailles (Charles Egbert
            Craddock, pseud.) (1850-1922)
        Amer. novelist
    Adelman—Famous p266
    Harkins—Famous p75-90
    Harkins—Little p75-90,por.
    Logan—Part p802,por.
    Maurice—Makers p7

Murphy, Emily (1868-1933)
        Can. politician, judge, author
    Innis—Clear p158-165,173-178,por.
    Sanders—Canadian p113-142,por.

Murphy, Florence Jones (fl. 1950's)
        Amer. legal secretary, aviatrix
    *May—Women p197

Murphy, Kathryn (n.d.)
        TV personality
    Blum—Television p151,por.

Murphy, (Eleanor) Patricia (c. 1911-   )
        Newfound, restauranteur,
            horticulturist
    Cur. '62 p313-315,por.

Murphy, Virginia Reed (fl. 1910's)
        Amer., daughter of "Donner" Reed
    Logan—Part p101

Murray, Alma (b. 1855
        Eng. actress
    Hammerton p1022

Murray, Augusta, Lady (d. 1830)
        Eng., wife of Augustus, Duke
            of Sussex
    Hasted—Unsuccess. p191-211,por.

Murray, Catherine Eliza.
    See Rush, Catherine Eliza Murray

Murray, Charlotte Wallace (m. 1915)
        Amer. singer, music teacher
    Cuney-Hare—Negro p378-379,por.

Murray, Elizabeth (fl. 1900's)
        Eng. painter
    Waters—Women p245-246

Murray, Esther Burke Higgins (1905-   )
        Amer. politician
    Roosevelt—Ladies p57-59

Murray, Evelyn fl. 1940's)
    Amer. employment consultant
    Epstein—People p58-73

Murray, Fanny (c. 1729-1778)
    Eng. courtesan
    Bleakley—Ladies p1-49,297-299,por.

Murray, Flora (fl. 1910's)
    Amer. physician
    Lovejoy—Women p291,293-296,298

Murray, Mrs. Frederick (fl. 1940's)
    Amer. mother of year
    Davis—Mothers p176-177

Murray, Judith Sargent ("Constantia")
        (1751-1820)
    Amer. author
    Benson—Women p171-172,175-177,
        192-193,215-216

Murray, Kathryn (1906-   )
    Amer. dancer
    TV—Person. (1) p38-39,por.

Murray, Mae (c. 1890-1965)
    Amer. dancer, actress
    CR '59 p539-540,por.
    Shickel—Stars p52-53,por.
    Stuart—Immort. p188-189,por.

Murray, Margaret Alice (1863-1963)
    Eng. Egyptologist
    Hammerton p1022

Murray, Margaret Ransone (fl. 1930's)
    Amer. biologist
    Women—Achieve. p138,por.

Murray, Mary Lindley (1720-1782)
    Amer. Rev. war patriot
    Green—Pioneer (3) p456
    Humphrey—Women p40-46

Murray, Mrs. (fl. 1600's)
    Eng. governess, mother of Lady
        Halket
    Stenton—English p159

Murray, "Nicky" (d. 1777)
    Scot., assembly director
    Graham—Group p149-164

Murray, Rosalind (b. 1890)
    Eng. author
    O'Brien—Road p123-134

Murray, Stella Wolfe (fl. 1920's)
    Brit. aviatrix
    Heath—Woman p41-69,por.

Murrell, Ethel Ernest (1909-   )
    Amer. organization official, lawyer
    Cur. Biog. '51 p450-451,por.

Murry, Kathleen.
    See Mansfield, Katherine Beauchamp

Murska, Ilma di (1835/43-1889)
    Croat. singer
    Klein—Great p80-88
    Lahee—Famous p150-157

Murtfeldt, Mary E. (1848-1913)
    Amer. entomologist
    Osborn—Fragments p165-166,por.

Muse, Maude B. (fl. 1920's-1930's)
    Amer. nurse, educator
    Pennock—Makers p83,por.
    Women—Achieve, p164,por.

Musgrave, Ruth (fl. 1910's-1940's)
    Amer. missionary
    They—Went p53-55

Mussey, Ellen Spencer (1850-1936)
    Amer. lawyer, club leader
    Irwin—Angels p177-178
    Logan—Part p479,749

Muzio, Claudia (1892-1936)
    It. singer
    Ewen—Ency. p338-339
    McCoy—Portraits p138,por.

Mydans, Shelley Smith (1915-   )
    Amer. journalist, author
    Cur. Biog. '45 p417-420,por.

Myddleton, Jane Needham (Middleton)
        (1645-1692)
    Eng. beauty
    Melville—Windsor p142-152

Myers, Carlene Brien (fl. 1930's)
    Amer. author
    Women—Achieve. p160,por.

Myers, Ella Burns (fl. 1930's)
    Amer. business executive
    Women—Achieve. p168,por.

Myers, Mrs. (fl. 1770's)
    Amer. Rev. war patriot
    Ellet—Women (2) p197-198

Myerson, Bess (n.d.)
    Amer. musician, TV personality,
        "Miss America"
    CR '63 p454,por.
    TV—Person (1) p65-66,por.

Myerson, Golda. See Meir, Golda

Mygatt, Tracy Dickinson (fl. 1930's)
    Amer. playwright, author
    Women—Achieve. p142,por.

Myra X. See X, Myra

Myrdal, Alva (1902-   )
      Swed. sociologist, U.N. official
      Cur. Biog. '50 p419-421,por.

Myrtis of Anthedon (fl. 500's-400's B.C.)
      Gr. poet
      Elson—Woman's p28

Mysz, Gmeiner, Lulu (1876-1948)
      Ger. singer
      McCoy—Portraits p138,por.

N

Naamah (1) (Biblical)
      daughter of Lamech
      Deen—All p284
      Lewis—Portraits p112-113

Naamah (2) (Biblical)
      one of Solomon's wives
      Deen—All p284

Naaman, wife of (Biblical)
      Deen—All p332
      Nelson—Bible p64-65

Naarah (Biblical)
      Deen—All p284

Nabbari (n.d.)
      Austral. native heroine
      *Deakin—True p217-231

Nadworney, Devora (1924-   )
      Amer. singer
      McCoy—Portraits p138,por.

Naidu, Sarojini (1879-1949)
      Ind. poet, patriot, lecturer, social
      reformer, politician, Gandhi
      follower
      Cur. Biog. '43 p548-551,por.
      *Kirkland—Good p25-31
      Stern—Women (see index),por.

Nain, Widow of (Biblical)
      Lewis—Portraits p191-192
      Lord—Great p148-159

Nairne, Caroline Oliphant, Baroness
      (Caroline Oliphant) (1766-
      1845)
      Scot. author
      Dorland—Sum p34
      Findlay—Spindle p114-152,por.
      Hammerton p1025

Najafi, Najmeh (fl. 1960's)
      Pers. teacher, humanitarian
      Spencer—Workers p80-93,por.

Namara, Marguerite (fl. 1940's)
      Amer. singer
      McCoy—Portraits p138,por.

Nam-Phuong (1915-1963)
      Annam empress
      Phila.—Women, unp.,por.
      Stiles—Postal p184

Naomi (Biblical)
      Buchanan—Women p44-46
      Deen—All p284-285
      Hammerton p1025
      Hughes—Mothers p104-105
      *MacVeagh—Champlin p426
      Mead—250 p73
      Nelson—Bible p35-36
      Schmidt—400 p266,por.
      Van der Velde—She p100-106

Napier, Sarah Lennox Bunbury, Lady
      (1745-1826)
      Eng. hostess, friend of George III
      Melville—Regency p22-30,por.
      Stenton—English p268-269

Narelle, Marie (c. 1874-1941)
      Austral. singer
      Cur. Biog. '41 p603

Narriman Sadek (1933-   )
      Egypt. queen
      Stiles—Postal p185

Naryshkin, Madame (fl. 1800's)
      Russ., mistress of Alexander I
      Kelen—Mist. p20

Nash, Alice Morrison (b.c. 1879)
      Amer. teacher
      *Fleming—Great p87-100

Nash, Clara Holmes Hapgood (b. 1839)
      Amer. lawyer
      Logan—Part p744

Nash, Eleanor Arnett (1892-   )
      Amer. author
      Warfel—Amer. p317-318,por.

Nash, Frances (fl. 1940's)
      Amer. pianist
      McCoy—Portraits p139,por.

Nash, Mary (b. 1885)
      Amer. actress
      Blum—Great p103,por.

Nash, Mary McKinlay (b. 1835)
      Amer. club leader
      Logan—Part p471

Nash family (Hannah, Deborah, Mehitabel,
      Elizabeth) (fl. 1640's)
      Amer. pioneers
      Fowler—Woman p48-51

Nasif, Melek Hifni (1886-1918)
      Egypt. author, feminist
      Schmitt—400 p119-120,por.

Nason, Emma Huntington (b. 1845)
    Amer. translator, poet
    Logan—Part p866

Nasser, Tahia Mahmoud (1923-   )
    Egypt., wife of Nasser
    Frederick—Ten p113-127,por.

Natalia (or Sabagotha)
    Sp. saint
    Englebert—Lives p287-288

Nataline (fl. 4th cent.)
    Fr. saint
    Englebert—Lives p422

Nathan, Adele Gutman (fl. 1930's)
    Amer. theatrical director, author
    Women—Achieve. p143,por.

Nathan, Maud (fl. 1930's)
    Amer. humanitarian, social worker
    Women—Achieve. p89,por.

Nation, Carry Amelia Moore (1846-1911)
    Amer. social reformer
    Aikman—Calamity p320-327
    Brown—Gentle p270-279,por.
    Carnegie—Little p77-80,por.
    Culver—Women p181
    Hammerton p1030
    Holbrook—Dreamers p97-105
    Irwin—Angels p204-206
    Jensen—Revolt p48-49,por.
    Johnson—Lunatic p207-221
    Rogers—Women p165,por.
    Ross—Charmers p173-195,por.

Natwick, Mildred (fl. 1920's)
    Amer. actress
    Ormsbee—Back. p271-272

Nau, Maria Delores Benedicta Josefina
        (1818-1891)
    Amer. singer
    McCoy—Portraits p139,por.

Naumburg, Elsie Margaret (fl. 1930's)
    Amer. ornithologist
    Women—Achieve. p89,por.

Navarre, Marguerite de.
    See Margaret of Navarre

Navarro, Mary de.
    See Anderson, Mary Antoinette

Nave, Anna Eliza Seamans (b. 1948)
    Amer. philanthropist
    Logan—Part p531

Nawkins, Angelina (1918-   )
    Amer. Salvation Army worker
    New Yorker Sept.21,1946 p34,por.
    (Profiles)

Nayyar, Sushila (fl. 1940's-1950's)
    Ind., co-worker of Gandhi
    Stern—Women p168-176,232-243,253-
    272

Nazimova, Alla (1879-1945)
    Russ.-Amer. actress
    Blum—Great p54,por.
    Cur. Biog. '45 p423
    Eustis—Players p47-58,por.
    Izard—Heroines p356-358
    Ormsbee—Back. p253-254,por.

Neagle, Anna 1904-   )
    Eng. actress
    Cur. Biog. '45 p423-427,por.

Neal, Alice B. (m. 1846)
    Amer. author, editor
    Hanaford—Dau. p233-234

Neal, (Jean) Frances (fl. 1850's)
    Amer. W. pioneer
    Sargent—Pioneers p15,19,por.

Neal, Grace Pruden (b. 1876)
    Amer. sculptor
    National—Contemp. p234

Neal, Josephine Bickney (1880-1955)
    Amer. physician
    Castiglioni—Hist. p1127

Neal, Patricia (1926-   )
    Amer. actress
    CR '59 p544-545,por.
    CR '63 p456,por.
    Cur. Biog. '64 p314-316,por.

Neale, Mary Peasley (fl. 1750's)
    Amer. colonial religious worker
    Jones—Quakers p300

Nealis, Jean Ursula (fl. 1910's)
    Amer. poet
    Logan—Part p838

Nearing, Elizabeth Custer (1900-   )
    Amer. novelist
    Warfel—Amer. p319-320,por.

Necker, Germaine (fl. 18th cent.) .
    Fr., daughter of Madame De Stael
    Kavanagh—Woman (2) p30-33

Necker, Suzanne Curchod, Madame (1739-
        1794)
    Fr. salonist, stateswoman, author,
        philanthropist, foundress
    Dorland—Sum p43,73,104,128
    Kavanagh—Woman (2) p24-33
    Schmidt—400 p180,por.
    Tallentyre—Women p62-112,por.

Necker de Saussure, Albertine Adrienne
  (1766-1841)
    Fr. educator
    Woody—Hist. (1) p70-76

Nedeva, Zlatina (fl. 1940's)
    Bulg. actress
    Phila.—Women unp.,por.

Nedwill, Rose (fl. 1930's)
    Amer. artist
    Women—Achieve. p99,por.

Nefertiti (c. 1390-1360 B.C.)
    Egypt. queen
    *Farmer—Book p1-12
    *Holmes—She p47-87,por.
    Phila.—Women, unp.,por.
    Schmidt—400 p113-114,por.
    Stiles—Postal p185
    Weigall—Person. p208-214

Neff, Mary (fl. 17th cent.)
    Amer., Ind. captive
    Bruce—Woman p14-16,
    Green—Pioneer (1) p376,379-380,
      382-383

Negri, Pola (1899-   )
    Pol. actress
    Lamparski—What. p36-37,por.
    Schickel—Stars p51,por.
    Wagenknecht—Movies p200-202,205

Negro, Teresa (fl. 1880's-1900's)
    It. artist, potter
    Waters—Women p246

Negrone, Carina, Marquise (fl. 1950's)
    It. aviatrix
    *May—Women p211

Nehru, Vijaya Lakshmi (n.d.)
    Ind., sister of J. Nehru
    Stern—Women p129-143

Nehushta (Nehusta), Queen (Biblical)
    Buchanan—Women p65-67
    Deen—All p285-287
    Lewis—Portraits p123-124

Neilsen, Alice (fl. 1910's-1920's)
    Amer. singer
    Lahee—Grand p359-362,por.

Neilson, (Lilian) Adelaide (1846/48-1880)
    Eng. actress
    Adelman—Famous p209-210
    Bodeen—Ladies p43-48
    Coad—Amer. p248,por.
    Dorland—Sum p50,168

Neilson, Frances Fullerton Jones (1912-)
    Amer. author
    Cur. Biog. '55 p441-442,por.

Neilson, Julia (1869-1957)
    Eng. actress
    Hammerton p1031,por.

Nelli, Herva (n.d.)
    It. singer
    Matz—Opera p142-145,por.

Nelli, Plautilla (b. 1523)
    It. painter, abbess
    Waters—Women p246-248

Nellis, Samantha Stanton (b. 1811)
    Amer. patriot
    Logan—Part p437

Nelson, Dorcas.
    See Richardson, Dorcas Nelson

Nelson, Harriet (n.d.)
    Amer. actress, singer
    Cur. Biog. '49 p451-453,por.
    TV—Person. (2) p97-99,por.

Nelson, Klondy Esmerelda (1897-   )
    Amer., Alaskan heroine
    *Deakin—True p136-151

Nelson, Lucy Grymes (m. 1762)
    Amer. patriot
    Green—Pioneer (3) p250-254

Nemcova, Bozena (1820-1862)
    Czech. novelist, poet, patriot
    Phila.—Women, unp.,por.
    Schmidt—400 p89,por.
    Stiles—Postal p186

Nemenoff, Genia (fl. 1930's)
    Fr. pianist
    Ewen—Living p224-225
    Saleski—Jewish p647-648,por.

Nemes-Ransonnett, Elisa, Countess (b. 1843)
    Aust. painter
    Waters—Women p248

Nemeth, Maria (fl. 1930's)
    Hung. singer
    McCoy—Portraits p140,por.

Nemiroff, Lorraine.
    See Hansberry, Lorraine

Nepean, Edith (fl. 1910's-1930's)
    Brit. author
    Hammerton p1032

Nerina, Nadia (1927-   )
    S. Afr. ballet dancer
    Cur. Biog. '57 p398-399,por.
    Fisher—Ball. p24,26,por.

Neruda, Wilma.
    See Hallé, Wilhelmina Maria
    Franziska Neruda, Lady

Nesbit, Edith (1858-1924)
    Eng. novelist
    Ducann—Loves p152-171,por.
    *Green—Authors p101-106,por.
    Hammerton p1033

Nesbit, Evelyn (Evelyn Thaw) (c. 1885-1967)
    Amer. dancer
    Jensen—Revolt p166-167,por.

Nesbitt, Cathleen Mary (1889-)
    Eng. actress
    CR '59 p546,por.
    CR '63 p457,por.
    Cur. Biog. '56 p459-461,por.

Nesle, Pauline Félicité de.
    See Vintimille, Pauline Félicité de Nesle

Nesle de, sisters (Mailly, Flavacourt, Vintimille, Tournelle, Lauraguais) (fl. 18th cent.)
    Fr., friends of Louis XV
    Kemble—Idols p64-69

Nethersole, Olga Isabel (1870-1951)
    Eng. actress, manager
    Coad—Amer. p293,por.
    Dorland—Sum p71,168
    Rogers—Women p154,por.
    Strang—Actresses p217-231,por.

Netmaker, Benedicta (fl. 1740's)
    Amer. colonial merchant
    Dexter—Colonial p23

Neuber, (Frederika) Caroline Weissenborn (b. 1697)
    Ger. pioneer, actress, manager
    Gilder—Enter p202-226,por.

Neuberger, Maurine (1907-)
    Amer. senator, politician
    CR '63 p457-458,por.
    Cur. Biog. '61 p339-340,por.
    Parshalle—Kash. p159-160,por.
    Roosevelt—Ladies p144-147
    U.S.—Women (87th) p5,por.
    U.S.—Women (88th) p1,por.

Nevada, Emma Wixom (1859/62-1940)
    Amer. singer
    Ewen—Ency. p342
    Lahee—Famous p230-236
    Logan—Part p766
    McCoy—Portraits p140,por.
    Marks—Glamour p320-321
    Wagner—Prima p79,246

Nevada, Mignon (b. 1887)
    Fr. singer
    McCoy—Portraits p140,por.

Nevelson, Louise (1900-)
    Russ.-Amer. sculptor
    Cur. Biog. '67 p314-317,por.

Nevill, Dorothy, Lady (1826-1913)
    Eng. social leader, hostess, author
    Furniss—Some p135-137
    Hammerton p1033,por.
    Wyndham—Chorus p40-41,81-82

Neville, Anne. See Anne Neville

Nevins, Georgia Marquis (fl. 1890's-1910's)
    Amer. philanthropist
    Logan—Part p547

Newberry, Clare Turlay (1903-)
    Amer. illustrator
    Mahony—Illus. p341

Newberry, Julia (1854-1876)
    Amer. heiress, diarist
    Dunaway—Treas. p30-34

Newbigen, Marion (d. 1934)
    Scot. geographer
    Hammerton p1034

Newby, Ruby Warren (fl. 1930's)
    Amer. artist, teacher
    Women—Achieve. p177,por.

Newcastle, Margaret, Duchess of (c. 1624-1673/74)
    Eng. author
    MacCarthy—Women p20-22, 81-93, 122-138,267-270
    Stenton—English p68,155-158,165, 192,265

Newcomb, Ethel (1879-1959)
    Amer. pianist
    McCoy—Portraits p141,por.

Newcomb, Maria Guise (b. 1865)
    Amer. painter
    Michigan—Biog. p227
    Waters—Women p248

Newcomer, Mabel (1891-)
    Amer. economist, educator
    Cur. Biog. '44 p491-493,por.

Newell, Harriet Atwood (1793-1812)
    Amer. missionary
    Dexter—Career p64-65
    Hanaford—Dau. p505-507
    Logan—Part p508
    Whitton—These p122

Newman, Angela F. (b. 1837)
    Amer. teacher, missionary
    Logan—Part p521-522

Newman, E. E. (fl. 1870's-1880's)
    Amer. clergyman
    Hanaford—Dau. p474

Newman, Frances (1788-1928)
Amer. novelist, librarian
Clark—Innocence p187-210,por.
Overton—Women p219-226

Newman, Henriette (fl. 1930's)
Amer. business executive, antique
dealer
Women—Achieve. p187,por.

Newman, Isadora (fl. 1930's)
Amer. artist, author, sculptor
Women—Achieve. p46,por.

Newman, Laura A. Mount (fl. 1860's)
Amer. Civil war nurse
Logan—Part p371

Newman, Pauline M. (fl. 1940's)
Amer. labor leader
Rogers—Women p70

Newman, Phyllis (n.d.)
Amer. actress
CR '63 p459,por.
Newquist—Show. p303-314,por.

Newmar, Julie (1935-   )
Amer. dancer, director
CR '63 p459-460

Newmarch, Rosa Harriet (1857-1940)
Eng. music writer
McCoy—Portraits p141,por.

Newport, Matilda (fl. 1820's)
Lib. patriot, heroine
Phila.—Women, unp.,por.
Stiles—Postal p187

Newsom, Ella King (fl. 1860's)
Amer. Civil war hospital manager,
nurse
Bruce—Woman p226
Simkins—Women p86,93

Newsome, Effie Lee (b. 1885)
Amer. poet
*Rollins—Famous p55-60,por.

Newstead, Helaine (1906-   )
Amer. educator
New Yorker Mr.30,1957 p39,por.
(Profiles)

Newton, Charlotte L. (fl. 1870's-1880's)
Amer. business woman
Hanaford—Dau. p610

Newton, Mary (fl. 1770's)
Amer. patriot, daughter of John
Jordan
Logan—Part p433

Ney, Elly (b. 1882)
Ger. pianist
Ewen—Living p259,por.
McCoy—Portraits p141,por.

New, Elizabeth (1830/33-1907)
Ger.-Amer. sculptor
Logan—Part p763
Michigan—Biog. p228
Taft—Women, Mentor (172) #1
Waters—Women p248-249,390

Ngo Dinh Nhu, Madame (Madame Nhu)
(n.d.)
Viet-Namese politician
Time August 9,1963 p21,por.(Cover)

Nicaula (fl. 980's-940's, B.C.)
Ethiop. queen
Boccaccio—Conc. p93-94

Nicholls, Rhoda Holmes (1854-1930)
Amer. painter
Adelman—Famous p290-291
Logan—Part p754-755
Michigan—Biog. p228-229
Waters—Women p249-250

Nichols, Alberta (n.d.)
Amer. composer
ASCAP p370

Nichols, Anne (n.d.)
Amer. playwright
Mantel—Contemp. p320

Nichols, Catherine Maude (fl. 1900's)
Eng. painter, illustrator
Waters—Women p250-252

Nichols, Clarinda Irene Howard (1810-
1885)
Amer. feminist, social reformer,
editor, lecturer
Brown—Gentle p250,por.
Hanaford—Dau. p366
O'Connor—Pioneer p86,152,182

Nichols, Edith Elizabeth (fl. 1930's)
Amer. singer, vocal teacher
Women—Achieve. p98,por.

Nichols, Elizabeth B. (fl. 1860's)
Amer. Civil war nurse
Logan—Part p335-336,371

Nichols, Marie (c. 1879-1954)
Amer. violinist
McCoy—Portraits p141,por.

Nichols, Mary Sargeant Neal (Mary Gove)
(1810-1884)
Amer. social reformer, feminist,
physician, author
Riegel—Amer. p130-134
Woodward—Bold p149-180

Nichols, Minerva Parker (1862/63-1949)
Amer. architect, lecturer
Logan—Part p786-787

Nichols, Rebecca Shepard Reed (1819-
1903)
Amer. poet
Hanaford—Dau. p269

Nichols, Ruth Rowland (1901-1960)
Amer. pioneer aviatrix
*Adams—Sky p87-113,por.
Earhart—Fun p162-165,por.
Heinmuller—Man's p338,por.
*May—Women p88-90,111,178,211
Planck—Women p65-69
*Stoddard—Top p56-66
Women—Achieve. p42,por.

Nicholson, Eliza Jane Poitevent (Pearl
Rivers, pseud.) (1849-1896)
Amer. poet, journalist, editor
Logan—Part p872-873

Nicholson, Margaret (1904-   )
Amer. editor, author
Cur. Biog. '57 p403-405,por.

Nicholson, Martha Snell (1886-c. 1951)
Amer. singer, poet
Miller—Handi. p60

Nickerson, Camille L. (fl. 1930's)
Amer. pianist, educator
Cuney-Hare—Negro p260

Nicks, Diana (fl. 1960's)
Amer. glider pilot
May—Women p227

Nicolau y Parody, Teresa (fl. 1900's)
Sp. painter
Waters—Women p252

Nicolette (fl. 12th cent.)
Saracen slave, friend of Aucassin
Davenport—Great p78-82

Nicolson, Marjorie Hope (1894-   )
Amer. educator
Cur. Biog. '40 p615-616,por.

Niculescu, Medea P. (fl. 1930's)
Rum. physician
Lovejoy—Women p207-208

Ni Dhuibh, Máire (fl. 18th cent.)
Irish poet
Concannon—Dau. p240-241

Niederhausen, Sophie (fl. 1890's-1900's)
Swiss painter
Waters—Women p252-253

Niehaus, Regina Armstrong (b. 1869)
Amer. author
Logan—Part p819

Nielsen, Alice (1876-1943)
Amer. singer
Cur. Biog. '43 p554
Ewen—Ency. p344-345
Logan—Part p783
McCoy—Portraits p141,por.
Strang—Prima p1-20,por.

Nielsen, Kay (b. 1886)
Dan. illustrator, painter
Mahony—Illus. p342

Nielsen, Nielsine Mathilde (gr. 1885)
Dan. pioneer physician
Lovejoy—Women p180-181

Niemack, Ilza (fl. 1920's)
Amer. violinist, composer
McCoy—Portraits p141,por.

Niemann-Raabe, Hedwig.
See Raabe, Hedwig

Nienhuys, Janna (m. 1937)
Nether. nurse
*McKown—Heroic p239-265

Niesen, Gertrude (1910-   )
Amer. singer, radio personality
Donaldson—Radio p22

Niggli, Josephina (1910-   )
Mex.-Amer. author
Cur. Biog. '49 p455-456,por.
Warfel—Amer. p320,por.

Nightingale, Florence (1820-1910)
Eng. nurse, philanthropist, social
reformer
Abbott—Notable p289-293
*Adams—Heroines p120-146,por.
Adelman—Famous p156-158
Balch—Modern p479-529
*Bolton—Lives p251-262,por.
*Borer—Women p92-112,por.
Bowie—Women p71-89
Carey—Twelve p81-106,por.
Castiglioni—Hist. p1084
Dark—More p239-259
Deen—Great p214-217
De Morny—Best p88-100
*Dodge—Story p15-37
Dolan—Goodnow's p221-233,255,257,
260,324,por.
Dorland—Sum p48,83,125-126,130
Douglas—Remember p139
Dunaway—Turn. p55-68
Fitzhugh—Concise p502-504
Furniss—Some p132-134,por.
*Galloway—Roads p174-196,por.
Golding—Great p290-295
Hammerton p1040-1041,por.
*Horowitz—Treas. p142-147
Hume—Great p48-83,por.
*Jones—Modern p238-247,por.

(Continued)

Nightingale, Florence (cont.)

Keyes—Lives p78-95
*Kirkland—Good p48-54
Lotz—Women p77-85
McKown—Heroic p51-75,por.
*MacVeagh—Champlin p435-436,por.
Massingham—Great p319-330
Meine—Great p298-302,por.
Miller—Ten p28-35
*Montgomery—Story p97-101
Muir—Women p162-166
Murrow—This (2) p204-205
*Nida—Pilots p315-319
*Nisenson—Minute p118,por.
100 Great p191-198
Pennock—Makers p19,por.
Phila.—Women, unp.,por.
*Pringle—When p117-131,por.
Reader's—Great p551-556
Schmidt—400 p155-157,por.
Sewell—Brief p143-144
Sitwell—Women p39-41,por.
*Steedman—When p309-314
Stenton—English p338,343-344
Stevens—Human p63-70,por.
Stiles—Postal p188
*Stone—Heroes p21-24
*Strong—Heroes p116-122
*Strong—Of p173-179
Thomas—Living Women p147-159, por.
Thomas—Modern p210-218
*Unstead—People p460-470
*Wright—Great p179-200
Young—Women p18-19,102-103

Nijinska, Bronislava (1891-   )
Russ. ballet dancer, choreographer
Beaumont—Complete p656-666,por.
Davidson—Ballet p208-211

Nikolaidi, Elena (1910-   )
Turk. singer
Ewen—Ency. p345-346

Nikolayevna-Tereshkova, Valentina.
See Tereshkova, Valentina Vladimirovna

Niles, Blair Rice (c. 1887-1959)
Amer. explorer, author
Warfel—Amer. p320-321,por.

Nilsson, (Märta) Birgit (1918-   )
Swed. singer
Cur. Biog. '60 p296-298,por.
New Yorker Oct.29,1966 p66-92,por. (Profiles)
Phelps—Men (2) p210-211
Wagner—Prima p246

Nilsson, Christine (1843-1921)
Swed. singer, violinist
Adelman—Famous p263-264
Davidson—Treas. p209-211

Ewen—Ency. p346
Hammerton p1041
Howe—Memories p224-226,por.
Klein—Great p66-79,por.
Lahee—Famous p157-168,por.
McCoy—Portraits p142,por.
Marks—Glamour p168-181,por.
Schmidt—400 p373-374,por.

Ni Mháille, Gráinne.
See (Ni) Mháille,Gráinne

Nin, Anais (1903-   )
Fr.-Amer. author, printer
Cur. Biog. '44 p493-495,por.
Warfel—Amer. p321-322,por.

Nina (Christiana) (fl. 4th cent.)
Russ. saint
Englebert—Lives p475-476

Nisbet, Noel Laura (b. 1887)
Eng. illustrator
Mahony—Illus. p342-343

Nisbett, Louise Cranston (1812-1858)
Eng. actress
Dorland—Sum p53,166

Nissen, Greta (fl. 1920's-1930's)
Nor.-Amer. actress
Herman—How p109,por.

Niswonger, Ilse W. (1900-   )
Ger.-Amer. sculptor
National—Contemp. p238

Nithsdale, Winifred Herbert Maxwell, Countess of (d. 1749)
*Unstead—People p339-347,350

Nixon, Thelma Ryan ("Pat") (1913-   )
Amer. teacher, wife of Richard Nixon
Phelps—Men (2) '59 p211-212
Time Feb.29,1960 p24,por.(Cover)

Nizia Floresta (Dio Nizia Pinto Lisboa) (1810-1855)
Brazil. author
Stiles—Postal p188

Nkrumah, Fathia Halim Ritzk (c. 1931-   )
Egypt., wife of G. Nkrumah
Frederick—Ten p128-137,por.

Noadiah (Biblical)
Deen—All p287
Lewis—Portraits p177-178

Noah, wife of (Biblical)
Deen—All p323
Lewis—Portraits p15-18

Noah, Myrtle Whaley (fl. 1920's-1950's)
    Amer. missionary
    They—Went p75-76

Nobili, Elena (fl. 1890's-1900's)
    It. painter
    Waters—Women p253

Noble, Edna Chaffee (b. 1846)
    Amer. educator
    Logan—Part p728

Noble, Esther Frothingham (fl. 1910's)
    Amer. club leader
    Logan—Part p465-466

Noble, Mrs. Frank (fl.c. 1660's)
    Amer. pioneer
    Fowler—Woman p44-46

Noble, Harriet L. (fl. 1800's)
    Amer. W. pioneer
    Ellet—Pioneer p388-396
    Logan—Part p96

Noble, Jeanne Lavetta (1926-   )
    Amer. educator
    *Cherry—Portraits p36-40,por.
    Robinson—Hist. p233

Nobles, Catherine (fl. 1890's)
    Amer. club leader
    Logan—Part p411

Noddack, Ida Eva (Ida Eva Tacke) (1896-)
    Ger. chemist
    Chambers—Dict. col. 336
    Weeks—Discovery p851-853

Noé, Emma (fl. 1940's)
    Amer. singer
    McCoy—Portraits p142,por.

Nofret (fl. 1900 B.C.)
    Egypt. queen-consort
    Schmidt—400 p108-109,por.

Nofretete. See Nefertiti

No-Fru (fl. 13th cent.)
    Babyl. singer, dancer
    Schmidt—400 p128,por.

Nolan, Helen (fl. 1920's-1930's)
    Amer. journalist
    Ross—Ladies p189-190

Nolan, Mae Ella (fl. 1920's)
    Amer. Congresswoman
    Paxton—Women p130

Nolan, Mary. See Robertson, Mary Imogene

Nolde, Frances (fl. 1940's)
    Amer. aviatrix
    *May—Women p185

Noni, Alda (1920-   )
    It. singer
    Dickinson—Treas. p211-213

Nonia Celsa (fl. 210's)
    Rom. empress, wife of Macrinus
    Serviez—Roman (2) p211-225

Nonna (c. 329-374)
    Turk., mother of Gregory the
        Divine
    Deen—Great p14-16

Nora Elizabeth (n.d.)
    Liech. princess, dau. of Joseph II
    Stiles—Postal p189

Norbertine, Sister (fl. 1840's)
    Amer. W. pioneer
    Ross—Heroines p126-155

Nordenflycht, Hedwig Charlotte (1718-
        1763)
    Swed. poet
    Schmidt—400 p366-367,por.

Nordia, Lillian, pseud. (Lillian Norton)
        (1859-1914)
    Amer. singer
    Adelman—Famous p248-249
    Davidson—Treas. p213-216
    Ewen—Ency. p346-347
    Hammerton p1043
    Klein—Great p113-129,por.
    Lahee—Famous p220-230,por.
    Logan—Part p766
    McCoy—Portraits p142,por.
    Pleasants—Great p263-270,por.
    Ulrich—Famous p19-24,por.
    Wagnalls—Opera p324-331,por.
    Wagner—Prima p85-86,246

Noréna, Eidé (Kaja Hansen Eide)
        (b. 1884)
    Nor. singer
    Ewen—Ency. p347
    Ewing—Living p260-261,por.
    McCoy—Portraits p142,por.

Norfleet, Helen (fl. 1940's)
    Amer. pianist
    McCoy—Portraits p142,por.

Noria, Jana (Josephine Ludwig) (fl. 1910's)
    Amer. singer
    Lahee—Grand p111-112,310

Norman-Neruda, Wilma.
    See Hallé, Wilhelmina Franziska
    Neruda

Normand, Henrietta Rae (Henrietta Ray)
        (1859-1928)
    Eng. painter
    Hammerton p1125
    Waters—Women p253-254

Normand, Mabel (1898-1930)
    Amer. actress
Cahn—Laugh. p91,98,100,103-104,
    por.
Stuart—Immort. p216-217,por.

Normandie, Elizabeth K. de (fl. 1870's-
        1880's)
    Amer. artist
Hanaford—Dau. p310-312

Norrell, Catherine D. (fl. 1950's-1960's)
    Amer. Congresswoman
U.S.—Women (87th) p31,por.

Norris, Deborah (1761-1839)
    Amer. colonial pioneer
Brooks—Colonial p245-284

Norris, Kathi (n.d.)
    Amer. TV personality
TV—Person (3) p147-148,por.

Norris, Kathleen (1880-1966)
    Amer. author
Collins—Biog. p326-327
CR '59 p552,por.
CR '63 p463,por.
Hammerton p1044
Jensen—Revolt p101,por.
Maurice—Makers p8,por.
Overton—Women p227-242
Taves—Success. p85-88,por.
Time Jan.28,1935 p65,por.(Cover)
Warfel—Amer. p323-326,por.

Norris, Mary. See Allerton, Mary Norris

Norris, Mrs. (1661-1683)
    Eng. actress
MacQueen—Pope p42-43
Wilson—All p173-175

North, Marianne (1830-1890)
    Eng. naturalist, painter
Adelman—Famous p211
Dorland—Sum p31,150,154

North, Sheree (c. 1932-   )
    Amer. dancer, actress
CR '63 p464,por.

Northampton, Aelfgifu of (fl. 1030's)
    Eng., mistress of Canute
Stenton—English p4-5

Northey, Carrie. See Roma, Caro

Norton, Andre (Alice Mary) (n.d.)
    Amer. author, librarian
Cur. Biog. '57 p411-412,por.

Norton, Caroline Elizabeth Sarah Sheridan
        (1808-1877)
    Eng. poet, novelist

Adelman—Famous p165
Courtney—Adven. p72-90,por.
Dorland—Sum p56,74,138
Hammerton p1046,por.
Iremonger—And. p101-122,por.
Stebbins—Victorian p22-25,197,206-
    207
Stenton—English p333-335

Norton, Charity. See Randall, Charity

Norton, Clara (fl. 1920's-1960's)
    Amer. artist
Bryant—Amer. p269

Norton, Eunice (fl. 1930's-1940's)
    Amer. pianist
Ewing—Living p261,por.
McCoy—Portraits p142,por.

Norton, Frances Freke, Lady (1640-1731)
    Eng. author
Fifty—Famous p209

Norton, Grace Fallow (1876-1926)
    Amer. poet
Smith—Women's p156

Norton, Jemima (1854-1937)
    Eng. servant
Martindale—Some p98-105,por.

Norton, Katherine Byrd Rodgers (fl. 1930's)
    Amer. business executive
Women—Achieve. p118,por.

Norton, Mary Teresa Hopkins (1875-1959)
    Amer. Congresswoman
Cur. Biog. '44 p500-503,por.
Cur. Biog. '59 p328
Paxton—Women p29-37,130,por.
Roosevelt—Ladies p152-167

Norton, Mrs. (fl. 1660's-1670's)
    Eng. actress
Wilson—All p175-176

Norton, Mrs. (1827-c. 1877)
    Eng. novelist, poet
Oliphant—Women p275-290

Norton, Mrs. Shubael H.
    See Colt, Susan; Vincent, Ellen M.

Nossis (fl. 3rd cent., B.C.)
    Eng. poet
Anthologia—Poets p94-96

Nosworthy, Meta (fl. 1930's)
    Amer. cosmetician, business
        executive
Women—Achieve. p59,por.

Nourse, Elizabeth (c. 1860-1938)
Amer. painter
Bryant—Amer. p230-231
Jackman—Amer. p218-219
Logan—Amer. p756
Michigan—Biog. p231-232
Waters—Women p254

Novaes (Pinto) Guiomar (1895-   )
Brazil. pianist
Cur. Biog. '53 p460-462,por.
Ewen—Living p261-262,por.
McCoy—Portraits p143,por.
Schonbery—Great p383-385

Novak, Kim (1933-   )
Amer. actress
Time July 29,1957 p53,por.(Cover)
CR '59 p553,por.
CR '63 p465,por.
Cur. Biog. '57 p412-414,por.
Schickel—Stars p247,por.

Novak, Nina (fl. 1940's)
Pol. ballet dancer
Atkinson—Dancers p119-122,por.

Novikoff, Olga Kireev (O.K., pseud.)
(1840-1925)
Russ. author
Hammerton p1047

Novotna, Jarmila (1906/11-   )
Czech. singer
Cur. Biog. '40 p620-621,por.
Ewen—Living p262-263,por.
McCoy—Portraits p143,por.
Matz—Opera p22-27,por.
Peltz—Spot. p67,por.

Noyes, Blanche Wilcox (1900-   )
Amer. aviatrix
*Adams—Sky p137-153,por.
Dwiggins—They p75,80,82-84,86-93
*May—Women p95,97-98,111,178,por.
*Peckham—Women p129
Planck—Women p83-84,por.

Noyes, Clara Dutton (1870-1936)
Amer. nurse, author
Pennock—Makers p50-51,por.

Noyes, Dorothy (fl. 1930's)
Amer. business executive,
advertising writer
Women—Achieve. p140,por.

Noyes, Ida E. Smith (m. 1879)
Amer. club leader
Logan—Part p475

Noyes, Mary Fish. See Silliman, Mary Fish

Noyes family (Charlotte, Harriet (1)(2)
(fl. 1840's)
Amer. religious worker
Holbrook—Dreamers p5-6,9,10-11

Noyes-Greene, Edith Rowena (b. 1875)
Amer. composer, music teacher,
pianist
Hipsher—Amer. p202-203
McCoy—Portraits p143,por.

Nugent, Luci Baines Johnson (1947-   )
Amer. daughter of Lyndon B. Johnson
Smith—White p177-200,por.
Time Aug. 5,1966 p19,por.(Cover)

Nugent, Maria, Lady (1771-1834)
Brit. author
Bottrall—Pers. p119-120,228-229

Nugent, Maude. See Jerome, Maude Nugent

Nuhn, Ruth. See Suckow, Ruth

Nunez, Maria (fl. 1590's-1600's)
Port. religious worker
*Levinger—Great p110-113

Nur Jahan (Nur Mahal; Jahangir) (d. 1645)
Ind. empress
Pool—Famous p89-105

Nura, pseud. See Ulreich, Nura Woodson

Nurse, Rebecca (1621-1692)
Eng. accused witch
Green—Pioneer (1) p227,231

Nuthall, Betty (1912-   )
Eng. tennis player
Hammerton p1047
New Yorker Aug. 23, 1930 p20,por.
(Profiles)
Time July 6, 1931,p42por.(Cover)

Nuthead, Dinah (fl. 1680's-1690's)
Amer. pioneer printer
Brigham—Journals p74
Club—Printing p11
Dexter—Colonial p166-167,174,178
Leonard—Amer. p119
Spruill—Women's p263
Woody—Hist. (1) p261

Nutt, Anna Rutter Savage (1686-1760)
Amer. colonial manufacturer
Leonard—Amer. p119

Nuttall, Zelia (1858-1933)
Amer. archaeologist
Adelman—Famous p305-306
Dorland—Sum p143
Mozans—Woman p322-324

Nutting, Mary Adelaide (1858-1948)
Amer. nurse, educator
Dolan—Goodnow's p258-259,306-307,
por.
Pennock—Makers p38-39,por.
*Yost—Nursing p3-21

Nutting, Mary Olivia (1831-1910)
  Amer. historian, teacher, librarian
  Dorland—Sum p33,78,175-176

Nuyen, France (1939-   )
  Chin.-Fr. actress
  CR '59 p554,por.
  CR '63 p465,por.

Nymphia (fl. 3rd cent.)
  It. saint
  Englebert—Lives p427

Nyswander, Marie 1919-   )
  Amer. psychiatrist
  New Yorker June 26,1965 p32,por.;
    July 3,1965,por.(Profiles)

Nzinga (fl. c. 1630's)
  Afr. queen
  Hahn—Love p73-88

O

Oakes, Betty (n.d.)
  Amer. singer, actress
  TV—Person (3) p42-43,por.

Oakley, Annie (Phoebe Anne Oakley
      Mozee) (1860-1926)
  Amer. markswoman
  Davis—100 p87-88,por.
  Holbrook—Little p1-7
  Izant—Ohio p52-62
  Muir—Women p211-215
  Rogers—Women p54,por.

Oakley, Violet (1874-1961)
  Amer. illustrator, designer, mural
      painter
  Adelman—Famous p316
  Jackman—Amer. p239-245
  Logan—Part p755-756
  Michigan—Biog. p232-234
  Waters—Women p254-256

Oatman, Olive (fl. 1850's)
  Amer. Ind. captive
  Peckham—Capt. p195-214

Ober, Mrs. Frank Somes.
  See Robb, Josephine

Ober, Margarete (b. 1885)
  Ger. singer
  McCoy—Portraits p143,por.

Oberdorfer, Anne Faulkner (fl. 1940's)
  Amer. musician, lecturer, author
  McCoy—Portraits p143,por.

Oberholtzer, Sara Louisa Vickers (1841-
      1930)
  Amer. poet, novelist
  Logan—Part p828

Oberon, Merle (1911-   )
  Tas. actress
  CR '59 p554,por.
  CR '63 p466,por.
  Cur. Biog. '41 p621-623,por.

Obolensky, Alice Astor (m. 1924)
  Amer., wife of Prince Obolensky
  Pearson—Marry. p199-207,por.
  Pearson—Pilgrim p209-214,por.

Obretenova, Tonka Tihovitza ("Baba
      Tonka") (1812-1893)
  Bulg. patriot
  Schmidt—400 p61-62,por.

O'Brien, Joan (1936-   )
  Amer. singer
  TV—Person (1) p9,por.

O'Brien, Kate (1897-   )
  Irish author
  Lawrence—School p243-247

O'Brien, Margaret (1937-   )
  Amer. actress
  CR '59 p555,por.
  CR '63 p467,por.
  Schickel—Stars p220,por.
  Wagenknecht—Movies p244

O'Brien, Margaret (fl. 1910's)
  Amer. librarian
  Logan—Part p621

O'Brien, Nelly (fl. 1768)
  Eng. courtesan
  Bleakley—Ladies p97,144,186-187,por.

O'Brien, Paulyna J. (fl. 1930's)
  Amer. publicity director
  Women—Achieve. p158,por.

O'Byrne, Stella Armstrong (n.d.)
  Amer. organization official
  Cur. Biog. '48 p477-479,por.

O'Carroll, Margaret (fl. 15th cent.)
  Irish heroine
  Concannon—Dau. p68-70
  McCraith—Romance p61-65
  Schmidt—400 p241-242,por.

Occidente, Maria del, pseud.
  See Brooks, Maria

Occioni, Lucilla Marzolo (fl. 1900's)
  It. painter
  Waters—Women p256

O'Connell, Eibhlin Dubh (fl. 1760's-1770's)
  Irish poet
  Concannon—Dau. p235-239

O'Connell, Frederique Emile Auguste Miene
(1823-1885)
Ger. painter
Waters—Women p256-160

O'Connell, Helen (n.d.)
Amer. singer
TV—Person. (1) p85,por.

O'Connell, Mary (1775-1836)
Irish patriot
Blunt—Great p320-340

O'Connor, Flannery (1925-   )
Amer. author
Cur. Biog. '58 p317-318,por.

O'Connor, Mary (fl. 1930's-1940's)
Amer. airline hostess
*May—Women p231-232,por.

O'Conor, Finola (d. 1493)
Irish patriot, wife of Niall Garbh
Concannon—Dau. p73-74

O'Crowley, Irene Rutherford (fl. 1930's)
Amer. lawyer
Women—Achieve. p121,por.

Octavia (c. 69-c. 11 B.C.)
Rom. empress, sister of Augustus
Balsdon—Roman p66-74,80,103,199,
201,256,por.
Hammerton p1049
McCabe—Empr. p80,86,95-97,99,
108-111,por.
*MacVeagh—Champlin p440
Serviez—Roman (1) p226-252

Octavia (42-62 A.D.)
Rom., daughter of Claudius
Balsdon—Roman p63,117-118,123-
124,126-127,152,177

Oda, of Odette (d. 713)
Irish saint
Englebert—Lives p452

O'Daniels, A. M. (b. 1828)
Amer. clergyman
Hanaford—Dau. p463-474

O'Day, Anita (n.d.)
Amer. singer
CR '63 p468,por.

O'Day, Caroline Goodwin (1875-1943)
Amer. Congresswoman, artist
Cur. Biog. '43 p563
Jensen—Revolt p59,por.
Paxton—Women p8-10,130

O'Dea, Anne Caldwell (1867-1936)
Amer. author, librettist
ASCAP p374

Odencrantz, Louise Christine (fl. 1930's)
Amer. vocational guidance director
Women—Achieve. p201

Odetta (Odetta Holmes Felious Gordon)
Amer. singer, guitarist
CR '63 p468,por.
Cur. Biog. '60 p300-301,por.

Odilla (Ottilia) (fl. 8th cent.)
Alsacian saint
Arsenius—Dict. p174,por.
Englebert—Lives p473
Phila.—Women, unp.,por.
Stiles—Postal p238

Odle, Dorothy.
See Richardson, Dorothy M.

Odlum, Hortense (fl. 1930's-1940's)
Amer. merchant
*Logie—Careers (2nd) p49-59

Odlum, Jacquelin.
See Cochran, Jacqueline

O'Doherty, Rosa, Lady (b. 1590
Irish patriot
Concannon—Dau. p180,201-204

O'Donnell, Finola O'Brien, Lady (d. 1528)
Irish patriot
Concannon—Dau. p74-75

O'Donnell, Gladys (fl. 1920's-1930's)
Amer. aviatrix
*Adams—Sky p257-266,por.
*May—Women p99
Planck—Women p84-86,88-90,93

O'Donnell, Mary (alias Stuart) (fl. 1600's)
Irish patriot
Concannon—Dau. p196-201

O'Donnell, Mary Agnes (d. 1938)
Amer. nurse
Pennock—Makers p44-45,por.

O'Donnell, Mary King (1909-   )
Amer. novelist
Warfel—Amer. p327,por.

O'Donnell, Nellie (b. 1867)
Amer. educator
Logan—Part p727-728

O'Donnell, Nuala (fl. 1600's)
Irish patriot
Concannon—Dau. p179-180,184-195
McCraith—Romance p140-153

O'Driscoll, Hannah (1892-   )
Irish-Amer. nurse
*Wright—Great p132-139

Oehler, Bernice Olivia (fl. 1930's)
Amer. artist
Women—Achieve. p52,por.

Oelheim, Helen (fl. 1930's)
Amer. singer
McCoy—Portraits p144,por.

Oemler, Marie Conway (1879-1932)
Amer. author
Overton—Women p243-244

Oerner, Inga (fl. 1910's)
Nor. singer
Lahee—Grand p330

Oettinger, Katherine Brownell (1903-   )
Amer. government official
Cur. Biog. '57 p418-420,por.

Ogden, Hannah. See Caldwell, Hannah

Ogden, Mrs. Robert (fl. 1770's)
Amer. pioneer
Green—Pioneer (3) p147

Ogilvie, Elisabeth May (1917-   )
Amer. author
Cur. Biog. '51 p466-467,por.
Warfel—Amer. p328,por.

Ogilvie, Elizabeth (fl. 1930's)
Amer. cosmetician, business
executive
Women—Achieve. p31-32,por.

Ogilvie, Gladys (fl. 1930's)
Amer. cosmetician, business
executive
Women—Achieve p31-33,por.

Ogilvie, Jessica (fl. 1930's)
Amer. cosmetician, business
executive
Women—Achieve. p31-32,por.

Ogilvie, Mary Helen Macaulay (fl. 1950's)
Eng. educator
Brittain—Women p145,220-221

Ogilvy, Margaret.
See Barrie, Margaret Ogilvy

Ogino, G. (fl. 1882's)
Japan. physician
Lovejoy—Women p236

O'Grady, Dorothy Pamela ("Sweet Rosie
O'Grady") (fl. 1940's)
Eng. eccentric, spy
Hoehling—Women p143-145
Singer—World's p254-257

O'Hagan, Anne (fl. 1930's)
Amer. journalist
Fairfax—Ladies p23,41-43,57-58

O'Halloran, Mary (fl. 17th cent.)
Irish nun, scholar
Concannon—Dau. p158-159

O'Hara, Dolores B. (c. 1935-   )
Amer. pioneer space nurse
Dolan—Goodnow's p343,por.

O'Hara, Mary (Mary Sture-Vasa)
Amer. author, composer
Burnett—Amer. p552,por.
Cur. Biog. '44 p512-513,por.
Warfel—Amer. p329,por.

O'Hara, Maureen (1921-   )
Irish-Amer. actress
CR '59 p559,por.
CR '63 p470,por.
Cur. Biog. '53 p462-464,por.

Ohe, Adele Aus der (1865-1937)
Ger. pianist, composer
McCoy—Portraits p5,por.
Schonberg—Great p247-249,por.

Ohl, Maud Andrews (b. 1862)
Amer. journalist
Logan—Part p866

Ohlson, Agnes (fl. 1950's)
Amer. nurse, organization official
Dolan—Goodnow's p301,341,por.

Ohms, Elizabeth (1896-   )
Nether. singer
McCoy—Portraits p144,por.

Oholibamah. See Aholibamah

O.K., pseud. See Novikoff, Olga Kireev

Okama, Mrs. Kyoko (fl. 1930's)
Amer.-Japan. medical missionary
Lovejoy—Women p235-236

O'Keefe, Georgia (1887-   )
Amer. painter
✱Clymer—Modern p41-47,por.
CR '63 p470,por.
Cur. Biog. '41 p634-636,por.
Cur. Biog. '64 p327-329,por.
Ency. Brit.—Amer. p89,por.
Frank—Time p31-35,por.
Jensen—Revolt p101,por.
New York. p146-153
New Yorker July 6, 1929 p21,por.
(Profiles)

Okey, Maggie (fl. 1930's)
Eng. violinist, composer
Elson—Woman's p144,por.

Olcott, Rita (fl. 1930's)
Amer. playwright, social leader
Women—Achieve. p43,por.

Olcott, Virginia (gr. 1909)
Amer. social worker, teacher, author
Women—Achieve. p201

Olden, Margarete (fl. 1940's)
Ger. singer
McCoy—Portraits p144,por.

Oldenbourg, Zoë (1916-   )
Fr. novelist
Peyre—French p429-430,459-460

Oldfield, Anne ("Nance") (1683-1730)
Eng. actress
Adelman—Famous p71
Dorland—Sum p27,164-165
Eaton—Actor's p195-197
Hammerton p1050
MacQueen—Pope p145-158,por.
Melville—Stage p11-31,por.

Oldfield, Pearl P. (fl. 1920's-1930's)
Amer. Congresswoman
Paxton—Women p130

Oldmixon, Mrs. George (d. 1836)
Amer. singer, actress
Coad—Amer. p37,por.

Oldmixon, Lady John (fl. 1740's)
Eng. actress
Dexter—Career p81-82

Olds, Helen Diehl (fl. 1930's)
Amer. author
Women—Achieve. p173,por.

Olds, Jessie Gouds (fl. 1930's)
Amer. journalist
Ross—Ladies p472-473

O'Leary, Lydia (fl. 1930's)
Amer. cosmetologist
Women—Achieve. p109,por.

Oleson, Rebecca Lemmon (fl. 1860's)
Amer. Civil war nurse
Logan—Part p372

Olga (d. 969/978)
Russ. princess, saint
Dorland—Sum p98-99
Englebert—Lives p266-267
Schmidt—400 p343,por.
*Windham—Sixty p233-240

Olga, Konstantinova (1851-1926)
Gr. queen
Phila.—Women, unp.,por.
Stiles—Postal p193

Olheim, Helen Marion (fl. 1930's)
Amer. singer
Ewen—Living p263,por.
Peltz—Spot. p103,por.

Oliphant, Carolina.
See Nairne, Carolina Oliphant, Baroness

Oliphant, Margaret Oliphant Wilson (1828-1897)
Scot. author
Dorland—Sum p36,198
Furniss—Some p35-36,por.
Hammerton p1051
Johnson—Women p188-199
Stebbins—Victorian p155-191,197,214-215

Olitzka, Rosa (c. 1873-1949)
Ger. singer
McCoy—Portraits p144,por.

Oliver, Anna (d. 1893)
Amer. clergyman, feminist
Culver—Women p214-215
Shaw—Story p123-124

Oliver, Edna May (1883-1942)
Amer. actress, comedienne
Cur. Biog. '43 p566
Marks—Glamour p321

Oliver, Grace Atkinson (1844-1899)
Amer. author
Logan—Part p818

Oliver, Sophia Helen (b. 1811)
Amer. poet
Hanaford—Dau. p264

Olivia (fl. 9th cent.)
It. saint
Englebert—Lives p225

Olivia, Edith (c. 1879-1948)
Eng. author
Millett—Brit. p402-403

Olivier, Frances (fl. 1930's)
Amer. cosmetician, business executive
Women—Achieve. p88,por.

"Ollia." See Poppaea Sabina

Olmsted, Elizabeth Martha (b. 1825)
Amer. poet
Logan—Part p818-819

Olmsted, Sophia Amson (fl. 1930's)
Amer. lawyer
Women—Achieve. p132,por.

Olney, Dorothy McGrayne (fl. 1930's)
Amer. concert manager
Women—Achieve. p201

Olnhausen, Mary Phinney von (1818-1902)
Amer. Civil war nurse, author
Dannett—Nobel p92-95,229-231
Young—Women p193-196,375-376

Olsen, Leonora Emelie (fl. 1930's)
　　Amer. insurance executive
　　Women—Achieve. p166,por.

Olsen, Mae (n.d.)
　　Amer. airline hostess, nurse
　　°Peckham—Women

Olson, Edith (n.d.)
　　Amer. electronics, miniaturization
　　　　expert
　　°May—Women p244-245

Olszewska, Maria (1892-   )
　　Ger. singer
　　Ewen—Living p263-264,por.
　　McCoy—Portraits p145,por.

Olympia Maldachini (fl. 17th cent.)
　　It., niece of Pope Innocent X
　　Ewart—World's p175-176

Olympias (360-408/10)
　　Gr. saint
　　Blunt—Great p38-40
　　Culver—Women p79
　　Deen—Great p314-315
　　Englebert—Lives p478
　　°McKown—Heroic p14

Olympias of Macedonia (d. 316 B.C.)
　　Gr., wife of Philip of Macedon
　　Boccaccio—Conc. p133-134

O'Mahoney, Katherine A. (fl. 1910's)
　　Irish-Amer. publisher, editor, club
　　　　leader, lecturer
　　Logan—Part p838

O'Malley, Grace (Ni Mháille, Grainne)
　　　　(fl. 1580's)
　　Irish heroine
　　McCraith—Romance p127-139

O'Malley, Patricia (fl. 1930's)
　　Amer. aviation author
　　Planck—Women p231,234-237,por.

O'Malley, Sallie Margaret (b. 1862)
　　Amer. poet, author
　　Logan—Part p838-839

Oman, Carola Mary Anima (1897-   )
　　Brit. author
　　Millett—Brit. p403-404

Omlie, Phoebe Fairgrave (1902-   )
　　Amer. pioneer aviatrix, aviation
　　　　instructor
　　°Adams—Sky p69-84,por.
　　Earhart—Fun p175-177
　　Knapp—New p157-168,por.
　　°May—Women p54-55,86-88,por.
　　°Peckham—Women p136-137,por.
　　Planck—Women p52-64,85

Onassis, Jacqueline.
　　See Kennedy, Jacqueline Lee Bouvier

O'Neal, Margaret ("Peggy") (m.1816)
　　Amer., friend of Sam Houston,
　　　　wife of Major Eaton
　　Parton—Dau. p423-429
　　Parton—Noted p546-552
　　Turner—Sam p8-11,por.

Onégin, Sigrid Hoffmann (1891-1943)
　　Swed. singer
　　Ewen—Ency. p354
　　Ewen—Living p264,por.
　　McCoy—Portraits p145,por.

O'Neil, Nance (b. 1874)
　　Amer. actress
　　Blum—Great p36,por.
　　Caffin—Vaud. p126-127,por.

O'Neill, Catherine, Countess (fl. 1600's)
　　Irish patriot
　　Concannon—Dau. p179-182

O'Neill, Eliza, Lady Becher (1791-1872)
　　Irish actress
　　Adelman—Famous p110-111
　　Dorland—Sum p35,165
　　MacQueen—Pope p298-301,por.
　　Wyndham—Chorus p14-16

O'Neill, Rose Cecil (fl. 1890's-1910's)
　　Amer. artist, illustrator
　　New Yorker Nov.24,1934 p22,por.
　　(Profiles)

O'Niel, Constance, Mary, Lady Annesley
　　　　(1895-   )
　　Irish actress
　　Wyndham—Chorus p125-127

Onions, Mrs. Oliver. See Ruck, Berta

Onis, Harriet Vivian Wishnieff de (1899-
　　　　1969)
　　Amer. translator, editor
　　Cur. Biog. '57 p420-421,por.

Oosterwisck, Maria (1630-1693)
　　Nether. painter
　　Waters—Women p260-261

Opie, Amelia Alderson (1769-1853)
　　Eng. novelist
　　Dorland—Sum p42,80
　　MacCarthy—Later p211-215
　　Stebbins—London p59-89

Opportuna (d. 770)
　　Fr. abbess, saint
　　Englebert—Lives p155

Orbiana, Barbia (fl. 200's-250's A.D.)
　　Rom. empress, wife of Hostilianus
　　Serviez—Roman (2) p312

Orcutt, Ruby R. M. (fl. 1930's)
    Amer. chemist
    Women—Achieve. p201

Orczy, Emmuska, Baroness (1865-1947)
    Eng. novelist, playwright
    Hammerton p1053

O'Reilly, Gertrude (fl. 1900's-1910's)
    Amer. artist
    Logan—Part p750-751

O'Reilly, Mary Boyle (b. 1873)
    Amer. humanitarian,
        philanthropist, police
        commissioner, author
    Logan—Part p839

Orelli, Susanna (1845-1939)
    Swiss feminist
    Phila.—Women, unp.,por.
    Stiles—Postal p194

Orestilia, Fabia (fl. 150's-230's)
    Rom. empress, wife of Gordianus,
        the Elder
    Serviez—Roman (2) p288

Orger, Mary Ann (1788-1849)
    Eng. actress
    MacQueen—Pope p301-303,por.

"Orinda." See Philips, Katherine Fowler

Oringa (Christina) (fl. 14th cent.)
    It. saint
    Wescott—Calen. p5

Orkney, Countess of.
    See Gilchrist, Constance

Orléans, Henriette-Anne, Duchess d' (1644-
        1670)
    Fr., daughter of Charles I
    Haggard—Remark. p92-100,106-111,
        113-119
    Hall—Moths p129-157,por.
    MacNalty—Princes p92-109
    Mayne—Enchant. p139-153,por.

Orleans, Maid of. See Joan of Arc

Orléans, Marie Therese Caroline Isabelle
        Louise d'
    Fr., daughter of Louis Philippe
    Haggard—Remark. p206-207

Ormerod, Eleanor Anne (1828-1901)
    Eng. entomologist
    Adelman—Famous p210-211
    Balch—Modern p531-541
    Dorland—Sum p57,77,149
    Hammerton p1055,por.
    Mozans—Woman p246-253

Ormsby, Mary Frost (b. 1852)
    Amer. author
    Logan—Part p819

Orpah (Biblical)
    Buchanan—Women p44-46
    Deen—All p287-288
    Mead—250 p74

Orr, Flora (fl. 1920's)
    Amer. journalist
    Ross—Ladies p358-359

Orr, Marion (fl. 1940's-1960's)
    Can. pioneer aviatrix
    *May—Women p206-207

Orrery, Countess of.
    See Monckton, Mary

Orrick, Mary Semmes (   )
    Amer. religious worker
    Logan—Part p622

Orsini, (Maria) Felice (1819-1858)
    It. revolutionist
    Blei—Fasc. p27-28,por.

Orth, Jane Davis (fl. 1920's-1930's)
    Amer. lecturer, traveler
    Women—Achieve. p94,por.

Orth, Lizette E. (d. 1913)
    Amer. composer, pianist
    McCoy—Portraits p145,por.

Ortiz de Dominguez, Josefa (1773-1829)
    Mex. heroine, patriot
    Arsenius—Dict. p145,por.
    Phila.—Women, unp.,por.
    Schmidt—400 p289-290,por.
    Stiles—Postal p194

Orton, Helen Fuller (1872-1955)
    Amer. author
    Cur. Biog. '41 p639-640
    Cur. Biog. '55 p468

Orvis, Mrs. (fl. 1870's-1880's)
    Amer. artist
    Hanaford—Dau. p295

Orzeszkowa (Orseszkowa), Eliza (1842-
        1910)
    Pol. author
    Nobel—Man p98,106
    Schmidt—400 p328,por.

Osanna, Andreasi (fl. 15th cent.)
    It. saint
    Wescott—Calen. p89

Osato, Sono (1919-   )
    Amer. dancer, actress
    Cur. Biog. '45 p440-442,por.

Osborn, Desire Allen (fl. 1850's-1860's)
Amer. whaling voyager
Whiting—Whaling p76-81,por.

Osborn, Lucy. See Hobart, Lucy M. P.

Osborn, Margaret (fl. 1670's-1690's)
Eng. actress
Wilson—All p176-177

Osborn, Sarah (b.c. 1714)
Amer. religious worker
Benson—Women p260-262

Osborn, Mrs. William Church (fl. 1870's)
Amer. nurse
Pennock—Makers p74-75,por.

Osborn-Hannah, Jane (1873-1943)
Amer. singer
Lahee—Grand p427-428

Osborne, Dorothy.
See Temple, Dorothy Osborne, Lady

Osborne, Ethel Florence Eliot (fl. 19th cent.)
Eng. accused criminal
Furniss—Some p217-218,por.

Osborne, Letitia Osborne Preston (1894-)
Amer. author
Warfel—Amer. p330,por.

Osborne, Susan M. (1858-1918)
Amer. philanthropist
Adelman—Famous p255

Osburn, Lucy (1837-1891)
Eng. pioneer nurse
Cope—Six p10-24,por.

Osburn, Mary (b. 1845)
Amer. social reformer
Logan—Part p670

Osenga, Giuseppina (fl. 1900's)
It. painter
Waters—Women p261-262

Osgood, Frances Sargent (1812-1849)
Amer. poet
Hanaford—Dau. p267

Osgood, Marion (fl. 1940's)
Amer. composer, violinist,
conductor
McCoy—Portraits p146,por.

O'Shea, G. Leona (fl. 1940's)
Amer. aviatrix
*Peckham—Women p35

Osipenko (Ossipenko), Pauline Denisovna
(1907-1939)
Russ. aviatrix
*May—Women p211
Phila.—Women unp.,por.
Stiles—Postal p194

Osser, Edna (1919-   )
Amer. composer, author
ASCAP p379

Ossoli, Marchioness D.'
See Fuller, (Sarah) Margaret

Ostenso, Martha (1900-1963)
Nor.-Amer. novelist
Overton—Women p245-252
*Richmond—Immig. p102-103
Thomas—Canad. p95
Warfel—Amer. p330-331

Ostertag, Blanche (fl. 1890's-1900's)
Amer. artist
Waters—Women p262

Osterzee, Cornelia van (b. 1863)
Batav. composer
McCoy—Portraits p146,por.

Ostman, Lempi (1899-   )
Amer. illustrator
Mahony—Illus. p343

O'Sullivan, Johanna MacSwiney (fl.c. 1585)
Irish patriot
Concannon—Dau. p173-175

O'Sullivan, Maureen (1911-   )
Irish-Amer. actress
CR '59 p565,por.
CR '63 p472,por.

Oswald, Elizabeth Holt (fl. 1790's)
Amer. printer
Dexter—Career p105,107

Oswald, Marina (1942-   )
Russ. wife of Lee Harvey Oswald
Time Feb.14,1964 p16,por.(Cover)

O'Tama-Chiovara (fl. 1900's)
Japan. sculptor, painter
Waters—Women p262-263

Otèro, Caroline (b. 1868)
Sp. courtesan
Skinner—Elegant p226-227,231,236-
244

Otero, Emma (fl. 1940's)
Cub. singer
McCoy—Portraits p146,por.

Otis, Amy (fl. 1930's)
Amer. painter
Michigan—Biog. p236

Otis, Eliza Henderson (1796-1873)
Amer. social leader
Amory—Proper p122-124,250,262,
268-269
Hanaford—Dau. p145-146
Irwin—Angels p112-113,152
Logan—Part p284

Otis, Emily Marshall (1807-1836)
Amer. social leader, beauty
Amory—Proper p120-122
Brooks—Young p269-287

Otis, Mercy. See Warren, Mercy Otis

Otis, Rebecca (fl. 1860's)
Amer. Civil war nurse
Logan—Part p372

O'Toole, Rosa (fl. 1580's)
Irish patriot
O'Cannon—Dau. p250-256

Ott, Elsie S. (n.d.)
Amer. nurse
Peckham—Women p21

Ott, Frances M. (fl. 1890's)
Amer. nurse
Pennock—Makers p79,por.

Ottaway, Ruth Haller (fl. 1940's)
Amer. pianist
McCoy—Portraits p146,por.

Otterson, Mrs. (fl. 1770's)
Amer. Rev. war heroine
Ellet—Women (1) p297-298

Ottilia. See Odilla

Ottman, Josephine Whitney (fl. 1930's)
Amer. club leader
Women—Achieve. p61,por.

Ouida, pseud. (Marie Louise de la Ramee)
(1839-1908)
Eng. novelist
Abbott—Notable p407-410
Adelman—Famous p215
Dorland—Sum p22,196
Furniss—Some p14-17,por.
Hammerton p1058,por.
*MacVeagh—Champlin p444

Ouseley, Lady William Gore (m. 1829)
Amer. social leader
Logan—Part p256

Ouspenskaya, Maria (fl. 1930's)
Russ.-Amer. dramatic teacher
Women—Achieve. p182,por.

Ouvaroff, (Uvarov) Countess P. S.
(b. 1870)
Russ. archaeologist
Schmidt—400 p347,por.

Ovando, Leonor de (d. 1613)
Dom. R. poet
Schmidt—400 p101,por.

Ovens, Florence Jane (fl. 1930's)
Eng.-Amer. child specialist, editor
Women—Achieve, p93,por.

Overstreet, Bonaro Wilkinson (fl. 1930's)
Amer. teacher, author
Women—Achieve. p158,por.

Owen, Bessie (fl. 1930's)
Amer. aviatrix
*May—Women p136

Owen, Mrs. James (fl. 1790's)
Amer. W. pioneer
Ellet—Pioneer p180

Owen, Jane Grafton Luce (fl. 1840's-1870's)
Amer. whaling voyager
Whiting—Whaling p215,284

Owen, Julia D. (fl. 1940's)
Amer. composer, singer, music
teacher
McCoy—Portraits p146,por.

Owen, Mary Alicia (b. 1858)
Amer. ethnologist
Dorland—Sum p143
Logan—Part p868

Owen, Ruth Brian (1885-1954)
Amer. diplomat, lecturer, author
Cur. Biog. '44 p522-525,por.
Cur. Biog. '54 p539
*Heath—Women (4) p32
Mears—They p15-18
Paxton—Women p4-6,130
Rogers—Women p66,por.
Roosevelt—Ladies p205-206
Women—Achieve. p39,por.

Owens, Marlene (n.d.)
Amer. beauty
*Cherry—Portraits p199

Owens, Mary (b.c. 1808)
Amer., friend of Abraham Lincoln
Barton—Women p187-209

Owens, Vilda Sauvage (fl. 1900's-1920's)
Welsh-Amer. poet
Smith—Women's p158

Owens-Adair, Bethenia.
See Adair, Bethenia Angelina Owens

Oxford and Asquith, Margot Tennant,
Countess of (1864-1945)
Brit. author
Asquith—Myself p9-39,por.
Cur. Biog. '45 p442
Gardiner—Por. p64-71
Hammerton p1061

Ozbirn, Catherine Freeman (c. 1900-   )
Amer. organization official
Cur. Biog. '62 p333-334,por.

P

Paas, Madeleine van de.
See Passe, madeleine van de

Paasikivi, Alli (fl. 1940's)
Fin., wife of Juho Kusti Paasikivi
Phila.—Women unp.,por.

Paca, Anne (d.c. 1780)
Amer. patriot
Green—Pioneer (3) p220

Paca, Mary Chew (m. 1763)
Amer. patriot
Green—Pioneer (3) p219-220

Pachler-Koschak, Marie Leopoldine (1792-
1855)
Aust. pianist
McCoy—Portraits p146,por.

Packard, Eleanor (1905-   )
Amer. journalist
Cur. Biog. '41 p647-648,por.

Packard, Ruth Mary (fl. 1930's)
Amer. fashion editor
Women—Achieve. p153,por.

Paczka-Wagner, Cornelis (b. 1864)
Ger. painter
Waters—Women p263-264

Paddleford, Clementine Haskin (1900-
1967)
Amer. journalist, food editor
CR '63 p474,por.
Cur. Biog. '58 p324-326,por.
Cur. Biog. '68 p460

Paddock, Josephine (fl. 1930's)
Amer. artist
Women—Achieve. p108,por.

Padmini of Chitore (fl. 14th cent.)
E. Ind. patriot, wife of Bhimsi
Pool—Famous p127-134
Schmidt—400 p233-235,por.

Paeff, Bashka (1893-   )
Russ.-Amer. sculptor
Michigan—Biog. p236-237
National—Contemp. p246

Pagan, Isobel ("Mother") (1741-1821)
Scot. poet
Graham—Group p215-230

Pagava, Ethery (1932-   )
Fr. ballet dancer
Davidson—Ballet p221-223

Page, Celeste Walker (fl. 1930's)
Amer. aviation writer
Planck—Women p239-240

Page, Elizabeth (b. 1889)
Amer. novelist
Warfel—Amer. p333,por.

Page, Elizabeth Whittredge (d. 1845)
Amer. teacher, religious worker
Hanaford—Dau. p635-636

Page, Fannie Pender (1870-1942)
Amer. missionary, teacher
Phillips—33 p108-113

Page, Geraldine (1924-   )
Amer. actress
CR '59 p568-569,por.
CR '63 p574,por.
Cur. Biog. '53 p468-470,por.
Ross—Player p424-428,por.

Page, Julia (fl. 1800's)
Amer. pioneer
Fowler—Woman p322-326

Page, Lucy Gaston (fl. 1910's)
Amer. social reformer, club leader
Logan—Part p412

Page, Marie Danforth (1870-1940)
Amer. artist
Cur. Biog. '40 p626
Jackman—Amer. p252-253

Page, Patti (1927-   )
Amer. singer, actress, TV
personality
CR '59 p569,por.
CR '63 p474,por.
Cur. Biog. '65 p309-311,por.
Popular Record, p100,por.
Stambler—Ency. p179-180
TV—Person. (3) p121-123,por.

Page, Ruth (c. 1903)
Amer. ballet dancer,
choreographer
Beaumont—Complete p776-779
Cur. Biog. '62 p334-336,por.

Page, Sarah Carlton (m. 1741)
Amer. patriot
Green—Pioneer (2) p131-132

Paget, Lady Arthur (1865-1919)
Eng.-Amer. social leader,
philanthropist, nurse
Adelman—Famous p259-260

Paget, Debra (1933-   )
Amer. actress
CR '59 p569,por.
CR '63 p475,por.
*Reed—Follow p51-57,por.

Paget, Della Mae Dale (fl. 1940's-1950's)
Amer. missionary
They—Went p125-126

Paget, Mary Fiske (Minnie) Stevens, Lady
  (1853-1919)
  Amer. heiress
  Eliot—Heiresses p86-95
  Pearson—Marry. p187-190

Paget, Violet. See Lee, Vernon, pseud.

Paige, Janis (1923-   )
  Amer. dancer, actress, comedienne
  CR '63 p475,por.
  Cur. Biog. '59 p341-342,por.
  TV—Person. (2) p14-15,por.

Paige, Mrs. Richard E. (fl. 1930's-1950's)
  Amer. business woman
  Fortune—100 p161-162

Pai Ku-Niang Pai (fl. 1930's)
  Chin. warrior
  Ayscough—Chinese p226

Paine, Eliza Baker (m. 1795)
  Amer. pioneer
  Green—Pioneer (3) p81-82

Paine, Harriet Eliza (Eliza Chester, pseud.)
  (1845-1910)
  Amer. author
  Logan—Part p850

Paine, Sarah (Sally) Cobb (m. 1770)
  Amer. patriot
  Green—Pioneer (3) p80-83,469

Painter, Hettie K. (fl. 1860's)
  Amer. Civil war patriot
  Young—Women p329-330

Paisley, Mary Neale (fl. 1750's)
  Amer. colonial evangelist
  Dexter—Colonial p147

Pak, Esther Kim (gr. 1900)
  Kor. pioneer physician
  Lovejoy—Women p240

Pakenham, Antonia (gr. 1950)
  Eng. author
  Brittain—Women p223-224

Pakington, Dorothy Coventry, Lady
  (d. 1679)
  Eng. author, scholar
  Fifty—Famous p310

Paldi, Mari (fl. 1940's)
  Amer. composer, music teacher
  McCoy—Portraits p147,por.

Palencia, Isabel de (b. 1881)
  Sp. auth., lecturer
  Cur. Biog. '41 p649-650,por.

Paley, Barbara Cushing (c. 1917-   )
  Amer. hostess, philanthropist,
    social leader
  CR '59 p570,por.
  CR '63 p476,por.

Palfrey sisters (fl. 1860's-1910's)
  Amer. hostesses
  Amory—Proper p138-141

Palladino, Eusapia (1854-1918)
  It. spiritualist
  Dingwall—Very p178-217,por.

Palmer, Mrs. A. M. (fl. 1910's)
  Amer. social reformer, sociologist
  Logan—Part p594

Palmer, Alice Freeman (1855-1902)
  Amer. educator
  Adelman—Famous p233
  Dorland—Sum p51,109-110
  *Fleming—Great p57-70
  Hammerton p1064
  *Heath—Woman p6
  *Kirkland—Good p32-40
  Lotz—Women p86-95
  Melikov—Immort. p102,179,por.
  *Moore—When p133-139
  Morello—Hall p50,por.
  *Palmer—Heroines p31-58,por.
  Schmidt—400 p23-24,por.
  *Vance—Lamp p225-254,por.

Palmer, Anna Campbell (1854-1928)
  Amer. poet
  Logan—Part p828

Palmer, Bernice (fl. 1940's)
  Amer. aircraft inventor
  *Peckham—Women p57

Palmer, Bertha Honoré (1851-1918)
  Amer. art collector, social leader
  Farmer—What p473,por.
  Irwin—Angels p214,234
  Logan—Part p291
  Schmidt—400 p20,por.

Palmer, Betsy (1926-   )
  Amer. actress, TV personality
  CR '63 p477,por.
  TV—Person. (3) p37,por.

Palmer, Caroline L. (fl. 1930's)
  Amer. editor
  Women—Achieve. p189,por.

Palmer, Fannie Purdy (1839-1923)
  Amer. author
  Logan—Part p829

Palmer, Gretta Brooker (1905-1953)
  Amer. journalist
  O'Brien—Road p29-56
  Ross—Ladies p433-434

Palmer, Hannah L. (fl. 1860's)
Amer. Civil war nurse
Logan—Part p363

Palmer, Hazel (1903-   )
Amer. lawyer
Cur. Biog. '58 p326-327,por.

Palmer, Lilli (1914-   )
Ger. actress
CR '59 p571,por.
Cur. Biog. '51 p471-474

Palmer, Lynde.
See Peebles, Mary Louise

Palmer, Mary E. (d. 1865)
Amer. Civil war humanitarian
Brockett—Woman's p640-642

Palmer, Miriam A. (fl. 1910's)
Amer. entomologist
Osborn—Fragments p86,262,300

Palmer, Phebe (1807-1874)
Amer. evangelist
Hanaford—Dau. p618

Palmer, Sophia F. (d. 1920)
Amer. nurse, editor
Dolan—Goodnow's p302-303,por.
Pennock—Makers p112-113,por.

Palmer, Susan (fl. 1910's-1940's)
Amer. restaurant owner
Taves—Success. p293-299
Women—Achieve. p179,por.

Palmerston, Emily Mary Lamb, Lady
(1787-1869)
Eng. hostess, wife of Lord
Palmerston
Guedalla—Bonnet p155-179,por.
Iremonger—And p220-224,por.
Lee—Wives p99-130,por.

Palms, Marie Martin (fl. 1910's)
Amer. religious worker
Logan—Part p622

Pamphile (fl. 20's A.D.)
Gr., daughter of Plates
Boccaccio—Conc. p95

Panayotatou, Alexandra (gr. 1896)
Gr. physician
Lovejoy—Women p212

Panayotatou, Angelique (gr. 1896)
Gr. physician
Lovejoy—Women p212

Pan Chao (Ts'ao Taku) (c. 50-112 A.D.)
Chin. educator, moralist, scholar
Ayscough—Chinese p228-263

Pan Chieh-Yü (fl. 30's, A.D.)
Chin. educator
Ayscough—Chinese p229-232,296

Pandit, Vijaya Lakshmi (1900-   )
Ind. politician, minister, co-worker
of Gandi
CR '59 p571-572,por.
Cur. Biog. '46 p451-453,por.
Stern—Women p280-289,por.

Pankhurst, Christabel (1880-1958)
Eng. feminist
Hammerton p1065-1066

Pankhurst, Emmeline Goulden (1858-1928)
Eng. feminist, social reformer
Adelman—Famous p289-290
*Borer—Women p151-171,por.
Canning—100 p240-248,por.
DeMorny—Best p163-170
Fellowes—Heroes p13-23,por.
Hammerton p1065,por.
Jensen—Revolt p53,por.
Lovejoy—Women p132-133,293-294
*MacVeagh—Champlin p447-448

Pankhurst, Sylvia (1882-1960)
Eng. feminist, social reformer
Asquith—Myself p259-312,por.
Hammerton p1066

Pannell, Anne Gary (1910-   )
Amer. educator
Cur. Biog. '50 p439-441,por.

"Pansy." See Alden, Isabella MacDonald

Pantaleoni, Helenka (Tradeuse Adamowski)
(1900-   )
Amer. organization official
Cur. Biog. '56 p479-481,por.

Paola, Donna Paola Margherita Maria
(1937-   )
Belg. princess
Stiles—Postal p198

Paoli, Betty, pseud.
See Gluck, Barbara Elisabeth

Paolozzi, Christina (1939-   )
Amer. model
CR '63 p477-478,por.

Pao Ssu (fl. 490's-480's B.C.)
Chin., concubine of Emperor Yu
the Gloomy
Llewellyn—China's p16-17

Papashvily, Helen Waite (1906-   )
Russ.-Amer. author
Ames—These p247-258
Cur. Biog. '45 p442-445,por.

Papegoija, Armegot (d. 1695)
Amer. pioneer landowner
Leonard—Amer. p119

Paper, Ernestine (gr. 1877)
It. physician
Lovejoy—Women p203

Papin, Theophile Emily Carlin (m. 1865)
Amer. religious worker
Logan—Part p622

Papira (fl. 220's-140's B.C.)
Rom., wife of L. Aemilius Pauulus
Balsdon—Roman p43,210-211

Papp-Vary, Sernea Sziklay (1881-1923)
Hung. poet, patriot
Schmidt—400 p232,por.

Pappenheim, Bertha (1859-1936)
Ger. humanitarian
Stiles—Postal p198

Parades y Flores, Mariana de Jesus (1618-1645)
Ecuad. saint, heroine
Englebert—Lives p203
Phila.—Women unp.,por.

Paradis (Paradies), Maria Theresia von (1759-1824)
Aust. blind singer, pianist, composer
Elson—Woman's p156-158

Paradis, Marjorie B. (fl. 1930's)
Women—Achieve. p87,por.

Pardo, Julia (1806-1862)
Eng. author
Dorland—Sum p33,72,113-114,174, 176

Pardo-Bazan, Emilia (1852-1921)
Sp. novelist, critic
Hammerton p1066-1067
Schmidt—400 p360-361,por.

Parepa-Rosa, Euphrosyne (1836-1874)
Scot. singer
Adelman—Famous p189
Lahee—Famous p111-113
McCoy—Portraits p148,por.
Marks—Glamour p153-167,por.

Park, Lucia Darling (fl. 1860's)
Amer. W. pioneer, teacher, vigilante
Towle—Vigil. p73-87,por.

Park, Maud Wood (1871-1955)
Amer. feminist
Irwin—Angels p261,374,377-379,412-414

Park, Rosemary (1907-   )
Amer. educator
CR '63 p478,por.
Cur. Biog. '64 p337-339,por.
*Seventeen—In p161-166,por.

Park, Ruth (c. 1920)
New Z. author, journalist
Hetherington—42 p201-206,por.

Parke, Lucy. See Byrd, Lucy Parke

Parke, Maria Hester (1755-1822)
Eng. singer, pianist
Elson—Woman's p132-133

Parker, Alice (b.1864)
Amer. lawyer, feminist
Logan—Part p745

Parker, Cornelia Stratton (b. 1885)
Amer. author
Hyde—Modern p23-40

Parker, Cynthia Ann (1827-1864)
Amer. Ind. captive, pioneer
*Johnson—Some p1-5,por.

Parker, Dorothy Rothschild (1893-1967)
Amer. author, humorist
Burnett—Amer. p552,por.
Burnett—This p1151-1152
CR '59 p572,por.
CR '63 p478-479,por.
Jensen—Revolt p171,por.
Lawrence—School p173-176
Loggins—Hear p299-303
*Millett—Amer. p162-163,521-522
O'Brien—50 p859
Rogers—Women p109,por.
*Witham—Pan. p310-311,por.

Parker, Eleanor R. (b. 1874)
Amer. home economist, editor, author
Logan—Part p839

Parker, Gladys (fl. 1930's)
Amer. fashion designer, cartoonist
Women—Achieve. p120,por.

Parker, Helen Almina (gr. 1885)
Amer. teacher
Logan—Part p727

Parker, Karla Van Ostrand (1894-   )
Amer. organization official
Cur. Biog. '47 p492-494,por.

Parker, Lottie Blair (d. 1937)
Amer. playwright, author
Logan—Part p790

Parker, Marjorie (n.d.)
Amer. educator, author
*Cherry—Portraits p45-48,por.

Parker, Ruth (fl. 1770's)
  Amer. Rev. war patriot, pioneer
  Green—Pioneer (2) p327

Parker, Suzy (1933-   )
  Amer. model
  CR '59 p572-573,por.
  CR '63 p479,por.

Parker, Valeria H. (1879-1959)
  Amer. physician, social hygiene
    worker
  Women—Achieve. p88,por.

Parkhurst, Helen Huss (b. 1887)
  Amer. educator
  Women—Achieve. p119,por.

Park-Lewis, Dorothea (fl. 1930's)
  Amer. cellist
  Women—Achieve. p121,por.

Parkman, Eliza W. S. (d. 1905)
  Amer., sister of Frances Parkman
  Pomeroy—Little p275-295

Parks, Elizabeth Richmond.
  See Robins, Elizabeth

Parlaghy, Vilma, Princess Lwoff (b. 1863)
  Ger. painter
  Waters—Women p264-265

Parlby, Irene (1878-1965)
  Can. politician
  Innis—Clear p171-172

Parlin, Lucy (fl. 1890's-1910's)
  Amer. patriot
  Logan—Part p438

Parloa, Maria (1843-1909)
  Amer. home economist, author
  Adelman—Famous p239

Parlow, Kathleen Mary (1890-1963)
  Can. violinist
  Adelman—Famous p324
  McCoy—Portraits p148,por.

Parma, Margerita, Duchess of (1522-1586)
  It., Nether. regent
  Schmidt—400 p251-252,por.

Parmelee, Ruth A. (fl. 1920's)
  Amer. physician, missionary
  Lovejoy—Women p341-343,347-351,
    por.
  Lovejoy—Women Phys. p143-145,
    173-184

Parmenter, Christine Whiting (1877-1953)
  Amer. author
  Binheim—Women p110,por.
  Warfel—Amer. p333-334,por.

Parnell, Eileen (1902-   )
  Irish-Amer. sculptor
  National—Contemp. p247

Parnell, Evelyn (fl. 1910's)
  Amer. singer
  Lahee—Grand p369

Parnis, Mollie (1909-   )
  Amer. fashion designer, business
    woman
  CR '63 p480,por.
  Cur. Biog. '56 p483-485,por.

Parr, Catherine (1512-1548)
  Eng. queen
  Dorland—Sum p34
  Fifty—Famous p199-203
  Hammerton p1068-1069,por.
  Sanders—Intimate p29-35,por.

Parrish, Anne (1760-1800)
  Amer. colonial philanthropist,
    educator
  Leonard—Amer. p53,119
  Woody—Hist. p202-207,por.

Parrish, Anne (1888-1957)
  Amer. illustrator, author
  Mahony—Illus. p343-344
  Overton—Women p253-356
  Warfel—Amer. p334-335,por.

Parrish, Frances G.
  See Knight, Frances Gladys

Parrish, Lydia G. (fl. 1860's)
  Amer. Civil war humanitarian
  Brockett—Woman's p362-373
  Dannett—Noble p326-328

Parrish, Mary Frances K.
  See Fisher, Mary Frances Kennedy

Parrish, Rebecca (1869-1952)
  Amer. physician
  Lovejoy—Women p242

Parry, Angenette (fl. 1920's-1930's)
  Amer. physician
  Lovejoy—Women p405
  Lovejoy—Women Phys. p53-54,por.

Parry, Blanche (d. 1589)
  Eng. maid of honor
  Stenton—English p135

Parsons, Alice Beal (1886-1962)
  Amer. author
  Warfel—Amer. p335-336,por.

Parsons, Augustina (fl. 1820's)
  Amer. publisher
  Brigham—Journals p78-79

Parsons, Edith Barretto Stevens (1878-1956)
Amer. sculptor
Jackman—Amer. p447-448
National—Contemp. p247

Parsons, Elizabeth Chase.
See Allen, Elizabeth Chase

Parsons, Elsie Clews (1875-1941)
Amer. anthropologist
Cur. Biog. '42 p642-643
Progress—Science p277

Parsons, Emily E. (fl. 1860's)
Amer. Civil war nurse
Brockett—Woman's p273-278,por.

Parsons, Harriet Oettinger (n.d.)
Amer. motion picture producer,
writer
Cur. Biog. '53 p470-473,por.

Parsons, Louella (1893-   )
Amer. journalist, columnist
CR '59 p573-574,por.
CR '63 p480,por.
Cur. Biog. '40 p631-632,por.
Ross—Ladies p410-411

Parsons, Mary L. (fl. 1910's)
Amer. pioneer journalist
Ross—Ladies p525-526

Parsons, Nancy (c. 1735-1814)
Eng. courtesan
Bleackley—Ladies p99-145,302-304,
por.

Parsons, Rose Peabody (1891-   )
Amer. organization official
Cur. Biog. '59 p344-346,por.

Parthenis (fl. c. 60 A.D.)
Gr. poet
Anthologia—Poets p97

Parton, Sara Payson Willis.
See Fern, Fanny, pseud.

Partridge, Deborah Cannon.
See Wolfe, Deborah Cannon Partridge

Pascal, Jacqueline (1625-1661)
Fr. prodigy
Corchran—Romance p123-124

Pasch, Ulricke Friederika (1735-1796)
Swed. painter
Waters—Women p265

Pascoli, Luigia (fl. 1870's-1880's)
It. painter
Waters—Women p265

Pasquali, Bernice de (fl. 1900's)
Amer. singer
Lahee—Grand p310-312,por.
McCoy—Portraits p148,por.

Passe (or Paas), Madeleine van de
(c. 1570/1600-   )
Nether. engraver
Waters—Women p265-266

Pasta, Guiditta Negri (1798-1865)
It. singer
Adelman—Famous p117
Derwent—Rossini p150,237-244,por.
Ewen—Ency. p382-383
Ferris—Great p171-196,por.(1)
Lahee—Famous p41-44
McCoy—Portraits p148,por.
Pleasants—Great p139-146,por.
Saleski—Wander. p419-420

Pasteur, Mrs. Louis (fl. 1830's-1880's)
Fr., wife of Louis Pasteur
Mozans—Woman p376-377

Paston, Anne (fl.c. 1470's)
Eng., sister of John II
Stenton—English p96

Paston, Elizabeth (f.c. 1440's)
Eng., sister of John I
Stenton—English p94

Paston, Margaret (fl. 1460's)
Eng., sister of John II
Stenton—English p9,95

Paston, Margaret Mauteby (1423-1484)
Eng. letter-writer
Bennett—Six p100-123
Stenton—English p92-96,98

Pastorelli, France (n.d.)
Fr. pianist
Eustace—Infinity p79-95,por.

Patch, Edith Marion (1876-1954)
Amer. entomologist
Osborn—Fragments p275,por.

Pater, Clara (fl. 1880's-1894's)
Eng. teacher
Brittain—Women p42-43,46,58,82,258

Paterson, Anne, pseud. (Anne Frances
Einselen)
Amer.author
Warfel—Amer. p337-338,por.

Paterson, Daphne (fl. 1920's)
Can. pioneer aviatrix
*May—Women p100

Paterson, Isabel Bowler (c. 1886-1961)
Amer. journalist, columnist
Bruère—Laugh. p230
Thomas—Canad. p97
Ross—Ladies p405-407

Patey, Janet Monach (1842-1894)
Scot.-Eng. singer
Klein—Great p162-166

Paton, Mary Anne (Mary Anne Paton Wood)
(1802-1864)
Eng. singer
Coad—Amer. p104

Patricia (d.c. 665)
Turk. saint
°Windham—Sixty p197-206

Patrick, Fannie Brown (b. 1864)
Amer. musician
Binheim—Women p141,por.

Patrick, Mary Mills (1850-1940)
Amer. educator, foundress
Cur. Biog. '40 p634

Pattee, Alida Francis (d. 1942)
Amer. dietician, lecturer,
publisher, author
Cur. Biog. '42 p648
Women—Achieve. p141,por.

Pattee, Elsie Dodge (b. 1876)
Amer. artist, illustrator
Women—Achieve. p126,por.

Patterson, Ada (fl. 1910's-1920's)
Amer. journalist
Ross—Ladies p65-73,por.

Patterson, Alicia (Alicia Guggenheim)
(1906-1963)
Amer. editor, publisher
CR '59 p577,por.
Cur. Biog. '55 p474-476,por.
Cur. Biog. '63 p316
Stewart—Makers p238
Time Sept.13,1954 p52,por.(Cover)

Patterson, Annie Wilson (1868-1934)
Irish organist, lecturer, author
McCoy—Portraits p148,por.

Patterson, Eleanor Medill (1884-1948)
Amer. editor, publisher
Cur. Biog. '40 p634-636,por.
Cur. Biog. '48 p493
Ross—Ladies p5,501-505,por.
Stewart—Makers p218,236-238

Patterson, Elizabeth (Elizabeth Bonaparte)
(1785-1879)
Amer. belle, wife of Jerome
Bonaparte
Brooks—Young p130-175
Logan—Part p253-254
Parton—Dau. p509-517,por.
Parton—Noted p509-517,por.
Pearson—Marry. p13-18,por.
Pearson—Pilgrim p5-7,por.
Sale—Old p259-272,por.

Patterson, Elizabeth Kelso (fl. 1940's)
Amer. singer, music teacher
McCoy—Portraits p149,por.

Patterson, Flora W. (b. 1847)
Amer. pathologist, botanist,
mycologist, editor
Logan—Part p878

Patterson, Jane C. (fl. 1870's-1880's)
Amer. clergyman
Hanaford—Dau. p452

Patterson, Jenny (fl. 1880's-1890's)
Eng., friend of George Bernard
Shaw
DuCann—Loves p57-72,por.

Patterson, Lillian D. (fl. 1930's)
Amer. business executive
Women—Achieve. p175,por.

Patterson, Mrs. Lindsay (fl. 1910's)
Amer. club leader
Logan—Part p480-481

Patterson, Martha Johnson (b. 1828)
Amer. social leader, daughter of
Andrew Johnson
Hanaford—Dau. p135-136
Jensen—White p96-98,por.
Truett—First p44,por.

Patterson, Mary J. (1840-1894)
Amer. teacher
Brown—Home. p145-146

Patterson, Nan (b.c. 1882)
Amer. actress, dancer
Rogers—Women p46,por.

Patterson, Sarepta C. McNall (fl. 1860's)
Amer. Civil war nurse
Logan—Part p372

Patti, Adelina (1843-1919)
It.-Sp. singer
Abbott—Notable p357-361,por.
Adelman—Famous p257-258,por.
Coad—Amer. p232,por.
Davidson—Treas. p216-221,por.
Dorland—Sum p70
Ewen—Ency. p383-384
Hammerton p1072,por.
Klein—Great p31-49,por.
Lahee—Famous p127-142,por.
McCoy—Portraits p149,por.
°MacVeagh—Champlin p450
Marks—Glamour p182-196,por.
°Nisenson—More Minute p104,por.
Pleasants—Great p104-211,por.
°Ulrich—Famous p11-16,por.
Wagner—Prima p6-8,13-15,31,40-41,
74-79,246

Patti, Carlotta (1840-1889)
    It. singer, music teacher
    Lahee—Famous p146-147
    McCoy—Portraits p149,por.
    Marks—Glamour p197-202,por.

Patti-Brown, Anita (n.d.)
    Amer. singer
    Cuney-Hare—Negro p234

Pattison, Dorothy Wyndlow.
    See Dora, Sister

Pattison, Helen Searle (fl. 1860's-1880's)
    Amer. painter
    Waters—Women p266-267

Patton, Abby Hutchinson (b. 1829)
    Amer. social reformer, singer
    Hanaford—Dau. p362-363
    Logan—Part p868-869

Patton, Frances Gray (1906-   )
    Amer. author
    Cur. Biog. '55 p476-477,por.
    Hoyle—Tar p131-135,por.

Patton, Marguerite Courtright (b. 1889)
    Amer. organization official
    Cur. Biog. '50 p441-442,por.

Pauker, Ana (c. 1894-   )
    Rum. foreign minister
    Cur. Biog. '48 p493-495,por.
    Time Sept.20,1948 p31,por.(Cover)

Paul, Alice (b. 1885)
    Amer. feminist, organization
        official
    Adelman—Famous p323
    Bruce—Woman p305-309,313,315-
        316
    Cur. Biog. '47 p499-500,por.
    Irwin—Angels (see index)
    Riegel—Amer. p181-182

Paul, Helene (fl. 1940's)
    Amer. astrologist
    Zolotow—Never p246-248

Paul, Mrs. Howard (fl. 1890's)
    Eng. actress
    Furniss—Some p147-148,por.

Paul, Nora Vincent (fl. 1930's)
    Amer. insurance executive,
        journalist
    Women—Achieve. p81,por.

Paula (347-404)
    Rom. saint, scholar, traveler
    Blunt—Great p36-37,397
    Culver—Women p78
    Deen—Great p28-33
    Dolan—Goodnow's p73-74,por.
    Englebert—Lives p35-36
    Mozans p31-34
    Wescott—Calen. p14

Paula, Mother (fl. 1910's)
    It. nun, missionary
    Elgin—Nun p126-127,por.

Paula Gambara (1473-1515)
    It. saint
    Englebert—Lives p33

Paulding, Virgilia.
    See Peterson, Virgilia

Paulee, Mona (n.d.)
    Can.-Amer. singer
    Peltz—Spot. p100
    Saleski—Jewish p607-608,por.

Pauli, Hanna Hirsch (fl. 1880's-1890's)
    Swed. painter
    Waters—Women p390

Paulina (1) (fl. 310's A.D.)
    Rom. empress, wife of Maximinus
    Serviez—Roman (2) p279-287

Paulina (2) (fl. 404 A.D.)
    Rom. saint
    *Windham—Sixty p130-136

Paulina (3) (fl. 20's B.C.-30's A.D.)
    Rom. beauty
    Boccaccio—Conc. p202-204

Paull, Grace A. (1898-   )
    Amer. illustrator
    Mahony—Illus. p344

Paulus, Käthe (fl. 1880's)
    Ger. parachutist
    *May—Women p49

Pauly, Rosa (1905-   )
    Czech. singer
    Ewen—Ency. p384
    Ewen—Living p271-272,por.
    McCoy—Portraits p149,por.

Pavloska, Irene (1889-1962)
    Can. singer
    McCoy—Portraits p149,por.

Pavlova, Anna (1881/86-1931)
    Russ. ballet dancer
    Adelman—Famous p323
    Beaumont—Complete p639-641,por.
    Clarke—Six p42-64,por.
    Davidson—Ballet p227-234,por.
    Galloway—Roads p105-122,por.
    Hammerton p1075,por.
    Haskell—Vignet. p13-15,por.
    Hurok—Impres. p56-88,por.
    Love—Famous p33
    *McConnell—Famous p36-48,por.
    *Muir—Famous p43-53,por.
    Schmidt—400 p348-349,por.
    *Terry—Star p112-121,por.
    *Trease—Seven Stages p168-194,por.

Pavlova, Karolina Karlovna Janisch (1807-
1893)
Russ. poet
Yarmolinsky—Treas. p298-299

Pavlovich, Nikola (1835-1894)
Bulg. painter
Stiles—Postal p200

Pax, pseud. See Cholmondeley, Mary

Paxinou, Katina (n.d.)
Gr. actress
Cur. Biog. '43 p572-574,por.

Paxton, Ethel (fl. 1930's)
Amer. artist, teacher, lecturer,
author
Women—Achieve. p90,por.

Paxton, Jean Gregory (fl. 1930's)
Amer. editor, author
Women—Achieve. p145,por.

Paybody, Elizabeth (fl. 1650's)
Amer. pioneer
Green—Pioneer (1) p130-131

Payne "Betsy" Johnson (fl. 1780's)
Amer. pioneer
Green—Pioneer (3) p403-404

Payne, Dorothy.
See Madison, Dorothy ("Dolly")

Payne, Martha (fl. 1800's)
Amer., mother of Daniel A. Payne
Brown—Home p1-12,por.

Payne, Nelle Maria de Cottrell (1900-   )
Amer. entomologist
Osborn—Fragments p275

Payne, Winona Wilcox (Mrs. Maxwell,
pseud.) (c. 1865-1949)
Amer. editor
Ellet—Women (2) p333-334
Ross—Ladies p553-554,por.cover

Payne-Gaposchkin, Cecilia Helena (1900-   )
Eng.-Amer. astronomer, educator,
author
Cur. Biog. '57 p421-423,por.

Payne-Townshend, Charlotte (b.c. 1857)
Brit., friend of George Bernard
Shaw
DuCann—Loves p172-201

Payson, Joan (1903-   )
Amer. philanthropist, baseball
team owner
CR '63 p483,por.

Pazzi, Maria Maddalena Caterina del
(1566-1607)
It. painter
Waters—Women p267

Peabody, Amelia (1890-   )
Amer. sculptor
National—Contemp. p253

Peabody, Elizabeth (c. 1800-1894)
Amer. bookseller
Dexter—Career p145

Peabody, Elizabeth Palmer (1804-1894)
Amer. author, educator
Adelman—Famous p183
Brooks—Three p83-153
Dorland—Sum p28,110-111
Douglas—Remember p236
*Fleming—Great p43-56
Hanaford—Dau. p240-242,530
Logan—Part p286-730
Whitton—These p205

Peabody, Elizabeth Smith Shaw (1750-
c. 1813)
Amer. Rev. war patriot
Logan—Part p181

Peabody, Josephine Preston (1880-1922)
Amer. poet, playwright
Adelman—Famous p266
Cook—Our p155-156
Logan—Part p791

Peabody, Lucy Evelyn (b. 1865)
Amer. scientist
Logan—Part p879

Peabody, Marian Lawrence (b. 1875)
Amer. sculptor
National—Contemp. p253

Peabody, Sophia (m. 1842)
Amer. artist
Whitton—These p194

Peake, Mary S. (1823-1862)
Amer. Civil war patriot, teacher
Hanaford—Dau. p208

Peale, Anna Claypoole (1791-1878)
Amer. painter
Waters—Women p267-268

Peale, Sara M. (1860-1885)
Amer. painter
Waters—Women p268

Pealer, Ruth M. Griswold (m. 1869)
Amer. genealogist
Logan—Part p435-436

Pearce, Alice (n.d.)
Amer. actress, comedienne, TV
personality
CR '63 p484,por.

Pearce, Louise (1886-1959)
Amer. pathologist
Castiglioni—Hist. p1127
*Fleming—Doctors p86-99

Pearce, "Mistress" (1607-1627)
Amer. pioneer gardener
Hollingsworth—Her p7-9

Pearce, Theodocia (1894-c. 1926)
Can. author, poet
Thomas—Canad. p98

Peare, Catherine Owens (1911-   )
Amer. author
Cur. Biog. '59 p349-350,por.

Pearl, Lee (1907-   )
Amer. author, song-writer
ASCAP p384

Pearsall, Rachel (fl. 1860's)
Amer. Civil war patriot
Andrews—Women p236-245

Pearse, Dorothy Norman Spicer (1908-   )
Eng. pioneer aeronautical
engineer
*Goff—Women p236-245

Pearse, Susan Beatrice (n.d.)
Eng. illustrator
Mahony—Illus. p344

Pearson, Beatrice (1920-   )
Amer. actress
Blum—Great p143,por.

Pearson, Evelyn Utter (fl. 1910's-1950's)
Amer. missionary
They—Went p50-51

Pearson, Flora (fl. 1860's)
Amer. W. pioneer
Brown—Gentle p13,234-235
*Miller—West. p150-164

Pearson, Joan D. M. (fl. 1940's)
Eng. WAAF heroine
*May—Women p162

Pearson, Sarah (fl. 1720's-1780's)
Amer., mother of Benjamin West
Bartlett—Mothers p39-42

Peary, Mary Wiley (1827-1900)
Amer., mother of Robert E. Peary
*Chandler—Famous p287-306

Pease, Jessie L. (fl. 1940's)
Amer. composer, pianist, teacher
McCoy—Portraits p150,por.

Pease, Parnell Smith (m. 1885)
Amer. whaling voyager
Whiting—Whaling p240-252,por.

Pease, Phebe Ann.
See Smith, Phebe Ann

Peasley, Mrs. (fl. 1880's)
Amer. businesswoman
Hanaford—Dau. p610

Peauly, Mary de. See Gower, Pauline

Pechey, Edith (fl. 1870's)
Eng. physician
Bell—Storm, p69-70,72-73,99-100,190

Pechova, Eliska.
See Krasnohorska, Eliska, pseud.

Peck, Anne Merriman (b. 1884)
Amer. illustrator, author
Mahony—Illus. p344-345

Peck, Annie Smith (1850-1933)
Amer. mountaineer, scholar,
lecturer, musician
Adelman—Famous p292-293
Logan—Part p880-881
Rogers—Women p135,por.

Peck, Willie (fl. 1930's)
Amer. airline hostess
Planck—Women p192

Peck, Winifred Frances Knox (gr. 1904)
Scot. novelist
Brittain—Women p116-117,119,125,
228,231,249

Peckauskas, Marija (1878-1930)
Lith. author
Schmidt—400 p283-284,por.

Peddle, Juliet (gr. 1922)
Amer. architect
Goff—Women p173-176

Peden, Katherine Graham (1926-   )
Amer. organization official,
business executive
Cur. Biog. '62 p337-338,por.

Peebles, Mary Louise ("Lynde Palmer")
(1834-1915)
Amer. author
Dorland—Sum p50,189

Peel, Beatrice.
See Lillie, Beatrice, Lady Peel

Peel, Julia Floyd, Lady (1795-1859)
Brit., wife of Lord Peel, prime
minister
Lee—Wives p44-62,por.

"Peggy of the Flint Hills."
See Greene, Zula Bennington

Peirce, Isabel (fl. 1930's)
    Amer. business woman
    Women—Achieve. p161,por.

Peixotto, Mary Hutchinson (m. 1897)
    Amer. artist
    Women—Achieve. p201

Peksen, Marija (1845-1903)
    Lat. pioneer playwright
    Schmidt—400 p273,por.

Pelagia (d. 304)
    Turk. saint
    Englebert—Lives p223
    Wescott—Calen. p157

Pelichy, Geertruida (1744-1825)
    Nether. painter
    Waters—Women p268

Pellegrino, Itala (b. 1865)
    It. painter
    Waters—Women p268-269

Pelletier, Marie de Sainte Euphrasie (1796-
    1868)
    Fr. saint
    Elgin—Nun p54-55,por.

Pellett, Miss (fl. 1850's)
    Amer. social reformer
    Aikman—Calamity p313-318

Peltier, Thérèse (fl. 1900's)
    Fr. sculptor, pioneer airplane
        traveler
    *Lauwick—Heroines p27
    *May —Women p60
    Planck—Women p14-15

Pelton-Jones, Frances (fl. 1940's)
    Amer. harpsichordist, pianist,
        organist
    McCoy—Portraits p150,por.

Peltz, Mary Ellie Opdycke (1896-   )
    Amer. journalist, author
    Cur. Biog. '54 p501-502,por.

Pember, Phoebe Yates (fl. 1860's)
    Amer. Civil war nurse, diarist
    Jones—Heroines p317-325,392-397
    Parton—Noted p309-321
    Simkins—Women p38,89,91

Pembroke, Anne.
    See Montgomery, Anne, Countess of

Pembroke, Marie de St. Pol, Countess of
    (d. 1377)
    Eng., great granddaughter of
        Henry III
    Sorley—King's p65-84

Pembroke, Mary Herbert Sidney, Countess
    of (5161-1621)
    Eng. author, literary patron
    Aubrey—Brief p138-140
    Hammerton p1079,por.
    Stenton—English p70,141
    Thomson—Queens p455-471

Penalosa, Dona Eufemia (fl. c. 1590's)
    Amer. colony co-sponsor
    Leonard—Amer. p119-120

Pendleton, Ellen Fitz (1864-1936)
    Amer. educator
    Logan—Part p733

Penelope (fl. 67 A.D.)
    It. saint
    *Windham—Sixty p19-27
    Davenport—Great p40-43

Penicke, Clara (1818-1849)
    Ger. painter
    Waters—Women p269

Penington, M. P. S.
    See Pennington, Mary Proude Springett

Peninnah (Biblical)
    Buchanan—Women p46-48
    Deen—All p288

Penn, Gulielma Maria Springett (1644-1694)
    Amer., first wife of William Penn
    Burt—Phila. p51-52
    Deen—Great p364-367
    Green—Pioneer (1) p365
    Lambert—Quiet p72-76

Penn, Hanna Callowhill (1671-1726)
    Amer., second wife of William
        Penn
    Burt—Phila. p49-50,52,94,142
    Green—Pioneer (1) p365
    Jones—Quakers p485-486
    Leonard—Amer. p120

Penn, Lucy. See Taylor, Lucy

Penn, Susan Lyme (b. 1741/42)
    Amer. patriot
    Green—Pioneer (3) p262-264

Pennell, Elizabeth Robins (1855-1936)
    Amer. author
    Dorland—Sum p173

Penney, Mary Frances Paxton (n.d.)
    Amer., mother of James Cash
        Penney
    Davis—Mothers p79-87

Penniman, Adelia (1801-1884)
    Amer. pioneer herbalist
    Hollingsworth—Her p50-53

Penniman, Fanny (1760-1834)
    Amer. pioneer herbalist
    Hollingsworth—Her p50-53

Penniman, Frances.
    See Allen, Frances Buchanan

Pennington, Mary Engle (1872-1952)
    Amer. bacteriologist, engineer,
        chemist, refrigeration specialist
    Goff—Women p183-214
    New Yorker Sept. 6, 1941 p23,por.
        (Profiles)
    Women—Achieve. p201
    *Yost—Women Sci. p80-98

Pennington (Penington), Mary Proude
        Springett (d. 1682)
    Amer. religious leader
    Lambert—Quiet p27-31

Pennock, Deborah (fl. 1870's)
    Amer. social reformer
    Hanaford—Dau. p376-377

Pennock, Grace Lavinia (fl. 1930's)
    Amer. editor
    Women—Achieve. p186,por.

Pennock, Meta (fl. 1930's)
    Amer. nurse, editor
    Women—Achieve. p84,por.

Pennoyer, Sara (fl. 1940's)
    Amer. retail executive
    Taves—Success. p150-159,por.

Pennybacker, Mrs. Percy V. (b. 1861)
    Amer. club leader
    Logan—Part p501
    Webb—Famous p375-384,por.

Penrose, Elizabeth.
    See Markham, Elizabeth

Penrose, Emily Dame (1858-1942)
    Eng. educator
    Brittain—Women (see index)

Penrose, Mary.
    See Wayne, "Polly" (Mary) Penrose

Pentry, Mrs. Edward (fl. c. 1672)
    Amer. pioneer
    Fowler—Woman p57-67

Pepoli, Countess.
    See Alboni, Marietta, Countess Pepoli

Peppercorn, Gertrude (fl. 1890's-1900's)
    Eng. pianist
    McCoy—Portraits p150,por.

Peyat, Mary (fl. 1750's)
    Irish printer
    Club—Printing p15

Pepys, Elizabeth Saint-Michel (1640-1669)
    Eng., wife of Samuel Pepys
    Bradford—Women p89-109,por.

Peralta, Angela (1845-1883)
    Mex. singer
    Schmidt—400 p292-293,por.

Peralta, Frances (d. 1933)
    Eng. singer
    McCoy—Portraits p151,por.

Percival, Mary Fuller (b. 1737)
    Amer. Rev. war patriot
    Green—Pioneer (3) p359-361

Percival, Susanna.
    See Verbruggen, Susanna P.

Percy, Anne, Lady (d.c. 1819)
    Eng.-Amer. beauty
    Smith—Originals p141-154,por.

Percy, Elizabeth, Duchess of Somerset
        (1666/67-1722)
    Eng. heiress
    Festing—On p91-179

Percy, Florence, pseud.
    See Allen, Elizabeth Chase

"Perdita."
    See Robinson, Mary Darby

Peregoy, Mary Cochran (fl. 1880's)
    Amer. W. pioneer
    Sargent—Pioneers p20,por.

Pereira, Irene Rice (1907-   )
    Amer. painter
    Cur. Biog. '53 p485-486,por.

Perelli, Lida (fl. 1880's)
    It. painter
    Waters—Women p269-270

Perelman, Laura (fl. 1930's)
    Amer. playwright
    Mantle—Contemp. p240

Perey, Marguerite (fl. 1930's)
    Fr. scientist
    Weeks—Discovery p866

Pereyaslawzewa, Sophia (fl. 1890's)
    Russ. biologist
    Mozans—Woman p244-245

Perez, (Barahona) Ernestina (gr. 1887)
    Chile. physician
    Lovejoy—Women p270-271

Perfield, Effa Ellis (fl. 1940's)
    Amer. educator, author, organist
    McCoy—Portraits p151,por.

Perham, Margery (gr. 1917)
 Eng. educator
 Brittain—Women p145,176,191,223,
  245

Périer, Jacqueline (fl. 1630's-1640's)
 Fr., sister of Pascal
 Corkran—Romance p139-140

Peritz, Edith (fl. 1930's)
 Ger.-Amer. surgeon
 Women—Achieve. p157,por.

Perkins, Anne (fl. 1860's)
 Amer. Civil war letter-writter
 Simkins—Women p224,226

Perkins, Elizabeth Peck (fl. 1770's)
 Amer. merchant
 Dexter—Career p154-155

Perkins, Frances (1882-1965)
 Amer. government official, social
  worker
 *Bolton—Lives p281-292,por.
 *Clymer—Modern p22-30,por.
 CR '63 p488,por.
 Cur. Biog. '40 p643-646,por.
 Cur. Biog. '65 p321
 Fisher—Amer. p171-173,por.
 *Heath—Women (4) p32,por.
 Huff—Famous (2nd) p411-418,por.
 Jensen—Revolt p62,por.
 New Yorker Sept.2,1933 p16,por.;
  Sept.9,1933 p20,(Profiles)
 Rogers—Women p66,por.
 Roosevelt—Ladies p187-195,282-283
 Time Aug.14,1933 p11,por. (Cover)
 Women—Achieve. p24,por.

Perkins, Sarah M. C. (b. 1824)
 Amer. lecturer, clergyman
 Hanaford—Dau. p342,452-453

Perley, Elizabeth Porter Putnam (1673-
  1746)
 Amer. mother of Israel Putnam
 Green—Pioneer (3) p489-490
 Root—Chapter p125-135

Perlman, Phyllis (fl. 1930's)
 Amer. publicity director, journalist
 Women—Achieve. p163,por.

Perman, Louise E. (fl. 1900's)
 Scot. painter
 Waters—Women p269-270

Pernel, Orrea (fl. 1940's)
 Eng. violinist
 McCoy—Portraits p151,por.

Perón, (María) Eva Duarte de (1919-1952)
 Argent., wife of Juan Perón
 Cur. Biog. '49 p477-478,por.
 Cur. Biog. '52 p467
 Phila.—Women unp.,por.

Robinson—100 p84-87,por.
Stiles—Postal p202
*Worcester—Makers p166-174,por.
 Time July 14,1947 p32,por.; May 21,
  1951 p42,por.(Covers)

Perovsky, Sophie (fl. 1870's)
 Russ. revolutionary
 Kelen—Mist. p140-144,151,155-156

Perozo, Evangeline Rodriguez (gr. 1919)
 Dom. R. pioneer physician
 Lovejoy—Women p274

Perpetua, Vivia (d. 202/03 A.D.)
 Carth. saint
 Blunt—Great p11-19
 Culver—Women p75-76
 Englebert—Lives p91-92
 Sharkey—Pop. p30-34

Perrault, I. Marie (fl. 1910's-1920's)
 Amer. painter
 Michigan—Biog. p247-248

Perrein, Michèle (1929-   )
 Fr. novelist
 Peyre—French p288,431

Perrers, Alice (d. 1400)
 Eng. criminal, mistress of
  Edward III
 Jenkins—Six p31-56

Perreton, Françoise (fl. 1840's)
 Fr. nun, missionary
 Elgin—Nun p98-101,por.

Perrier, Marie (fl. 1890's-1900's)
 Fr. painter
 Waters—Women p270-271

Perrin, Alice (1867-1934)
 Brit. novelist
 Hammerton p1083

Perry, Antoinette (1888-1946)
 Amer. actress, director, producer
 Cur. Biog. '46 p473

Perry, Clara Greenleaf (fl. 1900's)
 Amer. painter
 Waters—Women p271

Perry, Joanna (d. 1725)
 Amer. colonial bookseller
 Dexter—Colonial p30

Perry, Lilla Cabot (d. 1933)
 Amer. painter
 Waters—Women p271-272

Perry, Margaret (fl. 1920's)
 Amer. aviatrix, airport operator
 Planck—Women p188

Perry, Nora (1841-1896)
Amer. author, journalist
Adelman—Famous p202

Persiani, Fanny Tacchinardi (1812-1867)
It. singer
Ewen—Ency. p391
Lahee—Famous p79-80

Persis (Biblical)
Deen—All p288

Perugini, Caterina (Kate) E. Dickens
(1839-1929)
Eng. painter
Waters—Women p272-273

Peschka-Leutner, Minna (1839-1890)
Aust. singer
McCoy—Portraits p151,por.

Pessl, Yella (fl. 1930's-1940's)
Aust.-Amer.. harpsichordist
Ewen—Living p274,por.
McCoy—Portraits p151,por.

Pestalozzi, Anna (1738-1815)
Swiss humanitarian, philanthropist
Arsenius—Dict. p151,por.
Schmidt—400 p379-380,por.

Peter, Sarah (fl. 19th cent.)
Amer. pioneer industrial arts
teacher
Farmer—What p466-467

Peterborough, Countess of.
See Robinson, Anastasia

Peterkin, Julia Mood 1880-1961)
Amer. author
Clark—Innocence p213-231,por.
Loggins—Hear p216-224
*Millett—Amer. p525-526
Overton—Women p257-261

Peters, Anna 1843-1926)
Ger. painter
Waters—Women p273

Peters, Fannie Ledyard (c. 1754-1816)
Amer. Rev. war heroine
Green—Pioneer (3) p354,451
Root—Chapter p365-374

Peters, Roberta (1930-   )
Amer. singer
CR '59 p584-585,por.
CR '63 p489,por.
Cur. Biog. '54 p505-506,por.
Matz—Opera p281-284,por.
Seventeen—In p173-176,por.

Peter's wife (Biblical)
Deen—All p335
Nelson—Bible p96-97

Peter's wife, mother of (Biblical)
Nelson—Bible p98-100

Petersen, Agnes J. (fl. 1920's-1930's)
Amer. journalist, librarian
Ross—Ladies p475-476

Petersham, Maud Fuller (1889-   )
Amer. illustrator
Mahony—Illus. p345

Petersham, Miska (1888-1960)
Hun.-Amer. illustrator
Mahony—Illus. p345-346

Peterson, Alma (fl. 1940's)
Amer. singer
McCoy—Portraits p152,por.

Peterson, Betty (1918-   )
Amer. author
ASCAP p387

Peterson, Edna Gunnar (fl. 1940's)
Amer. pianist, music teacher
McCoy—Portraits p152,por.

Peterson, Esther Eggertsen (1906-   )
Amer. government official
Cur. Biog. '61 p358-360,por.

Peterson, Jane (fl. 1930's)
Amer. painter
Bryant—Amer. p276-278
Women—Achieve. p119,por.

Peterson, May (d. 1952)
Amer. singer
McCoy—Portraits p152,por.

Peterson, Miss (fl. 1840's)
Amer. pioneer
Logan—Part p104

Peterson, Virgilia (1904-1966)
Amer. lecturer, author, TV
personality
CR '59 p585,por.
CR '63 p490,por.
Cur. Biog. '53 p488-490,por.
Cur. Biog. '67 p481

Petherbridge, Margaret.
See Farrar, Margaret Fetherbridge

Petina, Irra (1911-   )
Russ. singer
McCoy—Portraits p152,por.
Peltz—Spot. p71,por.

Petit, Gabrielle (1893-1916)
Belg. heroine
Schmidt—400 p58-59,por.

Petite, Mademoiselle.
See Bari-Dussot, Countess

Petkere, Bernice (1906-   )
    Amer. composer, author, scenarist
    ASCAP p388

Petkevikaite, Gabriele (Petkevicaite-Bite)
    (1861-1943)
    Lith. stateswoman, author, patriot
    Arsenius—Dict. p152
    Phila.—Women unp.,por.
    Stiles—Postal p204

Petkova, Baba Nedelia (1826-1894)
    Bulg. pioneer, educator
    Schmidt—400 p62-63,por.

Petral (fl. 15th cent.)
    E. Ind., wife of Husain Khan
    Pool—Famous p121-126

Petronilla (fl. 1st cent.)
    Rom. saint
    Englebert—Lives p209
    Wescott—Calen. p79

Petrov, Yevdoklya (fl. 1950's)
    Russ., wife of Vladimir Petrov
    *May—Women p237-238

Petrova, Helene Assen (1872-1926)
    Bulg. educator
    Schmidt—400 p71,por.

Petrovna, Elisabeth (1709-1762)
    Russ. empress, foundress
    Arsenius—Dict. p57,por.
    Dorland—Sum. p54,108
    Phila.—Women unp.,por.

Petry, Ann (1911-   )
    Amer. author, journalist
    *Cherry—Portraits p145-147
    Cur. Biog. '46 p476-477,por.
    Richardson—Great p151-161,por.
    Robinson—Hist. p235-236,por.
    Warfel—Amer. p340,por.

Petry, Lucile (1903-   )
    Amer. nurse, educator
    Cur. Biog. '44 p545-546,por.
    Dolan—Goodnow's p327-328,por.
    *Yost—Nursing p176-197

Pettes, Mary Dwight (fl. 1860's)
    Amer. Civil war nurse
    Brockett—Woman's p385-389

Pettibone, Abigail.
    See Phelps, Abigail Pettibone

Pettigrew, Susan (fl. 1830's)
    Amer. traveler
    Woodward—Way p198-243

Pettit, Polly (fl. 1930's)
    Amer. business executive
    Women—Achieve. p183,por.

Petty, Mrs. (fl. 1670's-1680's)
    Eng. actress
    Wilson—All p181-182

Peycke, Frieda (n.d.)
    Amer. composer, pianist, music
        teacher
    McCoy—Portraits p152,por.

Peyser, Ethel R. (fl. 1910's-1930's)
    Amer. author, editor, music critic,
        lecturer
    Women—Achieve. p129,por.

Peyster, Mrs. D. E. (m. 1935)
    Amer. hostess
    Hellman—Mrs. p11-14

Peyton, Catherine (fl. 1750's)
    Amer. colonial religious worker
    Jones—Quakers p300

Pfeiffer, Ida Laura Reyer (1797-1858)
    Aust. traveler
    Adelman—Famous p132
    Dorland—Sum p23,114
    Fifty—Famous p169-176,por.
    Mozans—Woman p255-256
    Schmidt—400 p46,por.

Pfohl, Katherine Laughlin (b. 1867)
    Amer. religious worker
    Logan—Part p622

Pfost, Gracie Bowers (1906-1965)
    Amer. congresswoman
    Cur. Biog. '55 p485-488,por.
    Cur. Biog. '65 p321
    U.S.—Women (87th) p33,por.

Phanuel (Biblical)
    Deen—All p288-289

Pharailda (d. 8th cent.)
    Belg. saint
    Englebert—Lives p6

Pharaoh's daughter (Biblical)
    Buchanan—Women p27-28
    Deen—All p310-311
    Horton—Women p75-88
    Morton—Women p59-65

Phebe (Biblical)
    Deen—All p230-232

Phelps, Abigail Pettibone (1706-1787)
    Amer. patriot
    Green—Pioneer (3) p502
    Root—Chapter p238-255

Phelps, Almira Hart Lincoln (1793-1884)
    Amer. botanist, chemist, author,
        educator
    Hanaford—Dau. p286-287,528
    Logan—Part p796-797
    Weeks—Discovery p80

Phelps, Anna Elizabeth (fl. 1930's)
Amer. author, club leader
Women—Achieve. p54,por.

Phelps, Aurora (fl. 1870's-1880's)
Amer. philanthropist
Hanaford—Dau. p183

Phelps, Elizabeth Stewart.
See Ward, Elizabeth Stuart Phelps

Phelps, Elizabeth Stuart (H. Trusta)
(1815-1852)
Amer. author, lecturer
Dorland—Sum p28,195-196
Hanaford—Dau. p244-245,343

Phelps, Grace (fl. 1930's)
Amer. journalist
Ross—Ladies p182-183

Phelps, Mrs. John S. (fl. 1860's)
Amer. Civil war humanitarian
Brockett—Woman's p520-521

Phelps, Pauline (fl. 1910's)
Amer. playwright
Logan—Part p792-793

Philaneis of Samos (fl. 270 B.C.)
Gr. poet
Anthologia—Poets p97

Philbin, Mary (fl. 1920's)
Amer. actress
Herman—How p117,por.

Philenia, pseud.
See Morton, Sarah Wentworth

Philippa of Guelders (1462-1547)
Fr. saint, wife of René II
Englebert—Lives p79-80

Philippa of Hainault (c. 1314-1369)
Eng. queen, wife of Edward III
*Cather—Girlhood p103-118
Dark—More p37-57
Hammerton p1091
Unstead—People p167-175

Philippa of Lancaster (Filipa de Vilhena)
(1359-1415)
Port. patriot, queen
Arsenius—Dict. p195,por.
Phila.—Women unp.,por.
Stiles—Postal p205

Philips, Katherine Fowler ("Orinda")
(1631-1664)
Eng. poet
Aubrey—Brief p242
Dorland—Sum p56,179
Hammerton p1091
MacCarthy—Women p29-30
McQueen—Pope p127-128
Stenton—English p141,167-168,200

Philipse, Catharine Duval Van Cortland
(fl. 1690's)
Amer. colonial property manager,
philanthropist
Beard—Amer. p26-27
Dexter—Colonial p106-107

Philipse, Margaret Hardenbroeck DeVries
(d.c. 1690)
Amer. colonial shipper, business
woman
Dexter—Colonial p107-108
Earle—Colon. p73
Green—Pioneer (1) p187,197,222
Leonard—Amer. p97,120

Philipse, Mary (c. 1728-1822)
Amer. Rev. war heroine
Ellet—Women (1) p233-238,por.

Phillips, Abigail (m. 1769)
Amer. pioneer
Green—Pioneer (3) p482

Phillips, Adelaide (1833-1882)
Eng. singer
Dorland—Sum p22,163
Ewen—Ency. p394
Lahee—Famous p296-298
McCoy—Portraits p153,por.
Parton—Dau. p347-353,por.
Parton—Noted p347-353,por.

Phillips, Anita (fl. 1930's)
Amer. playwright
Mantle—Contemp. p209

Phillips, Anna Greene (fl. 1840's)
Amer. social reformer
Hanaford—Dau. p356-357

Phillips, Bessie I. (c. 1880-1954)
Amer. journalist
Ross—Ladies p446-447

Phillips, Bettie Taylor (fl. 1860's)
Amer. Civil war patriot
Andrews—Women p120-126

Phillips, Catherine Payton (1727-1794)
Eng.-Amer. colonial evangelist
Dexter—Colonial p147

Phillips, Elizabeth (fl. 1770's)
Amer. colonial producer, business
woman
Dexter—Colonial p48

Phillips, Emaline (fl. 1860's)
Amer. Civil war nurse
Logan—Part p370

Phillips, Eugenia Levy (fl. 1860's)
Amer. Civil war patriot
Simonhoff—Saga p14-20,por.

Phillips, Frances Lucas (fl. 1930's)
Amer. editor
Women—Achieve. p174,por.

Phillips, Irna (1903-   )
Amer. radio-script writer
Cur. Biog. '43 p590-591,por.

Phillips, Mrs. John (fl. 1940's)
Amer. mother of the year
Davis—Mothers p176

Phillips, Josephine (fl. 1860's)
Amer. Civil war patriot, author
Dannett—Noble p367-369

Phillips, Lena Madesin (1881-1955)
Amer. lawyer, lecturer, author,
editor
Cur. Biog. '46 p477-479,por.
Cur. Biog. '55 p488
Irwin—Angels p307-308,429
Women—Achieve. p52,por.

Phillips, Margaret (1925-   )
Welsh actress
Blum—Great p146,por.

Phillips, Marie Tello (1874-1962)
Amer. author
Smith—Women's p162

Phillips, Marion (1881-1932)
Brit. politician
Hammerton p1091

Phillips, Pauline Esther.
See Van Buren, Abigail

Phillips, Phebe (d. 1818)
Amer. philanthropist
Hanaford—Dau. p175-176

Phillips, Ruth (1903-   )
Amer. organization official
Cur. Biog. '59 p357-359,por.

Phillips, Thea (fl. 1930's)
Eng. singer
McCoy—Portraits p153,por.

Phillips, Velvalea (1925-   )
Amer. lawyer, politician
Cherry—Portraits p198

Phineas, wife of (Biblical)
Lewis—Portraits p169-170

Phippen, Laud German (fl. 1940's)
Amer. composer, music teacher,
pianist
McCoy—Portraits p153,por.

Phipps, Anne (1932-   )
Amer. student
Murrow—This (1) p135-136

Phoebe of Cenchrea (Biblical)
Buchanan—Women p106-107
Mead—250 p245
Nelson—Bible p123-125

Photina, Saint (Biblical)
Englebert—Lives p111

Phryne (fl. 4th cent. B.C.)
Gr. courtesan, model, beauty
Adelman—Famous p23
Hammerton p1092
Mozans—Woman p11

Phyfe, Mrs. Duncan (d. 1944)
Amer. recluse
Erskine—Out p236-244

Piaf, Edith (Giovanna Gassion) (1915-
1963)
Fr. singer
Beaton—Persona p78
CR '59 p587,por.
Cur. Biog. '50 p449-451,por.
Cur. Biog. '63 p326
Stambler—Ency. p183-185

Piatt, Sarah Morgan Bryan (1836-1919)
Amer. poet
Logan—Part p840-841

Piccard, Jeannette (fl. 1930's)
Fr. pioneer balloonist
*May—Women p31-35,por.

Piccolomini, Maria (1834-1899)
It. singer
Marks—Glamour p146-152,por.

Pichler, Karoline von Greiner (1769-1843)
Aust. salonist, novelist
Dorland—Sum p56,79,107,196
Schmidt—400 p44-45,por.

Pickard, Mae (m. 1914)
Eng. dancer
Wyndham—Chorus p134

Picken, Mary Brooks (b. 1886)
Amer. home economist, author
Cur. Biog. '54 p507-508,por.
Women—Achieve. p128,por.

Pickens, Jane (n.d.)
Amer. singer
Cur. Biog. '49 p484-486,por.

Pickens, Lucy Holcome (fl. 1860's)
Amer. Civil war heroine
Harkness—Heroines p3
Logan—Part p103

Pickens, Rebecca (Rebecca Calhoun)
(1745-1815)
Amer. pioneer
Green—Pioneer (2) p181-184

Pickersgill, Caroline (fl. 1810's)
Amer. flag-maker
*Carmer—Young p106-115

Pickett, LaSalle Corbell (b. 1843)
Amer. Civil war patriot, heroine,
diarist, lecturer
Harkness—Heroines p2-3
Jones—Heroines p240-247,por.
Logan—Part p845

Pickford, Mary (gr. 1906)
Eng. educator
Brittain—Women p117,250

Pickford, Mary Smith (1893-   )
Can.-Amer. actress
Adelman—Famous p324
CR '59 p588-589,por.
CR '63 p490,por.
Cur. Biog. '45 p467-470,por.
Hammerton p1093,por.
Herman—How p29,por.
Hughes—Famous p263-284,por.
New Yorker Apr.7,1934,p29,por.
(Profiles)
Rogers—Women p102-103,por.
Schickel—Stars p12,14,21,32-34,por.
Talmey—Doug. p29-39,por.
Wagenknecht—Movies p138-165,por.

Pickthall, Marjorie Lowry Christie (1883-
1922)
Can. author
Thomas—Canad. p98-99

Picon, Molly (1898-   )
Amer. actress
CR '63 p490-491,por.
Cur. Biog. '51 p488-490,por.

Picot, Eugenia (fl. 1170's)
Eng. heiress
Stenton—English p39-40

Picton-Turbervill, Edith (c. 1872-1960)
Welsh feminist, missionary, social
reformer
Asquith—Myself p313-360
Hammerton p1094

Pidgeon, Marie Kiersted (fl. 1930's)
Amer. librarian
Women—Achieve. p116,por.

Pier, Kate Hamilton (1845-1925)
Amer, lawyer, feminist
Logan—Part p745

Pierce, Anna Kendrick (fl. 1800's-1830's)
Amer., mother of Franklin Pierce
Hampton—Our p109-113

Pierce, Elizabeth F. (fl. 1910's)
Amer. club leader
Logan—Part p410-411

Pierce, Jane Means Appleton (1806-1863)
Amer., wife of Franklin Pierce
Farmer—What p85-86
Gerlinger—Mis. p46-47,por.
Hanaford—Dau. p90-91
Jensen—White p75
Logan—Ladies p77-79
Logan—Part p248-249
*McConnell—Our p147-155,por.
Prindiville—First p126-133
*Ross—Know p31,por.
Smith—Romances p195-203,por.
Truett—First p38,por.
Whitton—First p250-260,por.

Pierce, Sarah (Sally) (1767-1852)
Amer. educator
Dexter—Career p20-21
Woody—Hist. (1) p340-341,por.

Pierce, Tillie (fl. 1860's)
Amer. Civil war patriot
Young—Women p278-283

Pierpont, Laura (fl. 1910's)
Amer. actress
Caffin—Vaud. p127

Pierrebourg, Baroness de (fl. 1880's-1890's)
Fr. salonist
Skinner—Elegent p168-169

Pierrepont, Mary.
See Montagu, Mary Wortley, Lady

Pierson, Louise John Randall (1890-   )
Amer. author
Cur. Biog. '43 p596-599,por.

Pierson, Lydia Jane (fl. 1840's)
Amer. poet
Hanaford—Dau. p266

Pigott, Emeline (fl. 1860's)
Amer. Civil war heroine, spy
Harkness—Heroines p5
Simkins—Women p78

Piisimi, Vittoria (fl. 1570's)
It. actress
Gilder—Enter p63-64,68,74

Pilate's wife (Biblical)
Deen—All p205-208
Lewis—Portraits p62-63
Morton—Women p183-191
Nelson—Bible p93-95

Pillini, Margherita (fl. 1880's-1890's)
It. painter
Waters—Women p273

Pillsbury, Elinor (fl. 1920's-1930's)
Amer. journalist
Ross—Ladies p474

Piltz, Maria Puuohau (1877-1932)
    Amer. religious worker
    Phillips—33 p164-167

Pinchot, Ann (1910-   )
    Amer. novelist
    Warfel—Amer. p340-341,por.

Pinckney, Eliza Lucas (1723-1793)
    Eng.-Amer. agriculturist, author
    Beard—Amer. p33-41,86-87
    Brooks—Colonial p103-131
    Bruce—Woman p54-58
    Dexter—Colonial p119-125
    Douglas—Remember p43
    Earle—Colon. p76-83
    Hollingsworth—Her p39-49
    Leonard—Amer. p120
    Logan—Part p106-112
    Longwell—Amer. p56-90
    *McCallum—Women p49-64
    Spruill—Women's p59-60,103-105,
        144-145,157,206,308-311
    Whitton—These p21

Pinckney, Josephine (1895-1957)
    Amer. author
    Warfel—Amer. p341,por.

Pineda, Mariana (1804-1831)
    Span. heroine, martyr, author
    Phila.—Women unp.,por.
    Stiles—Postal p206

Pinero, Dolores M. (fl. 1940's)
    Puert. Ric. physician
    Lovejoy—Women p275

Pinkard, Edna Belle (1892-   )
    Amer. composer, author
    ASCAP p389-390

Pinkerton, Kathrene Sutherand (1887-1967)
    Amer. author
    Cur. Biog. '40 p653-654,por.
    Cur. Biog. '67 p481
    Van Gelder—Writers p208-211

Pinkert, Regina (fl. 1900's-1910's)
    Pol. singer
    Lahee—Grand p126,141-143

Pinney, Eunice (1770-1849)
    Amer. painter
    Lipman—Primitive p22-30

Pinney, Jean Burrows (fl. 1930's)
    Amer. editor, social hygiene worker
    Women—Achieve. p188,por.

Pinochet, Isabel Le Brun (fl. 1870's)
    Chile. educator, foundress
    Schmidt—400 p422,por.

Pinto, Apolonia (b. 1854)
    Brazil. actress
    Stiles—Postal p206

Pinto-Sezzi, Ida (fl. 1880's-1890's)
    It. painter
    Waters—Women p273-274

Piozzi, Hester Lynch Salusbury (1741-
        1821)
    Welsh author, friend of Samuel
        Johnson
    Adelman—Famous p97-98
    DeMorny—Best p224-230,por.
    Dorland—Sum p15
    Hammerton p1095,por.
    Stenton—English p271-315
    Thomson—Queens p341-367

Pipara (fl. 250's-260's)
    Daughter of Attalus, concubine
        of Gallienus
    Serviez—Roman (2) p319-320

Pisan, Christine de (1364-c. 1431)
    Fr. author
    Hammerton p1096
    Koven—Women p67-79,por.
    Mozans—Woman p53,106-108,134-135

Pisaroni, Rosamunda Benedetta (1793-
        1872)
    It. singer
    Pleasants—Great p213-215,por.

Pitcher, Molly (Mary Ludwig Hays
        McCauley) (1750/54-1832)
    Amer. Rev. war heroine
    Adelman—Famous p88
    *Carmer—Caval. p113-115,por.
    DAR Mag. July 1921 p382-383,por.
    *Dolin—World p36-39
    Green—Pioneer (2) p217-223,342
    Hanaford—Dau. p53
    *Horowitz—Treas. p11-14
    *Humphrey—Women p47-54
    Leonard—Amer. p118
    Logan—Part p162-165
    Muir—Women p144-146
    *Nida—Pilots p199-200
    *Stevens—Women p29-32
    Stiles—Postal p178
    *Strong—Of p102-105
    Whitton—These p16-17

Pitkin, Louisa Rochester (fl. 1900's-1910's)
    Amer. club leader
    Logan—Part p432

Pitkin, Martha.
    See Wolcott, Martha Pitkin

Pitt, Anne (fl. 18th cent.)
    Eng. sister of Lord Chatham
    Stenton—English p269-290

Pitt, Rosa Parks (1873-1959)
    Amer. missionary
    Phillips—33 p148-154

Pitts, Carol Marhoff (b. 1888)
    Amer. composer, conductor,
        educator
    McCoy—Portraits p154,por.

Pitts, Zasu (1900-1963)
    Amer. actress
    Cahn—Laugh p120,por.
    CR '59 p591,por.
    TV—Person (3) p26-27,por.

Pitzinger, Gertrude (1906-   )
    Czech. singer
    Ewen—Living p279-280,por.

Pix, Mary Griffith (1666-c. 1720)
    Eng. playwright
    MacQueen—Pope p130-132

Placida, Aelia Galla. See Galla Placidia

Placzek, Mrs. A. K. See Struther, Jan

Planer, Wilhelmina.
    See Wagner, Minna Planer

Plant, Jane (fl. 1930's)
    Amer. aviation instructor
    Planck—Women p159-160,243

Plantin, Arabella (fl. 1720's)
    Eng. novelist
    MacCarthy—Women p249-250

Plassmann, Martha Edgerton (b. 1850)
    Amer. author, W. pioneer
    Binheim—Women p133,por.

Platen, Countess von (fl. 18th cent.)
    Nor. social leader
    Trowbridge—Seven p61-62,por.

Plater, Emilja (1806-1831)
    Pol. soldier, patriot
    Schmidt—400 p324-325,por.

Platt, Aletha Hill (1861-1932)
    Amer. painter
    Michigan—Biog. p251

Platt, Emily (d. 1922)
    Amer., niece of Rutherford B.
        Hayes
    Smith—White p99-103,por.

Platt, Estelle Gertrude (fl. 1930's)
    Amer. singer, teacher, musical
        director
    Women—Achieve. p159,por.

Platz, Josephine. See Lawrence, Josephine

Plautia Urgulanilla (b.c. 84 A.D.)
    Rom. first wife of Claudius
    Balsdon—Roman p92,122

Plautilla (fl. 190-200 A.D.)
    Rom. empress, wife of Caracella
    Serviez—Roman (2) p168-181,189

Player, Willa (1909-   )
    Amer. educator
    °Cherry—Portraits p41-44,por.

Pleasants, "Mammy" E. (d. 1904)
    Amer., friend of John Brown
    Robinson—Hist. p109-110

Pleshette, Suzanne (1937-   )
    Amer. actress
    CR '63 p493,por.

Plessis, Rose Alphonsine.
    See DuPlessis, Marie

Pleyel, Marie Moke (1811-1875)
    Fr. pianist
    Schonberg—Great p192,por.

Plimpton, Hannah R. Cope (b. 1841)
    Amer. club leader
    Logan—Part p356-357

Plisetskaya, Maya Mikhailovna
    (1925/28-   )
    Russ. ballet dancer
    Cur. Biog. '63 p331-333,por.
    Swinson—Great p18,por.

Plongeon, Alice D. le (b. 1851)
    Amer. antiquarian, traveler
    Logan—Part p877

Plotina (d.c. 117 A.D.)
    Rom. empress
    Balsdon—Roman p133-139,194,251,
        257,306
    McCabe—Empr. p136-148,por.
    Serviez.—Roman (1) p360-388

Plowright, Joan (1929-   )
    Eng. actress
    Cur. Biog. '64 p351-353,por.

Plumb, Alma E. (fl. 1920's)
    Amer. educator
    Binheim—Women p126,por.

Plumb, Mrs. L. H. (b. 1841)
    Amer. social reformer, banker
    Logan—Part p899-900

Plumer, Eleanor (fl. 1940's)
    Eng. educator
    Brittain—Women p197,220-221

Plumer, Sally Fowler (fl. 1780's)
    Amer. pioneer, wife of Governor
        Plumer
    Green—Pioneer (3) p397-401,por.

Plummer, Edna Covert (fl. 1910's-1920's)
Amer. lawyer, banker
Irwin—Angels p300

Plummer, Electa Bryan (c. 1842-1912)
Amer. W. pioneer, vigilante
*Johnson—Some p76-79
Towle—Vigil p28-45

Plummer, Mary Elizabeth (fl. 1930's)
Amer. journalist
Ross—Ladies p209-210

Plummer, Mary Wright (1856-1916)
Amer. librarian, author
Bul. of Bibl. Jan.-Apr. '30 p1-3,por.
Marshall—Amer. p456

Plummer, Rachel (fl. 1830's)
Amer. W. pioneer, Indian captive
*Johnson—Some p2-3

Plunkett, Harriette Merrick Hodge
(b. 1826)
Amer. humanitarian, sanitation
reformer
Logan—Part p902-903

Pocahontas (Matoaka) (c. 1595-1617)
Amer. Ind. princess
Adelman—Famous p55-56
Arsenius—Dict. p155,por.
Bonte—Amer. p26-27,por.
*Carmer—Young p11-18
Deen—Great p354-355
Dolin—World p9-11,por.
Fifty—Famous p158-161,por.
Green—Pioneer (1) p9,69-109,por.
Hammerton p1103,por.
Hanaford—Dau. p32-33
Heiderstadt—Indian p3-9,por.
*Horowitz—Treas. p8-10
*Humphrey—Women p1-17
Logan—Part p19
*MacVeagh—Champlin p474
Muir—Women p141-143
Phila.—Women unp.,por.
*Power—More p84-100
Sale—Old p11-20,por.
Schmidt—400 p1,por.
*Stevens—Women p3-6,por.
Stiles—Postal p209
*Strong—Of p66-68

Poe, Elizabeth Arnold (d. 1811)
Eng. actress, mother of
Edgar Allen Poe
Coad—Amer. p66,por.

Poetting, Adrienne, Countess (b. 1856)
Bohem. painter
Waters—Women p274

Poinso-Chapuis, Germaine (1901-   )
Fr. government official
Cur. Biog. '48 p499-500,por.

Pointer, Augusta L. (1898-   )
Amer. sculptor
National—Contemp. p259

Pointevin, Madame (fl. 19th cent.)
Fr. parachutist
*May—Women p49

Pointing, Audrey (m. 1933)
Eng. dancer
Wyndham—Chorus p147

Poisson, Jeanne.
See Pompadour, Jeanne Antoinette
Poisson, Marquise de

Poitiers, Diane, Duchess de Valentinois
(1499-1566)
Fr., mistress of Francis I, Henry II
De Morny—Best p11-22,por.
Haggard—Remark. p15-17
Mayne—Enchant. p1-17,por.

"Poker Alice." See Tubbs, Alice Ivers

"Pola, La." See Salavarrieta, Policarpa

Polak, Jessamine, Baroness von Elsner
(b. 1869)
Amer. singer
Logan—Part p767

Polak, Mille Graham (n.d.)
Scot., Gandhi co-worker
Stern—Women p74-85

Polastron, Countess de.
See Polignac, Yolande Martine
Gabrielle de Polastron

Pole, Elizabeth. See Poole, Elizabeth

Poli-Gardner, Madame (fl. 1930's)
Fr. physician
Lovejoy—Women p256-257

Polignac, Yolande Martine Gabrielle de
Polastron, Duchess of (c. 1749-
1793)
Fr., friend of Marie Antoinette
Kavanagh—Woman p53-58
Trowbridge—Seven p249-279,por.

Polivanova, M. S. (fl. 1940's)
Russ. soldier, heroine
Stiles—Postal p210

Polk, Grace Porterfield (fl. 1940's)
Amer. composer, singer
McCoy—Portraits p156,por.

Polk, Sarah Childress (1803-1891)
Amer., wife of James K. Polk
Farmer—What p83,141-142
Gerlinger—Mis. p38-40,por.

(Continued)

Polk, Sarah Childress—*Continued*

    Hanaford—Dau. p86-87
    Jensen—White p69-70,por.
    Logan—Ladies p63-67
    Logan—Part p242-244
    *McConnell—Our p123-130,por.
    Means—Woman p74-93,por.,cover
    Prindiville—First p108-113
    Ross—Know p25,por.
    Smith—Romances p152-163,por.
    Truett—First p32-33,por.
    Whitton—First p200-217,por.

Polko, Elise Vogel (1823-1899)
    Ger. novelist, singer
    Dorland—Sum p42

Poll, Ruth (1899-   )
    Amer. author, song-writer
    ASCAP p391

Pollak, Anna (1915-   )
    Eng. singer
    Davidson—Treas. p228-231

Pollard, Carrie Wilkins (fl. 1860's)
    Amer. Civil war nurse
    Logan—Part p372

Pollard, Josephine (c. 1840-1892)
    Amer. journalist, author
    Dorland—Sum p36,117

Pollock, Anna. See Marble, Anna

Pollock, Louise (b. 1832)
    Amer. educator
    Logan—Part p712-713

Pollock, Mary B. (fl. 1860's)
    Amer. Civil war nurse
    Logan—Part p372

Pollock, Muriel (fl. 1930's)
    Amer. composer, pianist, organist
    ASCAP p392

Pollock, Roberta (fl. 1860's)
    Amer. Civil war heroine
    Andrews—Women p148-154

Polykoff, Shirley (fl. 1930's)
    Amer. advertising executive
    Women—Achieve. p124,por.

Pomeroy, Genie Clark (b. p1867)
    Amer. poet
    Logan—Part p826-827

Pomeroy, Lucy Gaylord(d. 1863)
    Amer. Civil war humanitarian
    Brockett—Woman's p691-696

Pompadour, Jeanne Antoinette Poisson,
    Marquise de (1720/21-1764)
    Fr., mistress of Louis XV
    Abbott—Notable p238-242,por.
    Adelman—Famous p76-77
    Armour—It p79-86
    Club—Printing p8
    Dark—More p177-198
    Dorland—Sum p18
    Haggard—Remark. p311-321,326-328,
      330-337,339-349
    Hammerton p1107,por.
    *Humphrey—Janes p82-102
    Kavanagh—Woman (1) p207-222,por.
    Kemble—Idols p69-75
    *MacVeagh—Champlin p477
    Muir—Women p115-119
    100 Great p169-174
    Russell—Glit. p177-182,por.

Pompeia (fl.c. 61 B.C.)
    Rom., 3rd wife of Julius Caesar
    Hammerton p1107

Pompeia, Paulina (fl. 60's A.D.)
    Rom., wife of Lucius Annaeus
    Seneca
    Boccaccio—Conc. p212-213

Pomponia Graecina (c. 43 A.D.)
    Rom. wife of Aulus Plautius
    Balsdon—Roman p248

Ponce de Leon, Dona Inés De.
    See De Ponce de Leon, Dona Inés

Pond, Cora Scott (b. 1856)
    Amer. philanthropist
    Logan—Part p540

Pond, Nellie Brown (b. 1858)
    Amer. actress
    Logan—Part p746

Ponisi, Elizabeth (1818-1899)
    Eng. actress
    Coad—Amer. p215,por.

Pons, Lily (1904-   )
    Fr.-Amer. singer
    CA '59 p592,por.
    CR '63 p494,por.
    Cur. Biog. '44 p546-548,por.
    Davidson—Treas. p231-233
    Eichberg—Radio p102-103,por.
    Ewen—Ency. p401
    Ewen—Living p281-282,por.
    Ewen—Men p41-47,por.
    McCoy—Portraits p156,por.
    Matz—Opera p207-210,por.
    New Yorker Jan.16,1932 p20,por.
    (Profiles)
    O'Connell—Other p17-33
    Peltz—Spot. p75,por.
    Rosenthal—Sopranos p78-79,por.

(Continued)

Pons, Lily—*Continued*

> Time Oct.17,1932 p37,por;
> Dec. 30, 1940 p30 (Covers)
> *Ulrich—Famous p103-108,por.
> Wagner—Prima p172,246
> Women—Achieve. p56,por.

Ponselle (Ponzillo), Carmela (1892-   )
> Amer. singer
> Ewen—Ency. p401-402
> Ewen—Living p282-283,por.
> McCoy—Portraits p156,por.

Ponselle (Ponzillo), Rosa Melba (1897-   )
> Amer. singer
> Davidson—Treas. p233-236
> Ewen—Ency. p402
> Ewen—Living p283-284,por.
> Hammerton p1107-1108
> McCoy—Portraits p156,por.
> Pleasants—Great p297-300,por.
> Time Nov.9,1931 p26,por.(Cover)
> Wagner—Prima p165,246

Ponsonby, Sarah (c. 1745-1831)
> Irish recluse
> Hammerton p1108

Pontes, Maria Rita. See Dulce, Sister

Ponzillo. See Ponselle, Rosa Melba

Pool, Maria Louise (1841-1898)
> Amer. novelist
> Dorland—Sum p52,197-198

Poole, Barbara (fl. 1930's)
> Amer. aviatrix
> Planck—Women p175-177

Poole, Edna (fl. 1930's-1950's)
> Amer. missionary
> They—Went p95-96

Poole (Pole), Elizabeth (1599-1654)
> Amer. colonial foundress
> Bell—Women p324-328
> Bruce—Woman p24-25
> Dexter—Colonial p103
> Earle—Colon. p51
> Farmer—What p37
> Leonard—Amer. p120

Poole, Fannie Huntington Runnells
> (fl. 1910's)
> Amer. poet, book reviewer
> Logan—Part p848

Pope, Amy Elizabeth (fl. 1890's-1900's)
> Can.-Amer. nurse
> Pennock—Makers p110,por.

Pope, Edith (1905-   )
> Amer. novelist
> Warfel—Amer. p343-344,por.

Pope, Jane (1742-1818)
> Eng. actress
> Dorland—Sum p36
> MacQueen—Pope p288-294,por.

Pope, Mildred Katharine (gr. 1893)
> Eng. teacher
> Brittain—Women (see index)

Pope, Sarah Lloyd Moore Ewing (fl. 1890's)
> Amer. club leader
> Logan—Part p470-471

Popelinière, Madame de la (fl. 18th cent.)
> Fr. foundress, art patron
> Kavanagh—Woman (1) p94-96

Popert, Charlotte (b. 1848)
> Ger. painter
> Waters—Women p274

Popkin, Zelda (1898-   )
> Amer. novelist
> Cur. Biog. '51 p492-494,por.
> Warfel—Amer. p344,por.

Popp, Babette (1800-c. 1840)
> Ger. painter
> Waters—Women p275

Poppaea Sabina, the elder (fl. 30's-60's)
> Rom., wife of Otho
> Balsdon—Roman p103-107,124-125
> Serviez—Roman (1) p307

Poppaea Sabina, the younger (d. 65/66 A.D.)
> Rom. empress, wife of Nero
> Balsdon—Roman p49,107-109,115,124-
> 129,195,251,258
> Hammerton p1109
> McCabe—Empr. p99,107-108,110-117,
> por.
> Serviez—Roman (1) p253-282

Poppe-Lüderitz, Elizabeth (b. 1858)
> Ger. painter
> Waters—Women p274-275

Poppenheim, Mrs. C. C. (fl. 1860's)
> Amer. Civil war patriot
> Andrews—Women p246-256

Poppenheim, Mary B. (1866-1936)
> Amer., organization official
> Logan—Part p384-385

"Poppy Lady." See Michael, Moina

Porcia (d. 42 B.C.)
> Rom., daughter of Marcus Cato
> Balsdon—Roman p50-51,59
> Boccaccio—Conc. p181-182

Poree, Caroline E. (b. 1842)
> Amer. librarian
> Logan—Part p296

Porphyrogenita, Zoë (978-1050)
    Byzant. empress, wife of Romanus
    Diehl—Portraits p231-275

Porter, Catherine (fl. 1920's-1930's)
    Amer. editor
    Women—Achieve. p54,por.

Porter, Charlotte Endymion (b. 1859)
    Amer. editor, poet
    Logan—Part p830

Porter, Delia Lyman (d. 1933)
    Amer. social reformer
    Logan—Part p841

Porter, Eleanor Hodgman (d. 1920)
    Amer. novelist
    Maurice—Makers p5,por.
    Overton—Women p262-264

Porter, Eliza C. (fl. 1860's)
    Amer. Civil war nurse, foundress
    Brockett—Woman's p161-171
    Logan—Part p311

Porter, Elizabeth Kerr (1894-   )
    Amer. organization official, nurse
    Curr. Biog. '52 p475-477,por.

Porter, Gene Stratton (1868-1924)
    Amer. author, ornithologist
    Adelman—Famous p273
    Hammerton p1110,por.
    Maurice—Makers p10,por.
    Overton—Authors p144-166
    Overton—Women p312-314

Porter, Jane (1776-1850)
    Eng. novelist
    Dorland—Sum p18,196
    Hammerton p1110,por.
    *MacVeagh—Champlin p479

Porter, Katherine Anne (1890/94-   )
    Amer. author
    Auchincloss—Pion. p136-151
    Burnett—This p1152-1153
    CR '59 p593,por.
    CR '63 p495,por.
    Cur. Biog. '40 p657-658,por.
    Cur. Biog. '63 p337-340,por.
    Millett—Amer. p528-529
    Van Gelder—Writers p42-44
    *Witham—Pan. p311-314,por.
    Writers—Paris p137-163,por.

Porter, Mary Ann (c. 1681-1765)
    Eng. actress
    Dorland—Sum p51,167
    MacQueen—Pope p159-161

Porter, Milicent.
    See Camp, Milicent Baldwin Porter

Porter, Mrs. (fl. 1780's)
    Amer. pioneer, heroine
    Fowler—Woman p93-94

Porter, Ruth Stephens (fl. 1940's)
    Amer. composer
    McCoy—Portraits p157,por.

Porter, Sarah.
    See Hillhouse, Sarah Porter

Porter, Sylvia Field Feldman (1913-   )
    Amer. journalist, financial
      columnist, author
    CR '59 p593-594,por.
    CR '63 p495,por.
    Cur. Biog. '41 p679-681,por.
    Time Nov.28,1960 p46,por.(Cover)

Portia. See Porcia

Portinari, Beatrice. See Beatrice Portinari

Portland, Margaret Harley, Duchess of
    (fl. 1730's)
    Eng. hostess
    Stenton—English p243-244,262,272

Portsmouth, Duchess of.
    See Kéroualle, Louise Renée de,
      Duchess of Portsmouth and Aubigny

Portuondo, Josephine B. Thomas (b. 1867)
    Amer. author
    Logan—Part p821

Possadnitza, Marfa (fl. 1910's)
    Russ. war heroine
    Dorland—Sum p98

Possanner-Ehrenthal, Garbrielle (gr. 1893)
    Aust. pioneer physician
    Lovejoy—Women p195

Posselt, Ruth (1916-   )
    Amer. violinist
    McCoy—Portraits p157,por.

Post, Amalia Barney Simons (m. 1864)
    Amer. feminist
    Logan—Part p588

Post, Cornelia S. (fl. 1860's)
    Amer. artist
    Hanaford—Dau. p301

Post, Emily Price (1873-1960)
    Amer. author, etiquette authority
    CR '59 p594-595,por.
    Cur. Biog. '41 p681-683,por.
    Cur. Biog. '60 p318
    New Yorker Aug.16,1930 p22-25,por.
    (Profiles)
    Women—Achieve. p76,por.

Post, Parthenia A. ((fl. 1880's)
    Amer. needlework artist
    Hanaford—Dau. p301

Postgate, Margaret J. (fl. 1920's)
    Amer. sculptor
    National Contemp. p264

Pote, Louise (fl. 1930's)
    Amer. aviatrix, aerial photographer
    Planck—Women p186-187

Potiphar's wife (Biblical)
    Deen—All p45-48
    Horton—Women p64-74
    Lewis—Portraits p143-144
    Lofts—Women p42-50
    Morton—Women p51-57

Potter, Beatrix (c. 1866-1943)
    Eng. author, artist, agriculturist
    Cur. Biog. '44 p548
    De Morny—Best p214-218
    *Green—Authors p44-49,por.

Potter, Mrs. Brown (fl. 1890's)
    Eng. actress
    Furniss—Some p63-64,por.

Potter, Ellen Culver (1871-1958)
    Amer. physician, public health
        worker
    Lovejoy—Women p380-381

Potter, Hester (fl. 1930's)
    Amer. journalist
    Ross—Ladies p460-461

Potter, Margaret Horton (1881-1911)
    Amer. novelist
    Logan—Part p861

Potter, Marguerite (fl. 1930's)
    Amer. singer
    Women—Achieve. p116,por.

Potter, Marion Craig (fl. 1930's)
    Amer. physician, gynecologist
    Women—Achieve. p202

Potter, Mrs. (fl. 1770's)
    Amer. Rev. war heroine
    Ellet—Women (1) p334-337

Potts, Anna M. Longshore (b. 1829)
    Amer. physician
    Logan—Part p742

Pouch, Helena R. (fl. 1890's-1930's)
    Amer. humanitarian, club leader
    Women—Achieve. p128,por.

Pougy, Liane de (Anne de Chassaigne)
        (fl. 19th cent.)
    Fr. courtesan
    Skinner—Elegant p231-237,por.

Poulett, Muriel, Countess of.
    See Ross, Oriel

Poulsson, Ann Emile (1853-1939)
    Amer. editor, author, illustrator
    Logan—Part p850

Powdermaker, Hortense (1900-   )
    Amer. anthropologist
    Cur. Biog. '61 p372-373,por.

Powell, Alma Webster (1874-1930)
    Amer. singer
    McCoy—Portraits p157,por.

Powell, Caroline Amelia (b. 1852)
    Irish illustrator
    Waters—Women p275

Powell, Cecile V. K. (fl. 1930's)
    Amer. radio personality
    Women—Achievement p156,por.

Powell, Dawn (Mrs. Joseph R. Gousha)
        (1900-   )
    Amer. author
    Mantle—Contemp. p322
    Van Gelder—Writers p132-134
    Warfel—Amer. p344-345,por.

Powell, Eleanor (1913-   ) TV
    Amer. dancer, actress, TV
        personality
    CR '63 p496,por.

Powell, Elizabeth M. (fl. 1870's)
    Amer. clergyman
    Hanaford—Dau. p476

Powell, Jane (c. 1928-   )
    Amer. singer, actress
    CR '59 p597,por.

Powell, Maud (1868-1920)
    Amer. violinist
    Adelman—Famous p262
    Dorland—Sum p160
    McCoy—Portraits p157,por.
    *Moore—When p140-146

Powell, Minna K. (fl. 1920's)
    Amer. journalist
    Ross—Ladies p572-575

Power, Edith Crane (b. 1869)
    Austral. actress
    Moses—Famous p307,por.

Power, Eileen (1889-1940)
    Eng. historian
    Hammerton p1111,por.

Power, Marguerite.
    See Blessinger, Marguerite Power,
        Countess of

Powers, Ada Weigel (fl. 1940's)
Amer. composer, pianist
McCoy—Portraits p157,por.

Powers, Lucy Gaylord (fl. 1860's)
Amer. Civil war patriot,
humanitarian
Hanaford—Dau. p209-210
Logan—Part p314

Powers, Marie (n.d.)
Amer. singer
Cur. Biog. '51 p494-495,por.

Powers, Mary Bullock ("Cousin Mamie")
(c. 1878-1948)
Amer. recluse
Erskine—Out p144-160

Powers, Rose Mills (fl. 1920's)
Amer. poet
Smith—Women's p165

Pownall, Mary Ann (Mary Ann Wrighton)
(1751-1796)
Amer. actress, singer, composer
Coad—Amer. p47,por.
Howard—Our p108-109

Praecia (fl. c. 78 B.C.)
Rom. courtesan, beauty
Baldsdon—Roman p53

Praed, Rosa Caroline Mackworth (1851-
1935)
Austral. novelist
Hammerton p1112
Roderick—20 p1-21

Prang, Mary Dana Hicks (b. 1836)
Amer. author, editor, art educator
Logan—Part p719

Pratt, Anne (1806-1893)
Eng. botanist
Dorland—Sum p22,150

Pratt, Elizabeth (b. 1750)
Amer. patriot
Green—Pioneer (2) p208-218

Pratt, Gladys Lynwall (fl. 1930's)
Amer. explorer, museum patron
Women—Achieve. p202

Pratt, Harriet Barnes (1910's-1930's)
Amer. horticulturist
Women—Achieve. p115,por.

Pratt, Mrs. Harry Rogers.
See Rothery, Agnes Edwards

Pratt, Malinda A. Miller (fl. 1860's)
Amer. Civil war nurse
Logan—Part p372

Pratt, Margaret (fl. 1740's-1760's)
Amer. colonial proprietor
Dexter—Colonial p8

Pratt, Ruth Sears Baker (1877-1965)
Amer. Congresswoman
New Yorker Apr. 24,1926 p21,por.
(Cover)
Paxton—Women p10-11,130

Pratz, Claire de (fl. 1900's-1910's)
Anglo-Fr. novelist
Hammerton p1112

Praxedes Carty, Mother (d. 1963)
Irish-Amer. nun
Logan—Part p618

Praxilla (fl.c. 450 B.C.)
Gr. poet, musician
Anthologia—Poets p81-82
Drinker—Music p103-104

Pray, Ada Jordan (fl. 1940's)
Amer. composer, pianist, teacher,
lecturer
McCoy—Portraits p157,por.

Pré, Julia du (fl. 1880's)
Amer. artist
Hanaford—Dau. p307-308

"Precious Pearl" (b. 1615)
Chin. empress
Llewellyn—China's p151-157

Predmore, Jessie (1896-   )
Amer. artist
Janis—They p213-215,por.

Prellwitz, Edith Mitchell (b. 1865)
Amer. painter
Michigan—Biog. p256

Prentice, Mrs. John (d. 1691)
Amer. colonial proprietor
Dexter—Colonial p5

Prentice, Marion (fl. 1910's-1920's)
Amer. composer, director, music
teacher
McCoy—Portraits p158,por.

Prentiss, Elizabeth Payson (1818-1878)
Amer. hymn writer
Deen—Great p305-306
Dorland—Sum p50,185,188

Prentiss, Harriet Doan (fl. 1930's)
Amer. poet, club leader
Women—Achieve. p79,por.

Prentiss, Henrietta (1880-1940)
Amer. educator, speech authority
Cur. Biog. '40 p662-663,por.

Prentiss, Paula (1939-   )
Amer. actress
CR '63 p498,por.

Prentner, Marie (fl. 1940's)
Aust. composer, violinist
McCoy—Portraits p158,por.

Preobrajenska, Olga (b. 1871)
Russ. ballet dancer
*Terry—Star p111,por.

Prescott, Hilda Frances Margaret (1896-)
Eng. novelist
Brittain—Women p126,223,251

Prescott, Rebecca.
See Sherman, Rebecca Prescott

Prestel, Maria Catharine (b. 1747)
Ger. artist
Waters—Women p275-276

Prestel, Ursula Magdalena (1777-1845)
Ger. painter
Waters—Women p276

Preston, Alice Bolam (1889-   )
Amer. illustrator
Mahony—Illus. p348-349

Preston, Ann (1813-1872)
Amer. pioneer physician
Adelman—Famous p184-185
Hanaford—Dau. p558-560
Irwin—Angels p43,49,133
Logan—Part p742
Lovejoy—Women p31-40,por.
Mead—Medical p26-29,por.

Preston, Frances Folsom Cleveland (1864-
1947)
Amer., wife of Grover Cleveland
Adelman—Famous p299-300
Sickels—Twelve p72-88,252-253

Preston, Lizzie (fl. 1870's)
Amer. W. pioneer
Parkhill—Wildest p14,56-58

Preston, Margaret Junkin (1820-1897)
Amer. Civil war letter-writer, poet
Logan—Part p811-812
Simkins—Women p223,247

Preston, Margaret Wickliffe (b. 1819)
Amer. pioneer
Logan—Part p69

Preston, Matilee Loeb- (fl. 1940s)
Amer. composer, cornetist
McCoy—Portraits p158,por.

Preston, May Wilson (1873-1949)
Amer. illustrator
Michigan—Biog. p257

Preuschen, Hermine von Schmidt (b. 1857)
Ger. painter
Waters—Women p276-277

Preuse, Madame E.
See Matzenauer, Margarete

Prévost, Françoise (1680-1741)
Fr. ballet dancer
*Terry—Star p22-25,por.

Prevost, Marie (d. 1934)
Can.-Amer. actress
Herman—How p125,por.

Prevost, Theodosia.
See Burr, Theodosia Provost Alston

Price, Eugenia (fl. 1950's)
Eng. author
Edman—They p114-119

Price, Florence B. Smith (1888-1953)
Amer. composer, pianist, organist,
educator
ASCAP p395
McCoy—Portraits p158,por.

Price, Goditha (fl. 17th cent.)
Eng. maid of honor
Melville—Windsor p129-133

Price, Hattie Longstreet (1891-   )
Amer. illustrator
Mahony—Illus. p349

Price, Joan Meakin (fl. 1930's)
Eng. glider pilot
*May—Women p221

Price, (Mary) Leontyne (1927-   )
Amer. singer
*Cherry—Portraits p82-84
CR '63 p500,por.
Cur. Biog. '61 p374-375,por.
Robinson—Hist. p239,por.
*Rollins—Enter. p87-93,por.
Time Mar.10,1961 p.58,por.(Cover)

Price, Margaret Bayne (1912-   )
Amer. politician
Parshalle—Kash. p141-143,por.

Price, Margaret Evans (b. 1888)
Amer. illustrator
Mahony—Illus. p349

Price, Mrs. (fl. 1670's-1680's)
Eng. actress
Wilson—All p182-183

Price, Rebecca L. (fl. 1860's)
Amer. Civil war nurse
Logan—Part p370

Prichard, Katharine Susannah (b. 1884)
Austral. author
Hetherington—42 p7-11,por.
Millett—Brit. p422-423

Prichard, Maude Hancock (b. 1876)
Amer. educator
Binheim—Women p149,por.

Prie, Jeanne Agnes Berthelot de Pléneuf,
Marquise de (1698-1727)
Fr., mistress of Bourbon
Haggard—Remark. p215-243
Kavanagh—Woman (1) p68-71
Trowbridge—Seven p7-15,por.

Priest, Ivy Baker (1905-   )
Amer. government official,
organization official, politician
CR '59 p600-601,por.
CR '63 p500-501,por.
Cur. Biog. '52 p477-479,por.
*Forsee—Women p101-126
Parshalle—Kash. p201-202,por.
Roosevelt—Ladies p247-252

Prigosen, Rosa Elizabeth (fl. 1930's)
Amer. bacteriologist, pediatrician
*Fleischman—Careers p456
Women—Achieve. p88,por.

Priley, Margaret Ann.
See Hubbard, Margaret Ann

Prim, Mary Elizabeth (fl. 1930's)
Amer. journalist
Ross—Ladies p485-486

Primus, Pearl (1919-   )
Brit. W. Ind. dancer
*Cherry—Portraits p112-116
CR '59 p602,por.
CR '63 p501,por.
Cur. Biog. '44 p551-553,por.

Prince, Joanna (fl. 18th-19th cent.)
Amer. religious worker
Hanaford—Dau. p635

Prince, Mary (fl. 1650's)
Amer. colonial religious worker
Jones—Quakers p36-39,46

Pringle, Angélique Lucille (1846-1920)
Brit. pioneer nurse
Cope—Six p35-46,por.

Pringle, Mary (b. 1833)
Amer. Civil war nurse
Logan—Part p333

Printemps, Yvonne (fl. 1910's-1930's)
Fr. actress, singer
Hammerton p1115
New Yorker Dec.18,1926 p29,por.
(Profiles)

Printz, Armegot (d. 1695)
Swed.-Amer. heiress, landowner
Burt—Phila. p31

Prior, Margaret B. (b. 1773)
Amer. philanthropist
Hanaford—Dau. p153-155

Prisca (1). See Priscilla

Prisca (Serena) (2) (fl. 310's A.D.)
Rom. empress, wife of Diocletian
Serviez—Roman (2) (see index)

Priscilla (Biblical)
Barker—Saints p13-21
Buchanan—Women p103-106
Culver—Women p55,57-60
Deen—All p227-230
Faulhaber—Women p198-204
Hammerton p104,1115
Lewis—Portraits p56-57
Lord—Great p185-196
Marble—Women Bible p220-223
Mead—250 p239
Nelson—Bible p111-114
Van Der Velde—She p242-249
Wescott—Calen. p9

Pritchard, Esther Tuttle (b. 1840)
Amer. editor, teacher
Logan—Part p737-738

Pritchard, Hannah Vaughan (1711-1768)
Eng. actress
Dorland—Sum p54,166
MacQueen—Pope p199-203,por.
Melville—Stage p111-122,por.

Proba, Anicia Faltonia (fl. 368-375)
Rom. poet, patriot
Blunt—Great p30-32,397-398

Prochazka, Anne (1897-   )
Amer. orthopedic nurse
*Yost—Nursing p135-154

Procla, Julia (fl. 230's-280's)
Rom. empress, wife of Probus
Serviez—Roman (2) p365

Procter, Adelaide Anne (1825-1864)
Eng. poet
Adelman—Famous p165
Dorland—Sum p19,179
Hammerton p1115
Parton—Dau. p213-218,por.
Parton—Noted p213-218,por.

Procter, Evelyn (gr. 1918)
Eng. educator
Brittain—Women p144,188,208,216,
245

Procter, Mary (fl. 1910's)
Amer. astronomer
Dorland—Sum p143

Proctor, Nina Gregory (fl. 1930's)
Amer. club leader
Women—Achieve. p56,por.

Proffitt, Josephine. See Dee, Sylvia

Prohme, Rayna (fl. 1920's)
Amer. journalist
Ross—Ladies p588

Prosper, Joan Dareth (fl. 1920's)
Amer. poet
Smith—Women's p168

Prosser, Anna Weed (b. 1866)
Amer. evangelist, missionary
Logan—Part p738

Prouty, Olive Higgins (b. 1882)
Amer. novelist
Overton—Women p265-268
Warfel—Amer. p348-349,por.

Provine, Dorothy (1937-   )
Amer. dancer, singer, TV
personality
CR '63 p501-502,por.

Provines, June (fl. 1920's-1930's)
Amer. journalist
Ross—Ladies p397-398

Provoost, Maria de Peyster Schrick Spratt
(Maria Spratt; Maria De Peyster)
(d. 1700)
Amer. colonial merchant
Dexter—Colonial p104-105
Green—Pioneer (1) p188,191-193
Leonard—Amer. p120

Prowse, Juliet (1936-   )
Brit. dancer
CR '63 p502,por.

Pruette, Lorine Livingston (1896-   )
Amer. psychologist, author
Women—Achieve. p202

Pruit, Willie Franklin (b. 1865)
Amer. philanthropist
Logan—Part p544

Pruszynska, Aniela (b. 1888)
Pol. illustrator
Mahony—Illus. p350

Pry, Polly (fl. 1870's-1890's)
Amer. journalist
Ross—Ladies p562-564

Pryor, Sara Rice (1830-1912)
Amer. Civil war heroine, author,
social leader
Jones—Heroines p265-270,313-316,
por.
Logan—Part p434-435
Simkins—Women p104,152-154,182,
184,221,245-246
Young—Women p29,31-32,37, 40-41,
330-331

Psibiliauskas, Sofija Ivanauskas (1867-1926)
Lith. author
Schmidt—400 p281-283,por.

Puah (Biblical)
Deen—All p289
Lewis—Portraits p212-213

Puehn, Sophie (b. 1864)
Ger. painter
Waters—Women p277

Pugh, Esther (fl. 1880's)
Amer. social reformer, publisher
Hanaford—Dau. p427

Pugh, Mary Williams (fl. 1860's)
Amer. Civil war diarist
Jones—Heroines p182-191

Pulcheria (Aelia Pulcheria Augustus)
(399-453 A.D.)
Byzant. empress
Beard—Woman p299-300
Culver—Women p80
Deen—Great p316-318
Englebert—Lives p345-346
McCabe—Empr. p317,332-339,por.

Pulitzer, Margaret Leetch.
See Leech, Margaret Kernochan

Pullman, Harriet Sanger (m. 1866)
Amer. humanitarian, philanthropist
Logan—Part p303

Purbeck, Frances Coke Villiers, Viscountess
(d. 1645)
Eng. hostess
Stenton—English p67

Purcell, Elinor (fl. 1750's)
Amer. colonial art teacher
Dexter—Colonial p93-94

Purcell, Mary (fl. 1750's-1770's)
Amer. colonial merchant
Dexter—Colonial p35-36

Purdy, Grace Bronson (fl. 1930's)
Amer. humanitarian
Women—Achieve. p118,por.

Pusey, Katrina (fl. 1930's)
Amer. aviatrix
Planck—Women p182-183

Putnam, Amelia. See Earhart, Amelia

Putnam, Brenda (1889/90-   )
Amer. sculptor
*Ferris—Girls p228-236
Jackman—Amer. p450-451
National—Contemp. p262
Taft—Women, Mentor (172) #2 p10

Putnam, Deborah Lothrop (1719-1777)
Amer. Rev. war patriot
Green—Pioneer (2) p124-130
Root—Chapter p136-148

Putnam, Elizabeth Porter.
See Perley, Elizabeth Porter Putnam

Putnam, Emily James (b. 1865)
Amer. author, educator
Adelman—Famous p301

Putnam, Georgiana Frances (1839-1914)
Amer. teacher
Brown—Home. p135-140

Putnam, Mary.
See Jacobi, Mary Corinna Putnam

Putnam, Mary Steiner (fl. 1910's)
Amer. club leader
Logan—Part p461

Putnam, Mary T. S. L. (1810-1898)
Amer. author
Adelman—Famous p177
Dorland—Sum p23,82

Putnam, Sarah Goold (fl. 1900's)
Amer. painter
Waters—Women p277-278

Putnam, Susannah French (fl. 1770's)
Amer. Rev. war humanitarian
Green—Pioneer (3) p522

Puyroche-Wagner, Elise (1828-1895)
Ger. painter
Waters—Women p278

Pyle, Gladys (fl. 1930s)
Amer. senator
Paxton—Women p130

Pyle, Katherine (d. 1938)
Amer. author, illustrator
Logan—Part p842

Pyles, Charlotta Gordon (1806-1880)
Amer. social reformer
Brown—Home. p34-45,por.

Pyne, Mable Mandeville (1903-   )
Amer. illustrator
Mahony—Illus. p350

Q

Quackenbush, Nancy.
See Van Alstyne, Nancy

Quant, Mary (1934-   )
Eng. fashion designer
Cur. Biog. '68 p322-325,por.

Queens. See names of queens

Queensberry, Catherine Hyde ("Kitty"),
Duchess of (d. 1777)
Brit. hostess
Graham—Group p128-148,por.
Stenton—English p253

Quellerie (Quellerius), Marie de la (1629-
1654/66)
S. Afr., wife of Jan van Riebeeck
Phila.—Women unp.,por.
Stiles—Postal p214

Querouaille, Louise.
See Kérouaille, Louise Renée de,
Duchess of Portsmouth and Aubigny

Questier, Catherine (fl. 1650's)
Nether. engraver, author
Waters—Women p278

Quezon, Aurora Aragon (1889-1949)
Phil. patriot, wife of Manuel
Quezon
Phila.—Women unp.,por.
Stiles—Postal p214

Quick, Alice (fl. 1750's-1760's)
Amer. colonial merchant
Dexter—Colonial p35

Quick, Dorothy (c. 1895-1962)
Amer. poet
Wagenkencht—When p193-199
Women—Achieve. p69,por.

Quick, Hazel Irene (gr. 1915)
Amer. engineer
Goff—Women p88-93

Quiggle, Dorothy (1903-   )
Amer. chem. engineer
Goff—Women p82-87

Quigley, Janet (fl. 1950's)
Eng. radio, TV editor
Winn—Queen's p157,159-174,por.

Quimby, Edith Hinckley (1891-   )
Amer. biophysicist, educator
Cur. Biog. '49 p492-493,por.
Women—Achieve. p131,por.
*Yost—Women Mod. p94-107,por.

Quimby, Harriet (1884-1912)
Amer. pioneer aviatrix
*Adams—Sky p3-26,por.
Dorland—Sum p101-102
Earhart—Fun p181-184,por.
Heinmuller—Man's p290,por.
Logan—Part p301
Maitland—Knights p160-161
*May—Women p66-69,por.
Planck—Women p18-24,por.

Quin, Mary. See O'Donnell, Mary King

Quinault, Mademoiselle (fl. 18th cent.)
Fr. actress
Kavanagh—Woman (1) p152

Quinby, Cordelia Adeline (fl. 1880's)
Amer. philanthropist
Hanaford—Dau. p182-183

Quincy, Abigail Phillips (m. 1769)
Amer. patriot
Green—Pioneer (3) p482-483

Quincy, Dorothy.
See Hancock, Dorothy Quincy

Quiner, Joanna (1796-1869)
Amer. sculptor
Hanaford—Dau. p320

Quinlan, Agnes Clune (d. 1949)
Irish composer, pianist, teacher,
lecturer, author
McCoy—Portraits p160,por.

Quinn, Carmel (1930-   )
Irish singer, TV personality
TV—Person (2) p92

Quinn, Edel (1907-1944)
Irish missionary, nun
Burton—Valiant p129-146
Graef—Mystics p195-216

Quinton, Amelia Stone (fl. 1870's-1880's)
Amer. humanitarian, club leader
Farmer—What p294,por.
Logan—Part p407

Quiroga, Margarita.
See Solis Quiroga, Margarita Delgado
de

Quisling, Maria (fl. 1940's)
Ger. spy
Singer—World's p128-139

Quiteria de Jesus Medeiros, Maria (d. 1853)
Brazil. heroine
Stiles—Postal p214

Quoirez, Françoise.
See Sagan, Françoise

R

Raab, Doris (b. 1851)
Ger. painter
Waters—Women p278

Raabe (Niemann-Raabe), Hedwig (1844-
1905)
Ger. actress
Dorland—Sum p48,71,166

Rabinoff, Sophie (1888-1957)
Russ.-Amer. physician
*Knapp—Women p123-136,por.
Women—Achieve. p95,por.

Rachel (1) (Biblical)
wife of Jacob
Buchanan—Women p20-23
Davenport—Great p54-56
Deen—All p28-36
Faulhaber—Women p26-44
Hammerton p1123
Horton—Women p48-63
Hughes—Mothers p65-75
*Levinger—Great p20-25
Lewis—Portraits p37-41
Lofts—Women p32-41
Lord—Great p35-46
MacCartney—Great p136-151
*MacVeagh—Champlin p486
Marble—Women p130-133
Mead—250 p29
Morton—Women p43-49
Ockenga—Women p29-42
Orr—Famous Affin. III p171-186
Pattee—Fem. p159
Schmidt—400 p264-265
Stiles—Postal p214
Van der Velde p53-57

Rachel (2) (Biblical)
wife of Akiba
*Levinger—Great p90-96

Rachel (3) (Elizabeth Rachel Felix)
(1821-1858)
Fr.-Swiss actress
Adelman—Famous p147-149
Coad—Amer. p210,por.
Dorland—Sum p42,165
Eaton—Actor's p136-154,por.
Hammerton p1123,por.
*Levinger—Great p117-120
*MacVeagh—Champlin p486-487
Orr—Famous p357-368
Parton—Dau. p362-371
Parton—Noted p425-434,por.
Stiles—Postal p214

Radcliffe, Ann Ward 176?-1823)
Eng. novelist
Adelman—Famous p106-107
Dorland—Sum p54,192
Hammerton p1124
Johnson—Women p54-59
MacCarthy—Later p162-182
*MacVeagh—Champlin p487

Radcliffe, Eleanor.
See Sussex, Eleanor, Countess of Sussex

Radegund (Radegonde) (518-587)
Ger. saint, queen, nun, nurse
Culver—Women p80-81
Deen—Great p321-322
Dolan—Goodnow's p89
Englebert—Lives p310-311
Hammerton p1124
*McKown—Heroic p15-16
Schmidt—400 p388,por.

Radovska, Annetta, Baroness (fl. 1880's)
It. painter
Waters—Women p278-279

Radziwill, Catherine (Catherine Kolb-Danvin)
Russ. princess, author, lecturer
Cur. Biog. '41 p694

Radziwill, Lee, Princess (1933-   )
Amer., sister of Jacqueline
Kennedy Onassis
CR '63 p506,por.

Rae, Henrietta.
See Normand, Henrietta Rae

Rae, Ishbel. See Ross, Ishbel

Rae, Melba (n.d.)
Amer. actress
TV—Person (3) p149-150,por.

Raedler, Dorothy Florence (1917-   )
Amer. theatrical producer
Cur. Biog. '54 p525-527,por.

Rafferty, Frances (1922-   )
Amer. actress
TV—Person (2) p127-128,por.

Raftor, Catherine.
See Clive, Catherine ("Kitty") R.

Ragan, Mrs. John (fl. 1870's)
Amer. pioneer
Logan—Part p102

Raguet, Anna.
See Irion, Anna Raguet

Ragusa, Eleanora.
See O'Tama-Chiovara

Rahab (1) (Biblical)
Buchanan—Women p31-32
Deen—All p65-69
Faulhaber—Women p144
Hammerton p1125
Horton—Women p89-103
Lewis—Portraits p213-216
Lofts—Women p51-56
McCartney—Great p43-59
*MacVeagh—Champlin p487

Marble—Women, Bible p228-232
Morton—Women p67-73
Nelson—Bible p33-34
Ockenga—Women p53-62
Singer—3000 p5-7
Spurgeon—Sermons p58-68
Van der Velde—She p86-92

Rahab (2) (Biblical)
wife of Salmon
Deen—All p290

Raiche, Bessica Faith (fl. 1910's)
Amer. pioneer aviatrix
*May—Women p65-66
Planck—Women p16-17

Raimond, C. E., pseud.
See Robins, Elizabeth

Rainbow(e), Rachel Allen (fl. 1620's)
Eng., mother of Edward
Rainbow(e) Bishop
Stenton—English p136-137

Rainer, Luise (1912-   )
Aust. actress
Lamparski—What. p174-175,por.

Raines, Ella (1921-   )
Amer. actress
TV—Person (2) p118-119,por.

Raingarda (fl. 630's-650's)
Fr. saint
Blunt—Great p151

Raisa, Rosa (1893-1963)
Pol. singer
Ewen—Ency. p414-415
McCoy—Portraits p160,por.
Saleski—Jewish p611-612,por.
Saleski—Wand. p423-426,por.

Raisbeck, Rosina (1918-   )
Austral. singer
Davidson—Treas. p238-240

Ralston, Esther (1902-   )
Amer. actress
Brundidge—Twinkle p157-168,por.
Herman—How p105,por.

Ralston, F. Marion (fl. 1940's)
Amer. composer, pianist, music
teacher
McCoy—Portraits p160,por.

Ramabai Sarasvati, Pandita (1858-1922)
Ind. missionary
Deen—Great p277-287
Miller—Ten p36-42

Ramann, Lina (1833-1912)
Ger., music educator, author
Elson—Woman's p239-240

Rama Rau, Santha (1923-   )
Inf. author, lecturer
CR '59 p607-608,por.
CR '63 p507,por.
Cur. Biog. '45 p482-484,por.
Cur. Biog. '59 p376-377,por.

Rambaut, Mary Lucinda Bonney (1816-1900)
Amer. educator
Logan—Part p711-712

Rambeau, Marjorie (1889-1970)
Amer. actress
Blum—Great p62,por.
Coad—Amer. p327,por.

Rambert, Marie, Dame (b. 1888)
Pol.-Brit. ballet dancer, teacher
Davidson—Ballet p240-247
Hammerton p1127
Haskell—Ballet p77-78,205-208,por.

Rambouillet, Catherine de Vivonne de Savelli, Marquise de (1588-1665)
Fr. salonist
Adelman—Famous p56-57
Beard—Woman p323
Dorland—Sum p30,105
Mozans—Woman p88-89
Schmidt—400 p173-174,por.
Snyder—Treas. p100-107

Ramée, Marie Louise de la. See Ouida

Ramsay, Elizabeth (fl. 1720's)
Eng., sister of Alexander Ramsay
Stirling—Odd p72-80

Ramsay, Margaret Jane (fl. 1750's)
Amer. pioneer
DAR Mag. July 1921 p380-381,
portrayal

Ramsay, Martha Laurens (1759-1811)
Amer. colonial horticulturist
Leonard—Amer. p120
Spruill—Women's p47-48,55,230-231

Ramsey, Grace Fisher (fl. 1930's)
Amer. club leader, author
Women—Achieve. p125,por.

Ramus, Anna Kolbjors (1665-1736)
Nor. heroine
Schmidt—400 p307,por.

Ranade, Mrs. Ramabai (1862-1924)
Ind. social reformer
Stiles—Postal p216

Ranavalona III (1864-1917)
Madag. queen
Hammerton p1128

Ranczak, Hildegarde (fl. 1940's)
Ger. singer
McCoy—Portraits p160,por.

Rand, Ayn (1904-   )
Russ.-Amer. author
CR '59 p608,por.
CR '63 p507-508,por.
Mantle—Contemp. p207-208
Warfel—Amer. p350,por.

Rand, Ellen Emmet (1876-1941)
Amer. artist
Cur. Biog. '42 p686
Jackman—Amer. p230-231

Rand, Sally (1904-   )
Amer. dancer
CR '59 p608,por.
CR '63 p508,por.
Lamparski—What. p14-15,por.

Randall, Charity (c. 1822-1905)
Amer. whaling voyager
Whiting—Whaling p33-34,36-38,189-193,276

Randall, Ollie Annette (fl. 1930's)
Amer. social worker, humanitarian
Women—Achieve. p99,por.

Randall, Ruth Elaine Painter (1892-   )
Amer. author
Cur. Biog. '57 p445-446,por.

Randolph, Anne Dillon (fl. 1920's)
Amer. nurse
Pennock—Makers p105,por.

Randolph, Frances Bland.
See Tucker, Frances Bland Randolph

Randolph, Lois (fl. 1920's)
Amer. educator
Binheim—Women p149,por.

Randolph, Martha Jefferson (1772-1836)
Amer., daughter of Thomas Jefferson
Brooks—Young p176-215
Donovan—Women p223-228,244-248,250-253,por.
Gerlinger—Mis. p13-14
Hanaford—Dau. p132-133
Jensen—White p19-20,por.
Logan—Part p217-220
Prindiville—First p27-35
Sale—Old p204-211,por.
*Sweetser—Famous p50-84,por.
Truett—First p12,por.

Randolph, Mary Isham.
See Keith, Mary Isham

Randolph, Nancy.
See Robb, Inez Callaway

Randolph, Virginia (c. 1874-1958)
Amer. teacher
Bowie—Women p112-119

Ranee of Jhansi (Lakshmi Bai) (1822-
1857)
Ind. soldier, heroine, patriot
Schmidt—400 p237-238,por.

Rankin, Jeannette (b. 1880)
Amer. pioneer congresswoman,
feminist
*Heath—Women (4) p32
Jensen—Revolt p62,por.
Paxton—Women p1-2,130

Rankin, Melinda (1811-1888)
Amer. missionary
Logan—Part p513-514

Rankin, Nell (1926-   )
Amer. singer
Matz—Opera p210-213,por.
Wagner—Prima p246-247

Ransford, Nettie (b. 1838)
Amer. club leader
Logan—Part p408

Ransom, Sarah (fl. 1870's-1880's)
Amer. artist
Hanaford—Dau. p320

Ranson, Ruth (fl. 1910's-1930's)
Amer. lawyer
Women—Achieve. p154,por.

Rao, Shanta (1930-   )
Ind. classical scholar
Cur. Biog. '57 p448-450,por.

Rapaelje, Sarah.
See Bogaert, Sarah Rapelje Bergen

Rapelje, Cataline de Trice (b. 1624)
Amer. pioneer
Green—Pioneer (1) p198

Rapin, Aimée (b. 1869)
Swiss painter
Waters—Women p279-282

Rapoport, Eda (1900-   )
Russ.-Amer. composer
Reis—Composers p290-292

Rapoport, Ruth (1900/01-1935)
Amer. composer
ASCAP p399

Rappard, Clara von (b. 1857)
Swiss painter
Waters—Women p282

Rappold, Marie Winteroth (1880-1957)
Amer. singer
Lahee—Grand p57-58,por.
McCoy—Portraits p161,por.
Saleski—Wander p426-427,por.

Rasche, Thea (fl. 1920's-1930's)
Ger. aviatrix
*May—Women p104-105

Rash, Doreen Wallace (gr. 1919)
Eng. novelist
Brittain—Women p144-251

Raskin, Judith (1928-   )
Amer. singer
Cur. Biog. '64 p366-368,por.

Raskovi, Marina (1912-1943)
Russ. aviatrix
Phila.—Women unp.,por.
Stiles—Postal p217

Ratchford, Fannie Elizabeth (b. 1887)
Amer. librarian, author, editor
Bul. of Bibl. May-Aug.1950 p31,por.

Rath, Henriette (1772-1856)
Swiss painter
Waters—Women p282

Rathbone, Eleanor F. (1872-1945)
Brit. politician, Parliament
member
Brittain—Women (see index)
Cur. Biog. '43 p611-612,por.
Cur. Biog. '46 p499

Rathbone, Josephine Adams (c. 1856-1941)
Amer. librarian, editor, educator
Bul. of Bibl. Sept.-Dec.'34 p81,por.
Cur. Biog. '41 p696
Marshall—Amer. p290-294,301-310,
457

Rathbone, Mary Jane (b. 1860)
Amer. zoologist, naturalist,
government employee, author
Logan—Part p878-879

Rathnell, Maria L. Moore (fl. 1860's)
Amer. Civil war nurse
Logan—Part p372

Ratliff, Beulah Amidon (fl. 1930's)
Amer. journalist, editor
Women—Achieve. p202

Ratnarajay Lakshmi (m. 1956)
Nepal queen
Stiles—Postal p217

Rau, Dhanvanthi Handoo Rama, Lady
Benegal Rama (1893-   )
Ind. organization official
Cur. Biog. '54 p527-529,por.

Rau, Santha Rama.
    See Rama Rau, Santha

Rauh, Bertha (b. 1865)
    Amer. club leader
    Logan—Part p650-651

Raunall, Sarah (fl. 1760's)
    Amer. colonial hostess
    Dexter—Colonial p9

Ravenel, Charlotte St. Julien (fl. 1860's)
    Amer. Civil war diarist
    Jones—Heroines p370-374

Raverat, Gwendolen Mary Darwin (1885-
    1957)
    Eng. illustrator
    Mahony—Illus. p350

Ravogli, Giulia (b. 1860)
    It. singer
    Klein—Great p171-176,por.

Rawalt, Marguerite (n.d.)
    Amer. organization official
    Cur. Biog. '56 p508-510,por.

Rawlings, Marjorie Kinnan (1896-1953)
    Amer. novelist
    Burnett—Amer. p553,por.
    Burnett—This p1153
    *Cournos—Famous p103-106,por.
    Cur. Biog. '42 p686-689,por.
    Cur. Biog. '54 p531
    *Scherman—Amer. p79-80
    Scherman—Literary p172-173
    Van Gelder—Writers p241-243
    Warfel—Amer. p350-351,por.

Rawson, Mary (fl. 1860's)
    Amer. Civil war diarist
    Jones—Heroines p335-341

Ray, Catherine (fl. 1750's-1760's)
    Amer., friend of Benjamin Franklin
    Donovan—Women p60-64

Ray, Charlotte E. (fl. 1870's-1880's)
    Amer. lawyer
    Hanaford—Dau. p669

Ray, Dixy Lee (1914-   )
    Amer., marine biologist
    *Poole—Outdoors p15-25,por.

Ray, Henrietta Cordelia (1849-1916)
    Amer. poet
    Brown—Home. p169-175

Ray, Martha (d. 1779)
    Eng. singer, mistress of Earl of
        Sandwich
    Jenkins—Ten p9-35,por.
    Stebbins—London p3-28

Ray, Renuka (fl. 1950's)
    Ind. religious worker
    Culver—Women p250

Rayburn, Kitty (fl. 1900's)
    Eng. actress
    Felstead—Stars p41

Raye, Martha (1916-   )
    Amer. singer, actress, comedienne
    Blum—Television p35,por.
    CR '59 p611-612,por.
    CR '63 p511,por.
    Cur. Biog. '63 p356-357,por.
    Donaldson—Radio p23
    TV—Person (1) p54-55,por.

Raymond, Maud (fl. 1890's-1900's)
    Amer. singer, actress
    Strang—Prima p233-238,por.

Raymond, Sarah E. (fl. 1870's-1880's)
    Amer. educator
    Hanaford—Dau. p548

Raymondi, Lillian (fl. 1940's)
    Amer. singer
    Peltz—Spot. p104,por.

Rea, Virginia (fl. 1930's)
    Amer. singer
    Women—Achieve. p70,por.

Read, Carrie R. (fl. 1910's)
    Amer. club leader
    Logan—Part p355

Read, Deborah.
    See Franklin, Deborah Read Rogers

Read, Elizabeth K. (fl. 1920's-1930's)
    Amer. journalist
    Ross—Ladies p514-515

Read, Gertrude Ross Till (m. 1763)
    Amer. patriot
    Green—Pioneer (3) p207,209-215

Read, Katherine S. (fl. 1930's)
    Amer. public health nurse
    Pennock—Makers p63,por.

Read, Mary M. (d. 1720)
    Eng. soldier, sailor, pirate
    *Deakin—True p264-280
    Hammerton p1132
    Rogers—Gallant p53-84
    Snow—Women p14-18

Reading, Martha Ann (fl. 1950's-1960's)
    Amer. aviatrix
    *May—Women p196-197

Reading, Sarah M. (fl. 1860's)
    Amer. Civil war nurse
    Logan—Part p372

Reading, Stella Charnaud Isaacs,
　　Marchioness of (1894-　　)
　　Brit. organization official,
　　　politician, social welfare leader
　Cur. Biog. '48 p517-518,por.
　Phelps—Men '58 (1) p211-212

Ready, Alice (fl. 1860's)
　　Amer. Civil war diarist
　Jones—Heroines p83-93

Réage, Pauline, pseud. (n.d.)
　　Fr. novelist
　Peyre—French p435-436,461

Ream, Vinnie. See Hoxie, Vinnie Ream

Reavey, Mrs. George.
　See Pereira, Irene Rice

Reavis, Babs H. (fl. 1930's)
　　Amer. lecturer, politician, club
　　　leader
　Women—Achieve. p40,por.

Reback, Mrs. Marcus. See Caldwell, Taylor

Rebe, Louise Christine (fl. 1940's)
　　Amer. composer, pianist, teacher
　McCoy—Portraits p162,por.

Rebecka (Biblical)
　Buchanan—Women p17-20
　Chappell—Fem. p36-48
　Culver—Women p19
　Deen—All p21-27
　Hammerton p1133
　Horton—Women p33-47
　Hughes—Mothers p57-64
　*Levinger—Great p11-19
　Lewis—Portraits p65-70
　Lofts—Women p23-31
　MacCartney—Great p121-135
　*MacVeagh—Champlin p491
　Marble—Women p125-130
　Mead—250 p25
　Morton—Women p35-41
　Nelson—Bible p21-23
　Schmidt—400 p264,por.
　Spurgeon—Sermons p33-57
　Van der Velde—She p45-51

Récamier, Jeanne Françoise Julie Adelaide
　　Bernard (1777/79-1850)
　　Fr. salonist, social leader,
　　　politician, beauty
　Abbott—Notable p232-237,por.
　Adelman—Famous p124-126,por.
　Collins—Biog. p314-323,por.
　De Morny—Beat p75-87,por.
　Dorland—Sum p36,77,106
　Hammerton p1133,por.
　*MacVeagh—Champlin p491-492,por.
　Muir—Women p125
　Phila.—Women unp.,por.
　Stiles—Postal p217
　Tallentyre—Women p134-152,por.

Terhune—Super. p230-249
Thomson—Queens p253-286,por.

Redden, Laura Catherine.
　See Searing, Laura Catherine Redden

Redell, Emma (d. 1940)
　　Amer. singer
　McCoy—Portraits p162,por.

Redempta (d.c. 580)
　　Rom. saint
　Wescott—Calen. p108

Redfield, Ann Maria Treadwell (fl. 1870's-
　　1880's)
　　Amer. zoologist
　Hanaford—Dau. p285-286

Redfield, Ethel (b. 1877)
　　Amer. educator, author
　Binheim—Women p126,por.

Redfield, Heloise Guillou (b. 1883)
　　Amer. painter
　Michigan—Biog. p263

Redgrave, Lynn (1943-　　)
　　Eng. actress
　Time Mar.17,1967 p80,por.(Cover)

Redgrave, Vanessa (1937-　　)
　　Eng. actress
　Cur. Biog. '66 p324-327,por.
　Time Mar.17,1967 p80,por.(Cover)

Redling, Netty Radvanyi.
　See Seghers, Anna, pseud.

Redmond, Frieda Voelter (fl. 1890's-1910's)
　　Swiss painter
　Waters—Women p282-283

Redmond, Mary (fl. 1770's)
　　Amer. Rev. war heroine, patriot
　Carmer—Young p55-61
　Ellet—Women (1) p196-197
　Green—Pioneer (2) p301-304
　Hanaford—Dau. p58-59

Redpath, Anne (1895-　　)
　　Scot. painter
　Cur. Biog. '57 p452-453,por.

Reece, Louise Goff (fl. 1950's-1960's)
　　Amer. Congresswoman
　U.S.—Women (87th) p35,por.

Reed, Anna Yeomans (b. 1871)
　　Amer. educator
　Women—Achieve. p111,por.

Reed, Caroline Keating (fl. 1910's)
　　Amer. musician, author
　Logan—Part p765

Reed, Catherine S. (fl. 1870's-1880's)
Amer. social reformer
Hanaford—Dau. p423

Reed, Donna (1921-   )
Amer. actress
CR '59 p613,por.
CR '63 p512,por.

Reed, Elizabeth Armstrong (1842-1915)
Amer. philosopher, religious
author
Logan—Part p861

Reed, Esther De Berdt (1746-1780)
Amer. Rev. war heroine, patriot,
philanthropist
Bruce—Woman p106-108
Ellet—Women (1) p47-70,por.
Green—Pioneer (2) p14,144-152
Hanaford—Dau. p55
Leonard—Amer. p120-121
Logan—Part p105-106

Reed, Florence (b. 1883)
Amer. actress
Blum—Great p73,por.

Reed, Helena D. (fl. 1930's)
Amer. banker
Women—Achieve. p82,por.

Reed, Ida L. (d. 1951)
Amer. hymn-writer
*Plumb—Lives p79-98

Reed, Janet (fl. 1940's)
Amer. ballet dancer
Atkinson—Dancers p127-130,por.
*Terry—Star p192-193

Reed, Margaret (fl. 1840's)
Amer. W. pioneer
*Miller—West. p45-63

Reed, Mary (1854-1943)
Amer. missionary
Logan—Part p515
Miller—Handi. p20-26,por.

Reed, Myrtle (1874-1911)
Amer. novelist
Dorland—Sum p19

Reed, Sarah (fl. 1840's)
Amer. pioneer
Whitton—These p234-235,237

Reed, Virginia (b. 1833)
Amer. W. pioneer, realtor
Brown—Gentle p13,94-100,por.
*Miller—West p45-63

Reed. See also **Read; Reid**

Reel, Estelle (m. 1910)
Amer. educator
Logan—Part p726

Rees, Elizabeth (fl. 19th cent.)
Welsh religious teacher
*Plumb—Lives p71-77

Rees, Mina S. (1902-   )
Amer. mathematician, educator,
government official
Cur. Biog. '57 p453-455,por.

Rees, Rosemary (fl. 1940's)
Amer. aviatrix, ballet dancer
*May—Women p142

Reese, Della (1932-   )
Amer. singer
*Cherry—Portraits p199
Stambler—Ency. p195

Reese, Lizette Woodworth (1856-1935)
Amer. poet
Cook—Our p200-201
*Logic—Careers p102-117
Love—Famous p29
*Millett—Amer. p536-537
Smith—Women's p170
Wagenknecht—When p449-460

Reeve, Ada (b. 1874)
Eng. actress
Caffin—Vaud. p164-167,por.

Reeve, Clara (1729-1807)
Eng. novelist
Dorland—Sum p51,192
MacCarthy—Later p137-142

Reeve, Winnifred Eaton Babcock (Onoto
Watanna, pseud.) (b. 1879)
Can. author
Thomas—Canad. p102-103

Reeves, Amber (fl. 1910's)
Eng. novelist
Johnson—Some Contemp. p107-115

Reeves, Anne (fl. 1670's)
Eng. actress
MacQueen—Pope p72-73
Wilson—All p183-184

Reeves, Margaret (1893-   )
Amer. child welfare worker
Binheim—Women p149,por.

Reggiani, Hilde (1914-   )
It. singer
Ewen—Living p292,por.
McCoy—Portraits p162,por.
Peltz—Spot. p98

Reginald (d.c. 251)
Alesian saint
Englebert—Lives p342-343

Regis, Emma (fl. 1900's)
Rom. painter
Waters—Women p283

Regnault, Jeanne.
See Bartet, Jeanne Julia Regnault

Régnier, Paule (fl. 1930's-1940's)
Fr. novelist
Peyre—French p279,281-183,436

Rehan, Ada (1860-1916)
Irish-Amer. actress
Adelman—Famous p251
Bodeen—Ladies p49-55
Coad—Amer. p260-262,por.
Dorland—Sum p168
Hammerton p1135,por.
Izard—Heroines p203-229,por.
Logan—Part p782-783
*Richmond—Immig. p108-109
Schmidt—400 p10,por.
Strang—Actresses p113-124,por.
Vance—Hear p68-80,por.

Reichardt, Gertrude (fl. 1800's)
Ger. nurse
Pennock—Makers p13,por.

Reicher-Kindermann, Hedwig (1853-1883)
Ger. singer
Klein—Great p208-210,por.
McCoy—Portraits p163,por.

Reid, Charlotte Thompson (1913-   )
Amer. Congresswoman, politician
U.S.—Women (88th) p21,por.

Reid, Christian.
See Tiernan, Francis Fisher

Reid, Frances (n.d.)
Amer. actress
TV—Person (2) p51-52,por.

Reid, Helen Rogers (b. 1882)
Amer. journalist, publisher
Cur. Biog. '41 p699-701,por.
Cur. Biog. '52 p492-494,por.
Ross—Ladies p25-26,135-141,458-459,
por.,cover
Time Oct.8,1934 p59,por.(Cover)
Women—Achieve. p95,por.

Reid, Margaret E. (1846-1923)
Amer. inn-keeper
Brown—Home. p154-155

Reid, Molly (fl. 1770's)
Amer. Rev. war patriot
Green—Pioneer (3) p468

Reigersberg, Maria Van (1589-1653)
Nether. patriot
Schmidt—400 p297-298,por.

Reiner, Max. See Caldwell, Taylor

Reinhardt, Aurelia Henry (1877-1948)
Amer. educator, religious worker
Cur. Biog. '41 p702-704,por.
Cur. Biog. '48 p518

Reinhardt, Sophie (1775-1843)
Ger. painter
Waters—Women p283-284

Reinhold, Eva (fl. 1900's)
Ger. singer
Wagner—Prima p247

Reisenberg, Nadia (1904-   )
Russ. pianist
Ewen—Living p293,por.
Saleski—Jewish p540-541,por.
Saleski—Wander. p380'por.

Reiset, Maria Felice de.
See Grandval, Marie Félicie Clemence
de Reiset, Viscomtesse de

Reitsch, Hanna (1912-   )
Ger. aviatrix, glider pilot,
helicopter pilot
Lauwick—Heroines p55-74,por.
May—Women p202,205,214-215,por.
Planck—Women p103

Réjane, Gabrielle Charlotte (1856/57-
1920)
Fr. actress
Adelman—Famous p261
Dorland—Sum p169
Hammerton p1136
Izard—Heroines p126-170,por.

Rembaugh, Bertha (1876-1950)
Amer. lawyer, author
Women—Achieve. p202

Rembrandt, Jeanne.
See Gerville-Réache, Jeanne

Remick, Bertha (fl. 1940's)
Amer. composer
Elson—Woman's p258
McCoy—Portraits p163,por.

Remick, Lee (1935-   )
Amer. actress
CR '59 p616,por.
CR '63 p515,por.
Cur. Biog. '66 p327-330,por.
Ross—Player p249-255,por.

Remington, Ann.
See Ellery, Ann Remington

Remington, Mrs. Mather (fl. 1870's)
Amer. business woman
Hanaford—Dau. p612

Remsen, Alice (1896-   )
Eng.-Amer. composer, author,
publisher
ASCAP p404

Rémusat, Claire Elisabeth, Countess de
(1780-1821)
Fr. author
Adelman—Famous p103

Remy, Marie (b. 1829)
Ger. painter
Waters—Women p284

Renan, Henriette (d.c. 1860)
Fr., sister of Ernest Renan
Cockran—Romance p215-234,por.

Renaud, Madeleine (1903-   )
Fr. actress
Beaton—Persona p80-81,por.
Cur. Biog. '53 p47-50,por.

Renault, Mary (n.d.)
Eng. author
CR '59 p616,por.
Cur. Biog. '59 p379-381,por.

Renée of France (1510-1575)
Fr. Christian, dau. of Louis XII
Blei—Fasc. p22-26,por.
Deen—Great p344-346

Rennes, Catherine van.
See Van Rennes, Catherine

Reno, Itti Kinney (b. 1862)
Amer. author
Logan—Part p872

Rensselaer, Mariana Griswold (1851-1914)
Amer. author
Adelman—Famous p248

Renvall, Aino. See Ackté-Jalander, Aino

Repplier, Agnes (1855-1950)
Amer. essayist
Adelman—Famous p285
Bruère—Laugh p67-68
Burnett—This p1153-1154
Logan—Part p864
*Millett—Amer. p537-539
Wagenknecht—When p327-337

Resnick, Rose (gr. 1934)
Amer. teacher of blind,
humanitarian
Murrow—This (1) p145-146

Resnik (Resniz), Regina (1922-   )
Amer. singer
Cur. Biog. '56 p512-514,por.
Matz—Opera p31-34,por.
Salenski—Jewish p615,por.

Respha, Queen (Biblical)
Faulhaber—Women p126-132

Respighi, Elsa Olivieri Sangiacomo
(b. 1894)
It. singer, composer
McCoy—Portraits p164,por.

Reszke, Josephine de (1855-1891)
Pol. singer
Davidson—Treas. p243-244,248-249

Rethberg, Elisabeth (1894-   )
Ger. singer
Davidson—Treas. p249-252
Ewen—Ency. p421
Ewen—Living p294-295,por.
McCoy—Portraits p164,por.

Rethy, Princess of.
See Mary Liliane, Princess of Rethy

Retzius, Anna (1841-1924)
Swed. feminist, foundress,
educator
Schmidt—400 p372-373,por.

Reumah (Biblical)
Deen—All p290

Reuss-Belce, Luise (b. 1860)
Aust. singer
McCoy—Portraits p164,por.

Reuter, Elizabeth (b. 1853)
Ger. painter
Waters—Women p284

Reuter, Gabriele (1859-1941)
Ger. author, feminist
Cur. Biog. '42 p691
Heller—Studies p273-274

Reuther, Anna Stoker (n.d.)
Amer., mother of Walter Reuther
Davis—Mothers p145-154

Reutiman, Gladys Harriet (fl. 1930's)
Amer. educator
Women—Achieve. p185,por.

Revell, Nellie (c. 1872-1958)
Amer. journalist, press-agent
Ross—Ladies p256-257

Revere, Anne (1903-   )
Amer. actress
Lamparski—What p126-127,por.

Revest, Cornelia Louisa (1795-1856)
Nether. painter
Waters—Women p284

Rex, Margery. See McCarthy, Julia

Rex, Peggy (fl. 1920's)
  Amer. patroness of aviation
  Planck—Women p46-47

Reyes, Doña Mercedes Abrego de
  (b.c. 1785)
  Col. heroine, patriot
  Schmidt—400 p79,por.

Reyner, Rebecca Hourwich (fl. 1930's)
  Amer. social worker, journalist
  Women—Achieve. p136,por.

Reynolds, Alice Louise b. 1873)
  Amer. educator
  Binheim—Women p178-179,por.

Reynolds, Anne Cannon (m. 1929)
  Amer., wife of Zachary Smith
  Reynolds
  Tebbel—Inher. p103-106

Reynolds, Belle (b. 1840)
  Amer. Civil war nurse, patriot,
  author
  Dannett—Noble p103-104,152-157
  Harkness—Heroines p13
  Moore—Women p254-277,por.
  Young—Women p94-95,159-167,171,
  376

Reynolds, Charlotte.
  See Hillman, Charlotte

Reynolds, Debbie (1932-   )
  Amer. actress
  CR '59 p618-619,por.
  CR '63 p516-517,por.
  Cur. Biog. '64 p368-370,por.
  Reed—Follow p9-13,por.

Reynolds, Helen Wilkinson (c. 1877-1943)
  Amer. author
  Cur. Biog. '43 p617

Reynolds, Jane Louisa (d. 1907)
  Eng. dancer
  Wyndham—Chorus p71

Reynolds, Libby Holman (fl. 1920's-1930's)
  Amer. singer
  Tebbel—Inher. p104-106,por.

Reynolds, Maria (fl. 1790's)
  Amer., friend of Alexander
  Hamilton
  Donovan—Women p270-278

Reynolds, Ruth (fl. 1920's-1930's)
  Amer. journalist
  Ross—Ladies p291-292

Rezia, Sultana (fl. 1220's-1230's)
  Ind., daughter of Altamish
  Pool—Famous p83-88

Rhoades, Cornelia Harsen (1863-1940)
  Amer. blind author
  Cur. Biog. '41 p707

Rhoda (Biblical)
  Deen—All p290-291

Rhode, Ruth Bryan Owen.
  See Owen, Ruth Bryan

Rhodes, Mary, Mother (fl. 1810's)
  Amer. foundress, nun
  Code—Great p120-151

Rhodes, Mrs. (fl. 1720's)
  Amer. colonial teacher
  Dexter—Colonial p88-89

Rhodes, Mrs. (Guy d'Hardelot, pseud.)
  (fl. 1930's)
  Fr.-Eng. composer, song-writer
  Elson—Woman's p149-150,

Rhondda, Margaret Haig Thomas (1883-
  1958)
  Eng. feminist, editor
  Brittain—Women p119-120,250
  Hammerton p1142,por.

Rhonie, Aline (1909-   )
  Amer. painter, aviatrix
  *May—Women p151,por.
  Taves—Success p305-320,por.

Rhys, Olwen (gr. 1903)
  Eng. educator
  Brittain—Women p160,244

Riabouchinska, Tatiana (b. 1918)
  Russ. ballet dancer
  Atkinson—Dancers p131-134
  Davidson—Ballet p250-254
  Haskell—Vignet. p23-26,31-33,por.
  *Terry—Star p138-141,por.

Riasanovsky, Antonina.
  See Fedorova, Nina

Ribla, Gertrude (n.d.)
  Amer. singer
  Saleski—Jewish p616-617,por.

Riccardo, Corona (fl. 1890's)
  It.-Amer. actress
  Strang—Actresses p147-155,por.

Ricci, Anne-Marie De (1820-1905)
  Fr., wife of Count Waleski
  Schmidt—400 p185-186,por.

Rice, Alice Caldwell Hegan (1870-1942)
  Amer. novelist
  Bruère—Laugh. p135
  Cur. Biog. '42 p691
  Hammerton p1143
  Maurice—Makers p4,por.
  Overton—Women p269

Rice, Anna Virena (fl. 1930's)
Amer. organization official
Women—Achieve. p89,por.

Rice, Mrs. Isaac L. (b. 1860)
Amer. social reformer, musician,
linguist, social leader
Logan—Part p602-603

Rice, Laura W. (fl. 1930's)
Hung.-Amer. designer
Women—Achieve. p80,por.

Rich, Barbara, pseud. See Riding, Laura

Rich, Gladys (1893-   )
Amer. composer
ASCAP p407

Rich, Helen Hinsdale (b. 1827)
Amer. poet
Logan—Part p868

Rich, Irene (1891/97-   )
Amer. actress
Donaldson—Radio p23-24
Herman—How p101,por.
Lamparski—What. p190-191,por.

Rich, Louise Dickinson (1903-   )
Amer. author
Cur. Biog. '43 p620-622,por.

Rich, Mary, Countess of Warwick (1625-
1678)
Eng. philanthropist
Aubrey—Brief p261-262

Richard, Hortense (b. 1860)
Fr. painter
Waters—Women p284-285

Richardis (Richilda) (d.c. 896)
It. saint, empress, wife of
Charles the Fat
Englebert—Lives p356

Richards, Anna Mary (b. 1870)
Amer. painter
Waters—Women p285-287

Richards, Ellen Henrietta Swallow (1842-
1911)
Amer. chemist, mineralogist,
sanitary engineer, pioneer
home economist
Adelman—Famous p244
Law—Civiliz. p286-289
Logan—Part p880
*Moore—When p147-154
Mozans—Woman p217-220
16 Amer. p57-60
Stern—We p118-144
*Yost—Women Sci. p1-26

Richards, Fannie M. (1840-1923)
Amer. teacher
Robinson—Hist. p116-117,por.

Richards, Henrietta King (fl. 1930's)
Amer. business executive
Women—Achieve. p202

Richards, Irene (m. 1917)
Eng. actress
Wyndham—Chorus p145-146

Richards, Janet Elizabeth Hosmer (d. 1948)
Amer. lecturer, feminist
Logan—Part p784-785

Richards, Laura E. (1850-1943)
Amer. author
*Benét—Amer. Poets p111-114,por.
*Benét—Famous Poets p66-72,por.
Cur. Biog. '43 p622
Logan—Part p857
Love—Famous p32
Rogers—Women p39,por.

Richards, Linda (Melinda) Ann (1841-
1930)
Amer. nurse
*Dodge—Story p88-103
Dolan—Goodnow's p248-249,252-253,
por.
Irwin—Angels p156,158,160
Lovejoy—Women p86
Pennock—Makers p30-31,por.
Schmidt—400 p399,por.

Richards, Maria M. C. Hall (fl. 1860's)
Amer. Civil war nurse
Logan—Part p371

Richards, Mary Virginia (b. 1855)
Amer. philanthropist
Logan—Part p535

Richards, Myra Reynolds (b. 1882)
Amer. sculptor
National—Contemp. p270

Richards, Rosa Coates (fl. 1930's)
Amer. dancer, poet
Women—Achieve. p48,por.

Richards, Wynn (fl. 1930's)
Amer. photographer
Women—Achieve. p137,por.

Richardson, Abby Sage (1837-1900)
Amer. historian, actress
Hanaford—Dau. p733

Richardson, Dorcas Nelson (c. 1741-1834)
Amer. Rev. war heroine
Ellet—Women (1) p299-310
Green—Pioneer (2) p420-427
Logan—Part p177-179

Richardson, Dorothy M. (Miriam
  Henderson; Dorothy Odle)
  (1872-1957)
  Eng. novelist
  Collins—Literature p96-115
  Hammerton p1144
  Johnson—Some Contemp. p131-146
  Millett—Brit. p432-433
  Ross—Ladies p260,551

Richardson, Ellen A. (1845-1911)
  Amer. artist, editor, author, club
  leader
  Logan—Part p848-849

Richardson, Emily Tracey Y. (1863-1892)
  Amer. translator, poet
  Logan—Part p872

Richardson, Florence (fl. 1920's-1930's)
  Amer. journalist, editor
  Women—Achieve. p123,por.

Richardson, Harriet (gr. 1896)
  Amer. biologist, author
  Logan—Part p879

Richardson, Henrietta (Henry Handel
  Richardson, pseud.)
  (1870/80-1946)
  Austral. author
  Cur. Biog. '46 p507
  Hammerton p1144
  Millett—Brit. p433-434

Richardson, Hester Dorsey (m. 1891)
  Amer. educator, author
  Logan—Part p718

Richardson, Jane. See McKinley, Jane

Richardson, Mary A. Ransorn (fl. 1860's)
  Amer. Civil war nurse
  Logan—Part p370

Richardson, Sarah (fl. 18th cent.)
  Amer. pioneer, mother of Leslie
  Coombs
  Logan—Part p75

Richey, Helen (fl. 1920's-1930's)
  Amer. pioneer aviatrix
  *Adams—Sky p186-193,por.
  Dwiggins—They p75,80-82,84,86,90
  May—Women p95-96,136-139,212
  Planck—Women p73,90,93,por.

Richier, Germaine (1904-)
  Fr. sculptor
  N. Y. Museum—New p38,por.

Richmond, Grace Louise Smith (1866-1959)
  Amer. novelist
  Overton—Women p270-271

**Richmond and Derby, Margaret, Countess
  of.** See Beaufort, Margaret, Countess of
  Richmond and Derby.

**Richmond and Lennox, Frances Teresa
  Stuart, Duchess of** (1648-1702)
  Eng., mistress of Charles II
  Dorland—Sum p17
  Hammerton p1146
  Melville—Windsor p183-209,por.

Richter, Ada (1944-)
  Amer. composer, educator,
  lecturer
  ASCAP p408
  McCoy—Portraits p165,por.

Richter, Gisela Marie Augusta (b. 1882)
  Eng.-Amer. archaeologist, museum
  curator, author
  Women—Achieve. p72,por.

Ricker, Marilla M. (1840-1920)
  Amer. lawyer
  Hanaford—Dau. p673

Ricketts, Cid.
  See Sumner, Bertha Cid Ricketts

Ricketts, Fanny L. (fl. 1860's)
  Anglo-Amer. humanitarian
  Brockett—Woman's p517-519
  Moore—Women p17-35,por.
  Young—Women p135-136,377,por.

Rictrude (c. 614-c. 688)
  Flem. saint, abbess
  Blunt—Great p150

Riddell, Charlotte Eliza Lawson Cowan
  (1832-1906)
  Eng. author
  Black—Notable p11-25,por.
  Furniss—Some p5-6
  Hammerton p1147

Riddle, Elizabeth (Eliza)
  Amer. actress
  Coad—Amer. p158,por.

Riddle, Estelle Massey (1903-)
  Amer. nurse
  *Yost—Nursing p96-118

Ridenour, Nina (1904-)
  Amer. psychologist
  Cur. Biog. '51 p520-523,por.

Rider-Kelsey, Corinne (1877-1947)
  Amer. singer
  McCoy—Portraits p166,por.

Ridge, Lola (1883-1941)
  Irish-Amer. poet
  Cook—Our p258-259
  Cur. Biog. '41 p713
  *Millett—Amer. p541-542

Ridgely, Sarah (fl. 1760's)
Amer. colonial midwife
Dexter—Colonial p66-67

Ridgeway, Ann (d. 1857)
Amer. social leader
Hanaford—Dau. p147

Ridgway, Phebe.
See Rush, Phebe Ann Ridgway

Riding, Laura (Laura Riding Gottchalk,
Barbara Rich) (1901-   )
Amer. author
*Millett—Amer. p542-543

Ridley, Catharine ("Kitty") Livingston
(1770-1780's)
Amer., friend of Alexander
Hamilton
Donovan—Women p256-258,280
Ellet—Women (2) p136-138
Green—Pioneer (3) p309-310

Ridley, Rebeccah C. (fl. 1860's)
Amer. Civil war diarist
Jones—Heroines p349-351

Riedesel, Frederica Charlotte Louisa
Massow, Baroness de (1746-
1808)
Amer. Rev. war heroine
Ellet—Women (1) p141-166,por.
Leonard—Amer. p121

Riego, Teresa. See Del Riego, Teresa

Ries, Therese Feodorowna (fl. 1900's)
Russ. sculptor
Waters—Women p287-289

Rigal, Delia (c. 1923-   )
Argent. singer
Matz—Opera p145-149,por.

Rigby, Cora (fl. 1910's-1920's)
Amer. journalist
Ross—Ladies p314,332-335,por.,cover

Rigg, Catherine, Lady Cavers (m. 1659)
Scot. covenanter
Anderson—Ladies p253-272

Riggs, Mary (1818-1852)
Amer. gardener, pioneer missionary
Hollingsworth—Her p67-70

Riggs, Sarah.
See Humphreys, Sarah Riggs

Riis, Mary Phillips (fl. 1930's)
Amer. business woman
Women—Achieve. p83,por.

Rijutine, Elisa (fl. 1890's)
It. painter
Waters—Women p289-290

Riker, Ina Ambrose (fl. 1930's)
Amer. club leader
Women—Achieve. p187,por.

Riker, Janette (fl. 1840's)
Amer. W. pioneer
Brown—Gentle p14,40-41
Fowler—Woman p449-452

Riley, Susan B. (1896-   )
Amer. educator, organization
official
Cur. Biog. '53 p527-528,por.

Rimini, Francesca da.
See Francesca da Rimini

Rincón de Gautier, Felisa.
See Gautier, Felisa Rincón de

Rind, Clementina (d. 1774)
Amer. publisher
Brigham—Journals p78
Dexter—Colonial p176
Spruill—Women's p265-266

Rinehart, Mary Roberts (1876-1958)
Amer. novelist, playwright
Breit—Writer p227-229
Carnegie—Little p195-198,por.
Hammerton p1149
*Kirkland—Writers p53-67
Logan—Part p792
Love—Famous p37
Mantle—Amer. p221-222
Mantle—Contemp. p271
Maurice—Makers #6,por.
Overton—Autors p262-276,por.
Overton—Women p272-285
Rogers—Women p108,por.
Stone—We p123-129
Taves—Success. p79-84,por.
Van Gelder—Writers p145-148
Warfel—Amer. p356-357,por.
Williams—Out p309-321

Ring, Barbara Taylor (1879-1941)
Amer. psychiatrist
Cur. Biog. '41 p713

Ring, Blanche (1872-1961)
Amer. actress
Blum—Great p50,por.

Ring, Montague. See Aldridge, Amanda Ira

Rio, Anita (b. 1873)
Amer. singer
McCoy—Portraits p167,por.

Ripley, Dorothy Brintnall (1737-1831)
Amer. Rev. war patriot
Root—Chapter p328-337

Ripley, Eliza. See Mayhew, Eliza

Ripley, Elizabeth Blake (1906-)
Amer. author, illustrator
Cur. Biog. '58 p360-361,por.

Ripley, Lucy Fairfield Perkins (d. 1949)
Amer. sculptor, painter
Taft—Women-Mentor (172) #2

Ripley, Lucy Norton (fl. 1850's)
Amer. whaling voyager
Whiting—Whaling p32-33,36-38

Ripley, Martha George (b. 1843)
Amer. physician, feminist
Logan—Part p744

Ripley, Mary A. (b. 1831)
Amer. poet, teacher
Logan—Part p817

Ripley, Sarah Alden (1793-1867)
Amer. educator
Bradford—Portraits p33-64

Ripperger, Henrietta Sperry (b. 1889)
Amer. novelist
Warfel—Amer. p357,por.

Rishel, Mary Anne (b.c. 1821)
Amer. patriot
Logan—Part p437

Risher, Anna Priscilla (b. 1875)
Amer. composer, organist,
conductor, music teacher
Elson—Woman's p261-262
Howard—Our p580
McCoy—Portraits p167,por.

Risley, Alice Carey Farmer (fl. 1860's)
Amer. Civil war nurse
Logan—Part p370

Ristori, Adelaide (1822-1906)
It. actress
Abbott—Notable p337-341
Adelman—Famous p207-208
Coad—Amer. p231,por.
Dorland—Sum p49,71,165
Hammerton p1149
Schmidt—400 p255-256,por.

Rita (1381-1457)
It. saint, foundress
Blunt—Great p123-147
Englebert—Lives p198
Stiles—Postal p239
*Windham—Sixty p322-327

Ritchie, Anna Cora O. Mowatt (1819-
1870)
Amer. actress, playwright
Dorland—Sum p35
Hanaford—Dau. p267

Ritchie, Anne Isabella Thackeray, Lady
(1837-1919)
Eng. novelist
Adelman—Famous p206
De Morny—Best p189-194
Hammerton p1149,por.

Ritchie, Jean (1922-)
Amer. folk-singer, folklorist, author
Cur. Biog. '59 p385-387,por.

Ritchie, Mrs. John (fl. 1890's)
Amer. club leader
Logan—Part p463-464

Ritner, Ann Gilliland (1906-)
Amer. author
Cur. Biog. '53 p528-529,por.

Rittenhouse, Anne (d. 1932)
Amer. journalist
Ross—Ladies p437

Rittenhouse, Constance Morgan (n.d.)
Amer. organization official
Cur. Biog. '48 p524-525,por.

Rittenhouse, Jessie Belle (1869-1948)
Amer. poet, critic
Cook—Our p146-149

Ritter, Irene Marschand (fl. 1940's)
Amer. composer, organist, pianist,
teacher
McCoy—Portraits p167,por.

Ritter, Margaret Tod (1893-)
Amer. poet
Binheim—Women p111,por.
Smith—Women's p174

Ritter, Thelma (1905-1969)
Amer. actress
CR '59 p626,por.
CR '63 p521,por.
Cur. Biog. '57 p467-469,por.

Rivé-King, Julia (1857-1937)
Amer. composer, pianist
Elson—Woman's p203-204,por.
McCoy—Portraits p168,por.
Schonberg—Great p249-250,por.

Rivera, Chia (n.d.)
Puert. Ric.-Amer. singer, dancer,
comedienne
CR '63 p521,por.

Rivers, Pearl.
See Nicholson, Eliza Jane Peitevent

Rivery, Aimée Dubuc.
See Dubucq de Rivery, Aimée

Rives, Amélie, Princess Troubetzkoy (1863-1945)
    Amer. author
    Adelman—Famous p298
    Clark—Innocence p73-84,por.
    Cur. Biog. '45 p617
    Logan—Part p816-817
    Maurice—Makers p5,por.

Rives, Hallie Erminie (n.d.)
    Amer. author
    Cur. Biog. '56 p514-515,por.

Rivet, Elise (1890-1945)
    Fr. heroine
    Stiles—Postal p222

Rizpah (Biblical)
    Buchanan—Women p51-52
    Deen—All p109-112
    Horton—Women p148-160
    Lewis—Portraits p83-85
    Marble—Women p141-144
    Mead—250 p103

Roach, Elizabeth Greenfield (fl. 1800's)
    Amer. philanthropist
    DAR Mag. July 1921 p387-388, portrayal

Roark, Helen Wills.
    See Wills, Helen Newington

Robb, Elizabeth B. (fl. 1930's)
    Amer. poet
    Women—Achieve. p165,por.

Robb, Inez Callaway (Nancy Randolph) (n.d.)
    Amer. journalist, columnist
    CR '59 p627,por.
    CR '63 p522,por.
    Cur. Biog. '58 p361-363,por.
    Ross—Ladies p450-453

Robb, Isabel Hampton (1860-1910)
    Amer. nurse, educator
    Dolan—Goodnow's p256-258,306,por.
    Pennock—Makers p33,por.
    Schmidt—400 p404-405,por.

Robb, Josephine (m. 1912)
    Amer. journalist
    Ross—Ladies p447

Robb, Louisa St. Clair (b. 1773)
    Amer. W. pioneer, patriot
    DAR Mag. July 1921 p385-386,portrayal
    Ellet—Pioneer p178-179
    Green—Pioneer (2) p198; (3) p464

Robbins, Margaret Dreier (fl. 1900's-1910's)
    Amer. sociologist
    Logan—Part p593

Robbins, Nancy (fl. 1790's)
    Amer. pioneer, heroine
    Green—Pioneer (2) p450-451

Robbins, Sara Franklin (fl. 1930's)
    Amer. psychologist, adult education pioneer
    Women—Achieve. p113,por.

Robert, Edwa. See Moser, Edwa Robert

Roberts, Abigail Hoag (d. 1841)
    Amer. clergyman
    Dexter—Career p58-59

Roberts, Dorothy James (1903-   )
    Amer. novelist
    Cur. Biog. '56 p521-522,por.
    Warfel—Amer. p359,por.

Roberts, Edith (1902-   )
    Amer. novelist
    Warfel—Amer. p360,por.

Roberts, Elizabeth Madox (1886-1941)
    Amer. novelist, poet
    Auchincloss—Pion. p123-135
    Cur. Biog. '41 p713-714
    *Millette—Amer. p544-545

Roberts, Emma (c. 1794-1840)
    Eng. traveler
    Courtney—Adven. p104-113

Roberts, Fannie (fl. 1870's)
    Amer. clergyman
    Hanaford—Dau. p476-480,668

Roberts, Florence (1861-1940)
    Amer. actress
    Cur. Biog. '40 p685
    Marks—Glamour p324

Roberts, Jane (b. 1809)
    Amer., wife of Liberian president
    Brown—Home. p46-49,por.

Roberts, Jewell Elizabeth Owen (m. 1934)
    Amer. missionary
    They—Went p104-106

Roberts, Kate Louise (d. 1941)
    Amer. librarian
    Cur. Biog. '41 p714

Roberts, Mary (d. 1761)
    Amer. colonial painter
    Leonard—Amer. p121

Roberts, Mary Fanton (d. 1956)
    Amer. editor
    Women—Achieve. p202

Roberts, Mary May (1877-1959)
    Amer. nurse, editor
    Dolan—Goodnow's p303,por.

Roberts, Widow (fl. 1740's)
    Amer. colonial inn proprietor
    Dexter—Colonial p12

Robertson, Agnes.
    See Boucicault, Agnes Robertson

Robertson, Alice M. (1854-1931)
    Amer. pioneer postmaster,
        Congresswoman
    DAR Mag. July 1921, p394, portrayal
    Paxton—Women p2-3,131

Robertson, Ann Lewis (fl. 1770's)
    Amer. pioneer
    Green—Pioneer (3) p125

Robertson, Charlotte Reeves (1751-1814)
    Amer. W. pioneer
    Ellet—Pioneer p63-78
    Green—Pioneer (3) p440-450
    Logan—Part p75-76

Robertson, Constance Noyes (Dana Scott)
        (1897-   )
    Amer. author
    Cur. Biog. '46 p511-512,por.
    Warfel—Amer. p362-363,por.

Robertson, Lucille (fl. 1930's)
    Amer. artist
    Women—Achieve. p155,por.

Robertson, Margaret.
    See Kendal, Margaret Robertson, Dame

Robertson, Marie. See Litton, Marie

Robertson, Mary Imogene (Mary Nolan)
    Amer. actress, dancer
    Brundidge—Twinkle p43-50,por.

Robesson, Eslanda Cardoza Goode (1896-
        1965)
    Amer. anthropologist, author
    Cur. Biog. '45 p505-506,por.

Robins, Elizabeth (C. E. Raimond,
        Elizabeth Raymond Parks)
        (1862/65-1952)
    Amer. novelist
    Hammerton p1154

Robins, Julia Gorham (fl. 1910's)
    Amer. author
    Logan—Part p731

Robins, Margaret Dreier (c. 1869-1945)
    Amer. social economist,
        organization official
    Cur. Biog. '45 p507
    Irwin—Angels p315-317,319-320

Robinson, Abbie C. B. (b. 1828)
    Amer. editor
    Logan—Part p871

Robinson, Adelaide Alsop (b. 1865)
    Amer. ceramic artist
    Jackman—Amer. p45-46

Robinson, Agnes Mary (b. 1857)
    Eng. author
    Hammerton p1154

Robinson, Anastasia, Countess of
        Peterborough (c. 1698-1755)
    Eng. singer
    McCoy—Portraits p168,por.
    MacQueen—Pope p163-165,por.
    Pleasants—Great p110,por.
    Wyndham—Chorus p31-32,por.

Robinson, Ann (n.d.)
    Amer., TV actress
    TV—Person (3) p113-114,por.

Robinson, Anna (m. 1905)
    Eng. actress
    Wyndham—Chorus p106-107,por.

Robinson, Carol (fl. 1930's)
    Amer. pianist
    Women—Achieve. p184,por.

Robinson, Corinne Roosevelt (1861-1933)
    Amer. poet, philanthropist, sister
        of Theodore Roosevelt
    Cook—Our p213-215

Robinson, Edna Mae Holly (n.d.)
    Amer. dancer, model
    °Cherry—Portraits p123-127,por.

Robinson, Elsie (1883-1956)
    Amer. journalist, columnist
    Ross—Ladies p384-386

Robinson, Evangeline (fl. 1930's)
    Amer. author
    Women—Achieve. p202

Robinson, Fannie Ruth (b. 1847)
    Amer. poet, educator
    Logan—Part p871

Robinson, Grace (fl. 1930's)
    Amer. journalist
    Ross—Ladies p7,270-280,por.,cover

Robinson, Hannah (fl. 1700's)
    Amer. colonial belle
    Bruce—Woman p59-64

Robinson, Harriet Hanson (b. 1825)
    Amer. feminist, merchant, author
    Dexter—Career p139,204-206,210-211,
        214-215
    Logan—Part p842-843

Robinson, Imogene Morrell (fl. 1870's)
    Amer. painter
    Waters—Women p290

Robinson, Irene Bowen (1891-   )
    Amer. painter
    Mahony—Illus. p353

Robinson, Jane Marie Bancroft (1847-1932)
    Amer. historian, philanthropist,
        foundress
    Dorland—Sum p130

Robinson, Josephine De Mott (d. 1948)
    Amer. circus performer
    °Ferris—Five p87-136,por.

Robinson, Judith.
    See Braxton, Judith Robinson

Robinson, Mabel Louise (d. 1962)
    Amer. author, educator
    Stoddard—Top. p131-143
    Warfel—Amer. p364,por.
    Women—Achieve. p202

Robinson, Margaret A. (fl. 19th-20th cent.)
    Can.-Amer. actress
    Marks—Glamour p324

Robinson, Martha Gilmore (fl. 1950's-
        1960's)
    Amer. club leader
    Parshalle—Kash. p57-58,por.

Robinson, Mary (fl. 1850's)
    Eng. nurse
    Dolan—Goodnow's p267

Robinson, Mary Darby ("Perdita") (1758-
        1800)
    Eng. actress, author
    Bottrall—Pers. p29-30,230
    Collins—Great p189-213
    Dorland—Sum p55-165
    MacCarthy—Later p82-86
    MacQueen—Pope p273-278
    Melville—More p171-196,por.
    Wyndham—Chorus p18-20

Robinson, Maude (fl. 1930's)
    Amer. ceramic artist
    Women—Achieve. p126,por.

Robinson, Nellie C. (fl. 1930's)
    Amer. patriot
    Women—Achieve. p91,por.

Robinson, Ophelia (1897-   )
    Amer. teacher, poet, educator
    Dreer—Amer. p51

Robinson, Pearle ("Perry") **Thurber** (n.d.)
    Amer. preflight aviation teacher
    °Peckham—Women p148-149,por.

**Robinson, Therese Albertine Louise von
        Jakob** (Talvj, pseud.) (1797-
        1869/70)
    Ger.-Amer. author, linguist,
        translator
    Dorland—Sum p44,177

Robinson-Duff, Frances (fl. 1930's)
    Amer. dramatic coach
    Women—Achieve. p83,por.

Robinson-Sawtelle, Lelia (d. 1891)
    Amer. pioneer lawyer
    Farmer—What p397,404-405

Robsart, Amy (c. 1532-1560)
    Eng., dau. of Sir John Robsart
    Hammerton p1155

Robson, Eleanor Elsie (1880-   )
    Eng. actress
    Blum—Great p27,por.
    °Kobbé—Homes p184-185,230-236,por.

Robson, Flora (1902-   )
    Eng. actress
    Blum—Great p129,por.
    Cur. Biog. '51 p528-530,por.
    Hammerton p1155

Robson, May (1865-1942)
    Austral.-Amer. actress
    Cur. Biog. '42 p697
    Marks—Glamous p325
    Strang—Actresses p323-338,por.

Robusti, Marietta (1560-1590)
    It. painter
    Waters—Women p290-292

Ruby, Ida Hall (b. 1867)
    Amer. pharmacist
    Logan—Part p898

Roby, Katie (b. 1812)
    Amer. friend of Abraham Lincoln
    Barton—Women p123-140

Roby, Lelia P. (b. 1848)
    Amer. philanthropist, foundress
    Logan—Part p375-376

Robyn, Louise (c. 1878-1949)
    Amer. composer, author, music
        teacher
    McCoy—Portraits p168,por.

Rocchi, Linda (fl. 1880's)
    It. artist
    Waters—Women p292

Rocco, Lili Rosalia (fl. 1880's)
    Sic. painter
    Waters—Women p292-293

Roche, Baroness de la (d. 1919)
    Fr. pioneer aviatrix
    Earhart—Fun p181
    °Lauwick—Heroines p27-28,30,por.
    Planck—Women p15,24

Roche, Josephine Aspinwall (b. 1886)
Amer. industrialist, lecturer
Beard—Amer. p428-432
Cur. Biog. '41 p723-725,por.
Rogers—Women p113,por.

Roche, Mazo de la.
See De la Roche, Mazo

Rochefort, Christiane (1917-   )
Fr. novelist
Peyre—French p287,438,461

Rock, Lillian (fl. 1920's-1930's)
Amer. lawyer
Women—Achieve. p63,por.

Rockefeller, Abby Aldrich (b. 1875)
Amer. social leader, wife of
John D. Rockefeller, Jr.
Time Jan.27,1936 p28,por.(Cover)

Rockefeller, "Bobo" (1917-   )
Amer. social leader, wife of
Winthrop Rockefeller
CR '59 p631-632,por.
CR '63 p527,por.

Rockefeller, "Happy" Margaretta Large
Fitler Murphy (n.d.)
Amer., 2nd wife of Nelson
Rockefeller
CR '63 p452,por.

Rockefeller, Mary Todhunter Clark
(1907-   )
Amer., 1st wife of Nelson
Rockefeller
Phelps—Men '58 (1) p217-218

Rockley, Alicia-Margaret Amherst, Baroness
(d. 1941)
Eng., author, gardener
Cur. Biog. '41 p730

Rockmore, Clara (1911-   )
Russ.-Amer. musician, thereminist
Saleski—Jewish p649-650,por.

Rockwell, Mabel MacFerran (1902-   )
Amer. electrical engineer
Goff—Women p94-112

Rodegunde (fl. 580's A.D.)
Fr. saint, queen
Blunt—Great p82

Rodger, Augusta M. (fl. 1870's-1880's)
Amer. inventor
Hanaford—Dau. p652

Rodgers, Irene (fl. 1940's)
Amer. composer, pianist
McCoy—Portraits p169,por.

Rodgers, Mary (1931-   )
Amer. composer
CR '63 p529-530,por.

Rodiana, Honorata (Onorata) (d. 1452)
It. artist, soldier, painter
Waters—Women p293-294

Rodman, Charity (1765-1823)
Amer. philanthropist
Hanaford—Dau. p166-168

Rodriguez, Marie Luisa Saldun de
(fl. 1950's)
Urug. physician
Lovejoy—Women p270

Rodriguez De Tió, Lola (1843-1924)
Puert. Ric. patriot, song-writer,
poet
Schmidt—400 p334-336,por.

Rodriguez de Toro, Luisa (fl. 1850's-1860's)
Span. painter
Waters—Women p294-295

Rodriguez-Dulanto, Laura Esther (gr.
1900)
Peru. physician
Lovejoy—Women p272

Roe, Dorothy (fl. 1920's-1930's)
Amer. journalist
Ross—Ladies p214-215

Roebling, Emily Warren (1843-1903)
Amer. Civil war patriot,
philanthropist, lawyer, club
leader, author
Logan—Part p297-299

Roebling, Mary Grindhart (1905/06-   )
Amer. banker
CR '59 p637,por.
CR '63 p530,por.
Cur. Biog. '60 p342-345,por.

Roeck, Marikka (fl. 1940's)
Ger. spy
Singer—World II p254-257

Roelofs, Henrietta (c. 1880-1942)
Amer. organization official
Cur. Biog. '42 p698

Roesgen-Champion, Marguerite (1894-   )
Swiss harpsichordist
Ewen—Living p299,por.

Rogé, Madame, pseud.
See Bates, Charlotte Fiske

Rogers, Abigail Dodge (fl. 1790's)
Amer. teacher
Dexter—Career p9-10

Rogers, Anne Hone (1929-   )
      Amer. animal handler
New York Apr.9,1960 p49 (Profiles)

Rogers, Annie Mary Anne Henley (1856-
      1927)
      Eng. educator, feminist
Brittain—Women (see index),por.

Rogers, Clara Kathleen (1844-1931)
      Eng.-Amer. composer
Howard—Our p363
McCoy—Portraits p169,por.

Rogers, Dale Evans (1912-   )
      Amer. singer, actress, wife of
            Roy Rogers
CR '59 p241,por.
Cur. Biog. '56 p525-527,por.
TV—Person (1) p138-139,por.

Rogers, Deborah.
See Franklin Deborah Read Rogers

Rogers, Edith Nourse (1881-1960)
      Amer. congresswoman, foundress
Cur. Biog. '42 p698-699,por.
Cur. Biog. '60 p344
Jensen—Revolt p59,por.
Paxton—Women p39-51,131,por.
Rogers—Women p65,por.

Rogers, Emma Winner (fl. 1910's)
      Amer. missionary
Logan—Part p817-818

Rogers, Ginger (1911-   )
      Amer. dancer, actress
CR '59 p637-638,por.
CR '63 p530,por.
Cur. Biog. '41 p730-732,por.
Cur. Biog. '67 p345-349,por.
Scheckel—Stars p141-142,por.
Time Apr.10,1939 p49,por.(Cover)

Rogers, Loula Kendall (fl. 1860's)
      Amer. Civil war patriot
Andrews—Women p286-302

Rogers, Mary (fl. 1890's)
      Brit. stewardess, sea heroine
*Deakin—True p203-216

Rogers, Mary Cecilia (1820-1841)
      Amer., heroine of Edgar Allen Poe
Wallace—Fabulous p172-215

Rogers, Mrs. (fl. 1790's)
      Amer. teacher
Dexter—Career p9-10

Rogers, N. (fl. 1930's)
      Amer. aviatrix
*May—Women p212

Rogers, Sara Jane ("Jennie") (fl. 1880's)
      Amer. W. pioneer
Parkhill—Wildest p40-49

Rogers, Tiana (d. 1838)
      Amer., 2nd wife of Sam Houston
Turner—Sam p21-24

Rogers, Vesta Marie (1909-   )
      Austral.-Amer. physician
Knapp—Women p17-31,por.

Roggero, Margaret (n.d.)
      Amer. singer
Matz—Opera p149-151

Rogner, Arveta (fl. 1920's)
      Amer. parachutist
*May—Women p56-57

Rohe, Alice (c. 1875-1957)
      Amer. journalist
Ross—Ladies p368-370

Rohe, Vera-Ellen. See Vera-Ellen

Rohlfs, Anna Katharine.
See Green, Anna Katharine

Rohlfs, Mrs. See Fenollosa, Mary McNeil

Rohrer, Gertrude Martin (fl. 1940's)
      Amer. composer, club leader
McCoy—Portraits p169,por.

Roland, Jeanne Manon Philipon, Madame
      (1754-1793)
      Fr. patriot, social leader, politician
Abbot—Notable p189-196
Abramowitz—Great p343-355
Adelman—Famous p94-96
Dobson—Four p31-59
Dorland—Sum p49-76
Fifty—Famous p121-125,por.
Hammerton p1158,por.
Jenkins—Heroines p473-520,por.
Kavanagh—Woman (2) p102,111-140,
      172-185,238,por.
*MacVeagh—Champlin p502
Muir—Women p119-122
Thomson—Queens p49-88

Rolanda (fl. 8th or 11th cent.)
      Ger. saint
Englebert—Lives p187

Rolfe, Pocahontas. See Pocahontas

Rollins, Charlemae (n.d.)
      Amer. librarian
*Hughes—First p45,por.
*Rollins—Famous p96,por.,cover

Roma, Caro (Carrie Northey) (1866-1937)
      Amer. composer, author, singer
ASCAP p418-419
McCoy—Portraits p170,por.

Roma, Lisa (fl. 1920's)
    Amer. singer
    McCoy—Portraits p170,por.

Romaine, Margaret (fl. 1910's)
    Amer. singer
    McCoy—Portraits p170,por.

Roman, Claire (d. 1939)
    Fr. pioneer aviatrix
    *Lauwick—Heroines p29

Roman, Mae (fl. 1930's)
    Amer. interior decorator, business
        executive
    Women—Achieve. p166,por.

Roman, Nancy Grace (1925-   )
    Amer. astronomer, space scientist
    Cur. Biog. '60 p345-347,por.
    *May—Women p244,por.
    Poole—Astronauts p29-31,33-34,40-43,
        por.
    Silver—Profiles p362-369,por.

Roman, Stella (fl. 1940's)
    Rum. singer
    McCoy—Portraits p170,por.
    Peltz—Spot. p77,por.

Romani, Juana (1869-1890's)
    It. painter
    Waters—Women p390-391

Rombauer, Irma von Starkloff (1877-
        1962)
    Amer. author
    Cur. Biog. '53 p544-545,por.
    Cur. Biog. '62 p363

Rombeau, Anne M. (n.d.)
    Amer. aviatrix, lecturer, traveler
    Murrow—This (1) p153-154

Rombout, Catheryna. See Brett, Catheryna

Romero family (fl. 1870's-1900's)
    Span. hermits
    Erskine—Out p136-143

Romic, Mary (n.d.)
    Amer. space scientist
    *May—Women p243

Roney, Marianne (1929-   )
    Ger. business executive
    Cur. Biog. '57 p115-117,por.

Ronner, Henriette (b. 1821)
    Nether. painter
    Waters—Women p295-297

Roobenian, Amber (1905-   )
    Amer. singer, organist, composer
    ASCAP p420

Rood, Helen Martin (1889-1943)
    Amer. author
    Cur. Biog. '43 p628

Roome, Mrs. Charle O.
    See Goertz, Arthémise

Roopnager (Rupnager), Princess of (fl.
        1860's-1730's)
    Ind., daughter of Emperor
        Aurangzeb
    Pool—Famous p75-82

Roosenboom, Margarite Vogel (1843-
        1896)
    Nether. painter
    Waters—Women p297-298

Roosevelt, Alice Lee.
    See Longworth, Alice Roosevelt

Roosevelt, Anna Eleanor.
    See Roosevelt, Eleanor

Roosevelt, Edith Kermit Carow (1861-
        1948)
    Amer., wife of Theodore Roosevelt
    Gerlinger—Mis. p81-84,por.
    Jensen—White p181-183,191,por.
    Logan—Ladies p139-145
    Logan—Part p282-283
    *McConnell—Our p243-252,por.
    Prindiville—First p195-202
    *Ross—Know p53,por.
    Smith—Romances p335-337,por.
    Truett—First p82,por.

Roosevelt, (Anna) Eleanor (1884-1962)
    Amer. humanitarian, lecturer,
        author, wife of Franklin Delano
        Roosevelt
    *Bolton—Lives p295-307,por.
    Bowie—Women p176-198
    CR '59 p644-645,por.
    *Commager—Crus. p229-233
    Cur. Biog. '40 p691-693,por.
    Cur. Biog. '49 p528-532,por.
    Cur. Biog. '63 p362
    *Curtin—Gallery p79,por.
    *Daugerty—Ten p136-147,por.
    Douglas—Remember p211-233,por.
    Fairfax—Ladies p199-201,206-209
    Fisher—Amer. p191-194,por.
    *Forsee—Amer. p159-181
    Gerlinger—Mis. p101-102,por.
    *Heath—Women (4) p27,por.
    Huff—Famous (2nd) p463-470,por.
    Jensen—Revolt p59,212,por.
    Jensen—White p238-239,por.
    Karsh—Faces p126,por.
    Kenworthy—12 p155-175,por.
    Lifton—Woman p267-287
    Logan—Ladies p193
    *McConnell—Our p305-317,por.
    Means—Woman p189-214,por.,cover

(Continued)

Roosevelt, (Anna) Eleanor—*Continued*

> Morris—400 p215-216
> Murrow—This (1) p155-156
> New Yorker June 12,1948 p30,por.;
>   June 19, 1948,p.30,por.(Profiles)
> Phelps—Men '59 (2) p242-244
> Phila.—Women unp.,por.
> Prindiville—First p245-264
> Reader's—Great p187-193,por.
> Robinson—100 p63-66,por.
> Rogers—Women p67,por.
> Roosevelt—Ladies p253-289
> *Ross—Know p65,por.
> Stiles—Postal p224
> Time Nov.20,1933 p12,por.;
>   Apr.17,1939 p21,por.;
>   Apr.7,1952 p4.2,por.Covers
> Truett—First p76,por.
> Women—Achieve. p23,por.

Roosevelt, Emily (1893-   )
> Amer. composer, singer
> McCoy—Portraits p170,por.
> Women—Achieve. p78,por.

Roosevelt, Martha Bulloch (m. 1853)
> Amer., mother of Theodore
>   Roosevelt
> Green—Pioneer (3) p323
> Hampton—Our p203-216

Roosevelt, Sara Delano (1855-1941)
> Amer., mother of Franklin Delano
>   Roosevelt
> Cur. Biog. '41 p732
> Love—Famous p19
> Time Mr.6,1933 p11,por.(Cover)

Root, Eliza H. (gr. 1882)
> Amer. physician
> Lovejoy—Women p92-93,97

Rope, Ellen Mary (b. 1855)
> Eng. sculptor
> Waters—Women p298

Roper, Margaret More (1505-1544)
> Eng. heroine, daughter of
>   Sir Thomas More
> Blunt—Great p197-223
> Cockran—Romance p129-134,por.
> Fifty—Famous p53-65,por.
> Hammerton p1163
> Muir—Women p87

Roquer, Emma de. See **Calvé, Emma**

Rorke, Kate (b. 1866)
> Eng. actress
> Hammerton p1163

Rosa, Aniella di (1613-1649)
> It. painter
> Waters—Women p298-299

Rosalba. See **Carriera, Rosalba**

Rosalita (d. 1160)
> It. saint
> Englebert—Lives p339
> Wescott—Calen. p134

Rosalita, Sister (fl. 1940's)
> Amer. missionary, nun
> Elgin—Nun p122-125,por.

Rosamond (c. 1140-c.1176)
> Eng. mistress of Henry II
> Hammerton p1163

Rosamund, Fair. See **Clifford, Rosamund**

Rosay, Françoise (1891-   )
> Fr. actress
> Ross—Players p207-214,por.

Rose, Ellen Alida (b. 1843)
> Amer. feminist, agriculturist,
>   business woman
> Logan—Part p897

Rose, Ernestine Louise Potowski (1810-
>   1892)
> Pol. social reformer, feminist
> Douglas—Remember p159-160
> O'Connor—Pioneer p74-75,141,162-
>   163,187,207,218-219,222-224
> Simonhoff—Jew. p315,por.

Rose, Laura Martin (b. 1862)
> Amer. club leader
> Logan—Part p300

Rose, Martha Parmelee (b. 1834)
> Amer. social reformer, sociologist,
>   art patron
> Logan—Part p595-596

Rose, Mary D. Swartz (1874-1941)
> Amer. nutritionist, government
>   official, author
> Cur. Biog. '41 p733
> Women—Achieve. p100,por.

Rose Marie, Baby (fl. 1930's)
> Amer. radio child actress
> Settel—Radio p75,por.

Rose of Lima (1586-1617)
> Peru. saint
> *Beebe—Saints p124-131
> Deen—Great p354
> Englebert—Lives p331-332
> Maynard—Saints p184-200
> Phila.—Women unp.,por.
> Sharkey—Pop. p157-161
> Stiles—Postal p239
> Wescott—Calen. p131
> *Windham—Sixty p350-355

Rose of Viterbo (1235-1253)
> It. saint
> Englebert—Lives p91
> Wescott—Calen. p67

Rosedale, Roxanne (n.d.)
    Amer. actress, TV performer
    TV—Person (1) p56-57,por.

Roselle, Anne (fl. 1930's)
    Hung. singer
    McCoy—Portraits p171,por.

Rosehill, Margaret Cheer, Lady (fl. 18th
    cent.)
    Amer. colonial actress
    Leonard—Amer. p121
    Spruill—Women's p261

Rosenberg, Anna Marie (1902-   )
    Hung.-Amer. government official
    CR '63 p535,por.
    Cur. Biog. '43 p631-634,por.
    Cur. Biog. '51 p538-540,por.
    Jensen—Revolt p60-61,por.
    New Yorker Apr.23,1938 p24,por.
    (Profiles)
    Phelps—Men's p59(2) p244-245
    Roosevelt—Ladies p198-205
    Women—Achieve. p202

Rosenberg, Beatrice (fl. 1930's)
    Amer. merchandise counselor
    Women—Achieve. p163,por.

Rosenberg, Ethel Greenglass (1915-1953)
    Amer. spy
    Singer—World's p70-89,por.

Rosenbery, Mollie R. M. (fl. 1910's)
    Amer. club leader, philanthropist
    Logan—Part p501

Rosenman, Dorothy Reuben (1900-   )
    Amer. housing expert
    Cur. Biog. '47 p549-551,por.

Rosenstein, Nettie (1897-   )
    Aust.-Amer. fashion designer,
      philanthropist, business executive
    CR '59 p643-644,por.
    New Yorker Oct.19,1940 p28,por.
    (Profiles)
    Women—Achieve. p167,por.

Rosenthal, Doris (n.d.)
    Amer. artist
    Ency. Brit.—Amer. p101,por.

Rosenthal, Jean (1912-   )
    Amer. theatrical lighting specialist,
      designer, consultant
    New Yorker Feb.4,1956 p33,por.
    (Profiles)

Rosmer, Ernst (Elsa Bernstein) (fl. 19th
    cent.)
    Ger. playwright
    Heller—Studies p293-294

Rosmond, Babette (1918-   )
    Amer. novelist
    Warfel—Amer. p365,por.

Ross, Anna Maria (fl. 1860's)
    Amer. Civil war philanthropist,
      nurse
    Brockett—Woman's p343-351
    Moore—Women p341-346

Ross, Anne Lawler (m. 1751)
    Amer. patriot
    Green—Pioneer (3) p207-209,280

Ross, Annie (fl. 1950's)
    Amer. singer
    Jazz—Panorama p157-160

Ross, Betsy (1) (fl. 1930's)
    Amer. aviatrix
    *Nida—Pilots p195-198
    Planck—Women p181-182

Ross, Betsy Griscom (Elizabeth Claypool;
    Elizabeth Grimke) (2)
    (1752-1832/36)
    Amer. pioneer flag-maker
    Adelman—Famous p88
    Bonte—Amer. p74,por.
    DAR Mag. July 1921 p382-383,portrayal
    *Dolin—World p30-35
    Green—Pioneer (3) p95-96,338-344
    *Humphrey—Elizabeths p39-55
    *Humphrey—Women p30-39
    Leonard—Amer. p113
    *MacVeagh—Champlin p507
    Muir—Women p146-148
    Phila.—Women unp.,por.
    Planck—Women p181-182
    *Stevens—Woman p23-26
    Stiles—Postal p225

Ross, Gertrude (fl. 1940's)
    Amer. composer, pianist
    McCoy—Portraits p171,por.

Ross, Ida Alena (b. 1885)
    Austral. novelist
    Hammerton p1428

Ross, Ishbel (1897-   )
    Scot.-Amer. author
    Beckwith—Contemp. p312-313
    Warfel—Amer. p365-366,por.

Ross, Ivy (d. 1933)
    Amer. journalist
    Ross—Ladies p444

Ross, Letitia Roano Dowdell (d. 1952)
    Amer. club leader
    Logan—Part p497-498

Ross, Mabel Hughes (m. 1929)
    Amer. missionary
    They—Went p126-127

Ross, Margaret Wheeler (d. 1953)
    Amer. pianist, music teacher,
        club leader
    Binheim—Women p7-8,por.
    McCoy—Portraits p171,por.

Ross, Martin. See Martin, Violet Florence

Ross, Mary (fl. 1920's-1930's)
    Amer. journalist
    Ross—Ladies p171

Ross, Myrta Pearson (m. 1917)
    Amer. missionary
    They—Went p52-53

Ross, Nancy Wilson (1907-   )
    Amer. author
    CR '63 p536
    Cur. Biog. '52 p505-506,por.
    Warfel—Amer. p366-367,por.

Ross, Nellie Tayloe (1880-1924)
    Amer. governor, government
        official
    CR '63 p536,por.
    Cur. Biog. '40 p697-699,por.
    *Heath—Women (4) p32,por.
    Roosevelt—Ladies p112-115

Ross, Oriel, Countess of Poulet (1907-   )
    Eng. actress
    Wyndham—Chorus p119-120

Ross, Rita (fl. 1910's-1930's)
    Amer., animal humanitarian
    New York. p85-97
    New Yorker May 14,1938 p21,por.
        (Profiles)

Rossel, Agda (Viola Jäderström) (1910-   )
    Swed. U.N. representative
    Cur. Biog. '59 p396-397,por.

Rossetti, Christina Georgina (1830-1894)
    Eng. poet
    Adelman—Famous p214
    Bald—Women p233-274
    *Benét—Famous Poets p36-48,por.
    Deen—Great p304
    Dorland—Sum p57,72,178
    *Green—Authors p133-135
    Hammerton p1165,por.
    Hubbard—Little p145-172,por.
    Moore—Disting. p43-58
    Schmidt—400 p159-160,por.
    Sitwell—Women p41-43,por.
    Untermeyer—Lives p527-531
    Winwar—Poor p22-30,35-37,109-111,
        302-306,309-314,385-386,por.

Rossetti, Elizabeth Siddal (fl. 19th cent.)
    wife of Dante Gabriel Rossetti
    Winwar—Poor p59-61,71-74,84-88,
        104-107,165-173,213-222,por.

Rossi, Properzia de (1490-1530)
    It. sculptor
    Waters—Women p299-301

Rosslyn, Countess of. See Robinson, Anna

Roswitha (Hrotswitha) (935-1002)
    Ger. poet, playwright, nun
    Deen—Great p326-327
    Dolan—Goodnow's p90
    Drinker—Music p199
    Gilder—Enter p18-45,por.
    Hammerton p785
    Koven—Women p11-12
    Mozans—Woman p43-45
    Schmidt—400 p190,por.
    Welch—Six p1-28,por.

Roth, Mrs. Frank C. (fl. 1930's)
    Amer. journalist
    Women—Achieve. p161,por.

Roth, Lillian (1911-   )
    Amer. actress, author
    CR '59 p649,por.
    CR '63 p537,por.

Roth, Vita F. (fl. 1940's)
    Amer. aviatrix
    *May—Women p162-163,184

Rothenberg, Rose (fl. 1930's)
    Amer. lawyer
    Women—Achieve. p116,por.

Rothery, Agnes Edwards (1888-1954)
    Amer. author
    Cur. Biog. '46 p523-524,por.
    Cur. Biog. '54 p547

Rothrock, Mary Utopia (1890-   )
    Amer. librarian, editor, author
    Bul. of Bibl. Sept.-Dec. '57 p73-75,por.

Rotky, Hanna, Baroness (b. 1857)
    Aust. painter
    Waters—Women p301

Roulet, Mary F. Nixon (fl. 1910's)
    Amer. author, journalist, musician,
        art critic, linguist
    Logan—Part p821

Round, Dorothy Edith (1909-   )
    Eng. lawn-tennis player
    Hammerton p1167

Roundtree, Martha (1916-   )
    Amer. radio, TV personality,
        journalist
    CR '63 p537,por.
    Cur. Biog. '57 p480-482,por.
    TV—Person (3) p29-30,por.

Rourke, Constance Mayfield (1885-1941)
Amer. author, critic, educator
Cur. Biog. '41 p736
*Millet—Amer. p172-173,556-557
Rourke—Roots p v-xii

Rousby, Clara Marion Jesse Dowse
(c. 1852-1879)
Eng. actress
Furniss—Some p45-47,por.

Rouse, Anna (fl. 1760's)
Amer. pioneer
Fowler—Woman p236-238

Rouse, Mrs. Benjamin (b. 1800)
Amer. Civil war humanitarian,
social reformer
Brockett—Woman's p544-545
Hanaford—Dau. p417-420

Rouse, Rebecca (fl. 1780's)
Amer. W. pioneer
Ellet—Pioneer p199-214
Logan—Part p60-63

Roussian, Tatiana (fl. 1960's)
Russ. aviatrix, helicopter pilot
*May—Women p208

Routt, Eliza Franklin (b. 1842)
Amer. social leader
Logan—Part p302

Routzahn, Mary Swain (m. 1914)
Amer. social worker
Women—Achieve. p174,por.

Rouverol, Aurania (1885-1955)
Amer. playwright, actress
Mantle—Contemp. p323

Rowden, Diana Hope (fl. 1940's)
Brit. spy
Hoehling—Women p128-132,por.
Singer—World's p228-229

Rowe, Elizabeth Singer (1674-1737)
Eng. author
MacCarthy—Women p251-286

Rowe, Fynette (1910-   )
Amer. novelist
Warfel—Amer. p368,por.

Rowe, Louise Jopling (1831-1884)
Eng. artist
Furniss—Some p83-85,por.

Rowe, Lucretia Olin (1896-   )
Amer. missionary, educator
They—Went p88-89

Rowland, Helen (n.d.)
Amer. journalist
Ross—Ladies p99,104,379-381,por.,
cover

Rowlandson, Mary White (c. 1635-1678)
Amer., Ind. captive, colonial
pioneer
Bruce—Woman p16-23
Dexter—Colonial p131-133
Earle—Colon. p23-24
Fowler—Woman p81-82
Leonard—Amer. p121
Peckham—Capt. p3-18

Rowson, Susanna Haswell (1762-1824)
Amer. actress, author, educator
Benson—Women p184-185,189-191
Coad—Amer. p41,por.
Dexter—Career p10-11,82-83,97-99
Leonard—Amer. p121
Papashvily—All p26-30,34
Rourke—Roots p75-87

Roxana (d.c. 309/311 B.C.)
Bactrian princess, wife of
Alexander the Great
Hammerton p1169

Roxburgh, May Goelet, Duchess of
(fl. 1890's)
Amer. heiress
Pearson—Marry. p208-213

Royall, Anne Newport (1769-1854)
Amer. journalist, author, editor,
publisher
Dexter—Career p110-115
Douglas—Remember p53-57
Ross—Ladies p27-30
Wallace—Square p243-266
Whitton—These p60-64,66
Woodward—Bold p8-23
Wright—Forgot p156-186

Royce, Sarah (fl. 1840's-1850's)
Eng.-Amer. W. pioneer
Brown—Gentle p37,108,191
Whitton—These p253-254,268

Royde-Smith, Naomi Gwladys (1875-1964)
Eng. novelist
Millett—Brit. p442-443

Roydne, Agnes Maude (1876-1956)
Eng. clergyman, author
Asquith—Myself p361-382,por.
Brittain p73,95-100,212,249
Cur. Biog. p719-720,por.
Cur. Biog. '56 p533
Gardiner—Por. p231-238
Hammerton p1169-1170
*Kirkland—Good p77-84
Lotz—Women p96-108

Royer, Clemence Augustine (1830-1902)
Fr. naturalist
Mozans—Woman p245-246

Roze, Marie Ponsin (1846-1926)
    Fr. singer
    Davidson—Treas. p259-261
    Ewen—Ency. p443-444
    Lahee—Famous p175-178,
    McCoy—Portraits p172,por.
    Wagner—Prima p51-52,247

Rubens, Maria (n.d.)
    Belg. heroine
    Schmidt—400 p56-57,por.

Rubinstein, Erna (1903-   )
    Hun. violinist
    McCoy—Portraits p172,por.
    Saleski—Wander. p240-242,por.

Rubinstein, Helena (Helen Gourielli)
    (c. 1871-1965)
    Pol.-Amer. cosmetician, business
        executive
    CR '59 p651-652,por.
    CR '63 p539-540,por.
    Cur. Biog. '43 p642-644,por.
    Cur. Biog. '65 p351
    New Yorker June 30, 1928 p20-23,por.
        (Profiles)
    Rogers—Women p199,por.
    Women—Achieve. p30,por.

Rubinstein, Ida (c. 1885-1960)
    Russ. dancer
    Hammerton p1171

Ruck, Berta (Mrs. Oliver Onions) (b. 1878)
    Eng. novelist
    Hammerton p1171

Rudd, Susan (fl. 1700's)
    Amer. social leader
    Hanaford—Dau. p143

Rudder, Madame de (fl. 1890's-1900's)
    Fr. embroidery artist
    Waters—Women p301-303

Rude, Ellen Sargent (b. 1838)
    Amer. poet
    Logan—Part p818

Rude, Sophie Fremiet (1797-1867)
    Fr. painter
    Waters—Women p303-304

Rudie, Evelyn (b.c. 1948-   )
    Amer. child TV actress
    Lamparski—What. p204-205,por.

Rudkin, Margaret Fogarty (1897-1967)
    Amer. bakery executive
    Cur. Biog. '59 p402-403,por.
    Cur. Biog. '67 p482
    New Yorker May 22,1948 p38,por.
        (Profiles)

Rudnick, Dorothea (1907-   )
    Amer. embryologist
    *Yost—Women Mod. p156-170

Rudnick, Elynor (fl. 1940's-1960's)
    Amer. aviatrix, helicopter pilot
    *May—Women p207

Rudolph, Wilma Glodean (1940-   )
    Amer. track athlete
    *Cherry—Portraits p174-177
    CR '63 p540,por.
    Cur. Biog. '61 p399-401
    *Gelfand—They p37-39,por.
    Gelman—Young p92-102,por.
    *Jacobs—Famous p80-86,por.
    Robinson—Hist. p247-248

Ruellan, Andreé (1905-   )
    Amer. artist
    Enc. Brit.—Amer. p102,por.

Ruffin, Josephine St. Pierre (1842-1924)
    Amer. feminist, Civil war patriot
    Brown—Home p151-153,por.

Ruffin, Margaret Ellen Henry (b. 1857)
    Amer. author
    Logan—Part p821

Rufina (1) (d. 257)
    Rom. saint
    Wescott—Calen. p99-100

Rufina (2) (d.c. 257/287)
    Span. saint
    Wescott—Calen. p105-106

Rufus, Maude Squire (b. 1880)
    Amer. aviatrix, "flying grandma"
    *May—Women p199-200
    *Peckham—Women p35
    Planck—Women p243,250-251,por.

Rufus' mother (Biblical)
    Deen—All p348-349

Rugerin, Anna (fl. 1480's)
    Ger. pioneer printer
    Club—Printing p10

Ruggles, Emily (b. 1827)
    Amer. business woman
    Hanaford—Dau. p608-609

"Ruhamah," pseud.
    See **Scidmore, Eliza Ruhamah**

Rukeyser, Muriel (1913-   )
    Amer. author
    Burnett—This p1155
    Cur. Biog. '43 p645-647,por.

Rule, Janice (1931-   )
    Amer. actress
    CR '63 p540-541,por.
    Ross—Player p351-358,por.

Rullann, Maria (fl. 1860's)
 Amer. teacher, philanthropist
 Hanaford—Dau. p210
 Logan—Part p314

Rumford, Marie Anne Pierrette Paulze
  Lavoisier, Countess (1758-
  1836)
 Fr. scientist
 Mozans—Woman p214-216

Rumsey, Elida.
 See Fowle, Elida B. Rumsey

Rumsey, Mary Ann (fl. 1820's)
 Amer. W. pioneer
 Ellet—Pioneer p376-381
 Logan—Part p95

Runbeck, Margaret Lee (1910-1956)
 Amer. author
 Cur. Biog. '52 p508-509,por.
 Cur. Biog. '56 p533
 Warfel—Amer. p368,por.

Runcie, Constance Owen (1836-1911)
 Amer. composer, pianist, club
  leader
 Elson—Woman's p258-259
 Hipsher—Amer. p321-322
 McCoy—Portraits p173,por.

Runeberg, Fredrika (1807-1879)
 Fin. author, feminist, pioneer
 Schmidt—400 p165,por.

Rünger, Gertrud (fl. 1940's)
 Pol. singer
 McCoy—Portraits p173,por.

Runkle, Bertha (d. 1958)
 Amer. novelist
 Harkins—Famous p331-343
 Harkins—Little p331-343
 Logan—Part p808

Rupnagar, Princess of.
 See Roopnager, Princess of

Rupprecht, Tini (b. 1868-   )
 Ger. painter
 Waters—Women p392

Rush, Julia Stockton (1759-1848)
 Amer. patriot
 Green—Pioneer (3) p136,169-174,por.

Rush, Phoebe Ann Ridgway (1797-1857)
 Amer. linguist, social leader
 Burt—Phila. p212-213
 Green—Pioneer (3) p174
 Logan—Part p283-284

Rusk, Mary F. Cleveland (d. 1856)
 Amer., wife of General Thomas
  Rusk
 Logan—Part p102-103

Ruskin, Margaret Cox (c. 1781-1871)
 Eng., mother of John Ruskin
 Peyton—Mothers p89-96
 Winwar—Poor p41-45,298

Russel, Mrs. Ezekiel (fl. 18th cent.)
 Amer. colonial printer, ballad
  writer
 Earle—Colonial p66-67

Russell, Anne (1911-   )
 Can. singer
 CR '59 p653,por.
 Cur. Biog. '54 p549-551,por.

Russell, Annie (1864-1936)
 Eng. actress
 Coad—Amer. p297,por.
 *Kobbé—Homes p95-137,por.
 Marks—Glamour p326
 Strang—Actresses p82-97,por.

Russell, E. Dilys Powell (gr. 1924)
 Eng. journalist
 Brittain—Women p177,252

Russell, Mrs. E. J. (fl. 1860's)
 Amer. Civil war nurse, teacher
 Brockett—Woman's p477-479
 Logan—Part p370

Russell, Elizabeth Mary Annette
  Beauchamp, Countess von Arnim
  (Elizabeth, pseud; Bettina,
  pseud.)
 Eng. novelist
 Adelman—Famous p285-286
 Cooper—Authors p1-18,por.
 Cur. Biog. '41 p743
 Dorland—Sum p35,173
 Hammerton p1173
 Hargrave—Some p155-203
 Lawrence—School p303-305

Russell, Elizabeth Shull (1913-   )
 Amer. zoologist, geneticist
 *Yost—Women Mod. p48-63,por.

Russell, Ella (1864-1935)
 Amer. singer
 McCoy—Portraits p174,por.

Russell, France ("Fanny"), Anna Maria
  Elliot, Countess (1815-   )
 Eng. patriot
 Lee—Wives p63-98,por.

Russell, Jane (1921-   )
 Amer. actress
 CR '59 p654,por.
 CR '63 p541-542,por.

Russell, Mrs. Joseph fl. 1770's)
 Amer. Rev. patriot
 Ellet—Women (2) p310-311

Russell, Lenie (fl. 1860's)
    Amer. Civil war heroine
Simkins—Women p72

Russell, Lillian (1861-1922)
    Amer. actress, singer
Adelman—Famous p267
Blum—Great p1,por.
Bodeen—Ladies p129-133
Caffin—Vaud. p78,por.
McCoy—Portraits p174,por.
Rogers—Women p45,por.
Strang—Prima p30-45,por.

Russell, Lois Hasselvander (m. 1920)
    Amer. missionary
They—Went p76-78

Russell, Martha M. (fl. 1910's-1920's)
    Amer. nurse
DAR Mag. Nov.1921 p644-645,por.

Russell, Penelope (fl. 1770's)
    Amer. printer
Club—Printing p12
Hanaford—Dau. p711

Russell, Rachel Wriothesley, Lady
    (1636-1723)
    Eng. author
Fifty—Famous p14-21,por.
Stenton—English p228-230

Russell, Rosalind (1911-   )
    Amer. actress
CR '59 p655,por.
CR '63 p542,por.
Cur. Biog. '43 p650-652,por.
Newquist—Show p387-401,por.
Time Mr.30,1953 p40,por.(Cover)

Russell, Sarah (fl. 1790's)
    Amer. printer, publisher
Dexter—Career p109

Russell, Tillie (fl. 1860's)
    Amer. Civil war heroine
Andrews—Women p145-147,413

Ruta, Gilda, Countess (fl. 1930's)
    It. pianist, music teacher, composer
Elson—Woman's p211-212

Ruth (Biblical)
Bowie—Women p3-4
Buchanan—Women p44-46
Culver—Women p29-30
Davenport—Great p60-62
Deen—All p81-87
Faulhaber—Women p144-146
Horton—Women p104-118
Hughes—Mothers p104-110
Levinger—Great p44-49
Lofts—Women p87-96
Lord—Great p71-82
MaCartney—Great p9-23
MacVeagh—Champlin p513

Marble—Women, Bible p183-188
Mead—250 p75
Morton—Women p75-83
*Nisenson—More Minute p123,por.
Ockenga—Women p75-89
Schmidt—400 p266,por.
Spurgeon—Sermons p107-146
Van Der Velde—She p107-113

Rutherford, Frances A. (fl. 1870's)
    Amer. physician
Hanaford—Dau. p669
Lovejoy—Women p101

Rutherford, Margaret (1892-   )
    Eng. actress
CR '59 p655-656,por.
Cur. Biog. '64 p383-385,por.

Rutledge, Ann (1816-1835)
    Amer., fianceé of Abraham Lincoln
Barton—Women p167-186

Rutledge, Elizabeth Grimke (d. 1792)
    Amer. Rev. war patriot
Green—Pioneer (3) p319-320

Rutledge, Henrietta Middleton (b. 1750)
    Amer. Rev. war patriot
Green—Pioneer (3) p264-266

Rutledge, Mary Shubrick Eveleigh
    (m. 1792)
    Amer. pioneer
Green—Pioneer (3) p265-266

Rutledge, Sarah Hert (Hext) (fl. 1730's)
    Amer. pioneer
Green—Pioneer (3) p320

Rutter, Margaret (fl. 1660's-1670's)
    Eng. actress
Wilson—All p184-185

Rutter, Ruth. See Hayward, Ruth Rutter

Ruys, A. Charlotte (gr. 1925)
    Nether. physician
Lovejoy—Women p184-185,por.

Ruysch, Rachel (1664-1750)
    Nether. painter
Adelman—Famous p72
Schmitt—400 p300-301,por.
Waters—Women p304-305

Ryan, Elizabeth ("Bunny") (fl. 1910's-
    1930's)
    Amer. lawn-tennis player
Hammerton p1175
New York Aug.22,1925 p9,por.
(Profiles)

Ryan, Harriet (fl. 1790's)
    Amer. hairdresser
Dexter—Career p38

Ryan, Ida Barry (fl. 1910's)
Amer. philanthropist
Logan—Part p536

Ryan, Mary P. Van Buren (fl. 1930's)
Amer. singer, music teacher,
accountant
Women—Achieve. p169,por.

Rybner (Rubner), Dagmar de Corval
(fl. 1910's)
Ger. composer
McCoy—Portraits p173,por.

Ryckoff, Lalla (fl. 1940's)
Amer. composer, pianist
McCoy—Portraits p174,por.

Ryder, Jeanette (fl. 1900's)
Cub., foundress
Stiles—Postal p228

Ryder, Theodora Sturkow (b. 1876)
Amer. composer, pianist, music
teacher
ASCAP p429

Ryerson, Margery Austen (b. 1886)
Amer. etcher, painter
Women—Achieve. p152,por.

Rysanek, Leonie (1928-   )
Aust. singer
CR '59 p656,por.
CR '63 p543,por.
Cur. Biog. '66 p347-348,por.

S

Saarinen, Aline Berstein Louchheim
(1914-   )
Amer. art critic, author
CR '63 p544,por.
Cur. Biog. '56 p534-535,por.

Sabagotha. See Natalia

Sabin, Florence Rena (1871-1953)
Amer. anatomist, author, educator,
scientist
Adelman—Famous p313
Castiglioni—Hist. p978,1127
Cur. Biog. '45 p527-529,por.
Cur. Biog. '53 p551
*Forsee—Women p127-151
Hume—Great p250,por.
Irwin—Angels p294
Logan—Part p729
Lovejoy—Women p109,126,por.
Rogers—Women p113,por.
16 Amer. p41-44
Women—Achieve. p60,por.
*Yost—Women Sci. p62-79

Sabin, Hannah. See Cooke, Hannah Sabin

Sabin, Pauline (Mrs. Charles) (m. 1916)
Amer. social reformer
Irwin—Angels p332-333
New Yorker Oct.22,1932 p20,por.
(Profiles)
Rogers—Women p159,por.
Time July 18,1932 p8,por.(Cover)

Sabina (fl. 117-138)
It. saint
Blunt—Great p7
Englebert—Lives p330

Sabina (fl. 3rd cent.)
Gr. saint
Wescott—Calen. p130

Sabina, Poppaea (d. 65)
Rom., wife of Nero
Boccaccio—Conc. p214-216

Sabina, Vibia (d.c. 138)
Rom., empress, wife of Hadrian
Balsdon—Roman p133,136,139-140,
194,257,por.
McCabe—Empr. p149-162,202,por.
Serviez—Roman (2) p3-17

Sable, Madeleine de Souvre, Marquise de
(1598/99-1678)
Fr. author, salonist
Dorland—Sum p23,104-105

Sablière, Marguerite de la.
See La Sablière, Marguerite de

Sabran, Madame de (1750-1827)
Fr. letter-writer
Kavanagh—Woman (1) p28

Sacajawea (Sakajawea) (c. 1787-1812)
Amer. Ind. pioneer, princess
DAR Mag. July 1921,p390-391,portrayal
*Deakin—True p297-315
Defenbach—Red p19-142,por.
*Dolin—World p59-67
Heiderstadt—Indian p45-53,por.
*Horowitz—Treas. p15-20
*Humphrey—Women p80-100
Logan—Part p20-21
Muir—Women p156-157
Ross—Heroines p34-51
Ross—Westward p93-99
Schmidt—400 p7-8,por.
*Sickels—Calico p125-139
*Stevens—Women p61-64,por.
Stiles—Postal p229
*Strong—Of p120-125
Whitton—These p269

Sachs, Emanie N. (m. 1917)
Amer. author
Overton—Women p291

Sachs, Evelyn (1924-   )
    Amer. singer
    Saleski—Jewish p618,por.

Sachs, Nelly (1891-   )
    Ger. poet, playwright
    Cur. Biog. '67 p365-367,por.

Sack, Erna (1908-   )
    Ger. singer
    Ewen—Living p307,por.
    McCoy—Portraits p175,por.

Sackett, Emma A. French (fl. 1860's)
    Amer. Civil war nurse
    Logan—Part p372

Sackville, Margaret, Lady (fl. 1910's-1930's)
    Eng. poet
    Hammerton p1176,por.

Sackville-West, Victoria (1892-1962)
    Eng. poet, novelist
    CR '59 p657-658,por.
    Lawrence—School p305-310
    Millett—Brit. p449-450
    Overton—Authors p66-80,por.

Sadako (1885-1951)
    Japan. princess
    Stiles—Postal p229

Sade, Laure de.
    See Chevigne, Laura De Sade,
    Comtesse de

Sadek, Narriman (1934-   )
    Egypt. queen, 2nd wife of Farouk
    Phila.—Women unp.,por.

Sadlier, Mary Anne Madden (1820-1903)
    Amer. novelist
    Blunt—Great p422-423

Safford, Mary Augusta (b. 1851)
    Amer. philanthropist
    Shaw—Story p142

Safford, Mary Joanna (d. 1891)
    Amer. Civil war humanitarian
    Brockett—Woman's p357-361,por.
    Logan—Part p844
    Young—Women p93-94,145,151-155,
        168,377,por.

Sagan, Françoise (1935-   )
    Fr. author
    CR '59 p658,por.
    Cur. Biog. '60 p355-355,por.
    Peyre—French p440,462-463

Sage, Florence (fl. 1940's)
    Amer. pianist, lecturer
    McCoy—Portraits p175,por.

Sage, Letitia Ann (fl. 1780's-1810's)
    Eng. pioneer balloon passenger
    °May—Women p11-13,por.
    Planck—Women p5

Sage, Margaret Olivia Slocum (1828-1918)
    Amer. philanthropist
    Adelman—Famous p253-254
    Fairfax—Ladies p72-73
    Logan—Part p545-547
    Rogers—Women p69,por.

Sager, Ruth (1918-   )
    Amer. geneticist
    Cur. Biog. '67 p367-370,por.

Saher, Lilla Van (fl. 1940's)
    Hung.-Amer. novelist
    Warfel—Amer. p435-436

Sahler, Helen (1877-1950)
    Amer. sculptor
    National—Contemp. p276
    Taft—Women, Mentor #6
    Women—Achieve. p114,por.

Saida, pseud.
    See Le Mair, Henriette Willebeek

Saint. See names of saints

Saint, Eva Marie (1924-   )
    Amer. actress
    CR '59 p659,por.
    CR '63 p545,por.
    Cur. Biog. '55 p524-525,por.
    TV—Person. (2) p67,por.

Saint Albans, Duchess of.
    See Mellon, Harriot, Duchess of
    St. Albans

Saint Augustine Mother (fl. 1830's)
    Fr.-Amer. nun
    Elgin—Nun p78-79,por.

St. Clair, Catherine N. (fl. 1850's)
    Amer. actress, theatrical builder,
        manager
    Coad—Amer. p181

St. Clair, Louisa.
    See Robb, Louisa St. Clair

St. Clair, Phoebe Bayard (fl. 18th cent.)
    Amer. pioneer
    Green—Pioneer (2) p197-198

St. Cyr, Lily (1920-   )
    Amer. burlesque queen
    CR '59 p659,por.
    CR '63 p545,por.

St. Damien, Sister (n.d.)
    Peru. nun
    Elgin—Nun p130-131

Salome (3) (1201-1269)
Hung. saint
Englebert—Lives p438

Salomon, Eliza (fl. 1860's)
Amer. Civil war philanthropist
Brockett—Woman's p613-614

Salomon, Leah (fl. 1800's-1830's)
Ger., mother of Mendelssohn
Bartlett—Mothers p46-50

Salomonsky, Verna Cook (fl. 1930's)
Amer. architect
Women—Achieve. p109,por.

Salonina, Cornelia (d. 268)
Rom. empress, wife of Gallienus
McCabe—Empr. p238-239,por.
Serviez—Roman (2) p316-317,322-323,
341-343

Salote Tubou (1900-1965)
Tonga queen
Arsenius—Dict. p169,por.
Cur. Biog. '53 p552-554,por.
Cur. Biog. '66 p470
Phila.—Women unp.,por.
Stiles—Postal p242

Salpe (fl. 1st cent. B.C.)
Gr. poet
Anthologia—Poets p97

Salsich, Margaret.
See Banning, Margaret Culkin

Salter, Mary Turner (1856-1938)
Amer. composer, singer,
song-writer
ASCAP p432
Howard—Our p564,598
McCoy—Portraits p176,por.

Saltza, Chris von (1944-   )
Amer. swimmer
*Gelman—Young p73-83,por.

Saltzman-Stevens, Minnie (b. 1878)
Amer. singer
Lahee—Grand p430-432

Salustia Barbia Orbiana (fl. 200's-230's A.D.)
Rom. empress
Serviez—Roman (2) p277

Salverson, Laura Goodman (1890-   )
Can. author
Cur. Biog. '57 p486-487,por.
Thomas—Canad. p109-110

Salvini-Donatelli, Fanny (fl. 19th cent.)
It. singer
Wagner—Prima p113,247

Salway, Ray (fl. 1940's)
E. Ind. airline hostess
*May—Women p239

Salyards, Christiana Stedman (1861-1951)
Amer. religious worker, author
Phillips—33 p95-101

Salzman, Pnina (1922-   )
Israeli pianist
Saleski—Jewish p709,por.

Samaria, woman of (Samaritan woman)
(Biblical)
Buchanan—Women p80-82
Deen—All p195-200
Faulhaber—Women p159-165
Lewis—Portraits p199-201
Lord—Great p123-134
Morton—Women p151-158
Van der Velde—She p205-211

Samaroff, Olga (1882-1948)
Amer. pianist, music teacher
Cur. Biog. '46 p531-534,por.
Cur. Biog. '48 p546
McCoy—Portraits p176,por.
Schonberg—Great p386-387,por.

Sammis-MacDermid, Sibyl (fl. 1940's)
Amer. singer, teacher
McCoy—Portraits p177,por.

Sammuramat. See Semiramis

Sampson, Deborah (1760-1827)
(Robert Shirtliffe, pseud.,
Deborah Gannett)
Amer. Rev. war soldier, heroine
Bruce—Woman p91-96
Ellet—Women (2) p143-158,por.
Fowler—Woman p402-408
Green—Pioneer (2) p265-279,por.
Hanaford—Dau. p50
Leonard—Amer. p115-116
Logan—Part p143-149
Schmidt—400 p12-13,por.
Whitton—These p14-16
Wright—Forgot. p94-120,por.

Sampson, Edith Spurlock (1901-   )
Amer. lawyer, U.N. delegate
*Cherry—Portraits p159-165,por.
Cur. Biog. '50 p511-513,por.
*Hughes—First p64,por.
Robinson—Hist. p248

Samson, Deborah.
See Sampson, Deborah

Samson's mother (Biblical)
Buchanan—Women p42

Samson's wife (Biblical)
Deen—All p326-328
Lewis—Portraits p43-45

Samuels, Margaret (fl. 1930's)
    Amer. librarian, teacher, author
    Women—Achieve. p203

Sanballat, daughter of (Biblical)
    Deen—All p315-316

Sanborn, Katherine (Kate) Abbott (1939-
            1917)
    Amer. teacher, essayist, lecturer,
        agriculturist
    Logan—Part p869

Sand, George, pseud. (Armandine Lucile
            Aurore Dupin Dudevant)
    Fr. novelist
    Abbot—Notable p402-406,por.
    Adelman—Famous p155-156,por.
    Blei—Fasc. p200-209,por.
    Bradford—Daughters p199-239,por.
    De Morny—Best p171-181,por.
    Dorland—Sum p42,192-193
    Dunaway—Treas. p143-146
    Hammerton p1183,por.
    *MacVeagh—Champlin p518,por.
    Maurice—Makers p12
    Moore—Disting. p81-95
    Muir—Women p176
    Orr—Famous Affin. IV p95-126
    Padover—Confess. p183-189
    Parton—Dau. p546-563,por.
    Parton—Noted p585-600,por.
    Ravenel—Women p64-89,por.
    Schmidt—400 p183,por.
    Sewell—Brief p122-123
    Sherman—World's p157-162
    Stiles—Postal p76
    Terhune—Super. p156-174

Sandberg, Marta Ehrlich (fl. 1930's)
    Ger.-Amer. chemist
    Women—Achieve. p186,por.

Sandell, Viola T. (fl. 1960's)
    Amer. aviatrix
    *May—Women p196

Sanders, Alma M. (1882-1923)
    Amer. composer
    ASCAP p434

Sanders, Harriet Fenn (1834-1909)
    Amer. pioneer
    *Johnson—Some p58-75,por.

Sanders, Sue A. Pike (fl. 1910's)
    Amer. club leader
    Logan—Part p350

Sanders, Mrs. Wilbur (d.c. 1909)
    Amer. W. pioneer, vigilante
    Towle—Vigil. p104-122,por.

Sanderson, Elizabeth (1825-1925)
    Eng. mother of Lord Haldane
    Wallace—Mothers p69-75

Sanderson, Julia (b. 1887)
    Amer. actress
    Blum—Great p71,por.
    Donaldson—Radio p25
    Eichberg—Radio p68-69,por.
    Settel—Radio p93,por.

Sanderson, Sybil (1865-1903)
    Amer. singer
    Davidson—Treas. p261-264
    Elson—Woman's p130,por.
    Ewen—Ency. p454
    Lahee—Famous p248-251
    Logan—Part p781
    McCoy—Portraits p177,por.

Sandes, Flora (fl. 1910's)
    Eng. nurse, heroine, soldier
    *Deakin—True p329-343
    Dorland—Sum p97

Sandoz, Mari (1901-   )
    Amer. author
    CR '63 p549,por.

Sanford, Amanda (gr. 1871)
    Amer. physician
    Irwin—Angels p136-137
    Lovejoy—Women p101-102
    Mead—Medical p48

Sanger, Margaret Higgins (1883-1966)
    Amer. social reformer, lecturer,
        author
    Adelman—Famous p323-324
    Allen—Advent. p52-68,por.
    CR '59 p665,por.
    CR '63 p549-550,por.
    Cur. Biog. '44 p585-589,por.
    Cur. Biog. '66 p470
    Holbrook—Dreamers p216-217
    Irwin—Angels p297
    Jensen—Revolt p83,por.
    Murrow—This (2) p130-131
    New Yorker Apr.11,1925 p11,por.;
        July 5,1930 p22,por. (Profiles)
    Rogers—Women p57,por.
    Stone—We p456-462
    Women—Achieve. p26,por.

Sangster, Margaret Elizabeth Munson
            (1838-1912)
    Amer. author, editor
    Adelman—Famous p217-218
    Dorland—Sum p18,78,181
    Logan—Part p869-870

San Martin, Romedios de Ascala de (1797-
            1823)
    Argent. patriot
    Schmidt—400 p33,por.

Sansbury, Angela, Mother (1795-1839)
    Amer. foundress
    Code—Great p230-253

Sans-Gêne, Madame (1774-1861)
Fr. adventuress
Hammerton p1184

Sansom, Emma (d. 1900)
Amer. Civil war heroine, diarist
Andrews—Women p278-283
Harkness—Heroines p6
Jones—Heroines p215-217
Logan—Part p304

Sansom, Odette.
See Churchill, Odette Mary Celine
Brailly Sansom

Santa Francesca Romana (1384-1440)
It. mother, protectress
Keyes—Three p41-123,por.

Santa Maria, Doña Manuela Sanz de (b. 1770)
Colom. patriot author
Schmidt—400 p78-79,por.

Santlow, Hester (fl. 1720's-1770's)
Eng. actress
MacQueen—Pope p113-117,por.

Santolalla, Irene Silva de (1904-   )
Peru. government official, educator, author, lecturer
Cur. Biog. '56 p542-544,por.

Santuccia Terrebotti (d. 1205)
It. foundress
Englebert—Lives p113

Sapho.
See Scudéry, Magdeleine de

Sapphira (Biblical)
Deen—All p213-217
Lewis—Portraits p171-172
*MacVeagh—Champlin p520
Marble—Women, Bible p104-105
Van der Velde—She p220-226

Sappho (fl.c. 600 B.C.)
Gr. poet
Adelman—Famous p19-20
Anthologia—Poets p79-81
Beard—Woman p312
Boccaccio—Conc. p99-100
Brown—Dark p91-159
Drinker—Music p104-107
Elson—Woman's p25-27
Ewart—World's p25-42
Hahn—Love p27-36
Hammerton p1185
*MacVeagh—Champlin p520
Maurice—Makers p12
Moore—Disting. p71-80
Mozans—Woman p5-8
Muir—Women p31-34
Schmidt—400 p211-212,por.
Sewell—Brief p2

Sarabhai, Anasuya (fl. 1930's-1940's)
Ind. Gandhi co-worker
Stern—Women p125

Saragossa (Saragoza), Augustina (1786-1857)
Span. patriot, heroine
Hammerton p1186
Schmidt—400 p355-356,por.

Sarah (1) (Sarai) (Biblical)
wife of Abraham
Buchanan—Women p13-16
Deen—All p8-16
Hammerton p11,1186
Horton—Women p16-32
Hughes—Mothers p34-57
*Levinger—Great p3-10
Lewis—Portraits p18-22
Lofts—Women p6-22
Lord—Great p23-24
*MacVeagh—Champlin p520
Marble—Women p119-124
Mead—250 p23
Morton—Women p17-27
Nelson—Bible p17-20
Ockenga—Women p19-28
Schmidt—400 p263-264,por.
Van der Velde—She p23-29

Sarah (2) (Biblical)
daughter of Asher
Deen—All p291

Sargent, Ellen C. (fl. 1910's)
Amer. social reformer

Sargent, Julia Amanda.
See Wood, Minnie Lee
Logan—Part p587-588

Sarnoff, Dorothy (n.d.)
Amer. singer
Saleski—Jewish p619,por.

Sarojini Nayadu.
See Naidu, Sarojini

Saroya, Bianca (fl. 1910's)
Amer. singer
McCoy—Portraits p178,por.

Sarraute, Nathalie (1900/02-   )
Fr. novelist
Cur. Biog. '66 p349-351,por.
Peyre—French p440-441,463

Sartain, Emily (b. 1841)
Eng.-Amer. painter, etcher, illustrator
Hanaford—Dau. p312-315
Logan—Part p757
Waters—Women p306

Sartain, Geraldine (fl. 1920's)
Amer. journalist
Ross—Ladies p220-224,por.cover

Sartain, Harriet (d. 1957)
Amer. artist, teacher
Logan—Part p757

Sartoris, Adelaide Kemble (1814-1879)
Eng. singer
Dorland—Sum p26

Sartoris, Ellen Grant (b. 1857)
Amer., daughter of Ulysses S. Grant
*Sweetser—Famous p212-229,por.

Saruya, Julia Salinger (fl. 1930's)
Amer. milliner, business executive
Women—Achieve. p169,por.

Sasa, Marie-Constance (1838-1907)
Belg. singer
McCoy—Portraits p178,por.

Saunders, Agnes Kelly (fl. 1920's-1930's)
Amer. museum director
Women—Achieve. p86,por.

Saunders, Aileen (fl. 1950's-1960's)
Amer. aviatrix
*May—Women p188

Saunders, Hortense (fl. 1910's-1930's)
Ross—Ladies p435-436

Saunders, Margaret (fl. 1700's-1740's)
Eng. actress
MacQueen—Pope p161

Saunders, Margaret Marshall (b. 1861)
Can. author
Adelman—Famous p295

Saunders, Marshall (1861-1947)
Can. author
Harkins—Famous p173-189,por.
Harkins—Little p173-189,por.
Thomas—Canad. p110-112

Saunders, Mary A. (b. 1849)
Amer. inventor, business woman
Logan—Part p897-898

Saunderson, Mary.
See Betterton, Mary Saunderson

Sauvageot, Marcelle (d. 1934)
Fr. novelist
Peyre—French p279-281

Savage, Augusta Christine (1900/10-   )
Amer. sculptor
*Cherry—Portraits p194-195
Cur. Biog. '41 p752-754,por.
Cur. Biog. '62 p372
Robinson—Hist. p248-249,por.

Savage, Elizabeth.
See Heyward, Elizabeth

Savage, Mary (fl. 1790's)
Amer. clergyman
Dexter—Career p59

Savery, Constance Winifred (1897-   )
Eng. author
Cur. Biog. '48 p548-549,por.

Savi, Ethel Winifred (b. 1865/86)
Eng. author
Hammerton p1188

Savigny, Anna Victorine (fl. 19th cent.)
("Madame de Thebes")
Fr. astrologist
Dorland—Sum p143

Saville, Frances (1862-1935)
Amer. singer
McCoy—Portraits p178,por.

Savina, Marie G. (1854-1915)
Russ. actress
Schmidt—400 p346,por.

Savitri (date uncertain)
E. Ind., dau. of Aswapati
Pool—Famous p46-58

Savord, Ruth (1894-1966)
Amer. librarian
Women—Achieve. p136,por.

Savoy, Maggie (n.d.)
Amer., Arizona's "Lady Fare"
CR '63 p551

Savoy, Marie Adelaide of (fl. 1700's)
Fr., friend of Louis XIV
Haggard—Remark. p180-182,184-187,
189-193,198-200

Savoy, Yolande (d. 1299)
It. saint
Englebert—Lives p231
Koven—Women p85-86

Sawin, Martha A. (1815-1859)
Amer. physician
Mead—Medical p45

Sawyer, A. R. (fl. 1870's-1880's)
Amer. artist
Hanaford—Dau. p320

Sawyer, Caroline Mehitabel Fisher (1812-
1894)
Amer. poet, editor, author
Hanaford—Dau. p265

Sawyer, Helen Alton (n.d.)
Amer. artist, teacher
Cur. Biog. '54 p556-557,por.

Sawyer, Lucy (fl. 1870's-1880's)
Amer. inventor
Hanaford—Dau. p644

Sawyers, Martha (fl. 1930's-1940's)
Amer. illustrator
Watson—40 p263-267,por.

Saxe Weimar, Duchess of. See **Anna Amalia**

Saxl, Eva R. (c. 1921-   )
Czech.-Amer. teacher, traveler,
lecturer, author
Murrow—This (1) p163-164

Sayao, Bidu (c. 1906-   )
Brazil. singer
Cur. Biog. '42 p735-737,por.
Ewen—Ency. p457
Ewing—Living p311-312,por.
McCoy—Portraits p178,por.
Peltz—Spot. p79,por.

Sayers, Dorothy Leigh (1893-1957)
Eng. author
Brittain—Women p122-124,156,213,
251,255
Hammerton p1190

Sayn-Wittgenstein, Carolyne (1819-1887)
Pol. princess, author
Hammerton p1190

Sayre, Ruth (fl. 1630's-1640's)
Amer. patriot
Green—Pioneers (3) p478-479

Sayre, Ruth Buxton (1896-   )
Amer. organization official
Cur. Biog. '49 p550-551,por.

Scalchi, Sofia (1850-1922)
It. singer
Ewen—Ency. p457
Klein—Great p167-170,por.
Lahee—Famous p300-302
McCoy—Portraits p179,por.
Wagner—Prima p61,247

Scales, Cordelia Lewis (fl. 1860's)
Amer. Civil war diarist
Jones—Heroines p179-182,203-207

Scarborough, Dorothy (d. 1935)
Amer. novelist
Overton—Women p292-293

Scarborough, Katherine (fl. 1910's)
Amer. journalist
Ross—Ladies p498-500

Scarlett, Rebecca.
See **Burt, Katharine Newlin**

Scarron, Madame.
See **Maintenon, Françoise D'Aubigne
Marquise de**

Schabanoff, Anna N. (gr. 1877)
Russ. physician
Lovejoy—Women p169

Schachter, Joan.
See **Edwards, Joan**

Schaefer, Maria (b. 1854)
Ger. painter
Waters—Women p306-307

Schaeffer, Mary (n.d)
Amer. composer, author, pianist,
organist
ASCAP p438

Schain, Josephine (n.d.)
Amer. consultant, social worker,
lecturer
Cur. Biog. '45 p532-534,por.
Women—Achieve. p108,por.

Schanne, Margrethe (fl. 1950's)
Dan. ballet dancer
Stiles—Postal p245

Scharibrook, Elizabeth (fl. 1760's)
Amer. colonial teacher
Dexter—Colonial p94-95

Scharlieb, Mary Ann Dacomb Bird, Dame
(1845-1930)
Eng. physician, gynecologist,
surgeon
Bell—Storm. p113-116,130-131,
169,por.
Hammerton p1191,por.

Scharr, Adela Rick (fl. 1930's)
Amer. aviation instructor
Planck—Women p165-166

Scharrer, Irene (b. 1888)
Eng. pianist
Hammerton p1191
McCoy—Portraits p179,por.

Schaumberj (Schaumberg), Emilie
(fl. 1860's)
Amer. social leader
Hanaford—Dau. p147
Logan—Part p295

Schechner-Waagen, Nanette (1806-1860)
Ger. singer
McCoy—Portraits p180,por.

Scheff, Fritzi (1879/82-1954)
Aust. singer, actress
Blum—Great p45,por.
New Yorker Nov.16,1929,p30,por.
(Profiles)

Scheffer, Caroline (d. 1839)
Nether.-Fr. artist
Waters—Women p307

Scheider, May (fl. 1900's-1910's)
Amer. singer
McCoy—Portraits p180,por.

Schell, Maria Margarethe Anna (1926-   )
 Aust. actress
 CR '59 p669,por.
 CR '63 p553,por.
 Cur. Biog. '61 p411-413,por.
 Ross—Player p224-230,por.
 Time Dec.30,1957 p40,por.(Cover)

Schelling, Karoline (1763-1809)
 Ger. scholar, essayist
 Dorland—Sum p36,173

Schemm, Mildred.
 See Walker, Mildred

Schenck, Alice.
 See Teller, Alice Schenck

Schenck, Hannah Brett (fl. 1790's)
 Amer. pioneer
 Green—Pioneer (1) p420,423-424

Schenck, Rachel Katherine (1899-   )
 Amer. librarian, educator
 Bul. of Bibl. Jan.-Apr.'62 p145-146,por.

Schervier, Frances (Franziska), Mother
 (1819-1876)
 Ger. nurse, nun, foundress
 Pennock—Makers p22

Schiaparelli, Elsa (c. 1907-   )
 It. fashion designer
 CR '59 p670,por.
 Cur. Biog. '40 p719-720,por.
 Cur. Biog. '51 p551-553,por.
 New York. p239-246
 New Yorker June18,1932 p19-23,por.
  (Profiles)
 Time Aug.13,1934 p49,por.(Cover)

Schidlowskaia, Olga (fl. 1910's)
 Russ. soldier, heroine
 Dorland—Sum p99

Schiff, Dorothy (1903-   )
 Amer. journalist, publisher
 CR '59 p670,por.
 CR '63 p553-554,por.
 Cur. Biog. '65 p364-366,por.

Schiffi, Chiara.
 See Clare (saint)

Schille, Alice (n.d.)
 Amer. painter
 Michigan—Biog. p279

Schiller, Charlotte Von (1766-1826)
 Ger., wife of Johann Schiller
 Schmidt—400 p197,por.

Schilling, Bertha.
 See Breval, Lucienne

Schimmoler, Laurette (fl. 1930's)
 Amer. aviatrix
 *May—Women p90-91
 Planck—Women p185-186

Schirmacher, Dora (b. 1862)
 Eng. composer
 Elson—Woman's p146

Schlamme, Martha (c. 1930-   )
 Aust. singer, actress
 Cur. Biog. '64 p392-393,por.

Schlauch, Margaret (1898-   )
 Amer. educator, author, philologist
 Cur. Biog. '42 p737-738,por.

Schlegel, Caroline (b. 1763)
 Ger. salonist
 Hargrave—Some p247-275,por.

Schleh, Anna (b. 1833)
 Ger. painter
 Waters—Women p307

Schlein, Miriam (1926-   )
 Amer. author
 Cur. Biog. '59 p405-406,por.

Schlesin, Sonya (n.d.)
 Scot.-Russ., co-worker of Gandhi
 Stern—Women p85-91

Schliemann, Sophia Kastromenos (d. 1932)
 Gr. archaeologist
 Mozans—Women p317-319

Schmäling (Schmeling), Mademoiselle.
 See Mara, (Gertrude) Elizabeth
 Schmeling

Schmitt, Edwienne (fl. 1930's)
 Amer. lawyer
 Women—Achieve. p203

Schmitt, Gladys Leonore (Gladys Goldfield)
 Amer. author, teacher, editor
 Cur. Biog. '43 p671-673,por.
 Warfel—Amer. p373,por.

Schmitt, Susan (fl. 1940's)
 Amer. composer, pianist, teacher
 McCoy—Portraits p182,por.

Schmitt-Schenkh, Maria (b. 1837)
 Ger. painter, designer
 Waters—Women p307

Schneider, Alma Kittredge (1901-   )
 Amer. government official
 Cur. Biog. '54 p559-561,por.

Schneider, Romy (1938-   )
 Aust. actress
 Cur. Biog. '65 p369-370,por.

Schneiderman, Rose (b. 1884)
Pol.-Amer. labor leader
Cur. Biog. '46 p538-541,por.
Fisher—Amer. p187-188,por.
Rogers—Women p68,por.

Schnitzer, Germaine (b. 1888)
Fr. pianist
McCoy—Portraits p182,por.
Saleski—Wander. p386-387,por.

Schnorr von Carolsfeld, Malwine (1832-1904)
Dan. singer
McCoy—Portraits p182,por.

Schnurer, Carolyn Goldsand (1908-   )
Amer. fashion designer
Cur. Biog. '55 p535-537,por.

Schoene, Lotte (fl. 1930's)
Aust. singer
McCoy—Portraits p182,por.

Schoenfeld, Julia (gr. 1897)
Amer. philanthropist
Logan—Part p648-649

Schoen-René, Anna Eugenie (1864-1942)
Ger.-Amer. voice teacher
Cur. Biog. '43 p673
Ewen—Ency. p462

Schoff, Hannah Kent (1853-1940)
Amer. editor, author, child-aid leader
Bennett—Amer. p139-160,por.
Cur. Biog. '41 p759
Logan—Part p403-405

Scholastica (480-547)
It. saint, sister of St. Benedict
Culver—Women p79,85
Dolan—Goodnow's p89,por.
Stiles—Postal p239

Scholl, Sophie (1921-1943)
Ger. patriot
Stiles—Postal p246

Scholte, Mareah (fl. 1840's)
Nether. immigrant, wife of Minister
Cavanah—We p181-194

Scholtz-Klink, Gertrud.
See Klink, Gertrud Schotz

Schoonhoven, Helen Butterfield (b. 1869)
Amer. lecturer, teacher
Women—Achieve. p165,por.

Schoop, Trudi 1903-   )
Swiss dancer, comedienne
Hurok—Impres. p171-173,por.

Schorr, Esther Brann (fl. 1930's)
Amer. artist, author
Women—Achieve. p203

Schram, Ann Maria B. (fl. 1860's)
Amer. Civil war nurse
Logan—Part p370-371

Schramck, Olga E. (fl. 1930's)
Amer. wedding counselor
Women—Achieve. p103,por.

Schratt, Katharina (1856-1940)
Aust. courtesan, mistress of Emperor Francis Joseph
Cur. Biog. '40 p720-721,por.
Kelen—Mist. p280-292,313-328,334-335,por.

Schreiber, Charlotte.
See Guest, Charlotte Elizabeth
Bertie, Lady Schreiber

Schreiner, Olive (Ralph Iron, pseud.)
Eng.-S. Afr. feminist, author
Adelman—Famous p262
Hammerton p1194,por.
Lawrence—School p126-156,por.
Stern—Women p61-73,91-101,por.
Wellington—Women p91-111

Schrick, Maria. See Provost, Marie

Schröder, Sophie Bürger (1781-1868)
Ger. actress
Dorland—Sum p38,69,165

Schröder-Devrient, Wilhelmine (1804-1860)
Ger. singer
Dorland—Sum p38
Ewen—Ency. p464
Lahee—Famous p77-79
McCoy—Portraits p183,por.
Pleasants—Great p152-157,por.

Schroeder, Louise (1887-1957)
Ger. mayor
Stiles—Postal p247

Schröter, Corona Von (1751-1802)
Ger. singer, composer
McCoy—Portraits p183,por.
Schmidt—400 p196,por.

Schubin, Ossip (Lola Kirschner) (fl. 19th cent.)
Ger. author
Heller—Studies p264-265

Schulenburg, Ehrengarde Melusina von der, Countess (Duchess of Kendal) (c. 1667-1743)
Eng., mistress of George I
Hammerton p845,1196
Trowbridge—Seven p61-95,por.

Schuller, Mary Craig.
 See McGeachy, Mary Agnes Craig

Schultz, Sigrid Lillian (fl. 1920's-1940's)
 Amer. journalist, author
 Cur. Biog. '44 p600-603,por.
 Ross—Ladies p365,376-377

Schultz-Adaievsky Ella von (1846-1926)
 Russ. composer, pianist
 McCoy—Portraits p184,por.

Schumann, Clara Josephine Wieck (1819-
  1896)
 Ger. pianist, composer, music
  teacher
 Adelman—Famous p199
 Brook—Masters p81-95,por.
 Dorland—Sum p55-56,78,160
 Elson—Woman's p90-110,por.
 Hammerton p1196,por.
 McCoy—Portraits p184,por.
 Schonberg—Great p223-230

Schumann, Elisabeth (1891-1952)
 Ger. singer
 Davidson—Treas. p267-269
 Ewen—Ency. p465
 Ewen—Living p318-319,por.
 McCoy—Portraits p184,por.
 Wagner—Prima p80-81,248

Schumann, Meta (fl. 1940's)
 Amer. composer, singer
 McCoy—Portraits p184,por.

Schumann-Heink, Ernestine Roessler (1861-
  1936)
 Bohem. singer
 Adelman—Famous p295
 Ewen—Ency. p466
 Fairfax—Ladies p141-144
 *Ferris—When p2-67,por.
 Huff—Famous (2nd) p517-528,por.
 Klein—Great p177-182,por.
 McCoy—Portraits p184,por.
 Mears—They p98
 New Yorker Mar.20,1926 p17,por.
  (Profiles)
 Pleasants—Great p279-283,por.
 Saleski—Jewish p622-624,por.
 Saleski—Wander. p431-436,por.
 Thomas—Living Women p245-257,por.
 *Ulrich—Famous p53-58,por.
 Wagner—Prima p223-248

Schupack, May (fl. 1930's)
 Amer. journalist, publicity director
 Ross—Ladies p517-518

Schurman, Anna Maria von (1607-1678)
 Nether. sculptor, feminist, linguist,
  wood & ivory carver, engraver
 Culver—Women p150
 Schmidt—400 p298-299,por.
 Stenton p128,173,183-184,193
 Waters—Women p207-311

Schurz, Mrs. Carl (fl. 1850's)
 Amer. pioneer kindergarten
  educator
 Irwin—Angels p128-129

Schuyler, Catherine Van Rensselaer (1733-
  1803/04)
 Amer. Rev. war patriot
 DAR Mag. July 1921 p371-372,por.
 Ellet—Women (1) p71-75,por.
 Green—Pioneer (2) p85-94,por.
 Hanaford—Dau. p141-142
 Leonard—Amer. p121
 Logan—Part p115-117,203
 *Sickels—Calico p97-110

Schuyler, Cornelia (fl. 1700's)
 Amer. colonial property owner,
  patriot
 Beard—Amer. p27
 Dexter—Colonial p108

Schuyler, Elizabeth.
 See Hamilton, Elizabeth Schuyler

Schuyler, Louisa Lee (b. 1840)
 Amer. Civil war philanthropist,
  social worker, humanitarian
 Adelman—Famous p275
 Brockett—Woman's p532,534,537
 Dolan—Goodnow's p251-252

Schuyler, Margaret.
 See Van Rensselaer, Margaret

Schuyler, Margaretta (fl. 1930's)
 Can.-Amer. retail manager
 Women—Achieve. p177,por.

Schuyler, Margaretta Schuyler (1701-1782)
 Amer. colonial administrator
 Benson—Women p281,305
 Leonard—Amer. p122

Schuyler, Philippa Duke (1931/32-1967)
 Amer. composer, pianist
 *Cherry—Portraits p72-76,por.
 Robinson—Hist. p249

Schwartz, Bertha (fl. 1930's)
 Aust.-Amer. lawyer
 Women—Achieve. p175,por.

Schwartz, Margaret (1900-   )
 Amer. sculptor
 National—Contemp. p286

Schwartze, Therese (or Teresa) (1852-
  1918)
 Nether. painter
 Dorland—Sum p155-156
 Waters—Women p392-394

Schwarzhaupt, Elizabeth (1901-   )
 Ger. government official
 Cur. Biog. '67 p375-376,por.

Schwarzkopf, Elisabeth (1915-   )
 Pol.-Ger. singer
 Brook—Singers p161-164,por.
 CR '59 p674,por.
 Cur. Biog. '55 p537-539,por.
 Davidson—Treas. p270-273,por.
 Rosenthal—Sopranos p80,89,por.

Scidmore, Eliza Ruhamah ("Ruhamah,"
 pseud.) (1856-1928)
 Amer. journalist, traveler
 Logan—Part p856

Sciffi, Clare Dei (1194-1253)
 It. nurse
 *McKown—Heroic p16

Scio, Julie Angélique (1768-1807)
 Fr. singer
 Pleasants—Great p108

Scofield, Edna May (fl. 1930's)
 Amer. meteorologist
 Planck—Women p223

Scoggin, Margaret Clara (1905-1968)
 Amer. librarian
 Cur. Biog. '52 p520-522,por.
 Cur. Biog. '68 p462
 Epstein—People p3-17

Scholastica (c. 480-543)
 It. saint
 Englebert—Lives p58-59
 Wescott—Calen. p23

Scotney, Evelyn (fl. 1910's)
 Austral. singer
 Lahee—Grand p391-392,415,por.

Scott, Abigail.
 See Duniway, Abigail Jane Scott

Scott, Barbara Ann (1928-   )
 Can. figure skater
 Cur. Biog. '48 p567-569,por.
 Time Feb.2,1948 p50,por.(Cover)

Scott, Blanche Stuart ("Betty") (fl. 1910's)
 Amer. pioneer aviatrix
 *May—Women p64-66,68-69,por.

Scott, Catherine Amy Dawson (1863-1934)
 Eng. author, feminist
 Hammerton p487
 Jones—Quakers p25,63,75-76,208

Scott, Catharine Marbury (fl. 17th-18th
 cent.)
 Amer. pioneer
 Green—Pioneer (1) p237; (3) p87

Scott, Charlotte Angas (1858-1931)
 Amer. mathematician
 Mozans—Woman p166

Scott, Dana.
 See Robertson, Constance Noyes

Scott, Dorothy.
 See Hancock, Dorothy Quincy

Scott, Elisabeth Whitworth (1898-   )
 Brit. architect
 Hammerton p1198

Scott, Elizabeth Thorn (fl. 1850's)
 Amer. pioneer school foundress
 Brown—Home p241

Scott, Emily Maria Spaford (1832-1915)
 Amer. painter
 Logan—Part p755
 Michigan—Biog. p281

Scott, Evelyn D. (1893-   )
 Amer. author
 Lawrence—School p241-243
 *Millett—Amer. p60-61,569-571
 Overton—Women p294-296

Scott, Harriet M. (fl. 1860's)
 Amer. Civil war nurse
 Dannett—Noble p343

Scott, Hazel Dorothy (1920-   )
 Trin.-Amer. pianist, singer
 *Cherry—Portraits p119-122
 CR '59 p675-676,por.
 CR '63 p557,por.
 Cur. Biog. '43 p677-680,por.

Scott, Mrs. Hector (fl. 1830's)
 Amer. W. pioneer
 Ellet—Pioneer p400
 Logan—Part p96

Scott, Helen Jo (fl. 1930's)
 Amer. educator
 Women—Achieve. p203

Scott, Jeannette (b. 1864)
 Can. artist, teacher
 Jackman—Amer. p212-213

Scott, Julia H. (b. 1809)
 Amer. poet
 Hanaford—Dau. p261

Scott, Kate Frances (1890-   )
 Amer. physician, organization
 official
 Cur. Biog. '48 p571-573,por.

Scott, Kate M. (d. 1911)
 Amer. Civil war nurse
 Logan—Part p361

Scott, Kathleen, Lady (fl. 1890's-1900's)
    Eng. diarist
    Dunaway—Treas. p436-439

Scott, Leader.
    See Baxter, Lucy E. Barnes

Scott, Linda (fl. 1960's)
    Amer. singer
    Kahn—Tops. p133

Scott, Malcomb (Maidie) (fl. 1910's)
    Eng. singer
    Felstead—Stars p154-155,por.

Scott, Maria D. Mayo (d. 1866)
    Amer., wife of Winfield Scott
    Logan—Part p256

Scott, Martha (1914-   )
    Amer. actress
    CR '59 p676,por.
    CR '63 p557,por.
    Women—Achieve. p203

Scott, Mary (fl. 1770's)
    Eng. poet
    Stenton—Eng. p297-298,305,308

Scott, Mary Anne (b. 1851)
    Amer. patriot
    Logan—Part p437

Scott, Mary Augusta (1851-1916)
    Amer. author, educator
    Logan—Part p720

Scott, Mary Sophie (b. 1838)
    Amer. author
    Logan—Part p898

Scott, Mrs. Matthew T. (fl. 1910's)
    Amer. club leader
    Logan—Part p441-453

Scott, Miriam Finn (1882-1944)
    Russ.-Amer. educator, lecturer,
        author
    Women—Achieve. p101,por.

Scott, Mrs. (fl. 1780's)
    Amer., W. pioneer
    Ellet—Pioneer p115-118

Scott, Natalie Anderson (Natalie B.
        Sokoloff) (1906-   )
    Russ.-Amer. advent. novelist
    Warfel—Amer. p376,por.

Scott, Patience (   )
    Religious worker
    Jones—Quakers p79

Scott, Rose (1847-1925)
    Austral. feminist, social reformer
    Schmidt—400 p38-39,por.

Scott, Sarah (m. 1726)
    Amer. colonial religious worker
    Jones—Quakers p208

Scott, Mrs. Taylor (fl. 1860's)
    Amer. Civil war patriot
    Andrews—Women p205

Scott-James, Anne (gr. 1933)
    Eng. journalist
    Brittain—Women p187,253

Scovil, Cora (fl. 1930's)
    Amer. inventor, business executive
    Women—Achieve. p185,por.

Scribonia (fl. 39 B.C.)
    Rom., 2nd wife of Emperor
        Augustus
    Balsdon—Roman p68,84,215,220

Scripps, Ellen Browning (1836-1932)
    Amer. journalist, philanthropist
    Ross—Ladies p534-535
    Time Feb.22,1926 p21,por.(Cover)

Scroggins, Eliza Anna Clark (1820-1912)
    Amer. religious worker
    Brown—Home. p81-83,por.

Scudder, Deborah.
    See Hart, Deborah Scudder

Scudder, Ida Scudder (1870-1960)
    Amer. physician, missionary
    Culver—Women p160-162
    *Knapp—Women p63-78,por.
    Lovejoy—Women p227-228,por.

Scudder, Janet (1873-1940)
    Amer. sculptor, painter
    Adelman—Famous p314-315
    Cur. Biog. '40 p721,por.
    *Ferris—When p70-133,por.
    Hyde—Modern p185-204
    Jackman—Amer. p408-409
    *Kirkland—Artists p86-97
    McSpadden—Sculptors p351-359
    Michigan—Biog. p281-282
    National—Contemp. p290
    Taft—Women, Mentor (172) #4 p4-5,
        por.
    Waters—Women p311-312

Scudder, Vida Dutton (1861-1954)
    Amer. author, educator
    Allen—Advent. p277-289,por.
    Logan—Part p793
    Wagenknecht—When p413-421

Scudéry, Madeleine (or Magdaleine) de
        (Sapho) (1607-1701)
    Fr. novelist, poet
    Adelman—Famous p63
    Hammerton p1201,por.
    Schmidt—400 p174-175,por.

Sczaniecka, Emilja (1804-1896)
Pol. patriot, humanitarian
Schmidt—400 p323,por.

Seacombe, Mrs. Charles M. (fl. 1930's)
Amer. critic, translator, lecturer,
actress, social leader
Women—Achieve. p58,por.

Seal, Elizabeth (fl. 1720's-1730's)
Eng. actress
MacQueen—Pope p203-204

Seaman, Elizabeth Cochrane.
See Bly, Nellie, pseud.

Searing, Annie Eliza Pidgeon (1857-1942)
Amer. author, feminist
Cur. Biog. '42 p748
Ross—Ladies p332

Searing, Laura Catherine Redden (Howard
Glyndon) (b. 1840)
Amer. journalist, author
Logan—Part p845

Searls, Fanny (1851-1939)
Amer. pioneer naturalist
Hollingsworth—Her p102-106

Sears, Eleanora (c. 1880-1968)
Amer. tennis player, pioneer
sportswoman
Rogers—Women p58-59,por.

Sears, Sarah C. (fl. 1890's-1900's)
Amer. painter
Waters—Women p312-313

Sears, Zelda (b. 1873)
Amer. playwright
Mantle—Amer. p307

Seaver, Blanche Ebert (1891-   )
Amer. composer, author
ASCAP p446

Seaver, Nancy B. (fl. 1880's)
Amer. educator
Hanaford—Dau. p530

Seawell, Molly Elliot (1860-1916)
Amer. novelist
Harkins—Famous p107-123,por.
Harkins—Little p107-123,por.
Logan—Part p803

Seay, Virginia (1922-   )
Amer. composer
Ewen—American p220-221,por.

Seberg, Jean (1939-   )
Amer. actress
CR '59 p677,por.
CR '63 p559-560,por.
Cur. Biog. '66 p360-363,por.

Sebel-Wongel (fl. 1530 A.D.)
Ethiop. empress
Stiles—Postal p248

Secunda (d. 257)
Rom. saint
Wescott—Calen. p99-100

Sedgwick, Anne Douglas (Anne de
Selincourt) (1873-1935)
Amer. novelist
Hammerton p1202
*Millett—Amer. p571-572
Overton—Women p297-309

Sedgwick, Catharine Maria (1789-1867)
Amer. novelist, educator
Brooks—Three p157-244
Dexter—Career p100-101
Dorland—Sum p26,112,198
Hanaford—Dau. p216-217
Logan—Part p870
Papashvily—All p41,43-44,47

Seebach, Marie (1830-1897)
Ger. actress
Dorland—Sum p50,129,166

Seefried, Irmgard (1919-   )
Ger. singer
Cur. Biog. '56 p561-562,por.
Ewen—Ency. p469
Rosenthal—Sopranos p90-91,por.

Seeley, Evelyn (fl. 1930's)
Amer. journalist
Ross—Ladies p216-220,por.,cover

Seeley, Mabel (1903-   )
Amer. novelist
Warfel—Amer. p378,por.

Seelye, Maria (fl. 1860's)
Amer. soldier
Fowler—Woman p425-428

Seghers, Anna, pseud. (Nettie Radvanti
Redling) (1900-   )
Ger. novelist
Cur. Biog. '42 p748-750,por.

Seibert, Katharine Burr (1897-   )
Amer. physicist
*Yost—Women Sci. p177-195

Seibold, Mrs. Louis.
See Hopkins, Jenny Lind

Seid, Ruth. See Sinclair, Jo

Seidler, Caroline Luise (1786-1866)
Ger. painter
Waters—Women p313

Seifert, Elizabeth (1898-   )
 Amer. author
 Cur. Biog. '51 p563-564
 Warfel—Amer. p379-380,por.

Seifert, Florence Barbara (1897-   )
 Amer. biochemist, pioneer scientist
 Castiglioni—Hist. p978,1127
 Cur. Biog. '42 p750-752,por.
 Gelfand—They p19-21,por.

Seifert, Marjorie Allen (fl. 1900's-1920's)
 Amer. poet
 Smith—Women's p176

Seifert, Shirley Louise (b. 1888/89)
 Amer. novelist
 Cur. Biog. '51 p564-566,por.
 Warfel—Amer. p380-381,por.

Seifullina, Lidiia V. (1889-1954)
 Russ. author
 Stiles—Postal p248

Seiler, Emma (1821-1866)
 Ger. musician, author, vocal
  teacher
 McCoy—Portraits p187,por.

Seitz, Helen (fl. 1930's)
 Amer. teacher, journalist
 Women—Achieve. p139,por.

Selassie, Tsahai Haíle (1919-1942)
 Ethiop. nurse
 *McKown—Heroic p213-238,por.

Selden, Gisella (b. 1884)
 Hung. composer
 McCoy—Portraits p187,por.

Selena, Countess of Huntingdon (1707-
  1791)
 Eng. hymn-writer
 Deen—Great p306

Selika, Marie (fl. 1870's-1880's)
 Amer. singer
 Cuney-Hare—Negro p222-224,por.

Selincourt, Anne de.
 See Sedgwick, Anne Douglas

Selinko, Annemarie (1914-   )
 Aust. author
 Cur. Biog. '55 p541-543,por.

Sell (Etta) Grace (1862-1938)
 Amer. W. pioneer
 Sargent—Pioneers p70-71,por.

Sell, Hildegarde Loretta. See Hildegarde

Sellers, Kathryn (1870-1939)
 Amer. lawyer, judge, bibliographer,
  librarian
 Irwin—Angels p300

Sellers, Marie (fl. 1930's)
 Amer. agriculturist, editor
 Women—Achieve. p152,por.

Sellew, Gladys (b. 1887)
 Amer. nurse
 Pennock—Makers p103,por.

Selznick, Irene (1910-   )
 Amer. theatrical producer
 CR '59 p680-681,por.
 CR '63 p561-562,por.

Sembrick, Marcella (Praxede Marcelline
  Kochanska) (1858-1935)
 Galic. singer
 Adelman—Famous p292
 Davidson—Treas. p276-279
 Ewen—Ency. p470
 Klein—Great p132-140,por.
 Lahee—Famous p212-215
 Lahee—Grand p4,137-138
 McCoy—Portraits p187,por.
 Marks—Glamour p327-328
 Pleasants—Great p278-279
 Ulrich—Famous p27-32,por.
 Wagnalls—Opera p392-401,por.
 Wagner—Prima p248

Semiramis (Sammuramat) (fl. 8th cent.,
  B.C.)
 Assyr. queen
 Adelman—Famous p17
 Boccaccio—Conc. p4-7
 Koven—Women p1-2
 *MacVeagh—Champlin p530
 Muir—Women p13-14
 Schmidt—400 p123-124,por.

Semmer, Marcelle (fl. 1910's)
 Fr. war heroine
 Dorland—Sum p97

Semmes, Myra E. (fl. 1860's)
 Amer. philanthropist
 Logan—Part p536

Semple, Ellen Churchill (1863-1932)
 Amer. anthropo-geographer,
  author
 Dorland—Sum p144
 Logan—Part p879-880

Sempronia (1) (fl. 70's B.C.)
 Rom., wife of D. Junius Brutus
 Balsdon—Roman p47-49,55,214,272,
  275
 Boccaccio—Conc. p173-175

Sempronia (2) (fl. 210's B.C.)
 Rom., dau. of Tiberius Sempronius
  Gracchus
 Boccaccio—Conc. p166-167

Sender, Toni (b. 1888)
   Ger.-Amer. labor leader
   Cur. Biog. '50 p525-527,por.
   Women—Achieve. p86,por.

Senesh, Hannah (1921-1944)
   Palest. parachutist, heroine, spy
   *Horowitz—Treas. p182-190
   *Strong—Heroes p166-176
   *Strong—Of p306-314

Senger-Bettaque, Katharine (b. 1862)
   Ger. ballet dancer
   Wagner—Prima p248

Senie, Claire M. (fl. 1930's)
   Amer. club leader
   Women—Achieve. p80,por.

Senkrah, Arma (b. 1864)
   Amer. violinist
   Erlich—Celeb. p196-197,por.

Senn, Margaret Lynch (b. 1882)
   Amer. author
   Logan—Part p822

Septimia (240-300)
   Palmyra queen
   Schmidt—400 p128,por.

Sera. See Sarah (2)

Serao, Matilda (1856-1927)
   It. novelist
   Hammerton p1204-1205

Seraphia (fl. 1st cent.)
   It. saint
   Englebert—Lives p330

"Seraphina" (Lorenza Feliciani) (fl. 1780's)
   It., friend of Cagliostro
   Bolitho—Twelve p177-200

Seraphina Sforza (1434-1478)
   It. saint
   Blunt—Great p164-165
   Englebert—Lives p343-344
   Wescott—Calen p136

Seredy, Kate (1896-   )
   Hung. illustrator
   Cur. Biog. '40 p724-725,por.
   Mahony—Illus. p357

Sergeant, Adeline (1851-1904)
   Eng. novelist
   Black—Notable p157-171,por.

Sergeant, Elizabeth Shepley (b. 1881)
   Amer. author
   Beckwith—Contemp. p307

Sergio, Lisa (1905-   )
   It.-Amer. radio personality
   Cur. Biog. '44 p603-606,por.

Seriramis. See Semiramis

Serrano y Bartolomé, Joaquina (fl. 1870's-
      1880's)
   Sp. painter
   Waters—Women p313

Servilia (fl. 80's B.C.)
   Rom., mother of Brutus, mistress of
      Caesar
   Balsdon—Roman p51

Seton, Anya (Anya Chase) (1916-   )
   Amer. author
   CR '63 p563,,por.
   Cur. Biog. '53 p566-567,por.
   Warfel—Amer. p382,por.

Seton, Elizabeth Ann Bayley, Mother
      (1774-1821)
   Amer. foundress, nun
   Blunt—Great p272-293
   Burton—Loveliest p20-38
   Code—Great p70-119,por.
   *Curtin—Gallery p87,por.
   Deen—Great p381-383
   Dolan—Goodnow's p203
   Elgin—Nun p84-87,por.
   Foster—Religion p57-87,por.
   Hanaford—Dau. p184
   Logan—Part p623-625
   Maynard—Great p99-109
   Pennock—Makers p25-26,por.

Seton, Grace Gallatin (1872-1959)
   Amer. author, feminist, book
      designer, geographer, lecturer
   Logan—Part p842
   Women—Achieve. p38,por.

Settle, Mary Lee (1918-   )
   Amer. author
   Cur. Biog. '59 p410-411,por.

Severa, Julia Aquilia (fl. 200's-220's)
   Rom. empress, wife of Heliogabulus
   McCabe—Empr. p216
   Serviez—Roman (2) p239-243

Severa, Marcia Otacilia (fl. 200's)
   Rom. empress
   McCabe—Empr. p237,por.

Severance, Caroline Maria Seymour
      (1820-1914)
   Amer. club leader, feminist, social
      reformer
   Bruce—Woman p239-241
   Hanaford—Dau. p359-360
   Logan—Part p413-419

Severina, Ulpia (fl.c. 270's)
   Rom. empress, wife of Aurelian
   Serviez—Roman (2) p355-360

Sevier, Catherine Sherrill ("Bonny Kate")
(c. 1754-1836)
Amer. W. pioneer
Dar Mag July 1921 p382,portrayal
Ellet—Pioneer p29-41
Green—Pioneer (3) p525-526
Logan—Part p72-75
*Stickels—Calico p111-124

Sevigné, Francoise Margaret de.
See Grignan, Francoise Margaret
de Sevigné

Sevigné, Marie de Rabutin-Chantel (1626-
1696)
Fr. letter-writer, salonist
Adelman—Famous p58-59
Blunt—Great p404-409
Bradford—Women p111-131,por.
Dorland—Sum p29
Hammerton p1206,por.
Koven—Women p262-300
*MacVeagh—Champlin p531
Moore.—Disting. p29-41
Phila.—Women unp.,por.
Ravenel—Women p118-145,por.
Schmidt—400 p179-180,por.
Stiles—Postal p249
Tallentyre—Women p204-222,por.
Thomson—Queen p179-206

Sewall, Lucy E. (fl. 1860's)
Amer. physician
Lovejoy—Women p82,86,145-146,148,
153,155,165

Sewall, May Wright (1844-1920)
Amer. feminist, club leader
Irwin—Angels p224-226,229-232,234
Logan—Part p580-581
Riegel—Amer. p114-115,por.

Seward, Anna (1747-1809)
Eng. poet
Dorland—Sum p18,178
Hammerton p1206
Stenton—English p298-299

Seward, Sara C. (d. 1891)
Amer. physician
Lovejoy—Women p221

Sewell, Amanda Brewster (d. 1926)
Amer. painter
Waters—Women p313-315

Sewell, Anna (1820-1878)
Eng. author
Adelman—Famous p179

Sewell, Helen Moore (1896-1957)
Amer. illustrator
Mahony—Illus. p359

Sewell, Mary (1797-1884)
Eng. author
Hammerton p1206

Sewell, (Emma) Winifred (1917-   )
Amer. librarian, organization
official
Cur. Biog. '60 p373-374,por.

Sexburga (d. 699)
Eng. (Kent) queen, saint
Blunt—Great p80

Seydel, Irma (fl. 1940's)
Amer. violinist
McCoy—Portraits p188,por.

Seydell, Mildred (fl. 1920's)
Amer. journalist
Ross—Ladies p595-596

Seydelmann, Apollonie (1768-1840)
It. painter
Waters—Women p315

Seyler, Athene (b. 1889)
Brit. actress
Hammerton p1206,por.

Seymour, Agnes Rogers (fl. 1940's)
Amer. missionary
They—Went p116-118

Seymour, Beatrice Kean Stapleton
(d. 1955)
Eng. novelist
Millett—Brit. p453-455

Seymour, Flora Warren (b. 1888)
Amer. author, lawyer, Indian
authority
Cur. Biog. '42 p753-755,por.

Seymour, Frances I. (fl. 1930's)
Amer. physician
Women—Achieve. p104,por.

Seymour, Harriet Ayer (c. 1876-1944)
Amer. musical therapist, piano
teacher, author
Cur. Biog. '44 p609
McCoy—Portraits p188,por.

Seymour, Mrs. Horatio (fl. 1860's)
Amer. Civil war humanitarian
Brockett—Woman's p79,590-592

Seymour, Jane. See Jane Seymour

Seymour, Laura (d. 1879)
Eng., friend of Charles Reade
Orr—Famous Affin. IV p169-186

Seymour, Louise (fl. 1890's)
Amer. nurse
Schmidt—400 p407,por.

Seymour, Mary Julia (1769-1808)
Amer. belle
Sale—Old p200-203,por.

Seymour, Tot (n.d.)
    Amer. song-writer
    ASCAP p448-449

Sforzia, Caterina Countess of Forli (1463-1509)
    It. stateswoman
    Dorland—Sum p17

Sforzia, Seraphina (b. 1434)
    It. saint, abbess
    Blunt—Great p164-165

Shacklock, Constance (1913-   )
    Eng. singer
    Brook—Singers p165-169.por.
    Davidson—Treas. p280-284,por.

Shadwell, Anne Gibbs. See Gibbs, Ann

Shafer, Helen Shafer (1839-1894)
    Amer. educator
    Logan—Part p729

Shafik, Doris Ahmad (1919-   )
    Egypt. feminist, journalist
    Cur. Biog. '55 p545-547,por.

Shagaret el-Dor. See Sheger-ed-Dur

Shaibany, Homa (fl. 1930's-1940's)
    Iran. pioneer surgeon
    Lovejoy—Women p215

Shakespeare, Mary Arden (m. 155&)
    Eng., mother of William
      Shakespeare
    *Chandler—Famous p21-39

Shankland, Eugenia (fl. 1910's)
    artist
    Logan—Part p752

Shannon, Effie (1867-1941)
    Amer. actress
    Strang—Actresses p187-192,por.

Shannon, Peggy (c. 1907-1941)
    Amer. actress, dancer
    Cur. Biog. '41 p776

Sharington (Sherington), Olive (d. 1651)
    Eng. hostess
    Aubrey—Brief p277

Sharlow, Myrna Docia (fl. 1940's)
    Amer. singer
    McCoy—Portraits p188,por.

Sharon, Florence (m. 1880)
    Amer. heiress
    Eliot—Heiresses p210-228,por.

Sharp, Evelyn, Dame (1869-1955)
    Eng. feminist, government official,
      author
    Brittain—Women p177,252
    Hammerton p1210

Sharpe, Jemima Alexander (m. 1748)
    Amer. Rev. war patriot
    Green—Pioneer (3) p470,473

Sharpe, Miss (fl. 1780's-1790's)
    Eng. governess to Jane Austen
    Howe—Galaxy p79-81

Sharpe, Mrs. R. M. (fl. 1950's)
    Eng. aviatrix
    *May—Women p198

Sharpless, Hattie R. (fl. 1860's)
    Amer. Civil war nurse
    Brockett—Woman's p741-743

Shatford, Vera V. (fl. 1930's)
    Amer. interior decorator
    Women—Achieve. p170,por.

Shattuck, Harriette Lucy Robinson (b. 1850)
    Amer. pioneer government clerk
    Logan—Part p843

Shattuck, Mrs. Job (fl. 1770's)
    Amer. Rev. war soldier
    Ellet—Women (2) p295-297
    Green—Pioneer (2) p332
    Hanaford—Dau. p56

Shaver, Dorothy (1897-1959)
    Amer. pioneer retail executive
    *Boynick—Pioneers p209-240
    Clymer—Modern p72-80,por.
    Cur. Biog. '46 p546-548,por.
    Cur. Biog. '59 p411
    Taves—Success. p141-150,por.

Shaver, Mary Mumpere (1883-1942)
    Amer. librarian, educator
    Cur. Biog. '42 p758

Shaw, Abigail. See Ellery, Abigail Carey

Shaw, Ann. See Carter, Ann Shaw

Shaw, Anna Howard (1847-1919)
    Eng.-Amer. physician, feminist,
      clergyman
    Adelman—Famous p258-259
    Beard—Amer. p105-113
    Bennett—Amer. p229-252,por.
    Brown—Gentle p249-250
    Cavanah—We p54-64
    Irwin—Angels p165-167,261,340,352,
      368-371
    *Kirkland—Good p10-18
    Logan—Part p581-583
    Lovejoy—Women p301
    *McCallum—Women p201-234
    O'Higgins—Amer. p277-299
    *Parkman—Heroines p151-181,por.
    Riegel—Amer. p179-182
    Rogers—Women p62,por.
    Shaw—Story p1-338,por.
    Webb—Famous p441-448,por.

Shaw, Annie Cornelia (1852-1887)
    Amer. painter
    Logan—Part p757
    Waters—Women p315-316

Shaw, Carolyn Hagner (c. 1903-   )
    Amer. publisher, social leader
    CR '63 p565,por.

Shaw, Elizabeth (1750-c.1816)
    Amer. Rev. war patriot
    Ellet—Women (2) p37-39

Shaw, Ellen Eddy (fl. 1930's)
    Amer. naturalist, lecturer, author
    Women—Achieve. p101,por.

Shaw, Flora Madeline (gr. 1896)
    Can. nurse
    Dolan—Goodnow's p255,por.
    Pennock—Makers p73,por.

Shaw, Lilian (fl. 1910's)
    Amer. actress
    Caffin—Vaud. p55-57

Shaw, Lucretia (c. 1737-1781)
    Amer. Rev. war patriot
    Green—Pioneer (3) p522-523
    Root—Chapter p91-100,por.

Shaw, Margaret Elizabeth (fl. 1940's-1950's)
    Amer. missionary, nurse
    They—Went p131-132

Shaw, Mary (1860-1929)
    Amer. actress
    Adelman—Famous p303
    Strang—Actresses p206-216

Shaw, Mrs. Quincy A. (fl. 1870's)
    Amer. pioneer kindergarten
        educator
    Irwin—Angels p129
    Shaw—Story p156

Shaw, Mrs. Stoddard (d.c. 1950's)
    Amer. recluse
    Erskine—Out p245-247

Shaw-Lefevre, Madeleine Septimia (1835-
        1914)
    Eng. educator
    Brittain—Women (see index),por.

Shay, Dorothy (n.d.)
    Amer. singer
    CR '63 p566,por.

Shay, Edith Foley (1894-   )
    Amer. author
    Cur. Biog. '52 p535-536,por.

Sheads, Carrie (fl. 1860's)
    Amer. Civil war heroine
    Brockett—Woman's p776-777
    Hanaford—Dau. p212

Moore—Women p238-244
Young—Women p274-276

Sheaffe, Susannah Child (fl. 1770's)
    Amer. colonial grocer
    Dexter—Colonial p25,183-184

Sheard, Virginia Stanton (d. 1943)
    Can. author
    Thomas—Canad. p114-115

Shearer, Moira (1926-   )
    Scot. ballet dancer
    Atkinson—Dancers p135-139,por.
    CR '59 p686,por.
    Cur. Biog. '50 p530-531,por.
    Davidson—Ballet p257-264
    Fisher—Ball. p20,por.
    Haskell—Ballet p11,por.
    Haskell—Vignet. p51-53,por.
    *McConnell—Famous p76-85,por.
    *Terry—Star p203-207,por.

Shearer, Norma (1904-   )
    Can.-Amer. actress
    Brundidge—Twinkle p231-240,por.231
    CR '59 p686-687,por.
    CR '63 p566,por.
    Hammerton p1212
    Herman—How p89,por.
    Hughes—Famous p285-306,por.
    Lamparski—What. p176-177,por.
    Schickel—Stars p60-61,por.

Sheba, Queen of (Biblical)
    Buchanan—Women p57-58
    Davenport—Great p63-65
    Deen—All p120-124
    Horton—Women p188-201
    Lewis—Portraits p137-138
    Lofts—Women p134-139
    *MacVeagh—Champlin p534
    Marble—Women, Bible p192-195
    Mead—250 p108
    Morton—Women p127-133
    Nelson—Bible p51-54
    Ockenga—Women p135-145
    *O'Clery—Queens p11-19
    Spurgeon—Sermons p160-195
    Stiles—Postal p250
    Weigall—Person. p9-15

Shedd, Margaret (1900-   )
    Amer. novelist
    Warfel—Amer. p383-384,por.

Sheger-ed-Dur (Shagaret el-Dor) (fl. 1250)
    Egypt. & Syr. sultana
    *Holmes—She p134-175

Sheilah (Biblical)
    daughter of Jephthah
    *Levinger—Great p38-43

Shelby, Sarah Bledsoe (m. 1784)
　　Amer. W. pioneer
　　Ellet—Pioneer p162-170
　　Logan—Part p59

Shelby, Susannah Hart (m. 1761)
　　Amer. patriot
　　Green—Pioneer (3) p484-485
　　Logan—Part p68

Sheldon, Hannah. See Chapin, Hannah

Sheldon, Lillian Taitt (1865-1925)
　　Amer. composer, organist
　　McCoy—Portraits p189,por.

Shell, Elizabeth Petrie (fl. 1770's-1780's)
　　Amer. Rev. war heroine
　　Fowler—Woman p126-127
　　Green—Pioneer (2) p436-440

Shelley, Gladys (1918-   )
　　Amer. author, lyricist, actress
　　ASCAP p452

Shelley, Mary Wollstonecraft (1797-1851)
　　Eng. author
　　Adelman—Famous p136-137
　　Dorland—Sum p45,193-194
　　Hammerton p1212,por.
　　Hubbard—Little p393-429,por.
　　MacCarthy—Later p182-183

Shelley, Mary Josephine (1902-   )
　　Amer. aviatrix
　　Cur. Biog. '51 p568-570,por.
　　*May—Women p191

Shelomith (1) (Biblical)
　　daughter of Dibri
　　Deen—All p292-293

Shelomith (2) (Biblical)
　　daughter of Zerubbabel
　　Deen—All p293

Shelomith (3) (Biblical)
　　daughter of Maachah and
　　　Rehoboam
　　Deen—All p293-294

Shelton, A. (fl. 1860's)
　　Amer. Civil war nurse
　　Moore—Women p519-522

Shelton, Emma Sanford (b. 1849)
　　Amer. social reformer
　　Logan—Part p665-666

Shelton, Louise (1867-1934)
　　Amer. author business woman
　　Hanaford—Dau. p615

Shelton, Mary E. (fl. 1860's)
　　Amer. Civil war philanthropist
　　Moore—Women p213-237

Shelton, Sarah. See Henry, Sarah Shelton

Shenton, Barbara. See Webster, Barbara

Shepard, Helen. See Gould, Helen Miller

Shephard, Esther (fl. 1920's)
　　Amer. author
　　Binheim—Women p202,por.

Shepherd, Ina (fl. 1910's)
　　Amer. bank secretary
　　Logan—Part p894

Shepherd, Theodosia Burr Hall (1845-1906)
　　Amer. florist, business executive
　　Hollingsworth—Her p107-120

Sheppard, Elizabeth Sara (1830-1862)
　　Eng. novelist
　　Dorland—Sum p43,196

Sheppard, Eugenia Benbow (c. 1910-   )
　　Amer. journalist, columnist
　　CR '63 p568,por.

Sheppard, Jeanie R. (fl. 1930's)
　　Amer. social worker, humanitarian
　　Women—Achieve. p142,por.

Shera, Florence B. (fl. 1950's)
　　Amer. printer, club leader
　　Club—Printing p6-7,por.

Sherah (Biblical)
　　Deen—All p294
　　Lewis—Portraits p221-222

Sheridan, Ann (1915-1967)
　　Amer. actress
　　CR '59 p689,por.
　　CR '63 p568,por.
　　Schickel—Stars p214,por.

Sheridan, Clare Consuelo Frewen (b. 1885)
　　Eng. sculptor, author
　　Cole—Women p233-260,por.
　　Hammerton p1215

Sheridan, Frances Chamberlaine (1724-
　　　1766)
　　Irish author
　　MacCarthy—Later p21-25

Sheriff, Hilla (fl. 1930's)
　　Amer. physician
　　Lovejoy—Women p353-354,356,358
　　Lovejoy—Women Phys. p189-197,por.

Sherington, Olive.
　　See Sharington, Olive

Sherman, Eleanor Boyle Ewing (1824-
　　　1888)
　　Amer., wife of General Sherman
　　Logan—Part p293

Sherman, Elizabeth Hartwell (d. 1760)
Amer. patriot
Green—Pioneer (3) p92-93

Sherman, Florence A. (fl. 1930's)
Amer. fashion, doll designer
Women—Achieve. p164,por.

Sherman, Margaret Stewart (m. 1848)
Amer., wife of John Sherman
Logan—Part p293

Sherman, Minna E. (fl. 1910's)
Amer. agriculturist, club leader,
lecturer, author
Logan—Part p906

Sherman, Rebecca Prescott (m. 1763)
Amer. Rev. war patriot
Green—Pioneer (3) p93-98

Sherman, Mrs. Sidney (d. 1865)
Amer. pioneer
Logan—Part p103

Sherrill, Catharine.
See Sevier, Catharine Sherrill

Sherven, Betty (fl. 1930's)
Nor.-Amer. physio-therapist
Women—Achieve. p92,por.

Sherwood, Emily Lee (1929/43-   )
Amer. journalist, author
Hanaford—Dau. p691
Logan—Part p814-815

Sherwood, Grace (d.c. 1733)
Amer. accused witch
Spruill—Women's p328-330

Sherwood, Kate Brownlee (b. 1841)
Amer. editor, organization official
Logan—Part p347-348,816

Sherwood, Margaret Pollock (1864-1955)
Amer. author
Women—Achieve. p153,por.

Sherwood, Mary Elizabeth (b. 1830)
Amer. author
Logan—Part p815-816

Sherwood, Mary Martha (1775-1851)
Eng. author
Dorland—Sum p36

Sherwood, Roberta (1913-   )
Amer. singer
CR '59 p689,por.
CR '63 p568,por.

Sherwood, Rosina Emmett (1854/57-   )
Amer. illustrator, painter
Logan—Part p752
Michigan—Biog. p285
Waters—Women p118

Sherwood, Ruth (b. 1889)
Amer. sculptor
National—Contemp. p294

Sherzer, Jane (fl. 1910's)
Amer. scholar
Logan—Part p729

Sheshan's daughter (Biblical)
Deen—All p313-314

Shiber, Etta (c. 1878-1948)
Amer. author
Cur. Biog. '43 p690-692,por.
Cur. Biog. '49 p567

Shields, Ella (c. 1879-1952)
Brit. actress
Felstead—Stars p101,por.

Shimeath (Biblical)
Deen—All p294

Shimrith. See Shomer

Shindler, Mary B. (1810-1833)
Amer. author
Hanaford—Dau. p243

Shinn, Florence Scovel (d. 1940)
Amer. illustrator, lecturer,
metaphysicist
Cur. Biog. '40 p732
Michigan—Biog. p286

Shinn, Milicent Washburn (1858-1940)
Amer. child psychologist
Cur. Biog. '40 p732

Shiphrah (Biblical)
Deen—All p294-295
Lewis—Portraits p212-213
Mead—250 p44

Shipley, Ruth Bielaski (1885-1966)
Amer. government official
Cur. Biog. '47 p571-572,por.
Cur. Biog. '67 p483

Shipman, Clare (fl. 1920's-1930's)
Amer. journalist
Ross—Ladies p557-558

Shipp, Mary (n.d.)
Amer. actress
TV—Person. (1) p37,por.

Shippen, Katherine Binney (1892-   )
Amer. author
Cur. Biog. '54 p569-570,por.

Shippen, Margaret.
See Arnold, Margaret Shippen

Shippen, Mrs. William Watson (fl. 1890's)
Amer. club leader
Logan—Part p468-469

Shipton, Mother (c. 1486-c. 1561)
Amer. prophetess
Hammerton p1216-1217

Shirley, Dame, pseud.
See Clappe, Louise Amelia Knapp
Smith

Shirley, Frances, Lady (b. 1707)
Eng. hostess
Stenton—English p285

Shirreff, Emily Ann Eliza (1814-1897)
Eng. pioneer educator
Dorland—Sum p45,110

Shirtliffe, Robert, pseud.
See Sampson, Deborah

Shishova, Zinaida (fl. 1940's)
Russ. poet
Yarmolinsky—Treas. p301

Shlonsky, Verdina (n.d.)
Russ.-Israeli composer, pianist
Saleski—Jewish p700-701

Shoda, Michiko (b. 1935)
Japan., friend of Prince Hirohito
Time Mar.23,1959 p24,por.(Cover)

Shoemaker, Gertrude Mae (fl. 1920's-
1950's)
Amer. missionary
They—Went p82-83

Shoff, Carrie M. (b. 1849)
Amer. artist
Logan—Part p752

Shomer (Biblical)
Deen—All p295

Shook, Virginia Nelson (fl. 1930's)
Amer. advertising manager
Women—Achieve. p143,por.

Shore, Dinah (Frances Rose) (1917-   )
Amer. singer, TV personality
Blum—Television p124,por.
CR '59 p690-691,por.
CR '63 p569-570,por.
Cur. Biog. '42 p762-764,por.
Cur. Biog. '66 p376-378,por.
Donaldson—Radio p26
Reed—Follow p33-41,por.
Settel—Radio p114,por.
Stambler—Ency. p212-213
TV Guide—Roundup p45-48,por.
TV—Person. (1) p77-78,por.
Wilson—NBC p52-65,por.

Shore, Jane (c. 1445-c.1527)
Eng., mistress of Edward IV
Hammerton p1217

Short, Marion (fl. 1910's)
Amer. playwright
Logan—Part p792-793
Mantle—Amer. p307

Shorter, Susie I. L. (1859-1912)
Amer. business woman
Brown—Home. p205-207,por.

Shotoku (fl. 770 A.D.)
Japan. empress, pioneer printer,
sponsor
Club—Printing p8

Shover, Felicia Lee Carey Thornton
(fl. 1860's)
Amer. Civil war heroine
Harkness—Heroines p7

Showalter, Edna Blanche (fl. 1940's)
Amer. singer, pianist, music
teacher, manager
McCoy—Portraits p189,por.

Shrewsbury, Elizabeth.
See Talbot, Elizabeth, Countess of
Shrewsbury

Shrimpton, Ada M. (fl. 1900's)
Amer. painter
Waters—Women p316

Shua (Biblical)
Deen—All p295

Shuard, Amy (1924-   )
Eng. singer
Davidson—Treas. p287-289
Rosenthal—Sopranos p92-93,por.

Shub-ad (c. 3000 B.C.)
Babyl. (Ur.) queen
Schmidt—400 p120-121,por.

Shubrick, Mary.
See Rutledge, Mary Shubrick Eveleigh

Shubrick, Mrs. Richard (fl. 1770's)
Amer. Rev. war patriot
Ellet—Women (2) p354-355
Hanaford—Dau. p62-63

Shuchari, Sadah (fl. 1920's)
Amer. violinist
McCoy—Portraits p189,por.

Shuck, Henrietta (1817-1844)
Amer. missionary
Hanaford—Dau. p512

Shuler, Evelyn (fl. 1920's)
Amer. journalist
Ross—Ladies p511-514

Shuler, Marjorie (fl. 1920's-1930's)
Amer. journalist, pioneer air
traveler
Ross—Ladies p130-131
Women—Achieve. p120,por.

Shull, Martha Arvesta (1902-   )
Amer. organization official,
educator
Cur. Biog. '57 p502-504,por.

Shumway, Naomi (1909-   )
Amer. librarian
O'Brien—50 p863

Shunammite woman (Biblical)
Deen—All p135-140
McCartney—Great p168-185
Harrison—Little p68-78
Lewis—Portraits p85-88
Marble—Women, Bible p235-239

Shute, Mrs. James (fl.c. 1670's)
Amer. pioneer
Fowler—Woman p41-44

Sibley, Mrs. George C. (fl. 1830's)
Amer. humanitarian
DAR Mag. July 1921 p388-389,portrayal

Sibley, Mrs. Harper (fl. 1940's)
Amer., mother of the year, religious
worker, teacher
Davis—Mothers p77,179

Sibley, Sarah Sproat (m. 1802)
Amer. W. pioneer
Ellet—Pioneer p215-225

Sibyllina Biscossi (1287-1367)
It. saint
Englebert—Lives p109

Siddal, Elizabeth.
See Rossetti, Elizabeth Siddal

Siddall, Louise (d. 1935)
Amer. composer, teacher
McCoy—Portraits p190,por.

Siddons, Belle. See Vestal, Belle

Siddons, Maria (fl. 1800's)
Eng., sister of Sally Siddons
Stebbins—London p97-116

Siddons, Sarah (Sally) Kemble (1755-
1831)
Eng. actress
Abbott—Notable p342-346,por.
Adelman—Famous p104-105,por.
Dorland—Sum p32,70,165
Eaton—Actor's p7-11,25
Fitzhugh—Concise p630-631
Hammerton p1218-1219,por.
MacQueen—Pope p316-330,por.
*MacVeagh—Champlin p537

Marinacci—Lead p51-77,por.
Melville—More p71-170,por.
Ormsbee—Back. p10-11,84,94-104,por.
Schmidt—400 p142-143,por.
Sitwell—Women p18,20,por.
Stebbins—London p90-116
Trease—Seven Stages p54-82,por.

Sidgwick, Ethel (b. 1877)
Eng. novelist
Johnson—Some Contemp. p95-106
Millett—Brit. p464-465

Sidney, Frances, Countess of Sussex
(d. 1588)
Eng. philanthropist
Sorley—King's p243-267

Sidney, Mary, Countess of Pembroke
(1555/61-1621)
Eng. poet
Pomeroy—Little p21-44,por.
Sitwell—Women p11,por.

Sidney, Sylvia (1910-   )
Amer. actress
CR '59 p692-693,por.

Sidon's wife (fl.c. 700 A.D.)
Phoenician religious worker
*Levinger—Great p101-104

Siebold, Charlotte von (1761-1859)
Ger. physician
Lovejoy—Women p190-191

Siegrist, Mary (c. 1881-1953)
Amer. poet, translator
Smith—Women's p179

Sieveking, Amalie (1794-1859)
Ger. nurse, humanitarian,
educator
Stiles—Postal p251

Sifton, Claire (1898-   )
Amer. playwright
Mantle—Contemp. p232

Sigmond, Anna (fl. 1920's-1930's)
Nor. dentist, educator
Women—Achieve. p203

Signoret, Simone (1921-   )
Fr. actress
Cur. Biog. '60 p381-382,por.
Ross—Player p399-403,por.

Sigouney, Lydia Howard Huntley (1791-
1865)
Amer. author
Adelman—Famous p130
Bacon—Puritan p43-72,por.
Dexter—Career p96-97
Dorland—Sum p58,78,174,178,187

(Continued)

Sigouney, Lydia—*Continued*

> Hanaford—Dau. p250,253
> Logan—Part p797
> Papashvily—All p41,46
> Whitton—Tyese p103-104

Silberta, Rhea (1900-   )
> Amer. composer, singer, educator
> ASCAP p457
> McCoy—Portraits p190,por.

Silcott, Jane ("Jane") (1842-1895)
> Amer. Indian heroine
> Defenbach—Red p227-290,por.

Silks, Mattie (Martha) (1846/48-1929)
> Amer. W. pioneer
> Parkhill—Wildest p14,207-286,por.

Sillman, Mary Fish (1736-1818)
> Amer. Rev. war heroine
> Green—Pioneer (3) p367-373,por.
> Root—Chapter p149-172,por.

Silva (540's-550's)
> It. saint, mother of Pope Gregory
> the Great
> Blunt—Great p42-43

Silva, Vierira da.
> See Vierira da Silva, Maria Helena

Silva de Santolalla, Irene.
> See Santolalla, Irene Silva de

Sime, Jessie Georgina (b. 1880)
> Can. author
> Thomas—Canad. p115-116

Simecek, Angeline Frances (fl. 1930's)
> Amer. physician
> Women—Achieve. p152,por.

Simidtchieva, Ekaterina A. (1872-1899)
> Bulg. patriot
> Schmidt—400 p69-70,por.

Simionato, Giulietta (1916-   )
> It. singer
> Cur. Biog. '60 p382-384,por.

Simkhovitch, Mary Melinda Kingsbury
(1867-1951)
> Amer. social worker, author
> Cur. Biog. '43 p696-699,por.
> Cur. Biog. '51 p588
> *Ferris—Girls p253-270
> Women—Achieve. p68,por.

Simmons, Alberta (fl. 1920's)
> Amer. pianist
> Jazz—Panorama p75-76

Simmons, Eleanor Booth (c. 1869-1950)
> Amer. journalist
> Ross—Ladies p119-124

Simmons, Jean (1929-   )
> Eng. actress
> CR '59 p695-696,por.
> CR '63 p572-573,por.
> Cur. Biog. '52 p542-543,por.
> Time June 28,1948 p54,por.(Cover)

Simmons, Lydia Avirit (1883-1934)
> Amer. pianist
> McCoy—Portraits p190,por.

Simms, Alice D. (1917-   )
> Amer. composer, author
> ASCAP p459

Simms, Ginny (Virginia) E. (c. 1915-   )
> Amer. singer, radio personality
> Donaldson—Radio p26

Simms, Hilda (1920-   )
> Amer. actress
> Cur. Biog. '44 p621-623,por.

Simms, Lu Ann (1932-   )
> Amer. singer
> TV—Person (1) p114,por.

Simms, Ruth Hanna McCormick (1880-
1944)
> Amer. congresswoman, daughter of
> Mark Hanna
> Cur. Biog. '45 p548
> Paxton—Women p6-7,130
> Time Apr.23,1928 p12,por.(cover)

Simms, Sarah Dickinson (fl. 1770's)
> Amer. Rev. war heroine
> Green—Pioneer (3) p517-518

Simon, Anna (fl. 1910's)
> Ger. printer
> Club—Printing p16

Simon, Charlie May (1897-   )
> Amer. author
> Cur. Biog. '46 p556-557,por.

Simon, Edith (1917-   )
> Ger. author
> Cur. Biog. '54 p572-573,por.

Simonds, Emma E. (d. 1893)
> Amer. Civil war nurse
> Logan—Part p334

Simone, Nina (1935-   )
> Amer. singer, composer, pianist
> Cur. Biog. '68 p365-368,por.

Simonetta (1922-   )
> It. fashion designer
> Cur. Biog. '55 p553-554,por.

Simpson, Adele Smithline (1903-   )
> Amer. fashion designer
> CR '63 p573,por.

Simpson, Annie (d. 1905)
    Amer. Civil war patriot
    Logan—Part p501

Simpson, Cora E. (fl. 1900's-1920's)
    Amer. nurse
    Pennock—Makers p116-117,por.

Simpson, Elizabeth (fl. 1940's)
    Amer. composer, pianist, music
        teacher, lecturer, author
    McCoy—Portraits p191,por.

Simpson, Harriette.
    See Arnow, Harriette Louise Simpson

Simpson, Helen de Guerry (1897-1940)
    Eng. novelist
    Brittain—Women p145-146
    Cur. Biog. '40 p739
    Hammerton p1222
    Roderick—20 p126-142

Simpson, Lucretia Harper (b. 1820)
    Amer. pioneer
    Brown—Home. p84-85,por.

Simpson, Lucy Faucett (fl. 1860's)
    Amer. Civil war patriot
    Simkins—Women p18

Simpson, Martha Ritchie (fl. 19th cent.)
    Amer. social leader, humanitarian
    Farmer—What p372-377

Simpson, Wallis Warfield.
    See Windsor, Wallis Warfield, Duchess
        of

Sims, Isabella (fl. 1770's)
    Amer. Rev. war heroine
    Ellet—Women (1) p296-297

Sims, Leora (fl. 1860's)
    Amer. Civil war diarist
    Jones—Heroines p69-71

Sims, Marian McCamy (1899-   )
    Amer. author
    Warfel—Amer. p387,por.

Sinclair, Adelaide Helen Grant MacDonald
        (1900-   )
    Can. government official, U.N.
        representative
    Cur. Biog. '51 p588-589,por.

Sinclair, Catherine (d. 1891)
    Eng.-Amer. actress-manager
    Bodeen—Ladies p31-35

Sinclair, Guinivere (m. 1925)
    Eng. dancer
    Wyndham—Chorus p152-153

Sinclair, Jo (1913-   )
    Amer. author
    Cur. Biog. '46 p557-559,por.
    Warfel—Amer. p388,por.

Sinclair, Margaret (1900-1925)
    Scot. nun
    Burton—Valiant p112-128

Sinclair, Mary (c. 1922-   )
    Amer. actress
    TV—Person. (1) p41,por.

Sinclair, May (c. 1865-1946)
    Eng. novelist
    Cur. Biog. '46 p559
    Hammerton p1223,por.
    Johnson—Some Contemp. p33-43
    Lawrence—School 268-272
    Millett—Brit. p465-468
    Wellington—Women p133-155

Sinclair-Cowan, Bertha Muzzy.
    See Bower, Bertha Muzzy, pseud.

Singer, Ava Hamilton (fl. 1930's)
    Amer. explorer, geographer
    Women—Achieve. p100,por.

Singer, Betty (fl. 1930's)
    Amer. business woman
    Women—Achieve. p157,por.

Singer, Caroline (m. 1921)
    Amer. journalist
    Ross—Ladies p585-586

Singleton, Angelica (d 1877)
    Amer., wife of Abram Van Buren
    Smith—White p51-54,por.

Singmaster, Elsie (1879-1958)
    Amer. novelist
    Overton—Women p310-311
    Warfel—Amer. p392-393,por.

Sink, (Mary) Virginia (1913-   )
    Amer. engineer, organization
        official
    Cur. Biog. '64 p417-419,por.

Sioussat, Helen J. (fl. 1930's)
    Amer. business executive
    Women—Achieve. p115,por.

Sipprell, Clara (fl. 1920's)
    Amer. photographer
    *Ferris—Girls p199-210

Siran, Elisabetta (1638/40-1665)
    It. painter
    Waters—Women p316-319

Sirch, Margaret Frances (fl. 1920's)
    Amer. nurse
    Pennock—Makers p106-107,por.

Sirikit Kitiyakara (1932-   )
 Thail. queen, consort of Rama IX
 Cur. Biog. '60 p387-388,por.
 Time May 27,1966 p28,por.(Cover)

Sirmen, Maddalena Lombardini (b. 1735)
 It. violinist, composer, singer
 Elson—Woman's p214

Sisera's mother (Biblical)
 Deen—All p339
 Lewis—Portraits p76-77

Sister of the Beguines of Flanders (fl. 1340's)
 Fr. nurse, nun
 Schmidt—400 p391,por.

Sita (B.C., date unknown)
 E. Ind., consort of Rama
 Pool—Famous p1-17

Sitgreaves, Beverley (1867-1943)
 Amer. actress
 Cur. Biog. '43 p702

Sitgreaves, Mary (b. 1774)
 Amer. pioneer
 Logan—Part p213

Sitt al-Mulk (fl. 1021-1025)
 Egypt. queen
 Schmidt—400 p115-116,por.

Sitterly, Charlotte Moore (1898-   )
 Amer. astrophysicist
 Cur. Biog. '62 p391-393,por.

Sittig, Margaret (fl. 1910's)
 Ger. violinist
 McCoy—Portraits p191,por.

Sitwell, Edith (1887-1964)
 Eng. poet, critic, novelist
 Beaton—Persona p86,por.
 CR '59 p698-699,por.
 Hammerton p1224,por.
 Millett—Brit. p468-470
 Untermeyer—Lives p690-692

Skarbek, Krystyna Gizycka Granville
 (1915-1952)
 Pol.-Brit. spy
 Hoehling—Women p133

Skelton, Betty (1926-   )
 Amer. aviatrix
 *May—Women p43,198-199

Skelton, Martha.
 See Randolph, Martha Jefferson

Skinner, Constance Lindsay (1879-1939)
 Can. author
 Thomas—Canad. p116-117

Skinner, Cornelia Otis (1901-   )
 Amer. actress, monologist
 *Benét—Humorists p173-177,por.
 Burnett—This p1160
 CR '59 p700-701,por.
 CR '63 p574,por.
 Cur. Biog. '42 p769-771,por.
 Cur. Biog. '64 p423-426,por.
 Dodd—Celeb. p81-85
 Taves—Success. p69-78,por.

Skinner, Eleanor Oakes (1911-   )
 Amer. organization official
 Cur. Biog. '51 p592-593

Skinner, Esther (c. 1731-1831)
 Amer. Rev. war patriot
 Ellet—Women (2) p195-197

Skolnik, Jenny (1896-   )
 Russ. violinist
 Saleski—Wander. p255,por.

Skorik, Irène (fl. 1940's-1950's)
 Fr.-Russ. ballet dancer
 Haskell—Vignet. p78-79,por.
 Swinson—Dancers p44-48,por.

Skujeniece-Dambekalne, Biruta (1888-1931)
 Lat. poet, actress
 Schmidt—400 p275,por.

Slack, Gene (fl. 1940's)
 Planck—Women p240

Slade, Barbara (fl. 1940's)
 Eng. spy
 Hoehling—Women p151-163,por.

Slade, Caroline (b. 1886)
 Amer. novelist, social worker
 Warfel—Amer. p393-394,por.

Slade, Elizabeth (fl. 1660's-1670's)
 Eng. actress
 Wilson—All p187-188

Slade, Madeleine (1892-   )
 Eng., Gandhi co-worker
 Stern—Women p150-157,180-199,207-
 214,246-272,por.,cover

Slade, Maria ("Molly") Virginia Dale
 (fl. 1860's)
 Amer. W. pioneer, vigilante
 Johnson—Some p79-84
 Towle—Vigil. p123-151

Sladen, Victoria (1910-   )
 Eng. singer
 Brook—Singers p174-177,por.
 Davidson—Treas. p291-293

Slator, Helen M. (fl. 1930's)
 Amer. public relations expert
 Women—Achieve. p127,por.

Slavenska, Mia (1917-   )
Yugoslav. ballet dancer
Atkinson—Dancers p144-146,por.
Cur. Biog. '54 p577-579,por.
Matz—Opera p284-287,por.

Sleeper, Ruth (1899-   )
Amer. organization official, nurse
Cur. Biog. '52 p543-545,por.

Slemmer, Caroline Lane Reynolds, Lady
Jebb (b. 1840)
Amer. patriot
Pearson—Pilgrim p241-257

Slenczynska, Ruth (1925-   )
Amer. pianist
CR '59 p701,por.
Ewen—Living p327-328,por.
McCoy—Portraits p192,por.

Slesinger, Tess (1905-1945)
Amer. author
*Millett—Amer. p586
O'Brien—50 p866

Slessor, Mary (1848-1915)
Scot. missionary
*Deakin—True p344-362
Deen—Great p266-273
Holmes—Seven p112-135
*Horowitz—Treas. p148-156
*Kirkland—Good p85-93
Miller—Ten. p20-27
*Parkman—Heroines p235-264,por.
*Strong—Heroes p137-147
*Strong—Of p234-242

Slidell, Mathilde Deslonde (m. 1835)
Amer. patriot
Logan—Part p258

Slingsby, Mary Aldridge, Lady (Mary
Aldridge Lee)
Eng. actress
Wilson—All p159-162

Slobodskaya, Oda (n.d.)
Russ. singer
Saleski—Wander. p427

Slocum, Caroline Edna (fl. 1930's)
Amer. business woman, club leader
Women—Achieve. p126,por.

Slocum, Catherine Luden (fl. 1930's)
Amer. aviatrix
Planck—Women p178-179

Slocum, Frances ("Maconaquah") (1773-
1847)
Amer. Ind. captive, pioneer
Ellet—Women (2) p200-205
Fowler—Woman p241-247
Peckham—Capt. p116-132

Slocum, Lillie (fl. 1870's)
Amer. business woman
Hanaford—Dau. p615

Slocum, Mary Hooks (1760-1836)
American Rev. war heroine
Ellet—Women (1) p347-376
Fowler—Woman p132-136
Green—Pioneer (2) p373-383
Logan—Part p165-169
Whitton—These p2,22

Slocum, Rosalie (1906-   )
Amer. illustrator
Mahony—Illus. p361

Sloop, Mary T. Martin (1873-1962)
Amer. physician, educator, social
worker, mother of the year
Davis—Mothers p124-130
*Kirkland—Good p111-120

Slosson, Anne Trumbull (1838-1926)
Amer. entomologist
Osborn—Fragments p208,por.

Slott, Molly (c. 1896-1967)
Amer. journalist, editor
Ross—Ladies p292-293

Slott-Möller, Agnes. See Möller, Agnes Slott

Slye, Maude (1879-1954)
Amer. pathologist
Castiglioni—Hist. p963-964,1117
Cur. Biog. '40 p743-745,por.
Cur. Biog. '54 p579

Small, Jerusha R. (fl. 1860's)
Amer. Civil war nurse
Brockett—Woman's p493-494

Smallwood, Delia Graeme (fl. 1910's)
Amer. club leader
Logan—Part p435

Smallwood, Hannah T. (fl. 1870's)
Amer. scientific artist
Hanaford—Dau. p279

Smart, Alice McGee (fl. 1950's)
Amer. sociologist, poet, teacher
Dreer—Amer. p63

Smart, Susannah Barnett (b. 1761)
Amer. pioneer, heroine
Green—Pioneer (2) p399-405

Smauley, Ann. See Story, Ann

Smedley, Agnes (1894-1950)
Amer. author, journalist, lecturer
Cur. Biog. '44 p627-629,por.
Cur. Biog. '50 p533

Smedley, Constance (Anne Constance
    Armfield) (1881-1941)
    Brit. playwright, author
    Cur. Biog. '41 p797
    Hammerton p1226

Smellie, Elizabeth (fl. 1910's-1930's)
    Can. nurse, WAC officer
    Dolan—Goodnow's p273,por.
    Pennock—Makers p52,por.

Smiley, Sarah Frances (b. 1830)
    Amer. clergyman, author,
        foundress
    Hanaford—Dau. p441

Smirnoff, Zoe (fl. 1910's)
    Russ. soldier, heroine
    Dorland—Sum p99

Smith, Abigail.
    See Adams, Abigail Smith

Smith, Ada. See "Bricktop"

Smith, Ada Clark (1871-1915)
    Can.-Amer. religious worker
    Phillips—33 p121-125

Smith, Adelaide W. (b. 1831)
    Amer. Civil war nurse
    Dannett—Nobel (see index)
    Young—Women p329-330,377-378

Smith, Mrs. Alexander.
    See Pleasants, "Mammy" E.

Smith, Alice Mary (1839-1884)
    Eng. composer
    Elson—Woman's p137-138

Smith, Amanda (1837-1915)
    Amer. evangelist, missionary
    Brown—Home. p128-132,por.
    Culver—Women p167-168
    Deen—Great p251-258
    Schmidt—400 p27-28,por.

Smith, Amy.
    See Jernegan, Amy Chase

Smith, Anita (1922-   )
    Amer. composer, author
    ASCAP p465

Smith, Anne.
    See Hopkins, Anne Smith

Smith, Barbara Leigh.
    See Bodichon, Barbara Leigh Smith

Smith, Bertha Madison (1843-1896)
    Amer. religious worker
    Phillips—33 p58-64

Smith, Bessie (c. 1896-1937)
    Amer. singer

*Hughes—Music p91-98,por.
    Shapiro—Jazz p127-140,por.
*Terkel—Giants p36-50,por.

Smith, Betty Wehner (1904-   )
    Amer. author
    CR '59 p703,por.
    CR '63 p576,por.
    Cur. Biog. '43 p704-706,por.
    Warfel—Amer. p395,por.

Smith, Blanche. See Chapman, Blanche

Smith, Cassie Selden (m. 1861)
    Amer. Civil war diarist
    Jones—Heroines p177-179

Smith, Charlotte Ann (fl. 1930's)
    Amer. editor
    Women—Achieve. p203

Smith, Charlotte Turner (1749-1806)
    Eng. novelist, poet
    Dorland—Sum p48,193
    MacArthur—Later p153-162,187-189

Smith, Clara Eliza (c. 1865-1943)
    Amer. mathematician, educator
    Cur. Biog. '43 p706
    Logan—Part p731-732,879

Smith, Cornelia (fl. 18th cent.)
    Amer. printer
    Club—Printing p12

Smith, Dodie.
    See Anthony, C. L., pseud.

Smith, Doris (fl. 1910's)
    Amer. feminist
    Holbrook—Dreamers p222-223

Smith, Eleanor (1858-1942)
    Amer. song-writer, composer
    Elson—Woman's p208

Smith, Eleanor (fl. 1860's)
    Eng. lecturer, dog fancier
    Brittain—Women p37-38,59,258

Smith, Eleanor Armor (m. 1745/46)
    Amer. patriot
    Green—Pioneer (3) p197-202

Smith, Eleanor Furneaux, Lady (1902-
        1945)
    Brit. novelist
    Cur. Biog. '45 p556

Smith, Elinor (1908-   )
    Amer. pioneer aviatrix
*Adams—Sky p179-184,por.
    Earhart—Fun p165-169
    Heinmuller—Man's p337,por.
*May—Women p94,98
    New Yorker May 10,1930 p28,por.
        (Profiles)

Smith, Elizabeth (fl. 1920's)
Amer. journalist
Ross—Ladies p235-236

Smith, Elizabeth Baker (fl. 1920's-1950's)
Amer. missionary
They—Went p89-90

Smith, Elizabeth ("Betty") Martin (d. 1778)
Amer. pioneer
Green—Pioneer (1) p283,387-397

Smith, Elizabeth N. (fl. 19th cent.)
Amer. pianist, linguist
Brown—Home. p18-22

Smith, Elizabeth Oakes Prince (1806-1893)
Amer. feminist, novelist, poet
Hanaford—Dau. p264
O'Connor—Pioneer p87,141
Pattee—Fem. p100-102
Riegel—Amer. p106-112

Smith, Elizabeth Quincy (c. 1722-1775)
Amer. Rev. war patriot, mother
of Abigail Adams
Ellet—Women (2) p31,37,por.

Smith, Elizabeth Rudel (1911-   )
Amer. government official
Cur. Biog. '61 p428-429,por.

Smith, Ella Huntley (m. 1863)
Amer., wife of Charles Emory
Smith
Logan—Part p296

Smith, Ella May (1860-1934)
Amer. composer, pianist, organist,
music teacher, author
McCoy—Portraits p192,por.

Smith, Emily Adella (fl. 1880's)
Amer. entomologist, author
Osborn—Fragments p185,por.

Smith, Emily L. Goodrich (b. 1830)
Amer. club leader
Logan—Part p863

Smith, Emma Elizabeth (1847-1918)
Amer. religious worker
Phillips—33 p70-73

Smith, Emma Hale (1804-1879)
Amer. religious worker, wife of
Joseph Smith
Deen—Great p198-203
Phillips—33 p18-27

Smith, Erminie Adelle Platt (1836-1886)
Amer. ethnologist, geologist
Adelman—Famous p210
Dorland—Sum p20,143,144

Smith, Eva Munson (b. 1843)
Amer. composer
Logan—Part p816

Smith, Eveline Sherman (b. 1823)
Amer. poet
Hanaford—Dau. p266

Smith, Fanny I. Burge (fl. 1870's-1880's)
Amer. author
Hanaford—Dau. p288

Smith, Georgina (fl. 1930's)
Amer. singer, organist
Cuney-Hare—Negro p221-222

Smith, Hannah (d. 1939)
Amer. composer, music teacher,
author
McCoy—Portraits p193,por.

Smith, Hannah Whitall (1832-1911)
Amer. religious leader, author
Deen—Great p397-398
Foster—Religion p160-178,por.

Smith, Helen (1840-1891)
Amer. missionary
Phillips—33, p48-52

Smith, Helen Evertson (b. 1839)
Amer. editor, journalist
Farmer—What p463,por.

Smith, Helen Grace (b. 1865)
Amer. poet
Logan—Part p822

Smith, Hilder Florentina (fl. 1910's)
Amer. parachutist
*May—Women p52

Smith, Ida B. Wise (b. 1871)
Amer. organization official, teacher,
business woman
Cur. Biog. '43 p715-716,por.
Cur. Biog. '52 p548
Huff—Famous (and) p567-574,por.

Smith, Isabel Elizabeth (1845-1938)
Amer. painter
Logan—Part p751

Smith, Mrs. J. Henry (fl. 1860's)
Amer. Civil war author
Andrews—Women p230-236

Smith, Mrs. J. Morgan (fl. 1910's)
Amer. club leader
Logan—Part p405

Smith, Jane Norman (1874-1953)
Amer. feminist
Women—Achieve p114,por.

Smith, Jean Kennedy (b. 1928)
Amer., daughter of Joseph
Kennedy
Time July 11, 1960 p19,por.(Cover)

Smith, Jessie Welborn (fl. 1900's-1920's)
Amer. poet
Smith—Women's p184

Smith, Jessie Willcox (d. 1935)
Amer. illustrator, painter
Adelman—Famous p320-321
Jackman—Amer. p253-254
Michigan—Biog. p293
Waters—Women p319-320

Smith, Julia (1911-)
Amer. composer
ASCAP p467-468
Hanaford—Dau. p372
Howard—Our p558

Smith, Julia Holmes (b. 1839)
Amer. physician, author
Logan—Part p815

Smith, Kate (1909-)
Amer. singer, radio and TV
personality
Blum—Television p177,por.
CR '59 p704,por.
CR '63 p578,por.
Cur. Biog. '40 p745-747,por.
Cur. Biog. '65 p390-393,por.
Donaldson—Radio p26
Eichberg—Radio p134-135,por.
*Forsee—Amer. p182-204
*Gelfand—They p29-32,por.
New Yorker Mar.3,1934 p25-29,por.
(Profiles)
Settel—Radio p67,80,114,por.
TV—Person (1) p72,por.
Women—Achieve. p101,por.

Smith, Kate Walsh Fitzroy, Countess Euston
(d. 1903)
Eng. dancer
Wyndham—Chorus p72-80

Smith, Keely (1932-)
Amer. singer, comedienne
CR '63 p578,por.

Smith, L. Virginia (fl. 1850's)
Amer. poet
Whitton—These p169-170

Smith, Letta Crapo (1862-1921)
Amer. painter
Michigan—Biog. p294

Smith, Lillian Eugenia (1897-1966)
Amer. author, editor, social worker
CR '59 p704-705,por.
CR '63 p578,por.
Cur. Biog. '44 p635-638,por.

Cur. Biog. '66 p471
Warfel—Amer. p397,por.

Smith, Louisa. See Vollmer, Luia

Smith, Lucy (fl. 1860's)
Amer. Civil war diarist
Jones—Heroines p165-168

Smith, Lucy Mack (1776-1855)
Amer. religious worker, wife of
Joseph Smith
Phillips—33 p11-17

Smith, Lucy P. See Vincent, Lucy P.

Smith, Lulu Gestis (fl. 1910's-1950's)
Amer. missionary
They—Went p9-10

Smith, Mabell Shippie Clarke (1864-1942)
Amer. educator, lecturer, author
Women—Achieve. p180,por.

Smith, Madeleine-Hamilton (1935-1928)
Eng. accused criminal
Furniss—Some p212-216,por.

Smith, Mamie (fl. 1920's)
Amer. musician
Jazz—Panorama p77-79

Smith, Margaret (fl. 1660's-1670's)
Amer. colonial religious worker
Jones—Quakers p109

Smith, Margaret Bayard Harrison (1778-
1844)
Amer. author, social leader,
hostess
Hanaford—Dau. p244
Stewart—Makers p35-36

Smith, Margaret Chase (1897-)
Amer. senator
Clymer—Modern p81-90,por.
CR '59 p705,por.
CR '63 p578-579,por.
Cur. Biog. '45 p559-561,por.
Cur. Biog. '62 p393-396,por.
Jensen—Revolt p60-61,por.
Lamson—Few p3-29,104
Murrow—This (2) p138-139
Parshalle—Kash. p61-65,por.
Paxton—Women p75-80,131,por.
Roosevelt—Ladies p177-186
Time Sept.5,1960 p13,por.(Cover)
U.S.—Women (87th) p7,por.
U.S.—Women (88th) p3,por.

Smith, Margaret Elizabeth Rusk
(c.1959-)
Amer., daughter of Dean Rusk
Time Sept.29,1967,p28,por.(Cover)

Smith, Margaret Nicholson.
See Nicholson, Margaret

Smith, Marion Couthouy (fl. 1920's)
 Amer. poet
 Smith—Women's p187

Smith, Martha Turnstall (fl. 1680's-1700's)
 Amer. colonial business manager
 Dexter—Colonial p55-56
 Leonard—Amer. p98

Smith, Mary Agnes Easby (b. 1855)
 Amer. author
 Logan—Part p822

Smith, Mary E. Webber (fl. 1860's)
 Amer. Civil war nurse
 Logan—Part p372

Smith, Mary "Sis" Hopkins (fl. 1900's-
  1940's)
 Amer. missionary
 They—Went p34-36

Smith, Mary Stuart (b. 1834)
 Amer. author, translator
 Logan—Part p815

Smith, Myrtle Lee (fl. 1820's-1950's)
 Amer. missionary, physician
 They—Went p93-95

Smith, Naomi Royde.
 See Royde-Smith, Naomi Gwladys

Smith, Nina G. (1886-1950)
 Amer. religious worker
 Phillips—33 p177-181

Smith, Phebe Ann (m. 1851)
 Amer. whaling voyager
 Whiting—Whaling p93-95,241

Smith, Polly (fl. 1860's)
 Amer., mother of Gipsy Smith
 Wallace—Mothers p76-81

Smith, Priscilla Allen (m. 1682)
 Amer. pioneer
 Green—Pioneer (1) p374

Smith, Quincy (fl. 1940's)
 Amer. aircraft inventor
 *Peckham—Women p57

Smith, Rebecca (1772-1837)
 Amer. belle
 Sale—Old p212-218,por.

Smith, Rebecca S. (fl. 1860's)
 Amer. teacher, Civil war nurse
 Brockett—Woman's p789
 Logan—Part p363

Smith, Ruth Lyman (1872-1926)
 Amer. child welfare worker,
  religious worker, author
 Phillips—33 p139-147

Smith, Mrs. S. E. D. (fl. 1860's)
 Amer. Civil war patriot
 Simkins—Women p87,221-222

Smith, Sarah. See Stretton, Hesba

Smith, Sarah E. (fl. 1870's-1880's)
 Amer. botanist, linguist
 Hanaford—Dau. p284-285

Smith, Sarah L. Huntington (b. 1802)
 Amer. missionary
 Fowler—Woman p366-369
 Hanaford—Dau. p508-509
 Logan—Part p511

Smith, Sarah P. Hickman (1811-1832)
 Amer. poet
 Hanaford—Dau. p264

Smith, Sarah Rozet (fl. 1890's-1920's)
 Amer. philanthropist
 Addams—Excellent p29-36

Smith, Sarah White (b.c. 1813-1855)
 Amer. pioneer
 Drury—First (3) p83-229,por.

Smith, Sheila Kaye.
 See Kaye-Smith, Sheila

Smith, Sophia (1796-1870)
 Amer. philanthropist, educator,
  foundress
 Adelman—Famous p149
 Dorland—Sum p40,77,108
 Douglas—Remember p94
 Hanaford—Dau. p183,540
 Jansen—Revolt p108,por.
 Logan—Part p711

Smith, Susan Hayes (m. 1784)
 Amer. pioneer, telegraph operator
 Sargent—Pioneers p51-53

Smith, Sydney (n.d.)
 Amer. TV personality
 TV—Person. (1) p107-108,por.

Smithson, Harriet Constance (Harriet
  Berlioz) (1800-1854)
 Irish actress
 Elson—Woman's p81-83

Smock, Rose Melville (b. 1873)
 Amer. actress
 Logan—Part p783

Smyth, Ethel Mary, Dame (1858-1944)
 Eng. composer, author, feminist,
  journalist
 Cole—Women p1-29,por.
 Cur. Biog. '44 p641
 De Morny—Best p149-156
 Elson—Woman's p140
 Ewen—Ency. p479
 Hammerton p1229,por.
 McCoy—Portraits p193,por.

Smythe, Amanda B. (fl. 1860's)
Amer. Civil war nurse
Logan—Part p371

Snead, Nell (fl. 1930's)
Amer. journalist
Ross—Ladies p571-572

Snell, Cornelia Tyler (fl. 1930's)
Amer. chemist
Women—Achieve. p149,por.

Snell, Sarah (fl. 1780's-1850's)
mother of William Cullen Bryant
Bartlett—Mothers p56-59

Snelling, Abigail Hunt (b.c. 1797/98)
Amer. W. pioneer
Ellet—Pioneer p305-337
Logan—Part p89-93
Whitton—These p208-210

Snethlage, Emilie (1868-1929)
Ger.-Brazil. zoologist
Schmidt—400 p421,por.

Snezhina, Elena (fl. 1940's)
Bulg. actress
Phila.—Women unp.,por.

Snipes, Esther Wacknitz (fl. 1920's-1950's)
Amer. missionary
They—Went p80-81

Snively, Mary Agnes (d. 1933)
Can. nurse
Dolan—Goodnow's p255,por.
Pennock—Makers p35,por.

Snodgrass, Louise Harrison (fl. 1940's)
Amer. pianist
McCoy—Portraits p193,por.

Snook, Neta (fl. 1930's)
Amer. aviatrix
°May—Women p112
Planck—Women p37-38

"Snooks, Baby."
See Brice, Fanny Borach

Snow, Alice Rowe (fl. 1880's)
Amer. seafarer
Snow—Women p167-195,por.

Snow, Anna Rablen (b. 1861)
Amer. pioneer
Sickels—Twelve p150-166,254

Snow, C. Georgia (fl. 1870's)
Amer. lawyer
Hanaford—Dau. p667

Snow, Carmel White (1890-1961)
Irish-Amer. editor, journalist
CR '59 p707-708,por.

Snow, Constantia (d. 1679)
Amer. pioneer
Green—Pioneer (1) p141
Logan—Part p33

Snow, Eliza Groxey (1804-1887)
Amer. W. pioneer, hymn-writer
Ellet—Pioneer p303-304
°Miller—West. p66-82

Snow, Emily Topple (fl. 1870's-1890's)
Amer. W. pioneer
Sargent—Pioneers p22-23,por.

Snowden, Ethel (1881-1951)
Eng. feminist
Hammerton p1230

Snyder, Alice Dorothea (1887-1943)
Amer. author, educator
Cur. Biog. '43 p719

Snyder, Grace McCance (b.c. 1783)
Amer. author
°Johnson—Some p150-165,por.

Snyder, Janet.
See Lambert, Janet Snyder

Soaemias, Julia, Woman of Emesa (fl. 200's)
Rom., mother of Heliogabalus
Boccaccio—Conc. p223-225
Serviez—Roman (2) p228-230,254

Sobieski, Maria Clementina (d. 1735)
Pol., wife of James Edward,
mother of Charles Edward
Hammerton p1230

Soederstroem, Elizabeth (1927-   )
Swed. singer
Wagner—Prima p166-167,248

Sofia of Chotek, Princess of Hohenburg
(d. 1914)
Aust. princess
Arsenius—Dict. p181,por.
Phila.—Women unp.,por.
Stiles—Postal p255

Soissons, Olympe Mancini, Comtesse de
(fl. 1640's-1670's)
Fr., niece of Cardinal Mazarin
Hall—Moths p190-210,por.

Sokalski, Annie Blanche (fl. 1860's)
Amer. W. pioneer
Brown—Gentle p14,59,61-64

Sokoloff, Natalie B.
See Scott, Natalie Anderson

Sokolova, Lydia (fl. 1920's)
Brit. dancer
Hammerton p1232

Sokolsky-Fried, Sara (1896-   )
 Pol. pianist
 Saleski—Wander. p391,por.

Solange (d. 880)
 Fr. saint
 Englebert—Lives p182

Soldat, Marie (b. 1864)
 Aust. violinist
 Erlich—Celeb. p257-259,por.
 McCoy—Portraits p194,por.

Soldene, Emily (c. 1845-1912)
 Eng. singer, actress, journalist,
  novelist
 Marks—Glamour p49-55,por.

Solis, Manuela (gr. 1889)
 Sp. pioneer physician
 Lovejoy—Women p205

Solis Quiroga, Margarita Delgado de
 (fl. 1920's)
 Mex. physician
 Lovejoy—Women p265-266,por.

Solovieff, Miriam (1921-   )
 Amer. violinist
 Saleski—Jewish p398-399,por.

Soltesova, Elena Marothy (b. 1855)
 Czech. author, educator, editor
 Schmidt—400 p90,por.

Somerset, Frances Howard Carr, Countess
 of (1594-1632)
 Eng. accused criminal
 Jenkins—Six p81-136

Somerset, Isabel, Lady Henry (1851-1921)
 Eng. heiress
 Bolton—Famous Leaders p250-271,por.
 Carey—Twelve p333-347,por.
 Cole—Women p31-64,por.
 Hammerton p1234

Somerville, Edith Anna Oenone (1861-
 1949)
 Irish novelist, artist
 Hammerton p1234

Somerville, Mary Fairfax (1780-1872)
 Scot. mathematician, physicist,
  author
 Adelman—Famous p123-124
 Coolidge—Six p25-26
 Dorland—Sum p24,83,141-142
 Hammerton p1234
 °Humphrey—Marys p110-128
 Mozans—Woman p157-161,211-212
 Parton—Noted p362-376,por.
 Stenton—English p180,328-332

Somigli, Franca (c. 1907-   )
 Amer. singer
 Ewen—Living p333-334
 McCoy—Portraits p194,por.

Sommerfield, Rose (fl. 1880's-1890's)
 Amer. religious worker, teacher
 Logan—Part p646-647

Sondergand, Gale (fl. 1920's-1930's)
 Amer. actress
 Lamparski—What p146-147,por.

Sone, Monica (1919-   )
 Japan.-Amer. author
 Hazeltine—We p196-206

Sonrel, Elizabeth (fl. 1890's-1910's)
 Fr. painter
 Waters—Women p320

Sontag, Henriette, Countess Rossi
 (Henriette von Lauenstein)
 (1806-1854)
 Ger. singer
 Adelman—Famous p133-134
 Ewen—Ency. p481
 Ferris—Great (1) p197-220,por.
 Howard—Our p204
 Lahee—Famous p45-47
 McCoy—Portraits p194,por.
 Marks—Glamour p119-126,por.
 Pleasants—Great p192-197,por.
 Schmidt—400 p199,por.

Sooja Bae (fl. 16th cent.)
 E. Ind. (Boondi) princess
 Pool—Famous p64-68

Soong, Mrs. Charles Jones (c. 1869-1931)
 Chin. Christian
 Deen—Great p294-298

Soong, Chingling.
 See Sun Yat-sen, Chingling Soong
 Madame

Soong, Kwei-Tseng Ni, Madame (c. 1869-
 1931)
 Chin., mother of Soong sisters
 Clark—Chiangs p27-30,,40-41,por.

Soper, Eileen A. (1905-   )
 Amer. illustrator
 Mahony—Illus. p361-362

Soper, Luella Hartt (fl. 1930's)
 Amer. lecturer, club leader
 Women—Achieve. p156,por.

Sophia (fl. 3rd cent. A.D.)
 Christian saint
 Englebert—Lives p355-356

Sophia (1630-1714)
    Ger. electress of Hanover
Dark—Royal p175-198,por.
Hammerton p1234,por.

Sophia Alekseevina (1657-1704)
    Russ. regent
Hammerton p1234

Sophia Charlotte (1668-1705)
    Ger., mother of Frederick the
      Great
Mozans—Woman p370-371

Sophia Dorothea (1666-1726)
    Ger. princess
Hammerton p1234

Sophia Dorothea Ulrike Alice (1870-1932)
    Ger. princess, Gr. queen
Phila.—Women unp.,por.
Stiles—Postal p255

Sophie May, pseud.
    See Clarke, Rebecca Sophia

Sophonisba (Sophoniba) (d.c. 203/204 B.C.)
    Carth., daughter of Hasdrubal
Boccaccio—Conc. p152-154
Hammerton p1235

Sorabji, Cornelia (c. 1866-1954)
    E. Ind. lawyer, author
Brittain—Women p73,84-85,212,248
Hammerton p1235

Soraya Esfandiari (1932-   )
    Pers. ex-queen
CR '59 p711-712,por.
Phila.—Women unp.,por.
Stiles—Postal p84

Sorel, Agnes (1409-1450)
    Fr., mistress of Charles VII
Hammerton p1235
Koven—Women p85-86,por.
Welch—Six p147-172,por.

Sorensen, Virginia (1912-   )
    Amer. author
Cur. Biog. '50 p538-539,por.
Warfel—Amer. p398-399,por.

Sosenko, Anna (1910-   )
    Amer. composer, author
ASCAP p471

Soss, Wilma Porter (c. 1902-   )
    Amer. public relations expert,
      economist, organization official
Cur. Biog. '65 p393-395,por.

Sothern, Ann (1912-   )
    Amer. actress, TV personality
Blum—Television p101,por.
CR '59 p712-713,por.
CR '63 p582,por.

Cur. Biog. '56 p595-597,por.
TV—Person (1) p17-18,por.

Souder, Emily Bliss (fl. 1860's)
    Amer. Civil war patriot, author
Dannett—Noble 249-p253,267-271
Young—Women p287,289,293-294

Soulage, Marcelle (1894-   )
    Fr. composer
McCoy—Portraits p194,por.

Soule, Aileen Riggin (1906-   )
    Amer. swimmer
*Jacobs—Famous p73-79,por.

Soule, Caroline A. (fl. 1870's-1880's)
    Amer. lecturer, social reformer,
      clergyman, author
Hanaford—Dau. p240,350,493-494,550

Soulsby, Elsie MacGill (gr. 1927)
    Can. electrical engineer, aeronaut
      pioneer, airplane builder
Goff—Women p45-49

Souray, Eleanor (m. 1910)
    Eng. dancer
Wyndham—Chorus p169-170

Souslova, Nadiejda (fl. 1860's)
    Russ. physician
Lovejoy—Women p167

South, Lillian H. (b. 1878)
    Amer. physician
Lovejoy—Women Phys. p211,por.

Southcott, Joanna (1750-1814)
    Eng. religious worker
Hammerton p1236

Souther, Marguerite (fl. 1940's)
    Amer. basketball coach, dancing
      teacher
Amory—Proper p288-290

Southey, Caroline Ann Bowles (1786-1854)
    Eng. poet
Courtney—Adven. p33-43

Southgate, Eliza (fl. 18th-19th cent.)
    Amer. educator
Woody—Hist. (1) p154-158

Southwick, Charlotte Augusta (fl. 1850's)
    Amer. social leader
Logan—Part p259-260

Southwick, Elsie Whitmore (fl. 1920's)
    Amer. painter
Michigan—Biog. p294

Southworth, Alice. See Bradford, Alice

Southworth, Ella (b. 1872)
Amer. artist
Janis—They p174-177,por.

Southworth, Emma Dorothy Eliza Nevitte
(1819-1899)
Amer. novelist
Dorland—Sum p34,80,194
Hanaford—Dau. p237
Logan—Part p813-814
Papashvily—All (see index)
Pattee—Fem. p122-124

Souza, Ernest, pseud.
See Scott, Evelyn D.

Souza-Botelho, Adèle Marie Émilie Filleul,
Marquise de (1761-1836)
Fr. novelist
Dorland—Sum p23,77,106

Sowerby, Amy Millicent (fl. 1940's)
Eng. illustrator
Mahoney—Illus. p362

Spain, Frances Lander (1903-   )
Amer. librarian, organization
official
Cur. Biog. '60 p392-393,por.

Spalding, Anne (fl. 1910's)
Amer. philanthropist
Logan—Part p536

Spalding, Catherine, Mother (1793-1858)
Amer. foundress
Code—Great p152-179,por.

Spalding, Eliza Hart (1807-1851)
Amer. W. pioneer, missionary
Brown—Gentle p13,15,100,158
Drury—First (1) p173-233
*Ross—Heroines p14,58-60,63-64,66,
88-89
Ross—Westward p23,26-27,34-37
Whitton—These p260-261

Spalding, Mrs. (fl. 1770's)
Amer. Rev. war heroine
Ellet—Women (1) p318-321
Fowler—Woman p493-494
Logan—Part p185-186

Spangberg-Holth, Marie (gr. 1893)
Nor. pioneer physician
Lovejoy—Women p178-179,por.

Spanò, Mario (b. 1843)
It. painter
Waters—Women p320

Sparkes, Leonora (fl. 1900's-1920's)
Eng. singer
Lahee—Grand p278,313
McCoy—Portraits p194,por.

Sparks, Ruth Sevier (d. 1824)
Amer. W. pioneer
Ellet—Pioneer p153-161

Sparks, Sarah (fl. 1930's)
Can.-Amer. personnel director
Women—Achieve. p203

Sparrow, Arianna Cooley (fl. 1860's)
Amer. singer
Cuney-Hare—Negro p220-221

Sparrow, Elizabeth (Betsy) Hanks (c. 1771-
1818)
Amer., sister of Lucy Hanks
Barton—Women p47-50

Spaulding, Jennie Tileston (fl. 1860's)
Amer. Civil war nurse
Brockett—Woman's p789

Speaks, Margaret (fl. 1930's)
Amer. singer
Ewen—Living p335-336,por.

Speare, Dorothy (1898-1951)
Amer. author, singer
Warfel—Amer. p399,por.

Speare, Elizabeth George (1908-   )
Amer. author
Cur. Biog. '59 p421-422,por.

Spears, Nanette M. (fl. 1950's)
Amer. aviatrix
*May—Women p194-195

Speed, Mrs. Joshua (fl. 1850's-1860's)
Amer. social leader
Logan—Part p285-286

Spence, Catherine Helen (1825-1910)
Scot.-Austral. journalist, social
reformer
Prout—Petticoat p164-170,por.
Schmidt—400 p38,por.

Spence, Geraldine (1931-   )
Eng. illustrator
Ryder—Artists p117

Spencer, Anne (b. 1882)
Amer. poet
Dreer—Amer. p47

Spencer, Cornelis, pseud. (Grace
Sydenstricker Yaukey) (1899-)
Amer. novelist
Warfel—Amer. p400,por.

Spencer, Eleanor (1890-   )
Amer. pianist
McCoy—Portraits p195,por.

Spencer, Elizabeth (1931-   )
Amer. novelist
Warfel—Amer. p401,por.

Spencer, Emily P. (fl. 1860's)
Amer. Civil war nurse
Logan—Part p372

Spencer, Ethel (fl. 1930's)
Amer. lawyer
Women—Achieve. p203

Spencer, Fleta Jan Brown (1883-1938)
Amer. composer, author
ASCAP p473

Spencer, Lilian White (c. 1873-1953)
Amer. author
Binheim—Women p111-112,por.

Spencer, Lily Martin (1847-1902)
Amer. artist
Hanaford—Dau. p304

Spencer, Mrs. R. H. (fl. 1860's)
Amer. Civil war nurse
Brockett—Woman's p404-415,por.

Spencer, Shirley (1897-   )
Amer. graphologist
New Yorker Dec. 24,1949 p26,por.
(Profiles)

Spender, Lily (1835-1895)
Eng. novelist
Hammerton p1239

Spens, Janet (fl. 1910's)
Eng. teacher
Brittain p95,124-125,147

Sperandia (d. 1276)
It. saint
Wescott—Calen. p138

Spewack, Bella Cohen (1899-   )
Hung. playwright, journalist
CR '59 p716,por.
CR '63 p584,por.
Gould—Modern p135-140,por.
Mantle—Contemp. p230-231,249

Speyer, Mrs. James (1862-1921)
Amer. philanthropist
Adelman—Famous p265

Speyer, Leonora Von Stosch (1872-1956)
Amer. poet
Cook—Our p314-316
Smith—Women's p190

Spicer, Charlotte (b. 1852)
Eng. social worker
Martindale—Some p23-30,por.

Spicer, Dorothy (fl. 1930's)
Amer. aviatrix
*May—Women p139

Spiegel, Clara Gatzert (Clare Jaynes, pseud)
Amer. author
Cur. Biog '54 p364-365,por.
Warfel—Amer. p228-229,por.

Spies, Hermine (1857-1893)
Ger. singer
McCoy—Portraits p195,por.

Spilimberg, Irene di (b. 1540)
It. painter
Waters—Women p320-321

Spilman, Mrs. Baldwin Day (fl. 1910's)
Amer. club leader
Logan—Part p463

Spirito, Yolanda (fl. 1930's-1940's)
Amer. aviation instructor
Planck—Women p162-163

Spitzer, Marian (fl. 1930's)
Amer. journalist
Ross—Ladies p259-260

Spofford, Grace (fl. 1940's)
Amer. music educator
McCoy—Portraits p195,por.

Spofford, Harriet Elizabeth Prescott (1835-1921)
Amer. novelist, poet
Hanaford—Dau. p246
Logan—Part p839

Spohr, Dorette Scheidler (fl. 1790's-1840's)
Ger. harpist
Elson—Woman's p80-81

Spooner, Winifred (fl. 1930's)
Eng. aviatrix
*May—Women p102-103

Sporborg, Constance Amberg (1879-1961)
Amer. organization official
Cur. Biog. '47 p599-601,por.
Cur. Biog. '61 p436

Spottiswoode, Alicia Ann (1811-1900)
Scot. song-writer
Hammerton p1242

Spottswood, Dorothea.
See Dandridge, Dorothea

Sprague, Kate Chase. See Chase, Kate

Sprague, Sarah J. Milliken (fl. 1860's)
Amer. Civil war nurse
Logan—Part p372

Sprague, Susannah (fl. 1860's)
Amer. Civil war nurse
Logan—Part p373

Spratt, Maria. See Proovost, Maria de
  Peyster Schrick Spratt

Spratt, Mary (Polly). See Alexander, Mary
  (Polly) Spratt Provoost

Spray, Ruth Hinshaw (b. 1848)
    Amer. teacher, philanthropist
  Logan—Part p531-532

Spring, Agnes Wright (fl. 1900's-1920's)
    Amer. journalist
  Binheim—Women p112,por.

Springer, Adele I. (1907-   )
    Amer. lawyer, organization official
  Cur. Biog '47 p601-603,por.

Springer, Mrs. C. R. (fl. 1860's)
    Amer. Civil war humanitarian,
      teacher
  Brockett—Woman's p639-640

Springer, Rebecca Ruter (1832-1904)
    Amer. author, poet
  Logan—Part p862

Springett, Gulielma.
  See Penn, Gulielma Maria Springett

Springfield, Laodicea (Dicey) Langston
    (Dicey Langston) (b. 1760)
    Amer. Rev. war heroine
  Ellet—Women (1) p323-331
  Fowler—Woman p127-130
  Green—Pioneer (2) p304-316
  Hanaford—Dau. p57
  Leonard—Amer. p122
  Sickels—Calico p85-95

Sproat, Florantha Thompson (b. 1811)
    Amer. W. pioneer, inn-keeper
  Sargent—Pioneers p33-37,por.

Sproull, Lillian R. (fl. 1950's)
    Amer. aviatrix
  *May—Women p195

Spry, Constance (1886-1960)
    Eng. horticulturist, author
  Cur. Biog. '40 p753-754
  Cur. Biog. '60 p397

Spurgeon, Caroline Frances Eleanor (1869-
    1942)
    Eng. educator
  Cur. Biog. '42 p790

Spurr, Gertrude E. (fl. 1900's)
    Eng. painter
  Waters—Women p321-322

Spyri, Johanna Heusser (1827-1901)
    Swiss author
  *Cather—Younger p73-95

Phila.—Women unp.,por.
Schmidt—400 p384-385,por.
Stiles—Postal p257

Squire, Mary E. (fl. 1860's)
    Amer. Civil war nurse
  Logan—Part p361

Staal (Stahl) Marguerite Jeanne Cordier
    Delaunay, Baroness de (1684-
    1750)
    Fr. politician, courtesan
  Dorland—Sum p15,106
  Kavanagh—Woman (1) p44,48,53-56
  Herold—Love p119-189,por.

Stacey, Anna Lee (fl. 1900's)
    Amer. painter
  Waters—Women p322-323

Stader, Maria (1915-   )
    Swiss singer
  Cur. Biog. '58 p405-407,por.

Stading, Evelina (1803-1829)
    Swed. painter
  Waters—Women p323

Staël, Albertine. See Broglie, Albertine Ida
  Gustavine de Staël, Duchesse de

Staël (Staël-Holstein), Anne Louise
    Germaine Necker, Baroness de
    (1766-1817)
    Fr. author
  Abbot—Notable p248-252,por.
  Adelman—Famous p111-112
  *Bolton—Lives p309-328,por.
  Coryn—Enchant. p127-154
  Dark—More p219-237
  De Morny—Best p68-75,por.
  Dorland—Sum p32-33,76,105
  Fifty—Famous p146-151,por.
  Fitzhugh—Concise p646-647
  Hammerton p1243,por.
  Hubbard—Little p213-249,por.
  Kavanagh—Woman (2) p71-74,por.
  *MacVeagh—Champlin p545-546
  Orr—Famous Affin. III p99-117
  Parton—Dau. p263-279,por.
  Parton—Noted p262-279,por.
  Ravenel—Women p90-117
  Schmidt—400 p181-182,por.
  Tallentyre—Women p113-133,por.
  Thomson—Queens p307-340
  Watson—Some p97-148,por.

Stafford, Jean (1915-   )
    Amer. novelist
  Auchincloss—Pion. p152-160
  Breit—Writer p223-225
  CR '59 p719,por.
  CR '63 p586,por.
  Cur. Biog. '51 p603-604,por.
  Warfel—Amer. p401,por.

Stafford, Jo (1918-   )
Amer. singer
CR '59 p719,por.
CR '63 p586,por.
Stambler—Ency. p222-223
TV—Person. (1) p12-13,por.

Stagg, Jessie A. (fl. 1920's)
Amer. sculptor
National—Contemp. p301

Stagg, Mary (fl. 1710's-1730's)
Amer. colonial actress, dancer,
dancing teacher
Dexter—Colonial p157
Spruill—Women's p95,259-260,287

Stagnero de Munar, Maria (1856-1922)
Urug. educator
Schmidt—400 p413-414,por.

Stahl, Lydia (n. d.)
Russ. spy
Singer—World's p320-321

Stahl, Madame de. See **Staäl, Marguerite
Jeanne Cordier Delaunay, Baroness de**

Stahl, Rose (b. 1870)
Can. actress
Blum—Great p53,por.

Stainville, Thérèse de (fl. 18th cent.)
Fr. Rev. martyr
Blei—Fasc. p165-167

Stair, Patty (1869-1926)
Amer. composer, pianist, organist,
teacher
McCoy—Portraits p196,por.

Stairs, Gordon, pseud. See **Austin, Mary
Hunter**

Stairs, Louise E. (fl. 1940's)
Amer. composer, pianist, organist,
teacher
McCoy—Portraits p196,por.

Stalina, Svetlana. See **Alliluyeva, Svetlana
Stalina**

Stam, Elizabeth ("Betty") (1906-   )
Amer. missionary
Miller—Ten p49-55

Stamper, Mrs. (fl. 1770's)
Scot.-Amer. colonial singer
Dexter—Colonial p164-165

Standerin, Ann Lee. See **Lee Ann**

Standish, Barbara (d.c. 1659)
Amer. Pilgrim, 2d wife of Miles
Standish
Green—Pioneer (1) p133
Marble—Women p98-100

Standish, Marian Eddy (fl. 1910's-1930's)
Amer. publicity director, journalist
Women—Achieve. p203

Standish, Rose (d. 1620)
Amer. Pilgrim, 1st wife of Miles
Standish
Bell—Women p19-20,24
Green—Pioneer (1) p133

Standish, Sarah Alden (d.c. 1688)
Amer. Pilgrim
Green—Pioneer (1) p133

Standring, Heather (1928-   )
Eng. illustrator
Ryder—Artists p119

Stanford, Jane Lathrop (1825-1905)
Amer. philanthropist
Adelman—Famous p234-235
Binheim—Women p10
Dorland—Sum p45,78-79,108,128
Logan—Part p543-544

Stanhope, Hester Lucy, Lady (1776-1839)
Eng. traveler, Arab. "queen"
Adelman—Famous p108-109
Blei—Fasc. p175-180,por.
De Morny—Best p43-53,por.
Dorland—Sum p29
Erskine—Out p267-281
Hammerton p1246,por.
Holmes—Seven p35-78
Holroyd—Fifty p189-193
Muir—Women p139-141
Schmidt—400 p147-148,por.
Sitwell—Women p26-27,por.
Stenton—English p272-277
Stirling—Odd p88-98

Stanislaus, Sister (fl. 1800's-1900's)
Amer. nun, nurse
Elgin—Nun p44-47,por.

Stanley, Cornelia M. Tomkins (fl. 1860's)
Amer. Civil war nurse
Logan—Part p373

Stanley, Dorothy, Lady (fl. 1900's)
Eng. painter
Waters—Women p323

Stanley, Esther (1697-1776)
Amer. Rev. war patriot
Root—Chapter p279-285

Stanley, Helen (1889-   )
Amer. singer
McCoy—Portraits p196,por.

Stanley, Imogene (fl. 1920's)
Amer. journalist, beauty
Ross—Ladies p281-290,por.,cover

Starr, Belle Shirley (1849-1889)
Amer. W. pioneer
Aikman—Calamity p158-206,por.
Horan—Desperate p201-226,por.
Rogers—Gallant p115-144

Starr, Cecile (1921-   )
Amer. film critic
Cur. Biog. '55 p573-575,por.

Starr, Frances (b.c. 1886)
Amer. actress
Blum—Great p58,por.
Coad—Amer. p310,por.

Starr, Mrs. Harold (fl. 1920's)
Amer. heroine
*Deakin—True p7-20

Starr, Kay (1923-   )
Amer. singer
CR '59 p721,por.
Stambler—Ency. p223-224

Starr, Lucy E. (fl. 1860's)
Amer. Civil war nurse
Brockett—Woman's p728-730

Starr, Stella (fl. 1900's)
Amer. milliner
Woodward—Way p366-372

Stastny, Olga (1878-1952)
Amer. physician
Lovejoy—Women p199,340
Lovejoy—Women Phys. p128,por.
Mead—Medical p67,por.

Statilia Messalina. See Messalina, Valeria

Stead, Christina (1902-   )
Austral. novelist
Roderick—20 p190-215

Stearns, Betsey Ann Goward (b. 1830)
Amer. inventor
Logan—Part p889

Stearns, Lutie Eugenia (1866-1943)
Amer. pioneer librarian
Marshall—Amer. p457-458

Stearns, Sarah Burger (b. 1836)
Amer. Civil war humanitarian,
feminist, social reformer
Brockett—Woman's p760
Moore—Women p382-386

Stebbins, Catherine A. F. (fl. 1870's-1880's)
Amer. social reformer
Hanaford—Dau. p372

Stebbins, Clara B. ("Callie") (1858-1958)
Amer. religious worker
Phillips—33 p89-94

Stebbins, Emma (1815-1882)
Amer. sculptor
Hanaford—Dau. p308-309
Tuckerman—Look p602-603
Waters—Women p323-324

Steber, Eleanor (1916-   )
Amer. singer
CR '59 p722,por.
CR '63 p587-588,por.
Cur. Biog. '43 p731-732,por.
Ewen—Ency. p484
McCoy—Portraits p197,por.
Matz—Opera p218-222,por.
Peltz—Spot. p81,por.
Rosenthal—Sopranos p94-95,por.
Wagner—Prima p82-83,248

Steeb, Olga (d. 1942)
Amer. pianist
McCoy—Portraits p197,por.

Steedman, Elsie V. (fl. 1930's)
Amer. anthropologist
Women—Achieve. p161,por.

Steel, Flora Annie Webster (1847-1929)
Eng. novelist
Adelman—Famous p279

Steel, Katharine Fisher (c. 1724-1785)
Amer. pioneer heroine
Green—Pioneer (2) p414-420

Steele, Ann (fl. 1840's)
Amer. author
Whitton—These p86-88

Steele, Anne (1716-1778)
Eng. hymn-writer
Deen—Great p305
Dorland—Sum p56,186

Steele, Elizabeth Maxwell (fl. 1770's)
Amer. Rev. war heroine
Dar Mag. July 1921 p381-382,portrayal
Ellet—Women (1) p339-343
Green—Pioneer (3) p344-348
Hanaford—Dau. p58

Steele, Helen McKay (n.d.)
Amer. illustrator
Michigan—Biog. p296

Steele, Norma Mitchell Talbot (m. 1932)
Amer. playwright
Mantle—Contemp. p236-237

Steen, Marguerite (1894-   )
Eng. author
Cur. Biog. '41 p819-821,por.

Stein, Camille L. (fl. 1940's)
Amer. airline executive
Peckham—Women p95-96

Stein, Charlotte von (1742-1827)
Ger. letter-writer
Hammerton p1249
Schmidt—400 p194-195,por.

Stein, Edith (1891-1942)
Ger. nun
Burton—Valiant p76-92

Stein, Gertrude (1874-1946)
Amer. author
Bruère—Laugh. p285
Cur. Biog. '46 p566
Ewen—Ency. p485
Hammerton p1249
Jensen—Revolt p100,por.
Loggins—Hear p323-328
*Millett—Amer. p94-95,593-596
*Muir—Writers p55-70,por.
Scherman—Literary p113
Stone—We p117-122
Time Sep.11,1933 p57,por.(Cover)
Untermeyer—Makers p458-467
Witham—Pan. p247-250,por.

Stein, Nanette (Maria Anna) (1769-1833)
Ger. pianist
Schonberg—Great p38-39

Steinbach, Sabina von (date unknown)
Ger. sculptor
Hanaford—Dau. p291

Steinberg, Maria Alice (fl. 1960's)
Amer. aeronautical research
engineer
*May—Women p197

Steinberg, Mrs. Saul. See **Sterne, Hedda**

Steiner, Emma (fl. 1930's)
Amer. composer
Elson—Woman's p205-206

Steinman, Mrs. John F. See **Watkins, Shirley**

Stella, Antoinette (1929-   )
It. singer
Cur. Biog. '59 p428-429,por.

Stellman, Maxine (fl. 1940's)
Amer. singer
Peltz—Spot. p102-103,por.

Steloff, (Ida) Frances (b. 1887)
Amer. bookseller
Cur. Biog. '65 p410-412,por.

Sten, Anna (1910-   )
Russ. actress
Lamparski—What. p134-135,por.

Sten, Suzanne (fl. 1940's)
Aust.-Hung. singer
McCoy—Portraits p198,por.

Stephanie de Beauharnais, Grand Duchess of Baden (1789-1860)
Ger., wife of Grand Duke Charles
Stiles—Postal p258

Stephens, Alice Barber (1858-1932)
Amer. illustrator
Michigan—Biog. p296
Waters—Women p324

Stephens, Anna Sophia Winterbotham
(Jonathan Slick (1810/13-1886)
Amer. author
Bruère—Laugh. p14
Dorland—Sum p34,196
Hanaford—Dau. p237-238
Papashvily—All p61,142-144,
Pattee—Fem. p124-125,por.
Stern—We p29-54

Stephens, Anne (fl. 1930's-1940's)
Eng. WAAF
*May—Women p189

Stephens, Catherine ("Kitty"), Countess of Essex (1794-1882)
Eng. singer, actress
MacQueen—Pope p263-264,por.
Wyndham—Chorus p11,41-43,46,por.

Stephens, Martha Stewart Elliot (fl. 1770's)
Amer. Rev. war patriot
Green—Pioneer (3) p323

Stephens, Nan Bagby (1892-   )
Amer. playwright
Mantle—Amer. p308

Stephenson, Geneva (n.d.)
Amer. author
Warfel—Amer. p405,por.

Stephenson, Sarah (1738-1802)
Eng. clergyman
Stenton—English p179-180

Sterling, Antoinette (1850-1904)
Anglo-Amer. singer
Dorland—Sum p31,163
Hammerton p1251
Klein—Great p183-185
McCoy—Portraits p198,por.

Sterling, Jan (1923-   )
Amer. actress
CR '59 p726-727,por.
CR '63 p590-591,por.

Stern, Daniel, pseud. See **Agoult, Marie Catherine Sophie de Flavigny Comtesse d'**

Stern, Elizabeth Gertrude Levin (Elsie-Jeab; Eleanor Morton, pseud.) (1890-1954)
Amer. author, editor
Women—Achieve. p103,por.

Stern, Gladys Bronwyn (1890-   )
    Eng. novelist
    Hammerton p1251
    Lawrence—School p198-203
    Millett—Brit. p477-479

Stern, Lucie (1913-1938)
    Lat. pianist
    McCoy—Portraits p199,por.

Stern, Marie Simchow (Masha, pseud.)
        (1909-   )
    Amer. illustrator
    Mahony—Illus. p362

Sternberger, Estelle Miller (b. 1886)
    Amer. humanitarian
    Women—Achieve. p131,por.

Sterne, Eva Rosine Ruff (b. 1810)
    Ger.-Amer., godmother of Sam
        Houston
    Turner—Sam p25-28,por.

Sterne, Hedda (1916-   )
    Rum.-Amer. artist
    Cur. Biog. '57 p529-531,por.

Sterne, Mabel Dodge. See Luhan, Mabel
    Dodge

Stetson, Charlotte. See Gilman, Charlotte
    Perkins
    National—Contemp. p306

Stetson, Katherine Beecher (b. 1885)
    Amer. sculptor
    National—Contemp. p306

Stetson, Martha A. (fl. 1870's-1880's)
    Amer. lecturer
    Hanaford—Dau. p345-346

Steuber, Lillian (fl. 1940's)
    Amer. singer
    McCoy—Portraits p199,por.

Stevens, Alice J. (b. 1860)
    Amer. editor, author
    Logan—Part p822

Stevens, Alzina Parsons (b. 1844)
    Amer. feminist, author, social
        reformer
    Logan—Part p903

Stevens, Augusta de Grasse (1865-1894)
    Amer.-Belg. author
    Black—Notable p270-285,por.

Stevens, Christine (1918-   )
    Amer. antivivisectionist
    CR '63 p591

Stevens, Connie (1938-   )
    Amer. actress, TV personality
    CR '63 p591-592,por.
    *Kahn—Tops p134,por.

Stevens, Mrs. E. H. (fl. 1910's)
    Amer. librarian, lecturer
    Logan—Part p786

Stevens, Edith Barretto (b. 1878)
    Amer. sculptor
    Waters—Women p324-325

Stevens, Emily (fl. 1910's)
    Amer. actress
    Izard—Heroines p364-365

Stevens, Georgia, Mother (d. 1946)
    Amer. nun, teacher
    Drinker—Music p242-243

Stevens, Grace. See Vanderbilt, Grace
    Wilson

Stevens, Helen B. (b. 1878)
    Amer. etcher
    Michigan—Biog. p298

Stevens, Helen Norton (b. 1868)
    Amer. editor
    Binheim—Women p202,por.

Stevens, Inger (1934-1970)
    Swed.-Amer. actress
    CR '63 p592,por.

Stevens, Lillian M. N. (1844-1914)
    Amer. social reformer,
        organization official
    Logan—Part p660-661

Stevens, Lucy Beatrice (b. 1876)
    Amer. illustrator
    Mahony—Illus. p362

Stevens, Margaret Dean. See Aldrich, Bess
    Streeter

Stevens, Mary (fl. 1900's)
    Eng. painter
    Waters—Women p325

Stevens, Mary E. (fl. 1870's)
    Amer. justice of peace
    Hanaford—Dau. p668

Stevens, Mary O. Townsend (fl. 1860's)
    Amer. Civil war nurse
    Logan—Part p371

Stevens, Minnie (d. 1919)
    Amer. heiress
    Pearson—Pilgrim p193-196

Stevens, Risë (1913-   )
    Amer. singer
    CR '59 p728,por.
    CR '63 p592,por.
    Cur. Biog. '41 p824-825,por.
    Ewen—Ency. p486

(Continued)

Stevens, Risë—*Continued*

 Ewen—Living p337-338,por.
 McCoy—Portraits p199,por.
 Matz—Opera p82-85,por.
 Peltz—Spot. p83,por.
 *Ulrich—Famous p111-116,por.
 Wagner—Prima p84,226,248

Stevenson, Elizabeth (1919-)
 Amer. author
 Cur. Biog. '56 p607-608,por.

Stevenson, Fay (1895-)
 Amer. journalist
 Women—Achieve. p179,por.

Stevenson, Margaret (fl. 1740's-1750's)
 Amer., friend of Benjamin Franklin,
  mother of Mary Stevenson
 Donovan—Women p68-69

Stevenson, Margaret Isabella Balfour
  (1829-1897)
 Scot., mother of Robert Louis
  Stevenson
 Peyton—Mothers p104-112

Stevenson, Mary ("Polly") (Mary Hewson)
  (fl. 1750's)
 Amer., friend of Benjamin Franklin
 Donovan—Women p68-74,por.

Stevenson, Matilda Coxe (d. 1915)
 Amer. ethnologist, anthropologist
 Dorland—Sum p144
 Logan—Part p881-882

Stevenson, Sara Yorke (1847-1921)
 Amer. archaeologist
 Adelman—Famous p264
 Dorland—Sum p143
 Mozans—Women p322-323

Stevenson, Sarah Hackett (1849-1910)
 Amer. physician, author
 Hanaford—Dau. p283
 Schmidt—400 p20-21,por.

Stevenson, Sophie (fl. 1860's)
 Amer. Civil war nurse
 Logan—Part p373

Steward, Ann Schiear (1898-)
 Amer. novelist
 Warfel—Amer. p408-409,por.

Steward, Susan S. McKinney (1848-1918)
 Amer. physician
 Brown—Home. p160-168,por.

Stewart, Anna Bird (n.d.)
 Amer. author, lecturer
 Cur. Biog. '48 p600-601,por.

Stewart, Clara (fl. 1950's)
 Eng. physician
 Lovejoy—Women p250-251

Stewart, Dorothy M. (1891/97-1954)
 Austral.-Amer. theatrical agent,
  composer, author, pianist
 ASCAP p483

Stewart, Eleanor, pseud.
 See Porter, Eleanor Hodgman

Stewart, Frances.
 See Stewart, (Frances) Maria W. Miller

Stewart, Frances.
 See Richmond and Lennox, Frances
  Teresa, Duchess of

Stewart, Isabel Maitland (b. 1878)
 Can.-Amer. nurse, educator
 Dolan—Goodnow's p228-306,por.
 Pennock—Makers p82,por.
 Women—Achieve. p177,por.
 *Yost—Nursing p61-76

Stewart, Kathleen. See Forrester, Maurine

Stewart, Mabel (n.d.)
 Amer. secretary
 *Ferris—Girls p63-73

Stewart, (Frances) Maria W. Miller
  (b. 1803)
 Amer. lecturer, social reformer
 O'Connor—Pioneer p53-55,126,137,
  142,145-146,169-170,178

Stewart, Mary E. Pearce (fl. 1860's)
 Amer. Civil war nurse
 Logan—Part p373

Stewart, Pamela.
 See Johnson, Pamela Hansford

Stewart, Priscilla (fl. 1850's)
 Amer. poet
 Brown—Home. p241-242

Stewart, Salome M. (fl. 1860's)
 Amer. Civil war nurse
 Logan—Part p361

Stewart, Sylvia (fl. 1940's)
 Amer. aircraft engine instructor
 *Peckham—Women p138

Stickney, Dorothy (1900-)
 Amer. actress
 CR '59 p731,por.
 CR '63 p594,por.
 Cur. Biog. '42 p518-521,por.

Stiebeling, Hazel Katherine (1896-)
 Amer. physical chemist,
  government official
 Cur. Biog. '50 p548-550,por.
 *Yost—Women Sci. p158-176

Stieglitz, Charlotte (1806-1834)
Ger. salonist
Hargrave—Some p277-287,por.

Stignani, Ebe (1907-   )
It. singer
Cur. Biog. '49 p592-593,por.
Davidson—Treas. p296-298

Stillings, Kemp (fl. 1930's)
Amer. violinist, teacher
Women—Achieve. p143,por.

Stillman, Marie Spartali (fl. 1860's-1870's)
Eng. artist
Waters—Women p325-326

Stillman, Sarah S. (fl. 1920's)
Amer. illustrator
Michigan—Biog. p298

Stilson, Ruth (fl. 1930's)
Amer. aviation instructor
Planck—Women p160-161

Stimson, Barbara Bartlett (1898-   )
Amer. physician, orthopedic
surgeon
*Knapp—Women p151-164,por.

Stimson, Julia Catherine (1881-1948)
Amer. nurse, educator
Cur. Biog. '40 p768-769,por.
Cur. Biog. '48 p601-602
Dolan—Goodnow's p311,325
Pennock—Makers p58-59,por.
Taves—Success. p240-252,por.

Stinetorf, Louise (fl. 1950's)
Amer. nurse, author
Dolan—Goodnow's p4-5

Stinson, Katherine (1896-   )
Amer. pioneer aviatrix,
aeronautical engineer
Adams—Sky p29-45,por.
Earhart—Fun p189-191
Heinmuller—Man's p295,por.
Maitland—Knights p163-164
*May—Women p73-76,83,100,211-212,
por.
*Peckham—Women p128-129
Planck—Women p27-32,118-120,por.

Stinson, Marjorie (c. 1896-   )
Amer. aviatrix
Earhart—Fun p191-193,por.
*May—Women p81-83,212
Planck—Women p27-28,32-33

Stinson, Virginia McCollum (fl. 1860's)
Amer. Civil war diarist
Jones—Heroines p277-285

Stirling, Anna Maria Wilhelmina Pickering
(fl. 1800's)
Eng. author
Stirling—Odd p152-168

Stirling, Catherine, Lady.
See Duer, Catherine (Kitty)

Stirling, Elizabeth (Elizabeth Syrling Bridge)
(1819-1895)
Eng. organist, composer
Elson—Woman's p133-134

Stirling, Mary. See Watts, Mary

Stirling, Mary Anne (Fanny) (Fanny
Clifton) (1813/15-1895)
Eng. actress
Dorland—Sum p55,79-80
Hammerton p1254,por.
MacQueen—Pope p336-343,por.

Stirling, Mrs. (Lady Cholmondeley)
(m. 1911)
Amer.-Eng. dancer
Wyndham—Chorus p121-123

Stirling, Sarah.
See Jay, Sarah Van Brugh Livingston

Stirling-Maxwell, Caroline Norton, Lady.
See Norton, Caroline Elizabeth Sarah
Sheridan

Stites, Mabel M. (fl. 1940's)
Amer. aviatrix
*May—Women p193

Stobart, Mabel Annie St. Clair (fl. 1860's)
Brit. hospital organizer
Hammerton p1254

Stöbe, Ilse (fl. 1940's)
Ger. spy
Singer—World's p233-234

Stober, Buena Rose (fl. 1920's-1950's)
Amer. missionary
They—Went p73-75

Stocks, Mary D. (fl. 1910's)
Eng. teacher, author
Brittain—Women p91,95-97,134,196

Stocks, Minna (b. 1846)
Ger. painter
Waters—Women p326-327

Stockton, Annis Boudinot (1736-1801)
Amer. colonial poet
Green—Pioneer (3) p132-139,169
Hanaford—Dau. p141
Leonard—Amer. p122

Stockton, Julia.
See Rush, Julia Stockton

Stockton, Louise (1839-1914)
  Amer. journalist, historian, author,
    social worker, critic
  Dorland—Sum p39,78,111,122,175
  Hanaford—Dau. p690

Stockton, Susan.
  See Cutbert, Susan Stockton

Stoddard, Dora V. (fl. 1870's)
  Amer. lecturer
  Hanaford—Dau. p346

Stoddard, Haila (1913-   )
  Amer. actress
  CR '63 p594,por.
  TV—Person. (1) p27,por.

Stoddard, Harriet B. (d. 1848)
  Amer. missionary
  Hanaford—Dau. p514

Stoessel, Mrs. Henry Kurt.
  See Chastain, Madye Lee

Stokes, Margaret McNair (1832-1900)
  Irish archaeologist
  Mozans—Woman p316-317

Stokes, Marianna (fl. 1880's-1890's)
  Ger.-Eng. artist
  Waters—Women p327-328

Stokes, Missouri (fl. 1860's)
  Amer. Civil war diarist, teacher

Stokowski, Olga Samaroff.
  See Samaroff, Olga

Stolberg Wernigerode, Juliana van
    (1506-1580)
  Nether., mother of Prince William
    of Orange
  Schmidt—400 p295-296,por.

Stolitza, Lubov Nikitishna (Yershova)
    (b. 1884)
  Russ. poet
  Yarmolinsky—Treas. p302-303

Stoltz, Rosine (1815-1903)
  Fr. singer
  Ewen—Ency. p486-487

Stolz, Mary Slattery (1920-   )
  Amer. author
  Cur. Biog. '53 p596-597,por.

Stolz, Teresa (1834-1902)
  Bohem. singer
  Ewen—Ency. p487

Stone, Anna (d. 1905)
  Chin. missionary leader
  Burton—Notable p233-271,por.

Stone, Carol (1916-   )
  Amer. actress
  Blum—Great p141,por.

Stone, Constance (gr. 1887)
  Austral. pioneer physician
  Lovejoy—Women p248-249

Stone, Cornelia Branch (b. 1840)
  Amer. Civil war patriot, club leader
  Andrews—Women p414-415,420-424
  Logan—Part p492-494

Stone, Grace Zaring (Ethel Vance, pseud.)
    (1896-   )
  Amer. author
  Millett—Amer. p598-599
  Van Gelder p274-277
  Warfel—Amer. p432,por.

Stone, Hannah Mayer (c. 1893-1941)
  Amer. pioneer physician
  Cur. Biog. '41 p835

Stone, Helen (1904-   )
  Amer. illustrator
  Mahony—Illus. p363

Stone, Lucinda Hinsdale (m. 1840)
  Amer. educator, feminist
  Dar Mag. July 1921 p394,portrayal
  Green—Pioneer (3) p507-508
  Hanaford—Dau. p737
  Logan—Part p412-413

Stone, Lucy (Mrs. Henry Brown Blackwell)
    (1818-1892)
  Amer. lecturer, feminist, social
    reformer
  Abbot—Notable p279-283
  Adelman—Famous p168-170
  Beard—Amer. p187-193
  *Bolton—Famous Leaders p212-249,por.
  Burnett—Five p129-176
  Culver—Women p172-173,177-178
  Dexter—Career p6
  Dorland—Sum p16,78,137
  Douglas—Remember p154-156,163-164
  Hammerton p1255
  Hanaford—Dau. p363-365
  Holbrook—Dreamers p175-178,183-
    189,192-199
  Irwin—Angels (see index)
  Jensen—Revolt p44,por.
  *Kirkland—Achieved p66-73
  Lader—Bold p56-57
  Logan—Part p562-566
  Love—Famous p7
  O'Connor—Pioneer (see index)
  Riegel—Amer. p83-95,por.
  Whitton—These p147-148

Stone, Margaret Brown (d. 1787)
  Amer. patriot
  Green—Pioneer (3) p220-225

Stone, Mary (Shih Mai-yu) (1873-1954)
Chin. physician
Burton—Notable p161-218,por.

Stone, Verlinda Cotton Burdette Boughton
(fl.c. 1650's)
Amer. colonial journalist, letter-
writer
Earle—Colon. p49
Leonard—Amer. p122

Stoothoff, Saartze Kierstede von Borsum
(d. 1693)
Amer. colonial interpreter
Leonard—Amer. p122

Stopes, Charlotte Carmichael (1841-1929)
Brit. author
Hammerton p1255

Stopes, Marie Carmichael (1880-1959)
Eng. paleobotanist, author
Hammerton p1355,por.

Storch, Despina Davidovitch (fl. 1910's)
Turk.-Ger. spy
Barton—Celeb. p189-198,por.
Hoehling—Women p92-93

Storer, Ann (m. 1798)
Amer. actress
Wright—Forgot. p55-57

Storer, Fanny (fl. 1790's)
Amer. actress
Wright—Forgot. p57-58

Storer, Maria (d. 1795)
Amer. actress
Wright—Forgot. p34-55

Storer, Maria Longworth (b. 1849)
Amer. artist
Logan—Part p758-759
Waters—Women p328-329

Storey, Sylvia, Countess Poulett (m. 1908)
Eng. actress
Wyndham—Chorus p119

Storey, Widow (fl. 1600's)
Amer. pioneer
Hanaford—Dau. p33-34

Storm, Gale (1922/24-   )
Amer. actress, singer
CR '59 p734,por.
CR '63 p596
TV—Person. (1) p67,por.

Storni, Alfonsina (c. 1892-1938)
Argent. poet
Rosenbaum—Modern p205-227

Story, Ann (Ann Goodrich) (1742-1817)
Amer. Rev. war heroine
Dar Mar. July 1921 p371,portrayal
Green—Pioneer (2) p427-431

Story, Josephine, pseud.
See Loring, Emilie Baker

Stotesbury, Louise (fl. 1930's-1940's)
Amer., 1st wife of Douglas
MacArthur
Tebbel—Inher. p144

Stotesbury, Lucretia Roberts Cromwell
(d. 1946)
Amer., wife of Edward Stotesbury
Tebbel—Inher. p142-147

Stout, Juanita Kidd (1919-   )
Amer. judge
*Cherry—Portraits p200

Stout, Penelope Van Princes (c. 1612-1712)
Amer. pioneer
Green—Pioneer (3) p388-391

Stout, Ruth Albertine (1910-   )
Amer. educator, organization
official
Cur. Biog. '59 p432-434,por.

Stovall, Kate Bradley (m. 1904)
Amer. club leader
Brown—Home. p243-247

Stover, Mary (fl. 1850's-1860's)
Amer. social leader
Hanaford—Dau. p136-137

Stover, Sarah (fl. 1860's)
Amer. soldier
Fowler—Woman p425-428

Stow, Freelove Baldwin (b. 1728)
Amer. patriot
Green—Pioneer (3) p509-510
Root—Chapter p338-441

Stowe, Emily Jennings (1831-1903)
Can. pioneer physician
Lovejoy—Women p111-114,por.

Stowe, Harriet Elizabeth Beecher
(1811-1896)
Amer. author, social reformer
Abbot—Notable p397-401
*Adams—Heroines p89-119,por.
Adelman—Famous p174,por.
America's 12 p41-43,por.
*Bolton—Authors p119-125
*Bolton—Lives p331-343,por.
Bradford—Portraits p99-130,por.
Bruce—Woman p185-186
Bruère—Laugh p18
Coad—Amer. p196-197,por.

(Continued)

Stowe, Harriet—*Continued*

    *Commager—Crus. p77
    Davis—Mothers p24-28
    *Dolin—World p84-91,por.
    Dorland—Sum p21,73,80,127
    Douglas—Remember p120-127,por.
    *Elson—Side (1) p271-277
    Farmer—What p197-198
    Fitzhugh—Concise p655-656
    Hammerton p1256,por.
    Hanaford—Dau. p221-223,737
    Harkness—Heroines p12
    *Heath—Authors p14,por.
    *Heath—Women p9,por.
    *Horowitz—Treas. p48-53
    *Humphrey—Women p132-153
    Jensen—Revolt p45,por.
    Lader—Bold p169-173,268
    Ladies'—Amer. p41-43,por.
    Logan—Part p808-809
    Lotz—Women p109-117
    Maurice—Makers p1-2,12
    Melikov—Immort. p75,155,por.
    *Moore—When p163-169
    Morello—Hall p40,por.
    Morris—400 p240
    Muir—Women p168-170
    *Nisenson—Minute p140,por.
    *Nisenson—More Minute p138,por.
    100 Great p182-190
    Papashvily—All p64-77,79-80,134-135,
      210
    Parton—Dau. p73-77,por.
    Parton—Noted p73-77,por.
    Pattee—Fem. p73-74,130-145,por.
    *Pringle—When p73-85,por.
    Reader's—Great p309-315,por.
    *Scherman—Amer. p42-43,por.
    Scherman—Literary p56-57,por.
    Sewell—Brief p138-139
    *Stevens—Human p47-50,por.
    Stevens—Women p89-91,por.
    *Strong—of p167-172
    *Vance—Lamp p66-91,por.
    Whitton—These p109-110,130-134
    Witham—Pan. p120-121,por.

Stowell, Louise M. R. (b. 1850)
    Amer. teacher, editor, author
    Logan—Part p880

Strabel, Thelma (n.d.)
    Amer. novelist
    Warfel—Amer. p413,por.

Strachan, Grace Charlotte (fl. 1900's)
    Amer. educator, philanthropist
    Logan—Part p616,732

Strahan, Elsie T. (fl. 1920's-1930's)
    Amer. dietician, home economist
    Women—Achieve. p143,por.

Strahan, Kay Cleaver (b. 1888)
    Amer. author
    Binheim—Women p165,por.

Stranahan, Clara Harrison (m. 1879)
    Amer. social leader
    Logan—Part p293-294

Stranahan, Marianne F. (fl. 1860's)
    Amer. Civil war humanitarian
    Brockett—Woman's p651-658,por.

Strange, Michael (Blanche Marie Oelrichs
    Twede) (1890-1950)
    Amer. author, poet, actress
    Women—Achieve. p51,por.

Strange, Ruth May (1895-   )
    Amer. educator, author
    Cur. Biog. '60 p405-406,por.

Strangeways, Susan Fox, Lady (m. 1764)
    Eng. dancer
    Wyndham—Chorus p12-13,por.

Strantz Führing, Anna von (fl. 1900's)
    Ger. actress
    Arsenius—Dict. p71,por.
    Phila.—Women unp.,por.

Strasberg, Susan Elizabeth (1938-   )
    Amer. actress
    CR '59 p735,por.
    CR '63 p596-597,por.
    Cur. Biog. '58 p418-420,por.

Straten, Florence van (1913-   )
    Amer. meteorologist
    *Yost—Women Mod. p124-139,por.

Stratton, Dorothy Constance (1899-   )
    Amer. naval officer
    Cur. Biog. '43 p742-744,por.
    *Stoddard—Top. p29-42

Stratton, Lavinia Warren, Countess Magri
    (1841-1919)
    Amer. heiress
    Eliot—Heiresses p150-153,por.

Stratton-Porter, Gene.
    See Porter, Gene Stratton

Straus, Flora B. S. (fl. 1930's)
    Amer. club leader
    Women—Achieve. p203

Straus, Geneviève (fl. 1840's-1850's)
    Fr. salonist
    Skinner—Elegant p169-171

Straus, Lina (fl. 20th cent.)
    Ger. philanthropist, humanitarian
    *Levinger—Great p148-152

Strauss, Anna Lord (1899-   )
    Amer. editor, club leader
    Cur. Biog. '45 p575-577,por.
    Women—Achieve. p74,por.

Strauss, Pauline de Ahma (m. 1894)
Ger. singer, wife of Richard
Strauss
Elson—Woman's p88-89
McCoy—Portraits p201,por.
Wagner—Prima p155-156,240

Strawbridge, Anne West (1883-1941)
Amer. aviatrix, author
Cur. Biog. '41 p841

Strawn, Julia Clark (d. 1942)
Amer. physician, surgeon
Schmidt—400 p546,por.

Street, Ann. See Barry, Ann Street

Street, Jessie Mary Grey (b. 1889)
Brit. U.N. official
Cur. Biog. '47 p617-618,por.

Streeter, Elizabeth M. (fl. 1860's)
Amer. Civil war humanitarian
Brockett—Woman's p659-664

Streeter, Ruth Cheney (1895-   )
Amer. aviatrix, marine officer
Cur. Biog. '43 p744-746,por.
*May—Women p158
*Peckham—Women p30

Streisand, Barbra (1942-   )
Amer. singer, actress
CR '63 p598,por.
Cur. Biog. '64 p438-440,por.
Stambler—Ency. p224-225,por.
Time Apr.10,1964 p62,por.(Cover)

Strepponi, Giuseppina (1815-1897)
It. singer
Ewen—Ency. p490

Stretton, Hesba, pseud. (Sarah Smith)
(1832-1911)
Eng. novelist
Dorland—Sum p28,195
Hammerton p1259

Stretton, Julia Cecilia Collinson (1812-
1878)
Eng. novelist
Oliphant—Women p204-210

Strickland, Agnes (1796-1874)
Eng. historian
Adelman—Famous p164-165
Dorland—Sum p50,79,175
Hammerton p1259,por.

Strickland, Catharine Parr (1802-1899)
Can. pioneer, author
Innis—Clear p42-73,por.

Strickland, Lily Teresa (b. 1887)
Amer. composer, author
ASCAP p489

Howard—Our p566
McCoy—Portraits p201,por.

Strickland, S. E. (fl. 1870's)
Amer. feminist, lecturer, teacher
Hanaford—Dau. p346-347

Strickland, Susanna (1802-1899)
Can. pioneer, author
Innis—Clear p42-73,por.

Stritch, Elaine (1925-   )
Amer. actress
CR '59 p737,por.
CR '63 p599,por.
TV—Person. (3) p152,por.

Strode, Muriel (m. 1908)
Amer. poet
Cook—Our p322-324

Strong, Anna Louise (b. 1885)
Amer. journalist, author
Cur. Biog. '49 p595-597,por.
Ross—Ladies p377-378

Strong, Betsy (fl. 1930's)
Amer. journalist
Ross—Ladies p587-588

Strong, Joanna. See Floyd, Joanna

Strong, May A. (fl. 1940's)
Amer. composer, singer, teacher
McCoy—Portraits p202,por.

Strong, Rebecca Thorogood (1843-1944)
Eng. pioneer nurse
Cope—Six p25-34,por.

Strong, Susan (fl. 1890's)
Amer. singer
McCoy—Portraits p202,por.

Stroup, Leora (fl. 1940's)
Amer. aviatrix, nurse
*May—Women p158
*Peckham—Women p20

Struther, Jan, pseud. (Joyce Anstruther)
(1901-1953)
Eng. author
Cur. Biog. '41 p842-843,por.
Cur. Biog. '53 p604
Van Gelder—Writers p102-104

Stryker, Helen (fl. 1930's)
Amer. radio actress
Eichberg—Radio p112

Stuart, Arabella Seymour, Lady (1575-1615)
Brit. princess
Fifty—Famous p100-107,por.
Hammerton p1260,por.
*MacVeagh—Champlin p553-554

Stuart, Cora Wilson (fl. 1920's)
    Amer. educator, social reformer
    Adelman—Famous p312-313

Stuart, Flora Cooke (fl. 1860's)
    Amer. Civil war heroine
    Harkness—Heroines p3

Stuart, Jane (1810-1888)
    Amer. artist
    Hanaford—Dau. p295

Stuart, Louisa, Lady (1757-1851)
    Scot. author, social leader
    Graham—Group p294-315,por.
    Stenton—English p252,264,267,269,
    290

Stuart, Mary (1).
    See Mary (Mary Stuart, Queen of
    Scots)

Stuart, Mary (2) (fl. 1950's)
    Amer. actress
    TV—Person. (2) p77-78,por.

Stuart, Mary Horton (1842-1925)
    Amer., mother of John Leighton
    Stuart
    Davis—Mothers p54-62

Stuart, Ruth McEnery (1849-1917)
    Amer. author
    Adelman—Famous p259
    Bruère—Laugh p37-38
    Harkins—Famous p255-265,por.
    Harkins—Little p255-265,por.
    Logan—Part p806

Stuart, Sarah M. (fl. 1840's)
    Amer. social reformer
    Hanaford—Dau. p373

Stuart-Wortley, Emmeline Charlotte
    Elizabeth Manners, Lady
    (1806-1855)
    Eng. traveler, author
    Courtney—Adven. p156-168,por.

Stubbs, Annie Bell (fl. 1860's)
    Amer. Civil war nurse
    Logan—Part p371

Studebaker, Mabel (1901-   )
    Amer. educator, organization
    official
    Cur. Biog. '48 p602-603,por.

Studer, Carmen (fl. 1940's)
    Aust. conductor, composer, author
    McCoy—Portraits p202,por.

Studholme, Marion (n.d.)
    Eng. singer
    Davidson—Treas. p298-300

Stueckgold, Grete (1895-   )
    Eng.-Ger. singer
    Ewen—Ency. p490
    Ewen—Living p344-345,por.
    McCoy—Portraits p202,por.

Stuerm, Ruza Lukavaska (fl. 1930's)
    Czech.-Amer. railroad executive,
    lecturer
    Women—Achieve. p98,por.

Stumm, Maud (fl. 1900's)
    Amer. painter
    Waters—Women p329-330

Sture-Vasa, Mary O'Hara Alsop.
    See O'Hara, Mary

Sturgis, "Mother" (fl. 1860's)
    Amer. Civil war nurse
    Moore—Women p478-484

Sturkow-Ryder, Theodora (fl. 1940's)
    Amer. composer, pianist
    McCoy—Portraits p202,por.

Stutz, Geraldine (1924-   )
    Amer. business woman, fashion
    expert
    CR '63 p599,por.
    Silver—Profiles p393-403,por.

Stuyvesant, Judith Bayard (fl. 1650's-
    1660's)
    Amer. pioneer, wife of Peter
    Stuyvesant
    Green—Pioneer (1) p197,222

Suba, Susanna (1913-   )
    Hung. illustrator
    Mahony—Illus. p363
    Taves—Success p261-274,por.

Subligny, Mademoiselle (1666-c. 1736)
    Fr. ballet dancer
    *Terry—Star p21-22,por.

Sucher, Rosa Hasselbeck (1849-1927)
    Ger. singer
    Ewen—Ency. p490-491
    Klein—Great p199-204,por.
    McCoy—Portraits p202,por.

Suckow, Ruth (1892-1960)
    Amer. author
    Lawrence—School p240-241
    *Millett—Amer. p602-603
    O'Brien—50 p856
    Warfel—Amer. p416-417,por.

Sues, Lea (fl. 1890's-1900's)
    It. painter
    Waters—Women p331-332

Sues, (Ilona) Ralf (n.d.)
    Pol. author
    Cur. Biog. '44 p665-668,por.

Suesse, Dana Nadine (1911-   )
　　Amer. composer, pianist, author
　　ASCAP p491
　　Cur. Biog. '40 p781-782,por.
　　Howard—Our p548-549

Sugg, Catharine Lee (m. 1819)
　　Amer. actress
　　Moses—Famous p145-146,161

Suggett, Jemima.
　　See Johnson, Jemima Suggett

Suggia, Guilhermina (1888-1951)
　　Port. violoncellist
　　Hammerton p1202,por.

Suggs, Louise (1923-   )
　　Amer. golfer
　　Cur. Biog. '62 p408-410,por.

Sugimoto, Etsu Inagaki (c. 1874-1950)
　　Japan. author
　　*Ferris—When p224-301

Suim, Kim (d. 1950)
　　N. Kor. spy
　　Singer—World's p181-183

Sullavan, Margaret (1911-1960)
　　Amer. actress
　　CR '59 p739-740,por.
　　Cur. Biog. '44 p668-671
　　Cur. Biog. '60 p412

Sullivan, Anne (Anne Sullivan Macy)
　　(1866-1936)
　　Amer. teacher of blind
　　Bartlett—They p76-80
　　Bowie—Women p160-175
　　Douglas—Remember p237-238,por.
　　Holbrook—Dreamers p274-275
　　Peterson—Great p5-12
　　Rogers—Women p38,por.
　　*Stevens—Women p151-155,por.

Sullivan, Betsy ("Mother") (fl. 1860's)
　　Amer. Civil war patriot
　　Andrews—Women p112-115

Sullivan, Leonor Alice Kretzger (n.d.)
　　Amer. congresswoman
　　Cur. Biog. '54 p590-591,por.
　　U.S.—Women (87th) p39,por.
　　U.S.—Women 88th p25,por.

Sullivan, Lydia Wooster (m. 1765)
　　Amer. pioneer
　　Green—Pioneer (2) p199-201

Sullivan, Marie (fl. 1930's)
　　Amer. aviation inspector, decorator
　　Women—Achieve. p203

Sullivan, Mary Agnes (c. 1879-1950)
　　Amer. policewoman, detective
　　Rogers—Women p118,por.

Sullivan, Mary Mildred Hammond (m. 1856)
　　Amer. Civil war patriot
　　Andrews—Women p428-448

Sulpicia (1) (fl. 100)
　　Rom. poet
　　Balsdon—Roman p273-274

Sulpicia (2) (fl. 186 B.C.)
　　Rom., aunt of Consul
　　Balsdon—Roman p38-40

Sulpicia (3) (fl. 63 B.C.-14 A.D.)
　　Rom. poet
　　Balsdon—Roman p273

Sulpicia (4) (fl. 390's)
　　Rom., wife of Fulvius Flaccus
　　Boccaccio—Conc. p146-147

Sumac, Yma (1927-   )
　　Peru. singer
　　CR '59 p741-742,por.
　　CR '63 p601,por.

Summerhayes, Martha (fl. 1870's)
　　Amer. W. pioneer
　　Brown—Gentle p4,44-45,143,161,por.

Summers, Quinneth C. (fl. 1930's)
　　Amer. business executive
　　Women—Achieve. p182,por.

Summerskill, Edith Clara, Baroness
　　(1901-   )
　　Eng. physician, gynecologist,
　　　member of Parliament
　　Cur. Biog. '43 p749-751,por.
　　Cur. Biog. '63 p408-410,por.
　　*Knapp—Women p33-45,por.

Sumner, Bertha Cid Ricketts (1890-   )
　　Amer. author
　　Cur. Biog. '54 p591-592,por.
　　Warfel—Amer. p418,por.

Sumner, Mrs. G. Lynn.
　　See Picken, Mary Brooks

Sumner, Jessie (fl. 1930's-1940's)
　　Amer. congresswoman, judge
　　Cur. Biog. '45 p579-581,por.
　　Paxton—Women p53-62,131,por.

Sumner, Mary.
　　See Newcomb, Mary Sumner

Sumter, Mary Canty Jeimesson (d. 1818)
　　Amer. pioneer
　　Green—Pioneer (2) p452

Sun, Chingling Soong.
　　See Sun Yat-Sen, Chingling Soong,
　　　Madame

Sundelius, Marie (1915-   )
    Swed. singer
    McCoy—Portraits p203,por.

Sunderland, Anne, Countess (fl. 1690's)
    Eng. letter-writer, politician
    Stenton—English p197

Sunderland, Dorothy Sidney, Countess
    (m. 1639)
    Eng. hostess
    Stenton—English p139-140,196,325

Sundquist, Alma (d. 1940)
    Swed. physician
    Lovejoy—Women p177,por.

Sundstrom, Anne-Marie (fl. 1960's)
    Swed. photographer, model,
      aviatrix, fashion writer
    *May—Women p236

Sundstrom, Ebba (fl. 1920's-1930's)
    Amer. conductor, violinist
    McCoy—Portraits p203,por.

Sunshine, Marion (1897-   )
    Amer. composer, author, actress
    ASCAP p492

Sun Yat-Sen, Chingling Soong, Madame
    (1890-   )
    Chin. political leader
    Clark—Chiangs p40-52,57-67,por.
    Cur. Biog. '44 p677-682,por.

Supervia, Conchita (1899-1936)
    Sp. singer
    Davidson—Treas. p300-302
    Ewen—Ency. p491-492
    McCoy—Portraits p203,por.

Suratt, Valeska (fl. 1910's)
    Amer. dancer
    Caffin—Vaud. p102,por.

Susan (fl. 238 A.D.)
    Rom. saint
    *Windham—Sixty p38-44

Susanna (1) (fl. 3rd cent.)
    Rom. saint
    Englebert—Lives p308-309
    Wescott—Calen. p120

Susanna (2). See **Anne** (Gr. saint)

Susanna (3) (Biblical)
    Culver—Women p47
    Deen—All p295
    Marble—Women, Bible p92-94

Sushila Nayyar. See **Nayyar, Sushila**

Susman, Karen (1942-   )
    Amer. tennis player
    CR '63 p601,por.

Sussex, Eleanor, Countess of (Eleanor
    Radcliffe) (d. 1666)
    Eng. wife of 6th Earl of Sussex
    Aubrey—Brief p252

Sussman, Cornelia. See **Jessey, Cornelia**

Sutherland, Anne (fl. 1870's-1940's)
    Amer. actress
    Marks—Glamour p331

Sutherland, Jane, Countess of (1545-1629)
    Scot. Amazon
    Graham—Group p27-28,38-56,por.

Sutherland, Joan (1929-   )
    Austral. singer
    CR '63 p602,por.
    Cur. Biog. '60 p414-416,por.
    Pleasants—Great p350-352,por.
    *Seventeen—In p77-80,por.
    Wagner—Prima p248

Sutherland, Lucy Stuart (gr. 1927)
    Eng. educator
    Brittain—Women p171,176,206,236,
    246,255

Sutherland-Hunter, Mary Y. (fl. 1900's)
    New Z. painter
    Waters—Women p167-170

Sutherlin, Mrs. W. T. (fl. 1860's)
    Amer. Civil War diarist
    Jones—Heroines p401

Sutliffe, Irene (d. 1936)
    Amer. nurse
    Pennock—Makers p34,por.

Sutor, Adele (fl. 1940's)
    Amer. composer, piano teacher
    McCoy—Portraits p203,por.

Sutphen, Olive.
    See **Fremstad, (Anna) Olive**

Sutro, Ottilie (fl. 1940's)
    Amer. pianist
    McCoy—Portraits p203,por.

Sutro, Rose Laura (1872-1957)
    Amer. pianist
    McCoy—Portraits p203,por.

Suttner, Bertha, Baroness von (Countess
    Kinsky) (1843-1914)
    Aust. novelist
    Adelman—Famous p247
    Dorland—Sum p15,128
    Hammerton p1266

(Continued)

Suttner, Bertha—*Continued*

*Meyer—Champions p27-45,por.
Nobel—Man p33-35,489-492
Phila.—Yomen unp.,por.
*Riedman—Portraits p15-16,18
Schmidt—400 p50-51,por.
Stiles—Postal p262

Sutton, Kate ("Ma") (fl. 1930's-1950's)
Amer. seafarer
Snow—Women p232

Sutton, May G. (fl. 1900's)
Amer. tennis player
Rogers—Women p60,por.

Suzman, Helen Gavronsky (1917-   )
S. Afr. Parliament member
Cur. Biog. '68 p389-390,por.

Suzuki, Pat (1931-   )
Amer. singer, actress
CR '59 p743,por.
CR '63 p602,por.
Cur. Biog. '60 p416-417,por.
Time Dec.22,1958 p42,por.(Cover)

Suzy, pseud. See Mehle, Aileen

Svetla, Karolina Rottova (1830-1899)
Czech. novelist, feminist
Schmidt—400 p91,por.

Svobodova, Ruzena Capova (fl. 1910's)
Czech. author, humanitarian
Schmidt—400 p91-92,por.

Swain, Clara A. (1834-1910)
Amer. physician, missionary
Deen—Great p399-400
*Fleming—Doctors p55-69
Hanaford—Dau. p285
Lovejoy—Women p220-221
Mead—Medical p70

Swain, Louisa Ann (fl. 1870's)
Amer. W. pioneer, feminist
Brown—Gentle p245,por.
Hanaford—Dau. 433

Swain, Meliscent Barrett (fl. 1770's)
Amer. pioneer
Green—Pioneer (2) p289-290

Swaine, Elizabeth W. (fl. 1930's)
Amer. organization official
Women—Achiev. p203-204

Swallow, Ellen (gr. 1873)
Amer. chemist
Irwin—Angels p127,132-133

Swallow, Frances (fl. 18th cent.)
Amer. colonial teacher, business
woman
Spruill—Women's p258,284,291

Swan, Annie S. (fl. 1880's-1930's)
Eng. author
Black—Notable p313-319,por.
Hammerton p1266

Swanger, Ludmilla E. (fl. 1930's)
Czech. club leader
Women—Achieve. p155,por.

Swann, Mary Lee (fl. 1930's)
Amer. editor
Women—Achieve. p204

Swanson, Gloria (1899-   )
Amer. actress
Cahn—Laugh. p95,por.
CR '59 p743-744,por.
CR '63 p603,por.
Cur. Biog. '50 p556-558,por.
Hammerton p1266
Herman—How p61,por.
Hughes—Famous p307-327,por.
New Yorker Jan.18,1930 p24,por.
(Profiles)
Schickel—Stars p14,48-49,51,por.
Talmey—Doug. p19-27,por.
Wagenknecht—Movies p208-210

Swanwick, Anna (1813-1899)
Eng. traveler, feminist
Adelman—Famous p135
Dorland—Sum p26,80,109,177
Hammerton p1266-1267

Swarthout, Gladys (1904-1969)
Amer. singer
CR '59 p744,por.
CR '63 p603,por.
Cur. Biog. '44 p682-685,por.
Ewen—Ency. p492-493
Ewen—Living p346-347,por.
McCoy—Portraits p203,por.
Peltz—Spot. p87,por.
Taves—Success. p160-174,por.
Women—Achieve. p77,por.

Swartz, Jeska (fl. 1910's-1940's)
Amer. singer
Lahee—Grand p369,por.
McCoy—Portraits p203,por.

Swartz, Nelle (fl. 1900's-1930's)
Amer. social worker
Women—Achieve. p101,por.

Swartz, Vesta M. (fl. 1860's)
Amer. Civil war nurse
Logan—Part p373

Swaythling, Lady.
See Knox, Jean, Lady Swaythling

Sweeney, Edith Igoe (fl. 1930's)
Amer. fashion designer
Women—Achieve. p128,por.

Sweeney, Genevieve Evelyn (fl. 1930's)
Amer. dancer
Women—Achieve. p204

Sweet, Ada Celeste (1853-1928)
Amer. journalist, editor, social
reformer, philanthropist, author
Dorland—Sum p102
Logan—Part p831

Sweet, Blanche (1895/96-)
Amer. actress
Lamparski—What. p82-83,por.
Wagenknecht—Movies p88-89,97-99,
por.

Sweet, Sophia Miriam (1855-1912)
Amer. author, editor
Dorland—Sum p54,119
Logan—Part p859

Swetchine, Anne Sophie Soymanov (1782-
1857)
Russ.-Fr. mystic, social leader
Adelman—Famous p131-132
Blunt—Great p408-417

Swift, Kay (1907-)
Amer. composer, pianist
ASCAP p493

Swinburne, Jane, Lady (fl. 1810's-1850's)
Eng., mother of Algernon
Swinburne
Winwar—Poor p129-132

Swinton, Sarah.
See McIntosh, Sarah Swinton

Swisshelm, Jane Grey Cannon (1815-
1884)
Amer. journalist, feminist, editor,
teacher
Adelman—Famous p167
Hanaford—Dau. p703
Holbrook—Dreamers p185,189-192
O'Connor—Pioneer p94-96
Riegel—Amer. p102-106
Ross—Ladies p16,323,326,por.,cover
Thorp—Female p56-106,por.
Whitton—These p138-140,211-212,
230

Switlik, Lottie (n.d.)
Amer. parachute jumper, business
executive
*Peckham—Women p85-86,por.

Switz, Marjorie (fl. 1950's)
Russ. spy
Singer—World's p225-227,por.

Switzer, Marguerite Birdelle (fl. 1890's)
Amer. journalist
Ross—Ladies p552-553

Switzer, Mary Elizabeth (1900-)
Amer. government official
Cur. Biog. '62 p412-414,por.

Swoboda, Josephine (b. 1861)
Aust. painter
Waters—Women p330

Swope, Ethel (fl. 1930's)
Amer. nurse
Pennock—Makers p122-123,por.

Swope, Kate (fl. 1880's-1890's)
Amer. painter
Waters—Women p330-331

Swormstedt, Mabel Godfrey (gr. 1890)
Amer. teacher, club leader
Logan—Part p465

Swynford, Catherine, Duchess of **Lancaster**
(c. 1350-1403)
Eng. governess
Hammerton p1269
Howe—Galaxy p18-22

Swynnerton, Annie Louisa (1844-1933)
Eng. artist
Hammerton p1269

Syamour, Marguerite (b. 1861)
Fr. painter
Waters—Women p332

Sychar, woman of (Biblical)
Chappell—Fem. p208-219

Sydney, Doris. See Keane, Doris

Sylva, Carmen.
See Elizabeth Amelia Eugenie

Sylva, Marguerite (fl. 1940's)
Belg. singer
Lahee—Grand p231-235
McCoy—Portraits p204,por.

Sylvia (fl. 398 A.D.)
Fr. saint
*Windham—Sixty p117-122

Symmes, Susannah (fl. 1770's)
Amer. patriot
Green—Pioneer (3) p306,308,310,312

Symons, Charlotte (fl. 1940's)
Amer. singer
McCoy—Portraits p204,por.

Symphorosa (d. 120)
Rom. saint
Blunt—Great p8-9
Wescott—Calen. p104

Syntyche (Biblical)
Deen—All p295-296

Syrkin, Marie (1900-   )
Swiss-Amer. editor, educator,
author
Ribalow—Auto. p312-330

Syro-Phoenician woman (Justa; Canaanite
woman) (Biblical)
Deen—All p189-192
Harrison—Little p103-111
Nelson—Bible p83-85
Van der Velde—She p190-197

Szabo, Violette (d. 1945)
Brit. spy
Hoehling—Women p117-123
Singer—World's p229

Szantho, Enid (fl. 1930's)
Hung. singer
Ewen—Living p347,por.
McCoy—Portraits p204,por.

Szcawinska, Wanda (gr. 1902)
Pol. physician
Lovejoy—Women p174

Szold, Henrietta (1860-1945)
Amer. religious leader
Cur. Biog. '40 p785-786,por.
Cur. Biog. '45 p589-590
Lownsbery—Saints p1-45,por.,cover
Stiles—Postal p263

Szumowska, Antoinette (Antoinette
Adamowska) (1868-1938)
Pol. pianist, music teacher
McCoy—Portraits p1,204,por.

Szymanowska, Marja (Maria) Agata
(1790/95-1831)
Pol. pianist, composer
Schmidt—400 p321,por.
Schonberg—Great p91-92

T

Taber, Gladys Leonae Bagg (1899-   )
Amer. author
Cur. Biog. '52 p574-575,por.
Warfel—Amer. p422-423,por.

Tabitha. See Dorcas

Tabor, Augusta Pierce (1833-1895)
Amer. W. pioneer
Parkhill—Wildest p151-173
Sickels—Twelve p90-109,253

Tabor, Elizabeth Bonduel McCourt ("Baby
Doe") (1854-1935)
Amer. pioneer, recluse
Erskine—Out p288-293
Parkhill—Wildest p152-174

Tabouis, Geneviève R. Le Quesne (1892-   )
Fr. journalist
Cur. Biog. '40 p786-787,por.

T'a Chi (date uncertain)
Chin., concubine of Emperor
Chou Hsin
Llewellyn—China's p16

Tadema, Alma.
See Alma-Tadema, Lady Laura Therese

Taft, Helen Herron (c. 1861-1943)
Amer. musician, teacher, wife of
William Howard Taft
Cur. Biog. '43 p751
Fairfax—Ladies p95-96
Gerlinger—Mis. p85-88,por.
Jensen—White p192-195,por.
Logan—Ladies p146-152
Logan—Part p283
*McConnell—Our p253-261,por.
Means—Woman p116-134,por.
Prindiville—First p203-210
*Ross—Know p55,por.
Smith—Romances p338-350,por.
*Sweetser—Famous p254-281,por.
Truett—First p64,por.

Taft, Louisa Maria Torrey (fl. 1840's-1860's)
Amer., mother of William
Howard Taft
Green—Pioneer (3) p451
Hampton—Our p217-229

Taft, Martha Wheaton Bowers (1889-1958)
Amer., wife of Senator Robert Taft
Mears—They p99

Taft, Mary (fl. 1920's)
Amer. journalist
Ross—Ladies p149-152

Taggard, Genevieve (1894-1948)
Amer. poet, educator
*Millett—Amer. p603-604
Women—Achieve. p204

Tagliafero, Magda (fl. 1940's)
Fr. pianist
Ewen—Living p349-350,por.
McCoy—Portraits p205,por.

Taglioni, Maria (1804-1884)
Swed.-It. ballet dancer
Adelman—Famous p143-144
Beaumont—Complete p287-295,por.
Clarke—Six p11-41,por.
Hammerton p1271
*McConnell—Famous p1-13,por.
Mayne—Enchant. p252-262,por.
*Muir—Famous p19-27,por..
*Terry—Star p57-65,por.

Tahpenes (Biblical)
Lewis—Portraits p138-139

Taigi, Anna Maria Giannetti (1769-1837)
It. religious worker
Blunt—Great p250-271

Tailleferre, Germaine (1892-   )
Fr. composer
McCoy—Portraits p205,por.

Tait, Maude (fl. 1930's)
Earhart—Fun p150

Talbert, Florence Cole- (fl. 1910's)
Amer. singer
Cuney-Hare—Negro p332,368-369,por.

Talbert, Mary Burnett (1862-1923)
Amer. club leader
Brown—Home. p217-219,por.
Robinson—Hist. p127-128,por.

Talbot, Catherine (1721-1770)
Eng. essayist
Stenton—English p288-292

Talbot, Elizabeth, Countess of Shrewsbury
(Bess of Hardwicke) (1518-1608)
Eng. hostess
Dorland—Sum p25
Hammerton p1217,por.
Stenton—English p57-60

Talbot, Ellen Bliss (b. 1867)
Amer. author, educator
Logan—Part p720

Talbot, Grace Helen (1901-   )
Amer. sculptor
National—Contemp. p314

Talbot, Nita (n.d.)
Amer. actress
TV—Person. (2) p59-60,por.

Talbot, Norma.
See Steele, Norma Mitchell Talbot

Tallchief, Maria (1925-   )
Amer. ballet dancer
Atkinson—Dancers p147-151,por.
Bakeless—In p39-44,por.
CR '59 p747-748,por.
CR '63 p605,por.
Crowle—Enter p137-150,por.
Cur. Biog. '51 p618-620,por.
Davidson—Ballet p277-279,por.
*McConnell—Famous p157-164,por.
*Muir—Famous p149-156,por.
Swinson—Dancers p27-32,por.
Swinson—Great p20,por.
*Terry—Star p213-220,por.

Tallchief, Marjorie (1927-   )
Amer. ballet dancer
Atkinson—Dancers p152-154,por.
Davidson—Ballet p279-281
Swinson—Great p22,por.
*Terry—Star p191

Talley, Marion Nevada (1907-   )
Amer. singer
Ewen—Ency. p496-497
Ewen—Living p350-351,por.
McCoy—Portraits p205,por.
New Yorker Feb.11,1928 p18,por.
(Profiles)
Time Mar.1,1926 p16,por.(Cover)

Talley, Mary (fl. 1940's)
N.Y. fortuneteller
Zolotow—Never p256-257

Talley, Susan Archer (fl. 1840's)
Amer. poet
Hanaford—Dau. p269

Talleyrand-Périgord, Anna Gould, Duchess
de (1876-1961)
Amer. heiress
Eliot—Heiresses p165-174,256,por.
Pearson—Pilgrim p127-140,por.
Skinner—Elegant p82-83,86-88

Talleyrand-Périgord, Catherine Noël Worlée
Grand de, Princesse de Beñévent
(1762-1835)
Ind. princess
Hahn—Love p265-285

Tallien, Jeanne.
See Chimay, Jeanne Marie Ionace
Therese de Cabarrus, Princess of

Tallmadge, Mary Floyd (1764-1805)
Amer. Rev. war patriot
Root—Chapter p256-278,por.

Talma, Louise (1906-   )
Amer. composer
Goss—Modern p383-391,por.
Reis—Composers p353-354

Talmadge, Constance (1900-   )
Amer. actress, comedienne
Lamparski—What. p184-185,por.
Talmey—Doug. p41-47,por.

Talmadge, Margaret (fl. 1900's-1920's)
Amer., mother of Constance,
Norma Talmadge
Talmey—Doug. p41-47,por.

Talmadge, Norma (1897-1957)
Amer. actress
Hammerton p1273,por.
Herman—How p73,por.
Schickel—Stars p58,por.
Stuart—Immort. p196-198,por.
Wagenknecht—Movies p177-178

Talmey, Allene (1903-   )
Amer. journalist
CR '63 p606,por.
Ross—Ladies p176-177

Talvj, pseud.
 See Robinson, Thérèse Albertine Louise
  von Jakob

Tamar (1) (Biblical)
  mother of Pharez, ancestor of David
  Deen—All p41-44
  Faulhaber—Women p143-144
  Lewis—Portraits p157-158

Tamar (2) (Biblical)
  daughter of David
  Deen—All p296-297
  Lewise—Portraits p109-110

Tamar (3) (Biblical)
  daughter of Absalom
  Deen—All p297
  Lewis—Portraits p110-111

Tamara (Thamar) (1160-1212)
  Asian Georgia queen
  Arsenius—Dict. p186,por.
  Phila.—Women unp.,por.
  Stiles—Postal p266

Tamiris, Helen (Helen Becker) (1905-)
  Amer. dancer
  *Maynard—Amer. p156-163,por.

Tandy, Jessica (1909-)
  Eng. actress
  CR '59 p749,por.
  CR '63 p606,por.
  Cur. Biog. '56 p619-620,por.
  Dodd—Celeb. p306-310
  Newquist—Show. p403-412,por.

Taney, Mary Florence (b. 1861)
  Amer. educator, journalist, editor,
   author, secretary
  Logan—Part p822

Tan Eyck, Melissa (fl. 1910's)
  Amer. dancer
  Caffin—Vaud. p108

Tanguay, Eva (1878-1947)
  Amer. actress, singer
  Caffin—Vaud. p36-42,por.

Tankersley, Ruth McCormick ("Bazy")
  Amer. editor, journalist,
   horsewoman
  CR '63 p606,por.

Tannehill, Arabella (fl. 1860's)
  Amer. Civil war nurse
  Brockett—Woman's p789

Tanner, Margo (fl. 1930's)
  Amer. aviatrix
  *May—Women p210-211

Tanner, Mero L. White (b. 1844)
  Amer. teacher, humanitarian
  Logan—Part p299-300

Tanner, Sarah Elizabeth (1804-1914)
  Amer. teacher, religious worker
  Brown—Home p32-33,por.

Tao Suranari ("Lady Mo") (fl. 1820's)
  Siam. military leader, heroine
  Stiles—Postal p264

Taphath (Biblical)
  Deen—All p297

Tappen, Cornelia.
 See Genet, Cornelia

Tappen, Elizabeth Harper (b. 1784)
  Amer. W. pioneer
  Ellet—Pioneer p274-280
  Logan—Part p85

Tapper, Bertha (1859-1915)
  Nor. composer, pianist, music
   teacher
  McCoy—Portraits p205,por.

Tara Bae (fl. 16th cent.)
  E. Ind., wife of Prithwi Raj.
  Pool—Famous p143-150

Tarbell, Ida Minerva (1857-1944)
  Amer. author
  Adelman—Famous p287
  Cur. Biog. '44 p687
  *Daugherty—Ten p123-135,por.
  Dorland—Sum p176
  Garraty—Unfor. p292-297
  Hammerton p1274,por.
  Hazeltine—We p55-64
  Irwin—Angels p274
  *Logie—Careers p2-11
  Mears—They p29-30
  Rogers—Women p57,por.
  Stone—We p354-363
  Women—Achieve. p112,por.
  *Yost—Famous p131-141,por.

Tarbox, Frances (fl. 1940's)
  Amer. composer, pianist
  McCoy—Portraits p205,por.

Tarr, Florence (d. 1951)
  Amer. author, radio personality
  ASCAP p494

Tarsilla (fl. 6th cent.)
  Fr. saint
  Wescott—Calen. p202

Tas, Helen Teschner (b. 1889)
  Amer. violinist
  Ewen—Living p351,por.
  McCoy—Portraits p206,por.
  Saleski—Wander. p256-257,por.

Tate, Caroline. See Gordon, Caroline

Tauber, Doris (1908-   )
  Amer. composer, pianist, singer
  ASCAP p495

Tauch, Waldine (fl. 1920's)
  Amer. sculptor
  National—Contemp. p314

Taussig, Helen Brooke (1898-   )
  Amer. physician
  *Clymer—Modern p91-98,por.
  Cur. Biog. '46 p50-53,por.
  Cur. Biog. '66 p401-403,por.
  Dolan—Goodnow's p291
  Hume—Great p249-250,por.
  Lovejoy—Women p386,por.
  Parshalle—Kash. p67-70,por.

Tawse, Sybil (fl. 1940's)
  Eng. illustrator
  Mahony—Illus. p363

Tayloe (Taylor), Ann (fl. 17th cent.)
  Amer. pioneer
  Green—Pioneer (3) p255

Tayloe (Taylor), Elizabeth.
  See Corbin, Elizabeth T.

Taylor, Alice (fl. 1860's)
  Amer. Civil war patriot
  Brockett—Woman's p239-240,768-769

Taylor, Alva (fl. 1920's)
  Amer. journalist
  Ross—Ladies p395-397

Taylor, Ann (1782-1866)
  Eng. poet
  *Benét—Famous Poets p17-19,por.

Taylor, Anna (fl. 1900's)
  Amer. stunt woman
  Muir—Women p194-195

Taylor, Catherine L. (fl. 1860's)
  Amer. Civil war nurse
  Logan—Part p360

Taylor, Effie J. (fl. 1920's-1930's)
  Can.-Amer. nurse, educator
  Dolan—Goodnow's p313-314,343,por.

Taylor, Elizabeth (fl. 1870's-1880's)
  Amer. printer
  Hanaford—Dau. p711

Taylor, Elizabeth ("Betty") (fl. 1820's-
    1830's)
  Amer., daughter of Zachary Taylor
  *Sweetser—Famous p154-177

Taylor, Elizabeth (1932-   )
  Eng. actress
  CR '59 p750-751,por.
  CR '63 p607-608,por.
  Cur. Biog. '52 p576-578,por.

Schickel—Stars p278,280,por.
  Time Aug.22,1949 p48,por.(Cover)

Taylor, Elizabeth Coles (1912-   )
  Eng. author
  Cur. Biog. '48 p613-614,por.

Taylor, Elizabeth V. (1890's-1900's)
  Eng. painter
  Waters—Women p332

Taylor, Estelle (c.1899-1958)
  Amer. actress
  Talmey—Doug. p121-127,por.

Taylor, Esther (gr. 1872)
  Amer. physician
  Hanaford—Dau. p563

Taylor, Euphemia J. (fl. 1900's-1920's)
  Can.-Amer. nurse
  Pennock—Makers p141-142,por.

Taylor, Harriet.
  See Mill, Harriet Hardy Taylor

Taylor, Isabel (1883-1947)
  Eng. government official
  Martindale—Some p52-60,por.

Taylor, Jane (1783-1824)
  Eng. poet
  *Benét—Famous Poets p17-19,por.
  Dorland—Sum p41,188

Taylor, Kathleen DeVere (fl. 1930's)
  Amer. feminist, stock-broker
  Women—Achieve. p109,por.

Taylor, Keturah Leitch (b. 1773)
  Amer. pioneer
  Logan—Part p67

Taylor, Laurette Cooney (1884-1946)
  Amer. actress
  Blum—Great p63,por.
  Caffin—Vaud. p140
  Coad—Amer. p327,por.
  Cur. Biog. '45 p594-596,por.
  Cur. Biog. '47 p630
  Marinacci—Lead. p241-268,por.

Taylor, Mrs. Lodusky J. (b. 1856)
  Amer. organization official
  Logan—Part p353

Taylor, Lucy Hobbs (d. 1910)
  Amer. pioneer dental surgeon
  Stern—We p95-117,por.

Taylor, Margaret Mackall Smith (1788-
    1852)
  Amer., wife of Zachary Taylor
  Farmer—What p83-84
  Gerlinger—Mis. p41-42

(Continued)

Taylor, Margaret—*Continued*

> Hanaford—Dau. p88
> Jensen—White p71
> Logan—Ladies p68-71
> Logan—Part p244-246
> *McConnell—Our p131-138,por.
> Prindiville—First p114-119
> *Ross—Know p27,por.
> Smith—Romances p167-178,por.
> Whitton—First p218-234

Taylor, Marian Young.
> See Young, Marian

Taylor, Nancy Savage (m. 1739)
> Amer. Rev. war patriot
> Green—Pioneer (3) p202-205

Taylor, Nellie Maria (fl. 1860's)
> Amer. Civil war nurse
> Brockett—Woman's p234-240,por.
> Logan—Part p311

Taylor, Pauline (fl. 1930's)
> Eng.-Amer. teacher
> Women—Achieve. p204

Taylor, Peggy Hammond (fl. 1930's)
> Amer. social consultant
> Women—Achieve. p92,por.

Taylor, Rebecca (fl. 19th cent.)
> Amer. nurse
> Dexter—Career p32-33

Taylor, Rosemary Drachman (1899-   )
> Amer. author
> Warfel—Amer. p423-424,por.

Taylor, Sarah Strother (fl. 1780's-1790's)
> Amer., mother of Zachary Taylor
> Hampton—Our p92-99

Taylor, Susan Lucy Barry (1807-1881)
> Amer. feminist, pioneer
> Logan—Part p69

Tchankova, Iordanka (fl. 1940's)
> Bulg. heroine
> Phila.—Women unp.,por.

Tcherniawaka, Glustchenko (fl. 1910's)
> Russ. soldier, heroine
> Dorland—Sum p99

Tead, Mrs. Ordway (fl. 1930's)
> Amer. educator
> Time Oct.8,1934 p59,por.(Cover)

Teal, Valentine (fl. 1940's)
> Amer. novelist
> Warfel—Amer. p425,por.

Teasdale, Sara (1884-1933)
> Amer. poet
> Adelman—Famous p322

> Brenner—Poets p207-242
> Cook—Our p31-40
> Dodd—Celeb. p258-262
> *Millett—Amer. p610-613

Teazle, Lady.
> See Darrach, Mrs. Marshall

Tebaldi, Renata (1922-   )
> It. singer
> Brook—Singers p184-186,por.
> CR '59 p753-754,por.
> CR '63 p610,por.
> Cur. Biog. '55 p599-600,por.
> Davidson—Treas. p318-320
> Ewen—Ency. p503
> Matz—Opera p222-226,por.
> Rosenthal—Sopranos p96-97,por.
> Time Nov.3,1958 p58,por.(Cover)
> Wagner—Prima p249

Teck, Mary Adelaide, Duchess of (b. 1833)
> Eng. philanthropist, mother of
>   Queen Mary
> Carey—Twelve p199-211,por.
> Hammerton p1278,por.

Tee-van, Helen Damrosch (fl. 1910's-1930's)
> Amer. artist, illustrator
> Women—Achieve. p66,por.

Teichner, Miriam (fl. 1910's)
> Amer. journalist
> Ross—Ladies p105-108

Tekakwitha, Kateri (1656-1680)
> Amer. Christian Indian
> Husslein—Heroines p157-176
> Maynard—Great p41-52

Tekoa, Wise woman of (Biblical)
> Lewis—Portraits p179-182

Telesilla (B.C. c. 51)
> Gr. poet, musician
> Anthologia—Poets p81
> Drinker—Music p103

Telkes, Mari de (1900-   )
> Hung. physical chemist, engineer
> Cur. Biog. '50 p563-564,por.

Teller, Alice Schenck (m. 1790)
> Amer. pioneer
> Green—Pioneer (1) p423-424

Teller, Margaret.
> See Van Kleeck, Margaret

Telva, Marion (1897-1962)
> Amer. singer
> Ewen—Ency. p504
> Ewen—Living p353,por.
> McCoy—Portraits p207,por.

Tempest, Mary (Marie) Susan Etherington,
    Dame (1864/66-1942)
    Brit. actress
    Blum—Great p24,por.
    Cur. Biog. '42 p823
    Hammerton p1278,por.
    Marks—Glamour p331-332
    Strang—Prima p222-232,por.

Tempest, Theresa.
    See Kent, Louise Andrews

Temple, Dorothy Osborne, Lady (1627-
    1695)
    Eng. letter-writer
    Balch—Modern p360-379,por.
    Bottrall—Pers. p121-122,229
    Hammerton p1279,por.
    Stenton—English p168-169

Temple, Hope, pseud. (d. 1938)
    Irish composer, pianist
    McCoy—Portraits p207,por.

Temple, Irene. See Bailey, Temple

Temple, Madge (fl. 1930's)
    Eng. singer
    Felstead—Stars p155-156

Temple, Shirley (1928-   )
    Amer. actress
    Blum—Television p252,por.
    CR '59 p755-756,por.
    CR '63 p610,por.
    Cur. Biog. '45 p597-599,por.
    Schickel—Stars p135,por.
    Tanner—Here p178-197
    Time Apr.27,1936 p36,por.;
        Jan.8,1945 p39,por.(Covers)
    Zierold—Child p56-96,por.

Templeton, Fay (1865-1939)
    Amer. actress
    Blum—Great p30,por.
    Caffin—Vaud. p66-71
    McCoy—Portraits p207,por.
    Marks—Glamour p332
    Strang—Prima p67-80,por.

Tempski, Armine von (1899-1943)
    Amer. author, lecturer
    Cur. Biog. '44 p687-688

Ten Broeck, Christina.
    See Livingston, Christina Ten Broeck

Tench, Mrs. Frank Murray (fl. 1930's)
    Amer. patriot, club leader
    Women—Achieve. p138,por.

Tencin, Claudine Alexandrine Guérin de
    (1685-1749)
    Fr. social leader, author, courtesan
    Haggard—Remark. p208-209,212,215-
        216,256
    Hammerton p1279

Herold—Love p3-59,por.
Kavanagh—Woman p66-68,72-73,96-
    99,193,por.

Tennant, Kylie (1912-   )
    Austral. author
    Hetherington—42 p133-139,por.
    Roderick—20 p305-323

Tennant, Margot.
    See Oxford & Asquith, Margot Tenant,
        Countess of

Tennyson, Emily (fl. 1820's-1870's)
    Eng., wife of Alfred, Lord
        Tennyson
    Guedalla—Bonnet p125-151,por.

Tennyson, Jean (fl. 1830's)
    Amer. singer
    Women—Achieve. p45,por.

Tentoni, Rosa (fl. 1930's)
    Amer. singer
    Ewen—Living p354-355,por.
    McCoy—Portraits p207,por.

Teodorini, Elena (1857-1926)
    Rum. singer
    Stiles—Postal p265

Terentia (1st cent. B.C.)
    Rom., wife of Cicero
    Balsdon—Roman p46,217

Teresa, M. Imelda, Sister (b. 1862)
    Amer. philanthropist, nun
    Logan—Part p536

Teresa. See also Theresa

Tereshkova, Valentina Vladimirovna
    (1937-   )
    Russ. cosmonaut
    Cur. Biog. '63 p417-419,por.
    Stiles—Postal p265

Terhune, Anice Stockton (fl. 1940's)
    Amer. composer, pianist, wife of
        Albert Payson Terhune
    McCoy—Portraits p207,por.

Terhune, Mary Virginia Hawes (Marion
        Harland, pseud.) (1830-1922)
    Amer. author
    Adelman—Famous p265
    Logan—Part p799-800
    Papashvily—All (see index)
    Whitton—These p190-191

Ternina, Milka (1863-1941)
    Croat. singer
    Ewen—Ency. p504-505
    Klein—Great p230-237
    McCoy—Portraits p207,por.

Terraube, Geneviève de Galard.
See Galard Terraube, Geneviève de

Terrell, Mrs. Alexander W. (fl. 1900's-
1910's)
Amer. pioneer
Logan—Part p103-104

Terrell, Ann (m. 1755)
Amer. religious worker
Jones—Quakers p296-297

Terrell, Mary Church (1863-1954)
Amer. feminist
Adams—Great p95,por.
Cur. Biog. '42 p827-830,por.
Cur. Biog. '54 p602
Robinson—Hist. p251

Terrington, Lady (m. 1927)
Amer. journalist
Ross—Ladies p296

Terry, Ellen Alicia, Dame (1847/48-
1928)
Eng. actress
Adelman—Famous p280-282
Bodeen—Ladies p117-128,por.
Coad—Amer. p294,por.
De Morny—Best p144-149
Du Cann—Loves p245-259,por.
Fitzhugh—Concise p679-680
Furniss—Some p67-76
Hammerton p1281-1282,por.
Izard—Heroines p93-125,por.
Love—Famous p35
MacQueen—Pope p355-368,por.
*MacVeagh—Champlin p564-565
Marinacci—Lead. p97-123,por.
Mears—They p83-84
Ormsbee—Back. p179-185,259-260,
por.
Schmidt—400 p161-162,por.
Sitwell—Women p44,por.
Wagenknecht—Seven p91-116,por.

Terry, Ellen F. (fl. 1860's)
Amer. Civil war humanitarian
Brockett—Woman's p546-547

Terry, Frances (fl. 1940's)
Amer. composer, pianist
Howard—Our p580
McCoy—Portraits p207,por.

Terry, Rose (b. 1827)
Amer. poet
Hanaford—Dau. p260

Terry-Lewis, Mabel (b. 1872)
Eng. actress
Hammerton p1282

Tertia Aemilia (fl. 230's-180's B.C.)
Rom., wife of Scipio Africanus,
the Elder
Boccaccio—Conc. p163-164

Terwangne, Anne Joseph.
See Théroigne de Mericourt, pseud.

Tesi, Vittoria (1700-1775)
It. singer
Pleasants—Great p100,102

Tesselschade, Maria (1594-1649)
Nether. poet, social leader
Phila.—Women unp.,por.
Stiles—Postal p266

Tester, Dorothy Julia, Marchioness of
(Dorothy Julia Ailesbury)
(m. 1884)
Eng. ballet dancer
Wyndham—Chorus p68-70

Tetisheri (1650-1575 B.C.)
Egypt. queen
Schmidt—400 p109-110,por.

Tetrazzini, Luisa (Madame Bazelli)
(1874-1940)
It. singer
Adelman—Famous p315
Cur. Biog. '40 p796,por.
Davidson—Treas. p320-324
Ewen—Ency. p505
Hurok—Impres. p134-135
Lahee—Grand p128-141,144,255-256,
por.
McCoy—Portraits p207,por.
*MacVeagh—Champlin p565
Pleasants—Great p289-292,por.
Wagner—Prima p92-93,106-107,
172-173, 249

Teurbe Tolón, Emilia (fl. 1840's-1850's)
Cub. patriot
Stiles—Postal p266

Textor, Katherine Elizabeth (fl. 1720's-
1750's)
Ger., author, mother of Goethe
Bartlett—Mothers p26-31

Teyte, Maggie, Dame (b. 1889)
Eng. singer
CR '59 p756,por.
Cur. Biog. '45 p601-604,por.
Davidson—Treas. p324-326
Ewen—Ency. p505
Lahee—Grand p432-433,por.
McCoy—Portraits p207,por.
Wagner—Prima p88-89,249

Thacher, Ella Hoover (fl. 1890's)
Amer. social reformer
Logan—Part p668

Thackrey, Dorothy Schiff (1903-   )
Amer. journalist, publisher
Cur. Biog. '45 p604-606,por.

Thaden, Louise McPhetridge (1906-   )
Amer. pioneer aviatrix
*Adams—Sky p117-133,por.
Dwiggins—They p75,80,83-93
Earhart—Fun p177-179,por.
Heinmuller—Man's p331,por.
*May—Women p94-96,111,132,182,por.
Planck—Women p70-74,85,108

Thaïs (1) (fl. 4th cent. B.C.)
Gr., courtesan, mistress of
Alexander the Great
Hammerton p1283-1284

Thais (2) (fl. 4th cent.)
Egypt. saint
Englebert—Lives p383

Thal, Augusta (fl. 1930's)
Amer. business woman
Women—Achieve. p176,por.

Thamar. See Tamar (1)

Thamyris (1) (Tomyris) (fl. c. 529 B.C.)
Scyth. queen
Boccaccio—Conc. p104-106

Thamyris (2) (fl. 400's-390's B.C.)
Gr. painter
Boccaccio—Conc. p122

Thane, Elswyth (1900-   )
Amer. author, playwright
Warfel—Amer. p427-428,por.

Thanet, Octave, pseud. (Alice French)
(1850-1934)
Amer. author
Hammerton p622
Harkins—Famous p157-171,por.
Harkins—Little p157-171,por.
Logan—Part p804
Maurice—Makers p5

Thant, Madame U.
See Daw Thein Tin

Tharp, Louise Marshall Hall (1898-   )
Amer. author, lecturer
Cur. Biog. '55 p600-602,por.

Thaulow, Alexandra (fl. 1900's)
Scan. artist, bookbinder
Waters—Women p332-333

Thaw, Evelyn. See Nesbit, Evelyn

Thaxter, Celia Laighton (1836-1894)
Amer. poet
Adelman—Famous p201
Benét—Amer. Poets p83-89,por.
Dorland—Sum p22,183
Hanaford—Dau. p260
Howe—Memories p129-131
Parton—Noted p159-171

Thaxter, Mabel. See Marchant, Mabel

Thayer, Deborah.
See Wheelock, Deborah Thayer

Thayer, Lizzie E. D. (b. 1857)
Amer. train dispatcher
Logan—Part p892

Thayer, Mary Appleton Shute (m. 1904)
Amer. social worker
Logan—Part p604

Thayer, Theodora W. (1868-1905)
Amer. painter
Michigan—Biog. p308

Theano (fl. 540-510 B.C.)
Crete philosopher, wife of
Pythagoras
Beard—Woman p313-314

Thebes, Madame de.
See Savigny, Anna Victorine

Thebes, Woman of (Biblical)
Culver—Women p26

Thebom, Blanche (1919-   )
Amer. singer
CR '59 p757,por.
CR '63 p611,por.
Cur. Biog. '48 p616-618,por.
Hurok—Impres. p290-291,por.
Matz—Opera p155-157,por.

Thecla (fl. 1st cent.)
Turk. saint
Deen—Great p311-312
Englebert—Lives p362-363
Hammerton p1284
Wescott—Calen. p144-145

Thelberg, Elizabeth B. (1860-1935)
Amer. physician
Lovejoy—Women p97,269,308,321,333
Lovejoy—Women Phys. p52-53,por.

Theoctista (c. 740-c. 801)
Turk., mother of Theodore of
Studion
Diehl—Portraits p106-124

Theodelina (Theodelinda) (568/580-628)
Lombard. queen, religious leader
Culver—Women p81
Deen—Great p322
Dolan—Goodnow's p90-91

Theodora (1) (c. 508-548)
Rom. empress, wife of
Justinian I, actress
Abbott—Notable p39-43
Adelman—Famous p30
Blei—Fasc. p3-15,por.

(Continued)

Thevenin, Marie Anne Rosalie (fl. 1840's-
    1860's)
        Fr. painter
    Waters—Women p333

Thible, Madame (fl. 1780's)
        Fr. pioneer aeronaut
    Planck—Women p1

Thirkle, Angela Margaret Mackail (1890-
    1961)
        Eng. novelist
    Breit—Writer p73-75

Thoburn, Isabella (1840-1901)
        Amer. missionary
    Deen—Great p401-402

Thom, Mrs. Douglas (m. 1919)
        Amer. model
    Time June 16,1958 p86,por.(Cover)

Thomas, Carrie A. (1839-1883)
        Amer. religious worker, poet,
            hymn-writer
    Phillips—33 p44-47

Thomas, Clara Chaplin (fl. 1920's)
        Amer. journalist
    Ross—Ladies p398-399

Thomas, Clara Fargo (fl. 1930's)
        Amer. painter
    Women—Achieve. p176,por.

Thomas, Dorothy (fl. 1930's)
        Amer. author
    Women—Achieve. p134,por.

Thomas, Mrs. E. (fl. 1860's)
        Amer. Civil war nurse
    Brockett—Woman's p496

Thomas, Edith Matilda (1854-1925)
        Amer. poet
    Adelman—Famous p272
    Cook—Our p211-213
    Dorland—Sum p53,181
    Logan—Part p811

Thomas, Flora (fl. 1930's)
        Amer. pianist
    Cuney-Hare—Negro p378

Thomas, Jane (Jane Black) (m. 1740)
        Amer. Rev. war heroine
    Bruce—Woman p112-113
    Ellet—Women (1) p285-295
    Green—Pioneer (2) p357-364
    Logan—Part p181-183
    Whitton—These p22

Thomas, Lida. See Larrimore, Lida, pseud.

Thomas, M. Louise (fl. 1870's)
        Amer. agriculturist
    Hanaford—Dau. p724-729

Thomas, Martha Carey (1857-1935)
        Amer. educator
    Adelman—Famous p289

Thomas, Mary (fl. 1850's)
        Amer. lecturer
    O'Connor—Pioneer p94,142-143,217-
        218

Thomas, Mary Frame (1816-1888)
        Amer. physician, editor
    Hanaford—Dau. p559
    Mead—Medical p27,por.

Thomas, Patricia (fl. 1930's)
        Amer. aviation instructor
    Planck—Women p166-167

Thomas, Sally (1769-1813)
        Amer. religious worker
    Deen—Great p380-381

Thomas Aquinas, Sister (1884-1957)
        Brit. nun
    Elgin—Nun p128-129,por.
    *Peckham—Women p150-152,por.

Thomas-Soyer, Mathilde (b. 1859)
        Fr. sculptor
    Waters—Women p333-334

Thompson, Alice (n.d.)
        Amer. publisher, editor
    Murrow—This (1) p181-182

Thompson, Alleen (1919-   )
        Amer. librarian
    Cur. Biog. '65 p422-424,por.

Thompson, Ann. See Gerry, Ann Thompson

Thompson, Caroline Wadsworth (b. 1856)
        Amer. author
    Logan—Part p823

Thompson, Charlotte (fl. 1910's)
        Amer. playwright, public relations
            counsel
    Logan—Part p788

Thompson, Charlotte Marson (fl. 1860's)
        Amer. Civil war nurse
    Logan—Part p373

Thompson, Dorothy (1894-1961)
        Amer. journalist
    Burnett—Amer. p555,por.
    CR '59 p759-760,por.
    Cur. Biog. '40 p798-800,por.
    Cur. Biog. '61 p453
    Drewry—Post p431-477
    Fisher—Amer. p275-277,por.
    *Muir—Writers p119-128,por.
    New Yorker Apr.20,1940 p24,por;
        Apr.27,1940 p24(Profiles)

(Continued)

Thompson, Dorothy—*Continued*

Rogers—Women p174,por.
Ross—Ladies p130,360-367,por.
Time June12,1939 p47,por.(Cover)
Women—Achieve. p25,por.

Thompson, Eliza J. (b. 1816)
Amer. social reformer
Hanaford—Dau. p412-417,por.
Holbrook—Dreamers p87-88

Thompson, Elizabeth.
See Butler, Elizabeth Southerden
Thompson

Thompson, Elizabeth Rowell (1821-1899)
Amer. philanthropist, social
reformer
Dorland—Sum p52,127,131,142

Thompson, Franklin, pseud.
See Edmonds, (Sarah) Emma

Thompson, Kay (1913-   )
Amer. singer, author
Beaton—Persona p90-91
CR '59 p760,por.
CR '63 p612,por.
Cur. Biog. '59 p449-451,por.

Thompson, Lydia (1836-1908)
Eng. actress
Coad—Amer. P230,por.
Furniss—Some p47,por.

Thompson, Maria Sanchez de (1786-1848)
Argent. patriot
Schmidt—400 p31-32,por.

Thompson, Mary Harris (1829-1895)
Amer. physician
Lovejoy—Women p88-91,por.
Mead—Medical p53-54,por.

Thompson, Mary Wolfe (b. 1886)
Amer. author
Cur. Biog. '50 p568-569,por.

Thompson, Mrs. (fl. 1850's)
Amer. W. pioneer
Sargent—Pioneers p15,18

Thompson, Myrtle Grey (fl. 1950's-1960's)
Amer. aviatrix, airport operator
°May—Women p197

Thompson, Ruth (b. 1887)
Amer. Congresswoman
Cur. Biog. '51 p620-621,por.

Thompson, Sarah (d. 1909)
Amer. Civil war spy
Hoehling—Women p18-44,por.

Thompson, Sarah, Countess Rumford
(d. 1852)
Amer. social leader, philanthropist
Hanaford—Dau. p139-140

Thompson, Sylvia Elizabeth (1902-   )
Brit. novelist, lecturer
Brittain—Women p177,251
Millett—Brit. p488-489

Thoms, Adah B. (gr. 1879)
Amer. nurse
Pennock—Makers p31-32,por.

Thomson, Mrs. Alexander (fl. 1940's)
Amer. mother of the year
Davis—Mothers p179

Thomson, Frances. See Marion, Frances

Thorborg, Kerstin (1906-   )
Swed. singer
Cur. Biog. '40 p803-804,por.
Ewen—Ency. p509-510
Ewen—Living p359-360,por.
McCoy—Portraits p209,por.
Peltz—Spot. p91,por.

Thoreau, Sophia (b.c. 1819)
Amer. sister of Henry Thoreau
Pomeroy—Little p251-274,por.

Thorn, Edgar. See Merrick, Mrs. C.

Thorn, Emily (b. 1865)
Amer. recluse
Erskine—Out p178-208

Thorndike, Sybil, Dame (b. 1882)
Eng. actress
CR '59 p761,por.
Cur. Biog. '53 p621-623,por.
Gardiner—Por. p261-268
Hammerton p1290

Thorne, Diana (1895-   )
Can.-Amer. painter
Mahony—Illus. p365

Thorne, Isabel (fl. 1870's)
Eng. physician
Bell—Storm. p69,92,106-107,110,142
Hume—Great p136,146,164,168,por.

Thorne, Marion, pseud.
See Thurston, Ida Treadwell

Thornton, Alice Wandesford (b. 1626)
Eng. eccentric
Stirling—Odd p69-71

Thornton, Hannah Jack (m. 1760)
Amer. patriot
Green—Pioneer (3) p16-18

Thornycroft, Mary Frances (1814-1895)
Eng. sculptor
Dorland—Sum p26,158
Waters—Women p334

Thornycroft, Rosalind (1891-   )
Eng. illustrator
Mahony—Illus. p365

Thorp, Sarah (fl. 1790's-1800's)
Amer. W. pioneer
Ellet—Pioneer p266-271

Thorpe, Cleta (n.d.)
Amer. teacher, author
Parshalle—Kash. p193-194,por.

Thorpe, Rose Hartwick (1850-1939)
Amer. author
Logan—Part p842

Thorpe, Sarah (fl. 1790's)
Amer. pioneer
Logan—Part p84-85

Thorward, Clara Schafer (fl. 1930's)
Amer. artist
Women—Achieve. p91,por.

Thouret, Jeanne Antide (1765-1826)
Fr. saint
Hammerton p1292
Schmidt—400 p394-395,por.

Thrale, Hester.
See Piozzi, Hester Lynch Salusbury

Threrwitz, Emily Geiger (b.c. 1760)
Amer. Rev. war heroine
Leonard—Amer. p122-123

Thukral, Sarla (n.d.)
E. Ind. aviatrix
*May—Women p239

Thumb, Mrs. Tom. See Warren, Lavinia

Thurber, Caroline Nettleton (fl. 1890's-
1900's)
Amer. painter
Waters—Woman p334-336

Thurber, Louise Lockwood (fl. 1930's)
Amer. humanitarian, feminist,
social worker
Women—Achieve. p142,por.

Thuria. See Turia

Thüringen, Elizabeth von (1207-1231)
Hung. princess
Schmidt—400 p223,por.

Thurlow, Lady.
See Bolton, Mary Katherine, Lady
Thurlow

Thurman, Lucy Smith (1849-1918)
Amer. social worker, club leader
Brown—Home. p176-177

Thursby, Emma Cecelia (1854-1931)
Amer. singer
McCoy—Portraits p209,por.

Thurston, Ida Treadwell (Marion Thorne,
pseud.) (d. 1918)
Amer. author
Logan—Part p854

Thurston, Lucy G. (1795-1876)
Amer. missionary
Deen—Great p383-385

Thurwanger, Felicité Chastanier (fl. 1850's)
Fr. painter
Waters—Women p336-337

Thynne, Frances, Countess of Hertford
Duchess of Somerset (d. 1754)
Eng. maid of honor
Melville—Maids p222-225

Tible (Thible), Marie (fl. 1780's)
Fr. pioneer balloon passenger
*May—Women p8-10

Tier, Nancy Hopkins (fl. 1930's)
Amer. aviatrix
Planck—Women p77

Tiernan, Francis Fisher (Christian Reid,
pseud.) (fl. 1910's)
Amer. novelist
Logan—Part p615-616,823

Tierney, Gene (1920-   )
Amer. actress
CR '59 p763-764,por.

Tietjens, Eunice (1884-1944)
Amer. poet, author
Cook—Our p329
Cur. Biog. '44 p692
Smith—Women's p194

Tietjens, Theresa (1831-1877)
Hung. singer
Adelman—Famous p188
Dorland—Sum p35,162
Hammerton p1295,por.
Klein—Great p15-30,por.
Lahee—Famous p108-109
McCoy—Portraits p210,por.
Marks—Glamour p142-145,por.
Wagner—Prima p249

Tiffany, Marie (fl. 1910's)
Amer. singer
McCoy—Portraits p210,por.

Tiffin, Pamela (1942-   )
Amer. actress
CR '63 p613,por.

Tighe, Dixie (c. 1905-1946)
 Amer. journalist
 Ross—Ladies p245-246,511

Tighe, Mary Blachford (1772-1810)
 Irish poet
 Dorland—Sum p34,179

Tii. See Tiy

Till, Gertrude. See Read, Gertrude Ross Till

Tillery, Merle Gulley (fl. 1940's-1950's)
 Amer. missionary
 They—Went p122-124

Tilley (or Tillie), Ann (fl. 1600's)
 Amer. Pilgrim
 Green—Pioneer (1) p146-147

Tilley, Bridget (fl. 1600's)
 Amer. Pilgrim
 Green—Pioneer (1) p146
 Logan—Part p34

Tilley, Elizabeth.
 See Howland, Elizabeth Tilley

Tilley, Vesta (Matilde Alice DeFrece, Lady)
 (c. 1864-1952)
 Eng. actress
 Caffin—Vaud. p156-161
 Felstead—Stars p100,por.
 Hammerton p491-1295
 Lerory—Music p51-52

Tillinghast, Mary Elizabeth (d. 1912)
 Amer. painter, stained-glass
 designer
 Michigan—Biog. p310

Tilton, Elizabeth Richards (1834-1897)
 Amer. wife of Theodore Tilton
 Irwin—Angels p253-254

Tilton, Harriet. See Cottle, Harriet N.

Tilton, Mary (fl. 1650's)
 Amer. colonial religious worker
 Jones—Quakers p225

Timna (Biblical)
 Deen—All p298

Timothy, Ann Donovan (fl. 1780's-1790's)
 Amer. colonial pioneer journalist,
 printer, editor, publisher
 Club—Printing p14
 Dexter—Career p102
 Dexter—Colonial p173-174
 Earle—Colonial p64
 Leonard—Amer. p123
 Spruill—Women's p264,278

Timothy, Elizabeth (fl. 1730's-1780's)
 Amer. colonial pioneer journalist,
 printer, editor, publisher

Brigham—Journals p74-75
 Club—Printing p14
 Dexter—Career p102
 Earle—Colon. p63
 Hanaford—Dau. p710-711
 Leonard—Amer. p123
 Spruill—Women's p263-264

Timothy, Mary (fl. 1730's-1740's)
 Earle—Colonial p64
 Jones—Quakers p225

Tinayre, Marcelle Chasteau (1873-1948)
 Fr. novelist
 Hammerton p1296

Tinee, Mae (fl. 1920's-1930's)
 Amer. journalist
 Ross—Ladies p410-412

Tingley, Katherine Augusta Westcott (1847-
 1929)
 Amer. theosophist leader
 Logan—Part p294

Tinné, Alexandrine (Alexine) (1839-1869)
 Nether. traveler
 Adelman—Famous p182-183
 Dorland—Sum p36,114
 Schmidt—400 p304-305,por.

Tirlinks, Liewena (fl. 1520's-1540's)
 Belg. painter
 Waters—Women p337-338

Tisdale, Doris H. (fl. 1930's)
 Amer. home economist, educator
 Women—Achieve. p76,por.

Titcomb, Louise (fl. 1860's)
 Amer. Civil war nurse
 Brockett—Woman's p461,463

Titheradge, Madge (c. 1887-1961)
 Brit. actress
 Hammerton p1298

Titiana, Flavia (fl. 140-180)
 Rom. empress
 McCabe—Empr. p190-191
 Serviez—Roman (2) p111-123

Titiens. See Tietjens

Titlow, Effie (fl. 1860's)
 Amer. Civil war heroine
 Brockett—Women's p522-767

Tito, Jovanka Broz (1924-   )
 Yugoslav. wife of Tito
 Frederick—Ten p97-110,por.

Tiy (Tii), Egypt. queen, (c. 1400 B.C.)
 mother of Aknaton
 Koven—Women p3
 Schmidt—400 p112-113,por.

Tjaden, Olive F. (fl. 1930's)
Amer. architect
Women—Achieve. p100,por.

Tobolowsky, Hermine D. (fl. 1950's-1960's)
Amer. feminist, lawyer
Parshall—Kash. p197-198,por.

Tocheva, Anastasia (1837-1915)
Bulg. educator
Schmidt—400 p64-65,por.

Todd, Ann (1910-   )
Eng. actress
CR '59 p765,por.

Todd, Helen (1912-1963)
Amer. novelist
Warfel—Amer. p428-429,por.

Todd, Jane Hedges (fl. 1930's)
Amer. social worker, politician
Women—Achieve. p175,por.

Todd, Mabel Loomis (1856-1932)
Amer. astronomer, author
Dorland—Sum p142

Todd, Mary. See Lincoln, Mary Todd

Todd, Sarah (1750's-1770's)
Amer. colonial merchant
Dexter—Colonial p35

Todd, Sarah (fl. 1730's)
Amer. colonial teacher
Dexter—Colonial p90

Tofts, Katherine (Catherine) (c. 1680-1758)
Eng. singer
Wagner—Prima p23,249

Toklas, Alice B. (1897-   )
Amer. hostess
CR '59 p766,por.
CR '63 p616,por.

Tokyo Rose. See Aquino, Iva Ikuko Toburi d'

Tollefsen, Augusta Schnabel (c. 1885-1955)
Amer. pianist
McCoy—Portraits p211,por.

Tolstoy, Alexandra Lvovna (b. 1884)
Russ. author, lecturer, social worker,
daughter of Leo Tolstoy
Cur. Biog. '53 p624-626,por.
New Yorker Mar.15,1952 p34,por.;
Mar.22,1952 p36(Profiles)

Tolstoy, Sophie Behrs (1844-1919)
Russ. diarist, wife of Leo Tolstoy
Dunaway—Treas. p122-129

Tomara, Sonia (fl. 1920's-1930's)
Russ.-Amer. journalist
Ross—Ladies p372-373

Tomasi, Mari (n.d.)
Amer. author
Cur. Biog. '41 p866-867,por.

Tomkins, Cornelia M. (fl. 1860's)
Amer. Civil war nurse
Brockett—Woman's p489-490

Tomkins, Miriam Downing (1892-   )
Amer. librarian, editor
Bul. of Bibl. Sept.-Dec. '43 p25-26,por.

Tomkins, Sally Louisa (1833-1916)
Amer. hospital foundress, Civil
war patriot
Andrews—Women p127-130
Dolan—Goodnow's p237-238
Simkins—Women p86

Tomkinson, Grace (fl. 1940's)
Can. novelist
Thomas—Canad. p126

Tompkins, Juliet Wilbor (1871-1956)
Amer. author
Women—Achieve. p184,por.

Tomyris (fl. 6th cent. B.C.)
Scythian queen
Muir—Women p34-36

Tonaillon, Christiane (1878-1928)
Aust. physician, feminist, author
Schmidt—400 p54,por.

Tong, Eleanore Elizabeth (fl. 1910's)
Amer. religious author
Logan—Part p823

Tonkin, Lois Coots (fl. 1940's)
Amer. aviatrix
*Knapp—New p34-46,por.

Tonkonogy, Gertrude (1908-   )
Amer. playwright
Mantle—Contemp. p207

Tormoċzy, Bertha von (b. 1846)
Aust. painter
Waters—Women p338

Toro, Petronella (fl. 1900's)
Amer. artist
Waters—Women p338

Torpadie, Greta (fl. 1940's)
Amer. singer
McCoy—Portraits p211,por.

Torre, Lillian de la.
See De la Torre (-Bueno), Lillian

Torre, Marie (1924-   )
Amer. journalist, TV personality
CR '59 p767,por.
CR '63 p616,por.

Torre, Marta de la (fl. 1940's)
Cub. violinist
McCoy—Portraits p211,por.

Torrey, Louisa Maria.
See Taft, Louisa Maria

Totten, Vichen von P. (b. 1886)
Swed.-Amer. sculptor
Natl.—Contemp. p317

Touchet, Marie (1549-1638
Fr., mistress of Charles IX
Imbert—Valois p281-282

Toumanova, Tamara (1917-   )
Russ. ballet dancer
Atkinson—Dancers p155-158,por.
Davidson—Ballet p281-285,por.
Haskell—Ballet p48-49,por.
Haskell—Vignet. p34-35,por.
Swinson—Dancers p71-75,por.
Swinson—Great p24,por.
*Terry—Star p127-133,por.

Tour, Francoise-Marie Jacquelin (1602-1645)
Fr.-Can. pioneer
Innis—Clear p3-24

Tourel, Jennie (1910-   )
Can.- singer
CR '63 p617,por.
Cur. Biog. '47 p641-643,por.
Ewen—Ency. p514-515
McCoy—Portraits p211,por.
Saleski—Jewish p629-630,por.

Tournelle, Marie Anne de la.
See Chateauroix, Marie Anne de
Mailly-Nesle, Duchess

Toussaint, Anna Luisa Geertruida (1812-1886)
Nether. author
Schmidt—400 p303-304,por.

Toussaint, Jeanne (n.d.)
Fr. jewelry designer
Cur. Biog. '55 p612-613,por.

Tovell, Ruth Massey (b. 1889)
Can. novelist
Thomas—Canad. p126

Towle, Katherine Amelia (1898-   )
Amer. marine officer
Cur. Biog. '49 p607-608,por.

Towner, Isabel Louise (fl. 1930's)
Amer. librarian
Women—Achieve. p128,por.

Townley, Elizabeth Smith Carteret (fl. 1710's)
Amer. colonial patriot
Leonard—Amer. p123

Townsend, Eliza L. (fl. 1860's)
Amer. Civil war nurse
Logan—Part p373

Townsend, Sally (1760-1842)
Amer. Rev. war heroine
*Stevens—Women p35-39,por.

Townsend, Virginia Francis (1830-1914)
Amer. author, editor
Dorland—Sum p36,119

Toynbee, Charlotte Atwood (d. 1931)
Eng. philanthropist
Brittain—Women p47,74,186,258

Tracey, Minnie (c. 1870-1929)
Amer. singer
McCoy—Portraits p212,por.

Tracey, Cateau Stegeman (fl. 1940's)
Amer. pianist, music teacher,
author, critic, lecturer
McCoy—Portraits p212,por.

Tracy, Hannah. See Grant, Hannah Tracy

Tracy, Louise (fl. 1960's)
Amer. humanitarian
Parshalle—Kash. p169-170,por.

Tracy, Martha (1876-1942)
Amer. physician
*Fleischman—Careers p334

Tracy, Susan E. (d. 1928)
Amer. nurse
Pennock—Makers p118-119,por.

Trader, Ella King (fl. 1860's)
Amer. Civil war nurse
Andrews—Women p131-144

Trader, Georgia (fl. 1910's)
Amer. philanthropist, humanitarian
Logan—Part p531

Tranchepain de Saint Augustine, Marie de,
Sister (d. 1733)
Amer. colonial foundress, nun
Leonard—Amer. p123

Tranquillina, Turia Sabina (fl. 230's-240's)
Rom. empress, wife of Gordianus III
Serviez—Roman (2) p295-296

Traphagen, Ethel (1882-1963)
Amer. fashion designer
Cur. Biog. '48 p628-630,por.
Cur. Biog. '63 p425
Parshalle—Kash. p137-139,por.

Trapp, Maria Augusta (1905-   )
Aust.-Amer. singer
CR '63 p618,por.
Cur. Biog. '68 p24-27,por.

Trask, Frances (fl. 19th cent.)
Amer. W. pioneer
Ellet—Pioneer p397-400

Traubel, Helen (1899/1903-   )
Amer. singer
CR '59 p770,por.
CR '63 p618-619,por.
Cur. Biog. '40 p813-814,por.
Cur. Biog. '52 p600-602,por.
Ewen—Ency. p515
Ewen—Living p366-367,por.
Ewen—Men p22-30
McCoy—Portraits p212,por.
O'Connell—Other p183-198
Peltz—Spot. p95,por.
Time Nov. 11, 1946 p61,por.(Cover)
Wagner—Prima p95-96,249

Trautmann, Marie (1846-1925)
Alsac. pianist
Schonberg—Great p188

Travell, Janet Graeme (1901-   )
Amer. physician
CR '63 p619,por.
Cur. Biog. '61 p457-459,por.

Traver, Ethel K.(fl. 1930's)
Amer. osteopath
Women—Achieve. p145,por.

Treadwell, Sophie (m. 1911)
Amer. playwright, journalist
Mantle—Contemp. p326
Ross—Ladies p583-585

Treat, Mary (b. 1830)
Amer. scientific author, naturalist
Hanaford—Dau. p288

Trebelli, Zelia (Zelie) (1838-1892)
Fr. singer
Klein—Great p89-101,por.
Lahee—Famous p298-300
McCoy—Portraits p213,por.

Treble, Lillian Massey 1854-1909)
Can. philanthropist
Adelman—Famous 39-240

Trébuchet, Sophie (Sofie) (1778-1821)
Fr., mother of Victor Hugo
Bartlett—Mothers p32-33
Schmidt—400 p184-185

Treby, Bridget (fl. 1760's)
Amer. colonial merchant
Dexter—Colonial p22-23

Tredwell, Gertrude (1840-c. 1933)
Amer. recluse
Erskine—Out p161-177

Tree, Helen Maude, Lady (b. 1863)
Furniss—Some p67,por.
Hammerton p1306,por.

Tree, Marietta (1917-   )
Amer. politician
CR '63 p619,por.
Cur. Biog. '61 p459-461,por.

Tree, Viola (b. 1884)
Eng. actress
Hammerton p1306

Treen, Mary (n.d.)
Amer. actress
TV—Person. (1) p15

Trefilova, Vera (fl. 1900's)
Russ. dancer
Hammerton p1306

Trefouret, Jeanne Alfrédine.
See Hading, Jane

Trehawke-Davies, Eleanor J. (d. 1915)
Eng. military aviatrix
Dorland—Sum p102

Tremaine, Marie (1902-   )
Amer. librarian, author, editor
Bul. of Bibl. Sept.-Dec. '49 p253-255,por.

Trémoille, Marie Anna de la, Princess des
Ursins (1642-1722)
Span. lady of court
Dorland—Sum p38

Tremouille, Charlotte de la, Countess of
Derby (fl. 1640's)
Eng. "warrior"
*Deakin—True p363-384

Trentini, Emma (1878-1959)
It. singer
Lahee—Grand p236-237

Tresidder, Mary Curry (n.d.)
Amer. business executive
Sargent—Pioneers p75-76,por.

Treu (Trey), Katharina (1742-1811)
Ger. painter
Waters—Women p338

Trevelyan, Hilda (1879-1959)
Eng. actress
Hammerton p1308

Trevelyan, Pauline (1905-   )
Eng. illustrator
Mahony—Illus. p366
Winwar—Poor p156-158

Treville, Yvonne de (fl. 1940's)
Amer. singer
Lahee—Grand p393
McCoy—Portraits p213,por.

Trey, Katharine. See Treu, Katharina

Triaria (fl. 1-50 A.D.)
> Rom. wife of Lucius Vitellius
> Boccaccio—Conc. p217-218

Trigère, Pauline (1912-   )
> Fr.-Amer. fashion designer
> CR '59 p771,por.
> CR '63 p620,por.
> Cur. Biog. '60 p434-436,por.

Trimmer, Sarah Kirby (1741-1810)
> Eng. author
> Stenton—English p299-302

Trimmer, Selina (1765-1829)
> Eng. governess
> Howe—Galaxy p59-78

Triolet, Elsa (1903-   )
> Russ.-Fr. novelist
> Peyre—French p444,464

Tripp, June Howard. See June

Tristan, Flora (1803-1844)
> Fr. revolutionary
> Goldsmith—Seven p67-89

Trivulzio, Cristina Belgiojoso (1808-1871)
> It. sociologist, author, journalist
>   editor
> Schmidt—400 p254-255,por.

Trix, Helen (1892-1951)
> Amer. composer, author, pianist,
>   singer, actress
> ASCAP p506-507

Troendle, Theodora (fl. 1940's)
> Amer. composer, violinist
> McCoy—Portraits p213,por.

Trollope, Frances Milton (1780-1863)
> Eng. author
> Abbott—Notable p421-425
> Courtney—Adven. p127-137
> Douglas—Remember p66-68
> Hammerton p1309
> Johnson—Women p145-148
> Parton—Dau. p332-344
> Parton—Noted p332-344
> Saturday Rev. p3-10
> Whitton—These p63-75,79

Trott, Dame. See Trotula of Salerno

Trotter, Ann. See Bailey, Ann

Trotter, Catharine (1679-1749)
> Eng. playwright, author
> MacQueen—Pope p130-132

Trotula of Salerno (Dame Trott) (fl.c.1000)
> It. physician, surgeon
> Castiglioni—Hist. p303
> Dolan—Goodnow's p92

Lovejoy—Women p4
Mozans—Woman p284-286

Troubetskoy, Princess.
> See Rives, Amelie, Princess Troubetzkoy

Trout, Evelyn ("Bobby") (1906-   )
> Amer. pioneer aviatrix
> Earhart—Fun p148
> Heinmuller—Man's p341,por.
> *May—Women p94
> Planck—Women p75-76,83-84,225-226,
>   por.

Trout, Grace Wilbur (d. 1955)
> Amer. lecturer, author, feminist,
>   club leader
> Logan—Part p408

Trowbridge, Sarah.
> See Ward, Sarah Trowbridge

Trujillo, Angelita (1939-   )
> Dom. R., daughter of Rafael L.
>   Trujillo
> Stiles—Postal p270

Trujillo, Julia Molina de (b. 1865)
> Dom. R., mother of Trujillo Molina,
>   wife of Trujillo Valdez
> Stiles—Postal p270

Trulock, Mussette Langford (n.d.)
> Amer. organization official, lecturer
> Cur. Biog. '57 p557-558,por.

Truman, Elizabeth ("Bess") Wallace
>   (1885-   )
> Amer. wife of Harry S. Truman
> Cur. Biog. '47 p646-647,por.
> Gerlinger—Mis. p103-105,por.
> Jensen—White p249-250,por.
> Logan—Ladies p194
> *McConnell—Our p319-324,por.
> Means—Woman p215-241,por.,cover
> Prindiville—First p265-278
> *Ross—Know p67,por.
> Truett—First p78,por.

Truman, (Mary) Margaret (1924-   )
> Amer. singer, daughter of Harry S.
>   Truman
> CR '59 p775-776,por.
> CR '63 p621,por.
> Cur. Biog. '50 p575-577,por.
> Jensen—White p249-250,262-263,por.
> Time Feb. 26, 1951 p38,por.(Cover)

Trumbull, Faith Robinson (1718-1780)
> Amer. Rev. war patriot
> DAR Mag. July 1921 p373-374
> Green—Pioneer (3) p290-300,por.
> Root—Chapter p1-16,por.

Trumbull, Florence (fl. 1940's)
> Amer. pianist
> McCoy—Portraits p213,por.

Trumbull, Mary. See Williams, Mary

Trumbull, Sabra.
   See Bissell, Sabra Trumbull

Truskolawska, Agnieszka Marunowska
      (1755-1831)
      Pol. actress
      Schmidt—400 p320,por.

Trusta, H.
   See Phelps, Elizabeth Stuart (1)

Truth, Sojourner (1797-1885)
      Amer. social reformer, feminist
      Adams—Great p25,por.
      Beard—Amer. p231-232
      Brown—Home. p13-17,por.
    *Cherry—Portraits p9-12
      Irwin—Angels p98-101
      O'Connor—Pioneer p45,88-89,180,194,
         202,221,224
      Robinson—Hist. p130-131,por.
      Schmidt—400 p26,por.

Tryphena (Biblical)
      Deen—All p298

Tryphosa (Biblical)
      Deen—All p298

Tsahai (1919-1942)
      Ethiop. princess
      Stiles—Postal p271

Ts'ao Taku. See Pan Chao

Tseu-hi. See Tzu Hsi

Tsianini, Princess (fl. 1940's)
      Amer. Ind. singer
      McCoy—Portraits p214,por.

Tua, Teresina (1866-1911)
      It. violinist
      Ehrlich—Celeb. p28-29,por.
      McCoy—Portraits p214,por.

Tubb, Carrie (fl. 1920's-1940's)
      Eng. singer
      Hammerton p1311
      McCoy—Portraits p214,por.

Tubbs, Alice Ivers ("Poker Alice") (1851-
      1930)
      Amer. poineer
      Aikman—Calamity p310-311

Tubman, Emily H. (1794-1885)
      Amer. philanthropist, religious
         worker, hostess
      Deen—Great p178-185

Tubman, Harriet Ross (1826-1913)
      Amer. social reformer, lecturer
      Adams—Great p24,por.
      Brown—Home. p55-68,por.

*Buckmaster—Women p99-121,por.
*Cherry—Portraits p13-17
*Commager—Crus. p77-79
   Culver—Women p181
*Deakin—True p32-43
*Dolin—World p105-110,por.
   Douglas—Remember p163
*Gersh—Women p205-224,por.
*Horowitz—Treas. p54-58
*Hughes—First p41-44
*Hughes—Negroes p35-42
   O'Connor—Pioneer p96,131
   Robinson—Hist. p131-132,por.
   Schmidt—400 p397-398,por.
*Sickels—Calico p221-237
*Stone—Heroes p19-20
*Strong—Of p180-184
*Woodward—Bold p237-267
*Yost—Famous p79-88,por.
   Young—Women p300-304,378

Tuchman, Barbara Wertheim (1912-   )
      Amer. historian, author
      Cur. Biog. '63 p426-428,por.

Tucker, Ann (fl. 1760's)
      Amer. colonial merchant
      Dexter—Colonial p70-71

Tucker, Augusta (1904-   )
      Amer. novelist
      Warfel—Amer. p430-431,por.

Tucker, Bertha Fain (1899-   )
      Amer. judge
      Cur. Biog. '57 p558-560,por.

Tucker, Charlotte Maria ("A.L.O.E.")
      (1821-1893)
      Eng. author
      Dorland—Sum p52,188
      Hammerton p1311-1312,por.
      Oliphant—Women p293-297

Tucker, Frances Bland Randolph (d. 1788)
      Amer. patriot
      Green—Pioneer (3) p463-464

Tucker, Lucy Dougherty (fl. 1770's)
      Amer. nurse, pioneer
      Green—Pioneer (3) p431-435

Tucker, Mary Elizabeth Logan (m. 1870)
      Amer. patriot
      Logan—Part p295-296

Tucker, Sophie (1884-1966)
      Amer. singer
      Beaton—Persona p91,por.
      CR '59 p776,por.
      CR '63 p622,por.
      Cur. Biog. '45 p626-630,por.
      Cur. Biog. '66 p472

Tudor, Tasha (1915-   )
      Amer. illustrator
      Mahony—Illus. p366

Tufts, Susannah Warner (1745-1832)
Amer. patriot
Green—Pioneer (3) p521

Tull, Jewell Bothwell (fl. 1920's)
Amer. poet
Smith—Women's p197

Tullia (1), (B.C. 79-45)
Rom. daughter of Cicero
Balsdon—Roman p179,187-188

Tullia (2) (fl.c. 534 B.C.)
Rom., daughter of Servius Tullius
Balsdon—Roman p26-28

Tully, Alice (fl. 1940's)
Amer. singer
McCoy—Portraits p214,por.

Tunnell, Barbara Madison.
See Anderson, Barbara Tunnell

Tunnicliff, Ruth (1876-1946)
Amer. bacteriologist, physician
Castiglioni—Hist. p1127

Tupper, Ellen S. (b. 1822)
Amer. bee-culturist
Hanaford—Dau. p722-724

Turchin, Nadine (1826-1904)
Russ.-Amer. Civil war patriot,
soldier, heroine
Brockett—Woman's p480,770-771
Hanaford—Dau. p192-194
Young—Women p94,321,378-379

Tureck, Rosalyn (1914-   )
Amer. pianist
Cur. Biog. '59 p456-458,por.
Ewen—Living p367-368,por.
McCoy—Portraits p214,por.
Saleski—Jewish p568-570,por.
Schonberg—Great p387

Turia (Thuria) (fl. 1st cent. B.C.)
Rom. matron
Balsdon—Roman p194,204-205,210
Boccaccio—Conc. p183-184

Turnbull, Agnes Sligh (b. 1888)
Amer. author
Warfel—Amer. p431,por.

Turnbull, Ruth (1912-   )
Amer. sculptor
National—Contemp. p317

Turner, Blanche (fl. 1950's)
Eng. singer
Davidson—Treas. p326-328

Turner, Eva (1892-   )
Eng. singer
Brook—Singers p187-191,por.
Davidson—Treas. p328-332,por,

Turner, Florence (fl. 1910's-1920's)
Amer. actress
Wagenknecht—Movies p44-46,48,por.

Turner, Frances (fl. 1930's)
Amer. journalist
Ross—Ladies p471-472

Turner, Helen M. (b. 1858)
Amer. painter
Bryant—Amer. p262-265
Michigan—Biog. p313

Turner, Lana (1920-   )
Amer. actress
CR '59 p777-778,por.
CR '63 p622,por.
Cur. Biog. '43 p776-779,por.
Schickel—Stars p214,por.

Turner, Lida Larrimore (1897/98-   )
Amer. author
Warfel—Amer. p258-259,por.

Turner, Lizabeth A. (d. 1907)
Amer. club leader
Logan—Part p351

Turner, Nancy Byrd (b. 1880)
Amer. poet, author
Smith—Women's p200

Turner, Rose (fl. 1940's-1960's)
Amer. club leader
Parshalle—Kash. p45-47,por.

Turner-Maley, Florence (fl. 1940's)
Amer. composer, singer
McCoy—Portraits p214,por.

Turnure, Pamela (1937-   )
Amer. press secretary
CR '63 p622-623,por.

Turpin, Edna Henry Lee (1867-1952)
Amer. author
Women—Achieve. p128,por.

Turrell (Turell), Jane Colman (1708-1735)
Amer. colonial poet
Dexter—Colonial p137-138
Leonard—Amer. p104-105,123

Tushingham, Rita (1942-   )
Eng. actress
Cur. Biog. '65 p427-429,por.

Tusnelda (fl. 9 A.D.)
Ger. heroine
Schmidt—400 p189-190,por.

Tusch, Mary E. Hall ("Mother") (c. 1875-1960)
Amer. aviation patron
Planck—Women p45-46,por.

Tussaud, Marie Gresholtz (1760-1850)
Swiss wax modeler
Adelman—Famous p122
Dorland—Sum p21
Hammerton p1315,por.

Tussenbroek, Catherine van (gr. 1880)
Nether. physician
Lovejoy—Women p184

Tuthill, Cornelia (1820-1870)
Amer. author
Hanaford—Dau. p243

Tuthill, Louisa Cornelia (1798-1879)
Amer. author
Hanaford—Dau. p238

Tuttiett, Mary Gleed.
See Gray, Maxwell

Tuttle, Florence Onertin (b. 1869)
Amer. politician, author
Women—Achieve. p183,por.

Tuttle, Marguerite (fl. 1930's)
Amer. business executive
Women—Achieve. p184,por.

Tutwiler, Julia Strudwick (1841-1916)
Amer. educator
Bennett—Amer. p181-205,por.
Irwin—Angels p131-132

Tweddle, Georgina Ogilvie (fl. 1930's)
Amer. cosmetician
Women—Achieve. p31-32,por.

Twede, Blanche Marie Louise.
See Strange, Michael

Tweedie, Ethel Brilliana (d. 1940)
Brit. artist, author, journalist,
social worker, traveler
Cur. Biog. '40 p817
Hammerton p1316

"Twiggy" (Leslie Hornby) (1949-   )
Eng. fashion model
Cur. Biog. '68 p407-409,por.

Twilford, Mrs. (fl. 17th cent.)
Eng. actress
MacQueen—Pope p121

Twining, Louise (1820-1912)
Eng. archaeologist
Mozans—Woman p316

Twining, Violet, Marchioness of Donegall
(m. 1902)
Amer. heiress
Eliot—Heiresses p195-199,por.

Twisleton, Ellen Dwight (c. 1829-1862)
Amer. social leader
Pearson—Marry. p28-51

Twomey, Kathleen (Kay) (1914-   )
Amer. author, designer, song-
writer
ASCAP p509-510

Twyford, Mrs. (fl. 1670's-1680's)
Eng. actress
Wilson—All p188-189

Tyler, Adaline, Sister (fl. 1860's)
Amer. Civil war nurse
Brockett—Woman's p241-250
Young—Women p53-54,379

Tyler, Alice Kellogg (fl. 1890's-1920's)
Amer. artist
Addams—Excellent p51-58

Tyler, Alice Sarah (1859-1944)
Amer. librarian, educator
Bul. of Bibl. Sept.-Dec.1927 p61,por.
Cur. Biog. '44 p696
Marshall—Amer. p458

Tyler, Elizabeth (d. 1850)
Amer., daughter of John Tyler
Smith—White p55-63,por.

Tyler, Julia Gardiner (1820-1889)
Amer., 2d wife of John Tyler
Gerlinger—Mis. p36-37,por.
Hanaford—Dau. p85-86
Jensen—White p64-67,por.
Logan—Ladies p59-62
Logan—Part p241-242
*McConnell—Our p117-121,por.
Prindiville—First p94-107
*Ross—Know p23,por.
Smith—White p65-79,por.
*Sweetser—Famous p131-153,por.
Truett—First p30,por.
Whitton—First p187-199,por.

Tyler, Letitia Christian (1790-1842)
Amer., 1st wife of John Tyler
Farmer—What p80-82
Gerlinger—Mis. p35-36,por.
Hanaford—Dau. p85-86
Logan—Ladies p56-58
Logan—Part p240-241
McConnell—Our p113-117,por.
Prindiville—First p94-101
Ross—Know p23,por.
Smith—Romances p142-148,por.
Whitton—First p177-187,por.

Tyler, Mary Armistead (fl. 1790's-1800's)
Amer., mother of John Tyler
Hampton—Our p81-85

Tyler, Odette (fl. 1880's)
Amer. actress
Strang—Actresses p285-290

Tyman, Mrs. See Jonas, Mrs. Tryntje

Tynan, Katharine (Katharine Hinkson)
(1861-1931)
Irish poet, novelist
Hammerton p1317,por.
Millett—Brit. p272-275

Tyndal, Margaret. See Winthrop, Margaret

Tynes, Mary ("Molly") Elizabeth (fl. 1860's)
Amer. Civil War heroine
Harkness—Heroines p6

Tyrrell, Catherine (fl. 1640's-1650's)
Irish patriot
Concannon—Dau. p258-260

Tyson, Laura R. Cotton (fl. 1860's)
Amer. Civil war nurse
Logan—Part p373

Tyson, Mildred Lund (1900-   )
Amer. composer
ASCAP p510

Tytler, Jane (fl. 1820's)
Scot.-Amer. pharmacist
Dexter—Career p38-39

Tzu Hsi (Tze-Hsi; Yehonala) (1835-1908)
Chin. empress
Adelman—Famous p238-239
*Boyd—Rulers p183-193
Ewart—World's p205-227
*Farmer—Book p170-183
Hammerton p1318,por.
Llewellyn—China's p181-202
Muir—Women p204-209

Tzvetayeva, Marina Ivanovna (1892-1942)
Russ. poet
Yarmolinsky—Treas. p305

U

Uccello, Ann (n.d.)
Amer. mayor, politician
Lamson—Few p197-215,por.

Ugalde, Delphine (1829-1910)
Fr. singer, music teacher
McCoy—Portraits p214,por.

Uggams, Leslie (1943-   )
Amer. singer, actress
Cur. Biog. '67 p421-423,por.

Ugon, Maria Armand (fl. 1910's)
Urug. physician
Lovejoy—Women p269

Ukrainka, Lesya, pseud. (Larissa Kossach
Kuitka) (1872-1913)
Russ. poet
Stiles—Postal p272

Ulanova, Galina Sergeyevna (1908/10-   )
Russ. ballet dancer
Clarke—Six p127-157,por.
CR '59 p778-779,por.
Cur. Biog. '58 p443-445,por.
Haskell—Ballet p195-196,por.
Swinson—Great p26,28,por.
*Terry—Star p207-211,por.

Ulfeld, Lenora Christine, Countess (1631-
1698)
Dan. author
Schmidt—400 p94-95,por.

Ullmann, Amelia (fl. 1850's)
Ger.-Amer. author
Marcus—Memoirs (2) p351-375

Ullman, Mrs. Edon Victor.
See Kennelly, Ardyth

Ulm, Mary Josephine (fl. 1930's)
Amer. aviatrix, mail pilot
*May—Women p212

Ulmar, Geraldine (1862-1932)
Amer. actress, singer
Hammerton p1319

Ulmer, Edith Ann (fl. 1930's)
Amer. teacher, author
Women—Achieve. p157,por.

Ulpia, Marciana. See Marciana, Ulpia

Ulreich, Nura Woodson (Nura, pseud.)
1899-1950)
Amer. illustrator
Mahony—Illus. p366-367

Ulric, Lenore (1894-   )
Amer. actress
Blum—Great p83,por.
Brown—Upstage p120-123
Coad—Amer. p328,por.

Umeki, Miyoshi (1930-   )
Japan.-Amer. singer, actress
CR '59 p779-780,por.
CR '63 p624,por.
Time Dec.22,1958 p42,por.(Cover)

Umiliana de Cerchi (fl. 13th cent.)
Christian saint
Wescott—Calen. p74

Ummidia Quadratilla (d. 107 A.D.)
Rom. philanthropist
Balsdon—Roman p277

Umphreville, Lucina (fl. 1830's)
Amer. feminist
Woodward—Bold p90-103

Underhill, Evelyn 1875-1941)
  Eng. poet, mystic
  Deen—Great p407-410
  Hammerton p1319
  Millett—Brit. p492-493

Underhill, Harriette (d. 1928)
  Amer. journalist, reviewer, critic
  Ross—Ladies p412-413,470

Underhill, Ruth Murray (b. 1884)
  Amer. anthropologist
  Cur. Biog. '54 p617-619,por.
  Parshalle—Kash. p129-130,por.

Underwood, Agness May Wilson (1902-)
  Amer. editor
  Parshalle—Kash. p23-25,por.

Underwood, Cecilia.
  See Inverness, Cecilia Laetitia
  Underwood, Duchess of

Underwood, Charlotte (Joan Charles, pseud.)
  Amer. novelist
  Warfel—Amer. p87,por.

Underwood, Edna Worthley (b. 1873)
  Amer. author, linguist, translator
  Women—Achieve. p154,por.

Underwood, Lillias (m. 1889)
  Amer. missionary, physician,
    pioneer
  Matthews—Daunt. p149-170

Underwood, Sophie Kerr.
  See Kerr, Sophie

Undset, Sigrid (1882-1949)
  Nor. novelist
  Cur. Biog. '40 p817-819,por.
  Cur. Biog. '49 p611
  Hammerton p1319
  McClintock—Nobel p611
  Nobel—Man p122-123
  Phila.—Women unp.,por.
  Stiles—Postal p273
  Van Gelder p108-110

Unger, Caroline (1803-1877)
  Aust. singer
  Ewen—Ency. p525

Unger, Gladys Buchanan (d. 1940)
  Amer. playwright
  Mantle—Amer. p310-311
  Mantle—Contemp. p326

Unger, Karoline (1803-1877)
  Hung. singer
  McCoy—Portraits p215,por.

Unschuld, Marie von (fl. 1900's)
  Aust. pianist, lecturer, author
  McCoy—Portraits p215,por.

Untermeyer, Jean Starr (b. 1886)
  Amer. poet
  Cook—Our p304

Unwin, Mary (1724-1796)
  Eng. nurse, friend of William
    Cowper
  Corkran—Romance p326-339,por.
  Fifty—Famous p282-284
  Hammerton p1319,por.

Unwin, Nora Spicer (1907-)
  Eng. illustrator
  Mahony—Illus. p367

Uphill, Susana, Lady Howard (fl. 1660's-
    1690's)
  Eng. actress
  MacQueen—Pope p65-66
  Wilson—All p189-191

Upjohn, Elizabeth P. (1876-1910)
  Amer. nurse
  Schmidt—400 p410,por.

Upton, Harriet Taylor (d. 1945)
  Amer. author, feminist
  Irwin—Angels p401,404

Urbanek, Carolyn (fl. 1930's)
  Amer. singer
  Ewen—Living p368,por.

Ureña de Henriquez, Salome (1850-1897)
  Dom. R. poet
  Stiles—Postal p273

Urmenyi, Baroness von.
  See Weidt, Lucie, Baroness von
    Urmenyi

Urrutia de Urmeneta, Ana Gertrudis de
    (1812-1850)
  Sp. painter
  Waters—Women p338-339

Ursins, Marie Anne de la Trémoille (1642-
    1722)
  Sp. politician
  Hall—Moths p291-318,por.
  Hammerton p1320

Urso, Camilla (1842-1902)
  Amer. violinist
  McCoy—Portraits p215,por.

Ursula (d. 238/283 or 451)
  Fr.-Eng. saint, daughter of
    King Donatus
  Arsenius—Saint p174,por.
  Hammerton p1320-1321
  Phila.—Women unp.,por.
  Stiles—Postal p240
  Wescott—Calen p165-166
  *Windham—Sixty p28-37

Ursuleac, Viorica (1899-   )
 Rum. singer
 Ewen—Ency. p526
 McCoy—Portraits p215,por.

Usher, Elizabeth Reuter (1914-   )
 Amer. librarian, organization
  official
 Cur. Biog. '67 p426-428,por.

Usher, Leila (fl. 1890's-1920's)
 Amer. sculptor
 National—Contemp. p319

Usher, Rebecca R. (fl. 1860's)
 Amer. Civil War nurse
 Brockett—Woman's p463
 Moore—Women p453-464

Utley, Freda (1898-   )
 Eng.-Amer. author, journalist,
  lecturer
 Cur. Biog. '58 p448-459,por.

Uttmann, Barbara (1514-1575)
 Ger. lace-maker
 Schmidt—400 p190-191,por.

Uvaroff, Countess.
 See Ouvaroff, Countess P.S.

Uzès, Duchess d' (b.c. 1847)
 Fr. sportswoman
 Skinner—Elegant p73-74,por.

V

Vaganova, Agrippina (1879-1951)
 Russ. ballet dancer
 Haskell—Ballet p202

Vail, Mrs. Laurence. See Boyle, Kay

Vail, Stella Boothe (fl. 1910's-1920's)
 Amer. nurse, author, social worker
 Pennock—Makers p101-102,por.

Vaka, Demetra (Demetra Vaka Brown)
 (1877-1946)
 Gr.-Amer. novelist
 Overton—Women p315-317

Valdi, Marguerite (fl. 1940's)
 Eng. singer
 McCoy—Portraits p215,por.

Valdo, Pat (b. 1887)
 Amer. circus personnel director
 New Yorker Apr.19,1952 p39,por.;
  Apr.26,1952 p43 (Profiles)

Valence, Mary.
 See Gates, Mary Valence

Valente, Caterina (1932-   )
 Fr. singer, actress
 Stambler—Ency. 235-236

Valentina (1904-   )
 Russ.-Amer. fashion designer
 CR '63 p627,por.
 Cur. Biog. '46 p607-609,por.
 Taves—Success. p115-128,por.

Valeria Galeria (d. 326)
 Rom. empress, wife of Galerius
 Balsdon—Roman p165-170,249
 McCabe—Empr. p256-257,259-264,por.
 Serviez—Roman (2) p367-371,377,
  382-383,391-402

Valeria Nessalina (fl. c. 40's A.D.)
 Rom. empress, wife of Claudius
 Serviez—Roman (1) p146-176

Valerie (fl. 3rd cent.)
 Fr. saint
 *Windham—Sixty p57-62

Valesh, Eva McDonald (b. 1866)
 Amer. printer, social reformer,
  feminist, journalist, labor leader
 Logan—Part p904-905
 Ross—Ladies p332

Valleria, Alwina Schoening (1848-1925)
 Amer. singer
 Ewen—Ency. p526-527
 McCoy—Portraits p216,por.

Valli, June (n.d.)
 Amer. singer
 TV—Person (3) p96,por.

Vallière, Mademoiselle.
 See La Vallière, Louise Baume Le
  Blanc de

Valois, Jeanne de.
 See La Motte, Jeanne de Saint-Rémy
  de Valois

Valois, Mademoiselle (d. 1722)
 Fr., friend of Duke of Richelieu
 Kavanagh—Woman (1) p36-37

Valois, Margaret of.
 See Margaret of Valois

Valois, Ninette de (1898-   )
 Irish ballet dancer
 Beaumont—Complete p758-770
 Davidson—Ballet p296-304
 Fisher—Ball. p6,por.
 Hammerton p1322

Van Alstine, Nancy (b.c. 1733)
 Amer. Rev. war patriot, heroine
 Fowler—Woman p114-120
 Green—Pioneer (2) p347-357
 Hanaford—Dau. p60-61

Vanamee, Grace Davis (1876-1946)
Amer. club leader, lecturer,
teacher, author
Women—Achieve. p136,por.

Van Blarcom, Carolyn Conat (fl. 1920's)
Amer. nurse
Pennock—Makers p92-93,por.

Van Brugh, Catharine.
See **Livingston, Catharine**

Vanbrugh, Irene, Dame (1872-1949)
Eng. actress
Asquith—Myself p383-397,por.
Hammerton p1322-1323,por.

Vanbrugh, Violet (1867-1942)
Brit. actress
Cur. Biog. '43 p779
Hammerton p1323
Marks—Glamour p333

Van Buren, Abigail ("Abby") (1918/19-)
Amer. journalist
CR '59 p783,por.
CR '63 p628,por.
Cur. Biog. '60 p442-444,por.

Van Buren, Alicia Keisker (1860-1922)
Amer. composer, singer, poet
McCoy—Portraits p216,por.

Van Buren, Angelica Singleton (c. 1820-
1878)
Amer., daughter-in-law of
Martin Van Buren
Gerlinger—Mis. p29-31,por.
Hanaford—Dau. p134
Jensen—White p57-58,por.
Logan—Ladies p49
Logan—Part p237-238
*Sweetser—Famous p116-130,por.
Truett—First p26,por.

Van Buren, Hannah Hoes (1783-1819)
Amer., wife of Martin Van Buren
Gerlinger—Mis. p29
Hanaford—Dau. p82
Logan—Ladies p46-48
*McConnell—Our p95-102,por.
Prindiville—First p77-82
*Ross—Know p19,por.
Smith—Romances p114-123,por.
Whitton—First p136-151,por.

Van Buren, Mary Hoes (fl. 1780's-1800's)
Amer., mother of Martin Van Buren
Hampton—Our p63-72

Vance, Ethel. See **Stone, Grace Zaring**

Vance, Eunice (fl. 1910's)
Amer. singer
Caffin—Vaud. p79-80,por.

Vance, Marguerite (1889-1965)
Amer. author
Cur. Biog. '51 p633-634,por.
Cur. Biog. '65 p429

Vance, Mary (fl. 1860's)
Amer., Civil war nurse
Brockett—Woman's p429-430

Vance, Vivian (1912-)
Amer. actress
TV—Person (3) p142-143,por.

Van Cleve, Edith (fl. 1930's)
Amer. dancer, actress
Women—Achieve. p204

Van Cortlandt, Annetje Lockermans
(m. 1642)
Amer. pioneer
Green—Pioneer (1) p184-185,187,196-
197

Van Cortlandt, Joanna Livingston
(Catharine Clinton) (b. 1752)
Amer. patriot
Green—Pioneer (2) p280

Van Cott, Maggie N. (fl. 1870's-1880's)
Amer. clergyman, evangelist
Hanaford—Dau. p344,480,482,por.

Vanderbilt, Alice Claypoole Gwynne (n.d.)
Amer. social leader
Tebbel—Inher. p111-112,115,123-124,
133-134,por.

Vanderbilt, Alva Smith Belmont (d. 1933)
Amer. social leader, feminist
Jensen—Revolt. p54-55,por.
Tebbel—Inher. p111-117,123-124,151-
152,por.

Vanderbilt, Amy (Mrs. Hans Knopf)
(1908-)
Amer. journalist, author, etiquette
authority
CR '59 p784-785,por.
CR '63 p628,por.
Cur. Biog. '54 p619-621
Fitzgibbon—My p201-208

Vanderbilt, Consuelo.
See **Balsan, Consuelo Vanderbilt**

Vanderbilt, Cornelia (b.c. 1900)
Amer. heiress
Tebbel—Inher. p121-122

Vanderbilt, Gertrude (c. 1899-1960)
Amer. actress, dancer
Caffin—Vaud. p29-32,por.
Tebbel—Inher. p115,129,131-132

Vanderbilt, Gladys Moore (m. 1908)
Amer. heiress
Tebbel—Inher. p.115,132,por.

Van Lew, Mrs. John (fl. 1860's)
Amer. Civil war spy
Kane—Spies p233-236,241

Van Loon, Emily Lois (1898-   )
Amer. physician
*Knapp—Women p95-108,por.

Van Meter, Pattie Field (fl. 1890's-1910's)
Amer. club leader
Logan—Part p437

Vannah, Kate (1855-1933)
Amer. composer, pianist, organist
Elson—Woman's p251-252
McCoy—Portraits p217,por.

Van Ness, Cornelia (m. 1831)
Amer. social leader
Hanaford—Dau. p144-145
Logan—Part p255-256

Van Ness, Marcia Burns (1782-1832)
Amer. philanthropist, social leader, patriot
DAR Mag. July 1921 p387,portrayal
Green—Pioneer (3) p500-502
Hanaford—Dau. p144-145
Logan—Part p262-263

Van Orroer, Beatrice (fl. 1950's)
Belg. printer
Club—Printing p10

Van Princes, Penelope.
See Stout, Penelope Van Princes

Van Rennes, Catherine (d. 1858)
Nether. composer
Elson—Woman's p217

Van Rensselaer, Euphemia (Sister Mary Dolores) (b. 1840)
Amer. nurse, nun
Dolan—Goodnow's p259-260,por.

Van Rensselaer, Margaret (m. 1783)
Amer. pioneer
Green—Pioneer (2) p93-95

Van Rensselaer, Mari Van Cortandt (1645-1689)
Amer. colonial administrator
Leonard—Amer. p123

Van Saher, Lilla.
See Saher, Lilla van

Van Sciver, Esther (1907-   )
Amer. author, song-writer
ASCAP p513

Van Stockum, Hilda (1908-   )
Nether. illustrator
Mahony—Illus. p367-368

Van Straaten, Florence Wilhelmina (1913-   )
Amer. physical chemist
Phelps—Men '58 (1) p250-251

Van Valkenburg, Catherine E. (b. 1880)
Amer. musician
Binheim—Women p127,por.

Van Vooren, Monique (1933-   )
Belg. actress
CR '59 p791,por.
CR '63 p632,por.

Van Vorst, Marie (1867-1936)
Amer. poet
Smith—Women's p205

Van Waters, Miriam (b. 1887/88)
Amer. penologist
Binheim—Women p91,por.
Cur. Biog. '63 p441-444,por.

Van Wyck, Margaret.
See Brett, Margaret

Van Zandt, Marie (1861-1919)
Amer. singer
Ewen—Ency. p527-528
Lahee—Famous p215-219
Logan—Part p767-768
McCoy—Portraits p217,por.
Wagner—Prima p79,250

Van Zandt-Vanzini, Jennie (fl. 1860's-1870's)
Amer. singer
McCoy—Portraits p217,por.

Vare, Glenna Collett (1940-   )
Amer. golfer
*Jacobs—Famous p87-96,por.

Varian, Dorothy (1895-   )
Amer. artist
Cur. Biog. '43 p782-783,por.

Varnay, Astrid (1918-   )
Swed.-Amer. singer
Cur. Biog. '51 p639-641,por.
Ewen—Ency. p528
McCoy—Portraits p217,por.
Matz—Opera p158-160
Peltz—Spot. p99
Rosenthal—Sopranos p98-100,por.

Varner, Margaret (1927-   )
Amer. tennis player
*Jacobs—Famous p97-103,por.

Varnhagen Von Ense, Rachel Levin (1771-1838)
Ger. salonist
Hargrave—Some p95-153,por.

Varnum, Molly (fl. 1770's)
Amer. Rev. war patriot
Green—Pioneer (3) p470,por.

Varsanof' Yeva, Vera Aleksandrovna
(1889-   )
Russ. geologist, social worker
U.S.—Biog. Soviet p99-100

Varsi, Diane (1937-   )
Amer. actress
CR '59 p791-792,por.

Varsova, Terezia (1857-1942)
Czech. author
Stiles—Postal p276

Vartenissian, Shakeh (fl. 1950's)
Armen. singer
Matz—Opera p48-50

Vashon, Susan Paul Smith (1838-1912)
Amer. teacher
Brown—Home p133-134,por.

Vashti, Queen (Biblical)
Buchanan—Women p67-69
Deen—All p298-300
Lewis—Portraits p130-131
Marble—Women, Bible p86-88
Mead—250 p158

Vassenko, Xenia (fl. 1940's)
Russ. singer, teacher
McCoy—Portraits p217,por.

Vaughan, Anne (1913-   )
Amer. illustrator
Mahony—Illus. p368

Vaughan, Anne, Lady.
See Bolton, Anne Vaughan, Duchess of

Vaudémont, Louise de.
See Louise de Vaudémont

Vaughan, Baroness de.
See Delacroix, Caroline, Baroness de
Vaughan

Vaughan, Hannah.
See Pritchard, Hannah Vaughan

Vaughan, Janet Maria, Dame (fl. 1940's)
Eng. educator, physician
Brittain—Women p57,101,145,207-208,
227

Vaughan, Kate (1852-1903)
Eng. actress
Furniss—Some p59-60,por.
Hammerton p1327,por.
Wyndham—Chorus p83-88,por.

Vaughan, Sarah Lois (1924-   )
Amer. singer
CR '63 p632-633,por.

Cur. Biog. '57 p562-564,por.
Stambler—Ency. p238

Vaupel, Ouise (fl. 1930's)
Amer. fashion designer, realtor,
singer, author
Women—Achieve. p160,por.

Vautrollier, Jeanne (fl. 1580's)
Eng. printer
Club—Printing p15

Vaz Ferreira, María Eugenia (b. 1875)
Urug. poet
Rosenbaum—Modern p49-54

Veitch, Marion Fairlie (1638-1693)
Scot. covenanter
Anderson—Ladies p159-180

Vejjabul, Pierra Hoon (1909-   )
Siam. pioneer physician
Lovejoy—Women p245-247,por.

Velasquez, Loretta Janeta (b. 1838)
Amer. W. pioneer, Civil war
diarist, spy
Brown—Gentle p14,129-130,223,por.
Jones—Heroines p290-298
Muir—Women p150
Simpkins—Women p81

Velez, Lupe (1910-1944)
Mex. actress
Brundidge—Twinkle p23-31,por.
Cur. Biog. '45 p643
Herman—How p49,por.
Stuart—Immort. p130-131,por.

Velhagen, Millicent H. (fl. 1920's)
Amer. politician
Binheim—Women p112,por.

Venable, Mary Elizabeth (d. 1926)
Amer. pianist, educator, author
McCoy—Portraits p217,por.

Venkova, Tota (1856-1921)
Bulg. pioneer physician
Schmidt—400 p66-67,por.

Venturini, Countess Mario (fl. 1910's)
Amer. artist
Logan—Part p769-770

Vera-Ellen (Vera-Ellen Rohe) (1926-   )
Amer. dancer
CR '59 p792-793,por.
Cur. Biog. '59 p463-465

Verbruggen, Susanna Percival (c. 1667-
1703)
Eng. actress
MacQueen—Pope p109-112,149
Wilson—All p177-181

Vercheres, Madeleine de (1678-1747)
Can. pioneer heroine
*Horowitz—Treas. p127-131
Schmidt—400 p73,por.
*Strong—Heroes p78-81
*Strong—Of p72-76

Verchinana, Nina (fl. 1930's)
Russ. dancer
Hammerton p1330

Verdon, Gwen (1925-   )
Amer. dancer, actress
CR '59 p793,por.
CR '63 p633,por.
Cur. Biog. '60 p446-448,por.
Phelps—Men '59 (2) p298-300
Time June 13,1955 p62,por.(Cover)

Verdugo, Elena (n.d.)
Amer. actress, TV personality
Blum—Television p97,por.
TV—Person. (2) p92-93,por.

Verelst, Marian (b. 1680)
Belg. painter
Waters—Women p339-340

Veres, Hermine Beniczky (1815-1895)
Hung. educator, feminist
Schmidt—400 p229-230,por.

Verginia (1) (fl.c. 449 B.C.)
Rom. maiden
Balsdon—Roman p28-29
Boccaccio—Conc. p128-130

Verginia (2) (fl.c. 308 B.C.)
Rom., wife of Lucius Volupinus
Boccaccio—Conc. p137-138

Verne, Adèla (1855/1877-1952)
Eng. pianist
Schonberg—Great p336

Verne, Mathilde (1865-1936)
Eng. pianist, teacher
McCoy—Portraits p218,por.
Schonberg—Great p336

Vernooy, Catharine (fl. 1770's)
Amer. Rev. war patriot
Ellet—Women (2) p207

Vernon, Elizabeth (fl. 1590's)
Eng., cousin of Earl of Essex
Brown—Dark p288-289,297-298,300,
305

Vernon, Mrs. Weston (b. 1873)
Amer. teacher
Binheim—Women p180,por.

Veronica (1) (Biblical)
Faulhaber—Women p184-188

Veronica (2) (Biblical)
Saint, daughter of Salome, the
dancer
Wescott—Calen. p19

Veronica (3) (1455-1497)
It. saint
Englebert—Lives p18
Wescott—Calen. p6
*Windham—Sixty p327-332

Veronica, M., Sister (fl. 1960's)
Amer. teacher, nun
*May—Women p245

Veronica Giuliani (1660-1727)
It. saint
Sharkey—Pop. p219

Verrett, Shirley (c. 1933-   )
Amer. singer
Cur. Biog. '67 p437-440,por.

Verrill, Virginia (fl. 1930's)
Amer. actress
Eichberg—Radio p139,por.

Verrue, Jeanne Baptiste (d'Albert de
Luynes), Countess de (1670-
1736)
Fr. art collector
Haggard—Remark. p220-221
Kavanagh—Woman (1) p60-61

Very, Lydia Louisa Ann (1823-1901)
Amer. poet
Hanaford—Dau. p256

Vesey, Elizabeth (c. 1715-1791)
Irish literary personality
Stenton—English p270-271,290

Vestal, Belle (Belle Siddons) (d.c. 1881)
Amer. W. personality
Parkhill—Wildest p3-12

Vestris, Lucia Elizabeth (Eliza Lucy)
(1797-1856)
Eng. singer, actress
Coad—Amer. p110,por.
Dorland—Sum p55
Furniss—Some p48-49,por.
Gilder—Enter. p258-291,por.
Hammerton p1335
Wyndham—Chorus p60

Vetsera, Marie Alexandrine, Baroness (1871-
1889)
Aust., mistress of Prince Rudolph
Davenport—Great p159-167
Kelen—Mist p298-311,por.

Vettori, Elda (fl. 1940's)
It. singer
McCoy—Portraits p218,por.

Veturia (fl. 5th cent., B.C.)
    Rom. heroine, mother of
      Coriolanus
    Boccaccio—Conc. p118-121
    Muir—Women p38-39

Viafora, Gina Ciaparelli (d. 1936)
    It. singer, teacher
    McCoy—Portraits p218,por.

Viani, Maria (1670-1711)
    It. painter
    Waters—Women p339

Viardot (Louise) Pauline Marie, Madame
      Heritte (1821-1910)
    Fr. composer
    Elson—Woman's p185

Viardot-Garcia, Marie Felicitas (fl. 1920's-
      1930's)
    Fr. singer, composer
    Elson—Woman's p184-185

Viardot-Garcia, Pauline (1821-1910)
    Sp.-Fr. singer
    Adelman—Famous p243
    Elson—Woman's p183-184
    Ewen—Ency. p532
    Lahee—Famous p53-57
    McCoy—Portraits p218,por.
    Pleasants—Great p216-223,por.
    Wagner—Prima p250

Viart, Guyonne (fl. 16th cent.)
    Amer. pioneer printer
    Club—Printing p10

Vibia Matidia, Sasina.
    See Matidia, Sabina

Vibia Perpetua (c. 181-203)
    Carth. martyr
    Deen—Great p3-7

Vicarino, Regina (fl. 1940's)
    Amer. singer
    McCoy—Portraits p218,por.

Vicario, Maria Leona (1787/98-1842)
    Mex. patriot, heroine
    Arsenius—Dict. p194,por.
    Phila.—Women unp.,por.
    Stiles—Postal p279

Vichy-Chamrond, Marie.
    See Deffand, Marie de Vichy-
      Chamrond, Marquise du

Victoire, Madame (1733-1799)
    Fr., Aunt of Louis XVI
    Haggard—Remark. p333-334

Victor, Metta Victoria Fuller (1831-1886)
    Amer. author
    Papashvily—All p144-145

Victor, Sally Josephs (1905-   )
    Amer. milliner, fashion designer
    CR '59 p793,por.
    CR '63 p634,por.
    Cur. Biog. '54 p623-625,por.
    Taves—Success. p133-140,por.

Victoria (1) (d.c. 250/253)
    Rom. saint
    Englebert—Lives p486

Victoria (2) (fl. A.D. 304)
    Sp. saint
    *Windham—Sicty p97-104

Victoria (3) (Vitruvia) (fl. 260's)
    Rom. empress, wife of Victorinus
    McCabe—Empr. p242-244
    Serviez—Roman (2) p331,338-340

Victoria (4) (1819-1902)
    Brit. queen
    Abbott—Notable p197-206,por.
    Adelman—Famous p229-233
    Armour—It p117-125
    Arsenius—Dict. p195,por.
    Benson—Queen p1-305,por.
    *Bolton—Famous Leaders p304-356,por.
    Boyd—Rulers p175-182,por.
    Canning—100 p94-99
    Carey—Twelve p15-77,por.
    Club—Printing p8
    *Coffman—Kings p123-128,por.
    Davenport—Great p168-176
    D'Humy—Women p179-226
    Dorland—Sum p17
    Dunaway—Treas. p104-114
    *Farjeon—Kings p78,por.
    *Farmer—Book p153-169
    Fitzhugh—Concise p706-708
    Hammerton p1336-1337,por.
    *Hayward—Book p211-228
    Hyde—Modern p307-317,por.
    *Jones—Modern p189-200,por.
    MacVeagh—Champlin p592-593
    Muir—Women p180-183
    Murrow—This (2) p207-209
    *Nisenson—Minute p147,por.
    *O'Clery—Queens p156-174
    Parton—Dau. p44-60,por.
    Phila.—Women, unp.,por.
    Reader's—Great p349-354,por.
    Sanders—Intimate p202-220,por.
    Schmidt—400 p151-152,por.
    Sewell—Brief p148-149
    *Steedman—When p296-302
    Stiles—Postal p279
    Thomas—Modern p200-209
    Thomas—Rulers p237-250,por.
    Thomas—Vital p461-463,por.
    Trease—Seven p179-212
    Wallace—Mothers p22-29

Victoria (5) (1840-1901)
    Eng. princess, Empress Frederick
      of Germany
    Benson—Queen (see index),por.
    Schmidt—400 p398

Victoria, Vesta (c. 1873-1951)
Eng. singer, actress
Caffin—Vaud. p161-164,por.
Felstead—Stars p12,36,79,82,por.

Victoria Alexandra Alice Mary (1897-   )
Eng. princess
Phila.—Women unp.,por.

Victoria Eugenia Julia (Ena) (b. 1887)
Sp. queen
Arsenius—Dict. p195,por.
Hammerton p1337
Phila.—Women, unp.,por.
Stiles—Postal p279

Victoria Kamanalu. See Kamanalu, Victoria

Videau, Mary. See Marion, Mary Videau

Viebig, Clara (1860-1952)
Ger. author
Heller—Studies p280-281

Vierira da Silva, Maria Helena (1908-   )
Port.-Fr. painter
Cur. Biog. '58 p450-452,por.
N.Y. Museum—New p105,por.

Vigée-Lebrun, Marie.
See Lebrun, Marie Louise Elizabeth
Vigée

Vigon, Ann (fl. 1930's)
Amer. retail buyer
Women—Achieve. p181,por.

Vigri, Caterina da (1413-   )
It. painter
Waters—Women p350-352

Vilhena, Filipa de.
See Philippa of Lancaster

Villa, Amelia Chopitea (d. 1942)
Bol. physician
Lovejoy—Women p272-273

Villani, Luisa (fl. 1900's)
Amer. singer
McCoy—Portraits p219,por.

Villiers, Barbara, Countess of Castlemaine
(1641-1709)
Eng., mistress of Chas. II
Hammerton p411,por.
MacQueen—Pope p61-62
Melville—Windsor p57-110,por.

Villiers, Vera de (fl. 1930's)
Amer. singer
McCoy—Portraits p219,por.

Vincens, Madame Charles.
See Arvede Barine, pseud.

Vincent, Abigail S. (fl. 1850's)
Amer. whaling voyager
Whiting—Whaling p43-45,136

Vincent, Ellen M. (fl. 1860's-1870's)
Amer. whaling voyager
Whiting—Whaling p194-195

Vincent, Lucy P. (1842-1933)
Amer. whaling voyager
Whiting—Whaling p159-177,199-208,
213-218,277-278

Vincent, Madame.
See Labille, Adelaide Vertus

Vincent, Mary Ann (1818-1887)
Amer. actress
Dorland—Sum p45,166

Vincent, Rebecca See Matthews, Rebecca

Vining, Elizabeth Janet Gray (1902-   )
Amer. author
Murrow—This (1) p183-184

Vining, Mary (d. 1821)
Amer., friend of Anthony Wayne
Burt—Phila. p308,310-311
DAR Mag. July 1921 p380,portrayal

Vining, Matilda Charlotte (Matilda Wood)
(1831/33-1915)
Eng.-Amer. actress
Coad—Amer. p226,por.
Hammerton p1417,por.

Vinsnes, Hanna (1789-1872)
Nor. author
Schmidt—400 p308,por.

Vintimille, Pauline Félicité de Nesle
(fl. 1720's-1730's)
Fr., mistress of King Louis XV
Haggard—Remark p263,265-272
Kavanagh—Woman (1) p108-109
Trowbridge—Seven p32-35,por.

Virgil, Antha Minerva (d. 1939)
Amer. composer, pianist, educator
McCoy—Portraits p219,por.

Virgin Mary.
See Mary (Biblical), mother of Jesus

Virginia, Sister (1575-1650)
It. nun
Ewart—World's p112-124

Viscario, Leona (d. 1842)
Mex. heroine, patriot
Schmidt—400 p291-292,por.

Vishnevskaya, Galina Pavlovna (1926-   )
Russ. singer
Cur. Biog. '66 p422-423,por.

Visscher, Anna (1584-1651)
    Nether. poet
    Waters—Women p352

Vitary, Laura (fl. 1930's)
    Amer. journalist
    Ross—Ladies p472,507-509

Vitruvia. See Victoria (3)

Vivian. See Bibiana

Vivian, Mrs. Thomas J. (fl. 1930's)
    Amer. club leader
    Women—Achieve. p204

Vix, Genevieve (1879-1939)
    Fr. singer
    McCoy—Portraits p220,por.

Vogl, Therese (b. 1845)
    Ger. singer
    Klein—Great p205-207

Voigt, Henriette (1808-1839)
    Ger. pianist, friend of Mendelssohn
        and Schumann
    McCoy—Portraits p220,por.

Vokersz, Veronica (fl. 1940's)
    Eng. aviatrix
    *May—Women p144

Vokes, Jessie.
    See Biddulph, Jessie Catherine Vokes

Vokes, Rosina (1858-1894)
    Eng. actress
    Coad—Amer. p245,por.
    Dorland—Sum p40,168

Vokes, Victoria (1853-1894)
    Eng. actress, singer
    Coad—Amer. p245,por.

Volkmar, Antonie Elizabeth Caecilia
        (b. 1827)
    Ger. painter
    Waters—Women p352

Volkonsky, Marie Raevsky (1806-1863)
    Russ. princess
    Schmidt—400 p344-345,por.

Volkova, Anna Aleksandrovna (1902-   )
    Russ. microbiologist
    U.S.—Biog., Soviet p215-216

Vollick, Eileen (fl. 1920's)
    Can. aviatrix
    *May—Women p100

Vollmar, Jocelyn (b. 1925)
    Amer. ballet dancer
    Atkinson—Dancers p163-165,por.

Vollmer, Luia (Louisa Smith) (1898-1955)
    Amer. playwright
    Mantle—Amer. p192-194
    Mantle—Contemp. p288-289

Volumnia (fl. 5th cent. B.C.)
    Rom. heroine, wife of Coriolanus
    Muir—Women p38-39

Von Arnim, Elizabeth.
    See Russell, Elizabeth Mary Arnette
        Beauchamp

Von Bronsart, Ingeborg.
    See Bronsart, Ingeborg von

Von Furstenberg, Betsy ("Madcap Betsy")
    Ger. actress
    CR '59 p796,por.
    CR '63 p635-636,por.

Von Hesse, Elizabeth F. (fl. 1930's)
    Amer. teacher, author, lecturer
    Women—Achieve. p50,por.

Von Kettler, Wanda (fl. 1930's)
    Can.-Amer. journalist
    Women—Achieve. p134,por.

Von Klenner, Katherine E. (fl. 1930's)
    Amer. author, translator
    Women—Achieve. p204

Vonnoh, Bessie Potter (1872-1955)
    Amer. sculptor
    Adelman—Famous p314
    Jackman—Amer. p433-434
    McSpadden—Sculptors p360-368
    Michigan—Biog. p321-322
    National—Contemp. p322
    Taft—Women, Mentor (172) #5 p5-6,
        por.
    Waters—Women p352-353

Von Tempski, Armine.
    See Tempski, Armine von

Vormelker, Rose Lillian (1895-   )
    Amer. librarian, editor, lecturer
    Bul. of Bibl. Sept.-Dec. '59 p217-219,
        por.

Vorse, Mary Heaton Marvin (b. 1881)
    Amer. author
    Bruère—Laugh. p79-80
    Overton—Women p318

Vos, Elizabeth (fl. 1830's)
    Amer. actress
    Coad—Amer. p158

Vose, Maria (b. 1824)
    Nether. painter
    Waters—Women p353

Votipka, Thelma (fl. 1920's)
Amer. singer
McCoy—Portraits p221,por.
Matz—Opera p161-164,por.
Peltz—Spot. p102,por.
Wagner—Prima p250

Voukotitch, Milena (1847-1923)
Monte. queen
Arsenius—Dict. p133,por.
Phila.—Women unp.,por.

Voyer, Jane (fl. 1740's)
Amer. colonial teacher
Dexter—Colonial p90-91

Vredenburgh, Dorothy McElroy (1916-   )
Amer. secretary, politician
Cur. Biog. '48 p649-651,por.

Vreeland, Diana (c. 1903-   )
Fr.-Amer., fashion editor
CR '63 p636,por.

Vreeland, Jeannette (d. 1939)
Amer. singer
McCoy—Portraits p221,por.

Vronsky, Vitya (1909-   )
Russ.-Amer. pianist
Ewen—Living p371-372

Vrooman, Angelica (fl. 1770's)
Amer. Rev. war heroine
Hanaford—Dau. p51

Vyroubova, Nina (1921-   )
Russ. ballet dancer
Haskell—Ballet p28-29,por.
Haskell—Vignet. p77-78
Swinson—Dancers p61-66,por.
Swinson—Great p29,por.

Vyvyan, Jennifer (1925-   )
Eng. singer
Brook—Singers p192-194,por.
Davidson—Treas. p332-334

W

Waddell, Charlotte Augusta Southwick
(fl. 1870's-1880's)
Amer. social leader
Hanaford—Dau. p147

Waddell, Helen (b. 1889)
Brit. author, scholar
Brittain—Women p175,252
Hammerton p1347

Wade, Jennie (fl. 1860's)
Amer. Civil war patriot
Brockett—Woman's p775-776
Hanaford—Dau. p211-212
Young—Women p285-286

Wade, Mary B. (fl. 1860's)
Amer. Civil war patriot
Brockett—Woman's p736,por.

Wadley, Sarah L. (fl. 1860's)
Amer. Civil war diarist
Jones—Heroines p195-197

Wadsworth, Elizabeth Bartlett (m. 1772)
Amer. patriot
Ellet—Women (2) p348-351

Wadsworth, Mary Ann (fl. 1930's)
Amer. aviatrix
Planck—Women p185

Waggoner, Electra (fl. 1930's)
Amer. sculptor
Women—Achieve. p84,por.

Wagner, Cosima (1837/40-1930)
Hung., 2nd wife of Richard
Wagner, music patron
Adelman—Famous p276
Downes—Olin p159-162
Elson—Woman's p88,por.
McCoy—Portraits p222,por.
Schmidt—400 p203-204,por.
Wagner—Prima p190-191,250

Wagner, Erica von (1890-   )
Aust. singer
Arsenius—Dict. p197,por.
Stiles—Postal p283

Wagner, Johanna (1826-1894)
Ger. singer
Ewen—Ency. p536

Wagner, Maria Dorothea Dietrich (1728-1792)
Ger. painter
Waters—Women p353 •

Wagner, Minna (Wilhelmina) Planer
(1809-1866)
Ger., 1st wife of Richard Wagner
Elson—Woman's p86-88

Wagstaff, Blanche Shoemaker (b. 1888)
Amer. poet, editor
Smith—Women's p211

Wailes, Marylin (fl. 1920's)
Eng. dancer, musician
Parkinson—Law p25-41,por.

Wainwright, Mehitable.
See Weare, Mehitable

Waite, Alice Vinton (1864-1943)
Amer. educator
Cur. Biog. '43 p799

Wake, Nancy (fl. 1940's)
Austral. spy
Hoehling—Women p141

Wakefield, Henrietta (fl. 1900's)
Amer. singer
Lahee—Grand p112

Wakefield, Priscilla (1751-1832)
Eng. author
Adelman—Famous p101

Walburga. See **Walpurgis**

Wald, Lillian D. (1866/67-1940)
Amer. social worker, nurse,
physician
Adelman—Famous p304
Bruce—Woman p338-340
Cur. Biog. '40 p833
Dolan—Goodnow's p271,273,314-315,
320,por.
*Dolin—World p162-172,por.
Douglas—Remember p147
*Forsee—Amer. p36-64
*Gersh—Women p49-74,por.
*Heath—Women (4) p22
*Horowitz—Treas. p100-108
Irwin—Angels p160
*Logie—Careers (2nd) p203-214
Lotz—Jews p10-20
New Yorker Dec. 14, 1929 p32-35,por.
(Profiles)
Pennock—Makers p56-57,por.
16 Amer. p61-64
*Strong—Of p284-292
Women—Achieve. p68,por.
*Wright—Great p162-176
*Yost—Nursing p22-41

Waldau, Margarethe (b. 1860)
Ger. painter
Waters—Women p394-395

Waldegrave, Frances Elizabeth Anne
Braham, Countess (1821-1879)
Eng. social leader
Wyndham—Chorus p53-54

Walden, Amelia Elizabeth (1909-   )
Amer. author
Cur. Biog. '56 p634-635,por.

Wales, Alexandra, Princess of (m. 1863)
Eng. daughter of Prince Christian
Carey—Twelve p171-195,por.

Wales, Marguerite (fl. 1920's-1930's)
Amer. public health nurse
Pennock—Makers p121,por.

Walewska, Marie, Countess (1787-1817)
Pol., mistress of Napoleon
Coryn—Enchant. p155-176
Orr—Famous Affin. II p111-132
Orr—Famous p231-247

Walford, Lucy Bethia Colquhoun (1845-
1915)
Scot. novelist
Black—Notable p26-36

Walker, Adeline (d. 1865)
Amer. Civil war nurse
Brockett—Woman's p457-458

Walker, Alice Brenard Ewing (fl. 1900's)
Amer. club leader
Logan—Part p462

Walker, Bertha (Bee) (1908-   )
Amer. composer
ASCAP p518

Walker, Edythe (1870-1950)
Amer. singer
Lahee—Grand p24-25,223
McCoy—Portraits p222,por.

Walker, Ethel, Dame (1867-1951)
Scot. painter
Hammerton p1452

Walker, Gertrude A. (d. 1928)
Amer. physician
Lovejoy—Women Phys. p38-41,45-46

Walker, Helen M. (fl. 1930's)
Amer. mathematician
Women—Achieve. p111,por.

Walker, Jane (fl. 1940's)
Eng. governess
Howe—Galaxy p193

Walker, Jean (fl. 1930's)
Amer. musician, poet
Women—Achieve. p69,por.

Walker, Mrs. John (fl. 1770's)
Amer. Rev. war patriot
Ellet—Women (2) p339

Walker, Maggie Lena (1867-1934)
Amer. banker, insurance agent
Adams—Great p69,por.
Daniel—Women p28-52,por.
Longwell—Amer. p185-205
Ovington—Por. p127-134
Robinson—Hist. p139,por.

Walker, Margaret Abigail (1915-   )
Amer. author, poet
Cur. Biog. '43 p799-801,por.
*Rollins—Famous p80-86,por.

Walker, Marietta Hodges (1834-1930)
Amer. religious worker
Phillips—33 p33-38

Walker, Mary Edwards (1832-1919)
Amer. physician surgeon, feminist,
inventor
Adelman—Famous p204-205
Douglas—Remember p144-145
Fairfax—Ladies p239
Logan—Part p579

(Continued)

Walker, Mary Edwards—*Continued*

   Mead—Medical p66
   Riegel—Amer. p127
   *Stevens—Women p99-101
   Woodward—Bold p281-298
   Young—Women p319-320,380

Walker, Mary Richardson (1811-1897)
   Amer. W. pioneer
   Drury—First, v.2 p21-44,71-118,por.
   *Johnson—Some p37-46,por.
   *Ross—Heroines p93-125
   Ross—Westward p53-76

Walker, Mildred (1905-   )
   Amer. author
   Cur. Biog. '47 p659-660,por.
   Warfel—Amer. p439-440,por.

Walker, Nancy (1922-   )
   Amer. actress
   CR '59 p799-800,por.
   CR '63 p638,por.
   Cur. Biog. '65 p441-443,por.

Walker, Nellie Verne (b. 1874)
   Amer. sculptor
   Michigan—Biog. p325
   National—Contemp. p323
   Taft—Women, Mentor (172) #2 p6-8

Walker, Norma Ford (1893-1968)
   Can. biologist, educator
   Cur. Biog. '57 p574-575,por.
   Cur. Biog. '68 p463

Walker, Rachel (fl. 1910's)
   Amer. singer
   Cuney-Hare—Negro p233-234

Walker, Mrs. Robert (d. 1695)
   Amer. colonial teacher
   Dexter—Colonial p85-86

Walker, Sarah Breedlove ("Madame" C. J.)
   (1869-1919)
   Amer. cosmetician, manufacturer
   Adams—Great p68,por.
   Brown—Home. p220-221,por.
   *Cherry—Portraits p21-23
   Robinson—Hist. p138,por.

Walker, Sarah L.
   See Cahier, Sarah Layton-Walker

Walker, Susan Hunter (m. 1904)
   Scot.-Amer. editor, author
   Logan—Part p865-866

Walker, Waurine Elizabeth (1911-   )
   Amer. teacher, organization official
   Cur. Biog. '55 p627-629,por.

Walker, "Widow" (fl. 1680's)
   Amer. colonial teacher
   Dexter—Colonial p79-80

Walkinshaw, Clementina (c. 1726-1802)
   Eng., mistress of Charles Edward
   Hammerton p1353

Wall, Florence Emeline (fl. 1920's-1930's)
   Amer. industrial chemist,
     cosmetician
   Women—Achieve. p138,por.

Wall, Mildred Ivy (fl. 1930's)
   Eng. fashion designer
   Women—Achieve. p179,por.

Wallace, Emma R. (d. 1911)
   Amer. club leader
   Logan—Part p350-351

Wallace, Grace (fl. 1910's)
   Amer. actress, ventriloquist
   Caffin—Vaud. p116-117

Wallace, Lila Bell Acheson (1889-   )
   Can.-Amer. editor, publisher
   Cur. Biog. '56 p637-640,por.
   Forsee—My p109-136
   Time Dec. 10 '51 p64,por.(Cover)

Wallace, Lurleen Burns (1926-1968)
   Amer. governor, politician
   Cur. Biog. '67 p447-450,por.
   Cur. Biog. '68 p463

Wallace, Mary. See Dickinson, Velvalee.

Wallace, Mary Ella (1855-1938)
   Amer. author
   Overton—Women p319-320

Wallace, Mildred White (b. 1889)
   Amer. composer, author, singer,
     publisher
   ASCAP p519

Wallace, Nellie (1882-1948)
   Brit. actress
   Hammerton p1354

Wallace, Susan Arnold (1830-1907)
   Amer. philanthropist, social leader,
     author
   Logan—Part p851

Wallace, Susan Binney (fl. 1810's-1830's)
   Amer., mother of Horace Binney
     Wallace
   Logan—Part p214

Wallace, Zerelda Gray (b. 1817)
   Amer. social reformer, feminist
   Logan—Part p575-576

Wallin, Mathilda K. (1858-1955)
   Swed.-Amer. physician
   Lovejoy—Women Phys. p42,53,por.

Walling, Harriet (fl. 1680's)
Amer. Puritan
Woodward—Way p47-66

Walling, Mary Cole (b. 1838)
Amer. lecturer, patriot
Logan—Part p376-377

Wallis, Mary D. (fl. 1870's)
Amer. traveler, author
Hanaford—Dau. p737

Waln, Nora (1895-   )
Amer. author
Cur. Biog. '40 p839-840,por.
Cur. Biog. '64 p457

Walpurgis (Walburga, Walpurga) (c.710-
777/779)
Eng. saint
Hammerton p1358

Walsh, Betty (fl. 1930's)
Amer. meteorologist
Planck—Women p224

Walsh, Blanche (1873-1915)
Amer. actress
Caffin—Vaud. p127-128
Strang—Actresses p72-81,por.

Walsh, Honor (fl. 1910's)
Amer. editor, author
Logan—Part p823

Walsh, Kate.
See Smith, Kate Walsh Fitzroy,
Countess Euston

Walsh, Mrs. Richard John.
See Buck, Pearl

Walsh, Stella (c. 1913-   )
Pol.-Amer. field and track athlete
Davis—100 p134,por.

Walter, Lucy (Mrs. Barlow)
(c. 1630-1658)
Eng., mistress of Charles II
Hammerton p1359,por.

Walter, Martha (fl. 1930's)
Amer. painter
Bryant—Amer. p266-267
Jackman—Amer. p245-246
Michigan—Biog. p325-326
Women—Achieve. p147,por.

Walter, Mary Jane (fl. 1910's)
Amer. social reformer, evangelist
Logan—Part p670

Walter, Rose (fl. 1940's)
Ger. singer
McCoy—Portraits p223,por.

Walton, Mrs. Austin.
See Darrach, Mrs. Marshall

Walton, Cecile (1891-   )
Scot. painter, illustrator, sculptor
Mahony—Illus. p368

Walton, Dorothy C. (d. 1800's)
Amer. patriot
Dar Mag July 1921 p375,380,portrayal
Green—Pioneer (3) p278-279

Walton, Mary. See Morris, Mary Walton

Waltrude (fl. 7th cent.)
Fr. saint
Blunt—Great p150

Walworth, Dorothy (Dorothy Crowell)
(1900-   )
Amer. novelist
Warfel—Amer. p441,por.

Walworth, Ellen Hardin (1832-1915)
Amer. patriot, foundress, club
leader, author
Green—Pioneer (3) p405-406
Logan—Part p441

Walworth, Ellen Hardin (the younger)
(b. 1858)
Amer. artist
Logan—Part p752

Walworth, Mrs. John (fl. 1800's)
Amer. W. pioneer
Ellet—Pioneer p271-272

Wambaugh, Sarah (1882-1955)
Amer. author, lecturer, consultant
Cur. Biog. '46 p619-621,por.
Cur. Biog. '56 p641

Wamsley, Lillian Barlow (fl. 1930's)
Amer. artist, ceramicist
Women—Achieve. p165,por.

Wanamaker, Pearl Aderson (1899-   )
Amer. educator
Cur. Biog. '46 p621-622,por.

Wanda, Queen (fl. 730's)
Pol. heroine, patriot
Schmidt—400 p315-316,por.

Wandling, Arlita R. (fl. 1930's)
Amer. child research worker
Women—Achieve. p111,por.

Wandru (d. 688)
Belg. saint
Englebert—Lives p138-139

Wang Ch'Iang (fl. 33 B.C.)
Chin. concubine
Llewellyn—China's p159-164

Ward, Barbara Mary (1914-   )
    Eng. editor, journalist
    Cur. Biog. '50 p593-595,por.

Ward, Dorothy (1890-   )
    Eng. actress
    Hammerton p1361

Ward, Miss E. (fl. 1900's)
    Amer. artist, sculptor
    Waters—Women p353

Ward, Elizabeth Stuart Phelps (1844-1911)
    Amer. philanthropist, author
    Adelman—Famous p244
    Dorland—Sum p38,196
    Hammerton p1361
    Harkins—Famous p11-26,por.
    Harkins—Little p11-26,por.
    Logan—Part p800

Ward, Fannie (1872-1952)
    Amer. actress
    Hammerton p1361

Ward, Geneviève (1837-1922)
    Eng. actress
    Furniss—Some p47-48,por.
    Hammerton p1361,por.
    Logan—Part p783-784

Ward, Henrietta Mary Ada (1832-1924)
    Eng. painter
    Waters—Women p353-355

Ward, Lydìa Avery Coonley (1845-1924)
    Amer. poet, philanthropist
    Addams—Excellent p113-120

Ward, Maisie (1889-   )
    Eng.-Amer. publisher, lecturer,
       author
    Cur. Biog. '66 p423-426,por.

Ward, Mary Alden (b. 1853)
    Amer. editor, club leader
    Logan—Part p849

Ward, Mary Augusta Arnold (Mrs.
       Humphrey Ward) (1851-1920)
    Eng. novelist
    Adelman—Famous p260-261
    Brittain—Women (see index)
    Furniss—Some p20-22,por.
    Hammerton p1361-1362,por.
    *MacVeagh—Champlin p599

Ward, Mary Jane (1905-   )
    Amer. novelist
    Cur. Biog. '46 p622-624,por.
    Warfel—Amer. p441-442,por.

Ward, Myrle Olive (fl. 1920's-1950's)
    Amer. missionary
    They—Went p92-93

Ward, Sallie (S.W.I.H.A. Downs)
    Amer. social leader
    Hanaford—Dau. p143-144
    Logan—Part p262

Ward, Sarah. See Knight, Sarah Kemble

Ward, Sarah Trowbridge (c. 1724-1788)
    Amer. pioneer, wife of Artemas
       Ward
    Green—Pioneer (2) p184-186

Warde, Beatrice Lamberton (1900-   )
    Brit. printer, typographer
    Club—Printing p16

Warde, Mary Xavier, Mother (1810-1884)
    Irish foundress
    Code—Great p358-378

Wardel, Elizabeth (fl. 1660's)
    Amer. religious worker
    Jones—Quaker p372

Wardel, Lydia (fl. 1660's)
    Amer. religious worker
    Jones—Quakers p372,379

Wardlaw, Elizabeth, Lady (1677-1727)
    Scot. poet
    Hammerton p1362

Ware, Harriet (1877-1962)
    Amer. composer, pianist
    ASCAP p521-522
    Elson—Woman's p253-254
    Hipsher—Amer. p360-361
    Howard—Our p567
    McCoy—Portraits p223,por.

Ware, Helen (fl. 1910's)
    Amer. actress
    Izard—Heroines p365

Ware, Helen (fl. 1910's)
    Amer. composer, violinist
    McCoy—Portraits p223,por.

Ware, Katharine A. Rhodes (1797-1843)
    Amer. poet
    Hanaford—Dau. p263

Ware, Mary Pickard (fl. 1810's)
    Amer. merchant, importer
    Dexter—Career p155

Warens, Louise Francoise Elenore, Baroness
       de (1699/1700-1762)
    Fr., friend of Jean Rousseau
    Blei—Fasc. p133-135,por.

Warfield, Sandra (n.d.)
    Amer. singer
    Matz—Opera p278-281,por.

Waring, Grace. See Martin, Grace

Waring, Mary D. (fl. 1860's)
Amer. Civil war diarist
Jones—Heroines p385-389

Warne, Margaret Vliet (fl. 1770's)
Amer. Rev. war patriot, physician
Green—Pioneer (3) p457

Warner, Anna. See Bailey, Anna Warner

Warner, Anna Bartlett (Amy Lothrop,
pseud.) (1820/27-1915)
Amer. novelist
Adelman—Famous p178
Dorland—Sum p43,83,185,189
Hollingsworth—Her p91-101
Papashvily—All p4,11-13,169-170
Pattee—Fem. p54-58,por.

Warner, Anne Richmond (Anne Warner
French) (1869-1913)
Amer. author
Dorland—Sum p43

Warner, Estella Ford (1891-   )
Amer. pioneer public health
surgeon
Lovejoy—Women p381

Warner, Harriet E. (fl. 1870's-1880's)
Amer. architect
Hanaford—Dau. p315-316

Warner, Jemima (fl. 1770's)
Amer. Rev. war soldier
Fowler—Woman p396-401

Warner, Marie Pichel (fl. 1930's)
Amer. gynecologist
Women—Achieve. p129,por.

Warner, Mildred.
See Washington, Mildred Warner

Warner, Susan Bogert (Elizabeth Wetherell,
pseud.) (1819-1885)
Amer. novelist
Adelman—Famous p177-178
Dorland—Sum p43,194-195
Hammerton p1363
Papashvily—All p1-14,95,106,169-170
Pattee—Fem. p54-58,por.

Warner, Susannah.
See Tufts, Susannah Warner

Warner, Sylvia Townsend (1893-   )
Eng. author
Millett—Brit. p495-496

Warnick, Polly (Mary D.) (m. 1830)
Amer., friend of Abraham Lincoln
Barton—Women p157-166

Warnock, Susan Mercer (fl. 1860's)
Amer. Civil war nurse
Logan—Part p373

Warr, Emma Louise (c. 1847-1937)
Amer. nurse
Pennock—Makers p76-77,por.

Warren, Althea Hester (1886-1958)
Amer. librarian, lecturer
Bul. of Bibl. May-August '42 p153-154,
por.
Cur. Biog. '42 p868-869,por.
Cur. Biog. '60 p448

Warren, Anne Wignell. See Merry, Anne

Warren, Constance (b. 1880)
Amer. educator
Murrow—This (1) p185-186
Women—Achieve. p204

Warren, Elinor Remick (1905-   )
Amer. composer, pianist
ASCAP p523
McCoy—Portraits p223,por.

Warren, Elizabeth (b. 1583-1673)
Amer. Pilgrim
Bell—Women p104-105
Marble—Women p93-94

Warren, Elizabeth Hooton (1598-1672)
Eng. clergyman
Culver—Women p145-146
Deen—Great p355-357
Green—Pioneer (2) p196-197
Jones—Quakers p105-107,111-112

Warren, Mrs. Fiske (fl. 1920's-1940's)
Amer. social leader
Amory—Proper p29,124-125,261

Warren, Lavinia (Mercy Lavinia Warren
Bumpus; Mrs. Tom Thumb)
(1841-1919)
Amer. circus midget
*Woodward—Bold p299-306

Warren, Mercy Otis (1728-1814)
Amer. patriot, author, poet, historian
Adelman—Famous p85
Beard—Amer. p56-59,77
Benson—Women p171,256-257
Coad—Amer. p23,por.
Dar Mag. July 1921 p380,portrayal
Dexter—Career p90-91
Dexter—Colonial p140,por.
Dorland—Sum p40,81,175
Ellet—Women (1) p91-126,por.
Farmer—What p38
Green—Pioneer (2) p7-8,19-20,25-26,
168-170
Green—Pioneer (3) p328-338,por.
Hanaford—Dau. p38-39,137-138
Leonard—Amer. p104,123-124
Logan—Part p124-128
Rourke—Roots p111-114
Schmidt—400 p5-6,por.
Whitton—These p8-9

Warrick, Mete Vaux.
　　See **Fuller, Meta Warrick**

Warth, Sally Fleehart (fl. 1790's)
　　Amer. W. pioneer
　　Ellet—Pioneer p191

Warwick, Anne, Countess of (fl.c. 1600's)
　　Eng. lady-in-waiting
　　Stenton—English p135-136

Warwick, Frances Evelyn Maynard,
　　　　Countess of (1861-1938)
　　Brit. humanitarian
　　Adelman—Famous p264
　　Hammerton p1364,por.

Waser, Anna (1679-1713)
　　Swiss painter
　　Schmidt—400 p378-379,por.

Washburn, Estella Hill (m. 1885)
　　Amer. W. pioneer
　　Sargent—Pioneers p61,por.

Washburn, Florinda (fl. 1850's)
　　Amer. pioneer, milliner, business
　　　　woman
　　Whitton—These p245-246

Washburn, Jean Linsey Bruce (1838-1904)
　　Scot.-Amer. poet
　　Sargent—Pioneers p31-32,59-61

Washington, Dinah (1924-1963)
　　Amer. singer
　　CR '63 p642,por.

Washington, Elizabeth ("Betty").
　　See **Lewis, Elizabeth ("Betty")
　　Washington**

Washington, Eugenia (d. 1900)
　　Amer. patriot, foundress, club
　　　　leader
　　Green—Pioneer (3) p405-406
　　Logan—Part p453

Washington, Frances. See **Ball, Frances**

Washington, Jane Elliott (d. 1830)
　　Amer. Rev. war patriot
　　Ellet—Women (2) p102-104

Washington, Lucy Payne (d.c. 1836)
　　Amer., sister of Dolly Madison
　　Smith—White p13-17,por.

Washington, Margaret Murray (1865-1925)
　　Amer. author, wife of Booker T.
　　　　Washington
　　Brown—Home. p225-230,por.
　　Schmidt—400 p27,por.

Washington, Martha Dandridge Custis
　　　　(1732-1802)
　　Amer., wife of George Washington
　　Abbott—Notable p426-433,por.
　　Adelman—Famous p85-86
　　Arsenius—Dict. p199,por.
　　Brooks—Colonial p133-167
　　Bruce—Woman p97-101,por.
　　Burt—Phila. p299-301
　*Cather—Girlhood p311-336
　　DAR Mag. July 1921 p370,portrayal
　　Donovan—Women p4,7,94,105-110,
　　　　115-129,131-149,330-332
　　Ellet—Women (2) p9-20,por.
　　Farmer—What p62-65,por.
　　Gerlinger—Mis. p3-7,por.
　　Green—Pioneer (1) por., front.
　　Green—Pioneer (2) p10,13,28,109,
　　　　117,119-120,128,150
　　Green—Pioneer (3) p165-166,238,337
　　Hanaford—Dau. p66-72,por.
　*Humphrey—Women p55-71
　　Leonard—Amer. p124
　　Logan—Ladies p11-14
　　Logan—Part p207-213
　*McConnell—Our p1-15,por.
　　Mears—Woman p3-28,por.
　　Minnigerode—Some p1-46,por.
　　Parton—Dau. p256-261
　　Parton—Noted p256-261
　　Phila.—Women, unp.,por.
　　Prindiville—First p3-13
　*Ross—Know p5,por.
　　Sale—Old p64-74,por.
　　Smith—Romances p24-25,por.
　*Stevens—Women p43-49,por.
　　Stiles—Postal p284
　　Truett—First p8,por.
　　Whitton—First p3-19,por.
　　Whitton—These p6-8

Washington, Mary Ball (1708-1789)
　　Amer., mother of George
　　　　Washington
　　Bartlett—Mothers p34-38
　*Chandler—Famous p41-59
　　DAR Mag. July 1921 p370,portrayal
　　Donovan—Women p4-11
　　Ellet—Women (1) p33-45,por.
　　Farmer—What p55,60-61
　　Green—Pioneer (1) p455-485,por.
　　Hampton—Our p3-14
　　Hanaford—Dau. p41-44,por.
　*Humphrey—Marys p40-65
　　Leonard—Amer. p124
　　Logan—Part p205-207
　　Love—Famous p18
　　Muir—Women p143-144
　　Peattie—Journey p48-62
　　Peyton—Mothers p36-42
　　Sale—Old p41-55,por.
　　Schmidt—400 p3-4,por.
　　Spruill—Women's p60-61
　　Wallace—Mothers p15-21
　　Whitton—These p3-6

Washington, Mildred
See Willis, Mildred Washington

Washington, Mildred Warner (fl. 1690's-
1730's)
Amer., grandmother of George
Washington
Green—Pioneer (2) p76,81

Washington, Mrs. (fl. 1840's-1880's)
Amer., mother of Booker T.
Washington
Wallace—Mothers p95-100

Washington, Rachel M. (fl. 1870's)
Amer. music teacher, pianist
Cuney-Hare—Negro p213

Wasilewska, Wanda (1905-1964)
Pol.-Russ. author, journalist,
politician
Cur. Biog. '44 p719-722,por.
Cur. Biog. '64 p457

Wason, Betty (1912-   )
Amer. journalist, author
Cur. Biog. '43 p806-808,por.

Wasser, Anna (1676/79-1713)
Swiss painter
Waters—Women p355-356

Watanna, Onoto.
See Reeve, Winnifred Eaton Babcock

Waterbury, Kate E. (fl. 1860's)
Amer. Civil war patriot
Brockett—Woman's p651,658

Waterhouse, Helen (fl. 1930's)
Amer. journalist, aviation editor
Planck—Women p237-239

Waterhouse, Jessie (fl. 1910's)
Amer. pharmacist
Logan—Part p907

Waters, Clara Erskine Clement (Clara
Clement) (1834-1916)
Amer. author
Hanaford—Dau. p292

Waters, Crystal (fl. 1920's)
Amer. singer
McCoy—Portraits p224,por.

Waters, Ethel (1900-   )
Amer. singer, actress
Adams—Great p136,por.
Blum—Great p126,por.
*Cherry—Portraits p135-139
CR '59 p809,por.
CR '63 p642-643,por.
Cur. Biog. '41 p899-901,por.
Cur. Biog. '51 p644-647,por.
*Hughes—First p45,por.
*Hughes—Music p109-114,por.

Jazz—Panorama p83-90
Robinson—Hist. p256-257,por.

Waters, Lydia (fl. 1850's)
Amer. W. pioneer
Brown—Gentle p109,111,114,144

Waters, Marianne (1906-   )
Amer. playwright
Mantle—Contemp. p327

Waters, Sadie P. (1869-1900)
Amer. painter
Waters—Women p356-358

Watkins, Carolyn Ellen (fl. 1930's-1950's)
Amer. missionary
They—Went p137-138

Watkins, Frances.
See Harper, Frances Allen Watkins

Watkins, Maurine Dallas (1900-   )
Amer. playwright
Mantle—Amer. p201-204
Mantle—Contemp. p299

Watkins, Shirley (1897-   )
Amer. author)
Cur. Biog. '58 p455-456,por.

Watkins, Susan (b. 1875)
Amer. painter
Michigan—Biog. p328

Watson, Ella ("Cattle Kate", Kate Maxwell)
(c. 1862-1889)
Amer. W. pioneer
Aikman—Calamity p128-157

Watson, Evelyn Mabel Palmer (b. 1886)
Amer. poet
Dreer—Amer. p78

Watson, Glenda Sawyer (fl. 1940's-1950's)
Amer. missionary
They—Went p134-135

Watson, Jennie (fl. 1870's-1880's)
Amer. botanist
Hanaford—Dau. p289

Watson, Louise (fl. 1930's)
Amer. business woman
Women—Achieve. p188,por.

Watson, Lucile (1879-1962)
Amer. actress
Cur. Biog. '53 p654-647,por.
Cur. Biog. '62 p450

Watson, Mabel Madison (fl. 1940's)
Amer. composer, pianist, violin
teacher
McCoy—Portraits p224,por.

Watson, Virginia Cruse (fl. 1930's)
Amer. author
Women—Achieve. p204

Watt, Agnes (c. 1846-1894)
Scot. pioneer missionary
*Matthews—Daunt. p124-148

Watteville, Benigna Zinzendorf (1725-1789)
Amer. colonial educator
Leonard—Amer. p124

Wattle, Mary (fl. 1870's)
Amer. pioneer lawyer
Hanaford—Dau. p668

Watts, Hannah. See Weston, Hannah Watts

Watts, Hazel Biven (fl. 1920's)
Amer. missionary
They—Went p69-70

Watts, Helen (1927-   )
Eng. singer
Brook—Singers p198-200,por.

Watts, Mary (fl. 1920's)
Amer. journalist
Ross—Ladies p431-432

Watts, Mary Stanbery (1868-1958)
Amer. novelist
Maurice—Makers p8,por.
Overton—Women p321-323

Watts, Mary Stirling (fl. 1770's)
Amer. patriot
Green—Pioneer (2) p154-156,158

Waugh, Dorothy (fl. 1930's-1940's)
Amer. illustrator, author
Jones—Quakers p36-39,46-47,51,73,
108,220
Mahony—Illus. p369

Way, Amanda M. (b. 1829)
Amer. clergyman, nurse, social
reformer, feminist
Hanaford—Dau. p475-476
Irwin—Angels p164

Wayles, Martha.
See Jefferson, Martha Wayles

Wayman, Agnes R. (fl. 1930's)
Amer. author
Women—Achieve. p204

Wayne, Mabel (1898/1904-   )
Amer. composer, pianist, song-
writer
ASCAP p525-526
Gammond—Dict. p241
Howard—Our p673

Wayne, "Pinky" (fl. 1920's-1930's)
Amer. journalist
Ross—Ladies p562,564-566

Wayne, "Polly" (Mary) Penrose (d. 1793)
Amer. pioneer, wife of Anthony
Wayne
Green—Pioneer (2) p172-178

Weafer, Elizabeth (1924-   )
Amer. organization official
Cur. Biog. '58 p459-460,por.

Weamys, Anne (fl. 1650's)
Eng. novelist
MacCarthy—Women p64-68,72

Weaver, Affie (1855-1940)
Amer. actress
Cur. Biog. '41 p903

Weaver, Anna K. (fl. 1870's)
Amer. business woman
Hanaford—Dau. p611

Weaver, Elizabeth (fl. 1660's)
Eng. actress
MacQueen—Pope p64-65

Weaver, Maurine Barr (fl. 1920's-1930's)
Amer. missionary
They—Went p86-87

Webb, Aileen Osborn (1892-   )
Amer. organization official
Cur. Biog. '58 p460-462,por.

Webb, Beatrice Potter (1862-1948)
Eng. author, wife of Sidney Webb
Bottrall—Pers. p84-85,233
Cole—Women p261-289,por.
Cur. Biog. '43 p808

Webb, Jane (d. 1740)
Eng. accused criminal
Jenkins—Six p137-176

Webb, Mary (1881-1927)
Scot. religious leader
Irwin—Angels p51-52
Lawrence—School p331-338

Webb, Mary Gladys Meredith (1881-1927)
Eng. novelist
Hammerton p1371,por.
Millett—Brit. p500-501

Webber, Irma Eleanor Schmidt (1904-   )
Amer. illustrator
Mahony—Illus. p369

Webber, Mary T. (fl. 1860's)
Amer. poet
Hanaford—Dau. p254-255

Weber, Caroline Brandt von (fl. 1790's-
1810's)
    Aust. singer
    Elson—Woman's p78-80

Webling, Peggy (fl. 1900's-1920's)
    Eng. novelist
    Hammerton p1372

Webster, Abigail Eastman (1737-1816)
    Amer. Rev. war patriot
    Green—Pioneer (3) p383-385
    Logan—Part p254
    Peyton—Mothers p18-23

Webster, Alice Jean (1876-1916)
    Amer. author
    Hammerton p1372

Webster, Augusta (fl. 1950's)
    Amer. physician, educator
    Lovejoy—Women p384,por.

Webster, (Julia) Augusta Davies (1837-
1894)
    Eng. poet, playwright
    Dorland—Sum p57,180
    Hammerton p1372

Webster, Barbara (1900-   )
    Amer. novelist
    Warfel—Amer. p445,por.

Webster, Caroline Leroy (fl. 1800's-1830's)
    Amer., wife of Daniel Webster
    Logan—Part p256

Webster, Elizabeth Vassall.
    See Holland, Elizabeth Vassal Webster

Webster, Harriet (m. 1862)
    Eng. actress
    Wyndham—Chorus p59

Webster, Margaret (1905-   )
    Amer. actress, theatrical director
    CR '59 p814,por.
    CR '63 p646,por.
    Cur. Biog. '40 p847-848,por.
    Cur. Biog. '50 p604-606,por.
    New Yorker May 20, 1944 p32,por.
    (Profiles)

Webster, Mary C. (fl. 1870's)
    Amer. clergyman, author
    Hanaford—Dau. p452

Wedgwood, (Cicely) Veronica (1910-   )
    Brit. historian, editor
    Brittain—Women p177,253
    Cur. Biog. '57 p581-582,por.

Weed, Marion (1870-1947)
    Amer. singer
    Lahee—Grand p26

Weeden, Elizabeth (fl. 1680's)
    Amer. colonial midwife
    Dexter—Colonial p63-64

Weekes, Marie (fl. 1920's)
    Amer. publisher, journalist
    Ross—Ladies p463-464

Weeks, Helen Weeks (fl. 1940's-1950's)
    Amer. missionary
    They—Went p115-116

Weeks-Shaw, Clara (fl. 1880's)
    Amer. nurse, author
    Dolan—Goodnow's p260,por.

Weeton, Ellen (b. 1776)
    Eng. governess
    Howe—Galaxy p83-92

Wegmann, Bertha (b. 1847)
    Swiss painter
    Waters—Woman p358-359

Weick, Louise (fl. 1930's)
    Amer. journalist
    Ross—Ladies p456-457

Weidt, Luci, Baroness von Urmenyi (1880-
1940)
    Aust. singer
    Lahee—Grand p329-330

Wei Fu-Jên (c272-350 A.D.)
    Chin. calligraphist
    Ayscough—Chinese p198-202

Weil, Lisl (1910-   )
    Aust.-Amer. artist, author
    Cur. Biog. '58 p462-463,por.

Weil, Simone (fl. 1930's-1940's)
    Fr. novelist
    Peyre—French p283-285

Weill, Blanche C. (fl. 1930's)
    Amer. psychologist
    Women—Achieve. p137,por.

Weiman, Rita (1889-1954)
    Amer. author, playwright
    Mantle—Amer. p311
    Mantle—Contemp. p327

Weimar, Anna Amalia, Duchess of (1739-
1807)
    Ger. wife of Duke Ernst Constantin
    Schmidt—400 p193-194,por.

Weingartner, Lucille.
    See Marcel, Lucille Wasself

Weis, Jessica McCullough (1901-1963)
    Amer. Congresswoman
    Cur. Biog. '59 p476-478,por.
    Cur. Biog. '63 p460
    U.S.—Women (87th) p41,por.

Weis, Rosario (fl. 1820's-1840's)
    Sp. painter
    Waters—Women p359

Weisner, Dorothy E. (fl. 1930's)
    Amer. statistician, social worker
    Women—Achieve. p205

Weiss, Soma (1899-1942)
    Amer. physician
    Cur. Biog. '42 p877

Weitbrecht, Oda (fl. 1910's)
    Ger. printer
    Club—Printing p16

Weitz, Alice C. (fl. 1920's)
    Amer. poet
    Smith—Women's p215

Weizmann, Vera Chatzmann (c. 1879-1966)
    Israeli, wife of Chaim Weizmann
    Lovejoy—Women p219,por.

Welby, Amelia Ball Coppuck ("Amelia")
        (1821-1852)
    Amer. poet
    Hanaford—Dau. p269
    Whitton—These p169

Welch, Ann (fl. 1930's)
    Eng. glider pilot
    *May—Women p221-222

Welch, Barbara (fl. 1940's)
    Amer. model
    Zolotow—Never p135-151

Welch, Mrs. E. Sohier (fl. 1930's)
    Amer. hostess
    Amory—Proper p270-272

Welch, Mabel R. (1871-1959)
    Amer. painter
    Michigan—Biog. p333-334

Welch, Nancy (fl. 18th-19th cent.)
    Amer. religious worker
    Hanaford—Dau. p635

Weld, Theresa (Theresa Blanchard) (1893-)
    Amer. ice skater
    *Jacobs—Famous p104-108,por.

Weld, Tuesday (1943-   )
    Amer. actress
    CR '63 p649,por.

Weldon, Catherine S. (fl. 1880's)
    Amer. W. pioneer
    *Johnson—Some p129-136

Welge, Gladys (fl. 1930's)
    Amer. orchestra conductor
    McCoy—Portraits p226,por.

Welitsch, Ljuba (1913-   )
    Bulg. singer
    Cur. Biog. '49 p629-631,por.
    Davidson—Treas. p337-339
    Rosenthal—Sopranos p101-103,por.
    Wagner—Prima p250

Weller, Beatrice Stuart (fl. 1930's)
    Women—Achieve, p64,por.

Wellerson, Mila (1910-   )
    Amer. cellist
    Saleski—Wander. p284-285,por.

Welles, Winifred (1893-1939)
    Amer. poet
    Cook—Our p252-254
    *Millett—Amer. p629

Wellington, Margaret (fl. 1870's-1880's)
    Amer. printer
    Hanaford—Dau. p713

Wellman, Louisa (fl. 1860's)
    Amer. soldier
    Fowler—Woman p420-425

Wells, Agnes Ermina (1876-1959)
    Amer. mathematician, astronomer,
        educator
    Cur. Biog. '49 p632-634,por.
    Cur. Biog. '59 p480

Wells, Ann Maria (b. 1797)
    Amer. poet
    Hanaford—Dau. p261

Wells, "Becky" (Mary) Davies (1781-1812)
    Eng. actress
    Collins—Great p245-262
    Jenkins—Ten p120-132,por.
    MacQueen—Pope p295-297

Wells, Bernice Young Mitchell (n.d.)
    Amer. author
    Dreer—Amer. p179

Wells, Carolyn (1869-1942)
    Amer. poet, author
    Bruère—Laugh. p107
    Cur. Biog. '42 p880

Wells, Charlotte Fowler (b. 1814)
    Amer. teacher, lecturer, journalist,
        business woman
    Hanaford—Dau. p611-612,702
    Logan—Part p902

Wells, Elizabeth.
    See Adams, Elizabeth

Wells, Goldie Ruth (fl. 1910's-1940's)
    Amer. missionary
    They—Went p58-59

Wells, Margaret Elizabeth (fl. 1930's)
Amer. educator
Women—Achieve. p132,por.

Wells, Mary Georgene Berg (1928-   )
Amer. advertising executive
Cur. Biog. '67 p450-453,por.

Wells, Phradie (fl. 1920's)
Amer. singer
McCoy—Portraits p227,por.

Wells, Rebecca (fl. 1750's)
Amer. colonial realtor
Dexter—Colonial p109

Wells, Sarah. See Bull, Sarah Wells

Wells, Mrs. Shepard (fl. 1860's)
Amer. Civil war humanitarian
Brockett—Woman's p497-498

Welsh, Mrs. Andrews, Sr. (fl. 1910's)
Amer. philanthropist
Logan—Part p622

Welsh, Elizabeth Knox (fl. 1570's-1600's)
Scot. covenanter
Anderson—Ladies p11-12

Welsh, Jane Baillie.
See Carlyle, Jane Baillie Welsh

Welty, Eudora (1909-   )
Amer. novelist
CR '59 p820,por.
CR '63 p650,por.
Cur. Biog. '42 p881-883,por.
*Muir—Writers p131-137,por.
Scherman—Literary p174-175
Van Gelder—Writers p287-290
Warfel—Amer. p447-448,por.

Wendell, Ella von Echtel (d. 1931)
Amer. recluse
Carnegie—Five p76-81
Erskine—Out p72-90

Wendell family (fl. 1900's-1930's)
Amer. recluses
Carnegie—Five p77-81

Wendt, Julia M. Bracken (b. 1871)
Amer. sculptor
Dorland—Sum p158
Michigan—Biog. p334
National—Contemp. p332
Taft—Women, Mentor (172) #2,4
Waters—Women p59-60

Wengerova, Isabella (fl. 1920's)
Russ.-Amer. pianist
McCoy—Portraits p227,por.
Saleski—Jewish p573,por.
Saleski—Wander. p390,por.

Wentworth, Bessie (d. 1900)
Eng. actress
Felstead—Stars p69-70,por.

Wentworth, Cecile de (c. 1853-1933)
Amer. painter
Michigan—Biog. p335
Waters—Women p360

Wentworth, Frances Deering, Lady
(d. 1813)
Amer. belle
Sale—Old p94-100

Werner, Kay (1918-   )
Amer. composer, author, singer
ASCAP p531

Werner, Sue (1918-   )
Amer. composer, author, singer
ASCAP p531

Wesendonk, Mathilde (1828-1902)
Ger. composer
McCoy—Portraits p227,por.

Wesley, Susanna Annesley (1669-1742)
Eng. religious worker, mother of
John Wesley
Adelman—Famous p69-70
Bartlett—Mothers p65-69
Bowie—Women p42-53
Culver—Women p151-152
Deen—Great p141-149
Foster—Religion p23-25,por.
Lotz—Women p118-126
Milller—Ten p7-13
Peyton—Mothers p82-88
Wallace—Mothers p7-14

West, Annie Blythe (1860-1941)
Amer. missionary
Cur. Biog. '41 p912

West, Claudine (c. 1884-1943)
Brit.-Amer. screen writer
Cur. Biog. '43 p816

West, Mrs. Cornwallis (fl. 19th cent.)
Eng. beauty
Furniss—Some p149-150,por.

West, Gertrude. See Eager, Gertrude

West, Jessamyn (1907-   )
Amer. author
CR '59 p821,por.
CR '63 p651,por.
*Muir—Writers p151-157,por.

West, Lydia (m. 1770)
Amer. whaling voyager
Whiting—Whaling p1-2

West, Mae (1892/93-   )
　　　Amer. actress, playwright, author
　　CR '59 p821,por.
　　CR '63 p651,por.
　　Cur. Biog. '67 p455-458,por.
　　Hammerton p1382
　　Mantle—Contemp. p327
　　New Yorker Nov.10,1928 p26,por.
　　　(Profiles)
　　Schickel—Stars p116-117,por.

West, Maria A. (fl. 1870's-1880's)
　　　Amer. missionary, author
　　Hanaford—Dau. p738

West, Mary Allen (fl. 1870's-1880's)
　　　Amer. educator, journalist
　　Hanaford—Dau. p547

West, Rebecca, pseud. (Cicely Isabel
　　　　Fairfield) (1892-   )
　　　Irish journalist, author, critic
　　Beaton—Persona p95-96
　　Church—British p120-122,por.
　　Collins—Literature p169-180,por.
　　CR '59 p822,por.
　　Cur. Biog. '68 p427-430,por.
　　Hammerton p1382
　　Millett—Brit. p508-510
　　Murrow—This p187-188
　　Overton—Authors p254-261,por.
　　Time Dec.8,1947 p108,por.(Cover)
　　Wellington—Women p175-189

West, Sarah Pearson (fl. 1740's-1760's)
　　　Amer., mother of Benjamin West
　　Peyton—Mothers p43-48
　　Wallace—Mothers p36-41

West, V. Sackville.
　　See Sackville-West, Victoria

Westbrook, Helen Searles (1898-   )
　　　Amer. composer, organist
　　ASCAP p532

Westcott, Cynthia (1898-   )
　　　Amer. plant pathologist
　　New Yorker July 26, 1952 p26,por.
　　　(Profiles)

Westcott, Jane Vlachos (1912-   )
　　　Amer. novelist
　　Warfel—Amer. p448-449,por.

Westgate, Elizabeth (fl. 1930's)
　　　Amer. personnel director, retailer
　　Women—Achieve. p44,por.

Westley, Helen (c. 1879-1942)
　　　Amer. actress
　　Cur. Biog. '43 p816
　　Frank—Time p63-68,por.
　　New Yorker Mar.27,1926 p15-16,por.
　　　(Profiles)

Westmeath, Lady (fl. 1850's)
　　　Eng. hostess
　　Stenton—English p334-335

Weston, Agnes E., Dame (c. 1840-   )
　　　Eng. philanthropist, social reformer
　　Carey—Twelve p255-276,por.
　　Hammerton p1383,por.

Weston, Bertine Emma (fl. 1930's)
　　　Amer. librarian
　　Women—Achieve. p112,por.

Weston, Christine Goutiere (1904-   )
　　　Eng.-Amer. author
　　Breit—Writer p111-113

Weston, Eunice.
　　See Moor, Eunice Farnsworth

Weston, Hannah Watts (1758-1855)
　　　Amer. Rev. war patriot, heroine
　　Green—Pioneer (3) p394-397
　　Logan—Part p158-159

Weston, Mary Pillsbury (fl. 1870's-1890's)
　　　Amer. artist
　　Hanaford—Dau. p307

Weston, Mildred (fl. 1940's)
　　　Amer. composer, music teacher
　　McCoy—Portraits p228,por.

Westray, Elizabeth (fl. 1810's)
　　　Amer. actress
　　Coad—Amer. p64

Wetché, Ludmila Vojáckova (fl. 1940's)
　　　Czech. pianist, music teacher
　　McCoy—Portraits p228,por.

Wethered, Joyce (1901-   )
　　　Eng. golfer
　　Hammerton p1383,por.

Wetherell, Elizabeth.
　　See Warner, Susan Bogert

Wetherell, June (1909-   )
　　　Amer. novelist
　　Warfel—Amer. p449-450,por.

Wetherhead, Mary (fl. 1650's)
　　　Amer. religious worker
　　Jones—Quakers p36-39,46-47,51,220

Wetherill, Louisa (fl. 1900's)
　　　Amer. W. pioneer
　　*Miller—West p206-221

Wetmore, Elizabeth Bisland (b. 1863)
　　　Amer. journalist, editor, traveler
　　Logan—Part p848
　　Ross—Ladies p61,592

Wettergren, Gertrud (1896)
Swed. singer
Ewen—Living p378-379,por.
McCoy—Portraits p228,por.

Whale, Winifred Stephens (fl. 1910's)
Eng. author
Hammerton p1384

Wharton, Anne Hollingsworth (1845-1928)
Amer. author
Adelman—Famous p278

Wharton, Edith Newbold Jones (1862-1937)
Amer. novelist
Adelman—Famous p296
Auchincloss—Pion. p20-55
*Bolton—Authors p167-174
Boynton—Some p89-107
Bruce—Woman p282-283
*Cournos—Famous p170-171
Green—Pioneer (3) p314
Hammerton p1384,por.
*Heath—Authors p27,por.
Heath—Women (4) p24,por.
Jensen—Revolt p100,por.
Jessup—Faith p14-33,119-121
Lawrence—School p256-259
Logan—Part p829-830
Loggins—Hear p179-188
Love—Famous p39
*MacVeagh—Champlin p606
Maurice—Makers #2,por.
*Millett—Amer. p24-25,86-87,633-639
Morgan—Writers p23-41
New Yorker Mar.2,1929 p26-28,por.
Overton—Authors p189-204,por.
Overton—Women p324-342
Rogers—Women p39,por.
Scherman—Literary p98-99
Van Doren—Amer. p95-104
Williams—Our p337-357
Witham—Pan. p200-202,por.

Wharton, Frankie (fl. 1930's)
Amer. airline hostess
Planck—Women p191

Wharton, Sarah Grace (fl. 1830's)
Amer. pioneer
Logan—Part p104

Wharton, Susannah Lloyd (d. 1772)
Amer. Rev. war patriot
Green—Pioneer (3) p313-314

Whateley, Anne, Sister (c. 1561-1600)
Eng., friend of Shakespeare
Brown—Dark p293-295

Wheatley, Mrs. John (d. 1774)
Amer. colonial benefactor, teacher
of Phillis Wheatley
Dexter—Colonial p140-141

Wheatley, Phillis (c. 1753-1784)
Amer. poet
Adams—Great p118,por.
Bacon—Puritan p1-42,por.
Brown—Home p5-10,por.
Cavanah—We p281-293
*Cherry—Portraits p4-8
Dexter—Colonial p140-142,por.
Douglas—Remember p43-44,por.
Dreer—Amer. p21-22
Hammerton p1385
Hanaford—Dau. p37
*Hughes—First p64,por.
*Hughes—Negroes p3-8,por.
Leonard—Amer. p104,124
Robinson—Hist. p27-38,por.
Rollins—Famous p18-21,por.
Schmidt—400 p25-26,por.
*Witham—Pan. p46-47,por.
Woody—Hist. (1) p132,por.

Wheatley, Mrs. Ross (fl. 1800's-1820's)
Amer. actress
Dexter—Career p83-84

Wheaton, Anne Williams (1892-   )
Amer. journalist, public relations
expert, government employee
Cur. Biog. '58 p468-470
Ross—Ladies p524-525

Wheaton, Elizabeth Lee (1902-   )
Amer. author
Cur. Biog. '42 p886-888,por.

Wheeler, Amey Webb (fl. 1880's-1890's)
Amer., wife of Benjamin Ide
Wheeler
Logan—Part p300

Wheeler, Anna Doyle (b. 1785)
Eng. feminist
Stenton—English p321-322

Wheeler, Candace (1827-1923)
Amer. artist, interior decorator
Logan—Part p753
Stern—We p273-303

Wheeler, Janet D. (fl. 1900's-1930's)
Amer. painter
Waters—Women p360-361

Wheeler, Mrs. Post.
See Rives, Hallie Erminie

Wheelhouse, M. V. (fl. 1940's)
Eng. illustrator
Mahony—Illus. p372

Wheelock, Deborah Thayer (1742/43-1815)
Amer. Rev. war patriot
Green—Pioneer (3) p485

Wheelock, Julia Susan (fl. 1860's)
Amer. Civil war nurse, author
Dannett—Noble p199-205,233,241-245,
284-287,380-381

Whetten, Harriet Douglas (fl. 1860's)
Amer. Rev. war patriot
Brockett—Woman's p301,316

Whetton, Margaret Todd (d. 1809)
Amer. Rev. war patriot
Green—Pioneer (3) p480-482

Whiffin, Blanche (1845-1936)
Eng.-Amer. actress
Adelman—Famous p278
Coad—Amer. p275,por.

Whipple, Katharine Moffat (fl. 1770's)
Amer. Rev. war patriot
Green—Pioneer (3) p14-16

Whipple, Maurine (1906-   )
Amer. author
Cur. Biog. '41 p912-914,por.

Whistler, Anna Matilda McNeill (1804-
1881)
Amer., mother of James Whistler
Davis—Mothers p181-191
Phila.—Women unp.,por.
Stiles—Postal p285

Whistler, Mrs. George (fl. 1890's)
Amer., wife of George Whistler
Arsenius—Dict. p199

Whitcher, Frances Miriam Berry (The
Widow Bedott) (1814-1852)
Amer. humorist, caricaturist,
author
Bruère—Laugh p6-7

Whitcomb, Catharine (1911-   )
Amer. novelist
Warfel—Amer. p450,por.

Whitcomb, Mildred E. (gr. 1919)
Amer. journalist, editor
Soper—These p27-38

White, Alice (fl. 1920's-1930's)
Amer. actress
Herman—How p57,por.

White, Ann (m. 1943)
Amer. seafarer
Snow—Women p240-250,por.

White, Armenia (fl. 1860's)
Amer. philanthropist, social
reformer, Civil war patriot
Hanaford—Dau. p457

White, Betty (n.d.)
Amer. actress, TV personality
TV—Person. (2) p151-152,por.

White, Callie (fl. 1870's)
Amer. printer
Club—Printing p16
Hanaford—Dau. p714

White, Carolina (1883-1961)
Amer. singer
Lahee—Grand p383,425-427,por.
McCoy—Portraits p228,por.

White, Carolina Earle (1833-1916)
Amer. philanthropist
Hanaford—Dau. p180
Logan—Part p537

White, Cynthia Elbin (fl. 1860's)
Amer. Civil war nurse
Logan—Part p374

White, Doris Pike (fl. 1950's)
Amer. club leader
Phelps—Men (2) '59 p310-311

White, Edith Hamilton (fl. 1930's)
Amer. humanitarian
Women—Achieve. p171,por.

White, Eirene Lloyd (1909-   )
Eng. Parliamentary member
Brittain—Women p177,253

White, Elise Fellows (b. 1873)
Amer. violonist, composer
Elson—Woman's p252-253

White, Ellen Gould (1827-1915)
Amer. religious foundress, leader
Culver—Women p190
Deen—Great p230-236

White, Florence (fl. 1890's-1900's)
Eng. painter
Waters—Women p361

White, Helen Constance (1896-   )
Amer. educator, author
Cur. Biog. '45 p668-670,por.
*Millett—Amer. p640
Warfel—Amer. p450-451,por.

White, Katherine Elkus (1906-   )
Amer. ambassador
Cur. Biog. '65 p454-456,por.

White, Margaret.
See Bourke-White, Margaret

White, Mary. See Morris, Mary

White, Maude Valerie (1855-1937)
Fr.-Eng. composer, song-writer
Elson—Woman's p150-151
Hammerton p1388
McCoy—Portraits p229,por.

White, Miss (fl. 1840's)
Eng. governess
Howe—Galaxy p117-119

White, Mrs. (fl. 1830's)
Amer. pioneer missionary
Fowler—Woman p382-392

White, Nancy (1916-   )
Amer. editor, fashion designer
CR '63 p652,por.

White, Nelia Gardner (1894-1957)
Amer. author
Cur. Biog. '50 p614-615,por.
Cur. Biog. '57 p588
Warfel—Amer. p452,por.

White, Nettie L. (fl. 1870's)
Amer. stenographer, government
employee
Logan—Part p893

White, Olive Bernardine (1899-   )
Amer. author, educator
Warfel—Amer. p452-453,por.

White, Pearl (1889-1938)
Amer. actress
Wagenknecht—Movies p57,72-73

White, Portia (1917-   )
Can. singer
Cur. Biog. '45 p670-671,por.

White, Rhoda Elizabeth Waterman
(fl. 1830's-1850's)
Amer. humanitarian, philanthropist
Logan—Part p258-259

White, Rose Rubin (fl. 1930's)
Russ.-Amer. author, translator
Women—Achieve. p105,por.

White, Susanna.
See Winslow, Susanna Fuller White

White, Tryphena (fl. 1800's) ›
Amer. pioneer, diarist
Whitton—These p41-42

Whitehall, Ann Cooper (d. 1797)
Amer. patriot
Green—Pioneer (3) p510-511

Whitehead, Reah (fl. 1920's)
Amer. lawyer
Binheim—Women p205,por.

Whiteman, Elizabeth A. O. (gr. 1940)
Eng. educator
Brittain—Women p247

Whiteman, Lydia L. (fl. 1960's)
Amer. Civil war nurse
Logan—Part p373

Whiting, Barbara (n.d.)
Amer. actress
TV—Person (3) p110-111,por.

Whiting, Lilian (1855/59-1942)
Amer. author, editor
Farmer—What p409,por.
Hammerton p1390
Logan—Part p849

Whiting, Margaret (1924-   )
Amer. singer
CR '59 p827,por.
TV—Person (3) p109-110,por.

Whiting, Martha (b. 1795)
Amer. educator
Hanaford—Dau. p529

Whitley, Mrs. (fl. 1770's)
Amer. Rev. war patriot
Ellet—Women (2) p304-306

Whitlock, Eliza Kemble.
See Kemble, Elizabeth

Whitman, Lucilla Mara de Vescovi,
Countess (1893-   )
It.-Amer. fashion designer,
business woman
Hellman—Mrs. p318-331

Whitman, Narcissa Prentiss (1808-1847)
Amer. W. pioneer, missionary
Beard—Amer. p114-116
Brown—Gentle p13,15,100,103-107,
161,163,196
Culver—Women p163-165
DAR Mag. July 1921 p393,portrayal
*Daugherty—Ten p48-62,por.
Deen—Great p204-213
Drury—First (1) p25-170,por.
*Johnson—Some p36,40
Peattie—Journey p192-206
Ross—Heroines p52-92
Ross—Westward p23-52
*Sickels—Calico p173-188
Thomas—Crusaders p282-308
Whitton—These p260-262

Whitman, Sarah de St. Crix (1842-1904)
Amer. painter
Waters—Women p361-362

Whitmer, Veneta Fern Viers (m. 1939)
Amer. missionary
They—Went p112-113

Whitmore, Frances Brooke, Lady (fl. 1640's)
Eng. beauty
Melville—Windsor p153-154,por.

Whitmore, Mrs. (fl. 1760's)
Amer. colonial midwife
Leonard—Amer. p124

Whitmore, Mrs. Thomas (fl. 1760's)
    Amer. colonial pioneer
    Dexter—Colonial p61

Whitney, Adeline Dutton Train (1824-1906)
    Amer. author
    Dorland—Sum p53,81,189
    Hanaford—Dau. p245

Whitney, Anne (1821-1915)
    Amer. artist, poet, sculptor
    Dorland—Sum p158
    Hanaford—Dau. p318-319
    Logan—Part p760-761
    Taft—Women, Mentor (172) #1,por.
    Tuckerman—Book p605
    Waters—Women p362

Whitney, Gertrude Vanderbilt (c. 1877-1942)
    Amer. sculptor
    Adelman—Famous p318
    Cur. Biog. '41 p914-916,por.
    Cur. Biog. '42 p890
    Jackman—Amer. p434-437
    Logan—Part p763
    Michigan—Biog. p337-338
    National—Contemp. p334
    Taft—Women, Mentor (172) #2,4,
      p10,por.

Whitney, Helen Hay (fl. 1900's-1920's)
    Amer. poet
    Smith—Women's p218

Whitney, Joan (1914-   )
    Amer. composer, author, singer,
      music publisher
    ASCAP p536-537

Whitney, Mrs. L. A. (fl. 1910's)
    Amer. pioneer airline passenger
    Planck—Women p38,por.

Whitney, Phyllis Ayame (1903-   )
    Amer. author
    Cur. Biog. '48 p673-674,por.

Whitson, Beth Slater (1879-1930)
    Amer. author, poet, song-writer
    ASCAP p537

Whittier, Abigail H. (fl. 1870's)
    Amer. religious worker
    Hanaford—Dau. p626

Whittier, Elizabeth Hussey (1815-1864)
    Amer. poet, religious worker
    Hanaford—Dau. p626
    Pomeroy—Little p115-142,por.

Whitton, Charlotte Elizabeth (1896-   )
    Can. mayor ,social worker,
      journalist, lecturer
    Cur. Biog. '53 p654-657,por.

Whitty, May, Dame (1865-1948)
    Eng. actress
    Cur. Biog. '45 p679-682,por.
    Cur. Biog. '48 p674
    Hammerton p1391

Whyte, Edna Gardner (fl. 1930's)
    Amer. nurse, aviatrix
    May—Women p134,162,186,205,por.

Wicjck, Cornelia van Asch van (fl. 1940's)
    Nether. religious leader
    Culver—Women p197

Wick, Frances Gertrude (1875-1941)
    Amer. physicist
    Cur. Biog. '41 p916

Wickens, Aryness Joy (1901-   )
    Amer. government official,
      economist
    Cur. Biog. '62 p462-464,por.

Wicker, Ireene (1905-   )
    Amer. singer, actress, radio script
      writer
    Cur. Biog. '43 p819,por.
    Eichberg—Radio p160-161,por.
    Settel—Radio p67,98,por.

Wickham, Anna (b. 1883)
    Brit. author
    Millett—Brit. p510

Wickham, Florence (1882-1962)
    Amer. singer, composer
    Lahee—Grand p312-313
    McCoy—Portraits p229,por.

Wickins, Margaret Ray (fl. 1910's)
    Amer. club leader
    Logan—Part p350

Widdemer, Margaret (b.c. 1880)
    Amer. author, poet
    Cook—Our p176-179
    Overton—Women p343-344
    Smith—Women's p220

Widener, Ella H. Pancoast (d. 1929)
    Amer. hostess
    Tebbel—Inher. p155-157

Widener, Josephine ("Fifi"), (fl. 1920's-1930's)
    Amer. hostess
    Tebbel—Inher. p155-157,por.

Widerström, Karolina (fl. 1880's)
    Swed. physician
    Lovejoy—Women p176-177

Wieck, Clara.
    See **Schumann, Clara Josephine Wieck**

Wieck, Dorothea (1907-   )
Swiss actress
Hammerton p1392

Wieck, Marie (b. 1819-   )
Ger. pianist
Elson—Woman's p91,por.

Wiedemann, Sarah Anna (fl. 1810's-1850's)
Eng., mother of Robert Browning
Bartlett—Mothers p51-55

Wieder, Gertrud (fl. 1940's)
Amer. singer
McCoy—Portraits p230,por.

Wiedhopf, Louise Bartling (fl. 1920's-
1930's)
Amer. teacher, business woman
Women—Achieve. p183,por.

Wiegmann, Marie Elisabeth Hanche (1826-
1893)
Siles. painter
Waters—Women p359-360

Wietrowetz, Gabriele (1866-1937)
Yugoslav. violinist
Erlich—Celeb. p262-264,por.
McCoy—Portraits p230,por.

Wiggin, Kate Douglas Smith (1859-1923)
Amer. author, educator
Adelman—Famous p269-270
Ames—These p69-78
*Cather—Younger p305-326
*Coffman—Authors p133-138,por.
Hammerton p1393
Harkins—Famous p191-203,por.
Harkins—Little p191-203,por.
Logan—Part p804-805
*MacVeagh—Champlin p610
Maurice—Makers #5 por.
*Moore—When p170-177
Overton—Women p345-349

Wiggin, Mary (fl. 1930's-1940's)
Amer. aviatrix, stunt flier
Planck—Women p74

Wight, Estella (1874-1955)
Amer. religious worker, journalist
Phillips—33 p155-158

Wightman, Hazel Hotchkiss (b. 1887)
Amer. tennis player
New Yorker Aug. 30,1952 p31,por.
(Profiles)

Wigman, Mary (b. 1886)
Ger. dancer
Hurok—Impres. p156-162,por.
*Maynard—Amer. p21-30

Wilbour, Charlotte B. (fl. 1870's-1880's)
Amer. social reformer, lecturer,
club leader

Hanaford—Dau. p371
Irwin—Angels p216,227-228

Wilbur, Bernice Marion (1911-   )
Amer. army nurse
Cur. Biog. '43 p820-822,por.

Wilcox, Ella Wheeler (1855-1919)
Amer. poet, journalist
Adelman—Famous p259
Cook—Our p172-174
Dorland—Sum p183
Hammerton p1394
Logan—Part p842
Rogers—Women p40,por.
Saturday Rev. p76-83
Schmidt—400 p18-19,por.

Wilcox, Mrs. G. Griffin (fl. 1860's)
Amer. Civil war diarist
Jones—Heroines p239-240

Wilcox, Mary R. (fl. 1910's)
Amer. club leader
Logan—Part p296-297

Wilcox, Molly Warren (fl. 1930's)
Amer. journalist, editor, publisher
Ross—Ladies p458-459

Wilde, Jane Francesca, Lady (1826-1896)
Irish poet, mother of Oscar Wilde
Furniss—Some p1-4,por.

Wilde, Jennie (fl. 1910's)
Amer. artist
Logan—Part p752

Wilde, Louise Kathleen (1910-   )
Amer. naval officer
Cur. Biog. '54 p645-646,por.

Wilde, Maud (b. 1880)
Amer. foundress
Binheim—Women p96,por.

Wilde, Miriam Leslie (b. 1851)
Amer. publisher
Pearson—Marry. p172-182

Wilde, Patricia (1928-   )
Can.-Amer. ballet dancer,
choreographer, teacher
Cur. Biog. '68 p432-435,por.

Wilder, Frances Farmer (1897-   )
Amer. radio executive
Cur. Biog. '47 p678-679,por.

Wilder, Jessie (fl. 1930's)
Eng.-Amer. poet, teacher, critic,
lecturer
Women—Achieve. p81,por.

(Continued)

Willard, Frances Elizabeth Caroline—
Continued

*Lamm—Biog. p101-102
Logan—Part p653-658,por.
Lotz—Women p127-137
*McCallum—Women p141-154
*MacVeagh—Champlin p611
Mears—They p73-74
Melikov—Immort. p81,161,por.
Miller—Ten p56-60
*Moore—When p178-185
Morello—Hall p64,por.
Morris—400 p269
Muir—Women p183-185
*Nisenson—More Minute p156,por.
*Parkman—Heroines p89-115,por.
Phila.—Women, unp.,por.
Rogers—Women p155,por.
Schmidt—400 p15-16,por.
Shaw—Story p155-156
Stiles—Postal p286
Stone—We p332-336
*Tappan—Heroes p132-139
Thomas—Living Women p179-191,
por.
*Vance—Lamp p197-224,por.

Willard, Luvia (fl. 1930's)
Amer. pediatrician
Women—Achieve. p125,por.

Willard, Mary Thompson Hill (b. 1805)
Amer., mother of Frances Willard
Logan—Part p288-289

Willcox, Mary Alice (1856-1953)
Amer. zoologist, teacher
Logan—Part p879

Willebrandt, Mabel Walker (1889-1963)
Amer. government official, lawyer
New Yorker Feb. 16,1929 p23,por.
(Profiles)
Rogers—Women p159,por.
Time Aug.26,1929 p13,por.(Cover)

Willemer, Marianne von Jung (1784-1860)
Ger. musician, friend of Goethe
Schmidt—400 p45,por.

Willet, Anna Lee (c. 1867-1943)
Amer. artist, designer of stained
glass windows
Cur. Biog. '43 p824

Willets, Georgiana (fl. 1860's)
Amer. Civil war nurse
Brockett—Woman's p791
Moore—Women p523-528,por.

Williams, Abigail (fl. 1710's-1740's)
Amer. pioneer
Green—Pioneer (1) p278

Williams, Anna May (c. 1895-   )
Eng. physician
Castiglioni—Hist. p1127

Williams, Anne Newton (fl. 1770's)
Amer. Rev. war patriot
Green—Pioneer (3) p457

Williams, Bertye Young (d. 1951)
Amer. poet
Smith—Women's p229

Williams, Blanche Colton (1879-1944)
Amer. author, educator
Women—Achieve. p94,por.

Williams, Camilla (n.d.)
Amer. singer
*Cherry—Portraits p77-81,por.
Cur. Biog. '52 p632-634,por.
New Yorker Jan.19,1952 p68,por.
(Profiles)

Williams, Cara (n.d.)
Amer. TV personality
CR '63 p658,por.

Williams, Cecilia (fl. 1800's)
Amer. actress, poet
Brown—Home. p242

Williams, Cicely D. (fl. 1950's)
Eng. physician
Lovejoy—Women p379-380,por.

Williams, Clara (fl. 1870's-1910's)
Amer. physician
Lovejoy—Women p322-324,329-330
Lovejoy—Women Phys. p87-91,por.

Williams, Clare (gr. 1931)
Amer. politician
Parshalle—Kash. p39-40,por.

Williams, Colleen (n.d.)
Amer. author, teacher
Dreer—Amer. p242

Williams, Esther (1923-   )
Amer. actress, business woman,
swimmer
CR '59 p833-834,por.
CR '63 p659,por.
Cur. Biog. '55 p651-653,por.

Williams, Esther (fl. 1700's)
Amer. pioneer, Ind. captive
Green—Pioneer (1) p272,274-275

Williams, Eunice (1696-1786)
Amer. pioneer, Ind. captive
Green—Pioneer (1) p241-280

Williams, Flos Jewell (1892-   )
Can. author
Thomas—Canad. p128-129

Williams, Frances (n. d.)
Welsh-Amer. composer
ASCAP p538-539

Williams, Frances Dighton (m. 1632)
Amer. patriot
Green—Pioneer (3) p477-478

Williams, Greta (fl. 1890's)
Eng. seafarer
Snow—Women p221-231

Williams, Hannah English (1692-1722)
Amer. colonial biologist
Leonard—Amer. p125

Williams, Helen Maria (1762-1827)
Eng.-Fr. poet, music writer,
politician
MacCarthy—Later p79-82

Williams, Irene (fl. 1940's)
Amer. singer
McCoy—Portraits p231,por.

Williams, Ivy (gr. 1899)
Eng. lawyer
Brittain—Women p73,156,176,249

Williams, Katherine Breed (d. 1953)
Amer. social leader
Jensen—Revolt p187,por.

Williams, Kathryn Taylor (fl. 1950's)
Amer. missionary
They—Went p145-146

Williams, Lorraine Anderson (1923-   )
Amer. educator, author
*Cherry—Portraits p49-53,por.

Williams, Margaret Lindsay (d. 1960)
Welsh painter
Hammerton p1404

Williams, (Helen) Maria (1762-1827)
Eng. author, poet, hymn-writer
Dorland—Sum p55,187

Williams, Maria Pray Mestayer (m. 1850)
Amer. actress
Coad—Amer. p210,por.

Williams, Mary (fl. 1810's-1830's)
Eng. pioneer missionary
*Matthews—Daunt. p102-123

Williams, Mary Ann Barnes (n.d.)
Amer. author, teacher, club leader
Parshalle—Kash. p149-151,por.

Williams, Mary Lou (1910-   )
Amer. composer, pianist
ASCAP p539
Cur. Biog. '66 p445-447,por.
New Yorker May 2, 1964 p52,por.
(Profiles)

Williams, Mary Trumbull (m. 1771)
Amer. patriot
Green—Pioneer (3) p100-103

Williams, Mattie (fl. 1920's-1930's)
Amer. club leader
Binheim—Women p8,por.

Williams, Pamela (b. 1785)
Amer. social leader
Hanaford—Dau. p143
Logan—Part p261

Williams, Rachel (1840-1908)
Brit. pioneer nurse
Cope—Six p47-56,por.

Williams, Rebecca (b. 1754)
Amer. W. pioneer
Ellet—Pioneer p171-178

Williams, Tessie (fl. 1920's-1950's)
Amer. missionary
They—Went p68

Williams, Theresa Amelia (b. 1853)
Amer. philanthropist, social
reformer
Logan—Part p665

Williamson, Pauline Brooks (fl. 1930's)
Amer. health worker
Women—Achieve. p150,por.

Williamson, Sophia Christiana Hopkey
(fl. 1730's)
Amer., friend of John Wesley
Wright—Forgot. p72-92

Willing, Ann. See Bingham, Ann Willing

Willing, Elizabeth (fl. 1780's-1800's)
Amer. belle, sister of Ann Willing
Sale—Old p175-176,por.

Willing, Jennie Fowler (b. 1834)
Amer. clergyman
Hanaford—Dau. p460-463,por.

Willis, Frances Elizabeth (1899-   )
Amer. ambassador
Cur. Biog. '54 p650-651,por.
*Heath—Women (4) p32

Willis, Mildred Washington (fl. 18th cent.)
Amer. pioneer
Green—Pioneer (2) p81

Willis, Olympia Brown (1835-1926)
Amer. feminist
Sickels—Twelve p168-187,254

Willis, Pauline (b. 1870)
Amer. religious worker, author
Logan—Part p823-824

Willis, Sara Payson. See Fern, Fanny

Willms, Emilie (fl. 1930's-1940's)
Amer. physician
Lovejoy—Women p348-351

Wills, Helen Newington (Helen Wills
Moody) (1905/06-   )
Amer. tennis player
*Cooper—Twenty p179-196,por.
Davis—100 p140-141,por.
Gallico—Golden p155-175,por.
Hammerton p1009
*Jacobs—Famous p109-118,por.
Jensen—Revolt p132,por.
Lamparski—What. p132-133,por.
New Yorker Aug. 27, 1927 p16,por.
(Profiles)
Rogers—Women p132,134,por.
Time July 26,1926 p22,por.;
July 1,1929 p50,por.(Covers)
Women—Achieve. p73,por.

Willson, Mary Ann (fl. 1810's-1820's)
Amer. painter
Lipman—Primitive p50-56

Willson, Mary Eleanor (fl. 1860's)
Amer. Civil war nurse
Logan—Part p374

Willson, Mary Elizabeth (b. 1842)
Amer. missionary
Logan—Part p517

Wilmarth, Mary Hawes (fl. 1890's-1920's)
Amer. social worker
Addams—Excellent p97-109

Wilson, Alice (1881-1964)
Can. geologist
Innis—Clear p260-278,por.

Wilson, Alice (m. 1918)
Amer. niece of Woodrow Wilson
Smith—White p157-159,por.

Wilson, Anne Maynard K. (fl. 1930's)
Amer. club leader
Women—Achieve. p205

Wilson, Augusta Jane.
See Evans, Augusta Jane

Wilson, Bess K. Kidston (m. 1909)
Can.-Amer. missionary
They—Went p36-38

Wilson, Bess M. (fl. 1930's)
Amer. journalist
Ross—Ladies p558-559

Wilson, Deborah (fl. 1660's)
Amer. religious worker
Jones—Quakers p108-109

Wilson, Dolores (fl. 1950's)
Amer. singer
Matz—Opera p231-233,por.

Wilson, Dorothy Clarke (1904-   )
Amer. author
Cur. Biog. '51 p666-667,por.
Warfel—Amer. p461-462,por.

Wilson, Edith Bolling Galt (1872-1961)
Amer., 2nd wife of Woodrow
Wilson
Gerlinger—Mis. p91,por.
Jensen—White p204-206
Logan—Ladies p159-165
*McConnell—Our p271-275,por.
Means—Woman p135-164,por.
Prindiville—First p215-220
Ross—Know p57,por.
Smith—Romances p361-363,por.
Smith—White p145-155,por.
Truett—First p68-69,por.

Wilson, Eleanor Randolph (m. 1914)
Amer., dau. of Woodrow Wilson
Smith—White p139-143,por.
*Sweetser—Famous p282-299,por.

Wilson, Ellen Louise Axson (1860-1914)
Amer., first wife of Woodrow
Wilson
Fairfax—Ladies p203-204
Gerlinger—Mis p89-90
Jensen—White p201-203,por.
Logan—Ladies p153-157
*McConnell—Our p263-270,por.
Prindiville—First p211-215
*Ross—Know p57,por.
Smith—Romances p354-360,por.
Truett—First p66,por.

Wilson, Elva (n.d.)
Amer. aircraft inventor
*Peckham—Women p56-57

Wilson, Enid (1910-   )
Eng. golfer
Hammerton p1406

Wilson, Florence.
See Austral, Florence Wilson

Wilson, Frances Seydel (fl. 1930's)
Amer. astronomer
Women—Achieve. p205

Wilson, Hannah. See Bartlett, Hannah Gray

Wilson, Harriet M. Howe (d. 1870)
Amer. religious worker
Hanaford—Dau. p620-621

Wilson, Harriette (1789-1846)
Eng. author, courtesan
Jenkins—Ten p133-150,por.
Melville—Regency p208-223,por.

Wilson, Janet Woodrow (fl. 1840's-1870's)
Amer., mother of Woodrow Wilson
Hampton—Our p230-239

Wilson, Jean (n.d.)
  Amer. helicopter pilot
  *May—Women p208,por.

Wilson, Jessie Woodrow (m. 1913)
  Amer. daughter of Woodrow
    Wilson
  Smith—White p133-137,por.
  *Sweetser—Famous p282-299,por.

Wilson, Julie (1925-   )
  Amer. singer
  CR '59 p841,por
  CR '63 p662,por.

Wilson, Justina Leavitt (fl. 1930's)
  Amer. feminist
  Women—Achieve. p140,por.

Wilson, Kathleen (fl. 1930's)
  Amer. radio actress
  Eichberg—Radio p109,112

Wilson, Lois (fl. 1920's)
  Amer. actress
  Herman—How p84,por.

Wilson, Louisa (fl. 1920's)
  Amer. journalist
  Ross—Ladies p171-174

Wilson, Louise Maxwell.
  See Baker, Louise Maxwell

Wilson, Mabel K. (fl. 1930's)
  Amer. aviatrix, airport manager
  Planck—Women p184-185

Wilson, Margaret (1667-1685)
  Scot. covenanter, martyr
  Anderson—Ladies p340-343
  Graham—Group p82-85
  Muir—Women p112-113

Wilson, Margaret Stevens (c. 1865-1943)
  Amer. librarian
  Cur. Biog. '43 p832

Wilson, Margaret Woodrow (1886-1944)
  Amer., dau. of Woodrow Wilson
  Logan—Ladies p158
  Sweetser—Famous p282-299,por.

Wilson, Marie (1917-   )
  Amer. actress, TV personality
  Blum—Television p102,por.
  CR '59 p841,por.
  CR '63 p663,por.

Wilson, Martha (b. 1758)
  Amer. Rev. war patriot
  Ellet—Women (2) p43-77,por.
  Logan—Part p131-136

Wilson, Mary (fl. 1870's)
  Amer. agriculturist
  Hanaford—Dau. p724

Wilson, (Gladys) Mary Baldwin (1916-   )
  Eng. wife of prime minister
  Frederick—Ten p38-52,por.

Wilson, Maude H. Mellish (d. 1933)
  Amer. nurse, editor
  Pennock—Makers p139-140,por.

Wilson, Melva Beatrice (1866/75-1921)
  Amer. sculptor
  Waters—Women p362-363

Wilson, Nancy (1937-   )
  Amer. singer
  Stambler—Ency. p252-253,por.

Wilson, Rachel (fl. 1760's)
  Eng. clergyman
  Spruill—Women's p253

Wilson, Rachael Bird (m. 1771/72)
  Amer. Rev. war patriot
  Green—Pioneer (3) p205-207

Wilson, Mrs. Robert (fl. 1720's)
  Amer. Rev. war patriot
  Hanaford—Dau. p62

Wilson, Romer pseud.
  See Muir, Florence Roma

Wilson, Sarah (fl. 1790's)
  Amer. W. pioneer
  Ellet—Pioneer p106-109
  Logan—Part p84

Wilson, Sarah (fl. 1770's)
  Eng.-Amer. accused criminal
  Earle—Colon. p167-172

Wilson, Mrs. Stewart (fl. 1770's)
  Amer. social leader, daughter of
    Charles Stewart
  Hanaford—Dau. p142

Wilt, Marie (1833-1891)
  Aust. singer
  Dorland—Sum p51,162
  McCoy—Portraits p231,por.

Wilton, Marie Effie.
  See Bancroft, Marie Effie Wilton, Lady

Winans, Mrs. Hubert Charles.
  See Brush, Katharine Ingham

Winans, Sarah D. (fl. 1910's)
  Amer. club leader
  Logan—Part p353-354

Winchell, Constance M. (1896-   )
  Amer. librarian
  Cur. Biog. '67 p465-468,por.

Winchelsea, Countess of.
　　See Finch, Anne, Countess of
　　　Winchelsea.

Winchester, Alice (1907-　　)
　　Amer. editor, author
　　Cur. Biog. '54 p658-660,por.

Winchilsea, Elizabeth Finch (d. 1914)
　　Eng. poet
　　Hammerton p1409

Windsor, Bessie Wallis Simpson, Duchess of
　　(1896-　　)
　　Amer., wife of Duke of Windsor
　　CR '59 p843-844,por.
　　CR '63 p664,por.
　　Cur. Biog. '44 p737-741,por.
　　Jensen—Revolt p187,por.
　　Pearson—Marry. p304-313,por.
　　Pearson—Pilgrim p239-240,328-330,
　　　por.
　　Time Jan. 4, 1937 p13,por.(Cover)

Windsor, Mary Catherine (1830-1914)
　　Amer. Civil war heroine, spy
　　Brown—Home p108-109

Wing, Anna Olsdotter (b. 1851)
　　Swed. immigrant
　　Cavanah—We p251-259

Wing, Helen (fl. 1940's)
　　Amer. composer, pianist, violinist
　　McCoy—Portraits p232,por.

Wingro, Effigene (fl. 1930's)
　　Amer. Congresswoman
　　Paxton—Women p131

"Wink, Josh". See Malloy, (Marie) Louise

Winn, Edith L. (d. 1933)
　　Amer. violinist, music teacher,
　　　author
　　McCoy—Portraits p232,por.

Winn, Marcia (fl. 1930's)
　　Amer. journalist
　　Ross—Ladies p546-547

Winning, Freda J. Gerwin (fl. 1930's)
　　Amer. teacher, home economist
　　Women—Achieve. p130

Winnocur, Perlina (fl. 1930's)
　　Argent. physician
　　Lovejoy—Women p267-268

Winona, Kim (n.d.)
　　Amer. actress
　　TV—Person. (2) p110-111

Winser, Beatrice (c. 1872-1947)
　　Amer. librarian
　　Marshall—Amer. p150-153,158-160

Winslow, Amy (1890)
　　Amer. librarian, director
　　Bul. of Bibl. Sept.-Dec. '52 p201-203,
　　　por.

Winslow, Anna Green (d. 1779)
　　Amer. colonial diarist
　　Benson—Women p147,293-294,305
　　Dexter—Colonial p65-66,139-140

Winslow, Anne Goodwin (b. 1875)
　　Amer. author
　　Cur. Biog. '48 p685-686,por.
　　Smith—Women's p232
　　Warfel—Amer. p464-465,por.

Winslow, Elizabeth Barker (d. 1621)
　　Amer. Pilgrim
　　Bell—Women p17,25
　　Green—Pioneer (1) p139
　　Logan—Part p32
　　Marble—Women p55-56

Winslow, Helen Maria (1851-1938)
　　Amer. author, editor, publisher
　　Logan—Part p850
　　Ross—Ladies p483-484

Winslow, Mary Chilton (c. 1608-1679)
　　Amer. Pilgrim
　　Bell—Women p11-14,21,24,26-27,118-
　　　119,213-216,308-314
　　Green—Pioneer (1) p129,147
　　Hanaford—Dau. p34
　　*Humphrey—Marys p27-39
　　Logan—Part p34
　　Marble—Women p80-85

Winslow, Phebe Horrox (b. 1760)
　　Amer., mother of Charles F.
　　　Winslow
　　Snow—Women p111-113

Winslow, Susanna Fuller White (d. before
　　1675)
　　Amer. Pilgrim
　　Bell—Women p41-43,119-120
　　Green—Pioneer (1) p136-138
　　Logan—Part p33
　　Marble—Women p62-67

Winslow, Thyra Samter (1893-1961)
　　Amer. journalist, author
　　Ross—Ladies p545-546
　　Women—Achieve. p105,por.

Winsor, Kathleen (1916/19-　　)
　　Amer. author
　　CR '59 p845-846,por.
　　Cur. Biog. '46 p651-652,por.
　　Warfel—Amer. p464-465,por.

Winter, Ella (1898-　　)
　　Austral. journalist, author
　　Cur. Biog. '46 p655-656,por.

Winter, John Strange, pseud.
See Stannard, Henrietta Eliza Vaughn
Palmer

Winterbotham, Ann Sophia.
See Stephens, Ann Sophia
Winterbotham

Winters, Midge (n.d.)
Amer. airline publicity director
*Peckham—Women p95

Winters, Shelley (1922-   )
Amer. actress
CR '59 p847-848,por.
CR '63 p665,por.
Cur. Biog. '52 p644-646,por.
Funke—Actors p295-329,por.
Martin—Pete p308-318
*Seventeen—In p35-39,por.

Winters, Mrs. Yvor. See Lewis, Janet

Winthrop, Elizabeth Temple (fl. 1780's)
Amer. social leader
Hanaford—Dau. p137

Winthrop, Hannah (c. 1726-1790)
Amer. Rev. war patriot
Green—Pioneer (3) p337,458
Hanaford—Dau. p138

Winthrop, Margaret (1591-1647)
Amer. colonial patriot
Bell—Women p195-197,271-280,367-
377
Earle—Colon. p110-111
Fowler—Woman p38-40
Green—Pioneer (1) p283-299
Leonard—Amer. p125

Winthrop, Mary. See Dudley, Mary

Winwood, Estelle (b. 1883)
Eng. actress, comedienne
CR '59 p848,por.

Wirth, Anna Marie (b. 1846)
Russ. painter
Waters—Women p363-364

Wise, Jessie Moore (1883-1949)
Amer. composer, author
ASCAP p543

Wise, Louisa fl. 19th cent.)
Amer. balloonist
*May—Women p19

Wiseman, Jane (fl. 18th cent.)
Eng. playwright
MacQueen—Pope p162

Wisinger-Florian, Olga (1844-1926)
Aust. painter
Waters—Women p364-465

Wister, Anne Lee Furness (1830-1908)
Amer. traveler
Dorland—Sum p17,177

Wister, Sarah ("Sally") (1762-1804)
Amer. Rev. war patriot
Brooks—Colonial p245-284
Burt—Phila. p275,281-282
Logan—Part p159-160

Wiswall, Hattie (fl. 1860's)
Amer. Civil war nurse
Brockett—Woman's p725-727

Witch of Endor. See Endor, Witch of

Witherell, Mrs. E. C. (fl. 1860's)
Amer. Civil war nurse
Brockett—Woman's p499-501

Witherington, Pearl (fl. 1940's)
Eng. spy
Hoehling—Women p136-138

Withers, Jane (c. 1926-   )
Amer. actress
Zierold—Child p97-106,por.

Witherspoon, Elizabeth Montgomery
(d. 1789)
Amer. Rev. war patriot
Green—Pioneer (3) p139-141

Witherspoon, Naomi Long (gr. 1945)
Amer. poet, journalist
Dreer—Amer. p84

Withington, Alfreda (1860-1951)
Amer. physician
Fabricant—Why p146-147
Stone—We p426-433

Withy, Mary (d. 1810)
Amer. inn-keeper
Dexter—Career p116,127

Witt, Estelle E. (fl. 1930's)
Amer. retail executive
Women—Achieve. p155,por.

Wittenmeyer, Annie T. (1827-1900)
Amer. Civil war humanitarian,
social reformer, lecturer, author
Brockett—Woman's p373-379
Dannett—Nobel p311-313,340-342
Hanaford—Dau. p344,394-399,por.
Logan—Part p349
Young—Women (see index)

Wittkowska, Marta (fl. 1910's)
Pol.-Amer. singer
Lahee—Grand p435-436,por.

Woffington, Margaret ("Peg")
Irish actress
Abbott—Notable p347-351,por.
Adelman—Famous p79-80
Collins—Great p141-158,por.
Dorland—Sum p49,69,129,166
Hammerton p1413,por.
MacQueen—Pope p186-198,por.
Marinacci—Lead. p23-49,por.
Melville—Stage p153-191,por.
Ormsbee—Back. p89-90
Terhune—Super. p41-67

Wolcott, Abigail.
See Ellsworth, Abigail Wolcott

Wolcott, Ann Louise (b. 1868)
Amer. archaeologist, educator
Logan—Part p718

Wolcott, Laura Collins (m. 1789)
Amer. Rev. war patriot
Green—Pioneer (3) p103-112

Wolcott, Lucy. See Barnum, Lucy Wolcott

Wolcott, Martha Pitkins (c. 1639-1719)
Amer. pioneer
Green—Pioneer (1) p328-340
Root—Chapter p173-185

Wolcott, Mary Ann.
See Goodrich, Mary Ann

Wolcott, Sarah Drake (m. 1702)
Amer. pioneer
Green—Pioneer (1) p336

Wolcott, Ursula. See Griswold, Ursula

Wolf, Anna D. (fl. 1930's-1940's)
Amer. nurse
Pennock—Makers p117,por.

Wolf, Constance (c. 1905-   )
Can. balloonist
*May—Women p37-38,por.

Wolfe, Catherine Lorillard (1828-1887)
Amer. philanthropist
Adelman—Famous p198

Wolfe, Deborah Cannon Partridge
(1916-   )
Amer. educator, government
consultant
Cur. Biog. '62 p469-471,por.

Wolfe, Lilian. See Lauferty, Lilian

Wolfe, Winifred Frances (n.d.)
Amer. radio actress
Eichberg—Radio p112

Wolff, Betty (fl. 1890's-1900's)
Ger. painter
Waters—Women p365

Wolff, Maritta M. (1918-   )
Amer. author
Cur. Biog. '41 p932-933,por.

Wolff, Mary Evaline.
See Madeleva, Mary, Sister

Wolkoff, Anna (fl. 1940's)
Rus.-Eng.-Ger. spy
Hoehling—Women p147-150
Singer—World's p235-241

Wollstein, Rose R. (fl. 1940's)
Amer. pianist, author, linguist
McCoy—Portraits p234,por.

Wollstonecraft, Mary.
See Godwin, Mary Wollstonecraft

Wolter, Annett (fl. 1930's)
Amer. dramatics teacher
Women—Achieve. p29,por.

Wolter, Charlotte (1834-1897)
Aust. actress
Adelman—Famous p227-228
Dorland—Sum p27,168

Wolters, Henrietta Van Pee (1692-1741)
Nether. painter
Waters—Women p365

Wong, Ah Mae (fl. 1920's-1930's)
Chin. physician
Lovejoy—Women p233

Wong, Anna May (1907-1961)
Amer. actress
CR '59 p849,por.
Hammerton p1416,por.
Stuart—Immort. p206-207,por.

Wong, Jeanyee (1920-   )
Amer. illustrator
Club—Printing p28

Wood, Anne. See Elderkin, Anne Wood

Wood, Beatrice (n.d.)
Amer. artist, ceramist
Parshalle—Kash. p19-20,por.

Wood, Caroline. S. (. 1900's)
Amer. sculptor
Waters—Women p365-366

Wood, Edith Elmer (b. 1871)
Amer. humanitarian, author
Logan—Part p854

Wood, Ellen Price (1814-1887)
Eng. novelist
Adelman—Famous p179
Dorland—Sum p39,115,194
Hammerton p1416-1417,por.
Oliphant—Women p175-192
Stebbins—Victorian p32-35,208

Wood, Ethel Pope (fl. 1930's)
Amer. author
Women—Achieve. p73,por.

Wood, Frances Gilchrist (b. 1859)
Amer. author
O'Brien—50 p855

Wood, Juliana Westray (1778-1836)
Amer. actress
Coad—Amer. p64,por.

Wood, Louise Aletha (1910-   )
Amer. organization official,
educator
Cur. Biog. '61 p480-481,por.

Wood, Mary Anne Paton.
See Paton, Mary Anne

Wood, Mary Elizabeth (1870-1950)
Amer. recluse
Erskine—Out p57-71

Wood, Mary Knight.
See Mason, Mary Knight

Wood, Matilda, Alice Victoria.
See Lloyd, Marie

Wood, Minnie Lee (Julia Amanda Sargent)
(fl. 1840's)
Amer. journalist
Ross—Ladies p558

Wood, Natalie (1938-   )
Amer. actress
CR '59 p850,por.
CR '63 p666,por.
Cur. Biog. '62 p472-474

Wood, Peggy (1892-   )
Amer. actress
Blum—Great p105,por.
Blum—Television p89,por.
Coad—Amer. p329,por.
CR '59 p850,por.
CR '63 p667,por.
Cur. Biog. '42 p894-896,por.
Cur. Biog. '53 p659-660,por.
Dodd—Celeb. p327-331
Hammerton p1417,por.
Murrow—This (1) p193-194
TV—Person. (1) p76-77,por.

Wood, Ruby Ross (fl. 1910's-1920's)
Amer. decorator
Taves—Success. p175-187,por.

Woodridge, Mary Ann (fl. 1870's)
Amer. social reformer
Hanaford—Dau. p386-387

Woodbury, Anna Lowell (fl. 1870's-1880's)
Amer. humanitarian, educator
Farmer—What p364-365

Woodbury, Marcia Oakes (1865-1913)
Amer. painter
Waters—Women p366

Woodeville, Elizabeth.
See Grey, Elizabeth, Lady

Woodham-Smith, Cecil Blanche Fitzgerald
(1896-   )
Eng. historian
Breit—Writer p175-177
Brittain—Women p145,251
Cur. Biog. '55 p656-657,por.

Wood-Hill, Mabel (1870-1954)
Amer. composer
Howard—Our p434-435

Woodhouse, Margaret Chase Going
(1890-   )
Amer. Congresswoman, economist,
educator, author
Cur. Biog. '45 p690-692,por.
Paxton—Women p117-121,131,por.

Woodhouse, Sophia (fl. 1810's)
Amer. inventor
Dexter—Career p173

Woodhull, Ruth Floyd (m. 1761)
Amer. Rev. war patriot
Green—Pioneer (2) p193-195

Woodhull, Victoria Claflin (1838-1927)
Amer. feminist, stock-broker
Davenport—Ladies p110-124
Douglas—Remember p164-165
Eliot—Heiresses p148-150,por.
Ewart—World's p243-260
Holbrook—Dreamers p196-206
Irwin—Angels p252-257
Jensen—Revolt p53,por.
Johnson—Lunatic p80-105
Pearson—Marry p183-187
Pearson—Pilgrim p188-193
Riegel—Amer. p144-150
Ross—Charmers p110-136,289-290,por.
Ross—Ladies p27-28,30-36,38,por.
Stern—We p251-272,por.
Wallace—Square p100-147,por.

Woodley, Emily E. Wilson (fl. 1860's)
Amer. Civil war nurse
Logan—Part p369

Woodruff, Hannah (1730-1815)
Amer. Rev. war patriot
Root—Chapter p305-314

Woods, Bertha Gerneaux Davis (1873-1952)
Amer. author
Logan—Part p842

Woods, Kate Tannatt (d. 1910)
Amer. author, club leader
Logan—Part p849

Woods, Margaret Louisa Bradley (1856-
1945)
Eng. poet, playwright
Hammerton p1418,por.

Woods, Mary A. (fl. 1910's)
Amer. dressmaker, flag-maker
Logan—Part p302-303

Woods, Mrs. (fl. 1770's)
Amer. Rev. war patriot
Ellet—Women (2) p314-316

Woodsmall, Ruth Frances (1883-/1963)
Amer. government official,
organization official, author
Cur. Biog. '49 p645-646,por.
Cur. Biog. '63 p476
Women—Achieve. p80,por.

Woodstock, Lenoir Carpenter (b. 1882)
Amer. religious worker, pioneer
Phillips—33 p173-176

Woodville, Elizabeth.
See Elizabeth Woodville

Woodward, Alice Bolingbroke (b. 1862)
Eng. illustrator
Mahony—Illus. p374,376

Woodward, Ann Aubertine (fl. 1870's-
1880's)
Amer. translator
Hanaford—Dau. p600

Woodward, Betsy (fl. 1950's-1960's)
Amer. glider pilot
*May—Women p220-221

Woodward, Dewing (1856-1950)
Amer. painter
Waters—Women p366-367

Woodward, Emily (fl.1920's-1930's)
Amer. editor, journalist
Ross—Ladies p596-597

Woodward, Helen (b. 1882)
Amer. advertising executive
*Logie—Careers p182-201

Woodward, Hildegard (1898-   )
Amer. illustrator
Mahony—Illus. p376

Woodward, Joanne (1934-   )
Amer. actress
CR '59 p851-852,por.
CR '63 p667-668,por.
Cur. Biog. '58 p481-482,por.

Woodward, Mary D. (fl. 1880's)
Amer. W. pioneer
Brown—Gentle p162-164,166,211

Woodworth, Mary A. E. K. (fl. 1860's)
Amer. Civil war nurse
Logan—Part p375

Wooley, Edna K. (fl. 1900's)
Amer. journalist
Ross—Ladies p554-555

Woolley (Wooley), Hannah b. 1623)
Eng. pioneer educator, governess
*Borer—Women p13-17
Howe—Galaxy p37-38
Stenton—English p188-191,214

Woolley, Mary Emma (1863-1947)
Amer. educator
Adelman—Famous p297-298
America's 12 p47-49,por.
Cur. Biog. '42 p896-898,por.
Cur. Biog. '47 p693
Fisher—Amer. p53-54,por.
Irwin—Angels p281,418-419
Ladies'—Amer. 12 p47-49,por.
Logan—Part p721
Lotz—Women p138-149
Schmidt—400 p547,por.

Woolf, Virginia (1882-1941)
Eng. novelist
Church—British p85-88,por.
Collins—Literature p187-190
Cur. Biog. '41 p935
Dunaway—Treas. p423-430
Johnson—Some Contemp. p149-160
Lawrence—School p373-382
Millett—Brit. p516-517
Sitwell—Women p47-48,por.
Time Apr. 12, 1937 p93,por.(Cover)

Woolsey, Abby (fl. 1860's)
Amer. Civil war nurse, author
Dannett—Nobel (see index)

Woolsey, Caroline Caisson (fl. 1860's)
Amer. Civil war nurse, author
Dannett—Nobel p29-31,264-265,364-
365,por.

Woolsey, Georgiana M. (fl. 1860's)
Amer. Civil war nurse
Brockett—Woman's p303,322-324,327-
342
Dannett—Nobel (see index)

Woolsey, Harriet (Hatty) Roosevelt
(fl. 1860's)
Amer. Civil war nurse, author
Dannett—Nobel p29-31,265,279-280,
358-360

Woolsey, Jane Newton (fl. 1860's)
Amer. Civil war nurse
Dannett—Nobel p29-31,120-122,277-
279,354-355,365-366

Woolsey, Jane Stuart (fl. 1860's)
　　Amer. Civil war humanitarian,
　　　　nurse, author
　　Brockett—Woman's p324,342,713
　　Dannett—Nobel (see index)
　　Pennock—Makers p27-29,por.

Woolsey, Maryhale (1899-　　)
　　Amer. song-writer, author
　　ASCAP p547

Woolsey, Sarah C. (fl. 1860's)
　　Amer. Civil war nurse
　　Brockett—Woman's p342

Woolsey sisters (fl. 1860's)
　　Amer. Civil war nurses
　　Brockett—Woman's p324-342
　　Young—Women p290-291,381-382

Woolson, Abba Louisa Goold (1838-1921)
　　Amer. author, educator, lecturer
　　Hanaford—Dau. p245,343

Woolson, Constance Fenimore (1848-1894)
　　Amer. novelist
　　Adelman—Famous p197
　　Dorland—Sum p57

Woolston, Beulah (1828-1886)
　　Amer. missionary
　　Logan—Part p516

Wooster, Lizzie E. (b. 1870)
　　Amer. editor, author
　　Logan—Part p861

Wooster, Lydia.
　　See Sullivan, Lydia Wooster

Wooster, Mary Clapp (1729-1807)
　　Amer. social leader
　　Green—Pioneer (2) p186-192
　　Hanaford—Dau. p139
　　Root—Chapter p101-124

Wootton, Barbara Frances, Baroness
　　　　(1897-　　)
　　Brit. social leader, economist,
　　　　educator, author, politician
　　Cur. Biog. '64 p468-470,por.

Worden, Helen (1896-　　)
　　Amer. author, journalist
　　Ross—Ladies p387-393,por.

Wordsworth, Dorothy (1771-1855)
　　Eng. author, sister of William
　　　　Wordsworth
　　Adelman—Famous p118
　　Corkran—Romance p185-214,por.
　　Dunaway—Treas. p115-121
　　Hammerton p1420,por.
　　Moore—Disting. p59-70
　　Pomeroy—Little p73-113,por.
　　Sitwell—Women p23-25

Wordworth, Elizabeth, Dame (1840-1932)
　　Eng. educator
　　Brittain—Women (see index),por.

Workman, Fanny Bullock (c. 1859-1925)
　　Amer. explorer, mountaineer
　　Adelman—Famous p298-299
　　Hammerton p1421,por.

Worman, Donna (fl. 1950's)
　　Amer. business woman
　　Fortune—100 p16-17

Wormeley, Katharine Prescott (1830-1908)
　　Eng.-Amer. author, translator, Civil
　　　　war patriot
　　Adelman—Famous p237
　　Brockett—Woman's p318-323
　　Dannett—Nobel p159-167,187-191,
　　　　194-196
　　Dorland—Sum p22,125,129-130,177
　　Young—Women p177-178,308,311,
　　　　382-383

Wormly, Mrs. (fl. 1870's-1880's)
　　Amer. artist, steel engraver
　　Hanaford—Dau. p315

Worrell, Mary.
　　See Knight, Mary Worrell

Worth, Amy (b. 1888)
　　Amer. composer, musical director,
　　　　pianist
　　ASCAP p547-548
　　McCoy—Portraits p235,por.

Worth, Elisabeth. See Lipei Naij

Worth, Irene (1916-　　)
　　Amer. actress
　　Cur. Biog. '68 p437-440,por.

Worth, Jane. See Harding, Jane

Worth, Mary Wesley Pease (fl. 1870's)
　　Whiting—Whaling p240

Worthington, Jane T. Lomax (d. 1847)
　　Amer. poet
　　Hanaford—Dau. p266

Wortley Montagu, Lady.
　　See Montagu, Mary Wortley, Lady

Wrede, Mathilda (1864-1929)
　　Fin. humanitarian
　　Kenworthy—12 p267-286,por.
　　Schmidt—400 p168-169,por.

Wright, Alice Morgan (b. 1881)
　　Amer. sculptor
　　Jackman—Amer. p418-420
　　National—Contemp. p338

Wright, Anna Maria Louisa Perrott Rose
    (1890-   )
    Amer. author
    Cur. Biog. '52 p650-651

Wright, Cobina (n.d.)
    Amer. hostess, singer, society
        leader, journalist
    CR '59 p853,por.
    CR '63 p668,por.
    Tanner—Here p143-164

Wright, Mrs. Crafts J. (fl. 1860's)
    Amer. Civil war humanitarian
    Brockett—Woman's p791-792

Wright, Mrs. David (fl. 1770's)
    Amer. Rev. war heroine
    Ellet—Women (2) p295-297
    Hanaford—Dau. p56

Wright, Mrs. Donald McCloud.
    See Meadowcroft, Enid La Monte

Wright, Elizabeth M. (b.c. 1863)
    Eng. author
    Brittain—Women p71-72

Wright, Emma Scholfield (b. 1845)
    Eng.-Amer. artist
    Logan—Part p753-754

Wright, Ethel (fl. 1890's-1930's)
    Eng. painter
    Waters—Women p367

Wright, Frances ("Fanny") D'Arusmont
    (1795-1852)
    Scot.-Amer. feminist, philanthropist,
        foundress, social reformer,
        author, lecturer
    Culver—Women p171
    Douglas—Remember p66-75,por.
    Hammerton p480,1424
    Holbrook—Dreamers p170-174
    O'Connor—Pioneer p12,47-53,126-127,
        135,137,143-145,163,194,208-209,216
    Riegel—Amer. p10-15,por.
    Whitton—These p64-66,94
    Woodward—Bold p24-52

Wright, Helen (1914-   )
    Amer. astronomer, author
    Cur. Biog. '56 p655-657,por.

Wright, Jane Cooke (1919-   )
    Amer. physician
    Cur. Biog. '68 p443-445,por.

Wright, Julia McNair (1840-1903)
    Amer. novelist
    Dorland—Sum p42,196-197

Wright, Kate Semmes (fl. 1910's)
    Amer. social leader
    Logan—Part p300

Wright, Katherine (1874-1929)
    Amer. aviation patroness, sister of
        Wright brothers
    Earhart—Fun p180
    Izant—Ohio p117-123
    *May—Women p60
    Planck—Women p39-41

Wright, Leonore Smith (fl. 1860's)
    Amer. Civil war nurse
    Logan—Part p374

Wright, Lucy (fl. 1780's-1820's)
    Amer. colonial religious leader
    Dexter—Colonial p153

Wright, M. Louise Wood (b. 1865/75)
    Amer. illustrator, painter
    Michigan—Biog. p343

Wright, Mabel Osgood (1859-1934)
    Amer. author
    Adelman—Famous p284

Wright, Martha (1926-   )
    Amer. singer, actress
    CR '63 p668-669,por.
    Cur. Biog. '65 p472-473,por.
    TV—Person (3) p55-56,por.

Wright, Martha Coffin Pelham (fl. 1840's-
    1860's)
    Amer. feminist, philanthropist
    Hanaford—Dau. p174-175
    O'Connor—Pioneer p89
    Riegel—Amer. p23-26,por.

Wright, Mickey (Mary Kathryn) (1935-   )
    Amer. golfer
    Cur. Biog. '55 p663-665,por.

Wright, N. Louise (fl. 1940's)
    Amer. composer, pianist, educator
    McCoy—Portraits p235,por.

Wright, Nancy (n.d.)
    Amer. singer
    TV—Person (1) p12,por.

Wright, Patience Lovell (1725-1785)
    Amer. colonial sculptor (wax-
        modeler)
    Jackman—Amer. p302-303
    Schmidt—400 p4-5,por.
    Taft—Women, Mentor #1
    Tuckerman—Book p49
    Waters—Women p367-369

Wright, Prudence Cumings (c. 1739-1823)
    Amer. Rev. war heroine
    Green—Pioneer (2) p316-336
    Leonard—Amer. p125

Wright, Rebecca (m. 1871)
    Amer. Civil war heroine,
        government employee
    Hanaford—Dau. p615
    Harkness—Heroines p10-11

Wright, Mrs. S. J. (m. 1883)
Amer. club leader
Logan—Part p405-406

Wright, Sophie (n.d.)
Amer. teacher
Bennett—Amer. p47-67,por.

Wright, Susan Catharine (fl. 1860's-1900's)
Amer., mother of Wright brothers
Davis—Mothers p63-73

Wright, Susanna (1697-1784)
Amer. colonial business woman,
poet
Hanaford—Dau. p605
Leonard—Amer. p125

Wright, Teresa (1918-   )
Amer. actress
CR '59 p853-854,por.
CR '63 p669,por.
Cur. Biog. '43 p847-849,por.

Wright, Zoe Harmon (1895-   )
Amer. librarian
Parshalle—Kash. p209-211,por.

Wrighten, Mary Ann.
See Pownall, Mary Ann

Wrinch, Dorothy M. (1894-   )
Eng. biochemist, mathematician
Cur. Biog. '47 p693-695,por.
Progress—Science p388-389,por.

Wriothesley, Elizabeth, Countess of
Northumberland (1647-1690)
Eng. heiress
Festing—on p89-179

Wroath (Wroth), Mary, Lady (c. 1586-
1640)
Eng. poet
MacCarthy—Women p47,53-64,72

Wrong, Rosalind Mary (gr. 1942)
Eng. teacher
Brittain—Women p247

Wu, Chien Shiung (c. 1912-   )
Chin. physicist
Cur. Biog. '59 p491-492,por.
Year—Pic. p215-217,por.

Wu, Eva (fl. 1950's)
Chin. spy
*Nolen—Spies p208-216

Wulfraat, Margaretta (1678-1741)
Nether. painter
Waters—Women p369

Wulfwaru (d.c. 984/1016)
Eng. landowner
Stenton—English p26

Wurdemann, Audrey May (1911-1960)
Amer. poet
*Millett—Amer. p660-661

Wurm, Mary (1860-1938)
Eng. composer, pianist, teacher
McCoy—Portraits p235,por.

Wu Y-Fang (1893-   )
Chin. educator, religious leader
Cur. Biog. '45 p696-698,por.

Wyatt, Edith Franklin (b. 1873)
Amer. author
Bruère—Laugh. p73

Wyatt, Euphemia Van Rensselaer
(fl. 1930's)
Amer. editor
Women—Achieve. p130,por.

Wyatt, Jane Waddington (1911/12-   )
Amer. actress, TV personality
CR '59 p854,por.
CR '63 p669-670,por.
Cur. Biog. '57 p598-600,por.
TV—Person. (1) p135-136,por.

Wyatt, Mary (c. 1611-1705)
Amer. colonial midwife
Dexter—Colonial p61

Wycherley, Margaret (c. 1884-1956)
Amer. actress
Coad—Amer. p323,por.

Wydville, Elizabeth.
See Elizabeth Woodville

Wylie, Elinor Morton Hoyt (1885-1928)
Amer. poet, novelist
Beckwith—Contemp. p118-133
Brenner—Poets p311-354
Clark—Innocence p167-183,por.
Cook—Our p249-251
Loggins—Hear p90-97
*Millett—Amer. p661-663
Moore—Disting. p219-233
New Yorker Mr. 19, 1927 p24,por.
(Profiles)
Overton—Women p350-352

Wylie, Ida Alexis Ross (1885-1959)
Eng. author
Lawrence—School p276-278

Wyllys, Ruth (fl. 1680's)
Amer. pioneer
Green—Pioneer (1) p283,340-357
*Sickels—Calico p31-40

Wyllys, Ruth Belden (1747-1807)
Amer. Rev. war patriot
Green—Pioneer (1) p353-354
Root—Chapter p17-30

Wyman, Jane (1914-   )
    Amer. actress ,TV personality
    CR '59 p856,por.
    CR '63 p670-671,por.
    Cur. Biog. '49 p647-648,por.
    TV—Person. (2) p52-53,por.

Wyman, Margaret Holmes (m.c. 1760)
    Amer. pioneer
    Green—Pioneer (3) p498

Wynflaed (d.c. 95)
    Eng. religious worker
    Stenton—English p25-26

Wynne, Madeline Yale (b. 1847)
    Amer. author, metal worker
    Logan—Part p861

Wynter, Dana (1932-   )
    Eng. actress
    CR '59 p857-858,por.

Wynyard, Diana (1906-   )
    Eng. actress
    Hammerton p1429

Wysor, Elizabeth (fl. 1930's)
    Amer. singer
    Women—Achieve. p59,por.

Wythe, Anne Lewis (b. 1726)
    Amer. patriot
    Green—Pioneer (3) p233-235

X

X, Hilda (Brandt, Hilda) (fl. 1940's)
    Russ. spy
    Singer—World's p29-39

X, Myra (fl. 1940's)
    Zionist spy
    Singer—World's p312-313

Xanthippe (Xantippe) (5th cent. B.C.)
    Gr., wife of Socrates
    Hammerton p1429
    *MacVeagh—Champlin p542

Y

Yadviga. See Jadwiga

Yandell, Enid (1870-1934)
    Amer. sculptor
    Logan—Part p763-764
    Michigan—Biog. p345
    National—Contemp. p340
    Taft—Women, Mentor (102) p10;#2
    Waters—Women p369-371

Yang, Kuei-Fei (b. 718)
    Chin. concubine, beauty
    Collins—Biog. p328-329
    Llewellyn—China's p92-101

Yardley, Temperance Flowerdew Yardley
        West, Lady (1593-1636)
    Amer. colonial patriot
    Green—Pioneer (1) p101-102
    Leonard—Amer. p125

Yarmouth, Amalie Sophie Marianne von
        Wallmoden, Countess of (1704-
        1765)
    Eng., mistress of George II
    Hammerton p1431

Yates, Elizabeth (1905-   )
    Amer. author
    Cur. Biog. '48 p696-698,por.
    Warfel—Amer. p471,por.

Yates, Josephine Silone (1852-1912)
    Amer. teacher
    Brown—Home. p178-181

Yates, Mrs. (fl. 1750's)
    Eng. actress
    MacQueen—Pope p222-224,por.

Yaukey, Grace Sydenstricker.
    See Spencer, Cornelis

Yeakley, Marjory Hall.
    See Hall, Marjory

Yeardley, Temperance.
    See Yardley, Temperance Flowerdew
        Yardley West, Lady

Yeats, Elizabeth Corbe (fl. 1900's)
    Irish printer
    Club—Printing p16

Yehonala. See Tzu Hsi

Yellin, Thelma (fl. 1930's)
    Eng.-Israeli violoncellist
    Saleski—Jewish p712

Yelverton, Marie Therese, Viscountess of
        Avonmore (fl 1870's)
    Irish author
    Sargent—Pioneers p27,35-36

Yenni, Julia Truitt (1913-   )
    Amer. novelist
    Warfel—Amer. p472,por.

Yermolova, Mariya Nikolayevna (Ermolova)
        (1853-1928)
    Russ. actress
    Phila.—Women, unp.,por.
    Stiles—Postal p290

Yermol'yeva, Ziraida Vissarionovna
(1898-   )
Russ. microbiologist, bacterio-
chemist
U.S.—Biog., Soviet p211-212

Yezierska, Anzia (b. 1885)
Pol.-Amer. author
Cooper—Authors p103-111,por.
Ribalow—Auto. p446-459

Yim, Louise (1904-   )
Kor. politician, educator, U.N.
official
Cur. Biog. '47 p695-696,por.

Ykens (Ijkens), (Laurence) Catherine
(b. 1659)
Belg. painter
Waters—Women p371

Yohé, May, Lady Francis Hope (c. 1869-
1938)
Amer. actress, singer
Furniss—Some p60-62
Marks—Glamour p337
Wyndham—Chorus p101-105,por.

Yolanda (or Helen) (d. 1299)
Hung. saint
Englebert—Lives p231

Yolanda of Aragon (fl. 15th cent.)
Sp. princess, countess, wife of
Louis of Provence and Aragon
*Cather—Girlhood p141-162

Yolanda of Montferrat (Irene, consort of
Andronicus II) (c. 1273-1317)
Byzant. empress
Diehl—Byzant. p276-286

Yolande of Savoy. See Savoy, Yolande of

Yonge, Charlotte Mary (1823-1901)
Eng. novelist, editor
Adelman—Famous p213-214
Brittain—Women p25,35,50,79
Dorland—Sum p19,74,115-116,188
Hammerton p1432,por.
Johnson—Women p199-203
*MacVeagh—Champlin p625

Yonis, Bathsheba (fl. 1910's)
Israeli physician
Lovejoy—Women p217

York, Anne, Duchess of (1637-1671)
Eng. beauty, daughter of Edward
Hyde
Melville—Windsor p17-56,por.

York, Elizabeth, Duchess of.
See Elizabeth, Queen of George VI

York, Elizabeth (n.d.)
Amer. actress
TV—Person (1) p83,por.

York, Frederica, Duchess of (d. 1767-
c. 1819/20)
Ger. daughter of William II of
Prussia
Hasted—Unsuccess p35-53,por.
Melville—Windsor p17-56,por.

Yorke, Sarah (m. 1831)
Amer., wife of Andrew Jackson, Jr.
Hanaford—Dau. p134
Smith—White p41-43,por.

Yoshioka, Yayoi (1871-1959)
Japan. physician
Lovejoy—Women p236-238,por.

Young, Ann Eliza Webb (bc. 1844)
Amer. feminist, religious worker,
pioneer
Brown—Gentle p14,248,265-268,por.
Woodward—Bold p307-333

Young, Barbara (b. 1878)
Amer. poet
Smith—Women's p234

Young, Carrie (fl. 1870's)
Amer. editor
Hanaford—Dau. p703

Young, Dorothy Lamb (fl. 1930's-1950's)
Amer. aviatrix, helicopter pilot
*May—Women p205-207,209

Young, Ella Flagg (1845-1918)
Amer. educator
Adelman—Famous p254
Bennett—Amer. p253-277,por.
Fleming—Great p101-114
Logan—Part p733
Mears—They p77-78
Moore—When p186-192
Webb—Famous p583-593,por.

Young, Emily Hilda (1880-1949)
Irish poet
Lawrence—School p299-301
Millett—Brit. p522

Young, Loretta (1913/14-   )
Amer. actress, TV personality
Blum—Television p196,por.
CR '59 p858-859,por.
CR '63 p674,por.
Cur. Biog. '48 p699-701,por.
Hammerton p1434
TV—Person (1) p84-85,por.

Young, Lucy A. Newton (fl. 1860's)
Amer. Civil war nurse
Logan—Part p374

Young, M. A. B. (d. 1865)
 Amer. Civil war nurse
 Brockett—Woman's p459

Young, Marguerite (fl. 1930's)
 Amer. journalist
 Ross—Ladies p352-354

Young, Marian (Martha Deane) (1909-)
 Amer. radio personality
 CR '63 p163,por.
 Cur. Biog. '52 p658-660,por.

Young, Mary Vance (1866-1946)
 Amer. educator
 Logan—Part p720

Young, Nancy Wilson Ross.
 See Ross, Nancy Wilson

Young, Pearl (fl. 1930's)
 Amer. aviation, technical editor
 Planck—Women p242

Young, Mrs. Poyner (fl. 1770's)
 Fr.-Amer. Rev. war patriot
 Ellet—Women (2) p199

Young, Rida Johnson (1869/75-1926)
 Amer. playwright, author, librettist,
  actress
 ASCAP p551
 Logan—Part p790

Young, Rose Emmet (1869-1941)
 Amer. author, editor, feminist
 Cur. Biog. '41 p942

Young, Ruth (1916-)
 Amer. labor union secretary
 Epstein—People p114-130

Younger, Mrs. (b. 1702)
 Eng. actress
 MacQueen—Pope p161-162

Yourcenar, Marguerite, Mademoiselle de
  Crayencour (fl. 1950's)
 Fr. novelist
 Peyre—French p447,465

Youse, Glad Robinson (1898-)
 Amer. composer
 ASCAP p552

Youville, Marie Marguerite (Marie
  Marguerite Dufrus de la
  Gesmerais) (1701-1771)
 Can. foundress, philanthropist, nun
 Schmidt—400 p73-74,por.

Yu Hsuan-Chi (d. 870)
 Chin. beauty, nun, poet
 Llewellyn—China's p114-126

Yu Kuliang (b. 1873)
 Chin. religious worker
 Burton—Notable p221-229,por.

Yuro, Timi (fl. 1960's)
 Amer. singer
 *Kahn—Tops p135-136

Yvette (1158-1228)
 Hung. saint
 Englebert—Lives p17

Z

Zabella-Vrubel, Madame (fl. 1890's-1900's)
 Russ. singer
 Schmidt—400 p349,por.

Zabriskie, Louise G. (1864-1963)
 Amer. nurse, social welfare leader
 Taves—Success. p252-260,por.

Zachs, Anna H. (fl. 1930's)
 Russ.-Amer. lawyer
 Women—Achieve. p189,por.

Zadek, Hilde (fl. 1940's-1950's)
 Ger.-Israeli singer
 Davidson—Treas. p342-344

Zaharias, Mildred ("Babe") Didrikson
  (1912/14-1956)
 Amer. athlete
 *Clymer—Modern p169-178,por.
 Cur. Biog. '47 p701-703,por.
 Cur. Biog. '56 p663
 Davis—100 p30-31,por.
 *Freedman—Teen. p143-169,por.
 Gallico—Golden p235-251,por.
 *Gelman—Young p26-37,por.
 *Gersh—Women p142-163,por.
 *Jacobs—Famous p23-30,por.
 Jensen—Revolt p132-133,por.
 *Meyers—Champ. p78-101
 *Moderow—People p221-241,por.
 Stiles—Postal p291

Zahle, Nathalie (b. 1827)
 Dan. educator
 Schmidt—400 p97-98,por.

Zaidens, Sadie Helene (fl. 1930's)
 Amer. physician, dermatologist
 Women—Achieve. p104,por.

Zakrzewska, Marie Elizabeth (1829-
  1902)
 Ger.-Amer. physician
 Castiglioni—Hist. p917
 Farmer—What p384
 *Fleming—Doctors p9-22
 Hanaford—Dau. p554-555
 Hume—Great p36-38,40-41,179
 Irwin—Angels p49-50,135-136

(Continued)

Zakrzewska, Marie Elizabeth—*Continued*

    Lovejoy—Women p54-59,62,81-82, 84-86
    Mead—Medical p31-33

Zakutu (c. 700-650 B.C.)
    Babyl. queen
    Schmidt—400 p126-127,por.

Zambrana, Luisa Pérez de (1835-1922)
    Cub. poet, novelist
    Schmidt—400 p84,por.

Zamir-Weinreich, Hanna (fl. 1930's-1940's)
    Russ.-Israeli singer
    Saleski—Jewish p712

Zand, Nathalie (fl. 1930's)
    Pol. physician, pathologist
    Lovejoy—Women p174

Zane, Elizabeth ("Betty") (1759-1847)
    Amer. Rev. war heroine
    Bruce—Woman p127-133
    *Carmer—Young p82-88
    DAR Mag. July 1921 p384,portrayal
    Ellet—Women (2) p319-324
    Fowler—Woman p89-90
    Green—Pioneer (2) p444-450
    Hanaford—Dau. p61
    *Humphrey—Elizabeths p76-88
    Logan—Part p160-162
    *Nida—Pilots p202-203

Zanft, Hattie Carnegie. See Carnegie, Hattie

Zanova, Aja (1934-   )
    Czech. skater
    CR '63 p675,por.

Zapolska, Gabryela (1860/80-1921)
    Pol. playwright, novelist, actress
    Schmidt—400 p329-330,por.

Zarephath, widow of (Biblical)
    Buchanan—Women p59
    Chappell—Fem. p115-127
    Deen—All p131-134
    Lewis—Portraits p158-160

Zarudny-Cavoss, Catherine S. (b. 1870)
    Russ. artist
    Schmidt—400 p347,por.

Zauditu (Zaudita; Zeodita), Judith Waiseru (1876-1930)
    Abyss. empress
    Arsenius—Dict. p204,por.
    Stiles—Postal p292
    Phila.—Women, unp.,por.

Zebudah (Biblical)
    Deen—All p300

Zefira, Bracha (fl. 1940's)
    Israeli singer
    Saleski—Jewish p712-713,por.

Zeisler, Fannie Bloomfield.
    See Bloomfield-Zeisler, Fannie

Zell, Katharina Schutz (1497-1562)
    Ger. religious leader
    Culver—Women p123

Zelle, Gertrud Margarete. See Hari, Mata

Zeller, Joan (fl. 1950's)
    Amer. airline hostess
    *May—Women p235-236

Zellers, Christine (fl. 1740's)
    Amer. colonial heroine
    Bruce—Women p71-72

Zelophehad, daughters of (Biblical)
    Deen—All p62-64

Zemaite (Zymantieni), Julija (1845-1921)
    Lith. author
    Arsenius—Dict. p205

Zemani, Mumtaza. See Mumtaz-Mahal

Zenaida (fl. 1st cent.)
    Turk. saint
    Englebert—Lives p386-387

Zenger, (Anna) Catherine (1704-1751)
    Amer. publisher
    Brigham—Journals p76
    Club—Printing p12-13,22
    Dexter—Colonial p169-171
    Earle—Colon. p68
    *Gersh—Women p118-141,por.
    Hanaford—Dau. p709
    Leonard—Amer. p125

Zenobia (fl. 3rd cent., A.D.)
    Palm. empress
    Abbot—Notable p44-49
    Adelman—Famous p26-27
    Balsdon—Roman p164-165
    Beard—Woman p283-284
    Boccaccio—Con. p226-230
    *Farmer—Book p31-41
    Hammerton p1439
    Koven—Women p2
    McCabe—Empr. p240-249,por.
    MacVeagh—Champlin p628,por.
    Muir—Women p55-57
    Serviez—Roman (2) p326-354
    Stiles—Postal p293
    Weigall—Person. p112-119

Zeresh (Biblical)
    Deen—All p300
    Lewis—Portraits p147-148
    Marble—Women, Bible p88-90
    Mead—250 p162

Zeruah (Biblical)
Mother of Jeroboam
Deen—All p300-301

Zeruiah (Biblical)
Half-sister of David
Deen—All p301-302
Lewis—Portraits p82-83

Zetkin, Clara Eissner (1857-1933)
Ger. teacher, politician, editor
Hammerton p1440
Stiles—Postal p293

Zhemaite (Zhemayte), **Yuliya Antanovna**
(1845-1921)
Lith. author
Stiles—Postal p293

Zibiah (Biblical)
Deen—All p302

Ziegler, Mrs. William (fl. 1910's)
Amer. philanthropist
Logan—Part p531

Ziesensis, Margaretta (fl. 18th cent.)
Dan. painter
Waters—Women p372

Ziglevice, Elza (1898-1919)
Lat. patriot, foundress
Schmidt—400 p276-277,por.

Zillah (Biblical)
Deen—All p302-303
Mead—250 p7

Zilpah (Biblical)
Deen—All p303
Mead—250 p31

Zilvé, Alida (fl. 1920's)
Nether.-Amer. sculptor
National—Contemp. p342

Zimand, Gertrude Folks (fl. 1930's)
Amer. club leader
Women—Achieve. p205

Zimantas, Julija (1845-1921)
Lith. author, patriot
Schmidt—400 p279-280,por.

Zimbalist, Mary Louise Curtis (fl. 1910's-
1920's)
Amer. music patron
McCoy—Portraits p237,por.

Zimmerman, Agnes (1847-1925)
Ger.-Eng. pianist, composer
Elson—Woman's p145

Zimmerman, Carma Russell (1904-   )
Amer. librarian, editor
Bul. of Bibl. May-Aug.1955 p145-147,
por.

Zimmerman, Helena (Helena Kintore),
Duchess of Manchester
(fl. 1900's)
Amer. heiress
Eliot—Heiresses p179-188,por.
Pearson—Pilgrim p147-149

Zimmern, Helen (1846-1934)
Eng. author
Hammerton p1440

Zinzendorff, Anna Caritas Nitschmann
(1715-1760)
Amer. colonial educator
Leonard—Amer. p125

Zipporah (Biblical)
Buchanan—Women p28-29
Deen—All p54-56
Hammerton p1441
Lewis—Portraits p58-59
Marble—Women, Bible p50-54

Zita (1218-1272/78)
It. saint
Englebert—Lives p162-163
Wescott—Calen. p60

Zita (1892-1922)
Aust. empress; Hung. queen
Arsenius—Dict. p206,por.
Phila.—Women unp.,por.
Stiles—Postal p294

Zmichowska, Narcyza (1819-1876)
Pol. poet
Schmidt—400 p326,por.

Zoe (date unknown)
Ger. saint
Englebert—Lives p259

Zoë, the Porphyrogenita (980-1050/56)
Byzant. empress
Diehl—Byzant. p136-173
Hammerton p1441

Zorbaugh, Geraldine Bone (1905-   )
Amer. radio, TV executive, lawyer
Cur. Biog. '56 p667-669,por.

Zorina, Vera (1917-   )
Ger.-Amer. dancer
CR '59 p864,por.
CR '63 p677,por.
Cur. Biog. '41 p946-947,por.

Zrini (Zrinyi), **Ilona** (Helen) (1643-1703)
Hunt. patriot, diplomat
Phila.—Women, unp.,por.
Stiles—Postal p294

Zucca, Mana (1891/94-   )
Amer. pianist, composer
Saleski—Wander. p96,por.